AMERICAN EPOCH

*A HISTORY
OF THE
UNITED STATES
SINCE
THE 1890's*

AMERICAN EPOCH

A HISTORY
OF THE
UNITED STATES
SINCE
THE 1890's

BY ARTHUR S. LINK

PROFESSOR OF HISTORY
NORTHWESTERN UNIVERSITY

NEW YORK / **ALFRED A. KNOPF** / 1962

L. C. catalog card number: 54-13244

© Arthur S. Link, 1955

THIS IS A BORZOI BOOK,
PUBLISHED BY ALFRED A. KNOPF, INC.

PUBLISHED 1955; REPRINTED 1956, 1958, (2), 1959, 1960, 1961, 1962, (2)

EDWARD MEAD EARLE

1894–1954

SCHOLAR AND FRIEND OF SCHOLARS

IN MEMORIAM

PREFACE

*T*HIS book is written for the general reader who shares my interest in one of the great epochs of modern history—the struggles, failures, and achievements of the American people in the twentieth century. I have tried to reconstruct the American experience since the 1890's in all its baffling complexity and to convey some understanding of the events and movements that have transformed American institutions and helped to catapult the American people into a position of leadership in world affairs. An outgrowth of fifteen years of research and teaching in the field of recent American history, this book embodies what I think is the essence of that history and my convictions concerning its long-run significance.

I have had so much help in writing *American Epoch* that I scarcely know how to begin to acknowledge my indebtedness. The "Suggested Additional Reading" is selective and does not convey my enormous debt to scholars in the field of recent American history who have enriched my knowledge and understanding and made my own researches more meaningful. I have said very little that is new. Indeed, I will be satisfied if I have succeeded in assembling, assimilating, and organizing the excellent sources and literature of this period.

And now I must acknowledge my debt to a host of friends who made writing *American Epoch* an unforgettable experience. At the House of Knopf, Mr. Alfred A. Knopf, head of the firm, has given more encouragement than he knows. Dr. Roger W. Shugg, formerly head of the College Department and now Director of the University of Chicago Press, conceived the idea of the book and helped me find my bearings. Mr. John T. Hawes, present head of the College Department, has been throughout a tower of strength and as fine a friend as one could have. Mr. Thomas A. Bledsoe, also of the College Department, edited the manuscript with skill and care.

Professors John M. Blum of the Massachusetts Institute of Technology, Frank Freidel of Stanford University, Henry Bamford Parkes of New York University, and Dr. Max Beloff, Nuffield Reader in the Comparative Study of Institutions at Oxford University, read the entire manuscript, gave their help unstintingly, and saved me from many errors. My good friend, Professor John Hope Franklin of Howard University, my colleagues at Northwestern University, Ray A. Billington, Roger Hackett, Franklin D. Scott, and

Ernest Samuels, and Mr. William Miller, formerly of the House of Knopf, read large portions of the manuscript and furnished me with indispensable materials. Messrs. William B. Catton, Gerald N. Grob, Naaman J. Woodland, Jr., and Justin L. Kestenbaum, graduate students at Northwestern University, helped with a hundred burdensome details. To Mr. Theodore R. Miller, both for his skill as a cartographer and his informed suggestions, goes most of the credit for the excellence of the graphs, charts, and maps. I am deeply indebted, also, to the National Industrial Conference Board, Inc., 247 Park Avenue, New York City, for permission to redraw their charts and graphs for use in this book. The photographs were furnished by Brown Brothers, 220 West 42nd St., New York City. I owe the greatest debt to my colleague, Richard W. Leopold, who not only read the entire manuscript with a watchful eye but also gave such assistance as only a friend can give, and to my wife, Margaret Douglas Link, who kept children from my study, read and edited during evenings uncountable, and yet preserved her sanity and serenity. Finally, I should like to think that the late Professor Edward Mead Earle of the Institute for Advanced Study would have liked this book. He was a generous friend and wise counselor.

A. S. L.

Evanston, Illinois
August 27, 1954

CONTENTS / *AMERICAN EPOCH*

x / *Contents*

PART TWO / *AN ERA OF WAR, PROSPERITY, AND*
DEPRESSION, 1914–1933

PART THREE / *THE DEMOCRATIC ERA, 1933–1953*

xiv / Contents

PHOTOGRAPHS

MAPS / PLANNED AND EXECUTED BY THEODORE R. MILLER

GRAPHS AND FIGURES / *BY THEODORE R. MILLER*

PART ONE

THE PROGRESSIVE GENERATION 1897-1914

IN WHICH the American people sur-mount the depression of the 1890's, find prosperity and peace at home, launch the progressive movement in city, state, and nation to restore representative govern-ment and subject organized wealth to their control, and, withal, become a world power with dominions beyond the seas.

CHAPTER 1 / *THE HERITAGE OF THE*
NINETEENTH CENTURY

O N September 6, 1901, an anarchist shot President William McKinley at Buffalo, New York, and by so doing helped inaugurate a new era in American history. The coming to national leadership of McKinley's successor, Theodore Roosevelt, marked not only a change of Presidents but also the beginning of a new epoch for a people standing on the threshold of the most momentous century in modern history. Rash is the man who undertakes to describe the aspirations and to chronicle the triumphs and failures of the American people during the past six decades. Yet knowledge of the follies and failures of history may yield wisdom and understanding for a generation ignorant of its own experiences and distraught by fear of an uncertain future.

1 / *The Economic and Political Revolution, 1861–1876*

To understand our recent history we must know something about the heritage that the nineteenth century bequeathed to the twentieth, for the framework of twentieth century American society was constructed during the Civil War and Reconstruction and shaped by a revolution in industry, agriculture, transportation, and politics. During the period 1861–1901 the United States emerged as the leading industrial and agricultural producer of the world. The statistics all add up to the same story of incredible growth and multiplying the examples would merely elaborate the obvious facts of economic development. More important is an understanding of the dynamics that produced this economic revolution, for the same forces that set the revolution in progress gathered momentum after 1900 and helped create the twentieth century American economic society.

To begin with, the three essential ingredients—natural resources, labor, and capital—existed in abundance in the United States after the Civil War. The development of vast new coal fields and iron mines in western Pennsylvania, for example, provided the basis for the growing American iron and steel industry. The expanding demand for labor was amply satisfied by masses of unskilled workers from at home and abroad. And over the long period from 1861 to 1901 profits were sufficiently large to make possible a steady expansion of plant and equipment.

Natural resources, labor, and capital were only the ingredients, not the dynamic causes of economic growth. The catalyst was the Civil War, which stimulated the first great boom in heavy industry in American history. War-time demand for clothing, shoes, ammunition, and iron products caused in four years an acceleration of economic growth that would have required probably twenty years for completion in the processes of normal development.

During the crisis of the Union, moreover, there occurred a shift in the balance of power in Washington and in many of the state governments that added a new impetus to the economic revolution then in progress by making the federal and state governments protectors and benefactors of the rising banking, industrial, and railroad interests. The Republican party in the Northeast, at least, had supplanted the Whig party as the political agent of the propertied interests, just as the Whigs had earlier supplanted the Federalists in this capacity. Before 1861 a tenuous alliance of the South and West in the Democratic party had held the non-agrarian interests in check and had prevented them from using the federal government to underwrite their program. The withdrawal of the southern delegations from Congress in 1860–1861, however, threw political control into the hands of the Republican agents of the business classes.

The result was that the Reconstruction of the United States got under way even before the first guns were fired on Fort Sumter. The passage of the Morrill tariff law of 1861 was the first sign that control of the federal government had passed from the agricultural sections to the industrial North-east. Under the guise of war necessity, the industrial-financial leaders of the Republican party carried forward this reconstruction of federal policies at a rapid pace—through land grants to railroads, a national banking system, introduction of contract labor from Europe and Asia, and further tariff increases.

When the war ended and an assassin's bullet placed Andrew Johnson of Tennessee in the White House in 1865, the struggle for control of the federal government entered a new phase. The object of Johnson's plan of Reconstruction was to bring the former Confederate states back into the Union as speedily as possible, without changing the agrarian control of the southern states. When the Republican leaders realized that the outcome of Johnson's plan might well be to restore dominance in the federal govern-ment to the agrarian South and West, they moved quickly to overturn Johnsonian reconstruction and to inaugurate their own so-called Radical program. Conceived in the interest of the business classes and justified in the name of humanitarianism, Radical Reconstruction stirred passions North and South without effecting any lasting changes in the southern economy or social order. Negroes were enfranchised and given a small measure of civil rights, but control of the land and other means of production was left securely in the hands of the whites. And when, for a number of reasons, the Radicals abandoned their southern program in 1877, the southern whites at once resumed sovereignty in local affairs.

Radical Reconstruction was, therefore, but an interlude in southern history; but the reconstruction of national politics that began in 1861 had fully accomplished its objectives by 1877. Without altering the structure of American political institutions, the business classes had executed a bloodless revolution. They had, in brief, wrested control of the political institutions from the agrarian majority and changed the character, but not the forms, of representative government in the United States.

2 / The Captains of Industry

In the final analysis, the transformation of the American economy was effected, not by impersonal forces, but by men. The character and methods of the new captains of industry and transportation offer, therefore, another key to understanding the development of politics and business during America's so-called Gilded Age. The new economic leaders who rose to power during and after the Civil War were a remarkable group—sometimes ruthless and dishonest, often no worse than their fellow Americans, yet extraordinarily bold and resourceful. Like most other businessmen of their day, they conceived of economic activity as warfare, in which only the strong survived and the weak perished. In a generally acquisitive age, the acquisition of wealth was their goal, money their standard. Monopoly, the subversion of representative government, the corruption of private and public morals—these were often necessary means in the fierce struggle for wealth and power. One historian has called them Robber Barons and likened them to the freebooters of the Middle Ages who pillaged the countryside. Another writer has compared them to the gangsters of the 1920's.

The comparisons, however engaging, are essentially unfair, because, for all their faults, most of the captains of industry were men of enormous constructive energy and in the final analysis reflected the standards of their age. For every Daniel Drew, who bankrupted railroads for his own enrichment, there were a dozen Thomas A. Scotts, James J. Hills, and Edward H. Harrimans, who laid the gleaming rails across plains and mountains to the Pacific Coast. The character, methods, and achievements of these men who used freedom to win unparalleled economic power can best be read in the career of the pre-eminent captain of industry and master monopolist, John D. Rockefeller.

Born in upstate New York in 1839, Rockefeller moved with his family to Cleveland, Ohio, in 1853, and two years later went to work as a bookkeeper in a commission firm. In 1859 he formed a partnership and opened a commission house to deal in agricultural products. In the same year that young Rockefeller set out upon his business career, 1859, oil was discovered in western Pennsylvania and America's first oil boom soon developed in that area. Since Cleveland was on the main line of an East-West railroad and had direct rail connections with the oilfields after 1863, it rapidly emerged as the center of the new petroleum refining industry. Rockefeller went into the oil business in 1863, at the same time that dozens of other refineries were being built in and around the city.

By 1867 Rockefeller's firm was the largest refinery in Cleveland, and in that year he began his long career of sharp practices that brought eventual domination of the American oil industry. He made his first rebating agreement with the railroads. Under this arrangement Rockefeller received not only a rebate of fifteen cents a barrel on the oil that he shipped, but also a similar amount for every barrel of oil that his competitors shipped. Given Rockefeller's energy and daring, he could not fail to prosper with such an advantage. In 1870 his firm was reorganized and capitalized at $1,000,000. Two years later Rockefeller began buying other refineries in Cleveland. In 1873 he acquired a large distributing company, started building his own pipe lines, and purchased refineries in New York. Later he moved on to Philadelphia, Baltimore, and the Middle West and Southwest.

By 1904 Rockefeller's Standard Oil Company was refining more than 84 per cent of the crude oil in the United States, producing more than 86 per cent of the illuminating oil, and controlling 86 per cent of the export trade in illuminants. Standard's pipe lines, moreover, carried nearly 90 per cent of the crude oil of the older fields and 98 per cent of the output of the new Kansas fields. So profitable was the oil monopoly that Rockefeller's wealth increased almost by a geometric ratio, and by the turn of the century he was worth probably a billion dollars.

While Rockefeller was the most successful of the captains of industry, he was only one of many who contrived to acquire for themselves and their families large portions of the land, the timber, the railroads, the mineral resources, and the industrial wealth of the United States. The Rockefellers in oil, the Carnegies and Fricks in steel, the Morgans in banking, or the Harrimans and Hills in railroading—these were the men who dominated the Republican party and usually the Democratic party as well from 1865 to 1901. They financed political campaigns and received their rewards from government in the form of utilities franchises, land bounties, freedom from taxation, or tariff protection.

3 / Consequences of the Economic Revolution

The most significant consequence of the economic revolution was the creation of modern America, of a powerful productive economy that in spite of its limitations provided an increasingly rich material life for a majority of the citizens. Few would gainsay this generalization, yet the industrialization of the United States took place in such a way as to create extraordinary economic and social problems for twentieth century Americans.

For one thing, freedom from public control allowed businessmen to engage in ruthless economic warfare, the end result of which was often the destruction of competition and the establishment of monopoly. By 1901 big business was either monopolistic or quasi-monopolistic in many of the basic industries, while new enterprises were encountering grave difficulty in entering the field. Moreover, even before the turn of the century investment bankers had begun to extend their control over railroads and industries and to build interlocking financial empires. In other words, an economic oligarchy dominated the American economy by 1900.

In the second place, the economic revolution had created social problems of enormous magnitude—cities that grew too fast, where millions of people lived amid squalor and misery; the exploitation of women and children; and a whole complex of problems caused by unemployment, illness, and perilous old age. These were the social, the human costs of rapid and uncontrolled industrialization; and a growing body of thoughtful Americans realized that a continuation of such unrestrained exploitation could only result in the degradation of the masses.

Finally, the manner in which the economic revolution took place meant that by the turn of the century the American people had been deprived of a large part of their great heritage of land, timber, and mineral resources by the railroads and the captains of industry. Wealthy men had entered politics and dominated city, state, and federal governments to bring this about. How to recover that lost heritage, restore representative government, and subject great wealth to a measure of public control would constitute the paramount domestic challenge of the twentieth century.

4 / *The Agricultural Problem, 1861–1900*

While a new industrial and urban economy was advancing with gigantic strides, agriculture remained the principal means of livelihood for the American people. During the last four decades of the nineteenth century, however, American agriculture went through a revolution as significant as the revolution that occurred in transportation and industry. Improved transportation facilities, the invention of agricultural machinery, and the opening of vast new farm areas all combined to hasten the shift which began in the 1850's, from subsistence agriculture to commercial agriculture, from production for the home and local market to production for the world market.

During the Civil War and afterward, until the late 1860's, American farmers generally prospered during a period of inflation and high production. About 1869, however, they entered a quarter century of declining prices, during many years of which they produced at an actual loss. The result was the creation of America's most serious domestic problem from 1870 to 1897—the farm problem.

The most obvious causes of the farmer's steady march toward economic ruin were overproduction and declining prices, as agricultural production in the United States, indeed in all the world, far outstripped demand.

For example, wheat, which brought $1.21 a bushel in 1879, was worth 61 cents in 1894; corn fell from an average of 50 cents in 1879 to 34 cents in 1896, cotton from 20 cents a pound in 1873 to 5 and 6 cents in 1893.

As if to compound the farmer's troubles, the twin evils of excessive freight rates and interest charges on the money he borrowed also beset him. Railroad freight rates, which were fixed on the principle of charging what the traffic would bear, were in many areas exorbitant, while discriminations in rates and services, the granting of secret rebates to favored shippers, pooling agreements to eliminate competition, and the improper influencing of legislatures and judges were common practices of the railroad managers. As for the burden of carrying their debt load, farmers in most areas had to pay usury instead of interest. This problem was most serious in the South, where the cotton and tobacco crops were financed by outside credit and where interest charges usually consumed profits before the crops could be harvested.

5 / *The Agrarian Revolt, 1870–1890*

The consequences of the long depression in agriculture can be read clearly in the efforts farmers made to use political instrumentalities to extricate themselves from the slough of despair. Most of the important legislative and political battles from 1873 to 1897 revolved directly or indirectly around the agrarian campaign for relief, and out of the ferment of agrarian revolt emerged a political philosophy and program that would have profound significance for the development of twentieth century American politics.

The Granger movement was the first organized attempt of the farmers to strike back at the railroads and industrial monopolies. Begun in Washington in 1867 as an organization designed to ameliorate the social drabness of rural life, the Grange spread rapidly through the West and South and by 1875 had a national membership of over 800,000. When farmers got together they inevitably discussed common grievances and means of remedying them, and it was not long before they went into politics. In the Middle West, for example, they won control of the legislatures in Iowa, Illinois, Wisconsin, and Minnesota and attempted to establish fair railroad rates and practices. In the end the Granger movement fell victim to the Panic of 1873, but a beginning toward concerted farmer political organization had been made, and farmers had recovered their political consciousness.

Leadership in articulating and marshaling agrarian discontent passed in the 1880's from the Grange to a new and more aggressive movement—the farmers' alliances. In the late '70's and early '80's there were a number of alliances, but by 1890 they had coalesced into three powerful groups, the Northwestern Alliance, the Southern Alliance, and the Colored Alliance, all actively at work arousing farmers to a consciousness of the agrarian crisis.

From the outset, the alliances plunged into politics with a vehemence that startled and frightened the business interests, capturing state after state in the South and West and sending eloquent spokesmen to state legislatures and to Washington. More important for the future of American politics than the mere fact of this agrarian revolt, however, was the program that the Alliance leaders advocated, and the philosophy that underlay that program. Economic adversity and a sense of baffling frustration impelled the farmers to abandon *laissez faire* as the right rule of political practice and to espouse a program envisaging far-reaching governmental intervention in economic affairs. The conversion of the great masses of farmers to this new philosophy called progressivism made it a political force that could not long be ignored by the two major parties.

The consummation of the agrarian revolt was the organization of the Populist party in 1892 and the effort of William Jennings Bryan and his agrarian followers to win control of the federal government in 1896. Before this last campaign occurred, however, the agrarian reformers, by their efforts to solve the railroad problem and obtain an ample supply of money and credit, had already sounded the death-knell of *laissez faire*.

The idea of public regulation of railroads was an outgrowth mainly of the Granger movement. In the early 1870's Illinois, Wisconsin, Minnesota, and Iowa attempted to prescribe equitable rates by direct legislation and established state commissions to compel nondiscriminatory services. Except for Illinois, however, these states failed to accomplish any lasting reform because the railroad interests either regained control of the legislatures and obtained repeal of the regulatory laws or else fought the railroad commissions to a standstill in the state courts. A much more promising movement for railroad reform got under way in Georgia and California in 1879, when both states established expert railroad commissions empowered to set rates.

After the failure of the so-called Granger railroad laws, the midwestern farm organizations came out for federal regulation. This shift was occasioned in part by the general conviction that the railroad problem was beyond the competence of the individual states. It was more immediately a result of the Supreme Court's opinion, rendered in the Wabash case of 1886, that Congress alone could regulate interstate rates and services.

The Wabash decision, therefore, provided the final impetus for an already strong movement for federal legislation. In 1887 Congress passed the Interstate Commerce Act, which decreed that rates should be fair and just, outlawed discriminatory practices, and established the Interstate Commerce Commission. It was an epochal turning point in American political history: the first important turning away from the *laissez-faire* philosophy that had so long prevailed among federal lawmakers. Even so, it soon became evident that the Commerce Act conferred no real authority on the Commission; and the railroad problem was far from being settled when the agrarian revolt of the 1890's exploded in full force.

Obtaining an adequate money supply without wrecking the national financial structure was an even more perplexing problem than railroad regulation. Yet to the embattled farmers, who saw the prices of their commodities decline, the value of their properties shrink, and the burden of their debts grow heavier, this became the vital issue of the last quarter of the nineteenth century.

The money question had its origin in the manner in which the federal government financed the Civil War. During that conflict the Treasury issued about $450,000,000 in greenbacks with no gold backing. The greenbacks depreciated in value and contributed to the inflation of the war period, but they also helped make money plentiful. Once the war was over, however, the business and banking interests demanded and obtained a reduction in the greenback currency and a return to the gold standard in 1879. One result of this deflation was that the per capita circulation declined almost 50 per cent between 1865 and 1879; and as money became dearer the prices of commodities declined. Farmers who had incurred large mortgages during the prosperous years soon found themselves in the position of having to repay the same debts with commodities worth about half as much as when they had borrowed the money.

During the '70's and early '80's the debtor classes viewed the greenback as the means of their salvation; but after 1882 they abandoned paper money and seized upon silver as the most likely instrument of inflation. The reason for this sudden shift in allegiance is not hard to find. Until about 1865 so little silver was mined in the United States that the established ratio between silver and gold of 16 to 1 undervalued silver and drove it out of circulation as money. During the 1860's and early 1870's, however, immense deposits of silver were discovered in the Rocky Mountain region, and production increased so rapidly that by 1879 the old ratio of 16 to 1 greatly overvalued silver and made it the perfect tool of the inflationists. In contrast to greenbacks, silver satisfied the demand that the currency have a metallic basis, while coining silver at the ratio of 16 to 1 would ensure an expanded money supply and increased commodity prices without causing runaway inflation.

From the mid-seventies to about 1898, therefore, the western and southern farmers demanded free and unlimited coinage of silver at the ratio of 16 to 1. In 1878 their representatives in Congress overrode a presidential veto to pass the Bland-Allison Act, which required the Secretary of the Treasury to purchase not less than two nor more than four million dollars of silver monthly. Farm prices rose during the early '80's and the silver agitation subsided; but drought and hard times in the last years of the decade stimulated renewed agitation by the Alliances for free coinage at 16 to 1. So powerful was this demand that Congress in 1890 passed the Sherman Silver Purchase Act, which provided for the purchase by the federal government of almost the entire domestic production. As it turned out, however, the economic dislocations were too fundamental to be corrected by such a simple expedient, and with the coming of the Panic of 1893 the farmers' plight grew infinitely worse.

6 / The Populist Revolt and the Battle of the Standards, 1890–1896

The passage of the Sherman Purchase Act did not halt a sharp new downward spiral of commodity prices that began in 1891. Money was tight, credit almost inflexible, banking facilities woefully inadequate. But since the industrial and banking interests controlled the national leadership of both major parties the farmers could expect little relief from either of them.

In these circumstances the final revolt of the farmers developed with astonishing rapidity. In 1890 the Alliances captured the Democratic party in Tennessee, Georgia, and South Carolina, and by cooperating with the Democrats in the midwestern and Plains states won control of Kansas, Nebraska, South Dakota, and Minnesota. Convinced that the two major parties were beyond the hope of reform, the Alliance leaders next launched their own party—the People's, or Populist party—at Omaha on July 4, 1892. Thus, after nearly two decades of discontent, agrarian unrest finally took shape in political action on a national scale.

The Populist platform, written by Ignatius Donnelly of Minnesota, sounded the battle cry of revolt and set forth a program around which the farmers could rally. It demanded the free and unlimited coinage of silver at the ratio of 16 to 1. At the insistence of southern Alliancemen, it endorsed the so-called sub-treasury plan to establish a federal commodity loan system, under which farmers might borrow against their crops. It demanded also a graduated federal income tax, postal savings banks, public ownership of railroads, telegraph, and telephones; prohibition of alien land ownership and recovery from the railroads of land illegally held; immigration restriction; the eight-hour day for industrial workers, and prohibition of the use of private armies against strikers. Finally, to enable the people to win control of the political machinery and to restore representative government, the Populists demanded the direct election of senators, the initiative and referendum, and the secret ballot.

The adoption of the Populist platform marked the end of an era when practically all Americans put their trust in the English Liberal ideal of a free, competitive economy, operating automatically in the general interest without decisive and planned intervention by government. The adoption of this platform heralded the coming triumph of a new progressive faith—a faith in the ability of men working together to overcome economic adversity and rectify social injustice by legislative action. The later progressive movement went far beyond the Populist charter in elaborating specific remedies, but the spirit, purpose, and assumptions of progressivism were inherited directly from the Populists, the advance guard of a new reform movement.

The Populists did not expect to win the election of 1892, but their beginning was auspicious enough. Indeed, they might well have displaced the Democratic party had the eastern, conservative element continued to dominate that party. Unforeseen events, however, wrecked the existing political alignment and in the end destroyed Populism as an independent movement.

Soon after the Democrat, Grover Cleveland, was inaugurated President in 1893, one of the worst depressions of the nineteenth century began. Convinced that the chief cause of the depression was a lack of confidence in the ability of the Treasury to maintain the gold standard, a lack of confidence induced by the Sherman Purchase Act,[1] Cleveland called Congress into special session in 1893 and obtained repeal of that measure. By this Act, which was accomplished with the help of Republicans, the President split his own party and embittered the agrarian Democrats. Next, Cleveland tried to get honest tariff reform and failed. In 1894 he broke a railroad strike in Chicago by using federal troops and imprisoning the strike leaders. Finally, he further antagonized farmers and debtors by entering into an alliance with Wall Street bankers to keep the government on the gold standard. Cleveland saved the gold standard and disrupted the Democratic party in the process. When the Democrats met in national convention in Chicago in the summer of 1896, the leaders of the southern and western majority took control of proceedings and read Cleveland and his following out of the party. United and aggressive, the agrarians found their new leader and spokesman in William Jennings Bryan, a young congressman-editor from Omaha, who captured the convention by defying Wall Street and demand-

---

[1] This Act required the Treasury to purchase 4,500,000 ounces of silver monthly and to pay for the silver, at the market price, with Treasury notes. The Secretary of the Treasury, moreover, was instructed to redeem these Treasury notes in gold or silver coin.

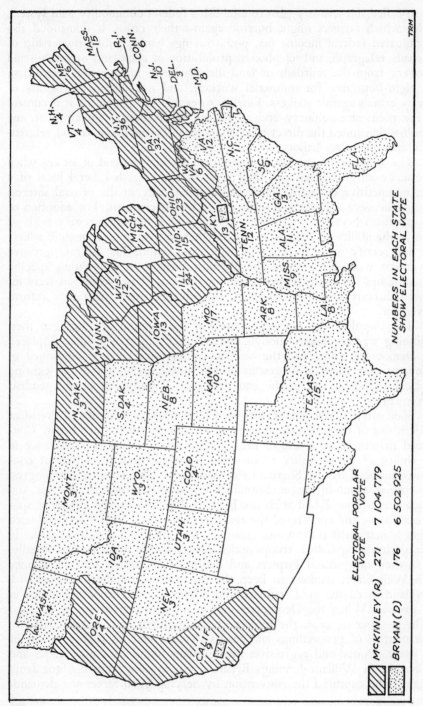

1. *The Election of 1896*

NUMBERS IN EACH STATE
SHOW ELECTORAL VOTE

	ELECTORAL VOTE	POPULAR VOTE
MCKINLEY (R)	271	7 104 779
BRYAN (D)	176	6 502 925

ing the free and unlimited coinage of silver. The toiling producers of America—the farmers and workers—he intoned, must not be crucified upon a Cross of Gold!

Although he was an ardent silverite and a low tariff advocate, Bryan was not yet a radical of the Populist stripe. Moreover, the Democratic platform was neither as well integrated nor as advanced as the Populist platform of 1892. But the Democrats offered enough to the more radical Populists to make fusion inevitable: tariff reform, a graduated income tax, vigorous prosecution of the trusts, and, of course, the free coinage of silver. Thus the agricultural sections, the South and West, united in order to capture control of the federal government from the manufacturing East.

Against the young orator from Nebraska the Republicans pitted William McKinley of Ohio, a spokesman of the business interests and a reluctant champion of the gold standard.

With so much at stake, the business interests rallied behind McKinley and his campaign manager, Mark Hanna. All the influence money could buy was brought to bear against Bryan. Workers by the hundreds of thousands were told not to return to work after election day if the Democrats won. An enormous propaganda, depicting Bryan and his friends as anarchists, seditionists, and potential despoilers, was set in motion. In doubtful states like Indiana, Hanna spent money on a lavish scale.

With all the influence of organized wealth and respectable society marshaled against the Democrats, their defeat was almost inevitable. But Bryan polled 6,503,000 votes, to 7,105,000 for McKinley, and carried the South and many of the states west of the Mississippi. His defeat by such a narrow margin signified that the kind of progressivism he advocated would hereafter be a major force in American politics.

7 / Political and Social Theories, 1865–1900

The political, industrial, and agricultural revolutions from 1865 to 1900 were accompanied by a profound change in the attitudes of thoughtful people toward government and the role it should play in human affairs. Most of the intellectual and literary history of this period is beyond the scope of this discussion. Twentieth century progressivism had deep nineteenth century roots, however, and these we will attempt to describe and analyze. To put it simply, from 1865 to 1900 political and economic thinkers were divided roughly in two major groups: on the one hand, persons who attempted to justify unbridled capitalism and the reign of big business, on the other, those dissident voices who attempted emotionally and intellectually to justify the revolt against *laissez faire*.

The dominant economic interests found their chief justification in the theories of classical economics, the gospel of wealth, and social Darwinism. An intellectual outgrowth of the English commercial and industrial revolutions, so-called classical economics taught that the highest social good could be achieved only by allowing men to pursue their self interests untrammeled by governmental restrictions and unaided by governmental favors. Economists of this school worked out an elaborate body of theory to prove this point and before 1885, at least, a large majority of economists in the United States expounded their doctrines.

The gospel of wealth accepted the classical economic assumptions and attempted to find moral and social justification for the leadership of the captains of industry. Success and the acquisition of wealth, so the argument ran, were the just rewards of industry, thrift, and sobriety, while the great mass of humanity remained poor because of their own indolence and natural inferiority. Government, the propounders of the gospel of wealth argued, should merely preserve order and protect property; it should leave control over the economy to the natural aristocracy, who won and held their leadership in competitive struggle. On the other hand, these natural aristocrats owed large obligations to society, precisely because they were the stewards of the national wealth.

Social Darwinism, however, was probably the most important economic and social philosophy in the last third of the nineteenth century. As an integrated system, it was largely the product of the fertile brain of Herbert Spencer, an English political philosopher. Profoundly impressed by Darwin's findings in the field of biology, Spencer attempted to construct his system on the principles of survival of the fittest and the evolution of organisms from the simple to the complex. Darwin had seen in the animal world a fierce struggle for survival that destroyed the weak, rewarded the strong, and produced evolutionary change. Struggle, destruction, and the survival of the fit, Spencer contended, were essential to progress in human society as well. The weak stood athwart the high road to progress and deserved to perish. The strong survived because they were superior. As this was an elemental law of social development, it was futile for government to try to help the weak survive.

As social Darwinism so obviously repudiated the humane and Christian principles upon which the American democratic tradition rested, how can we account for Spencer's great popularity in the United States? To begin with, he offered to intellectuals of the period a scientific system to replace the shattered orthodox Christian cosmogony. As one historian has pointed out, Spencer offered "a comprehensive world-view, uniting under one generalization everything in nature from protozoa to politics."[2] In the second place, Spencer's philosophy was easily understood; it made a philosopher of the crossroad sage because it confirmed his own deductions. Finally, social Darwinism was made to order to suit the needs of the ruling business oligarchy. In the name of progress it justified economic warfare, poverty, exploitation, and suffering. And there was nothing organized society, that is, government, could really do, because attempts at amelioration would only create graver social problems.

The opposite concept of positive government found its prophet in Henry George, author of *Progress and Poverty*, published in 1879, and many other tracts, and best known for his proposal of a single tax on unearned increments in land values. But the single tax was not the concept that changed men's lives and stimulated a whole host to undertake a crusade for social and economic reform. The significant feature of George's philos-

[2] Richard Hofstadter, *Social Darwinism in American Thought, 1860–1915* (Philadelphia, 1944), p. 18.

ophy was his assertion that men could reconstruct society by collective political action. In place of the complacency of social Darwinism, he offered confidence in a future bright with the promise of social and economic betterment. As the leading democratic philosopher of the Gilded Age, Henry George became the chief link between the reform movements of the antebellum period and the progressive movement of the twentieth century.

On the other hand, the task of converting American intellectuals to a positive concept of the state fell mainly to a sociologist, Lester Frank Ward, who published his major work, *Dynamic Sociology*, in 1883. Ward was a social evolutionist like Spencer, but he drew a sharp difference between purposeless animal evolution and human evolution, which he said could be decisively modified by artificial control of natural phenomena. In brief, *Dynamic Sociology* was essentially an argument for controlled social and economic development. Although few among his generation ever heard Ward's name, his influence on a large school of young sociologists and economists exceeded that of any other contemporary American.

American economists could also boast of their own revolt against Spencer and William Graham Sumner, the chief American expositor of social Darwinism. Most of the young insurgents who repudiated their classical masters had been trained in the historical school of economics, either in Germany or at the new Johns Hopkins University in Baltimore. Gathering at Saratoga, New York, in the autumn of 1885, they organized the American Economic Association and adopted a statement of principles that was tantamount to a declaration of war against the classical school. Asserting that the positive intervention of the state was one of the indispensable conditions of human progress, they went on to declare that changing economic conditions must be met by changing progressive legislation.

Finally, there could be no real mass support for the new progressive concepts until the religious leaders of the United States had awakened to the challenge of social Darwinism and joined in the movement to make the industrial-financial regime responsible to the people. Accompanying the revolt against *laissez faire* among political and intellectual leaders went a humanitarian movement in American Protestantism called the social gospel, which we will review in a later chapter. So powerful was this movement that by 1900 most of the large denominations had moved well along the road toward social Christianity.

8 / *The End of An Era*

The last four years of the nineteenth century witnessed the return of prosperity and confidence and the ending of a long era of relative isolation from international politics by the United States. A number of factors combined to produce the economic upswing. To begin with, McKinley's election in 1896 assured the business and financial communities that the federal government would continue to pursue friendly policies and would not tamper with the currency. In the second place, the Russian wheat crop of 1896–1897 was short to the point of famine, and western Europe had to buy more wheat than usual in the United States. The American wheat crops of 1897 and 1898 were abnormally large; but the pressure of European buying drove the price from 78 cents a bushel in 1896 to 95 cents in 1897 and 1898. Thirdly, governmental spending and recruitment of manpower during the War with Spain in the spring and summer of 1898 added yet another stimulus to economic activity. Fourthly, there occurred at the same time a spectacular increase in the world's gold production, which stimulated world-wide inflationary tendencies.

With an increased money supply and a spurt of new industrial activity, bank clearings increased one-third from 1898 to 1899, steel rails doubled in price between February and August of the latter year, while wholesale prices increased 23 per cent between 1896 and 1900. With the return of prosperity, agrarian discontent subsided almost at once, and, as the flames of Populism died, a new fever seized upon the American people—a fever of imperialism, of a new kind of manifest destiny to extend civilization to the so-called backward peoples of the earth. Allegedly to save the Cubans from Spanish brutality and tyranny, Americans righteously went to war with Spain in 1898; and after a short and glorious adventure they awoke to find themselves a world power with a colonial empire in the Caribbean and the Far East.

By the Treaty of Paris of 1898 the United States took possession of Puerto Rico and the Philippine Islands and assumed responsibility for the government of Cuba as well. Although the Democrats had enough votes in the Senate to defeat ratification of the Treaty, their leader, Bryan, persuaded them to ratify the peace settlement and to try to make imperialism the paramount issue of the impending presidential campaign.

The campaign of 1900, which for a second time pitted McKinley against Bryan, was bitterly fought. Joined by Boston and New York anti-imperialists, the Democrats contended that democracy and imperialism could not coexist in the same political system and that the United States would abandon its moral leadership of the world if it went into the business of governing alien peoples. On the other hand, strident young expansionists like Theodore Roosevelt, Henry Cabot Lodge, and Albert J. Beveridge replied by defending "the national honor" and pointing to a new destiny for the American people. McKinley won a sweeping victory, but it is doubtful if the voters rendered any verdict on imperialism. A majority of them probably voted against Bryanism and for prosperity.

At the turn of the century, therefore, Americans were both in an exuberant and an uncertain mood. They entered the new century confident of their ability to make things work out at home, but the venture into imperialism had raised grave misgivings for the future of the American democracy. Although a majority would probably have denied it, their long isolation was now shattered and their government would have to play an active role in world affairs in the years to come. What the future would bring no man could foretell; but all thoughtful observers agreed that one era was dead beyond recall and that a new epoch in America was just beginning.

CHAPTER 2 / *THE AMERICAN PEOPLE BEFORE THE FIRST WORLD WAR*

*T*HE YEARS from 1897 to 1914 were a golden period of American development. They were usually prosperous years, marked by solid progress in living standards for most classes. It was, moreover, a comfortable, hopeful age. Confident they had the ability to set aright the social and economic injustices inherited from the nineteenth century, Americans in the early 1900's launched a virtual crusade on all levels of government to revitalize democracy, bring the economic machinery under their control, and find an answer to the twin evils of special privilege and poverty.

The years before the First World War were, finally, a period when Christian moralism subdued the crass materialism of the Gilded Age, and morality and righteousness became the keynotes of politics. The YMCA movement swept through the colleges and universities, and social Christianity triumphed over Calvinism, as man's first duty became love of man instead of God. Drunkenness, prostitution, the exploitation of women and children, stock watering—these and other evils must fall before the reformer's trumpet blast!

9 / *The American People, 1900–1910: a Demographic View*

From 1900 to 1910 the population of the United States increased 21 per cent, from 75,994,575 to 91,972,266 souls. Although 70 per cent of the people lived east of the Mississippi River in 1910, the most spectacular growth had occurred in the West. The Pacific states, for example, grew 73.5 per cent over the decade, as contrasted with a growth of 25 per cent among the Middle Atlantic states between 1900 and 1910.

The most striking trend in American population from 1900 to 1910, however, was the steadily increasing migration of people from the countryside to the cities. Urban population grew by 34.8 per cent from 1900 to 1910, a rate of increase three times that of the rural areas. In 1900, 40.5 per cent of the people lived in towns and cities over 2,500. By 1910, on the other hand, the percentage of town and city dwellers was 46.3; and, if we include persons living in incorporated towns under 2,500, the percentage of urban

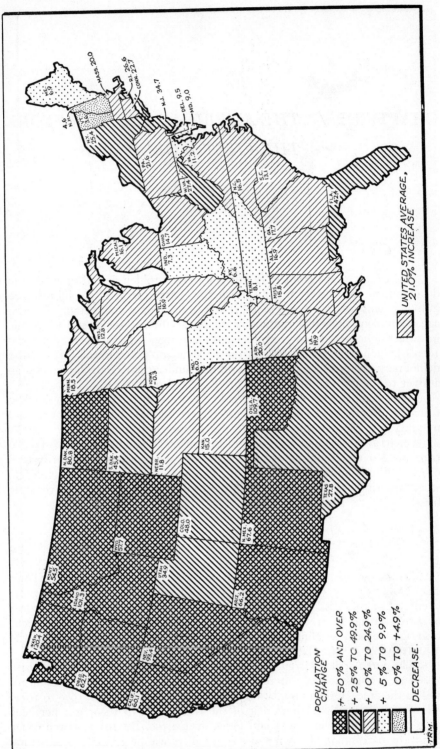

POPULATION
CHANGE

+ 50% AND OVER
+ 25% TC 49.9%
+ 10% TO 24.9%
+ 5% TO 9.9%
0% TO +4.9%

DECREASE.

UNITED STATES AVERAGE,
21.0% INCREASE

2. *Population Change, 1900–1910*

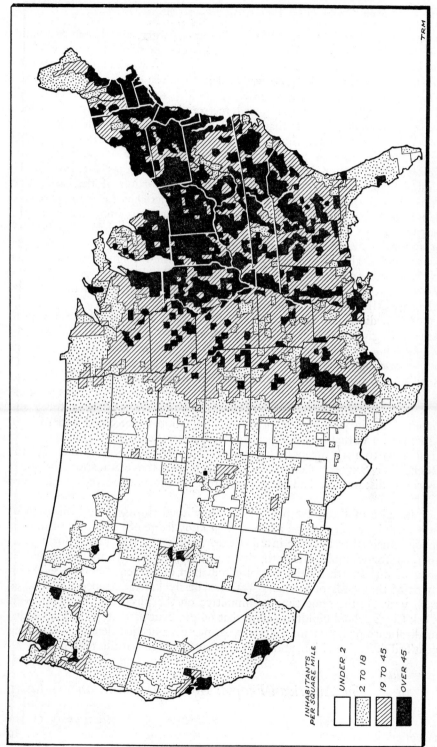

INHABITANTS
PER SQUARE MILE.

UNDER 2

2 TO 18

19 TO 45

OVER 45

3. *Population Density in 1910*

population was actually 55.1. As the cities grew larger, they began to acquire a different character, more and more becoming centers of commerce and industry, where people from outlying areas went to work and then returned to suburban homes. This trend was evidenced in the growth of the so-called metropolitan districts, that is, cities of 200,000 or over with a number of outlying suburbs. There were 25 such metropolitan districts in 1910, in which 22,088,331 people, or more than one-fifth of the total population, resided.

What were the racial and national origins of the American people in 1910? Most of them—88.9 per cent, to be exact—were white. There were almost half a million Indians and Orientals and 9,827,763 Negroes in the United States, but Negroes were a smaller proportion of the population in 1910 than they had been in 1900. Most Americans in 1910 were also native-born; but under the impact of the tremendous immigration of the past decade the numbers of the foreign-born had increased from 10,341,276, or 13.6 per cent of the total population, in 1900 to 13,515,886, or 14.7 per cent of the total in 1910. Nearly 85 per cent of the foreign-born lived either in the North or Middle West, but 89 per cent of the Negroes lived in the South, with the highest concentration in South Carolina, Georgia, Florida, Alabama, Mississippi, and Louisiana.

As medical knowledge expanded through experience and research, Americans grew healthier every year from 1900 to 1914. Indeed, the progress of medicine in overcoming the ancient ravagers of mankind during this period was spectacular. The death rate in areas where reliable statistics were kept declined from 19.7 per thousand in 1900 to 15.3 per thousand for whites, and from 33.3 to 26.8 per thousand for Negroes. In part this progress was made possible by a sharp decline in deaths from typhoid fever and tuberculosis, in part by the practical elimination of smallpox and malaria. Moreover, a virtual physiological revolution was accomplished in the South from 1909 to 1914 through the work of Doctor Charles W. Stiles and the Rockefeller Sanitary Commission in beginning the eradication of hookworm, a disease that had long enervated a large portion of the southern people.

In spite of the great progress accomplished through the utilization of new techniques, drugs, and a broadening knowledge of the causes of disease, much remained to be done in this field by the eve of the First World War. In 1909, for example, one authority concluded that the death rate could be reduced one-fourth by the partial elimination of preventable diseases. Hundreds of thousands of workers were needlessly killed, maimed, or disabled each year. At the same time a committee on the physical welfare of New York City's school children found that 66 per cent of these children needed medical care or better nourishment, 40 per cent needed dental care, 31 per cent had defective vision, and 6 per cent suffered from malnutrition.

10 / *The American People: Income, Wealth, and Industry*

The most striking economic phenomenon of the first years of the twentieth century was the steady increase in the wealth and income of the people of the United States. Adjusted to fluctuations in the cost of living, the total national income increased from $16,158,000,000, or $480 per capita, at the turn of the century, to $31,213,000,000, or $565 per capita, on the eve of the World War. The economic progress of the period can also be read in the steadily increasing volume of industrial production. To state the

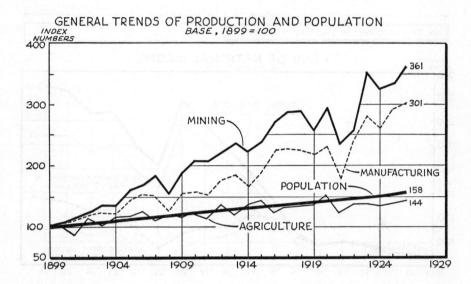

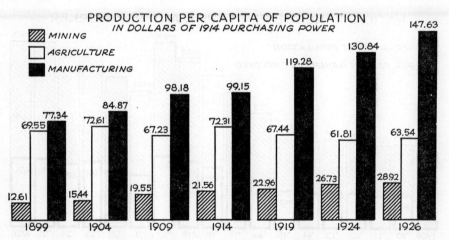

1. *The Economic Growth of the United States, 1899–1926*

matter briefly, during the decade 1899–1909, when population increased by only 22 per cent, the number of manufacturing establishments increased 29.4 per cent; the capital invested, 105.3 per cent; the average number of wage earners, 40.4 per cent; and the value of products turned out, 76.6 per cent.

The major manufacturing industries in 1909 were still the enterprises that furnished the basic necessities—meat packing, iron and steel, foundries and machine shops, lumbering, milling, clothing, textiles, printing and publishing, and tobacco. By 1914, however, signs of the future development of a new technology were already evident. The automobile industry, with a

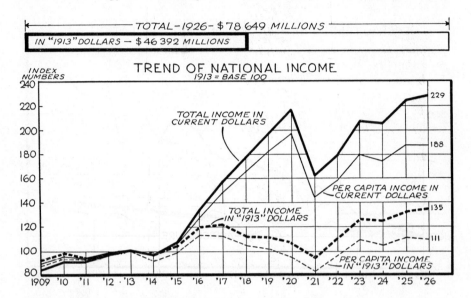

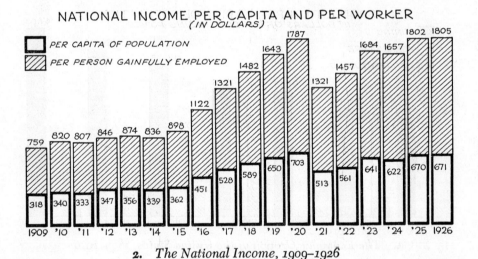

2. *The National Income, 1909–1926*

total product valued at $503,230,000 in 1914, ranked eighth in importance. Although the petroleum industry did not yet rank among the major enterprises, the production of oil and oil products was rapidly increasing.

Out of a total population in 1910 of 71,580,270 persons ten years of age and over, 30,091,565 men and 8,075,772 women were gainfully employed.

Among this working force the carpenters, painters, brickmasons, printers, and other skilled and organized craftsmen enjoyed the shortest working hours and the highest wages. But only 500,000 persons in nonagricultural pursuits worked 48 hours a week or less, while 4,000,000 worked between 54 and 60 hours a week, almost 500,000 between 60 and 72 hours, and over 100,000 more than 12 hours a day, six and seven days a week.

Generally speaking, the prewar years were marked by steady employ-ment and a rising material standard of living for most classes. Yet the benefits of prosperity were not always distributed evenly, and the process of the concentration of incomes and wealth in fewer hands went on apace. Accord-ing to the best estimates, the richest families, constituting 1.6 per cent of the population, received 10.8 per cent of the national income in 1896 and 19 per cent in 1910. Moreover, the wealthiest 1 per cent owned about 47 per

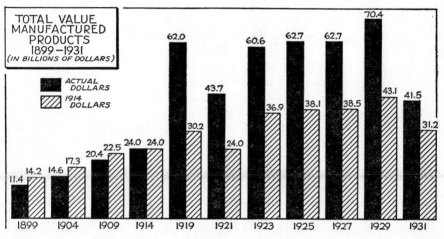

3. *The Growth of American Manufactures, 1899–1931*

cent of the national wealth and received about 15 per cent of the national income in 1910. In short, although the poor were not becoming poorer, the rich were gaining faster than the lower and middle classes.

11 / *American Agriculture Finds Stability*

During this period of industrial expansion, American agriculture enjoyed such stability and prosperity as it had not known since 1865. From 1900 to 1910 the rural population increased by 11.2 per cent, acreage under cultiva-tion by 15.4 per cent, and gross farm income by more than 100 per cent.

One result of this phenomenal increase in farm income was unparalleled prosperity for farmers during a period when what they received for the products they sold equaled what they paid for the goods they purchased. Another result was a general increase of more than 100 per cent in the value of farm property.

Although the doubling of the value of farm property added to the wealth and security of the landowning class, it also made the acquisition of land more difficult, at a time when the supply of free arable land was about exhausted. Thus, while the number of farm owners increased 8.1 per cent from 1900–1910, the number of tenants increased 16.3 per cent. In 1910 37 per cent of all farms were operated by tenants, as contrasted with 35.3 per cent in 1900 and 25.6 per cent in 1880.

Farm tenancy, especially sharecropping, was so common in the South that its prevalence in that region evoked little comment. But the spread of tenancy through the heartland of the Middle West during the two decades before the First World War was so rapid as to raise the question of whether a large minority of midwestern farmers were not rapidly approaching a condition of peasantry. In 1914 one authority concluded that 40 per cent of the farms in the corn belt were operated by tenants. In 1910 38 per cent of the farms in the rich state of Iowa were worked by tenants.

12 / The Changing Tide of Immigration

Down to the outbreak of the First World War immigration was the most persistent and one of the most important forces in American history, for the development of the United States was in large measure governed by the ebbing and onrushing tide of alien peoples to the Atlantic shores. Between 1860 and 1900 almost 14,000,000 immigrants came to the United States, and over 14,500,000 followed from 1900 to 1915. The majority of immigrants after 1860 came from England, Ireland, Germany, and Scandinavia, people akin culturally and historically to Americans. Around 1880, however, there began an immigration of peoples heretofore unfamiliar to most Americans—Italians, Slavs, Magyars, and Jews from southern and eastern Europe. This so-called "new" immigration accounted for only 18.3 per cent of the total in the decade from 1881 to 1890, but it soon became a rushing stream. From 1891–1900 almost 52 per cent of the immigrants were from southern and eastern Europe, and from 1901–1910 the proportion grew to 72 per cent. Let us examine the three major groups of "new" immigrants and ascertain the causes for their coming to a country with a civilization so different from their own.

The Italians. Italian emigration to the United States began slowly in the 1880's and reached important proportions about 1900. From 1901 to 1910 more than 2,000,000 Italians came to the United States, and an additional 1,100,000 entered during the four years before the war. The high mark was reached in 1907, when over 292,000 passed through the gates at Ellis Island.

Of all the western nations, Italy alone deliberately encouraged emigration and used it as an instrument of national policy to rid herself of surplus population and increase the supply of gold from abroad. The great majority of Italian immigrants came from Sicily and the southern provinces, where living standards were lowest and estates were largest. The Italian peasant, moreover, faced the unpleasant prospect of serving two years in the army as a conscript. Finally, to aggravate an already unhappy situation, the Italian birthrate was one of the highest in Europe, so that only an extraordinary death rate kept population from increasing to the point of disaster. To escape the lash of the landlord and the army officer and starvation as well, therefore, millions of Italians fled to the United States, Argentina, Brazil, and Uruguay.

The Slavs. The migration of the Slavic peoples of eastern Europe to the

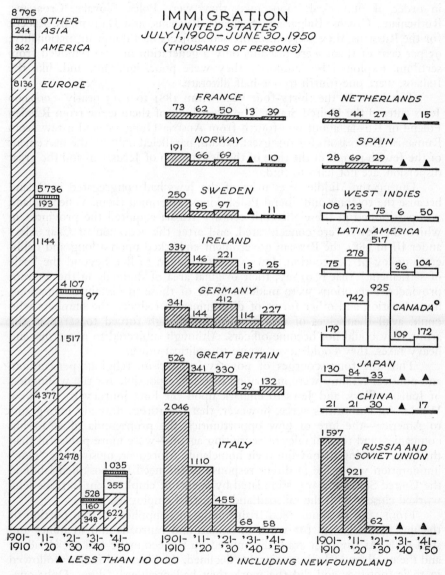

IMMIGRATION
UNITED STATES
JULY 1, 1900 – JUNE 30, 1950
(THOUSANDS OF PERSONS)

▲ LESS THAN 10 000   ○ INCLUDING NEWFOUNDLAND

4. *Immigration, 1900–1950*

United States exceeded even the outpouring of the Italians and constituted the major element in the "new" immigration. From Austria-Hungary and Russia, which governed most of the Slavic peoples before the First World War, there came 619,000 immigrants during the decade 1881–1890, 1,191,000 from 1891–1900, and over 5,500,000 from 1900 to 1914. As these figures include about 1,500,000 Jews, we must reckon the total Slavic immigration to the United States from 1881 to 1914 at about 6,000,000.

Who were they, these peoples from central and eastern Europe? Ranked in order of numerical importance, they were Poles, Slovaks, Croatians, Ruthenians, Czechs, Bulgarians, Serbians, Russians, and Dalmatians. Except for the Russians, they were all oppressed subjects of a dominant nationality; 95 per cent of them were peasants only a generation or two removed from serfdom. Exploited by landlords, they were poor, ignorant, and, like the Italians, were one-fourth to one-half illiterate.

The Jews. In the thirty-four years from 1881 to 1915 nearly 2,000,000 Jews entered the United States. The great bulk of them came from Russian Poland or Russia, about one-fourth from Austria-Hungary, and a few from Rumania. The reasons for this great exodus, paralleled only by the movement of the Jewish people at the time of the destruction of Jerusalem and the great dispersion, are not hard to find.

During the Middle Ages most of the Jews had congregated in Poland because the tolerant and liberal Polish kings welcomed them. When Poland was partitioned in the eighteenth century Russia acquired the provinces in which the Jews were concentrated, and after the accession of Czar Alexander III in 1881 the Russian government embarked upon a long and deliberate policy of persecution. Jews were forbidden to live beyond the "pale of settlement," that is to say, their original area of domicile in the western provinces. Exceptions were made in favor of those in certain occupations, but education and other forms of discrimination reduced the numbers who could avail themselves of this privilege. Although forced to serve in the army, they could not become officers. Although subjected to numerous and heavy taxes, they could never aspire to political office.

Thus the four scourges of poverty, militarism, religious persecution, and political tyranny were in varying degrees responsible for the willingness of Italians, Slavs, and Jews to embark upon the long journey to the New World. All authorities agree, however, that the forces drawing immigrants to America—the lure of new opportunities, the propaganda of steamship companies, and the tall tales of recruiting agents—were more powerful than the forces driving them from their homelands. Moreover, most of the "new" immigration was made in direct response to the need for unskilled labor in the United States and was stimulated by agents of employment bureaus who worked closely with the railroad and industrial employers.

From 1846 to about 1890 Irish immigrants supplied a large portion of the unskilled laborers for work on canals and railroads and in mines and steel mills. As the Irish gradually moved up the economic and social ladder and the numbers of Irish immigrants declined, the Slavs and Italians followed in their footsteps and did the work they had previously done. Only one-sixth of the Italians, 3 to 5 per cent of the Ruthenians, Croatians, Rumanians, and Slovaks, and 8 to 10 per cent of the Magyars and Poles were skilled workers when they came to the United States. Invariably they went to the industrial areas of the East and Middle West and found employment on the railroads, in the textile factories of New England, in the steel mills of Pittsburgh and Chicago, in the stockyards of the Middle West, and in coal mines from Pennsylvania to Colorado. By 1914 they constituted the bulk of the working force in the basic industries. Although as poor as other eastern European immigrants, the Jews brought with them a high degree of skill and experience in the trades. They congregated in the garment sweat-shops of New York, Chicago, and other large cities mainly because they found Jewish employers in the clothing industry.

13 / The Social Impact of the New Immigration

The fact that the American society absorbed this transfusion of new and different national strains without violent reactions was testimony to its growing maturity and adaptability. And yet it was everywhere evident that the processes of social assimilation, which had on the whole worked admirably among the Germans, Irish, and Scandinavians, practically ceased to operate among the newer immigrants. Older Americans viewed them suspiciously and thought they were an inferior people, incapable of understanding American ideals.

This hostility was evidenced in the formation in 1887 of the American Protective Association, an anti-Catholic organization much like the Know-Nothing party of the 1850's, and in the spreading fear that the "new" immigration would undermine Anglo-American institutions and eventually dilute the old American racial stock. It was reflected, also, in the absence of any governmental effort to protect the immigrant from exploitation and thievery. But the worst aspect of the record was the exploitation of these immigrants by the railroads and industries. Surveying the American scene in 1915, the Commission on Industrial Relations noted that two-thirds of the immigrant families lived on a subsistence level or below.

Before 1882 all foreigners, regardless of race, nationality, or physical and moral condition, could enter the United States. In that year, however, the first general federal immigration act was passed, and the process of restriction was begun when, at the insistent demand of Californians, Chinese were excluded for ten years. Re-enacted from time to time, the Chinese Exclusion Act was made permanent in 1902. No sooner had the fears of Californians been quieted regarding the prospect of a Chinese inundation than another and more alarming prospect arose—the specter of an invasion of the state by Japanese workers and farmers. There were only 2,000 Japanese subjects in the United States in 1890, but two decades later their number had increased to 110,000. Agitation for exclusion of the Japanese, powerful and well organized, led to the negotiation by the State Department in 1907 of an agreement with the Japanese government that virtually ended Japanese immigration to the continental United States.

Thus by 1907 almost complete exclusion of Orientals had been accomplished. Moreover, the doors had been shut against paupers, the sick and diseased, polygamists, prostitutes, contract laborers, anarchists, and convicts. By this time, however, the demand for a severe restriction, if not outright exclusion, of most European immigrants was mounting on all sides. Organized labor, for example, asserted that heavy immigration depressed wages and impeded the progress of unionization; and this assertion was confirmed by the federal Immigration Commission appointed in 1907. The weapon the exclusionists advocated at this time was a literacy test. President Cleveland had vetoed a bill imposing such a test in 1897. In 1913 and again in 1915 such a measure passed Congress only to be nullified by the vetoes of Presidents Taft and Wilson. Finally, in January 1917, the exclusionists in Congress mustered sufficient strength to pass an immigration bill that imposed the literacy test over Wilson's veto. Thus, the open door to America—for centuries the gateway of opportunity for countless millions—was partially closed.

14 / *American Negroes, 1897–1914*

The most tragic aspect of the American social scene during the years before the First World War was the condition of Negroes in the United States. Foreign observers could never cease to wonder how Americans could boast of democracy and at the same time deny essential democratic privileges to one-tenth of the population. The great paradox was not resolved during the progressive period. In fact, by and large the social and political status of Negroes worsened from 1897 to 1914, while their economic status only slightly improved.

Optimists, to be sure, could point to a few signs of progress since 1865. Demonstrating a passion for education in the face of incredible obstacles, Negroes had reduced their illiteracy rate from 95 per cent in 1865 to 44.5 per cent in 1900. And even greater progress was made during the decade 1900–1910. The illiteracy rate among Negroes 10 years of age and over declined to 30.4 per cent in 1910, while illiteracy among Negro children 10 to 14 years of age declined from 30.1 per cent in 1900 to 18.9 per cent in 1910.

The Negro's progress toward education had been accomplished before 1900 with the help of the northern philanthropists and churches and only slightly with the aid of the southern states. After 1900, however, there was an increasing awareness throughout the white South, especially in the border states, of the need for greater public aid to Negro education. Even so, no southern state on the eve of the World War was making a serious effort to provide adequate or anywhere near equal educational opportunities for its Negro youth. In 1910, for example, there were only 141 Negro high schools, with 8,251 pupils, in all the states from Maryland to Texas.

Meanwhile, social and political forces had been at work in the South to make the progressive era a time of profound discouragement for Negroes. For one thing, the Civil War and Reconstruction had not altered southern race concepts or southern determination to keep the Negroes in an inferior status. For another, slavery had given way to sharecropping, so that the vast majority of Negroes found not economic freedom after 1865 but merely another form of bondage. As a substitute for the social controls of slavery, which went by the board in 1865, the southern whites after Reconstruction substituted a legal caste system that prohibited intermarriage and established a severe pattern of segregation for schools, public places, and transportation facilities. Informal race controls, moreover, were tightened, and many a

Negro suffered the extreme penalty for violating the rules of racial etiquette. Finally, in the late 1870's and early 1880's many southern states began gradually to make voting by Negroes difficult. The southern legislatures acted cautiously in this regard, however, and as late as the 1890's large numbers of Negroes voted in many southern states.

During the Populist revolt a genuine political division among the white voters occurred for the first time since 1860, and both Democrats and Populists bid for Negro votes. This resurgence of Negro political activity frightened both agrarian and conservative Southerners and led them to conclude that the Negro must be removed forever as a dynamic factor in southern political life.

In 1890 Mississippi had pointed the way to disfranchise the great mass of Negro voters—by use of the literacy test, the poll tax, provisions requiring an understanding of the Constitution, and long residence requirements for registration—without openly violating the Fifteenth Amendment. Then, as an aftermath of the revival of Negro political activity during the Populist upsurge, from 1895–1907 all the southern states except Maryland, Tennessee, and Kentucky disfranchised their Negro voters.

The one man who, more than any other person, brought peace between the races in the South after this bloody decade of conflict was Booker T. Washington, whose rise to leadership of the Negro people was one of the most dramatic episodes in the history of the United States. Born a slave in Franklin County, Virginia, in 1856 and educated at Hampton Institute in his native state, Washington founded Tuskegee Institute in Alabama in 1881 as a school where Negro boys and girls might learn to become useful members of southern communities as teachers, farmers, and tradesmen. By 1895 Washington was recognized as the preeminent spokesman of American Negroes, and it came as something of an official pronouncement when, at the height of the disfranchisement movement, he counseled them to eschew politics and learn to become good citizens. His program of vocational education and political quiescence for Negroes was seized upon by whites all over the country as a formula for racial peace.

This so-called Washington Compromise found favor among conservative Southerners and won their support for Negro education. But it did not operate to diminish the anti-Negro passions of the southern masses. The Populist revolt brought to the fore a new leadership of violent men. Some, like Cole L. Blease of South Carolina, were sheer demagogues; others, like Hoke Smith of Georgia, had many qualities of statesmanship. All of these new leaders, however, rose to power on a wave of anti-Negroism that found expression in violence in many forms. The last sixteen years of the nineteenth century had witnessed more than 2,500 lynchings, and the century had ended with a race riot in Wilmington, North Carolina, the climax of the disfranchisement campaign in that state. This was followed in the twentieth century by other riots, the worst of which occurred in Atlanta in September 1906, which degenerated into a mass slaughter. Moreover, lynching continued in the twentieth century to be an important aspect of race control, as more than 1,100 Negroes fell victims, from 1900 to 1914, to mobs that often discarded the rope for the faggot.

To Negroes, however, the most frightening development of this period

was the way in which the southern race concepts and the southern techniques of violence spread to the North and Middle West. Southern orators
like Ben R. Tillman of South Carolina carried the message of white supremacy to northern audiences and stimulated latent prejudices. The most
effective southern propagandist, however, was Thomas Dixon, an erstwhile
Baptist minister of North Carolina, whose novels, *The Leopard's Spots*
(1902) and *The Clansman* (1905), were calculated to arouse the basest racial
prejudices of white readers and which sold by the hundreds of thousands.
The Clansman was made into a motion picture, "The Birth of a Nation," in
1915, and was a powerful factor in stimulating race riots in the North and
Middle West during and after the First World War.

Small wonder it was, therefore, that the progressive era was a dreary
period for sensitive Negroes, ambitious for the advancement of their race.
There was, however, one ray of hope: the development of an aggressive
and advanced leadership among both races. Foremost among the militant
Negroes was a young scholar, William E. B. DuBois, a native of Massachusetts with a doctor's degree in history from Harvard University. In June
1905 DuBois and a small group of Negro intellectuals met at Niagara Falls,
Canada, adopted a platform demanding political and economic equality for
black men, and announced to the world their determination to begin a new
war for emancipation. Meeting the following year at Harpers Ferry, West
Virginia, the site of John Brown's raid, the Niagara Movement, as the
DuBois group was called, reiterated its resolves and renewed its courage.

Progressives and champions of social justice in the North, however, at
first paid scant attention to the Niagara rebels. Then, in August 1908, an
anti-Negro riot occurred in Springfield, Illinois, within half a mile of Lincoln's home, and humanitarians in the North at last awoke to the imminent
threat of the southernizing of their section. The following February, on
Lincoln's birthday, the young Negro rebels and a distinguished group of
white educators, clergymen, editors, and social workers met in New York
City and organized the National Association for the Advancement of Colored
People, pledged to work for the abolition of all forced segregation, equal
justice for Negroes, and enlarged educational opportunities for Negro children. The only Negro official of the NAACP during its formative period
was DuBois, who was director of publicity and research and editor of the
Association's monthly magazine, *The Crisis*. But the selection of DuBois as
the official spokesman of the organization signified that the revolt against the
Washington Compromise had at last found powerful support among progressive groups in the North and held promise for the day when the northern
people would rediscover their equalitarian heritage.

15 / *The Growth of American Education*

At the turn of the century the federal Commissioner of Education could
boast of the steady development of educational institutions since 1890 and
of an increase of 19.2 per cent in the numbers of children enrolled in public
and private schools and institutions of higher learning. These general national
statistics, however, obscure the details of the educational picture in the

various regions. Progress in the North and Midwest, for example, was even more substantial than they would indicate. On the other hand, the situation in the South in 1900 was so gloomy that leaders of the region wondered if there were any hope at all. Southern children received on an average three years of public schooling, as compared with an average of nearly seven years for northern children. The southern states spent an average of $9.72 per pupil in 1900, as compared with an expenditure of $20.85 per pupil in the North Central states. To use the words of a contemporary southern educator, the situation in his region was "sad beyond expression."

The general educational picture had improved perceptibly by the eve of the First World War, but the most significant advances are not revealed by general statistics. To begin with, the growth of kindergartens since 1900 had evidenced the expanding influence in America of the champions of the child of pre-school age. In 1900 only about 250 cities had established kindergartens. By 1914, on the other hand, there were almost 9,000 separate kindergartens, with nearly half a million children enrolled. Even more important, however, was the remarkable expansion of the public high schools from 1900 to 1914. In 1900 there were about 6,000 public high schools in the United States, with 500,000 pupils. In contrast, by 1914 there were 11,500 such high schools, with 1,218,807 students.

The most important educational revolution in this period occurred, however, in the South. Under the spur of publicists like Walter H. Page and philanthropic agencies like the Southern Education Board, political leaders launched virtual crusades for education in the southern states. The result was a mass awakening in the South from 1902 to about 1910, comparable to the educational revival that swept through the North and Middle West before the Civil War. In the short span of a decade, appropriations for school purposes by the southern states doubled, the enrollment of white children increased almost a third, and the average length of the school term lengthened from five to six months. Southern illiteracy, moreover, by 1910 had declined from 11.8 to 7.7 per cent of the native whites over 10 years of age and from 48 to 33.3 per cent of the Negroes 10 years of age or older.

While the nation was annually recording progress in all areas of public education from the late '90's to 1914, a revolution in the theory and practice of education was also getting under way. By the turn of the century the theories of educational psychologists and experimentalists were undermining older pedagogical theories and stimulating a new scientific attitude toward children. In the years before the war these so-called progressive theories gained wider acceptance, especially after the philosopher, John Dewey of Columbia University, assumed leadership of the movement.

Dewey set out to fulfill the American dream of a public school system that was the chief training ground for democracy. Repudiating the classical tradition that emphasized formal and polite learning, he advocated a curriculum that had meaning for an urban age and prepared the child to live in a democratic society. He taught, moreover, that curriculum and subject matter should be adapted to the needs and capabilities of children and not of adults; that the learning process should be centered around the child's own experiences; and that "learning by doing" should supplant memorization of data that had no meaning to the child. Although his theories were assailed by traditionalists and sometimes violently abused by his own disciples, Dewey left such a deep imprint on American educational theory and practice that it can be said that he, almost single-handed, accomplished one of the significant cultural revolutions of his time.

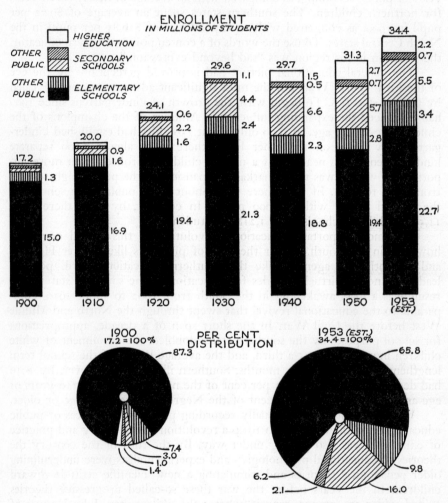

5. American Public Education: a Half Century of Growth, 1900–1953

Meanwhile, important developments were also taking place in higher education in the United States. For one thing, the formation of the Association of American Universities in 1900 and of regional associations soon afterward marked the beginning of a concerted campaign to raise academic standards all over the country. The result was an actual decrease in the number of colleges and universities from 1900 to 1914, at the same time that their enrollment increased from 109,929 to 216,493. Other important changes were taking place in this field: facilities for graduate and specialized training were enormously improved; there was a significant development of technical education and growth of private institutions like the Massachusetts Institute of Technology and state engineering and agricultural colleges; new methods of teaching were introduced; the states expanded their aid to universities, colleges, and junior colleges; and there was the beginning of an important adult education movement. By the eve of the First World War all Americans could rejoice in the tremendous advancement of their colleges and universities since 1897. No longer was the United States a cultural appendage of Europe in the field of higher learning. No longer did Americans have to go to Germany for graduate training. In fact, the day was not far distant when American scholarship could claim preeminence in many fields.

16 / *Religious Institutions and Movements, 1897–1914*

The most important social phenomenon of the prewar period was the survival of religion after the violent storms of the last quarter of the nineteenth century. The growth of skepticism, the war between the Darwinists and the fundamentalists, and the spread of new philosophies like Marxian scientific materialism and social Darwinism had so promoted the growth of secularism that by 1914 probably a large majority of American intellectuals would have disavowed Christian beliefs. Yet Christian ethics and ideals not only survived but found wider acceptance and fuller meaning. American Protestantism largely abandoned literal fundamentalism and rediscovered the ancient Christian message of social justice, while the Roman Catholic Church expanded its ministrations to the poor.

For all religious groups the years before the taking of the religious census in 1916 were a period of substantial growth in numbers, influence, and wealth. All told, the Protestant bodies enrolled 26,205,039 members in 1916, as compared with 20,857,303 in 1906, and among the Protestant denominations the Baptist and Methodist bodies were easily the most numerous and powerful. But the most spectacular religious development during the period 1890–1916 was the tremendous growth of the Roman Catholic Church in the United States, the result chiefly of the "new" immigration. From 1890 to 1916 this Church grew from 7,343,186 to 15,721,815 members, a gain of 114.1 per cent. The great expansion of Catholicism occurred, however, before 1906. From 1906 to 1916, when Protestant bodies increased about 23 per cent, the Catholic Church grew by only 10.6 per cent.

During its period of rapid growth the Roman Catholic Church was neither torn by internal dissensions nor concerned with theological disputes. There was a movement in the late nineteenth century to "Americanize" the Catholic Church in the United States by bringing it into close cooperation with other religious groups. This effort was ended by Pope Leo XIII's firm stand in 1899 in behalf of traditional practice. Any trend toward modernism in the Church, moreover, was firmly suppressed by Pope Pius X in 1907. Thereafter, modernism simply did not exist in American Catholicism.

The decision to adhere to traditional Catholic doctrines and practices did not, however, signify any diminution of the social conscience of the

Catholic Church. As the shepherds of most of the "new" immigrants and a large portion of the submerged urban masses, Catholic priests and bishops knew what poverty and suffering were. During the 1880's James Cardinal Gibbons of Baltimore had been one of the leading champions of the Knights of Labor, and his attitude was probably decisive in the issuance in 1891 of Pope Leo XIII's encyclical, *Rerum Novarum,* one of the most important assertions of the rights of labor. In the twentieth century, moreover, Catholic laymen and priests, like Father John A. Ryan of the Catholic University of America, figured prominently in the movement for the passage of social and economic legislation.

For American Protestantism, on the other hand, the progressive era was a time of change on all sides. That the old divisive forces that had kept the Protestant groups separated were still at work was evidenced by the steady offshooting of new sects from the parent bodies. The most notable of these new movements was Christian Science, founded around the turn of the century by a remarkable Bostonian, Mrs. Mary Baker Eddy. Denying the existence of death, evil, or the material world, Mrs. Eddy worked out a new science from the Scriptures by asserting that disease did not exist. By the First World War Christian Science had gained almost 100,000 adherents and was growing rapidly. The most numerous of the new sects, however, were the various holiness, or pentecostal, bodies, most of which came out of Methodism and taught a primitive fundamentalism.

Furthermore, Protestantism was still suffering the effects of the profound division in its ranks between the traditionalists, who adhered steadfastly to ancient creeds and confessions, and the modernists, who ranged theologically all the way from liberal orthodoxy to outright humanism, but who usually emphasized the social mission of the church at the expense of exegesis. There could be no doubt that the modernists were in the ascendancy from 1900 to 1916. The northern Presbyterian Church preserved the purity of its doctrines at the cost of expelling several of its most distinguished ministers and of losing control of its leading seminary, Union, in New York City. The Lutherans generally remained impervious to the new intellectual currents. But the northern Methodists, the northern Baptists, and the Congregationalists were by and large captured by the modernist clergy.

In spite of these divisive forces, there were numerous signs during the first years of the twentieth century that the forces drawing Protestant bodies together were at last beginning to prevail. Even the great division between the traditionalists and the modernists was a cohesive force, since it cut across denominational barriers and drew men together on one side or the other. Within the denominations, too, the unifying forces gathered strength. The union of the northern Presbyterian and Cumberland Presbyterian bodies in 1906, for example, healed an old wound in the ecclesiastical body. The northern Baptist groups gradually came together in close cooperation, while the three principal Methodist bodies set under way a movement for unification that would come to fruition years later.

Among the denominations, moreover, subordination of minor theological differences and cooperation on various levels of church activity became the prime objective of Protestant leaders after 1900. Unity came first on the local level, in the formation of city, county, and state federations of churches, and in organizations like the Young Men's Christian Association, the Young Women's Christian Association, the International Sunday School Association, and the American Bible Society. The dream of the champions of Protestant unity was finally realized in 1908, with the formation of the Federal Council of Churches of Christ in America. Sharing common beliefs and purposes, spokesmen of thirty-three evangelical bodies and 17,000,000 members united to proclaim their faith in the ecumenical church.

The successful launching of the Federal Council in 1908 also signified the triumph in American Protestantism of the social gospel, a movement designed to revitalize the church and proclaim Christianity's message to an industrial society. It was not the first time the Protestant Church in America had set out to reform society. At least since the advent of Methodism in the eighteenth century there had always been a strong, socially-minded left wing of Protestantism in America. By 1865 the church had subdued the older frontier areas and overcome slavery, only to be confronted afterward by a host of new and less obvious challenges—social Darwinism, the triumph of materialism, and new forms of bondage.

How would the church meet the issues of a new day? Perhaps a majority of urban Protestant churches fell under the control of businessmen concerned mainly with laying up treasures on earth; perhaps their ministers glorified the captains of industry as fervently as did the college professors and editors of the day. Yet the years from 1870 to 1890 were a time also of the awakening of the social consciousness of Protestantism. An increasing number of clergymen began to measure the competitive, exploitative *Zeitgeist* by the Christian standard and found the new values wanting. Some of these pioneers found an answer in Christian Socialism; others rejected socialism but sought to resurrect the old Christian doctrine of brotherhood. In any event, out of the widespread discussion of the 1870's and 1880's there emerged the first articulation of social Christianity. By 1890 it was evident that Protestantism was changing, that it was becoming less other-worldly in outlook and beginning to view salvation in social and ethical, as well as in theological, terms.

If the two decades from 1870 to 1890 were a time of awakening among the urban Protestant leaders, the years from 1890 to 1915 saw the social gospel come of age. The 1890's witnessed the wholesale acceptance of the theory of evolution by liberal theologians; and the consequent accommodation of religion to Darwinism was accompanied by the elevation of three ancient Christian concepts to new prominence in American religious thought. They were, first, the concept that God is everywhere present and works through human institutions; second, the concept of the fatherhood of God and the brotherhood of man; third, the concept that the Kingdom of God is now and that the chief duty of the Church is the extension of that Kingdom. Together, these concepts constituted a frame of reference and a point of departure for the proponents of social Christianity.

From 1890 until the First World War the hosts of the social gospel preachers increased and their good works multiplied, until it seemed that urban Protestantism had truly been transformed. At the same time Christian Socialism became respectable and commanded the sympathy, if not the allegiance, of an increasing number of clergymen. The Salvation Army, founded by William Booth in London in 1878, spread to the United States in 1880 and after 1890 expanded its relief and rehabilitation work among the outcasts of society. So-called institutional churches, which sponsored hospitals, missions, social and relief agencies, and boys' and girls' clubs, spread through the great cities. Finally, around 1900 most of the major denominations officially recognized their social mission by establishing commissions of social service.

Among the champions of the social gospel one man emerged as leader and spokesman—Walter Rauschenbusch, for many years professor of church history at the Rochester Theological Seminary. A socialist, Rauschenbusch reserved his severest criticism for industrial capitalism, a "mammonistic organization with which Christianity can never be content." For the law of competition he proposed to substitute cooperation, collectivism, and democracy and thus to hasten the consummation of the Kingdom of God on earth. The publication of Rauschenbusch's eloquent *Christianity and the Social Crisis* in 1907 immediately established him as the major prophet of the social gospel movement.

A year after the publication of *Christianity and the Social Crisis* the social gospel achieved its fulfillment in the formation of the Federal Council of Churches, for from the beginning the movement for Protestant unity had stemmed more from social action impulses than from any desire to achieve doctrinal accord. At its first meeting in Philadelphia, the Council adopted a ringing manifesto, "The Church and Modern Industry," which placed official Protestantism squarely behind the movement to end exploitative capitalism through social welfare legislation and the strengthening of labor unions.

For all its power and commanding influence, the social gospel movement was a development in urban Protestantism. It was in the campaign to end the liquor traffic that urban and rural Protestants found a common outlet for mutual social energies and impulses. The later excesses of the prohibitionists and their failure to change the habits of a nation should not obscure the fact that in the beginning, at least, the temperance and prohibition movements were responses to one of the major social challenges of the time.

A child of the humanitarian awakening of the 1840's and 1850's, the crusade against Demon Rum had culminated in the adoption of prohibition by many northern and midwestern states by 1861. The movement, however, lost its strength during the Civil War; most of the states repealed their prohibition laws; and it seemed the experiment had failed. Between 1860 and 1880, on the other hand, the liquor problem grew to menacing proportions, as investment in the liquor business increased 700 per cent, saloons multiplied in the cities, and intemperance everywhere increased. Moreover, the liquor interests entered into cooperation with vice rings and corrupt politicians, so that saloons were often the fronts for houses of prostitution, and liquor dealers' associations and brewers worked hand in glove with city bosses.

The answer of the aroused church membership to this, as they thought, dire threat to the home and family was immediate and emphatic. The Protestant churches, containing most of the nondrinking population, went directly into politics in the 1880's and 1890's. On the local level they smashed saloons and elected city councils opposed to the liquor dealers. On the county and state levels they organized alliances and leagues to work for local option and state-wide prohibition. Leadership in the temperance agitation in the North and Middle West was taken by the Methodists, often more socially alert than other Protestant groups; in the South the Methodists and Baptists joined hands in the movement.

The Women's Christian Temperance Union, founded by Frances Willard in 1874, was the first successful attempt to marshal the ranks of Protestantism against the liquor traffic; but effective organization of the church forces on a national scale came only in 1893, with the formation of the Anti-Saloon League at Oberlin, Ohio. Under the aegis of the League, the Methodist, Baptist, Presbyterian, and Congregational churches went into politics with such determination that in many southern and midwestern states the division between church and state almost ceased to exist. In many states the Leagues—with their general superintendents, organizers, and hosts of speakers—became the most powerful factors in politics.

At first the goal of the Anti-Saloon leaders was local option or state-wide prohibition, and by 1917 three-fourths of the American people lived in dry counties, while two-thirds of the states had adopted prohibition. As the movement gained power, however, it assumed more and more the character of a religious crusade. The Anti-Saloon leaders lost sight of their original objective after 1913 and began to agitate for national prohibition by constitutional amendment. In 1913 the powerful Anti-Saloon lobby in Washington obtained passage of the Webb-Kenyon Act, which prohibited transportation of alcoholic beverages into dry states. Three years later a prohibition amendment received a majority vote, though not the necessary two-thirds, in both houses of Congress. And when Congress imposed prohibition on the District of Columbia in 1917, it was evident the day was not far distant when Protestantism's crusade would culminate in nation-wide prohibition by federal amendment.

17 / *The Power of the Press*

From 1897 to 1914 that other agency of social education, the press, grew more powerful and wielded greater influence among the masses of people than ever before. Indeed, one cannot recount the history of the progressive awakening without acknowledging that the newspapers and magazines of the period were in large measure responsible for generating the reform movement. And this was true because American journalism was literally transformed and recreated, because newspapers and magazines ceased to serve only the educated middle and upper classes and became a vital force in the lives of the masses.

This transformation occurred not accidentally, but because newspaper publishers adopted new techniques to increase the circulation and power of their journals. The pioneer was Joseph Pulitzer, a Hungarian immigrant, who settled in St. Louis in 1865 and soon became active in politics and journalism. In 1878 Pulitzer purchased the bankrupt *St. Louis Dispatch* and made it a going concern. In 1883 he bought the New York *World* from Jay Gould and moved to the great metropolis. Soon Pulitzer had made the *World* the first modern American newspaper. Its news coverage was generally excellent; its aggressive support of labor and reform causes made it easily the commanding progressive spokesman in the East. Even more important in the *World's* rise to pre-eminence was the fact that its cartoons, features, stories, and the like made it attractive to the mass of readers.

If Pulitzer's leadership in the American newspaper world was the most important journalistic phenomenon of the early twentieth century, because he established the pattern that most city newspapers followed after 1900, the most spectacular development was the entrance of William Randolph Hearst into the Fourth Estate and the consequent building of his vast empire and newspapers. With the support of a rich father, Hearst bought the New York *Journal* in 1895 and launched a new and violent experiment in journalistic techniques. Pulitzer had made the *World* acceptable to the masses by giving them illustrations, crusades, and a modicum of sensationalism. Hearst, however, used all the techniques of yellow journalism and proved that they would pay handsomely. Pulitzer struck back by adopting Hearst's methods, and from 1896 to 1898 the two publishers engaged in a mad rivalry for circulation and power. By their combined efforts they stirred American passions against Spain, then attempting to suppress a rebellion in Cuba, to fever pitch; and they helped drive an unwilling President to war in order to increase their circulations. After the war, however, Pulitzer repented, abandoned yellow journalism to its master, and made the *World* a model liberal, if overly partisan, newspaper.

Fortunately for the American people, the great majority of publishers followed Pulitzer rather than Hearst after 1900. By 1914 every city had its little New York *World*, and American journalism had advanced to a new level of usefulness. The Associated Press, reorganized in 1900, and the United Press, the second of its name, formed in 1907, furnished an abundance of reliable domestic and foreign news. The Sunday editions added magazine sections, cartoons, and, in a few cases, book review sections, while special columns by humorists and feature writers provided entertainment.

With the enormous growth of circulation after 1900 the metropolitan dailies grew into big businesses. Advertising was the main source of publishing revenue, to be sure; but as advertising followed circulation the large newspapers attained a position of security and independence in the business world they had never known before. Nor is there convincing evidence that prosperity caused newspaper publishers to align themselves on the side of big business and the special interests. Even more important was the fact that practically all newspapers, except the Hearst chain, whether conservative or progressive in editorial policy, tried honestly and accurately to report the news.

Along with growing circulation and wealth during the progressive period went consolidation and the new phenomenon of chains of newspapers under the control of single owners. The most important of these chains was of course the Hearst press, consisting of two magazines and nine newspapers in 1914. An even larger, if less powerful, consolidation was effected by E. W. Scripps, who by 1914 controlled thirty-four dailies, mainly in the smaller cities. Another important entrepreneur was Frank A. Munsey, who in

1908 owned five large newspapers in Boston, New York, Philadelphia, Baltimore, and Washington.

The same trends evident in the newspaper world were operating to transform the weekly and monthly magazines from journals of pure literature and sophisticated opinion into mass media of new ideas and originators of new movements. Technological improvements in printing made possible the mass production of magazines, and this in turn stimulated the beginning in the 1890's of a number of periodicals cheap in price but often high in quality. By 1905, for example, *Munsey's Magazine, McClure's Magazine, Cosmopolitan, Collier's, Saturday Evening Post*, and *Everybody's* enjoyed circulations in the hundreds of thousands or millions. At first featuring popular fiction, most of these journals became outlets for the reform literature of the early progressive period. On the other hand, the older literary journals, like the *Century, Scribner's, North American Review*, and *Harper's*, lost heavily in circulation and maintained a precarious existence, while the three leading journals of opinion, the *Nation*, the *New Republic*, and the Chicago *Public*, were kept alive only by generous subsidies.

The glaring contrast between the wealth of the popular journals and the penury of the journals of literature and comment did not signify literary decadence. On the contrary, it only emphasized the fact that by 1914 middle class Americans were buying and reading magazines that satisfied their longing for excitement and adventure and enlarged their understanding of the political and economic developments of the time.

18 / Main Trends in Literature

Regenerative forces combined from about 1897 to 1914 to produce a literary flowering in the United States and to lay the foundations for new trends in American creative writing. It was a productive and fertile period. Traditionalism survived under new forms; a new literary *genre*, naturalism, reached its apogee in the works of Theodore Dreiser, while literary pre-eminence passed from the East to the Middle West and, to a lesser degree, to the South.

By the turn of the century the Victorian giants were either dead or dying. Henry James, who had discovered reality in the drawing room, had fled America for the more congenial British *milieu*. His creative energies were almost spent by 1900. William Dean Howells lived on until 1920, a friend of many young authors; but his great work was also done. Mark Twain, the novelist of American boyhood, survived like a ghost from the nineteenth century past until 1910. His only significant work after 1900 was *The Mysterious Stranger*, published posthumously.

For all their realism, the realists like James and Howells lived in a moral universe. Realism to them meant probing into human character and mirroring life as they found it. Their subjects may have been drab or driven by greed, but they were above all else human beings with will, spirit, and purpose. Their work was taken up in the early twentieth century by a goodly company—Ellen Glasgow of Virginia, Willa Cather of Nebraska,

Dorothy Canfield of Kansas and Vermont, Ole Rølvaag of Minnesota, and Edith Wharton of New York—who depicted life in the New South, the Middle West, or in New York drawing room society, in all its stark drabness, irony, and tragedy. As realists, however, they also knew the other side of the picture. And in the end they glorified the human spirit, magnified the struggle against evil, and thus carried on the humane tradition.

Meanwhile, in the 1890's a new literary movement, naturalism, was beginning to make its first impression on American writers. The leading French naturalist, Émile Zola, enunciated the philosophy of the new school. The writer, he said, must study human nature as the biologist studied the animal world and describe sheerly natural phenomena without compassion and without applying moral criteria. It was a discipline too strong for most Americans, and the early so-called naturalists like Jack London, Frank Norris, Hamlin Garland, Ambrose Bierce, and Stephen Crane were more harsh realists than true disciples of Zola.

The publication in 1900 of Theodore Dreiser's *Sister Carrie*, however, marked a real turning point in American literary history. Here was a genuine effort to discover a new view of humanity based upon the findings of science, to discern a theory of existence divorced from religious beliefs. In biology Dreiser found an answer to the search for truth. Man is an animal driven by instincts to struggle for survival in an impersonal universe. In his striving for wealth, power, or sexual satisfaction, he reverts to his true animal nature and the façade of civilization falls away. Social forces, moreover, are impersonal and drive the weak, who cannot outwardly defy social conventions, to crime and violence.

The American public was not yet ready for such strong literary fare when Dreiser published *Sister Carrie* in 1900, and Dreiser bided his time without compromising his integrity. When he published *Jennie Gerhardt* in 1911 he won, not popular acclaim, but acceptance by a wide circle of intellectuals. Dreiser's leadership of the naturalistic school was firmly secured with the publication of *The Financier* in 1912 and *The Titan* in 1914. Although naturalism had not become an obsession among American writers by 1914, it clearly commanded the allegiance of a majority of serious young writers; and the day could not be far distant when it would become the dominant theme in American literature.

The years before the First World War witnessed, too, a remarkable outburst of poetic creativity. As the Victorian era gave way to the modern age, the genteel tradition survived in a simpler form; new poetic forms emerged; and poetic themes varied from the very abstruse to the homely and common aspect of life. But, withal, a real renaissance occurred, and America recovered her poetic voice again.

The two poetic giants of the early years of the twentieth century, William Vaughan Moody and Edwin Arlington Robinson, were both traditionalists who wrote in the genteel manner. A professor at the University of Chicago, Moody was an idealist outraged by the social and economic injustices of his time and by his country's venture into imperialism. His "Ode in Time of Hesitation" (1900) and "Gloucester Moors" and "On a Soldier Fallen in the Philippines," both published in 1901, were prophetic expressions of the American social consciousness. Robinson, however, dealt with a simpler and more abiding theme—the individual searching for God and truth in darkness and suffering. To Robinson, life and human destiny remained mysterious; he could not fathom their secrets. Yet in the "black and awful chaos of the night" he felt "the coming glory of the Light." His first collected works, *Children of the Night*, appeared in 1897. *The Town Down the River*, published in 1910, and *The Man Against the Sky*, published in 1916, established him as the pre-eminent man of letters among a remarkable generation of poets and novelists.

Robinson was in some respects a latter-day Puritan, in others, a Transcendentalist. Such could not be said, however, of the new school of Chicago poets, who first came upon the literary horizon with the publication in 1912 of *The Lyric Years*, an anthology of contemporary verse, and the printing of the first issue of *Poetry: A Magazine of Verse*. The editor of *Poetry*, Harriet Monroe of Chicago, was certain that traditionalism was passing and urged poets to write about contemporary life. The Chicago poets, Lindsay, Masters, and Sandburg, replied enthusiastically. Vachel Lindsay's "General William Booth Enters into Heaven," published in the first issue of *Poetry*, marked the beginning of his ecstatic glorification of the common people and their destiny. Edgar Lee Masters, a Chicago lawyer who wrote poetry as an avocation, laid bare the alleged sham and moral shabbiness of small-town America in *Spoon River Anthology*, published in 1915. On the other hand, Carl Sandburg, whose first volume appeared in 1916, magnified Chicago, the roaring, brawling butcher and steel-maker to the world.

The fourth of these poets of the common people, Robert Frost, was not a Chicagoan, found his first literary acceptance in England, and refused to identify himself with any movement. But he was the poet of the farmers and workers of New England, and his quiet free verse mirrored the staid New Hampshire countryside. The publication in England of his *A Boy's Will* in 1913 and *North of Boston* a year later immediately established his eminence among the "new" poets.

While the Chicago poets were writing poetic sagas of the common man, another revolt against the genteel tradition was brewing far to the east, among a group of American and English poets in London. These were the so-called imagists, under the leadership of Ezra Pound, Amy Lowell, and later of T. S. Eliot, who were striving toward a new verse form and new artistic standards. Asserting that the poet's purpose was to recreate impressions caught in the fleeting image, they rejected the metrical form and rhyming as artificial and posing obstacles to the creation of the pure image. Rejecting also romanticism as being the literary expression of a decadent humanistic culture, the imagists sought merely to recreate the impressions of everyday life.

The work of these novelists and poets raised American literature to a new eminence and gave it a standing in the western world it had not enjoyed since the 1840's and 1850's. But none of the truly creative writers of the early twentieth century enjoyed material success or popular acclaim. Except for the few who had independent incomes or other professions, they lived in obscure poverty, like Edwin Arlington Robinson, who was rescued by Theodore Roosevelt and given a sinecure in the New York Customs House, or Vachel Lindsay, who earned his bread by touring the country as a vagabond minstrel. By 1914 Americans were actually reading and buying more books than ever before; but the reading public rewarded the sentimentalists and the romanticists who amused and entertained them without questioning their virtue.

19 / Philosophy and the Arts

Out of the late nineteenth century struggle between the social Darwinists and the idealists emerged an American, William James, who rejected both schools and in so doing founded a philosophical system of his own. Denying the validity of all absolutes and fixed principles and building upon the ideas of an earlier philosopher, Charles S. Peirce, James conceived a system, pragmatism, in which the truth or value of an idea or act was measured by its workability and its consequences. It was a philosophy of ultimate individualism, to be sure, since each man had to establish pragmatic values for himself. It was also a philosophy that easily became the intellectual tool of progressivism, for pragmatism evaluated legislation on a basis of whether such legislation would meet the test of practicability and whether it would benefit the greatest numbers.

Although William James was the founder of the pragmatic school, the task of converting his philosophy into an instrument of progressive change fell to one of his disciples, John Dewey of Columbia University. Whereas James had emphasized the individual, Dewey emphasized the mass and sought to make philosophy an instrument of social action. As he became more and more the social prophet and the advocate of a hundred causes, however, Dewey became less the pragmatist and more the absolutist—a believer in the absolute value of tolerance, experimentation, free expression, and democratic collectivism.

Against the relativistic philosophy of James and Dewey the dissent of one idealist was clearly heard in the years before the war. He was Josiah Royce, professor of philosophy at Harvard University, who published his major work, *The Philosophy of Loyalty*, in 1908. To a generation obsessed either with a mechanistic or a pragmatic view of society, Royce asserted the supreme importance of ideals. Measuring the new against the eternal, he chose the eternal and the absolute. And the ideal that raised man above the level of animal was the ideal of loyalty—of devotion, selflessness, and sacrifice. These were the ideals, the reality, he said, that would give an impelling quality and a sense of direction to democracy.

Although they varied in method and approach, it is significant that the three leading American philosophers of the early twentieth century—James, Dewey, and Royce—all sought to formulate a creed for a democracy that would cast off the paralyzing view that mankind could not work out answers to fundamental problems. They offered hope and confidence for a world then in process of being born.

In contrast to the American achievement in literature and philosophy during the period 1897 to 1914, achievement in the field of traditional music was slight, although the growing number of music schools, opera houses, symphony orchestras, and civic music federations evidenced a considerable increase in popular appreciation of classical music. This was the period, also, when Victor Herbert and Sigmund Romberg, who combined the semi-classical form with popular themes, were writing their best operettas and adding dozens of songs to the American repertoire. The most important musical development lay not in this field, however, but in the creation of a new music for the people: rag-time, the ancestor of the modern popular music. With Irving Berlin and George M. Cohan setting the pace, a whole new school of musical writers burgeoned forth with tunes for musical comedies and the phonograph. Negro musicians, principally in New Orleans, were also experimenting with jazz, a musical form even more rhythmic and dissonant than rag-time; but jazz had made its way northward only to St. Louis and Memphis by about 1914.

In American painting, also, there were signs of new vigor and expanding horizons after 1897. Among the leaders of the "American" school of the late nineteenth century, Winslow Homer, George W. Bellows, and Thomas Eakin survived into the twentieth century and continued to shock respectable folk with scenes of the sea, the ring, and the operating room. Two Americans, John Singer Sargent and James M. Whistler, were pre-eminent among the portrait painters of the world.

The future in painting, however, belonged not to the older generation of artists but to the young rebellious American followers of the French impressionists and postimpressionists, Van Gogh, Cézanne, Matisse, and Gauguin—modernists who abandoned the "imitation of nature" for painting that reflected the artist's own reactions and conceptions. A small advance guard, including Alfred Henry Maurer, John Marin, and Charles Demuth, studied in France during the years before the First World War and brought the new postimpressionistic concepts home with them. A real turning point in the history of American art came in February 1913, when the advance guard gathered what modern French and American paintings they could find and displayed them before a shocked public in the New York Armory. From this time forward at least until the early 1930's, modernism in its many forms would be dominant in American artistic endeavor.

While American painters were thus responding to the dynamic artistic impulses of their time, American sculptors were raising their art to a new eminence. The leader of the group was Augustus Saint-Gaudens, whose wide variety of statuary, including the haunting figure of Grief at the grave of Mrs. Henry Adams, marked him as one of the great artists of his age. And there were other American sculptors who nearly attained Saint-Gaudens' high level of achievement during this period, like Daniel Chester French, whose tragic figure of the seated Lincoln in the Lincoln Memorial is beloved by millions of Americans.

In the field of architecture, also, Americans demonstrated vitality and a new vision. By 1900 the Victorian era of the brownstone front, the gimcrack house, and the "dumbbell" tenement had happily passed. In the cities new housing codes required light, ventilation, and fireproof construction in large apartment houses, and the day of tenement construction was over. In the suburban areas the Victorian styles gave way before a craze for colonial, Dutch, and southern styles. Advanced architects condemned them as archaic, but they were a vast improvement over the Victorian architectural chaos.

During the years before the First World War, moreover, Louis Sullivan, Frank Lloyd Wright, Ernest Wilby, and other pioneers were beginning a movement to give functional and social meaning to architectural forms.

The most notable architectural development of the period, however, was the perfection of the skyscraper, which made possible a virtual revolution in American urban life. The first important work was done by a group of Chicago architects, Le Baron Jenney, Louis Sullivan, Daniel Burnham, and John W. Root, who by 1900 had demonstrated the potential uses to which the steel structure could be put. However, the completion of the Woolworth Building, designed by Cass Gilbert, in New York in 1912 ended a decade during which the eastern metropolis took leadership from Chicago in the building of skyscrapers.

CHAPTER 3 / ASPECTS OF ECONOMIC DEVELOPMENT, 1897–1914

*B*y the end of the progressive period pride in the nation's economic growth since the end of the depression of the 1890's had in large measure given way to foreboding among many thoughtful Americans, for along with growth had come a steady movement toward concentration of economic power in fewer and fewer hands. This movement, in industry, finance, and transportation, was one of the most powerful and significant forces in recent American history. For one thing, it completely transformed the American economy from an economy of relatively small competitive producers into one dominated and to a degree controlled by an oligarchy of giant corporations. For another, many of the domestic problems of this century, at least before 1917, arose from the obvious necessity either of halting the movement toward monopoly or oligopoly—that is, domination of an industry by a few large producers—or else of bringing the great corporations, banks, railroads, and public service monopolies under effective public control.

No other question received as much attention or stimulated as many investigations and proposals for amelioration. Journalists, publicists, and politicians described the changes taking place: big business was becoming monopolistic, or nearly so, while the few men who dominated Wall Street were also extending their control into industry and transportation. As the statistics were plain enough for all to read, the people reluctantly agreed that the old promise of American life—the promise of equality of opportunity and a fair field for all comers—was rapidly becoming an anachronism. How to revitalize this promise, in brief, how to bring the great new aggregations of economic power under social control—this constituted progressivism's greatest challenge and dilemma.

This question, which perplexed the progressive mind and agitated the American people, is beyond the scope of the present chapter. Here we are concerned only with the development and progress of the concentration movement—how it came about and where it seemed to be heading.

20 / The Emergence of the Modern Corporation

The most obvious, yet the most important development in American industry after the Civil War was the rise of the corporation as the dominant type of industrial organization. Before 1865 the corporate form was used extensively only in transportation, insurance, banking, and, to a lesser degree, in textiles. With the enlargement of industrial units, the spread of mass production techniques, and the growth of the trust movement after 1865, however, the corporation rapidly displaced the proprietorship and partnership as the chief agency for combining capital and labor. By 1899 66 per cent of all manufactured products were turned out by corporations. Ten years later the proportion had increased to 79 per cent.

During the latter part of the nineteenth century the men who managed American corporations and made the important decisions owned the properties they controlled. From 1900 to 1914, however, the domination of corporations by men who owned them gradually gave way in the face of a new trend: the emergence of the giant, super-corporation, the ownership of which was so widely dispersed that there could be no real correlation between ownership and management. In other words, one consequence of the emergence of the large corporation was the establishment in power of a professional managerial class who were only theoretically accountable to the stockholders. Another consequence of this development was the rise of investment bankers as the ultimate powers in industry and transportation from about 1901 to 1929. What were the developments that stimulated the growth of the super-corporations?

The important factor was the movement of the bankers into the transportation and industrial fields. The process first began on a large scale during and after the Panic of 1893, when J. P. Morgan & Company and Kuhn, Loeb & Company, the two leading Wall Street investment firms, set about reorganizing and consolidating bankrupt railroad properties. So successful was Morgan in rehabilitating insolvent railroads that he began to cast about for an opportunity to extend his control into industry. His chance came when a bitter rivalry between Carnegie and the producers of finished steel products, with whom Morgan was associated, threatened to plunge the entire steel industry into a chaotic price war. At this juncture Morgan came forward with a plan to combine 60 per cent of the iron and steel producers into one giant corporation. The result was the creation in 1901 of the United States Steel Corporation, the retirement of Carnegie, the great entrepreneur, and the establishment of the House of Morgan as the dominant power in the industry. This event was a turning point in modern American history, but it was only a beginning. As Morgan combined more and more industries and railroads after 1901 his power grew almost by geometric ratio. He was not merely the organizer and consolidator; he also underwrote the floating of securities that launched the new corporations on their way; and through his representatives on the boards of directors, and because he controlled the sources of credit, he was able to exercise a decisive voice in the corporations' policies.

Although the process of banker consolidation and control did not culminate until the 1920's, the effects of this revolution in the character, ownership, and control of the large corporations was already well apparent by the outbreak of the First World War. By 1914 the super-corporations dominated many fields of American enterprise: steel and iron, railroads, anthracite coal, agricultural machinery, copper, the telephone and telegraph, and public utilities. Hundreds of thousands of shareholders now owned these properties, but control had passed from the owners to a managerial class responsible to a board of directors, who in turn were often beholden to investment bankers.

Undergirding this economic revolution was a body of state law that afforded a legal means of effecting consolidations and assuring managerial-banker control. New Jersey took the lead in 1888 and did a bargain counter business in charters until 1913. As New Jersey's treasury overflowed with corporation fees and taxes, other states entered the competition. The key provision in all the state corporation codes was the clause allowing one corporation to hold stock in other corporations. The invention of an ingenious New York lawyer, James B. Dill, this, the holding company device, was first incorporated into the New Jersey code in 1888 and was refined and clarified in 1889, 1893, and 1896. The holding company form offered a simple means of effecting a huge combination or acquiring monopolistic control. Indeed, it soon became the legal form of practically all the giant corporations. In addition to providing a legal structure for the combinations, many state corporation codes endowed boards of directors with control over property without imposing obligations to the stockholders. Finally, these codes made no effort to cause the nominal and the actual capital of a corporation to coincide, which encouraged stock watering and fleecing of innocent investors.

21 / The Consolidation Movement in Industry, 1879–1903

The movement toward concentration of control in industry went through two major phases before the First World War: first, the trust movement, which began in 1879 and ended about 1890; second, the consolidation movement from 1897 to 1903, in which combinations were mainly constructed through the use of the holding company form. After 1903 the process of concentration went steadily forward, but at a much slower pace, until the 1920's.

Most of the trusts of the first period of combination were organized by the manufacturers and businessmen directly involved, without the intervention of professional promoters or underwriting bankers. The trust was simply an extra-legal arrangement by which competing manufacturers pooled their properties to achieve a monopoly. The Standard Oil Trust of 1879, superseded by the Trust Agreement of 1882, affords a good example of how this was done. First, the Trust Agreement was approved by the stockholders and owners of forty-odd oil companies, which together controlled over 90 per cent of the refining industry and an almost equal proportion of the pipe lines. Second, a valuation of the properties and assets of the member corporations was made, and on the basis of this valuation trust certificates with a par value of $100 each were issued in exchange for the property. Finally, the combined properties were managed by nine trustees elected on a basis of stock ownership. Following Standard Oil's lead, similar trusts were organized in other important branches of industry, while other combinations, organized by purchase or as holding companies, were also launched in the late 1880's and early 1890's.

The use of the trust form to achieve monopoly was abandoned in the 1890's, and for a time the combination movement came almost to a standstill. The Panic of '93 was in part responsible, but an even more important factor was the enactment of sweeping laws against conspiracies in restraint of trade by Congress and many state legislatures. Few manufacturers were willing to risk heavy damages and dissolution by federal and state courts. The situation changed drastically in 1895, however, when the Supreme Court decreed that the federal antitrust law did not apply to combinations in the field of manufacturing.

The apparent removal of the formidable federal barrier to industrial combinations, the election of McKinley in 1896, and the return of prosperity in 1897 all combined to clear the way for a second consolidation movement that lasted until 1904. So great was this movement that the consolidations of the earlier period pale into insignificance. All told, not more than twelve important combinations, with a total capitalization of under $1,000,000,000, had been organized from 1879 to 1897. Yet the Census of Manufactures in 1899 reported some 185 combinations with a total capital of over $3,000,-000,000, which accounted for nearly one-third the entire capitalization of all manufacturing industries in the country. In 1904 a comprehensive survey of American corporations listed 305 industrial combinations, with an aggregate capital of nearly $7,000,000,000, in operation. In addition, thirteen important combinations, with a capital of $500,000,000, were in process of reorganization; and combinations controlled fully two-fifths of the manufacturing capital of the United States.

The momentum of the consolidation movement during the period 1897–1903 can best be illustrated by pointing again to the statistics. Of the 318 giant corporations in operation or in process of reorganization on January 1, 1904, 236, with a total capitalization of over $6,000,000,000, had been organized since January 1, 1898. This generalization, however, conveys only half the truth about the power of the movement. With 95 per cent of the nation's mileage under the control of six groups, concentration in railroads had reached an even more spectacular level than in industry. Moreover, some 1,330 public service corporations had been consolidated into a few holding companies that had a combined capitalization of three and three-quarter billion dollars.

The reasons for this tremendous number of consolidations are not hard to find. Having acquired a violent dislike for competition during the depression of the 1890's, manufacturers were easily persuaded that combination offered a sure means of controlling the price of their products. The fact that the three most important monopolies—Standard Oil, American Sugar, and American Tobacco—had prospered and paid dividends while the rest of industry struggled through destructive price wars was not lost upon the business community. Manufacturers, moreover, anticipated increased profits through the vertical integration of plants to achieve a continuous industrial process, large-scale production, the exploitation of the national market, and the utilization of by-products. But certainly an important incentive to combination was the desire to achieve stability through considerable control of prices.

The moving agent in the later consolidation movement, however, was not the manufacturer but the professional promoter and investment banker. He it was who brought competitors together, harmonized their differences, and worked out schemes of financing and marketing the new securities. A favorite method of financing the combination was to issue bonds and preferred stock to compensate the owners of the properties being consolidated. In addition, a bonus in common stock as large as the market would bear would be awarded to the promoter and the corporation. The classic example of this method of financing was the manner in which Morgan worked out a financial structure for United States Steel in 1901. The corporation was capitalized at $1,400,000,000, divided as follows: $362,000,000 in bonds, $510,000,000 in preferred stock, $508,000,000 in common stock, and $22,000,000 in cash. As the actual value of the corporation's assets was only $682,000,000, all the common and about one-fourth of the preferred stock— about half the capitalization—was pure water. Yet the Morgan firm was able to dispose of these securities on the Stock Exchange and to realize a profit of $62,000,000 as a fee for organizing and underwriting the corporation.[1]

The consolidation movement came to a halt in 1904, chiefly because about every branch of industry susceptible of combination had been combined. But the activation of the federal antitrust law by Theodore Roosevelt and his successor, William H. Taft, was also an important factor in bringing the movement to an end. In fact, from 1904 to 1914 the federal government on the whole succeeded in compelling the great corporations to comply with the provisions of the antitrust law. Most of the genuine monopolies were dissolved. Other combinations, like the International Harvester Company, the New Haven Railroad, and American Telephone and Telegraph, voluntarily acquiesced in reorganization plans approved by the Attorney General. By 1911 the era of monopoly in American industry had passed and a new economic structure was emerging. It was an oligopolistic structure, in which a few giant corporations dominated their branches of industry and determined price and wage policies. We will examine this new development in greater detail in a future chapter.

22 / The Emergence of the Financial Empires

As the wealth of the United States increased during the two decades before American intervention in the First World War, the savings of the middle and upper classes began to flow into banks and insurance companies. All American financial institutions combined had assets and resources of only

[1] It is only fair to add, however, that by 1916 the directors of United States Steel, through wise management and prudent reinvestment, had built the corporation's assets to the point where the common stock was no longer watered.

$9,000,000,000 in 1899; by 1911 the country could boast of savings and liquid capital of nearly $28,000,000,000.

As a result of this growth of capital resources, the entrepreneurs of the money market, the investment bankers, assumed leadership after 1897 in marshaling and allocating capital for industrial, railroad, public utility, and other forms of expansion. As we have seen, they were also the chief agents in promoting and financing the new consolidations. But the portentous fact was not the growth of American wealth, for that reflected an expanding and healthy economy; it was the startling concentration of control that took place among the banks and insurance companies and the transformation of the leading investment bankers from entrepreneurs of capital into dominant forces in the American economy.

So swift was this process of concentration of control of the nation's credit resources that by 1904 there were two financial empires in Wall Street: the House of Morgan and the Rockefeller group. With its profits from railroad reorganization and the promotion of large corporations, the Morgan firm bought control of the National Bank of Commerce and partial ownership of the great First National Bank of New York City. From this vantage point, Morgan rapidly extended his control over other banks and trust companies in New York, Philadelphia, and Chicago. Moreover, the House of Morgan was represented in the counsels of the United States Steel, the International Mercantile Marine, the International Harvester, the General Electric, and other large corporations. By 1904 it controlled, besides, the Southern, the Reading, the Northern Pacific, the Great Northern, the New Haven, the Erie, and other railroads, whose total mileage was over 47,000 and whose combined capital amounted to nearly one-fourth of the group railroad capital in the United States. Such an empire might have satisfied a man of modest ambition. Around 1900, however, Morgan set out to win the richest prize of all—the large New York insurance companies. Control of their huge resources would open up an almost unlimited market for securities. Morgan won the New York Life and Mutual Life by interlocking their directors into his own system. Finally, in 1910 he bought a controlling interest in the Equitable Life. By 1913 these three companies had assets of nearly $2,000,000,000 and some $70,000,000 of new money every year for investment.

On the other side of Wall Street was the far-flung Rockefeller group and its allies—the National City Bank, the Hanover National Bank, the Farmers Loan and Trust Company, and lesser banks; the Standard Oil Company; the Union Pacific, Southern Pacific, and nine other major railroads, managed by Edward H. Harriman; and Morgan's rival in the investment and promotion fields, Kuhn, Loeb & Company, headed by Jacob H. Schiff. The normal process of concentration had been reversed to construct this financial imperium: the industrialists in the Standard Oil monopoly had channeled their excess profits into investment and promotion.

Around the Morgan and Rockefeller empires clustered a number of smaller kingdoms, and before 1907 they were all allied in a loose confederation. "These two mammoth groups jointly . . . constitute the heart of the business and commercial life of the nation," one financial expert wrote in 1904, "the others all being the arteries which permeate in a thousand ways our whole national life, making their influence felt in every home and hamlet, yet all connected and dependent on this great central source, the influence and policy of which dominates them all."[2]

The two major financial alliances, however, did not always live in peace before 1907. Their rivalry for control of railroads, corporations, and insurance companies was sometimes bitter and on one memorable occasion reached the point of open war, the stakes of which were nothing less than control of most of the western transcontinental railroads. By 1900 Morgan and his ally, James J. Hill, controlled the two northern transcontinental systems, the Northern Pacific and the Great Northern. On the other hand, Edward H. Harriman and Kuhn, Loeb & Company controlled the central and southern systems, the Union Pacific and Southern Pacific. Neither group, however, controlled the outlet to Chicago, the Burlington, that the Hill lines used. When Hill persuaded the owners of the Burlington to sell their railroad to the Northern Pacific and Great Northern in 1901, Harriman and Schiff executed a daring flank attack by attempting to buy control of the Northern Pacific. The ensuing battle in the New York Stock Exchange drove the price of Northern Pacific common from $100 to over $1,000 a share, and when the smoke had cleared it was discovered that, although Harriman and Schiff owned a majority of the shares of Northern Pacific, Hill and Morgan still controlled a majority of the voting stock. So costly was the battle, however, that the rivals agreed to terms of peace. They formed the Northern Securities Company, which controlled the Northern Pacific and Great Northern lines, and Harriman and Schiff were given minority representation on the board of directors. In addition, Harriman was awarded a seat on the board of the Burlington.

Morgan's pre-eminence was further demonstrated during the Panic of 1907, when he dramatically marshaled Wall Street's resources to prevent total demoralization of the securities markets. After this demonstration of power, the Rockefeller-Kuhn, Loeb group concluded that further opposition to the Morgan combination was futile. Thus from 1907 to 1913 the Morgan and Rockefeller groups were merged into one confederated association by interlocking directorates and purchases of one another's stocks.

The power of the Morgan-Rockefeller confederation was dramatically revealed through the careful investigation of a House sub-committee—the Pujo Committee—in the early months of 1913. This committee found that by consolidating bank and trust companies, by gaining control over insurance companies, and by interlocking their directorates among the boards of railroads and industrial and public utility corporations, the Morgan-Rockefeller community of interest had achieved a nearly monopolistic control of the credit resources of the nation. How deeply this control extended into almost every phase of American economic life was illustrated by the fact that the Morgan-Rockefeller group had

118 directorships in 34 banks and trust companies, with total resources of over $2,500,000,000;

30 directorships in 10 insurance companies, with total assets of over $2,000,000,000;

[2] John Moody, *The Truth About the Trusts* (New York, 1904), p. 493.

105 directorships in 32 transportation systems, with a total capitalization of more than $11,000,000,000;

63 directorships in 24 producing and trading corporations, with a total capitalization of over $3,000,000,000; and

25 directorships in 12 public utility corporations, with a combined capitalization of over $2,000,000,000.

In brief, on January 1, 1913, the House of Morgan and its allies had 341 directorships in 112 banks, railroads, industries, and other corporations with aggregate resources or capitalization of more than $22,000,000,000.

The question whether a "money trust" existed as a result of the aggrandizement of power by the Wall Street bankers was hotly debated before the Pujo Committee. The committee did not claim that the Morgan empire had established an absolute monopoly of credit. It revealed beyond cavil, however, the vast and growing concentration of control of money and credit in the hands of a few men. And the significance of the committee's findings was not lost upon the American people. How could genuine economic freedom and equality of opportunity exist in such circumstances? "This is the greatest question of all," Woodrow Wilson observed, "and to this statesmen must address themselves with an earnest determination to serve the long future and the true liberties of men."

23 / The American Railroad Empires, 1897–1914

The same processes of consolidation and concentration that were being used to construct the empires of industry and finance we have just described were also employed, often by the same bankers and promoters, to consolidate America's greatest single property interest, the railroads. By 1897 the task of linking all sections was accomplished, although railroad mileage grew at a steady pace, from 198,964 miles in operation in 1900 to 251,984 by 1914, while railway capital and the volume of passenger and freight traffic practically doubled during the same period.

Growth, however, was accompanied by consolidation and an increasing degree of banker control. Leadership in the consolidation movement was taken, as we have seen, by the Morgan firm during and after the Panic of 1893.

Morgan's dominance in the transportation field, however, was challenged by the rise of Edward H. Harriman, easily the boldest railroad promoter of the early twentieth century. Associated with Kuhn, Loeb & Company in managing the Illinois Central, Harriman and his Wall Street allies bought control of the bankrupt and worn-out Union Pacific in 1897. Harriman personally supervised the rebuilding of this system, which soon became immensely profitable. In 1901 Harriman and Kuhn, Loeb & Company bought control of an even greater system, the Southern Pacific which, together with several other western lines, gave them control over most of the railroads of the Southwest and a monopoly of the transportation facilities of the entire West Coast from Canada to Mexico.

Beyond the Mississippi only three railway systems challenged the domination of that vast area by the Morgan-Hill and Kuhn, Loeb-Harriman interests. They were the Santa Fe Railroad, the Gould system, and the consolidation built around the Rock Island Railroad. The Santa Fe, financed by independent Boston and London banking interests, ran from Chicago to southern California and was never associated with the Gould or Harriman interests. The Gould system included the Missouri Pacific, the Denver and Rio Grande, the Texas and Pacific, and the Western Pacific. The Rock Island system was consolidated from 1901 to 1911 by a group of speculators out of the Rock Island, the St. Louis and San Francisco, and the Chicago and Alton.

The traffic of the East and eastern Middle West was dominated by the New York Central and Pennsylvania, allied with the Morgan interests, which controlled the Chesapeake and Ohio, the Baltimore and Ohio, and the Norfolk and Western. Under Morgan's direction, moreover, the New Haven bought control of the Boston and Maine, the trolley lines of New England, and even the Long Island Sound steamship companies. Thus, by 1906 about two-thirds of the nation's railroad mileage was controlled by four gigantic communities of interest: the Morgan-Hill-Vanderbilt-Pennsylvania; the Harriman-Kuhn, Loeb & Company; the Gould; and the Rock Island groups. Obviously, the process of consolidation could not have been carried much farther.

Along with consolidation in the railroad field went banker control on a scale exceeding that prevailing in industry. How did the bankers use their power—to promote the public interest, or to enrich themselves and expand their holdings? The answer is clear. The bankers sought primarily their own and their stockholders' gain, though this often meant charging exorbitant rates for poor service, bankrupting railroad properties, or debauching the politics of the states. Indeed, the mismanagement of America's greatest single property interest from 1897 to 1914 reached such a point that only federal rehabilitation and operation of the railroads during the First World War saved the industry from virtual bankruptcy.

Harriman's and Kuhn, Loeb & Company's use of the Union Pacific provides a good illustration of the way promoters manipulated a profitable railroad to build up a vast empire. By completely rebuilding the Union Pacific and managing it efficiently, Harriman made the line immensely profitable. But most of the cost of rebuilding was charged to operation and maintenance, while the company's excess profits were used to acquire control of the Southern Pacific and to purchase large interests in numerous other lines. All told, by 1907 the Union Pacific had "invested" more than $331,000,000 in this fashion; and, while Harriman constructed his empire, Kuhn, Loeb & Company reaped huge profits as his middlemen.

Harriman repeatedly violated the antitrust law, to be sure, but he did not wreck railroad properties. The most important case of railroad mismanagement during this period involved J. P. Morgan's use of the New Haven to acquire a complete monopoly over all forms of transportation in New England. From 1903 to 1912, when Morgan pursued his relentless campaign, the capitalization of the New Haven was increased from $93,000,000 to about $417,000,000. More than two-thirds of the increased capitalization was used, however, not to improve or purchase railroad property, but to achieve a monopoly of all transportation facilities. In the process, the New Haven directors debauched politicians, bribed editors, and in the end helped bring the economy of New England to the brink of ruin.

24 / The United States and the World Economy, 1897–1914

Since colonial times foreign trade had been the lifeblood of the American economy. Reflecting the profound changes taking place in the domestic economy, however, the volume and character of foreign trade underwent important changes from 1897 to 1914. For one thing, foreign trade expanded at a faster pace during this period than at any time since the Civil War. Exports increased from $1,394,000,000 in 1900 to nearly $2,500,000,000 by 1914, while imports rose from $850,000,000 to $1,800,000,000 during the same period. Secondly, an important shift in the character of exports and imports took place. In 1900 agricultural products constituted 60 per cent of the nation's exports, manufactured products only 35 per cent. By 1914, however, manufactured products accounted for nearly 49 per cent of American exports. At the same time, the development of new industries at home lessened American demand for manufactured goods from abroad and stimulated increased demand for raw materials like rubber, tin, and manganese.

The rapid growth of American exports of manufactured goods and capital before 1914 foretold the coming of the day when the United States would occupy a commanding position in the world economy. Before 1915, however, London was still the center of international exchange, and the United States continued to occupy its traditional status as debtor to Europe. In 1897 Europeans held American securities, over half of them in railroads, valued at nearly $3,500,000,000. By the eve of the First World War, European investments in the United States, direct and indirect, had more than doubled. In part this was offset by American investments abroad, but the balance of payments still ran heavily against the United States.

None the less, the two most significant trends during the period 1897–1914 were the growth of American exports of manufactured goods and the rapid increase in the export of American capital abroad. The first was achieved in spite of the lack of a sizable American merchant marine, of experience in doing business in foreign countries, or of a well organized governmental program to support foreign trade. The growth of American investments abroad, on the other hand, took place under the guidance of experienced bankers and often with the support of the State Department.

When the United States went to war with Spain in 1898 it was the richest and industrially the most powerful nation in the world. Up to this time, however, practically every available dollar had gone into building the railroads, opening the West, and constructing industries at home. On the eve of the Spanish-American War, American investments abroad totaled only $684,500,000. Yet by 1914 this figure stood at $3,513,800,000. Except for $692,000,000 invested in Europe and $246,000,000 in the Far East, American capital, however, had not ventured far from home. American capitalists had invested $867,200,000 in Canadian mines, industries, and railroads. The encouragement given foreign investors by the seemingly stable Díaz govern-

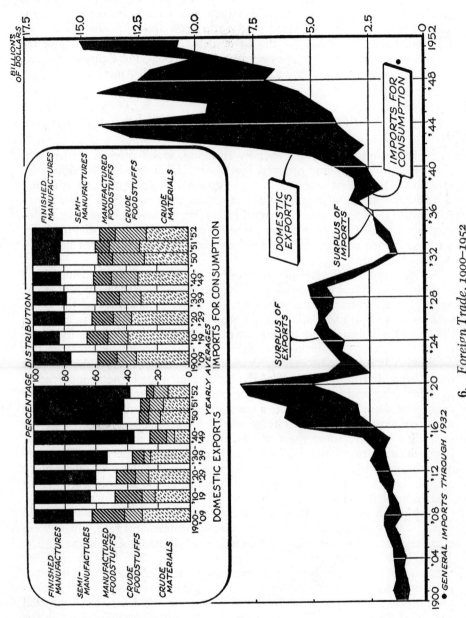

6. *Foreign Trade, 1900–1952*

ment of Mexico from 1877 to 1911 had attracted $854,000,000 from the United States, most of which was invested in railroads, mines, ranches, and oil. American investments in Cuba, which was a quasi-protectorate of the United States during the period 1898–1914, grew from $50,000,000 in 1897 to $200,000,000 by 1914. By the latter date Americans had also invested $136,000,000 in the other Caribbean islands, $93,000,000 in Central America, and $366,000,000 in the more stable countries of South America.

25 / *The Conditions and Hazards of Labor, 1897–1914*

The period 1897–1914, generally speaking, was a time of relative stability but slow economic progress for labor. Real wages of all workers increased at the rate of one-half of 1 per cent a year from 1897 to 1914 and would have increased considerably more had there not been a rise of 39 per cent in the cost of living for workers during the same period. The factor that saved them from serious retrogression during these years of prosperity for businessmen and farmers was not important wage increases but generally full employment.

This picture of increasing and steadier employment, accompanied by a slight increase in real wages, did not, however, encourage the friends of labor. Surveying the industrial scene in 1915, the majority members of the Commission on Industrial Relations, appointed by President Wilson to ascertain the causes of industrial unrest, observed that "a large part of our industrial population are . . . living in a condition of actual poverty. How large this proportion is can not be exactly determined, but it is certain that at least one-third and possibly one-half of the families of wage earners employed in manufacturing and mining earn in the course of the year less than enough to support them in anything like a comfortable and decent condition."[3] The social consequences of this state of affairs were ominous: children of the poor died at three times the rate of children of the middle classes; in six large cities 12 to 20 per cent of the children were underfed and undernourished; only one-third of all children enrolled finished elementary schools; less than 10 per cent of the children in public schools were graduated from high schools.

Although the existence of a large mass of submerged and unprotected workers disheartened students of the labor problem in 1914, there were other and more encouraging developments that offered hope for the future. To begin with, some progress had been made since 1897 toward reducing the hours of labor in industry and transportation. Average hours in industry fell from 59.1 a week in 1897 to 55.2 in 1914. These general averages, however, obscure the important differential in hours worked between organized and unorganized labor. The movement for shorter hours had begun in the building, printing, and other skilled and organized trades and was most successful among them. One survey, for example, revealed that in six unionized industries average weekly hours declined from 53.4 in 1897 to 48.8 in 1914.

[3] *Final Report of the Commission on Industrial Relations* (Washington, 1915), p. 10.

In contrast, average weekly hours in eight unorganized industries declined from 61.9 to 58.2 during the same period.

Secondly, during the years from 1907 to 1914 the first real progress was made toward reducing the hazards of labor. Statistics of industrial accidents are unreliable for this period, but an incomplete survey in 1907 revealed that at least 500,000 American workers were either killed, crippled, or seriously injured. As late as 1913, according to a more reliable survey, 25,000 workers were killed on their jobs and another 700,000 were seriously injured.

Before 1907 the sporadic efforts made by several states to reduce the industrial accident rate had been unproductive, but between 1907 and 1914 the public awakened to the fact that human resources were being uselessly squandered and that the national efficiency was gravely impaired by industrial deaths and accidents. The beginning of the safety movement came in 1907, when the United States Steel Corporation inaugurated a comprehensive campaign to reduce the accident toll. So successful was this program that a few other leading corporations and railroads, notably the International Harvester Company and the Chicago and North Western Railroad, instituted safety campaigns before 1914.

Thirdly, the reports of social workers and factory inspectors in many states also focused public attention on the social necessity of providing healthful working conditions in industry. The problem was most acute in factories in which large numbers of women and children were employed—in the textile mills and garment sweatshops. In fact, nowhere in the country were working conditions so incredibly bad as in the garment sweatshops of New York City, most of which were located in tenements that were literally firetraps. The Triangle Shirtwaist Factory fire on the East Side in 1911, in which 148 women lost their lives, however, stimulated the appointment of a Factory Investigating Commission and a thorough revision of New York's factory code between 1912 and 1914.

Finally, the urgency of eliminating occupational diseases like phosphorous and lead poisoning was brought home to employers and the public in a number of ways from 1900 to 1914. Medical research provided the essential knowledge, while state and national reform groups, like the American Association for Labor Legislation, carried on the necessary propaganda work. A campaign against phosphorous matches, for example, resulted in the enactment of a federal statute in 1912 forbidding their manufacture. Lead poisoning in its various forms was partially eliminated. But the greatest progress came when the American Medical Association joined hands with the American Association for Labor Legislation to begin a comprehensive campaign against industrial diseases.

26 / *The Rise of the American Federation of Labor*

Nothing so well illustrates the precarious position that workers occupied in the American society during the half century between the Civil War and the First World War than the story of labor's attempts to achieve some measure of protection through organization. Organized labor passed through several phases during this long period and was confronted at times with almost insurmountable obstacles. None the less, labor organizations won a larger degree of recognition than ever before in American history; and although labor's great goal—the unionization of all workers—was unrealized by 1914, the necessary, solid foundations of a strong labor movement had been well laid.

There were two initial attempts at labor organization on a national scale between 1865 and the late 1880's, before the dominant pattern of unionization was established. The first, the National Labor Union, founded in 1866, was a loose aggregation of trade unions and assorted reform groups which was practically defunct by 1872. More important was the Knights of Labor, organized in Philadelphia in 1869, which attempted to organize workers along industrial, rather than craft lines, and without regard to sex or race. Although the union won a few spectacular strike victories and attained a membership of over 700,000 in 1885, it rapidly disintegrated after newspapers and employers charged it with responsibility for a serious riot in Chicago in 1886.

At the time the Knights of Labor was enjoying momentary success, the leaders of the cigar makers' union, Samuel Gompers and Adolph Strasser, were at work building the first powerful trade union in American history. In 1881 other unions federated with the cigar makers in a Federation of Organized Trades, and in 1886 the union was reorganized as the American Federation of Labor. Under the leadership of Samuel Gompers, who dominated the organization until his death in 1924, the AF of L for the most part spurned the ideal of industrial unionism, that is, unionism that groups all workers in a single industry into a single organization, and built upon the foundation of craft and trade unions. The AF of L, moreover, from its beginning eschewed utopianism and was avowedly opportunistic and practical in objectives.

The essential strength of the AF of L and the soundness of its policies were demonstrated when it weathered the defeat of the steelworkers' and miners' unions in major strikes in 1892 and 1894 and came out of the depression in 1897 with 265,000 members. From this point, and with the return of prosperity, the AF of L soon fought its way to dominance in the American labor movement. By 1900 its membership had climbed to 548,000. There were spectacular gains until 1904, when membership reached 1,676,000. Then, under the hammer blows of an organized employer campaign, the AF of L's membership declined until 1911, when it began slowly to mount again. On the eve of the First World War the union's membership stood at a little over 2,000,000.

Standing apart from the AF of L as an independent force in the labor movement were the four railroad brotherhoods—the conductors, engineers, trainmen, and firemen—who since the 1880's had been the best paid workers in the country, a labor aristocracy conscious of their power and privileged position. By the threat of strikes the brotherhoods had won the ten-hour day throughout the country by 1910. Then in 1916 the four unions, 400,000 strong, combined to do battle for their next objective, the eight-hour day, which they won with the passage by Congress of the Adamson Act, establishing the eight-hour day as the standard for all workers engaged in interstate railway transportation.

27 / *The Progress of Unionization in the Coal Industry, 1897–1914*

From the end of the Panic of 1893 to the First World War was a time of labor's first concerted striving toward the goal of industrial democracy. Many factors combined to give the AF of L opportunities and advantages its predecessors had not enjoyed: superb *esprit de corps* accompanied by a feeling of solidarity, wise leadership, and a public opinion that was growing less hostile to the labor movement. Building largely on foundations already laid, from 1897 to 1914 Gompers and his colleagues were successful in expanding membership and winning collective bargaining, higher wages, and shorter hours in most of the building trades and the skilled crafts. On the other hand, labor's new militancy was matched by an equally aggressive determination on the part of management to prevent unionization in the mass industries. This, therefore, was the crucial issue: could the AF of L carry the fight into the basic industries and win the victory over great aggregations of power?

The first test came in the struggle of the United Mine Workers of America, an industrial union affiliated with the AF of L, to organize the coal industry. Decisively beaten in a general coal strike in 1894, the UMW by 1897 had only 10,000 members and was apparently dead. In spite of their apparent impotence, the leaders of the union in that year demanded increased wages and recognition. When the operators refused, the United Mine Workers ordered a general strike in the bituminous fields for July 4, 1897. During the ensuing struggle the strikers were organized and magnificently led by the UMW, and in September 1897 the operators in the bituminous fields of western Pennsylvania, Ohio, Indiana, and Illinois surrendered. It was a notable victory, not merely because the miners won recognition, higher wages, and other demands, but also because it was a spur and an inspiration to the entire labor movement.

Emerging from the strike of 1897 well organized and over 100,000 strong, the United Mine Workers now turned their sights on the anthracite coal industry, centered in five counties of northeastern Pennsylvania and controlled by nine railroad companies. When the president of the UMW, John Mitchell, authorized the calling of a strike on September 12, 1900, 150,000 anthracite miners walked out of the pits. The union had demanded recognition, the establishment of labor-management committees to settle petty disputes, a wage increase, and the right of the miners to employ check-weighmen. Before the strike was over, Mitchell waived the demand for recognition and suggested that the remaining issues be arbitrated. And when the operators granted a 10 per cent wage increase and made other concessions in October 1900, Mitchell gladly called off the strike. Although the UMW won only part of its demands, it had succeeded in accomplishing its major objective—the thorough organization of the anthracite industry.

Although the UMW had thoroughly organized the anthracite region during the strike of 1900, the operators refused even to discuss wage rates with UMW officials in 1902, and Mitchell called a second strike that began on May 14. Public opinion strongly favored the miners and veered even more sharply in their favor as the result of an incident that occurred in August. A citizen of Wilkes-Barre appealed in the name of Christianity to George F. Baer, president of the Reading Railroad, to end the strike by giving in to the union. In a letter that was subsequently published, Baer replied that the interests of the miners would be protected, "not by the labor agitators, but by the Christian men to whom God, in His infinite wisdom, has given control of the property interests of the country."

As the strike dragged on into the autumn of 1902 coal prices sky-rocketed and the eastern cities faced the possibility of a serious coal famine. President Roosevelt summoned Mitchell and the leading operators to a White House conference on October 3, 1902. Mitchell agreed to submit the issues to arbitration and to end the strike, but the operators denounced the UMW as a lawless body and declared they would never arbitrate. Convinced that the safety of the nation was imperiled and that the operators were now solely responsible for prolonging the strike, Roosevelt prepared to take drastic measures. First, he issued secret orders to the army to move 10,000 troops into the anthracite region, seize the mines, and operate them as receiver for the government. Secondly, he sent Secretary of War Elihu Root to New York City to warn J. P. Morgan, who had close financial ties with the operators, of the impending seizure. Morgan and Root at once sketched out a plan of mediation, which the operators accepted with the reservation that no labor official should be appointed to the arbitration commission. Mitchell approved the plan, insisting only that the President be given complete freedom in selecting the commission; and Roosevelt added a humorous touch, which he greatly enjoyed, by appointing the former head of the conductors' brotherhood to the commission in the capacity of "sociologist."

Roosevelt's decisive intervention and the subsequent arbitration of the anthracite dispute constituted one of the most important landmarks in American labor history. For the first time the federal government had looked at an industrial dispute on its merits, without automatically taking management's side. From the commission's award the miners won the nine-hour day, a 10 per cent wage increase, the right to select check-weighmen, and a permanent board of conciliation. Not until 1916 did the UMW finally win recognition and the right to bargain collectively with the anthracite operators; even so, the gains from the victory of 1902 were enormous indeed.

Thus, by 1903 the UMW had organized the eastern and midwestern bituminous areas and the entire anthracite industry. On the troubled frontiers of coal, however, they met fierce resistance and defeat that spelled eventual disaster for the union. West Virginia was the key to long range success or failure, for so long as the West Virginia fields were unorganized the UMW and the northern operators could never be protected from the competition of this low-wage and low-cost area. In 1900 and again in 1902 the UMW executed full-scale campaigns to organize the state and failed because all the powers of management, the state, and the courts combined against it. Meanwhile, as new coal fields were opened in Virginia, Kentucky, Tennessee, and Alabama, the task of organizing the southern area became increasingly important and difficult. In 1912–1913 the UMW launched a third great strike in West Virginia but was only partially successful. So long as West Virginia and the other southern fields remained unorganized there could be neither stability in the coal industry nor security for the UMW.

In the meantime, on another frontier of the coal industry, Colorado, the miners suffered other and bloodier defeats. A strike called by the UMW against Rockefeller's Colorado Fuel and Iron Company and other operators in 1903–1904 ended in a rout for the union and the deportation of many of the strikers. Ten years later, in September 1913, the UMW again attempted to overcome the Colorado coal companies, and the state was torn by violent civil war, set off when National Guard troops attacked and burned a strikers' tent colony at Ludlow on April 20, 1914, killing eleven women and two children.

The Ludlow Massacre and civil war in Colorado horrified the nation, provoked investigations by a congressional committee and the Industrial Relations Commission, and set off a wave of sympathy for the strikers. But John D. Rockefeller, Jr., who controlled the Colorado Fuel and Iron Company, refused to surrender to the UMW, rejected President Wilson's plan of settlement, and insisted upon instituting a labor relations program, the chief feature of which was the formation of a company union, that retained for management full power over policies affecting the workers. None the less, the American people had been taught a tragic lesson in the consequences of industrial despotism and absentee capitalism.

28 / "As Steel Goes"

Time and again during the period 1897–1914 socialists and other left-wing elements in the labor movement charged that Gompers and the AF of L represented only the aristocracy of labor and were indifferent to the necessity of organizing the basic industries that employed the mass of workers. These critics, however, ignored some important facts. This was a period when organized labor progressed from impotence to a position of considerable power, in spite of the absence of any favorable legislation or any effective public support in behalf of the labor movement. To say that Gompers and his leaders did not recognize the importance of unionizing the basic industries, like iron and steel, textiles, and lumber, is simply not true. But Gompers knew the AF of L's weakness as well as its strength, and he knew the time had not yet come for an all-out campaign against the mass industries.

The wisdom of Gompers' view was confirmed many times during the progressive period. For example, the UMW's leadership of the Colorado miners in the bloody strike of 1913–1914 was heroic, to be sure; but the long battle was costly, and defeat left the entire union severely weakened. The AF of L's most discouraging and significant reversal, however, was its failure to organize the steel industry, for all during the period under discussion steel stood as an anti-union bastion, setting an open shop pattern for the other mass industries and providing anti-union leadership for thousands of small manufacturers.

During the Homestead strike of 1892 in the Carnegie steel mills Carnegie defeated the Amalgamated Iron, Steel and Tin Workers but did not destroy the union, which then included only skilled workers. When the Carnegie plants were merged into the United States Steel Corporation in 1901 the union officials decided they now had no alternative but to attempt to organize all the workers, skilled and unskilled. First, however, the Amalgamated demanded that the union scale of wages be paid in all plants of the American Sheet Steel, American Steel Hoop, and American Tin Plate companies, all of them subsidiaries of United States Steel. The directors of the corporation offered a compromise that would have halted the progress of unionization. The union officials refused and on August 10, 1901, called a general strike against all plants of the Steel Corporation. A majority of workers walked out, but for a number of reasons the strike was doomed from the beginning. In the end the Amalgamated surrendered unconditionally. The corporation agreed to pay union wages, but the wage rate was no longer an important issue. In return, the union withdrew from fourteen mills, agreed neither to seek to extend its influence nor even to welcome new members, and conceded the corporation's right to discharge workers for union activities.

For a time after their victory of 1901 the officials of United States Steel made no direct assaults upon the carcass of the Amalgamated. Instead, they undertook a series of innovations designed to win the loyalty of the workers: profit-sharing, begun in December 1902; an employee-safety program, launched in 1906–1907; and finally a workmen's compensation and old age pension program, inaugurated in 1910. Meanwhile, in June 1909 the American Sheet and Tin Plate Company, the last of the unionized subsidiaries of the corporation, posted notices announcing it would begin an open shop policy on July 1, 1909. When the protests of the Amalgamated were not acknowledged, the union called a second general strike against the corporation. The workers responded *en masse* throughout the far-flung steel empire; the AF of L joined the struggle with financial support; but the strikers never had a chance. After holding out for fourteen months they surrendered on August 23, 1910.

Thus, after 1909 the United States Steel Corporation boasted an open shop throughout its vast domain. Moreover, the ally of United States Steel, the Lake Carriers' Association, destroyed the Lake Seamen's Union during a long and bitter strike from 1909 to 1912. The establishment of management's absolute authority in all branches of the steel corporation had been accomplished, in short, by relentless warfare against the union; by the use of spies and the blacklisting of strike leaders; by the domination of local governments; and by a welfare program that undermined the union's appeal. Until 1937 United States Steel remained the citadel of anti-unionism in the mass industries.

29 / *Left-Wing Unionism and the Rise of Socialism*

Left-wing unionism first developed on an important scale, not in the teeming cities of the East, but in the mining regions of the western slope of the Rockies. Here raw industrial absolutism provoked brutal retaliation by frontier miners. The result was nonideological class warfare on a grand and violent scale. Out of this morass of class conflict there emerged in 1905 an organization that assumed leadership of the frontier miners, migratory workers, lumber workers, and unskilled and unprotected laborers of all types. It was the Industrial Workers of the World, called the IWW, a coalition of the Western Federation of Miners, its ally, the socialistic American Labor Union, and the Socialist Trade and Labor Alliance. Organized along industrial lines, the IWW in the beginning was frankly revolutionary, with sabotage and strikes its weapons and the abolition of the wage system and the establishment of a proletarian commonwealth its objectives.

Within a year after its formation, however, the IWW showed signs of coming apart at the seams. The basic difficulty was dissension between the leaders of the Western Federation, who were more interested in promoting labor's immediate goals than in building the socialistic state, and the leader of the Socialist Trade and Labor Alliance, Daniel De Leon. A dogmatic Marxian theorist, De Leon had tried to wrest control of the AF of L from Gompers and when this campaign failed had organized his own Socialist Trade and Labor Alliance in 1895. He tried to win control of the IWW but failed and was unceremoniously expelled in 1908. From this time on the IWW was an untheoretical champion of lower class workers.

In the West the IWW fought the battles of the lumbermen, the migratory workers, and the frontier miners. Its emphasis on direct action—the strike and sabotage—brought it into collision with employers, the police, and the courts and prevented any systematic organizational campaigns. In the East the IWW provided leadership for unskilled workers that the AF of L had ignored. In 1912 it led a strike in Lawrence, Massachusetts, against the American Woolen Company and won a wage increase. In Paterson and Passaic, New Jersey, the IWW took command of rebellious silk workers and led them successfully in a strike in 1912 and 1913.

While the IWW was careening from one bloody conflict to another, the political counterpart of left-wing unionism, socialism, was struggling for a program and a means of expression. During the 1890's the socialists were united in the Socialist Labor party, which Daniel De Leon ruled until his inflexible Marxist dogma provoked a rebellion in 1899–1900 by a moderate element. Meanwhile, in 1897 the midwestern labor leader, Eugene V. Debs, had founded a potential rival, the Social Democracy, dedicated to advancing the public ownership of railroads, utilities, and industrial monopolies. In 1901 the anti-De Leon faction in the Socialist Labor party, headed by Morris Hillquit of New York and Victor Berger of Milwaukee, joined the Debs group in Indianapolis to launch the Socialist Party of America.

The Socialist party included visionaries and dogmatic Marxians, but it was so completely dominated by the moderates—Debs, Hillquit, and Berger

—that it was more the left-wing of progressivism than a revolutionary workers' party. By 1908 the party had a membership of over 58,000; four years later the figure stood at nearly 126,000. The party's influence during this period, however, was far greater than its small membership would indicate. By 1912 Socialist administrations governed Milwaukee, Schenectady, and Berkeley, California; one of the party's leaders, Victor Berger, sat in the House of Representatives and was soon joined by another Socialist from New York City's East Side, Meyer London; and in the presidential election of 1912 the Socialist candidate, Debs, polled over 897,000 votes.

30 / *The Counteroffensive of the Employers*

For a time at the turn of the century it seemed the lion and the lamb might lie down together, when the National Civic Federation, the first important attempt to bring peace out of the prevailing chaos of industrial relations, was formed in 1900. Founded to prove that "organized labor cannot be destroyed without debasement of the masses," the Federation's leaders included industrialists like Mark Hanna and George W. Perkins, bankers like J. P. Morgan, and labor spokesmen like Samuel Gompers and John Mitchell. Dedicated to advancing the cause of industrial peace and offering its mediation if strikes occurred, the Federation for a few years rendered service to the labor movement by lending a sort of respectability to the AF of L.

That the Federation represented only a minority of employers, however, was demonstrated by a significant movement that was already getting under way when the Federation was organized. It was a mass offensive of employers to destroy unionism altogether and to establish an open shop pattern throughout American industry. Management's counterattack opened in 1900 in Dayton, Ohio, where the union movement had made considerable progress. Within two years the local employers' association had driven the unions out of town. Flushed with their victory, propagandists went out of Dayton to arouse employers in other cities to the defense of what they called "the American Plan"—that is, the open shop. So successful were employers' associations in Dayton, Chicago, Beloit in Wisconsin, and Sedalia in Missouri, that the leaders of the open shop crusade received appeals for assistance from employers' groups all over the country.

Obviously, what most industrialists and businessmen wanted was destruction of the labor movement. In 1903 the National Association of Manufacturers, under the presidency of David M. Parry, took command of the open shop campaign and formed the Citizens' Industrial Association for the purpose of forming employers' associations throughout the country. The Citizens' Industrial Association also sponsored a propaganda campaign to rally public opinion behind the American Plan. Appealing to the average citizen's individualism and prejudices, these propagandists defended the right of Americans to work when and where they pleased, depicted labor organizers as agitators and socialists, and portrayed employers as champions of free enterprise and ancient American liberties.

This counteroffensive did not destroy unionism, but it struck such a heavy blow that between 1904 and 1910 the AF of L not only failed to grow but actually lost membership. Nor can it be doubted that the Citizens' Industrial Association and its several hundred local branches succeeded in engendering widespread popular hostility to the very concept of unionism. President Charles W. Eliot of Harvard, for example, glorified the strikebreaker as an "American hero," while President Woodrow Wilson of Princeton avowed himself a "fierce partisan" of the open shop.

The employers' counteroffensive would not have succeeded so well, however, if labor had been able to come into the court of public opinion with clean hands. The middle class would never support the labor movement until it was certain that labor sought the general good instead of class privileges and had repudiated violence as an instrument of industrial warfare. In so far as Gompers and his associates were able to identify unionism with democracy and to remove the stigma of alien origin from the AF of L, they made a lasting contribution to the advancement of American democratic institutions. Unfortunately, however, anti-union spokesmen were able to point with telling effect to many examples of violence, irresponsibility, and corruption among the ranks of organized labor during the years before the First World War.

31 / *The Courts, Injunctions, and the AF of L in Politics, 1900–1914*

During the political upheaval of the 1890's Gompers had fought off those idealists who advocated aligning the AF of L with the Socialist Labor party, the Populists in 1892, and with the Democrats during the great battle of 1896. As the progressive movement gathered strength after 1900, however, it is doubtful that Gompers could have preserved inviolate the policy of nonpartisanship, or that the AF of L could have avoided taking a stand on the issues of the day. In any event, the entrance of the AF of L into national politics in 1906 and its subsequent campaign for a specific legislative program was necessitated and certainly hastened by a development that seemed to threaten the very existence of the labor movement.

This development was the entrance of the federal courts into labor disputes in a decisive way. The phenomenon began during the Chicago railroad strike of 1894, when the Attorney General of the United States obtained an injunction against Eugene V. Debs and other leaders of the American Railway Union for conspiring to restrain trade and obstruct the movement of the mail. The theory upon which this and later injunctions were issued was that the prohibitions against restraint of trade embodied in the Sherman antitrust law of 1890 applied as well to labor and farm unions as to corporations. The effect of this doctrine, which was confirmed by the Supreme Court in 1895, was not to outlaw unions, *per se*, as illegal conspiracies, but to forbid union practices that might be construed to be unreasonable, or illegal, restraints upon trade.

Before 1901 the Sherman Act was used, not against illegal industrial combinations, but to neutralize labor's allegedly illegal weapons—mass picketing, the sympathetic strike, the secondary boycott, and the blacklisting of goods manufactured by anti-union employers. It was the continued intervention of the federal courts after 1901 that finally compelled Gompers and the AF of L to take an active role in national politics. The immediate provocation, however, arose out of two cases involving the boycott of non-union products: the Danbury Hatters' case and the Buck's Stove and Range Company case.

In 1902 the United Hatters of North America called a strike against a hatmaker of Danbury, Connecticut, D. E. Loewe and Company, and declared a nation-wide boycott of Loewe's products. The officials of the company struck back by organizing the American Anti-Boycott Association and suing the United Hatters in 1903 for triple damages of $240,000 under the Sherman Act. Five years later the Supreme Court confirmed the judgment of the lower courts that the boycott was a conspiracy in restraint of trade; the district court thereupon awarded the company full damages and made the members of the union personally responsible for payment of the claim. In the second case, the Buck's Stove and Range Company in 1907 obtained an injunction in a federal court ordering the officials of the AF of L to end a boycott against the company's products. When Gompers and the executive committee of the AF of L ignored the injunction, the federal court sentenced them all to jail for terms ranging from six months to one year. The Supreme Court in 1914 upheld the injunction but removed the penalties on a technicality.

The effect of the rulings in these two test cases was to establish the doctrine that all of labor's strike activities fell within the purview of the federal courts and that union leaders and members were liable to jail terms and loss of property if they defied injunctions. In short, labor might wage industrial warfare only if the federal courts approved. Obviously, the AF of L's surest means of protection against such judicial interference was to obtain amendment of the Sherman law to give labor unions immunity from its prohibitions.

From 1900 to 1906 the leaders of the AF of L tried in various indirect ways to force the desired changes in the Sherman Act, but their pressure, as contrasted with the growing political power of the NAM, was pitifully weak. In 1906 Gompers and his associates decided the time had come to begin an all-out political campaign. First they presented to President Roosevelt and Congress a Bill of Grievances, demanding, among other things, amendment of the Sherman law and relief from judicial interference; second, they entered the congressional campaign of 1906 and helped elect six union members to the House of Representatives. In 1908 Gompers presented the AF of L's demands to the platform committees of the Republican and Democratic national conventions. The Republicans refused to make any concessions or promises, while the Democrats adopted a disingenuous platform plank that seemed to promise substantial relief. Taking what they could get, Gompers and his colleagues openly campaigned in behalf of the Democratic ticket headed by Bryan.

The decisive Republican victory in 1908 was only a momentary reversal, for the political situation from 1910 to 1912 seemed to offer the AF of L an opportunity finally to achieve its goal. Internal warfare split the Republican party and made certain a Democratic victory in 1912. And when the Democrats nominated a progressive, Woodrow Wilson, and reaffirmed the promises they had made to labor four years before, Gompers and his executive committee campaigned openly and effectively for the Democratic ticket. Wilson won a sweeping victory in the Electoral College; the Democrats won control of both houses of Congress; and it seemed that labor's friends were finally in control of the federal government.

And in large measure labor's hopes were realized during the period of Wilson's first administration, from 1913 to 1917. The new Secretary of Labor, William B. Wilson, was a former secretary-treasurer of the UMW; some fifteen union members sat in the House of Representatives, while the new President was considerably more susceptible to labor pressure than Roosevelt or Taft had been. The changed climate was everywhere evident in Washington—in the exposure by a congressional committee in 1913 of a NAM lobby; in the forthright way in which the House labor committee and the Industrial Relations Commission investigated the Colorado coal strike in 1914; in the enactment in 1915 of the Seaman's Act, sponsored by Gompers and Andrew Furuseth of the International Seamen's Union, which freed sailors from bondage to their labor contracts; in the passage of the Smith-Hughes Act in 1916, providing for federal aid to state vocational schools; and in the passage of the Burnett immigration bill, which established a literacy test for immigrants, over Wilson's veto in 1917.

Even so, the AF of L's chief objective was amendment of the Sherman law to give unions immunity from prosecution for using illegal strike weapons. In their campaign to obtain what was essentially class legislation, Gompers and the AF of L lobby ran head on into the stubborn opposition of President Wilson and the Democratic majority in Congress.

The issue of labor exemption first arose decisively in the new administration during the preparation of new antitrust legislation, the Clayton bill, in 1914. As it emerged from the House judiciary committee, this measure included no provisions for labor's benefit. Gompers and his powerful lobby at once descended upon Congress and the White House; labor spokesmen in the House threatened to oppose the Clayton bill; and there were many stormy conferences between the labor leaders and administration spokesmen. So firmly did the administration stand, however, that Gompers had to accept a compromise that denied the AF of L its supreme objective. The House committee added sections to the Clayton bill providing for jury trials in criminal contempt cases and circumscribing the issuance of injunctions in labor disputes. Another provision declared that neither farm nor labor unions should be construed to be illegal combinations, *per se*, in restraint of trade; but as the courts had repeatedly declared that labor unions were not unlawful combinations, this declaration by Congress conferred no new benefit. A final provision legalized strike activities that the courts had heretofore approved.

President Wilson and the chairman of the House committee that framed the labor sections of the Clayton bill frankly declared that the bill did not give labor unions the privilege of using illegal strike weapons or immunity from prosecution for violating the antitrust law. But Gompers hailed the Clayton Act as labor's "Magna Charta" and announced that the AF of L had finally won freedom from judicial interference under the Sherman law. As we will see in a later chapter, the Supreme Court thought otherwise.

CHAPTER 4 / THE PROGRESSIVE MOVEMENT

*I*T is impossible to comprehend within the bounds of a few generalizations any phenomenon so complex and far-reaching as the progressive movement in the United States. Much confusion can be avoided, however, if from the outset the reader bears several fundamental principles in mind.

To begin with, there was no such thing as *a* progressive movement, that is, no organized campaign uniting all the manifold efforts at political, social, and economic reform. On the contrary, there were numerous progressive movements operating in different areas simultaneously. There was, for example, the effort of social workers and students of the labor question to bring the power of the state and national governments into the economic struggle on the side of women, children, and other unprotected groups. This movement for social justice was often, but not always, independent of the movement for political reform. Or, there was the far-reaching campaign, getting under way about 1900, to restore representative government to the cities and to end the reign of corruption in them. Next came a movement to bring state governments out of their subservience to railroads and corporations and to make them instruments for advancing social welfare. Finally, there was a progressive movement on the national level, which took form in attempts to subject railroads, industrial corporations, and banks to effective public control.

In the second place, the progressive movement, in its political manifestations, was essentially a revolt of the middle classes—the small businessmen and bankers, prosperous farmers, editors, clergymen, and other professional groups—against a state of affairs that seemed to guarantee perpetual control to the privileged few who owned the wealth of the United States. Although it drew support from organized labor, the movement had no solid basis of popular support among the masses of workers, nor was it particularly sympathetic to labor's needs. Moreover, while leadership in the reform movement of the 1890's had been largely agrarian, after 1897 farm unrest subsided. Leadership in the revolt against the *status quo* passed, therefore, to the cities and small towns, and progressivism ceased to be agrarian in outlook and objectives.

Thirdly, the degree to which progressives were united in a common cause with well-defined objectives varied from movement to movement and from area to area. The social justice champions, for example, were organized in state and national associations and united behind common programs. Although the city and state reformers never formally combined regionally or nationally, they all faced the same problems, attacked them in much the same way, and profited from one another's experiences. In the arena of national politics, moreover, progressives in both parties often fought for the same goals.

None the less, until 1916 there was a profound divergence in progressive attitudes toward the paramount questions of corporation control and of how far federal legislation should be employed for the benefit of workers and farmers. The dominant tradition of American democracy had been the Jeffersonian tradition of the neutral, umpire state, which gave special favors to no class or interest. Many progressives, including most Democrats, thought the federal government should do no more than destroy the system of protection for business that the Republicans had constructed since 1861. Others, including Theodore Roosevelt and many progressive Republicans after 1908, argued that the federal government should play a dynamic, positive role by directly regulating business activities and giving special protection to labor and farmers. As we will later see, this dilemma was not resolved until 1916.

With these generalizations made by way of introduction, let us now examine one of the most significant and fruitful reform movements in American history.

32 / The Social Justice Movement

The social justice movement was the first large-scale attempt to palliate the grosser aspects of American life—the miserable living conditions of the city masses, the exploitation of women and children in industry, and the degradation of the submerged, unprotected workers. The vanguard in the effort to alleviate the sufferings of the poor were the priests and ministers who worked in the slums. During the 1890's, however, there developed a separate class of social workers, usually employed by charity organizations and settlement houses. After 1900 the social workers constituted a growing and vociferous element in the American society. With the support of philanthropic foundations, they made intensive surveys of labor conditions, the causes of poverty, and means of alleviating social distress. As this time passed, moreover, the social workers became departmentalized, some concerned with the care of immigrants, some with the problems of labor, some with juvenile delinquency.

By 1900 the leaders of the social justice movement had gone far beyond the concept of private amelioration and were beginning to evolve ambitious new schemes of social salvation. What they now envisaged was nothing less than using the state police power to accomplish rearrangement of economic relationships. In other words, the state governments, and later the federal government, should enter the battle to protect the weak—first by legislation based upon the investigations of the social workers, and then by employing the social workers as the agents of enforcement.

First to come under the concerted attack of the social justice forces was the old problem of child labor, which posed the most poignant challenge. By 1900 probably 1,700,000 children under sixteen were employed in the cotton mills of New England and the South, in the berry fields of New Jersey, and on the farms of the country. In the early years of the twentieth century, moreover, the problem was growing worse as the textile industry advanced in the South.

The child labor movement of the twentieth century opened simultaneously on two fronts—in the Southeast in 1901 with the introduction of child labor bills in the legislatures of the Carolinas, Georgia, and Alabama; and in the North, with the adoption of pioneer legislation by New Jersey, New York, and Illinois in 1903–1904. In 1904 the southern and northern wings of the movement came together in the National Child Labor Committee, which by 1910 had twenty-five branch committees in twenty-two states.

The accomplishments of this dedicated band constituted perhaps the greatest single triumph of the social justice movement before the First World War. In 1900 twenty-four states and the District of Columbia made no provision for a minimum age for workers. By 1914, on the other hand, every state but one had established a minimum age limit, usually fourteen, while many states had prohibited children between fourteen and sixteen from working at night and in dangerous occupations.

The movement for a federal child labor law did not reach serious proportions until near the end of the progressive period. Senator Albert J. Beveridge of Indiana introduced the first federal bill in 1906, but the National Child Labor Committee refused to endorse it on the ground that it was best to work for a while longer in the states. In 1914, however, when conditions seemed ripe for federal action, the Committee sponsored the introduction of a bill in Congress, which prohibited the shipment in interstate commerce of goods manufactured in whole or in part by children under fourteen and of products of mines or quarries where children under sixteen were employed. After passing the House of Representatives in 1914, the measure languished in the Senate, while spokesmen of the NAM and the southern textile interests denounced it as an unconstitutional invasion of the police power of the states. Then, in the summer of 1916, President Wilson pushed the bill, now called the Keating-Owen bill, through the Senate in order to enhance the chances of a Democratic victory in the impending elections, and the most significant victory of the social justice advocates on the national level was won.

A second major objective of the social justice crusade was the protection of women in industry by limiting the number of hours they might work. Illinois enacted the first enforceable eight-hour law for women in 1893— the result of the labors of Florence Kelley of Chicago's Hull House. Two years later, however, the state Supreme Court nullified the Illinois statute, and leadership in this campaign passed to the East, where the standard of reform was carried by Consumers' Leagues, organizations of socially-minded women. Beginning with the enactment of statutes by New York in 1896 and Massachusetts in 1900 limiting women's hours to sixty a week, the movement spread slowly to Nebraska, Michigan, Colorado, Oregon, Washington, and Tennessee. When the United States Supreme Court in 1908 swept away all doubt as to the constitutionality of women's hours legislation, it seemed the floodgates retarding reform had been opened. Between 1909 and 1917 thirty-nine states enacted hours legislation for the first time or strengthened existing laws.

A third, and perhaps the most ambitious, social justice objective was minimum wage legislation for women workers. By enacting the first legislation in this field from 1896 to 1909, Australia and Great Britain provided inspiration to American reformers. An even more important impetus came from governmental and private investigations in the United States from 1911 to 1914, revealing that large numbers of women received wages entirely inadequate to maintain a decent standard of living. In 1910 the National Consumers' League made minimum wage legislation part of its long-range program; the following year the Women's Trade Union League joined the fight, and the campaign had begun.

The allied reform groups scored their first victory in 1912, when the Massachusetts legislature established a wage commission empowered to recommend minimum wages for women and to expose employers who refused to conform. The year following the enactment of this pioneer law saw the adoption by eight midwestern and western states of statutes that went the whole way and empowered wage commissions to establish binding minimum wage rates. After 1913, however, the movement lost most of its strength. Between 1914 and 1923 only six additional states, the District of Columbia, and Puerto Rico joined the states that sought to protect the living standard, and therefore the health and morality, of their women workers.

The last major objective of the champions of social welfare was the establishment of public systems of industrial accident insurance. By 1900 the western European nations had long since demonstrated the excellence and feasibility of such systems; but in the United States the common law rules relating to industrial accidents still governed the payment of damages.

The obvious injustice of throwing practically the entire financial burden of industrial accidents and deaths on the workers and their families—for that was usually the result of the application of the common law rules[1]—led to an early movement to abrogate or modify these doctrines. By 1910 most states had modified the common law rules in favor of the injured worker; even so, he was little better off than before because he still had to sue to recover damages. From 1902 to 1909 Maryland, Montana, and the federal government experimented with crude and limited systems of accident insurance, but this represented all that had been accomplished. From 1909 to 1913 came a brief but intense period of official investigation into the entire subject. All commissions concluded that the prevailing compensation system had collapsed and recommended the enactment of accident insurance laws. As the people learned the facts, a wave of protest and legislation swept over the country. Ten states established insurance systems in 1911 and twenty states, three territories, and the federal government followed suit from 1912 to 1916.

---

[1] Briefly stated, under these common law rules the injured employee was not entitled to compensation if he had willingly assumed the risks of his job, if he was himself negligent, or if his injury had been caused by a fellow worker's negligence. Moreover, in most cases the injured employee had to sue for damages and prove that he had suffered as a direct result of his employer's negligence.

Thus it was that the professional social workers, students of the labor problem, and leaders of advanced social opinion grew strong during the progressive era, emerged as a redemptive element in the American democracy, and banded together in crusades to transform an individualistic and competitive society into something approximating the welfare state. There were dozens of organizations and more campaigns for social reforms than we have the space to relate. Some social justice advocates went far beyond the objectives we have described and set under way discussions of social security, unemployment relief, and laws designed to advance the interests of organized labor. These pioneers on the advanced social frontier failed to obtain the legislation they advocated. Their failure, however, was only momentary, for they were laying the necessary groundwork for the time when the social justice movement would come to fruition in the 1930's. The line of descent between the social justice movement of the early 1900's and the New Deal is, therefore, clear and straight.

33 / *The Supreme Court and Social Legislation*

Beset by the opposition of employers and other representatives of uncontrolled economic interests, the social justice advocates at times faced even more formidable opposition from yet another source—the bench and bar of the United States. Reared on the Anglo-American legal tradition that often valued liberty above justice and the rights of property above the interests of society, the great majority of American lawyers and judges at the turn of the century believed firmly in the automatic operation of economic laws, cherished a strong hostility to the concept of public control, and were usually ranged on the side of the railroads and large corporations.

The implications of this fact for the social justice movement become at once apparent when one recalls the peculiar power of judges in the American constitutional system. Unlike their counterparts elsewhere in the western world, American judges had established the privilege of determining whether legislation violated the provisions of written state and federal constitutions. As judges nowhere rendered decisions in an intellectual vacuum tube, their own preconceived notions of the proper function of government invariably affected their legal judgments. In rendering decisions in cases involving social legislation, therefore, judges often unconsciously allowed inherited prejudices, instead of sound legal precepts, to control the decisions they gave.

Although the proponents of social welfare legislation occasionally ran afoul the verdicts of state judges, the federal courts and eventually the United States Supreme Court posed the greatest threat to the success of their efforts. This was true during the progressive period, not because that court always nullified state efforts at social amelioration, but rather because the federal courts insisted upon exercising the privilege of reviewing state regulatory legislation to determine whether it violated the Fourteenth Amendment's dictum that no state should deprive a person of life, liberty, or property without due process of law. As the Supreme Court in the 1880's had established the doctrine that corporations were persons within the meaning of the Fourteenth Amendment, corporations were at liberty to appeal to the federal courts for protection against unfair and discriminatory state regulation.

It was not, however, until 1898 that the Supreme Court rendered its first important decision involving state labor legislation. In Holden *v.* Hardy the court upheld a Utah statute establishing the eight-hour day for miners. The court also expounded in forceful language the legal theories underlying all social legislation by the states, namely, that it was the duty of the state to protect the health and morals of its citizens; that this protection could be afforded by a proper use of the police power; and, finally, that such use of the police power was not an unlawful infringement of the freedom of contract guaranteed by the Fourteenth Amendment. While this decision clearly established the right of the states to limit the hours of labor in dangerous occupation, it did not affirm the constitutionality of hours legislation for any and all occupations. In fact, no one was quite sure how far the states might go in this field until the Supreme Court rendered its decision in Lochner *v.* New York in 1905.

The Lochner case involved the constitutionality of a New York statute limiting the hours that bakers could work to ten a day and sixty a week. Counsel for the state argued that the bakers' law protected the public's food supply; Lochner's counsel, on the other hand, contended that the law unduly violated the freedom of employer and employee to make a labor contract. A bare majority of the court decided the time had come to call a halt to improper use of the state police power. Asserting that the bakers' trade was not particularly unhealthy, the majority concluded that "Statutes of the nature of that under review, limiting the hours in which grown and intelligent men may labor to earn their living, are mere meddlesome interferences with the rights of the individual." In other words, a state could not contravene the freedom of contract unless there were obvious and compelling reasons for exercising the police power.

Moreover, the Lochner decision created grave doubt as to the constitutionality of legislation restricting the hours of labor merely on the basis of sex. This issue arose in 1907, when an employer challenged the Oregon ten-hour law for women. Perceiving that this was a supreme crisis in the life of the social justice movement, Mrs. Florence Kelley, chief Factory Inspector of Illinois, and Josephine Goldmark, the driving spirit in the National Consumers' League, moved to obtain a distinguished attorney to defend the Oregon statute in this test case. First they turned to Joseph H. Choate, leader of the American bar, but Choate refused, saying he could see no reason why "a big husky Irishwoman should not work more than ten hours a day in a laundry if she and her employer so desired." The next day Mrs. Kelley and Miss Goldmark asked Louis D. Brandeis of Boston to defend the law, and Brandeis gladly agreed.

Easily the most socially conscious lawyer of his generation, Brandeis had long protested that the law had not been altered to fit the new conditions of American economic and social life. The trouble was, he said, that neither lawyers nor judges knew anything about the economic and social conditions out of which cases arose. Thus in place of a stale legal traditionalism he proposed the development and application of a sociological jurisprudence.

As Brandeis put it, "A lawyer who has not studied economics and sociology is very apt to become a public enemy."

The Oregon case gave Brandeis an opportunity to put his theory of a sociological jurisprudence to practical use and to demonstrate it before the whole body of lawyers. In preparing his brief, he gave only two pages to conventional legal reasoning and citation of precedents. But he used more than one hundred pages to demonstrate the economic and social consequences of long hours of work by women; and by citing evidence drawn from hundreds of sources he proved that long hours were dangerous to women's health and morals and that reasonable hours produced tangible social benefits. Before this time no lawyer had ever submitted such a brief, for cases had always been argued on a basis of abstract logic and by an appeal to precedents. "There is no logic that is properly applicable to these laws," Brandeis replied, "except the logic of facts."

When the case, Muller v. Oregon, was argued before the Supreme Court in January 1908, plaintiff's counsel asserted that women, equally with men, were endowed with a freedom of contract which no legislature could impair. To this Brandeis responded with a masterful array of facts. Although the court was dominated by traditionalists, Brandeis' argument won the day. In upholding the constitutionality of the ten-hour law, the Court for the first time admitted the need for facts to establish the reasonableness or unreasonableness of social legislation.

It was an epochal victory for the social justice movement; but even more important was the fact that Brandeis' technique of marshaling economic and social data in defense of social legislation soon became ordinary legal practice. From 1908 to 1915 four additional cases involving women's hours legislation reached the Supreme Court. In each case the court adhered to the principle set forth in Muller v. Oregon, approving even a comprehensive California eight-hour law for women.

During the period 1898–1915 the Supreme Court also reviewed a number of state child labor laws. In no field of social legislation were reformers on surer constitutional ground, for the court consistently affirmed the right of the states to protect their children—by prohibiting work in hazardous occupations or at an age that was prejudicial to their health and morals. Before 1918, however, it was still a moot question whether Congress could use its control over commerce to regulate the labor of children.

Obviously, the court had been profoundly influenced by the progressive temper of the time. The extent of that influence was demonstrated in 1917, when the court passed judgment on almost all forms of labor legislation. In Bunting v. Oregon, the justices tacitly reversed their decision in Lochner v. New York by approving an Oregon ten-hour law for men in industry. In Wilson v. New the court narrowly sustained the Adamson Act, which established the eight-hour day for railway workers engaged in interstate commerce. In Stettler v. O'Hara an evenly divided court upheld an Oregon statute establishing minimum wages for women. Finally, the court upheld the constitutionality of the three systems of industrial accident insurance then in effect in various states. Indeed, it seemed as if sociological jurisprudence had at last found acceptance by the highest court of the land.

34 / *The Muckrakers*

At about the same time that the social workers were beginning their investigations and formulating their programs, a revolution in the field of journalism was also slowly taking form. It featured the emergence of a group of reporters, called muckrakers, who dedicated themselves to the task of awakening the public to the fact that American representative government had ceased to be either representative or democratic; that the old promise of equality of economic opportunity was rapidly becoming an anachronism in view of developments in business and finance; that uncontrolled railroads, insurance companies, and meat packing houses were levying tribute from the people and endangering their lives; and that the ideal of social equality was on all sides being destroyed by the treatment accorded immigrant groups and Negroes.

These publicists who probed all the dark corners of American life did not make the progressive movement. The social justice movement and the campaign to clean up the cities and states, for example, were well under way when they entered the battle. However, by exposing the shame and corruption of American public life the muckrakers fired the righteous indignation of the middle classes and by so doing helped to make the progressive movement a national uprising instead of a series of sporadic campaigns.

A medium for the muckrakers came with the development in the 1890's of the cheap magazine. By 1900 *Cosmopolitan, Munsey's,* and *McClure's* were already in the field, catering to the reading habits of the middle classes. The leader of the three, *McClure's,* was the creature of S. S. McClure, an ebullient but erratic Irishman, who was evolving a novel concept of the cheap magazine as the nineteenth century ended. Understanding the agitation over the growth of railroad and industrial combinations, he decided to publish articles of contemporary economic and social significance. Giving complete freedom and generous financial support to his writers, McClure imposed only two standards—accuracy and readability.

To Ida M. Tarbell, a young writer on his staff, McClure in 1896 assigned the task of writing a history of the Standard Oil Company. He expected that her series would begin the following February; Miss Tarbell, however, spent five years in hard research and writing before her work was completed. Her *History of the Standard Oil Company,* which began in *McClure's* in November 1902 and ran for the following fifteen months, virtually took the country by storm. Although she was coldly objective and a master of the evidence, Miss Tarbell fully revealed the methods Rockefeller and his partners had used to build the oil monopoly.

At about the time Miss Tarbell was completing her study a courageous circuit attorney in St. Louis, Joseph W. Folk, was exposing the corruption of the local Democratic boss. McClure's managing editor, Lincoln Steffens, went to investigate; and that was how one of the best reporters of the twentieth century began his remarkable career as a muckraker. From St. Louis, Steffens went on to investigate political conditions in Minneapolis, Cleveland,

New York, Chicago, Philadelphia, and Pittsburgh. Everywhere he found essentially the same story of government by corrupt alliances of politicians and businessmen, and he returned to write about them in *McClure's.*

After his exposure of municipal corruption, Steffens next studied political affairs in several states, and his findings were embodied in a second series in *McClure's* in 1905 and 1906. As a movement to end the corporation-boss alliances and restore representative government was well under way when Steffens wrote these articles, he found evidence that an aroused citizenry could demand and obtain honest and efficient government.

The third of the trinity of McClure's great muckrakers was Ray Stannard Baker, a young journalist from the Middle West who investigated social and economic problems. He explored the labor problem, for example, and wrote for *McClure's* a revealing account of the Colorado coal strike of 1903–1904. His scholarly and convincing indictment of railroad malpractices, *The Railroads on Trial*, strengthened President Roosevelt's hand in the battle to enlarge the powers of the Interstate Commerce Commission. His *Following the Color Line* was a pioneer study of prevailing racial attitudes, North and South.

Of the other writers on *McClure's* staff who followed in the footsteps of Tarbell, Steffens, and Baker, two were notable: Burton J. Hendrick, who in 1906 publicized the revelations of corruption and mismanagement among the New York insurance companies that the commission headed by Charles Evans Hughes had brought to light the year before; and George Kibbe Turner, whose articles in 1909 on the alliance between the Chicago police and organized prostitution led to a famous vice commission's report on the midwestern city in 1911.

McClure's experiment soon proved that the public would buy a magazine devoted to serious discussions of contemporary problems, and other publishers were not long in following his example. *Collier's*, under the editorship of Norman Hapgood, led crusades against twin evils: the patent medicine fraud and the fraud of William Randolph Hearst. Charles Edward Russell's exposure of the beef trust, published in *Everybody's* in 1905, was another notable contribution.

It was inevitable, however, that the muckraking technique should be adopted by publishers and writers of dubious integrity and exploited merely for financial gain. As muckraking turned into yellow journalism around 1906, public interest was at first tremendously stimulated. But soon readers tired of the excitement; and by 1908 the entire muckraking movement was discredited.

The first of the yellow muckrakers was Thomas W. Lawson, a stock market gambler and former president of the Amalgamated Copper Company, whose series, "Frenzied Finance," in *Everybody's* in 1905 allegedly exposed the insides of the monster, high finance. His revelations of financial corruption were lurid and highly exaggerated, but they had a tremendous impact. The circulation of *Everybody's* jumped in one year from 150,000 to over 750,000; and there can be no doubt that his series contributed to the public demand for control of the stock market that culminated in the Pujo committee's investigation of 1913.

A sure sign that muckraking was heading for the gutter came in 1906 when William Randolph Hearst announced that his *Cosmopolitan* would soon publish a series of exposures that would be "the most vascular and virile" of them all. What Hearst had in mind was a series entitled "The Treason of the Senate" that the novelist, David Graham Phillips, was then writing. As it turned out, Phillips combined truth, fiction, and outright prevarication; but his indictment of the business domination of the Senate added a powerful impetus to the movement for direct election of senators.

35 / The Literature of Revolt

Contemporaneous with muckraking in journalism was the proliferation of a fictional literature dedicated to advancing the cause of democracy. Social and economic criticism ran the gamut from harsh exposés to frank appeals for a proletarian revolution. Frank Norris' *The Octopus* and *The Pit* told the story of the Southern Pacific Railroad's domination of the politics of California and the grain speculators' control of the wheat market. The naturalist, Theodore Dreiser, contributed two powerful socio-economic studies, *The Financier* and *The Titan,* based on the career of Charles T. Yerkes, a traction magnate of Chicago in the 1890's. David Graham Phillips exploited the theme of the corrupting power of money in *The Great God Success* and *The Second Generation,* while his *Susan Lennox, Her Fall and Rise* analyzed the social forces that drove a country girl in the city to prostitution. Robert Herrick's *The Memoirs of An American Citizen* and *Clark's Field* were impressive portrayals of the rise of men of wealth in an acquisitive society.

Socialist literary critiques of the shortcomings of the American democracy were, if anything, even harsher than the works already cited. Robert Hunter's *Poverty* and Ben. B. Lindsey's *The Beast,* for example, indicted capitalism for making greed, exploitation, poverty, and corruption inevitable. In *The Bitter Cry of the Children,* John Spargo offered a moving plea for child labor reform and a damning indictment of a system that consumed its young. Jack London, like Spargo a leader in the Socialist party, was easily the most violent literary radical of his time. His *The Iron Heel* portrayed the capitalistic system at its worst—brutal and repressive. In *The War of the Classes* and *Revolution,* however, London affirmed his faith in the ultimate triumph of the workers.

Foremost in influence among the Socialist critics was Upton Sinclair, whose most important work during the progressive period was *The Jungle,* published in 1906, a story of a Lithuanian immigrant in the Chicago packing houses. Intended as a plea for socialism, *The Jungle* is a moving indictment of an economic system that allegedly brought hunger and misery to great masses of people. As Sinclair later lamented, however, *The Jungle* appealed to the stomachs and not to the hearts of the American people, who ignored what he said about socialism but were revolted by his descriptions of the filthy conditions of the slaughtering houses. The novel was, therefore, a powerful factor in compelling passage of the Pure Food and Drug Act in 1906.

The political novelists of the first decade of the twentieth century were more prolific, if less critical of American institutions, than the socio-economic writers. Alfred Henry Lewis' *The Boss*, based upon the career of Richard Croker of Tammany Hall, and Elliott Flower's *The Spoilsman* portrayed in fictional form the political corruption that Lincoln Steffens knew so well. From his experiences in the government of Toledo, Ohio, Brand Whitlock added two powerful novels to the literature of exposure—*The Thirteenth District* and *Forty Years Of It*. In *The Gentleman from Indiana, In the Arena*, and other novels, Booth Tarkington exploited the theme of the corruption of the political life of a state by the railroad and business interests.

The most popular of these political novelists was Winston Churchill of New Hampshire, whose *Coniston* and *Mr. Crewe's Career* sold by the hundreds of thousands. Somehow Churchill thought all that was necessary to effect a regeneration of American politics was for the sturdy, plain people to turn the rascals out and elect honest men. Much in the same vein was William Allen White's *A Certain Rich Man*, a collection of platitudes with an incredible ending. If Churchill and White illustrated the shallowness of many of the political writers, David Graham Phillips exemplified in fictional form the strenuosity of this literary movement. In *The Plum Tree* Phillips attempted to expose the system of corruption and special privilege everywhere in the United States.

Whether profound or shallow, however, these leaders of the literary revolt against the *status quo* made a considerable contribution to the progressive movement. They wrote on subjects ranging from child labor to the use of state troops to break strikes; and their achievement in highlighting corruption in politics and the darker phases of American society furnished a basis in conviction for the national effort to achieve government representative of the people and responsive to their social and economic needs.

36 / *Intellectual Progressivism*

Every movement of vitality eventually reaches a point where it spawns philosophers who attempt to systematize its thought and formulate a philosophy justifying its practical program. Although the progressive movement was no exception to this rule, its intellectuals had to do more than merely construct a new philosophy. They first had to overturn the whole structure of ideas upon which the defenders of the *status quo* rested their arguments: social Darwinism and individualism; the cult of hostility to government; the belief that the Constitution was an inspired document and that the Supreme Court was the interpreter of divine judgment; and, finally, the idea that the railroad builders, financiers, and captains of industry were heroes, who had made a great contribution to the nation's economic progress. By 1900 these concepts had become so firmly embedded in the popular mind that together they constituted the American creed—a creed that first had to be destroyed before progressive concepts could find wholesale acceptance.

Inherent in practically every aspect of the progressive offensive, furthermore, was the ultimate objective of planting in the popular mind a faith in the efficacy of public measures of amelioration and control. The students of labor legislation, the champions of social justice measures, and the expounders of the new sociological jurisprudence, for example, were all trying to build a basis in economic and social fact for the necessity of positive government. So also were the social gospel leaders, when they preached doctrines of social salvation, or sociologists, when they urged the necessity of thinking of wrongdoing in social as well as individual terms.

The most significant formulation of the progressive political theory came from the pen of Herbert Croly, a New York journalist, whose major works, *The Promise of American Life,* published in 1909, and *Progressive Democracy,* published in 1914, at once established him as the intellectual leader of the progressive forces. Moreover, as editor of the *New Republic* from 1914 to 1930, Croly gathered around him most of the leading young social and economic thinkers of the time. Since Croly's writings provided progressives with their most cogent arguments in behalf of positive legislation, it is important that we understand his main argument.

Croly began by demonstrating that the main American political tradition was the Jeffersonian tradition of distrust of government and extreme individualism in economic affairs. In contrast, the Hamiltonian tradition of strong government had been closely identified in the popular mind with special privileges for the upper classes. Most Americans still believed that the promise of American life could be realized only if the golden age of competition could be restored by the withdrawal of all special privileges to the business classes. The fact was, however, Croly warned, that such a policy of *laissez faire* and drift in an age of big industry and big finance could only carry the nation to inevitable ruin—to the aggrandizement of power by the special interests and the degradation of the masses.

Who could save the nation from such peril? How could the American dream of democracy and equality of opportunity be fulfilled? The answer, said Croly, was clear. Progressives must abandon their romantic Jeffersonian concepts and support a program of positive and comprehensive state and federal intervention on all economic fronts. This would mean, for one thing, that progressives would have to abandon their opposition to class or special interest legislation. Such a philosophy had perhaps served a useful purpose at one time, but now it was the chief intellectual stumbling block to the progressive movement.

The important task ahead, Croly declared, was first to define the national interest and then to achieve fulfillment of it by careful planning and legislation. The important question, of course, was, who would define the national interest? Croly answered by calling for a new nationalism that would attract the leadership of the "best minds" in the task of reconciling planning and positive government with the democratic tradition.

The year 1912 saw the publication of a second significant plea for a new political positivism—Walter Weyl's *The New Democracy.* In contrast to Croly's mystical faith in the "national interest" and the "best minds," Weyl made self-interest the motivation for his program of social and industrial democracy. In brief, he said, a democracy could not allow large groups to be degraded and exploited because in the end these same groups would resort to violence and perhaps destroy society. Supplementing the arguments of Croly and Weyl was Walter Lippmann's *Preface to Politics,* published in 1913. Lippmann, then a young socialist, assumed the necessity of collectivism, but his major argument was the need for objective, scientific legislation unencumbered by sheerly moral criteria.

Another important component of the intellectual attack on the conservative ideology was the discrediting of the divine-origin theory of the Constitution, which was often invoked by opponents of the direct election of senators and other progressive proposals. Discontent over the undemocratic features of the Constitution was as old as the document itself, but not until the progressive period did scholars and politicians evolve the thesis that the Constitution had been written deliberately to frustrate the democratic movement.

This thesis was first systematically developed by Walter Clark, Chief Justice of North Carolina, in an address at the University of Pennsylvania Law School in 1906. The following year, in *The Spirit of American Government*, Professor J. Allen Smith of the University of Washington repeated Clark's contention that a minority had conceived the Constitution in class interest and imposed it upon the people in order to thwart their aspirations. An attempt to prove this argument was made by a young historian at Columbia University, Charles A. Beard, who had discovered Marx and Engels in England around the turn of the century. Beard went to work to prove that the Constitution was written to protect the interests of the merchants, great landowners, money-lenders, and speculators. His findings, embodied in *An Economic Interpretation of the Constitution*, shocked and horrified conservatives in 1913. Progressives, however, now had convincing proof that the Constitution, which had so often stood in the way of their reforms, was no more sacred than any other part of the American past.

As a final blow, intellectual progressives applied the full weight of their scholarship and sarcasm toward discrediting the belief that the railroad builders, the financiers, and the captains of industry were heroes and contributors to American progress. The most trenchant of the critics of the moneyed classes was Thorstein Veblen, a strange quondam economics professor, whose economic theory had much greater impact in the 1930's than during his own day. His most widely read work, *The Theory of the Leisure Class*, 1899, was a wholesale attack against the standards and practices of the contemporary American business civilization.

The most prolific of the debunkers of the plutocracy, however, was Gustavus Myers, a socialist, who set to work with unflagging zeal to discover the manner in which great fortunes in the United States had been aggrandized. His *History of the Great American Fortunes*, published in three volumes in 1909–1910, confirmed the old charge that the large American fortunes had been made through plunder and pre-emption of natural resources. Myers' work came as a climax to a number of shorter excursions into the same subject, and the truth is that he simply buried the corpse of the benevolent plutocrat.

There were, of course, many other leaders equally prominent in this extraordinary and far-reaching revolt of the intellectuals. Beginning with Lester F. Ward and the young economists who organized the American Economic Association in 1885, their numbers multiplied and their influence grew as the years passed. While we cannot measure their contribution precisely, their part in making the progressive movement a permanent force in

American life was not small. Their great contribution lay in discrediting the conservative ideology and in laying a philosophical basis for development toward the social welfare state. In this respect and for this reason, therefore, the intellectuals were the true leaveners of progressivism.

37 / *The Shame of the Cities*

Through the agitation of their political leaders and the exposures of the muckrakers, the American people from about 1900 to 1908 discovered the shocking fact that representative institutions had broken down almost completely in the area of municipal government. Instead of government through representatives impartially chosen, most American cities were ruled by organizations called machines, which in their hierarchical structure resembled the modern corporation. In the bottom rank was the precinct captain, who organized a small district and dispensed small favors. Above the precinct captain was the ward leader, or heeler, who was a lieutenant of the boss and helped manage campaigns and make important decisions. Often the ward heeler held an important office, such as the position of alderman or water commissioner. Together with the boss and his immediate assistants, the ward leaders constituted the inner circle of the organization, called "the ring."

The head of the machine was known as the "boss," "big man," or "leader." Because of his unsavory reputation with the people, usually he held no office. Almost invariably he had risen from the ranks after years of service in the organization. The boss operated like a general in charge of field forces. His orders were commands, passed down from the "ring" to its hundreds or thousands of workers. Occasionally, however, the boss' authority was challenged by a rising politician or faction in the machine; and if tensions mounted too high the organization would split into rival forces. These were exceptional cases, however, for the machines were usually superbly organized and smoothly run—the invisible governments of great cities, controlling the destinies of millions of people.

How does one account for this peculiarly American phenomenon, the city machine? Where did it derive its strength and resources? What kept it running, in spite of persistent attack?

Woodrow Wilson once declared that the prevailing form of American city government had been constructed as if to make the usurpation of power by an extra-constitutional organization inevitable. Wilson's statement was essentially correct. When city charters were granted or rewritten during the high tide of Jacksonian democracy, their framers deliberately dispersed power and responsibility among numerous agencies—the mayor, a two-house council, and sometimes among independent boards and commissions. The result was not democratic government but a form under which responsible government was nearly impossible, because the agencies for achieving it did not exist. Into the power vacuum created by the system of checks and balances and division of authority moved the kind of political machine just described. For all its sins, the machine did have enough cohesion and concentration of authority to govern.

Even when forms of government were changed, however, the machine survived. A more important reason for its existence and power, therefore, was the fact that it rendered service to large numbers of people. The majority of voters in 1900 asked not whether the organization was corrupt but whether it did something for them. And the machine made it a point to do things for them. Its agents met the friendless immigrant at the dock and helped him find shelter and work. The precinct captains provided coal and food for Widow Flanagan or Mrs. Moskowitz when they were in need. There was nothing scientific about the machine's charity, to be sure; but so long as the submerged third lived in slum areas and poverty, they cared little about honesty and efficiency. They wanted social services which the machines knew how to give and which progressives had not yet developed.

The machine survived also because it was held together by the twin cords of patronage and loyalty. The chief source of livelihood of lesser dignitaries was petty office and graft, and so long as the boss had offices and favors to bestow he could command a host of willing workers. Loyalty and friendship also played an important role in keeping the organization intact. Organization politics, moreover, afforded social and political opportunities for immigrant and minority groups such as they could never find in "respectable" society. In fact, the machine was one of the few cohesive and unifying forces in the social chaos of metropolitan life.

The oil best calculated to lubricate the political machine was the bribes it received from various sources. On the lower levels, bribery—in the form of money paid to politicians and policemen by criminals, prostitutes, saloonkeepers, and others—was extremely widespread, highly organized, and fabulously profitable. The Chicago Vice Commission reported in 1911, for example, that the annual profit from vice in that city was $15,000,000, and that one-fifth of this sum was paid to the police in the form of graft.

Although the system of police graft was everywhere prevalent, the most dangerous kind of bribery was the money paid by businessmen for protection, special privileges, and public rights. To begin with, the great economic interests in the cities turned "their dollars into votes and their property into political power," as one writer has observed, by buying control of the political machines. It was inevitable that so long as businessmen wanted exemption from equitable taxation, for example, there would be corruption. In addition, in large and rapidly growing cities there were numerous opportunities for bribery of another kind—the purchase of franchises and contracts. New city railway lines had to be constructed; sewerage, gas, electrical, and water lines had to follow new areas of development. By virtue of his control over the city council, the boss usually had franchises and contracts at his disposal; and even perpetual franchises could be bought. It was top level bribery of this kind that was most dangerous to the public interest and most profitable to the machine.

This, therefore, was the "System," as Lincoln Steffens called it. This was the pattern of corruption that permeated American municipal politics. Some cities, to be sure, outshone the others in the fine art of misgovernment. In St. Louis, for example, the Democratic boss systematically sold franchises, licenses, and exemptions to the respectable leaders of the business community. The boss of Minneapolis operated the most spectacular system of police graft in the country. In Pittsburgh two Republican leaders owned the city council and grew rich on contracts and utilities. Philadelphia presented the sorriest sight of all—a place where the citizens cheerfully acquiesced in the total subversion of representative government.

38 / *The Municipal Reform Movement*

The general prevalence of municipal corruption and misrule stimulated the first important political development in the progressive movement—the crusade for municipal reform. It began in a sporadic way in the 1890's, with the temporary overthrow of Tammany Hall by organized reform forces in 1894 and with the formation of civic leagues in various cities. The years 1896–1897, however, seem to mark a dividing line between an era of spasmodic uprisings and the time of widespread revolt. The first of these uprisings occurred in Chicago, where the city council was busily selling the public's most valuable rights to Charles T. Yerkes, the utilities magnate. As protests against the corrupt selling of franchises began to swell, some 232 civic leaders met in 1895, organized the Municipal Voters' League, and launched a nonpartisan campaign to clean up the city government. By pitilessly exposing the records of corrupt aldermen, the League won control of the city council in the aldermanic elections of 1896 and 1897. In the latter year, moreover, the League helped elect a progressive mayor, Carter Harrison, and Chicago was saved from the grafters. So vigilant was the League in following years that when Lincoln Steffens visited Chicago in 1903 he could find no evidence of a machine or of grafting on a large scale.

The reform movement in Chicago was illustrative of what could be accomplished by an aroused citizenry, without any outstanding single leader. Elsewhere the municipal reform movement followed a similar pattern. Various nonpartisan good government leagues combined in New York City in 1913, for example, to overthrow Tammany rule and elect a young Democratic reformer, John Purroy Mitchel, mayor. In Minneapolis, an energetic citizens' committee and a fearless grand jury exposed the rotten system of police graft operated by Mayor A. A. Ames and put Ames and his henchmen in prison.

The dominant pattern of municipal reform, however, was redemption through the leadership of some dynamic and often colorful popular tribune. Indeed, the rise of a whole group of these city reformers around the turn of the century in part signaled the beginning of the progressive revolt.

The most famous and influential member of this group was Tom L. Johnson of Cleveland. A successful street railway operator and steel manufacturer, who had learned the secrets of monopoly at an early age, Johnson became a convert to Henry George's philosophy in the late 1880's. Elected to Congress in 1890 and 1892, he fought vainly for free trade. In 1897 he assisted Henry George in his unsuccessful campaign for the mayoralty of New York City. Returning to Cleveland, Johnson was elected mayor in 1901 on a platform demanding equal taxation and the three-cent fare on trolley lines.

Gathering about him some of the ablest young municipal administrators in the country, Johnson first moved against the inequalities of the tax lists. Next, he opened fire on the railroads and utilities, which owned extensive property in Cleveland but paid hardly any taxes. In 1903–1904 the state legislature doubled railroad taxes, while the utilities consented to a doubling of their assessments. All these battles, however, were mere skirmishes as compared to the great campaign Johnson waged for the three-cent fare. The climax of the controversy came when Johnson and his council established competing trolley routes and invited outside capitalists to bid for them. The local traction interests appealed to the state Republican ring for protection. The state ring, in turn, appealed to the Supreme Court of Ohio, which declared that all the charters of Ohio cities were void because they had been created by special legislation. With all city governments of Ohio thus destroyed, the ring called the legislature into special session to adopt a uniform municipal code, which replaced the old system of concentrated power that had prevailed in Cleveland with government by divided authorities and independent boards.

Such tactics did not daunt Tom Johnson. He kept on appealing to the people and winning mayoralty campaigns. Eventually he concluded that public ownership of utilities and traction properties was the only way to eliminate the worst source of municipal corruption. Johnson was finally beaten in 1909, less than a year before his death; but his program was saved by the election of his chief lieutenant, Newton D. Baker, as mayor in 1911. Of all the host of city crusaders, Tom Johnson was the greatest, not only because of his dauntless spirit and determination to protect the people's interests, but also because he set new standards of efficiency for municipal administrators all over the United States. By making Cleveland "the best governed city," he proved that reformers were not necessarily incompetent and politically naive.

Such, therefore, was the kind of man who led the progressive movement in the cities. All these municipal reformers fought common enemies, entrenched and corrupt politicians allied with privileged business and criminal elements, and sought the same goals—impartial government, fair taxation, regulation of public service companies, and expanded social services for the lower classes. These remained always the chief objectives. But progressives soon learned that it was not enough to throw the rascals out and inaugurate a program of economic and social reform. Politics remained; and so long as the bosses controlled the party structure, reformers could never rest secure. Thus inevitably progressives turned also to the task of changing the political mechanisms, in the hope that greater popular participation in and control over the political processes would lay a secure basis for the economic and social reforms already begun.

Progressives in the cities, therefore, joined hands with other reform groups in a frontal assault on bosses and machines by establishing the direct primary for nominating candidates and adopting the short ballot, the initiative, referendum, and recall. As these campaigns were part of the progressive movement on the state-wide level, we will relate them elsewhere in this chapter.

Municipal reformers fought hard, moreover, to obtain home rule and an end to legislative interference in municipal administration. As Tom Johnson and other progressives soon discovered, the city machines were invariably components of the state rings. After smashing the local machine, it profited progressives little if the state ring, acting through the legislature, could nullify all their gains. And this often happened because in most states the city governments were creatures of and completely under the control of the legislature.

In their struggle to be free from legislative interference the municipal reformers were not notably successful, because rural and small-town legislators were loath to yield their control over metropolitan revenues. Four states, Missouri, California, Washington, and Minnesota, had granted home rule to cities by the turn of the century. From 1900 to 1914 eight other states granted this coveted privilege, but only two of them, Michigan and Ohio, had any large cities of consequence.

The most far-reaching progressive proposal for institutional change struck at the heart of the problem of municipal government and seemed to offer the greatest hope of saving the cities. It was the plan to abolish the old mayor-council system entirely and to substitute instead government by a commission of nonpartisan administrators. The commission form developed quite accidentally. On September 8, 1900, a hurricane and tidal wave devastated Galveston, Texas. With the corrupt city council utterly incapable of facing the tasks of reconstruction, the leading property owners of Galveston appealed to the state legislature to assume the government of the city. The legislature responded by establishing a government by five commissioners elected, after 1903, by the people.

The commission was so successful in rebuilding Galveston and rehabilitating its finances that Galveston not only retained its new form of government but also soon exported it to Houston, Dallas, Fort Worth, Austin, and El Paso. Nor was it long before other cities awoke to the advantages of the new system. It had often been impossible to fix responsibility for bribery on any particular individual under the old council system. Under the commission form, however, all responsibility, as well as all authority, was concentrated in five men, each of whom had charge of a single department of the city government.

The commission plan first won nation-wide prominence when the Iowa legislature in 1907 adopted a more elaborate version of the Texas model. The Iowa statute allowed cities over 25,000 to adopt the commission form; more important, it incorporated the initiative, referendum, and recall as part of the machinery of city politics and provided for the nomination of commissioners in nonpartisan elections. At once Des Moines adopted the commission form, and thereafter it was known as the "Des Moines Idea." By 1910 more than one hundred cities had adopted commission government; by the eve of the First World War the number had passed four hundred—chiefly medium sized cities in the Middle West, New England, and the Pacific States.

Experience, however, soon demonstrated that the commission form had inherent weaknesses that were not evident at the outset. It failed really to concentrate responsibility for administration, since there was no guarantee that the commissioners would be expert managers. Slowly progressives evolved a refinement of the commission form. The final product was the city manager plan, first adopted in its complete form by Dayton, Ohio, in

1913, after a great flood had inundated the city and the mayor and council could not cope with the emergency. This innovation preserved the best features of the commission plan and eliminated most of its weaknesses. All authority was vested in a board of commissioners, elected on a nonpartisan basis, who made laws and policies for the city. The commissioners appointed a city manager, usually a trained expert, to administer the various departments of the government, and the city manager, in turn, was responsible in all matters to the commissioners.

The new form seemed such a logical way to achieve responsible and expert administration without sacrificing the principle of democratic control that it spread rapidly and soon displaced the commission form in many cities. By 1923 more than three hundred cities had adopted the city manager plan.

Thus the progressive movement in the cities stimulated the rise of a host of new popular leaders and the development of political institutions calculated to facilitate popular rule and responsible and enlightened government. To charge, as certain critics have done, that the city reformers did not abolish all evils and bring the millennium is at best naive. For the most part they were tough-minded men, who well knew that venality and corruption would survive, regardless of the form of government, so long as men profited thereby. They must be judged, therefore, on a basis of the obstacles they faced and what they accomplished, not condemned for failing to change human nature or reconstruct society. Surveying the American scene at the end of the progressive period, competent authorities concluded that the municipal reformers had in large measure succeeded. By and large, the era of flagrant corruption had passed; cities were governed more efficiently than a decade before; and a new class of professional municipal administrators were in training throughout the country. In short, if the city was not yet the hope of American democracy, it was no longer democracy's nemesis.

39 / The Shame of the States

Corruption and special privilege held sway in practically every state around the turn of the century, in the same manner and for the same purpose that they reigned in the cities. Just as the city machine was the medium through which corrupt businessmen obtained contracts, franchises, and immunities from the city government, so also was the state machine, or ring, the medium through which such favors were bought on the state-wide level.

The boss system in the states varied so much from state to state and from party to party that it is difficult to generalize about its structure. The city organizations usually formed the basis for the state machine, although in rural states the county courthouse rings were the important components. In states with a tremendous concentration of population in one metropolis, the boss of the great city machine was often head of the state organization. In other states, political power was more widely dispersed. In any event, party authority was concentrated in the state committee, headed by a state chairman who represented the dominant leader or leaders in the state. It was the state chairman who usually organized the legislature, controlled legislation, and made deals with railroad and corporation lobbyists.

Two states, Missouri and New Jersey, afford exaggerated but vivid illustrations of how the so-called "System" operated in most states of the Union at the turn of the century. In Missouri the bribery, or "boodle," system worked at peak efficiency to govern the state in the interest of railroads and corporations. The corrupting agency was the lobby at the state capital, representing the important railroad and business interests of the state. The medium through which the lobby worked in this case was the party caucus in the legislature. Because the lobby bought control of the caucus, even honest legislators were caught in its net and forced to do its bidding. In Missouri, as in many other states, the lobby was the real, the living government that operated behind the façade of constitutional forms.

The control of state politics by a corporation-machine alliance reached its apogee in New Jersey. Because the leaders of the business and financial communities were also often the leaders of the dominant Republican party, it was usually unnecessary for businessmen to corrupt legislators and state officials. The railroad lobby in 1903, for example, furnished the chief justice of the state, the attorney general, the state comptroller, the commissioner of banking and insurance, and one of the members of the state board of taxation. It was no coincidence that railroads at that time paid only one-third of their just share of the tax burden. In 1903, moreover, both United States senators from New Jersey were interested in public utilities, while the retiring attorney general was on the boards of three public service corporations. It was not surprising that public utilities in the state enjoyed immunity from equitable taxation and public regulation.

In Missouri the methods the business interests used were cruder and more flagrantly corrupt than in New Jersey, but the techniques and objectives of corporation control were the same throughout the country. Who could tell how far the process of corporation dominance of state politics would go, or where it would end?

40 / *The Progressive Movement in the States*

Like the municipal reform movement, the great revolt against the "System" in the states was a culmination rather than a beginning. In the South and West agrarian unrest metamorphosed into progressivism from 1896 to 1900, as urban spokesmen assumed leadership in the struggle against railroad and corporation dominance. The Middle West, where the dominant GOP was firmly controlled by the vested interests at the turn of the century, was convulsed by a series of spectacular revolts from 1900 to 1908. Under insurgent leaders like Robert M. La Follette of Wisconsin, Albert B. Cummins of Iowa, and Albert J. Beveridge of Indiana, the midwestern states were transformed from bastions of Old Guard Republicanism into strongholds of progressivism. In the East the progressive revolt had a more decided urban complexion, as it often grew out of earlier campaigns in the cities. But progressivism was no less spectacular in the East than in the Middle West. Charles Evans Hughes' election as Governor of New York in 1906 and 1908 and his courageous battles for the direct primary and public regulation of utilities and railroads; the so-called New Idea movement in New Jersey, which began in 1906 as a rebellion within the Republican party and culminated in the election of a Democrat, Woodrow Wilson, as governor in 1910; and the sweeping triumph of progressivism in Ohio, with the adoption of a new constitution and the election of a Democratic progressive, James M. Cox, as governor in 1912—these developments, among others, signified the power and strength of eastern progressivism. The politics of the Pacific Coast states, too, was transformed by the triumph of such reform leaders as Hiram W. Johnson of California and William S. U'Ren of Oregon.

Obviously, therefore, what we are dealing with here was no minor phenomenon but a political revolt of national proportions and momentous consequences for the future of American politics. So successful were the progressive leaders in the several states by 1912 that all observers agreed that a thoroughgoing revolution had been accomplished since 1900. In most states the power of the bipartisan machines had been shattered or else curtailed. State governments were more representative of the rank and file and more responsive to their economic and social needs. Even more important, moreover, was the fact that by 1912 progressivism had spread into the arena of national politics, subverted ancient party loyalties, and caused such a political commotion as the country had not seen since 1896.

"Give the government back to the people!"—the battle cry of progressivism in the states—not only reflected the conviction that the state governments had ceased to be representative but also pointed up the major objective of the movement. But how could the "System" be destroyed? What were the processes and techniques of this counterrevolution against privilege?

The first, indeed the absolutely essential, ingredient was leadership. In every state in which progressivism triumphed there was some aggressive leader who carried the fight to the people and, after winning, provided responsible and effective government. Indeed, it is now evident that the progressives' most lasting contribution to American political practice was not the mechanical changes they instituted but rather the fact that they awakened the American people to the necessity for responsible leadership in a democracy.

Progressive leaders in the states, moreover, made a concerted campaign to overhaul the existing structure of political institutions. If representative government had broken down under the old forms, progressives argued, then new institutions must be devised to facilitate popular control of parties and governments. Invariably, the first objective of reform leaders was the inauguration of the direct primary system of nominating candidates and party officials. This objective took priority because the old system of nomination by conventions seemed to afford the bosses an easy means of perpetuating their control. Before 1900 practically all city and state elective officials were nominated at party conventions on district, county, and state-wide levels. Normally such conventions were easily bought or controlled; usually they were well oiled cogs in the machine. By heroic efforts the reform forces might capture the conventions and momentarily subdue the bosses, but it was an extraordinarily difficult undertaking.

The progressive remedy was simple and direct—to make it easier for the voters and more difficult for the bosses to control the party by instituting a system of nominating candidates directly by the people. The direct primary apparently originated in Pennsylvania in the 1840's, but it was not until the 1890's that it was used extensively on the local level, mainly in the South. Mississippi in 1902 was the first state to adopt a compulsory, state-wide primary law. The following year Wisconsin enacted similar legislation as the first major item in Governor La Follette's reform program. From this time on the system spread rapidly through all sections, so that by 1916 only Rhode Island, Connecticut, and New Mexico had failed to enact primary legislation of some kind.

After winning the direct primary, state progressives usually campaigned next for a variety of institutional reforms: the short ballot, to reduce the number of elective officials and concentrate responsibility in government; corrupt practices legislation, to control and limit campaign contributions and expenditures; and the direct election of United States senators by the people instead of by the state legislatures. Progress in the field of short ballot reform was notable only in the area of municipal government, with the rapid spread of the commission and city manager forms. Practically every state adopted stringent corrupt practices laws, while Congress in 1907 and 1909 prohibited corporations, insurance companies, banks, and railroads from contributing to campaign funds in federal election contests. For many years, however, the reactionary forces in the Senate would not allow a constitutional amendment for direct election of senators to pass. Many states, therefore, turned to an indirect method of electing senators directly—by requiring senatorial candidates to be nominated in primary elections and candidates for the state legislature to swear that they would vote for the senatorial candidate thus nominated by the people. Finally, after a scandal involving the election of William Lorimer, Republican boss of Illinois, to the Senate in 1909, the upper house approved the Seventeenth Amendment for the direct election of its members in 1912. It became a part of the Constitution on May 31, 1913.

The direct primary, corrupt practices laws, the short ballot, and the popular election of senators were all designed to purify politics, assure popular control over all stages of the electoral process, and strengthen representative government. But many skeptical progressives refused to agree that these reforms sufficed. Convinced that representative government might become subverted by the forces of privilege under the new and more democratic forms, they proposed to give the people an alternative and a last resort —the initiative and referendum.[2] The initiative and referendum were used most widely in the West, where South Dakota first adopted them in 1898. During the next ten years only Utah, Oregon, Nevada, Montana, and Oklahoma joined South Dakota in experimenting with direct legislation; but from 1908 to 1915 fifteen other states, including several in the East and

---

[2] The initiative is a device whereby the electorate may enact legislation against the will of the legislature. Upon petition of a stipulated percentage of the voters, the legislature must consider the measure that the petitioners propose. If the legislature refuses to approve the bill it must call a special election in which the voters may enact or reject the measure. The referendum, on the other hand, is a device whereby a measure already approved by the legislature may be rejected by the voters.

South, adopted the measures. Indeed, so great was the popular enthusiasm for these innovations that for a time, from 1912 to 1914, it seemed direct legislation might supplant legislation by representative assemblies in almost every state. The movement came to a virtual standstill in 1915, however, as conservatives launched a vigorous counterattack and experience soon proved that the mass of voters were not competent to deal with technical matters of legislation.

As a further safeguard of the popular interest, advanced progressives championed the recall, a device that afforded the voters a handy means of removing unsatisfactory elective officials. First used in Los Angeles in 1903, the recall found widest acceptance in cities that adopted the commission and city manager forms. Oregon made the recall applicable to elective state and local officials in 1908, and from 1911 to 1915 nine other states, most of them in the West, followed suit. The recall provoked strenuous opposition from conservatives, to be sure; but the defenders of the *status quo* saved their choicest invectives for those progressives who advocated the recall of judges. If the people could remove judges for making unpopular decisions, then what minority and property rights would be safe from the assaults of an irrational majority? Seven states—Oregon, California, Arizona, Nevada, Colorado, Kansas, and North Dakota—adopted the recall of judges; but the violent controversies over the measure at the time seem now rather pointless, as not a single judge of a superior or state supreme court has been removed since the recall of judges was first proposed. As an alternative means of protecting the right of the states to use the police power for social and economic ends, Theodore Roosevelt in 1912 proposed the recall of judicial decisions that nullified such legislation. Only Colorado, in 1913, adopted this measure, and the Colorado supreme court in 1921 declared the statute unconstitutional.

These, then, were the changes in political practice and institutional structure that progressives championed from 1900 to 1914. Critics have accused progressive leaders of naively believing that representative and truly democratic government could be restored by such alterations in the mechanics of politics. The charge reveals a profound ignorance of the progressive era. There were undoubtedly fools among the leaders of the reform movement in the states. The great majority of the progressive leaders, on the other hand, were realistic politicians who well knew that the changes they proposed were merely instruments to facilitate the capture of the political machinery by spokesmen of the majority. They used these instruments, therefore, to gain and hold power; and they must be judged for what they accomplished or failed to accomplish on the higher level of substantive reform.

Their achievements in the realm of social and economic legislation were imposing indeed. We have already related the progress of the movement in the states for social justice legislation. In the realm of strictly economic legislation, moreover, progressive leaders in the states made substantial progress toward subjecting railroads and public service corporations to effective public control. Beginning with the Georgia railroad commission of 1879 and culminating in the adoption by the Wisconsin legislature of Governor La Follette's bill for a railroad commission in 1905, the movement for state regulation advanced steadily. Indeed, so effective was it by 1914 that the railroad managers were then begging Congress to free them from harassment by state commissions. It was during the progressive era, too, that the movement for expert regulation by state commissions of the rates and services of public service corporations began and reached its first culmination.

These were all important substantive reforms and together constitute an imposing record. But in assessing progressivism's achievement one should not dismiss lightly the political changes it effected. By their emphasis on simplified forms of government, greater popular participation in and control over the electoral process, and responsible leadership, the progressive leaders transformed the theory and practice of politics in the United States. Looking back in 1913 upon his hard battles for the people as Governor of Wisconsin, Robert M. La Follette penned a fitting epilogue, not only for the progressive movement in Wisconsin, but for progressivism in many other states as well:

"This closes the account of my services in Wisconsin—a time full of struggle, and yet a time that I like to look back upon. It has been a fight supremely worth making, and I want it to be judged, as it will be ultimately, by results actually attained. If it can be shown that Wisconsin is a happier and better state to live in, that its institutions are more democratic, that the opportunities of all its people are more equal, that social justice more nearly prevails, that human life is safer and sweeter—then I shall rest content in the feeling that the Progressive movement has been successful."[3]

[3] *Autobiography of Robert M. La Follette* (Madison, Wis., 1913), pp. 368–369; see also Belle Case La Follette and Fola La Follette, *Robert M. La Follette* (2 vols., 1953), I, 192. Used by permission of Miss Fola La Follette.

CHAPTER 5 / POLITICS AND PROBLEMS OF
THE REPUBLICAN ERA, 1901–1910

ALTHOUGH the progressive movement began in the cities and states, it was inevitable that it should soon spread into the larger arena of national politics. This was true because in the American system there is no real dividing line between state and federal politics. It was true even more because the spread of the railroad, financial, and industrial networks across state boundaries created important problems with which the federal government alone could constitutionally cope.

This and following chapters relate the impact of the progressive upheaval upon national politics and policies. At the beginning of the twentieth century the dominant Republican party was controlled by men who frankly urged a program of generous assistance to the business interests and who abhorred the very concept of public regulation. Under William Jennings Bryan, the minority Democrats were cautiously moving toward a more advanced position, but they had matured no comprehensive and rational attack on the system of privilege. Within less than a decade, however, the progressive ferment had wrought an almost miraculous change in the American political scene. Advanced progressives, who sought to make the federal government a positive, regenerative force, were nearly dominant in the Republican party by 1910. Under new leadership, moreover, the Democrats were united behind a far-reaching program of reform. In brief, the progressive movement, which had already brought important changes in federal policies, stood on the verge of culmination and fulfillment.

41 / Theodore Roosevelt and the Progressive Movement[1]

No account of the development of national progressivism would be complete without some note of its most extraordinary leader. Catapulted into the presidency by a tragic circumstance, Theodore Roosevelt presided over the nation's destinies during the time of agitation and development of a

[1] Parts of the following section first appeared in Arthur S. Link, "Theodore Roosevelt in His Letters," *Yale Review*, xliii (Summer, 1954), 589–598; reproduced by permission of the Editors of the *Yale Review*.

national reform program. He opportunely adapted his policies to meet the changing configurations of political power; he was, however, no mere creature of circumstance, but rather a prime moving force in history.

Born on October 27, 1858, the scion of a well-to-do mercantile and banking family, he was reared in the genteel Knickerbocker traditions of New York City. Afflicted with a frail body and weak eyes, as a youth he determined to make himself physically strong. By the dint of exhausting labors he overcame his weakness and ever afterward gloried in the strenuous life and manly virtues. Whether as cowboy and gunfighter, Rough Rider during the Spanish-American War, or big game hunter in Africa, Roosevelt proved that physically he was as good as the best and that he did not know the meaning of fear.

The urge to be always doing combined with a first-rate intellect to produce a man of broad interests and intellectual creativity. Although he was not a trained historian, he wrote good history and, besides, read widely in the field of literature. A biologist and student of nature, he spent considerable time as President exposing nature-fakers. These were a few of his peripheral interests. His profession was the practice of politics and diplomacy, and in this calling he displayed intelligence and skill.

From his social environment and especially from his father, Roosevelt inherited a compulsion to do good for people less fortunate than himself. While most persons of his class gave money to settlement houses or home missions, Roosevelt went into politics after being graduated from Harvard in 1880. Part of his motivation must have been the strong moral sense he acquired from his Reformed religion and its Calvinistic emphasis upon righteousness. In any event, Roosevelt usually viewed political contests as struggles between the forces of good and of evil and, like Wilson and Bryan, he became a preacher at large to the American people.

Background, training, temperament, and personal associations all combined in Roosevelt to produce a fundamentally cautious and conservative, rather than a doctrinaire, approach to politics. Justice to all classes, and therefore legislation in the general interest, became his guiding principle. A patrician, he viewed with righteous anger the vulgarity and materialism of the newly-rich captains of industry, the financiers, and the railroad speculators. Yet experience and his sense of justice prevented him from condemning whole classes or accepting the socialist dictum that it was the economic system that was alone responsible for social wrongdoing. Roosevelt's conservatism, moreover, was manifested in his insistence upon continuity, in his abhorrence of men who advocated unnatural change. Believing that progressive adaptation to new circumstances could not occur unless order and social stability first existed, he feared a mob as much as he feared the malefactors of great wealth.

In the practice of politics Roosevelt was as hard-headed a realist as ever sat in the presidential chair. He was a realist because he recognized and respected power. Thus he worked with the Republican boss of New York, when he, Roosevelt, was governor of that state. When he assumed the presidency in 1901 he found political power in the Republican party concentrated in the state organizations and exercised by their representatives in Congress. He did not attempt to destroy the party hierarchy; indeed, he worked with and through it. The important point, however, is that Roosevelt not only accepted the existing power structures as he found them in New York and Washington but that he also became a master politician, able to use his party for his own and the country's interests.

Indeed, in the way in which he conceded the smaller points in order to win the important objectives and mastered the political game without yielding his own integrity, Roosevelt symbolized the moral man confronted by the dilemmas that an immoral society creates. Doctrinaire reformers demanded the whole loaf of reform and denounced Roosevelt when he accepted a half or two-thirds of the loaf. Roosevelt knew, however, that he could not transform society and politics by one bugle blast; he knew that men are usually governed by selfish motives and that politics is fundamentally not a moral profession. Knowing these things, he tried to use selfishness to achieve moral ends—the advancement of human welfare; and he also tried to strengthen altruistic tendencies whenever he found them.

These, then, were some of the features of Roosevelt's personality and philosophy. There was, however, another trait that to a varying degree dominated all the rest—his love of power, which mounted as the years passed and at times verged on megalomania. Love of his own opinions often obscured the truth in Roosevelt's mind and generated the feeling that he was above the law and ordinary conventions. Yet his confidence was as much a source of strength as of danger, giving him the strength essential to leadership; combined with intelligence and energy, it made him a superb administrator, precisely because he was bold enough to do unprecedented things.

Yet while Roosevelt enjoyed power as did no other President in the twentieth century except his nephew-in-law Franklin D. Roosevelt, he also recognized the dangers and corrupting potentialities of power. "There is not one among us in whom a devil does not dwell," he wrote near the end of his life; "at some time, on some point, that devil masters each of us; he who has never failed has not been tempted." Much as he enjoyed the presidency, he voluntarily gave it up. "I believe in a strong executive," he wrote in 1908; "I believe in power; but I believe that responsibility should go with power, and that it is not well that the strong executive should be a perpetual executive. . . . The Presidency . . . can only be saved from abuse by having the people accept as axiomatic the position that one man can hold it for no more than a limited time."

Personal judgments of Roosevelt will vary, but no one should make the mistake of not taking him seriously. Because he was a powerful personal leader, it was given to him to make a large contribution to the progressive movement, to the art of government in the United States, and to advancing the diplomacy of his country. In fact, since Lincoln only two other Presidents, Wilson and Franklin Roosevelt, have made comparable contributions.

Theodore Roosevelt's most lasting contribution to American political practice was his exercise of leadership and the way in which he revitalized the Presidency. From 1865 to 1901 a long line of second-rate politicians had occupied the White House. With the exception perhaps of Cleveland, they were not even leaders of their own party, much less of the country. Because of the entrenched position of the Old Guard professionals in Congress,

Roosevelt was never able to dominate the legislators, as Wilson could do because he had a pliant congressional majority between 1913 and 1917. But Roosevelt made himself the one great popular spokesman in the country and was therefore able to bend a stubborn Congress to his purpose. Because he exploited some of the powers inherent in the Presidency, he proved that effective national leadership was possible in the American constitutional system.

Roosevelt's contributions to the science of administration alone would entitle him to distinction among the Presidents. Perceiving that the only alternative to rule by private wealth was the development of a strong, efficient administrative state, democratically controlled but powerful enough to make important economic decisions, he advanced the science of administration as no President before him had done. He and his able associates strengthened the Civil Service, put the consular service on a professional basis, modernized the army's command structure, and brought the navy to an unprecedented peak of efficiency. Moreover, he helped broaden the powers of an old agency, the Interstate Commerce Commission, and created a new one, the Bureau of Corporations, which in 1914 was metamorphosed into the Federal Trade Commission. In brief, during the Roosevelt era democracy learned to become efficient.

A third contribution is almost as important as Roosevelt's development of the presidential power. It was his vindication of the supremacy of the national, or public, interest over all private aggregations of economic power. The open contempt that bankers, monopolists, and railroad managers displayed toward the law and the high-handed manner in which they dealt with the people filled him with loathing and anger. He retaliated by asserting the supremacy of the people over private interests in three far-reaching ways—first, by withdrawing more than 200,000,000 acres of public lands to curb the plunder of a great national heritage; second, by activating the Sherman Act and beginning a movement that succeeded in curbing industrial monopoly in the United States; and, third, by forcing the passage of the Hepburn Act of 1906, which deprived the railroads of ultimate sovereignty in the rate-making process. In the anthracite coal strike of 1902, he was prepared to go the full limit in asserting the public interest, by seizing and operating the coal mines if the operators should refuse to mediate the controversy. Such actions marked the momentous beginnings of legislation and administration that culminated in the New Deal and the concept of the democratic welfare state.

With this brief introduction to Theodore Roosevelt, let us now see in larger detail the way in which he helped to change the course of American political history after 1900.

42 / *Roosevelt and the Republican Party, 1900–1904*

The leaders of the Republican party laid their plans carefully for the election of 1900. President William McKinley was of course the inevitable presidential choice of the GOP. The death of the Vice President, Garret A. Hobart, in 1899, however, left the second place on the ticket open and created an unusual opportunity for Thomas C. Platt, Republican boss of New York State. In 1898 Platt had nominated Theodore Roosevelt, the hero of San Juan Hill, for Governor of New York in order to win. Elected easily, Roosevelt attacked corruption with vigor and championed social legislation and was consequently soon at odds with Platt. Hobart's death offered a dignified yet final method of getting Roosevelt out of New York. By elevating him to the vice presidency, the Republican Old Guard could silence the Rough Rider, and Platt would be saved the embarrassment of having to nominate him again for governor in 1900.

When Platt first presented his plan to McKinley and his manager, Mark Hanna, they responded coldly. "Don't any of you realize," Hanna is later alleged to have remarked, "that there's only one life between this madman and the White House!" But Platt was so persistent that Hanna finally gave in. With his usual perception, Roosevelt at once saw through Platt's scheme. He had grave misgivings about accepting his consignment to oblivion; but his friends suggested that he would be the logical presidential candidate in 1904, and he could think of no alternative but to accept the nomination if it were offered to him.

The Democrats nominated Bryan for a second time, and the Nebraskan made his campaign chiefly on the issues of imperialism and trust control. As we have said, Bryan soft-pedaled the silver issue and tried to make the election a solemn referendum on imperialism. As one diplomatic historian has shown, however, the election was more a repudiation of Bryanism and a thumping endorsement of prosperity than a popular expression on colonial policy. McKinley was elected by an even greater majority than in 1896.

On March 4, 1901, therefore, McKinley and Roosevelt were inaugurated. Platt said a pleasant good-by; Hanna stood at McKinley's right hand, and businessmen thanked God that all was right with the world. In September 1901, however, the point of Platt's joke was lost when an assassin mortally wounded McKinley at Buffalo. "That damned cowboy," as Hanna called Roosevelt, was now President of the United States!

Those impatient reformers who expected Theodore Roosevelt at once to reorganize the Republican party and assume control of Congress understood neither the political situation nor the new President. During the years since the Civil War the great industrial and financial interests had constructed an organization within the Republican party that could not be overthrown by direct assault. The pre-eminent leader of the party was Mark Hanna of Ohio, McKinley's friend and adviser and member of the Senate. Nearly equal to Hanna in power was Senator Nelson W. Aldrich of Rhode Island, the avowed spokesman of Wall Street. Allied with Hanna and Aldrich in the upper house were John C. Spooner of Wisconsin, William B. Allison of Iowa, and Orville H. Platt of Connecticut. Together they and other Old Guardsmen controlled the Senate and protected the industrial, financial, and railroad interests. Furthermore, the Old Guard were firmly entrenched in the House of Representatives. After 1902 the Speaker was Joseph G. Cannon of Illinois, a reactionary extraordinary, who ruled the House with rural wit and an iron hand. As Cannon not only appointed all committees but was also chairman of the rules committee that determined the priority of bills, he was able personally to block "dangerous" legislation.

Congressional supremacy was not merely a slogan in 1901. It had been so much a reality since Lincoln's death that Presidents, except perhaps for Cleveland, had been creatures of the congressional machine. McKinley's death did not alter the configuration of political power. Power in the Republican party still resided with the state organizations and their representatives in Congress.

From all sides in the autumn of 1901 came advice to Roosevelt to move slowly. The advice did not fall on deaf ears, but it was unnecessary. As he was in no position to challenge the Old Guard, Roosevelt determined to work with them for a time. Immediately after his accession, the new President announced that he would continue McKinley's policies and retain his Cabinet. Obviously, Roosevelt was feeling his way and assuring his nomination in 1904. Not yet ready to make war on the Old Guard, he came to terms with them. In August 1902 he went to Aldrich's home in Rhode Island and a short time later conferred at Oyster Bay, Long Island, with the leading Republican senators. The upshot of these negotiations was that the President agreed to leave the protective tariff system and the monetary structure essentially undisturbed. The senators, in return, agreed to give Roosevelt freedom of action in other matters.

The enormous agitation for railroad regulation and the destruction of the so-called trusts, however, was beginning to have a significant impact on the Middle West, where a popular revolt against the policies of Hanna and Aldrich was getting under way. The first signs of this upheaval were the election of Robert M. La Follette as Governor of Wisconsin in 1900, on a platform demanding the direct primary and effective railroad regulation, and the rise of Albert Baird Cummins as the dominant political leader in Iowa in 1901. Roosevelt realized far better than Aldrich and his friends the necessity of appeasing midwestern opinion. His first move was to instruct the Attorney General in February 1902 to announce that he would soon institute proceedings to dissolve the Northern Securities Company, the gigantic railroad combination J. P. Morgan had recently formed.

The midwestern progressives, however, could not be propitiated by this one act alone. They demanded drastic tariff reductions, federal regulation of railroad rates, and more vigorous action against the large corporations. In August 1902 Roosevelt made a tour through the Middle West; the following year, in April, he returned to the region. And the more he said the more it was clear he understood and sympathized with the midwestern antagonism to Hanna and the Wall Street crowd.

43 / *The Election of 1904*

As the time for the national conventions of 1904 drew near, Roosevelt laid careful plans for winning his chief objective: the chance to be President in his own right. Quietly but surely he retired Hanna as chief dispenser of the patronage and made his own alliances with the dominant state organizations, especially in the South. Hanna was Roosevelt's only serious rival, but the Ohioan died on February 15, 1904, and no one stood in Roosevelt's way. Surely the old order was changing as the President made plans to seize control of the GOP. Hanna and Matt Quay, Pennsylvania Republican boss, were dead; Boss Platt had been shorn of his power over the New York State Republican organization; Spooner of Wisconsin would pass from the scene in 1905 and be replaced in the Senate by La Follette.

Roosevelt, therefore, received the nomination at the Republican convention on June 23, 1904, without even a show of opposition. Having twice failed with Bryan, the Democrats decided to try a conservative to offset the impulsive Roosevelt. They nominated Judge Alton B. Parker of New York, an obscure and ineffectual third-rate politician. Except for Roosevelt's speeches the campaign would have been a drab affair. Near the end of the campaign, however, Parker enlivened the contest by charging that Roosevelt was blackmailing Wall Street into supporting his candidacy.

The charge was false, but somehow Roosevelt had become badly frightened by rumors that certain Wall Street interests were pouring huge sums into the Democratic war chest. Rejecting the suggestion that he appeal directly to the people for small contributions, Roosevelt allowed his manager, George B. Cortelyou, to raise money in the usual way.[2] The voters could not have taken Parker's blackmail charge seriously, for they elected Roosevelt by the largest popular majority that had ever been given a presidential candidate. Roosevelt was actually stunned by the landslide. "The election results," he wrote on November 10, 1904, "are really astounding, and I am overwhelmed by them. . . . I frankly confess that I do not understand it."

44 / *The Emergence of a Progressive Leader*

Events soon proved that Roosevelt had given no hostage to Wall Street by accepting its lavish campaign contributions. On the contrary, by 1904 he had won more real power with the people than any President since Lincoln. The wine of victory exhilarated him and strengthened his determination to be the real leader of the country, the spokesman of the majority. His Annual Message of 1904 gave hints of an advanced position, but it was in his address before the Union League Club of Philadelphia, delivered in January 1905, that the President blazoned his new progressivism. Great industries and wealth, he warned, must submit to public control; specifically, the public interest demanded effective regulation of railroad rates.

From this time forward, the pressure on Roosevelt from the Republican Middle and Far West to support such causes as railroad regulation, the direct election of senators, and corporation control mounted incessantly. Moreover, Bryan and progressive Democrats were charging that the President talked loudly but was essentially a straddler. Roosevelt, however, did not merely give in to these pressures. Haunted by the fear that failure to appease the popular demand would provoke revolution, he took personal

---

[2] Edward H. Harriman, the railroad magnate, contributed $50,000 personally and collected $200,000 more from other sources. J. P. Morgan gave $150,000 and the three life insurance companies he controlled added another $148,000. Two Standard Oil partners, H. H. Rogers and John D. Archbold, gave $100,000; and although Roosevelt demanded that this gift be returned, his managers quietly ignored his request. In all, corporations contributed nearly three-fourths of the $2,195,000 collected by the Republican committee.

control of the reform movement in the summer and fall of 1905. He launched an attack on the meat packers, beginning with a thorough investigation of the industry. And when Congress assembled in December 1905, he demanded a stringent railroad regulation law, a pure food and drug law, publicity for campaign contributions, and additional conservation legislation.

The more vigorously Roosevelt asserted leadership, the more successes he won. He got a pure food and drug law; he forced the passage of a railroad regulation bill in 1906; and through executive action he advanced the cause of conservation. Moreover, he attacked the so-called trust problem with renewed vigor, not only by many dissolution suits, but perhaps even more effectively through a number of searching exposures by federal agencies. He recognized the intensity of the midwestern demand for tariff reduction, but he never thought the tariff was an important factor in preserving the system of privilege. He knew, also, that the country needed currency reform and more effective regulation of the banking system, but he never pressed these issues before Congress and the country.

Day in and day out during 1906 and most of 1907, however, Roosevelt gave eloquent voice to the demand for an extension of the public authority over great aggregations of wealth. It is easy to condemn Roosevelt for not doing more than he did—for not fighting hard for tariff and banking reform, for example. It is also easy to forget that the national progressive movement was only yet in the making, that Roosevelt did not control Congress, and that his leadership of the reform cause was courageous and bold.

Roosevelt, however, was forced to restrain his reform energies during the last months of 1907 as a consequence of a severe panic in Wall Street. Bankers and railroad men blamed the administration for loss of public confidence, but the panic was brought on by a world-wide credit stringency and by the very speculative excesses that Roosevelt had condemned.

Depressed economic conditions only momentarily paralyzed Roosevelt's reform impulses. He knew that the popular desire for progressive change was as strong as ever and bound to grow. Thus while congressional leaders awaited his abdication in pleasant anticipation, Roosevelt intensified his propaganda for reform. In a special message to Congress on January 31, 1908, he sounded the keynote of a campaign for advanced national legislation that would culminate in a political revolt in 1912 and the enactment by Congress of most of the program afterward. Outraged by the Supreme Court's nullification of the federal Employers' Liability Act of 1906, Roosevelt demanded new legislation and urged the states to adopt accident compensation systems. Moreover, he condemned the courts for using injunctions merely to protect property in labor disputes; urged Congress to empower the Interstate Commerce Commission to make a physical valuation of railroad property and supervise the financial operations of the railroads; suggested closer supervision of corporations, either through federal licensing, "or in some other way equally efficacious"; and denounced speculators and dishonest businessmen. "The Nation," he warned, "will not tolerate an utter lack of control over very wealthy men of enormous power in the industrial, and therefore in the social, lives of all our people. . . . We strive to bring nearer the day when greed and trickery and cunning shall be trampled under feet by those who fight for the righteousness that exalteth a nation."

45 / The Election of 1908

By the end of 1907 Roosevelt was the spokesman of the masses of Republican voters and the real leader of his party. Even the special interests who could delay or defeat his program in Congress could not have prevented his renomination in 1908. Roosevelt enjoyed being President and delighted in the thought of another four years at the helm. But he had given a pledge after the election of 1904 that he would not run again, and an inner compulsion urged him to stand by his promise.

It was the most fateful decision of Roosevelt's career and perhaps the unwisest. By refusing to heed the popular call in 1908 he denied himself the opportunity to render his greatest service to the Republican party, for a Roosevelt in the White House from 1909 to 1913 might well have averted the disastrous rupture that occurred in 1912. In any event, he had the power to name his successor and was determined to use it.

The ablest member of the constellation around the President was Elihu Root, who had served as Secretary of War from 1899 to 1904 and as Secretary of State since John Hay's death in 1905. Although he was tempted to make this able corporation lawyer his successor, Roosevelt knew the Middle West would never accept Root because of his Wall Street connections. New York's reform governor, Charles Evans Hughes, was another possibility; but Hughes was strangely cold to the President's advances. Finally Roosevelt turned to William Howard Taft of Ohio, his Secretary of War, who was one of his stanchest supporters in the Cabinet, and settled the succession on him. Taft had made a distinguished record as federal judge, Governor General of the Philippines, and Secretary of War. He had good family connections and an eastern education, an excellent mind and unquestioned integrity. But, most important, he seemed certain to carry forward the Roosevelt policies.

In January 1908 Roosevelt began to set in motion all the machinery of the party organization to assure Taft's nomination. Asserting publicly that the Republican convention should be free to choose its candidate, Roosevelt was privately boasting by the end of May that he had prevented his own renomination and could dictate the naming of Taft. At the Republican convention that met in Chicago in June, therefore, the Ohioan was nominated on the first ballot on a platform that promised, among other things, tariff revision and a federal system of postal savings banks.

Meeting in Denver, the Democrats in this year of Rooseveltian supremacy turned again to Bryan. Although he was by now something of a perennial candidate, the Nebraskan at least seemed able to save his party from another such disaster as it had suffered in 1904. Bryan had come a long way on the road toward progressivism since 1896. Perhaps he was not a man of great intellect, but he had a keen ear for the voice of the people and was free from any connection with special privilege. He made his campaign largely on the tariff and trust questions and, promising relief from indiscriminate injunctions, made a frank appeal for labor support. Taft, on the other hand, attacked Bryan as a demagogue, pledged himself to continue the Square

Deal policies of substantial justice to all classes, and promised tariff revision.

As all observers predicted, Taft won easily; but it was significant that Bryan increased the Democratic vote by a million and a third over 1904 and carried the South, Oklahoma, Colorado, Nevada, and Nebraska. More significant for the future of the country, however, was the marked rise of Republican insurgency in the Middle West. Heretofore the midwestern progressive Republican bloc in Congress had been a small minority. In the Sixty-First Congress, which would meet in 1909, they would be a powerful force in both houses. Upon Taft's ability to reconcile the conservative and progressive factions would depend the fate of the GOP.

46 / *Republican Troubles Under Taft*

Soon after Taft's inaugural, Roosevelt left the United States to hunt big game in Africa and for an extended tour of Europe. His going was applauded in financial circles, where many men wished luck to the lions. Conservatives, generally, were sure that Taft would align himself with the Old Guard in Congress. Progressives, on the other hand, were certain he would come to their support. What manner of man was he, who seemed all things to all men as he took the oath of office on March 4, 1909?

It would be unjust to say that Taft took the presidency under false pretenses. On the eve of his magistracy he thought he was a progressive. He shared Roosevelt's belief in the supremacy of the public over the private interest. He helped advance the cause of railroad regulation, for example, pursued a ruthless campaign against monopolies, and continued Roosevelt's policy of preserving the nation's heritage of natural resources. In a normal period of political quietude he would have been a beloved President. The years of Taft's reign, however, were highly abnormal. It was a time of agitation and revolt, when civil war within the Republican party impended.

Open party warfare could be averted only by bold presidential leadership, but Taft was temperamentally unfitted to play the role that history demanded. He could not lead in a time of trouble, because leadership in such circumstances required whole-hearted commitment and abandonment of the judicial quality that was dominant in his character. Taft was a philosophical progressive, but he could not get on with the progressive leaders in Congress because they were too sweeping in their denunciations, too impatient, too willing to experiment with untried measures.

At the beginning of the special session which convened in March 1909 to consider tariff revision, the new President was forced to choose between the Old Guard leadership in Congress and the insurgent Republican bloc. As the Republicans now had a majority of only forty-seven in the House of Representatives, the insurgent leaders concluded that the time had come to combine with the Democrats to unhorse the tyrannical Speaker, Joe Cannon. When it seemed the insurgents were bound to succeed, the Speaker appealed to Taft for support, promising to support the President's legislative program in return. In a perplexing dilemma because he did not like Cannon yet needed his cooperation, Taft made his first mistake: he endorsed Cannon and hinted that the insurgents should give up their campaign if they wanted a share in the patronage. In the end it was the defection of a group of southern and Tammany Democrats, not Taft's opposition, that frustrated the insurgents' *coup d'état,* but many progressives suspected that the President had betrayed them.

This incident only marked the beginning of the alienation of the progressives from the President. Effective White House leadership in the future could easily have repaired the damage done during the fight over the speakership. Instead of leading boldly, however, Taft soon blundered again—in a battle over tariff revision that split the Republican party in the spring of 1909.[3]

There is no doubt that Taft sincerely desired substantial tariff reductions. But he erred in the beginning by refusing to interfere in the fight in Congress and failing to rally public opinion behind the cause of tariff reform. When he finally did intervene, moreover, he acted in such a manner as to cause the midwestern insurgents, who were leading the fight for tariff reduction, to believe he had deserted them and surrendered to special privilege. And although the President won a few noteworthy concessions, the bill that he signed—the Payne-Aldrich Act—represented a substantial victory for the eastern manufacturers. By this time—the late summer of 1909—the Middle West was seething with rebellion. Although few men realized the fact, the doom of the Taft administration had been sealed.

In an attempt to assuage the popular discontent, Taft embarked in September 1909 upon a 13,000 mile speaking tour from Boston to the West Coast. Instead of calming the storm, however, he arrayed the insurgent masses decisively against him by making a series of indiscreet speeches. He publicly eulogized Nelson W. Aldrich of Rhode Island, leader of the Old Guard in the Senate, rebuked the midwestern senators who voted against the tariff bill, and climaxed his blunders by declaring at Winona, Minnesota, that the measure was the best tariff act the Republican party had ever passed. After the Winona address, Midwesterners were certain Taft had deserted to the Old Guard.

No sooner had public agitation over the Payne-Aldrich débâcle quieted than a worse catastrophe befell the administration and completed the alienation of the progressives. This was the Ballinger affair, which grew out of a feud between the Secretary of the Interior, Richard A. Ballinger, and the chief of the Forestry Service in the Department of Agriculture, Gifford Pinchot. The root of the trouble was the fact that Pinchot was a conservationist and Ballinger was not. When an investigator in the Interior Department, Louis R. Glavis, told Pinchot that Ballinger had connived with the Morgan-Guggenheim syndicate to validate certain withdrawals of Alaskan coal lands, Pinchot believed the accusation. Pinchot, moreover, urged Glavis to present his evidence to the President and publicly denounced Ballinger as a traitor to the cause of conservation.

Glavis presented his indictment to the President, who accepted Ballinger's rebuttal and authorized the Secretary to dismiss Glavis for insubordination. Pinchot, however, refused to halt his attack and virtually forced Taft to remove him from the Forestry Service in January 1910. Meanwhile, the controversy had developed into a national *cause célèbre,* with conserva-

---

[3] For details of this epochal conflict, see below, pp. 105–106.

tives defending the administration and progressives charging treachery and fraud.

The climax of the affair came when the Democrats and insurgent Republicans in Congress combined to force an investigation of the Interior Department. A committee packed by administration leaders voted Ballinger a clean bill of health. But the trenchant questions asked by Louis D. Brandeis, who represented Glavis, exposed Ballinger, not as a corrupt public official, but as an opponent of conservation and a champion of the far western demand for rapid distribution of the remaining public domain. Instead of dismissing Ballinger and appointing a genuine conservationist in his stead, Taft continued stubbornly to defend him and thus exacerbated popular discontent.

By the early months of 1910 the progressive Republicans in the House of Representatives were ready to try again to shear Speaker Cannon of his dictatorial control over legislation. Aware of the impending attack, the Speaker struck back by declaring he would fight to the end. In March 1910 an insurgent-Democratic coalition, led by George W. Norris of Nebraska, deposed the Speaker from the rules committee and deprived him of the power to appoint the members of standing committees. Certainly Taft secretly approved, for he well knew what a liability the Illinoisian was. And yet because he had done nothing by word or deed to encourage the insurgents, the country concluded that Taft was on Cannon's side.

The misunderstanding about Taft's position in the fight against Cannon caused a final and complete break between the administration and the insurgents. They quarreled with Taft over the terms of a bill to strengthen the powers of the Interstate Commerce Commission; they accused him of conniving with Wall Street when he proposed the establishment of a postal savings system. Convinced that the insurgents were maneuvering in every possible way to destroy him politically and goaded by incessant and often unfair attacks, Taft turned fiercely on the progressives and joined the Old Guard in a powerful campaign to destroy insurgency. In March 1910 Taft, Aldrich, and Cannon conferred and formulated a plan of attack. It involved using money and patronage, first to build up strong conservative organizations in the Middle West, and then to defeat the insurgents for renomination in the impending spring primary elections. The plan was quickly carried out. Patronage in the midwestern states was given to supporters of the President, while Old Guard spokesmen descended upon the region and exhorted the voters to support administration candidates.

The insurgents fought bitterly for their political lives and in so doing virtually declared their independence of the party dominated by Taft, Aldrich, and Cannon. It was a momentous battle, for its outcome would determine the fate of the GOP, not only in the Middle West, but in the nation as well. The railroad, industrial, and financial interests of the Midwest supported the administration almost solidly, but in every state the people supported their rebel leaders. Nothing was more indicative of the inevitable doom of the Taft administration than the failure of its midwestern campaign. The flames of midwestern progressivism had grown into a raging prairie fire of insurgency. Already insurgents were talking of organizing a new party if Taft were renominated; already the eyes of the Middle West were turning to Theodore Roosevelt for leadership in the impending battle for control of the Republican party. Before we discuss these events, however, let us turn back and see the way in which political leadership confronted the issues that agitated the American people during the Republican era.

47 / Struggles for Tariff and Tax Reform, 1897–1913

No public question was more potentially explosive and at the same time more perpetually discussed after the Civil War than the issue of a tariff and tax policy for the United States. By the turn of the century, the elaborate system of tariff protection and relative immunity from taxation that wealth enjoyed had become to progressives the very symbol of the control of the federal government by the allied industrial and banking interests.

During the second Cleveland administration, the Democrats had made a fumbling effort at tariff and tax reform. The outcome of their labors, the Wilson-Gorman Tariff Act of 1894, represented at best a feeble effort at downward revision and left the protective structure essentially unimpaired. But a coalition of western and southern representatives succeeded in forcing into the tariff bill an amendment levying a 2 per cent tax on all net incomes of individuals and corporations over $4,000.

By a strained and obviously class conscious opinion, however, a bare majority of the Supreme Court ruled the income tax unconstitutional in 1895. It would be many years before progressives were strong enough to overcome the Old Guard's opposition to an income tax amendment. Meanwhile, the Republicans would have spared themselves much future trouble if they had left well enough alone in tariff legislation. Anxious to propitiate the agrarian Middle West after his close victory over Bryan in 1896, however, McKinley called a special session of Congress in March 1897 to consider tariff revision. The President desired only a moderate revision of the Wilson-Gorman rates; but the senators from the western states held the balance of power and forced a substantial increase in duties on agricultural raw materials like wool and hides. Eastern senators, in turn, obtained increased duties on woolens, silks, and other manufactured products. The upshot of this log-rolling was the Dingley Tariff, the highest tariff in American history to that time.[4]

For twelve years after the adoption of the Dingley Act, the manufacturing interests and western agricultural producers were able to forestall any attempt at general revision. Only one breach was made in the protective structure during the early progressive period: the reciprocity treaty of 1903 with Cuba, providing for mutual tariff reductions of from 20 to 40 per cent. At the same time conservatives kept an equally firm hand on tax policy.

[4] The Dingley Act, however, authorized the President to negotiate reciprocal agreements on certain enumerated articles principally in the French and Latin American trade. Such agreements were later made with France, Italy, Brazil, and other nations. Section 4 of the Dingley Act, moreover, authorized the President to negotiate commercial treaties under which the American tariff might be reduced up to 20 per cent in return for reciprocal benefits. These treaties had to be approved by both houses of Congress and could not run for more than five years. The State Department subsequently negotiated eleven such treaties, none of which Congress approved.

During the Spanish-American War, Congress had imposed a moderate estate tax; but this impost was repealed in 1902, and the federal government reverted to its usual practice of obtaining revenue almost entirely from consumption taxes—customs duties and excise taxes on tobacco and alcoholic beverages—that fell most heavily on the lower and middle classes.

Nevertheless, strong forces were at work during the first years of the twentieth century that would eventually culminate in an irresistible movement for tariff and tax reform. First, the passage of the Dingley Act at the beginning of the period of frantic industrial combination lent apparent proof to the charge, often pressed by Bryan and other Democrats, that the high protective system stimulated the growth of monopolies and super-corporations at home. Secondly, the cost of living increased nearly one-fourth between 1897 and 1907, and the average consumer saw a close relation between high tariffs and high prices, although there was often no connection between the two. Thirdly, widespread discussion of the increasing concentration of incomes and wealth alarmed the middle class and stimulated the conviction that only income and inheritance taxes could reverse a process that seemed to threaten the future of American democracy.

The most significant factor in the beginning of a powerful movement for tariff and tax reform was the awakening of the Middle West. After an epochal struggle in 1902, the Iowa Republicans nominated the progressive Albert B. Cummins for governor and wrote into their platform his proposal to remove all duties on articles manufactured by the so-called trusts. Thereafter the "Iowa Idea," as Cummins' suggestion was called, became a stock feature of most midwestern state Republican platforms. And although the movement for downward revision soon became nation-wide and included many small businessmen, the midwestern insurgents remained the most consistent advocates of tariff reduction in the GOP.

As he recognized the potential danger of the popular discontent, Roosevelt was tempted to take leadership of the movement for tariff revision. He failed to act, however, because the Old Guard leaders warned that such a move would disrupt the party and, more important, because he did not think the tariff really mattered. By 1908, on the other hand, both Roosevelt and Taft agreed that the issue could no longer be evaded. At their insistence, a plank declaring "unequivocally for the revision of the tariff" was written in the Republican platform. By 1908, moreover, both Roosevelt and Taft had come out squarely for graduated federal estate, gift, and income taxes.

Thus it seemed the movement for genuine tariff and tax reform had reached a point of culmination when President Taft called Congress into special session in March 1909 to consider tariff revision. Sponsored by Sereno Payne of New York, chairman of the House ways and means committee, the administration's tariff bill put a number of important raw materials on the free list and substantially reduced rates on iron and steel products, agricultural implements, sugar, and lumber. The measure, moreover, included a federal inheritance tax ranging from 1 to 5 per cent. Although the Democrats made an unsuccessful effort to add an income tax amendment to the Payne bill and voted against it for party reasons, they, like the midwestern insurgents, were pleasantly surprised by the substantial revision it attempted.

The chief defenders of the privileged were in the Senate. There Senator

Aldrich and his finance committee took the Payne bill in hand and on April 12, 1909, reported it with 847 amendments, the majority of which effected increases, and with the provision for an inheritance tax eliminated. Instead of lowering the Dingley rates, as the Rhode Island senator claimed, the Aldrich bill actually increased the *ad valorem* duties from 40.21 to 41.77 per cent.

As the colossal nature of Aldrich's cynical betrayal of his party's pledges became evident, a wave of indignation swept over the country and especially the Middle West. In the Senate a group of insurgent Republicans conferred and pledged themselves to make an open fight against the Aldrich amendments. Opposing the Rhode Island senator were La Follette of Wisconsin, Jonathan P. Dolliver and Albert B. Cummins of Iowa, Albert J. Beveridge of Indiana, Joseph L. Bristow of Kansas, and Moses E. Clapp of Minnesota. Each of these Midwesterners took an important section of the tariff bill and discussed it in a lengthy and bitter speech. At the same time, they joined the Democrats to obtain an income tax amendment as a substitute for the discarded inheritance tax. So effective was their campaign that Aldrich headed it off only by accepting Taft's proposal for a 2 per cent tax on the net incomes of corporations and by agreeing to the passage of an income tax amendment to the Constitution.

With the administration's support in the violent intra-party battle in the Senate, Aldrich rallied his forces and put his bill across on July 8. It included the corporation income tax, restored the duties on hides, iron ore, and lumber, and greatly increased the Payne rates on a number of manufactured products. The final struggle came when the conference committee met shortly afterward. Finally bestirring himself in behalf of lower rates, Taft forced the committee to accept free hides and reductions in the prevailing duties on shoes, lumber, coal, and iron ore. None the less, the bill that the committee approved and Taft signed was a victory for the manufacturing East and an affront to the insurgent Middle West.[5]

The Payne-Aldrich débâcle had profound and almost immediate repercussions. For one thing, it further widened the gulf between the insurgents and the Taft administration. For another, it enabled the Democrats to capture the House of Representatives in the congressional elections of November 1910. Following hard on the heels of this disaster for the GOP, Taft proceeded further to alienate midwestern opinion by driving for reciprocity with Canada.

Confronted with an impending trade war between the United States and her northern neighbor, the State Department in January 1911 concluded a reciprocal trade agreement with the Canadian government that promised to draw the two nations into an economic union. The agreement placed all important agricultural products, industrial raw materials, and raw lumber and wood pulp on the free list. Moreover, it substantially reduced prevailing rates on many manufactured products. The President presented the agreement to Congress on January 26, 1911, for approval by joint resolution;

[5] As the matter of tariff rates is infinitely complicated, it is almost impossible to say what the average rates of the Payne-Aldrich bill were. The figure usually given by the authorities is 37 per cent. The measure also established a Tariff Board to make scientific studies of various phases of the tariff question and to advise Congress and the President.

ABOVE: *John D. Rockefeller on his way to the oil investigation*
BELOW: *Andrew Carnegie, William Jennings Bryan, James J. Hill, and John Mitchell*

Nelson W. Aldrich

William Howard Taft

Elihu Root

Henry Cabot Lodge

J. P. Morgan

Edward H. Harriman

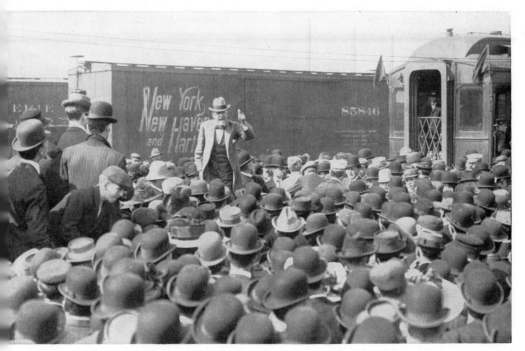

Eugene Debs campaigning from the Red Special *in 1912*

Samuel Gompers

Robert M. La Follette

Louis D. Brandeis

Lincoln Steffens and Clarence Darrow

Theodore Roosevelt

Woodrow Wilson

Albert J. Beveridge

Gifford Pinchot

Hiram Johnson

George W. Perkins

OVE: *Battleships of the Great White Fleet*
OW: *Social Life with the Early Model T*

John Dewey

Walter Rauschenbusch

Joseph Pulitzer

Edward Arlington Robinson

and when the Senate refused to act before the regular session ended, Taft called Congress into special session for the first week in April.

In the subsequent battle over reciprocity that raged from April nearly to August, the traditional alignment of progressive Republicans and Democrats against administration and Old Guard Republicans was totally destroyed. The Democrats joined with Taft's friends in Congress in supporting the agreement—because it represented a tremendous victory for free trade. For the same reason the Old Guard fought the measure. The midwestern insurgents, on the other hand, accused the administration of sacrificing midwestern farm interests in order to widen the foreign market for eastern manufactured products. They fought the treaty, therefore, even more bitterly than did the Old Guard. For once, however, Taft exerted himself strenuously and with the nearly solid support of the Democrats won the fight in Congress. The House approved the agreement on April 21, the Senate on July 22, 1911. But it seemed Taft could not succeed, even when he did the statesmanlike thing. Aroused by talk in the United States of annexation, the Canadian voters on September 21, 1911, repudiated the Liberal government that had negotiated the reciprocity agreement and prevented its ratification.

The insurgent-Old Guard anti-reciprocity coalition was short-lived. In fact, while the battle over reciprocity was raging the insurgents combined with the Democrats to pass three tariff bills—a farmers' free list bill, which removed duties from about one hundred articles that the farmer bought; a wool and woolens bill; and a bill reducing duties on iron and steel products, cotton goods, and chemicals. Taft vetoed these measures on the ground that they were not "scientific." During 1911 and 1912, moreover, progressive Democrats and Republicans joined hands throughout the country to obtain ratification of the Sixteenth, or income tax, Amendment, which Congress had submitted to the states in 1909. The first chapter in the history of twentieth century tax reform was completed on February 25, 1913, when the amendment became a part of the Constitution. By the inauguration of the Wilson administration on March 4, 1913, therefore, the road seemed clear ahead for the fulfillment of the progressive demand for downward tariff revision and the beginning of a democratic federal tax policy.

48 /   The Railroad Problem

Agitation for effective public control of railroad rates and services was as old as the progressive movement in the United States. First came efforts by the midwestern and southern legislatures during the 1870's and 1880's to institute regulation, either by statute or commission. Some of these attempts succeeded partially; others failed completely. In any event, during the 1880's the conviction grew that only Congress could deal effectively with rebating, stock watering, pools that destroyed competition, and exorbitant rates for goods and passengers in interstate commerce. Experience and the Supreme Court's decision in the Wabash case of 1886, forbidding the states to regulate interstate rates, demonstrated that the really important railroad evils were beyond the jurisdiction of the states.

As a result of the Wabash decision and long years of agitation, the American people by 1886 had firmly determined to institute federal regulation and bring the reign of unbridled freedom in the field of transportation to an end. The legislative response to this overwhelming demand, the Interstate Commerce Act of 1887, was avowedly tentative in character. It specifically forbade pooling, discrimination, rebating, and higher charges for a short haul than a long one. As for rates, it declared that all charges should be reasonable and just and required railroads to publish their rate schedules. Finally, the measure established the Interstate Commerce Commission, the first federal regulatory agency, to administer the law. The passage of the Commerce Act, unenforceable though it turned out to be, marked a turning point in the exercise of federal power in the United States. For the first time the federal authority had been extended into an important area of hitherto private economic activity.

For a brief time after the adoption of the Act of 1887 the railroad managers seemed eager to abide by the law. When the ICC tried to stamp out rebating, however, it ran head on into the refusal of the railroad managers to testify; and it required years of adjudication to establish the Commission's authority to compel testimony. But it was the Supreme Court's narrow interpretation of the Commerce Act that deprived the ICC of any real power. In the maximum freight rate cases of 1896 and 1897, the Court ruled that the Commission did not have the power to fix rates; and in the latter year, in the Alabama Midlands case, that tribunal practically emasculated the prohibition against discrimination in charges for long and short hauls. Indeed, after these decisions the ICC became nothing more than a fact-finding body and openly confessed its inability to cope seriously with the problem of regulation.

The significance of these developments is, of course, at once apparent: By 1900 the whole problem of federal railroad regulation had to be fought out all over again in Congress and the country. The first amendment to the Interstate Commerce Act, the Elkins Act of 1903, was adopted, ironically enough, in response to the pleas of the railroad managers themselves. The rebating evil, they warned, had grown to such monstrous proportions that it threatened to bankrupt the railroads. Congress responded at once with the Elkins Act, which outlawed any deviation from published rates.

The "railroad senators" who framed the Elkins Act, however, carefully avoided giving the ICC any authority over the rate making process. And yet it was obvious on all sides that this was what the great majority of farmers and businessmen wanted most. At this high point of public agitation, Theodore Roosevelt took leadership of public opinion. In his Annual Message of December 1904, he recommended that the ICC be empowered, upon complaint of shippers, to fix maximum rates, subject to the review of the courts. In response, the House passed the Esch-Townshend bill, implementing the President's suggestion, by the impressive majority of 326 to 17. Seeking to delay or postpone further action, the Republican leaders in the upper house instructed the Senate commerce committee to investigate the railroad problem during the spring and summer of 1905. As it turned out, the committee's investigation was no whitewash but rather uncovered a far-flung propaganda campaign by the railroads against federal regulation.

Armed with this new evidence of railroad misdoing, Roosevelt pressed hard his campaign for legislation all during the summer and fall of 1905. And so enthusiastic was the popular response that even the railroad senators began to tremble. The House of Representatives quickly passed the administration's measure, the Hepburn bill, in February 1906. Although it fell short of what advanced progressives wanted, the bill went straight to the core of the railroad problem by empowering the ICC, upon complaint by shippers, to lower rates already established. It was not all that Roosevelt wanted, either, but he was certain it was the most he could get.

In the Senate the Hepburn bill was referred to the commerce committee, the chairman of which was the multimillionaire Stephen B. Elkins of West Virginia, who, along with Aldrich, was the leader of the railroad senators. Realizing he could not control the administration majority on the committee, Aldrich allowed the committee to report the Hepburn bill unamended. In order to outflank the committee, however, Aldrich maneuvered so that the fiery Democrat, Ben Tillman of South Carolina, would report the bill and defend it on the Senate floor. At this stage, moreover, the astute Rhode Islander proposed amendments to cripple the bill. The most important of these was an amendment to endow the courts with sweeping authority to review and nullify the rate decisions of the Commissions.

For two months debate raged in the Senate over Aldrich's amendment. Contending that judicial review should be limited solely to determining whether the ICC had exercised due process in fixing rates, Roosevelt fought with unusual resourcefulness for a time. Then, when it seemed that a coalition of Democrats and administration Republicans could put the measure across without Aldrich's consent, several Democrats deserted the coalition. At this point—that is, early May 1906—Roosevelt executed a brilliant maneuver. Instead of going down to defeat with the progressives who still demanded narrow court review, Roosevelt maneuvered Aldrich into accepting a middle-of-the-road solution. A compromise amendment, framed by Aldrich, sponsored by William B. Allison of Iowa, and approved by the President, was accepted, and the Hepburn bill became law on June 29, 1906.

Progressives like La Follette charged that Roosevelt had betrayed the cause of railroad regulation, but was their accusation just? The verdict in this historic dispute must go to Roosevelt. The Allison amendment authorized district courts to issue interlocutory, or suspensive, injunctions against the ICC's decisions, it is true; but it also provided for speedy appeals to the Circuit and Supreme courts. Moreover, only the Circuit courts and the Supreme Court could reverse the Commission's rulings; and these high courts were instructed to pass upon such rulings with the same seriousness that they would pass upon acts of Congress, with the presumption always in favor of the ICC. Thus so-called broad court review was hedged about with such effective limitations that judicial nullification of the Hepburn Act was well nigh impossible.

Furthermore, an examination of the general provisions of the Hepburn Act emphasizes the dimensions of Roosevelt's victory in this struggle. To begin with, the ICC was empowered, upon complaint, to investigate and lower rates. In other words, control over rates was taken from private hands and given to an agency of the people. The Commission, in addition, was given jurisdiction over express and sleeping car companies, switches and spurs, and pipe lines. Finally, the Act required a uniform system of cost accounting by the railroads, eliminated the old free pass evil, and required that railroads after 1908 divest themselves of outside properties. The latter provision was aimed chiefly at the anthracite coal monopoly controlled by nine eastern railroads.

The effect of the broadening of the ICC's power was at once apparent. Within two years after the passage of the Hepburn Act, shippers made more than 9,000 appeals to the Commission, while the railroad managers seemed almost in a chastened mood. Suddenly in 1908, however, the railroad managers began to challenge the ICC, and their action in turn caused a crowding of the dockets of the Circuit courts. Moreover, in 1909 the railroads made general rate increases, and the masses of people realized for the first time that the Commission could deal only with specific increases, upon complaint, and did not have the power to suspend or revoke general rate advances.

The railroads' resistance to regulation and the general rate increases of 1909 at once stimulated increased agitation for a further strengthening of the ICC's power. In response, President Taft, in the summer of 1909, requested Attorney General George W. Wickersham to prepare a new railroad bill. The measure that Wickersham drafted greatly enlarged the Commission's rate-making power and established a Commerce Court, which would have original jurisdiction in appeals from the rulings of the ICC. The midwestern insurgent senators were disappointed because the Wickersham draft made no provision for valuation of railroad property by the Commission, and they strongly disapproved the proposal for a Commerce Court, with power of broad review. Even so, the insurgents' opposition to the President's bill might have been less violent had it not seemed that Taft was willing to change the measure to satisfy the demands of the railroad spokesmen. After a conference with six railroad presidents early in January 1910, and before the measure was introduced in the House, Taft changed the bill to allow railroads to acquire competing lines. To progressives, this looked suspiciously like collusion; and when Senator Aldrich announced that he would support the bill, they were certain some evil scheme was being plotted.

Introduced in the House of Representatives in January 1910 as the Mann bill, the President's measure at once fell under the control of a progressive Republican-Democratic coalition, which struck out the provision allowing mergers of competing lines, added amendments for physical valuation and equality in charges for long and short hauls, and brought telephone and telegraph companies under the jurisdiction of the Interstate Commerce Commission. Meanwhile, in the Senate the insurgents had launched a violent attack on the President's bill, which the commerce committee reported without amendments. When Taft made the measure a test of party loyalty, the insurgents joined the Democrats and threatened to rewrite the bill altogether. After the progressive coalition struck out the provisions contrary to the Sherman Act, Aldrich turned to the Democrats. If they would support the administration's railroad bill, Aldrich said, the administration would agree to pass statehood acts for New Mexico and Arizona. As this seemed a cheap way of getting four new Democratic senators, the Democrats sealed the bargain. Thus the progressive Republican-Democratic coalition changed into a Democratic-Regular Republican majority, and the administration bill passed the Senate essentially intact.

None the less, the bill that emerged from the conference committee and Taft approved as the Mann-Elkins Act represented more a victory for the progressives than for Aldrich and Taft. The new legislation empowered the ICC to suspend general rate increases and to revise rates on its own initiative. It also established a Commerce Court to hear appeals directly from the Commission. These provisions had been originally parts of the President's bill. On the other hand, all the important progressive amendments, except the provision for physical valuation, were retained by the conference committee. Railroads were not allowed to acquire competing lines. Telephone, telegraph, cable, and wireless companies were defined as common carriers. The prohibition in the Act of 1887 against discriminations in charges for long and short hauls was effectively implemented. As a result of the hard fight progressives made in support of these amendments, the Mann-Elkins Act of 1910 had become legislation not merely supplementary, but comprehensive in character.

With the passage of the Mann-Elkins Act, progressives in Congress redoubled their efforts to obtain physical valuation as the basis for rate-making by the Commission. Valuation of railroad property would enable the Commission to fix rates on a basis of the true value of railroad property, rather than on a basis of watered capitalization. This was the chief reason progressives supported and railroad spokesmen opposed the proposal. To conservatives, moreover, physical valuation seemed to be the first step in eventual nationalization. None the less, the insurgent-Democratic congressional coalition won this last objective in the closing months of the Taft regime. The Physical Valuation Act of 1913 required the Interstate Commerce Commission to report the value of all property owned by every common carrier subject to its jurisdiction, including the original cost, the cost of reproduction new, and the cost of reproduction, less depreciation. When completed, the Act declared, such valuations were to be accepted as *prima facie* evidence of the worth of the property in all actions by the Commission.

49 / *The Federal Antitrust Policy, 1890–1913*

Almost simultaneous with the beginning of the agitation for railroad regulation there developed a widespread movement in the 1870's and 1880's to destroy the infant industrial combinations of that day, the trusts.[6] By 1890 at least fourteen states and territories had written antitrust provisions into their constitutions, while thirteen others had adopted antitrust laws. Almost without exception, these were western and southern states—a reflec-

[6] For a discussion of the origins and progress of the trust movement in the United States, see above, pp. 47–49.

tion of the impact of the agrarian crusade against railroads and monopolies. And from 1890 to 1900 the antitrust crusade gained new momentum. By the turn of the century forty-two states and territories attempted to outlaw monopolies, either by constitutional provision or by statute.[7]

It became increasingly obvious that sporadic and uncoordinated action by the states could neither destroy monopoly nor restore competition, especially when New Jersey in 1888 permitted the legal incorporation of trusts as holding companies. By 1888 the popular agitation had reached such a high pitch that both major parties incorporated antitrust planks in their platforms. And when President Benjamin Harrison, in his Annual Message of December 1889, endorsed the demand for a federal antitrust law, Congress did not dare refuse to act.

Congress' response, the Sherman Antitrust Act of 1890, was brief and to the point. The core of the statute was embodied in Section 1, which prohibited "every contract, combination in the form of trust or otherwise, or conspiracy, in restraint of trade or commerce among the several States, or with foreign nations," and which provided punishment for such restraint of trade. Section 7, moreover, provided that any person injured by illegal combinations or conspiracies might sue under the provisions of the Act and recover threefold damages and the cost of the suit.

No statute ever enacted by Congress more clearly reflected an overwhelming popular demand for the inauguration of a strong federal policy than did the Sherman law of 1890. Yet after several prosecutions by the Harrison administration, the law fell into neglect and general contempt until Theodore Roosevelt revived it in 1902. Effective enforcement of the law depended largely upon the Justice Department; and the Attorneys General during the Cleveland and McKinley administrations did little to carry out the popular mandate to destroy the trusts because neither Cleveland nor McKinley had any sympathy for the objectives of the Sherman Act—except in so far as it might be applied against labor unions.

A case in point was E. C. Knight v. the United States, 1895, in which the government protested the monopoly recently acquired by the American Sugar Refining Company of Philadelphia. Instead of vindicating the Sherman law, Cleveland's Attorney General, Richard Olney, presented the government's case in such a manner that the Supreme Court had to declare that the Sherman Act did not apply to combinations in manufacturing. The consequences of Olney's calculated subversion of the Act were far reaching and disastrous, but we should not fall into the common error of thinking that the Supreme Court entirely emasculated the antitrust law. As we will later see, on every opportunity afforded by the government that tribunal evidenced a sincere desire to carry out the mandate embodied in the statute.

As the new century opened, therefore, it was obvious that all that was necessary to make the Sherman law a really effective weapon was a Presi-

---

[7] Practically all these states and territories prohibited restraint of trade contrary to the public interest. Some twenty-nine states prohibited suppression of competition through pools, agreements to limit quantity or divide sales territories, price fixing agreements, and so on. A number of states, moreover, attempted to outlaw cutthroat competitive practices, such as price cutting to destroy competition, so-called tying contracts, and discriminations in prices made for the purpose of destroying competition.

dent's determination to give teeth to the measure. Because he understood the dimensions of the popular fear of the "trusts," abhorred monopoly, and personally resented the power that uncontrolled wealth exercised over the nation's destinies, Theodore Roosevelt resolved to vindicate the national sovereignty by bringing great combinations to book. His chief weapons were publicity and the Sherman law. Publicity and investigations of mergers and so-called trusts he assured on a systematic scale with the establishment of the Bureau of Corporations in the Department of Commerce and Labor in 1903.

In the form of direct attack, the Justice Department under Roosevelt instituted eighteen proceedings in equity, obtained twenty-five indictments, and participated in one forfeiture proceeding. Beginning with his first prosecution, the suit to dissolve the Northern Securities Company in 1902, Roosevelt pressed relentlessly forward against other combinations. Later in 1902 the President ordered prosecution of the Swift, Armour, and Nelson Morris companies—the so-called Beef Trust—for organizing the National Packing Company to acquire control of independent packing firms in the Middle West. The Supreme Court rendered a unanimous verdict for the government in 1905; but the packers continued to defy the government, and it was not until 1920 and 1921 that competition was effectively restored to the meat industry. The climax of Roosevelt's campaign came with sweeping indictments by the Justice Department of the Standard Oil Company in 1907 and of the American Tobacco Company in 1908. These two cases, the most important in the history of the antitrust movement before 1945, did not reach final settlement until 1911.

In spite of Roosevelt's effort and achievement, his contribution to the antitrust cause has been derided by most historians. Their failure to understand his contribution stems, among other things, from a faulty appreciation of his objectives. Unlike some progressives, who would have limited the size of corporations, Roosevelt never feared bigness in industry—unless bigness was accompanied by monopolistic control and a disposition on the part of management to defy the public interest. Thus, he never moved against two prominent combinations, United States Steel and International Harvester, because he never had good evidence to prove they were monopolies or were illegally suppressing competition. The Taft administration later instituted dissolution proceedings against these two corporations, but in both cases the Supreme Court confirmed Roosevelt's judgment.

Roosevelt's aggressive program of publicity and prosecution was carried forward at an even more intensive pace by President Taft and his Attorney General, George W. Wickersham. When Congress refused to enact Taft's proposal for federal incorporation, a corporation commission, and a means to end stock watering, the Taft administration moved in a wholesale way against combinations. All told, Taft instituted forty-six proceedings for dissolution, brought forty-three indictments, and instituted one contempt proceeding. His two most important cases, against United States Steel and International Harvester, ended in failure. His two most important victories, against Standard Oil and American Tobacco, were scored in proceedings that Roosevelt had instituted.

After five years of legal warfare, the government seemingly won complete victory in 1911, with the Supreme Court's order for the dissolution of the gigantic oil and tobacco monopolies. The Court implicitly repudiated the Knight decision and made it plain that the holding company form could not be used to evade the Sherman law. And yet in both cases the government accepted dissolution plans prepared by the corporations' lawyers, plans that provided for the re-establishment of the constituent companies and a *pro rata* distribution of shares in the new companies on the basis of ownership of shares in the old holding companies. As time passed, the new companies did in fact emerge as independent concerns, while the tremendous expansion of the oil and tobacco industries during the First World War helped create a new competitive situation. At the time the dissolution decrees were issued in 1911, however, progressives indignantly protested they were a sham and a fraud.

None the less, by the end of the Taft administration the primary objectives of the antitrust movement had been fairly accomplished. There was no longer any constitutional doubt that the federal government possessed ample power to prevent monopoly and suppress unfair trade practices in the day to day operations of businessmen. Because of Roosevelt's and Taft's vigorous prosecutions, moreover, the age of monopoly was over. Great corporations remained and dominated certain industries, but these oligopolies existed by the sufferance of public opinion and a government that jealously guarded their smaller competitors.

50 / The Supreme Court and Economic Policy Before the First World War

In the American constitutional system Congress proposes and the Supreme Court disposes. The phrase is of course a hyperbole, but it points up a problem that continually perplexed progressives who were struggling to extend the boundaries of governmental power. Unlike their counterparts in other countries, American reformers in state and nation were never free to develop at will a system of administrative regulation. For one thing, they were bound by a written Constitution capable of being construed as the bulwark of a *laissez-faire* policy. For another, they were restrained by the fear that a conservative Supreme Court, which insisted upon having the final word, would not tolerate the extension of governmental power they sought to accomplish. As we will see, by the outbreak of the First World War the courts had effected a remarkable accommodation of constitutional doctrine to most progressive concepts. In the last years of the nineteenth century, however, reformers might well have believed such a development was impossible.

To begin with, by 1900 the Supreme Court had established the right to review all state attempts to regulate railroads and corporations. This power the Court had assumed as a result of one of the most important revolutions in judicial theory in American history, which came about in the following manner. When the Granger legislature of Illinois, in the early 1870's, established a schedule of charges for grain elevators, one of the elevator owners appealed to the federal courts for protection. The Illinois statute, he averred, deprived his corporation of property without due process of law and thus violated the Fourteenth Amendment. In an epochal opinion, in Munn *v.* Illinois, 1877, Chief Justice Morrison R. Waite upheld the Illinois law and declared that the determination of a reasonable rate was a legislative and not a judicial function. This doctrine was reaffirmed soon afterward in a series of so-called Granger cases and seemed to be firmly established as a basic principle of American constitutional law. And yet between 1886 and 1898 the Supreme Court completely reversed Waite's doctrine and transformed the Fourteenth Amendment into an instrument for the protection of corporations and railroads against "unreasonable" regulation by the states. Let us see how this startling reversal occurred.

While arguing the case of San Mateo County *v.* Southern Pacific Railroad before the Supreme Court in 1882, Roscoe Conkling, counsel for the railroad, asserted that the congressional committee that framed the Fourteenth Amendment had intended to include corporations within the meaning of that amendment. As Conkling had been a member of the committee and produced its secret journal, the Court listened carefully to his argument, although it did not take judicial cognizance of it. In Santa Clara County *v.* Southern Pacific Railroad, 1886, and the Minnesota Rate Case, 1889, however, the Court accepted Conkling's reasoning and declared that corporations were federal citizens, entitled to the protection of the Fourteenth Amendment against action of the states that would deprive them of property, or income, without due process of law. Finally, in Smyth *v.* Ames, 1898, the Supreme Court reached the last stage in its journey away from the doctrines expounded in Munn *v.* Illinois. Nebraska had established maximum charges on freight carried entirely within the state. Overturning the Nebraska statute, the Court reaffirmed the federal citizenship of corporations, declared that rates must be high enough to guarantee a fair return to the railroads, and warned state legislatures that the courts existed, among other reasons, for the purpose of protecting property against unreasonable legislation.

In none of these cases did the Supreme Court deny the right of the states to regulate railroads and other corporations. It only insisted that state regulation be reasonable and just and not invade the jurisdiction of Congress. Until a body of doctrine defining due process regarding state regulation had been built, however, the effect of the Court's new departure was to create a twilight zone of authority. Judges of the numerous federal district courts could prevent the states from acting; and the states had no recourse but to await the verdict of the high tribunal.

Progressives, therefore, charged that the Supreme Court had usurped the administrative function of the states and imposed its own notion of due process and reasonableness on state commissions. They resented even more bitterly the systematic manner in which the Court narrowed the authority of the ICC under the Act of 1887 and even reduced that great statute to an unenforceable generalization. As we have seen, the Court's decision in the Alabama Midlands Case of 1897 nullified the prohibition against discrimination in charges for long and short hauls. In 1896 and 1897, moreover, in the so-called maximum freight rate cases, the Court denied that Congress had conferred rate-making authority on the Interstate Commerce Commission. In view of the absence of any specific delegation of the rate-making authority to the Commission by the Commerce Act, the Court could probably not have ruled otherwise. Impatient progressives, however, found the Court a more vulnerable scapegoat than Congress.

Progressives were on more solid ground when they denounced the Supreme Court's nullification of the income tax provision of the Wilson-Gorman Tariff Act of 1894. By a five to four decision in Pollock *v.* Farmers' Loan and Trust Company, 1895, the Court reversed precedent by declaring that the income tax was in part indirectly a tax on land and would therefore have to be apportioned among the states according to population. It was easily the most unpopular judicial ruling since the Dred Scott decision set the nation afire in 1857. For one thing, the income tax decision effectively blocked the movement for a more democratic tax policy until a constitutional amendment could be adopted. For another, the Court's majority had obviously made a political rather than a judicial judgment. Coming as it did in the same year in which the Court upheld the conviction of Debs and other officials of the American Railway Union for violating the Sherman law, the income tax decision only deepened the popular conviction that the Supreme Court had become the tool of railroads, corporations, and millionaires.

Popular distrust of the Court was further intensified in 1895 when that tribunal, in the case of E. C. Knight *v.* the United States, seemingly emasculated the Sherman Act's prohibition against industrial monopoly. That the Court was actually anxious to interpret the Sherman Act liberally was demonstrated, however, in a series of important antitrust cases from 1897 to 1899. In the Trans-Missouri Freight Association case of 1897, the Court affirmed that the Sherman law applied to railroads and outlawed a pool of railroads operating south and west of the Missouri River. The following year, in the Joint Traffic Association Case, the Court reaffirmed this judgment. Moreover, in the Addyston Pipe Company case, 1899, the justices made it clear that the Sherman law applied also to manufacturers who combined in pools to eliminate price competition.

Thus by the turn of the century the Supreme Court had firmly established the rule that combinations formed directly to suppress competition in the transportation and distribution of products were illegal. Promoters of industrial combinations and their lawyers, however, continued to assume that manufacturing consolidations did not fall under the prohibitions of the antitrust act. This illusion the Court finally and completely shattered in its decisions in the Standard Oil and American Tobacco cases, rendered in 1911. Without openly repudiating the Knight decision, the tribunal declared that industrial combinations formed for the purpose of achieving monopoly were outlawed by the Sherman Act and that the holding company form did not confer legality on otherwise illegal consolidations.

The Standard Oil and Tobacco decisions represented, therefore, a complete accommodation of legal doctrine to prevailing antitrust sentiment. But even more important was the fact that they marked the end of a long struggle within the Court over the basic meaning of the Sherman Act. Did that statute forbid all restraints of trade, or did it prohibit only unreasonable, that is, direct and calculated, restraints? Before 1911 the Supreme Court's majority had consistently ruled that the Sherman law proscribed all restraints, reasonable and unreasonable.[8] In the Trans-Missouri Freight Association case of 1897, however, Justice Edward Douglas White had vigorously dissented, declaring that the framers of the antitrust law had intended to outlaw only unreasonable restraints. Over the years White had reiterated his position and won converts to it. In 1911 White, now Chief Justice, finally won a majority to his side and wrote the "rule of reason" into American legal doctrine. The Sherman law, he declared, prohibited only unreasonable restraints of trade.

Actually, the "rule of reason" was the only standard by which the antitrust law could be enforced, as the Court had tacitly admitted years before. By winning his campaign to interpret the law in the light of common law doctrine, Chief Justice White enabled businessmen to conduct their normal operations without fear of reprisal and the government in good conscience to enforce the statute. All the same, the promulgation of the new rule set off an incredible furor. The great mass of people thought the Court had drawn a distinction between reasonable, or "good," trusts and unreasonable, or "bad," trusts. Immediately a number of Democratic congressmen introduced bills to outlaw White's interpretation. The Supreme Court had ruled wisely, but the Taft administration failed to explain to the people that the Court's decisions in the Oil and Tobacco cases and the promulgation of the "rule of reason" represented the greatest victory thus far accomplished in the long fight to destroy monopoly in the United States.

[8] In common law doctrine a reasonable restraint of trade is any restraint that is ancillary to an otherwise legal contract. Almost any form of contract involves such reasonable restraint of trade. By agreeing to sell his product to one person, for example, a manufacturer restrains trade to the extent that he cannot sell the same goods to another person. An unreasonable restraint of trade, on the other hand, occurs when businessmen enter into an agreement, the objective of which is to restrain trade. Thus conspiracies to control prices, restrict production, divide markets, and so on are unreasonable restraints of trade.

CHAPTER 6 / WOODROW WILSON AND THE FLOWERING OF THE PROGRESSIVE MOVEMENT, 1910–1916

*T*HE years from 1910 to 1917 were a time of culmination and fulfillment for American progressivism. We have seen how the reform movement in the cities and states came to fruition during this period. In addition, a virtual revolution took place in the more important area of national politics. Convulsed by internal schisms, the Republican party suffered a violent rupture from 1910 to 1912; and in the latter year Theodore Roosevelt attempted to rally progressives of all parties under the banner of a third party. As the Democrats now had a reform leader of their own in Woodrow Wilson, Roosevelt failed to build either a solid progressive phalanx or a permanent party. Instead, he split the Republican majority and enabled the Democrats to capture control of the presidency and of Congress.

But Roosevelt did more than make possible a Democratic victory in 1912. By championing an advanced program of federal economic and social regulation, he also pointed up the major dilemma confronting American progressives. Could national regeneration be achieved, as most Democratic progressives thought, merely by destroying special privilege and applying the rule of equity to all classes? Or could the promise of American life be fulfilled only through a positive program of federal intervention and participation in economic and social affairs, as Roosevelt and Herbert Croly contended?

All during the period of the first Wilson administration, from 1913 to 1917, the advocates of these two concepts of progressivism battled to shape the form and character of federal legislation. As the new President exercised an extraordinary control over Congress, the outcome of the conflict—in fact, the future destiny of the progressive movement—was largely in his hands. Let us now see how progressivism came to the season of flowering, how Wilson guided it from one channel into another, and how the foundations for a later and bolder program of federal action were laid by the time the United States entered the First World War.

**51 / *The Disruption of the Republican Party and the
Reorganization of the Democracy***

There were numerous warnings in all parts of the country during the
spring and summer of 1910 that a violent storm impended in the Republican
party. The most portentous was the near hurricane velocity of the insurgent
revolt in the Middle West. After the failure of his campaign to purge the
midwestern progressives in the primary campaigns of 1910, President William
Howard Taft hastily sought to make peace with his enemies and save his
party from disaster. By now determined to seize control of the GOP and
prevent Taft's renomination in 1912, the insurgent leaders rebuffed the
President's overtures and began a search for a leader of their own.

A second signal of Republican distress was the estrangement between
Roosevelt and Taft that was fully evident by the time the former President
returned from Europe in June 1910. The coolness that Roosevelt felt toward
his former intimate friend was partly the outgrowth of incidents like the
Ballinger affair, but above all of Roosevelt's growing conviction that Taft
had allowed the Old Guard to maneuver him into a position that made the
revolt of the insurgents inevitable. Although he was firmly committed to
the progressive cause, Roosevelt tried hard to bring the warring factions in
his party together. Feeling rebuffed by the administration when he endeavored to mediate between conservatives and progressives in New York State,
Roosevelt set out in the summer of 1910 upon a speaking tour to kindle the
flames of progressivism. So enthusiastic was the popular response that
Roosevelt was catapulted into a reluctant leadership of the rebellion against
Taft and the Old Guard.

In the congressional and gubernatorial elections of November 1910 the
Democrats harvested the fruits of Republican dissension and the popular
protest against the Payne-Aldrich tariff and the Ballinger affair. The House
of Representatives went Democratic for the first time since 1892, while
Democratic governors were elected in many normally Republican states in
the East and Middle West. There could be no doubt that progressive agitation was rising to flood tide, or that a Republican party dominated by Taft,
Aldrich, and Cannon faced almost certain defeat in 1912.

The Republican insurgents, on the other hand, were determined to win
in 1912, but to win with a ticket of their choosing and a platform embodying
their objectives. In 1910 and early 1911 many signs pointed to Senator
Robert M. La Follette of Wisconsin as the leader of the rebels, especially
after prominent insurgents formed the National Progressive Republican
League in January 1911 to fight for the senator's nomination. La Follette
had the support of a small and dedicated band of idealists, but the great
mass of Republican progressives wanted Roosevelt. Convinced that his party
faced certain defeat if Taft were renominated and persuaded that La Follette
could never be nominated, Roosevelt at last gave in to the pleas of his friends
and announced his candidacy for the Republican nomination on February
24, 1912.

The battle for control of the GOP that occurred from March through

May 1912 was bitter and violent. In the thirteen states that held presidential primaries, Roosevelt won 278 delegates, as compared to 48 for Taft and 36 for La Follette. On the other hand, Taft controlled the southern states, had the support of Old Guard-dominated states like New York, and dominated the Republican National Committee. Thus, the Taft forces organized the national convention that met in Chicago on June 18, awarded themselves 235 of the crucial 254 contested seats, and proceeded ruthlessly to renominate the President on the first ballot on June 21.

Meanwhile, over three hundred Roosevelt delegates had stormed out of the convention and in consultation with Roosevelt had decided to return to Chicago and form a new party dedicated to advancing the cause of progressivism. The outgrowth of the insurgents' anger and dedication was the Progressive party, organized in Chicago on August 5 and 6, 1912. Feeling, he said, like a bull moose, Roosevelt came in person on August 6 and delivered his acceptance speech, "A Confession of Faith."

The drama and high excitement of these events at Chicago should not be allowed to obscure their significance or the importance of the platform that the Progressive convention adopted. As it erected mileposts that the American progressive movement would follow for the next fifty years, the Progressive credo was the most important American political document since the Populist platform of 1892. It approved all the objectives of the social justice reformers—minimum wages for women, child labor legislation, workmen's compensation, and social insurance; endorsed demands for the initiative, referendum, and recall, the recall of judicial decisions, the nomination of presidential candidates by preferential primaries, and women's suffrage; and demanded the establishment of powerful new federal agencies—a federal trade commission and a federal tariff commission—to regulate business and industry. In brief, because the Progressive platform envisaged the transformation of the state and federal governments into positive, dynamic agencies of social and economic regeneration, it was the high point of the progressive movement to that time.

In the meantime, an equally crucial struggle had been occurring for control of the Democratic party. Although Bryan remained titular head of the party, he announced soon after the elections of November, 1910, that he would not be a candidate for a fourth nomination, and a host of new leaders rose to claim his mantle. Woodrow Wilson, who had made a brilliant campaign for the governorship of New Jersey, quickly emerged as the most formidable Democratic claimant. Hard on the heels of his election in November 1910, Wilson drove ahead from one triumph to another. First, he broke with the Democratic state boss who had nominated him, and led a popular fight to prevent the boss's election to the United States Senate. Then, in a spectacular display of leadership, Wilson forced through an unwilling legislature a series of measures—a direct primary system, corrupt practices legislation, workmen's compensation, and effective state regulation of railroads and public utilities—that implemented the program for which New Jersey progressives had been fighting for almost a decade. As a consequence of these triumphs, by the summer of 1911 many progressive Democrats throughout the country were thanking God they had a new leader and spokesman. For his part, Wilson threw himself into the movement for his nomination for the presidency with such vigor that at the beginning of 1912 it seemed he would easily win leadership of the Democracy.

Wilson's apparent success in the Democratic prenomination campaign, therefore, made the meteoric rise of his chief rival, Champ Clark of Missouri, Speaker of the House of Representatives, all the more surprising. In contrast to the New Jersey governor, who represented the newcomer and the nonprofessional in politics, Clark was an old-line politician who had served without distinction in the House since the 1890's. Temperamentally and intellectually unfitted to be President, Clark none the less knew better than Wilson how to play the game of politics. He inherited most of Bryan's following in the West, made alliances with a number of eastern and southern state organizations, and won the support of William Randolph Hearst and his chain of newspapers.

Thus, while Wilson campaigned fervently and won not quite one-fourth the delegates to the Democratic national convention, Clark negotiated shrewdly and harvested a crop nearly twice as large. To make matters worse for Wilson, Oscar W. Underwood of Alabama, chairman of the House ways and means committee and the pre-eminent Democratic tariff reformer, had entered the contest and won over one hundred southern delegates that would have otherwise gone to Wilson. By the end of the preconvention campaign, therefore, the Wilson movement seemed on the verge of collapse.

It was a critical moment in the life of the Democratic party and, indeed, in the history of the country, when the delegates assembled in national convention in Baltimore on June 25, 1912. As nothing less than control of the federal government was at stake, the convention was a bitter affair from the beginning. The outcome of preliminary contests over organization, in which Bryan and the Wilson forces were defeated by the conservative leaders with the help of the Clark delegates, seemed to forecast Clark's impending victory. In the early balloting, moreover, Clark took a commanding lead; and when the ninety Tammany-controlled New York delegates went to the Speaker on the tenth ballot, giving him a majority—but not the then necessary two-thirds—his nomination seemed almost inevitable.

Yet the expected Clark landslide did not materialize; in fact, on the next few ballots Clark lost votes. Then followed a long and grueling battle in which the Wilson managers gradually undermined Clark's strength and finally won a two-thirds majority for the New Jersey governor on the forty-sixth ballot.

How was this seemingly impossible miracle accomplished? Many historians have mistakenly assumed that Bryan's action in changing his vote from Clark to Wilson on the fourteenth ballot was the decisive factor. Actually, a number of other circumstances were more responsible for Wilson's victory. In the first place, at the beginning of the balloting the Underwood and Wilson managers agreed to stand together, and their solid front broke the force of Clark's main assault, on and immediately after the tenth ballot. In the second place, much of Clark's support was more superficial than real, and in the protracted battle the Wilson leaders were able to capture many of the Speaker's delegates. But most important was the fact that Wilson's managers were finally able to win Roger Sullivan, Illinois Democratic boss, to their side. Going to Wilson on the forty-second ballot, the fifty-eight Illinois votes gave Wilson a majority for the first time and set in motion a landslide that finally developed when the Underwood delegates came to the New Jersey governor four ballots later.

If Bryan did not dictate the nomination, he at least dominated the writing of the historic Democratic platform of 1912, a document that represented the final maturing of the Bryan-progressive Democratic tradition. It denounced the Payne-Aldrich tariff and promised honest downward revision; demanded legislation to destroy the so-called trusts and to establish a decentralized banking system free from Wall Street control; held out the hope of early independence to the Filipinos; approved the income tax and direct election of senators amendments; and favored exempting labor unions from the application of the Sherman law. Although it was more ambiguous and neither as advanced nor as nationalistic as the Progressive "Contract with the People," the Democratic platform did promise at least the destruction of the system of special privileges for business that Republicans had carefully erected since 1861.

52 / *The Campaign and Election of 1912*

During the presidential campaign of 1912 there was, for the first time since 1896, a meaningful division in American politics, for the four parties and tickets in the field offered programs that well reflected the existing divisions of political sentiment. Although the Republican platform contained concessions to the dominant progressive sentiment, the voters understood that Taft's re-election would mean a continuation of Old Guard leadership and policies. In contrast to Taft and the regular Republicans stood Eugene V. Debs, the Socialist candidate, and his party. Offering a program envisaging the gradual nationalization of resources and major industries, Debs campaigned as if he thought he had a chance to win.

The campaign, however, soon turned into a verbal duel between Roosevelt and Wilson. Both men were progressives, yet in their respective programs and philosophies they reflected a significant ideological divergence in the progressive movement. As the next four years would witness a momentous contest between these two philosophies for control of federal policy, it would be well to understand clearly what Roosevelt and Wilson stood for in that memorable summer and autumn of 1912.

Roosevelt's program, the New Nationalism, represented the consummation of a philosophy that had been maturing in his mind at least since 1908. Like Herbert Croly, Roosevelt called upon progressives to examine their basic political assumptions and to realize that the historic American democratic creed, which was intensely individualistic, no longer sufficed to meet the problems of an urbanized and industrialized society. What did this mean, practically? It meant, Roosevelt declared, that progressives must abandon *laissez faire* for democratic collectivism and be willing to use the federal government as a regulator and protector of business, industry, and workers.

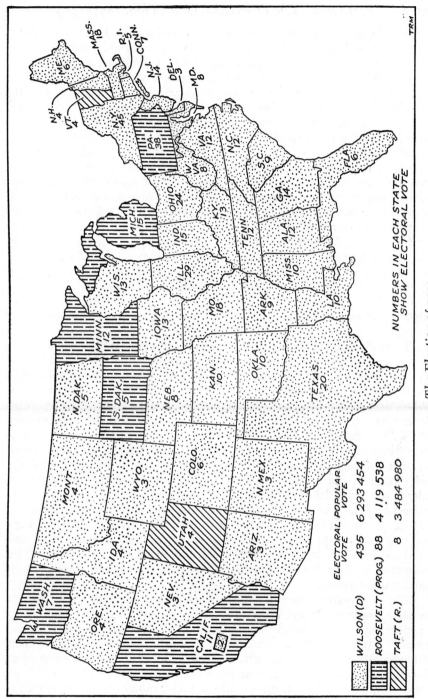

NUMBERS IN EACH STATE
SHOW ELECTORAL VOTE

	ELECTORAL	POPULAR VOTE
WILSON (D)	435	6 293 454
ROOSEVELT (PROG.)	88	4 119 538
TAFT (R.)	8	3 484 980

4. *The Election of 1912*

It meant, in brief, that progressives must surrender their hostility to strong government and espouse instead a New Nationalism that would achieve democratic ends through Hamiltonian, or nationalistic, means.

Expounding this philosophy in the campaign of 1912, Roosevelt advocated a policy toward big business that was entirely at variance with the individualistic tradition. Let us recognize, he said, that concentration and bigness in industry are in many fields inevitable. At the same time, let us subject the large corporations to comprehensive public control through a powerful federal trade commission. Let us also recognize that the great mass of American workers, especially women and children, are powerless to protect themselves, Roosevelt continued, and hence let us use the state and federal governments to improve their lot—by a program embracing minimum wages for women, workmen's compensation, federal prohibition against child labor, and expanded public health services.

In contrast, Wilson had no such well-constructed program when the campaign began. A recent convert to progressivism, he was still imbued with nineteenth century *laissez-faire* concepts and the Democratic state rights belief that the federal authority should be used only to destroy artificial barriers to the full developments of individual energies, not to rearrange social and economic relationships or to give protection to special classes.

Thus, during the presidential campaign of 1912, Wilson promised to destroy the Republican system of tariff protection as the first step in restoring competition in American industry. Following the suggestion of Louis D. Brandeis, who became his most important adviser during the campaign, Wilson next moved to what he called the fundamental issue of the campaign —the emancipation of American business and labor from monopolistic control. Lashing out at Roosevelt's proposals for social legislation and corporation control, Wilson asserted that the New Nationalism could end only in control of the federal government by big businessmen and the consequent enslavement of the workers. In contrast, he would destroy monopoly and unleash the potential energies of businessmen by restoring the conditions under which competition could flourish—by specifically outlawing unfair trade practices and by then relying upon the courts to enforce an amended and strengthened Sherman law. This program Wilson called the New Freedom. In brief, it envisaged the destruction of special privileges, the restoration of the reign of competition, and reliance for future progress on individual enterprise.

The most striking fact of the campaign was Roosevelt's failure to split the Democratic ranks and create a solid progressive coalition. The results, therefore, were obvious long before election day. Wilson polled 6,286,214 popular votes; Roosevelt, 4,126,020, Taft, 3,483,922; and Debs, 897,011. Although Wilson received slightly less than 42 per cent of the popular votes, his victory, because of the multiple division of votes in the Electoral College, was overwhelming. The disruption of the GOP, moreover, gave the Democrats a large majority in the House and a small but workable majority in the Senate.

All observers agreed that the election of 1912 demonstrated that the

American people were in an overhelmingly progressive, if not rebellious, mood. Had progressive Republicans and progressive Democrats been able to unite behind a single ticket and platform, progressivism's triumph would have been even more spectacular. As it was, the Democrats would control the federal government chiefly because of the division among their opponents. Upon Wilson's ability to bring the reform program to fulfillment and unite the two divergent wings would depend the future of the progressive movement in the United States.

53 / Woodrow Wilson and the Progressive Movement

What manner of man was he, this new leader who would preside over the federal government during eight of the most fateful years in the nation's history and leave such a strong imprint on his period that future historians would call it the "Wilson Era"?

No man in American history before 1910 had such a meteoric rise to political pre-eminence as Woodrow Wilson. Born in a Presbyterian manse in Staunton, Virginia, on December 28, 1856, he grew to boyhood in a South convulsed by Civil War and Reconstruction. After being graduated from Princeton University in 1879, Wilson studied law at the University of Virginia and tried unsuccessfully, in 1882 and 1883, to practice law in Atlanta. Embittered and disillusioned by his failure, he entered the new Johns Hopkins University in Baltimore and won his doctor's degree in political science and history in 1886. Denied the political career he desired, Wilson taught successively at Bryn Mawr College, Wesleyan University, and Princeton from 1885 to 1902; but he found an outlet for his political energies in lecturing and writing, and above all in analyzing the weaknesses inherent in the structure of the national government. The basic cause of the failure of leadership in the American political system, he asserted in his most famous work, *Congressional Government*, 1885, lay in the separation of executive from legislative leadership.

Wilson's election as president of Princeton University in 1902 gave him his first opportunity to practice the principles of leadership that had for many years been maturing in his mind. Visualizing himself a prime minister, he put into operation a reorganized curriculum and a new method of undergraduate instruction, the preceptorial system of guided study. As he emerged as an educational leader of national prominence, he also became increasingly articulate as a spokesman of Democratic conservatism.

Probably Wilson would not have allowed his suppressed political ambitions to revive again had events continued to go well for him at Princeton. In 1906 and 1907, however, he attempted to reorganize the social life of the undergraduates by abolishing their eating clubs and substituting quadrangles, or residential colleges, in their stead. Intellectually and academically the proposal was sound, but the students and alumni were so bitterly opposed that the trustees felt compelled to withdraw their approval of the quadrangle plan. This first reversal was so humiliating that Princeton's prime minister nearly resigned. But the really crushing blow, the event that made him willing to embark upon an uncertain political career when the opportunity arose in 1910, was Wilson's defeat in a personal controversy in 1909 and 1910 with the trustees and the Dean of the Graduate School over the establishment and control of a Graduate College.

In the spring of 1910 George Harvey, editor of *Harper's Weekly*, persuaded the leading Democratic boss of New Jersey, James Smith, Jr., to nominate Wilson for the governorship. Wilson accepted the nomination chiefly because the situation at Princeton had become personally intolerable to him. Once in politics, however, he refused to play the role that Harvey and Smith had cut out for him. Sensing that the progressive movement in his state was at flood tide, he came out squarely behind the progressive program and, with the support of insurgent Republicans, won a startling victory in November, 1910. As we have seen, during the following six months he boldly seized control of the Democratic party in New Jersey, pushed a comprehensive reform program through an Assembly heretofore dominated by bosses and lobbyists, and then undertook a nation-wide campaign that carried him into leadership of the Democratic party in 1912 and the White House in 1913.

For the next four years Wilson occupied the same position with regard to the progressive movement that Theodore Roosevelt had occupied from 1905 to 1909. But changed circumstances and differences in personality made Wilson's role in the development of the movement considerably different from Roosevelt's. Unlike Roosevelt, Wilson had not helped to make the progressive movement or to mature its philosophy. In Trenton and later in Washington he was given leadership of movements ripe for fulfillment. All that was required of him was to act as the catalytic agent of his time— to rally and strengthen his forces, to synthesize ideas and proposals, and then to use his incomparable powers of articulation and leadership to translate these ideas into statutory realities.

Roosevelt had never mastered the powerful and entrenched Old Guard machine in Congress. By appealing to the country he had forced Congress to act, but he never led it. In contrast, Wilson found a congressional situation in 1913 that afforded a unique opportunity for a strong executive. For one thing, there was no Democratic machine in Congress; for another, after wandering in the wilderness for twenty years, Democratic leaders were determined to make good and to cooperate for the success of their program and party. Wilson was thus privileged to be the best and most effective kind of leader in the American system—the parliamentary leader of a cooperative congressional majority, not the antagonist of a congressional machine. A strong believer in party government and responsibility, Wilson prepared a legislative program, personally guided congressmen in the preparation of measures, and mediated among the various factions when disputes inevitably arose over principles and details.

Wilson's first and most important contribution to the national progressive movement, therefore, was his strengthening and extension of the power of the presidency. By his own example he demonstrated that the President has it in his power not only to represent the majority opinion, as Roosevelt had done, but also to destroy the wall between the executive and legislative branches. His second great contribution was a more immediate one—the manner in which he used this leadership to bring the national progressive movement to legislative consummation.

Men followed Wilson because he was determined to fulfill party pledges, to act for the good of the country, and especially because he gave eloquent voice to high ideals and aspirations. Except among a select circle, however, Wilson was usually cold and perfunctory. For this reason men never loved Wilson as they loved the warm and outgoing Roosevelt. Wilson's leadership was of the mind and spirit, not of the heart. It succeeded only so long as he had a willing majority, and it collapsed in the face of adversity. This paradox —Wilson's demonstration of high qualities of leadership and his ultimate failure as a political leader—points up the essential defects of his character and the fundamental causes of his failure. The most striking of these defects was a tendency to value his own intuitive and moralistic judgments over conclusions deduced from an analysis of cold and sometimes unpleasant facts. Moreover, because he defined friendship in terms of personal loyalty, Wilson was an extraordinarily poor judge of men. He broke with advisers who disagreed with him on fundamental issues and retained friends who followed him blindly. Finally, because he interpreted partisan opposition as opposition to him personally, Wilson was never charitable toward Republicans who differed with him. In fact, so deep and bitter were his personal and partisan prejudices that after the political tide turned against him in 1918 he was no more capable of providing a truly national leadership than his worst detractors.

54 /   *The New Freedom*

When Wilson took the oath of office on March 4, 1913, he thought he saw the path of progressive duty clear before him. The Democratic party should destroy the Republican system of special privilege—by revising the tariff to eliminate all features of favoritism to domestic producers, by bringing the national banks into effective cooperation and freeing them from alleged Wall Street control, and by working out a new code to restore competition in industry and make impossible the misuse of power by the large corporations. This, in brief, was the core of the New Freedom program. It was a program based squarely on the assumptions implicit in Wilson's campaign addresses of 1912: that the country could be set free by simply unleasing individual energies and by strengthening the altruistic tendencies in the business community.

The first item on Wilson's reform schedule was tariff revision, for so long as the Payne-Aldrich Act, the symbol of business privilege, remained in force, Democratic promises would be hollow. On the day of his inauguration, therefore, Wilson called a special session of Congress; and on April 8, he went in person before the two houses. By breaking the precedent established by Jefferson and destroying the wall between the executive and legislative branches, Wilson asserted his personal leadership in legislation and focused the attention of the country on Congress. Even more, he conferred frequently with Chairman Oscar W. Underwood while the House ways and means committee prepared the new tariff bill.

The measure that Underwood presented to the House on April 22, 1913, represented an honest fulfillment of Democratic promises of tariff reform. It was not a free trade bill but rather an attempt to place American industries in a genuinely competitive position with regard to European producers. All products manufactured by the so-called trusts, such as iron and steel products and agricultural machinery, were placed on the free list, while most raw materials, clothing, food, shoes, and other such items were either placed on the free list or given only incidental protection. The general average of the Underwood duties was about 29 per cent, as contrasted with the 37–40 per cent level of the Payne-Aldrich Act. Finally, to compensate for the anticipated loss of revenue, the ways and means committee added a provision drafted by Representative Cordell Hull of Tennessee, levying a graduated but slight tax on incomes.[1]

The Underwood bill passed the House by a thumping majority on May 8, but the battle for tariff reform had only just begun. By insisting on free sugar and free wool, Wilson had antagonized the Democratic senators from states like Louisiana, Montana, and Colorado, and a change of three Democratic votes in the upper house could change a Democratic majority into a minority. It was a dangerous situation, but the President took unprecedented steps. First he applied heavy personal and political pressure on wavering Democrats. Then, on May 26, he issued a statement to the country denouncing the swarms of lobbyists who infested Washington and were hard at work to defeat tariff reform.

This bold strategy succeeded far beyond the President's expectations. In response to Wilson's indictment of the lobbyists, La Follette and other progressives in the Senate instituted a searching inquiry into lobbying and compelled senators to reveal personal property holdings that might be affected by tariff legislation. Under such penetrating publicity the opposition of the Democratic senators, except for the two Louisianans, vanished, and the road was clear ahead for honest reform. In fact, by putting food and other farm products on the free list, the Senate finance committee actually effected a reduction of 4 per cent in the Underwood rates. Moreover, a threatened rebellion of progressive senators of both parties forced the finance committee to increase the levy on incomes from a maximum of 4 per cent to a maximum of 7 per cent.[2] The Senate approved the tariff bill on September 9, 1913; the House conferees accepted the Senate amendments; and Wilson signed the revised and strengthened Underwood bill on October 3.

It was fortunate for Wilson that he emerged from this first and crucial test stronger than before, for at the moment he signed the Underwood Act a controversy provoked by his attempt to reorganize the national banking and currency systems was brewing. Practically every authority recognized the imperative need for speedy reform, lest the entire awkward banking

[1] The Hull provision levied a flat tax of 1 per cent on all personal and corporate incomes over $4,000 and an additional surtax of 1 per cent on incomes from $20,000 to $50,000, 2 per cent on incomes from $50,000 to $100,000, and 3 per cent on incomes over $100,000.

[2] The Senate bill, to which the House agreed, levied an income tax of 1 per cent on incomes over $4,000 and an additional surtax ranging from 1 to 6 per cent.

structure collapse in the event of another depression.[3] The trouble was that different interests and groups demanded different kinds of legislation. Almost unanimously the banking community and conservative Republicans supported the plan proposed by the Aldrich Commission, appointed in 1908 to study banking reform, to establish a great central bank, with branches, controlled by the dominant banking interests. Although the Democrats condemned the Aldrich plan in their platform of 1912, they were well nigh fatally divided. The progressive-Bryan faction demanded the establishment of a reserve system and a currency supply owned and controlled by the government and pointed to the revelations of the Pujo committee, which investigated the so-called Money Trust in early 1913, to prove that only decisive public control could destroy the existing concentration of credit resources in Wall Street. On the other hand, conservative Democrats, still fearful of Bryan's monetary heresies, proposed a decentralized reserve system, free from Wall Street domination, but owned and controlled by private interests.

It was amid such confusing and divided counsels that Wilson tried to steer a middle course and evolve a policy that would be acceptable to all factions. He commissioned Carter Glass of Virginia, chairman of the House banking committee, to prepare a preliminary bill. As Glass was a leader of the conservative Democratic faction, he came forward with a measure that would have established a system of as many as twenty reserve banks, under private control and without central direction. At Wilson's insistence, Glass added a provision for a central governing board, on which bankers should have minority representation, to coordinate the far-flung reserve system.

The publication of the original Glass bill set off a controversy in administration circles that for a time threatened to disrupt the Democratic party. Bryan, Secretary of the Treasury William G. McAdoo, and Robert L. Owen, chairman of the Senate banking committee, led progressive Democrats in demanding a reserve and currency system owned and controlled entirely by the government. In addition, agrarian spokesmen in the House denounced the Glass bill because it made no provision for destroying the Money Trust or furnishing credit to farmers. Confronted by a seemingly impossible situation, Wilson moved serenely but decisively. Upon the advice of Louis D. Brandeis, the President decided that the bankers should be denied representation on the proposed Federal Reserve Board and that the Federal Reserve currency should be the obligation of the United States. At Bryan's urging, he allowed the agrarian faction to amend the Glass bill to provide short-term credit facilities for farmers in the new system. On the other hand, private banking interests would own and largely control the Federal Reserve banks. Thus Wilson's mediating leadership in this first great crisis in banking reform

[3] The banking and currency systems established by the Civil War legislation were totally unfitted to the needs of a great industrial and commercial nation. For one thing, the currency was based upon the bonded indebtedness of the United States and was therefore inflexible; worse still was the fact that the national banking structure was without any effective central control or workable machinery for mobilizing banking reserves. The Panic of 1907 had prompted Congress to enact the Aldrich-Vreeland Act of 1908, which allowed banks to issue emergency currency against securities and bonds, but this measure proved to be almost unworkable.

enabled the progressive, agrarian, and conservative Democratic factions to find an acceptable compromise they could all support.

No sooner had the controversy within the administration been quieted, however, than another and more violent storm burst upon the country. Bankers and their spokesmen were up in arms, denouncing the revised Glass bill as harebrained, socialistic, and confiscatory. All during the late summer and autumn of 1913 organized banking groups and banking journals raged, but gradually the preponderant opinion turned in the administration's favor. The Glass bill passed the House in September by a large majority; considerably revised, it passed the Senate on December 19, and the President signed it four days later.

The Federal Reserve Act established twelve Federal Reserve Banks owned by the member banks[4] and controlled by boards of directors, the majority of whom were chosen by member banks. As central banks of their various districts, the Reserve banks held a portion of member banks' reserves and performed other central banking functions. The Glass measure also created a new currency, Federal Reserve notes, issued by the Reserve banks to member banks on the basis of collateral consisting of commercial and agricultural paper and a 40 per cent gold reserve. This Federal Reserve currency, moreover, was flexible, that is, it would expand or contract in volume in direct relation to the needs of the business community. Uniting and controlling in a limited fashion the entire system was the Federal Reserve Board of seven members, appointed for long terms by the President with the consent of the Senate.

Thus, the creation of the Federal Reserve System provided a means of mobilizing the major part of the banking reserves of a region and of the entire country, if that were necessary; created a new and flexible, yet absolutely sound, currency; effectively destroyed the concentration of credit resources in a few financial centers; and reinforced private control on the local level, tempered by a degree of public supervision and national coordination. Extreme progressives like La Follette denounced the Federal Reserve Act because it did not provide for comprehensive federal control or ownership and operation of the national banking system. Yet the framers of the measure never intended to implement such a far-reaching progressive policy. In the spirit of Wilson's New Freedom they conceived a banking and currency system in which the private interest would predominate and the public interest would enjoy only a supervisory function.

55 / *The Turning Point in Wilsonian Progressivism*

The writing and adoption of the Federal Reserve Act marked the high tide of the New Freedom doctrines expounded by the Democratic candidate during the campaign of 1912. Throughout 1913 and the early months of 1914 Wilson gave numerous evidences of his determination to adhere strictly to his limited reform program and his resolution not to surrender to the movements then on foot to commit the federal government to advanced

[4] All national banks were required to join the Federal Reserve System. State banks were free to join the system but were not compelled to do so.

social and economic legislation. The root of the disagreement between the President and the agrarian, labor, and social justice reformers stemmed from divergent conceptions of the proper role the federal government should play. Like Theodore Roosevelt, advanced progressives championed measures to use the federal authority to benefit special, if underprivileged, classes. Thus controversy inevitably arose when Wilson invoked the New Freedom concepts to halt the progress of these powerful pressure groups.

So resolutely did the President stand in defense of the New Freedom, in fact, that for a time he thwarted or refused to encourage the fulfillment of a large part of the progressive program. We have already seen the manner in which he blocked the AF of L's campaign to obtain immunity for labor unions from the application of the antitrust laws to their illegal strike activities.[5] In the same manner, in the spring of 1914, Wilson prevented passage of a bill that would have established a system of long-term rural credits financed and operated by the federal government. Or, again, when the National Child Labor Committee's child labor bill passed the House in 1914, Wilson refused to fight for its passage by the Senate because he thought it unconstitutional, just as he refused to support a women's suffrage amendment because he thought suffrage qualifications should be determined by the states.

Three other incidents revealed the extent to which the President failed to share the advanced progressive sentiments of the time. The first was the manner in which he opposed and momentarily obstructed the movement to reduce the number of immigrants coming to American shores. Restriction, or outright exclusion, of immigration had long been an objective of the AF of L, many sociologists, and many social workers. The instrument proposed by these groups, the literacy test, was embodied in the Burnett immigration bill that passed Congress on January 2, 1915. Wilson vetoed this measure, and his veto held. Two years later, in January 1917, Congress overrode his veto of a similar bill.

The second illuminating incident was the manner in which Wilson nearly vetoed the La Follette seamen's bill in March 1915. Sponsored by Andrew Furuseth, president of the International Seamen's Union, this measure imposed rigorous safety requirements on all vessels in the American maritime trade. More important, it freed American and foreign sailors on vessels coming to American ports of their bondage to labor contracts. At first Wilson supported the seamen's bill, as it conferred no special privileges and did no more than place maritime workers on an equal footing with other workers. The State Department, however, strongly opposed the measure because it unilaterally abrogated some thirty treaties with the maritime powers. After much soul-searching, and after Senator La Follette agreed to give the State Department ample time to renegotiate the treaties, Wilson approved the seamen's bill on March 4, 1915. Obviously, however, it was not an administration measure.

The third incident was perhaps the most revealing. It came early in the New Freedom dispensation, when Wilson allowed his Secretary of the Treasury and Postmaster General to undertake a policy of segregating Negro

---

[5] See above, p. 67.

and white workers in their departments. This triumph of white supremacy in the nation's capital provoked such a storm of protest from Negroes and from white progressives in the North that the administration reversed the segregation policy late in 1914. The incident, none the less, revealed the absence in administration circles of any strong obsession for social justice.

When the President and his leaders in Congress set out during the early months of 1914 to prepare antitrust legislation, however, the first important turning point in Wilsonian progressivism occurred. Advanced progressives demanded the establishment of an independent trade commission armed with authority to oversee business activities and suppress unfair trade practices. At the outset of the discussions, on the other hand, Wilson insisted upon a solution more in accord with the New Freedom doctrine of limited intervention. His original antitrust program was embodied in two measures, the Clayton bill and the Covington interstate trade commission bill. The former enumerated and prohibited a series of unfair trade practices, outlawed interlocking directorates, and gave private parties benefit of decisions in antitrust suits originated by the government. The Covington bill created an interstate trade commission to supplant the Bureau of Corporations. The new commission, however, would have no independent regulatory authority but would act merely as a fact-finding agency for the executive and legislative branches.

The publication of the administration's proposed antitrust bills provoked such a storm of confusing dissent that it seemed for a time there might be no legislation at all. Because the Clayton bill failed to provide immunity from antitrust prosecution for labor unions, spokesmen of the AF of L were up in arms. Because the measure attempted to enumerate every conceivable restraint of trade, advanced progressives in both parties denounced it as futile. Because it did not attempt to destroy the oligarchical financial and industrial structure, agrarian radicals from the South and West claimed the Clayton bill was a betrayal of Democratic pledges. Wilson was visibly shaken by these attacks, but in the confusion of voices he did not know where to turn.

In April 1914, when the President seemed most uncertain, his adviser, Louis D. Brandeis, came forward with an alternative that involved virtually abandoning the effort to prohibit unfair trade practices by the statutory method. Instead, Brandeis proposed outlawing unfair trade practices in general terms and then establishing a federal trade commission endowed with ample authority to suppress restraints of trade whenever they occurred. Brandeis' solution had been embodied in the federal trade commission bill, offered earlier by Representative Raymond B. Stevens of New Hampshire.

Although Brandeis' proposal envisaged such a positive regulation of business as Roosevelt had advocated and Wilson had condemned in 1912, it seemed the only practical answer to an otherwise insoluble problem. Thus Wilson at once made the Stevens bill the cornerstone of his new antitrust policy. As administration leaders in Congress sidetracked the Covington bill and pressed the Stevens measure instead, Wilson lost all interest in the Clayton bill, except to maintain his inflexible opposition to granting labor unions the privilege of using illegal strike weapons. In consequence, the Clayton bill was cut adrift in the Senate, where most of its strong provisions were fatally weakened; and the measure that Wilson signed on October 15, 1914, was, Senator James A. Reed of Missouri complained, "a sort of legislative apology to the trusts, delivered hat in hand, and accompanied by assurances that no discourtesy is intended."

Meanwhile, Wilson bent all his energies toward obtaining congressional approval of the Stevens trade commission bill. After a hard battle he won a sweeping victory, for the Federal Trade Commission Act that he approved on September 26 committed the federal government to a policy of vigorous regulation of all business activities. In sweeping terms it outlawed but did not attempt to define unfair trade practices. Moreover, it established a Federal Trade Commission armed with authority to move swiftly and directly against corporations accused of suppressing competition—first by issuing cease and desist orders and then, if that recourse failed, by bringing the accused corporations to trial.

Wilson's complete reversal on antitrust policy represented an important turning point in the American progressive movement. It was the first important sign that the President might be willing to abandon his New Freedom concepts and surrender to the rising progressive demands for bold social and economic legislation in other fields. Any such surrender, however, must come in the future, for the passage of the Clayton and Federal Trade Commission acts in the autumn seemed to signal the completion of the President's reform program. In a public letter to Secretary of the Treasury McAdoo on November 17, Wilson declared that the legislation of the past eighteen months had destroyed the Republican system of special privilege and ended the antagonism between business and the public. The future, Wilson wrote, would be a time in which businessmen would adapt themselves to changed conditions and the nation would enter a new era of "cooperation, of new understanding, of common purpose." In brief, the progressive movement was over; reform would now give way to readjustment.

56 / *The Triumph of the New Nationalism*

As it turned out, Wilson's forecast of future political developments was naive. By the time the President wrote his letter to McAdoo a profound upheaval in American politics—the virtual disappearance of the Progressive party—had occurred during the congressional elections of November 3, 1914. The outbreak of war in Europe a few months before had diverted American attention from the campaign and evoked a general disposition to stand by the President. Even so, the Democratic majority in the House of Representatives was reduced from seventy-three to twenty-five; Republicans swept back into power in key states like New York, Pennsylvania, Illinois, and New Jersey; and so powerful was the tide that it seemed a general Republican victory in 1916 was probable.

The months passed and the nation was convulsed by alarms of war with Germany and a great debate over preparedness. By January 1916 it was obvious Theodore Roosevelt would abandon his third party and join with his erstwhile enemies to drive the Democrats from power. If he succeeded in leading most Progressives back into the Republican camp, Democratic defeat in the impending presidential campaign was virtually inevitable. The urgent necessity confronting Wilson and his party at the beginning of 1916, therefore, was to find some means of luring at least a large minority of the former Progressives into the Democratic ranks. This strategy offered the only possible hope of converting a normal Democratic minority into a majority in November, 1916. To execute the strategy, however, Wilson and the Democratic party had to cast off the shackles of state rights and *laissez-faire* doctrines and convince the doubtful Progressives that they offered the only hope of positive economic and social reform.

Although adopting advanced progressive concepts and legislation required the total abandonment of the philosophy upon which the New Freedom rested, Wilson did not shrink from the necessity confronting him. Beginning in January, 1916, he embarked upon a new course of action, and because his new departure seemed to offer the only hope of staying in power, most Democrats in Congress followed him willingly. Let us see how this startling metamorphosis developed.

The first sign of Wilson's change was his appointment on January 28, 1916, of Louis D. Brandeis to the Supreme Court. Progressives of both parties were delighted, for Brandeis was perhaps the leading exponent of social and economic reform in the country. Shortly afterward the President called the sponsors of the much controverted rural credits bill to the White House and told them he would support their measure. He was as good as his word, and the Federal Farm Loan Act passed Congress in May.[6] A few months later, after the presidential campaign had begun, spokesmen of the social justice forces informed Wilson that the pending child labor and federal workmen's compensation bills were the real tests of his progressivism. Before the warning was delivered Wilson had said not a word in behalf of the measures. Reversing his position, he immediately applied heavy pressure on Democratic leaders in the Senate and obtained passage of the crucial measures in August.[7]

The extent of Wilson's commitment to advanced progressivism can best be understood when we perceive the long-run significance of the Child Labor Act of 1916. By this measure, for the first time in an important way, Congress used its power over interstate commerce to control conditions under which employers might operate their industries. Did this signify the beginning of a new and enlarged federal regulation under the commerce clause, as the spokesman of the NAM declared, "of any commodity produced in whole or in part by the labor of men or women who work more than eight hours, receive less than a minimum wage, or have not certain educational qualifications"? Progressives hoped and conservatives feared that

[6] This measure established twelve Federal Farm Loan Banks capitalized at $750,000 each, which should extend long-term credit to farmers on a basis of land and improvements. It also created a Federal Farm Loan Board to supervise the new system.

[7] Drafted by the American Association for Labor Legislation, the Kern-McGillicuddy Compensation Act established a model workmen's compensation system for federal employees. The Keating-Owen child labor bill, sponsored by the National Child Labor Committee, forbade the shipment in interstate commerce of goods manufactured by children under fourteen, of products of mines and quarries involving the labor of children under sixteen, and of any products manufactured by children under sixteen employed more than eight hours a day.

it did. In any event, it seemed a constitutional way had been found to extend federal control over all phases of the manufacturing process.

Nor did the foregoing measures alone represent the full extent of Wilson's espousal of the program embodied in the Progressive platform of 1912. Echoing a proposal Roosevelt had made in 1912, Wilson in 1916 sponsored and obtained passage of a bill to establish an independent tariff commission, allegedly to remove the tariff issue from politics. Moreover, in language that Roosevelt might have used, the President publicly reversed the historic Democratic policy and approved rational protection. Finally, he sponsored but did not obtain adoption until January 1918 of the Webb bill to allow American manufacturers to combine for the purpose of carrying on an export trade.

Thus it was that the exigencies of a changing political situation compelled a President and party who had taken office in 1913 for the purpose of effectuating a limited reform program to sponsor and enact the most far-reaching and significant economic and social legislation in American history before 1933. Looking back in 1916 upon the development of the progressive movement since 1912, observers might well have been puzzled by the revolution that had occurred. On the one hand, Wilson and his party had tacitly abandoned the New Freedom, and the President could with justice claim that Democrats were also Progressives and boast that his party had enacted practically all the Progressive platform of 1912. On the other hand, the great expounder of the New Nationalism in 1912 had by 1916 abandoned his platform to the Democrats and was striving mightily to defeat the party that had carried out his proposals. Whether the acceptance of the New Nationalism signified a fundamental change in the philosophy of the Democratic party, only the future could reveal. Much, of course, depended upon the verdict of the voters in the impending presidential election.

CHAPTER 7 / THE RISE OF THE UNITED
STATES AS A WORLD POWER,
1898–1916

*D*URING the period from the end of the Napoleonic Wars in
1815 to the outbreak of the Spanish-American War in 1898, the American
people enjoyed such freedom from foreign vexations as they had never
known before 1815 and would not experience in the twentieth century. Not
only was the United States not a world power in the conventional sense of
the word before 1898; the American people did not want to sit in the councils of the mighty, nor engage in the scramble for colonies and concessions,
nor play the game of power politics. They desired only to be let alone.
They were determined to defend the Monroe Doctrine, the cornerstone of
their foreign policy, to be sure; but defense of the Western Hemisphere was
defense of America's splendid isolation.

Yet a people are not isolated and apart merely by wishing to be. In fact,
the high tide of American insularity, 1865–1898, came at a time when forces
were at work that would soon make continued isolation impossible. One of
these forces was the emergence during this period of the United States as
the dominant industrial power in the world. American financiers and manufacturers were beginning to export capital and goods, to acquire markets
and interests abroad that their government could not ignore. Because of
their strategic economic position, moreover, the American people would
find it well nigh impossible to avoid involvement in a future general European war. Thus, although few Americans realized the fact in 1900, the
United States had a vital stake in the peace of Europe. Secondly, swift technological advances during the half century before the First World War
were drawing the world closely together and diminishing the strategic
value of America's oceanic defensive barriers. Finally, the rise of Germany
as the dominant military power in Europe and Japan as an aspiring power
in Asia during the last quarter of the nineteenth century upset the old
balance of power upon which American security had in large measure
depended.

While these great forces would in time inevitably have caused the

American people to burst the bonds of provincialism, the emergence of the United States as a world power in 1898 was largely the result of historical accident. The Democrats who framed the Wilson-Gorman Tariff Act of 1894 had no intention of setting off a chain reaction that would culminate in war and overseas expansion. Yet by nullifying the reciprocity treaty of 1891 with Spain and placing high duties on Cuban sugar, that tariff law ruined Cuban prosperity and helped set off a revolt against Spanish rule in 1895. As the Spaniards employed brutal measures to suppress a brutally executed revolution, anti-Spanish sentiment in the United States was inflamed by such yellow newspapers as the New York *World* and New York *Journal*. President Cleveland stubbornly resisted the mounting demands for war; his successor, William McKinley, could not. After the American battleship *Maine* was mysteriously sunk in the Havana harbor on February 15, 1898, the popular demand for war became irresistible. On April 11 McKinley capitulated and asked Congress for a war declaration, two days after the Spanish government had surrendered to the American demand for an immediate armistice in Cuba.

57 / The Acquisition and Administration of the American Colonial Empire, 1898–1916

The American people entered blithely upon the War with Spain only for the purpose of freeing Cuba from Spanish tyranny. Indeed, by the Teller amendment to the war resolution, Congress solemnly pledged its word that the United States would not annex Cuba. Even so, a few thoughtful leaders of the war movement like Theodore Roosevelt and Henry Cabot Lodge of Massachusetts welcomed the war for the opportunity it offered to acquire bases in the Caribbean and the Pacific. Looking toward the day when the United States would construct an isthmian canal and would need naval bases to guard its approaches, they urged the annexation of Puerto Rico, Spain's other Caribbean possession, and the retention of naval bases in Cuba. As for the Pacific, they urged and won the annexation of Hawaii a few months after the War with Spain began. As Assistant Secretary of the Navy, Roosevelt, on February 25, 1898, had instructed Commodore George Dewey, commanding the Asiatic Squadron then at Hong Kong, to prepare to attack the Spanish fleet in Manila Bay in the event war occurred. But neither Roosevelt nor any other responsible spokesman of the administration contemplated taking the Philippine Islands.

And yet at the peace conference that met in Paris from October 1 through December 10, 1898, the American commissioners demanded and won, not only Cuba's freedom and the transfer of Puerto Rico to the United States, but also the cession of Guam and the entire Philippine archipelago. By this act, the United States extended its frontiers far out into the Pacific and assumed the burden of pacifying and then defending the Philippines against future aggression.

What men, or what forces and events, were responsible for this decision to launch the United States as a major Asiatic power? The decision was made by McKinley and his Cabinet, apparently without seriously consider-

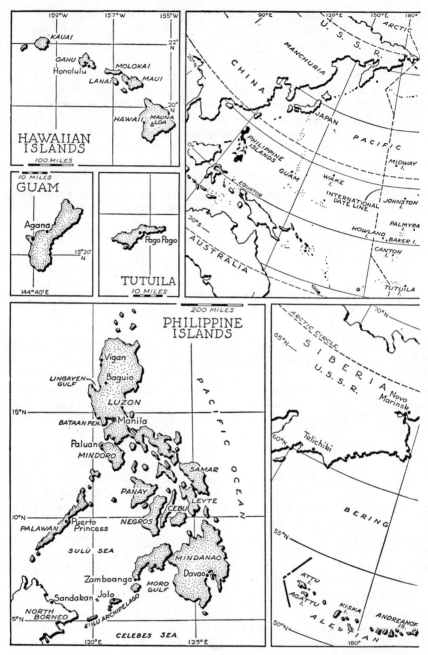

5. *The Territorial Possessions*

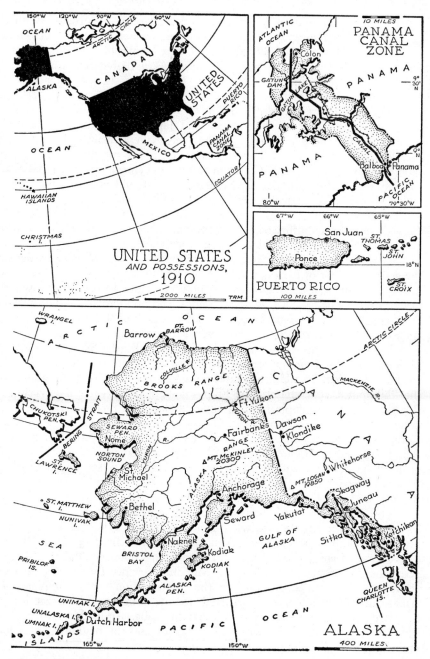

UNITED STATES
AND POSSESSIONS,
1910

2000 MILES   TRM

PANAMA
CANAL
ZONE

10 MILES

ATLANTIC
OCEAN

Colon

GATUN
DAM

GATUN LAKE

PANAMA

9°
30'
N

CANAL

PANAMA

Balboa   Panama

9°
N

PACIFIC
OCEAN

80°W   79°30'W

67°W   66°W   65°W

San Juan

ST.
THOMAS

ST.
JOHN

Ponce

18°N

ST.
CROIX

PUERTO RICO

100 MILES

ALASKA

400 MILES

of the United States in 1910

ing whether the choice was strategically sound or in accordance with the long-run national interest. Other forces and events, instead, dictated the decision. On May 1, 1898, Dewey sailed into Manila harbor and destroyed the decrepit Spanish fleet anchored there. As a native revolt against the Spaniards was also in progress in the Philippines, it was apparent that Spanish sovereignty in the islands was doomed. The German government dispatched a squadron larger than Dewey's to Manila to give force to German hopes of annexation. The British and Japanese governments were also concerned over the islands' fate. Thus it was evident Spain could not retain the Philippines even if the United States did not want them. At the same time, Dewey's victory set off a tremendous movement in the United States for annexation. Jingoists declared that the flag should not be hauled down; church leaders expounded upon America's moral duty to the "little brown brothers," the Filipinos; most important, businessmen, who at the outset had viewed the war unenthusiastically, now talked of converting Manila into a great *entrepôt* for the American Far Eastern trade.

As a result, McKinley instructed his peace commissioners to demand the cession at least of Luzon, the largest of the Philippine islands. But it soon became evident that the United States could not take Luzon and allow some other power to occupy the adjacent islands; and on October 28 the President instructed the commissioners to demand the cession of the entire archipelago. As a consolation prize, Spain was given $20,000,000.

After the ratification of the Treaty of Paris by the Senate in 1899 and McKinley's second victory over Bryan in 1900, the issue of imperialism was for a time settled. The United States would continue to hold and administer the Philippines, at least until the Filipinos were ready for self-government. But the American people soon discovered that it is far easier to acquire a colonial empire than to govern it. On the outbreak of the War with Spain, Commodore Dewey and the American Consul at Singapore had helped a Philippine leader, Emilio Aguinaldo, return to Luzon to help lead a revolt against the Spanish authority. Aguinaldo succeeded so well that when American troops occupied Manila, Aguinaldo and his forces were besieging the city.

The Filipinos wanted independence, not merely a transfer of sovereignty to a new foreign master. And when it became obvious that the United States intended to impose its authority, Aguinaldo and his rebel forces, on February 4, 1899, raised anew the standards of revolt. So stubbornly did the Filipinos resist the American occupation that McKinley eventually sent some 70,000 troops to the islands, and before the "pacification" was completed the American commanders had resorted to the same primitive tactics the Spaniards had unsuccessfully employed in Cuba. Aguinaldo's capture on March 23, 1901, signaled the end of resistance and the beginning of a long era of peaceful development of the islands.

Even before the Aguinaldo rebellion was suppressed, the McKinley administration began to work out plans for a permanent government. On July 4, 1901, a civilian administration, headed by William Howard Taft as civil governor, supplanted military rule. The following year, on July 2, 1902, Congress passed the first Organic Act for the Philippines and established a government for the islands that survived until 1916. While the Act reflected the conviction that the Filipinos were not yet ready for autonomy, it also bore witness to the American intention to give the Philippine peoples an opportunity to learn the difficult art of self-government.[1]

During the remaining years of the Republican era, Presidents Roosevelt and Taft acted as if the islands were their personal trust. The results of superb administration, generous appropriations by Congress, and the determination of the American leaders to lay a solid foundation for self-government in the Philippines were spectacularly evident by 1913. By this date, four out of the nine members of the Commission, 71 per cent of the classified employees in the civil service, 92 per cent of the teachers, and all governors of the Christian provinces were Filipinos. The Philippine government, moreover, had established a splendid system of schools and other public services, dispensed impartial justice, and carried out important land reforms.

It is not surprising, therefore, that Roosevelt and Taft shuddered when the Democrats came to power in 1913, for during every presidential campaign since 1899 the Democrats had advocated independence for the Filipinos. Elected in 1912 on a platform that reiterated this position, Woodrow Wilson was confronted with the necessity of finding a solution that would please his party and yet not give the Republicans a major issue for 1916. The large majority of Democrats wanted to give the Filipinos independence at a specified date. On the other hand, Wilson's Secretary of War, the Bureau of Insular Affairs in the War Department, which had charge of Philippine matters, and Wilson himself all agreed that the Filipinos were not yet ready for independence.

Actually, the cleavage in the administration was not profound, and the new Organic Act for the Philippines that Congress passed on August 29, 1916, the Jones Act, fell little short of giving the Filipinos dominion status. This measure created an elective Senate to supplant the Commission as the upper house of the Philippine legislature, lowered suffrage requirements, and provided that the Governor-General should appoint heads of executive departments, except the head of the Department of Public Instruction, with the consent of the Philippine Senate. The Jones Act, however, reserved ultimate sovereignty to the United States.

With a view toward hastening the day of independence, Wilson's Governor-General, Francis Burton Harrison, cooperated with the native Nationalist leaders, Sergio Osmeña and Manuel Quezon, in transferring power to the native department heads and to the leaders of the Assembly and Senate. By the end of the Wilson era, Filipinos were running their own affairs so well that Governor Harrison and the President urged Congress to grant them independence at once. Even though the Republicans, who controlled Congress, refused the request and soon afterward attempted to restore a larger measure of American control over the islands, it was evident

[1] The Organic Act made Filipinos citizens of the Philippine Islands; created an executive branch consisting of the Governor-General and a Commission, to be appointed by the President with the consent of the Senate; established an Anglo-American system of courts; and provided for the establishment of a two-house legislature, the lower house to be elected by the Christian tribes and the upper house to consist of the Commission.

that the logic and application of American policy since 1901 could culminate only in one solution—independence.

Pacifying Cuba and establishing a stable government in the island was considerably less difficult than the task that confronted Americans in the Philippines. For one thing, a large group of educated Cubans stood ready to cooperate with the American forces who occupied the country in 1898; for another, the fact that the United States had given a pledge of no annexation prevented the native aristocracy from leading the masses in a revolt against the American troops. From 1898 to May 20, 1902, an American military government did heroic work in repairing the damage of the civil war, building roads and schools, cleaning up the cities, and establishing order in the rural districts. Meanwhile, in 1900, the military governor, General Leonard Wood, had arranged the election of a constituent convention, which in due time adopted a frame of government for the new republic.

The American government was now ready to withdraw its forces and leave the Cubans to manage their own affairs. But President McKinley and Secretary of War Elihu Root agreed that the United States bore a special responsibility to itself, the world, and to the Cubans themselves for the future behavior of Cuba. The administration, therefore, determined to draw the Cuban republic into a special relationship with the United States. The Platt Amendment to the army appropriations bill of 1901, which spelled out this relationship, stipulated that Cuba should make no treaties with other powers that might impair its independence, should not assume debts it could not pay, should carry on the sanitation program begun by the military government, and should lease naval bases to the United States. Most important was the provision that authorized the United States to intervene in Cuba, if that were necessary to the maintenance of orderly government and the discharging of Cuba's international obligations.

Because they had no other alternative and because the Americans held out the hope of tariff reciprocity, the Cubans wrote the Platt Amendment into their Constitution in 1902 and signed a treaty with the United States in 1903 that embodied its provisions. For a brief time peace and prosperity reigned in the island, especially after the Cuban-American reciprocity treaty of 1903 opened the American market to Cuban sugar. After the second national elections in December 1905, however, widespread rioting against the government broke out and President Tomás Estrada Palma appealed for American intervention.

Roosevelt was reluctant to undertake the thankless task. After repeated warnings to the insurgents and attempts at mediation had failed, he finally sent troops into the island in 1906 and established a provisional government under Charles E. Magoon, Governor of the Canal Zone. There was some talk in administration circles at this time of making Cuba a permanent protectorate, but Roosevelt repudiated it angrily. After new elections were held and a government was formed, the Americans withdrew in January 1909. From that time on the State Department intervened frequently, but on a diplomatic level, in Cuban affairs, and American troops were sent into the republic to preserve order only in 1911 and 1917. On each occasion the troops were soon withdrawn.

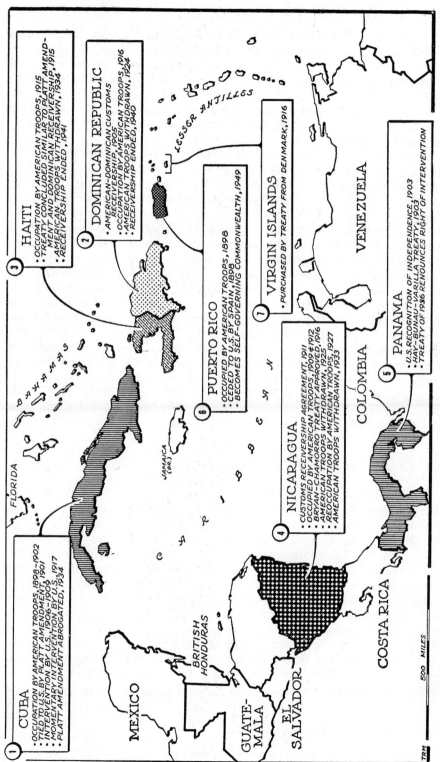

CUBA
- OCCUPATION BY AMERICAN TROOPS, 1898-1902
- TIED TO U.S. BY PLATT AMENDMENT, 1901
- INTERVENTION BY U.S., 1906-1909
- MOMENTARY INTERVENTION BY U.S., 1917
- PLATT AMENDMENT ABROGATED, 1934

HAITI
- OCCUPATION BY AMERICAN TROOPS, 1915
- TREATY CONCLUDED SIMILAR TO PLATT AMEND-MENT AND DOMINICAN RECEIVERSHIP, 1915
- AMERICAN TROOPS WITHDRAWN, 1934
- RECEIVERSHIP ENDED, 1941

DOMINICAN REPUBLIC
- AMERICAN-DOMINICAN CUSTOMS RECEIVERSHIP, 1905
- OCCUPATION BY AMERICAN TROOPS, 1916
- AMERICAN TROOPS WITHDRAWN, 1924
- RECEIVERSHIP ENDED, 1940

VIRGIN ISLANDS
- PURCHASED BY TREATY FROM DENMARK, 1916

PUERTO RICO
- OCCUPIED BY AMERICAN TROOPS, 1898
- CEDED TO U.S. BY SPAIN, 1898
- BECOMES SELF-GOVERNING COMMONWEALTH, 1949

NICARAGUA
- CUSTOMS RECEIVERSHIP AGREEMENT, 1911
- OCCUPIED BY AMERICAN TROOPS, 1909 #1912
- BRYAN-CHAMORRO TREATY APPROVED, 1916
- AMERICAN TROOPS WITHDRAWN, 1925
- REOCCUPATION BY AMERICAN TROOPS, 1927
- AMERICAN TROOPS WITHDRAWN, 1933

PANAMA
- U.S. RECOGNITION OF INDEPENDENCE, 1903
- HAY-BUNAU-VARILLA TREATY, 1903
- TREATY OF 1936 RENOUNCES RIGHT OF INTERVENTION

FLORIDA

BAHAMAS

JAMAICA (BR.)

CARIBBEAN

MEXICO

BRITISH HONDURAS

GUATE-MALA

EL SALVADOR

COSTA RICA

COLOMBIA

VENEZUELA

LESSER ANTILLES

500 MILES

TRM

6. *The Rise and Fall of the American Empire in the Caribbean*

The governing of America's other major island dependencies[2] proved a relatively simple task. Annexed by joint resolution of Congress on July 7, 1898, Hawaii was made an incorporated territory on April 30, 1900, and thereafter enjoyed all the rights of self-government of a territory. Puerto Rico, occupied by the American army in July 1898, was given civil government by the Foraker Act in 1900 and a large measure of self-government by the Jones Act of 1917, which also granted American citizenship to inhabitants of Puerto Rico.

After 1900, the chief diplomatic objective of the American government became, as we will see more fully in a later section, the building of an isthmian canal and the establishment of naval supremacy in the Caribbean. As the British withdrew the larger units of their West Indian squadron in 1904–1905, the United States was in fact the dominant power in the Caribbean after this date. But there was always the danger, often more illusory than real, that Germany would attempt to establish naval bases in the area, possibly by acquiring the Danish West Indies or by obtaining a base in the splendid harbor at Môle St. Nicholas in Haiti. Secretary of State Bryan tried to purchase a site for a naval base at Môle St. Nicholas in 1913; although the Haitians refused to sell, they agreed not to alienate the site to any other power. In 1902 Secretary of State John Hay negotiated a treaty with Denmark for the purchase of the Danish West Indies, or Virgin Islands; but the Danish Parliament, acting, Americans suspected, under pressure from Germany, refused to ratify the treaty. When the Danish government in 1916 offered to sell the islands at the inflated price of $25,000,000, the American government concluded the deal without haggling. The islands were transferred to American sovereignty on March 31, 1917, and were governed by the Navy Department until 1931.

58 /   *The Panama Incident and Two Hemispheric Disputes*

From the War with Spain until the outbreak of the First World War the building and defense of a canal linking the Atlantic and Pacific oceans became the chief objective of American diplomacy. The dramatic voyage of the battleship *Oregon* from Puget Sound around Cape Horn to the Caribbean in 1898 underscored the absolute strategic necessity of a canal, while the development of the West Coast and the anticipation of a great American trade with the Far East highlighted the economic need. Once the canal was begun it became potentially America's naval and economic life line. Protection of this life line, as we will see, necessitated the absolute supremacy of American naval power in the Caribbean, while this development was in turn accompanied by a new and more aggressive diplomacy.

At the end of the War with Spain the agitation for building a canal was so strong that the McKinley administration could not ignore it. A diplomatic

[2] It should be noted that by 1900 the United States had also acquired a string of coaling stations in the Pacific beyond Hawaii: Midway Island, acquired in 1867; the Samoan Islands, occupied jointly with Germany and Great Britain from 1889 to 1899 and divided between Germany and the United States in the latter year; Guam, ceded by Spain in the Treaty of Paris of 1898; and Wake, acquired formally in 1899. All these islands were governed by naval officers acting under orders from the Navy Department.

obstacle, however, stood athwart the fulfillment of the public demand—the Clayton-Bulwer Treaty of 1850, in which the United States and Great Britain agreed not to construct a canal without the other's participation. Embroiled in a costly and embarrassing war with the Boers in South Africa and anxious to win American friendship, the British government gave up its right to participate in building the canal in the first Hay-Pauncefote Treaty, negotiated at Washington in 1900. This Treaty, however, forbade the United States to fortify the canal. As a nonfortified canal would have been at that time a canal under British control in the event of an Anglo-American war, because of British supremacy on the seas, the Senate refused to ratify the treaty without amendments providing for fortification. It was obvious the Americans meant to build and fortify their canal, even if they had to denounce the Clayton-Bulwer Treaty. The British, therefore, went the whole way, and the second Hay-Pauncefote Treaty, concluded on November 18, 1901, acknowledged the right of the United States exclusively to build and fortify the canal.

Discussion in Washington now centered upon the proper route. President Roosevelt and a large majority of Congress favored the Nicaraguan route; the Isthmian Canal Commission, which McKinley had appointed, recommended the Nicaraguan route in November 1901; and on January 9, 1902, the House of Representatives approved the Commission's recommendation. In the meantime, however, Philippe Bunau-Varilla and William Nelson Cromwell, agents of the French New Panama Canal Company, had been working assiduously to sell their company's rights to the route across the Isthmus of Panama.[3] Faced with the possibility of losing everything, the directors of the French company hastily cut the price for their rights from $109,000,000 to $40,000,000. Their bargain offer, the advantages of the Panamanian route, and the providential eruption of a volcano in Nicaragua caused Roosevelt, the Commission, and Congress to change their minds. The Spooner Act, approved by Roosevelt in June 1902, stipulated that the Panamanian route should be used, provided a satisfactory treaty could be concluded with Colombia, which owned the Isthmus, within a reasonable time. Otherwise, the Act declared, the Nicaraguan route must be chosen.

During the following months the State Department applied extraordinary pressure on the Colombian government to obtain a treaty authorizing the construction of the canal. After the Colombian Minister left in disgust for home, Secretary Hay signed a treaty with the Colombian Chargé, Tomás Herrán, on January 22, 1903, which authorized the United States to build a canal across the Isthmus of Panama in return for the payment of $10,000,000 and an annual rental of $250,000. Colombia agreed, moreover, not to conduct independent negotiations with the New Panama Canal Company—in other words, not to demand a share of the $40,000,000.

---

[3] In 1879 the builder of the Suez Canal, Ferdinand de Lesseps, organized a French company for the construction of a Panamanian Canal. By 1889 over $250,000,000 had been wasted in a vain attempt to conquer tropical diseases and the jungle, and the French company went into bankruptcy. In 1894 the New Panama Canal Company was organized to take over the assets of the bankrupt corporation. Bunau-Varilla, formerly chief engineer of the old company, was a large stockholder in the new concern. Cromwell was a prominent New York attorney with large influence in Republican circles.

The American Senate approved the Hay-Herrán Treaty on March 17, 1903. The Colombian government, however, balked. Public opinion in Colombia opposed the treaty because it impaired the nation's sovereignty in the proposed Canal Zone, but Colombia's leaders had an additional reason for refusing to ratify the treaty. The French company's concession would expire in 1904, when all its rights and property would revert to Colombia. Thus, by delaying action for only one year, the Colombian government would be in a position to demand the $40,000,000 that would otherwise be paid to the French company.

Although the Colombian government was acting well within its rights, its refusal to ratify the Hay-Herrán Treaty infuriated Roosevelt. It was, he said, as if "a road agent had tried to hold up a man," and Colombians were "entitled to precisely the amount of sympathy we extend to other inefficient bandits." He made plans, therefore, to seize the Isthmus and to justify such action by the Treaty of 1846 between the United States and New Granada (Colombia), under which the former guaranteed the neutrality and free transit of the Isthmus.

Meanwhile, Bunau-Varilla was setting plans on foot that would render unnecessary such violent action by the United States. Working through his agents in Panama, the astute Frenchman organized a Panamanian "revolution" against Colombia. While the State Department took no part in these intrigues, Bunau-Varilla informed the President and Secretary of State of the plot and could deduce from what they said that Colombia would not be allowed to suppress a revolution. The President, moreover, dispatched the U.S.S. *Nashville* to Colón, on the Atlantic side of the Isthmus. The *Nashville* arrived at Colón on November 2, 1903; the following day the army of patriots rebelled at Panama City, on the Pacific side, whereupon the commander of the *Nashville* landed troops at Colón and forbade Colombian troops in the city to cross the Isthmus and suppress the rebellion. In fact, in return for a generous gift from Bunau-Varilla's agent, the Colombian commander agreed to take his troops back to Colombia.

At 11:35 on the morning of November 6 the American Consul at Panama City informed the State Department that the revolution had succeeded. At 12:51 p.m. Secretary Hay instructed the Consul to extend *de facto* recognition to the new government of Panama. Fearful that the Panamanians would now demand a share of the $40,000,000, Bunau-Varilla persuaded Roosevelt to receive him as the Minister from Panama. On November 18 he signed a treaty with Secretary Hay that conveyed to the United States in perpetuity a zone ten miles wide across the Isthmus, for which the United States agreed to pay $10,000,000 in cash and a rental of $250,000 a year. As Panama's independence could be maintained only by the military power of the United States, the leaders of the new republic had no choice but to ratify this treaty.

On May 4, 1904, the American government took possession of the Canal Zone and set to the task of preparing to excavate the great ditch. Before work could proceed, however, Colonel William C. Gorgas, one of the conquerors of yellow fever, first cleaned up the region and subdued the fever-carrying mosquitoes. In 1906 Congress approved a plan for a lock canal; the following year Roosevelt reorganized the Canal Commission by putting it in the hands of the Army Engineers. Under the direction of Colonel George W. Goethals, chief engineer, operations proceeded steadily and smoothly. The first ship passed through the Canal on January 7, 1914; seven months later, on August 15, 1914, the Canal was opened to the commerce of the world. The cost of the project to the United States had been approximately $375,000,000.

After agreeing that the construction of the Panama Canal was a great boon to all mankind, many thoughtful Americans regretted the means Roosevelt employed to accomplish the objective. Criticism of Roosevelt's Big Stick diplomacy in Panama was bitter in 1903 and 1904, and as more details were revealed, especially by a congressional committee in 1912, the American public began to suffer from acute pangs of conscience. On the other hand, never once did Roosevelt admit that he had perhaps acted unwisely or wrongly. Every action of his administration in the Panamanian affair, he once wrote, had been "in accordance with the highest, finest, and nicest standards of public and governmental ethics." In fact, as the years passed Roosevelt grew bolder in his own defense, until finally in 1911 he spoke the truth: "I am interested in the Panama Canal because I started it. . . . I took the Canal Zone and let Congress debate; and while the debate goes on the Canal does also."

Two other diplomatic incidents, the Venezuelan blockade and Canadian-American boundary disputes, revealed the arrogance, strident nationalism, and growing concern for American supremacy in the Western Hemisphere that characterized Roosevelt's diplomacy during the first years of his presidency. The Venezuelan trouble began when the dictator of that republic, Cipriano Castro, refused even to acknowledge his country's indebtedness to European creditors. In desperation, and after obtaining the State Department's approval, Great Britain and Germany, later joined by Italy, instituted a blockade of Venezuela in December 1902. American public opinion, which from the beginning of the affair had viewed the intervention suspiciously, became greatly agitated when the Germans bombarded Fort San Carlos and destroyed a Venezuelan town in January 1903. Meanwhile, Castro had signified his readiness to submit the debt question to the Hague tribunal.

The German bombardment inflamed American opinion and caused Roosevelt to suspect German intentions. When it seemed the German government would refuse Castro's offer of mediation, Roosevelt, in February 1903, called in the German Ambassador and told him that he had put Admiral Dewey in charge of the Atlantic Fleet for its annual maneuvers in West Indian waters; public opinion was so aroused, he went on regretfully, that he would be obliged to use force if the Germans took any steps toward acquiring territory in Venezuela or elsewhere in the Caribbean.

Roosevelt's warning was probably unnecessary, for the Germans then had no desire to risk a serious incident with the United States. They and the British gladly accepted arbitration to escape from a potentially dangerous situation. The Venezuelan blockade incident was significant, however, first because it emphasized the danger of any such future European interventions and led soon afterward to the adoption of a new Caribbean policy by the Roosevelt administration; and second because the European powers had tacitly recognized the Monroe Doctrine and openly admitted the supremacy of the United States in the Caribbean.

The boundary dispute with Canada, which involved the long finger of Alaska that runs from Alaska proper down the Pacific Coast to the latitude 54° 40', first became acute when gold was discovered in the Canadian Klondike region in 1896. Because it seemed clear the United States had an airtight case, for several years the State Department refused to arbitrate the conflicting claims.[4] At first inclined to let the matter rest, Roosevelt studied the case and concluded that the Canadians had completely fabricated their claim. Secretary of State John Hay, therefore, negotiated a convention with the British government in 1903 providing that six impartial jurists—three appointed by the President and three by the King of England—meet in London and settle the question by majority vote. When the tribunal convened in London in September 1903 it soon became evident that the Americans would vote as a bloc, that the two Canadian members would support their country's claims, and that the decision would rest with the British commissioner, Lord Chief Justice Alverstone. Meanwhile, Roosevelt had already decided to ask Congress for authority to run the boundary line himself if the tribunal did not endorse the American claims. After the tribunal convened, Roosevelt carefully repeated this threat in conversations and letters for the benefit of the British Foreign Office. Whether Lord Alverstone was more influenced by the President's threat than by the merits of the American case, we do not know. In either event, to the disgust of the Canadians he voted consistently with the American commissioners and thus helped cement Anglo-American friendship.

59 / *The Roosevelt Corollary to the Monroe Doctrine*

On the day before the Senate ratified the Hay-Bunau-Varilla Treaty the Hague Court rendered a verdict that contained significant implications for the United States. That tribunal ruled that Germany, Great Britain, and Italy, the very powers that had used force against Venezuela, were entitled to the first claim on payments by Venezuela to European creditors. In brief, the Hague Court's decision put a premium on intervention, at a time when American security interests in the Caribbean were being multiplied by the decision to construct the Panama Canal.

After the Venezuelan blockade affair, Roosevelt knew that the United States could not hereafter tolerate European armed intervention on a major scale in the Caribbean. On the other hand, he knew also that he could not command sufficient naval power to stand off Europe by announcing a policy of nonintervention by outside powers in the Western Hemisphere. Some other way of reconciling American security interests with European economic interests in the Caribbean had to be found. In 1902 the British Prime

---

[4] The Canadians claimed that the line should run 30 miles inland in a straight line from the sea and should not be adjusted to the heads of the bays and inlets. The Americans argued that the boundary should run along a line 30 miles inland from the heads of these bays and inlets.

Minister, Arthur Balfour, had suggested one solution to the dilemma. Britain, Balfour intimated, would support the Monroe Doctrine and abstain from intervening in the New World if the United States would guarantee that the necessity for such intervention should not arise.

Two years later, in 1904, a situation developed in the Caribbean republic of Santo Domingo that compelled Roosevelt to work out some kind of policy. After prolonged civil war, that island republic defaulted on its foreign debt of $32,000,000. Roosevelt was extremely reluctant to intervene. "If I possibly can I want to do nothing . . . ," he wrote on February 23, 1904. "If it is absolutely necessary to do something, then I want to do as little as possible." As there was a strong probability that the European powers would intervene if he did not, Roosevelt sent Admiral Dewey and the Assistant Secretary of State to Santo Domingo to investigate. The latter recommended the establishment of an American receivership to collect and disburse the Dominican customs. As this course was soon agreed upon, the American representatives in the Dominican capital, on January 20, 1905, signed a protocol with Dominican officials stipulating that the United States should collect the Dominican customs, turn over 45 per cent of the receipts to the local government, and apply the balance to the liquidation of Santo Domingo's foreign debt. When this original agreement provoked severe opposition in the American Senate, the State Department negotiated a more restricted protocol the following month, but it, too, failed to obtain the two-thirds vote necessary for ratification. Then Secretary Root concluded a new treaty, one less sweeping in its guarantees to Santo Domingo, on February 8, 1907, and the Senate concurred shortly afterward. Meanwhile the President had established and operated the receivership under an executive agreement.

So smoothly did Roosevelt and Root put the new arrangement into operation that neither Dominican pride nor the sensitivity of the rest of Latin America was offended. The American Receiver General, moreover, persuaded Santo Domingo's creditors to scale down their claims from $32,000,000 to $17,000,000, while the new debt was refunded at a lower rate of interest. More important was the fact that, as the customs houses were no longer prizes to be won by successful revolutionists, the little republic enjoyed such peace and prosperity as it had never known before.

The manner in which Roosevelt solved the Dominican dilemma revealed that he had no real imperialistic ambitions in the Caribbean; that is, he desired no new territories or bases. He intervened reluctantly and in a limited way only to avert European intervention that might threaten the security of America's Panamanian life line. The incident was additionally important because Roosevelt seized the opportunity it offered to announce a new Caribbean policy—the Roosevelt Corollary—to Latin America and the world.

Roosevelt forecast his Corollary in a public letter to Secretary Root on May 20, 1904, and articulated it more fully in his Annual Message in the following December. Chronic wrongdoing by an American republic might require intervention by some civilized nation, he said on the latter occasion; and "the adherence of the United States to the Monroe Doctrine may force the United States, however reluctantly, in flagrant cases of such wrong-doing or impotence, to the exercise of an international police power." In other words, the President declared that since the Monroe Doctrine pro-hibited European intervention in the Western Hemisphere, the United States owed it to the European powers to guarantee that no cause for intervention should arise.

As scholars have emphasized, the Roosevelt Corollary was based upon false assumptions and bad history, for no American statesman, not even Roosevelt, had ever before construed the Monroe Doctrine to forbid tem-porary European interventions to compel Latin American states to pay their debts or discharge their international obligations. The truth was that Roose-velt was invoking the sanction of a historic doctrine to justify a major and necessary change in American foreign policy: hereafter the United States would tolerate no further European interventions in the Caribbean region.

60 / *Theodore Roosevelt and the New Diplomacy in Europe and Asia*

The years from 1901 to 1909 were a period of mounting tension in Europe and the Far East. In Europe, Germany's simultaneous determination to dominate the continent and challenge Britain's naval supremacy had brought about a diplomatic revolution by forcing Britain to seek a *rap-prochement*, first with France and then, in 1907, with Russia as well. In the Far East the old balance of power was upset by the rise of Japan and by Russia's determination to control Manchuria and Korea. It was a time of danger to the peace of the world, but because he was neither naive nor unresourceful Theodore Roosevelt was privileged to exercise large influence in world affairs. With refreshing realism and boldness, he confronted the diplomatic revolutions of his time to help preserve the balance of power in the Far East and avert a general European war into which the United States might be drawn. That the attainment of these objectives required abandon-ment of traditional isolationist principles did not deter Roosevelt. He played the game of power politics as if he were a divine right monarch, but he played it well and for the peace of the world.

Roosevelt's chief objective in European affairs was to play the role of impartial friend so as to relieve the growing tension between Britain and France on the one hand and Germany on the other. Friction between Ger-many and France during the early years of the twentieth century centered in part on Morocco, where France was closing the doors to German and other foreign merchants. When France's ally, Russia, became embroiled in a war with Japan in 1904, the Kaiser and his Foreign Office saw an oppor-tunity to call France's hand and perhaps also to break the newly formed Anglo-French *entente*. In 1905 the Kaiser demanded the convoking of an international conference to define the status of Morocco. When the French Foreign Office refused the demand, the Kaiser appealed to Roosevelt for support. Although he was extremely reluctant to intervene, Roosevelt knew that war impended unless the French gave in. In order to avert a general war into which his country might be drawn, therefore, the President brought such pressure to bear on England and France that they consented to attend a conference to determine Morocco's status.

The Kaiser had won the first round. But when the conference met at Algeciras, in southern Spain, in early 1906, the Germans were confronted by a solid Anglo-French bloc, which usually had the support of the American delegates. The General Act of Algeciras, signed on April 7, 1906, represented superficially a victory for commercial freedom in Morocco; it gave the French such control over the sultanate, however, that they were able quietly to close the door to non-French trade. But that was in the future. At the moment when a general war seemed probable, Roosevelt had intervened decisively and had helped Europeans find a peaceful alternative.

Working out a viable Far Eastern policy posed an even greater challenge to Roosevelt's skill. The basic American objectives in the Far East had been defined by Secretary Hay in 1899 and 1900—to preserve the commercial Open Door to China and the territorial integrity of that country, and to protect the vulnerable Philippines from Japanese attack. By 1905, moreover, the American emotional investment in China was considerable as a result of the tremendous growth of American missionary, medical, and educational endeavors in that country. Indeed, by this time most Americans regarded their government as China's defender against the alleged rapacity of imperialistic European powers.

The chief threat to the peace of the Far East in the late 1890's and early 1900's was Russian expansion into Manchuria and Korea. In order to halt Russian expansion, the British concluded an alliance with Japan in 1902, and when war broke out between Japan and Russia in 1904, American sympathy went to the Nipponese. Convinced that Japan was playing America's game by curbing and offsetting the growing Russian preponderance of power in the Far East, Roosevelt supported the Japanese, even to the extent of warning Germany and France that he would not countenance their going to the support of Russia.

By the spring of 1905 the Japanese had won a series of spectacular victories on land and sea, but the Empire was so exhausted that it could not long continue the war. On April 18, 1905, therefore, the Japanese Cabinet opened secret negotiations with the President looking toward ending the conflict through his mediation. Reluctant to undertake what was bound to be a thankless task, yet realizing that a Japanese victory was essential to the maintenance of the existing power balance in the Far East, Roosevelt, on June 8, invited the belligerents to come to a peace conference to end the "terrible and lamentable conflict." With the Kaiser's help, the President persuaded the Czar to accept.

The conference opened at the Portsmouth, New Hampshire, Navy Yard on August 9, 1905. Not satisfied with winning control of southern Manchuria, Korea, and the southern half of Sakhalin from Russia, the Japanese commissioners also demanded a huge monetary indemnity. The latter demand caused American opinion to turn sharply against Japan, and the Japanese leaders, realizing they had gone too far, yielded the point rather than risk a resumption of hostilities. Ignorant of the tremendous assistance Roosevelt had given their government and groaning under a heavy tax burden, the

Japanese people concluded that the President had denied them their indemnity.

The Treaty of Portsmouth of 1905 in effect preserved the balance of power in the Far East that Russian expansion had threatened to destroy. Russia remained an important Pacific power, but to offset Russia Japan now stood as an effective counterpoise. Whether this configuration would protect American interests in the Far East depended upon many factors, the most important of which was the future conduct of the Japanese government. It was not within Roosevelt's power to control Japanese policy, but he could try to channel it in a direction advantageous to the United States. If this involved recognizing Japan's new position, then Roosevelt would not shrink from the necessity. Even before the Portsmouth Conference opened, he sent Secretary of War Taft, then in Manila, to Tokyo to come to an immediate understanding with the Imperial Cabinet. On July 25, 1905, Taft concluded with the Prime Minister, Taro Katsura, an executive agreement under which the United States recognized Japan's suzerainty over Korea and Japan disavowed any designs on the Philippines.

The Japanese welcomed America's recognition of the new status in the Far East, but events were developing in the United States that threatened to impair good relations between the two countries. For one thing, there was a great deal of irresponsible talk about the "Yellow Peril," and the Hearst press day in and day out stimulated fears of future Japanese aggression. The most dangerous trouble, however, was brewing in California on account of Japanese immigration into that state.[5] Following the Russo-Japanese War, it seemed that the relatively small stream of Japanese immigrants would become a rushing tide. With Congress indifferent to the problem, Californians organized to take matters into their own hands. As the first step in the anti-Japanese campaign, the San Francisco Board of Education on October 11, 1906, adopted an order requiring the segregation of all Oriental school children.

Still flushed with their victory over the largest power in Europe, the Japanese people were in no mood to let this insult pass. The Japanese Ambassador lodged a formal protest with the Secretary of State on October 25, 1906, while irresponsible newspapers in both countries tried to stir war passions. It was a dangerous situation, but Roosevelt acted with superb caution and good sense. He did not ignore the fact that war was a possibility, but he was certain the segregation order violated the Japanese-American Treaty of 1894, which guaranteed most favored treatment to Japanese subjects in the United States. Determined if necessary to use the army to protect the rights of the Japanese in California, Roosevelt at the same time understood that Japanese immigration was the root of the trouble and resolved to bring such immigration to an end.

By a judicious mixture of courtesy and sternness, Roosevelt solved the difficulty. At his invitation the Mayor and Board of Education of San Francisco came to the White House in February 1907. Roosevelt promised

[5] There were 12,000 Japanese in California in 1900. In that year the Japanese government announced that it would cease issuing passports to laborers who wished to go to the continental United States. Japanese kept coming to California, however, at the rate of 500 to 1,000 a year until 1905.

to use diplomacy to stop Japanese immigration; in return the School Board revoked the segregation order. Then the President negotiated, in 1907 and 1908, the so-called Gentlemen's Agreement with the Japanese, by which the Imperial government promised to issue no more passports to peasants or workers coming directly to the continental United States.

In order to disabuse the Japanese of any notion that he had acted out of fear of them, Roosevelt decided in the summer of 1907 to send an American fleet of sixteen battleships on a cruise around the world, first by way of the Pacific. Leaving Hampton Roads in December 1907, the fleet steamed to Australia and then to Japan, where it was received with an overwhelming demonstration of goodwill. From Yokohama, the fleet sailed through the Indian Ocean, the Mediterranean, and the Atlantic, and arrived at Hampton Roads on February 22, 1909. The 46,000-mile voyage had demonstrated American naval power and efficiency; more important, the fleet's visit to Japan had evoked demonstrations of Japanese-American friendship. Looking back over his administration a few years later, Roosevelt concluded that sending the fleet on its long cruise had been his most important contribution to the cause of peace.

While the fleet was on its epochal voyage, the Japanese Foreign Minister instructed his Ambassador in Washington, Baron Takahira, to open negotiations with the State Department looking toward a comprehensive understanding with the American government on all phases of the Far Eastern question. The outcome of these conversations was the Root-Takahira Agreement of November 30, 1908, by which Japan and the United States agreed to help maintain the *status quo* in the Pacific, to respect each other's territorial possessions, and jointly to support the Open Door in China and the independence and territorial integrity of that country. Here indeed was a program of cooperation which, if faithfully adhered to, might provide a *modus vivendi* by which the two nations could live in peace for all time to come.

Thus when Roosevelt left the White House in 1909 the United States was a world power in fact as well as in name. By blunt and sometimes stern diplomacy, Roosevelt had established unquestioned American supremacy in the Caribbean area. By abandoning old traditions against interference in non-American affairs, he had helped preserve the peace of Europe. And by a policy of realism, he had supported the rise of Japan and come to friendly understanding with that power. It was unfortunate for the United States and the world that he could not transmit his wisdom and skill to his successors.

61 / Taft and "Dollar Diplomacy" in the Caribbean and the Far East

Unfitted and unprepared to play the role of strong leader in world affairs, Taft abandoned Roosevelt's policy of active intervention in European politics and blundered into a partial reversal of Roosevelt's policy of maintaining Japanese good will. On the other hand, Taft and his Secretary of

State, Philander C. Knox, could not reverse Roosevelt's policy of securing American supremacy in the Caribbean area without endangering national security. In fact, they went far beyond the limited kind of intervention that Roosevelt and Root had employed and devised a new policy to strengthen American power in the approaches to the Canal. Called "dollar diplomacy," Taft's policy involved, on the one hand, using private American banking resources to displace European concessionaires and creditors in the Caribbean republics, and, on the other, using military force, if that were necessary, to maintain American supremacy in the Caribbean region, where, as Knox said, "the malady of revolutions and financial collapse is most acute precisely . . . where it is most dangerous to us."

Soon after he took office in 1909, Knox tried to persuade American bankers to take over the debt owed by the Central American republic of Honduras to British investors. In 1911 the Secretary signed a treaty with the Honduran Minister providing for a refunding of that country's foreign debt by American bankers and the establishment of an American receivership of the customs. The government of Honduras, however, refused to ratify the convention. Again, in 1910, Knox persuaded four New York banking firms to invest in the National Bank of the Republic of Haiti in order to help the Negro republic stabilize its currency.

These activities were merely a prelude to Knox's most important action in the Caribbean area, his intervention in Nicaragua. In this affair the administration tried to use American dollars to stabilize and control Nicaraguan finances, to be sure; but it also went far beyond "dollar diplomacy" and launched a new and even more drastic policy of armed intervention. As the Nicaraguan intervention established a pattern that the Wilson administration followed, it would be well to examine it in some detail.

At the beginning of the Taft administration Nicaragua was ruled by the dictator José Zelaya, who at the time was nursing a grudge against the United States. He vented his anti-American spleen on the United States-Nicaragua Concession, a mining company owned by Pittsburgh capitalists, and even went so far as to make plans to offer an option on the Nicaraguan canal route to the Japanese government.

When officials of the company helped engineer a revolution against Zelaya in 1909, the State Department sent marines to the Nicaraguan city of Bluefields to protect foreign nationals and property. As a consequence of Knox's interference, Zelaya was overthrown; and after a period of confusion Adolfo Díaz, formerly secretary of the United States-Nicaragua Concession, was installed in 1911 as President with the State Department's blessing.

Knox now moved swiftly to bring Nicaragua completely under American control. On June 6, 1911, the Secretary signed a treaty with the Nicaraguan Minister providing for a refunding of the Nicaraguan foreign debt by two New York banking firms and the establishment of an American receivership of the customs. Democrats in the Senate blocked ratification of this, the Knox-Castrillo Treaty. At the request of the State Department, however, the New York bankers lent $1,500,000 to stabilize Nicaragua's finances temporarily and received in return the majority control of the state railways and the National Bank of Nicaragua. Later in the same year an

American receiver-general of the Nicaraguan customs was appointed by the banking houses and approved by the two governments.

As it turned out, the new Díaz government did not have the support of a majority of Nicaraguans, who, in defiance of the State Department, continued to look to Zelaya and his Liberal party for leadership. The Liberals raised the standards of revolt in 1912 and Díaz would have fallen had not Taft rushed 2,700 marines to Nicaragua to suppress the uprising. So bitter was anti-Díaz and anti-American sentiment that the marines continued to occupy the country for many years.

The American intervention and occupation, however, did not solve Nicaragua's most pressing requirement—her need for financial assistance in refunding the foreign debt and paying the claims arising from the revolutions of 1909 and 1912. Chiefly to satisfy the national treasury's need for ready cash, Secretary Knox signed a treaty in 1913 with the Nicaraguan Minister for the payment by the United States to Nicaragua of $3,000,000. In return, Nicaragua granted to the United States an exclusive option on its canal route, the privilege of establishing a naval base on the Gulf of Fonseca, on the Pacific side, and a ninety-nine-year lease on the Great Corn and Little Corn Islands in the Caribbean. The treaty was negotiated too late to be ratified before the Sixty-Second Congress expired on March 4, 1913, and the Wilson administration inherited the unpleasant task of persuading the Senate to ratify the convention.

If the prime objective of "dollar diplomacy" in the Caribbean was the protection of America's strategic interests in that region, the objectives of the new policy as it was applied in the Far East were nearly as ambitious. Toward the end of the Roosevelt administration a clique in the State Department headed by a young career diplomat, Willard Straight, was maturing plans to sponsor American investment in Manchuria to offset Japanese influence in that province. Restrained by Roosevelt's firm hand, Straight and his colleagues came into control of Far Eastern policy when Knox took the reins as Secretary of State. Their opportunity to obtain a more aggressive Chinese policy came in 1909, when a consortium of British, French, and German bankers signed a contract with the Chinese government to build a network of railways in central and southern China.

Arguing that American participation in the consortium was necessary to enable the United States to defend the Open Door and the territorial integrity of China, Straight and his friends in the Far Eastern Division easily won Knox to their side. Accordingly, the State Department in 1909 demanded that American bankers be allowed to participate in making the loan. Finally, in May 1911, an American banking syndicate formed by J. P. Morgan & Company was admitted to the consortium, along with Japanese and Russian bankers. For various reasons the project never prospered, and in March 1913 President Wilson announced the withdrawal of the American group.

After demanding the admission of American bankers to the consortium, Secretary Knox pressed on in another and more reckless move. Alarmed by the consolidation of Japanese and Russian influence in Manchuria, he proposed, in November and December 1909, the internationalization of the Manchurian railways. As the British were encouraging Japanese expansion in Manchuria in order to keep the Japanese a safe distance from the British sphere of influence, they promptly rebuffed Knox's suggestion. The Japanese, on the other hand, regarded Knox's proposal as an attempt to undermine their influence in an area that Roosevelt had tacitly recognized as being within the Japanese orbit. In short, Knox's proposal was ill-conceived and naively made. It angered the British, drove the Japanese and Russians into an anti-American bloc, and even alienated the American banking group. It was a blunder that Roosevelt and Root would not have made.

The historian must conclude that, on the whole, Taft's record of achievement in foreign affairs was even more barren than his record in domestic politics. The most important outcome of "dollar diplomacy" in the Caribbean was an armed intervention in Nicaragua that was strategically unnecessary, that intensified anti-American feeling in Latin America, and that failed to bring peace to that unhappy country. The result of "dollar diplomacy" in the Far East was an embittering of Japanese-American relations without any benefit to the United States. For the failure of his foreign policy Taft had only himself and his Secretary of State to blame. Where Roosevelt had been wise and far-sighted, Taft was indolently ineffectual; where Root had been suave, Knox was often offensive. The contrast goes far toward explaining the unsatisfactory state of American foreign relations when Woodrow Wilson took office on March 4, 1913.

62 / *The New Freedom Abroad*

Humanitarians hailed the inauguration of the Wilson administration in 1913 as beginning a more idealistic era in American foreign relations. Since 1901 most Democrats had consistently condemned Roosevelt's and Taft's policies of military intervention, quasi-protectorates, and "dollar diplomacy" in Central America and the Caribbean region, had stood for early independence for the Filipinos, and had fought for the adoption of a moderate naval building program designed, they thought, only to implement a diplomacy of defense.

Even more encouraging to idealists than the Democratic record were the character and views of the new makers of American foreign policy. No public leader of his generation gave more eloquent expression of the liberal, idealistic international program than Woodrow Wilson. Long before he became the prime exponent of international organization and collective security, Wilson had articulated and championed a diplomacy that sought the good of mankind above the selfish interests of the United States. Moreover, Wilson's Secretary of State, William Jennings Bryan, was easily the leading opponent of imperialism and navalism and a pioneer in the movement to advance peace through arbitration and conciliation.

The first sign of the New Freedom in foreign policy came with the launching of Bryan's ambitious plan for peace, which was based upon assumptions that most progressives and humanitarians of that day shared. There were no disputes among nations, progressives argued, that could not be settled by reasonable discussion; no people in command of their reasoning faculties would allow their government to go to war if such a course could honorably be avoided. The obvious and easiest way to avoid war in the future, therefore, was to construct some machinery for the peaceful settlement of disputes.

In its practical aspects, Bryan's solution was based upon the experience of his predecessors in trying to steer arbitration treaties through a Senate jealous of its partial control over foreign relations. Secretary of State John Hay had negotiated a series of arbitration treaties that excluded all disputes involving vital interest and national honor. When the Senate in 1905 amended these treaties to make its consent to each arbitration necessary, Roosevelt withdrew them. Three years later, in 1908, Secretary Root persuaded Roosevelt to yield to the Senate's demand and negotiated twenty-five limited arbitration agreements in 1908 and 1909. However, when President Taft and Secretary Knox signed treaties with Britain and France in 1911 that provided for the arbitration of all justiciable questions, including disputes affecting national interest and honor, the Senate again rebelled. It ratified the treaties in 1912 but exempted all important questions from possible arbitration. In disgust, Taft refused to promulgate the mutilated treaties.

With the memory of Knox's failure fresh in his mind, Bryan found a solution that he thought would achieve the goal of unlimited arbitration without provoking the Senate's suspicions. Bryan's treaties provided, not for arbitration, but for the submission of all disputes to permanent commissions for investigation for a period of one year. During this interval of investigation and "cooling off," neither party would resort to war or increase its armaments. After the investigation was completed, the parties might accept or reject the commission's findings. And although both countries would then also be free to go to war, Bryan was confident that in such circumstances war could not occur.

Bryan signed the first conciliation treaty with El Salvador on August 7, 1913, and during the following year negotiated twenty-nine other such agreements with Great Britain, France, Italy, and lesser powers. Although realists like Theodore Roosevelt condemned Bryan's plan as futile and dangerous, the truth was that he had constructed workable machinery that nations might use if momentary but dangerous crises ever arose to menace the peace.

Further evidence of the New Freedom's idealism in foreign affairs was the administration's withdrawal of the American banking group from the six-power consortium that had been formed in 1911 to finance the construction of the Hukuang Railway in China. As Wilson explained in a public statement on March 18, 1913, the United States could not approve the loan agreement because it would lead to intolerable outside interference in Chinese affairs. The manner in which missionaries and the religious press applauded the President's statement was evidence of the revulsion that all idealists felt against what seemed to be an insidious scheme to control the government of China. And a few weeks later, as if to emphasize his determination to cut the United States loose from all such imperialistic conspiracies, Wilson recognized the new Republic of China without first consulting the other powers.

A third demonstration of idealistic diplomacy was Wilson's settlement of the Anglo-American dispute provoked when Congress, in August 1912, exempted American ships engaged in the coastwise trade from the payment of Panama Canal tolls and when the British Foreign Office soon afterward protested that the exemption violated the Hay-Pauncefote Treaty of 1901, which promised equal rates for the ships of all nations. Although he had unthinkingly approved exemption during the campaign of 1912, Wilson concluded even before he was inaugurated that the British were right. He could not run the risk of splitting his party so long as the tariff and banking bills pended; but on January 28, 1914, after these measures were safely passed, he met with the Senate foreign relations committee, reviewed the critical state of American foreign relations, and urged repeal of the exemption provision as a means of restoring fully cordial relations with the British government. On March 5, 1914, moreover, the President reiterated his plea before a joint session and ended with the cryptic warning that if Congress did not grant his request he would not know how to deal with other and more difficult matters. The House of Representatives repealed the exemption provision on March 31, 1914; and when administration leaders finally obtained a Senate vote on June 11, the advocates of repeal won an easy victory for national integrity and good faith.

A fourth illustration of Wilson's and Bryan's determination to do the moral, if the unpleasant, thing in foreign affairs was the treaty of reparation they negotiated with the Colombian government during 1913 and 1914. Secretaries Root and Knox had earlier but unsuccessfully sought to restore good relations with Colombia. Wilson and Bryan succeeded because they were willing to go the whole mile in making amends for Rooseveltian sins of the past. In a treaty signed at Bogotá on April 6, 1914, the United States expressed "sincere regret" for incidents that had interrupted good relations between the two countries, agreed to pay an indemnity of $25,000,000 to Colombia for the loss of Panama, and gave the government of Colombia free use of the Canal and Colombian citizens equality of treatment with Americans in the Canal Zone.

The publication of the treaty provoked an explosion of rage by Roosevelt that was heard from one end of the country to the other. His friends in the Senate blocked ratification in 1914 and again in 1917, although on the second occasion Secretary of State Robert Lansing declared ratification was essential to national security. In spite of the Senate's refusal to ratify, the Washington administration's intentions had been clearly demonstrated. The idea of the great government of the United States apologizing to a helpless neighbor stirred a wave of warm and cordial feeling toward the United States throughout Latin America.[6]

63 / *New Troubles with Japan, 1913–1917*

The record of the Wilson administration's troubled relations with Japan from 1913 to 1917 reveals that good intentions alone do not always suffice to settle delicate international disputes. Storm warnings were raised in California during the campaign of 1912, when Democrats and Progressives

---

[6] In 1921 the Harding administration negotiated a new treaty that awarded the Colombian government $25,000,000 but omitted the specific apology.

launched a campaign in that state to obtain passage of a law prohibiting Japanese ownership of land. Instead of perceiving the dangers inherent in such discriminatory legislation, Wilson conferred at length with the California leaders and even volunteered a means by which the Japanese might be excluded from land ownership without violating the Japanese-American Treaty of 1911. Acting upon the President's suggestion, the California Assembly on April 16, 1913, passed an alien bill that prohibited Japanese ownership of land in an indirect manner.

Wilson and Bryan were, therefore, totally unprepared for the crisis that suddenly erupted when the Japanese government, press, and people learned of the action of the California Assembly, and when the California Senate, on April 21, added to the tension by adopting an alien land bill that was openly anti-Japanese. A rising war fever in Japan at once brought Wilson to his senses and compelled him to act. He first addressed a public appeal to the Californians, urging them not to make their alien land bill openly discriminatory, and then sent Bryan to Sacramento to plead for caution.

Wilson's and Bryan's supplications, however, did not budge the California leaders from their determination to humiliate the Japanese people. On May 9, 1913, the legislature adopted a bill excluding from land ownership persons "ineligible to citizenship"—words hateful to the Japanese. And in spite of last minute appeals from Wilson and Bryan, Governor Hiram W. Johnson signed the measure. On May 9 the Japanese Ambassador lodged a strong protest with the State Department; in Japan public opinion was at a dangerous point of anger. So explosive was the situation, in fact, that on May 13 and 14 the Joint Board of the Army and Navy warned the President that war with Japan was "not only possible, but even probable." The Joint Board, besides, urged the President to transfer American warships in Chinese waters to the Philippines to help avert a surprise Japanese attack on those islands.

It was a dangerous situation, but Wilson and Bryan kept their heads. Correctly assuming that the Japanese Cabinet did not want war, they rejected the Joint Board's advice and resorted instead to diplomacy to settle the issue. Many notes passed between Tokyo and Washington during the remainder of 1913 and the first months of 1914. The Japanese government proposed a treaty guaranteeing the mutual right of land ownership; in reply, Wilson and Bryan promised to negotiate such a treaty when it was politically possible to obtain ratification. But that time never came, and, in June 1914, the new Japanese Foreign Minister, Baron Kato, abruptly terminated the negotiations. Thus relations between the two governments were gravely unsettled when the war in Europe spread to the Far East and raised new difficulties in that area for the United States.

The grave danger, which Wilson and Bryan perceived, was that Japan would take advantage of Europe's adversity to upset the balance of power in the Far East. When Japan entered the war on the side of the Allies and seized the German naval base and concession in the Shantung Province of China, the American leaders were disturbed but helpless to prevent such action. When the Japanese government proceeded in the early weeks of 1915 to attempt to impose a treaty embodying twenty-one demands on China, adherence to which would have made China virtually a satellite of Nippon, Wilson and Bryan entered the ensuing controversy as defenders of the integrity and independence of China and voiced their opposition to the secret Japanese demands in a series of statements to the press and notes to the Japanese and Chinese governments during April and May 1915. Moreover, the British Foreign Office had meanwhile become aroused and applied heavy pressure on the Tokyo Cabinet in favor of a policy of moderation. The upshot of these Anglo-American protests was that for the time being the Japanese government abandoned its plan to bring China under its control.

Following the settlement of the crisis over the twenty-one demands, the Japanese pressed forward to consolidate their economic position in China by offering capital that European bankers could no longer supply. At the urgent prompting of the British Foreign Office and the State Department, Wilson finally reversed his position on the consortium. On November 9, 1917, therefore, Secretary of State Robert Lansing, who had succeeded Bryan in 1915, announced that the American government was contemplating the creation of a new four-power consortium of American, British, French, and Japanese bankers for the purpose of supplying capital that the Chinese desperately needed.

Actually, the State Department's determination to use American capital to preserve an economic balance of power in China was evident months before Lansing's announcement of November 9, and prompted the Japanese government to ask the Washington leaders for a frank avowal of their policy in China. When correspondence failed to yield a satisfactory understanding, the Japanese Foreign Office sent a special envoy, Viscount Kikujiro Ishii, to Washington; and from September 6 to November 2, 1917, Ishii and Lansing discussed the Chinese problem. The extent of their divergence became evident when Ishii insisted that the United States recognize Japan's paramount interest in China, in the same way that Japan had recognized the paramount American interest in Mexico, and when Lansing replied that Japan should reaffirm her allegiance to the principle of the Open Door and promise to help maintain the independence of China.

Unable to come to clear and firm agreement, the two men resorted to ambiguous language to break the deadlock. In an agreement signed on November 2, 1917, the United States recognized that Japan had special interests in China, especially in provinces contiguous to Japanese possessions —presumably Manchuria and the Shantung Province. In return, Japan reaffirmed her support of the Open Door and the territorial and administrative independence of China. By a secret protocol, moreover, Japan promised not to take advantage of the war situation to seek special rights in China that would abridge the interests of citizens of other friendly powers.

The negotiation of the Lansing-Ishii Agreement brought to an end one era in Japanese-American relations and marked the beginning of a new period of strain and crisis. Although the Japanese publicly boasted that Lansing had recognized their controlling interest in China, actually he had done nothing of the kind. Without in any way abandoning the historic American insistence upon the Open Door and the independence of China, Lansing had used ambiguous language to create a *modus vivendi* that would thwart Japanese claims and ambitions until the war with Germany was over. At that time the United States would be free to use its full naval and military strength to demand the erection of a new power structure in the Far East.

Looking back over the Far Eastern policy of the United States during the first four and a half years of the Wilson era, the astute observer might well have concluded in 1918 that there was little that was new about New Freedom diplomacy in this area. To be sure, Wilson and Bryan had handled the crisis over the California land law of 1913 with far less vigor and astuteness than Roosevelt and Root displayed in dealing with an earlier Japanese-American crisis. The Wilson administration, moreover, had repudiated Taft's and Knox's policy of economic penetration of China. None the less, in the face of an expansive and encroaching Japanese imperialism, which threatened to upset the Far Eastern balance and establish Japan as the master of eastern Asia, the Wilson administration not only revived "dollar diplomacy" but also came to a firm defense of American interests in China. And in thus refusing to abandon the policy begun by Secretary John Hay in 1899, Wilson, Bryan, and Lansing set the stage for future and more portentous conflicts with Imperial Japan.

64 / Further Penetration of Central America and the Caribbean

In contrast to Wilson's and Bryan's promises of a new policy of non-intervention toward northern Latin America stands a record of wholesale diplomatic and military interference in the affairs of neighboring states unparalleled at any time in the annals of American diplomacy. How can this contradiction between promise and performance be explained?

To begin with, the Wilson administration inherited a foreign policy, the chief objective of which was the protection of the future Panamanian life line, which could not be reversed without abandoning what seemed to be the cornerstone of the American security system. Actually, however, the Democratic leaders believed as implicitly in the necessity of preserving American supremacy in the Caribbean and Central American areas as did Roosevelt or Taft and were willing to undertake even bolder programs than their Republican predecessors had envisaged.

In the second place, although Bryan and the Democratic party had solemnly condemned so-called "dollar diplomacy" as insidious financial imperialism, circumstances compelled the new Secretary of State to use the instrument he had formerly denounced. In the beginning, however, Bryan had other plans. To free Latin America from the snares of foreign concessionaires and bankers, Bryan proposed a far-sighted plan, one that envisaged the assumption and refunding by the United States government of the external debts of the small Latin American states. But Wilson rejected this proposal as being too "radical," and Bryan concluded that he had no alternative but to continue to use private capital to extend American influence in a vital area.

Wilson's and Bryan's determination to safeguard the approaches to the Canal and the seeming necessity of continuing to use private capital to strengthen American influence in the Central American and Caribbean areas in part explain why there was no change in the Latin American policies of the United States in 1913. But the motives for their extension of the

Roosevelt-Taft policy lay deeper than the desire to protect American security interests. Moved by the missionary's desire to do good, Wilson and Bryan sincerely wanted to help the neighboring peoples of Mexico, Nicaragua, Haiti, and Santo Domingo find peace and develop democratic institutions. Thus they intervened, not to subjugate and enslave, but to liberate and enlighten.

The formulation of the Wilson administration's Nicaraguan program provides an excellent illustration of how these factors all combined to shape and control policy. Bryan could not withdraw American troops from Nicaragua without inviting civil war and the inauguration of a bitterly anti-American regime in an area close to the Canal. He continued, therefore, to support the Díaz government, which the Nicaraguan people would have overthrown had they been free to rebel.

Having concluded that it was necessary to control the government of Nicaragua, Bryan was also willing to go the whole way and regularize Nicaragua's special relation to the United States in treaty form. On June 9 and 11, 1913, counsel for the Nicaraguan government presented to the State Department the draft of a treaty that was later known as the Bryan-Chamorro Treaty. Like the agreement that Secretary Knox had negotiated and the Senate had refused to ratify a few months before, the Bryan-Chamorro Treaty provided for American purchase of an option on the Nicaraguan canal route for $3,000,000, an American lease on the Great Corn and Little Corn Islands in the Gulf of Mexico, and cession to the United States of the right to build a naval base in the Gulf of Fonseca, on the Pacific side. Unlike Knox's treaty, however, the Bryan-Chamorro Treaty also empowered the United States to intervene in Nicaragua to preserve order, protect property, and maintain Nicaraguan independence.

Republicans hailed the administration's extension of Taft's policy. Old-line Democrats on the Senate foreign relations committee, however, refused to change their principles; and the Senate approved the treaty on February 18, 1916, only after the provision authorizing American intervention in Nicaragua's internal affairs had been removed. Actually, the deletion of the objectional provision made no difference in State Department policy, which continued to be one of active interference in all phases of Nicaraguan politics.

The Bryan-Chamorro Treaty only marked the beginning of a further penetration of the Caribbean area that culminated in the occupation of the two island republics of Santo Domingo and Haiti. This final penetration occurred, not because the Wilson administration sought imperialistic advantage or feared immediate European intervention, but rather because intervention and American control seemed the only way to save the peoples of Santo Domingo and Haiti from anarchy and sheer starvation.

By the summer of 1914, Santo Domingo was approaching a condition of anarchy as a result of recurrent revolutions, and officials in the Latin American Affairs Division of the State Department argued that only full-scale military occupation would save the Dominican people from chaos. Wilson intervened, first, by trying to persuade the warring chieftains to lay down their arms, agree upon a provisional president, and allow the United States to assume control of the Dominican finances and police force. The

Dominican leaders consented to the first two proposals but would not sign a treaty making their country a virtual protectorate of the United States. But when the leader of the strongest rebel band launched a new revolution in 1916, Wilson decided the time for drastic action had come. Acting under his orders, American marine and naval forces seized the capital on May 15, 1916, and took control of the government. And when the Dominican chieftains still refused to ratify the proposed treaty, the American naval commander established a military government on November 29, 1916. For the next six years American naval forces governed the country, built schools and roads, carried through sanitation projects, and trained a native constabulary to preserve order. Neither Dominican nationalists nor American anti-imperialists approved, but the Dominican people lived in peace and prosperity for the first time in many years.

Although the Haitians had also indulged frequently in the revolutionary habit, before 1915 they had contrived to pay their external debts and to escape foreign intervention and control. During 1914 and 1915, however, the political situation in the Negro republic grew so anarchic that the State Department concluded that the only way to remove the incentive to revolution was to establish American control of the Haitian customhouses. An excuse for intervention presented itself when a new revolution exploded in June 1915. On July 28 American marines and bluejackets seized Port-au-Prince; on August 9, 1915, the American naval officer in command took control of the Haitian government and soon afterward compelled the National Assembly to elect a pro-American, Sudre Dartiguenave, as President of Haiti. The State Department, moreover, now pressed a treaty—revised to provide not only American supervision of Haitian finances but also the disbanding of the so-called army and the establishment of a native constabulary —upon the puppet regime.[7]

To such extremes did the desire to protect American interests and end the reign of tyranny and anarchy in the Caribbean and Central American regions bring the administration of Woodrow Wilson. The one feature of this policy that prevented it from becoming imperialistic was the idealism that prompted Wilson and especially Bryan to adopt it. Instead of using American diplomatic and military power to promote the exclusive material interests of American citizens, Bryan guarded the interests of the people of Nicaragua, Haiti, or Cuba as vigilantly as he guarded the welfare of the American people. On numerous occasions, for example, he prevented corrupt Latin American politicians from selling special rights and resources to American bankers.

Wilson and Bryan climaxed their hemispheric policy from 1914 to 1917 by attempting to unite the American republics in a Pan-American Alliance, binding them to respect one another's territorial integrity, to guarantee one another's political independence, and to settle all disputes by peaceful methods. Practically all the small states approved the proposed Pact, and

[7] When Dartiguenave balked at signing away his country's independence, Secretary of State Lansing threatened either to find a new President of Haiti or else to establish complete military government. Dartiguenave signed the treaty on September 16, 1915; it was ratified by the Haitian Senate on November 12, 1915, and by the United States Senate on February 28, 1916.

Brazil enthusiastically supported it. Argentina, on the other hand, was not pleased, while Chile was positively opposed to any treaty that would bind her hands in her old border dispute with Peru. As American diplomats were never able to overcome Chile's opposition, Wilson's plans for a hemispheric League of Nations collapsed.

65 / Wilson and the Mexican Revolution, 1913–1917

The crucial test of New Freedom diplomacy came when Wilson sought to apply a policy of helpfulness through interference in Mexico from 1913 to 1917. As we will see, he desired only to help the Mexicans establish a constitutional government responsive to the needs of the masses. But in attempting to help he forgot that Mexico was a nation with a proud tradition of independence, and his efforts provoked crises that twice brought the two nations to the brink of war.

The background of the story can be briefly told. The old regime of Porfirio Díaz had been overthrown in 1911 by the reformer, Francisco I. Madero. Because Madero tried to destroy the special privileges of the upper classes he provoked the inevitable counterrevolution, during which the head of the army, Victoriano Huerta, seized control of the Mexican government on February 18, 1913, and murdered the deposed President five days later. The Taft administration did not recognize Huerta as the provisional President, because it planned to use recognition as a bargaining weapon to obtain favorable settlement of certain outstanding disputes. On the other hand, Britain, France, Germany, Japan, Russia, and the other great powers extended recognition to the new regime.

This was the situation when Wilson was inaugurated in March 1913. In spite of appeals from representatives of American investors in Mexico to accord immediate de facto recognition of Huerta's government, Wilson hesitated because he feared that recognizing Huerta and his "government of butchers" would imply approval of the means Huerta had used to rise to power. Another development, however, caused him to hesitate further. It was the beginning of a movement in the northern states of Mexico, led by the Governor of Coahuila, Venustiano Carranza, to depose Huerta and restore constitutional government. Wilson, therefore, waited to see whether Huerta could consolidate his power.

By the middle of June, 1913, Wilson had decided upon a policy. The United States, the Secretary of State informed Huerta on June 14, would attempt to mediate between Huerta's forces and the followers of Carranza, called Constitutionalists, if Huerta would hold early constitutional elections and agree not to be a candidate for the presidency. A short time later, President Wilson recalled the American Ambassador from Mexico City and sent John Lind, former Governor of Minnesota, to confer with the Mexican leaders. Lind's objectives, in brief, were to obtain Huerta's elimination and the establishment through Wilson's mediation of a constitutional government that the United States could recognize and support.

Wilson of course assumed that the Mexicans would welcome his assistance. The fact was, however, that all factions, Constitutionalists as well as

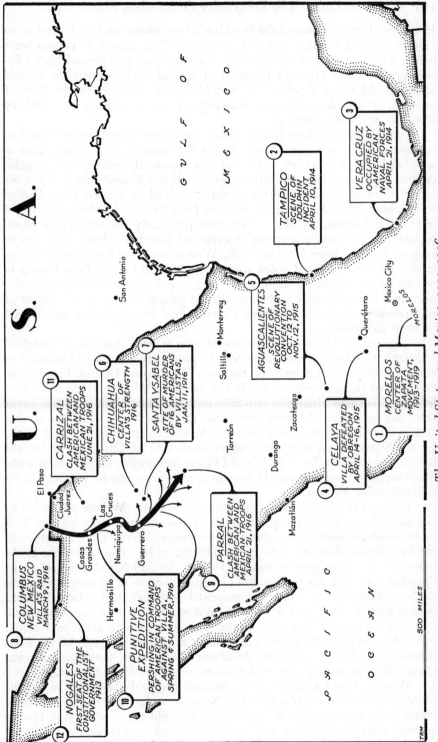

7. *The United States and Mexico, 1913–1916*

Huertistas, bitterly resented the President's interference and applauded when Huerta rejected Wilson's offer of mediation. Thus rebuffed, Wilson went before a joint session of Congress on August 27, 1913, explained his mediation proposal and Huerta's rejection of it, and declared that the United States would adopt a policy of "watchful waiting," prevent the flow of arms to either side in Mexico, and urge American citizens to withdraw from the war-torn country.

During the next four or five weeks the situation in Mexico seemed to improve. Huerta was not a candidate for President in the national elections scheduled for October 26, 1913, and was apparently willing to relinquish control to a candidate entirely acceptable to the United States. Then Sir Lionel Carden, the new British Minister, arrived in Mexico City. Carden was an intimate of S. Weetman Pearson, Lord Cowdray, who had large oil interests in Mexico. As Mexico was then practically the sole source of oil for the Royal Navy, one major objective of British foreign policy was to keep oil flowing from Mexican wells. Wilson suspected that Cowdray controlled Huerta and that Carden was sent to Mexico City to keep Huerta in power. In any event, on October 10, 1913, the day before Carden officially presented his credentials at the presidential palace, Huerta arrested most of the members of the Chamber of Deputies and inaugurated a full-fledged military dictatorship.

Angered by Huerta's usurpation, Wilson at once abandoned "watchful waiting." As a first step, he informed the powers that he would proceed to employ "such means as may be necessary" to depose Huerta. In addition, he prepared an angry note to the British Foreign Office, accusing the British leaders of keeping Huerta in power against his wishes. The note was never sent, but in subsequent correspondence the President made it clear that Britain would have to choose between the friendship of Huerta and of the United States. In view of the then perilous state of European affairs, the British Foreign Secretary, Sir Edward Grey, had no alternative but to withdraw support from Huerta. Wilson in return promised to protect British concessions in Mexico.

Having cut Huerta off from all foreign support, Wilson proceeded to the second step in his campaign to drive the dictator from power. This move involved nothing less than the cooperation of the United States and the Constitutionalists in a war against Huerta, to be followed by the establishment of a new government in Mexico. In mid-November, 1913, the President sent an agent to Carranza's camp with an offer of cooperation and support. Wilson was, therefore, surprised and indignant when Carranza replied that the Constitutionalists did not want American support, would oppose the entry of American troops into Mexico with arms, and would proceed to establish their own government in their own way. All the Constitutionalists desired from the American government, Carranza said, was the privilege of buying arms and ammunition in the United States.

Wounded by Carranza's reply, Wilson withheld aid from the Constitutionalists for two months after the Nogales conference. But as it became increasingly apparent that the revolutionists could never overthrow Huerta without a larger supply of war *matériel,* Wilson on February 3, 1914, revoked the arms embargo that Taft had applied. None the less, the speedy triumph of the Constitutionalists that Wilson confidently expected did not occur. In fact, by the beginning of April, 1914, Huerta was stronger than he had been before the American President lifted the arms embargo.

For Wilson, this was a catastrophic development, because the United States would now have to use force to fulfill the President's pledge to depose Huerta. Yet how could this be done without provoking war also with the Constitutionalists? There seemed no way out of the dilemma until a trivial incident at Tampico on April 10, 1914, offered an excuse for drastic action. A *Huertista* colonel arrested the paymaster and several of the crew of the U.S.S. *Dolphin* when they landed their whaleboat behind the lines at Tampico, then under attack by the Constitutionalists. When the *Huertista* commander in Tampico heard of the incident he at once ordered the release of the American sailors and sent an apology to Admiral Henry T. Mayo, commander of the American fleet off Veracruz.

That would have been the end of the matter had not Mayo rejected the apology and demanded a twenty-one-gun salute to the American flag and had not the President backed up Mayo's demand. When Huerta agreed to render the salute only provided an American warship returned a simultaneous volley, Wilson drew war plans with his Cabinet and military and naval advisers. Then, on April 20, he went before a joint session and asked for authority to compel Huerta to respect the honor of the United States. Before Congress could act on the President's request, however, news arrived in Washington of the impending arrival at Veracruz of a German merchant ship, the *Ypiranga*, with a load of ammunition for the Huerta government. Without waiting for congressional sanction, Wilson on April 21 ordered the fleet to occupy Veracruz and prevent the *Ypiranga* from unloading her cargo. By April 22 Veracruz was in American hands.

Did this aggression signify the beginning of a full-scale American invasion of Mexico? Wilson may have had such a plan in mind when he began the Veracruz operation, but unforseen events soon compelled him to change plans. For one thing, humanitarians in the United States were astonished and embittered by the President's belligerence and demanded that he find a peaceful solution. For another, Carranza denounced the Veracruz occupation as wanton aggression and threatened to resist the American forces if they attempted to move against Mexico City.

But how could the United States withdraw without losing face? How could war with Mexico be averted so long as American troops remained on Mexican soil? There seemed to be no answer to these questions until the Argentine, Brazilian, and Chilean envoys in Washington, on April 25, offered to mediate the dispute. In mutual relief Wilson and Huerta accepted the offer. It seemed somewhat incongruous for the United States to confer with a government it was endeavoring to destroy. The truth was, however, that Wilson planned to use the so-called mediation to eliminate Huerta and establish a government controlled by the Constitutionalists.

The American and Mexican delegates met under ABC auspices at Niagara Falls, Canada, from May 20 until July 2, 1914. As the days passed Huerta's power waned and the Constitutionalists drove closer to Mexico City. The only significant aspect of the conference, therefore, was Wilson's effort to persuade the Constitutionalists to accept American guidance in establishing a new government. Carranza at last sent commissioners to Niagara Falls, but they made it plain to the American delegates that they wanted no help from the United States either in conquering or governing their country. There was nothing Wilson could do except to acquiesce and to warn Carranza that he would tolerate no mass executions or confiscations. Huerta abdicated on July 15, 1914, after taking one parting shot at the "Puritan" in the White House; Carranza and his armies entered the City of Mexico on August 20.

Huerta's retirement, however, did not signal the beginning of peace in Mexico, for immediately after his downfall a rupture in the Constitutionalist ranks plunged Mexico anew into civil war. The chief cause of the schism was the rivalry between the First Chief of the Revolution, Carranza, and his most successful general, Francisco, or "Pancho," Villa. Ignorant and unfitted for political leadership, Villa gathered around him many of the worst elements in Mexico. In contrast, Carranza was scholarly, idealistic, and dedicated to the revolutionary cause as he understood it. Around him, therefore, gathered most of the young liberal reformers of Mexico.

That a break between the two leaders impended was evident as early as April 1914, when American diplomatic officers in Mexico prevented an open rupture until Huerta could be overthrown. Into this critical and delicate situation the American government moved with an extraordinary plan: to support Villa, depose Carranza, and obtain the establishment of a new provisional revolutionary government subject to American control.[8] In August 1914 the Washington administration launched its new policy by sending an agent, first to Villa's headquarters in Chihuahua and thence to Mexico City, to propose the calling of a convention of the revolutionary leaders and the subsequent establishment of a new provisional government which, as the agent later said, "would place Villa in control." Carranza and his generals approved the American plan and Carranza agreed to retire, provided Villa also gave up his command. That Villa had no intention of withdrawing, however, was evidenced when he declared war on the First Chief on September 23, 1914, three weeks before the convention was to meet.

In spite of this evidence of Villa's bad faith, the convention assembled at Aguascalientes from October 12 through November 12, 1914. By securing the admission of delegates from the forces of Emiliano Zapata, a free lance rebel in the State of Morelos, Villa controlled the convention and established a provisional government that for a time enjoyed the support of the United States. However, Carranza's leading generals, Álvaro Obregón and Pablo Gonzáles, withdrew and joined Carranza in his new headquarters at Veracruz, recently evacuated by the American forces.

Thus it was that the civil war began again between the constructive wing of the Revolution headed by Carranza and the plundering elements under Villa's control. While Villa waited for the *Carrancistas* to collapse,

---

[8] The reasons for the adoption of this ill-fated policy do no credit to Wilson's and Bryan's judgment. On the one hand, Villa had been depicted in a friendly American press as a genuine social reformer; more important, he had made it clear to Wilson that he would welcome the support and guidance of the United States. On the other hand, Carranza had already demonstrated that in no circumstances would he welcome American advice or reciprocate the friendship Wilson had earlier proffered.

Carranza broadened his reform program, strengthened his armies, and began a military campaign in January 1915 that drove Villa and his forces northward from the capital. Then in one last great battle at Celaya from April 14 to 16, 1915, Obregón destroyed Villa's offensive power, and the bandit chietain sought refuge in his native stronghold of Chihuahua.

The swift destruction of Villa's government compelled the Wilson administration to revert to a policy of neutrality in the Mexican conflict. At the same time, the renewal of the civil war increased the destruction of foreign property and the suffering of the Mexican people and set off a vociferous demand in the United States by jingoists and spokesmen of the Roman Catholic Church that Wilson intervene to stop the carnage. For a time Wilson resisted these counsels of war and demanded that the Mexicans be allowed to settle their problems in their own way. Gradually, however, his resistance weakened, and on June 2, 1915, he warned the rival factions to compose their differences or else expect corrective measures by the United States. Two months later, furthermore, Wilson and his new Secretary of State, Robert Lansing, sought the assistance of the leading Latin American envoys in Washington in formulating a plan to eliminate Carranza and create a new provisional government in Mexico.

Events over which Wilson had no control, however, again intervened to alter the direction of his Mexican policy. In the first place, while Wilson and Lansing talked, Carranza acted; and by August 1915 it was evident that Carranza's power was growing daily and that intervention by the United States would provoke a general war with the Mexican people. In the second place, during the summer of 1915 the United States became embroiled in a serious diplomatic controversy with Germany over the use of submarines against Allied merchant ships. As the possibility of war with Germany increased, Wilson's and Lansing's willingness to risk war with Mexico diminished. And finally, the two American leaders learned that the German government was actively intriguing to provoke a war between Mexico and its neighbor, in order to lessen American pressure against the unrestricted use of submarines. Revelation of the German intrigues caused the Washington government at once to abandon all plans for intervention.

As the only alternative to intervention was recognition and support of Carranza, Lansing swiftly reversed American policy, persuaded his Latin American conferees to cooperate, and on October 19, 1915, extended *de facto* recognition to Carranza's provisional government. During the next three months relations between the United States and the *de facto* regime were friendly, and had no untoward events occurred Wilson's troubles would have been at an end. As it turned out, the President's worst perplexities were just beginning.

The chief troublemaker was Villa, whose evil genius concocted mad schemes to provoke the United States into war. On January 11, 1916, a band of *Villistas* stopped a train at Santa Ysabel, fifty miles west of Chihuahua City, removed seventeen Americans, and shot sixteen of them on the spot. When this massacre failed to provoke American military intervention, Villa made a bold raid on Columbus, New Mexico, on March 9, 1916, burning the town and killing nineteen inhabitants.

No longer could the President refuse to act. At once he ordered army commanders in Texas to assemble an expedition for the pursuit of Villa; at the same time he sought and seemingly obtained the consent of the leaders of the *de facto* government for the entry of an American force into Mexican territory. Finally, on March 18 he sent a Punitive Expedition, under the command of Brigadier General John J. Pershing, across the border. Although Mexicans resented this violation of their sovereignty, the sending of the Punitive Expedition would have provoked no crisis if Villa had been quickly apprehended. However, Villa cunningly led them deep into Mexico. By April 8, 1916, the Punitive Expedition had penetrated more than 300 miles into the heart of Mexico, but Villa was still defiantly at large. At this point the Expedition halted and became an army of occupation.

Ignoring the advice of his military advisers, the President refused to withdraw Pershing's command. He made this fateful decision partly for political reasons but also because the State Department was not convinced that Carranza was either able or willing to control the bandit gangs that menaced the American border. On the other hand, the Mexican leaders were beginning to suspect that Wilson intended permanently to occupy northern Mexico; and as this suspicion grew, they gave less attention to pursuing Villa and began to prepare for an inevitable showdown with the United States.

Neither government wanted war, to be sure, yet a situation was developing that could lead only to hostilities. On April 12 occurred a skirmish between American and Mexican troops at Parral in which forty Mexicans were killed. Such a wave of anger swept over Mexico that Carranza could do nothing less than demand the prompt withdrawal of the Expedition. When the Washington government refused, Carranza took two steps preparatory to the final reckoning: first, on May 22 he addressed a bitter note accusing the United States of warlike intentions; second, he ordered his field commanders to resist the American forces if they moved in any direction but toward the border. Wilson replied by calling practically the entire National Guard to the border on June 18 and by sending a stinging note to Carranza on June 20, declaring that the United States would not withdraw the Expedition and warning that any attacks by the *de facto* troops on American soldiers would lead to "the gravest consequences."

The *casus belli* occurred only a few hours after Lansing's note of June 20 was delivered in the Mexican capital. On June 21 an American patrol tried to force its way through a Mexican garrison at Carrizal, in northern Chihuahua. The Mexicans lost thirty men but killed twelve and captured twenty-three Americans. As the first reports to Washington told of a treacherous ambush, Wilson demanded the immediate release of the prisoners and prepared a message to Congress asking for authority to occupy northern Mexico, action that could have resulted only in full scale war. But he did not deliver the message, because on June 26 the newspapers published an account of the Carrizal incident written by an American officer on the scene, which revealed that the Americans had aggressively attacked the Mexican forces. Immediately, a wave of revulsion swept through the American people; Wilson was bombarded with appeals for peace from leaders in all walks of life; and almost at once the war fever passed from Washington.

The upshot of the Carrizal affair was the eventual settlement of the most troubling phase of the Mexican-American trouble. When Carranza, on July 4, suggested the appointment of a Joint High Commission to investigate and recommend, Wilson agreed; and from September 6, 1916, through January 15, 1917, American and Mexican commissioners met and pondered all aspects of the Mexican problem. The Americans insisted on discussing internal conditions and especially the protection of American and British oil interests in Mexico; the Mexicans, on the other hand, pressed for the immediate and unqualified withdrawal of the Punitive Expedition. Under heavy American pressure the Mexican delegates signed an agreement on November 24, 1916, for the withdrawal of the Expedition within forty days, but only provided conditions in northern Mexico justified such withdrawal. Carranza, however, rejected the protocol.

The Joint High Commission broke up, therefore, without agreement on January 15, 1917, and Wilson now had to choose between surrendering to Carranza's insistent demand for withdrawal or accepting the possibility of war with Mexico. As events were inexorably drawing the United States into the European war, the President had no alternative but to yield. On January 27 the withdrawal was begun, and a nearly tragic chapter in the history of American foreign relations was happily ended.

The withdrawal of the Punitive Expedition and Wilson's *de jure* recognition of Carranza's new constitutional regime on March 13, 1917, marked a momentous turning point in modern Mexican history. Henceforward the Mexican people could carry forward their difficult progress toward democratic institutions free from outside control. In large measure Wilson had made this great opportunity possible. Single-handed he prevented the European powers from coming to Huerta's aid, assisted the Constitutionalists in deposing the usurper, and stood off powerful forces in the United States that sought the downfall of the Revolution. The tragedy was that while striving for worthy objectives Wilson interfered so often and in the wrong way that he lost the friendship of the Mexican people and aroused the deepest suspicions of their leaders.

PART TWO

AN ERA OF WAR, PROSPERITY, AND DEPRESSION, 1914-1933

IN WHICH the American people engage in a crusade for democracy, reject world leadership, find unrivaled prosperity, are beset with new intellectual and social tensions, and struggle vainly to prevent the Great Depression from engulfing themselves and the world.

CHAPTER 8 / *THE ROAD TO WAR, 1914–1917*

*O*N the eve of the most frightful holocaust in history to that time, Americans thought they were still living in a secure international community, in which a benevolent British sea dominion and a fine world balance of power operated almost automatically to protect the Monroe Doctrine without the maintenance of a huge American naval and military establishment. Then, in 1914, the Germans set out to destroy the power structure that had operated so advantageously to American interests since 1815. The German armies destroyed the balance on the Continent; German submarines threatened to destroy British control of the seas. And with the collapse of the established international community Americans found themselves at a crossroads in their history. Upon their policies regarding the First World War depended not only the fate of Europe but the destiny of the United States as well.

This great crisis occurred when the American people were only beginning to awaken from a long slumber of isolation. Psychologically and historically unprepared to know and understand either the issues of the war or their own stake in its outcome, most Americans assumed that national interest demanded a policy of complete neutrality. And because their leaders failed to tell them the facts of international life, the American people struggled desperately to keep from assuming obligations they could not safely avoid. In the end the United States entered the war, but in a blundering way and for reasons that had no realistic meaning.

66 / *American Neutrality, 1914–1915*

To Americans who confidently believed that a general war was virtually impossible, the outbreak of the First World War came, as one North Carolinian wrote in November 1914, "as lightning out of a clear sky." The dominant American attitude in August 1914 stemmed from relief and unconcern—relief that America was far removed from the scene of conflict coupled with the conviction that the United States had no vital stake in the outcome of the conflict. Thus, when President Wilson issued an official proclamation of neutrality on August 4 and two weeks later urged Americans to be impartial in thought as well as in deed, even ardent believers in the

Allied cause approved. Moreover, when the President failed to protest Germany's violation of Belgian neutrality, no American objected at the time.

To be sure, many Americans were unable to follow the President's injunction to be impartial in thought. From 1914 to 1917 the United States was deluged with propaganda in behalf of the opposing alliances. Probably a majority of thoughtful Americans, concluding that Germany and Austria were primarily responsible for the war's outbreak, desired an Anglo-French victory. This generalization, however, obscures some important facts: First, Americans were not nearly so naive from 1914 to 1917 as a later generation believed; many leaders of opinion recognized the complexity of the causes of the war, and a large number of spokesmen argued that Germany, along with Great Britain, was least responsible for beginning hostilities. Second, the Germans had a full and free opportunity to present their cause before the American public and did so as skillfully as circumstances would allow. Third, Allied atrocity charges against the Germans played a minor role in shaping American opinion. Fourth, American opinion was influenced not so much by propaganda as by certain obvious facts: Germany's and Austria's refusal to submit the Serbian question to arbitration, German violation of Belgian neutrality and ruthless destruction of passenger liners, and German conspiracies and intrigues against American neutrality. Fifth, the fact that a majority of Americans were pro-Allied did not mean they also wanted to enter the war. On the contrary, before 1917 the overwhelming majority of Americans desired only to live at peace with Germany.

The sudden threat and then the outbreak of war in Europe in late July and early August of 1914 set off an economic panic in the United States and compelled the Wilson administration to take drastic steps to protect the domestic economy. To prevent unloading of securities by Europeans and a panic in Wall Street, the Stock Exchange was closed on July 31. To provide tonnage to carry American products to Europe, Congress amended the ship registry law to allow foreign ships to hoist the American flag.[1] Finally, in order to protect the nation's gold reserve the administration adopted a policy of discouraging loans by American bankers to the belligerents. The President, however, allowed Secretary Bryan to say that the administration disapproved of loans to belligerent governments because such loans violated the spirit of neutrality.

On the whole, therefore, the administration acted vigorously to withstand the first shock of the war. Meanwhile, the President had also begun negotiations to protect the right of Americans to engage freely in neutral trade. As the British soon swept German raiders from the seas and began slowly but inexorably to extend far-reaching controls against neutral trade with the Central Powers, the Washington government's early difficulties were all with Great Britain. By the end of March 1915, when the British

---

[1] It should be added that Congress also established a War Risk Insurance Bureau to provide marine insurance at standard rates to American shippers and that the administration attempted to obtain passage of a bill creating a federal shipping corporation capitalized at $30,000,000 and empowered to build or purchase ships and operate them in international trade. The House approved this, the so-called ship purchase bill; but Republican leaders in the Senate successfully blocked the bill, in February and March of 1915, on the grounds that it was socialistic and that federal operation of merchant ships might provoke a serious diplomatic crisis with Great Britain.

system of maritime controls was fairly complete, the British Admiralty had mined the North Sea, laid down a long-range naval blockade of Germany and neutral Europe, and seized American ships carrying noncontraband[2] to Italy, Holland, and other European neutrals.

The crucial question during the first months of the war was, therefore, whether the United States would accept the British maritime system, many aspects of which went far beyond the bounds of international law, or what neutrals had traditionally considered to be the laws governing war at sea, or would insist to the point of war upon freedom of trade with Germany in noncontraband materials. The reaction of the United States as the principal neutral power was further complicated by the inapplicability of many of the traditional rules to new weapons such as the mine and the submarine. Wilson's first reaction to the British measures was to insist sternly upon full respect for American commercial rights; but his most trusted adviser in foreign affairs, Colonel Edward M. House, persuaded him not to take a position that might provoke a serious crisis with the British Foreign Office. Instead, the President endeavored in a friendly way to persuade the British government to adhere to the Declaration of London.[3] When the Foreign Office refused to abide by that Declaration, the President acquiesced and allowed the State Department to lodge firm but friendly protests that reserved American rights for future adjudication.

The result of the President's decision to accept the British maritime system was the same as if the United States had imposed a blockade on all trade with Germany. Under British control of the Atlantic, American trade with Germany and Austria declined from $169,289,775 in 1914 to $1,159,653 in 1916; during the same period American trade with the Allies increased from $824,800,237 to $3,214,480,547. In other words, because the Washington government chose to accept the British blockade rather than to challenge it, the United States became virtually an Allied warehouse, from which munitions, food, and other vital raw materials flowed in an increasing stream.

Nor was this the only consequence of the American acquiescence in the British sea blockade. As Allied, and particularly British, purchases began to assume enormous proportions in the spring and summer of 1915, the system of international exchange began to collapse under the heavy burden of financing the war purchases. Normally, American bankers would have extended the credit necessary to finance the excess Allied purchases. As it became evident that continued adherence to Bryan's ban against loans would destroy the only important foreign trade in which Americans could then engage, the administration, including Bryan himself, began gradually to

---

[2] Under traditional international law, during wartime goods fall into three categories: (1) absolute contraband, that is, materials destined directly for the use of military forces; (2) conditional contraband, that is, goods susceptible of being used by military forces; and (3) noncontraband, or food, raw materials, and goods destined only for use by civilians. Under traditional law, a belligerent could seize and confiscate absolute contraband, had to prove that conditional contraband was destined for military forces in order to confiscate it, and was required to allow noncontraband to pass to its enemy.

[3] This was a code of maritime warfare drawn up by representatives of the maritime powers at London in 1908 and 1909 that imposed severe limitations on the use of sea power against neutral trade. It was never ratified by the British and American governments and did not, therefore, become a part of international law.

retreat. On March 31, 1915, Bryan opened the door to large scale loans by declaring that the State Department would not oppose a $50,000,000 commercial credit "loan" by the House of Morgan to the French government.

Bryan's approval of the French commercial credit in effect reversed the State Department's ban on loans, but the issue was raised even more squarely when an Anglo-French commission came to the United States in September 1915 to negotiate an unsecured loan of $500,000,000. By announcing that it had no objections to the loan, the State Department specifically reversed the Bryan ban, and the United States soon became the arsenal of credit as well as of war *matériel* for the Allies. During the next eighteen months American bankers advanced an additional $1,800,000,000 to the Allied governments to finance the war trade. Unlike the first Anglo-French loan, however, all the later loans were secured 100 per cent by high grade American and South American securities, and none was sold by public campaign.

These were some of the ties of trade and credit that bound the United States to the Allies by the autumn of 1915. It is important that we understand why the President approved policies that operated so powerfully to the advantage of one alliance. Certainly one decisive factor in Wilson's decision to acquiesce in the British maritime system was his conviction, shared by many Americans in 1914 and 1915, that German methods and objectives were morally reprehensible and that the triumph in Europe of Imperial Germany, militaristic and expansive, would constitute a potential threat to the security of the United States.

Another factor shaped Wilson's neutral policies even more decisively than his desire for an Allied victory. It was the fact that Wilson had virtually no choice but to accept British sea measures and allow the United States to become an arsenal of the Allies. What was the situation confronting the President in 1914 and early 1915? On the one hand, the Germans had used their superior land power to overrun Belgium and the industrial areas of France. On the other, Great Britain had used her superior sea power to control the Atlantic and to keep open her indispensable sources of supply. In accomplishing these objectives both Germany and Great Britain violated traditional international law but operated within a familiar framework. Because the United States was not prepared to halt the German invasion of Belgium, the President withheld any condemnation of this gross violation of the European treaty system. Because he had no desire to insure a German victory, the President acquiesced in the British maritime system. Only if Great Britain had been fighting for objectives dangerous to American security would Wilson have been justified in attempting to deny to the British the advantages inherent in their control of the seas.

67 / *The German Submarine Challenge, 1915*

So long as Germany carried on her military operations within the traditional framework there could have been no possibility of conflict with the United States. When Germany used a new weapon, the submarine, to challenge British control of the seas, however, Wilson was compelled to re-

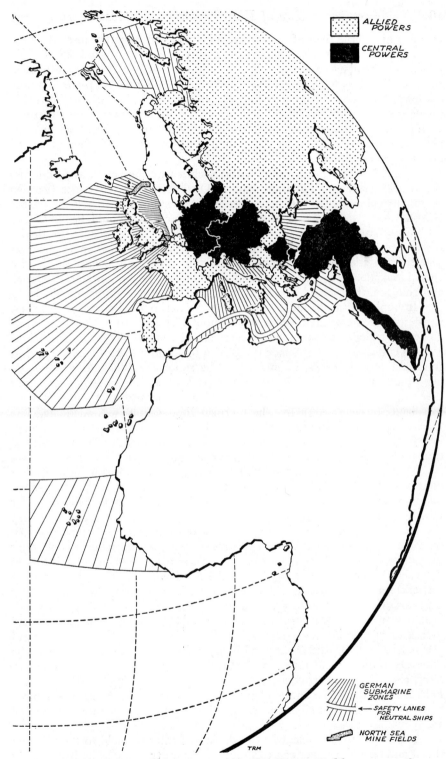

ALLIED
POWERS

CENTRAL
POWERS

GERMAN
SUBMARINE
ZONES

SAFETY LANES
FOR
NEUTRAL SHIPS

NORTH SEA
MINE FIELDS

TRM

8. *German Submarine Zones and Allied Mine Fields, 1915–1918*

examine his whole plan of neutrality. This was necessary because, after the German government raised the submarine challenge, the United States could no longer acquiesce in the British blockade without impairing friendly relations with Germany. Nor, on the other hand, was it possible for the United States to acquiesce in the German submarine blockade without impairing friendly relations with the Allies and perhaps also guaranteeing a German victory. In other words, the United States could not be impartial in these new circumstances; either way it turned it was bound to give an advantage and impose a disadvantage.

The submarine issue was raised in such a way, however, as to confuse the American people and their leaders. On February 4, 1915, the German Admiralty announced the inauguration of a submarine blockade of the British Isles. All enemy vessels in a broad war zone would be destroyed without warning; even neutral vessels would not be safe, because the British often used neutral flags. The Imperial government, German spokesmen explained, had adopted this extreme measure in retaliation against the British food blockade. If the British abandoned their campaign to starve women and children, they added, Germany would abandon her submarine blockade.

In reply, Wilson addressed a note to Berlin on February 10, 1915, warning that the United States would hold Germany to a "strict accountability" for illegal destruction of American ships and lives. At the same time, Wilson endeavored to persuade the British to abandon their blockade against food and raw materials. Even though the submarine blockade was 90 per cent bluff at this time, the British agreed to allow foodstuffs to enter Germany, provided the Germans would abandon use of U-boats against merchant shipping. Actually, the German food supply was adequate. The German government insisted, therefore, that the British allow the free entry into Germany of raw materials as well as food. The British of course refused thus to destroy the effectiveness of their maritime system.

When the submarine bluff failed to frighten the British into yielding control of the sea lanes, the Imperial government embarked upon a general terror campaign of sinking, without warning, unarmed British passenger vessels in the North Atlantic. The great German-American crisis of 1915 revolved entirely around the alleged right of Americans to travel in safety on these British liners. This issue was raised when a submarine sank without warning the British liner *Falaba* on March 28, 1915, and one American was drowned. During the next five weeks the President and his advisers tried to formulate a policy that would protect American rights without provoking a serious crisis with Germany. Bryan argued that the American government should warn its citizens against traveling on belligerent merchantmen and give Germany the same freedom to violate international law that it had granted Britain. On the other hand, Robert Lansing, then Counsellor of the State Department, and the Joint Neutrality Board, speaking for the State, War, and Navy departments, contended that the sinking of the unarmed *Falaba* was such a flagrant violation of international law that the United States could not avoid taking a firm stand, even if a strong protest provoked a diplomatic crisis.

In essence, the President had to decide whether to yield to the German threat and abandon American technical rights on the seas, as he had already done in the case of the British blockade. It was a decision he did not want to make. However, on May 7 an event occurred that forced him to meet the German challenge to freedom of the seas—the sinking without warning of the British liner *Lusitania* off the coast of Ireland, with the death of more than 1200 noncombatants, including 128 Americans.

Americans were horrified, but few of them wanted to go to war; and they applauded the President when he declared on May 10, "There is such a thing as a man being too proud to fight." From all over the country came fervent appeals to the White House for peace; from Democratic leaders in Congress came a warning that Wilson probably could not obtain passage of a war resolution. These appeals and warnings only strengthened Wilson's determination to find a peaceful solution. In his first *Lusitania* note of May 13, 1915, he invoked the rights of humanity in virtually demanding that the Imperial government forego its campaign against unarmed merchantmen. When the German Foreign Office replied evasively, Wilson called upon the Imperial government to renew its allegiance to "the rights of humanity." And when the German government replied equivocally for a second time, Wilson was both conciliatory and stern in his third *Lusitania* note. On the one hand, he admitted that submarine operations might be conducted within traditional rules, provided the U-boat commanders warned their victims and provided for the safety of passengers and crews; on the other, he declared that the United States would regard a repetition of ruthless sinkings as "deliberately unfriendly."

Thus, as a result of the *Lusitania* incident, Wilson stood firm against the German attempt to terrorize the sea lanes and drive Americans from Allied passenger ships. So anxious was Bryan to avoid doing anything that might conceivably lead to war with Germany that he resigned rather than sign the second *Lusitania* note. In contrast, Wilson was willing to run the risk of war to avoid cooperating with Germany's attempt to disrupt the North Atlantic trade. When a submarine sank the White Star liner *Arabic* on August 19, 1915, with the loss of two American lives, the President and his new Secretary of State, Lansing, determined to obtain a showdown with the German government or else to break diplomatic relations. This new crisis forced the German government to reveal that it had issued secret orders to U-boat commanders on June 6 to spare large passenger liners; it also compelled the German Emperor on August 26 to order a total abandonment of unrestricted submarine operations against all passenger ships. On September 1, 1915, therefore, the German Ambassador in Washington informed Lansing that unresisting liners would not be sunk without warning and without provision being made for the safety of passengers and crew.

The *Arabic* pledge preserved peace between the United States and Germany and was a diplomatic achievement for the President. None the less, he could not have been encouraged by the perilous state of American foreign relations and the signs of disunity and confusion at home during the summer of 1915. There were numerous evidences of German conspiracies against American neutrality and of German intrigues to provoke conflict between the United States and Mexico. Moreover, the secrets of the German propaganda organization in New York were revealed in August 1915, when the head of that organization left a brief case full of documents on an elevated train and the contents were published in the newspapers. Such exposures naturally intensified anti-German sentiment, which had grown by leaps and bounds since the sinking of the *Lusitania*. On the other hand, the great mass of Americans were still stubbornly opposed to a belligerent policy, while a minority, led by the Hearst press and Irish- and German-American organizations were loudly demanding the imposition of an embargo on the shipment of munitions to the Allies and the warning of American citizens against traveling on Allied ships.

68 / The Diplomacy of Mediation, 1915–1916

What could the President do in the face of the strong demands at home both for a stern defense of American rights on the seas and for the preservation of peace almost at any price? With customary wisdom, the President's adviser, Colonel House, recognized that the surest way to end this dilemma and to create a situation subject to positive control was to end the war through Wilson's mediation.

Ever since the outbreak of hostilities spokesmen of the opposing alliances had talked of peace. In September and December 1914, for example, the German Ambassador hinted that his government might be willing to evacuate and indemnify Belgium. The British Foreign Secretary, in turn, intimated that the Allies would not refuse a reasonable German offer. At Wilson's request, therefore, Colonel House went to Europe in January 1915 to explore the possibility of mediation. He found British officials willing to discuss peace terms, provided the Germans consented to evacuate Belgium, disarm after the war was over, and give definite guarantees of a future peaceful policy in Europe. But the Germans would make no promises, for they had decided to retain control of Belgium and, if possible, to destroy British naval power. House's first peace mission ended in failure.

The German refusal to cooperate in peace plans and the subsequent submarine controversy and revelations of German intrigues in the United States convinced House and Lansing that the triumph of Germany in Europe would gravely imperil future American security. Unlike Lansing, however, House had no desire to destroy German power in Europe, for he regarded Germany as a bulwark against Russia. During the autumn of 1915 he concluded that circumstances compelled nothing less than positive action by the United States that would end the war and create a new international structure that would safeguard American security. He thought these goals could be accomplished through the cooperation of the United States and the Allied governments in a drive for a reasonable peace.

House first revealed his plan to Wilson in October 1915 and with Wilson's consent broached the matter to Sir Edward Grey soon afterward. When Grey replied that the Allies might be willing to consider a negotiated peace if the United States were prepared to join a postwar League of Nations, Wilson decided to send House to Europe to begin secret negotiations. In brief, Wilson's and House's strategy envisaged close Allied and American cooperation in forcing Germany to come to the peace table. If the Germans refused even to negotiate, the United States would probably enter the war on the side of the Allies. If, on the other hand, the German government agreed to negotiate, the United States would cooperate with the Allies at the peace conference in attempting to compel Germany to accept a reasonable settlement. Finally, if Germany withdrew from the conference and renewed hostilities, the United States would probably join the war on the side of the Allies. Although Wilson and House did not discuss possible terms of peace before House went to Europe, they both thought in terms of the *status quo ante* and the establishment of an international system that would guarantee freedom of the seas and provide for general disarmament.

Wilson certainly and House probably thought of armed intervention only as a last, desperate resort. They knew there was grave danger of war if they continued to allow the German Admiralty indirectly to determine American foreign policy. They thought the chances of obtaining a reasonable settlement through the President's mediation were good. But, they reasoned, even should the United States have to enter the war under House's plan, the nation would at least be acting on its own volition and in behalf of a cause worth fighting for—a just settlement and an effective postwar international organization. At least Americans would not be fighting merely to vindicate technical rights on the seas.

To carry forward his peace project House arrived in London on January 6, 1916. After preliminary conferences with Grey and other British leaders, he went to Berlin and Paris, where talks with German and French officials convinced him that mediation was impossible until the summer campaigns had ended. In London again in February, House moved to bring the British to a definite agreement. The Cabinet declared that autumn would be the best time to talk of peace, and on February 22, 1916, House and Grey initialed a memorandum embodying their understanding: the President was ready to move for peace when the Allied governments gave the signal, and—although this was implied by what Grey said and was not included in the memorandum—the Allies presumably would welcome Wilson's mediation according to the plan worked out by Colonel House.

While House was concluding these negotiations, Wilson and Lansing had embarked upon a separate diplomatic campaign that nearly wrecked House's labors, threatened to draw Germany and the United States together, and caused such a controversy in Congress that Wilson nearly lost control of American foreign policy. The immediate background of this episode was the nearly successful conclusion in January and early February 1916 of Lansing's negotiations with the German government for a settlement of the *Lusitania* affair. Although the Germans were unwilling to admit the outright illegality of the sinking of the liner, they assumed liability for the loss of American lives and offered a suitable indemnity.

The issue that set off a diplomatic and political explosion, however, was a larger controversy over armed merchant ships. Months before the submarine challenge was raised, the State Department had issued regulations classifying defensively armed merchant ships as peaceful vessels. But when the British during 1915 not only armed merchant ships but also ordered them to attack submarines, Wilson and Lansing began to wonder whether it was fair to require submarines to surface and warn such ships before they attacked. Convinced that the American people did not want to go to war over the submarine issue, Lansing—with the President's approval—decided to come to a comprehensive understanding with the German government. On January 18, 1916, he issued to the Allied governments a proposal for a new *modus vivendi* to govern maritime warfare. Repeating the German argument that any armed merchant ship was offensively armed in relation to the submarine, Lansing suggested that the Allies disarm their merchant ships and warned that the American government was considering classifying armed merchantmen as auxiliary cruisers.[4]

Coming at the time when House was in London promoting intimate Anglo-American cooperation for peace, Lansing's *modus vivendi* struck like a bolt from a clear sky in the British capital. Sir Edward Grey protested that the United States was proposing nothing less than the destruction of the entire British merchant marine. The incongruity of his government proposing a close *entente* with Great Britain on the one hand and threatening to adopt a policy that might lead to Britain's defeat on the other was at once apparent to Colonel House, who urged Lansing to hold his proposal in abeyance. Before Lansing could withdraw his *modus vivendi*, however, the German government announced on February 10, 1916, that its submarines would sink all armed merchant ships without warning beginning February 29.

Instead of acquiescing in the new German campaign, Lansing announced, on February 15, 1916, that the United States would not warn its citizens against traveling on ships armed for defense. Baffled by the administration's swift reversal and alarmed by the thought of going to war to protect the right of Americans to travel on armed belligerent merchantmen, Democratic leaders in Congress went to the White House on February 21 to protest. But Wilson stood firm and declared he would hold Germany to strict account. News of the President's position provoked a panic in the House of Representatives. The Democratic members of the foreign affairs committee agreed unanimously to demand prompt action on a resolution previously offered by Representative Jeff McLemore of Texas, warning Americans against traveling on armed ships, while the Democratic leaders in the House visited the President again in the morning of February 25 to warn that the McLemore Resolution would pass by a two to one margin. Moreover, Senator Thomas P. Gore of Oklahoma introduced an identical resolution in the upper house soon after the Democratic House leaders returned from their conference with the President.

In this crisis in his leadership, Wilson acted with his usual boldness, and after a bitter fight his supporters in both houses tabled the Gore and McLemore resolutions. The tragedy was that because the President refused to explain the reasons for his position on the armed ship issue many Democratic leaders began for the first time to suspect that he was maneuvering to lead the country into the war. Actually, Wilson had repudiated Lansing's proposed *modus vivendi* because he realized that he would destroy com-

---

[4] Such action by the United States government would in effect have excluded armed merchantmen from American ports, for under the rules of international law belligerent warships could stay only twenty-four hours in a neutral port and could purchase only enough fuel to reach their home ports.

pletely his standing as a mediator among the Allies and give a tremendous military advantage to Germany if he insisted upon its adoption. But he could not explain these good reasons to congressional leaders for fear of wrecking House's delicate negotiations.

Events soon gave Wilson an opportunity to force a final reckoning with Germany without making an issue of armed ships alone. On March 24, 1916, a submarine torpedoed without warning the unarmed Channel packet, the *Sussex,* with eighty casualties. After agonizing deliberation, Wilson appeared before a joint session of Congress on April 18 and read the terms of an ultimatum he had just sent to Berlin: if the Imperial government did not at once abandon its unrestricted submarine operations against all shipping, belligerent and neutral, armed and unarmed, the United States would sever diplomatic relations with the German Empire.

In Germany Wilson's ultimatum brought to a head a controversy over submarine policy then going on between the military-naval and the civilian branches of the government. Convinced the Admiralty did not have enough submarines to conduct a successful blockade and to justify bringing the United States into the war, the Emperor on May 1 announced his submission to the President's demands. On May 4, therefore, the German Foreign Office informed the State Department that henceforth submarine commanders would observe the rules of visit and search before sinking merchant vessels. But the note ended with a warning that Germany reserved freedom of action and might adopt a different policy if the United States did not compel the British to observe international law.

So complete was the German surrender that the tension between the two governments diminished almost at once. And as the months passed, official and public opinion in the United States became increasingly aroused against the Allies. Before we discuss this development and its consequences, however, we must first consider two important and closely related domestic events, the preparedness controversy and the presidential campaign of 1916.

69 /   *The Preparedness Controversy, 1914–1916*

The crisis in German-American relations in 1915 and early 1916 had an impact on the American people more powerful than the shock caused by the war's outbreak. For one thing, among a small minority it stimulated the conviction that the United States could not safely allow the triumph of German militarism in Europe and the destruction of British sea power. But much more important was the fact that the submarine crisis caused many Americans to realize for the first time that they lived in a chaotic international community; that force, not reason, was the final arbiter in disputes between nations; and that because of its military weakness the United States was practically powerless to affect the outcome of the war in Europe or even to protect its own security.

In fact, an important public debate over military and naval policy had begun even before the submarine controversy arose. During the autumn of 1914 Theodore Roosevelt, the Army League, the Navy League, the newly formed National Security League, and a small group in Congress tried vainly to tell the people of their military weakness, but the public was apathetic and the administration was opposed to increased armaments. However, after the submarine controversy began, the advocates of preparation poured forth a flood of books and articles depicting the nation's military impotence and forecasting the invasion of the United States by hostile forces.

Wilson and his advisers knew the administration could not continue to oppose the preparedness movement without giving the Republicans a formidable issue for the presidential campaign of 1916. It would, however, be unfair to say that the President shifted his ground for political reasons. It was, rather, the submarine crisis, the knowledge that the United States possessed no military strength to give force to its demands, and a fear of an uncertain postwar future that caused Wilson to change his mind. On July 21, 1915, therefore, he requested his Secretaries of War and of the Navy to recommend programs that would satisfy the needs of national security.

The General Board of the Navy proposed the adoption of a long-range construction program that would give the United States naval equality with Great Britain by 1925. The Army War College proposed a substantial increase in the regular army, the scrapping of the National Guard, and the creation of a volunteer national reserve force—a so-called Continental Army—of 400,000 men as the first line of defense. In an address in New York City on November 4, 1915, the President presented this, the administration's, program and set off one of the most violent battles of the decade.

The issues of this controversy went deeper than any mere difference of opinion over military policy. Obsessed with a passion for domestic social and economic reform and convinced that wars were always caused by bankers, industrialists, and scheming diplomats, the great majority of American progressives viewed the preparedness movement and the President's proposals with startled indignation. To them the President was at best a dupe, ready to betray the cause of progressivism to his enemies and to convert the country into an armed camp. Led by Bryan and numerous peace organizations, the anti-preparedness spokesmen launched a campaign that drew nearly every progressive-humanitarian to their side and had a powerful appeal to workingmen and farmers.

In Congress a group of some thirty to fifty Democrats, most of them Southerners and Westerners, formed an anti-preparedness bloc to wrest control of policy from the President. Through Claude Kitchin of North Carolina, the House majority leader, the Democratic rebels were able to pack and control the key House military affairs committee in December 1915. And when Secretary of War Lindley M. Garrison urged the most important feature of the Army's reorganization plan—the abandonment of the National Guard and the creation of a new national reserve force, the Continental Army—he ran into a wall of opposition. Army spokesmen asserted that the National Guard of the states could never be effectively integrated into the national defense structure because of constitutional limitations. The military affairs committee denied the assertion and came forward with a plan to "federalize" the National Guard, that is, subject the state forces to comprehensive federal control, and to scrap entirely the Continental Army plan.

By the middle of January 1916 the administration and the House Democratic leaders were in a hopeless deadlock. Stung by critics who charged he had abandoned leadership of the preparedness movement, Wilson went directly to the people in late January and early February. In New York City and the major cities of the Middle West he urged preparedness as a national cause and pleaded for the Continental Army plan. He returned to Washington on February 4, however, to find his Democratic opponents more inflexible than before. In order to obtain any legislation whatever, Wilson surrendered to the House leaders and allowed Secretary Garrison to resign on February 10, 1916.

The army reorganization bill that the House adopted on March 23, 1916, merely increased the strength of the regular army from 100,000 to 140,000 men and enlarged and brought the National Guard under the control of the War Department. The month following the passage of the House bill was the time of the *Sussex* crisis. As the nation waited for word from Berlin that would mean peace or war, preparedness champions in the Senate pushed through a measure that embodied most of the War College's proposals and established a Continental Army. By the time the House and Senate conferees resolved their differences in mid-May, however, the *Sussex* crisis had passed, and the measure they approved embodied mutual concessions. The Army Reorganization bill, which Wilson subsequently signed, increased the regular army to 11,327 officers and 208,338 men; integrated the National Guard into the national defense structure and increased its authorized strength; and permitted the War Department to establish a number of volunteer summer training camps.

Meanwhile, the naval affairs committees of the two houses had been biding their time until the army issue was settled. Although most progressives in principle opposed unusual naval expansion, they concentrated their main energies on the army bill. On June 2, 1916, therefore, the House approved a bill that ignored the administration's request for a five-year building program but actually provided more tonnage than Secretary of the Navy Josephus Daniels had requested for the first year. The Senate went even further and adopted a bill on July 21 that provided for the completion of the five-year building program in three years. Up to this time the President had not interfered in the course of naval legislation; now, however, he applied the full force of his personal and political pressure to persuade the House leaders to accept the Senate bill. On August 15, 1916, the House capitulated and accepted the important provisions of the Senate measure without altering a word.

Three days later, on August 18, 1916, the President rounded out his preparedness program when the Senate approved a much revised and strengthened shipping bill. In contrast to the ship purchase bill of 1915, which provided merely for federal ownership and operation of a shipping line, the Merchant Marine Act of 1916 authorized the appointment of a United States Shipping Board, empowered not only to own and operate merchant ships but also to regulate the rates and services of all vessels engaged in the interstate, coastwise, and foreign commerce of the United States. Moreover, as the measure forbade the Shipping Board to purchase belligerent merchant ships, there could be no chance of provoking a crisis with Great Britain by the purchase of German vessels in American harbors.

By the late summer of 1916 the President had had his way in naval and merchant marine policies, but the last victory belonged to the anti-preparedness radicals. It involved the question of finding new revenues to pay for military and naval expansion. If conservatives had controlled Congress the entire cost of the new armaments would have been met by a bond issue and increased consumption taxes. Rejecting the suggestion of a bond issue, Secretary of the Treasury William G. McAdoo presented a tax plan in November 1915 that threw the burden of paying for preparedness as much on the lower and middle classes as on the rich.

No sooner had the newspapers published McAdoo's proposed tax bill than the spokesmen of progressive, farm, and labor groups demanded that the wealthy classes, whom they blamed for forcing preparedness on the country, pay the full bill. This ground swell had an immediate impact on the southern and western Democrats who controlled the House ways and means committee, and the measure presented by the committee and adopted by the House on July 10 was a far cry from the administration's original proposal. It doubled the normal income tax, without lowering exemptions; raised the maximum surtax from 6 to 10 per cent; levied a tax of from 1 to 8 per cent on the gross receipts of munitions manufacturers; imposed a new federal estate tax ranging from 1 to 5 per cent; and repealed the consumption taxes of the emergency tax act of 1914. In the Senate, midwestern progressives like George W. Norris of Nebraska and Robert M. La Follette forced even further changes,[5] so that the Revenue Act of 1916 represented a frank effort to "soak the rich." It was Populism and Bryanism finally triumphant—an important victory in the equalitarian attack on privileged wealth in the United States.

70 / The Campaign and Election of 1916

Not since 1910 had the American political scene seemed so confused as during the early months of 1916. The President's preparedness program and armed ship stand had nearly disrupted the Democratic party; Bryan was in a rebellious mood, threatening to bolt the party if Wilson made further warlike moves. On the other hand, the Republicans were even more divided than their opponents. The eastern wing of the GOP were demanding tremendous military and naval increases, while the eastern leaders, Roosevelt, Elihu Root, and Henry Cabot Lodge, were beginning a fierce denunciation of the President for his allegedly cowardly refusal to defend American rights on the seas and in Mexico. In contrast, the great majority of midwestern Republican voters and leaders bitterly opposed further preparedness and were overwhelmingly for a maintenance of peace, even at the price of abandoning American rights on the seas.

After Wilson's surrender to the Westerners and Southerners during the House battle over the army bill and the peaceful settlement of the *Sussex*

[5] The Senate increased the surtax to a maximum of 13 per cent, levied a new tax on corporation capital, surplus, and undivided profits, increased the estate tax to a maximum of 10 per cent, and increased to 12½ per cent the maximum tax on munitions manufacturers. All these amendments were accepted by the House.

crisis, however, the Democrats closed ranks. By the middle of May it was obvious there would be no Democratic rupture, although it was not yet clear what position that party would take on foreign policy during the coming campaign. The one great question that held the key to the future was whether the mass of former Progressives would follow Roosevelt back into the Republican party or would be won to the Democratic party by Wilson's espousal of advanced progressive measures.[6]

The chief task before the Republicans was to find a candidate and write a platform that would hold the conservative East without alienating the progressive, pacifistic Midwest and West. When the Republicans met in national convention in Chicago on June 8, 1916, the party managers rejected Roosevelt, who had made a hard fight for the nomination, and chose instead Charles Evans Hughes, former Governor of New York and now an Associate Justice of the Supreme Court. The nomination of the progressive Hughes and the adoption of a platform that demanded "a straight and honest neutrality" and only "adequate" preparedness was, therefore, an outright repudiation of Roosevelt's demands for a strong policy toward Germany, an effort to appease the Middle West, and a sop to the important German-American element. Disgruntled and disappointed though he was, Roosevelt was so eager to avoid another four years of what he called Wilson's cowardly infamy that he disbanded his Progressive party and took to the field for Hughes.

Soon afterward, on June 14, the Democrats assembled in national convention in St. Louis. They dutifully approved the platform Wilson and his advisers had prepared;[7] and they willingly renominated the President on June 15. But otherwise Wilson's plans for the convention went awry. Before the convention met, Wilson gave orders that the Democrats should make "Americanism" and patriotism their keynotes. Instead, the convention gave one long and tremendous ovation for peace, as delegates stormed and demonstrated when speakers extolled Wilson's success in keeping the country out of war.

The campaign that followed was full of strange surprises, but soon a clear pattern of issues emerged. Trying to avoid a straightforward discussion of the question of neutrality and unable to attack the Democratic reforms of the past three years without seeming reactionary, Hughes finally concentrated his main fire on Wilson's Mexican policy and alleged Democratic inefficiency. Everywhere he spoke he made votes for Wilson by his petty criticisms and his failure to offer any constructive alternatives. While Hughes was thus trying to hold the Middle and Far West for the GOP, Roosevelt was barnstorming the East, calling for universal military training and a heroic defense of American rights.

Wilson was unable to enter the campaign until September because a threatened nation-wide strike for the eight-hour day by the railroad brother-

---

[6] See above, pp. 133–135.

[7] The Democratic platform made an open bid for Progressive support by promising the adoption of an advanced program of federal social legislation, endorsed a neutral foreign policy, and commended the administration's program of "reasonable" preparedness. It also endorsed the proposal then being put forward by various groups for the establishment of a postwar League of Nations.

hoods demanded all his energies. He averted this catastrophe by forcing through Congress the Adamson Act, which established the eight-hour day as the standard for all interstate railroad workers. But when this crisis was over, Wilson on September 23 began a series of speeches that left the Republicans dazed. When Hughes denounced the Adamson Act as a craven surrender to the railroad workers, Wilson replied that the eight-hour day was the goal for which all workers should strive. When Hughes denounced the Democrats for lacking a constructive program, Wilson replied by pointing to the most sweeping reform program in the history of the country.

Hughes' straddling and Wilson's bold defense of progressivism caused such a division on domestic issues as the country had not seen since 1896. The left wing of the progressive movement, including many Socialists, single taxers, sociologists, social workers, and intellectuals and their journals, moved *en masse* into the Wilson ranks. Most of the leaders of the Progressive party repudiated Roosevelt and came out for the President. The railroad brotherhoods, the AF of L, and several powerful farm organizations worked hard for the Democratic ticket. Finally, practically all important independent newspapers and magazines came to Wilson's support. Thus, as a result of Wilson's and the Democratic party's straightforward espousal of reform legislation, a new political coalition that included practically all independent progressives came into being during the campaign of 1916.

To interpret the campaign of 1916 solely in terms of domestic issues, however, would be to miss its chief development: the fusion accomplished by the President and his campaigners of the ideal of progressive democracy with the peace cause. Profoundly impressed by the peace demonstrations at St. Louis at the same time that he was growing suspicious of the Allies, Wilson took personal leadership of the peace movement. Charging that the Republicans were a war party and that Hughes' election would mean almost certain war with Mexico and Germany, Wilson by implication promised to keep the country out of war. So overwhelming was the response in the Middle West to the peace appeal that Democratic orators took up the battle cry. "He kept us out of war" became the constant refrain of campaign speeches and the chief theme of Democratic campaign literature.

In spite of the power of the peace issue, which drew progressives into the Democratic camp as powerfully as did Wilson's espousal of advanced reform, and the momentum of Wilson's campaign, it seemed at first the President had not performed the miracle of converting the normal Democratic minority into a majority.[8] Early returns on election night, November 7, revealed that Hughes had made a clean sweep of the East, except for New Hampshire, and of the eastern Middle West. But as returns from the trans-Mississippi West began to come in, the tide turned suddenly in Wilson's favor. To the core of the Solid South Wilson added New Hampshire, Ohio, Kansas, Nebraska, North Dakota, Montana, Wyoming, Colorado, New Mexico, Arizona, Utah, Nevada, Idaho, Washington, and California—for a total of 277 electoral votes and a majority of twenty-three. Wilson received 9,127,695 popular votes, as against 8,533,507 for Hughes; it was a gain for the President of nearly 3,000,000 votes over 1912.

[8] In 1912 Taft and Roosevelt had received a combined vote 1,323,728 larger than Wilson's total vote.

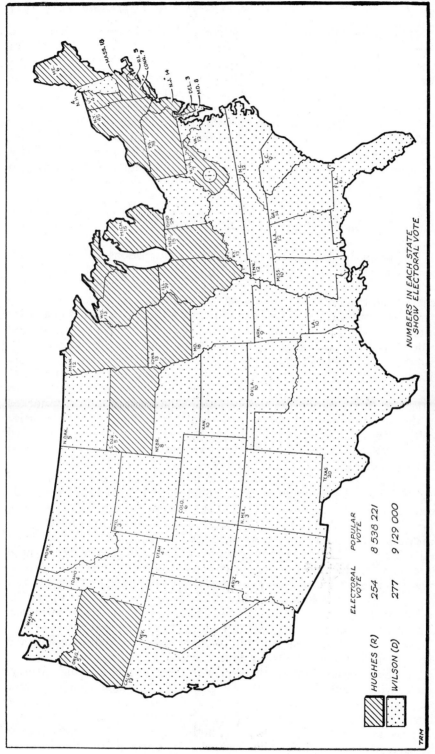

NUMBERS IN EACH STATE
SHOW ELECTORAL VOTE

	ELECTORAL VOTE	POPULAR VOTE
HUGHES (R)	254	8 538 221
WILSON (D)	277	9 129 000

9. *The Election of 1916*

The causes of Wilson's breath-taking victory became apparent soon after the returns were in. The key factor was the Democratic promise of continued peace, prosperity, and progressive policies. These were the issues that won most independents, a large minority of former Progressives, women voters in the suffrage states, and the left-wing element that usually voted the Socialist ticket. The defection to Wilson of some 400,000 persons who had voted Socialist in 1912 was alone sufficient to give the President a majority in key states like California. Added to the normal Democratic minority, these advanced progressives gave Wilson a bare majority and enabled the Democrats narrowly to control Congress for another two years.

71 / The United States Enters the War

Let us now go back to the story of American relations with the belligerents where we left it at the end of the *Sussex* crisis and review briefly the important diplomatic events of the summer of 1916. The *Sussex* pledge greatly relieved the tension in German-American relations, and events soon afterward cast a dark shadow over relations between the United States and Great Britain. To begin with, during the spring and summer Sir Edward Grey made it plain that so long as the Allies had any hope of achieving a military victory they would not permit the President's mediation. To Wilson and House this was a crushing blow, almost a betrayal; in consequence they began to suspect that the Allies desired a vindictive peace, not a righteous settlement. In the second place, American opinion was profoundly shocked by the ruthless manner in which the British army suppressed the abortive Irish Easter Rebellion of April 24, 1916. "The Dublin executions," observed the *New Republic*, "have done more to drive America back to isolation than any other event since the war began."

The really dangerous tension in Anglo-American relations occurred during the summer and autumn, when the British intensified their economic warfare in a supreme effort to bring all neutral commerce and shipping under their control. These new measures included seizure of parcels in the American mails; publication of a "blacklist" of firms in the United States and the rest of the neutral world suspected of trading with the Central Powers, with which no British subject could deal in any way; and, finally, an attempt to compel American shipowners to submit their operations to the control of the British Admiralty in return for the privilege of buying coal in British ports. Against these new infringements of American neutral rights the State Department protested in menacing language, while in September the President obtained from Congress power to retaliate against any nation that discriminated against American commerce.

While the nation was in the throes of a presidential campaign Wilson could neither take steps to bring the British to book nor launch a peace campaign of his own. Once the election was over, however, he faced a situation that demanded speedy and decisive action. After the failure of the German and Allied offensives of 1916, both sides resolved to use their most desperate weapons to break the deadlock. For Great Britain this involved further intensification of economic warfare. For Germany it meant abandoning the *Sussex* pledge and launching a wholesale submarine campaign against maritime commerce.

To preserve American neutrality in the face of an all-out struggle on the seas would be virtually impossible, and yet that was what the American people wanted Wilson to do. The only course of peace and safety, the President thought, was to bring the war to an end. Yet how could this be done in view of continued British hostility to peace negotiations? Obviously, Wilson had no alternative but to seek peace through cooperation with the German government which, since the end of the *Sussex* crisis, had been urging him to take leadership in a drive for peace. On November 14 and 15, 1916, the President informed House and Lansing that he had decided to try to end the war. But, House and Lansing asked, what if the Germans agreed to a reasonable settlement and the Allies refused? In that event would not the United States be forced into a sympathetic alliance with Germany against the Allies? Wilson replied that he was willing to run this risk.

While Wilson continued these discussions in Washington, civilian and military leaders in Berlin concluded that the success of their recent campaign in Rumania had created a situation favorable to a peace move. They drafted terms that would have left Germany the master of Europe; agreed that Wilson should be used only to force the Allies to the peace table and then ignored during the actual conference discussions; and resolved to begin an all-out submarine campaign if their peace move failed. When Wilson did not move quickly enough, moreover, the German government on December 12 invited its enemies to a peace conference.

Wilson backed up the German overture on December 18 by calling upon the belligerents to define the objectives for which they were fighting. He next undertook highly secret negotiations with the German and British governments looking toward peace. While the British Cabinet sent word that it was willing to negotiate on liberal terms, the German Foreign Office was evasive and finally informed the President that it did not desire his presence at the peace table. Meanwhile, on January 22, 1917, Wilson went before the Senate to clarify the American position and to explain what kind of a peace settlement the United States would be willing to help enforce. It must be a peace among equals, he said, a "peace without victory," without indemnities and annexations.

The tragic irony was that the kind of settlement Wilson outlined was possible only if the German leaders had been willing to accept a draw and cooperate with Wilson in forcing the Allies to abandon their own extreme objectives. Unfortunately, the men in control of the German government desired victory and domination, not negotiations and the friendship of the United States. They gave their answer to Wilson's appeal on January 31, 1917: after February 1 submarines would sink without warning all ships, belligerent and neutral, in a broad zone around Great Britain, France, and Italy, and in the eastern Mediterranean. The German Admiralty, however, would allow one American ship to sail weekly between New York and Falmouth, England, provided the ship were suitably marked.

Wilson had no alternative but to break diplomatic relations with Germany. This he did on February 3, 1917; but he was still hopeful that the

Germans would not carry out their threats against American commerce. During the remainder of February he continued to pray that events would not force the nation into war. Meanwhile, as more and more ships stayed at their berths and goods began to pile up in warehouses and on wharves, the demand for the protective arming of American ships grew on all sides. At first Wilson stubbornly resisted these demands and asserted that the country was not willing to run the risk of war. However, on February 25 he received a message from Ambassador Walter Page in London that removed all his doubts as to German intentions. It was a dispatch transmitting a message, intercepted and deciphered by the British, from the German Foreign Secretary, Alfred Zimmermann, to the German Minister in Mexico City. In the event Germany and the United States went to war, Zimmermann's message read, the Minister should propose to the Mexican government an alliance by which Mexico would join the war against the United States and receive as reward "the lost territory in Texas, New Mexico, and Arizona." Moreover, the Minister should request President Carranza to invite Japan to join the new anti-American coalition.

On February 26, the day after the receipt in Washington of Zimmermann's instructions, Wilson asked Congress for authority, first, to arm American ships for defense and, second, to employ other measures to protect American commerce on the high seas. There was little objection in either house to giving the President authority simply to arm merchantmen, but there was an overwhelming opposition to empowering him to wage an undeclared naval war. To compel Congress to act, Wilson gave the Zimmermann message to the Associated Press, which published it on March 1. A tremendous surge of anger swept over the country, but a small group of western and southern radicals in the Senate were unmoved. Refusing to abdicate the war-making power to the President, this "little group of willful men," as Wilson called them, insisted on talking the armed ship bill to death in the closing hours of the Sixty-Fourth Congress.

From this point on, however, events led straight to war. On March 9 the President announced that he would put guns and naval crews on merchant vessels and called Congress into special session for April 16. On March 18 German submarines sank three American merchant vessels without warning and with great loss of life. The demand for war, which had heretofore been largely confined to the East, now spread to the South and West. And at this moment of tension occurred the first Russian Revolution, which overthrew the autocratic government and established a liberal regime. To those Americans who had feared Russian anti-Semitism and despotism more than German militarism, the news from Petrograd ended all doubts as to the issues of the war.

As the country tottered on the brink of war, Wilson brooded in despair. The German submarine campaign was obviously succeeding; the Allies were on the verge of financial and military collapse. And yet the President hesitated. War, he told a friend, would brutalize the American people and cause them to forget that tolerance and mercy ever existed. Much of his despair stemmed from his knowledge that events beyond his control were pushing the country blindly into war merely to defend American rights on the seas. In other words, the American people, without knowing what the war was about or what its outcome would be, were going to war to defend the right to be neutral!

Yet Wilson accepted the decision for war that his advisers were urging upon him. Having moved up the date for the convening of Congress, he went before the joint session on April 2 and asked for a resolution recognizing that a state of war existed as a result of the actions of the Imperial government. After recounting the German aggressions against American neutrality, he tried to find moral justification for leading the American people into "the most terrible and disastrous of all wars." The world, he declared, must be made safe for democracy and led to a universal dominion of righteousness through a concert of free peoples.

Thus Wilson did not urge American participation on the ground that such participation was essential to preserve American security; rather, he sounded a belated clarion call for a crusade to free mankind from the twin scourges of war and political oppression. In spite of the opposition in both houses by the anti-war progressives, the Senate on April 4 and the House on April 6 approved the war resolution.

Who willed American participation? Radicals and Socialists gave an answer in 1917 that was reiterated many times in the 1930's: The United States had been driven along the road to war by businessmen, bankers, and munitions manufacturers. These enemies of the people had worked in devious ways to protect their profitable trade and their enormous investments in an Allied victory. Moreover, the argument went on, Americans had been deceived by cunning propagandists into believing that the Allies were fighting for democratic and righteous objectives. The basic trouble, professors of international law added, was that the American government had not been truly neutral.

Obviously no such simple generalizations explain the complex causes for the decision for war in 1917. There is no evidence that bankers and businessmen affected that decision in any important way, and the effectiveness of the propagandists has been vastly overrated. In the final analysis it was Wilson, influenced by public opinion and his own conception of right and duty, who made the important decisions that shaped American policy. In the beginning he pursued a course favorable to the Allies. Then, as the British rejected his leadership in his drive for peace in the spring and summer of 1916, the President moved nearer to a position of genuine neutrality. And if the Germans in 1916–1917 had desired a reasonable settlement and evinced a readiness to cooperate in building a peaceful and secure postwar world, they would have found a friend in the White House eager to join hands with them.

In view of the pacifistic state of American public opinion and Wilson's own convictions at the beginning of 1917, it is reasonable to assume that there would have been no war between Germany and the United States had the German government stayed at least technically within the bounds of the *Sussex* pledge. The German leaders knew this just as they knew that the kind of warfare against all commerce they contemplated would inevitably bring the United States into the war. But they rejected American friendship and cooperation and chose deliberately to bring the United States into the war, because they thought they could win total victory before American military power made any difference on the field of battle. In short, the German military and naval chieftains decisively willed American participation, precisely because their plans, essential for victory and domination, made American participation inevitable.

CHAPTER 9 / *THE AMERICAN DEMOCRACY*
AT WAR

O N a Wilsonian note of idealism the American people entered the First World War, not knowing what the struggle was about or the objectives for which their new friends and enemies were fighting. For this appalling public ignorance the President had been largely responsible. He had refused to take sides, to awaken the people to the grave threat that German domination of Europe posed to their long range interests. Instead he had allowed events to overpower and to push the country into war merely to defend outmoded neutral rights. A recognition of this fact caused him to attempt to give a moral and altruistic meaning to American participation, to depict intervention in terms of the strong and pure democracy putting on the breastplate of righteousness to do battle for the Lord.

For Wilson's failure to educate the people to a realization of their vital stake in the outcome of the war, the American people paid a fearful price in divisions and doubts and organized efforts to sell the war to them. Nearly fatal was the almost utter lack of readiness for a great military and industrial effort. American unpreparedness and inability to retaliate had been the key factor in the German decision to launch unrestricted submarine warfare in 1917. And the inability of the United States to throw a powerful army without delay into the battle in France prolonged the war and increased the danger of German victory.

In a stumbling manner, however, the American democracy organized for war. The industrial and military mobilization thus hastily accomplished produced the food, *matériel*, ships, and manpower that tipped the balance and broke the deadlock on the western front in 1918. Let us now see how this was done, and at what price.

72 / *Raising an Army to Save the Allies*

Neither Wilson nor his military advisers understood the weakness of the Allied military situation in the spring of 1917. Since 1914 Americans had assumed as a matter of course that the Allies would win; and even after it became evident that the United States would enter the war, most Americans visualized their contribution in terms only of shipping, naval support, credit, and materials. Soon after the United States declared war, however, the Allied governments sent war missions to Washington to explain their critical need of men as well as of credit and material aid.

Wilson and his advisers were shocked when the Allied generals revealed that their governments were beginning to draw upon their last reserves. Fortunately, however, the Army War College had made plans on paper for raising a large American army; the question of how this army should be raised had been hotly debated in Congress during the months preceding the adoption of the war resolution; and administration and army officials, as well as a large segment of thoughtful opinion, had agreed that conscription offered the only rational and democratic method. Even so, the selective service bill, presented to Congress soon after the adoption of the war resolution, set off a bitter struggle in the House of Representatives. But Wilson insisted that conscription was essential to victory; in the end he had his way, although there was a hard struggle over age limits, whether the army should be forced to accept volunteer units, and whether alcoholic beverages should be sold at or near army camps. In the measure that Wilson signed on May 18, 1917, the House won its fight to set the minimum age at twenty-one instead of nineteen, as the army demanded, and the Anti-Saloon League won another victory over Demon Rum.

The issue of accepting volunteer units, however, set off a violent partisan storm because Theodore Roosevelt had already made plans to recruit a full division under his command and to take it to France at once. The Rough Rider was fifty-eight and half blind but still full of courage, and the French were eager to welcome his division to the western front. Determined the army should not be plagued with political generals, Wilson and Baker were unmoved by Roosevelt's pleading. Roosevelt then appealed to his friends in Congress to force Wilson to accept his division; but the Selective Service Act merely authorized without compelling the President to accept up to 500,000 volunteers.

Remembering the widespread rioting and bloodshed that accompanied the draft in 1863, Secretary of War Newton D. Baker enlisted the cooperation of state and local officials and leaders in making the first registration on June 5, 1917, a nation-wide demonstration of patriotism. On that date 9,586,508 men between the ages of twenty-one and thirty-one registered without commotion, riot, or organized resistance. On August 31, 1918, Congress expanded the age limits to include all men between eighteen and forty-five. All told, the draft boards registered 24,234,021 men, of whom 6,300,000 were found to be available and 2,810,296 were inducted into the army. In addition, volunteer enlistments in the army, navy, and marine corps brought the total number of men and women under arms by November 1918 to 4,800,000.

Experience soon proved that it was easier to raise a vast new army than to equip it. Before 1917 military leaders had thought and planned in terms of an emergency force of 500,000 men. Thus at the outbreak of the war the army had on hand only 600,000 Springfield rifles, some 2,000 machine guns, and 900 pieces of field artillery. There were ample facilities in the United States in 1917 to supply all the munitions, small arms, and machine guns the army needed. But with artillery and other heavy equipment it was a different story, and had not British and French producers been able to fill these vital needs the American army would have been miserably equipped. American factories were converted to the production of heavy guns on a large scale, but production did not reach high gear until after the Armistice; and only 500 of the 3,500 artillery pieces used by the American forces in France were produced in the United States. Moreover, American manufacturers were totally unprepared to produce those new weapons of war, the tank and the airplane, and the much-vaunted Yankee ingenuity did not effect the miracle circumstances demanded. By the end of the war only sixty-four small six-ton tanks had been produced in the United States. After several bad starts and innumerable crises, the Aircraft Production Board concentrated on the manufacture of a redesigned De Haviland bomber, 1,185 of which had been shipped to France by November 1918, and an all-purpose airplane engine— the twelve-cylinder Liberty motor—5,460 of which had been delivered by the end of the war.

73 / The American Military Contribution

As commander of the projected American Expeditionary Force the President and Secretary of War ignored the army's outstanding general, Leonard Wood, who, they wrongly thought, was an insubordinate trouble maker. They turned instead to Major General John J. Pershing, who had recently commanded the Punitive Expedition in Mexico. It was a fortunate choice, for Pershing soon revealed qualities of quiet yet stubborn greatness. Arriving in Paris on June 14, 1917, to establish the headquarters of the A.E.F., Pershing quickly realized that the Allies were militarily almost bankrupt and obsessed by a passion for defense. He looked forward to the day when he would command a great fresh army that would lead the British and French out of their trenches.

Refusing to believe that a large American force could either be assembled or transported to the front for many months to come, the Allied military leaders argued that available American troops should be integrated into the existing defensive structure and subordinated to Allied field commanders. However, Pershing stubbornly insisted on preserving the identity and integrity of his command and even demanded a share of the front. As they could not refuse, the Allied generals gave him the small and quiet Toul sector east of Verdun to defend with his initial force of 14,500 men.

In October 1917 the Germans began a series of heavy blows that pointed up the urgent need of large American reinforcements and forced the Allied governments to unite effectively for the first time. Following a near rout of the Italian armies by the Germans came the triumph in November of the Bolsheviks in Russia, which meant that Russia would soon withdraw from the war. Assembled in extraordinary conference at Rapallo, Italy, in November 1917, the Allied Prime Ministers created the Supreme War Council to sit at Versailles and coordinate and direct military operations. During the next few months Pershing and President Wilson were subjected to heavy

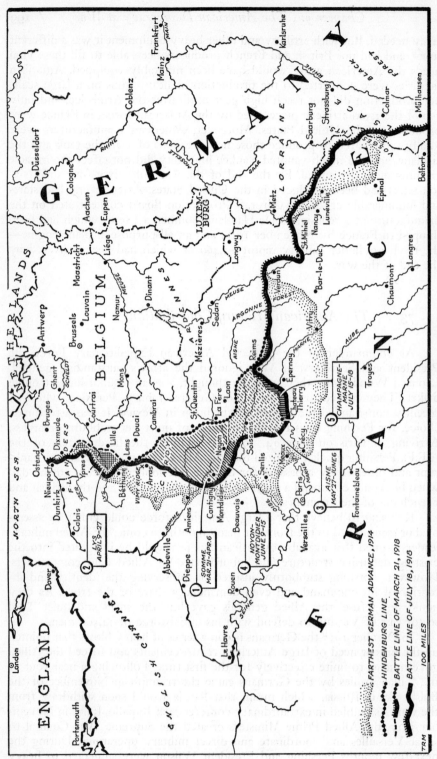

10. *The Five Great German Offensives of 1918*

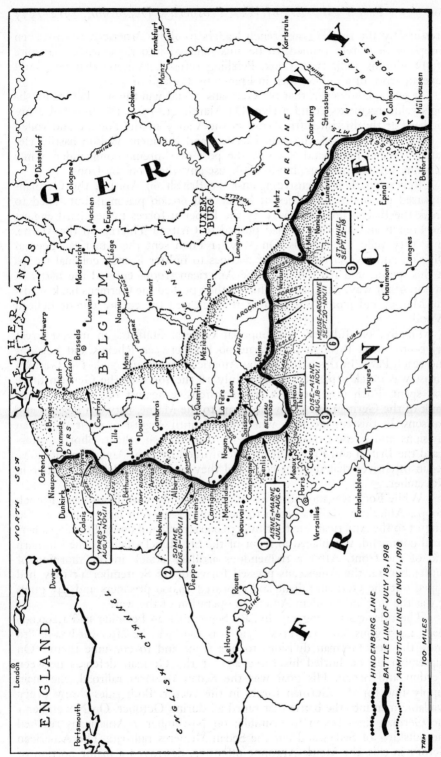

11. *American Participation in the Allied Offensives of 1918*

pressure by the British and French leaders to allow American troops, even troops inadequately trained, to be amalgamated into their armies. In spite of the gloomy military outlook, Pershing refused, replying that he would have an army of a million men in France by the end of 1918.

It seemed, however, that the Germans would win the war before Pershing's reinforcements could arrive. On March 21, 1918, the Imperial army hit hard at the British Fifth Army in the Valley of the Somme and rolled it back. On March 26, the Allied leaders and President Wilson hastily elevated Marshal Ferdinand Foch to the post of supreme commander, while Pershing offered his four divisions for use anywhere on the front.

Renewing their offensive against the British on April 9, the Germans captured enormous quantities of booty and 60,000 prisoners but failed to break the British lines. On May 27 the Imperial forces turned hard against the French and by May 30 had pushed to Chateau Thierry on the Marne, only fifty miles from Paris. On May 31 Foch sent the American Second Division and several regiments of marines to bolster French colonial troops in this sector, and for the first time American troops entered the battle in an important way. At Chateau Thierry they pushed the Germans back across the Marne; and from June 6 to 25 they cleared the enemy out of Belleau Wood.

Finally, on July 15, the Imperial General Staff began its last great drive—to break through the Marne pocket between Rheims and Soissons and reach Paris. In this battle 85,000 Americans were engaged. The German thrust was quickly parried, and by July 18 the force of the German drive was spent. Foch then began a counteroffensive against the weak western flank of the German line from the Aisne to the Marne, between Rheims and Soissons. In this engagement, which lasted until August 6, eight American divisions and French troops wiped out the German salient. Shortly afterward the British and French armies, reinforced by new American divisions, began offensives that did not end until they neared the Belgian frontier in November.

While Foch was mounting his offensive mainly with British and French troops, American soldiers began to pour into France in large numbers. On August 10 the American First Army, 550,000 strong and under Pershing's personal command, was placed in front of the St. Mihiel salient at the southern end of the front. After a tremendous artillery attack in the morning of September 12, the Americans pressed forward; by September 15 they had wiped out the German salient and captured 16,000 prisoners and 443 guns. It was the first independent American operation of the war.

The tide was turning rapidly. By September 26 Pershing had 1,200,000 men, 2,417 guns, and 324 tanks, and was eager, as he afterward said, "to draw the best German divisions to our front and to consume them." On September 26 he hurled his force against the German defenses between Verdun and Sedan. His goal was the Sedan-Meziéres railroad, the main supply line for the German forces in this sector. Both sides threw every available man into the battle that raged all during October. On November 1 the German lines began to crumble; on November 7 Americans reached the outskirts of Sedan and cut the Sedan-Meziéres railroad. The American victory in this, the Meuse-Argonne offensive, destroyed a major portion of the German defenses and, coupled with British and French successes in the central and northern sectors, brought the war to an end.

Thus was the military strength of the American democracy organized and brought to bear in the last phases of the war. An American tempted to exaggerate his country's contribution to the victory is less inclined to boast, however, when he recalls that only 50,280 Americans gave their lives in action, as compared with 1,700,000 Russians, 1,385,300 Frenchmen, and 900,000 Britons. It was the European Allies who bore the brunt of the German attack and made it possible for the United States to make any contribution at all. Yet belated though it was, the American contribution came perhaps in the nick of time to enable the Allies to withstand the last great German assault. On April 1, 1918, at the beginning of the German drive and before the American build up in France, the Germans had a superiority of 324,000 infantrymen on the western front. By June, however, American reinforcements gave the Allies a majority in manpower. By November the Allied preponderance was more than 600,000 men, enough to overwhelm the German defenses. Americans could rightly say, therefore, that their contribution had at least been decisive. They could also take pride in the courage and fighting effectiveness of their fighting men. As General Pershing put it, "Their devotion, their valor and their sacrifices will live forever in the hearts of their grateful countrymen."

74 / The United States Navy and the War

As the U-boats set out in February 1917 to destroy all sea-borne commerce, the most dangerous threat to the Allied cause came first not on land but on the seas. The German Admiralty had calculated that sinkings at the rate of 600,000 tons a month would bring England to her knees within six months, and for a time it seemed the promise of the U-boat champions would be fulfilled. Submarine sinkings totaled 540,000 tons in February, 593,841 tons in March, and 881,027 tons in April. All told, during 1917 submarines destroyed more than 6,500,000 tons of shipping, while all American, Allied, and neutral shipyards combined built only 2,700,000 tons. "They will win, unless we can stop these losses—and stop them soon," Admiral Jellicoe, First Sea Lord of the Admiralty, told the American liaison admiral in London, William S. Sims, in mid-April, 1917. "The British transport of troops and supplies is already strained to the utmost, and the maintenance of the armies in the field is threatened," Ambassador Page cabled the President from London on April 27. "There is food enough here to last the civil population only not more than six weeks or two months."

The adoption of the war resolution found the American navy ready to join in the campaign against the submarines. On April 10 and 11, 1917, Secretary Daniels and his staff conferred with British and French admirals and mapped out a preliminary division of duty: The American navy would defend and patrol the Western Hemisphere, while the British fleet would carry the brunt of the anti-submarine campaign in waters around the British Isles with what help the American navy could spare. American assistance was not long in coming. On May 4 the first six destroyers reached Queenstown, Ireland; by July 5 there were thirty-five American destroyers stationed at that base; and by the end of the war 383 American craft were overseas.[1]

In April 1917 the British system of defense against submarines consisted of dispersing sea traffic widely and then channeling merchant ships through heavily patrolled waters around the British Isles. The system created a positive death trap for merchantmen, as there simply were not enough ships to patrol the area. To the obvious alternative—the convoy system—British naval planners and masters of merchant ships objected, on the ground that convoys were slow and merchant ships could not stay in formation. But as the submarine toll mounted, a minority in the Admiralty joined Secretary Daniels and Admiral Sims in virtually demanding the use of convoys. Even after the feasibility of the plan had been demonstrated in the latter part of May 1917 by two experimental convoys from Gibraltar and Hampton Roads, the Admiralty contended that it did not have ships available to use the system generally. The American reinforcement of destroyers in July, however, turned the tide, and convoys for merchant ships were begun.

The intensified anti-submarine campaign and inauguration of the convoy system during the summer of 1917 were the two decisive factors that brought the submarines under control. Shipping losses fell from 881,027 tons in April to half that figure in December 1917; and after April 1918 British losses never ran above 200,000 tons a month. As an additional measure, the American Navy Department advocated laying a mine barrage between the coasts of Scotland and Norway to bottle up the submarines. The British Admiralty promptly rejected the plan as impractical, but the Navy Department kept at work on the project. With the development of a mine that was discharged when a submarine brushed against its antenna firing device, the British gave their approval; and in March 1918 the two navies began the undertaking. By the end of the war the North Sea barrage was not yet completed, but some 70,000 mines had been laid and German difficulties at sea had at least been compounded.

After helping to bridle the submarines, the American navy's chief task was the transporting and supply of the A.E.F. On July 1, 1917, the Navy Department had on hand seven troop and six cargo ships, totaling 94,000 tons; by November 1918 the Department had created a Cruiser and Transport Force of 143 vessels, aggregating 3,250,000 tons, which carried 911,047 soldiers to France. In addition, when the need for American manpower grew acute in 1918, every available British transport was pressed into service in the Atlantic Ferry. A little over 1,000,000 soldiers were carried by British vessels. So fast and closely guarded by naval escorts were these troop carriers that only two of them, both British vessels, were sunk on the eastward voyage.

With more than 2,000 vessels and 533,000 officers and men in service at the end of the war, the American navy had attained unparalleled size and fighting effectiveness. By November 1918, American ships were patrolling the reaches of the Western Hemisphere and cooperating with Japanese and British forces in the Far East, while 834 vessels and 200,000 men were either

---

[1] The administration immediately suspended the large building program authorized by the legislation of 1916 and adopted plans in May 1917 for the construction of 250 destroyers and 400 sub-chasers.

serving in European waters or else transporting troops and supplies to
France. By insisting on the adoption of the convoy system and the laying of
the North Sea mine barrage, American naval strategists had made a significant contribution to the operations that assured an Allied-American victory
at sea. By throwing its destroyers into the campaign against the submarines,
the American navy perhaps turned the tide against the U-boats in the first
Battle of the Atlantic. And by transporting nearly half the A.E.F. and
almost all the army's cargo to France, the navy made possible the defeat of
Germany in 1918 instead of 1920, as the Allied leaders had originally planned.

75 / The Triumph of a Democratic Tax Policy During Wartime

Americans entered the First World War without the slightest conception of the costs of participation. When a learned professor at Columbia
University suggested that the war would cost the United States at least
$10,000,000,000 during the first year, administration and congressional
leaders smiled in unbelief. Although predictions as to the long-run costs
were impossible, two facts became almost at once apparent and demanded
quick action. First, British spokesmen and Ambassador Page in London made
it clear that unless Britain and France received huge credits—not a piddling
few hundred million dollars—the structure of international exchange would
collapse and the European Allies would be in desperate straits. Second, the
Revenue Act of March 1917, which had increased taxes slightly, was grossly
inadequate to meet war needs and a new war tax would have to be adopted.

Without opposition a startled Congress, on April 23, 1917, passed the
first War Loan Act authorizing the Treasury to issue $2,000,000,000 in
short-term notes and $5,000,000,000 in bonds, three billions of which should
be lent to the Allies. Remembering the controversy provoked by President
Cleveland's negotiations with Wall Street bankers, Congress also stipulated
that the bonds should be sold through popular subscription. As the needs
of the American and Allied governments grew, Congress added subsequent
authorizations, so that by 1920 the government had borrowed $23,000,000,000
on a long-term basis. In order to sell these bonds to the public and not to
private bankers, the Treasury staged four Liberty Loan campaigns and one
Victory Loan drive after the war was over.

Out of the $33,500,000,000 that is reckoned as the cost of the war to
the American people by 1920, therefore, some $23,000,000,000 was charged
to future generations and about $10,500,000,000 was raised by taxes. Deter-
mining how much should be borrowed and how much raised by taxes set
off protracted struggles in Congress. Conservatives of both parties advocated
recourse to consumption taxes, borrowing, and perhaps slight increases in
income taxes. Progressives and radicals, on the other hand, believed that the
wealthy classes who had allegedly driven the country to war should be
forced to bear practically the entire costs through extraordinary income,
inheritance, and excess profits taxes.

Between these two extremes stood the President, the Secretary of the
Treasury, and a large majority of Congress. At first McAdoo thought that

half the war costs could be met by taxation; but as expenditures skyrocketed he revised his figure downward to 35 per cent. Discarding the emergency Revenue Act of March 3, 1917, congressional leaders finally agreed upon a new War Revenue bill, which Wilson signed on October 3, 1917. It imposed a graduated excess profits tax ranging from 20 to 60 per cent; reduced income tax exemptions from $3,000 to $1,000 for unmarried persons and from $4,000 to $2,000 for married persons; increased the normal income tax from 2 to 4 per cent; and increased the maximum surtax to 63 per cent. The measure, moreover, increased excise taxes and imposed new ones on luxuries, services, and facilities. Finally, it increased the estate tax to a maximum of 25 per cent.

Although the War Revenue Act of 1917 imposed 74 per cent of the financial burden of the war on large individual and corporate incomes alone, radicals in the Senate denounced the measure as a betrayal of the people because it failed to confiscate all incomes over $100,000. The appalling way in which expenditures mounted during the early months of 1918 convinced Wilson and McAdoo that their radical critics had at least been partially right. On May 27, 1918, soon after the beginning of the German offensive on the western front, the President appeared before a joint session and urged the imposition of additional levies on incomes, profits, and luxuries. The House on September 20 passed a revenue bill to provide $8,182,000,000 of the $24,000,000,000 that the administration estimated would be required for the current fiscal year. By the time the Senate set seriously to work on the measure, however, the war was over, and McAdoo had lowered his request for revenue from eight to six billions.

Even so, the Revenue Act of 1918, approved by the President on February 24, 1919, increased the prevailing tax burden by almost 250 per cent and put four-fifths of the load on large incomes, profits, and estates. Exemptions were unchanged from the Act of 1917, but the normal tax on individual net incomes up to $4,000 was increased to 6 per cent, while all net incomes above $4,000 had to pay a normal tax of 12 per cent.[2] An additional surtax ranging up to 65 per cent brought the total tax on the largest incomes to 77 per cent. In addition, the excess profits tax was increased to a maximum of 65 per cent.

The effect of the war revenue legislation can best be seen by comparing the status of the wealthy classes with that in which other groups found themselves during the war period. The average annual *real* earnings of workers in manufacturing, transportation, and coal mining in 1917 were 14 per cent higher than in 1914 and 20 per cent higher in 1918 than in 1914. As a result of a rapid increase in agricultural prices farmers also found a new prosperity. The real income, after taxes, of all persons engaged in farming was 25 per cent higher in 1918 than in 1915, while the number of farmers earning $2,000 or more a year increased from 2 per cent of the total in 1913 to 29 per cent in 1918.

It is instructive to contrast these spectacular economic gains by the large majority of low income receivers with the fortunes of the upper classes during the war period. To be sure, there were notable cases of "swollen" profits among certain industries, particularly munitions, shipbuilding, and

---

[2] This rate applied only for the balance of 1918. For subsequent years the normal rate would be 4 per cent on net incomes up to $4,000 and 8 per cent on all incomes above that figure.

steel; and the number of persons reporting incomes—*before taxes*—of between $50,000 and $100,000 increased from 5,000 in 1914 to 13,000 in 1918. But the gains of the wealthy classes as a whole were far less important than a few sensational figures would indicate. Total disbursements to owners in manufacturing, measured in terms of real income, increased hardly at all from 1913 to 1916. Real income from property increased about 30 per cent in 1917 and then fell back in 1918 almost to the level of 1916. But since the recipients of this income from property paid about seven-eighths of the total personal income taxes in 1917 and 1918, it is evident that they suffered a sizable economic loss as a result of the war.

The old picture of the American upper classes fattening on the nation's misery during wartime is, to say the least, overdrawn. The effect of the tax policies shaped by a progressive administration and majority in Congress was greatly to lighten the relative share of the tax burden carried by the overwhelming majority of Americans and sharply to increase the burdens of that small minority who before 1916 had paid hardly any taxes at all. Thus progressives could boast in 1918 that while Americans were fighting to save democracy in Europe, their leaders were putting democracy to work at home, and with a vengeance.

76 / The Mobilization of Industry

Preliminary groundwork for a mobilization of industry had fortunately been laid before the United States entered the war. As part of the preparedness legislation of 1916, Congress had established the Council of National Defense, composed of six Cabinet members, and the Council's working body, the Advisory Commission, made up of business, industrial, railroad, and labor representatives. Armed only with limited authority, the Council proceeded to take a complete inventory of America's industrial plant and then to establish, on March 31, 1917, a Munitions Standards Board to standardize the manufacture of munitions.

The Munitions Standards Board was reorganized shortly afterward as the General Munitions Board and given control over the purchase and supply of ammunition for the armed forces. But the new agency never established its authority over the armed services and the Allied purchasing commissions, and it was evident by the early summer of 1917 that only a central authority, with far-reaching control over American industry, could bring order out of the prevailing chaos. On July 28, 1917, therefore, the Council of National Defense abolished the General Munitions Board and created in its place the War Industries Board, to serve as a clearing house for purchases, to allocate raw materials and control production, and to supervise labor relations.

Although the WIB made rapid progress in many fields of industrial mobilization, it failed to coordinate military purchases because it lacked direct authority over the War and Navy departments. The Board's first chairman, Frank A. Scott, broke down under the strain and retired on October 17, 1917. And when his successor, Daniel Willard, president of the Baltimore & Ohio Railroad, left the agency on January 16, 1918, the critical moment in the nation's industrial mobilization had come. On all sides it seemed as if the war effort at home were collapsing. The winter of 1917–1918 was terribly severe. Heavy snows blocked the railroads so frequently that there were fuel shortages in the East and a decline in steel production.

Rumors of inefficiency led the Senate military affairs committee to begin a searching investigation of the mobilization effort in December 1917, which revealed a near breakdown in railroad transportation, confusion in the War Department, and failure to provide soldiers in cantonments with adequate shelter and clothing. "The Military Establishment of America has fallen down," exclaimed the Democratic chairman of the committee, George E. Chamberlain of Oregon, on January 19, 1918. ". . . It has almost stopped functioning . . . because of inefficiency in every bureau and in every department of the Government."

The exposures of the Chamberlain committee shocked the country and led Republicans to demand the establishment of a coalition War Cabinet to take control of the war effort out of the President's hands. Wilson's answer to this challenge to his leadership was as usual bold. He wrote out a measure —the so-called Overman bill—conferring on himself practically unlimited power to organize and direct the nation's resources. As Congress did not adopt the Overman bill until April, the President summoned Bernard M. Baruch, a Wall Street broker who had been Scott's and Willard's chief assistant, to the White House on March 4, 1918, and made him chairman of the WIB. Acting under his emergency war powers, the President also granted sweeping new authority to the agency—authority to conserve resources, advise purchasing agencies as to prices, make purchases for the Allies, and, most important, to determine priorities of production and distribution in industry.

Gathering about him one hundred of the ablest businessmen in the country, Baruch soon established the WIB as the most powerful agency in the government, with himself as economic dictator of the United States and, to a large extent, of the Allied countries as well. And before many months had passed the Board had harnessed the gigantic American industrial machine and brought such order into the mobilization effort that criticism almost vanished.

77 / *The Mobilization of Agriculture and Fuel Supplies*

An urgent need in the spring of 1917 was an increased flow of food from the United States to provide the margin between life and death for the British, French, and Italian armies and peoples. On May 19, 1917, the President announced the inauguration of a food control program under Herbert Hoover, recently director of the Belgian Relief Commission. At first Hoover's agency acted without legal authority as a sub-committee of the Council of National Defense. On August 10, 1917, however, after a lengthy and bitter debate, Congress passed the Lever Act, giving the President sweeping authority over the production, manufacture, and distribution of foodstuffs, fuel, fertilizers, and farm implements. The measure also empowered the President to institute a limited price control over certain scarce commodities. On the day the bill became law Wilson created the Food Administration and delegated full authority to Hoover.

The most pressing task in the summer of 1917 was the production and control of wheat. Bad weather and an epidemic of black stem rust had caused a sharp decline in American production in 1916; and by January 1917, the domestic supply was nearly exhausted and the price of wheat was skyrocketing. The Lever Act fixed a minimum price of $2.00 a bushel in order to stimulate production; and the Food Administration, on August 30, 1917, offered to buy the 1917 crop at $2.20 a bushel and established the United States Grain Corporation to purchase and distribute wheat. But 1917 was another poor wheat season, and stocks of bread grains abroad fell below the danger point in early 1918. Only by loyal cooperation from American housewives and the severest economies and controls was Hoover able to find enough wheat to carry Britain and France through the winter. Nature was more bountiful in 1918, however, and the bumper wheat crop of that year assured a plentiful supply of bread.

The Food Administration's second major objective was increased production of hogs, as pork was another important staple of the Allied diet. When Hoover's agency began its work in the spring of 1917 the slaughtering of hogs was running 7 to 10 per cent below the figure for a corresponding time in 1916. The Food Administration solved the problem in November 1917 by setting hog prices so high—at $15.50 per hundredweight—that farmers outdid themselves and nearly doubled production in 1918 and 1919.

The Food Administration's third major problem was finding a way to stimulate the production of sugar, which was in exceedingly short supply in 1917, and to assure fair distribution to consumers. On July 11, 1918, after several unsuccessful attempts, Hoover established the Sugar Equalization Board, which purchased the entire Cuban and American crops at a guaranteed price and in turn resold the sugar to the British government and to American refiners. No system of direct rationing was instituted, but grocers were allowed to sell only two pounds a month to each individual.

For over-all accomplishment with a minimum of confusion and direct controls, the Food Administration rivaled the reorganized WIB under Baruch's direction. By appealing to American pride and patriotism, Hoover persuaded the people to tighten their belts on meatless and breadless days. The result was that the United States was able to export 12,326,914 tons of food in 1917–1918 and 18,667,378 tons in 1918–1919, as compared with an average for the three prewar years of 6,959,055 tons. And these products of the American soil were as instrumental in saving the Allies from disaster as were the American doughboys fighting in the trenches on the western front.

The basic problem with regard to fuel was how to encourage the mining of marginal coal lands that were not usually exploited in peacetime. Empowered by the Lever Act to fix a price that would bring marginal mines into production, the President, on August 23, 1917, established the Fuel Administration, with his old friend, Harry A. Garfield, president of Williams College, as administrator. The Fuel Administration obtained the increased output it demanded by pegging the price of coal at a high level; but a near breakdown in railroad transportation caused distribution to become incredibly snarled in December 1917 and January 1918. In order to clear the railroad lines and supply ships waiting in ports on the East Coast, Garfield ordered all manufacturing firms, except vital war plants, to operate on a limited basis for the period January 18–22, 1918, and for nine subsequent Mondays. The order set off a wave of indignant protest but got the country through the crisis.

78 / Shipping and Railroads

A few days after the American declaration of war, the British Prime Minister, David Lloyd George, told a group of Americans in London: "The absolute assurance of victory has to be found in one word, ships, in a second word, ships, and a third word, ships." And so it seemed in that gloomy April of 1917, as submarines took a fearful toll on the seas. The Washington administration, however, promised "a bridge of ships" and on April 16 chartered the Emergency Fleet Corporation, a subsidiary of the United States Shipping Board, to build ships faster than submarines could sink them.

Beginning with a great flourish, the government's shipbuilding program ran afoul a combination of adversities and in the end became the most important failure of the American war effort. To begin with, the heads of the Shipping Board and the Emergency Fleet Corporation quarreled so violently that small progress had been accomplished when the President removed them both in July and gave full power to Edward N. Hurley, energetic chairman of the Federal Trade Commission. Moving with great speed, Hurley began construction of new shipyards along the Atlantic coast that contained ninety-four ship ways and were supposed to produce 15,000,000 tons of shipping. By September 1918, the Emergency Fleet Corporation had delivered only 465,454 tons of new shipping, while the first ship from the Corporation's largest shipyard—at Hog Island, near Philadelphia—was not delivered until December 3, 1918.

Meanwhile, the Shipping Board had moved in more productive directions to marshal an American merchant marine. First, it seized and repaired ninety-seven German ships in American harbors, totaling more than 500,000 tons, and put them into service. Second, on August 3, 1917, Hurley commandeered for the Shipping Board the 431 ships, totaling 3,000,000 tons, then under construction in private shipyards. Finally, in March 1918, he seized over half a million tons of Dutch shipping then in American ports. Through purchase, seizure, and requisition, therefore, by September 1, 1918, the Shipping Board had acquired the large fleet without which the A.E.F. could never have been transported to France and supplied.

The task of organizing American railroads to meet the strain of wartime demands was assumed during most of 1917 by a voluntary Railroads War Board that worked in cooperation with the Council of National Defense to divide traffic and move troops and army supplies. Struggling under an extraordinary burden and lacking any unified control, the railroads seemed near collapse in December 1917, when snows blocked lines and cold weather froze switches and impeded the operation of terminals. By Christmas conditions in the eastern freight yards and ports were nearly chaotic. On December 28, 1917, therefore, the President put all railroad transportation under the control of a United States Railroad Administration headed by William G. McAdoo, who resigned as Secretary of the Treasury to become Director-General of the Railroads. By controlling traffic on a rational, nation-wide scale, spending more than $500,000,000 for long needed improvements and equipment, and subordinating passenger traffic to war needs, the Railroad Administration created an efficient national transportation system that met fully the demands of the great military effort of 1918.

79 / *Government and Labor During Wartime*

In no area of public policy was the Wilson administration's determination to reinforce democracy at home during wartime better illustrated than in the field of labor policy. Rejecting proposals to conscript labor and refusing to allow the machinery of the labor market to regulate wages and hours, the President and his advisers embarked upon what soon became a comprehensive program designed to guarantee a full utilization of manpower without depriving labor of rights and living standards it had already won.

Like most other wartime policies, the administration's labor program evolved slowly in response to need, experience, and the administration's maturing social conscience. Because they had the most immediate and the largest interest in uninterrupted production and could wield direct power over manufacturers and contractors, the War and Navy departments moved quickly into the field of labor relations during the first months of the war. A Cantonment Adjustment Commission, established by the War Department on June 19, 1917, set wage and hours policies for workers engaged in constructing army camps. A Board of Control for Labor Standards, established on July 20, 1917, by Secretary of War Baker, regulated clothing manufacturers who supplied army uniforms. Nor was the Navy Department any less active in establishing wage commissions in navy shipyards and private firms. Even more important was the President's Mediation Commission, the driving spirit of which was Felix Frankfurter, who was also Baker's labor adviser in the War Department.

In order to achieve unified policies and direction of the labor administration, the President established the National War Labor Board on April 8, 1918, as a supreme court for labor controversies. Under the joint chairmanship of Frank P. Walsh, a distinguished labor lawyer, and former President William H. Taft, the WLB heard 1,251 cases affecting 711,500 workers and averted numerous strikes. Lacking any legal authority, the Board enforced its ruling through the President's war powers. For example, when the Smith & Wesson Arms factory at Springfield, Massachusetts, refused to accept the WLB's decision, the War Department simply commandeered the plant. On the other hand, when workers in the munitions factories in Bridgeport, Connecticut, threatened to strike rather than accept the Board's award, the President wrote a sharp letter to the Machinist's union at Bridgeport, telling the workers they could either work or fight.

The members of the WLB soon discovered that they were actually more a policy making than an arbitral body; yet they often had to decide labor policies on a basis of insufficient information and without knowing the needs of the country as a whole. To fill the need for a scientific agency to determine general policies, President Wilson in May 1918 created the War Labor Policies Board. Under the direction of Felix Frankfurter, the new agency undertook the gigantic task of surveying the whole labor field, standardizing wages and hours, and giving a central direction to the economy. One result of the Board's work, for example, was the establishment in the Department of Labor of a United States Employment Service that registered over 5,000,000 workers and placed 3,700,000 of them in vital industries.

This, then, was the administrative machinery that mobilized American manpower and inaugurated the most significant and far-reaching social experiment in the history of the United States to that time. What were the principles that guided this unprecedented extension of the federal authority into every aspect of industrial relations? How did labor fare in consequence?

In general, the government threw its war power to labor's side and accomplished such sweeping social gains as to warrant the conclusion that a virtual revolution was effected during wartime. A few particulars will illustrate the generalization. All the various administrative boards, for example, recognized and protected the right of workers to organize and bargain collectively. As a result, the membership of the AF of L grew from 2,072,702 in 1916 to 3,260,168 in 1920, while union membership in industries engaged in war production increased at an even faster rate. In the second place, the administration compelled the adoption of the eight-hour day when it was possible to do so without disrupting industrial operations. The result was a sharp decline in the hours of labor, from an average of 53.5 per week in 1914 to 50.4 in 1920, while the proportion of wage earners in manufacturing who worked 48 hours or less a week rose from 11.8 per cent in 1914 to 48.6 per cent in 1919. In the third place, the War and Navy departments and the various labor boards worked diligently to improve the conditions of labor and to prevent the exploitation of women and children by manufacturers with government contracts. Moreover, when the Supreme Court in 1918 invalidated the Child Labor Act of 1916, Congress responded immediately by levying a prohibitive 10 per cent tax on products manufactured in whole or in part by children under fourteen. Fourthly, the federal administrators attempted to guarantee all workers under their jurisdiction a living wage, that is, an income sufficient to provide a minimum of health and decency. In the face of a 50 per cent increase in the cost of living from 1914 to 1918, such a program involved heroic efforts to keep wages abreast the rising level of prices. Because of full employment and the vigilance of the war labor agencies, however, the average annual *real* income of labor increased 14 per cent above the prewar level in 1917 and 20 per cent above the prewar level in 1918.

These efforts to control the war economy in order to protect and advance the economic status of the working classes involved such federal intervention as few progressives had dreamed of before 1917. Under the guise of war necessity, an advanced element in the administration had demonstrated that public control of hours, wages, and working conditions could be effected without enslaving the workers or causing undue hardship on management. The experiment was abandoned after the war, to be sure, but a precedent for future action in another dire emergency had been laid.

80 / *Public Opinion and the War*

Seven days after the adoption of the war resolution, President Wilson signed an executive order creating the Committee on Public Information to mobilize public opinion behind the war effort. Before we examine this agency's work, however, let us consider why the President thought it necessary to embark upon a campaign of propaganda to convince the American people that their cause was just.

The answer lies chiefly in the fact of the profound division in sentiment over the question of American participation in the war. There was no frontal attack on American territory in 1917 to solidify public opinion and convert the opposition. On the contrary, Wilson and Congress decided to go to war only after protracted hesitation and painful deliberation. It is impossible to estimate the extent of the opposition to the war resolution. Probably a majority reluctantly accepted it as the only solution, but there were millions of Americans—Socialists, extreme radicals, many progressives, and tens of thousands of German- and Irish-Americans—who still believed on April 6 that American intervention was the work of an unneutral President and great evil forces that abetted him.[3]

It was to convert this still hostile opinion and to educate all Americans to an understanding of American objectives that Wilson created the Committee on Public Information. As head of the committee, the President named George Creel, a progressive journalist from Denver, who had come into the intimate Wilson circle during the campaign of 1916. One of Creel's first official acts was to establish a system of voluntary press censorship that worked remarkably well. He next turned to the more difficult task of making Americans war conscious, and before the war had ended he had 150,000 lecturers, writers, artists, actors, and scholars engaged in perhaps the most gigantic propaganda campaign in American history.

As a consequence, an official line was sold to the American people. One side of the propaganda glorified American participation in terms of an idealistic crusade to advance the cause of freedom and democracy throughout the world—a concept that the President constantly iterated in 1917 and 1918. The other side portrayed the German menace in the most lurid colors, in terms of the Hun attempting to despoil Europe and extend his dominion to the Western Hemisphere. Although the Creel Committee rejected the cruder atrocity stories, it appropriated and spread many of the official Allied atrocity charges.

The Creel Committee's efforts to make Americans war- and security-conscious came at a time when they were already distraught by rumors of

[3] Before its suppression, the Socialist party was the only important organization that opposed the war effort. In 1917 Socialist mayoralty candidates polled 22 per cent of the popular vote in New York City, nearly 34 per cent in Chicago, 44 per cent in Dayton, Ohio, and 25 per cent in Buffalo—an impressive indication of the extent of popular feeling against participation.

disloyalty, espionage, and sabotage. The result of Creel's propaganda and even more of the irresponsible agitation of volunteer organizations like the National Security League and the National Protective Association was to stimulate such an outbreak of war madness as the country had never before witnessed. There were numerous spy scares, and large organizations of patriots sprang up to catch enemy agents and domestic traitors.

Most of the hysteria was turned against German-Americans, all things German, and anti-war radicals and progressives. Each state had a committee of public safety, with branches in every county and city; and in many areas these committees were not much better than vigilante groups. It was they who conducted reigns of terror against German-Americans, especially in Montana, Minnesota, and Wisconsin. As the leader of the progressives who voted against the war resolution, La Follette was burned in effigy in Madison, expelled from the Madison Club, and publicly censured by most of the faculty of his beloved University of Wisconsin. The climax of the anti-La Follette campaign came when the Minnesota Public Safety Committee demanded the senator's expulsion from the upper house.

As one historian has shrewdly observed, in their hatred of things German the majority of Americans lost not only their tolerance but their sense of humor as well. Statues of heroes like Von Steuben and Frederick the Great were taken from their pedestals. Many states forbade the teaching of German or church services conducted in German. Sauerkraut was renamed "liberty cabbage," German measles, "liberty measles"; but the crowning blow came when Cincinnati ruled pretzels off free lunch counters in saloons.

81 / Civil Liberties During Wartime

During extreme crises all governments take means to protect themselves against enemies from within as well as from without. To Wilson and other administration leaders it was an absurd situation when the federal government could force men to fight and give their lives for their country and yet could not punish persons who attempted to obstruct the war effort at home or gave aid and comfort to the enemy without violating the law of treason.[4] The President's answer to opponents of the war was the Espionage Act of June 15, 1917, which provided imprisonment up to twenty years and/or a fine up to $10,000 for persons who willfully made false reports to help the enemy, incited rebellion among the armed forces, or attempted in any way to obstruct recruiting or the operation of the draft. An equivalent of censorship appeared in a section empowering the Postmaster General to deny the use of the mails to any matter which, *in his opinion*, advocated treason, insurrection, or forcible resistance to the laws of the United States.

Postmaster General Albert S. Burleson of Texas had been a stanch supporter of Wilson's policies, but he was neither tolerant nor discriminating in judgment, and he used his vast new power to establish a capricious cen-

---

[4] Several Civil War statutes, still on the books in 1917, prohibited conspiracies to resist recruiting and persuade men to resist the draft; but these laws did not affect individuals. The only statute applying to individuals was the treason law, which applied only to treasonable acts and not utterances and was extremely difficult to enforce.

sorship. Soon after the passage of the Espionage Act, for example, he banned the *American Socialist* from the mails; in August and October 1917 two other leading Socialist publications, *The Masses* and Victor Berger's daily *Milwaukee Leader*, fell under the Texan's ban. In addition, he suppressed all anti-British and pro-Irish publications and banned an issue of the single tax organ, *The Public*, for suggesting that more revenue should be raised by taxes.

In effect, the Espionage Act became a tool to stamp out dissent and radical, but never conservative, criticism. As one authority has observed, "It became criminal to advocate heavier taxation instead of bond issues, to state that conscription was unconstitutional though the Supreme Court had not yet held it valid, to say that the sinking of merchant ships was legal, to urge that a referendum should have preceded our declaration of war, to say that war was contrary to the teachings of Christ. Men have been punished for criticising the Red Cross and the Y.M.C.A."[5] A movie producer, Robert Goldstein, was sentenced to prison for ten years for displaying a movie about the American Revolution that allegedly incited hostility against an ally of the United States. The most famous case involved Eugene V. Debs, the leader of the Socialist party. After expressing his frank revulsion at the war in a speech before a Socialist convention in Canton, Ohio, on June 16, 1918, Debs was speedily brought to trial and sentenced to a term of ten years in federal prison.

In all fairness, it should be said that neither the administration nor the Justice Department was responsible for the length to which this legal witchhunt was carried. It was largely the outcome of the hysteria and maelstrom of hatred which converted district attorneys, judges, and juries into persecutors of the dissenting minority. During the Civil War federal judges in the North had stood forthrightly, although usually vainly, in defense of civil liberties against encroachments by the military commanders. During the First World War, however, the federal courts provided no effective defense against the momentary madness of the majority. None of the sedition cases reached the Supreme Court until after the war was over. But in Schenck *v.* United States, 1919, Justice Oliver Wendell Holmes, speaking for a unanimous Court, upheld the Espionage Act by inventing a new constitutional doctrine. Schenck had admittedly counseled resistance to the draft. In ordinary times, Holmes said, such action would have been legal. In wartime, however, Congress had the power to prevent utterances that might constitute a "clear and present danger" and provoke evils that Congress had a right to prevent. Actually, Holmes was trying to limit repression of free speech by imposing the "clear and present danger" test; but as interpreted by other judges the doctrine became the death knell of the long American tradition of free and unbridled criticism of public policies.

As the war progressed, the power of the government over thought and utterance was gradually enlarged, not diminished. The Trading-with-the-Enemy Act of October 6, 1917, empowered the President to censor all international communications and gave the Postmaster General sweeping powers of censorship over the foreign-language press in the United States. And still

[5] Zechariah Chafee, Jr., *Freedom of Speech in the United States* (Cambridge, Mass., 1941), p. 51; by permission of the author and the Harvard University Press.

the Attorney General claimed he lacked power to check disloyalty and asked Congress for broader authority. Congress moved again in April and May 1918, but not so much in response to the Attorney General's request as in reaction to two developments that had shaken the country during the preceding months.

The first of these developments was the government's suppression of the Industrial Workers of the World, a left-wing union which, as we have seen, worked mainly among western lumbermen, miners, and agricultural workers. During the first eight months of 1917 the IWW conducted a violent campaign against the copper companies, especially the Anaconda in Montana and Arizona. When the production of vital copper began to decline precipitously, the Justice Department moved swiftly. On September 5, 1917, federal agents raided IWW offices throughout the West and arrested the union's leaders, nearly one hundred of whom were subsequently tried, convicted, and imprisoned.

The second development that led Congress to tighten the laws against disloyalty in the spring of 1918 was the mounting of the war hysteria during the preceding winter, especially in states like Montana and Minnesota, where the IWW and German-Americans were an important element. In February 1918, the Montana legislature met in special session to consider the crisis; and on February 21, Governor Samuel V. Stewart signed a criminal syndicalism act that opened a new chapter in American legal history. It prohibited any language calculated to bring the American form of government, Constitution, flag, and armed forces into disrespect or contempt.

Spurred by appeals from the West, Congress succumbed to the demands for legislation against sabotage and sedition. The Sabotage Act, approved April 20, 1918, was aimed at the IWW and made willful sabotage of war materials, utilities, and transportation facilities a federal crime. The Sedition Act, signed by the President on May 16, 1918, was modeled after the Montana statute and supported chiefly by senators from the Rocky Mountain states. Whereas the Espionage Act had empowered the government to punish seditious utterances only if it could prove that injurious consequences would result directly from such utterances, the Sedition Act extended the power of the United States over speech and printed opinion, regardless of consequence. It forbade disloyal, profane, scurrilous, or abusive remarks about the form of government, flag, or uniform of the United States, or any language intended to obstruct the war effort in any way. In addition, the Postmaster General was empowered to deny the use of the mails to any person who, *in his opinion,* used the mail service to violate the Act.

All told, 1,532 persons were arrested under the Espionage and Sedition Acts for seditious utterances, sixty-five for threats against the President, and only ten for actual sabotage. But this reckoning gives little indication of the extent to which the suppression of dissent was carried out on the local level by organized bands who lynched, whipped, tarred and feathered, or otherwise wreaked vengeance on labor radicals, German-Americans, or any persons suspected of disloyalty. As Wilson had predicted in April 1917, many Americans forgot mercy and tolerance and compassion. In retrospect, the war hysteria seems the most fearful price the American people paid for participation in the First World War.

CHAPTER 10 / *THE GREAT CRUSADE ENDS IN A SEPARATE PEACE*

WE can see in retrospect that the participation of the United States in the First World War restored a preponderance of power to the Atlantic powers and enabled them to break the deadlock on the western front; that Britain and France were more severely weakened by the war than was Germany; and that a future preponderance of the Atlantic community depended upon the continued active participation of the United States in the western coalition. In other words, the future peace of the world depended upon the willingness of the American people to maintain a new Anglo-American-French preponderance of power, at least until a genuine world concert could come into being.

Wilson and perhaps a majority of thoughtful Americans realized this fact in 1919 and 1920. Unhappily, however, many Americans were unprepared to assume the duties of leadership that circumstances demanded. When the Paris Peace Conference gave birth, not to a Wilsonian millennium, but instead to a settlement that seemed to embody many of the old evils they had fought to destroy, American crusaders by the thousands turned into cynics and wished only to abandon Europe to an inevitable self-destruction. But this disillusionment over the Versailles Treaty was not the only factor in the rejection by the American people of leadership in world affairs. Once the war was over, historic and powerful isolationist sentiments revived in full force and provided an ideological frame of reference to which opponents of the Treaty could appeal. All the old anti-British animosities found a more virulent expression for having been suppressed during the war, while various national groups rebelled against aspects of the Treaty. But the most fatal and decisive development was the manner in which the question of a peace settlement was subordinated, by Democrats and Republicans alike, to partisan ambitions. This was the factor chiefly responsible for the failure of the Treaty in the United States.

The story we are about to relate has about it many elements of high tragedy. A concert of free peoples and the greatest aggregation of military power the world had yet seen ended in bitter and inglorious rupture and a chain of events was set in motion that led to a Second World War. Let us now see how this came about, and why.

82 / The Formulation of the Liberal Peace Program

The formulation of the liberal peace program illustrates the way in which thoughtful minorities affect the course of history. Soon after the outbreak of the war, groups of intellectuals and humanitarians in all the western nations set to the task of preventing future wars and elaborated a peace program to which liberals throughout the world subscribed. This program called for open diplomacy, an end to antagonistic balances of power, no postwar indemnities or annexations, self-determination for subject nationalities, the right of people to control the foreign policies of their governments, freedom of the seas, and disarmament on land. In other words, the liberal humanitarian peace advocates would substitute an idealistic and democratic system of international relationships for the old European system that they thought had caused the war in 1914.

In all countries these peace elements were small minorities of intellectuals and pacifists. In the United States they enjoyed complete freedom of action and propaganda before April 6, 1917. In England their meetings were broken up and banned; in Germany they encountered similar obstacles. But somehow they met and published their literature; and their ideas were causing a tremendous ferment throughout the western world by the spring of 1916.

Meanwhile, another peace organization had come into existence in the United States in June 1915. It was the League to Enforce Peace, which numbered among its leaders former President Taft, President A. Lawrence Lowell of Harvard, and Hamilton Holt, editor of the *Independent*. Because the League plan envisaged the use of force through a powerful international organization to preserve peace, many pacifists opposed it. Even so, the League advocates included an important segment of the leadership of the liberal peace movement and helped in a significant way to build its program.

The most important moment in the peace movement before 1917 came when Wilson espoused the League idea and the liberal peace program. Before 1916 the President had refused to make any public comment on the causes of the war or proposals for a settlement. In a speech before the League to Enforce Peace in Washington on May 27, 1916, on the other hand, he came out boldly in support of American participation in a postwar association to maintain the freedom of the seas and the territorial integrity of its members. When this momentous declaration evoked much favorable comment and little criticism, Wilson incorporated the League concept in the Democratic platform and made it a leading issue in the ensuing presidential campaign of 1916.

Encouraged by a favorable popular response, Wilson took the next step toward international leadership when he conjoined the League concept to the liberal peace program in his "Peace without Victory" speech to the Senate on January 22, 1917. In this declaration he reaffirmed his belief that the American people were prepared to join a postwar League of Nations and help maintain peace. He went further, however, and for the first time outlined in general terms the kind of peace settlement the American people would be willing to help enforce. It was a settlement giving liberty to the Poles and autonomy to oppressed nationalities, guaranteeing freedom of the seas, destroying the old system of a divided Europe and substituting instead a world community of power: a peace without great indemnities, without annexations, except—and this could only be inferred from the address—perhaps to return Alsace-Lorraine to France and to give Russia free access to the Mediterranean.

There can be no doubt that Wilson believed this was the only kind of peace worth fighting for because it was the only kind of peace that would endure. Yet he lost the opportunity given him to obtain such a settlement—not at Versailles, when it was more difficult to obtain, but during the anxious two months before he asked Congress for a war resolution. Instead of using American intervention as a diplomatic weapon to accomplish a great end, by attempting to compel the Allies to agree to a peace settlement the United States could approve, Wilson allowed the country to drift into war merely to defend highly questionable maritime rights.

This was Wilson's first mistake. His second was like unto it, and nearly as damaging. From the beginning of American belligerency, Wilson insisted on maintaining the fiction that the United States was carrying on a private war with Germany, as an associate but not an ally of the *Entente*, and presumably free to withdraw from the war when it had won its objectives. This thinking was unrealistic, for after April 6, 1917, the United States and the Allied countries had to make war together, win together, and make peace together.

This fact became apparent soon after the American declaration of war, when the President and the Allied leaders first discussed a possible settlement. Certainly after his and Colonel House's talks with the British Foreign Secretary, Arthur Balfour, in late April 1917, Wilson knew the terms of the secret treaties that the Allied governments had concluded for the division of German and Austrian territory and colonies. He knew also that the British and French planned to exact huge indemnities from Germany and that he faced an inevitable showdown on the whole subject of peace terms. On several occasions Wilson attempted to broach the subject with the British and French and was frightened from his effort by warnings that such talk would cause a fatal division in the face of the impending German onslaught on the western front. Wilson comforted himself, however, with the delusion that after the war was over he could *force* Britain and France to accept his terms. "By that time," he predicted, "they will among other things be financially in our hands."

Unable, as he thought, to come to definite agreement with the Allied governments and acting in response to demands at home and abroad for a clear statement of war aims, Wilson proceeded to launch his own campaign for a liberal and just peace settlement. The climax of this campaign, the Fourteen Points, came in response to the direst catastrophe that had befallen the Allies since the beginning of the war. In November 1917, the Bolsheviks overthrew the socialistic Kerensky government, appealed to the war weary peoples to put an end to the fighting, and announced their intention of exposing the hypocrisy of the Allied governments by publishing their secret agreements on war aims. Failing to receive any response to these moves, the Bolsheviks opened separate peace negotiations with Germany.

Some answer had to be made. The American people, Wilson said, would not fight for "any selfish aim on the part of any belligerent." After trying vainly to persuade the Interallied Conference in Paris to formulate a reply, Wilson set independently to the task on January 5, 1918. Three days later he appeared before a joint session of Congress to tell the world in precise terms, enumerated in fourteen points, the peace program for which the United States and the Allies were fighting. The first five points were general and called for open diplomacy, freedom of the seas, "alike in peace and in war," removal of artificial trade barriers, reduction of armaments, and an "absolutely impartial adjustment of all colonial claims." Point 6 demanded the evacuation of Russia by German forces and self-determination by the Russian peoples. Points 7 and 8 demanded the evacuation by Germany of Belgium and France and the return of Alsace-Lorraine to France. Point 9 called for the readjustment of Italy's boundary along the clear line of nationality, Point 10 for autonomy for the subject nationalities of Austria-Hungary, Point 11 for the evacuation and restoration of Rumania, Serbia, and Montenegro, Point 12 for autonomy for the subject peoples of the Ottoman Empire, and Point 13 for the creation of a free and independent Poland with access to the sea. For the end the President saved the capstone, Point 14: "A general association of nations . . . affording mutual guarantees of political independence and territorial integrity to great and small states alike."

The Fourteen Points at once became the great manifesto of the war. Enthusiastically received by liberal and labor groups in the United States and the Allied countries, they also made a powerful appeal to the German people, for Wilson had promised not the destruction of Germany but the welcoming of a democratized Reich into the new concert of power. Although the Allied leaders used the Fourteen Points as a weapon of war, they gave no indication they were willing to adopt them as a basis for peace. None the less, all during the spring and summer of 1918 Wilson maintained his campaign for a liberal peace and laid plans for forcing the Allies to accept his program.

83 / Armistice: 1918

Wilson's opportunity to take leadership in peace negotiations arose as a result of the weight of the Allied-American offensive on the western front that began in July 1918. On September 29 and October 1 General Ludendorff, one of the German supreme commanders, demanded that the Imperial civil authorities obtain an armistice immediately. A new Chancellor, Prince Max of Baden, a liberal anti-militarist, was at this moment in process of forming a new government. Could the army not hold a little longer, he asked, to give him time to prepare the way at home and abroad for an end to the fighting? When the High Command replied that no time could be lost, Prince Max addressed an appeal to President Wilson on October 3 for an armistice based upon the Fourteen Points and other pronouncements.

In the face of demands for driving straight to the Rhine, Wilson resolved to end the fighting, provided an effective German surrender could be obtained. Actually, Ludendorff and the other German leaders hoped to use the supposedly simple Wilson to win the respite they needed in order to prepare for a defense of the Fatherland. Wilson's reply to Prince Max's appeal, however, revealed that the President understood German purposes. The United States was ready to consider peace negotiations, Wilson wrote on October 8, but only if the Central Powers would evacuate Belgium and France and give adequate guarantees that they would not resume hostilities—in other words, if Germany were prepared to admit defeat. Furthermore, Wilson added, he would negotiate only with a responsible, legitimate civilian government, not with the military masters of Germany.

Prince Max replied on October 12, assuring Wilson that he spoke in the name of the German people, accepting the Fourteen Points, and suggesting that a mixed commission be established to supervise the evacuation of France and Belgium. The President responded shrewdly on October 14. Rejecting the suggestion of a mixed commission, he made it clear that the only kind of armistice he would approve was one that guaranteed the present supremacy of the American and Allied armies. This note fell like a bolt in Berlin. The German commanders were now all for fighting to the last man rather than surrender. At the same time, it was evident that the morale of the German people was destroyed beyond repair, and the civilian government finally took control. On October 20 Prince Max informed Wilson that Germany accepted the President's conditions.

Convinced that the German peace appeal was sincere, Wilson replied on October 23 that he would transmit that appeal to the Allied governments and discuss with them the question of an armistice. Among the Allied-American prime ministers and commanders only Pershing opposed the cessation of hostilities on satisfactory military terms. By the evening of November 4, therefore, agreement on the military and naval terms had been reached by the Supreme War Council, the Interallied Naval Council, and Colonel House and the British, French, and Italian premiers. In the meantime, events were transpiring within Germany that made inevitable acceptance of almost any terms by the German authorities. Wilson's message of October 23 to Prince Max had contained the hint that a German Republic would fare better at the peace conference than an Imperial Germany. Feeling in civilian and military circles reached such a point that the Emperor abdicated and fled to Holland on November 8. The lowering of the Imperial standards so shattered the army's morale that Germany was afterward incapable of waging even a purely defensive war.

Meanwhile, discussions in the Allied camp had brought sharply into the open Allied and American differences over the nature of the peace settlement that must soon be made. Believing he had now or never to win Allied approval of his peace program, Wilson sent Colonel House to Paris to force a showdown with the Allied Premiers. At the first conference on October 29 the Allied spokesmen claimed they did not know what the Fourteen Points were, and House read them. David Lloyd George, the British Prime Minister, refused point blank to accept Point 2 regarding freedom of the seas; the French and Italian leaders concurred. House replied that if his colleagues refused to accept the Fourteen Points the President might feel compelled to lay the matter before the American people and make a separate peace. The following day he reiterated this warning and headed off a whole host of French and Italian objections.

In the face of this threat, the Allied leaders surrendered for the moment, but in return the President agreed that the British might reserve freedom of action on Point 2 and that the Germans should be told they would be required to pay reparations for all civilian damages caused by their aggression. On November 4 the Supreme War Council approved the compromise. The following day Wilson informed the German government that Marshal Foch was ready to receive its representatives. The German delegates met the French Marshal and a British naval representative in Foch's headquarters in a railroad car in Compiègne Forest on November 8; and at 5:15 on the morning of November 11 they signed articles providing for a rapid withdrawal of the German armies beyond the right bank of the Rhine, the surrender of a huge quantity of *matériel* and 150 submarines, and the withdrawal of the German surface fleet to the Baltic.

Thus the end of the war saw no such capitulation of the German forces as the Allied armies could have soon compelled, but rather an agreement by both sides to quit fighting on terms that would prevent Germany from renewing hostilities and, more important, on the basis of a solemn promise by the American and Allied governments that Germany could expect a peace based upon the Fourteen Points, with the two reservations noted.

84 / *Preliminaries to the Peace Conference*

In the months following the Armistice the President would need the full support of the American people if he were to win the peace settlement he had set his heart upon. But he could have overwhelming support at home only if he continued to be the spokesman of the entire country, of Republican moderates as well as Democrats of good will. In this situation, which demanded adroit and national leadership, Wilson not only failed to unite the country but moved from one blunder to another; and when the peace conference opened it was doubtful whether he spoke for a majority of his people.

He made his first mistake even before the guns were silenced on the western front, at the close of the hotly contested off-year congressional campaign. Importuned on all sides by Democratic congressional and senatorial nominees for individual endorsements such as he had given many times before, Wilson decided to issue a blanket appeal to the country. Instead of asking the voters to elect candidates who would support him regardless of party affiliation, he made a frankly partisan appeal for a Democratic Congress on October 25, 1918. "The return of a Republican majority to either House of the Congress," he added, "would . . . certainly be interpreted on the other side of the water as a repudiation of my leadership." It was an invitation to disaster. By attempting to make political capital out of foreign policy, Wilson outraged the numerous Republicans whose support had made his war measures possible and threw the question of the peace settlement into the arena of partisan discussion. Even worse, Wilson had declared that he would stand repudiated in the eyes of the world if the people did not vote the Democratic ticket; he had asked for a vote of confidence when he should have known that such a vote is impossible in the American constitutional system.

The irony is that Wilson's appeal probably had little effect on the outcome of the elections on November 6. Other factors—business resentment against high taxes, the disaffection of the western wheat farmers because the administration had put ceilings on wheat prices and allowed cotton prices to rise uncontrolled, all the large and petty irritations that stemmed from the war, and the normal inclination of a majority to vote Republican—these, rather than Wilson's ill-timed and futile appeal, accounted for the Republican victory.[1] In any event, Wilson now stood repudiated by his own people, as he said he would be if the Republicans won, on the eve of his most important undertaking.

And now we come to that phase of Wilson's career when ordinary historical interpretation fails to yield an understanding of his motivation and actions. After the elections of November 6 he acted as if he were an absolute monarch instead of a President who had to win the approval of two-thirds of the Senate for any peace treaty he might conclude. How can we explain his blindness and folly? Not on grounds of ignorance, for the author of *Congressional Government* assuredly knew the Senate's jealous power in foreign relations. Not on the grounds of ordinary stupidity, for Wilson was obviously intelligent and often an astute political strategist. The only explanation that makes sense is a psychological one. Wilson was temperamentally incapable of working with Republicans because many Republicans, he was sure, had in the past opposed him out of spite and meanness and wanted only to wreck his peace plans. How this conviction governed his future actions will soon become apparent.

On November 18, 1918, Wilson announced that he would go to the peace conference in Paris as head of the American delegation. Believing as he did that only he could prevail against the forces of greed at Paris and that the fate of the liberal international program depended upon his presence at the peace conference, Wilson thought he had no choice in the matter. He went to Paris because stern duty called him there, and whether his decision was a mistake is at least debatable.

Wilson's choice of the peace commissioners, however, was a blunder of the first magnitude. In addition to the President, the commissioners were Colonel House, Secretary of State Lansing, General Tasker H. Bliss, a member of the Supreme War Council, and Henry White, an experienced Republican diplomat. All of them were able men, to be sure, but in the situation more than ability was required. Other considerations aside, political necessity demanded the appointment of a peace commission that was broadly representative, for Wilson would fail in the critical period after the peace conference if he could not command the support of the Senate and a large minority of Republicans. Wilson ignored the Senate because he knew he would have to include Henry Cabot Lodge of Massachusetts if he appointed

---

[1] In the next, or Sixty-Sixth Congress, the Republicans would outnumber the Democrats in the House of Representatives 237 to 190 and have a majority of two in the Senate.

any senators at all, and he thought Lodge was utterly without scruple or character. On the other hand, why Wilson ignored a host of other prominent Republican leaders—men like William H. Taft, Elihu Root, or Charles Evans Hughes, who would have worked loyally with him at Paris—is more difficult to understand. Probably the President was determined to impose his own personal settlement and wanted a compliant, rubber-stamp commission. But by refusing to include prominent Republicans in the commission Wilson offended the great body of moderate Republicans and lent validity to the charge then current that he intended to maintain an exclusive Democratic monopoly on peace-making. It was an inauspicious beginning for one of the most fateful undertakings in American diplomatic history.

85 / *The Versailles Compromise*

On the morning of December 4, 1918, Wilson, the peace commissioners, and a large body of technical experts sailed from New York aboard the *George Washington*. The voyage was a tonic to the President and afforded him an opportunity to reflect soberly on the task ahead. Already he was beginning to think of himself as a Messiah, who would deliver Europe from the tyranny of history. The American delegation, he told the assembled experts on board, would be the only disinterested spokesmen at the conference; the Allied leaders did not even represent their own people. "Tell me what's right and I'll fight for it," he promised.

The situation in Europe did not, however, portend easy sailing for one who wished merely to fight for the right. England was in the throes of a parliamentary campaign that found Lloyd George and his Conservative-dominated coalition obliged to give hostages to the aroused passions of the electorate. The French were in a state of postwar shock and clamoring for fearful retribution. Italians expected compensation for their losses in the form of large accretions of Austrian territory. Behind the lines, Germany was torn by revolt, and the old Austro-Hungarian Empire was crumbling into pieces. Moreover, the meeting place of the Conference, Paris, was a hotbed of anti-German hatred. The crippling terms which the Germans had imposed on the Russians in the treaty of Brest-Litovsk in March 1918 could be used to put aside arguments in favor of greater leniency. At the same time, consideration of long-term issues was handicapped by the immediate fears of the spread of Bolshevism into central and even western Europe.

After making triumphal tours of Paris, London, and Rome, Wilson returned to Versailles on January 12, 1919, for discussions with the Allied leaders, who made plans for the first Plenary Session six days later. So unwieldy was the conference that important questions were referred to a Council of Ten representing Great Britain, France, Italy, the United States, and Japan, while the detail work was divided among sixty commissions on which the small nations were represented. In order to hasten the conference's work, the Council of Ten was abolished on March 24 and the so-called Big Four—Wilson, Lloyd George, Premier Georges Clemenceau of France, and Prime Minister Orlando of Italy—began a long series of private discussions. At the same time, the Council of Five, consisting of the foreign ministers of the five great powers, was established to discuss matters of subordinate importance.

By the end of April 1919 a treaty for Germany had been hammered out and presented to the government of the new German Republic. On May 7 the German Foreign Secretary appeared before a Plenary Session to receive the Treaty; on May 29 the German delegates presented a comprehensive reply; and the German National Assembly at Weimar approved the Treaty on June 23. The formal ceremony of signing was held five days later in the Hall of Mirrors of the Versailles Palace, where the German Empire had been proclaimed forty-eight years before.

This chronology ignores the thousand small details and the writing of the treaties with the other Central Powers. What concerns us most at this point, however, is understanding what Wilson accomplished by his labors at Paris. How did his liberal peace program fare, in spite of the high passions that pervaded the deliberations? The answer is that Wilson accomplished less than he fought for and a great deal more than his critics later admitted. The Versailles Treaty was a compromise between the Fourteen Points and what the Allied, and especially the French, peoples demanded.

The foremost problem before the conference was security against future German aggression in the West. Foch and Clemenceau proposed tearing the west bank of the Rhine from Germany and creating buffer states under French control. With Lloyd George's help, Wilson resisted this demand. Instead, France had to be satisfied with the return of Alsace-Lorraine, which was in accord with the principle of self-determination and the Fourteen Points; with the permanent demilitarization and a fifteen-year occupation by Allied forces of the west bank of the Rhine; and with an Anglo-French-American treaty of mutual defense against Germany. It was this promise of a triple defensive alliance that persuaded Clemenceau to abandon his demand for the creation of buffer states in the Rhineland. Finally, the German army and navy were so severely limited in size that a future German war of aggression was to be impossible. On the whole, Wilson, Lloyd George, and Clemenceau succeeded in erecting an intelligent defensive structure which, if maintained in full vigor, might have preserved the peace of Europe. Certainly it did not violate the Fourteen Points in any important way.

In the second place, Wilson found the spokesmen of Britain, the Dominions, Japan, and Italy determined that Germany should not recover her overseas colonies. In the face of their inflexible position, he gave in, but not without gaining important concessions. For one thing, although Japan received title to German economic rights in the Shantung Province, she promised to return that province to the political control of China. For another, the former German colonies were not awarded outright to new masters but were made mandates of the League of Nations and given in responsible trusteeship to Great Britain, the Dominions, and Japan. Whether this arrangement represented the "absolutely impartial adjustment of all colonial claims" that Wilson had demanded in Point 5 would in large measure depend upon the development of the mandate system.

A third major problem was the creation of a Polish state and the establishment of a Polish-German boundary that would give Poland access to the sea and the Polish provinces of Germany and Austria without violating unduly the principles of self-determination. Standing firm against Clemenceau and the Polish representatives, Wilson and Lloyd George won a settlement that vindicated the liberal program. Poland was given a corridor to the Baltic, and the Port of Danzig was established a free city under the jurisdiction of the League of Nations.

The fourth important issue—how much Austrian territory Italy should receive—involved the validity of the secret Treaty of London of 1915, by which Italy was brought into the war and promised the Trentino, the Austrian Tyrol, and a strip of the Dalmatian coast along the Adriatic. Impressed by the plea that control of the Brenner Pass in the Tyrol was absolutely essential to Italian security, Wilson agreed that this area, which contained 200,000 Germans, should go to Italy. The Italians demanded also a long strip of the Dalmatian coast, including the important Port of Fiume. Arguing that Fiume was the only possible outlet to the sea for the new state of Yugoslavia and pointing out that the Treaty of London had awarded the disputed port to Yugoslavia, Wilson successfully resisted Italian demands.

In the struggle over the fifth great issue, reparations, Wilson made his most disastrous concessions. During the pre-Armistice negotiations he had agreed that Germany should be compelled to pay for all civilian damages incurred by the Allied countries during the war—alone a staggering sum. At the conference, he agreed that Germany should also be forced to bear the cost of separation allowances and pensions for Allied veterans. Although he was ill at the time and acted through Colonel House, the President later approved Article CCXXXI of the Treaty, in which Germany acknowledged responsibility for all losses incurred by the Allied governments and peoples during the war. Wilson agreed, besides, that the Allies might occupy the Rhineland until the potentially astronomical reparations bill was finally paid. Nor was this all. In compensation for the wanton destruction of French mines by the retreating German armies, France was given ownership of the mines in the Saar Province of Germany, and the territory was to be governed by a League of Nations commission for fifteen years. At the end of that period the people of the Saar might vote to join the Fatherland. Finally, the Treaty compelled the Germans to pay to Britain, France, and Belgium an enormous quantity of reparations in kind—merchant shipping, coal, livestock, and the like. Inexplicably, Wilson made hardly any effort to prevent this, the grossest violation of the Fourteen Points and the Pre-Armistice Agreement with Germany.

In Wilson's mind, however, the first, last, and overriding issue was the creation of an international organization to create a concert of world power and preserve the peace. From the outset of the conference he insisted that the Covenant, or constitution, of the League of Nations be firmly embedded in the Treaty and that the execution of the Treaty be entrusted to the League. Clemenceau was not opposed to the League, but he insisted that the organization would be powerless to maintain peace unless it had a powerful army and navy at its command. Convinced such a proposal was politically impossible, Wilson and the British delegates created a League that would depend for its effectiveness upon the wholehearted support of its leading members. As Clemenceau thought he had obtained security for his beloved France by other means, he was willing to let Wilson write any kind of Covenant he desired.

Looking back over his labors at Paris and remembering the tense sessions, the bitter complaints of Orlando, the barbed remarks of Clemenceau, and the compromises that he inevitably had to make, Wilson was none the less certain he had helped to write a Treaty and create a postwar peace structure that would endure. The Treaty was not perfect, he knew; but he was sure time would heal many wounds and that the United States could work successfully within the League for modifications.

Critics, contemporary and historical, have castigated Wilson in general for failing to win the liberal peace program at Paris and in particular for bargaining all his Fourteen Points away in order to win a League of Nations. Such criticism can come only from one who has never bothered to read the Fourteen Points, for actually that document was honored more in the observance than in the breach. Wilson's chief failures—on the colonial question and reparations—were perhaps inevitable; but the damage done was not irreparable, given forceful American leadership in the League of Nations and the Reparations Commission. Nor did Wilson fail to obtain a vindication of the principle of freedom of the seas. This was true because during the conference he finally realized that freedom of the seas was a part of the old system of neutrality and that in future wars neutrality would be impossible.

Wilson's critics, not content with exaggerating his failures, have also minimized his difficulties. He did not write the Treaty alone but in collaboration with three able and determined negotiators. To be sure, Wilson could have withdrawn from the conference, as on one occasion he seriously threatened to do; but the results of American withdrawal would have been even worse than an unsatisfactory settlement. Furthermore, Wilson's difficulties at Paris were compounded by the virulent opposition to his peace program in the United States. Senator Lodge, for example, did not lighten the President's burdens by writing to Clemenceau that Wilson did not speak for the American people, who, Lodge declared, desired a harsh and punitive settlement.

Finally, the historian must ask, what kind of a peace treaty would have been written if Wilson had not been at Paris and had not won British support for most of his principles? Together Wilson and Lloyd George prevented the dismemberment of Germany and compelled a redrawing of the map of Europe that did not unnecessarily violate the principle of self-determination. As the spokesman of the only disinterested nation represented at the conference, Wilson emerged from the fiery trial with the greatest stature because of what he was able to accomplish in spite of stupendous obstacles.

86 / First Phases of the Treaty Fight

Long before the end of the Peace Conference there were signs that Wilson would encounter strong opposition in the Senate if he insisted on incorporating the League Covenant in the Treaty. Returning briefly to Washington in the latter part of February 1919, the President conferred with the members of the House and Senate foreign relations committees in an effort to meet the rising tide of criticism. Many nonisolationist senators, he learned, objected because the Covenant contained no explicit recognition of the Monroe Doctrine, did not specifically exclude internal affairs from the jurisdiction of the League, and made no provision for the right of a member nation to withdraw. On March 4, 1919, just before Wilson was to return to France, moreover, Senator Lodge presented to the upper house a round robin drawn up by Republican leaders warning that the Covenant, "in the form now proposed," was unacceptable. It was signed by thirty-nine senators or senators-elect, considerably more than the one-third plus one necessary to defeat ratification.

Instead of turning the other cheek, Wilson was defiant in response. When he brought the Treaty back with him, he boasted at the Madison Square Garden on March 4, the Covenant would be so embedded in the Treaty that the two could never be separated. Back in Paris, however, Wilson obtained changes in the Covenant to meet the moderate criticisms noted above. Returning to the United States on July 8, he formally presented the Treaty to the Senate two days later. "Our isolation was ended twenty years ago," he declared. ". . . There can be no question of our ceasing to be a world power. The only question is whether we can refuse the moral leadership that is offered, whether we shall accept or reject the confidence of the world."

Wilson spoke confidently of the great new role of "service and achievement" that lay ahead for the American people, whose destiny had been disclosed by the very hand of God. His poetic phrases, however, suggested a unanimity that did not exist. No one could yet say how large a part of the population the critics of the Treaty represented, but by the time Wilson returned to the United States they were already well organized and exceedingly vociferous. Leading the opposition were a small group of extreme isolationists in the Senate, the chief among whom were Hiram W. Johnson of California, William E. Borah of Idaho, and James A. Reed of Missouri. Convinced that membership in the League would violate wise and historic policy, these irreconcilables pledged themselves to the cause of keeping America free from the entanglements of Europe. Although sincere conviction, and not petty hatred of Wilson, caused them to raise the standards of battle, they fought bitterly and unscrupulously. Not truth but misstatements, perversions of fact, and false alarms were their chief weapons.

Perhaps even more bitter in opposition to the Treaty were the so-called hyphenates, their newspapers, and their chief journalistic allies, the Hearst publications. German-Americans protested that the Treaty was a base betrayal of the Pre-Armistice Agreement. Italian-Americans were sulking over Wilson's refusal to award Fiume to Italy. But the most virulent opposition came from the Irish-Americans, who were up in arms because Wilson had refused to press the cause of Irish independence at Versailles or throw the weight of the United States behind the Irish rebellion then in progress.

The opposition of isolationists and hyphenates was powerful, to be sure; but if all Americans who believed in the liberal international program had stood firmly together, the President might yet have triumphed. Unfortunately for the President, such a solid phalanx did not materialize. In the first place, many cautious liberal internationalists—men like Elihu Root and Henry L. Stimson, who put their faith in international law and arbitration—feared Wilson was going too far too fast in breaking with ingrained American traditions. In the second place, many independent progressives and radicals, who had followed Wilson during the war and shared his noble dream of a new world order, drew back in revulsion when the terms of the Treaty were published. "The European politicians who with American complicity have hatched this inhuman monster," exclaimed the *New Republic*, the leading liberal internationalist journal, "have acted either cynically, hypocritically, or vindictively." The *Nation* and other such liberal journals were equally bitter.

The greatest obstacles to ratification of the Treaty, however, were personal and partisan rivalries and prejudices, the ingrained tradition of apartness, and the absence in 1919 and 1920 of any popular conviction that membership in the League was essential to American security. Germany had been decisively beaten and disarmed; Russia was in chaos. No war clouds darkened the horizon; no nation menaced the peace and security of the United States. Men might warn of the perils of the future, but who would believe them when it was obvious there could never be another war?

After Wilson presented the Treaty to the Senate on July 10, the vortex of the struggle over ratification shifted to the upper house, which in the past had upset the plans of less distinguished Presidents than Woodrow Wilson. By midsummer of 1919 a fairly distinct alignment was already evident. There were some twelve to fifteen bitter-end isolationists, who would vote against the Treaty in any form so long as it contained the Covenant. They were a small minority, to be sure, but they dominated the foreign relations committee and were able to influence the committee's chairman, Lodge, by their frequent threats to bolt the Republican camp. On the other hand, at least forty-three of the forty-seven Democrats would follow Wilson's leadership, while the great majority of the forty-nine Republicans favored ratification after making certain reservations to safeguard American interests. Thus considerably more than the necessary two-thirds in the Senate favored ratification of the Treaty and membership in the League. The main task of statesmanship in the months ahead, therefore, would be to find common ground upon which this preponderant majority could stand.

Much, of course, would depend upon the ability of leaders of both parties to suppress partisan ambitions and prejudices and to pull together for the good of the country. The Republican leader in the Senate was Henry Cabot Lodge, a Boston Brahmin, long an intimate of Theodore Roosevelt, and a man of great intellect. Although he had supported a postwar League in 1915 and 1916, Lodge reversed himself after Wilson linked the League plan with the concept of a "peace without victory." Exactly where he stood on the League of Nations in the summer of 1919, however, it is impossible to say. One historian has recently suggested that Lodge was not an irreconcilable but rather that he was intent upon taking leadership in the Treaty struggle out of Wilson's hands and winning credit for ratification for himself and the Republican party.

Lodge's position, admittedly, was extraordinarily difficult. As leader of his party in the Senate he had to preserve some semblance of harmony among the three Republican factions—the irreconcilable isolationists, the so-called "mild reservationists," and the majority who favored strong reservations. Naturally he was buffeted about and appeared all things to all men. But never during the Treaty fight or afterward did he act like a sincere friend of the League or a statesman who had been able to exalt the national interest above his consuming personal hatred of Wilson and the Democratic party. On the contrary, moving from one calculated step to another, he acted as if his chief purpose was to embarrass the President and prevent ratification of the Treaty.

Public sentiment in July 1919 was running so strongly in favor of the Treaty that Lodge knew he could not defeat it outright. Thirty-two state legislatures and thirty-three governors had endorsed the League; leaders of the League to Enforce Peace were now actively campaigning throughout the country in behalf of unconditional ratification; and a poll of the nation's press indicated that an overwhelming majority of newspapers favored American membership in the League. It was evident to the Massachusetts senator, therefore, that he must work indirectly—first, by packing the foreign relations committee with enemies of the League; and second, by appending such strong reservations to the Covenant that the President would refuse to accept them.

Meanwhile, Lodge desperately needed time to allow the opponents of the League to agitate. Time he easily obtained, by reading aloud all of the 264 pages of the Treaty, which consumed two weeks, and then by holding public hearings on the Treaty for another six weeks. In the meantime, the bitter-enders, liberally supplied with funds by the steel manufacturer, Henry C. Frick, and the banker and aluminum monopolist, Andrew W. Mellon, flooded the country with anti-League propaganda.

By September 1919 opponents of the Treaty were gaining momentum. At the same time, a series of convulsive strikes had diverted Wilson's attention and prevented him from giving his customary leadership to the League forces. He had, it is true, appeared before Lodge's committee on August 19 and conferred individually with some twenty Republican senators, most of them "mild reservationists." But the more he conferred with senators the more he realized the situation was passing from his control. Under these circumstances Wilson decided upon bold steps. First, he announced on September 3 that he would not oppose interpretative reservations that did not impair the integrity of the Covenant or require new diplomatic negotiations. Second, he decided to carry his fight for the League to the people. He would purify the wells of public sentiment poisoned by the irreconcilables; he would tell the people the truth about their stake in preserving peace through the League of Nations.

No act of his public career so dramatically demonstrated Wilson's sincerity than his decision to undertake this campaign. His health had been poor since he narrowly escaped a stroke at Paris; he was now weak and exhausted, and his physician warned that a long speaking tour might take his life. He gladly took the risk, however, thinking he could arouse such a ground swell of support for the League that his senatorial opponents could not resist it. For three weeks in September he traveled more than 8,000 miles through the Middle and Far West and delivered some thirty-seven addresses. The strain on his meager physical resources was great, but the total effect of his outpouring to the people of the West was magnificent. And the deeper Wilson moved into the West the larger and more enthusiastic the crowds became. In fact, the irreconcilables were so alarmed by the President's triumphal procession that they sent their two best speakers, Senators Johnson and Borah, to trail him.

The effects of the strain began to tell on Wilson before the tour was half over. He began to have blinding headaches and to show signs of exhaustion. On September 25 he delivered one of his longest and most important speeches at Pueblo, Colorado. "It always seems to make it difficult for me to say anything, my fellow citizens, when I think of my clients in this case," he exclaimed with tears in his eyes. "My clients are the children; my clients are the next generation. . . . I intend to redeem my pledges to the children; they shall not be sent . . . [to France]." After this address the President was so near collapse that his physician canceled the remaining speeches and sped the presidential train straight to Washington. On October 2, 1919, Wilson suffered a stroke that paralyzed the left side of his face and body, and for days his life hung in a precarious balance.

87 / *The Triumph of Partisanship*

Meanwhile, the battle in the Senate had begun when the foreign relations committee reported the Treaty on September 10, 1919, with forty-five amendments and four reservations. With the help of some twelve Republican "mild reservationists," the Democrats defeated all the amendments, whereupon Lodge, on November 6, presented for his committee a series of fourteen reservations. Most of them merely underlined existing provisions of the Covenant and provided that the United States could take no action in important matters without the consent of Congress. The fourth reservation reserved control over all domestic affairs exclusively to the United States; the fifth removed all questions arising under the Monroe Doctrine from the jurisdiction of the League; the sixth declared that the United States withheld assent from the articles of the Treaty relating to Shantung. The most important reservation, however, was the second, which had been suggested by Elihu Root on June 21, 1919. It asserted that the United States assumed no obligations under Article X of the Covenant to preserve the territorial integrity or political independence of any country, to interfere in controversies between nations, or to use its armed forces to uphold any article of the Treaty for any purpose, unless Congress by joint resolution so provided. After a bitter partisan battle, the Senate approved twelve of Lodge's reservations and added two others.

The next move was up to the ailing President and his Democratic colleagues in the Senate. Colonel House and other friends of the League begged the President either to compromise on Lodge's terms or else to accept the senator's reservations entirely, if that were necessary to get the United States into the League. But when Gilbert M. Hitchcock of Nebraska, Democratic leader in the Senate, was allowed to visit Wilson in his sickroom on November 7 and 17, he found the President determined never to surrender and disposed to compromise only on his own terms—by accepting reservations that he thought did not impair the obligations of the United States under the Covenant. On November 18, furthermore, in a public letter to Hitchcock, Wilson declared that the Lodge reservations provided for nullification, not ratification, of the Treaty; and he virtually ordered Democratic senators to vote against Lodge's reservations.

The first showdown came the following day, November 19, 1919, when the Senate voted on the Treaty. On a resolution to ratify with the Lodge reservations, the irreconcilables combined with a nearly solid Democratic phalanx to defeat ratification by a vote of thirty-nine ayes to fifty-five nays. Immediately afterward, a Democratic resolution to ratify without any reservations failed by a vote of thirty-eight ayes to fifty-three nays. Obviously, Wilson's strategy of splitting the "mild reservationists" from the Republican bloc had failed.

Yet it was apparent from the two test votes that seventy-seven senators, considerably more than the necessary two-thirds, favored ratification and joining the League, with or without reservations. What chance was there for compromise between the two factions? After the first Senate vote it was clear that Lodge would never surrender and that if Wilson wanted ratification he would have to compromise largely on the senator's terms. Colonel House advised the President to wash his hands of responsibility and let the Senate decide; but House was now *persona non grata* at the White House, and his letters were not even acknowledged. William J. Bryan urged immediate ratification, even with reservations, and most Democratic senators privately agreed. The French and British leaders were, if anything, more frightened by the prospect of the Treaty's defeat than were Wilson's friends. The British government sent Sir Edward Grey, former Foreign Secretary, as a special Ambassador to Washington to plead for compromise. The President, however, refused to see Grey and was outraged when Grey later issued a public statement declaring that the League would fail without the United States and that the Allies would accept the Lodge reservations without requiring a reopening of negotiations.

Public sentiment in the United States, moreover, refused to accept the Senate's vote on November 19, 1919, as final. The leaders of the League to Enforce Peace, now called the League of Free Nations Association, appealed for ratification with necessary reservations; newspaper spokesmen were up in arms. On January 13 and February 9, 1920, the representatives of twenty-six organizations representing some 20,000,000 members demanded that Lodge and Wilson compromise their differences. But the aged and weary man in the White House paid scant heed to this ground swell, if, indeed, his wife and physician told him of it. As the days passed he grew more bitter and all the more determined to accept defeat of the Treaty rather than surrender. In a public letter to the Democrats assembled at a Jackson Day Dinner in Washington on January 8, 1920, he gave his answer to friends and foes. He was certain, Wilson asserted, that the overwhelming majority of Americans desired prompt ratification without crippling reservations. If, however, the Senate refused thus to ratify, then the presidential election of 1920 would be a "great and solemn referendum" in which the voters could decide the issue.

In the face of what seemed to be an overwhelming demand at home and abroad for ratification, the Senate agreed to reconsider and began debate anew in mid-February 1920. While Democratic leaders in the Senate tried desperately to find common ground with the Republicans, the President, now vastly improved in health and mental vigor, loosed blast after blast at the Lodge reservations and even intimated that he would refuse to proclaim the Treaty if the Senate adopted them. The Treaty came up for vote on March 19. One reservation, favoring Irish independence, had been added by the Democrats in an effort to embarrass Lodge, while the second reservation regarding Article X had been made even more sweeping than before.

Practically all Democratic senators desperately wanted to accept the reservations, but a majority of them were literally too afraid of Wilson to oppose him; and twenty-three Democrats joined the irreconcilables to defeat approval by a vote of forty-nine ayes to thirty-five nays. A change of only seven Democratic votes would have put the United States in the League of Nations! To end the state of hostilities, Congress, on May 15, 1920, adopted a joint resolution repealing the war resolutions against Germany and Austria-Hungary and reserving to the United States all rights under the Treaty of Versailles. Declaring he would not be party "to an action which would place ineffable stain upon the gallantry and honor of the United States," Wilson vetoed the resolution on May 27.

It was the end, although the tragedy was prolonged during the "great and solemn referendum" that was no referendum at all. Who was responsible for American refusal to enter the League of Nations and for the "ineffable stain" of a separate peace? Certainly Lodge and his Republican friends must share a large measure of the guilt for one of the most tragic episodes in American history. Had they been less interested in the election of 1920 and more concerned with their country's good, they would have suppressed personal and partisan ambitions and met the champions of the League half way. In addition, the irreconcilables, who used every device to defeat ratification, must share a large part of the guilt, for their unscrupulous propaganda helped confuse the public as to the implications of American membership in the League.

On the other hand, what shall we say of Wilson's conduct in this, his greatest and most fateful battle? Because of his consuming hatred of Lodge he, too, refused to compromise; he ignored the advice of his best counselors and threw away the only possible chance for ratification. He, therefore, shared with Lodge and other Republicans responsibility for breaking the heart of the world. Moreover, those Democratic senators who voted against ratification with reservations out of fear of the Wilsonian wrath served neither the national interest nor the cause of international peace.

Whatever the causes for the great betrayal of 1919–1920, the consequences remained. The American people were perhaps not yet ready to assume leadership in world affairs, but their leaders denied them an opportunity even to learn the duties of leadership or to grow in wisdom and experience. More important were the catastrophic effects of the American rejection on the infant League and upon the future development of European politics. Given American leadership in the postwar era, the League might have developed into the association of free peoples of which its founders had dreamed, and become more efficient in dealing with the maladjustment of European society.

CHAPTER 11 / *DEMOBILIZATION AND THE TRIUMPH OF NORMALCY, 1918–1923*

*A*LL postwar periods in American history have been times when partisanship runs at fever pitch and passions generated by the war drive the people to acts of violence. So it was during the years following the Armistice, as the war hysteria found new victims in "Reds," foreigners, Jews, Negroes, and Catholics. As if further to confuse the domestic scene, labor unrest during 1919 and 1920 was at its highest peak since the 1890's, as labor leaders faced the postwar future determined to launch grandiose plans for industrial reorganization. On the other hand, employers in many areas were determined to recover the ground they had lost and to restore their exclusive control over labor policies.

Politically, the postwar era was marked by extraordinary partisanship. Centering at first on the struggle over ratification of the Versailles Treaty, this partisan conflict culminated in 1920, when a reunited Republican party smashed the old progressive coalition and swept into control of the federal government. The election results were convincing evidence that the people were determined to put an end to the division of control in the federal government and to return, as the Republican candidate in 1920 said, to "normalcy," to the good days of prosperity and peace.

88 / *Demobilization, 1918–1920*

Just as it had adopted the war resolution without any effective preparation for a great war effort, the American government found itself on November 11, 1918, without any plan for facing the demobilization and reconstruction that lay ahead. Indeed, the sudden and unexpected German collapse came at a time when American leaders were planning, not for peace, but for an invasion of Germany in 1919.

In his Annual Message to Congress in December 1918, the President aptly described the manner in which demobilization took place: "The moment we knew the armistice to have been signed we took the harness off."

And that is about what happened. The A.E.F. was brought home and quickly broken up. At the same time, the various war agencies began to wind up their affairs. For example, the War Industries Board, refusing to believe there were any problems of demobilization that the business world could not solve, abandoned its control of industry once the fighting stopped. "The magnificent war formation of American industry was dissipated in a day," writes the Board's chief historian.

The truth was that the President and his leaders in Congress expected the country to return quickly to normal without the benefit of governmental controls and planning. However, by the time Wilson returned from Paris for the first time in February 1919, prices were rising so fast that either large scale unemployment or an outbreak of industrial conflict was inevitable. Unable to obtain legislation from the lame-duck session, Wilson prepared for the impending crisis as best he could. Calling governors and mayors to the White House on March 3, he warned them of the dangers ahead. In addition, he established an Industrial Board to coordinate the various purchasing agencies of the government in an effort to hold down prices. The Industrial Board, however, had neither statutory authority nor prestige in the business world; it disbanded in May 1919, after the Railroad Administration refused to permit it to fix prices for steel.

For the most part, therefore, the administration was powerless to meet the larger problems of postwar inflation, business readjustment, and industrial conflict. On the other hand, the period 1919–1920 was not as chaotic or unproductive as this generalization might suggest. For one thing, there were specific problems of demobilization so urgent that Congress could not ignore them. For another, the last two years of the Wilson era witnessed the adoption by Congress of significant measures that brought several phases of the progressive movement to final culmination.

The first requirement was the most urgent—to provide the government with funds to liquidate the war effort at home, to care for wounded soldiers and sailors, to bring the A.E.F. back from France, and to provide relief for Europe. In spite of demands for immediate tax reduction, the lame-duck session courageously adopted a War Revenue bill in February 1919 that increased the tax burden, especially on business and the upper classes.[1]

The second problem involved the disposition of the railroads, which were still under the control of the Railroad Administration at the beginning of 1919. While McAdoo recommended a five-year experiment in public operation and Congress deliberated during the summer of 1919, a movement for nationalization gained the support of AF of L unions and the railroad brotherhoods. It was the so-called Plumb Plan, suggested by Glenn E. Plumb, a lawyer for the brotherhoods, to nationalize the railroads and give the workers a share in their management and profit. Wilson took no part in the controversy; he simply announced on December 24, 1919, that unless Congress decided otherwise he would return the railroads to their owners on March 1, 1920.

Congress responded with the Transportation Act of 1920, drawn largely

---

[1] For the provisions of this measure see above, p. 206.

by two midwestern progressive Republicans, Representative John J. Esch of Wisconsin and Senator Albert B. Cummins of Iowa, and approved February 28, 1920. Perhaps the most significant measure of the postwar era, the Transportation Act marked the complete fulfillment of the movement for thoroughgoing federal control of railroads. Stopping only short of nationalization, the Act gave the ICC complete control over rates, even those set by state commissions; authorized the Commission to supervise the sale of railroad securities and the expenditure of the proceeds; permitted railroads to pool traffic in the interest of economy; and empowered the ICC to consolidate existing lines into a limited number of systems. The measure constituted a thoroughly progressive solution of a difficult problem.

The third issue of demobilization was the disposition of the huge fleet of merchant vessels that the Shipping Board had purchased, confiscated, or built during and after the war. No one wanted to junk a merchant marine that totaled some 15,000,000 tons by 1920; yet Congress was unwilling to embark upon a long-range program of public operation. A compromise solution was embodied in the Merchant Marine Act of 1920, which directed the Shipping Board to sell as many vessels as possible to corporations of predominantly American ownership and authorized the federally owned Merchant Fleet Corporation to open new shipping lines and operate surplus vessels. As it turned out, the Shipping Board's low prices on easy terms and guarantees against operational losses to private firms lured considerable private capital into the shipping industry and kept a sizable merchant marine afloat in the 1920's. By the end of 1930 the privately owned American merchant marine totaled over 7,000,000 tons.

Four measures—the General Leasing and Water Power acts of 1920 and the women's suffrage and prohibition amendments—rounded out the postwar legislative program, brought several phases of the progressive movement to culmination, and revealed that the reform spirit was by no means dead. The General Leasing Act kept large naval oil reserves from private exploitation but empowered the Secretary of the Interior to lease other public lands containing mineral and oil deposits to private parties on terms that safeguarded the public interest. The Water Power Act established a Federal Power Commission, composed of the Secretaries of War, the Interior, and Agriculture, to license the building and operation of dams and hydroelectric plants on navigable rivers and nonnavigable streams in the public domain. Although experience proved that effective federal control of electric rates and services was almost impossible under this legislation, it was significant as the beginning of federal regulation of the expanding electric power industry.

We will reserve our discussion of national prohibition for a later chapter. The point here is, however, that Congress acted promptly and, it thought, effectively in the postwar period to implement what many progressives hailed as the greatest triumph for morality since the abolition of slavery. Another important objective of the progressive movement, women's suffrage, also came to fulfillment in the postwar years. In June 1919 Congress approved the Nineteenth Amendment, which forbade denying the right to vote on account of sex, and the thirty-sixth state ratified it in August 1920.

89 / *Postwar Inflation and Labor Troubles*

During the early months of 1919, leaders in Washington and the states prepared clumsily to cope with the mass unemployment they were certain would follow in the wake of demobilization of the armed forces and a sudden ending of war production. The crisis they anticipated never came. To be sure, industrial production declined slightly from October 1918 to July 1919, and unemployment reached a level of 3,000,000 in February 1919; but at no time during the months immediately following the Armistice were there any signs of acute economic distress. Then, during the summer of 1919 a boom got under way, and by the following October industrial production was well above the wartime peak.

A number of forces—among them being continued heavy governmental spending, the release of pent-up consumer demand and savings, a rapid resumption of industrial and home construction, increased production in the automobile industry, and a continuation of exports financed in part by American loans to the Allied governments—contributed to the postwar boom. In the face of what seemed to be an insatiable demand, prices began to rise in the spring of 1919 and continued to mount until the autumn of 1920. Prices of manufactured goods rose from 198.4 in 1918 (100 representing average prices in 1913) to 239.5 in 1920, while prices of processed farm products increased from 201.1 to 241.9 during the same period. To put it more comprehensively, the cost of living rose to 77 per cent above the prewar level in 1919 and to 105 per cent above the prewar level in 1920.

The postwar inflation most adversely affected public employees, white collar workers, and persons living on fixed incomes; but its chief significance lay in the fact that it combined with other forces to set off an unprecedented outbreak of labor troubles. All told, during 1919 there were 2,665 strikes involving more than 4,000,000 workers, as organized labor fought to preserve wartime gains and embarked upon ambitious new projects of unionization.

The wave of strikes began four days after the Armistice, when the Amalgamated Clothing Workers in New York and Chicago struck for the forty-four-hour week and a 15 per cent wage increase. Victory for the union was followed by the adoption of the new wage and hours scale in the entire clothing industry. Then followed in rapid succession strikes by textile workers in New England and New Jersey, a general strike in Seattle, strikes by New England telephone operators and by telegraph operators throughout the country, by the printers' union, the longshoremen of New York, and switchmen in the Chicago railroad yards. Practically all these strikes, and hundreds of others, succeeded, and organized labor was able not only to hold its own against rising prices but also to win an increase in real income.

This outbreak of industrial unrest, however, occurred at a time when the American people were disturbed by a new hysteria—the so-called "Red" scare. Most of the strikes of 1919 were waged successfully in spite of a growing popular suspicion that they were being provoked by Communist agents and would culminate in a general labor uprising. On the other hand, organized labor's most important effort in 1919, the AF of L's drive to estab- iish collective bargaining in the steel industry, ran afoul the "Red" hysteria.

Since 1901 the United States Steel Corporation had stood as the chief barrier to unionization of the steel industry and many other basic industries as well. Encouraged by the friendly attitude of federal authorities and what they thought was a sympathetic public opinion, the AF of L convention, in June 1918, directed its executive committee to undertake "one mighty drive to organize the steel plants of America"—the first attack in a general offensive against the mass industries. On August 1 the union's president, Samuel Gompers, appointed a National Committee for the Organizing of the Iron and Steel Industry, with William Z. Foster, a left-wing syndicalist, as secretary.

All during the autumn and winter of 1918 and 1919 Foster and his committee organized the steel workers, and by June 1919 the reorganized steel workers' union claimed a membership of 100,000 and was ready to test its strength in battle. Although the union included a minority of the steel workers, no impartial observer could doubt that it voiced the protests of the overwhelming majority against old and rankling grievances. Steel workers everywhere lived under the tyranny of petty bosses, and even mild complaints often brought prompt dismissal. Moreover, about half the iron and steel employees worked from eleven to fourteen hours a day, an addi- tional quarter worked between ten to twelve hours daily, while a minority worked twenty-four hours a day every other Sunday.[2] In spite of long hours, wage rates were so low in 1919 that 60 per cent of all steel workers and their families lived below or barely above a minimum subsistence level.

In August 1919 union officials presented their demands—recognition, the eight-hour day, "an American living wage," and reinstatement of work- ers discharged for union activities—to Judge Elbert H. Gary, head of United States Steel. When Gary refused to negotiate, some 343,000 workers in the plants of United States Steel went on strike on September 22; and three days later the walkout spread to plants of Bethlehem Steel. The ensuing struggle was marked by widespread violence in which eighteen strikers were killed, the use of state and federal troops to prevent picketing, and stern suppres- sion of civil liberties in all the strike districts except West Virginia. Perhaps the most significant aspect of the conflict was management's use of new propaganda techniques learned during the war. By raising and reiterating the false alarm of Bolshevism, management and the vast majority of news- papers diverted public attention away from the workers' grievances to the false issue of communism. The result was that in this most crucial battle the workers lost the support of public opinion.

With a large segment of public opinion and most state officials arrayed against them, the strikers could not win, for the steel companies had emerged from the war with full treasuries and resources adequate for a long struggle. The first break came when United States Steel officials imported tens of thousands of strikebreakers and put them to work under military guard. By November, for example, the large United States Steel works at Gary, Indiana,

[2] The average work week in the steel industry in 1919 was 68.7 hours, as compared with a work week of 67.6 hours in 1910.

were operating at 75 per cent capacity. The struggle dragged on into January 1920, when it was officially ended by the unconditional surrender and submission of the AF of L.

While the steel strike was getting under way, there occurred in Boston a police strike that gave further evidence of deep social unrest and incidentally catapulted an obscure Governor of Massachusetts into the presidency of the United States. Like most other public employees during the postwar inflation, the police of Boston were struggling to survive on prewar salaries. When the police authorities refused to raise wages and correct other grievances, the policemen's organization, the Boston Social Club, obtained a charter as an AF of L local in August 1919 and threatened to strike. A hastily appointed Mayor's Citizens' Committee was conciliatory and proposed a settlement that would have granted most of the union's demands, except recognition. The Police Commissioner, however, not only rejected the proposed settlement but also summarily dismissed nineteen leaders of the local.

Thus goaded, the policemen abandoned their posts on September 9, 1919. When a volunteer force of prominent citizens and Harvard students were unable to control the gangs of looters that menaced the city, Governor Calvin Coolidge called out the Boston companies of the National Guard and took personal command. The strike was quickly broken; the rebel policemen were dismissed; and a new police force was assembled. And when Gompers appealed to Coolidge to persuade the Boston authorities to reinstate the strikers, the Governor replied with a cryptic rebuke that made him at once nationally famous: "There is no right to strike against the public safety by anybody, anywhere, any time."

The last important strike of the immediate postwar era, the short-lived bituminous coal strike of November 1919, was notable in that it provoked the first test of strength between the federal government and the new president of the United Mine Workers of America, John L. Lewis. Of all workers in the country, the bituminous miners probably had the best grounds for discontent. In August 1917 the UMW had concluded a no-strike agreement —the so-called Washington Agreement—with the Fuel Administration. Although the anthracite miners later received substantial wage increases, the bituminous miners received none after August 1917. After the Armistice the UMW contended that the Washington Agreement was dead; government spokesmen, on the other hand, pointed to the fact that the Agreement would not expire until March 31, 1920.

As prices continued to soar after the Armistice, agitation among the bituminous miners mounted in the spring and summer of 1919, and it was only by extreme threats that UMW officials ended an insurgent strike in the Illinois district in August. When the UMW met in national convention in Indianapolis the following month, bituminous miners throughout the country were on the verge of rebellion. Their representatives at Indianapolis adopted a bold program demanding immediate abrogation of the Washington Agreement, a six-hour day and five-day week, and wage increases of 60 per cent. And when the operators refused to negotiate until the Washington Agreement had expired, Lewis called a nation-wide bituminous strike for November 1. Meanwhile, Wilson's Attorney General, A. Mitchell Palmer, had tried vainly to persuade the UMW to cancel the strike order, which, he claimed, was in violation of the Lever Act.

Faced with a complete shutdown of the mines, Palmer obtained one injunction on November 8 from the federal district court in Indianapolis ordering Lewis and other UMW officials to cease all strike activity and another injunction soon afterward commanding the union officials to cancel the strike order by November 10. "We cannot fight the government," Lewis declared as he called off the strike. None the less, the miners refused to go back to work until the government, a month later, ordered an immediate 14 per cent wage increase and established an arbitration commission to consider the union's demands. After extended hearings, the commission awarded the miners another 27 per cent increase in pay, without changing the hours of work.

90 / The First Red Scare

The triumph and establishment of the Bolshevik dictatorship in Russia in November 1917, the ensuing spread of communism into Germany, Hungary, and other parts of Europe, and especially the formation in Moscow on March 2, 1919, of the Third International, or Comintern, as it came to be known, dedicated to stimulating an immediate world proletarian revolution, set off a wave of new hysteria in the United States. No other development of the postwar era so well reflected the insecurity of the American people as the way in which they reacted to fantastic rumors of an equally fantastic Bolshevik uprising in their midst.

An early sign of the excited state of public opinion was the trial of Victor Berger, Socialist congressman from Milwaukee, for conspiracy under the Sedition Act. Re-elected to the House in November 1918 after his indictment, Berger was tried in Chicago in the following December, convicted, and sentenced to prison for twenty years. He was released on bail pending appeal, but denied his seat in the lower house when Congress met in special session in May 1919. Re-elected in a special election, Berger was again denied his seat in January 1920.

Berger's conviction was the first manifestation of the postwar hysteria that developed during the following months into the first Red scare. Perhaps the story can best be told by a narration of the events that set off the scare. On February 6, 1919, workers in Seattle, Washington, staged a general strike that brought industry to a standstill and seriously crippled operation of utilities and transportation services. Asserting that the strike was the work of Bolsheviks and the IWW, Mayor Ole Hanson warned the country that the Seattle general strike was the beginning of a workers' uprising. At the same time, committees of the United States Senate and the New York legislature began investigations of Bolshevik activities, while on February 11 the Justice Department rounded up fifty-three alien Communists on the West Coast and shipped them to New York for deportation. A week later a naturalized citizen was quickly acquitted in Indiana for killing an alien who had shouted, "To hell with the United States!"

The climax came in April 1919, with the discovery of a plot to assassinate governors, judges, Cabinet members, and other public officials. On April 28 a large bomb was found in Mayor Hanson's mail; the following day the Negro maid of Senator Thomas W. Hardwick of Georgia opened a package in the senator's Atlanta home and had her hands blown off. Immediate investigation in the New York Post Office uncovered sixteen bomb packages addressed to such persons as Attorney General Palmer, Postmaster General Burleson, Justice Oliver Wendell Holmes, J. P. Morgan, and John D. Rockefeller. Some twenty other missiles were discovered elsewhere in the mails. Although this plot failed, the residences of Attorney General Palmer and two judges were partially destroyed by bombs later in the spring.[3]

Popular retaliation against the April bomb plot came quickly and indiscriminately. The California legislature outlawed membership in organizations that advocated use of violence. In the wake of the investigations of its Lusk Committee, the New York legislature enacted similar, if less drastic, legislation.[4] On May 1, 1919, a group of some four hundred soldiers and sailors invaded the offices of the New York *Call*, a Socialist daily, and beat up several May Day celebrants. And in other parts of New York and in Boston and Cleveland there were clashes between May Day paraders and servicemen and police. The most serious outbreak occurred in the lumber town of Centralia, Washington, on the following Armistice Day. Members of the newly organized American Legion attacked the local headquarters of the IWW, and four of the attackers were killed in the ensuing fracas. In swift reprisal, enraged townspeople lynched one of the defenders; police officials raided IWW headquarters throughout the state, arresting more than one thousand leaders of the union; and soon afterward eleven IWW members involved in the Centralia affair were convicted of murder and sentenced to long prison terms.

Scare headlines and sensational newspaper reports magnified these events and stimulated a widespread public alarm.[5] What basis was there for such panic? Was there any likelihood of a proletarian revolution in the United States in 1919? The answer is clear: Never was a great nation so afraid of phantom invaders and so agitated by groundless fears.

To be sure, there was widespread labor unrest during 1919. But there was no evidence of any important Communist infiltration of labor unions, and all the great strikes of 1919–1920, except perhaps the Seattle general strike, were caused by the usual grievances. The end of wartime restraints saw a revival of the radical press, but as always these sheets spoke for an infinitesimal fraction of the people. In the Northwest and along the Pacific

---

[3] The worst outrage, incidentally, occurred more than a year later, in September 1920, when a wagonload of explosives was set off in front of the offices of J. P. Morgan & Company in New York City. Thirty-eight people were killed, more than 200 were injured, and property damage ran to more than $2,000,000.

[4] Vetoed by Governor Alfred E. Smith, the New York anti-Communist bill was re-enacted and signed by Smith's Republican successor in 1921.

[5] One good index of the state of public opinion was the adoption by state legislatures in 1919 and 1920 of laws outlawing display of the Red flag, prohibiting membership in organizations that advocated the violent overthrow of the government, and forbidding seditious utterances. During 1919 thirty-four states and two territories enacted such statutes; in 1920 two states adopted such legislation.

Coast the IWW struggled for rebirth through One Big Union. And in the large cities there were a few anarchists, some of whom probably perpetrated the bomb outrages. These disparate and fractional groups offered no threat to the public safety that ordinary law enforcement agencies could not control.

Any threat to the established order, therefore, would have to come from the newly organized Communist parties, the alleged spearheads of the revolution. What was the situation here? Shattered by internal dissensions, the Socialist party met in emergency convention in Chicago on August 30, 1919, to take stock and reform ranks. Under Victor Berger's leadership, the moderates controlled the convention, and the left-wingers withdrew. Rebuffed by the Communists, the left-wing Socialists formed the Communist Labor party on August 31. A day later, on September 1, 1919, other left-wing groups met in Chicago and organized the Communist Party of America. By the end of 1919 the Socialist party had a membership of 39,000, the Communist party, between 30,000 and 60,000, and the Communist Labor party, between 10,000 and 30,000—at most not more than two-tenths of 1 per cent of the population.

In view of the weakness of the parties of the Left, the danger of social upheaval in 1919 seems exceedingly remote. The Wilson administration, however, acted as if the menace were dire and launched such a campaign against civil liberties as the country had not witnessed in peacetime since 1799. Leadership was taken by the Attorney General, A. Mitchell Palmer of Pennsylvania, who thought he had a good chance to become the next resident of the White House. Palmer not only set the entire Federal Bureau of Investigation to work ferreting out Communists and boring into their organizations; he also reported to Congress on radical activities and urged the adoption of a measure that went so far as to punish persons guilty even of inciting sedition.

When Congress refused to enact Palmer's sedition bill, the Attorney General undertook his own private campaign to purge the country. The Labor Department had rounded up some 249 known Russian Communists and shipped them to Finland, on December 21, 1919. But Palmer was after bigger game. Without informing the Secretary or Assistant Secretary of Labor of his plan, Palmer obtained warrants for the arrest of some three thousand alien members of the Communist and Communist Labor parties from an agent in the Labor Department. On New Year's Day, 1920, thousands of federal agents and local police executed a gigantic simultaneous raid on Communist headquarters throughout the country. Some six thousand persons, many of them non-Communists and American citizens, fell into the net and were hurried off to jails and bull pens. In Hartford, Connecticut, persons visiting prisoners were arrested on the ground that they, too, must be Communists.

Eventually, one-third of the victims were released for lack of evidence. American citizens suspected of membership in a Communist party were turned over to local authorities for indictment and prosecution under state syndicalism laws. But for the aliens it was a different story. Outraged by Palmer's procedure, Secretary of Labor William B. Wilson, a stout Scotch-

Irish Presbyterian, took charge of the deportation proceedings and saw that justice was done. Only 556 aliens, all of them proved members of the Communist party, were deported.

Although Palmer continued to warn of gigantic Red plots, he executed no more raids. The scene now shifted to the states, with the investigations by the Lusk Committee of the New York legislature and the subsequent expulsion of five Socialist members of the New York Assembly for no crime except membership in the Socialist party; with the arrest and conviction of two Massachusetts anarchists, Nicola Sacco and Bartolomeo Vanzetti, for the alleged murder of a paymaster in a South Braintree shoe factory; and with the growth everywhere of demands for conformity. As we will see in a later chapter, the postwar era bequeathed to the 1920's a heritage of hatred and hysteria that permeated and disturbed every aspect of life and thought.

91 / Troubled Race Relations

This summer of the first Red scare was also a time of tribulation for American Negroes, as postwar intolerances found yet other victims and another form of expression. Tensions generated by the migration of Negroes northward and by large-scale Negro participation in the war burst into the most awful outbreak of interracial warfare in the history of the United States. What were the causes for this unrest on America's most troubled social frontier?

To begin with, a decline in immigration from a little over 1,218,000 in 1914 to 327,000 in 1915 created a scarcity of unskilled labor in the North and stimulated the first large-scale migration of Negroes from the southern countryside to northern and midwestern industrial centers. This stream of black workers swelled in response to increased demands in 1917 and 1918. The several hundred thousand Negroes who went to the North found no warm welcome awaiting them. Forced to crowd into the worst areas, they became the object of the suspicion and hatred of white unskilled workers, most of them immigrants themselves, who resented Negro competition and *mores*.

At the same time, Negro-white relations were considerably worsened by the Negroes' participation in the war. Some 400,000 Negroes served in the armed forces, about half of them overseas, where they were accorded an equality they had never known in their native South. Terrified at the thought of so many Negro men learning the use of firearms and the ways of equality, white Southerners were prepared in 1919 to use the rope and the faggot to remind returning Negro veterans that the Great Crusade was no war for racial democracy in the South.

Thirdly, while the war heightened anti-Negro sentiments North and South, the Negro people of America and their spokesmen were beginning to demand higher wages, immunity from acts of violence, and larger participation in politics. Now under the control of the militant element, the National Association for the Advancement of Colored People was especially active during the war; and during the Peace Conference the NAACP's leader, William E. B. Du Bois, convoked a Pan-African Congress in Paris to speak for Negroes throughout the world.

In the South these tensions burst into wholesale violence as southern white men resorted to traditional weapons to purge the Negro communities. Lynchings increased from thirty-four in 1917 to sixty in 1918, and to more than seventy in 1919. Ten Negro veterans, several of them still in uniform, were lynched in 1919; fourteen Negroes were burned publicly. Southern white terrorism, however, found expression in a form more ominous than these individual acts of violence—in the rapid spread, especially through the Southwest, of the newly revived Ku Klux Klan. During 1919 the Klan grew from insignificance into a thriving organization of more than 100,000 members with cells in twenty-seven states. Defying law enforcement officials, hooded Klan night-riders flogged, tarred, and hanged their victims in many southern and southwestern communities.

Even worse travail awaited Negro Americans, in the outbreak of the most fearful race riots in American history. The riots began in July 1919 in Longview, Texas, and spread a week later to the nation's capital, where mobs composed principally of white servicemen pillaged the Negro section. The worst riot, however, began in Chicago on July 27, 1919, after an altercation between whites and Negroes on a Lake Michigan beach. For thirteen days mobs roamed the slum areas of the city, burning, pillaging, and killing, with the National Guard unable to subdue them. When it was over fifteen whites and twenty-three Negroes were dead; 178 whites and 342 Negroes were injured; and more than 1,000 families were homeless. During the next two months major riots broke out in Knoxville, Omaha, and Elaine, Arkansas, and by the end of 1919 the final reckoning revealed some twenty-five riots, with hundreds dead and injured and property damages running into the millions.

Negroes and liberal whites were dismayed and reacted in varied ways. The NAACP and other militant Negro groups counseled resistance and undertook in 1919 a campaign against lynching that culminated in the passage by the House of Representatives of the first anti-lynching bill in 1921. Endorsed by twenty-four governors and an overwhelming northern opinion, this measure was defeated by a southern filibuster in the Senate. In the South the most significant reaction was the final awakening of the southern conscience and the organization in Atlanta in 1919 of the Commission on Interracial Cooperation, which became the spearhead of a growing southern liberal movement in the 1920's and 1930's.

The mass of Negroes, however, were not inspired by anti-lynching campaigns or encouraged by the beginning of an organized southern effort to combat racial intolerance. They were simply overwhelmed by the events of 1919 and ready to follow any leader who promised escape. Such a Moses was Marcus Garvey, a Jamaican, who organized his Universal Negro Improvement Association in 1914 and who moved to New York City two years later. A chauvinist and a charlatan, Garvey appealed to Negroes to take pride in their allegedly superior race and culture and to follow him back to Africa, there to erect a "free, redeemed and mighty nation." In the racial upheaval of the postwar years, Garvey's schemes stimulated visions of a grand new destiny in the minds of countless Negroes. Claiming 4,000,000 followers in 1920 and 6,000,000 in 1923, Garvey proclaimed himself provisional president of an African Empire in 1921 and raised funds to buy a Black Star steamship line and carry his people home. The empire crumbled in 1923, however, when the black Moses was convicted in federal court on charges of using the mails to defraud and sentenced to the Atlanta penitentiary for a five-year term. American Negroes, obviously, would not go back to Africa, but the manner in which so many of them rallied to Garvey's standard was vivid illustration of their feeling of hopelessness.

92 / The Election of 1920

During this season of social conflict and racial unrest the politicians began their quadrennial preparations for the coming presidential campaign. As it was obvious by the beginning of 1920 that any passable Republican candidate would win the presidency, there was much activity in the GOP camp. Absent or in retirement, however, were the commanding figures who had led the party since 1900. Theodore Roosevelt, who might have had the nomination by default, had died on January 6, 1919. Charles Evans Hughes, the party's nominee in 1916, adamantly refused to run and would not even participate in the national convention.

Into the fight for leadership, therefore, rushed a number of lesser dignitaries. General Leonard Wood, who inherited most of Roosevelt's following, made the most formidable campaign for the Republican nomination. Wood was forthrightly independent of the party bosses, intensely nationalistic, and a champion of universal military training. Nearly as popular was Frank O. Lowden, former congressman and Governor of Illinois in 1920, who had the support of the business and farm interests of the Middle West. On the periphery were Senator Hiram Johnson of California, vainly trying to rally the old insurgents; Senator Robert M. La Follette of Wisconsin, always a hopeful but never a successful contender; Herbert Hoover, who announced that he was a Republican and would accept the nomination; and a number of favorite sons, including the distinguished Nicholas Murray Butler of New York and the nondescript Warren G. Harding of Ohio.

When the Republicans met in national convention in Chicago on June 8, 1920, the Wood and Lowden managers battled fiercely during the first six ballots. But Wood could not gain more than one-third of the delegates and Lowden's managers stubbornly refused to surrender. Fearing a deadlock over the week-end, Chairman Henry Cabot Lodge adjourned the convention at seven o'clock on Friday evening, June 11. It was the signal for the execution of a bold plan to thwart the will of the Republican majority, who wanted a moderately progressive candidate, and to secure control of the next administration in the hands of a political clique intimately associated with the great industrial interests.

Dominating the Republican National Committee and controlling the convention machinery were a group of senators and their political and business allies—among them being Lodge; Senator Boies Penrose of Pennsylvania; Will H. Hays, national chairman; George Harvey, the caustic New York editor who had turned savagely against the President during the war; and

Harry Sinclair, Edward L. Doheny, and other businessmen. This clique wanted neither Wood nor Lowden but instead a President they could control. How they found their candidate and foisted him upon the convention constitutes one of the most interesting chapters in the history of American politics.

All during the evening of Friday, June 11, the senatorial clique conferred in Harvey's suite in the Blackstone Hotel. They eliminated the strong candidates one by one and then settled upon Senator Warren G. Harding of Ohio, a party hack who met all the qualifications of a perfect dark horse. Harding had many friends and no enemies in the party, had voted for the Lodge reservations, and, most important, was controllable. By eleven o'clock the decision was made and relayed to other party leaders. At about two o'clock in the morning of Saturday, June 12, Harvey called Harding to his room, told him of the decision, and asked if there was any reason the party should not nominate him. After meditating privately in an adjourning bedroom for ten minutes, Harding returned to reply that there was no reason why he should not be President. On the convention floor the following morning, the enraged Wood and Lowden managers battled furiously, but they could not hold their delegates, and Harding won in a landslide on the tenth ballot. For Vice President the senatorial clique had named Senator Irvine L. Lenroot of Wisconsin; however, in an unexpected burst of independence the weary delegates nominated instead Governor Calvin Coolidge, the hero of the recent Boston police strike.

The Republican platform gave notice of the GOP's intention to destroy Wilsonianism and all its works. It promised tariff increases, tax reductions, immigration restriction, vigorous aid to farmers, and, by implication, an end to further federal social legislation. On the League issue, the framers of the platform made room both for the irreconcilables and Republican League men; the platform condemned Wilson's League but approved membership in the World Court and "agreement among nations to preserve the peace of the world."

Meanwhile, the Democrats had been engaged in a preconvention contest even more confused than the struggle that preceded the Republican convention. The chief cause of the Democratic uncertainty was the President himself, for after his partial recovery during the early months of 1919 Wilson acted very much like a receptive if silent candidate. He had dismissed Secretary of State Lansing and taken charge of the government in February; and just before the Democratic convention met in June he called photographers to the White House and gave an important interview to the press. Whether Wilson wanted a third nomination will probably never be known. He may well have refused to disavow third-term ambitions in order to preserve his influence over the coming convention.

In any event, Wilson's potential candidacy cast a long shadow over the aspirations of his son-in-law, the chief contender for the nomination, William G. McAdoo. As a gesture of filial respect, McAdoo "withdrew" from the race on the same day, June 18, that Wilson's interview appeared in the press. McAdoo's strongest rival was the Attorney General, A. Mitchell Palmer, who was still battling ferociously for Americanism. Among the favorite sons, Governor James M. Cox of Ohio had the greatest potential strength. Three times elected governor of a doubtful state, he had an excellent progressive record, had survived the Republican victory of 1918, and was more acceptable to the city bosses than McAdoo or Palmer because of his opposition to prohibition.

Because of the division in the Wilsonian ranks, the Democratic convention that opened at San Francisco on June 28 was no less bossed and in the beginning no less confused than its Republican counterpart. The Irish bosses who controlled the Massachusetts, New York, New Jersey, Indiana, and Illinois delegations held the balance of power and in the end named the candidate in the same manner that the senatorial clique had done at Chicago. For thirty-seven weary ballots the McAdoo and Palmer forces fought to a standstill. On the thirty-eighth ballot Palmer released his delegates; but as most of them went to Cox, a McAdoo drive fizzled, and Cox was named on the forty-fourth roll call on July 5. Cox's choice for running-mate was Franklin D. Roosevelt of New York, Assistant Secretary of the Navy, a prominent Wilsonian and League supporter.

Meanwhile the convention had adopted a platform that sidestepped the prohibition question, extended sympathy to Ireland, and promised tax reductions and independence for the Philippines. On the all-important League issue the platform was at the same time straightforward—reflecting Wilson's demands—and evasive—reflecting the arguments of Democrats who wanted to accept the Lodge reservations. We advocate immediate ratification of the Treaty without crippling reservations, the platform declared; but we do not "oppose the acceptance of any reservations making clearer or more specific the obligations of the United States to the League associates."

In spite of the convention's straddle, Cox and Roosevelt labored heroically during the ensuing campaign to make the election a "great and solemn referendum" on the League and to warn the voters that the reactionary business interests would control the government if Harding were elected. Harding's managers, on the other hand, wisely decided that the less Harding said the better his chances would be. Hence the Republican candidate made no long tours like Cox but rather stayed at home in Marion, Ohio, and greeted delegations on his front porch. A perfect tool in the hands of his advisers, he talked about getting away from nostrums and back to "normalcy," about a general association of nations based on justice, which the United States might join, and the like. But where Harding stood on any specific issue it was impossible to conclude from his sonorous homilies. Isolationists were certain he would keep the country out of the detested League. On the other hand, a group of thirty-one distinguished pro-League Republicans, including Charles Evans Hughes and Elihu Root, assured the voters that Harding's election was the first necessary step in ratification with reservations.

Harding's ambivalent speeches and the statement of the thirty-one Republican internationalists so confused the voters that it is doubtful if the League was the paramount issue of the campaign. On the contrary, long before election day it was evident that the Republicans were capitalizing on an accumulation of grievances going back all the way to the progressive legislation of 1916 and the adoption of the war resolution. The disparate elements opposed to Democratic policies—the Irish- and German-Americans,

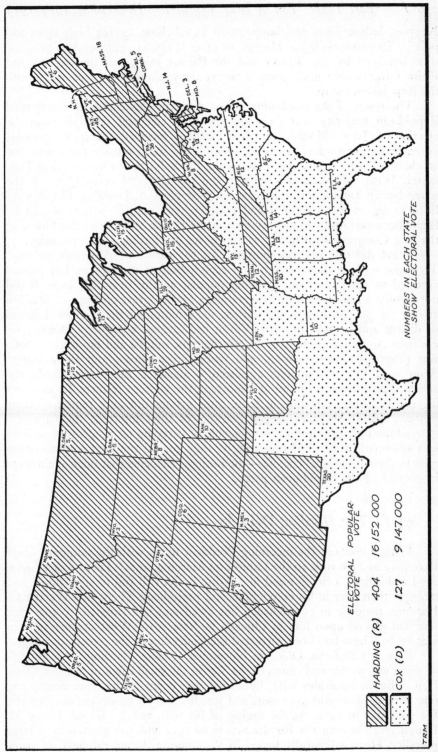

	ELECTORAL VOTE	POPULAR VOTE
HARDING (R)	404	16 152 000
COX (D)	127	9 147 000

NUMBERS IN EACH STATE SHOW ELECTORAL VOTE

12. The Election of 1920

Negroes, industrialists and businessmen in rebellion against high taxes and policies favorable to labor, champions of civil liberty, independent progressives outraged by the Treaty and the Palmer raids, and midwestern and Plains farmers then undergoing a severe depression—moved *en masse* into the Republican camp.

The result of the combining of the dissident elements with the normal Republican majority was the most smashing electoral triumph since the election of James Monroe in 1820. Harding received 16,152,000 popular votes, or 61 per cent of the total; won all the states outside the South, for an electoral vote of 404; and even broke the Solid South by carrying Tennessee. With only 9,147,000 popular and 127 electoral votes, Cox was the worst beaten Democratic candidate since Stephen A. Douglas. The Republican sweep in the senatorial and congressional contests—there would be Republican majorities of twenty-two in the Senate and 167 in the House in the next Congress—was nearly as impressive as Harding's own majority.

What did this landslide portend for the future of American politics? To begin with, it did not signify a repudiation of the League but instead revealed the confusion and growing popular apathy over that issue. It did not signify a repudiation of progressivism or any great collapse of idealism among the people. It signified, rather, the triumph of the combined forces of dissent and protest. In 1916 Wilson had created a majority Democratic coalition composed principally of Southerners, middle and far western anti-war progressives and farmers, and workingmen throughout the country. After 1916 Wilson's policies consistently alienated the independents, the anti-war progressives, and, most important, the western farmers. By destroying the Wilsonian coalition in 1920, these groups not only registered their protests against Wilson's alleged betrayal of their interests; they also destroyed the only political alliance capable of carrying on progressive policies in a systematic way. And unwittingly, they turned the next administration over to their traditional enemies—the business elements that once again were in control of the Republican party.

93 / *The Harding* Débâcle

What a contrast the incoming President made with the outgoing Chief Executive as they rode to the Capitol on March 4, 1921! There was Wilson, aged and infirm, a living mind in a dying body, still full of high hopes and stronger than ever in his convictions and prejudices. There was Warren G. Harding, majestic in countenance but awed and still stunned by the trick fate had played upon him in Chicago in June 1920. What manner of man was he, to whom had been entrusted the leadership of the American people?

Born at Caledonia, Ohio, on November 2, 1865, Harding for a number of years was owner and editor of the *Star* in the small town of Marion, Ohio. Driven by an ambitious wife, he served two terms in the State Senate and one term as lieutenant governor, and was his party's unsuccessful candidate for governor in 1910. At the urging of his wife and his friend, Harry M. Daugherty, Harding ran for the Senate in 1914 and was elected by a large plurality. He was blissfully happy in Washington during the next six years.

Realizing his own limitations, he did not want the presidency but allowed his manager, Daugherty, to maneuver him into a position where he could not refuse the nomination in 1920.

A man of average mental endowment can fulfill the duties of the presidency if his will power and character fortify his determination to rule wisely. It was an unkind act of fate, however, that made Harding President, for he had only average talents, no will power, and a striking inability to discriminate between right and wrong. Easy-going and affable, he drank too much and possessed an uncanny ability to draw into his personal circle men utterly unworthy of his confidence. There is also strong evidence that Harding was adulterous.

The contrast between Wilson and Harding was no more vivid than the dissimilarity between the outgoing administration and many of the men surrounding the new President. Most of the members of the Wilson circle were able public servants, honest and disinterested. They had carried the nation through a great war effort and spent billions of the public money, and hardly any of them had been guilty of theft or of using their office for private gain. In contrast stands a record of fraud and corruption in high places during the brief Harding regime unparalleled since the Grant era. Not all the thieves who moved in on the public treasury in 1921 were from Ohio, but the ringleaders were. Let us look briefly at the men Harding appointed to office—the so-called "Ohio Gang" and the more honorable leaders of the administration.

The "Ohio Gang" were as avaricious a group as ever moved in high circles in Washington. The leader was Harding's old Ohio crony, the unsavory politician and lobbyist, Harry M. Daugherty, whom the new President made Attorney General. As Secretary of the Interior, Harding appointed his old Senate intimate, Albert B. Fall of New Mexico. The President made a crony from Ohio and former Sheriff of Pickaway County, "Ed" Scobey, Director of the Mint; his brother-in-law, a missionary of the Adventist Church, Superintendent of Federal Prisons; Daniel R. Crissinger, a second-rate lawyer from Marion, Comptroller of the Currency and afterward Governor of the Federal Reserve Board; Charles R. Forbes, head of the Veterans' Bureau; and Thomas W. Miller, prominent in the American Legion, Alien Property Custodian. These were the leaders of the "Ohio Gang."

The opportunity to honor old friends and have them as drinking and poker companions warmed the President's heart. But when he was about halfway through his list Harding resolved to find the best men in the Republican party for the remaining and most important posts. Thus he chose as Secretary of State Charles Evans Hughes, as Secretary of the Treasury the Pittsburgh industrialist and banker, Andrew W. Mellon, as Secretary of War former Senator John W. Weeks of Massachusetts, as Secretary of Agriculture the distinguished Iowan, Henry C. Wallace, and as Secretary of Commerce Herbert Hoover. These able conservatives not only lent distinction to the new administration but also saved their departments from the pillaging of the "Ohio Gang."

Until his death in August 1923 Harding presided over the government of the United States with outward dignity. He abdicated leadership of legislative and foreign policies to Congress and his Cabinet, but this was what the leaders of the Republican party wanted him to do. On the other hand, he performed three acts of his own that revealed the generous side of his nature and indicated a certain courage. The first was his pardoning, in 1921, of Eugene V. Debs, who had spent three years in the Atlanta penitentiary and polled over 900,000 votes as Socialist candidate for President in 1920. The second was bringing the heads of the steel industry to the White House and persuading them to institute the eight-hour day. The third was his defiance of the American Legion lobby in his veto of the soldiers' bonus, or adjusted compensation, bill in 1922. On important matters of policy, however, Harding was ignorant and confused and yielded where the pressure was strongest.

Meanwhile, under the President's myopic eyes his cronies were engaging in a mad scramble for bribes and as much loot as they could lay their hands upon. The first scandal involved Jesse Smith, an old-time friend of Daugherty's, who had moved to Washington with the Attorney General and who soon became the liaison between the Department of Justice and violators of the prohibition laws, income tax evaders, and "fixers" of all kinds. When rumors of Smith's corruption reached Harding, the President told Daugherty that Smith must go back to Ohio. Smith went home for a while but could not bear his exile. He returned to Daugherty's apartment and killed himself on May 23, 1923.

Smith's suicide was the first event in a chain that culminated in Harding's death soon afterward. While Harding probably never knew the details of Smith's activities, he did learn about the gross corruption that prevailed in the Veterans' Bureau under the direction of Charles R. Forbes; and what he discovered filled him with presentiment of impending doom. Harding had a profound concern for the nation's disabled veterans and especially for the mental and tubercular cases for which the government was caring. As director of the Veterans' Bureau, established by Congress in August 1921, Forbes supervised the building of hospitals and the expenditure of hundreds of millions of dollars. A bustling, energetic person with a convincing tongue, he gave the impression of an efficient administrator. But he could not resist the temptation to make money on the side, and before he was dismissed he had stolen or squandered nearly $250,000,000.

Late in 1922 Daugherty learned of the corruption in the Veterans' Bureau and told Harding the rumors he had heard. Learning a part of the truth from Forbes himself, the President allowed Forbes to go abroad and resign on February 15, 1923. Soon the rumors reached the Senate, which began an investigation on March 2. Twelve days later the legal adviser to the Veterans' Bureau, Charles F. Cramer, committed suicide. Eventually, after Harding's death, the Senate committee exposed the extent of Forbes' corruption and Forbes was convicted of defrauding the government and sentenced to a two-year term in the Leavenworth penitentiary.

Meanwhile, Harding's Secretary of the Interior, Albert B. Fall, was executing one of the most daring steals in American history. In 1921 he persuaded the President to transfer control over the naval oil reserve lands at Elk Hills in California and Teapot Dome in Wyoming from the Secretary of the Navy to the Interior Department. Soon afterward, on April 7, 1922,

Fall secretly leased Teapot Dome to the Mammoth Oil Company, owned by Harry F. Sinclair. The following December the Secretary secretly leased Elk Hills to the Pan-American Petroleum Company, owned by Edward L. Doheny.

News of the leases leaked out at once; and in answer to a Senate inquiry Fall declared that he had leased Teapot Dome to Sinclair in the interest of national preparedness and was about to lease Elk Hills to Doheny. In October 1923 a sub-committee of the Senate public lands committee, headed by Thomas J. Walsh of Montana, began an investigation that was continued the following year by a special commission. These investigations revealed that Sinclair had given Fall $223,000 in government bonds, $85,000 in cash, and a herd of cattle for his ranch at the time the lease for Teapot Dome was negotiated; and that Doheny had also "lent" $100,000 to Fall at the time the lease on Elk Hills was being concluded.

Eventually—in 1927—the government won its suit to cancel the leases, while Doheny, Sinclair, and Fall were tried for conspiracy to defraud the government and acquitted, although Sinclair spent a term in jail for tampering with the jury. In October 1929, however, Fall was convicted of bribery, fined $100,000, and sentenced to a year in jail. After many delays, the former Secretary went to jail in July 1931 and thus became the first corrupt Cabinet member in American history to receive something like his just reward.

During the furor raised by the revelations of the oil scandal in 1923 and 1924 Attorney General Daugherty refused to resign from the Coolidge Cabinet and turned the FBI on senators and other public leaders who were unearthing the details of the corruption. Then a scandal involving the return of the American Metal Company to its German owners by the Alien Property Custodian, Thomas W. Miller, broke early in 1924. It came out that a highly placed New York Republican who engineered the deal had paid $50,000 to Miller and another $50,000 to Jesse Smith, who deposited his share in an account that he held jointly with Daugherty. When Daugherty refused to testify before a Senate committee of investigation in March 1924, Coolidge dismissed him. Brought to trial in New York in 1926, Daugherty again refused to testify, saying his personal relations with President and Mrs. Harding made it impossible for him to do so. After deliberating nearly three days the jury disagreed because Harding's good name seemed at stake. The following year Miller was tried, convicted, and sent to jail.

94 / *The Death of President Harding*

Early in 1923 Harding made plans for a speaking tour through the West and a vacation in Alaska. Before he and his party left Washington on June 20 the President had learned enough of the corruption of his friends to make him sick at heart. "My God, this is a hell of a job," he told William Allen White shortly before he left on his western trip. "I have no trouble with my enemies. . . . But my damned friends, my God-damn friends, White, they're the ones that keep me walking the floor nights!"[6]

[6] *The Autobiography of William Allen White* (New York, 1946), p. 619. Quoted by permission of the Macmillan Company, publishers.

All during the long trip across the continent Harding was physically exhausted and depressed. Instead of bringing rest, the trip to Alaska further tired the President. Returning to Seattle on July 27, he stood bareheaded under the sun to make a speech. Several times he faltered, and members of his party feared he would collapse. That evening Harding suffered intense pain. His physician said he had ptomaine poisoning from eating spoiled crabs.

From Seattle the presidential party went to San Francisco on July 29. Harding insisted on walking unaided from the station to his car, but he went at once to bed and developed pneumonia the following day. Just when it seemed he was on the road to recovery he suffered a stroke and died at 7:30 in the evening of August 2, 1923. As the funeral train bearing the President's body made its way slowly across the country, millions of Americans paid their respects to the man they thought Harding had been.

It was not long, however, before the American people learned the details of the scandals of the Harding administration, read the accusations of Harding's alleged mistress, Nan Britton, and heard the charge that Harding had been poisoned by his wife. In consequence, the deflation of Harding's reputation came at once, not slowly. The people forgot his simplicity and kindliness and remembered only that he had connived with thieves and sheltered scoundrels. And during a later period, when the Republican leadership of the twenties stood discredited in the public mind, "normalcy" became a term of opprobrium and the scandals of the Harding era, compounded with the Great Depression, became a heavy liability to the GOP.

CHAPTER 12 / *THE SURVIVAL OF PROGRESSIVISM: POLITICS AND PROBLEMS OF THE 1920's*

*D*ID the return of Republican rule in 1921 signify the end of progressivism on the national level and usher in an era in which reactionaries controlled the federal government?

It is not easy to give a categorical answer. To be sure, Presidents Harding and Coolidge and their spokesmen in Congress were avowed champions of business and financial enterprise. Believing that American prosperity depended upon the prosperity of the upper classes, they sponsored tariff and tax policies designed to promote special interests, brought the federal administrative agencies into close cooperation with the business community, and opposed measures that would have discouraged investment or carried the government into new areas of regulation. But to stop at this point would be to give a grossly distorted view of American politics in the 1920's. The fact was that conservative Republicans gained and held power in the executive branch because of the peculiar character of the American political system and because progressives were divided, not because they were weak. When the progressive coalition of 1916 was destroyed in 1920, progressives reverted to their traditional voting habits in the national elections of 1920, 1924, and 1928 and were never able to combine to capture the presidency. On the other hand, they combined in Congress to control the legislative branch during practically all the 1920's, to thwart the conservative executive leadership, and to push through a remarkable progressive legislative program, the most advanced parts of which were nullified by presidential vetoes.

Thus, as the following sections will attempt to reveal, the political development of the period 1920–1928 refuses to accommodate itself to sweeping generalizations or pat theories. As we will see, there were numerous conflicts, cross-currents, and elements of confusion; but withal progressivism as an articulate expression of social and economic aspiring not only survived but also widened its horizons.

95 /   The Anomaly of American Politics, 1921–1928

Those business leaders and men of wealth who poured nearly $8,000,-000 into the Republican campaign coffers in 1920 soon realized part of the expected return on their investment. Through the powerful Senate clique, they controlled the President and had a decisive voice in shaping federal policies, both administrative and legislative. The time seemed ripe for the complete fulfillment of the business-sponsored program—economy, drastic tax reductions, and sound financing; a return to tariff protection; control of federal regulatory agencies by men friendly to the business interests; and an end to the quasi-socialistic experiments launched during the war. At the very moment conservatives were enjoying the election returns on November 2, 1920, however, disruptive economic forces were at work that soon robbed them of many of the legislative fruits of victory. For during the autumn and winter of 1920–1921 agricultural prices were falling hard and fast, and a political rebellion, nearly equal in strength to the insurgent revolt of 1910–1912, was brewing.

Congress met in special session in April 1921, business leaders thought, to take the country back to "normalcy." If the President had controlled the enormous Republican majorities in both houses he could have put his program across with ease. As it turned out, the agrarian revolt developed so rapidly that the conservatives could not command even a bare majority for measures to which the agrarian insurgents objected.

A month after the special session convened, a group of midwestern farm spokesmen in Congress, led by Senators William S. Kenyon of Iowa and Arthur Capper of Kansas, met in the Washington offices of the new and powerful Farm Bureau Federation to consider means of meeting the agricultural crisis. Agreeing upon a program of extensive legislation, they at once organized the so-called Farm Bloc for independent, nonpartisan action. And by combining with southern Democrats, the Midwesterners were able not only to put a part of their program across but also to block the administration's efforts at substantial tax reductions.

The following year, 1922, agricultural prices recovered slightly, and business and industry began to recuperate from the sharp depression of 1921. But with returning prosperity, progressive discontent also increased. Republican insurgents made almost a clean sweep in the Republican primary campaigns through the Middle and Far West in the spring and summer of 1922. Even more discouraging to administration leaders were the results of the congressional election in November. Republican majorities in the Senate and House were reduced to eight and eighteen respectively, and so many insurgents were elected that the administration lost its small measure of control over Congress.

The congressional election of 1922 not only stimulated hopes of a general progressive revival but also heartened the leaders of the Farm Bloc in Congress. When the lame duck session convened in December 1922, Midwesterners organized a new and stronger bloc and adopted a platform that appealed as much to independents and workers as it did to farmers. Insurgent leaders insisted they were merely protesting against conservative Republican policies, not contemplating a campaign to unite the disparate progressive elements in a third party. And yet even as they spoke there were numerous signs that the rebellion among farmers and organized workers was growing to such large proportions that a nation-wide independent movement might be possible in 1924.

The most important sign of revolt was the sudden revival of the Non-Partisan League after 1919. Organized among the wheat growers of North Dakota in 1915, the Non-Partisan League advocated a program that was re-markably advanced for its day—state ownership and operation of farm credit agencies, warehouses, and grain elevators; minimum wages; and stringent control of railroads, banks, and private businesses. Capturing the state gov-ernment of North Dakota in 1916, the League organizers expanded into Minnesota, Iowa, Montana, Idaho, and other states in 1917 and 1918. In 1920 the League joined with a number of radical remnants to form the Farmer-Labor party and took second place in Minnesota, South Dakota, and Wash-ington.

As the sharp agricultural and industrial depression of 1920–1922 inten-sified discontent, the leaders of the railroad brotherhoods called a Conference for Progressive Political Action to meet in Chicago in February 1922 and consider independent political action. Represented at this first conference were the brotherhoods and many other unions, the Non-Partisan League, the Socialist party, and numerous splinter groups. Instead of launching a third party, however, the Conference decided to endorse congressional and senatorial candidates and to await the outcome of the fall elections.

Encouraged by the success of insurgent Republican and Farmer-Labor candidates, Senator La Follette, in December 1922, convoked an assemblage of progressive politicians, editors, and labor leaders in Washington. Shortly afterward the Conference for Progressive Political Action met for a second time in Cleveland. The upshot of these two gatherings was an agreement to campaign for La Follette's nomination on the Republican ticket in 1924 and, that failing, to launch a third party.

"The Midwest," said William Allen White, "is on the rampage again"; and remembering the insurgent revolt of 1910, progressives believed a second upheaval impended. Much, of course, depended upon the Democrats, for the insurgents alone could never capture the government. If the Democrats could find a strong new leader and unite behind a progressive program, they might win the independents, the labor vote, and the insurgents and rebuild their party into the powerful progressive coalition it had been in 1916.

This is what the Democrats did in 1932. In 1923 and 1924, however, the Democracy offered little hope of again becoming the instrument of the pro-gressive movement. Since the Civil War it had been a coalition of divergent elements; after 1920 it became so fragmentized that it ceased to be a national party. The majority Democratic element, the southern Methodists and Bap-tists, demanded vigorous enforcement of the Eighteenth Amendment. On the other hand, Democratic organizations in the northern cities represented wet constituencies who demanded repeal of that Amendment. Southern and midwestern Democrats either supported or feared the Ku Klux Klan, while most northern Democrats were Catholics or foreign-born citizens, opposed to all the Klan stood for. Finally, these two wings of the Democracy were hopelessly divided on the leading questions of the day. Southerners still supported the League of Nations; the northern Irish bosses wanted to forget the issue. Southerners demanded radical aid to farmers but were unfriendly to labor, uninterested in social reform, and anti-Negro. In contrast, the northern Democratic organizations opposed radical farm support but sponsored advanced labor legislation and were beginning to develop strength among Negro voters.

The unbridgeable gulf separating southern and northern Democrats was revealed at the Democratic national convention that met in New York City from June 24 to July 10, 1924. During the preconvention contest William G. McAdoo had won the support of the South and West and, although he openly repudiated it, the endorsement of the Ku Klux Klan. He might have won the nomination had he not become linked to the Teapot Dome scandal as Edward L. Doheny's lawyer and consequently lost support among progressives. His chief and only serious rival was Alfred E. Smith, Governor of New York, a Roman Catholic and avowed enemy of prohibition and the Klan, who had the support of the Irish and Catholic-dominated eastern and midwestern machines. For ninety-five weary ballots the McAdoo and Smith forces fought it out and in their struggle revealed the tensions that divided their party. On the ninety-sixth ballot both men withdrew by agreement; and on the one hundred and third the convention turned to John W. Davis, a lawyer for corporation and banking interests. As a sop to the agrarian element, the convention chose Governor Charles W. Bryan of Nebraska, a brother of the former Secretary of State, as Davis' running-mate.

The Democrats found it as difficult to agree upon a platform as upon a candidate. The worst fight centered around a resolution sponsored by the Smith forces, which condemned the Klan as un-American. It failed by a vote of 543 to 542. Nor could Northerners and Southerners agree on prohibition; the platform merely condemned the Republicans for failing to enforce the Eighteenth Amendment. Refusing to approve American membership in the League of Nations, the convention called for a public referendum on the issue. Except for denouncing the Fordney-McCumber tariff and promising independence to the Philippines, the Democratic platform differed little from its Republican counterpart.

In the meantime, the insurgent Republicans had been pressing their campaign to capture the Republican party. The futility of this endeavor had become so apparent by the spring of 1924, however, that La Follette withdrew from Republican presidential primaries in Wisconsin, North Dakota, and Michigan. Control of the party had passed to Harding's successor, Calvin Coolidge, a dour, taciturn man, who was even more intimately associated with big business than Harding had been.

Coolidge and his conservative allies, therefore, completely dominated the Republican convention that opened in Cleveland on June 10, 1924. Only the Wisconsin and South Dakota delegates objected when the President was nominated almost by acclamation on the first ballot. Rejecting a progressive platform submitted by the Wisconsin delegation, the convention adopted instead a platform promising economy, tax reduction, and limited aid to farmers, and approving American membership in the World Court.

Soon afterward, on July 4, the insurgent Republicans and their Conference for Progressive Political Action allies, representing organized labor, disgruntled western farmers, Socialists, and independent progressives, met in Cleveland.[1] The Communists, who had tried to control the Conference for Progressive Political Action, were unceremoniously excluded. Agreeing that both major parties were hopelessly corrupt and reactionary, the delegates formally organized the Progressive party, nominated La Follette for President,[2] and adopted a brief platform that demanded nationalization of the railroads, public ownership of water power and the development of a great public utilities system, abolition of the use of the injunction in labor disputes, the right of Congress to overrule decisions of the Supreme Court, and the direct nomination and election of the President.

Appealing chiefly to midwestern farmers and urban workers, La Follette made a strenuous campaign. But he was hampered by lack of funds, a gradual withdrawal of AF of L support, refusal of most midwestern Republican leaders to support his party, and most of all by a considerable increase in farm prices a month before the election. President Coolidge took practically no part in the campaign, but the other Republican leaders were generously supplied with funds[3] and made a vigorous campaign. Practically ignoring Davis and Bryan, Republicans concentrated heavy fire against La Follette, who, they asserted, was un-American and a front for the Third International. Davis tried to make a campaign on the issues of corruption and Coolidge's intimate association with big business, but his appeals were lost in the anti-Red clamor.

The question whether La Follette would draw enough votes away from Coolidge to throw the election into the House of Representatives was answered emphatically on election day, November 4, 1924. Coolidge received 15,725,000 popular and 382 electoral votes; Davis, 8,387,000 popular and 136 electoral votes; and La Follette, 4,823,000 popular votes and the thirteen electoral votes of Wisconsin.

Outwardly, the results constituted a thumping endorsement of the Coolidge policies of *laissez faire* and do-nothingism. Actually, few presidential elections in American history have meant so little. In his effort to unite progressives, La Follette had frightened numerous voters from Davis to Coolidge. But it was not La Follette's candidacy that caused the Democratic *débâcle*. It was internal dissension, failure to adopt a boldly progressive platform, Davis' inherent weakness as a leader of the forces of discontent, and his failure to appeal to the urban, Catholic, and immigrant voters that wrecked Democratic hopes in 1924. The fact that only 52 per cent of the voters went to the polls was a striking commentary on Democratic failure to rally the people either behind a candidate or a platform.

The following four years were a prosperous interlude during which Coolidge asserted no leadership in legislation and set about quietly to gain

---

[1] The principal groups represented at the Progressive convention were the Socialist party, the Farmer-Labor party, the Non-Partisan League, the railroad brotherhoods, and the AF of L.

[2] The National Committee later named the Montana Democrat, Senator Burton K. Wheeler, as La Follette's running-mate.

[3] According to the best estimates the Republicans spent nearly $6,000,000, the Democrats, $1,614,762, and the Progressives, $236,963.

control of the administrative agencies. Although the Republicans controlled the Sixty-Ninth Congress from 1925 to 1927 by large majorities and the Seventieth Congress during the following two years by a slight margin, they were constantly at war with one another and with the President. After La Follette's death in 1925, the Farm Bloc in Congress regrouped and put across two advanced progressive measures in 1927 and 1928—the McNary-Haugen farm relief bill and a measure for governmental operation of the Muscle Shoals dam—both of which were nullified by Coolidge's vetoes.

We have thus reviewed in outline the anomalous pattern of American national politics from 1920 to 1928. The pattern was anomalous because conservative administrations, seemingly overwhelmingly endorsed by the American people in 1920 and 1924, were counterbalanced by progressive coalitions in Congress that perpetuated the progressive tradition in legislative policy. How this came about will become more apparent as we discuss the legislative problems and policies of the period in detail.

96 / Tariff, Tax, and Bonus Battles of the Twenties

The first item on the Republican agenda after the election of 1920 was upward revision of the tariff, chiefly to meet the demands of midwestern agrarian congressmen. In the lame duck session of the Sixty-Sixth Congress in the winter of 1920–1921, eastern Republicans gladly joined Midwesterners in adopting an emergency tariff bill that imposed high duties on meat and major farm staples. Warning that farmers needed new markets for their products, not futile tariff protection, Wilson vetoed this measure on March 3, 1921.

When the Sixty-Seventh Congress met in special session on April 11, 1921, however, the midwestern spokesmen obtained the immediate re-enactment of the emergency tariff bill, which Harding signed on May 27. In the meantime, Chairman Joseph W. Fordney of Michigan and his ways and means committee set to work on a general overhauling of the Underwood rates. The measure that Fordney reported on June 29 and the House approved three weeks later incorporated the emergency increases for agricultural products and effected moderate increases in rates on most industrial products. The Senate finance committee, headed by Porter J. McCumber of North Dakota, deliberated during the summer and autumn of 1921 and reported the Fordney bill with over two thousand amendments in April 1922.

Approved by the President on September 19, 1922, the Fordney-McCumber Tariff Act to a limited degree revived the historic Republican policy of economic nationalism. It represented, first of all, a clear-cut victory for the newly-formed Farm Bloc, as duties on farm products—including reindeer meat and acorns—were higher than the Payne-Aldrich rates, while agricultural implements, wagons, and boots and shoes remained on the free list. For the rapidly expanding chemical industry, the Act provided the protection it needed to withstand the destructive competition of the German dye trust. For producers of silk and rayon textiles, toys, chinaware, cutlery, guns, and other items produced more cheaply by the Japanese and Germans, the measure offered almost prohibitive duties. Finally, for the great mass of industrial products the Act provided only moderate protection in order to equalize differences in cost of production at home and abroad.

As it turned out, the Fordney-McCumber Act was not nearly so disastrous to foreign trade as Democrats at the time asserted. Except for sugar and wool, the protection afforded agricultural products was more illusory than real. The protection given the chemical industry was important, but it represented fulfillment of a policy begun by the Wilson administration in 1916. The chief significance of the Act of 1922, however, was the manner in which its framers attempted to carry on the Underwood policy of fixing rates for the mass of industrial products to equalize differences in costs of production in the United States and abroad. In addition, the Tariff Commission was instructed to study relative production costs and recommend changes to the President, who might then raise or lower rates by as much as 50 per cent.

Although Democrats voted against the Fordney-McCumber bill, the measure was such a satisfactory compromise that for the next four years, at least, the tariff issue ceased to be important in national politics. Meanwhile, Harding and Coolidge also left well enough alone. Upon recommendation of the Tariff Commission, they made thirty-seven unimportant changes in rates. On the other hand, when the Commission suggested lowering the sugar duty in 1924, Coolidge discreetly buried the report.

The great majority of businessmen were clamoring more for a reduction in federal expenditures and drastic tax cuts than for a return to a McKinley-type protection in 1921 and 1922. As the first step toward economy, Congress, in May 1921, enacted the nonpartisan Budget and Accounting Act, establishing a Director of the Budget in the executive department and a Comptroller General as a watchdog for Congress to oversee the expenditure of funds. As the first step toward tax reduction, the spokesmen of the industrial and banking interests in the GOP insisted that Harding name Andrew W. Mellon as Secretary of the Treasury. Although he had never heard of Mellon, Harding did as his advisers requested.

What Mellon's appointment signified was clear to all who knew him. Head of the aluminum monopoly and a financial-industrial empire, he was the personification of the American self-made man and reactionary extraordinary. His philosophy was honest and simple, if devoid of foresight or undisturbed by qualms of social conscience. Believing in the sacredness of debts, he demanded the full payment by the former Allied governments of their debts to the United States. Sharing the Hamiltonian trickle-down theory of prosperity, he advocated low taxes on wealth and noninterference by government in business affairs. Let us see how he finally reversed progressive tax policy and imposed his fiscal theories on Congress.

During 1920 businessmen had launched a powerful campaign against the excess profits tax and the extremely high surtaxes that still prevailed under the War Revenue Act of 1918–1919. Reiterating business demands to the special session of 1921, Mellon recommended repeal of the excess profits tax, a slight increase in the corporation tax, reduction of the combined normal and surtaxes on incomes from a maximum of 73 per cent to 40 per cent for 1921 and 33 per cent thereafter, the repeal of war luxury taxes, and imposition of a new federal tax on automobiles. The House of Representatives and the Senate finance committee approved a bill embodying Mellon's program. In the Senate, however, the midwestern Republicans joined with the Democrats to write a tax measure of their own. Commanding a solid majority, these "wild asses of the desert," as the insurgents were derisively called at the time, defied the House, the President, and the Secretary of the Treasury and warned that there would be no tax legislation at all unless their bill prevailed. The President signed their measure on November 23, 1921.

The Revenue Act of 1921 was significant, not only because it attested to the power of the combined Farm Bloc and the Democratic minority, but even more because it gave evidence of the strong survival of advanced progressive tax theories. The measure repealed the excess profits tax entirely— progressives and conservatives alike agreed that it was an unnecessary burden on business during peacetime—but in the critical battle over the income tax the insurgent senators won all their demands. The Act of 1921 continued the rates under the War Revenue Act for the balance of 1921, set the maximum surtax thereafter at 50 per cent, increased the tax on net corporation incomes from 10 to 12½ per cent, and left estate taxes unchanged.

Meanwhile, the American Legion had launched a campaign to force Congress to provide additional compensation for men who had served in the armed forces while civilians enjoyed wartime prosperity at home. A measure to provide "adjusted compensation" passed the House in May 1920 but was killed by the Senate finance committee. But the agitation for adjusted compensation redoubled; and in March 1922 Chairman Fordney of the House ways and means committee introduced a revised "bonus" bill that provided payment of twenty-year endowment policies to veterans on a basis of $1.00 a day for service in the United States and $1.25 a day for service overseas. Even after the measure passed both houses by large majorities, Harding vetoed it on September 19, 1922.

The tax reduction of 1921 caused a decrease the following year of $1,500,000,000 in ordinary federal revenues; yet Mellon was able to reduce the public debt by almost two billions and to report a surplus of $310,-000,000 on hand at the end of the fiscal year. In December 1923, therefore, he reopened the tax battle by urging Congress to cut the maximum surtax on incomes from 50 to 25 per cent, decrease proportionately the normal tax on small incomes, and reduce drastically the federal estate tax. Again, however, insurgent Republicans and Democrats in Congress took control of tax policy. Their Revenue Act of 1924 cut the maximum surtax from 50 to 40 per cent and slashed in half the normal tax on small and middle incomes. To compensate for these reductions, they increased the maximum estate tax from 25 to 40 per cent and imposed a new gift tax. President Coolidge and Secretary Mellon were disgusted, but the President signed the measure on June 2, 1924. In a second display of defiance, Congress in the spring of 1924 reenacted the adjusted compensation bill over Coolidge's indignant veto.

Drastic tax reduction remained the chief objective of the business and propertied classes. They poured nearly $6,000,000 into the Republican campaign fund in 1924 to elect Coolidge and a friendly Congress; and after the election they began a strong propaganda to stimulate a clamor for tax reduction. When the Sixty-Ninth Congress met on December 7, 1925, the insurgent-Democratic coalition finally surrendered control of fiscal policy to the administration. So prosperous was the country and so relatively slight were the needs of the Treasury that only a tremendous increase in federal expenditures for public works, housing, and farm relief would have justified a maintenance of the prevailing high tax structure. And such a program was far beyond the ken of most progressives at the time.

The Revenue Act that Congress adopted on February 12, 1926, therefore, reduced the normal tax on small incomes, cut the maximum surtax from 40 to 20 per cent, abolished the gift tax, and slashed the estate tax in half. One further tax measure—the Revenue Act of 1928, which left income taxes undisturbed but reduced slightly corporation and consumption taxes—rounded out Mellon's fiscal program. He had failed only to obtain complete repeal of the federal estate levy. Organized wealth and its political allies, nevertheless, had for a time succeeded in repudiating the democratic tax policy inaugurated by Claude Kitchin and the anti-preparedness radicals of 1916.

97 / *The Farm Problem, 1920–1928*

The most important domestic economic problem of the 1920's was the agricultural depression that began in the summer and fall of 1920 and continued intermittently until 1935. Most of the farmers' troubles were caused by over extension, inflation, and too much spending during and immediately following the war. This development would not have had serious consequences if the prices of agricultural products had remained at the high level of 1919, for the farmers' position relative to the rest of the economy had not changed since 1914. However, when foreign demand decreased sharply in 1920 and the government withdrew price supports from wheat on May 31, 1920, the farmers' happy economic world came tumbling down. By the autumn of 1921 the price of wheat had dropped to approximately 40 per cent of its highest price in 1920, of corn to 32 per cent, and of hogs to 50 per cent.

Although agricultural prices recovered slightly during the years from 1921 to 1929, they never reached a level that made agriculture a really profitable enterprise. In fact, except during 1925 and 1929, farmers operated at a net capital loss during the entire period 1921–1929. A few statistics will illustrate the difficulties confronting these agrarian producers. Total cash farm income declined from $17,000,000,000 in 1919 to $13,600,000,000 in 1920 and to nearly $9,000,000,000 in 1921; it increased to nearly $10,000,-000,000 in 1922 and ran between eleven and twelve billions from 1923 through 1929. Farmers received 16 per cent of the national income in 1919 and only 8.8 per cent a decade later.

The first sharp decline in agricultural prices coincided with the return of the Republican party to national power and, as we have seen, stimulated the formation of the Farm Bloc in Congress. By operating as a nonpartisan pressure group, the Farm Bloc took control of agricultural policy between 1921 and 1924 and pushed through Congress the most advanced agricultural program in American history to that time.

The adoption of high tariff protection for agricultural products, which

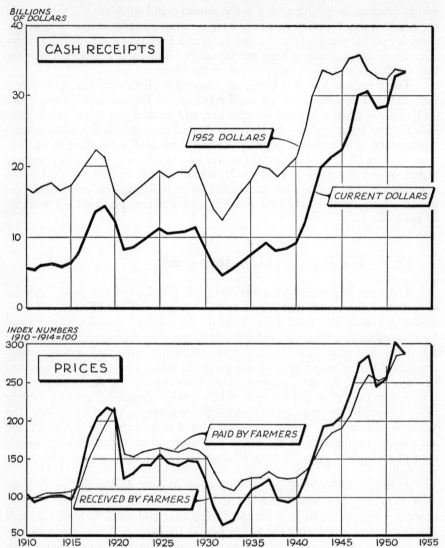

BILLIONS
OF DOLLARS

INDEX NUMBERS
1910–1914=100

7. The Economic Fortunes of American Farmers: Cash Incomes
and Prices, 1910–1952

we have already discussed, was the least important item in the agrarian reform program. A more urgent Farm Bloc goal in 1921 was legislation to subject the meat packers and stockyards to rigorous federal control. The Federal Trade Commission had made a thorough investigation in 1920, which stimulated a widespread demand for federal ownership and operation of the stockyards; and Attorney General Palmer shortly afterward had compelled the packers to accept a consent decree that ended their control over the stockyards. All that remained was to preserve competition in the packing industry and to maintain close public scrutiny over the stockyards.

These objectives the Farm Bloc accomplished in August 1921 with the passage of the Packers and Stockyards Act, which empowered the Secretary of Agriculture to issue cease and desist orders to preserve competition among packers and to compel commission merchants and the stockyards to charge only reasonable rates.

Nor was this all the Farm Bloc won during the hectic special session of 1921. First, Congress extended for three years the life of the War Finance Corporation, established in 1918 to supply capital for war industries, and authorized it to lend up to $1,000,000,000 to stimulate the export of agricultural commodities. Second, the lending operations of the Federal Farm Loan System were expanded by increasing the capital of the land banks. Thirdly, the Farm Bloc obtained passage of the Grain Futures Act, which gave the Secretary of Agriculture sweeping control over the grain exchanges. In addition, in 1922 Congress added an agricultural representative to the Federal Reserve Board and approved the Capper-Volstead bill exempting farm cooperatives from the prohibitions of the antitrust laws.

The Farm Bloc's most important triumph in the early twenties, however, was the enactment in March 1923 of the Agricultural Credits Act—the culmination of a searching inquiry into the farm problem by a joint congressional commission established in 1921.[4] This measure established twelve Intermediate Credit Banks, financed by the Treasury and operated in conjunction with the Federal Land Banks, to make loans to organized groups of farmers for periods running from six months to three years. In addition, the Act authorized the creation of National Credit Corporations, or private agricultural banks, to serve the special needs of livestock producers.

These were all important measures that greatly strengthened the agricultural program begun by the Wilson administration; and because they involved further extension of the federal power to uplift a now depressed minority they must be counted as gains for the progressive movement. But all the agricultural measures of 1921–1923 were based upon the assumption of full recovery in farm prices. When that recovery did not occur, then farm leaders moved further along the road toward advanced governmental support of agriculture.

The chief problem was to find a way to control the surpluses so that farmers might enjoy the benefits of tariff protection. Senator George W. Norris of Nebraska came forward in 1921 with a plan to establish a public corporation to buy up the surpluses, send them abroad on ships owned by the United States Shipping Board, and own and operate warehouses and elevators in the United States and selling agencies abroad. Bitterly opposed by the administration and failing to win the support of the Farm Bloc, the Norris bill was never approved by the Senate agriculture committee. But the idea inherent in the plan, namely, that of segregating the surplus from that portion of the crops sold within the United States, took firm hold in the

---

[4] The farmer's long- and short-term credit needs, the commission revealed, had been amply satisfied by the Federal Reserve and Federal Land Bank systems. What the farmer needed most, therefore, was an intermediate credit system enabling him to borrow against his products and land for periods running from six months to three years. With such new credit resources, farm spokesmen argued, cooperatives could withhold surpluses from the market during periods of deflation and thus prevent violent price fluctuations.

minds of agrarian leaders. It soon returned in a more pretentious form in the McNary-Haugen farm relief plan.

The McNary-Haugen plan was the invention of George N. Peek and Hugh S. Johnson, two farm machinery manufacturers of Moline, Illinois, whose business had been hard hit by the depression of 1920–1921. In a pamphlet entitled *Equality for Agriculture*, published in 1922, Peek and Johnson first explained the objective and operation of their proposal. The objective—a "fair exchange value" for farm products—would be achieved by segregating the exportable surplus so that the domestic market would not be governed by world prices. How this would be done can be illustrated by a familiar example: During the 1920's the United States annually produced about 800,000,000 bushels of wheat, of which about 650,000,000 bushels were consumed at home. If the world price were $1.00 a bushel, then in a free market American farmers would receive $800,000,000 for the wheat crop. Let us assume, however, that the Peek-Johnson plan were in operation. In this event, a federal board would buy wheat at a price that would yield a "fair exchange value," presumably the world price plus the tariff on wheat, which after 1924 would total $1.42 a bushel. Farmers would thus receive a gross of $1,136,000,000 for 800,000,000 bushels of wheat. The board, however, would sell the surplus of 150,000,000 bushels abroad at the world price of $1.00, and its loss of 42 cents a bushel, or $63,000,000, would be assessed in the form of an "equalization fee" against the farmers. Thus under the plan the farmers would receive a net of $1,073,000,000 for the wheat crop, instead of $800,000,000 if the wheat had been sold in a free market at world prices.

The Peek-Johnson proposal seemed such an easy and sensible way of assuring equitable farm prices that it was embodied in the form of the McNary-Haugen bill in 1924 and endorsed by more than 200 farm organizations and many state legislatures and chambers of commerce throughout the Middle West and Northwest. Violently opposed by eastern Republicans and President Coolidge, the measure was defeated by the House on June 3, 1924. This first defeat, however, only spurred farm leaders to redouble their propaganda and seek new allies. In 1926 Midwesterners won the support of the southern farm organizations by including cotton, tobacco, and rice in the proposed system; and a southern-western coalition pushed a revised McNary-Haugen bill through Congress in February 1927. Coolidge replied on February 25 with a caustic veto message that denounced the measure as unconstitutional special interest legislation. Re-enacted in May 1928, the McNary-Haugen bill drew a second veto from the President.

Organized farmers, therefore, failed to commit the federal government to the most advanced farm program yet seriously proposed. But they failed only because the eastern business wing of the GOP dominated the presidency. Actually, by 1929 the Farm Bureau Federation and other organizations in the forefront of the agricultural relief movement had scored one of the most important victories in the history of American progressivism. They had succeeded not only in uniting farmers throughout the country into a solid front; more important, they had compelled the conservative majority in the Republican party to approve a federal farm program that included strict control of grain exchanges, stockyards, and packing houses, support for agricultural cooperatives, and credit facilities on every level. From this advanced program there could be no turning back; in fact, the pathway of progressivism pointed straight ahead to other advanced measures built upon the foundations laid during the 1920's.

98 / The Triumph of the Movement for Immigration Restriction

One of the oldest objectives of the progressive movement was the exclusion of Oriental immigration to the West Coast and restriction of the numbers of Europeans who came to the United States before the First World War. Rightly or wrongly, leaders of organized labor believed that large-scale immigration depressed the domestic labor market and impeded the progress of unionization. Also, most sociologists and social workers believed that the immigration of eastern and southern Europeans created insoluble social problems. Finally, since most of the "new" immigrants were either Catholics or Jews, their coming aroused fear among Protestant Americans, especially in the rural areas, of a Catholic and Jewish inundation.

Before the United States entered the First World War the restrictionists sought to accomplish their objective by imposing a literacy test in 1917, which they thought would exclude large numbers of peasant immigrants from Eastern Europe. But the literacy test was only a slight deterrent, as immigrants who went to the trouble to seek a new home were also willing to learn enough to pass a simple test in reading and writing. In 1920 some 908,000 immigrants poured into the eastern ports, and American consuls throughout Europe warned that millions more were preparing to leave their war-ravaged districts.

Labor leaders and social workers found so many new allies in 1920 and 1921 that the movement for restriction became irresistible. For one thing, many leaders of communist and other radical groups were eastern Europeans; and employers, heretofore the chief opponents of restriction, now joined the movement for new legislation. For another, the Ku Klux Klan was beginning a powerful campaign aimed at Jews and Catholics. It is only fair to say, however, that the restrictionists would have succeeded without the assistance of the extreme nativistic element, for the preponderant majority had decided to end the historic policy of free and almost unlimited immigration.

Congress, therefore, acted with dispatch in 1920 and 1921. The House approved a bill sponsored by Representative Albert Johnson of Washington to suspend immigration for one year. Amended in the Senate to limit the number of immigrants to 3 per cent of the various foreign-born elements in the United States in 1910, the measure was approved by Congress in the closing days of the lame duck session. When Wilson refused to sign the bill, congressional leaders swiftly pushed it through the special session and Harding approved the measure on May 19, 1921. As a consequence of this emergency legislation, the number of immigrants declined from 805,228 for the fiscal year ending June 30, 1921, to 309,556 during the following fiscal year.[5]

Although the reduction effected was obviously drastic, the restrictionists and especially the champions of religious and nationalistic bigotry were still not satisfied. Congress responded in 1924 with a new and comprehensive immigration statute that satisfied even the exclusionists. Known as the National Origins Act, it prohibited Oriental immigration and limited the total number of European immigrants to 2 per cent of the foreign-born according to the census of 1890—a stipulation that reduced the total number of immigrants to 164,000, discriminated heavily in favor of Great Britain, Ireland, and Germany, and cut the flow of Italians, for example, to less than 4,000 a year. The Act provided, however, that after July 1, 1927, immigration should be further reduced to a maximum of 150,000, apportioned on a basis of the national origins of the American people in 1920.

The application of the new quota system based upon the national origins of the American people was postponed beyond 1927 because of the difficulty of determining what those origins were; but on July 1, 1929, the quotas finally went into effect. In 1931, moreover, President Herbert Hoover drastically reduced the quotas, so that more foreigners left the United States than entered in 1932. And during the thirties the number of immigrants in any one year never exceeded 100,000, while the total net immigration for the entire decade was only 68,789.

99 / The Power Controversy of the Twenties

The survival of progressivism in the 1920's was nowhere more significantly illustrated than in the battles that progressives waged, first, to obtain either municipal ownership and operation of electric power facilities or effective state regulation of the electric industry and, second, to commit the federal government to the operation of important power projects. If progressives in the 1920's did little more than awaken the public and lay the foundations for action, they gave further evidence that success in great movements comes only after decades of hard struggle.

Compared to the railroads, the electrical industry was still young in the 1920's, but its rise had been as rapid as it was important. Between 1902 and 1929 the production of electric power increased from 6,000,000,000 to 117,000,000,000 kilowatt hours. And expansion had been accompanied by the consolidation of small operating companies into large systems and of large systems into great holding company aggregations, so that by 1930 eleven well-defined holding company groups controlled 85 per cent of the installed capacity of the industry.

The movement to regulate this vast private interest, the second most important industry in the country, went through the same stages and encountered the same obstacles as did the earlier movement for railroad regulation. The establishment of public utility commissions with rate-making authority in Virginia in 1901 and in Georgia, Wisconsin, and New York in

[5] It should be noted, however, that neither this measure nor the National Origins Act of 1924 limited immigration from any countries of the western hemisphere.

1907 marked the beginning of the movement on the state level. In spite of public apathy caused by high pressure utilities propaganda and a downward trend in rates, many state commissions effected a reasonable degree of control over rates and services. On the other hand, probably a majority of the state commissions were timid and incompetent and more often than not controlled by the utilities interest. In the 1920's, therefore, progressives not only sought to strengthen the state commissions but also joined a movement for municipal ownership of power plants and distribution facilities.[6]

Like the railroads decades before, the power companies during the twenties fought to protect their privileged position, preserve their immunity from effective regulation, and prevent public ownership. By a gigantic advertising campaign that cost between $28,000,000 and $35,000,000 a year, the utilities influenced public opinion, indirectly controlled the editorial policies of hundreds of newspapers, and sometimes bought control of leading dailies. Working in practically every state on orders from the textbook committee of the National Electric Light Association, "Information Bureaus" brought pressure on school boards to force the abandonment of civics texts that condemned stock-watering and exorbitant rates and explained the benefits of regulation or public ownership. Moreover, the power interests quietly hired a number of college professors and sent them out to speak, subsidized the General Federation of Women's Clubs, controlled bankers through judicious use of deposits, bribed leaders of farm organizations, and worked relentlessly to control local and state politicians and commissions.

The first serious attempt at federal regulation came with the passage of the Water Power Act of 1920, enacted after a long controversy over policy toward the licensing of dams on public lands, reservations, or navigable rivers. This Act created a Federal Power Commission, composed of the Secretaries of War, Interior, and Agriculture, which was empowered to license the building of hydroelectric projects on sites within the jurisdiction of the federal government. Although such leases ran for fifty years, the government might purchase the entire property at net cost at the expiration of the lease. In addition, the Commission was authorized to regulate the rates, services, and financial operations of companies operating under its license, unless such companies were subjected to state regulation.

Between 1920 and 1930 the Federal Power Commission licensed 449 projects with 2,489,978 installed horsepower capacity; but because of inadequate staff and the pressure of private interests, it did practically nothing to protect the public interest. At President Hoover's request, Congress in 1930 created a new and independent Federal Power Commission but refused to endow it with additional authority for fear the President would pack the new agency with men friendly to the power interests. As Hoover soon justified congressional suspicions, effective federal regulation was postponed until the inauguration of an administration less concerned with preserving private enterprise in the production of electricity.

More significant than these largely ineffective efforts at federal regulation was the development of an organized campaign during the 1920's to

[6] By 1930 Los Angeles, Seattle, Tacoma, and some 2,000 other cities and towns owned generating plants or distribution facilities.

commit the federal government to the building of large hydroelectric projects in the Tennessee Valley, the Columbia River watershed, the Southwest, and on the St. Lawrence River. These regional developments, progressives asserted, would assure an abundance of cheap power for millions of consumers and also provide "yardsticks" for rates throughout the country. Only one of the proposed projects was begun during the Republican era— Hoover, or Boulder, Dam[7]—but around another proposed development centered one of the most crucial battles of the twenties. It was the struggle for control of a large federally-owned dam and nitrogen plants at Muscle Shoals, Alabama, which in time became the focus of the entire controversy over public ownership and operation of power plants.

The background of the Muscle Shoals episode can be briefly told. As part of the preparedness legislation of 1916, Congress had empowered the President and War Department to construct a plant to manufacture nitrates and thus relieve the United States of its dependence upon German and Chilean supplies. In 1918 two nitrate plants, with a combined annual capacity of 154,000 tons, were built at a cost of over $80,000,000 at Muscle Shoals, on the Tennessee River in Alabama. At the same time, the War Department began construction at this site of the gigantic Wilson Dam to provide electric power for the nitrate plants. The war's end found the nitrate plants completed but not yet in production and the dam about three-quarters finished.

Soon after Harding's inauguration in 1921, the new Secretary of War announced that he would recommend that Congress appropriate additional funds to complete the dam if some private company would lease the Muscle Shoals properties and guarantee a fair return on the government's investment. During the next two years a number of power companies and industrial corporations submitted bids, but it was the proposition made by Henry Ford, the automobile manufacturer, that excited the greatest enthusiasm. Offering to lease the Muscle Shoals facilities for one hundred years, to pay an annual rental of $1,500,000, and to produce at least 40,000 tons of nitrates annually for cheap fertilizers, Ford also promised to build a city seventy-five miles long in the Tennessee Valley and to devote the entire undertaking to the service of the American people.

Ford's proposal was enthusiastically supported by the Harding and Coolidge administrations and farm groups, and on March 10, 1924, the House approved a bill authorizing acceptance of Ford's bid. In the Senate, however, the Muscle Shoals offers had been referred to the agriculture committee, headed by George W. Norris. From 1921 to 1924 Norris investigated;

[7] The passage of the Boulder Dam Project Act by Congress in December 1928 represented a compromise between private power interests and the southwestern states and municipalities in a long battle for control of the water and water power resources of the lower Colorado River.

The Act provided for the construction of a dam 726 feet high and 1,244 feet long in the Black Canyon of the Colorado River on the Arizona-Nevada boundary. The cost of the dam and power plant, $108,000.000, was to be repaid out of revenues from the sale of falling water. In addition, the Act authorized the building of the so-called All-American Canal to divert water from the Colorado River to the Imperial and Coachella Valleys in California. The cost of this seventy-five-mile canal, $38,500,000, was to be paid by the users of the water.

and he soon concluded that Ford, the power companies, and other industrialists were deceiving the American people in an attempt to steal one of the nation's greatest natural assets—the potentially enormous hydroelectric resources of the Tennessee Valley. As early as 1922 a bold alternative began to take shape in Norris' mind: the creation of a public corporation to control the waters of the Tennessee Valley—and afterward of other such watersheds—for flood control and the production of vast quantities of cheap electric power.

Norris' first move was to push a bill through Congress in 1922 for completion of Wilson Dam, his second, to persuade the Senate agriculture committee, in May 1924, to approve a bill for governmental operation of the Muscle Shoals properties. When the Nebraskan presented his measure to the Senate on December 3, 1924, Senator Oscar W. Underwood of Alabama countered with a substitute providing for private operation, and the battle was joined. The ship of state, Norris exclaimed, referring to Coolidge's support of the Underwood bill, was "headed straight for Wall Street" and carried "a deed of conveyance . . . for one of the greatest inheritances of unborn generations of American citizens."

Norris' invective, however, could not stem the tide. On January 14, 1925, the Senate approved the Underwood bill; and two weeks later a conference committee met to iron out differences between the Senate and House measures. Just when it seemed the Senate would approve the conference report, on February 19, Norris made what was probably the most important parliamentary point of order in American history by protesting that the conference committee had improperly added new provisions to the Muscle Shoals bill. When the conference committee reported a new bill on February 26, Norris was able to prevent a vote by threat of filibuster.

Nor did he relax his vigilance during the next two years, and with new allies among the southern senators he won the Senate's approval, on March 13, 1928, of his bill for governmental operation of the Muscle Shoals power plant. Soon afterward insurgent Republicans and Democrats in the House adopted a measure that was in many respects superior to the Norris bill. It provided for the creation of a federal corporation to operate Wilson Dam and the nitrogen plants and for the construction of an additional dam at Cove Creek, Tennessee, to ensure flood control and a steady flow of water through the Muscle Shoals turbines. It was this House measure that the conference committee reported that the two houses approved in the latter part of May 1928.

The issue was now clearly drawn between the private interests and the advocates of public power, and the spokesmen of a large part of the business community appealed to Coolidge to prevent such a far-reaching experiment in socialism. Coolidge did not disappoint his friends; he gave the Muscle Shoals bill a pocket veto. In spite of President Hoover's avowed opposition, Norris and the progressive coalition adopted a second Muscle Shoals bill in February 1931. When Hoover replied on March 3 with a ringing defense of private enterprise, the fight to launch one of the most significant progressive experiments in American history was again momentarily defeated by a conservative President. Even so, Norris and progressives in Congress had saved Muscle Shoals and the water power resources of the Tennessee

Valley for the American people, and the time was not far distant when this aspect of the progressive movement would come to fruition.

100 / The Supreme Court and Social and Economic Policy, 1918–1929

The conflict between conservative and progressive theories was as evident in the Supreme Court as in the political arena. On the whole, the conservative philosophy prevailed in the judicial arm, chiefly because Chief Justice Edward D. White and a majority of the old conservative justices had refused either to die or to resign and allow Wilson to appoint a progressive majority.[8] On the other hand, the two great progressive jurists, Oliver Wendell Holmes and Louis D. Brandeis, remained on the bench during the twenties, and Harlan F. Stone, appointed by Coolidge in 1925, shocked his conservative friends by joining Holmes and Brandeis in numerous dissents.

From 1909 to 1917 the Court had validated a whole series of advanced social and economic legislation.[9] Then, beginning with the child labor case in 1918, discussed below, reaction against advanced progressivism set in and was enormously strengthened by the appointment of a new conservative majority between 1921 and 1930. So retrogressive, in fact, was the new court that on occasion it tended to be blindly reactionary in cases involving economic and social policies. And this attempt to roll back the progressive tide provoked violent attacks by reform groups and numerous proposals to curb the Court's authority. The causes for this progressive anger can best be demonstrated by a discussion of the trend of the Court's decisions in the fields of civil rights, social and economic legislation, the legal status of organized labor, and limitations on the regulatory power of the state and federal governments.

The decade from 1919 to 1929 was no time of triumph for defenders of the American tradition of civil rights. On the contrary, the prevailing demand for conformity and suppression of radical ideas was in part reflected in a series of Supreme Court decisions that destroyed old judicial barriers against assaults on the right of free expression. In Schenck v. United States and two other decisions rendered in 1919, a unanimous Court agreed that the government had the right to suppress sedition during wartime, on the ground that sedition constituted a "clear and present danger" to national security. In Abrams v. United States, 1919, and other cases, Holmes and Brandeis tried to persuade their colleagues to accept a narrow interpretation of the "clear and present danger" doctrine; but the bars were down, and the two dissenters pleaded in vain for a return to the old freedom. Moreover, in Gitlow v. New York, 1925, and Whitney v. California, 1927, the Court— with Holmes and Brandeis again eloquently dissenting—upheld criminal anarchy and syndicalism laws of New York and California. The effect of

---

[8] During his eight years as President, Wilson appointed only three justices. During his two and one-half years in office, Harding appointed a Chief Justice and three associate justices.

[9] See above, p. 74.

these decisions, in brief, was to give federal and state officials practically unlimited discretion in determining what constituted a "clear and present danger."

In the protection of racial and religious minorities, on the other hand, the Court exhibited a larger degree of boldness. In 1923 it overturned state wartime statutes forbidding the use of foreign languages in schools.[10] Two years later, in a momentous decision—Pierce v. Society of Sisters—the Court unanimously outlawed a Klan-sponsored Oregon statute designed to destroy parochial schools by requiring all children between the ages of eight and sixteen to attend public schools. Finally, when the Texas legislature excluded Negroes from the Democratic primary and soon afterward authorized the Democratic state committee to exclude Negro voters, the Court, in 1927 and again in 1932, nullified the statutes on the ground that they obviously violated the Fourteenth and Fifteenth Amendments.[11] In other cases, however, the Court vacillated between a firm defense of civil rights and a willingness to condone new means of violating them. On the one hand, it condemned the illegal seizure of evidence; on the other, it sanctioned the admission of evidence obtained by wire-tapping, approved western state statutes excluding Orientals from land ownership, and upheld the denial of citizenship to immigrants who refused to take an oath promising to bear arms in defense of the United States.

As for social and economic policies, it would be an exaggeration to say that the Court set out willfully during the period under discussion to overturn the whole body of progressive state and federal statutes. But on two important frontiers of the social justice movement the Court not only called a halt to reform but also completely nullified gains already made. The first controversy involved the constitutionality of the Child Labor Act of 1916. By a five to four decision in Hammer v. Dagenhart, 1918, the Court declared that the Act involved an unconstitutional invasion of the police powers of the states—in other words, that Congress could not use its power over interstate commerce to regulate the conditions of labor. When Congress early the following year levied a prohibitive tax on products manufactured in whole or in part by children, the Court, in Bailey v. Drexel Furniture Company, 1922, again applied its veto. Congress, the majority declared, could not use the taxing power to accomplish an unconstitutional regulation.

The Court's inflexible opposition to any form of *federal* regulation of hours, wages, and the conditions of labor—for such opposition was clearly implied in the child labor decisions—was discouraging enough to social justice reformers with ambitious plans for extensive federal regulation through the commerce power. Even more disheartening, however, was the Court's destruction of all *state* efforts to regulate the wages of women workers. In 1923 the case of Adkins v. Children's Hospital, involving the constitutionality of a District of Columbia minimum wage statute for women, came before the new conservative Court. Defending the District

[10] In Meyer v. Nebraska, 1923, and Barteis v. Iowa, 1923, both involving the use of German in parochial schools.

[11] In 1935, however, the same conservative Court, in Grovey v. Townsend, allowed the Democratic state convention of Texas to exclude Negroes from party membership and the privilege of voting in the party primary election.

minimum wage statute, Felix Frankfurter marshaled economic and social data to prove a direct connection between the wages women received and their health and morality. Brushing aside these arguments as irrelevant, Justice George Sutherland, speaking for the majority, resurrected the decision in Lochner v. New York and declared that state efforts to regulate the wages of grown women violated their freedom to make a labor contract. Indeed, Herbert Spencer or William Graham Sumner could not have been more eloquent in defense of *laissez faire.*

Enraged by this reversion to obsolete interpretations, progressives launched a propaganda attack that seriously weakened the Court's prestige and did not subside until the justices had specifically repudiated Hammer v. Dagenhart and Adkins v. Children's Hospital. Meanwhile, another long and bitter controversy was set off when the Court denied that the labor provisions of the Clayton Act of 1914 had conferred any substantial new benefits and privileges on labor unions. The question, in essence, was: Did the Clayton Act give unions immunity from prosecution and injunctions against methods of industrial warfare—the secondary boycott, the "blacklist," and mass picketing, among others—that the courts had earlier outlawed under the Sherman Act?

In a number of decisions in the 1920's, the Court ruled that the Clayton Act had neither conferred upon labor unions immunity from prosecution for violating the antitrust laws nor legalized labor practices that were illegal before the Clayton Act was adopted. Although the majority correctly interpreted the intentions of the framers of the Clayton Act,[12] Justices Holmes, Brandeis, and John H. Clarke dissented and lent authority to the AF of L's contention that organized labor had been unjustly deprived of the benefits of its "Magna Carta."

Continuing a policy begun in the 1880's, the Supreme Court during the 1920's insisted on wielding the power to review state action regulating economic enterprises. Generally speaking, however, Supreme Court policy concerning state regulation was neither capricious nor reactionary. The Court readily acknowledged the right of the states to regulate businesses clothed with a public interest; at the same time, it insisted that such regulation be nondiscriminatory and according to due process of law. By the 1920's railroad regulation, both state and federal, had become in practice thoroughly institutionalized. But state regulation of public utilities was not as well developed by precedent and experience, and there was considerable confusion over the proper constitutional basis for rate-making. The state commissions usually determined rates on a basis of original cost; during the prosperous twenties, on the other hand, public utilities companies contended that the cost of reproducing the properties was the proper basis. Although the Court usually accepted the latter contention before 1933, it did not evolve any definite formula for determining the basis for a fair return.

As for federal regulation, there occurred a relentless expansion of the federal power during the 1920's, in spite of the conservative temper of the men who determined Republican policies and controlled the Supreme

[12] See above, p. 67.

Court. In Massachusetts *v.* Mellon, 1923, the Court upheld the system of federal grants-in-aid to the states and repudiated Massachusetts' argument that such grants unduly infringed upon the police power of the states because of the conditions attached to the acceptance of such grants. The result of the decision was a significant erosion of state sovereignty. Moreover, in all cases in which the United States could demonstrate that the regulated activity was interstate in character the Supreme Court sanctioned an expansion of federal authority. In Stafford *v.* Wallace, 1922, for example, the Court upheld the Packers and Stockyards Act, which subjected the meat packing industry to strict federal control. While nullifying the Grain Futures Act in 1923 because Congress had used the taxing power to regulate the grain exchanges, the Court declared that Congress might use its commerce power to accomplish the same result. When Congress established the Federal Radio Commission and gave it complete control over the airways, the Court agreed in 1933 that such regulation was proper and constitutional.

Moreover, the Supreme Court's interpretation of the antitrust laws in the 1920's was consistent and straightforward. In United States *v.* United States Steel Corporation, 1920, and United States *v.* International Harvester Company, 1927, for example, the Court declared that mere bigness was no violation of the antitrust laws. In a number of cases involving the activities of trade associations, the Court outlawed any practices that might lead to price-fixing or restriction of production. In dealing with cases arising from the efforts of the Federal Trade Commission to suppress unfair trade practices, the Court always insisted upon the privilege of determining what an unfair trade practice was. It was true, as progressives lamented, that such broad review seriously hampered the work of the Commission. Progressives forgot, however, that the framers of the Federal Trade Commission Act of 1914 had explicitly given the Court broad review over the Commission's actions in order to prevent the Commission from ever becoming arbitrary, capricious, or independent of judicial limitations.

CHAPTER 13 / FOREIGN RELATIONS
OF THE 1920's

HE DEVELOPMENT of American foreign policy during the years between the Armistice and the Great Depression presents an anomaly between the popular desire for extrication from entangling obligations on the one hand and the necessary adoption of measures of cooperation on the other. In brief, during the 1920's the United States largely abandoned isolation and sought to strengthen and protect the peace structure of the world. At the same time it sought the advantages of peace without being willing to assume obligations to preserve peace. And because of this fact, new masters of aggression were able to make a hollow mockery of these vain efforts in the following decade.

Events of the thirties lay in the distant future, however, as the Harding administration set about in the spring of 1921 to extricate the United States from obligations Wilson had assumed. First, the new President made it clear that the United States would not join the League of Nations—"We do not mean to be entangled," he declared in his inaugural address. Second, the administration moved to end the state of war between the United States and the Central Powers. Soon after Congress, on July 2, 1921, approved a joint resolution declaring the war with Germany at an end, the new Secretary of State, Charles Evans Hughes, negotiated separate peace treaties with Germany, Austria, and Hungary that gave the United States the benefits without the responsibilities of the Versailles Treaty.

By concluding a separate peace with Germany, the Harding administration made it clear that the United States would assume no responsibility for enforcing the peace it had helped impose. Meanwhile, however, a crisis of dangerous magnitude among the United States, Great Britain, and Japan was nearing culmination just as Harding took office. Let us now examine the causes of this menace to peace and see the way in which the new administration met the first challenge to its leadership and courage.

101 / War Clouds over the Pacific

The reader will recall that Japanese-American relations on the eve of America's entrance into the First World War were troubled and that the effort of Viscount Ishii and Secretary of State Lansing to come to comprehensive understanding on all aspects of the Far Eastern question in October and November 1917 had brought no real relief from the tension. Events following the negotiation of the Lansing-Ishii Agreement only further embittered relations. For one thing, in order to halt Japanese economic penetration of northern China and Manchuria, Wilson revived the international banking consortium that he had roundly condemned in 1913. For another, as a result of the Russian Revolution and the ensuing civil war, Japanese and American troops had been brought face to face in Siberia. In the summer of 1918 the American and Allied governments agreed to send an expedition to Vladivostok to rescue a sizable Czech army from the Bolsheviks. President Wilson sent an expedition of 9,000 men under General William S. Graves to Vladivostok in August 1918. At the same time, the Japanese army dispatched some 73,000 troops and within a short time controlled all the strategic centers of eastern Siberia. Perceiving that the Japanese meant to seize the Russian Maritime Province, Lansing at once brought heavy pressure on the Imperial government for withdrawal of most of its troops.

Japanese-American relations were further embittered at the Paris Peace Conference, when the Japanese failed to secure the inclusion of a provision in the League Covenant affirming the principle of racial equality. Even more important were the controversies between Wilson and the Japanese delegates over the disposal of the former German-owned Marshall, Mariana, and Caroline islands and the Shantung Province of China, all of which Japan had occupied in 1914.

The Marshall, Mariana, and Caroline islands lay directly athwart the sea lanes between Hawaii and the American outposts in Guam and the Philippines. By fortifying their new island possessions, therefore, the Japanese could render American protection of the Philippines virtually impossible. Unable to win British and French support, Wilson had to agree that the disputed islands should be mandated to Japan but never fortified.[1]

Although he realized the strategic importance of this concession, Wilson made a much harder fight to force the Japanese out of the Shantung Province than out of the Marshalls, Marianas, and Carolines. He was fighting from a position of extreme weakness, however, for Britain and France had earlier agreed that Japan should retain the former German leasehold on Kiachow Bay and former German economic interests in the Shantung Province. Supported by a rising anti-Japanese sentiment in the United States, the President pressed his fight to the verge of disrupting the conference; he gave in only at the last moment because he had no alternative. None the less, American opinion was bitter, and the Japanese left the conference convinced Wilson had tried to thwart their legitimate expansion and challenge their predominant position in the Far East.

The series of Japanese-American controversies from 1913 to 1919 built up a cumulative mutual bitterness, but the event that made the tension immediately dangerous was the development of a naval race among the United

---

[1] Wilson, however, refused to concur in the conference's decision to mandate the island of Yap to Japan. Yap, which lay west of Guam and the Carolines, was an important center for the Pacific cables. Wilson entered a reservation to protect American rights in the island.

States, Britain, and Japan at the end of the war. As it threatened to disrupt good relations between America and Britain and perhaps to lead to a war in the Pacific, it would be well to understand the background of this, the direst menace to the peace of the world in the immediate postwar years.

When the United States entered the war in 1917 the Navy Department shelved its plans to build the great new fleet authorized by Congress in 1916 and concentrated all its resources on the construction of destroyers and anti-submarine vessels. At the end of the war the United States had but sixteen battleships, as compared with Britain's forty-two. Soon after the Armistice, however, the Navy Department prepared to resume construction of the ships authorized in 1916,[2] completion of which would give the Unitted States a dreadnought and battle cruiser fleet nearly equal to Britain's. In addition, in December 1918 the Department presented to Congress plans for a second three-year building program, which, if completed, would have given the American navy definite superiority over the British fleet.

Actually, the President introduced the second three-year building program in order to increase his bargaining power with the British at the peace conference and abandoned it in return for British support for the League of Nations. In December 1919, however, the Navy Department's General Board presented a new one-year program for the construction of two battle-ships, one battle cruiser, and lesser craft, completion of which would give the United States command both of the Atlantic and Western Pacific. Rebuffed by Congress, the General Board returned the following year to urge a new three-year program. Although Congress in 1920–1921 rejected this latest recommendation, the Navy's plans for a fleet as large and powerful as the British had considerable support in the American press.

The fear of an uncontrollable upsurge of navalism in the United States alarmed British leaders as no other event had done since Germany set out in the 1890's to challenge the mistress of the seas. "Great Britain would spend her last guinea to keep a navy superior to that of the United States or any other Power," Prime Minister Lloyd George had told Colonel House; and in March 1921 the British government revealed plans to resume construction on a large scale. Japanese leaders were equally alarmed, and by 1920 the Diet had authorized a construction program that would give the Empire a force of twenty-five capital ships by 1927. More immediately disturbing to the Japanese than the threat of new American naval construction was the stationing by the end of 1919 of an American fleet in the Pacific nearly as powerful as the entire Japanese navy, together with the development of plans by the Navy Department to enlarge naval bases in Hawaii and the Philippines and to fortify Guam.

102 / *The Washington Conference*

If the naval chieftains had had their way, the naval race would have gone merrily on. But they did not have their way because moderate opinion

---

[2] Ten dreadnoughts and six battle cruisers were authorized by the naval bill of 1916; in addition, the Navy Department had not yet completed construction of three dread-noughts authorized in 1914 and 1915.

in the United States, Britain, and Japan rose against a senseless arms rivalry. In no country was this popular uprising more powerful than in the United States. After the Armistice the old anti-preparedness bloc in Congress revived and forced drastic cuts in the naval programs of 1919 and 1920. In the winter of 1920–1921, moreover, the anti-navy elements coalesced into a strong movement for an international conference for naval disarmament; and despite the vigorous opposition of the Harding administration, the Senate on May 25 and the House on June 29, 1921, overwhelmingly approved Senator William E. Borah's resolution requesting the administration to begin negotiations with Britain and Japan looking toward disarmament.

Meanwhile, the achievement of a naval agreement with the United States had become one of the principal objectives of the British Foreign Office. The British were as anxious as ever to maintain naval superiority; but the prospect of an arms race with the United States caused British leaders to count the costs of attempting to maintain sea supremacy. Convinced the costs were exorbitant, the British Foreign Office informed the State Department that it would make the first move for disarmament if the Department did not. On the same day, July 8, 1921, that this message reached Washington, Harding and Secretary Hughes agreed that action could no longer be postponed. After preliminary overtures met with friendly responses, Hughes on August 11 issued formal invitations to Britain, Japan, China, France, Italy, Belgium, the Netherlands, and Portugal, all with interests in the Far East, to join the United States in a conference at Washington in November 1921.

Hughes next set to work to find a disarmament formula that would not impair American security on the one hand or, on the other, threaten the security of Japan and Great Britain. Rejecting the General Board's suggestion that the United States agree to halt construction after the building program already authorized was completed, Hughes concluded that the only hope for agreement lay in persuading the powers to agree, first, to abandon their present building plans and, second, to set a definite ratio for capital ships based roughly upon existing strength. When the conference assembled for its first session in Continental Hall on November 12, 1921, Hughes avoided generalities and went straight to the point. The only way to end the naval race, he asserted, was to end it now and not sometime in the future. He then outlined a bold plan: a ten-year holiday in the construction of capital ships; the scrapping by the United States of 845,740 tons, by the British of 583,375 tons, and by the Japanese of 448,928 tons of capital ships already built or under construction; and agreement to set the maximum capital tonnage of the United States, Britain, and Japan during the next ten years at 500,000 tons for the two Atlantic powers and 300,000 tons for Japan.

When the British, American, and Japanese delegates announced agreement on all essential points on December 15, observers concluded that Hughes' difficulties were over. When the Secretary tried to persuade the French and Italians to accept a maximum of 175,000 tons of capital ships, however, he ran into a host of troubles with the French. Offended by their exclusion from the three-power discussions and by an offensive remark by Hughes about their inability to pay their debts, the French demanded a quota of 350,000 tons of heavy ships. Only by appealing over the heads of the French delegates to Premier Aristide Briand and by marshaling world opinion was Hughes able to persuade the French to agree to his proposed limit.

Thus the Five Power Naval Treaty, signed in Continental Hall on February 1, 1922, not only ended the naval armaments race in capital ships but also preserved a balance of power in the Far East that left the relative security of the great powers unimpaired. Under the Treaty the naval powers agreed to abandon capital ship construction for ten years, to follow with a few exceptions Hughes' proposal for the destruction of existing tonnage, and to limit auxiliary craft to 10,000 tons and aircraft carriers to 27,000 tons.[3] In addition, Japan, the United States, and Great Britain promised not to fortify further their outlying island possessions in the Western Pacific.

The first agreement in modern history by which major powers undertook disarmament of any kind, the Five Power Naval Treaty represented a remarkable triumph of reason over selfish nationalism. But it was not enough. The naval arms race had in large measure reflected America's quest for security in the Pacific and Japan's fear of future American encroachments in the Far East. Any agreement for naval disarmament would soon prove worthless unless the causes for mutual distrust were removed, unless the three major powers were willing to forego future aggression and live at peace with one another.

Such an understanding was achieved at Washington because Britain and the United States desired only to preserve a *status quo* that safeguarded their interests in the Far East, but above all because the existing government of Japan sought the friendship of the democracies of the West. To Americans the chief obstacle to a comprehensive understanding was the Anglo-Japanese Alliance, which obligated Britain to assume a benevolent neutrality toward Japan in the event of a Japanese-American war. Months before the Washington Conference met, when renewal of the Alliance was under consideration, Hughes had brought strong pressure upon the British Foreign Office for abrogation or modification of the treaty. The Dominion governments were even more insistent upon abrogation than was the United States.

Japan and Britain were willing to abrogate the Alliance, which had now seemingly outlived its original purpose of restraining Russian expansion in the Far East, provided they could obtain a new security system that included the United States. Rejecting an Anglo-Japanese suggestion of a triple alliance, Hughes insisted upon bringing France into the new understanding and upon avoiding binding obligations. The outcome was the Four Power Treaty, presented to a plenary session of the conference on December 10, 1921, by Senator Lodge of the American delegation. It pledged Britain, America, Japan, and France to respect each other's possession in the Pacific area and to confer jointly if disputes among them or outside aggressors threatened the peace. The Treaty provided also that the Anglo-Japanese Alliance would be abrogated upon ratification of the Four Power pact.

There yet remained on the conference's agenda the question of China's

---

[3] Each signatory, however, was permitted to convert two capital ships to aircraft carriers as large as 33,000 tons. This provision was inserted to permit the American navy to convert the battle cruisers *Lexington* and *Saratoga* into carriers.

status and of Japan's intentions toward that so-called republic. Under steady Anglo-American pressure, the Japanese yielded their imperialistic ambitions and approved an agreement that reaffirmed the historic American policy of the Open Door and noninterference. Signed on February 6, 1922, by representatives of the United States, Britain, Japan, France, Italy, China, the Netherlands, Belgium, and Portugal, the Nine Power Treaty pledged the signatories to respect the sovereignty, independence, and integrity of China; to give China a full opportunity to establish a stable government; to uphold the Open Door in China; and to refrain from seeking special rights and privileges in China that would impair the rights of friendly states.

Nor was this all, though it represented the most sweeping affirmation of self-denial that Japan had yet made. Hughes meanwhile had been hard at work on the Japanese and Chinese delegates to effect a direct settlement of the Shantung question. Actually, the Japanese were more reasonable than the Chinese; and the Treaty concluded on February 4, 1922, conceded everything Hughes had asked—restoration of full Chinese sovereignty over Shantung and the sale by Japan to China under certain safeguards of the Shantung Railroad. Finally, as if to demonstrate their determination to liquidate all sources of potential trouble, the Japanese promised to evacuate Siberia, conceded the American demand for special cable rights on the island of Yap, and joined the United States in abrogating the Lansing-Ishii Agreement.

Years later it became fashionable in the United States to condemn the Harding administration for surrendering naval supremacy and for failing to obtain ironclad guaranteees against future disturbers of the peace. Such criticism, however, ignores some large historical facts. In the first place, in the Five Power Naval Treaty the United States yielded not actual but potential naval supremacy, which could have been achieved only if the American people had been willing to maintain a long and costly arms race. But were the people and Congress willing to support such an effort? The evidence is overwhelming that they were not, for until 1938 Congress refused even to maintain the fleet at the authorized treaty strength. In the second place, although the absence in the Washington treaties of any enforcement machinery undoubtedly weakened them, enforcement would have involved the giving of guarantees that the Senate would never have approved. In spite of the omission of any such guarantees, in ratifying the Four Power Treaty in March 1922 the Senate insisted upon declaring that the United States had made "no commitment to armed force, no alliance, no obligation to join in any defense."

The expressed determination of the American people to avoid a naval rivalry and even the suggestion of binding obligations to preserve the peace was a compelling historical reality to which Hughes had to yield. But by yielding what did he obtain? He obtained for his country parity in capital ships with Great Britain and considerable supremacy over Japan under an agreement that ended the most dangerous phase of the naval race for a decade. He cleared the air of suspicion and distrust; he won the abrogation of the Anglo-Japanese Alliance. Best of all, he helped erect a new peace structure for the Far East that seemed to make it possible for Britain, the

United States, and Japan to live and work together in mutual trust and respect.

103 / *The Japanese-American Crisis of 1924*

For a short time after the Washington Conference relations between Japan and the United States were unusually cordial, especially when a great earthquake in 1923 evoked an outpouring of American aid to the stricken Japanese people. Then in 1924 occurred a catastrophic event—the passage by Congress of legislation prohibiting Japanese immigration—that renewed the Yellow Peril agitation in the United States and poisoned the wells of sentiment against the United States in Japan.

Japanese immigration to the United States since 1907 had been regulated by the Gentlemen's Agreement.[4] Although the Agreement had worked reasonably well, it ended neither Japanese immigration nor the agitation on the Pacific Coast for frank and total exclusion. When the House immigration committee in 1923 began work on a permanent immigration bill to supplant the emergency measure of 1921, the AF of L, the American Legion, and other organizations joined Californians in what seemed to be an overwhelming demand for statutory exclusion. News of the impending legislation prompted the Japanese Embassy to remind the Secretary of State of the dangers it would raise; Hughes, in turn, urged the House leaders to put Japanese immigration on the quota basis, which would have permitted only 246 Japanese to enter a year, and pleaded on the high ground of national interest against insulting the Japanese people by an open and invidious exclusion. Disregarding this solemn advice, the House committee reported a bill forbidding the immigration of persons "ineligible to citizenship"—words hateful to the Japanese.

This was the situation in March 1924, when the Secretary called in the Japanese Ambassador, Hanihara, and asked him to write a letter summarizing his government's attitude toward the Gentlemen's Agreement. This Hanihara did on April 10; but in closing he warned that "grave consequences" would follow the enactment of the House immigration bill. Hughes read the letter before it was published and unwisely let the words "grave consequences" pass without comment. Published in the press with Hughes' approval, Hanihara's letter provoked a storm of comment. Declaring that it represented a "veiled threat" to the United States, the aged Senator Lodge persuaded the Senate to reject an amendment tacitly extending the Gentlemen's Agreement. On April 16, 1924, the senators approved the House bill 71 to 4 and Coolidge reluctantly signed it after vainly attempting to persuade the conference committee to delete the controverted provision.

It is no exaggeration to say that Congress' action in this episode virtually nullified all the progress Hughes and the moderate Japanese leaders had made since 1921 in restoring cordial relations between their two countries. "Our friends in the Senate have in a few minutes spoiled the work of years and done a lasting injury to our common country," Hughes wrote in disgust on April 24, 1924. Unfortunately, reaction in Japan fully justified the Secre-

---

[4] For the negotiation and provisions of this Agreement, see above, pp. 152–153.

tary's gloomy observation. The day upon which the immigration law went into effect was a day of national mourning and humiliation, and millions of Japanese lived thereafter in shame and anger.

104 / The United States and the World Economy, 1919–1929

While international political developments in the early 1920's refused to allow the American people to revert to isolation, they were projected into the arena of world affairs by still another force—the dissipation of European economic power during the war and the sudden emergence of the United States as the chief source of capital for so-called backward areas and the debt-ridden countries of Europe. By 1914, American citizens had invested some

PRINCIPAL CONSTITUENTS

VISIBLE ITEMS	SERVICES	SECURITIES TRANSACTIONS
MERCHANDISE	COMMERCIAL	INTEREST AND CURRENT ITEMS
GOLD	PERSONAL	CAPITAL MOVEMENT

EXPORTS AND OTHER CREDITS, $9 115 000 000

PER CENT   55.2   4.3 3.7 3.7 11.8   21.3

IMPORTS AND OTHER DEBITS, $9 121 000 000

PER CENT   49.2   2.5 3.3 12.5 3.1   29.4

8. *International Payments of the United States, 1927*

$3,500,000,000 abroad but still owed to Europe a net debt of $3,686,000,000. As a consequence of the disgorging of 70 per cent of British- and French-owned American securities between 1914 and 1919, the aggregate investment of foreigners in the United States was reduced from a little over seven to nearly four billion dollars; during the same period private American investments abroad increased to nearly $7,000,000,000. On December 31, 1919, therefore, foreigners owed Americans a net private debt of nearly three billions. In addition, European governments owed the United States $10,351,-000,000 borrowed during the war and post-Armistice periods.

This fundamental shift in the world's economic balance of power demanded bold American leadership in establishing a workable system of international exchange. Unfortunately, the American leaders and people were too inexperienced to be far-sighted in meeting this, the most important economic challenge of the postwar era. Instead of insisting upon the mutual cancellation of all intergovernmental debts and reparations, which were the most disturbing factors in the postwar international economy, the United States insisted upon their full payment of war debts. Instead of lowering tariffs to enable Europeans to pay their private debts in goods, Congress increased tariff rates. Instead of using the resources of the federal government to stabilize the European economies, administrations from Wilson to Hoover withdrew as completely as possible from the making of important international economic decisions and threw the burden of readjustment upon private bankers.

The result was the development in the 1920's of a structure of international exchange that, in spite of its superficial appearance of stability, was entirely dependent for its continued prosperity upon the maintenance of a high level of American export of capital. During the twenties the United States bought raw materials and other goods on the world market in large

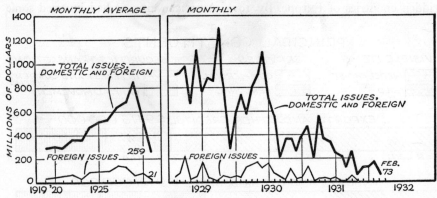

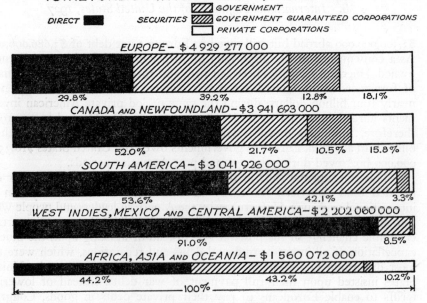

9. *Foreign Investments by American Citizens, 1919–1932*

quantities—total imports in the peak year exceeded $4,625,000,000. On the other hand, Americans consistently sold more abroad than they bought, the excess ranging from a low of $375,500,000 in 1923 to a high of slightly over $1,000,000,000 in 1928.

How did foreigners find dollars to meet these trade deficits and pay their war debts to the United States? The manner in which this was done in 1929 was typical for the decade. In 1929 the United States had a "favorable" trade balance of $842,000,000 and received as well about $800,000,000 from payments on war debts. Europeans met this aggregate deficit of $1,642,000,000 in a variety of ways—by the expenditure of $500,000,000 by American tourists abroad, the remittance of $200,000,000 to Europe by immigrants in the United States, and by dollar earnings from the carrying trade, foreign investments in the United States, and the like. The remaining deficit was supplied by American investments abroad of $1,037,000,000. Thus in 1929 foreign bankers and merchants actually accumulated a surplus of 508,000,000 *dollars*. And so it went throughout the 1920's. By the annual export of about $1,000,000,000 between 1919 and 1930 American bankers and businessmen supported the huge volume of American foreign trade and the world economy as well. The fatal weakness of the system was that its maintenance depended upon a continuing flow of American dollars in the form of purchases and investments abroad. As long as the system lasted, however, it seemed to work admirably and well.

105 / American International Economic Policy, 1919–1930

The Harding, Coolidge, and Hoover administrations followed the policy begun by the Wilson administration of withdrawing the federal government from the realm of international economic activity. At the same time, the State and Commerce departments worked vigorously and often successfully to protect economic interests abroad and to expand the frontiers of American foreign trade and investments. One notable victory was the Nine Power Treaty, which for a time preserved an area of freedom for American merchants and capitalists in China. Another was the State Department's effort to prevent the confiscation of American mining and oil properties in Mexico by the government of that country. More important, perhaps, was Secretary Hughes' fight to break the monopoly over the oil reserves of the Middle East that the British, French, and Dutch governments had established at the end of the World War. In 1925 seven American oil companies were given a quarter share in the future exploitation of oil in Iraq as a result of Hughes' intervention. In all these and other economic aspects of diplomacy the State Department continued the well-established policy of opposing special concessions and exclusive rights for Americans and insisting only upon equal commercial opportunity abroad.

The most perplexing international economic issues of the 1920's were the war debts and reparations questions; and the stubborn refusal of American leaders to work out an enlightened solution disturbed the economies of Europe and engendered antagonisms that persisted until the Second World War. The United States lent the Allied governments a little over $7,000,-

000,000 during the war and an additional $3,250,000,000 in cash and supplies during the months immediately after the Armistice. But this was only one aspect of the complicated structure of intergovernmental debts. The British, for example, had lent more than $4,000,000,000 to seventeen creditor nations; the French had lent to ten nations.

At the end of the war Allied leaders began a concerted campaign for the cancellation of all intergovernmental debts as the first step in restoring a healthy international economy. As for the Allied war debts to the United States, Europeans pointed out that practically every dollar borrowed had been spent in America for food and munitions; that Europeans had contributed their sons and Americans their money in a common cause; and that, in any event, American tariff and shipping policies prevented Europeans from paying these war debts in goods and services, the only kind of payment they could offer.

In retrospect, these arguments seem realistic, reasonable, and morally sound. To Americans of the 1920's and 1930's, however, they represented a shocking attempt to escape a just debt. When the British at Versailles suggested either mutual cancellation of intergovernmental debts or else a linking of reparation and war debt payments, Wilson replied coldly; and his insistence upon full payment without any reference to reparations receipts established a policy to which all administrations from Harding to Franklin D. Roosevelt adhered.

In February 1922 Congress established a World War Foreign Debt Commission to negotiate long-term funding agreements with the European debtors. With their reputation for financial integrity at stake, the British in June 1923 agreed to pay $4,600,000,000 in principal and accrued interest over a sixty-two-year period at 3 per cent for the first decade and 3½ per cent thereafter. The French and Italians, however, at first refused to acknowledge either the moral or financial validity of their indebtedness to the United States. The State Department retaliated by imposing a ban on all private loans to citizens and governments in default; and under this pressure the French and Italians finally surrendered in 1925 and 1926.[5] In the same manner the smaller nations of Europe were brought to terms.

Thus did the United States bludgeon Europeans into obligating themselves for a debt they could never possibly pay from their own resources through the normal channels of exchange. In the end a solution was found, but not before the American government had intervened decisively though unofficially to help settle the most perplexing issue of all—the question of Germany's reparations payments, upon which the structure of intergovernmental payments was based. Let us review briefly the background of this story.

On May 1, 1921, the Reparations Commission presented to the German Republic a reparations bill of $33,000,000,000, in addition to the total Belgian

---

[5] The Italians reached agreement with the War Debt Commission in November 1925. The Italian debt was funded at $2,042,000,000, at two-fifths of 1 per cent interest, to be paid in installments over a sixty-two-year period. The French acknowledged an indebtedness of $4,025,000,000, at an average interest rate of 1.64 per cent, to be paid over a sixty-two-year period. The French Chamber of Deputies did not ratify this agreement, however, until July 1929.

war debt and the costs of the armies of occupation. Forced at the point of a gun to accept responsibility for this sum, the German government tried to make payments but had to default in 1922. In retaliation, the French occupied the Ruhr, the center of German industry and coal mining, whereupon the Germans inaugurated a program of passive resistance that soon resulted in a spectacular inflation of the German currency. By the end of 1923 the German government was bankrupt and the Reich tottered upon the brink of total economic ruin. Alarmed by the prospect of chaos in central Europe, Secretary Hughes intervened to find a solution for the impasse. After patient negotiations with the French government, in which he had the full support of the British, Hughes persuaded the Reparations Commission to attempt to work out a plan of reparations payments based upon Germany's capacity to pay.

The upshot was that the Reparations Commission in November 1923 appointed a committee upon which two Americans, Charles G. Dawes and Owen D. Young, served unofficially. In April 1924 this, the so-called Dawes Committee, submitted a plan that saved Europe from financial collapse. It provided elaborate financial machinery to collect and distribute reparations payments, established a schedule of payments that Germany could bear, and arranged for a gold loan of $200,000,000 by American bankers to the German government to stabilize the German currency on a gold standard. In 1929 a new committee of experts, headed by Owen D. Young, re-examined the reparations question, set the total bill at a little more than $2,000,000,000, exclusive of interest, and provided for an end of payments by 1988.

The significant point of this somewhat complicated story is the manner in which the American government and private bankers intervened to help establish a system of intergovernmental debt and reparations payments that worked so long as the dynamic factor in the system continued to operate. That dynamic factor was private American loans to the central government, states, municipalities, and corporations of Germany totaling some $2,500,-000,000 from 1924 to 1930. During the same period Germany in turn made reparations payments under the Dawes Plan totaling nearly $2,000,000,000, while the former Allies paid to the United States on their war debt accounts $2,606,000,000, or about the same amount American bankers had lent to Germany. Thus, in spite of the refusal of the State Department ever to admit the fact, the payment of war debts under this complicated structure became contingent upon the payment of reparations by Germany, which in turn depended upon a maintenance of the flow of dollars from the United States.

106 / *The Further Search for Peace, 1924–1930*

Peace was the prevailing passion of the American people in foreign affairs in the 1920's. A small but influential minority of public leaders continued to agitate for entrance into the League of Nations, but probably a majority preferred to advance the cause through less entangling means— disarmament, membership in the World Court, cooperation with the League, treaties outlawing war, and the like. After the Washington Conference the popular obsession for peace continued unabated, while events in Europe—the settlement of the reparations imbroglio, the Locarno treaties of 1925, and Germany's admission to the League in 1926—raised bright hopes for the future. But the American peace sentiment was conceived in naiveté concerning European affairs and born of a romantic delusion as to the manner in which the United States could best serve mankind. Americans wanted peace, to be sure, but they were unwilling to assume obligations to enforce an international system. Moreover, as the Immigration Act of 1924 revealed, Americans were not yet ready to forego nationalistic prejudices that impaired international friendship. It is against this background climate of opinion that we must consider the further search for peace without obligations.

One significant manifestation of this search was the campaign for American membership in the World Court waged by Presidents and Secretaries of State from Harding and Hughes to Roosevelt and Cordell Hull. It was a project upon which both advanced and cautious internationalists could agree, for the Permanent Court of International Justice was an agency apart from the League and membership did not carry with it any obligation to help enforce the Court's decisions. In February 1923 Hughes won Harding's approval for membership and began a campaign to stimulate public discussion. By the summer of 1924 sentiment was so aroused that both major parties endorsed membership, and the following March the House of Representatives adopted a resolution approving a membership protocol. Bitter-end isolationists like Senator Borah failed to prevent passage of the resolution by the Senate on January 27, 1926, but they forced adoption of a reservation restricting the right of the Court to render advisory opinions. When the member nations refused to accept the reservation, Presidents Hoover and Roosevelt, in 1930 and 1935,[6] again vainly urged membership in the Court. Meanwhile, a number of distinguished Americans, including Charles Evans Hughes, John Bassett Moore, and Frank B. Kellogg, served as judges on the tribunal.

A second manifestation of the American search for peace in the 1920's was the gradual change in official policy toward the League of Nations. During the early months of the Harding administration the State Department not only refused to cooperate with the League's nonpolitical agencies but also failed, either accidentally or deliberately, even to acknowledge communications from the League's Secretariat. Evidence indicates that Hughes was cautiously avoiding giving offense to the Senate isolationists while devising a means by which the United States might cooperate with the League's humanitarian endeavors.

In any event, in the spring and summer of 1922 the Secretary launched a new policy of cooperation by sending "unofficial observers" to speak for the United States in various League agencies and commissions. As this policy developed and the American government cooperated in conferences to

[6] Isolationists made an especially bitter campaign against American membership in the World Court in 1934–1935. In spite of an outpouring of public support, the Franklin Roosevelt administration was unable to muster a two-thirds majority when the Senate, by a vote of fifty-two yeas to thirty-six nays, refused to approve a membership protocol on January 29, 1935.

control the traffic in arms, women, and opium, in the work of the Reparations Commission, in the League Health Organization, and in the International Labour Organization, Senator Borah and other irreconcilables charged that the Harding, Coolidge, and Hoover administrations were taking America into the League through the back door. In a sense the charge was justified, for by 1930 the United States had participated in some forty League conferences and had five permanent representatives stationed at Geneva, Switzerland, headquarters of the League. Even more important was the fact that the State Department had constructed machinery through which it could cooperate with the League Council in any crisis menacing the peace of the world.

Even so, there were few indications by the late twenties that the American people were willing to undertake responsibilities for preserving the peace in times of crisis. This fact was vividly revealed by events culminating in the signing of the Kellogg-Briand Pact in 1928. During the early twenties the American peace organizations voiced the passion for peace but could not agree on the most crucial issue, American membership in the League of Nations. In 1921, however, Salmon O. Levinson, a Chicagoan interested in the peace cause, devised a program upon which all the disparate and sometimes warring peace elements could unite—a program to outlaw war as an instrument of national policy. Gathering around him a group of idealists and pacifists, Levinson formed the American Committee for the Outlawry of War. Levinson's crusade became all the more formidable when he won the support of Nicholas Murray Butler and James T. Shotwell, two officials of the Carnegie Endowment for International Peace.

In March 1927 Shotwell visited the French Foreign Minister, Aristide Briand, in Paris and suggested that the French government could best allay American fears of French militarism by taking leadership in the movement to outlaw war. Perceiving an opportunity to draw the United States and France together in a sympathetic alliance, Briand addressed an open letter to the American people on April 6, 1927, proposing that the two countries join hands in a pact forever outlawing war between them. Briand's message went virtually unnoticed in the American press until Butler called attention to it in a letter published in the *New York Times* on April 25. At once the various peace organizations and Senator Borah took up the hue and cry for a peace pact.

Secretary of State Frank B. Kellogg, who had succeeded Hughes in March 1925, had often expressed a profane contempt for the "fools" and "pacifists" leading the outlawry movement and at first planned to ignore Briand's appeal. Then, on May 21, 1927, the young American flier, Charles A. Lindbergh, landed his *Spirit of St. Louis* outside Paris after making the first nonstop flight from New York. Lindbergh's feat provoked such a demonstration of Franco-American friendship and so stimulated the peace forces in America that the adminstration had to capitulate. Unwilling to sign a bilateral pact with France, which they regarded as a negative military alliance,[7] Coolidge and Kellogg countered on December 28, 1927, by proposing that France and the United States invite the other powers to join them in

[7] In other words, an alliance requiring the United States to remain neutral in the event France had to go to war under her far-flung military alliance system.

a treaty renouncing war as an instrument of national policy. It was not altruism that motivated the explosive Secretary of State; it was a desire to appease the American peace forces who, Kellogg thought, had been playing Briand's game.

Kellogg's counterthrust came as an alarming move to Briand, who knew that France's security rested upon her willingness to go to war to preserve her dominant position in Europe. Once the State Department made it clear that the proposed pact should outlaw only aggressive war and not legitimate defensive efforts, however, negotiations proceeded smoothly. Finally, on August 27, 1928, representatives of all the great powers except Russia, which later ratified, signed the Pact of Paris in the French capital. "The High Contracting Parties," it read, "solemnly declare in the names of their respective people that they condemn recourse to war for the solution of international controversies, and renounce it as an instrument of national policy in their relations with one another."

Although idealists romanticized the significance of the Pact of Paris and cynics sneered at what they called an "international kiss," its negotiation constituted another milestone along the road away from isolation that the American people were traveling. To be sure, the Treaty established no enforcement machinery and would be only as effective as the signatories made it. But it was not meaningless. For one thing, by outlawing aggressive war it changed international law in an important way. For another, it brought the United States, however tenuously, into the peace system established by the Treaty of Versailles and the Locarno treaties. While the American government assumed no legal obligations under the Pact of Paris to defend that peace system, it did assume large moral obligations to cooperate with the League in the event some aggressor violated the Pact. As Briand wisely observed, the Pact was "a beginning, not an end."

107 / Continued Efforts at Naval Disarmament

The Five Power Treaty of 1922 ended the rivalry in the construction of battleships and aircraft carriers; and it seemed for a short time after the Washington Conference that the signatory powers would also refrain from expanding their fleets of cruisers, destroyers, and submarines. In 1924, however, Great Britain launched a new construction program by laying keels for five heavy cruisers of 10,000 tons each and the following year adopted a program calling for the building of nine 10,000-ton and seven 8,000-ton cruisers. The Japanese countered by beginning construction of four heavy cruisers, while the American Congress in December 1924 authorized the President to undertake, prior to July 1, 1927, construction of eight 10,000-ton cruisers. Obviously, by 1927 the major naval powers stood on the verge of another costly naval race that threatened to upset the fine balance established so auspiciously at Washington.

In response to urgings by the House of Representatives and peace organizations in the United States, President Coolidge issued a hasty call, on February 10, 1927, for a five-power naval disarmament conference to meet at Geneva the same year. Alleging that they preferred to work for general disarmament through the League, the French refused to attend; and the French refusal gave the Italians good excuse for staying away. Thus only the three major naval powers sent delegates to the conference that met at Geneva from June 20 to August 4, 1927. Because the State Department had made no diplomatic preparations for the meeting, negotiations went badly from the outset. The British were willing to accept parity in heavy cruiser tonnage with the United States; but the two delegations were never able to agree upon the limitation of light cruisers, and the conference broke up in complete disagreement.

Public opinion in the United States and Britain refused to accept the Geneva failure as final, despite the passage by Congress in February 1929 of a second and larger cruiser bill. The coming to power of the Hoover administration in the United States and the Labour Cabinet under Ramsay MacDonald in Great Britain in 1929 raised new hopes of Anglo-American accord, as MacDonald and the new American Ambassador, Charles G. Dawes, set to work to prepare the way for an understanding. By July 26, 1929, the two governments had agreed on equality in combat strength, to be determined in all categories of fighting ships.

Only minor details remained for discussion, therefore, when Hoover invited MacDonald to visit the United States for final talks preparatory to the calling of a new five-power naval conference. At the President's fishing camp at Rapidan, Virginia, the two leaders agreed to end "all competitive building"; and speaking before the Senate on October 7, the Prime Minister ended all doubts about British willingness to go all the way. On the same day the British government invited the other four naval powers to send delegates to a conference in London the following year.

At the conference that opened in London on January 21, 1930, the American, British, and Japanese representatives readily agreed to extend the construction "holiday" on capital ships for five years and to scrap a total of nine battleships. The Japanese insistence upon greater cruiser strength than the 10:10:6 ratio would allow, however, threatened for a time to disrupt negotiations. In the end the Japanese accepted a compromise by which they obtained a 10:10:6 ratio for heavy cruisers, a 10:10:7 ratio for light cruisers and destroyers, and equality in submarines. In addition, the representatives of the three major naval powers fixed a definite tonnage quota based upon these ratios for cruisers, destroyers, and submarines.[8]

The French, on the other hand, worried as to what parity with Italy would mean locally in the Mediterranean, refused to accept any limitation that did not carry with it an Anglo-American guarantee of security; and when President Hoover flatly refused to make any such commitment, the French—and the Italians also—refused to approve the important provisions of the naval treaty completed on April 22, 1930. In view of the French attitude, the British insisted upon the insertion of a so-called "escalator" clause allowing the signatories to expand their fleets if their national security were threatened by the naval construction of some outside power.

[8] Under this quota the United States was awarded 325,000 tons of cruisers, 150,000 tons of destroyers, and 52,700 tons of submarines; Great Britain, 339,000 tons of cruisers, 150,000 tons of destroyers, and 52,700 tons of submarines; Japan, 208,850 tons of cruisers, 105,500 tons of destroyers, and 52,700 tons of submarines.

Coming at the end of a decade of popular agitation, the London Treaty was a striking victory for the peace movement[9] and further evidence of the determination of the British and American peoples to live in close friendship. As President Hoover declared in 1930, the alternative to naval agreement was mutual "suspicion, hate, ill-will and ultimate disaster." The British, American, and Japanese governments chose mutual trust instead, at least for a moment, in this, the last successful effort to preserve the peace system of the postwar era.

108 / Toward a New Latin American Policy

When Harding took office in 1921 the relations of the United States with Latin America were at probably the bitterest point in American history. American troops stationed in Nicaragua were sustaining a minority government in that country; American naval commanders were running the governments of Santo Domingo and Haiti; and the State Department and the government of Mexico headed by Álvaro Obregón were not even on speaking terms.

It was ironic that the Republican administrations of the 1920's, allegedly the protectors of American investors, should have reversed Wilsonian interventionism and set in motion the liquidation of a good part of the American imperium in the Caribbean area. For this phenomenon a number of factors were responsible. First and most important was the elimination of every threat to American security in the approaches to the Panama Canal, which meant that the American government could afford to be less sensitive to revolutions and debt repudiations after 1920. A second factor shaping the new policy was the accidental manner in which Wilsonian interventionism became an important issue in the campaign of 1920. The indiscreet boast by the Democratic vice presidential candidate, Franklin D. Roosevelt, that the United States would control twelve Latin American votes in the League Assembly, and his inaccurate brag that he had written the Haitian constitution, provoked Harding to give a sweeping pledge of nonintervention toward the Caribbean republics.

A third and certainly not unimportant factor was the character and attitude of the new Secretary of State, Charles Evans Hughes. Viewing with abhorrence the Wilsonian assumption that Americans knew more about the good government of neighboring countries than the leaders of those countries knew, Hughes determined to withdraw American power as fast as circumstances would permit. The new Secretary was also fortunate in finding an able young career diplomat, Sumner Welles, at the Latin American desk in 1921. Welles left the Department the following year but returned on several occasions to help implement the policy of withdrawal.

Santo Domingo became the first testing ground of the new policy. Convinced that Dominicans were ready to resume the powers of self-government, Hughes superintended the holding of elections and the forma-

[9] We should note one other important article of the Treaty—Part IV, which outlawed unrestricted submarine warfare against merchant shipping and which France and Italy, as well as the three great naval powers, approved.

tion of a native government from 1922 to 1924. After the inauguration of President Horatio Vásquez on July 12, 1924, the American occupation forces were gradually withdrawn; and, except for the American customs receivership, Dominicans were once again masters in their own house. Planning to restore self-government also to the Haitians, the Secretary sent a special commissioner to the black republic in 1922 to work with local leaders. When the commissioner warned that renewed anarchy would follow American withdrawal, and a special Senate committee confirmed his findings, Hughes had to postpone the day of liberation.

Nicaragua, however, seemed at last ready to stand on its own; and Hughes withdrew the United States marine guard at Managua in August 1925, after the Liberal, Carlos Solórzano, won the presidency in 1924. Immediately afterward, however, the Conservative leader, Emiliano Chamorro, forced Solórzano out of office and installed himself in the presidential palace. When the United States withheld recognition, the Nicaraguan Congress, in October 1926, elected Adolfo Díaz, another Conservative and long-time friend of the United States, to the presidency. Secretary of State Kellogg unwisely accorded immediate recognition.

At this point the exiled Liberal Vice President, Juan B. Sacasa, returned to Nicaragua and raised a general revolt against the Díaz government. In response to frenzied appeals from Díaz, President Coolidge dispatched some 5,000 marines to suppress the uprising early in 1927. The President's action evoked a storm of protest in the United States; and when it soon became evident that the Liberals would not tamely submit, Coolidge sent Henry L. Stimson to Nicaragua to mediate. By tact and patience Stimson persuaded the Liberals to give up the fight. In return, Stimson guaranteed a fair presidential election—under American military supervision—and compelled Díaz to admit Liberals to his Cabinet.

The result of Stimson's mediation became apparent when the Liberals, General Moncado and Sacasa, were elected to the presidency in 1928 and 1932. From 1909 to 1927 the United States had used military force to keep unpopular but pro-American Conservative governments in power, in defiance of the wishes of a large majority of Nicaraguans. When Stimson offered impartiality in return for the cooperation of the Liberals, he was in effect reversing the historic policy of the State Department. American troops remained in Nicaragua to help the government suppress the bandit leader, Augusto Sandino, and were gradually withdrawn from 1931 to 1933.

Setting the withdrawal from Santo Domingo, Haiti, and Nicaragua in motion was easy compared with the task of re-establishing Mexican-American relations on a friendly basis. The high tension between the two countries provoked by Wilson's interventions was increased during the war by American charges that Mexico was a hotbed of German espionage and especially by Carranza's decree of February 19, 1918, applying Article XXVII of the Mexican Constitution of 1917. This highly controverted article vested ownership in the Mexican people of all subsoil rights to oil and mineral properties acquired by foreigners before 1917 and required foreign owners of such properties to obtain new concessions from the revolutionary government. Vigorous protests from the United States and Great Britain forced Carranza to postpone operation of the decree.

In April 1920 a revolution headed by General Álvaro Obregón deposed Carranza and put Obregón and a less anti-American group in power in Mexico City. The Wilson administration refused recognition because Obregón would not promise to respect American holdings in Mexico, and diplomatic relations were thus in a ruptured state when Hughes assumed office in the spring of 1921. By firm but cordial dealing, Hughes won all his demands[10] and recognized the Obregón regime in 1923. With the accession to the presidency in 1924 of Plutarcho Elias Calles, however, a more radical wing of the revolutionary party came to power, and relations between Mexico and the United States suddenly worsened. Calles threatened to overturn the Mexican-American agreement of 1923 by requiring American owners of oil lands to exchange their titles for fifty-year leases. He also launched a bloody campaign against the Catholic Church that greatly inflamed Catholic opinion in the United States.

Relations were brought to a crisis point early in 1927 when Secretary of State Kellogg foolishly charged that the Calles government was working with Russian agents to establish a "Mexican-fostered Bolshevik hegemony intervening between the United States and the Panama Canal." Although Kellogg's sensational charge stimulated a serious war scare, the State Department was actually then preparing a new campaign to win Mexican friendship. In September 1927 President Coolidge inaugurated this campaign by sending as Ambassador to Mexico City Dwight Morrow, a partner of Morgan & Company and a man of extraordinary tact and ability. By offering genuine friendship, Morrow won the affection of the Mexican people. By his shrewd handling of Calles, he won also a compromise settlement of the oil lands dispute, a surcease of the anticlerical campaign, and a new Mexican-American accord.

While Republican leaders began the retreat from empire in the Caribbean area, they also set in motion a repudiation of the Roosevelt Corollary to the Monroe Doctrine, which Theodore Roosevelt had devised in 1905 to justify a policy of intervention.[11] Hughes began the reversal in 1923 by attempting to explain to the American people that the Monroe Doctrine was exclusively a policy of self-defense and neither infringed upon the independence of any American state nor warranted interference by the United States in the affairs of neighboring countries.[12] That such an interpretation did not imply American abandonment of the alleged right to intervene, however, was dramatically revealed at the Pan-American Conference at Havana in January 1928, when Hughes, as head of the American delegation, stubbornly refused to give in to an overwhelming Latin American

[10] They were compensation for or return of American-owned land seized by the revolutionary government before May 1, 1917; validation of the title to mineral and oil properties owned by Americans in Mexico before 1917; and the establishment of a joint commission to consider claims of American losses suffered during the Revolution.

[11] See above, pp. 148–150.

[12] This position was later affirmed by the State Department in 1930, when it published a _Memorandum on the Monroe Doctrine_, prepared in 1928 by J. Reuben Clark. The _Memorandum_ did not renounce the alleged right of the United States to intervene in the affairs of neighboring states but pointed out that such intervention could not be justified by the Monroe Doctrine.

demand that his country subscribe to an unequivocal pledge of nonintervention.

None the less, there were numerous signs from 1928 to 1933 that the United States could not long maintain its traditional position in the face of a growing Latin American demand. Before his inauguration in 1929, Hoover made a good will tour of Latin America and a few weeks after his accession promised never to intervene to protect American property rights abroad. And when the depression set off a wave of revolutions and debt repudiations throughout Latin America, Hoover and his Secretary of State, Henry L. Stimson, courageously honored the promise. Little wonder it was, therefore, that relations between the United States and Latin America were on a more cordial basis when Hoover left office than they had been at any time since 1901. The Good Neighbor policy of the Franklin Roosevelt administration was possible only because preceding Republican administrations had laid the groundwork in theory and practice for the American retreat from dominion through force.

CHAPTER 14 / ECONOMIC TRENDS
IN THE 1920's

*T*HE DECADE 1919–1929 was a period of rapid economic development that brought the standard of living of the American people to a level hitherto unknown in history. Even so, the economic progress of the twenties lacked the over-all solidity of the economic growth from 1900 to 1914. The prosperity of the twenties was more urban than general, more confined to certain industries than to others. More dangerous still was the fact that the resources of commercial banks were used to finance a runaway speculative boom in real estate and the stock markets.

Yet these were signs seen only by the wisest economists. Standing on the verge of the depression in the autumn of 1929, the American people could look back over a decade during which they had revitalized an old economy and assumed the financial leadership of the world. Blissfully unaware of the impending disaster, most of them saw no reason why the golden age should not continue forever.

109 / The American People, 1920–1930

This was a decade of revolutionary changes affecting the growth, distribution, and composition of the American people. For one thing, the decline in the birth rate, which had begun a century before, became really precipitous after 1915. It fell from 25.1 per 1,000 in 1915, to 23.7 in 1920, and to 18.9 in 1930; and the rate of population increase from 1920 to 1930 was only 16.1 per cent, as compared to an increase of 21.2 per cent from 1900 to 1910. Offsetting this declining birth rate, however, was a nearly phenomenal improvement in the health of the American people, which caused the death rate in areas furnishing reliable statistics to fall from 17.6 per thousand in 1900 to 11.3 per thousand in 1930 and the life expectancy for males to increase from forty-six years in 1901 to fifty-eight years in 1930.

Nearly 89 per cent of the 122,775,046 persons in the United States in 1930 were either white or native-born, but the severe restriction and selection of European immigration effected by the legislation of the twenties was beginning to affect the composition of the American people and help accelerate the decline in population growth by 1930. Total net immigration declined from a prewar peak of 815,303 in 1913 to 173,789 in 1930; but as these figures include Canadians and Mexicans unaffected by restrictions, they fail to describe the way in which the quota system affected immigration from Europe. One example must suffice. From 1900 to 1914 Italian stock in the United States increased in numbers from 727,844 to 3,336,941. But the net immigration of Italians from 1920 to 1924 was only 224,000, and from 1925 to 1929 27,000 more Italians left than entered the United States. Obviously, the operation of the quota system meant the eventual elimination of the foreign-born as an important element in the American population.

To stop at this point would be to ignore certain important demographic changes that took place in the 1920's. The most notable were the practical surcease of the westward land movement, the decline in farm population, and, above all, the acceleration of the growth of cities and towns. From 1900 to 1920 continued land settlement caused the entire area west of the hundredth meridian to grow at a much faster pace than the older sections. From 1920 to 1930, however, growth in the West depended more upon industry, oil, the tourist trade, and highly specialized agriculture than upon general farming. California, Oregon, Texas, and Arizona grew rapidly, but the remaining agricultural states of the West either lost population or else increased by less than 10 per cent.

This phenomenon was merely additional evidence of the most important internal demographic change of the decade—the increasing movement from the countryside to the cities. From 1920 to 1930 some 6,000,000 persons moved from farms to cities; it was so tremendous a migration that the farm population, for the first time, sustained a net loss of 1,200,000 persons during the decade. One of the most important changes in the American social fabric during the first three decades of the twentieth century can be read in the following generalization: In 1900 nearly 60 per cent of the American people lived in the country and in small towns under 2,500; by 1930 44 per cent of the people lived in rural areas, while only 26 per cent actually lived on farms.

In contrast was the accelerated growth of American cities in the 1920's. The five cities of 1,000,000 inhabitants or over, for example, alone absorbed more than one-third the total urban increase of 14,600,000 during the decade; and the so-called satellite cities surrounding the metropolises grew at twice the speed of nonsatellite cities of similar size. In 1910 the Census Bureau listed twenty-five so-called metropolitan districts, in which more than 20 per cent of the American people lived. In 1930, on the other hand, the Bureau could count ninety-six such metropolitan districts, in which 44.6 per cent of the people lived.

A final significant internal population change was the steady migration of Negroes from the South to the North and Middle West, which began in serious volume around 1915. In 1910 89 per cent of all Negroes lived south of the Mason and Dixon Line, which was only three units lower than the corresponding percentage on the eve of the Civil War. By 1930, however, 20 per cent of the Negroes lived in the North and Middle West; and 88 per cent of these lived in urban centers.

POPULATION CHANGE

+ 50% AND OVER

+ 25% TO 49.9%

+ 10% TO 24.9%

+ 5% TO 9.9%

0% TO +4.9%

DECREASE

WASH. 5.2
OREG. 21.8
CALIF. 44.1
NEV. 17.6
IDAHO 3.0
UTAH 13.0
ARIZ. 30.3
MONT. 2.1
WYO. 6.0
COLO. 10.2
N.MEX. 17.5
N.DAK. 5.3
S.DAK. 8.8
NEBR. 6.3
KAN. 6.3
OKLA. 18.1
TEXAS 24.9
MINN. 7.4
IOWA 2.8
MO. 6.6
ARK. 5.8
LA. 16.9
WIS. 11.7
ILL. 17.7
MICH. 32.0
IND. 10.5
OHIO 15.4
KY. 8.2
TENN. 11.9
MISS. 12.2
ALA. 12.7
GA. 0.4
FLA. 51.6
S.C. 3.3
N.C. 23.9
VA. 4.9
W.VA. 18.1
PA. 10.5
N.Y. 21.2
VT. 0.2
N.H. 5.0
ME. 3.8
MASS. 10.3
R.I. 13.7
CONN. 16.4
N.J. 28.1
DEL. 6.9
MD. 12.5

UNITED STATES AVERAGE, 16.1% INCREASE

13. *Population Change, 1920–1930*

TRM

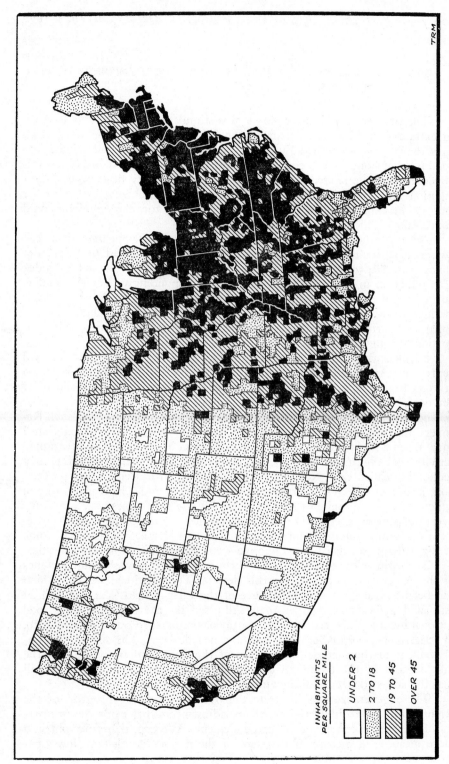

INHABITANTS
PER SQUARE MILE

UNDER 2

2 TO 18

19 TO 45

OVER 45

14. *Population Density in 1930*

TRM

110 / *The American People, 1920–1930: Income, Wealth, and Industry*

The prewar American economy was stimulated from 1914 to 1917 by an extraordinary European demand for food and war materials and from 1917 to 1919 by continued European purchases, enormous federal war expenditures at home, and a concomitant expansion in bank credits. Then followed, as we have related in a preceding chapter, a dizzy postwar period of inflation and intense economic activity, stimulated chiefly by a further increase in exports and a high domestic demand for clothing, household goods, automobiles, and housing.

Actually, the postwar boom of 1919–1920 was more apparent than real, except in agriculture. National income, adjusted by the cost of living, declined from $64,500,000,000 in 1918 to $57,884,000,000 in 1920, and the index of production in the basic industries fell correspondingly. Yet the decline during 1920 was not precipitous in manufacturing or trade, nor was it marked by any large number of business failures. The greatest shock was the collapse in farm prices that began in the late spring and reached panic proportions during the autumn.

By the spring of 1921, however, the recession had become a full-fledged depression. American foreign trade declined in value from $13,500,000,000 in 1920 to less than $7,000,000,000 in 1921; wholesale prices declined 21 per cent; and unemployment reached a peak of 4,754,000. Actually, what was occurring was a general readjustment to a lower world price level. Recovery set in at the beginning of 1922 and was steady on all fronts until 1927, when a slight recession was followed by an intensification of economic activity that continued until 1929. This was the period that contemporary economists called the "New Economic Era," when it seemed that production, prices, and wages had reached an equilibrium and a high plateau upon which the economy might run indefinitely. While such hopes were obviously overly confident, the 1920's were none the less a time of marked advancement on most economic fronts. Let us now consider in greater detail some of the general aspects of the economic scene during the prosperity decade.

To begin with, there was a steady increase in the wealth and incomes of the American people during this decade. Total national wealth, which had been $192,000,000,000 on the eve of the First World War, reached an estimated $367,000,000,000 in 1929. Adjusted by the cost of living, total national income increased from $65,093,000,000, or $620 per capita, in 1919, to $82,810,000,000, or $681 per capita, a decade later. The spectacular improvement in the material well being of the American people during the first decades of the twentieth century becomes apparent when we recall that the adjusted per capita income in 1900 was $480.

These generalizations illustrate the over-all economic progress of the twenties but fail to indicate internal maladjustments that made the prosperity of the period ephemeral for large elements. We can, therefore, obtain a more meaningful picture of the state of the nation during the New Eco-

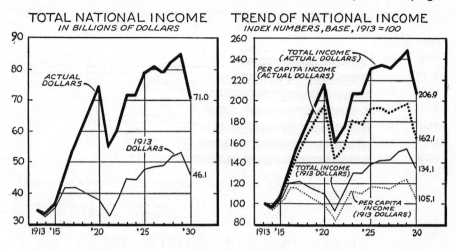

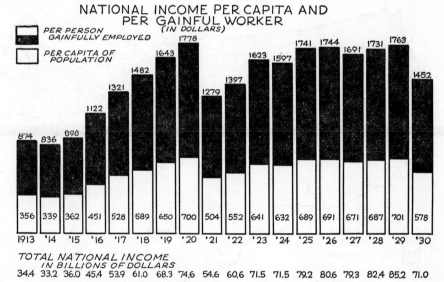

10. *The National Income of the United States, 1913–1930*

nomic Era by seeing the important changes in the relative economic status of the major groups that occurred from 1923 to 1929.

As we have already seen, farmers suffered a severe deflation in 1920 and 1921. In spite of some recovery in prices from the depression level of 1921, farmers never recovered the fine balance relative to other groups they had enjoyed in 1914 and 1919. The share of agriculture in the national private production income in 1919 had been 22.9 per cent; in 1929 it was 12.7 per cent.

In contrast, the condition of most workers in industry substantially improved in almost all aspects during the 1920's. Over the decade 1919–1929

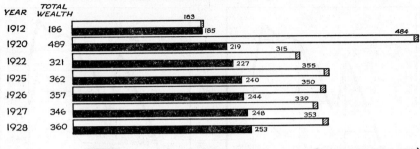

TOTAL NATIONAL WEALTH FOR SPECIFIED YEARS
(IN BILLIONS OF DOLLARS)

YEAR	TOTAL WEALTH			
1912	186	183	185	484
1920	489	219	315	
1922	321	227	355	
1925	362	240	350	
1926	357	244	339	
1927	346	248	353	
1928	360	253		

☐ WEALTH DISTRIBUTABLE BY STATES (CURRENT DOLLARS)
■ " " " " (1913 DOLLARS)
▨ WEALTH NOT DISTRIBUTABLE BY STATES (INCLUDED IN "TOTAL WEALTH IN CURRENT DOLLARS")

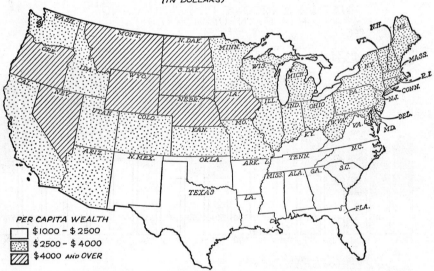

PER CAPITA WEALTH FOR STATES, 1928
(IN DOLLARS)

PER CAPITA WEALTH
☐ $1000 – $2500
▨ $2500 – $4000
▨ $4000 AND OVER

11. *The National Wealth of the United States, 1912–1928*

there was a rise in annual real earnings of 26 per cent, which was perhaps the largest decennial increase up to that time. During the period of greatest expansion, 1923–1929, the number of wage earners increased only about .5 per cent, but average hourly wages increased 8 per cent, average real earnings increased 11 per cent, while the average work week decreased from 47.3 to 45.7 hours.

A basic stimulant of prosperity in the 1920's was expansion in the construction industry after 1918. Because of stable costs and a continued high demand, especially for residential construction, the industry recorded one large gain after another from 1922 to 1928, when it began to slacken. The estimated value of construction, based on the value of materials used, rose from a little over $12,000,000,000 in 1919 to a peak of nearly $17,500,000,000 in 1928. In 1926 the industry paid 7.5 per cent of all wages and salaries and nearly equaled agriculture and transportation in importance.

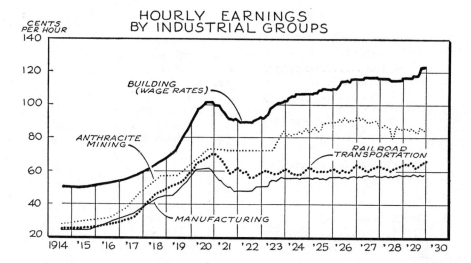

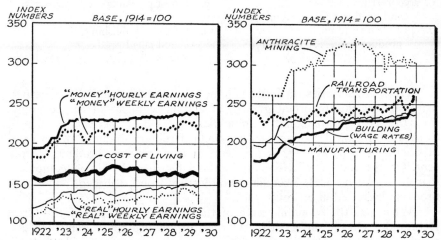

12. Money and "Real" Earnings, 1914–1930

Manufacturing enjoyed an even more significant expansion during the prosperity decade. The number of manufacturing establishments declined through consolidation and elimination of small producers from 274,598 in 1919 to 210,959 in 1929; the number of wage earners declined during the decade from 9,041,311 to 8,838,743. At the same time, there was an increase of 64 per cent in manufacturing output, chiefly because of a 40 per cent increase in labor's productivity. The following table illustrates the general character of the shifting pattern of production:

THE TEN LEADING AMERICAN INDUSTRIES, RANKED ACCORDING TO VALUE
OF PRODUCTS, 1919 AND 1929

	1919			*1929*	
		Value of Product			*Value of Product*
		(in thousands			*(in thousands*
Rank	*Industry*	*of dollars)*	*Rank*	*Industry*	*of dollars)*
1.	Food and allied industries	$12,748,348	1.	Food and allied industries	$12,023,589
2.	Textiles and textile products	9,210,933	2.	Textiles and textile products	9,243,303
3.	Iron and steel and products	5,887,844	3.	Iron and steel and products	7,137,928
4.	Transportation equipment, including automobiles	5,627,623	4.	Machinery	7,043,380
5.	Machinery	4,768,673	5.	Transportation equipment, including automobiles	6,047,209
6.	Chemicals and allied products	3,803,753	6.	Chemicals and allied products	3,759,405
7.	Forest products	3,113,460	7.	Petroleum and coal products	3,647,748
8.	Leather and its products	2,613,217	8.	Nonferrous metals and products	3,597,058
9.	Nonferrous metals and products	2,519,032	9.	Forest products	3,591,765
10.	Petroleum and coal products	2,289,170	10.	Printing, publishing, and allied products	3,170,140

These are statistics of dollar volume of production and therefore partially obscure the important growth of certain segments of the economy. Thus the actual production of automobiles increased 255 per cent from 1919 to 1929; of chemical products, 94 per cent; of rubber products, 86 per cent; of printing and publishing, 85 per cent; of iron and steel products, 70 per cent. On the reverse side, the production of coal and railroad equipment sharply declined, while production of leather, food, tobacco, and textile products increased at a slower pace.

What was the economic state of the nation on the eve of the Great Depression? On the surface, the American people had never seemed so economically healthy. And yet their prosperity was so unevenly divided that it could not long continue without some readjustment. This was true primarily because such an increasing share of the national income was going to industry and finance that workers relatively lost ground and farmers suffered an absolute retrogression. For example, corporate profits and dividends increased 62 and 65 per cent, respectively, from 1923 to 1929, while workers enjoyed an 11 per cent increase in real income. The result was that by the end of the prosperity decade such a large portion of the national income was being funneled off at the top by receivers in restricted geographical areas that the producers who worked on America's assembly lines and farms were finding it difficult to purchase what they produced. By 1928, for example, there were indications of overproduction in residential housing and automobiles.

This fundamental maladjustment is dramatically revealed by the following analysis: In 1929 there were nearly 27,500,000 families in the United States. Nearly 6,000,000 families, or more than 21 per cent of the total, had incomes less than $1,000; nearly 12,000,000, or more than 42 per cent, had incomes under $1,500; nearly 20,000,000 families, or 71 per cent, had incomes under $2,500, which was the sum estimated as being necessary for a decent living standard. On the other hand, the 36,000 wealthiest families received an aggregate income in 1929 nearly equal to the total income received by the 11,653,000 families receiving less than $1,500 a year. Or, to put it another way, 16,000,000 families, or nearly 60 per cent of the total number, received an aggregate income of $18,300,000,000. These families, experts estimated, were living either on or below a subsistence level. In contrast, the remaining 11,000,000 families, or 40 per cent of the total, received an aggregate income of $58,900,000,000.

111 / The Technological Revolution

Underlying the increased industrial output of the 1920's was a revolution in industrial management and technology that made possible the production of larger numbers of units by a smaller number of workers at a lower cost. Of all the causes of America's industrial development in the twentieth century, the technological revolution was most basic and therefore most significant, for without the techniques it afforded the mass production age could never have come. Like other economic developments of the 1920's, the technological revolution had its roots deep in the American past and its greatest impact after 1920. Let us look briefly at the background.

During the 1880's and 1890's a young industrial engineer, Frederick W. Taylor, turned to a study of scientific shop management and evolved his theory of scientific management, namely, that engineers by objective analysis could determine the reasonable capacities of men and machinery. The publication of his "Piece-Rate System" in 1895 and "Shop Management" in 1903 at once established him as the leading industrial engineer in the United States, if not in the world. So successful were Taylor and his disciples that scientific management had been accepted to a varying degree by almost every branch of business and industry by the early 1920's and had become an integral part of the curricula of engineering and business schools, which were graduating a new generation of managers.

While Taylor was waging his campaign another and equally important development was maturing—mass production by the assembly line technique and the production of interchangeable parts by automatic precision machinery.[1] The use of interchangeable parts had begun in the late eighteenth century,[2] but the introduction of the assembly line, or progressive line production, technique was a twentieth century phenomenon, first developed by

---

[1] A whole series of inventions between 1865 and 1900, particularly the micrometer caliper and other measuring devices, the automatic turret lathe, and hard alloys for cutting purposes, contributed to this development.

[2] By 1900, for example, interchangeable parts were being used in the manufacture of firearms, agricultural machinery, sewing machines, typewriters, and bicycles.

Henry Ford in the automobile industry from 1908 to 1914. From 1908 to 1913 Ford used a stationary assembly line. From 1913 to 1914, however, he reorganized the assembly process in a revolutionary way—by introducing the moving assembly line, which reduced the labor required for the assembly of an automobile chassis from fourteen to less than two man-hours. In the effort to increase production during the First World War, the assembly line technique was applied to shipbuilding, the manufacture of airplane engines, and the production of munitions. And by the early 1920's the new method was firmly established in many branches of industry.

Another important component of the technological revolution was industrial research, which had been carried on in a crude manner in the United States before the First World War and did not reach an important position until the 1920's. The establishment of the Mellon Institute of Industrial Research at Pittsburgh in 1913 marked the first systematic beginning; the creation of the National Research Council by the National Academy of Sciences in 1916 marked the first effort to stimulate and organize research on a national scale. The war of course gave the largest stimulus, and by 1920 many corporations had established independent research laboratories. By 1927 at least 999 corporations were carrying on either independent or cooperative research for the improvement of product or service, reduction of production costs, development of by-products and new products, and the like. Data on total expenditures are unavailable, but 208 firms reported expenditures aggregating nearly $12,000,000. This was a significant beginning, but industrial research was still in its infancy. Ten years later, for example, American industrialists were spending $180,000,000 annually for research.

A fourth aspect of the technological revolution paid largest dividends in human health and happiness. It was the growing acceptance and application of the theory that conditions affecting the health, comfort, and safety of workers had a direct influence on production and productivity. So successful was the safety-in-industry campaign before the First World War that practically every factory erected during the 1920's was constructed according to modern safety standards, while many old factories were modernized in this regard. A study of industrial accidents about 1928 revealed that only 10 per cent of them were caused by lack of mechanical safeguards.

The fifth and also the most basic factor in the increased productivity and output of the 1920's was a phenomenal growth in power per worker. During the decade 1919–1929 horsepower per worker increased nearly 50 per cent in manufacturing, 62 per cent in agriculture, 60 per cent in mines and quarries, and 74 per cent in the railroad industry. In manufacturing much of this increase was made possible through a threefold increase in the use of electric power[3]; in agriculture, through the first important use of tractors.[4]

In a more advanced stage the technological revolution worked the miracle in production that revitalized the American economy after the Great

[3] By 1929 70 per cent of all industries were electrified, as compared with 30 per cent in 1914.

[4] The horse and mule yielded to the tractor grudgingly, however. In 1919 there were 26,436,000 horses and mules and 147,600 tractors in the United States. A decade later 19,476,000 horses and mules and 852,989 tractors were in use on American farms.

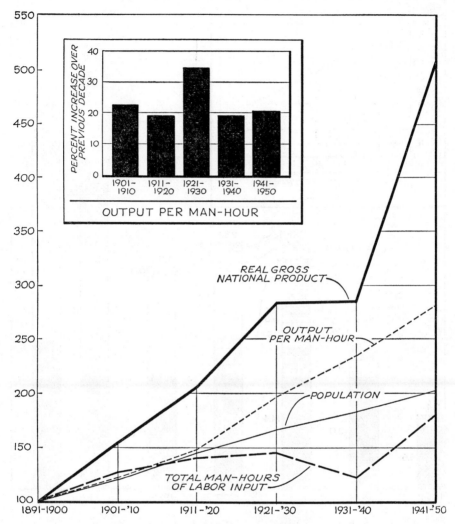

13. *The Increase in Productivity in the United States, 1891–1950,*
by Decades

Depression. But even by 1929 that revolution had proceeded so far as to cause observers to think that they, too, were living in an age of miracles. We will see shortly some of the more tangible results of the technological revolution in the 1920's. It suffices here to say that that revolution, in its first culmination from 1919 to 1929, caused a gain of productivity of 40 per cent in manufacturing and of 26 per cent in agriculture—as contrasted with gains in productivity from 1899 to 1909 of 7 per cent in manufacturing and 6 per cent in agriculture—and that the ability of American industry and agriculture to produce a larger volume with considerably fewer workers made possible a richer material life and the diminution of back-breaking labor for millions of Americans.

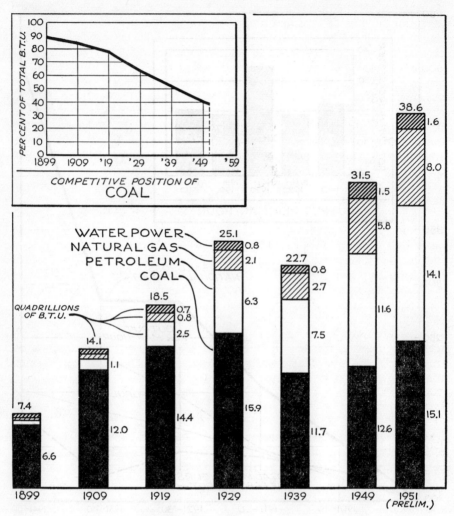

14. *Sources of Energy in the United States, 1899–1951*

112 / *The Rise of New Industries*

Several industries, in their infancy when the decade began, emerged to positions of key importance during the 1920's. They were not only dynamic economically, in that they stimulated other segments of the economy; they were also the prime movers of a revolution in living habits and social attitudes that was taking shape by 1929. Let us now review their rise, their economic importance, and their impact upon the American people.

The Rise of the Automobile. The historian feels almost at a loss for words to relate the story of the rise of the automobile or to convey some intimation of its economic and social significance in recent American history.

As two students of American sociology have put it, "It is probable that no invention of such far reaching importance was ever diffused with such rapidity or so quickly exerted influences that ramified through the national culture, transforming habits of thought and language."

For almost a century Europeans experimented with self-propelled carriages, until Carl Benz, a German, built the first automobile powered by a gasoline engine in 1884. In 1892 Charles and Frank Duryea of Springfield, Massachusetts, and in 1893 Henry Ford of Detroit built the first successful gasoline-driven carriages in the United States. At about the same time a number of other men were experimenting with automobiles driven by steam and electricity. By the turn of the century there were some 8,000 automobiles in the United States. During the next quarter century some 181 companies entered the field; but by 1930 the three major concerns, Ford, General Motors, and Chrysler, produced 83 per cent of the output.

All during this period the leader was Henry Ford who, after experimenting with low-priced cars, introduced the Model T in the autumn of 1908. By concentrating on this single unlovely but enduring model and by introducing the assembly line process and scientific management, Ford not only realized his dream of producing automobiles for the masses but also dominated the industry for twenty years. His closest rival in the fierce struggle for supremacy was the General Motors Corporation, organized by William C. Durant in 1908, which fell under the control of the DuPont and Morgan interests in 1921 and produced a wide number of lines, ranging from the luxurious Cadillac to the low-priced Chevrolet. A third but much smaller competitor was the Chrysler Corporation, organized in 1923, which acquired Dodge Brothers in 1928 and Plymouth in 1929.

Meanwhile, the automobile industry had emerged as the largest single manufacturing industry in the United States. Production of automobiles increased from 4,000 in 1900, to 1,518,061 in 1921, to 4,794,898 in 1929; and by the latter date there were over 26,500,000 automobiles, trucks, and busses in operation in the United States. In 1919 the automotive industry employed 343,115 workers, who earned $491,122,000 in wages and turned out products valued at two and a third billion dollars. In 1929 the industry employed 487,448 workers, paid $733,082,000 in wages, and manufactured products with an aggregate value of $3,722,793,000. Its importance in the economy as a whole can be seen by the fact that in 1929 it used 15 per cent of the steel and four-fifths of the rubber processed in the United States, employed 7.1 per cent of the manufacturing wage earners, paid 8.7 per cent of the manufacturing wages, and produced 12.7 per cent of the total product value of all manufacturing concerns.

Indeed, it is no exaggeration to say that the manufacture of automobiles was in large measure responsible for the intense economic activity of the 1920's. According to one estimate, it gave employment, directly or indirectly, to 3,700,000 persons by 1929, for use of the automobile gave rise to the construction and maintenance of hard-surfaced highways, the operation of garages and filling stations, the maintenance of tourist camps to accommodate the millions of Americans who annually took to the roads in the 1920's, the operation of fleets of motor trucks and busses, and the like. By the end of the 1920's, for example, county, state, and federal authorities were spending nearly $2,000,000,000 annually for the construction, maintenance, and financing of highways and bridges alone.

Electric Power, Machinery, and Appliances. In a preceding chapter we noted the rise of the electric power industry, but it might be well at this point briefly to summarize the story. From 1900 to 1929 the electric power industry rose from comparative insignificance to the status of the second most important economic interest in the United States. Between 1902 and 1929 production increased from 6,000,000,000 kilowatt hours to nearly 117,000,000,000; capital invested in the industry grew to nearly $12,000,000,-000 and total income to nearly $2,000,000,000. In 1912 only 16 per cent of American homes were electrified; by 1929 nearly 70 per cent used electric power.

Almost overnight, also, the manufacture of electric turbines, motors, supplies, and appliances grew into an industry of the first importance. The decade 1919–1929 was the period of greatest growth, as the value of products of this industry increased from $997,968,000 to $2,300,916,000. Even by the late twenties, however, the appliance industry still concentrated on a few standard items like irons, washing machines, and vacuum cleaners. By January 1928, for example, only 775,000 mechanical refrigerators were in use.[5]

The Radio Industry. Although most of the inventions basic to the construction of radio transmitters and receivers had been perfected before the First World War, it was not until 1919 that the federal government lifted its ban on the private operation of sets. During the next decade a great new industry came into being. In 1919 the General Electric and Westinghouse companies organized the Radio Corporation of America, obtained control of patents by cross-licensing agreements, and began manufacturing radio parts on a small scale.

Before 1922 RCA did not offer the basic component of the radio receiver, the vacuum tube, to the public; but in response to tremendous demand the Corporation began manufacturing receivers and parts on a large scale in 1922. At about the same time the patents on tubes expired, and a number of other concerns entered the field. As radio soon became a virtual obsession with the American people, the production of sets increased by leaps and bounds. In 1921 sales of radio parts totaled a mere $10,646,000. By 1929 the product value of the industry totaled $411,637,412; and the census reporters discovered the following year that 12,078,345 American families, or 40 per cent of the total number, had radio sets.

Meanwhile, radio broadcasting had evolved from a sport into a big business. The first regular broadcasting station was KDKA at East Pittsburgh, which began daily operation on November 2, 1920. Between 1920 and 1924 the number of stations grew to 562. In the latter year RCA organized the National Broadcasting Company, arranged with the American Telephone & Telegraph Company to transmit programs over telephone lines, and began

[5] The Census of Manufactures, 1929, does not give over-all statistics for the appliance industry. There must have been considerable expansion during 1928 and 1929, as that inquiry revealed that mechanical refrigerators totaling $161,566,000 in value were produced in 1929.

the first nation-wide broadcasting service. Three years later the Columbia Broadcasting System was established on a similar nation-wide scale.

The Aviation Industry. Although two Americans, Wilbur and Orville Wright, built and flew the first successful airplane at Kitty Hawk, North Carolina, on December 17, 1903, leadership in aviation soon moved across the Atlantic. After the outbreak of the war, Europeans swiftly developed the flying machine as a powerful fighting weapon. When Congress adopted the war resolution in 1917, however, the American army had on hand no combat planes and only a few inefficient observation craft. The government at once began a gigantic program to train thousands of pilots and established the Aircraft Production Board to build thousands of engines and aircraft.

Although there were twenty-four plants in the United States capable of producing 21,000 planes annually when the Armistice was signed, the government hastily canceled its orders, and the entire industry practically collapsed. European governments kept their aviation industries alive through generous mail subsidies, but it was many years before Congress followed suit. In 1918 the Post Office Department established a daily airmail service between New York and Washington with its own planes and pilots; and six years later it began regular airmail service between New York, Chicago, and San Francisco. The following year, 1925, Congress authorized the Post Office Department to let contracts for carrying mail to private companies and in 1926 enacted the Air Commerce Act, vesting control of commercial aviation in the Commerce Department.

As a result of this legislation, scheduled commercial air service first began in 1926; and by the end of their first year of operation eighteen airlines had carried 5,782 passengers over routes totaling 3,715 miles. By 1930 the aviation industry was firmly established, with 122 airlines in operation over routes covering nearly 50,000 miles.[6]

The Motion Picture Industry. The story of the rise of the motion picture industry from humble beginnings to a position of major importance in American life is one of the great sagas of the twentieth century. By 1896 Thomas A. Edison and others had constructed machines capable of taking motion pictures and projecting them on a screen. For the next few years short feature films were shown in vaudeville houses, and in 1903 the first movie that told a story, "The Great Train Robbery," was produced.

The motion picture industry had its first real beginning in 1905—when a Pittsburgh promoter rented a warehouse and displayed one-reel shows for a nickel. Within two years there were some 5,000 "nickelodeons," as these first movie theaters were called, in all parts of the country. From this time on progress in technique and technology was substantial; and on the eve of the First World War promoters began constructing large and ornate theaters.

Rapid technological developments, the most important of which were sound movies and Technicolor, brought the industry to full maturity by the end of the 1920's. By 1930 the motion picture industry had a capital invest-

[6] In 1930 commercial airlines carried 417,505 passengers, as contrasted with 49,713 passengers carried the year before. By 1930, moreover, there were 560 municipal and 564 commercial and private airports in operation, 15,280 licensed pilots, and 7,354 licensed aircraft in the United States.

ment of some $2,000,000,000 and gave employment to 325,000 persons. In every town and city there were motion picture theaters—some 23,000 of them, with a seating capacity of approximately 11,300,000. During 1930 total weekly attendance averaged perhaps 115,000,000 and total admissions ran to $1,500,000,000. So important a part of American social and cultural life had motion pictures become that even the depression did not halt the growth or impair the prosperity of the industry.

113 / The Age of Big Business

In spite of antitrust crusades, the consolidation movement in industry proceeded inexorably, through Democratic and Republican administrations, through eras of reform and reaction.[7] It slackened from 1904 to 1917, but revived on a large scale at the end of the First World War. A few statistics will illustrate the general trend. In 1909 the assets of the two hundred largest nonfinancial corporations totaled $26,000,000,000; in 1919, $43,718,000,000; in 1929, $81,074,000,000. The startling fact was that the growth of the two hundred giants had been two and one-half times faster than the growth of smaller corporations during the period 1909–1929, and three times faster during the years 1924–1928. By the end of the prosperity decade, these two hundred corporations controlled 49 per cent of all corporate wealth and received 43 per cent of the corporate income. Or, to illustrate the degree of concentration in another way, in 1929 the largest 1,349 corporations had a combined income of about $7,000,000,000, while all the rest had an aggregate income of only $1,740,000,000.

The favorite instrument of consolidation in the 1920's was the holding company, which enabled an individual or group of men with comparatively small resources to control a utility or railroad empire.[8] Samuel Insull, the Chicago utilities magnate, was most adept at the game. Indeed, so far-flung

[7] The industrial expansion from 1900 to 1929 was in large measure financed by the savings of the rank and file, rather than by the investments of a few promoters and industrial leaders. The result was a wide spread in the ownership of America's factories, banks, railroads, and insurance companies and a consequent separation between ownership and management. The 4,000,000 owners of corporate stocks in 1900, for example, grew to a mighty throng of 20,000,000 by 1930.

This divorcement of ownership from control in industry, which began around 1900, reached major proportions in the 1920's, as the component parts of the dissolved "trusts" developed into independent concerns and as more and more companies sold stock to the public. Consequently, there developed a significant managerial revolution, in which control passed from single owners or partners and even from boards of directors to a salaried bureaucracy, highly trained in production and distribution. In fact, by 1929 American industry was so thoroughly bureaucratized that the large majority of routine decisions were made by plant managers and shop foremen even in corporations controlled by owners.

[8] The technique is known as pyramiding and works in the following manner: Using a small investment a promoter might organize a holding company and gain control of it by owning a majority of the voting common stock. By using the proceeds from the sale of the bonds, preferred stock, and nonvoting common stock of this first holding company, the organizer would buy control of operating utility companies. And by following the same method the promoter might pyramid one holding company on top of another almost indefinitely.

and complicated was his utilities network by 1930—it had combined assets of $2,500,000,000 and produced one-eighth of the electric power in the United States—that it is doubtful whether even he understood its structure. Beginning by controlling the Nickel Plate Railroad before the First World War, Oris P. and Mantis J. Van Sweringen of Cleveland used the holding company device from 1925 to 1929 to acquire control of the Chesapeake & Ohio, the Pere Marquette, the Erie, and the Missouri Pacific railroads.

To what degree had the American industrial economy become consolidated by 1930? Obviously to a large degree, but not in the manner that the bare statistics might imply. Actually, by 1930 few vestiges of industrial monopoly remained,[9] while many important industries, notably textiles, clothing, furniture, and bituminous coal, remained fiercely competitive. On the other hand, oligopolies, that is, oligarchies of a few large producers, dominated many branches of industry in 1930. For example, nine large companies controlled approximately 82 per cent of the total productive capacity of the steel industry; three corporations controlled 83 per cent of the automobile output; four meat packing concerns produced 70 per cent of the product of that industry; the four largest rubber companies turned out 66 per cent of the tires and other rubber products; four tobacco companies produced 94 per cent of the cigarettes.

This trend toward oligopoly, however, did not necessarily signify a diminution of competition. On the contrary, it meant the restoration of competition in several important branches of industry. In 1901, for example, United States Steel controlled about 60 per cent of the steel ingot capacity of the country. The corporation grew steadily, so that its net assets totaled nearly $2,500,000,000 in 1929. But its rivals grew even faster; and in 1930 United States Steel controlled only 39 per cent of the total steel ingot capacity of the industry. At the time of its dissolution in 1911, the Standard Oil Company of New Jersey enjoyed a virtual monopoly over the refining of petroleum in the United States. The dissolution of the holding company into its constituent corporations was followed by the gradual emergence of these companies as independent concerns. Meanwhile, tremendous new amounts of capital entered the oil refining field; and by 1930 all the former members of the Standard Oil Trust combined did only about 50 per cent of the oil business of the country. In retailing, also, the rise of mail-order houses and chain stores, which did 25 per cent of the retail business in 1929, gave a powerful stimulus to competition in the distribution field. In thousands of small towns the hegemony of the local merchant was destroyed; he now had to compete, and competition often meant drastically lower prices for consumers.

We could multiply these examples to show that the trend toward oligopoly from 1910 to 1930 actually strengthened competition in many branches of industry in which competition had not existed before 1910. The important phenomenon in this regard, however, was the manner in which competition itself changed during the two decades before 1930. Historic

[9] The Texas Gulf Sulphur Company and the Freeport Sulphur Company controlled virtually the entire sulphur production of the United States, while the Aluminum Company of America enjoyed a monopoly in the production of bar aluminum. But these were the only important industrial monopolies remaining by 1930.

price competition remained in many branches of industry and was always a potential threat in others. But more and more producers in a given branch of industry tended to follow the price leadership of the largest manufacturer and to concentrate on improving and advertising their products.

114 / *The Regulation of Business, 1919–1929*

During the ten years following the Armistice there was considerable diminution of the antitrust energies of the Justice Department.[10] But to say that this decline of regulation occurred merely because the Harding and Coolidge administrations were friendly to the business world would be to reduce a complicated subject to a crude generalization. We can understand the evolution of federal control of business during the 1920's only if we bear in mind a few fundamental facts.

The first and most important is the fact that the main thrust of the antitrust movement before 1917 was aimed only at destroying monopoly and preventing the subversion of competition. As Wilson and Theodore Roosevelt often affirmed, the antitrust campaign was not aimed at bigness, *per se,* or even at oligopoly—so long as large producers did not use their power to destroy competitors. From 1911 to 1930 there was a strong trend away from monopoly toward competition, while large corporations practically abandoned the old and now outlawed methods of destructive competition. Consequently, the problem of regulation was considerably different in the 1920's from what it had been in the early progressive period.

The second fundamental is that the Harding-Coolidge policy of beneficent regulation represented the maturing of policies begun by the Wilson administration. The authors of the Federal Trade Commission bill intended that the FTC should prevent destructive competition and the growth of monopoly, it is true; but they also envisaged the Commission as the protector of small business and the friend and champion of all legitimate business enterprise. By 1921, the FTC had failed to become a strong arbiter of business affairs. This was true in part because Wilson had packed the Commission with conservatives, in part because the objective of governmental control had changed from the destruction of monopoly to the preservation of competition and conditions in which industry could expand and grow. And the tremendous expansion of the American economy from 1919 to 1929, the strengthening of competition through the growth of oligopoly, and the emergence of new industries seemed to confirm the wisdom of the moderate Wilsonian program and lessened the tension between the rank and file of the people and the business community.

The most important problem of business control in the 1920's was the rapid growth of new concepts and practices involving a diminution of price

[10] That is, as compared with the antitrust activities of the Roosevelt and Taft administrations. Actually, the Harding-Coolidge record of antitrust action surpassed the record of the Wilson administration. Under Wilson, the Justice Department entered twenty-seven consent decrees and instituted ninety-seven criminal and equity cases under the antitrust laws. Under Harding and Coolidge, the Justice Department entered forty-eight consent decrees and instituted 130 criminal and equity proceedings.

competition and envisaging instead close cooperation in purchasing, selling, and price fixing through trade associations, that is, organizations of producers in competitive industries. By 1921 some 2,000 of these trade associations were in operation.

It was many years before the various governmental agencies and departments agreed upon a common policy toward this new cooperation. The confusion was compounded by the fact that before 1921, and especially during the war, the Federal Trade Commission had given open endorsement to the trade associations; because many progressives, notably Justice Louis D. Brandeis, hailed the new cooperation as the salvation of small business enterprise; and because Secretary of Commerce Herbert C. Hoover sponsored the formation of trade associations and approved their activities. On the other hand, from 1921 to 1925 the Trade Commission and the Justice Department sought to prevent such collusion as the Commerce Department was encouraging, and were sustained by the Supreme Court.

The appointment of former Representative William E. Humphrey of Washington as chairman of the Federal Trade Commission in 1925, however, gave conservative Republicans control of the Commission and resulted in an important shift in the agency's attitudes and tactics. Hereafter, at least until 1933, the Commission encouraged the trade associations and approved agreements by business men for the elimination of cutthroat competition in advertising and pricing. At the same time, the Commerce Department helped the trade associations find a way to circumvent the Court's objections to exchange of information. Manufacturers submitted information on costs, production, and sales to the Department, and the Department assembled the information and distributed reports among producers in various fields. In 1925 the Court approved this new procedure, on the ground that it involved no conspiracy to fix prices or limit production.

The Commission's change of front in 1925 provoked bitter criticism from agrarian spokesmen in Congress, who asserted that the agency had become the tool of big business. Actually, the Commission was simply fulfilling one of the major purposes of its founders—the regulation of competition to prevent the ruthless, cutthroat trade practices that in the past had been the chief weapons of would-be monopolists. In brief, the Commission effectively suppressed fraudulent advertising, price cutting, and commercial bribery without attempting to destroy the gigantic oligarchical structure of the American industrial economy.

115 / *Trends in Banking and Finance, 1919–1929*

The industrial growth of the period 1919–1929 was accompanied by a rapid extension of the banking and financial resources of the American people. Bankers, security promoters and salesmen, and managers of other financial institutions had never before been as numerous or prosperous and had never received such a large share of the national income.[11] Nor had the

[11] In 1919 financial institutions earned 2.2 of the total private production income. A decade later, on the other hand, finance's share had increased to 4.6 per cent.

financial structure of the country ever seemed more solvent. As we will see, however, there were forces at work changing the character of the banking structure and undermining its foundations.

From 1919 to 1929 the total number of banks in the United States declined from 29,123 to 25,330. Although there were a number of significant mergers during the twenties, the principal reason for the decline was the steady failure of banks in the rural areas and in Florida following the collapse of the land boom in that state in 1926. All told, from 1921 through 1929 5,714 banks closed their doors. On the other hand, from 1919 to 1929 total bank capital and surpluses increased nearly 100 per cent, while total banking resources grew from $47,615,400,000 to over $72,000,000,000.

The statistics yield numerous other evidences of the steady accretion of American financial wealth during the decade. Thus life insurance companies, which had now emerged as the chief depositories of the people's savings, grew in resources much faster than the banks. From 1919 to 1929 life insurance income and policies in force increased nearly 300 per cent, and the aggregate resources of life insurance companies grew from $6,759,000,000 to $17,482,000,000. During the same period, Americans also increased their savings in banks from $13,040,000,000 to $28,218,000,000 and in building and loan associations from $2,126,620,000 to $8,695,154,000.

Along with this expansion of resources came a movement toward consolidation and the growth of large institutions. By 1929, for example, 250 banks, or 1 per cent of the total, controlled more than 46 per cent of the nation's banking resources, while some 273 chains controlled 18 per cent of the total banking resources. In addition, there were a number of mergers in Wall Street that greatly concentrated the banking resources of the nation's financial center.

Such consolidations were spectacular, but the most important financial trend of the 1920's was the profound change that occurred in the character and functions of the great commercial banks. In the past the chief function of commercial banks had been to make short-term loans to care for the needs of industry and commerce. The high prosperity of the period from 1922 to 1929 caused corporations to rely increasingly upon profits and proceeds from the sale of securities for expansion or even for current needs. Thus new capital issues increased from a total of $3,577,000,000 in 1921 to a record high of $10,183,000,000 in 1929, while business concerns piled up surplus cash reserves in the form of time deposits that increased from $3,500,000,000 in 1921 to nearly $9,000,000,000 by 1929.

As a consequence, bank loans during the prosperity decade did not keep pace with the rising level of economic activity, and there was no inflation either of bank credit or of the money supply.[12] Coming at a time when banking resources were greatly expanding, this phenomenon caused the managers of the great commercial banks to look elsewhere than to business and industry for ways to use their resources profitably. Consequently, they increased bank purchases of stocks and bonds by two-thirds and expanded bank loans against real estate by about 350 per cent. Most important, they

[12] National banks increased their loans and discounts from $11,980,000,000 in 1921 to $14,811,000,000 in 1929; the total money in circulation actually declined slightly during the period—from $4,911,000,000 in 1921 to $4,746,000,000 in 1929.

allowed their surplus funds to be used to finance the most reckless speculative campaign in American history. By the autumn of 1929 loans to brokers
against stocks and bonds stood at the astounding total of $8,500,000,000.

The role of the commercial banks in abetting the Wild Bull Market
did not end at this point, for practically all large commercial banks established investment affiliates, hired thousands of salesmen, organized huge
speculative campaigns, and did a flourishing business so long as the upward
surge continued. In 1927, for example, these security affiliates participated
in the floating of $19,000,000,000 of issues.

Meanwhile, the great financial leaders—Kuhn, Loeb & Company, the
House of Morgan, and their allies—not only survived but also prospered
and grew larger during the New Economic Era. They continued to dominate the financial operations of the railroads, in spite of the efforts of the
Interstate Commerce Commission to break their control. They took leadership in the organization and underwriting of the utility holding companies.
They continued to do the major share of the business of marketing securities
and wielded a certain influence in the industrial field through interlocking
directorships in corporations. And yet events and developments of the twenties changed and greatly weakened the Morgan-Kuhn, Loeb & Company
imperium. Until his death in 1913 the elder J. Pierpont Morgan had dominated Wall Street through sheer will power. His son, the young J. Pierpont
Morgan, Jr., was no such dominant leader; and control in the House of
Morgan shifted to partners and became institutionalized in various departments. But it is doubtful that the elder Morgan could have retained the
power that he wielded before 1913 during the 1920's. There was too much
competition in the money markets as new financial centers emerged and old
ones grew in power, corporations were too independent and prosperous,
and there was too vast a growth of the financial machinery to allow the
continued domination by Wall Street or by one man, even if that man were
the great J. Pierpont Morgan.

CHAPTER 15 / SOCIAL AND CULTURAL TRENDS, 1917–1930

*T*HE AMERICAN society between the Spanish-American and First World wars was bound together by common moral and political standards, but it was an exciting and hopeful time. The decade between the Armistice and the depression was also a period of social and intellectual ferment. But it was ferment of a different kind, marked by changes in moral standards, the rise of new faiths among intellectuals, and the flowering of a literary revolt against the polite tradition in letters. To what degree this revolt of the intellectuals affected the masses it is impossible to say. The significant fact was that a large segment of the molders of thoughtful opinion repudiated traditional values and thereby destroyed the ideological unity of the prewar period.

As we will see, however, the 1920's were a decade of social and artistic accomplishment, as well as a time of revolt and repudiation. The decade witnessed the first important beginnings of American literary criticism; a burgeoning that gained new eminence for American literature; a flowering of American scholarship and research; and the development of new vogues in music, art, and architecture. In addition, Americans poured out money to improve and expand public schools and to construct the most extensive system of higher education in the world. Finally, churches not only survived but grew in social usefulness. Thus, far from being barren of social and cultural accomplishment, the twenties were a time of enduring achievement and bright promise for the future.

116 / The Revolution in Morals and Customs

The most astonishing aspect of the revolution in manners and moral standards that occurred after 1918 was the rapidity with which forces that had long been eroding the historic Christian standard suddenly destroyed that code among an influential element. In its ethical aspects the Christian system taught respect for parental authority, idealized the husband-father as the master of the family, and required premarital chastity and marital fidelity. Before the First World War this code provided the basic way of life for most Americans. It was often violated, to be sure; but most middle class Americans accepted it as a standard perhaps unattainable yet practically and morally sound.

The postwar rebellion against the Christian standard was first evidenced by a revolt among young people, especially among the "flaming youth" on college and university campuses, against the rules governing sexual relations. Wartime excitement broke down the barriers, but other forces kept them down during the 1920's. For one thing, the automobile extended the frontier of love-making far beyond the sitting room. For another, the increased drinking among middle class women and young people that accompanied prohibition played a large role in weakening inhibitions. But even more important was the phenomenal spread of the teachings of Sigmund Freud, a Viennese psychoanalyist, whose writings were popularly misinterpreted to mean that the main cause of maladjusted personality was the suppression of the sexual desire and that a free expression of the libido, or sexual energies, promoted mental health.

Whatever the causes—and we have mentioned only the most important —the breakdown of the Christian moral standard was widespread. F. Scott Fitzgerald's *This Side of Paradise*, a story of undergraduate life at Princeton, and Charles C. Wertenbaker's novels about students at the University of Virginia undoubtedly drew exaggerated pictures; but "petting," promiscuity, and drinking among college students became to a degree fashionable. High school students, too, indulged in the new freedom on such a scale as to shock their parents.

Indeed, if there was any single striking social phenomenon of the twenties, it was the popular obsession with sex. While highbrows read James Branch Cabell's erotic novels and applauded Eugene O'Neill's powerful dramas written around Freudian themes, the common people found excitement in a new form of literature, the confession magazines, that featured lurid stories by fallen women or high school girls who had "gone wrong."[1] The motion pictures, also, played upon the sex theme; and it was revealing that the maidenly Mary Pickford was supplanted as "America's sweetheart" by the voluptuous Clara Bow, the "It" girl of the 1920's.

A second phenomenon illustrating the revolution in morals and manners was the rise during the 1920's of new forms of ballroom dancing, as the waltz and more decorous forms gave way to the fox-trot, the Charleston, and other fast steps. To defenders of the outmoded forms, the modern dance was simply another evidence of the general breakdown of sexual standards; and church groups launched heroic but vain attacks upon what they called the "syncopated embrace." The modern dance, exclaimed the Reverend John William Porter of Kentucky in his tract, *The Dangers of the Dance* (1922), is based upon and stimulates the sexual instinct. "If this be not true, why is it that women do not dance with women, and men with men? . . . The mix-up is the magnet. A man dancing with a man is about as satisfactory as near-beer to the old drunkard." The elders cried in vain, however; and before the decade was over parents were dancing quite as fast and as artfully as their children, and American morality seemed destined

[1] *True Story*, the most successful of these new periodicals, for example, began with a small circulation in 1919 and approached the 2,000,000 mark seven years later.

to survive in spite of the close embrace and frenzied rhythm of the new dance forms.

In the long run the most important aspect of the revolution in social life in the 1920's was the change that occurred in the status of women. Political equality was achieved with the adoption of the Nineteenth Amendment, and the twenties saw women not only voting but also holding offices high and low.[2] Although female spokesmen claimed that employers discriminated against women in the matter of wages and salaries, women found far larger economic opportunities in the 1920's than ever before. There was a sharp decline in the number of women employed in industry, farming, and domestic service. On the other hand, the rapid expansion of female employment in public schools, the service trades and professions, and business enterprise more than compensated for the decline in other fields. By 1930 the 10,546,000 women gainfully employed constituted nearly 22 per cent of the entire working force of the nation, as contrasted with 17.7 per cent in 1900.

This expansion of economic opportunities for middle class women was in large measure responsible for the revolution in feminine manners during the 1920's and the increase in the laxity of traditional sexual *mores*. Masculine supremacy had been based upon man's economic leadership in the family; it rapidly deteriorated as spinster sisters moved into apartments of their own, unmarried daughters went into school teaching or office work, and wives gained independence either by going to work or threatening to do so. As a consequence, women married at a later age, had fewer children, and were more willing to dissolve the marriage bonds. The number of divorces per 1,000 marriages, for example, increased from 81 in 1900 to 163 in 1929; and over 71 per cent of the divorces in the latter year were granted to wives.

The outward signs of the so-called emancipation were even more frightening to persons who believed in the old way of life. As women went to work in larger numbers they began to discard the historic badges of femininity and, ironically, sought to make themselves over in the image of man. The first casualty of feminine independence was the traditional dress that covered the neck and arms and assiduously hid the ankles from masculine view. In 1919 the average skirt was about six inches from the ground. From this time on the ascent was spectacular, until by 1927 the skirt had reached the knees or even above. At the same time women discarded their corsets and de-emphasized the upper reaches of their anatomy, and the result was fearful to behold. Finally, to complete the de-feminization, women sheared their tresses and wore their hair straight and short.

Nor was this the end of the revolt against femininity. As the barriers fell on all sides, women began smoking cigarettes and, what seemed worse to traditionalists, demanded and asserted the right to drink with men. On

---

[2] There were, for example, two women governors during the decade and one female United States senator. Mrs. Miriam A. ("Ma") Ferguson served as Governor of Texas from 1925 to 1927. Mrs. Ferguson represented her husband, former Governor James E. Ferguson, who had been impeached and removed from office in 1917. Her administration did not bear out feminine claims that women in office would purify politics. Mrs. Nellie T. Ross succeeded her husband upon his death in 1924 as Governor of Wyoming and served until 1927. Mrs. Rebecca L. Felton of Georgia, appointed to the United States Senate in 1922 to complete the term of Thomas E. Watson, was the first woman senator.

the other hand, there was one curious exception to this revolt. The shorter skirts and hair became the more women used cosmetics—lipstick, rouge, and mascara. It seemed as if the face had become the last refuge of femininity.

By 1930 the revolution in morals and customs had run its full course, and there were certain signs of returning sanity. Experience soon taught that free expression of the libido produced not mental health but psychological and moral degeneracy. After trying to act and look like men, women finally admitted that there were, after all, certain physical differences between the sexes and discovered that they did not have to yield their beauty in order to retain the large measure of independence they had won. Most men accepted the new order; in fact, many husbands abandoned authority and responsibility for the rearing of children to their wives. If, as Frederick Lewis Allen has observed, the American people were beginning by 1929 to build a new code on the shambles of the old system and learning to live gracefully again, then that effort would consist mainly of salvaging the enduring values of the Christian system.

117 / *Main Currents in American Thought*

Deep and sometimes bitter currents of intellectual unrest converged and swelled into a revolt of considerable proportions in the early 1920's. It is not difficult to understand why this happened. During the progressive period, intellectuals had made a deeply personal commitment to the democratic cause. Most of them, like the group that wrote for the *New Republic*, had answered Wilson's call for an application of the progressive ideal to international life during the war. After Versailles and the subsequent treaty fight the dream was shattered. Like the Confederate veteran on the way home from Appomattox, who said he would be damned if he ever loved another country, many intellectuals were damned if they would ever love another ideal.

As it turned out, the reaction against the Versailles settlement was merely the beginning of the disillusionment. Intellectual progressives, who before the war had advocated the extension of governmental authority, saw that same authority being used after 1918 to deprive a minority of the privilege of deciding whether they would drink alcoholic beverages. Intellectual progressives had glorified the people and championed the adoption of democratic political reforms before 1917. In the 1920's, on the other hand, these same people were demanding and enforcing conformity of thought, joining anti-democratic organizations like the Ku Klux Klan, and even attempting to forbid the teaching of evolution in the public schools in many states.

Were the old assumptions about the innate virtue of the people and the desirability of more democracy therefore wrong? Many intellectuals thought they were and turned in anger and disgust against the democratic ideal. Thus during the 1920's there developed an intellectual leadership at war with the middle classes, apart from the people, tired of crusades and talk about moral idealism and service. Turning from the pursuit of social and economic justice, they sought refuge in developing their individuality through sexual freedom, esoteric literary and artistic forms, or bitter attacks upon developments at home. Some of them, but not a large number, repudiated democracy altogether and hailed the Soviet Communist system as the answer to a dying bourgeois democracy. The importance of the defection of this element from the progressive movement can hardly be overestimated: It was as if the spark plugs had been removed from the engine of reform.

In essence, the revolt of the intellectuals was a rebellion against what they thought was the cant, hypocrisy, and low cultural level of American life. "This so-called 'moral idealism,'" cried Harold Stearns in 1921, "is merely what any good psychiatrist would immediately recognise as the morbid perversities which conventionally accompany a deeply dissatisfied human life." The young intellectual of the early twenties simply did not like the society in which he thought he lived. He objected to the "morbid perversities"—the anti-intellectualism of the small towns, the "shoddy, cheap" newspapers that gave more space to baseball than to the theater, the demand for conformity, the emphasis upon the utilitarian virtues, the "democracy of mountebanks." He felt rejected, unwanted, and overborne by the crowd. He wanted freedom to experiment, to drink, to dream, to write like James Joyce and paint in cubes. If he were impecunious he sought fellowship in Greenwich Village in New York City; if he had an independent income he moved to the Left Bank in Paris to find freedom and cultural refreshment with fellow expatriates.

It will perhaps suffice to illustrate the revolt by pointing to Henry L. Mencken, the chief intellectual rebel of the decade. A native of Baltimore, Mencken received his literary training as a reporter for the Baltimore *Sun*, wrote an excellent study of the American language, and for a brief time edited a "little" magazine, *The Smart Set*, with George Jean Nathan. Then, in collaboration with Alfred A. Knopf, Mencken and Nathan began publication in 1922 of the *American Mercury*, a monthly addressed to the intellectual rebels.

Because of Mencken's barbed and pungent observations on the American scene, the *American Mercury* soon became the Bible of the "lost generation." He ridiculed idealism, democracy, organized religion, prudery, cant, prohibition, and ignorance. To Mencken, morality and Christian marriage, for example, were absurdities; patriotism was imbecilic; the American people were mainly a vast collection of peasants, boobs, and hillbillies. Ironic and revealing it was that such a purveyor of intellectual snobbishness and anti-democratic views should have become, as Walter Lippmann observed in 1927, the most powerful influence on the contemporary generation of educated people.

To stop at this point, however, would be to give the impression that American intellectuals during the period did nothing but scoff and condemn. Actually, the twenties witnessed the flowering of the American mind in many fields of intellectual endeavor. It was, for example, a period adorned by important accomplishments in the social sciences. Historians abandoned their earlier preoccupation with political institutions and advanced the frontiers of scholarship deep into the fields of intellectual, social, and economic history. The advance of American scholarship into new fields of study, aided by the expansion and growing endowments of the country's academic institutions, gave American historiography a breadth which no single European country could match. Sociologists broke loose from the subjective, inductive method, developed new objective criteria, and launched new studies of ecology, urbanization, population, and race relations. The study of anthropology in the United States became an integral part of university curricula rather than an avocation of museum scholars. Social psychology became an independent discipline. Abandoning the old preoccupation with economic "laws," a whole host of economists set to work to analyze, describe, and dissect the American economic system.

American accomplishment in the physical sciences during the 1920's was on the whole perhaps less impressive than in the social sciences, mainly because the most important theoretical work was still being done by Europeans. The twenties saw the culmination and complete acceptance of new theories of matter, energy, and the structure of the universe fully as revolutionary in meaning as the Copernican and Newtonian theories had been. Robert A. Milliken of the California Institute of Technology and Arthur H. Compton of the University of Chicago won the Nobel Prize in 1923 and 1927 for their contributions to the new concepts; but leadership still rested with Europeans like Albert Einstein and Niels Bohr.

On the other hand, American chemists made extraordinary progress in a seemingly more practical field—the production of synthetic chemical fibers, plastics, and products from coal and oil. In biology, Americans like Edmund B. Wilson, T. H. Morgan, and H. J. Muller enlarged man's knowledge concerning heredity, mutations, and the transmission of characteristics from one generation to the next. Following the lead of Europeans, American psychologists abandoned the study for the laboratory, there to attempt to discover the biological bases of human behavior. And although the 1920's witnessed no spectacular new discoveries in the field of medicine, it was none the less a time of steady advancement in knowledge, improvement of medical schools and the construction of great medical centers, the development of new X-ray and surgical techniques, and the growth of the branch of medicine devoted to the treatment of mental illness.

118 / *The Triumph of Naturalism in Literature*

The conjunction at the end of the First World War of a complex of circumstances and intellectual currents produced one of the most significant literary developments in American history—the flowering of the naturalistic revolt against the genteel and Christian traditions in literature among a new group of writers called the "Lost Generation." Frank Norris, Theodore Dreiser, Jack London, and Edgar Lee Masters had raised the standards of the revolution before the war and pointed the way ahead for writers of the twenties. To the historian, the significant fact was the incredible vogue of the new standards among both writers and readers. For a time it seemed as if literary America had repudiated all the ideals and values of the past.

In trying to discern the causes for such revolutionary changes in literary standards the historian sees through a glass darkly. Yet writers not only create; they also reflect the intellectual and spiritual standards and voice the perplexities and doubts of their time. The "Lost Generation" of the 1920's were the creatures of an age characterized on the higher levels of thought by determinism in the physical sciences and relativism in ethical philosophy. Naturalism in literature—the study of man as a biological creature in an amoral universe—was nothing more than the literary reflection of a science that had removed the Creator from the universe, reduced man to a laboratory case study, solemnly declared that human emotions stemmed from the viscera, and avowed that the sexual act was on the same level as eating and drinking. The disillusionment of the "Lost Generation" was, moreover, reflected in a dozen other currents of national thought.

In any event, the converging of naturalistic concepts with the sharp moral deterioration that followed the war set the literary revolution in motion. Inevitably there was a spate of war novels and plays depicting the misery of trench warfare and the complete moral and spiritual bankruptcy of the soldiers. Among the early war novels the most notable was John Dos Passos' *Three Soldiers*, published in 1921, the theme of which was aptly expressed by one of the leading characters: "This ain't a war, it's a goddam madhouse."

Combining protest against Victorian prudery with a lusty naturalism, Ernest Hemingway wrote a series of stories and novels that set new standards of style in fictional writing. His most notable work during these years, *A Farewell to Arms*, 1929, summarized a decade of revulsion against the sham idealism of the war. But in a number of earlier short stories and novels —*The Sun Also Rises*, 1926, and *Men Without Women*, 1927, for example— he voiced the "Lost Generation's" revolt against allegedly false ideals.

Meanwhile, naturalism as a literary form found its apogee in a number of other American writers. In *Winesburg, Ohio*, 1919, *Poor White*, 1920, *Many Marriages*, 1923, and other novels and stories, Sherwood Anderson attempted to unmask the alleged perversities of the small town Middle West. Anderson, however, had too deep a sympathy with his tragic characters to be a true naturalist. More in the mainstream were Ring Lardner and Erskine Caldwell, whose stories about small town and country people of the Middle West and South were marked only by a morbid interest in the diseased in mind and body and the damned. And it was fitting that in this decade of naturalism Theodore Dreiser, one of the founders of the movement in the United States, should have written his most popular work. His *An American Tragedy*, published in 1925, was even more perfectly mechanistic than *Sister Carrie*, *Jennie Gerhardt*, *The Financier*, and *The Titan* had been.

Preoccupation with sex, which they often glorified as the primeval drive, was characteristic of all the naturalists and quasi-naturalists. There was, however, considerable difference in emphasis. To writers like Dreiser and Sherwood Anderson, sex was only one of the important drives that determined man's behavior. On the other hand were a group who played upon the sexual theme almost to the point of obsession. One of these was James Branch Cabell, author of *Jurgen*, 1919, *Figures of Earth*, 1921, and *Something About Eve*, 1927, whose vivid symbolism drew the fire of professional defenders of American morality. More indirect was F. Scott Fitzgerald, a superb story-teller and one of the most talented writers among the "Lost Generation." In *This Side of Paradise*, 1920, *The Beautiful and the Damned*,

1922, and *The Great Gatsby*, 1925, Fitzgerald chronicled the moral and spiritual dissolution of the "lost generation," to whom, as he said, all gods were dead, all wars fought, all faiths shaken.

While Fitzgerald described the moral crack-up of eastern upper class society, William Faulkner of Oxford, Mississippi, depicted the decay of the old southern aristocracy and the allegedly false ideals by which it lived. His early novels, *The Sound and the Fury*, 1929, *As I Lay Dying*, 1930, and *Sanctuary*, 1931, were written in an experimental stream of consciousness form often beyond the comprehension of the average reader; but in them the preoccupation with abnormality and morbidity found their most powerful literary expression.

As the decade drew to a close another southern rebel gave promise of offsetting Faulkner's extreme negation. He was Thomas Wolfe, a North Carolinian, whose *Look Homeward, Angel*, published in 1929, was the expression of a young tortured soul in rebellion against the materialism of his mother and, as it seemed to him, the narrow provincialism of his home town of Asheville. But Wolfe was no naturalist; he was too adolescent, too romantic, too fond of life to be always morbid and introspective, as his later novels, *Of Time and the River*, 1935, *The Web and the Rock*, 1939, and *You Can't Go Home Again*, 1940, revealed.

The most widely read and universally acclaimed American novelist of the 1920's, Sinclair Lewis, stands almost alone as the connecting link between the muckraking novelists of the progressive era and the social novelists of the New Deal period. In depicting the drabness of small town midwestern life, the provincialism and smugness of the business booster, and the moral sham and materialism of his time, Lewis could be harsh and almost captious. *Main Street*, 1920, *Babbitt*, 1922, *Arrowsmith*, 1925, *Elmer Gantry*, 1927, and *Dodsworth*, 1929, presented caricatures of types of middle class Americans and won for their author in 1930 the first Nobel Prize in literature ever awarded an American.

Confronted by the seemingly irresistible vogue of naturalism and negation, the traditionalists not only survived but also waged a rear-guard action against the younger generation. It is interesting that most of the novelists among the traditionalists were women. Edith Wharton continued writing her satires of the life and manners of the New York aristocracy. Dorothy Canfield Fisher defended morality and integrity. Ellen Glasgow of Richmond continued her series on life among Virginians high and low. But the greatest of these gentle realists was Willa S. Cather, who found nobility and spiritual grandeur in human tragedy and divine grace. Her *Death Comes for the Archbishop*, 1927, was not only her finest work but also one of the American novels of the 1920's most likely to endure.

In the field of literary criticism the traditionalists were more articulate and aggressive. The leaders in a new humanistic movement, Paul Elmer More, Irving Babbitt, William C. Brownell, and Stuart P. Sherman, met their antagonists, Mencken, Van Wyck Brooks, and Harold E. Stearns, in a great battle of the books. The neo-humanists condemned not only the naturalists' disdain of graceful style and form; they also boldly championed the Christian ethic and the western cultural tradition. And if they did not convert the writers of the twenties, they founded a school and laid the foundations for a later and broader humanistic revival in letters. Thus, on both sides there was an energy and activity that made the twenties exciting, creative, and fertile.

Nor did the poetic revival, which had begun so auspiciously during the years before the First World War, abate. Among the poets of the people, Vachel Lindsay and Edgar Lee Masters produced little of consequence; but Robert Frost and Carl Sandburg did not lose their voice during the twenties. In *New Hampshire*, 1923, and *West-Running Brook*, 1928, Frost again expressed his deep love of nature and a sharpened sympathy for man. After securing his reputation with *The Man Against the Sky*, 1916, Edwin Arlington Robinson continued his search for meaning in a trilogy based upon the Arthurian legend, *Merlin, Lancelot*, and *Tristram*, 1917–1927. He was, in the eloquent words of one critic, "the solitary poet who absorbed into his thought and art the best of the old in American poetry and became the first of his generation to understand, however darkly, the new."[3]

Meanwhile, leadership among the young intellectual poets who called themselves imagists was shared by two American expatriates, Ezra Pound and T. S. Eliot. Pound had deserted the imagist group in London before the war, spent four years in Paris, and finally settled in Rapallo, Italy. During the 1920's and 1930's he wrote seventy-one *Cantos*, brilliant word pictures often devoid of meaning. Although isolated from British and American friends, he continued to have great influence among the young poets.

Born in St. Louis and educated at Harvard, T. S. Eliot moved to London after the outbreak of the war. Convinced that poetry should convey a sense of the complexity of life, Eliot wrote poetry difficult to understand. But hidden by the shimmering imagery of his words were certain profound convictions, especially a belief that life without faith is vain foolishness. *The Waste Land*, 1922, Eliot's most important work of the decade, revealed the proportions of his break with the imagists and his conviction that the word image was futile unless it conveyed essential meaning about life. It also heralded his later conversion to Anglo-Catholicism and his metamorphosis into the chief religious poet of a later generation.

More accurately reflecting the dominant naturalistic temper among American writers was Robinson Jeffers, who wrote romantic poetry before the war and then in the mid-twenties turned savagely against humanity. His *Tower Beyond Tragedy* and *Roan Stallion*, 1925, and *The Women at Point Sur*, 1927, expressed his conviction that violence, sexual perversion, and inhumanity characterized all human behavior and that the natural world alone had grandeur and dignity.

Convincing proof of the continued vitality of the poetic tradition in the United States was the rise of a generation of young new poets in the 1920's. There was, for example, Pound's and Eliot's disciple, Hart Crane; a group of southern regionalists at Vanderbilt University—John Crowe Ransome, Robert Penn Warren, and Allen Tate—who combined a romantic love of the southern past with experiments in new forms; Edna St. Vincent Millay, whose sonnets expressed the youthful revolt against Victorian man-

---

[3] Stanley T. Williams, "Edwin Arlington Robinson," in Robert E. Spiller *et al.*, *Literary History of the United States* (New York, 1953), p. 1170; used by permission of the Macmillan Company, publishers.

ners; and Archibald MacLeish, who began a distinguished literary career by voicing the dominant mood of discontent. Or, again, there was the experimentalist, e. e. cummings, whose strange style almost obscured the simple romantic themes of his poems; and Conrad Áiken, William Carlos Williams, Marianne Moore, and Wallace Stevens, among a host of others. The most widely read of the young poets, Stephen Vincent Benét, found his theme in the great crisis of the Union. His *John Brown's Body*, 1928, an epic poem, depicted the passions and experiences of the American people during the Civil War more convincingly than most social histories have done.

Important though these developments in fictional and poetical writing were, the most significant literary development of the 1920's was the flowering of a native American drama. The movement to create a new American theater had its beginnings around 1915, when young intellectuals established little theaters at Provincetown, Massachusetts, and in New York City and began to experiment for their own pleasure. The New York group reorganized in 1919 under the name of Theater Guild, acquired a theater of its own, and began presenting the plays of contemporary European dramatists.

Meanwhile, out of the Provincetown group had emerged Eugene O'Neill, whose one-act *Bound East for Cardiff* was first produced by the Provincetown Players in 1916. During the next six years O'Neill gained distinction as the only American dramatist of any consequence to that time. Then, in *Desire Under the Elms*, 1924, *Strange Interlude*, 1928, and *Mourning Becomes Electra*, 1931, he turned to Freudian themes in an attempt to understand human motivation.

O'Neill was beyond cavil the pre-eminent American dramatist of his generation; but he was joined by such a goodly company after 1922 that almost overnight an American drama of genuine literary significance came into being. Moreover, the American public evinced an encouraging interest in the stage and a willingness to accept experimental forms; and this interest was reflected not only on Broadway but on college campuses and in little theater groups in a hundred American cities. This renaissance first began with the production of Elmer Rice's *The Adding Machine* in 1923 and Maxwell Anderson's and Laurence Stallings' *What Price Glory?*, Sidney Howard's *They Knew What They Wanted*, and John Howard Lawson's *Processional* in 1924–1925. From this beginning progress was rapid. Although S. N. Behrman and Philip Barry enlivened the theater with sophisticated comedies and Paul Green and Hatcher Hughes tried vainly to stimulate interest in folk drama, the large majority of young playwrights simply mirrored the contemporary determinism, disillusionment, and preoccupation with sex. Not until the depression would the stage become a sounding board for the American social conscience.

119 / *The Growth of American Music, Art, and Architecture*

Americans who, at the end of the First World War, lamented the absence of any strong musical and artistic traditions and bemoaned the public's indifference to these important manifestations of culture might well have been encouraged by developments during the twenties. Not only did American musicians and artists enjoy unprecedented prestige and acceptance; there were also numerous signs of the development of a genuine interest in music and art among the masses of people.

This fact was manifested in the field of music particularly in the spread of music by the phonograph and radio and in the growth of music education, symphony orchestras, and choral groups. By 1930, for example, practically every elementary and high school in the country offered some form of musical training, and there were 35,000 orchestras in the public schools alone. At the same time, there were seventy-three permanent symphony orchestras, fifty-five chamber music groups, and 576 choral societies. Even more important was the development of music schools and conservatories from 1914 to 1930. Indeed, by the latter date there were probably more able teachers in the United States than in Europe.

This musical awakening stimulated a love for music among millions of Americans, provided a broad economic base for the musical profession in the United States, and gave rise to a host of young composers. Between 1865 and 1917 America had produced a number of serious composers—Edward MacDowell, Edgar S. Kelley, Frank van der Stucken, Charles M. Loeffler, to mention a few of them. Except for MacDowell, however, their works made slight impression on the American musical public. In contrast, by 1930 American music critics and listeners were celebrating the accomplishments of their serious composers.

Deems Taylor was easily the most popular of this group. His *Through the Looking Glass*, written from 1917 to 1919, sparkled with wit and brilliance. His *The King's Henchmen*, completed in 1927, was produced at the Metropolitan Opera House and won enthusiastic acclaim. Ernest Bloch, a Swiss composer who came to the United States in 1916, abandoned Jewish themes to write *America*, a symphony built around American musical traditions. Howard Hanson, director of the Eastman School of Music at Rochester, New York, was perhaps the most gifted and technically competent of the young composers. His opera, *Merry Mount*, based upon an old American story, was produced by the Metropolitan Opera Company in 1934.

Important though the work of the serious composers was, American musicians during the period 1914–1930 made their most original contribution to the musical tradition by developing an old form, folk songs, and elaborating a new one, jazz. In the nineteenth century folk music voiced the yearnings of the slave, the patriotism and ideals of Northerners and Southerners during the Civil War, and other more homely aspects of life. In the early twentieth century the form and themes of folk music changed, from haunting melodies into so-called "ragtime," from themes of country life into themes reflecting an urban civilization. George M. Cohan, Irving Berlin, and George Gershwin were the chief writers of the new folk ballads. Berlin's *Oh How I Hate to Get Up in the Morning* and Cohan's *Over There*, for example, expressed the American spirit of 1917, just as *Dixie* and *The Battle Hymn of the Republic* had done in 1861.

During the 1920's hundreds of other popular song writers expressed in a hundred different ways the foolishness and wisdom, the gaiety and pathos of the time. Especially noteworthy were the musical plays like Jerome Kern's and Oscar Hammerstein II's *Show Boat,* 1927, that gave birth to many of the best songs of the decade. Noteworthy also was the rise of the Negro "blues" songs, best exemplified by W. C. Handy's *Memphis Blues* and *St. Louis Blues.* But more important was the phenomenal spread of Negro jazz, which had originated in the early years of the century in New Orleans and made its way to Chicago by 1915–1916. A highly sophisticated musical form, jazz spread rapidly over the country after 1916, especially after Paul Whiteman demonstrated the wide potentialities of the new form in the early twenties, and Gershwin combined the syncopation of jazz with the symphonic form in a successful way in *Rhapsody in Blue,* 1927, and *An American In Paris,* 1928.

If the period 1900–1917 witnessed the first important beginnings of American public interest in paintings and sculptures, then the years between 1917 and 1930 saw the full maturing of a genuine appreciation. This phenomenon was manifested in many ways: in increased artistic creativity, in the introduction of art subjects in public school and college curricula, and especially in the creation of art museums in all sections of the country, not merely in Boston, New York, and Philadelphia. By 1930, for example, the aggregate holdings of American art museums were valued at $2,000,000,000, and Europeans often had to come to the United States to study the works of the masters.

During the twenties, as before the war, American painters continued more to follow the Continental lead than to develop techniques and forms of their own. The reaction against impressionism, in the form of a movement toward abstraction and primitivism which had got under way in France just before the war, came to full flower in Europe and America after 1920. At the same time, abstraction metamorphosed into cubism, surrealism, and other "modern" forms among an advanced artistic guard. Among the notable exponents of abstraction in the United States were John Marin, who revealed great versatility in other forms, particularly in water colors, Max Weber, Maurice Prendergast, and Charles R. Sheeler. Not all American artists of the period abandoned the concrete for the purely intellectual, however, as a large group persevered in the realistic tradition and left a memorable graphic record of various aspects of American social life. George Bellows continued to paint powerful scenes of the ring; Edward Hopper, Rockwell Kent, Ernest Lawson, John Sloan, and other artists of the "Ash Can School" painted "drunks and slatterns, pushcart peddlers and coal mines, bedrooms and barrooms."[4] These artistic rebels shocked many genteel folk but left a vivid pictorial record of the seamy side of American life.

In sculpture one trend of the twenties was away from the idealistic realism of prewar masters like Augustus Saint-Gaudens and Daniel Chester French toward abstract symbolism and primitivism, as exemplified in the work of William Zorach, Arnold Ronnebeck, Robert Garrison, and others. On the other hand, Jacob Epstein, Trygve Hammer, and Gaston Lachaise did memorable work in the realistic tradition, while the most widely ac-

[4] Oliver W. Larkin, *Art and Life In America* (New York, 1949), p. 336.

claimed sculptor of the decade, Gutzon Borglum, chiseled monuments on Stone Mountain in Georgia and Mount Rushmore in South Dakota that were as realistic as they were massive.

Meanwhile, the period 1914–1929 also witnessed the maturing of a new and immensely popular art form—the motion picture—the artistic possibilities of which were first demonstrated by David W. Griffith's "The Birth of a Nation," produced in 1915. Although "The Birth of a Nation" was a piece of violent anti-Negro propaganda, it was a milestone in motion picture history because Griffith surmounted the limitations and conventions of the stage and utilized large numbers of actors, panoramic scenery, the close-up, the fade-out, and the switch-back.

From 1915 to 1929 the motion picture medium came to full maturity as an art form. Griffith subsequently produced other great historical films, notably "Intolerance"—as penance for "The Birth of a Nation"—and "America"; Cecil B. de Mille used thousands of actors and spectacular sets and scenery in his religious dramas, "The Ten Commandments," "The Flood," and "The King of Kings"; and other spectacles like "The Covered Wagon," "The Four Horsemen of the Apocalypse," "The Big Parade," "Quo Vadis," and "Ben Hur" employed diverse themes but used all the new artistic techniques and helped make the twenties a memorable motion picture decade. Moreover, as Hollywood salaries lured many of the best actors of the period from the legitimate stage, acting became an art that the masses of people, rather than the privileged few, could enjoy. Charlie Chaplin and Harold Lloyd, for example, were not only the pre-eminent film comedians of the twenties; they were superb creative artists as well.

In architecture Americans, at least since the eighteenth century, had exhibited a boldness and willingness to experiment that was not always characteristic of their European contemporaries. As we have seen, the pioneer work in the 1890's of a group of Chicago architects had culminated by 1914 in the perfection of the skyscraper form. During the 1920's the building of skyscrapers went on apace in all large cities, but especially in New York, where the form was used for apartments as well as office buildings.

In domestic architecture, the trend toward the colonial and Dutch farmhouse types, which had begun before 1914, continued to predominate in the twenties. The movement toward functionalism—toward simplicity in style and greater use of glass and open spaces—had also been begun in the United States by Louis Sullivan and Frank Lloyd Wright before the war. Wright continued his work in the twenties, but the American people still clung to traditional forms and steadily resisted the innovators.

Of greater immediate significance in the 1920's was the movement for city planning and the development of great parkway systems to facilitate traffic between the city and outlying areas. The movement to establish city planning commissions began in 1905 but did not gain momentum until after 1914. Before 1914 there were only seventeen such agencies; between 1914 and 1930 more than 750 planning commissions were established. In the wake of this development also followed campaigns to zone cities into exclusively industrial, commercial, and residential areas, to improve building codes, and to clean up slums—in general to clear away what had been the jungle growth in American city life.

ABOVE: *President Wilson reading his War Message to Congress*
BELOW: *The President leading a parade on Fifth Avenue*

The Big Four at Wilson's Paris home during the Peace Conference: Mr. Lloyd George, Signor Orlando, M. Clemenceau, and President Wilson

Warren G. Harding

Andrew Mellon

President Hoover opening the baseball season, 1932

ABOVE: *Sacco and Vanzetti*
BELOW: *The Ku Klux Klan*

ABOVE: *Assembly line at Ford's River Rouge Plant*
BELOW: *The tractor displaces the horse*

Helen Breaker

Ernest Hemingway

Eugene O'Neill

Sinclair Lewis and his first wife in a Model T

President Coolidge in the Black Hills

Al Capone and the Law

Wall Street, October 24, 1929

Apple sellers in New York, 1931

ABOVE: *A Hooverville—Grant's Tomb, Riverside Church, and uptown New York skyline in background*

BELOW: *Breadline, 1932*

120 / *School and Church in the Twenties*

For more than a century Americans had glorified public schools as the chief instruments of democracy and equality of opportunity; and from the Civil War to 1910 progress in expanding and improving free education had been steady and substantial. The prosperity of the war period and the twenties, however, stimulated such achievement as had not been recorded in any earlier comparable period. The following generalizations illustrate the main trends: From 1910 to 1930 the number of pupils enrolled in public schools increased from nearly 18,000,000 to over 25,500,000. Total expenditures for education in the United States grew during the same two decades from $426,250,000 to $2,316,790,000, the value of school property from $1,000,-000,000 to over $6,000,000,000, and per capita expenditure per pupil from $23.93 to $90.22. From 1910 to 1930, moreover, illiteracy declined generally from 7.7 per cent of the total population to 4.3 per cent, and among Negroes from 30.4 per cent to 16.3 per cent.

By 1910 the goal of a free education for all children in elementary schools had been fairly accomplished, and except for expansion in kindergartens and schools for Negro children the progress accomplished in the elementary field from 1910 to 1930 came more from improved instruction, longer terms, and the like, than from any great expansion in sheer numbers. For one thing, state departments of education assumed responsibility for licensing teachers and began to require the completion of a four-year college course as a prerequisite for a teaching certificate. For another, as schools of education broke away from the formal, classical tradition, the "progressive" methods advocated earlier by John Dewey and others found wider acceptance. Although conservatives bemoaned the neglect of the genteel subjects, there can be little doubt that the increased emphasis upon experimentation and participation by the children and the widespread use of workshops, laboratories, and other material equipment were not only better adapted to the capacities of children but also were indispensable instruments of mass education.

During the two decades under discussion, however, Americans made their greatest relative progress in secondary and higher education. From 1910 to 1930 the number of children enrolled in all high schools increased over 400 per cent, from 1,111,393 to 4,799,867. And along with growth came important changes in curriculum as high schools ceased to prepare children exclusively for college. Thus, in 1928 only 22 per cent of the high school pupils studied Latin, as contrasted to nearly 50 per cent in 1910. On the other hand, music, manual training, home economics, typewriting, agricultural science, and other vocational subjects, most of which had not even been offered in 1910, were beginning to overshadow the so-called classical offerings. Accelerated by the Smith-Lever and Smith-Hughes Acts of 1914 and 1917, which provided federal support for agricultural and vocational education, this movement toward more practical training for the large majority of high school students who would not go to college was a frank recognition of the state's enlarged social responsibilities.

The prosperity of the 1920's and especially the great increase in high school enrollment in turn stimulated an unprecedented expansion of American colleges and universities. The following statistics illustrate the general trends. From 1910 to 1930 the number of students enrolled increased from 266,654 to 924,275, of instructors from 33,631 to 71,722, of total endowments from $273,423,328 to $1,347,676,000, and of total receipts exclusive of endowments from $78,873,000 to $567,618,000.

This extraordinary growth raised serious new problems concerning the role of higher education in a democracy and inevitably compelled college and university leaders to modify methods and objectives. In other words, colleges and universities ceased to prepare students almost exclusively for the professions and became also training schools where young men and women prepared for careers in industry, business, and other walks of life. This fact did not signify any diminution of advanced professional training, research, and writing. On the contrary, graduate schools grew even more rapidly than undergraduate departments,[5] while the growth of medical, law, and other professional schools was substantial if not as spectacular.

Although the state universities grew faster in enrollment and income during the twenties, private colleges and universities continued to provide leadership in academic innovation. In an attempt to break away from the emphasis on mere lecture courses, Harvard, Swarthmore, and a number of other institutions followed Princeton's earlier example and introduced the tutorial system and honors programs. Following a plan proposed by Woodrow Wilson in 1906, Harvard and Yale constructed undergraduate colleges, in which upperclassmen and faculty members lived together. In Florida, Hamilton Holt founded Rollins College and abandoned the lecture system for the conference method of instruction, while Arthur E. Morgan introduced the so-called "in and out" system at Antioch College in Ohio, in which students alternated between attendance at college and work outside. There were of course retrogressive trends—periodic assaults upon freedom of teaching by religious and nationalistic groups, attempts by reactionary trustees to control academic policies, and the like. Such efforts to bring higher education under reactionary religious and economic control, however, were the exception rather than the rule. By and large, college and university faculties enjoyed greater respect and freedom than ever before in American history.

How fared the churches, the other great agencies of moral and social enlightenment, during this period? Protestant, Roman Catholic, and Jewish churches continued to grow in membership and wealth during the decade between the religious censuses of 1916 and 1926. Increasing urbanization and the use of the automobile caused the elimination of many small rural churches and the consolidation of others, and the building of churches and synagogues proceeded at a much slower pace than the growth in the general population. But church membership in the United States increased more rapidly than the population—from a total of 43,311,647 to 54,576,346; and churches increased their expenditures by 149 per cent during a decade when national income increased 98 per cent.

[5] For example, there were 9,370 students enrolled in graduate schools and 409 Ph.D. degrees conferred in 1910; in 1930 there were 47,255 graduate students enrolled and 2,024 Ph.D. degrees conferred.

Even more than during the first decade of the twentieth century, the United States was predominantly a Protestant country in the 1920's. Total Protestant membership grew from 26,205,039 in 1916 to 31,890,101 in 1926, Catholic membership from 15,722,000 to 18,605,000 over the same decade. But adult Protestant membership increased 46 per cent between 1906 and 1926, as compared with an increase of 25 per cent among adult Roman Catholics. Among the more than two hundred Protestant bodies in 1926, the Baptists, with nearly 8,500,000 members, and the various Methodist bodies, with an aggregate of 8,000,000 adherents, continued to command a large superiority in numbers and to account for the greatest increases in membership.

These statistics would seem to warrant the conclusion that organized religion not only survived the disillusionment of the 1920's but also grew to a position of unrivaled pre-eminence among American social institutions. Moreover, there is no convincing evidence that the religious faith of the masses of people was substantially weakened by the erosion of antagonistic concepts like Freudianism, scientific materialism, and behaviorism. A poll of 250,000 newspaper readers and 36,000 college students taken in 1927 revealed that young people were even more orthodox than their parents and that an overwhelming majority at least of the middle classes adhered to traditional Judaeo-Christian beliefs.

How can we reconcile the survival of religion in the 1920's with the apparent dominance of hostile faiths? Obviously, the advanced intellectuals, in their search for new gods, in large measure lost communication with the masses. Their deviation from the Christian tradition was significant, to be sure, but it was not symptomatic of any mass deviation. On the other hand, there could be little doubt that the Protestant churches were changing in an important way under the impact of new concepts and challenges. Long before the First World War, the Darwinian hypothesis and higher criticism had caused a large minority of Protestant clergymen to abandon belief in the inerrancy of the Scriptures and many tenets of the historic Christian creed. During the 1920's that so-called liberal minority became probably a majority among Protestant churchmen and controlled at least the Methodist and Congregational churches. Varying in their liberalism all the way from unitarianism to liberal fundamentalism, this majority abandoned an exclusive emphasis on theology and gave larger emphasis to the gospel of social service. They also met the advanced intellectual liberals on their own ground by marshaling the findings of anthropology, social psychology, and history to prove that the Judaeo-Christian ethical system was the way of life that could best stand the pragmatic test of long-run human experience.

121 / *Trends in American Journalism, 1914–1929*

From 1914 to 1929 newspapers grew in size and circulation and continued to rival schools and churches as the chief instruments of mass education and the dissemination of ideas. At the same time, there were signs that trends evident well before 1914 were culminating in the 1920's to alter the character and practice of journalism and newspaper publishing in the United States.

For one thing, there was a striking trend toward consolidation in ownership, a consequent decline in the number of newspapers published, and the further extension of the influence of the metropolitan press through rural areas. Daily newspapers declined in number from 2,514 in 1917 to 2,268 in 1931, weekly newspapers from 16,323 in 1915 to 12,825 in 1929. Cities having only one daily newspaper increased from 504 in 1910 to 913 in 1930. By the latter year, moreover, there were sixty newspaper chains, publishing some 300 newspapers, with over one-third the total daily circulation in the United States.

Among the large newspaper publishers, William Randolph Hearst was still the leader. From 1914 through 1929 he added twenty-seven dailies to his newspaper realm and in addition owned two wire news services, King Features, six magazines, a newsreel, a motion picture company, and a weekly supplement. Having abandoned his simulated progressivism of the prewar period, in the 1920's Hearst became openly reactionary and was as stridently nationalistic as ever. The Scripps-McRae chain, which published twenty-three newspapers in 1914, became the Scripps-Howard chain in 1922 and absorbed an additional eighteen dailies from 1921 through 1929. In upstate New York Frank E. Gannett established a chain of fifteen dailies, while James M. Cox, Democratic presidential candidate in 1920, went into the newspaper business in 1923 and bought control of a newspaper chain in Ohio, to which he later added the Atlanta *Journal* and the Miami (Florida) *News*.

As newspapers declined in number and came increasingly under outside control, they inevitably became capitalistic enterprises representing often the investment of several million dollars. In form and content, however, most American newspapers changed little after 1914. For the most part they used standardized news and features; became decidedly less partisan in politics; and grew more dependent upon advertising for revenue. In other words, running a great newspaper became a highly institutionalized and departmentalized function and often a highly profitable business. Consequently, the editor not only lost his independence but also the great prestige he had once enjoyed as a tribune of the people. Old-fashioned editors like Josephus Daniels of the Raleigh *News and Observer* and William Allen White of the *Emporia* (Kansas) *Gazette* survived; but they were prototypes of a vanishing race of men who dominated their newspapers and made them extensions of their personalities.

Although a majority of newspapers continued to adhere to the traditions of public service and honest and dignified reporting established earlier by Joseph Pulitzer and Adolph S. Ochs, the most notable journalistic development of the 1920's was the rise of the so-called tabloid. Imitating Lord Northcliffe's *Daily Mirror* of London, Robert R. McCormick and Joseph Medill Patterson in 1919 established the New York *Daily News*, a morning newspaper of sixteen four-column pages. Featuring sensational sex and crime stories and filled with pictures and features, the *News* attained the largest circulation in the country in 1924. Embittered because the owners of the *News* surpassed him in the art of yellow journalism, Hearst established his own tabloid in 1924, the New York *Daily Mirror*. And when Bernarr Macfadden entered the competition a few months later with the New York

Graphic, there began such a frenzied newspaper war as New Yorkers had not seen since Hearst and Pulitzer fought it out in 1898. Meanwhile, the tabloids spread to numerous other cities, and the result was the worst wave of yellow journalism in modern American history. However, a public reaction against journalistic obscenity set in about 1929, and the tabloids gradually changed into small newspapers with little news and many pictures, features, and cartoons.

Throughout the twenties and afterward, weekly and monthly magazines remained an important medium of opinion, news, and entertainment. The two chief organs of progressive ideas, the *Nation* and *New Republic*, maintained their subsidized existence. The *Saturday Evening Post, Collier's,* and the women's magazines combined light fiction with articles of contemporary interest and continued to enjoy mass circulations. On the other hand, journals like the *Outlook, World's Work,* and *Independent*, which appealed to more limited audiences by combining serious fiction with news and opinion, declined in the 1920's. Faced with a sharp rise in paper and printing costs and unable to adapt themselves to mass reading habits, these journals passed from the American journalistic scene during the depression.

Meanwhile, the most important revolution in magazine publishing since the advent of the popular magazine in the 1890's, the rise of the weekly news and picture magazines, was taking shape in the brain of Henry Luce, the most daring magazine publisher since S. S. McClure. In 1925 Luce began publication of *Time*, a weekly devoted exclusively to news in concise form, cryptic style, and ostensibly objective views, which became the leading American news weekly within a decade. In 1930 he opened a new field with the publication of *Fortune*, a monthly addressed to business leaders and intellectuals. But his greatest triumph came in 1936, with the publication of *Life*, a weekly news-picture magazine, which enjoyed immediate success. The subsequent rise of rival magazines like *Newsweek* and *Look*, founded in 1933 and 1937, only emphasized the dimensions of the journalistic revolution that Luce had accomplished by 1940.

CHAPTER 16 / TENSIONS OF THE 1920's

A NUMBER of developments combined at the end of the war to intensify old religious, social, and ideological discords and to cause new insecurities. The clash of scientific materialism and materialistic evolution with religious orthodoxy produced a remarkable fundamentalist counterattack. Patriotic organizations revived the strident nationalism and intolerance of the war period and inflamed religious prejudices. By attempting to suppress the traffic in alcoholic beverages, the Protestant majority outraged intellectuals, embittered the urban masses, and provoked a campaign of resistance to the federal authority.

In a varying degree the American people were affected by the tensions and conflicts we are about to describe, but withal democracy survived its periodic testing. Perhaps the foibles and failures of the American people in the 1920's will afford hope for the future to a generation distraught by new insecurities.

122 / The Anti-Evolution Crusade

The anti-evolution crusade was the last organized uprising of fundamentalist America against the complex of materialistic concepts that seemed to remove God from the process of creation, deny His dominion over human affairs, and attempt to destroy an ethical system based upon divinely revealed principles. It was fitting that William J. Bryan, the spokesman of rural, Protestant America, should have taken leadership in the anti-evolution crusade, which drew most of its recruits from the rural areas. The spread of scientific materialism and especially of the belief in the materialistic origins of man presented a personal challenge to Bryan. Investigation convinced him that the teaching of evolution caused students first to lose faith in the verbal inspiration and inerrancy of the Scriptures and later to repudiate Christianity altogether. What Bryan dreaded most was the prospect that atheistic evolutionists would be graduated from the colleges, invade the public schools as teachers, and undermine the Christian faith of American school children.

Bryan sounded the first note in his campaign to purge the public schools and colleges with addresses at the University of Wisconsin in April 1921 and before the General Assembly of Kentucky in January 1922. "They have taken the Lord away from the schools," he cried again and again. "Shall teachers paid by taxation be permitted to substitute the unproven hypothesis of scientists for the 'Thus saith the Lord' of the Bible, and so undermine the faith of the children of Christian taxpayers?" The answer, of course, was obvious: legislators should forbid the teaching of evolution in the public schools and institutions of higher learning in the state. From this beginning, Bryan's campaign soon became a nation-wide crusade. He turned his monthly magazine, *The Commoner*, into a fundamentalist sheet; spoke before state legislatures through the South and Middle West; and carried his fight to the General Assembly of the northern Presbyterian Church, where he failed to win adoption of an anti-evolution resolution in 1923. But he had succeeded in beginning one of the liveliest controversies of the decade; already legislatures in many states were being pressed to enact anti-evolution laws. Let us now look at some of the results of Bryan's agitation.

Although Bryan's campaign had significant reverberations in the Middle West, only in the South did it meet with strong popular support and a measure of success. Leadership and support for the movement in that region came largely from the Baptists and the Presbyterians. There was, however, no uniformity of religious opinion in the so-called Bible Belt. The Baptists, for example, were badly split by the evolution issue, while the Methodist Episcopal Church, South, and the Episcopal Church taught theistic evolution and refused to be drawn into the controversy.

But Bryan's call to battle in 1921 was answered by a large number of southern fundamentalist leaders. There was, for example, the Reverend J. Frank Norris of Fort Worth, Texas, the *enfant terrible* of the southern Baptist church, who undertook a reign of terror against science teachers at Baylor University in Waco and published a weekly newspaper, *The Search-light*, devoted to exposing atheists and evolutionists. Or there was the Reverend T. T. Martin, an itinerant Baptist evangelist, author of *Hell in the High Schools*, one of the leading anti-evolution tracts. From 1921 to 1925 they and their cohorts carried on vigorous campaigns in most southern and south-western states. At the same time, liberal leaders in church, school, and journal-ism met the fundamentalists head on, fought courageously for academic freedom, and on the whole won the first round of the battle.

In fact, the only state in which the anti-evolutionists had won a decisive victory by 1925 was Tennessee.[1] In the spring of 1923 academic circles in the United States were shocked by the dismissal from the University of Tennessee of a professor of genetic psychology for using James Harvey Robinson's *Mind in the Making*. At the end of the college year, five other professors were dismissed from the faculty for teaching the evolutionary hypothesis. Two years later, when an anti-evolution bill was introduced in

[1] The fundamentalists, however, won qualified victories in Florida, North Carolina, and Texas. Without forbidding the teaching of evolution, the Florida legislature in May 1923 adopted a resolution advising that "Darwinism, Atheism, and Agnosticism" should not be taught as truths in the public schools of the state. On January 22, 1924, the North Carolina State Board of Education forbade the teaching in public schools of any form of evolution affirming that man descended from a lower order of animals. In October 1925 the State Textbook Board of Texas ordered the deletion of all references to evolution in books adopted for the public schools of the state.

the Tennessee legislature, Bryan and a powerful Baptist lobby descended upon Nashville. The legislature and governor surrendered by approving a measure forbidding any teacher in the state's schools and colleges to teach any theory denying the biblical account of creation or asserting that man had descended from a lower order of animals.

At once the American Civil Liberties Union offered to finance the defense of any Tennessee teacher who would test the constitutionality of the statute. A young high school biology teacher in Dayton, John Thomas Scopes, volunteered and a friendly case was begun in May 1925. When the state's counsel invited Bryan to join the prosecution, the Commoner accepted joyfully, declaring, "This is a matter for the nation." At the same time, the famed trial lawyer, Clarence Darrow, joined the defense counsel, and the stage was set for one of the great forensic battles of the century.

As the opening day of the trial, July 14, 1925, drew near, the little mountain town of Dayton, Tennessee, was crowded with evangelists, traveling performers, and newspaper correspondents from all over the United States and the western world. Bryan was greeted by huge crowds and ovations; in response he pledged himself to undertake a campaign to amend the Constitution to prohibit the teaching of evolution anywhere in the United States. Once the trial began the presiding judge, John T. Raulston, a Methodist lay preacher, did his best to preserve a semblance of decorum; but the trial soon degenerated into a public circus after the court obligingly adjourned to a vacant lot in order to accommodate the huge crowds. When Raulston refused to admit expert testimony concerning the validity of the Darwinian hypothesis, the proceedings became a verbal duel between the agnostic Darrow and the fundamentalist Bryan.

It did not take long to prove that Scopes had violated the law, since he admitted as much. The Supreme Court of Tennessee later rescinded the fine that Raulston had imposed but upheld the conviction and the anti-evolution law. But the anticlimax came a few days after the Scopes trial, on July 26, 1925, when Bryan died, from exhaustion and overeating, at the scene of his attempt to defend the faith.

The Scopes trial and Bryan's death stimulated a momentary revival of the anti-evolution crusade—especially after the formation of the Supreme Kingdom, the Bible Crusaders, the Bryan Bible League, and other fundamentalist organizations. Modeled after the Ku Klux Klan and dedicated to obtaining adoption of an anti-evolution constitutional amendment, the Supreme Kingdom functioned in sixteen states, published a monthly magazine, *Dynamite*, and established a rest home in Florida for "those who grow old in the war against evolution."

Of all the anti-evolution organizations, the Bible Crusaders were best organized and the most formidable. Under the leadership of T. T. Martin, they formed mobile squadrons that went from one state capitol to another and applied pressure upon legislatures. Descending upon the Mississippi legislature in 1926, for example, they obtained passage of an anti-evolution law before the liberal forces of the state could counterattack. After encountering defeat in Louisiana, the Bible Crusaders moved next to North Carolina. In this leading progressive southern state the fundamentalists, mainly Presbyterians, had already organized to work for passage of an anti-evolution bill. The fight that ensued was bitter and prolonged, but liberal spokesmen struck back hard and prevented passage of a measure in 1927.

Defeat in North Carolina seemed to break the back of the entire fundamentalist crusade. In one state after another—in Georgia, Kentucky, Florida, South Carolina, and Oklahoma—the anti-evolutionists met with subsequent defeats. They had one last, curious triumph in Arkansas, and then the movement died almost entirely. After the Arkansas legislature several times had refused to adopt an anti-evolution bill, the fundamentalists obtained adoption of their measure in 1928 by using the initiative to bypass the legislature. For the first time in the history of the world the sovereign people by direct legislation decreed that Darwin was wrong!

Thus ended one of the most significant and also one of the most tragic social movements in American history. Southern Protestants who participated in the anti-evolution crusade thought they were fighting to preserve the best features of the American heritage—a belief in the spirituality of the universe and in the God-like character of man. Instead of defending this heritage, however, the anti-evolution crusade tended to identify organized religion with bigotry and ignorance instead of freedom and learning. In several states and many communities fundamentalists instituted witch-hunts and inquisitions, the effects of which were felt for many years afterward. On the other hand, the anti-evolution movement had one beneficial effect: Its great challenge to academic freedom revealed the South's intellectual backwardness and compelled the rising body of southern liberals to take a firm stand against intolerant obscurantism. Their victory in most states was, therefore, all the more significant for the future.

123 / The Growth of Nativism and Intolerance

There were, unhappily, numerous other manifestations of a growth of intolerance, bigotry, and nationalism among all classes and in all sections during the decade following the First World War. Reflected on all sides by the fear of "Reds," an intensification of anti-Semitism, organized campaigns against Roman Catholics, and, on the federal level, by legislation practically to end immigration from southern and eastern Europe, the champions of arrogant nationalism and religious bigotry seemed for a time to speak for the American people.

The popular fear of communism was reflected in different ways on different levels. Following a policy set by the Wilson administration, the Republican administrations refused to enter into diplomatic relations with the Soviet Union. In order to prevent the dissemination of revolutionary propaganda, the New York legislature in 1921 required all nonchurch private schools to obtain approval of their curricula by the Board of Regents. When the Socialist party's Rand School refused to apply for a license, the state began proceedings to close that institution.[2] In California, from 1919 to 1924, state officials carried on a ruthless campaign to destroy the Industrial Work-

---

[2] After the election of Alfred E. Smith as governor in 1922, this legislation was repealed and the proceedings against the Rand School were dropped.

ers of the World; and 504 persons were arrested and 264 alleged subversives were tried under the state's criminal syndicalism law for committing sabotage and advocating the violent overthrow of the government.

The case that aroused the most violent controversy, however, involved two obscure Italian-born anarchists, Nicola Sacco and Bartolomeo Vanzetti. Arrested in 1920 for the alleged murder of a paymaster in South Braintree, Massachusetts, Sacco and Vanzetti were tried the following year by a judge, Webster Thayer, who publicly vented his contempt for anarchism and allowed the state's attorney to make the defendants' radicalism a cornerstone of his case. Sacco and Vanzetti were convicted and sentenced to death, but throughout the United States and western Europe radical and liberal groups believed the two men had been sentenced, not for murder, but for anarchism.[3] In spite of mass demonstrations abroad and fervent appeals at home, Governor A. T. Fuller allowed Sacco and Vanzetti to die in the electric chair on August 23, 1927.

Anti-Semitism, always a latent menace, was exacerbated by the identification of many Jewish radicals first with opposition to the war and then with the Communist party and other radical groups. It was also intensified by the fact that many Jews were recent immigrants, as yet not "Americanized" during a decade when the great majority demanded unquestioning adoption of American manners and customs. It was, moreover, nurtured and used as a rallying cry by the leaders of the Ku Klux Klan, who resurrected discredited charges of an international Jewish conspiracy to control the world. These charges were echoed by Henry Ford's newspaper, the *Dearborn Independent*, until Ford was threatened with court action and repudiated the accusation.

An uncritical nationalism, stimulated by postwar disillusionment and bitter European criticisms of American life, also seized millions, if not a majority, of Americans during the twenties. Agitated by the Hearst newspapers and the *Chicago Daily Tribune*, public officials in New York and Chicago investigated school textbooks to root out works that failed properly to glorify the American past and damn the British. Oregon and Wisconsin forbade the use of history texts that defamed American heroism in the Revolution and the War of 1812, while organizations like the American Legion, the Daughters of the American Revolution, and the Ku Klux Klan maintained a steady pressure for "one hundred per cent Americanism," that is, unqualified acceptance of middle class standards. And nationalism often shaded into racism, as Madison Grant and Lothrop Stoddard, among others, in their *Passing of the Great Race* and *The Rising Tide of Color* popularized the contemporary view that the Nordic type was inherently superior to other so-called races.

The most sinister development of the 1920's, however, was the rise to power in many states of the Knights of the Ku Klux Klan, the American counterpart of the Italian Fascists and the German Nazis. Organized by William J. Simmons, a former lay preacher and history teacher, under a blazing cross on Stone Mountain near Atlanta in the autumn of 1915, the Klan was modeled after the hooded organization that had terrorized the

---

[3] It might be added that since 1921 this belief has grown into a firm conviction among lawyers and historians who have studied the case.

South during Reconstruction. By the end of 1919 Simmons had established a few chapters in Georgia and Alabama, but loss of membership seemed to threaten his organization with early extinction.

Early in 1920, however, two expert organizers, Edward Y. Clarke and Mrs. Elizabeth Tyler, rescued the Klan from oblivion. Simmons had constructed an imposing empire headed by himself as Imperial Wizard, but with only a few thousand subjects of dubious loyalty. Recognizing the rich financial opportunity at hand, Clarke and Mrs. Tyler increased the initiation fee to $10.00 and established an imperial promotion department, known as the imperial kleagle, with door-to-door solicitors and heads of state promotion departments.

By a vigorous promotional campaign, the Klan gained 100,000 new members in 1920, and growth was steady the following year. In 1922 the impractical Simmons was ousted as Imperial Wizard and replaced by Hiram W. Evans, a Texas dentist with a bent for making money, and the Klan began its first important expansion. It moved first into the Southwest and stirred violent political storms. In Texas the venerable statesman, Charles A. Culberson, who had served in the United States Senate for twenty-four years, was defeated for renomination in 1922 by a Klan-supported candidate because of his opposition to the Klan. In Oklahoma civil war nearly ensued when Governor J. C. Walton put the state under martial law on September 15, 1923, and called all citizens into military service in his campaign to exterminate the Klan. In retaliation, the Klan-dominated legislature impeached Walton and removed him from office on November 18, 1923.

From the Southwest the Klan penetrated rapidly into California and then into Oregon, where a Klan-supported governor and legislature were elected in 1922 and proceeded to attempt to destroy Catholic parochial schools. Moving at the same time into the Middle West, Klan organizers soon gained a large constituency in this stronghold of democratic idealism. In Indiana, for example, the leading klansman, David C. Stephenson, captured control of the Republican state organization, cowed Indiana's two senators into submission, and installed his henchman, Ed. Jackson, as governor in 1925.[4]

In summary, when the Klan reached the peak of its strength in 1925 it had a membership throughout the country, but chiefly in the Southwest, Far West, and Middle West, of approximately 5,000,000. At one time or another and to a varying degree, it controlled or had powerful influence in the governments of Texas, Oklahoma, Arkansas, California, Oregon, Indiana, Ohio, and other states. Wherever it went it carried bigotry, violence, and corruption and, as we will see, posed a dire threat to democracy. How can we explain the success in a country with strong democratic traditions of a movement so obviously anti-democratic and hostile to religious freedom? In short, what were the appeal, the program, and the tactics of the Klan that explain its momentary triumph?

The membership of the Klan was drawn largely from lower middle

[4] Stephenson's downfall, however, came swiftly. After a sordid affair in which he kidnaped and assaulted a secretary and caused her to commit suicide, Stephenson was convicted of second degree murder on November 14, 1925, and sentenced to life imprisonment. His crony, Jackson, was indicted for bribery in September 1927; and the Klan was disgraced and destroyed as a political and social force in Indiana.

class old American stock, chiefly in small towns and cities, who were intensely suspicious of anything foreign or different and who responded to bombastic expressions of patriotism. As only native-born white Protestants were allegedly "racially" capable of comprehending Americanism, the Klan excluded Catholics, Jews, Negroes, and most aliens. And the same sort of people who followed demagogues, went to revival meetings, and tried to suppress the teaching of evolution joined the Klan.

The Klan's chief appeal outside the South was anti-Catholicism. In the Middle and Far West its program was devoted almost exclusively to destroying the parochial schools, thwarting the Catholic hierarchy's alleged plot to capture the United States, and preventing the Pope from moving the Holy See to Georgetown. If there was any single issue on which small-town, Protestant Americans could be easily aroused, it was this Catholic issue, and the Klan thus gained members and power by appealing to historic fears and perpetuating the strong anti-Catholic tradition that went back to the colonial period of American history.

The Klan was not officially anti-Semitic, but in practice it was almost invariably so, because Jews were not only not Protestants but were also, for the most part, aliens from southern and eastern Europe. However, the Klan stood avowedly for white supremacy and for keeping the Negro "in his place." Indeed, the most important impetus for the rise of the Klan in the South was the white fear of returning Negro veterans and the troubled condition of race relations from 1919 to 1921.

Aside from its anti-Catholic program, the Klan's strongest attraction was its ritual, secrecy, and regalia and the fact that it was for a time a going concern. Americans have always been a nation of joiners and have loved especially a high-flown ritual. But the Klan also allowed its members to wear weird looking white robes and hoods, and any ordinary person could pay his ten dollars, become an exalted Knight of the Ku Klux Klan, and parade in exciting anonymity.

Because the imperial headquarters exercised absolutely no control over the klaverns, or local chapters, the tactics of the Klan varied from community to community. The coming of the Klan to the Southwest in 1920–1921, for example, was accompanied by a wave of murders, floggings, kidnapings, and other outrages. And thus it went, though on a lesser scale, wherever the Klan penetrated. Klan leaders piously protested that criminals using the Klan costume were always responsible for the outrages. Klan opponents replied that the Klan was essentially a lawless, terroristic organization, whose chief purpose was the subversion of orderly constitutional government.

At the end of the 1920's Fascism was triumphant in Italy and the forces of reaction were gathering strength in Germany. In the United States, on the other hand, the Ku Klux Klan stood exposed and discredited, its membership reduced to perhaps 100,000. For this failure of fascism in the United States the American people had to thank their traditions, a free press, and courageous leaders all over the country. Everywhere progressive editors, politicians, clergymen, and other public spokesmen recognized the Klan for what it was. They took the Klan's measure and threw themselves into what seemed in the beginning a losing fight; and in the end they triumphed because they fought to preserve traditions that the overwhelming majority of Americans, even most klansmen, cherished.

124 / Prohibition: the "Noble Experiment"

By the eve of American participation in the First World War the prohibition movement had gained such momentum that the day could not be far distant when the Anti-Saloon leaders would campaign for a constitutional amendment outlawing the manufacture and sale of alcoholic beverages in the United States.[5] By the end of 1914 fourteen states had adopted prohibition; and by the end of 1918 over three-fourths of the people lived either in dry states or counties. Prohibition, obviously, was not the product of sudden impulse or wartime hysteria. On the contrary, it was an important component of the modern reform movement and demonstrated better than any other aspect of that movement the naive progressive faith in the efficacy of legislation in accomplishing fundamental social change.

On the other hand, the Anti-Saloon League might never have won the Eighteenth, or prohibition, Amendment had not the entrance of the United States into the war coincided with the high tide of prohibition agitation, for many champions of local option and state rights had consistently opposed such a far-reaching extension of the federal authority as national prohibition would compel. Because the Anti-Saloon spokesmen succeeded in identifying prohibition with patriotism these conservative voices were momentarily stilled. And thus the dry leaders were able to carry the government and people from one step to another in their relentless progress toward a constitutional amendment.

To begin with, the Anti-Saloon lobbyists forced the adoption of an amendment to the Conscription Act of 1917 forbidding the sale of alcoholic beverages at or near army camps and naval bases. Secondly, to conserve desperately needed grain, the Lever Act prohibited the use of grain for distilling and brewing and empowered the President to ban the manufacture of other alcoholic beverages. Thirdly, on December 18, 1917, Congress passed and submitted to the states the Eighteenth Amendment, which prohibited, one year after ratification, the manufacture, sale, or transportation of alcoholic beverages in the United States. Fourthly, in October 1919 Congress passed over Wilson's veto the Volstead Act extending the wartime ban on distilling and brewing, defining alcoholic beverages as any containing more than one-half of 1 per cent alcohol by volume, and prohibiting the manufacture or sale of any such beverages after the Eighteenth Amendment had gone into effect in January 1920.

Meanwhile, in a wave of idealism all the states except Connecticut and Rhode Island approved the Eighteenth Amendment. Nebraska, the home of Bryan, one of the prime leaders of the prohibition crusade, appropriately made the thirty-sixth ratification on January 16, 1919. Nation-wide prohi-

[5] For the origins of the prohibition movement, see above, pp. 36–37.

bition went into force a year later; but as the country had in effect been dry since the summer of 1917 there were few protest demonstrations. Bryan held a victory celebration in New York in March 1920 and announced that the liquor issue was as dead as slavery. The Commissioner of Internal Revenue predicted that the American people would soon forget what liquor looked like, while the first Prohibition Commissioner later promised that no liquor would be manufactured, "nor sold, nor given away, nor hauled in anything on the surface of the earth or under the earth or in the air."

Of course it did not turn out that way. Strict enforcement was impossible unless the government put a million agents in the field and sternly suppressed personal liberty. Partial enforcement was possible only if a large majority of the people were determined to exterminate the liquor traffic. In rural and strongly Protestant areas like the South and Middle West, where public opinion generally supported state and federal enforcement authorities, there was probably a considerable decline in drinking and the liquor traffic. In fact, throughout the country prohibition was accompanied by a sharp decline in the measurable results of drinking—arrests for drunkenness and deaths from alcoholism.

From the outset, however, the difficulties of enforcement were enormous. Throughout the twenties, the politically dry majority in Congress followed the advice of the Anti-Saloon League in making appropriations and tightening the enforcement laws. Even so, such provisions were hopelessly inadequate without the full support of local officials and public opinion. There were only 1,520 agents in the Prohibition Bureau in 1920 and 2,836 ten years later. As a consequence, enforcement was spasmodic, largely ineffective in areas where public opinion was hostile to the Eighteenth Amendment, and often violent and corrupt because of the bad character of many agents and their strong-arm methods.

The chief obstacles to effective enforcement were the determined resistance of large and important segments of the population and the fanaticism of the dry leaders. Probably a majority of the people in states with large foreign-born populations—like Massachusetts, New York, New Jersey, Maryland, Illinois, Ohio, and Wisconsin—would have voted against prohibition in a national referendum. Certainly the overwhelming majority in the large cities, native- and foreign-born alike, thought they had a natural right to drink. Consequently, neither local nor state officials, nor the masses of people in these states and cities supported enforcement. Instead, they rallied behind organizations like the Association Against the Prohibition Amendment and political leaders like Governor Albert C. Ritchie of Maryland and Governor Alfred E. Smith of New York, committed to the repeal of the Eighteenth Amendment.

In the main prohibition might have succeeded had the dry leaders realized that most of the opposition to the Eighteenth Amendment stemmed from the ban on the sale of beer and light wine. Immediately after the ratification of the Amendment, the legislatures of Wisconsin, Massachusetts, New York, Maryland, and New Jersey adopted laws outlawing the saloon and the sale of hard liquors but permitting the sale of light beer. Instead of accepting this slight deviation from perfection, the Anti-Saloon lobbyists forced the adoption of the Volstead Act and successfully challenged the constitutionality of the beer laws of these states. The result was that officials and masses of people in the "wet" states not only refused to respect prohibition but began a relentless war against the dry regime.

Such, therefore, were some of the problems and difficulties of enforcing legislation that a large minority refused to respect. The consequences of this ambitious experiment in federal social control were as remarkable as the difficulties that the effort raised. For one thing, prohibition also brought in its wake a series of social innovations among the "wet" minority. Speakeasies instead of saloons, hip flasks at football games, "bathtub" gin, and the cocktail party—these were some of the social side products of the "noble experiment." Another phenomenon was an increase in drinking by women. Before the war saloons had been exclusively male preserves in which no respectable woman would be seen. In contrast, after 1919 mixed drinking in the home and speakeasy became the rule—another sign of the emancipation of the so-called weaker sex.

The most disastrous consequence of prohibition was the tremendous increase in bootlegging that followed the adoption of the Eighteenth Amendment, which in turn led to the organization of underworld gangs that went into rackets of various kinds, bought control of city governments, and in general posed a serious challenge to democratic government in American cities during the 1920's and early 1930's. Prohibition alone was not responsible for this development. Organized vice and gambling had long been the curse of American cities; and gangsterism, racketeering, and organized blackmail developed almost in direct proportion to the speed of the automobile and the ease with which criminals could purchase weapons of wholesale slaughter like the Thompson submachine gun. The fact remains, none the less, that bootlegging was the chief livelihood and source of income of the gangs.

The truth of this generalization can be demonstrated by pointing to the rise to power of the Capone gang in Chicago, the most important underworld association of the twenties. The story begins in 1920 when young Alphonse, or Al, Capone moved to Chicago after serving a brief apprenticeship in the Sicilian underworld of New York City. Within a few years he was not only master of his own gang but was also the leading bootlegger and gambling and vice operator in the Chicago area, with a gross income by 1927 of $60,000,000 a year. Ironically, most of Capone's income from bootlegging came from the sale of beer. With a private army of from 700 to 1,000 gangsters at his command, he ruthlessly crushed rivals who dared challenge his sovereignty; and Chicago witnessed pitched battles and mass gang killings that made its name a byword and a hissing in the civilized world. Capone was toppled from his high eminence only when a federal agent worked his way into the organization and obtained evidence that led to the gangster's conviction for federal income tax evasion in 1931.

Sporadic and unorganized at the beginning of the 1920's, opposition to the Eighteenth Amendment mounted in intensity after New York repealed its enforcement laws in 1923 and the Democratic party in the eastern states assumed leadership of the anti-prohibition movement. From 1920 through 1932 the Republicans continued to support the "noble experiment," as Herbert Hoover characterized the prohibition effort, without any important division in their ranks. On the other hand, the Democrats were so badly split over prohibition, among other issues, that they practically ceased to be a national party in the twenties.

The end of the "noble experiment" came not long after the people had seemingly given it a sweeping endorsement in the presidential election of 1928. Soon after his inauguration, President Hoover appointed a commission headed by former Attorney General George W. Wickersham to investigate the problems of enforcement. The commission's report, presented in 1931, revealed what most informed Americans already knew—that the whole process of enforcement had broken down and that it was virtually impossible to impose aridity upon a determined minority. Moreover, the conviction grew and was shared by many persons who originally had approved the experiment that prohibition simply was not worth the political and social costs—among others, the disruption of the Democratic party, the subversion of the right of the states to control social customs, the widespread contempt for law that prohibition had bred, and, most important, the stimulus that it gave to organized crime and bootlegging.

By 1932, when problems of relief and recovery from the depression overshadowed all other issues, a reunited Democratic party came out frankly for repeal of the Eighteenth Amendment and resumption of state control over the liquor traffic. And after the smashing Democratic victory in November 1932, the deed was quickly done. The lame duck session in February 1933 passed and submitted to the people the Twenty-First Amendment, which repealed the Eighteenth Amendment and prohibited the transportation of liquor into any dry state or territory. The lame duck session of Congress also legalized the sale of light beer in March 1933. By the following December three-fourths of the states had ratified the Twenty-First Amendment, and the "noble experiment" was over.

125 / The Decline of Organized Labor, 1920–1930

As we have seen earlier, the postwar decade was in the main a time of prosperity and economic advancement for American workers. This generalization, however, obscures the important exceptions, for economic sickness in the textile and coal mining industries stimulated labor tensions of fierce intensity that culminated in numerous outbreaks of industrial warfare. Moreover, in spite of steady employment and increases in real wages, the 1920's witnessed a steady decline in the numbers and power of organized labor.

For the anomalous phenomenon of the decline of organized labor during a prosperous period, both employers and trade union leaders were responsible. To begin with, in 1920 state manufacturers' associations and the NAM began a vigorous campaign to restore the open shop through the "American Plan."[6] Invoking sentiments of individualism and winning the support of the American Bankers' Association and the National Grange, open shop associations in every city and state pressed the attack with considerable success.

[6] This was the name given to the open shop movement by a conference of the leaders of twenty-two state manufacturers' associations in Chicago in January 1921.

Management's offensive in the twenties had another side—a positive, constructive effort, called "welfare capitalism," aimed at eliminating the causes of industrial unrest by substituting cooperation for conflict in the field of industrial relations. Accepting the relatively new concept, first expounded by Henry Ford, of full production and consumption through high wages, advanced industrialists took labor policy out of the hands of tyrannical foremen, established expert departments of labor relations, and sought to win labor's good will by recreational programs, profit sharing, stock distribution, group health and life insurance programs, and even plans for retirement benefits. Such employers, in addition, usually established elaborate machinery, ranging from shop grievance committees to company unions, by which workers might voice complaints and seek rectification of injustices.

All employers in the 1920's did not approve these new concepts and practices, but it was significant for the future that a large majority of the men who determined the policies of the great corporations began to think of the needs and aspirations of their workers. Organized labor, moreover, usually heartily reciprocated management's good will. In fact, when management accepted the principle of collective bargaining, labor leaders often went to unusual lengths to prove that cooperation was more profitable than conflict. A union-management plan adopted in the shops of the Baltimore and Ohio Railroad in 1922–1923, for example, so improved efficiency and reduced labor unrest that the Chicago and North Western Railroad, the Milwaukee Road, and the Canadian National Railway adopted it soon afterward. The Amalgamated Clothing Workers of America willingly assumed responsibility for shop discipline, encouraged plans to increase efficiency, and even lent money to clothing manufacturers in distress.

With several notable exceptions, tensions between management and organized labor after 1921 lessened perceptibly in the wake of these developments. The average number of strikes per year declined from 3,503 for the period 1916–1921 to 1,304 during the years 1922–1925 and to 791 from 1926 through 1930. In addition, as organized labor's wartime idealism cooled, the AF of L became increasingly "conservative," in the sense that the union's leadership accepted the concept of "welfare capitalism" when it was accompanied by recognition and the right to bargain collectively; fought hard and successfully to prevent Communist infiltration; and generally refused to launch movements to organize the great basic industries.

Little wonder it was, therefore, that liberal critics of the AF of L and the railroad brotherhoods charged that organized labor had ceased to speak for the great mass of workers and had become the bulwark of the established order instead of an agency for progressive change. Little wonder it was, also, that organized labor not only did not grow but instead declined in numbers and influence during the 1920's. From 1920 to 1930 trade union membership declined progressively from 5,110,800 to 3,407,600, membership in the AF of L from 4,079,000 to 2,961,000. Part of this loss resulted from the AF of L's failure to consolidate gains hastily made from 1917 to 1920; part of it was caused by the employers' counteroffensive. But an even more important factor in the AF of L's decline was cautious and unaggressive union leadership.

The violent experiences of workers in the coal mining and textile industries during the decade 1920–1930 stand in striking contrast to the generalizations of the foregoing discussion. Textiles and coal mining remained highly competitive, unstable, and plagued by overproduction and dislocations resulting from the movement of these industries into the low-wage area of the South. To a large degree frontier social conditions still prevailed in mining areas and mill towns. Low wages and attempts by employers to preserve an industrial absolutism stimulated efforts at unionization; in turn these organizational campaigns were accompanied by the kind of violent warfare that had been often characteristic of the American industrial scene before the First World War.

The United Mine Workers of America emerged from the bituminous coal strike of 1919 superficially defeated but actually strengthened by the award of the Bituminous Coal Commission and by simultaneous negotiations with the anthracite operators. Along the frontier of the bituminous industry in West Virginia and eastern Kentucky, however, occurred an outbreak that ended in disastrous defeat for the UMW. The union's attempt to organize mines in West Virginia in 1919 and 1920 provoked fierce resistance by the operators and pitched battles between striking miners and imported mine guards. The governor declared martial law in the strike area, and state and federal troops momentarily stopped the fighting. Then violence broke out anew in 1921, after the miners organized an army of 4,000 men and began to invade the strike zone. The uprising quickly collapsed, however, when President Harding dispatched 2,100 troops to the area and state authorities arrested the strike leaders on charges of treason, murder, and conspiracy.

The West Virginia civil war marked the beginning of a decade of conflict in the troubled coal fields. When negotiations for new contracts with bituminous and anthracite operators failed in early 1922, President John L. Lewis of the UMW called miners out in the greatest coal strike in American history to that time. There was no violence until the Southern Illinois Coal Company, in Williamson County, Illinois, imported strikebreakers and attempted to resume operations on June 21, 1922. The killing of two strikers by mine guards brought swift retaliation at Herrin, when enraged miners charged a stockade and slaughtered nineteen strikebreakers. After the Herrin massacre tempers subsided and then ensued a test of endurance between the UMW and the operators. In the late summer the operators gave in.

Although Lewis forced the operators to renew their contracts in 1924, a series of catastrophes soon befell and nearly wrecked the UMW. For one thing, increased competition from nonunion operators in the South and West forced northern and midwestern operators to cut wages. For another, progressive and Communist elements in the UMW in 1926 began a vigorous campaign to destroy Lewis' allegedly dictatorial and corrupt control. Although the movement failed, it seriously weakened the UMW and led to the formation of two rival unions, the Reorganized United Mine Workers and the Communist-controlled National Miners' Union. Lewis saved the UMW and preserved a semblance of collective bargaining in the coal industry by accepting wage reductions during contract negotiations in 1927. But by 1929 the once proud UMW was so weakened, both from within and from without, that it would be helpless to cope with the depression.

Tensions and conflicts also plagued the textile industry during the 1920's. Pleading southern competition and depressed economic circumstances, the New England manufacturers cut wages about 20 per cent in 1921. When they attempted to raise hours and impose another 20 per cent wage cut early the following year, however, the mill owners provoked a series of strikes by the United Textile Workers and left-wing unions that forced a restoration of the old wage and hours scales. Three years later the scene shifted to Passaic, New Jersey, after the large woolen textile mills cut wages 10 per cent in September 1925. A United Front Committee under Communist leadership began a strike in January 1926 that soon spread to all the large mills and engendered such disturbances as northern New Jersey had not seen since the IWW's Paterson strike of 1912. After the Communists withdrew from leadership in the strike, the United Textile Workers took control and brought it to a successful conclusion in March 1927.

By such violent reprisals the northern textile workers staved off wage reductions after 1921. But the rise of southern manufacturers to dominance in the textile industry and the movement of New England mills to the South in the 1920's not only dislocated the economy of New England; it also posed a serious menace to the union textile wage structure of the North. Obviously, the northern workers' only safety lay in eliminating the sectional wage differential by unionizing the southern mills and imposing a uniform national wage scale.

After a brief and unsuccessful attempt to organize the southern mills in 1919, the United Textile Workers again invaded the South in 1927 and 1928. They found the mass of workers bitter and resentful over long hours, low wages, the "stretch-out," and above all, the high profits of the manufacturers. They found, also, a virtual textile barony allied with local police and state officials ready to use any means to prevent unionization. The result of the union's campaign, therefore, was one of the bloodiest outbreaks of labor violence in recent American history.

The disturbances began in March 1929, when more than 5,000 rayon textile workers in Elizabethton, Tennessee, struck against a low wage scale. Local vigilante groups combined with company guards, state troops, and the courts to drive the United Textile Workers organizers out of the mills. A month later the Communist-controlled National Textile Workers' Union began a strike against the largest cotton mill in Gastonia, North Carolina, the center of the textile industry. The strike collapsed after the conviction, in October 1929, of seven of the Communist leaders for the second-degree murder of the Gastonia chief of police. At the same time, a Textile Workers strike in Marion, North Carolina, ended with the slaughter of five and the wounding of nineteen unarmed pickets by a sheriff's posse. The United Textile Workers made their most formidable effort at the Riverside and Dan River Mills in Danville, Virginia, in the autumn of 1930; but the owners stubbornly refused either to bargain with the union or to submit to arbitration, and the strikers had to surrender to avoid starvation.

Although the decade ended with labor tension running at its highest point since 1919, there were a few signs that official and public opinion was finally beginning to veer strongly in labor's favor. In 1930, for example, the Senate refused to confirm the nomination of Circuit Court Judge John J. Parker to the Supreme Court, in part because Parker had upheld the use of injunctions to prohibit union organizers from attempting to unionize workers who had signed a "yellow dog" contract.[7] Then in March 1932 Congress passed the Anti-Injunction Act sponsored by Representative Fiorello La Guardia and Senator George W. Norris. This measure made "yellow dog" contracts unenforceable in federal courts; forbade the issuance of injunctions against a number of hitherto outlawed union practices; and guaranteed jury trials in cases involving violations of criminal injunctions.

126 / *The Election of 1928*

As we have seen, the conflicts over the Klan and prohibition so rent the Democrats that they ceased to be an effective opposition from 1924 to 1928. That these same tensions would weaken the Democracy during the campaign of 1928 became apparent long before the national convention met in Houston, Texas, on June 26, 1928. Although Governor Alfred E. Smith emerged as the only Democrat of presidential stature and won most of the non-southern states during the preconvention campaign of 1928, he had failed utterly to win any popular support in the South. Indeed, all signs pointed to a southern rebellion of large proportions if the northern and western majority insisted upon nominating the New York governor and standing for repeal of the Eighteenth Amendment.

After struggling vainly in the Houston convention to prevent Smith's nomination, the Southerners surrendered only after the northern managers had agreed to yield their demand for a platform plank favoring repeal of the controverted Amendment. Without this concession, the southern politicians warned, they could not hold their constituents in the party. Ignoring these warnings, Smith notified the convention that although he would enforce the prohibition laws if elected, he also reserved the right to advocate and work for repeal of the Volstead Act and perhaps also of the Eighteenth Amendment.

Meanwhile, the Republicans had met at Kansas City on June 12 and nominated Secretary of Commerce Herbert C. Hoover, the most distinguished representative of the business leadership of the Harding-Coolidge administrations and a pre-eminent champion of individualism and regulated and orderly private enterprise. During the ensuing campaign Hoover reiterated his frank opposition to all advanced progressive proposals like the pegging of agricultural prices, public power projects, and special interest legislation in organized labor's behalf. Time and again, also, he reiterated his conviction that only a continuation of the Harding-Coolidge policies could make prosperity permanent. "We in America today are nearer to the final triumph over poverty than ever before in the history of any land," he exclaimed in his acceptance speech. "The poorhouse is vanishing from among

---

[7] An agreement between employer and employee by which the latter promised not to join a union in return for the privilege of employment.

us. We have not yet reached the goal, but, given a chance to go forward with the policies of the last eight years, we shall soon, with the help of God, be in sight of the day when poverty will be banished from this nation."

In contrast to the Republican candidate, Smith had a moderately progressive platform upon which to campaign[8] and a distinguished record as a champion of civil rights and social legislation. But progressives who expected him to revive and rally their scattered forces must have been badly disappointed. Although he advocated federal operation of Muscle Shoals and development of power projects in the West, and accepted the principle of the McNary-Haugen plan, Smith's campaign was thoroughly conservative in tone. He discussed almost exclusively the evils of prohibition and religious bigotry, while his peripheral remarks were aimed at convincing the voters that a Democratic victory would not endanger prosperity. For chairman of the Democratic National Committee, moreover, Smith chose John J. Raskob, a prominent Catholic layman, chairman of the finance committee of General Motors, and an official of other corporations and banks, who only a year before had given his party affiliation as Republican and his occupation as "capitalist." Moving the Democratic headquarters to the General Motors Building in New York City, Raskob boasted proudly whenever a banker or corporation official came out in support of Smith.

Although Smith campaigned vigorously he could never overcome the obstacles confronting him. His attacks on prohibition cost him more votes in the South and Middle West than he gained in the East. The fact that he was a devout Roman Catholic stirred bigots and Protestant leaders who feared the aggrandizement of Catholic power. Republicans and Hoover Democrats in the South blamed the New Yorker for all the misdeeds of Tammany Hall. Worst of all, social snobs whispered that Smith and his wife would not grace the White House because they had risen from New York City's East Side.

This invocation of religious bigotry and social snobbishness and the charge that Smith would restore saloons and debauch American youth had a powerful appeal all over the country. But in the South the campaign to defeat the Democratic nominee assumed the proportions of a religious crusade. Throughout that region the Protestant clergy and laity were up in arms, chiefly because of Smith's opposition to the Eighteenth Amendment. This is not to say that Catholicism was not an issue in the campaign in the region. Catholicism was a powerful issue, but it was used more by the Republican managers and the remnant of the Klan than by Bishop James Cannon, Jr., of the Methodist Episcopal Church, South, who formally organized southern opposition to Smith.

Cannon's anti-Smith campaign broke the Solid South and carried Virginia, North Carolina, Tennessee, Florida, Kentucky, Oklahoma, and Texas for Hoover. Even so, the results of the election would not have been meas-

---

[8] The Democratic platform promised farm relief without specifying details, approved collective bargaining and the passage of an anti-injunction act, demanded strict control of hydroelectric power, and promised immediate independence for the Philippines. It did not mention the League of Nations or demand drastic tariff reductions. The Republican platform approved prohibition and the protective tariff and promised sane farm relief without artificial price supports.

urably different had Smith been a Baptist deacon and a stanch supporter of the Eighteenth Amendment. Outside the South, Smith carried only Massachusetts and Rhode Island. His combined popular vote was 15,016,443, as compared with Hoover's 21,392,190 popular votes.

The truth was that the prevailing prosperity, more than the liquor and religious issues, was the decisive factor in the election. There was still acute unrest in the farm areas, especially in the western Middle West. In Minnesota, Nebraska, North Dakota, Wisconsin, and Washington insurgent Republicans, who violently opposed the conservative leadership of their party, were elected by large majorities. These were signs for the future, to be sure; but the large majority of the urban middle classes in the autumn of 1928 desired only a continuation of the leadership and policies that had seemingly accomplished economic stability and offered the promise of even better times ahead.

CHAPTER 17 / *HOOVER AND THE GREAT DEPRESSION, 1929–1932*

*T*HE GREAT DEPRESSION brought an end to a long era of economic expansion and social progress since the 1890's. There had been momentary recessions in 1907, 1913, and 1921, to be sure; but never had these reversals been severe enough or long enough to shake the deeply rooted popular confidence in the American economic system or to generate any comprehensive national discontent.

It would be inaccurate to say that the depression that began in 1929 destroyed the faith of the American people in the essential worth of the capitalistic system or the enduring value of democratic institutions. Like the depression of the 1890's, however, the Great Depression caused widespread suffering and profound discontent among all classes in all sections, which in turn revived the American progressive movement in full strength. Thus the chief consequence of the Great Depression was not the havoc that it wrought for a decade but rather the impetus it gave for completion of the metamorphosis in popular attitudes regarding the role of government in the economy.

The depression not only caused deflation at home but also stimulated the withdrawal of American capital from abroad, which culminated in the collapse of the international economy in 1931. In this chapter we will attempt to tell why and how this happened, and why political leadership seemed incapable of overcoming this most serious crisis since the First World War.

127 / Underlying Causes of the Depression

After the election of Herbert Hoover in November 1928, the American people reveled in the prospects of the economic millennium that lay just around the corner. The campaign had been scurrilous and unpleasant; but it had been a passing if necessary episode in the march of the people toward their economic destiny. As the year 1929 opened all seemed well with the Republic: the government was in safe hands and a great engineer, pledged to abolish poverty and carry on the policies that had made America prosperous, would soon occupy the White House. Except for a speculative boom in Wall Street, there were few obvious signs of impending disaster. And yet more discerning eyes could see subtle signs of weakness in the economy, apart from the dangerous stock market boom. In themselves these weaknesses in the internal and international economies did not set off the depression; but once the stock market collapse destroyed business confidence and caused huge withdrawals of capital, the subsidiary economic strains combined to prolong and intensify the severity of the depression.

The first and perhaps the most important economic maladjustment of the 1920's was the unstable nature of the international economy, stemming from a complex of difficulties reviewed in an earlier chapter.[1] The outpouring of American dollars helped western Europe meet its trade deficits and war debt and reparations obligations; and Europe's recovery from 1925 to 1930 in turn stimulated American prosperity. The fundamental weakness of the new international exchange system, however—Europe's financial dependence upon the United States—proved fatal when the wellsprings of American credit dried up.

In the second place, the long depression in agriculture that began in 1920 impoverished American farmers and caused them to operate at a net capital loss during most of the decade. The effects of this agricultural depression were everywhere apparent—in the decline in farm incomes, values, and purchasing power and in the failure of thousands of country banks. Even conservative Republican leaders admitted that the situation could not long continue without impoverishing the nation. When nothing really effective was done after 1929 to halt the downward plunge of farm prices, the farmers dragged the rest of the nation with them in their decline.

In other ways, too, the American economy was badly out of joint by 1929. Concentrated and bureaucratized, large segments of American industry were able to maintain wages and prices at artificially high levels for a time after the depression began. Abnormally high industrial profits and a federal tax policy that favored the rich aggravated a maldistribution of incomes that in 1929 gave 26 per cent of the national income to the top 5 per cent of the income receivers. At least two years before the stock market crash occurred, these internal maladjustments were beginning to impair the health of the economic system. Even so, the development that threw the financial machinery out of gear and set off the cumulative forces of dissolution was the stock market boom that ended in the crash of October 1929.

128 / *The Wild Bull Market: Boom and Bust*

The speculative mania that seized a large minority of the American people in 1927 was by any reckoning one of the most remarkable developments in the nation's history. It seemed as if the mania for quick profits had infected all the people and institutions, from bank presidents to street-corner grocers and school teachers.

One of the most startling aspects of the wild bull market was the sud-

[1] See above, pp. 283–287.

denness with which it developed. In response to increased business activity and rising profits, trading on the New York Stock Exchange increased from 236,000,000 shares in 1923 to 451,000,000 in 1926, while the average price of twenty-five representative industrial stocks rose from $108 to $166 a share, or nearly 70 per cent. This forward movement represented only the normal response of the market to high earnings in industry. Then in 1927 the tremendous upward surge of the market began. Brokers' loans—that is, loans with stock for collateral—increased from a little over $3,000,000,000 in January 1927 to nearly $4,500,000,000 by the end of December, while the volume of shares traded on the New York Stock Exchange rose from 451,000,000 in 1926 to 577,000,000 in 1927.

Obviously, a boom was developing; and conservative bankers, sensing a disastrous inflation of stock prices, urged caution. For a brief time in the early weeks of 1928 it seemed the market might break. Instead, it held firm when Treasury officials and President Coolidge declared that the volume of brokers' loans was not too great and that the country had never been more soundly prosperous. Thus reassured, on March 3, 1928, a group of the largest operators on the Stock Exchange opened a gigantic buying campaign in the stock of General Motors and the Radio Corporation of America. As the price of these and other stocks rose, the fever spread and the wild bull market had begun.

The first phase of the speculation lasted until nearly the middle of June 1928, when prices declined slightly. During the next sixteen months rallies alternated with recessions, but prices always recovered and surged on to new heights. By the beginning of 1929 the boom was totally out of control. Industrial issues were selling in January 1929, for example, at more than sixteen times their earnings, although the traditional safe ratio was ten to one.

The following summary statistics illustrate the dimensions of the stock market inflation that occurred from 1927 to September 1929: The market value of all stocks listed on the New York Stock Exchange increased from $27,000,000,000 in 1925 to a peak of $87,000,000,000 on October 1, 1929. The average price of common stocks increased nearly 300 per cent, and the volume of trading on the Exchange rose from 454,000,000 shares in 1925 to 1,125,000,000 shares in 1929. Brokers' loans, which were used to finance the speculation, rose from $3,500,000,000 in January 1926 to $8,500,000,000 on September 30, 1929.

It is easier to describe the proportions of the wild bull market than to say precisely why the speculative fever developed when it did. Certainly the large commercial banks bore a share of the responsibility, for they not only financed the speculation through loans to brokers and individuals but also participated directly in the market through active trading, underwriting of speculative issues, and formation of investment trusts and pools. By its approval of an unsound inflation, the United States Treasury gave an early impetus to the speculative movement. After the runaway boom had begun, the Federal Reserve Board tried vainly to check it by selling government securities and increasing the discount rate. But it was too late. By the summer of 1928 speculation was so profitable that money was flowing into New York from London and Paris and from the treasuries of American corporations.

Banks with surplus cash paid no heed to the Federal Reserve Board's warnings and proceeded blindly to abet the speculation.

In any event, by the summer of 1929 the boom had reached such irrational proportions that a collapse was inevitable. Prices could not rise forever, and the financial structure was so precarious that even a slight recession would create a panic. The first storm signals came from London, when the Bank of England on September 26, 1929, raised the rediscount rate, or the interest rate for banks, to 6½ per cent in order to halt the outward flow of gold and protect the pound in international exchange. The withdrawal of

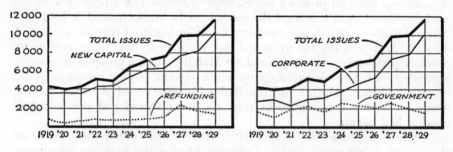

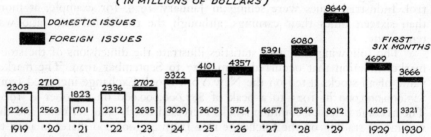

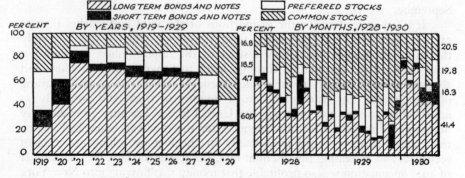

15.   *Total Security Issues in the United States, 1919–1929*

at least several hundred millions of dollars from New York to London caused prices to decline on September 30; but during the next two weeks the market rallied. Then, on October 15, dissolution and withdrawal began, gradually at first, as the large operators unloaded discreetly. On October 24, 1929, "Black Thursday," however, total panic seized the stock market. Nearly 13,000,000 shares changed hands and prices fell so rapidly that the tickers could not keep pace with their descent.

The panic subsided momentarily in the afternoon of "Black Thursday," when J. P. Morgan & Company and other large banks formed a $240,000,000 pool and bought heavily to buoy the market and protect their loans and investments. Thousands of brokers and hundreds of thousands of petty speculators had been ruined by the end of the day, to be sure; but Treasury officials, leading economists and bankers, and the metropolitan press all hastened to assure the public that the decline in stock prices would have a healthy effect on the economy by freeing more money for genuine investment purposes. "The fundamental business of the country, that is, production and distribution of commodities," said President Hoover on October 25, "is on a sound and prosperous basis."

Hoover's reassurance was echoed a hundred times in the inner circles of Wall Street. None the less, when the bottom again dropped out of the market on October 29 the bankers let prices slide. Nearly 16,500,000 shares changed hands in the wildest trading in the Stock Exchange's history, and the average price of fifty leading stocks declined almost forty points under the pressure. During the remaining weeks of 1929 and afterward, rallies alternated with declines, but always the declines were greater than the subsequent advances, until it seemed as if there were no end but a final smashup of the entire financial system.

129 / *The Progress of the Depression, 1929–1932*

The tremendous decline in stock values—a loss of some $40,000,000,000 during the last four months of 1929 alone—set off intricate forces that interacted to carry the United States into the depths of industrial and financial stagnation. The essential fact was that American prosperity was in large measure dependent upon the smooth functioning of the basic cogs of the economic machinery—world trade, investment in capital plant and equipment, the construction industry, and the production of automobiles. The oil that lubricated this economic machinery was confidence that goods could be sold and investments would yield a profitable return.

The stock market crash did not at once utterly destroy but it did severely shake the confidence of the business community, weaken the financial institutions, slow down industrial expansion, and cause a diminution in American purchases and investments abroad. The practical withdrawal of the American dollar props from beneath the foundations of the international economy in turn precipitated a severe financial crisis in Europe in 1931, which Europeans met only by adopting policies that virtually destroyed the system of international exchange. The European collapse in turn caused further strain on American banks and deepened the industrial and business depression. Thus, like a great avalanche, the forces of dissolution gained power and momentum as they interacted to speed the downward plunge.

The progress of the depression and its effect on the basic generative components of the economy are revealed by the following statistics: New capital issues, representing the investment of the American people in indus-

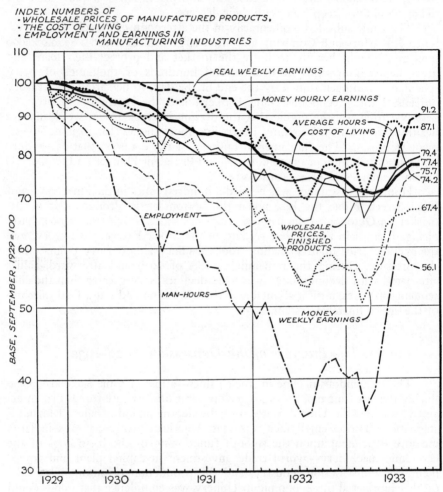

16. *The Progress of the Great Depression, 1929–1933*

trial, railroad, public utility, and other stocks and bonds, declined from $10,000,000,000 in 1929 to $7,000,000,000 a year later, to $3,000,000,000 in 1931, and to a little over $1,000,000,000 in 1932. Obviously, not enough new capital was being invested by 1932 even to maintain the domestic industrial plant. Foreign capital issues, governmental and corporate, declined from a high of nearly $1,500,000,000 in 1928 to a paltry $88,000,000 in 1932. American imports dropped from nearly $5,500,000,000 in 1929 to $1,735,000,000 in 1932, exports from $4,625,000,000 to $1,497,000,000. At home the two basic industries of construction and automobiles declined even more alarmingly.

The progressive slowing down of these important cogs in the economic machinery of course had an immediate and catastrophic effect on all other segments of the economy—the stock market, the financial and business communities, railroads, industrial production and employment, and agriculture. The depression's course can be at least partially comprehended when we examine its impact on these major aspects of economic life.

We might begin our review with a survey of the decline of stock prices. Twenty-five representative industrial stocks fell from an average closing price of $366.29 a share in 1929 to $96.63 a share in 1932. The decline in other shares was even more severe. From 1929 to 1932 twenty-five railroad stocks declined in average closing prices from $136 to $22 a share, twenty public utilities stocks from $142 to $28 a share, and the stock of twenty New York banks from $358 to $68 a share.

Another barometer of economic decline was the increasing frequency with which banks and business firms went to the wall. In 1929, 659 banks, with deposits of nearly $250,000,000, and in the following year 1,352 banks, with deposits of $853,000,000, failed. In 1931, when the European financial crisis intensified the crisis, a total of 2,294 banks, with aggregate deposits of nearly $1,700,000,000, closed their doors. After the Reconstruction Finance Corporation reinforced the sagging financial structure in 1932, the process of financial dissolution was halted; only 1,456 banks, with deposits of nearly $750,000,000, failed in that year. Equally dismal was the record of 109,371 commercial failures, with aggregate liabilities of nearly $3,000,000,000, from 1929 through 1932, and the decline in the net profits of all private corporations from $8,400,000,000 in 1929 to —$3,400,000,000 in 1932.

The decline in economic activity provoked an even more serious crisis among the railroads. Sound and prosperous in 1929, they staggered under heavy blows, and from 1929 to 1933 such great systems as the Wabash, Chicago and North Western, Missouri Pacific, Milwaukee, and New Haven, with some 45,000 miles, passed into receivership. Moreover, only the timely federal assistance saved other large systems from bankruptcy. As freight shipments and carloadings declined approximately 50 per cent from 1929 to 1932, net operating railroad income fell from $1,262,636,000 to $325,332,000. In addition, the railroads laid off men by the hundreds of thousands, reduced the work week of employees, and practically stopped buying new equipment.

The cumulative momentum of the depression can perhaps best be illustrated by the statistics on industrial production and unemployment for the period under discussion. By the last quarter of 1930 industrial production in the United States was 26 per cent below the peak level of 1929. By midsummer of 1932, however, the production curve had declined 51 per cent below the level of the peak year. In response, unemployment grew by the month and year: 3,000,000 by April 1930, 4,000,000 by October 1930, almost 7,000,000 in October 1931, nearly 11,000,000 a year later, and from 12,000,000 to 14,000,000 during the first months of 1933. Moreover, workers fortunate enough to find or retain employment suffered severely from wage reductions, especially after 1931. From 1929 to 1933 total labor income fell from

$53,000,000,000 to $31,500,000,000; manufacturing wages, from nearly $12,000,000,000 to approximately $7,000,000,000.

Already in desperate economic straits by 1929, American farmers lost more in cash income and general economic standing during the depression

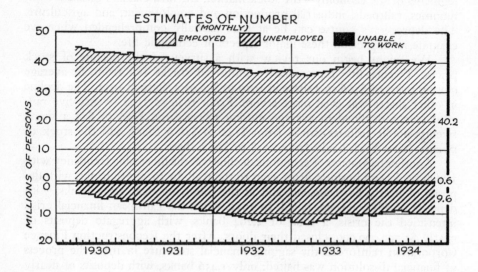

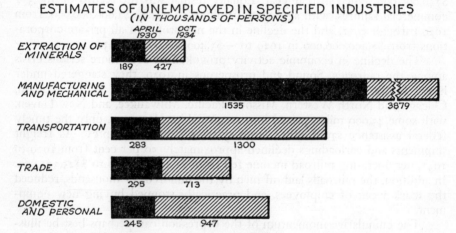

17. *Employment and Unemployment in the United States, 1930–1934*

years than any other important group. Between 1929 and 1932 gross farm income shrank from $11,941,000,000 to $5,331,000,000.

The dimensions of the economic misfortune that befell the American people from 1929 to 1933 can best be comprehended by the following summary view: National income declined from $81,000,000,000 in 1929 to $49,000,000,000 in 1932; adjusted for the cost of living, per capita income declined from $681 to $495. Salaries decreased 40 per cent, dividends nearly

57 per cent, and manufacturing wages 60 per cent. The total picture of these years of the locusts, therefore, is one of extreme deflation everywhere save in the debt structure. As the American people struggled to save their financial system, interest payments on long-term debts declined only 3.3 per cent from 1929 to 1933.

130 / *The Social Impact of the Depression*

The social impact of the depression could be seen in all aspects of life. The first place affected was the home, to which women formerly employed returned by the hundreds of thousands, even though the incidence of unemployment was less among women than among male workers. Most middle class families had to dispense with domestic servants; and women responded to "live at home" appeals by gardening, canning, making soap, and the like.

The American people acted sometimes curiously under the impact of the shattered economic situation. They practically stopped buying new automobiles, to be sure, but they stubbornly refused to give up their old ones; and gasoline consumption increased slightly from 1929 through 1933. Jewelry sales declined precipitously; but women would not give up silk and rayon hosiery or even radios, for the "soap operas" were just coming into vogue. And never would the people give up the joy of smoking. Cigarette consumption, in fact, rose steadily during the depression years, as if the nervous strains engendered by the distress demanded a sedative.

One of the most unfortunate social effects of the depression was the severe increase that it caused in family tensions and the way in which it affected the marriage and birth rates. Tens of thousands of families were forced to double up in homes and apartments, and tensions between fathers and sons increased as the latter found it impossible to find work and had to stay at home all day. Young people out of work married later and had fewer children. Thus the number of marriages declined from 1,232,000 in 1929 to 981,903 in 1932, and the birth rate declined from 19 to 17.4 per thousand. Moreover, as family tensions mounted in the first two years of the depression, the number of divorces per 1,000 marriages increased from 163 in 1929 to 173 in 1931.[2]

Schools and colleges were of course profoundly affected, but until 1932 the people struggled successfully to maintain school plant, equipment, and salaries. In 1932 the tide began to turn, and by the end of the school year 1933–1934 the retreat had turned into a rout on all educational fronts. From 1930 to 1934 expenditures for school purposes declined from $1,844,000,000 to $1,500,000,000 or about 18 per cent. But in many states the decrease exceeded 30 per cent, and in Michigan and Mississippi it was 41 and 52 per cent, respectively. During the same period, capital outlay for new school buildings declined 84 per cent; many rural counties reduced school terms from one-fifth to one-half; all states except Rhode Island decreased salaries, and the decreases in rural southern and western states ran as high as 43 per cent and averaged more than 30 per cent.

[2] There was, however, a sharp decline in the number of divorces to 163 per 1,000 marriages in 1932.

Colleges and universities experienced even greater adversity. Between 1931 and 1934 total enrollment in institutions of higher learning declined 8.5 per cent throughout the country. Generally speaking, state colleges and universities were hardest hit, suffering a 31 per cent decline in income from state appropriations, as compared with a 19 per cent decline in income from endowments owned by private institutions.

Perhaps the most important, because it was the most lasting, social effect of the depression was the manner in which it operated to cause a shift in responsibility for taking care of social distress from private to public agencies and resources. Almost at once city and state governments formed emergency relief administrations and took over the burden of relief and public health services from old philanthropic agencies. In spite of early optimism, excellent administration, and the cooperation of federal authorities, however, the cities and states could not meet the relief emergency after 1931. Staggering under financial burdens they could not bear, forced to default on obligations and pay public employees in script, the cities and states simply could not borrow the money necessary to meet the elemental needs of the unemployed. Appeals for private support yielded only paltry sums; "give-a-job" campaigns, "block aid" programs, and so on, were largely futile.

By the winter of 1932 the impossibility of using only private, city, and state resources to meet the crisis had been amply demonstrated by social workers and statisticians. Across the nation the destitute congregated in cardboard shacks in so-called "Hoovervilles" on the edges of cities; hundreds of thousands of the unemployed roamed the country on foot and in boxcars in futile search of jobs. There was perhaps little outright starvation but much hunger; and the malnutrition rate among patients admitted to certain community health centers in New York City and Philadelphia increased 60 per cent. Nor were hunger and malnutrition confined to the great cities, for five-cent cotton meant a lean diet of salt pork and hominy for southern poor whites and Negroes, and unemployment in the mining areas brought destitution unequaled on a large scale anywhere in the cities.

131 / *Rumblings of Social Discontent*

Americans were baffled by the anomaly of a country with abundant resources, the largest force of skilled labor, and the most productive plant in the world being unable to find the right formula for getting the wheels of industry turning once again. Moreover, it was difficult to understand why millions of people should go hungry in a country groaning under the burden of huge food surpluses. As they are wont to do during periods of economic distress, the people searched for scapegoats and soon concluded that the speculators and bankers in Wall Street had been responsible for the catastrophe.

This discrediting of an economic leadership hitherto warmly admired did not, of course, occur all at once. Until the summer of 1931 probably a majority of the people believed the assurances of Republican spokesmen and financial leaders, who since the stock market crash had predicted that the economic system would soon right itself again. As the European collapse caused more banks to fail and bread lines to lengthen, and as the Senate banking committee in the winter of 1931–1932 exposed corruption and malfeasance in the banking community, however, public confidence in the economic leadership and the Hoover administration sagged and then, during the summer of 1932, nearly collapsed.

After the spring of 1931, therefore, the rumblings of discontent grew from a scarcely audible whisper into a mighty chorus. In the late summer of 1931, for example, a commission of the Federal Council of the Churches of Christ in America prepared a statement to be read from pulpits on Labor Sunday. One of the most sweeping indictments of American capitalism ever drawn by a middle class group, the statement demanded the reconstitution of the economic order to assure security for the masses. Seconding the Federal Council's indictment, the bishops of the Episcopal Church issued a pastoral letter demanding that employers abandon the profit motive for the ideal of service to mankind.

Alarmed by the menace of revolutionary upheaval and moved by the misery of the lower classes, many businessmen abandoned their faith in automatic mechanisms and began to doubt the worth of an economy in which there could be so much abundance and misery. One of the most startling proposals for amelioration, in fact, came from Wall Street. It was a suggestion by Gerard Swope, president of the General Electric Company, that industrial leaders cooperate to increase production and protect workers against unemployment and poverty. Swope's warning that government would surely assume this responsibility if industry did not was echoed by the banker-industrialist, Owen D. Young, and by the president of the United States Chamber of Commerce.

During the first two years of the depression the leaders of the AF of L had cooperated with the President's plan to prevent strikes for higher wages and had waited patiently for the return of prosperity. By the autumn of 1931, however, unrest among AF of L membership was so great that the spokesmen of organized labor could no longer remain silent. In October 1931, the executive committee of the AF of L prepared a statement declaring that the prime cause of the depression had been the unequal distribution of wealth and incomes and calling upon President Hoover to convoke a great national economic conference to consider ways and means of combating the foe from within.

These protests and proposals were, of course, more a reflection of the important ideological upheaval that was transforming popular attitudes toward government and the economy than manifestations of outright social discontent. Signs of dangerous social eruption, actually, were few.

The only outbreak that threatened to get out of hand was the descent of the so-called "Bonus Expeditionary Force" of some twelve to fourteen thousand unemployed and homeless veterans on Washington in May and June 1932. Demanding the passage of the Patman bill providing immediate and full payment of the bonus by the issuance of $2,400,000,000 in paper money, the bonus marchers built a shanty town on the Anacostia Flats outside the capital and threatened to sit it out all summer. Under strong presidential pressure, the Senate refused to approve the Patman bill; but when Congress appropriated funds to provide transportation home for the veterans, about half of them gave up. Some five or six thousand veterans, many with wives and children, remained: gaunt spokesmen of the millions of destitute in every state and section.

On July 28, 1932, a riot occurred when the police force attempted to clear a throng of bonus marchers out of a construction area and two veterans were killed and several policemen were injured. After the District commissioners warned that they could not preserve order without the extensive use of force, President Hoover at once called upon the army to control the situation.[3] Assembling a formidable small army with machine guns and tanks, the Army Chief of Staff, General Douglas MacArthur, dispersed the bonus marchers from Anacostia Flats and, accidentally or deliberately, burned the shanty town. The very "institutions of our Government" would have been severely threatened, MacArthur declared, if the President had not acted decisively.

No doubt the General exaggerated the dimensions of the threat. There was much talk of revolution if Hoover were elected again, to be sure, but it never got beyond street-corners. Actually, the wonder is that there were so few organized uprisings like the "Bonus March," that the people suffered so much without losing their sense of humor or falling prey to the agitation of Communist and fascist agitators. Because the people never lost the hope of finding a democratic solution through new political leadership, the American democracy survived one of its severest testings.

132 / Hoover and the Crisis of American Capitalism

No man ever came to the presidency with a broader experience in world and domestic affairs than Herbert Clark Hoover. He was a self-made man, whose success story should become as much a part of the American legend as Horatio Alger's tales of boys who made good. Born of Quaker parents on an Iowa farm in 1874, Hoover migrated in his youth to Oregon, attended the newly-established Stanford University, and was graduated with an engineering degree in 1895. He proved to be resourceful and hard-working, in fact, a sheer genius at running large enterprises. Rising from one high position to another, by 1914 Hoover had won an international reputation and amassed a large personal fortune.

In London on the outbreak of the First World War, Hoover was given charge of the Belgian Relief Commission and did an extraordinary job. Called to Washington to head the Food Administration when his country entered the war, Hoover mobilized food resources and housewives and made his agency the most efficiently managed of all the war bureaus.

Appointed Secretary of Commerce by Harding in 1921, Hoover served in this post until his nomination for the presidency in 1928. During a decade when the businessman was the hero of the urban middle classes, Hoover was the chief spokesman of free regulated enterprise, mass consumption, and welfare capitalism. Although he was never intimate with professional

[3] In a public statement issued on July 28, 1932, President Hoover declared that Communists and persons with criminal records were stirring the bonus army to violence.

politicians, so overwhelming was the popular demand for his nomination in 1928 that the professionals could not deny him the honor.

Hoover must have idealized the presidency as the culmination of his long career of service to the people of the world. As one historian has put it, "Hoover the engineer would be the symbol of the coming age of material fulfillment, as Jefferson had been of democracy and Lincoln of emancipation." With supreme confidence that his administration would witness the maturing of humanitarian capitalism, he entered the White House with such popular approval as few Presidents have ever enjoyed. He left office, on the other hand, despised and rejected as few Presidents have been, his name an article of common sneering and associated with horse-drawn carts and assemblages of human misery.

What was wrong? How can we account for this almost total deflation of a great reputation? Why was it that a great engineer and expert in alleviating human suffering should have failed to provide the leadership and techniques so desperately needed in this interval of domestic crisis?

In the first place, great administrator though he was, Hoover was an exceedingly inept politician. All his life he had held positions of command and had grown accustomed to obedience. In his rigorously honest and orderly mind he probably had contempt for mere politicians, for men who consulted only the popular will. Thus, when it came to dealing with Congress, and particularly with a hostile Congress from 1931 to 1933, he was poorly equipped to furnish dynamic leadership. He could command men's respect in times of prosperity but not their love and devotion to a great vision during times of adversity.

Hoover's chief handicap, however, was a rigid, unyielding mental quality that made it difficult for him to adapt to new circumstances and undertake unusual experiments. Out of long experience and careful thought he had come to certain convictions concerning government and the economy. No *laissez-faire* economist of the classical school, he approved regulation of business enterprise clothed with the public interest and championed order and efficiency in business rather than destructive competition. On the other hand, he believed fervently that American progress and prosperity depended upon the combined outpouring of private initiative and striving. Thus he opposed all measures, like federal operation of Muscle Shoals, that would diminish private energies or impede private investment and enterprise. A sincere believer in democracy and the inherent goodness of the American people, Hoover just as strongly opposed any measures that would transfer responsibility for social alleviation from localities and states to the federal government.

With Hoover these principles not only constituted a political philosophy but a religious faith as well. During his own lifetime the American system of comparatively free enterprise had combined with private initiative and what he called "rugged individualism" to work the greatest material miracle of the modern age. Free capitalism, unhampered by binding controls, had brought the good material life within the reach of the average man; and Hoover saw no reason why it should not continue to carry the masses ever upward toward a higher standard of living. When the stock market crash set off a business depression, he refused to believe that the downswing was anything more than a passing phase in the business cycle, like the Panic of 1907 or the depression of 1921–1922.

After the recession of 1929–1930 turned into a full-fledged depression in 1931, Hoover was forced to recognize that the alternative to positive and unprecedented action by the federal government was complete economic ruin. Abandoning momentarily the main tenets of his philosophy, he approved ambitious measures to save the economy. At the same time, he never lost confidence in the inherent soundness of American economic institutions or in the altruism of the businessmen and bankers. Recovery was bound to come, he was certain, if only the federal government did not destroy business confidence by tampering with the gold standard or by launching wild measures of control.

133 / *The Hoover Policies: Agricultural Stabilization*

Disturbed by the rising spirit of insurgency in the Middle and Far West and maneuvering to head off the movement for the McNary-Haugen plan, Hoover and other GOP spokesmen promised sane farm relief and upward revision of the tariff rates on agricultural products during the campaign of 1928. Soon after his inauguration Hoover called the Seventy-First Congress into special session for April 15, 1929, to redeem these campaign pledges. Farm leaders still contended that only the McNary-Haugen or some other price-fixing plan would give agriculture parity with industry, and they had serious doubts that higher tariff rates would mean higher agricultural prices at home. But the President had his way, and Congress approved his two measures for farm relief—the Agricultural Marketing Act of June 15, 1929, and the Hawley-Smoot Tariff Act of June 17, 1930.

The draft of the Agricultural Marketing bill that Hoover presented to Congress provided a remedy that would not, the President explained, undermine the initiative of the individual farmer or involve the government in any schemes of price control. It created a nonpartisan Federal Farm Board and gave it the use of a revolving fund of $500,000,000 to be lent to agricultural marketing cooperatives, to enable them to market products efficiently, build warehouses, and hold farm products in the event of a price decline. In order to win the support of the Senate, however, the President made one concession that changed the character of the proposed stabilization program. It was an amendment authorizing the Federal Farm Board to establish corporations to stabilize farm prices through direct intervention in the market.

The Agricultural Marketing Act, therefore, launched the federal government upon the most ambitious program of agricultural stabilization and support in American peacetime history to that date. From 1929 to 1931 the Federal Farm Board organized the producers of the major staples into national cooperatives and established corporations to stabilize farm prices through large scale market operations. By lending to cooperatives and buying wheat and cotton in large quantities, the Board maintained domestic farm prices a little above the world price level until the summer of 1931. However, when the financial crisis in Europe caused a sudden shrinking of foreign markets for American agricultural exports and dumping by Russia, Argentina, and Australia drove prices to fantastically low levels, the Board was powerless to prevent the collapse of the price structure at home. Wheat, which sold at an average price of $1.05 a bushel in 1929, declined to 68 cents in 1930, and then plummeted to 39 cents in 1931 and 1932. From 1929 to 1932, moreover, corn fell from 81 cents to 33 cents a bushel, cotton from 17 cents to 6 cents a pound, and tobacco from 19 cents to 10 cents a pound.

During a time of relative stability or rising farm prices, the Federal Farm Board might have achieved its chief objective of underwriting efficient and economical marketing. Launched instead at the onset of a great depression, with a consequent demoralization of commodity markets throughout the world, the Board's program was doomed to futility. And this was true chiefly because the Board had no authority to compel farmers to limit production to achieve domestic price stability. In 1930 the Board launched a campaign for the reduction of wheat and cotton acreage; the following year it undertook a nation-wide campaign to achieve a general 30 per cent reduction in staple crops. But for every farmer who cooperated there must have been one who increased his plantings. The index of agricultural production fell two points in 1930, but only because of a severe drought; in 1931 production exceeded even the 1929 level.

As early as 1931 the members of the Federal Farm Board recognized their inability to cope with the situation; by the summer of 1932 the Board had lost some $354,000,000 in market operations and admitted its helplessness; and on December 7, 1932, the Board urged Congress to establish an effective system for regulating acreage and production as the only alternative to continued agricultural bankruptcy. Hoover's ambitious experiment obviously failed; but out of failure came experience and a profound conviction that cooperation and voluntary action would not suffice. The transition from the Hoover stabilization program to the bolder and more advanced New Deal measures was as natural as it was inevitable.

Hoover's program of tariff relief for agriculture was an even greater fiasco than his ill-fated effort at stabilization. Although the tariff had not been a partisan issue in the campaign of 1928, Hoover appealed to Congress in 1929 to give agriculture the same measure of protection that domestic manufacturers already enjoyed. His intentions undoubtedly were excellent, but once work on a tariff bill was begun all the old lobbies and pressures set diligently to work. The result was the Hawley-Smoot tariff bill of 1930, which provided about seventy-five increases for farm products and 925 for manufactured commodities.[4]

As a device for supporting domestic agricultural prices, the Hawley-Smoot Tariff was completely futile, except, perhaps, with regard to meat and dairy products. Moreover, its sheerly economic effect on foreign trade was probably unimportant. Its psychological impact abroad, however, was

---

[4] This measure increased the average level of agricultural duties from 20 to 34 per cent and the general average of all duties from 33 to 40 per cent. As a result of the Hawley-Smoot Act, moreover, the average *ad valorem* duties on imports subject to the tariff increased from 26 per cent for the period 1921–1925 to 50 per cent for the period 1931–1935.

unfortunate, as it seemed to signal a revival of economic nationalism in the United States just at the moment when the world desperately needed enlightened leadership. In an urgent appeal to the President to veto the Hawley-Smoot bill, more than one thousand members of the American Economic Association pointed out this elemental fact. Their warning was unheeded but justified. The British in 1932, for example, adopted protection and a system of imperial preference. The following year Germany embarked upon a program of autarchy that severely damaged world trade. The passage of the Hawley-Smoot bill was not responsible for the international economic demoralization that occurred in 1931 and afterward, but its enactment set a bad example for the rest of the world.

134 / The Hoover Policies: Combating the Depression

During the first and relatively mild phase of the depression, from October 1929 to the spring of 1931, Hoover moved with a new kind of presidential boldness to combat the recession he knew was bound to follow the stock market crash. On November 19 he met with railroad presidents and obtained their promise to proceed with normal construction. Calling leaders of finance, industry, and trade to the White House two days later, Hoover frankly warned them that a serious recession would follow in the wake of the storm in Wall Street. In response to Hoover's urgent pleading, the leaders of American business agreed to maintain production and refrain from severe wage reductions, provided labor leaders would cooperate by withdrawing demands for wage increases. The same afternoon the President obtained from labor leaders a promise of full cooperation. The following day, November 22, Hoover met with leaders in the construction industry and won their promise to maintain current wages and hours standards. Then on November 23 he called upon governors and mayors throughout the country to join with the federal government in increasing expenditures for public works. In addition, in December the President convened again with larger groups of business and labor leaders and warned them that the responsibility for averting a major catastrophe was primarily theirs.

By the spring of 1930 it seemed Hoover's program of cooperation had carried the country through the worst phase of the storm. Bankers had reduced brokers' loans from eight and a half to three billion dollars; the index of industrial employment, which had stood at 99 in December 1929, dropped only two and a half points during the next four months. A nationwide census of unemployment the following April revealed that only 2,500,000 workers were unable to find jobs. Congressional action in the spring of 1930, authorizing the expenditure of $145,000,000 for rivers and harbors improvements, $530,000,000 for public buildings, and $75,000,000 for highways, also had a steadying effect.[5] Moreover, employers were honor-

---

[5] Actually, federal expenditures for public works totaled $493,000,000 in 1930, as compared with $384,000,000 in 1929. State and municipal expenditures totaled $2,838,000,-000 in 1929 and $3,054,000,000 in 1930.

ing their pledges not to cut wages and workers their promise not to strike.[6]

Then, beginning in May and June 1930 employers began slowly to reduce production, at first without seriously cutting wages. From April to November 1930 the index of industrial employment fell from 96.3 to 84.6 and of payrolls from 97.7 to 76.8. When unemployment reached about 4,000,000 in October, Hoover appointed a Committee for Unemployment Relief and called upon city and private agencies to redouble their relief efforts; stopped immigration; and declared he would ask Congress for larger appropriations for public works.

Meanwhile, Democratic leaders had begun the congressional campaign of 1930 with such confidence as they had not felt since Wilson's first administration. Aided by a mounting public fear and by a "smear" campaign against Hoover personally, the Democrats for the first time since 1916 rolled back the Republican tide in the November elections.[7] The election was no landslide or mass repudiation of Hoover's leadership. Yet by giving control of the legislative branch to the President's political foes on the eve of a presidential election, it divided responsibility in the federal government and led inevitably to bitter wrangling.

In fact, there were numerous manifestations of tension between Hoover and the progressive bloc in Congress during the lame duck session of the Seventy-First Congress that sat from December 1930 to March 1931. The progressives, Republican and Democratic, demanded that the President abandon his voluntary program and take leadership of a movement to meet the crisis boldly—by a federal relief program, part payment of the veterans' bonus, and federal development of the Muscle Shoals facilities. Arguing that private and local relief resources were still ample, Hoover set himself sternly against any projects for direct federal relief. He successfully vetoed the Norris bill for federal operation of Muscle Shoals, but Congress overrode his veto of a bill allowing veterans to obtain half the value of their certificates in cash.

At the same time, it seemed again that the President's policies had turned back the depression tide and set the nation on the road to recovery. Beginning in February 1931 the indices of employment, payrolls, and production steadied and then rallied slightly until about the first of June. Bank failures abated; unemployment slackened. Did these encouraging developments signify that the recession was nearly over? So many observers thought.

Unhappily, the second and catastrophic phase of the depression was now about to begin in the United States as the result of a financial panic in Europe that paralyzed the international economy. Since 1927 central

---

[6] Only 7 per cent of firms reporting to the Bureau of Labor Statistics reduced wages during 1930.

[7] The Democrats elected seventeen governors, the Republicans twelve. The GOP lost some forty seats but on the surface retained control of the House of Representatives by a plurality of one. When the Seventy-Second Congress met in December 1931, however, enough Republican incumbents had died to give control to the Democrats. The new Senate consisted of forty-eight Republicans, forty-seven Democrats, and one Farmer-Laborite; but so many Republican senators were midwestern insurgents that an insurgent-Democratic coalition easily controlled the upper house.

European and South American countries had been borrowing heavily in short-term loans to compensate for a drying up of the sources of long-term credit.[8] In March 1931 French bankers, who held large sums of German and Austrian short-term notes, demanded immediate payment, partly for political reasons. To avert bankruptcy, Germany and Austria appealed to London and New York for aid. British bankers did what they could, but it was not enough, and on May 11, 1931, the Kreditanstalt of Vienna, the largest bank in Austria, was "reorganized." Its virtual failure stimulated such heavy withdrawals of gold from Germany that by June the Republic was unable to meet reparation payments, much less its short-term obligations. Desperately, almost pathetically, the aged President of Germany, Paul von Hindenburg, on June 18 appealed personally to Hoover for immediate assistance.

Hoover and his advisers, meanwhile, had been contemplating proposing a one-year moratorium on all intergovernmental debt and reparations payments. As these obligations would total about $1,000,000,000, any attempt to force payment would bankrupt Germany and cause the entire international economy to collapse. After delaying too long for fear of political repercussions, Hoover proposed the moratorium on June 21, 1931. Britain and Germany accepted at once; but the French government balked for two weeks, and further withdrawals from Germany compelled the German government to adopt severe measures to stave off repudiation.

No sooner had the German crisis passed, however, than French bankers began withdrawing large sums of gold they had earlier deposited in British banks. On August 1 the Bank of England negotiated a short-term gold loan in France and the United States and another in the United States at the end of the month. But the withdrawals were so heavy that on September 21, 1931, the Bank of England defaulted on gold payments, and the British Cabinet took the government off the gold standard. Within six months only the United States, France, Italy, Belgium, Holland, and Switzerland remained on that standard.

The financial crises of the spring and summer of 1931 virtually destroyed the existing system of international exchange and trade and set off a sharp depression in western Europe. More significant for our story was the manner in which the European crisis deepened the depression in the United States. For one thing, before the European crisis erupted, British, French, and other European nationals and banks had deposited some $1,500,000,000 in gold in American banks, and the American banks in turn had lent most of this money. When the crisis came in the spring of 1931, Europeans demanded payment of most of this gold, and the American depositories had to call in domestic loans. In the second place, American banks held more than $1,000,000,000 of German short-term trade paper and bank acceptances. Fear that these obligations could not be paid caused American bankers further to call loans to amass liquid reserves. Third, the panic in Europe led foreigners to unload large quantities of securities on the New York

---

[8] By March 1931 Germany alone had more than $4,000,000,000 short-term debts outstanding. Normally, short-term loans are made to finance business and trade operations. The Germans, however, had invested the money in a variety of nonliquid assets. Any crisis leading to demand for payment of these obligations would, therefore, immediately imperil the entire German financial structure.

Stock Exchange. Finally, devaluation and demoralization of exchange caused a virtual stoppage of foreign trade, the consequences of which were catastrophic for the commodity markets.

These and other factors combined during the summer of 1931 to destroy all the encouraging progress toward recovery the American economy had made since January and to plunge the country deeper into depression. Contraction of loans set off panic, hoarding of cash, and "runs" by depositors; and bankers in turn had to contract further. Dumping of securities drove the price of stocks and bonds to new depths. The loss of foreign markets caused agricultural prices to fall to very low levels. Above all, fear seized the American business and financial communities. Men began hoarding instead of spending; employers cut production and wages; investors tried to recover money instead of investing it. The downward spiral is well illustrated by the following table:

1931	*Index of Employment* *(Monthly average 1923– 1925 = 100)*	*Index of Payrolls* *(Monthly average 1923– 1925 = 100)*	*Number of Bank Failures*
May	80.1	73.4	91
June	78.4	69.7	167
July	77.0	66.2	93
August	77.1	65.9	158
September	77.4	63.4	305
October	74.4	61.3	522
November	71.8	58.1	175
December	71.0	57.6	358

Convinced that a natural and unrestrained liquidation would lead to a total collapse of the American financial structure, Hoover now determined to marshal the nation's resources to prevent collapse and inevitable social upheaval. Still hoping to win his campaign by voluntary cooperation of the business community, he called some thirty leading New York bankers and insurance executives to a secret conference on October 4, 1931. He wanted the banks to form an emergency credit pool of $500,000,000 and the insurance companies to agree not to foreclose mortgages when creditors were in honest straits; and he warned he would call Congress into special session if the financial leaders did not cooperate. The warning sufficed to bring early compliance. Two days later, October 6, the President met with congressional leaders of both parties and won their promise of support in the impending Seventy-Second Congress.

When Congress convened in early December, moreover, Hoover outlined the recovery program upon which he had been working since September—drastic reductions in administrative expenditures and an expansion of federal public works; expansion of the lending powers of federal farm banks; creation of a system of home-loan banks to prevent foreclosures; and a gigantic emergency reconstruction corporation to strengthen the entire economy. Obviously, fear of national collapse had forced the President to abandon old assumptions about the sufficiency of voluntary measures and to support a progressive program that implied more extensive federal intervention than had ever been attempted in peacetime.

The next seven months were marked by bitter wrangling between the President and Congress and among the leaders of the two houses. While unemployment mounted and huge withdrawals of gold by French banks threatened to drive the country off the gold standard, Congress for weeks and months delayed urgently needed legislation. Many Democrats acted as if they feared recovery would come before the presidential election in November 1932. Other Democrats and progressive Republicans supported Hoover's program but also demanded that the government extend as much relief to farmers and the unemployed as it gave to financial institutions and the railroads. In spite of wrangling and delay, Congress had approved a comprehensive recovery program by the time it adjourned in July 1932.

The main cog of the recovery machinery was the Reconstruction Finance Corporation, chartered by Congress on January 16, 1932, with a capital of $500,000,000 and authorized to borrow up to $1,500,000,000 more in tax-free obligations. Immediately the RFC opened offices in thirty cities and set to work to save banks, railroads, building and loan associations, and other financial institutions. In all, during 1932 the RFC lent $1,500,000,000 to more than 5,000 concerns, restored a large measure of public confidence, and successfully halted the undermining of the financial structure.

Through other measures the President and Congress cooperated to strengthen the financial machinery. Thus the Glass-Steagall Act of February 27, 1932, made government bonds and new classes of commercial paper acceptable as collateral for Federal Reserve notes. This measure not only permitted the Federal Reserve Banks to expand the currency but, more important, released $1,000,000,000 in gold to meet foreign withdrawals. The Federal Home Loan Bank Act of July 22, 1932, established home loan banks with a total capital of $125,000,000 to enable building and loan associations, savings banks, and insurance companies to obtain cash without foreclosing on home owners. In addition, an Act of January 23, 1932, provided additional capital for Federal Land Banks.

These were on the whole nonpartisan measures, passed after a minimum of bickering. Conflicting relief proposals, however, engendered bitter controversies between the administration and Democratic and progressive Republican leaders in Congress. Many of the progressives were frank inflationists, who proposed to extend direct aid to the unemployed by printing paper money, but Hoover blocked their efforts at almost every turn. A case in point was the controversy provoked by the agitation for full and immediate payment of the so-called bonus. On June 15, 1932, the House passed the measure sponsored by Representative Wright Patman of Texas, providing for full payment of the bonus with $2,400,000,000 in paper money. Under threat of a presidential veto, the Senate rejected the Patman bill on June 19.

Progressives, besides, demanded adoption of a large scale public works and direct relief program, to be financed through borrowing. Hoover was not callous to the suffering of the unemployed; but he insisted that relief was a local problem and that the federal government could serve the people best by working through the cities and states. When Congress, in early July, passed the Garner-Wagner relief bill providing direct aid to individuals and a vast expansion of public works, therefore, Hoover vetoed the measure on July 11, calling it "impractical," "dangerous," and "damaging to our whole conception of governmental relations." Congress then followed his advice and passed a new relief bill on July 16, authorizing the RFC to lend $300,000,000 to states whose resources were exhausted and an additional $1,500,000,000 to states and municipalities for self-liquidating public works.

In summary, what shall we say of Hoover's program for relief and recovery? To repeat the generally accepted story that Hoover fiddled while the country burned would be merely to add undue dignity to an important part of the American mythology. Hoover was obviously no old-fashioned conservative, no social Darwinist, willing to allow the depression to run its full course and confident that the automatic machinery of the economy would eventually start the wheels rolling again. On the contrary, he was a cautious progressive, whose campaign for recovery after the spring of 1931 was grounded ideologically on the assumption that only strong federal intervention would suffice to carry the people through the storm. His philosophy and policies after the acute phase of the depression set in represent, therefore, a turning point, a transition toward a future characterized by a larger measure of federal leadership.

While saving the capitalistic structure, Hoover also lost the confidence of a large majority of the American people. This was true in part because he had the misfortune of being President during a time of increasing social and economic misery, in part because he saved the financial structure but would not approve bold and direct measures of federal social alleviation. In the minds of most thoughtful Americans, Hoover's program seemed inadequate and too heavily weighted in favor of the upper classes. The majority of people demanded not a holding action but a thoroughgoing overhauling of the economic machinery. Unlike Hoover, who talked only of reviving the business civilization of the 1920's, millions of Americans had turned their eyes toward a new and, they hoped, brighter future in which they, not businessmen and bankers, would make the important economic decisions.

PART THREE

THE DEMOCRATIC ERA, 1933-1953

IN WHICH the American people reform their economic and political institutions in a flowering of reform under the New Deal, help to fight and win the Second World War, recover material prosperity and expand the progressive movement at home, and are beset by the perils of world leadership in the postwar years.

CHAPTER 18 / THE FIRST NEW DEAL:
EXPERIMENT IN COMPROMISE

*B*y the summer of 1932 the Hoover administration had seemingly halted the most destructive processes of economic dissolution, but most Americans were tired of talk about prosperity around the corner. Farmers in debt, workers without jobs, and bankrupt businessmen demanded bolder federal action than Hoover had been willing to approve. Rejecting the President and the now discredited business leadership, the disparate forces of discontent coalesced into a new progressive alliance in November 1932 and turned the government of the United States over to a new leader and a party long out of power.

On March 4, 1933, therefore, began the New Deal and the Age of Franklin D. Roosevelt. The key to understanding the period lies in realizing that there was no single set of Roosevelt policies carried out according to a prearranged plan but rather that there were two New Deals, which differed in ideology and objectives. The period of the First New Deal from 1933 to 1935 was a time of transition from a cautious progressivism, such as Wilson and Hoover had espoused, to new programs with expanded social and economic horizons. In the Second New Deal, from 1935 to 1939, the American progressive movement found fulfillment.

135 / The Election of 1932

While Republican fortunes declined in direct ratio to the intensity of the economic distress after 1930, Democratic leaders looked forward with growing confidence to victory in the new presidential election. Alfred E. Smith of New York was still titular head of the Democratic party, but as hopes of victory multiplied a number of other contenders entered the preconvention contest for the Democratic presidential nomination.

Among the Democratic aspirants, Franklin D. Roosevelt was easily Smith's most dangerous rival. Elected Governor of New York in 1928, Roosevelt was re-elected in 1930 by 725,000 votes, the largest majority ever given a gubernatorial candidate in his state. The magic of this majority at once made him a leading contender for the Democratic nomination in 1932;

but the situation in New York was discouraging, for Tammany Hall, the New York City Democratic organization, was still loyal to Smith. Therefore, Roosevelt's managers—Louis M. Howe, his secretary, and James A. Farley, a former Smith lieutenant who had come into the Roosevelt camp in 1929—began to build strength in the South and West. They succeeded so well that they had amassed a majority of the delegates, but not the then necessary two-thirds, for the New York governor by the time the Democratic national convention opened in Chicago on June 27, 1932. Instead of showing his full strength on the first ballot, Farley held off part of his delegates and added them to the Roosevelt column on the second and third ballots in order to create the impression of a landslide. On the fourth ballot on June 30, Farley swung Texas and California, whose votes he had obtained in exchange for the vice presidential nomination for Speaker John N. Garner, into line, and the battle was won. Only Smith's Tammany followers refused to make the nomination unanimous.

Flying to Chicago to accept the nomination in person, Roosevelt went down the planks in the platform, endorsing them one by one. "I pledge you, I pledge myself, to a new deal for the American people," he concluded on a high note of dedication. ". . . This is more than a political campaign; it is a call to arms." Roosevelt's promise of work, security, and a fairer distribution of incomes encouraged the country, but what it foretold no man could say. Moreover, a reading of the Democratic platform would neither have yielded knowledge nor provided inspiration. Indeed, in view of later New Deal policies, it was a poor prophecy.[1]

The Republicans, meanwhile, had assembled at Chicago on June 14 and renominated President Hoover on the first ballot. But the Republican convention was gloomy, and it seemed the delegates knew they were going through the necessary motions. Most of the speeches and a good part of the platform[2] were devoted to proving that the depression was the product of outside forces and that Hoover had met the enemy on home ground and conquered him through bold measures of relief and reconstruction.

In the ensuing campaign the Republican leaders fought like men with their backs to the wall, but their effort was hobbled from the outset by its defensive character. First, they tried to restore public confidence in the President, by portraying him as a shy but kindly man; as the pilot who had kept eternal vigil on the bridge, fighting through the storm; as the great

[1] The Democratic platform was brief but neither radical nor bold. Among other things, it demanded repeal of the Eighteenth Amendment; promised to balance the budget and reduce federal expenditures by 25 per cent; demanded the removal of government from all fields of private enterprise, "except where necessary to develop public works and natural resources"; promised to maintain "at all hazards" a sound currency and reform the banking system; advocated lending money to the states to care for the unemployed; endorsed unemployment and old age insurance "under state laws"; and promised lower tariffs and "effective control of crop surpluses" without specifying the nature of such controls.

[2] The Republican platform, among other things, advocated emergency relief loans to states unable to cope with the unemployment crisis, economy, maintenance of the gold standard, and banking reform; endorsed cooperative efforts by farmers to control agricultural production and the maintenance of tariff protection; and approved a constitutional amendment to allow the states to resume control of the liquor traffic.

engineer, whose genius would lead the people to safety. Second, Republicans tried to absolve their party of responsibility for the depression, convince the voters they were capable of bringing recovery, and restore public confidence in the GOP as the party of all the people, not merely of the business and financial interests.

Hoover also campaigned vigorously; but he spoke gravely, recounting the things he had done to combat the depression, "the battles on a thousand fronts, . . . the good fight to protect our people in a thousand cities from hunger and cold." To the unemployed he declared that he would mobilize the nation's resources rather than allow any one to starve. To farmers he promised enlarged tariff protection and additional federal credit. To investors he promised maintenance of the gold standard. And to the country at large he promised abundance if the Republicans won and warned that grass would grow "in the streets of a hundred cities, a thousand towns" if Roosevelt were elected.

In sharp contrast to Hoover's ineffective defense was Roosevelt's confident campaign. Although he said many things about economy and a balanced budget that he must have afterward regretted, he also outlined, with the help of his advisers, called the Brains Trust, at least the shadow of future New Deal policies. Thus on September 14, at Topeka, Kansas, he sketched the outline of a crop control measure, which farm leaders had agreed upon. At Portland, Oregon, he promised federal hydroelectric projects. Before the Commonwealth Club of San Francisco he demanded that businessmen work together to assure full production and employment. To millions of investors who had been fleeced by Wall Street operators he promised to bring the stock exchanges under strict control. To the unemployed he declared that he was "utterly unwilling that economy should be practiced at the expense of starving people." Strange to say, organized labor was the only group to which Roosevelt did not promise some specific benefit.

We can read Roosevelt's speeches, but how can we estimate the effect of his contagious smile, assuring voice, and ability to inspire confidence that things would turn out right? Whether he assured his election by his strenuous campaign is doubtful, for any Democrat could probably have won in that autumn of depression. There is no doubt, however, that Roosevelt's personality helped make the election of 1932 one of the most impressive mandates in American history.

Retaining business and a large middle class support, Hoover received 15,761,841 votes and carried Pennsylvania, Connecticut, Delaware, Maine, New Hampshire, and Vermont. In contrast, Roosevelt received 22,821,857 popular votes, carried the electoral votes of the rest of the states, and helped give the Democrats staggering majorities in both houses of Congress. Certainly the revolution of 1932 was as sweeping as any Democrat could have wished for.[3]

[3] In spite of a vigorous campaign and a comprehensive program for combating the depression, the Socialist candidate, Norman Thomas, polled only 884,781 votes. The Communist candidate, William Z. Foster, enjoyed considerable support in intellectual and literary circles. But he also failed utterly to profit by the prevailing discontent and polled a mere 102,991 votes.

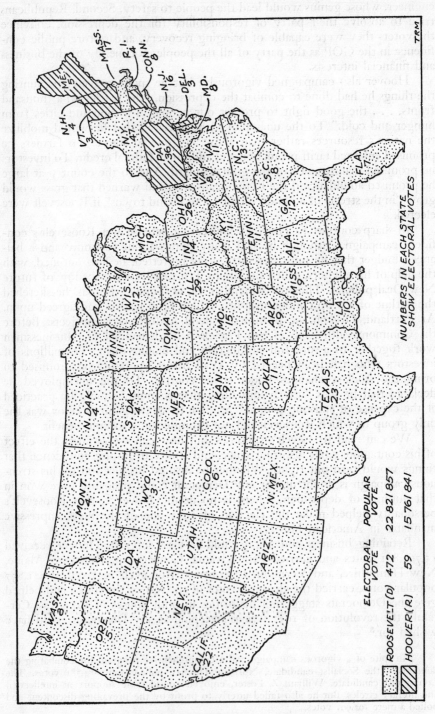

15. *The Election of 1932*

136 / *Franklin D. Roosevelt and the Progressive Movement*

No man, except perhaps Washington, Lincoln, and Truman, ever assumed the duties of President with more baffling problems than Franklin D. Roosevelt. But if the tasks were overwhelming, the opportunity for bold leadership was also great. That opportunity arose not only from the weakness of the Republican opposition and the strength of Roosevelt's forces in Congress after 1932. It arose even more importantly because of the strong survival in the 1930's of the progressive movement, especially in its economic and social manifestations. Divided and thwarted in the 1920's, the various components of progressivism came tenuously together in 1932. Roosevelt's most urgent political task, therefore, was to weld disparate groups that had not been able to cooperate effectively for long into a solid majority coalition.

In the dire emergency of 1933 this task proved deceptively easy, for practically all classes and interests demanded action. Once the worst phase of the depression had passed, however, large conservative and business elements deserted the New Deal coalition and Roosevelt had to fashion a new alliance and a new program. Abandoning many of his early policies, he resurrected the Jacksonian alliance of farmers and workingmen in 1935, added to it the social justice forces and the mass of the unemployed, and then set in motion the most far-reaching program of federal social and economic legislation in American history.

It was ironic that Roosevelt in 1932 neither foresaw nor planned this culmination of the American progressive movement. And yet when necessity compelled a new departure he took firm control of the progressive-democratic forces and won congressional approval for a program that satisfied their historic demands. This, in brief, was his chief contribution to the progressive movement in the United States.

What manner of man was he who guided the destinies of the American people from the Great Depression to victory in global war and became almost the personal embodiment of the democratic movement? Walter Lippmann's classic observation, written in January 1932—that Roosevelt was a "pleasant man who, without any important qualifications for the office, would very much like to be President"—was undoubtedly overdrawn. Even so, it would have required a soothsayer in 1932 to predict the shape of things to come.

Roosevelt came up the easy way, at least before 1921. Born at Hyde Park, New York, on January 30, 1882, the son of James Roosevelt and Sara Delano, Franklin received a proper education at Groton and Harvard without demonstrating either ambition or intellectual promise. After being graduated from Harvard in 1904, he moved to New York City, studied in a desultory way at the Columbia University Law School, married his distant cousin, Anna Eleanor Roosevelt, in 1905, and settled down in 1907 for a comfortable career with a prominent New York law firm.

Following the example of his uncle-in-law and fifth cousin, Theodore Roosevelt, Franklin went into politics in 1910 by accepting the Democratic nomination for the State Senate in a Hudson Valley district that had gone Republican in every election but one since the Civil War. By virtue of a split in the Republican party and hard campaigning he won this first election. At Albany in 1911 he led a small group of anti-machine Democrats in a fight to prevent the election of the Tammany leader, William F. Sheehan, to the United States Senate. Seeming success in this first skirmish brought Roosevelt a measure of national publicity; soon afterward he organized the anti-Tammany Democrats in support of Wilson's candidacy for the presidential nomination in 1912.

Appointed Assistant Secretary of the Navy in 1913 by Wilson at the suggestion of Josephus Daniels, who remembered that Theodore Roosevelt had used the same office as a stepping stone to the presidency, Franklin Roosevelt was an able administrator and popular in the second rank of the Wilson circle from 1913 to 1920. Coming to friendly terms with the new young leaders of Tammany Hall, Roosevelt supported Alfred E. Smith in Smith's first bid for the governorship in 1918 and won the Democratic vice presidential nomination in 1920 because he was the leading New York Wilsonian acceptable to Tammany.

Roosevelt lost the election, to be sure, but he gained invaluable experience, a host of friends, and a position of considerable prominence in Democratic councils. In brief, he was rapidly changing from a patrician reformer into a practical politician with a bright future. Then disaster struck in August 1921, when an attack of polio laid Roosevelt low. Courageously he fought to regain his strength and use of his withered legs; slowly, painfully he won a partial victory. Meanwhile, his wife and his devoted secretary and adviser, Louis M. Howe, stayed by his side and helped him extend his influence among Democratic politicians through voluminous correspondence.

By 1924 Roosevelt had recovered sufficiently to nominate Smith for the presidency at the Democratic convention in New York's Madison Square Garden. By 1928 he had discarded his crutches in public and had achieved maximum recovery when he placed Smith's name before the national convention at Houston. During succeeding months, the New York leaders begged Roosevelt to accept the gubernatorial nomination and pleaded that his name would greatly strengthen the national ticket in the state. At first he declined, saying he needed another year for complete recovery and thinking that 1928 was a Republican year. But when Smith appealed to him on a personal basis, Roosevelt could not refuse.

During the campaign that followed, Roosevelt surprised friends and opponents by his vigor; except for Smith he was the best vote-getter the Democrats had in 1928. And when the campaign was over a phenomenal thing happened on election day: Smith lost New York by a narrow margin, but enough Republicans voted for Roosevelt to give him the governorship by a plurality of 25,000.

We have seen how Roosevelt won the presidency in 1932 and established himself as the spokesman of a large part of the American people. During the fateful years of his tenure he abandoned old policies and adopted new ones, and he emerged with greater stature during war than in peace. But throughout the conflict and turmoil he remained remarkably the same man.

Roosevelt's personality was extraordinarily complex; he had many sides, and the whole is not equal to the sum of its parts. Personally, he was urbane and witty; yet for all his patrician upbringing he had a deep affection for people as individuals, not *en masse*. This was true in part because his long illness and fight for recovery purged him of any social snobbishness he might once have had and stirred a deep compassion in his heart for the physically afflicted and troubled in spirit. However, he so much wanted people to like him that he often gave the impression of duplicity because he found it difficult to disagree with a good friend. And in spite of his great courage in times of national peril, he rarely had the heart to dismiss a loyal but incompetent friend. Thus he was often a poor administrator.

Roosevelt's religious beliefs underlay all his attitudes toward men and society. He believed in a personal God, an absolute ethic, and in the integrity of his fellow men. Hence his views toward government and what govern- ment should do for people stemmed from his belief in decency, justice, and fair play. To his friends he was radiant and warm, and few could resist his charm, which he used in the confidence he could "get through" to any person. Toward his enemies, on the other hand, he could appear vain, decep- tive, petty, and vindictive.

Intellectually, Roosevelt was narrow—poorly read, averse to hard, logi- cal thinking, preferring intuition to reason in solving difficult problems. He was not an original thinker, but he had great capacity for learning and for thinking in broad terms and a willingness to try almost any experiment in order to achieve his goals. In economic matters Roosevelt was almost totally deficient. Ignorant himself of economic theory and history, he was at the mercy of his advisers in formulating economic policies and often approved inconsistent measures.

In spite of all his shortcomings, Roosevelt won such affection and loyalty from the American people as few Presidents have earned. He was the champion campaigner of American history, the President for life after 1932. In brief, Roosevelt succeeded, first, because he was able to communi- cate—either in person, over the radio, or in newsreels—directly with indi- viduals and to radiate his warmth and confidence into the hearts and minds of all manner of men. He succeeded, secondly, because he was able to express great ideas in simple language, in other words, to express the hopes and aspirations of the average man in homely yet moving words. He succeeded, above all, because he possessed an uncanny ability to know and understand what the people wanted and the courage to defy powerful forces of privilege and fight for measures of social and economic justice.

137 / *Interregnum: the Banking Panic and the Change of Government*

The development that gave the new administration its tremendous emergency power was the practical collapse of the banking structure of the United States in the months immediately preceding Roosevelt's inauguration. Most of the country's banks, especially the great metropolitan institutions, had stood impregnable during the first phase of the depression. From 1929 to June 1931 aggregate banking resources declined only $2,000,000,000—

from $72,172,500,000 to $70,209,000,000; but after the European collapse in the summer of 1931 American banking strength began to give way. Between June 30, 1931, and June 30, 1932, total bank resources declined from $70,209,000,000 to $57,245,100,000, while bank deposits shrank nearly $9,000,000,000.

Thus by the summer of 1932 the forces of dissolution were beginning to imperil the foundations of American capitalism. Whatever the cause, fear spread and grew into panic in January 1933. The strain of runs and heavy withdrawals was too great for the banks to bear. The first sign of crisis came on October 31, 1932, when the Governor of Nevada declared a twelve-day banking holiday in his state to avert the failure of an important chain of banks. On February 4, 1933, Governor Huey P. Long closed the banks of Louisiana; ten days later the Governor of Michigan declared a banking moratorium for a week. Then, during the ensuing three weeks, state after state succumbed, until the climax of the crisis came in the early morning of March 4, when Governor Herbert H. Lehman closed the New York banks for two days. By the hour of Roosevelt's inaugural, banks were either closed or doing business under severe restrictions in forty-seven states.

Meanwhile, President Hoover had been trying to win Roosevelt's approval for policies that would stabilize the financial situation and restore public confidence. In private conference and by letter Hoover exhorted the President-elect to announce that he would balance the budget, maintain the dollar at its current value in gold, and cooperate with the European powers in stabilizing currencies and exchange rates. Roosevelt refused, not only because he had already decided to inflate the currency, but also because he suspected that Hoover was trying to transfer some of his own unpopularity to the incoming administration. Thus irreconcilable differences over policy prevented effective teamwork between the two men, although Treasury officials worked loyally with the Secretary of the Treasury-designate and his subordinates.

Meanwhile, Roosevelt was at work constructing his administration. For Secretary of State he chose Senator Cordell Hull of Tennessee, probably the most influential Democrat in the upper house. As Secretary of the Treasury Roosevelt wanted Senator Carter Glass of Virginia, author of the Federal Reserve bill and former head of the Treasury under Wilson, whose financial orthodoxy would reassure the banking interests. Glass, however, refused because Roosevelt would not promise to eschew inflation. The post fell, therefore, to William H. Woodin of New York, president of the American Car & Foundry Company, a friend of Raymond Moley, head of the "Brains Trust," and a heavy contributor to the Democratic party. The secretaryships of Agriculture and of the Interior went to two midwestern progressive Republicans, Henry A. Wallace of Iowa and Harold L. Ickes of Chicago, who had helped swing their section to Roosevelt during the campaign. By selecting Frances Perkins, a social worker with long experience in New York, as Secretary of Labor, the President-elect honored women and accorded signal recognition to the men and women who had been pressing the cause of social and labor reform. The important job of dispenser of the patronage, otherwise known as the Postmaster General, went to the astute Jim Farley, while the remaining Cabinet appointees were an assortment of party hacks and wheelhorses.

The men who stood close to Roosevelt and with his approval made the important decisions, however, were not the Cabinet, although a few Cabinet members were in the charmed circle. They were Roosevelt's unofficial advisers—the earlier Brains Trust, by March 1933 considerably enlarged in number: Raymond Moley, Rexford G. Tugwell, Hugh S. Johnson, George N. Peek, Louis M. Howe, Samuel I. Rosenman, and others, all of whom were given posts in various agencies and on the White House staff.

It was a gloomy day, March 4, 1933, when Franklin Delano Roosevelt took the oath as President of the United States. The economic machinery of the country was almost at a standstill, and people looked toward Washington for some word of hope. Striking at the frights and tensions of the last three years, the new President called out defiantly: "This great Nation will endure as it has endured, will revive and will prosper. So, first of all, let me assert my firm belief that the only thing we have to fear is fear itself." He was ready, he declared, to assume supreme command, and he called upon the people to follow him as if he were their commander in chief in battle. There were many urgent tasks ahead, Roosevelt continued. People must be put to work; the banking, credit, and currency systems must be overhauled and strengthened; the nation had to learn to use its resources wisely. If Congress failed to provide adequate remedies, he warned, he would ask Congress for "broad Executive power to wage a war against the emergency, as great as the power that would be given to me if we were in fact invaded by a foreign foe."

The meaning of this pronouncement was not lost upon the people of the United States as they sat huddled around their radios. They knew little about the finely-spun rationalizations of the orthodox economists and understood even less the abstruse mathematical logic of the new school who talked of managed currency. They did not have to know or understand these things in order to sense that this day, March 4, 1933, was a fateful moment in the nation's history, that one order was dead beyond recall and that another, ill-defined and uncertain though it was, had been born.

138 / *Financial Reinforcement and Reform Under the New Deal*

So desperate was the crisis on March 4, 1933, and so frightened were congressmen and the people that Roosevelt possessed a power unprecedented in American peacetime history. Had he harbored imperial ambitions, he probably could have obtained dictatorial powers from Congress. Had he been a socialist, he might have nationalized the banks and set the country upon the road toward extreme collectivism. However, Roosevelt was neither a fascist, socialist, or Communist. He was simply an old-fashioned American with traditional views on the benefits of the system of private enterprise and ownership of property, who believed the capitalistic system was worth saving. And the manner in which he and his helpers accomplished this objective revealed the true character of the First New Deal.

The hope for national salvation, Roosevelt thought, lay in quick action to overcome the menace of national economic collapse. On March 6, 1933, he closed all banks for a four-day period and forbade all gold payments and exports. Three days later Congress met in special session and enacted within four hours the Emergency Banking bill that Moley, Woodin, and spokesmen of the banking community had agreed upon. Signed by the President before nine o'clock in the evening of March 9, the Emergency Banking Act revealed that the administration had decided to restore and strengthen private ownership and management in the financial field. The measure authorized Federal Reserve banks to issue currency against bank assets, empowered the Reconstruction Finance Corporation to provide liquid funds to banks by buying their preferred stock, and directed Treasury officials to supervise the reopening of banks.[4]

Coupled with the passage of the Economy Act on March 11, which drastically reduced federal expenditures in an effort to balance the budget, swift Treasury action under the Emergency Banking Act at once restored the confidence of the business classes. On March 12 the President had his first "fireside chat," or direct radio talk, with the American people, explaining what the government had done and appealing for public confidence in the banking system. The response was immediate. By the first week in April more than a billion dollars in currency had flowed back to the banks; hoarders returned gold to the Federal Reserve banks; and Treasury officials had to issue only a small amount of new Federal Reserve currency.

Once the crisis had passed, the Treasury began the immense task of strengthening weak banks and eliminating unsound ones. First, between March 1933 and July 1935 the RFC extended more than $1,000,000,000 in aid to 6,468 banks that were deemed essentially sound. Second, during the same two-year period Treasury and state officials liquidated 2,352 banks, with aggregate deposits of $2,756,946,000. Hence the administration strengthened and restored to private hands the most vital and sensitive part of the capitalistic economy. As Moley observed, "The policies which vanquished the bank crisis were thoroughly conservative policies. The sole departure from convention lay in the swiftness and boldness with which they were carried out."[5]

In fulfilling his promise to reform the financial system, the President merely encouraged a bipartisan congressional determination that the speculative *débâcle* of 1929 should never happen again. Thus the Glass-Steagall Act, or Banking Act of 1933, sought to prevent banks from using the resources of the Federal Reserve System for speculation—chiefly by compelling the absolute divorcement of commercial banks from their investment affiliates.[6] Moreover, the Truth-in-Securities Act of 1933 and the Securities Exchange Act of 1934 left operation of stock exchanges in private hands but compelled all underwriters and brokers to furnish complete information regarding the true value of securities being offered for sale and the arrangements under which the sale was being made. To the Securities and Exchange

---

[4] Treasury officials divided banks into four classes, on a basis of relative soundness. Over half the banks, with 90 per cent of the deposits, were given a clean bill and allowed to reopen by March 15, 1933.

[5] Raymond B. Moley, *After Seven Years* (New York, 1939), p. 155.

[6] For a discussion of the growth of these investment affiliates and their contribution to the speculation of the late 1920's, see above, pp. 316–317. At the insistence of southern and western Democrats, the Banking Act of 1933 also established the Federal Deposit Insurance Corporation which insured deposits, first up to $2,500, then up to $5,000 in 1935, and finally up to $10,000 after the Second World War.

Commission, a nonpartisan agency established by the Act of 1934, was entrusted the task of preventing and helping to punish misrepresentation and fraud.

After the banking crisis had been liquidated, administration leaders set to work to prepare a comprehensive banking measure to supplant the temporary Banking Act of 1933. The result, the Banking Act of 1935, was the first fundamental overhauling of the Federal Reserve Act since its adoption in 1913. In contrast to the Wilsonian legislation, which had widely diffused power within the Federal Reserve System and given little direct authority to the central board, the Act of 1935 concentrated enormous authority in the central board, now called the Board of Governors. The Board was given for the first time direct authority over discount, or interest, rates, reserve requirements, and the open market operations of the Federal Reserve Banks. In addition, a number of highly technical provisions established new classes of securities and commercial paper against which Federal Reserve currency might be issued.

Roosevelt's own contribution to this edifice of financial reform—the Holding Company Act of 1935—was the center of a long and bitter battle in Congress and the country. During the 1920's, ambitious monopolists had used the holding company device to create far-flung and often irrational public utilities systems.[7] Conservatives and New Dealers alike approved the President's plan to bring the holding companies under rigorous federal control, but controversy arose when Roosevelt insisted upon incorporating a provision imposing the "death sentence" upon the gigantic holding companies.

The battle over the President's bill raged in Congress during the spring and summer of 1935. In their efforts to force congressmen and senators into line, administration spokesmen stirred hot resentment. The utilities companies spent hundreds of thousands of dollars in a spectacular lobbying campaign that also backfired. The upshot was a compromise, embodied in the Public Utility Holding Company Act of August 26, 1935, which gave to the Securities and Exchange Commission, or SEC, complete supervisory control over the financial operations of holding companies, compelled the destruction of the giant utilities empires within five years, but allowed small holding companies controlling single, integrated operating systems to survive.

With Roosevelt's substantial victory in the battle against the utilities giants, the task of reforming the country's financial institutions was fairly complete. To progressives the changes accomplished were good because they transformed financial operations from a private into a quasi-public business. At long last the populistic demand for complete federal control of banks and the money supply had been satisfied.

Two other aspects of the First New Deal's program to save the capitalistic structure remain to be noted here: the administration's efforts, first, to enable homeowners to refinance and adjust their debt burdens and, second, to spur a revival of private home construction through federal support of the mortgage market. The first objective was accomplished by the establishment on June 13, 1933, of the Home Owners Loan Corporation. Authorized to borrow up to $2,000,000,000, later increased to $4,750,000,000, the HOLC set to the task of refinancing the mortgages of home owners in dire peril of

[7] For an elaboration of this matter, see above, pp. 312-313.

foreclosure. During the three years of its life the agency lent more than $3,000,000,000 to more than 1,000,000 home owners and assumed about one-sixth of the entire urban mortgage load. Secondly, to stimulate the nearly defunct housing construction industry,[8] Congress on June 28, 1934, established the Federal Housing Administration, which insured mortgages for new construction and home repairs. By establishing a system of long-term repayment at low interest rates, the FHA played a large role in the resumption of private home construction. Between 1934 and 1940 it insured 2,300,000 loans totaling $945,000,000 for home repairs and 554,000 loans totaling $2,300,000,000 for new construction.

139 / *The Problem of Recovery and an Unsuccessful Experiment*

The philosophy underlying the administration's recovery program was compounded of a curious mixture of pessimism about the future of the economy and naive faith in the ability of government to work miracles by easy solutions. To begin with, Roosevelt and his advisers accepted the then popular view that the American economy had reached a stage of full maturity, that the closing of the agricultural frontier, the restriction of immigration, and the sharp decline in the birth rate had removed the self-generating mechanisms from the economy. The age of expansion and confidence, when businessmen invested in the future and expanded the nation's economic frontiers, was allegedly over. Indeed, Roosevelt several times observed, the American industrial plant was overbuilt because it could produce more than the people could consume.

The chief task ahead, therefore, was to conserve human and natural resources, restore prices to a level that would yield profits to farmers, manufacturers, and businessmen, and assure a fair distribution of goods and incomes. This task could be accomplished, not by stimulating foreign trade and encouraging new investment, but by close cooperation among workers, farmers, businessmen, and government to raise prices, increase purchasing power through shorter hours and higher wages, and limit production to actual needs.

This is not to say, however, that Roosevelt took the helm with any grand plan for recovery, for his most elaborate undertakings, the National Recovery Administration and the Public Works Administration, were afterthoughts and improvisations. The administration's original program was aimed chiefly at stimulating recovery by raising the prices of agricultural products through restriction of output and by increasing the general price level through controlled inflation.

Roosevelt took the first step toward controlled inflation on March 6, 1933, by prohibiting the redemption of currency in gold coin and the export of gold without the Treasury's approval. Subsequent presidential decrees and acts of Congress nationalized gold and forbade the fulfillment of private and public contracts calling for payment of debts in yellow coin. This action took the country off the traditional gold standard at home but retained a

---

[8] Urban home construction numbered only 60,000 units in 1933, as compared with 900,000 units in 1925.

gold bullion backing for the currency and allowed limited gold payments in international exchange.

By mid-May 1933, the dollar had fallen in value to 85 cents in gold on international exchanges. As a result, wholesale prices in the United States were rising and the entire economy seemed on the verge of invigoration. Having apparently set recovery in motion, would the President now agree to stabilize the gold content of the dollar, or would he embark upon a course of frank inflation?

This was perhaps the most important question confronting the administration in the late spring of 1933. On the one hand, an overwhelming majority of Congress favored outright inflation through the issue of paper currency.[9] On the other, an international conference would meet in London in June 1933 for the purpose of lowering tariffs, stabilizing currencies, and finding other means to stimulate a revival of international economic activity. Thus by the end of May the President was caught in an embarrassing dilemma. He had pledged support for the London Conference, yet he was not willing to stabilize the gold content of the dollar and forego the advantages of further inflation.

By the time the London Conference met, Roosevelt had been converted to the so-called "commodity dollar" theory and had decided upon further inflation. Advocates of the "commodity dollar" argued, and Roosevelt agreed, that the best hope for sound recovery lay in devaluing the dollar to its 1926 purchasing power by decreasing its gold value by 43 per cent. Such inflation, these economists further contended, would not only stimulate production through substantial price increases but would also enable the American people better to carry their debt burdens.

Before acting, however, the President first waited to see how far the dollar would fall naturally in the exchanges and whether the recovery that had set in would last. By October the dollar had depreciated about 30 per cent and commodity prices had risen 19 per cent. Meanwhile, the country had gyrated from depression to near recovery and back to depression again, as the following statistics reveal:

1933	Manufacturing Production*	Employment*	Payrolls*	Wholesale Prices†
March	56	58.8	37.1	60.2
April	65	59.9	38.8	60.4
May	77	62.6	42.7	62.7
June	93	66.9	47.2	65
July	101	71.5	50.8	68.9
August	91	76.4	56.8	69.5
September	83	80	59.1	70.8
October	65	79.6	59.4	71.2

* Monthly average 1923–1925 = 100.
† 1926 average = 100.

[9] It required all the President's influence to restrain these congressional demands but he won control over monetary policy with the passage of the Thomas Amendment to the Agricultural Adjustment Act of May 12, 1933. The Thomas Amendment authorized but did not require the President to increase the money supply by six different methods, including the printing of $3,000,000,000 in paper currency, the free coinage of silver at 16 to 1, the lowering of Federal Reserve requirements, and devaluation of the gold content of the dollar up to 50 per cent.

Resolved to try any expedient rather than allow the nation to suffer through another winter of subdepression, Roosevelt decided the time had come to put the "commodity dollar" theory to work. In a "fireside chat" on October 22, 1933, he announced his decision; three days later he instructed the RFC to purchase gold, then selling at $29.80 an ounce, at $31.36 an ounce.[10] During ensuing months the President gradually increased the price of gold until he had finally achieved the "commodity dollar," theoretically equal in purchasing power to the dollar of 1926. Now willing to stabilize, he persuaded Congress to establish a new gold reserve standard[11] and on January 31, 1934, set the price of gold at $35.00 an ounce and the gold content of the dollar at 59.06 per cent of its pre-1933 value.

What shall we say about Roosevelt's efforts to achieve recovery through monetary manipulation? The most important fact was that his program failed to accomplish its announced objective. Prices refused to rise significantly because devaluation was not accompanied by a large increase either in the money supply or in bank credit and because the European nations quickly adjusted their currencies to the inflated American dollar. Moreover, the costs of devaluation were so great as to overshadow any temporary benefits. For one thing, devaluation in part cost the President the friendship of a number of close advisers and turned conservative Democrats against the administration. Worse still, European leaders interpreted Roosevelt's refusal to stabilize the dollar and his subsequent devaluation as a declaration of economic warfare. Inevitably, they retaliated in kind.

After stabilizing the dollar, however, the President eschewed any further financial legerdemain. Perhaps he realized recovery could not be bought so cheaply; certainly he began to recognize his mistake in thinking the depression was almost entirely domestic in origin and that recovery could come without a vigorous revival of foreign trade. In any event, henceforward his economic policies were aggressively internationalistic: tariff reductions, international currency stabilization, and revival of foreign trade were the order of the day.[12]

140 / *The NRA: Unsuccessful Experiment in a Planned Economy*

The Roosevelt administration had no unique plan for industrial recovery when it came into power. To be sure, such a plan—the National Industrial Recovery Act—was soon devised and became the spearhead of the New Deal's recovery effort. But it was improvised in haste in order to head off a movement in Congress to take control of the recovery effort out of the

[10] The pre-1933 price had been $20.67 an ounce.

[11] In the Gold Reserve Act, passed on January 30, 1934. This measure nationalized all gold in Federal Reserve banks, authorized the President to set the gold content of the dollar at between 50 and 60 per cent of its pre-1933 value, made gold bullion an unredeemable reserve against Federal Reserve notes, and established from the "profits" of devaluation a fund of $2,000,000,000 to be used to stabilize the dollar in international exchanges.

[12] For a more extended discussion of the administration's international economic policies, see below, pp. 460–463.

administration's hands. Let us look briefly at events that compelled the administration to embark upon an uncharted course in the sea of political economy.

The first stimulus came from organized labor and its spokesmen in Congress. In December 1932, Senator Hugo L. Black of Alabama introduced a bill sponsored by the AF of L to limit hours of labor in industry to thirty a week. Although Roosevelt's advisers regarded the Black bill as a dangerous threat to recovery, they were so engrossed in the banking crisis that they paid scant attention to the congressional situation. When the Senate passed the measure on April 6, however, the President commissioned Secretary Perkins to prepare an administration alternative. A few days later, therefore, Miss Perkins went before the House labor committee, half-heartedly approved the thirty-hour principle, and suggested the addition of provisions for minimum wages and federal control of production. When leaders of the business community protested, Roosevelt asked Moley to find out what they wanted.

Since 1931 the Chamber of Commerce of the United States had been at work on a plan for recovery. It proposed the creation of a national council of industrialists and businessmen empowered to work through trade associations to control production, raise prices, and stabilize wages. Adoption of this plan would of course necessitate relaxing the antitrust laws, although the business leaders were not ready before 1933 to admit the necessity of governmental supervision.

While Congress debated the Black bill, Moley, Hugh S. Johnson, and Rexford G. Tugwell set to work to reconcile the Chamber of Commerce plan with the principle of federal control. When the Chamber of Commerce met in Washington on May 3, 1933, Moley and Johnson presented a draft of their recovery bill to the business leaders. Although it included substantial concessions to labor, the Chamber of Commerce approved it as the only acceptable alternative to the Black-Perkins plan. Thus fortified, the administration presented its measure, the National Industrial Recovery Act, to Congress on May 15, 1933.

The NIRA was the most pretentious piece of legislation ever presented to Congress to that time. Its objectives were to end cutthroat competition, to raise prices to a profitable level by limiting production to actual needs, and to guarantee a reasonable work week and a living wage to labor. These aims would be accomplished through the adoption of codes for all branches of industry and business by committees representing management, labor, and the public. In the event of irreconcilable disagreement, the President might intervene and impose a code of his own making. Section 7a of the bill—added, incidentally, at the insistent demand of Secretary Perkins and William Green, president of the AF of L—affirmed labor's right to organize and bargain collectively. All these provisions were included in Title I of the measure. Title II, which appropriated $3,300,000,000 for a public works program, was incorporated in the measure at the last minute.

For several weeks the two houses held slipshod hearings and debates on the bill. A few senators were skeptical; but business, labor, and the administration united in a solid front, and Congress willingly concurred. On June 16, 1933, Roosevelt signed, as he called it, "the most important and far-reaching legislation ever enacted by the American Congress"; on the same day he established the National Recovery Administration and appointed Hugh S. Johnson Administrator, empowered to supervise the writing and enforcement of the codes.

With great energy and bustle Johnson set to his task. To provide for the interim period during which specific codes would be drawn up, he proposed the adoption of a blanket code. And to spur compliance, Johnson allowed employers who cooperated to display the Blue Eagle—the NRA emblem—and sponsored Blue Eagle parades reminiscent of the preparedness, draft, and war loan parades of the Wilson era. Within a few weeks almost 2,500,000 employers with 16,000,000 workers had signed the blanket code, and the NRA was on its way.

Now began the laborious task of preparing individual codes to fit the needs of every industry and trade in the United States. Theoretically the code-making process involved a mutualization of the interests of management, labor, and the consuming public. In actual practice, however, it was the trade associations, dominated usually by their large members, which wrote the codes in the first instance. After hasty reviews by the Code Analysis Division and various advisory boards, these codes were adopted as bodies of law governing the industries or trades involved.

From October 1933 to February 1934, when the code-making process was completed, the NRA approved 557 basic codes and 208 supplementary codes. All of them contained provisions confirming labor's right to organize and establishing minimum wage and maximum hours scales. But in making these concessions business leaders obtained far-reaching benefits from the government: price stabilization,[13] production controls,[14] and the outlawry of allegedly unfair competition. More important, business leaders won the right to govern themselves, for each code was administered by a code authority, almost invariably composed of trade association officials representing the large corporations. Finally, businessmen won another long-sought objective —exemption from antitrust prosecution for restrictive practices heretofore deemed illegal by the courts.

How did "self regulation" of industry work out? In the beginning all went smoothly on the surface, so long as the NRA gave businessmen a free hand. By the spring of 1934, however, Johnson had assembled a staff of experts to run the NRA. They soon discovered the obvious fact that the codes discriminated against small producers, especially in pricing and sales policies. But the codes were already written and in force. All the NRA staff could do was to try to compel the code authorities to implement the broad objectives of the NIRA, an effort that brought the NRA into increasingly

[13] Although the NRA tried to discourage outright price fixing, the bituminous coal, petroleum, and lumber codes contained schedules of minimum prices; most of the codes forbade sales below cost; and over half the codes required the establishment of the open-price system, that is, a system of prices openly published and adhered to.

[14] Production control was achieved in various ways in the codes. The petroleum, copper, and lumber codes, for example, set definite production limits and assigned quotas to individual producers. The cotton textile code limited mills to two eight-hour shifts daily. Other codes forbade the expansion of plant without approval of the code authority.

frequent and bitter conflict with business leaders. As if to compound the NRA's perplexities, the opposition of small businessmen and manufacturers to codes written and administered by big business swelled into a mighty storm of protest in the late winter of 1934. To palliate their discontent, Roosevelt appointed a National Recovery Review Board, headed by the famed criminal lawyer, Clarence Darrow, to investigate and recommend. Instead of trying to evaluate impartially, Darrow dealt with the NRA as if he were the prosecutor in a murder trial.

The fortunes of the NRA fell hard and fast after Darrow's pillorying. In the face of mounting criticism, the President asked Johnson to resign, abolished the office of National Recovery Administrator, and, on September 27, 1934, created a National Industrial Recovery Board composed of representatives of management, labor, and the public. Any overhauling of the codes, however, had to await congressional sanction, as the NIRA's life of two years would soon expire. Before Congress could respond to the President's request for extension of the measure, the Supreme Court ended the discussion on May 25, 1935, by declaring the NIRA unconstitutional.

Economists and historians agree that by and large the NRA failed to accomplish the objectives of the Act that gave it birth. What was wrong? Why did so hopeful an experiment end so ingloriously? In the final analysis the NRA failed because it was based upon false assumptions concerning human nature and the American economy. The framers of the Recovery Act assumed, for example, that businessmen would use the power of "self regulation" to promote the general interest. As any good Calvinist could have predicted, businessmen used the NRA for other purposes, and when they could not control the NRA they opposed it. More important, the NIRA was based upon the assumption that full production and employment could be achieved by outlawing price competition and either limiting or discouraging full production. Here was the basic contradiction and the most egregious error. What the United States needed in 1933 was new investment and a tremendous increase in production. Because the NRA discouraged both prerequisites of prosperity it impeded rather than stimulated recovery.

141 / *Relief, Labor, and the First New Deal, 1933–1934*

In no area of federal action was the basically conservative and emergency character of the First New Deal more fully revealed than in the matter of relief policies. So long as Roosevelt's original advisers had the President's ear, the administration rejected long-range comprehensive plans and followed Hoover's policies of public works and indirect relief through the cities and states.

From the outset, however, Roosevelt was more responsive to the needs of the millions in distress than Hoover had been. For example, Roosevelt came forward with a new plan to save both human and natural resources. It was the Civilian Conservation Corps, authorized by Congress in late March and put into operation on April 5, 1933. With an initial grant of

$300,000,000, the CCC enrolled 250,000 young men from relief families[15] in some 1,500 camps under the direction of the War Department and set them to the useful work of reforestation, flood control, and soil conservation. By 1935 the CCC had reached a maximum strength of 500,000; by 1940, when the project was ended, more than 2,250,000 youths had served in the undertaking.

The administration's first concern, however, was the plight of the 15,000,000 unemployed and the survival of the nearly 6,000,000 persons on city and state relief rolls in the spring of 1933. In response to the President's appeal, Congress, on May 12, 1933, approved the Federal Emergency Relief Act and appropriated $500,000,000, one-half of it to be given outright to impoverished states and the balance to other states on a basis of one federal dollar for every three dollars spent by states and municipalities. Creating the Federal Emergency Relief Administration, Roosevelt appointed Harry L. Hopkins, chairman of the New York Temporary Emergency Relief Administration, as Administrator. At the same time, the President made it clear that he agreed with Hoover that relief was primarily the responsibility of the cities and states.

Actually, the President regarded these measures as stopgaps to keep people from starving until recovery had set in. The administration's ace in the hole was a gigantic public works program to be launched with the NRA and used to stimulate depressed industries not immediately affected by the main recovery program. Title II of the NIRA, which established the Public Works Administration and appropriated $3,300,000,000 for the program, gave specific authorization.

Had this huge sum been poured immediately into the economy the effect might have been invigorating. Instead, fearing that Johnson was too unstable to spend the money wisely, the President separated the PWA from the NRA and gave control of the PWA to Secretary of the Interior Ickes. Determined that not one cent of the $3,300,000,000 should be stolen or wasted, Ickes insisted upon scrutinizing the details of all projects. In the form of new highways, hospitals, university buildings, municipal water works, and the like, the result was magnificent; but as a recovery device PWA was a failure. By the end of September 1933 the false boom of the spring and summer had ended; the PWA was mired in red tape; and millions of families faced the coming winter with no hope of employment.

It was during this crisis that Harry Hopkins first had decisive influence in the administration. He saw the President on about November 1 and urged him to launch a vast program of work relief—a kind of primitive public works on a direct basis—for 4,000,000 of the unemployed. Readily concurring, Roosevelt created the Civil Works Administration with Hopkins as Administrator and took $400,000,000 from PWA funds to get the program under way. Within thirty days the CWA was a thriving concern and a means of living for 4,000,000 men and their families.

Did Roosevelt's approval of the CWA signify that he had capitulated to what was then considered a radical doctrine—that every man was en-

---

[15] Men between the ages of eighteen and twenty-five, who were in need and capable of performing hard labor, were eligible. They received subsistence and $30 a month, $25 of which was sent to their families.

titled to a job, not merely a dole, and that it was the federal government's duty to provide work if private industry did not? So it seemed for a time. Then, in response to bitter Republican criticism of waste and the advice of conservative Democrats, Roosevelt, in mid-January 1934, told Hopkins he would have to end the CWA. In February Hopkins obtained an additional $450,000,000 from Congress to carry the agency through the winter; and in March and April he liquidated his CWA projects. The burden of relief for the balance of 1934, therefore, fell again on the FERA, for which Hopkins had obtained an additional $500,000,000 from Congress on February 15, 1934.

An experimental pattern and indecision over general objectives also characterized the New Deal's labor program during the NRA period. Administration leaders sincerely wanted to help labor, and to a degree they succeeded. But in their eagerness to win the cooperation of employers, the administration left the power to frustrate labor's strivings in management's hands. Not until the NRA and the First New Deal were dead did the President and his supporters make the sort of wholesale commitment that labor needed for the success of its ambitious plans. Let us see, meanwhile, how labor fared under the Blue Eagle.

To begin with, the adoption of labor provisions in all NRA codes won immediate gains that organized labor in its then weakened position could not have won on its own. The forty-hour week was established by codes covering 13,000,000 workers, while the average work week for all industries fell from 43.3 hours in June 1933 to 37.8 hours the following October. All the codes, moreover, contained provisions outlawing child labor and establishing minimum wages, ranging generally from 30 to 40 cents an hour. Finally, the adoption of the codes helped stimulate an increase in the index of factory employment from 62.6 in May 1933 to 80 in September and in the index of pay rolls from 42.7 to 59.4 during the same period. But between October 1933 and May 1935, when the NRA experiment was ended, there occurred little change in hours and wages, in spite of a 14 per cent increase in manufacturing output.

More important to labor in the long run was Section 7a of the Recovery Act, which asserted that workers should have the right to organize and bargain collectively "through representatives of their own choosing," outlawed the "yellow-dog" contract, and declared that workers should not be required to join a company union as a condition of employment. Experience soon demonstrated that Section 7a was more an affirmation than a grant of essential protection. None the less, it marked an epochal turning point: for the first time the federal government endorsed organized labor's historic objectives in general legislation.

Under the aegis of Section 7a, the AF of L roused with new hope and vigor. From 1933 to 1935 AF of L membership increased from 2,127,000 to 3,045,000, while membership in all unions grew from 2,857,000 to 3,728,000 during the same two years.

Substantial though it was, organized labor's progress under the NRA came in spite of the strong opposition of a large segment of management. A minority of employers, particularly in the building trades and the coal and garment industries, tried faithfully to honor Section 7a. For the most part, however, management was as determined as ever to prevent unionization, and employers by the thousands defied the NRA in labor disputes and harassed it by frequent appeals to the courts.

Labor's striving and management's continued determination to preserve the open shop inevitably collided; and a wave of bloody strikes followed the adoption of the NRA codes. Most of the disputes of 1933 and 1934 were not protracted, but they were exceedingly numerous and frequently violent, particularly in the southern textile region. To help bring peace to the industrial world, the President, on August 5, 1933, established a mediation commission to cooperate with the NRA—the National Labor Board, composed of distinguished labor leaders and industrialists, with Senator Robert F. Wagner of New York as chairman.

During the ensuing year the National Labor Board settled many disputes by common sense, persuasion, and an ability to find a compromise. More important was the fact that for the first time since 1915 a group of public leaders studied the whole problem of industrial relations and learned the full extent of management's opposition to the principle of collective bargaining. They also learned that many employers would use almost any method, including the use of labor spies and force, to prevent unionization.

Experience soon convinced Senator Wagner that the labor movement could never prevail until the federal government came to labor's support in the struggle for unionization. When an employer refused to recognize a union or to bargain in good faith, for example, there was nothing the National Labor Board could do but appeal to the NRA and the courts for uncertain redress. Following a wave of strikes in the spring of 1934, the President abolished the National Labor Board and established the National Labor Relations Board, a three-man commission empowered to hold elections to determine the right of unions to conduct collective bargaining. Wagner vainly tried to persuade the President and Congress to give the new Board authority to prevent so-called unfair practices by management. Lacking such authority, the National Labor Relations Board was even less successful in settling disputes than its predecessor had been.

What shall we say in summary about the First New Deal's labor policies? In part they represented the fulfillment of the most advanced objectives of the social justice program—abolition of child labor, minimum wages, and maximum hours. Long overdue though they were, these reforms were not enough. In the final analysis, industrial democracy could be achieved only by the workers themselves, not by a beneficent government. In refusing to give the protection and positive support that organized labor needed for the full success of its movement, the President acted in the spirit of compromise that permeated the First New Deal.

142 / *Toward Agricultural Stability, 1933–1935*

Farmers everywhere were on the verge either of despair or rebellion by the spring of 1933, but in no section was agrarian discontent so intense and dangerous as in the corn belt of the Middle West. Radical farm sentiment found expression in the so-called Farm Holiday Association, organized by the fiery president of the Iowa Farmers' Union, Milo Reno, to persuade farmers to withhold agricultural products from the market until prices equaled cost of production. In August 1932 mobs of farm strikers tried to prevent food from entering Sioux City and Des Moines; on March 12–13, 1933, representatives from most of the midwestern and Plains states met in a national convention of the Farm Holiday Association in Des Moines and threatened to call a nation-wide strike if the new Roosevelt administration did not meet its demands by May 3, 1933.

Actually, the farmers' most immediate concern was not low prices but the threat of foreclosure. Everywhere in the Middle West farm owners banded together to save their farms, either by direct action or through their state governments. The legislature of Minnesota enacted a two-year moratorium on foreclosures; the Governor of North Dakota forbade forced sales of farm properties. Vigilante committees threatened to shoot bank or insurance agents and went *en masse* to foreclosure sales and bought back properties for nominal sums. The most famous outbreak occurred at Le Mars, Iowa, on April 27, 1933, when some six hundred enraged farmers dragged a foreclosing judge from his bench and beat him into unconsciousness.

In this crisis the Roosevelt administration acted quickly to save the farmers and avert the likelihood of even more violent revolt. On March 27, 1933, the President consolidated all federal agricultural credit agencies into the Farm Credit Administration; shortly afterward Congress provided abundant new credit.[16] Moreover, in response to radical farm demands, Congress on June 28, 1934, adopted the Frazier-Lemke Farm Bankruptcy Act, which enabled farmers to recover lost property on easy terms.

These, however, were all stop-gap measures. The major task was devising a long-range program for agricultural recovery. Here the difficulty lay not in originating measures but in persuading agricultural spokesmen to unite upon a common plan. Speaking for tenants and subsistence farmers, the National Farmers' Union and the Farm Holiday Association demanded direct relief and inflation and opposed production controls. By the beginning of 1933, on the other hand, the more influential spokesmen of the large farmers—the Farm Bureau Federation and the National Grange—had settled upon the so-called domestic allotment plan, which called for federal payments to farmers who cooperated in limiting the production of basic staples.

On March 6, 1933, the new Secretary of Agriculture, Henry A. Wallace, began a series of conferences with farm leaders, the outgrowth of which was the Agricultural Adjustment Act, approved by Congress on May 10, 1933, and signed by the President two days later. It was easily the most ambitious agricultural legislation in the history of the country, but all its major features had long been discussed and advocated by important farm groups. Thus it represented, not a new departure, but a logical culmination of policies begun by the Wilson administration and carried forward by subsequent Republican Presidents and Congresses.

[16] The Emergency Farm Mortgage Act of May 12, 1933, for example, authorized emergency loans to save farmers in immediate peril. Within less than two years the Farm Credit Administration had refinanced one-fifth of all farm mortgages in the United States. The Farm Credit Act of June 16, 1933, moreover, established a system of production credit corporations to extend short-term loans to farmers and livestock producers.

Lest there be misunderstanding as to the intentions of the framers, the Act announced their objectives in clear language: to establish and maintain such a balance between the production and consumption of agricultural commodities that farm income would have the same relative purchasing power that it had enjoyed during the stable period from 1909 to 1914. To achieve so-called "parity" prices, the Act authorized the imposition of various production controls[17] on the major staples. The money to finance the program would come from taxes levied on the processing of agricultural commodities and from customs duties on certain enumerated commodities.

While farm leaders and administration spokesmen were agreeing upon the domestic allotment plan, the Agricultural Department received frightening reports of bountiful crops for the coming summer and autumn of 1933. In response, Wallace and George N. Peek, the new head of the Agricultural Adjustment Administration, put into effect a remedy that caused more criticism than anything the AAA ever did. They sent agents through the South and Southwest, who persuaded farmers to plow under 10,000,000 acres, or one-fourth, of the cotton crop in return for benefit payments. In addition, the AAA bought 220,000 sows and over 6,000,000 pigs for immediate slaughter. A similar destruction of part of the wheat crop was averted only by weather reports that indicated there would be drastic natural reductions in that staple.

Although cotton farmers plowed under with a vengeance, they fertilized the remaining crop so heavily that total output in 1933 was 13,047,000 bales, as compared with 13,002,000 bales in 1932. The following year, therefore, Congress adopted the Bankhead Cotton Control Act, which permitted the AAA to assign marketing quotas to large producers.[18] In consequence, cotton production fell to 9,636,000 bales in 1934 and to 10,638,000 bales in 1935.

Meanwhile, the AAA used its vast powers in other ways to restrict production and restore prices. After the "plow-under" and the slaughter of the pigs, the AAA set production goals for 1934 in the major staples and sent 100,000 agents into the agricultural regions to persuade farmers to sign contracts. When prices did not rise sufficiently in the autumn of 1933, the AAA established the Commodity Credit Corporation in October to enable cotton and corn producers to borrow against their crops and hold them until prices rose to higher levels.

Through these and other measures the AAA worked almost an economic miracle until the Supreme Court called a halt in January 1936. In the case of cotton and tobacco, the effects of the AAA program were direct and calculable. Cotton acreage, for example, was cut one-third during the period 1933 to 1935; had controls and price supports not been in effect the price of cotton would not have risen much above the depression level. On the other hand, the effects of the AAA program on the important midwestern and western staples of corn, wheat, and livestock are more difficult to calculate, but it seems likely that the droughts of 1933 and 1934 caused vastly greater

[17] Among them were benefit payments for voluntary crop reduction, commodity loans to farmers who cooperated, marketing agreements and quotas, export subsidies, and purchase of surpluses by the Department of Agriculture.

[18] The Kerr-Smith Tobacco Control Act, also approved in 1934, gave the AAA similar powers of control over tobacco growers.

reductions than could ever have been accomplished by crop controls. It was as if nature cooperated with the AAA to end for a time the problem of uncontrollable surpluses in the basic food commodities.

Whatever the cause, farmers were well on the way toward stability and parity by the end of 1935. When net farm income rose from $1,235,000,000 in 1932 to $3,090,000,000 in 1935, the results were startling indeed. For one thing, the ratio of farm prices to prices the farmer paid for manufactured goods rose from 61 per cent in 1932 to 86 per cent in 1935.[19] For another, moderate prosperity and increased governmental credit enabled farmers not only to hold their own in the battle against bankruptcy but even to turn the tide for the first time since 1920, by reducing the total farm mortgage load from $9,214,278,000 in 1930 to $7,645,091,000 in 1935.

In the long run, however, the economic results of the first AAA program were not as significant as its political implications. Acting on the assumption that a bankrupt agriculture could mean only an impoverished economy, the representatives of the urban majority in Congress converted agriculture into a subsidized industry by taxing consumers and diverting a portion of the national income to the farming minority. To be sure, the organized farmers who benefited most from the AAA program were a powerful pressure group, able almost to impose demands on the two parties. Even so, the first AAA stemmed as much from genuine progressive convictions concerning government's duty toward submerged groups as from considerations of the political advantage.

[19] 100 equals the ratio prevailing during the parity period 1909–1914.

CHAPTER 19 / THE SECOND NEW DEAL: THE CULMINATION OF AMERICAN PROGRESSIVISM

*T*HE FIRST NEW DEAL coalition of businessmen, workers, and farmers came apart at the seams in the spring and summer of 1934, as a large part of the business and industrial leadership came out in opposition to the administration's program and the masses of voters—the workers, farmers, and the unemployed—rallied more overwhelmingly to Roosevelt's support in the congressional election in the autumn of 1934 than they had done two years before. Roosevelt had neither foreseen nor desired the realignment in American politics that occurred as the nation divided roughly into a Right and a Left during the last months of 1934 and the early part of 1935. Yet the realignment occurred, and spokesmen of labor, the unemployed and destitute, and the aged were beginning campaigns to commit the federal government to new and often absurd schemes. Indeed, by January 1935 it was evident that the administration must undertake measures to allay the forces of discontent or else run serious risk of being overwhelmed by those forces.

With remarkable agility Roosevelt moved swiftly to construct a new coalition and program in order to bring the political situation under his control. Gradually discarding conservative advisers, he gathered a new retinue of rasher friends and espoused a program designed to ameliorate the misfortunes of the masses through deficit spending, redistribution of wealth, and the most far-reaching program of social and economic legislation in American history. This was the Second New Deal, the full flowering of social justice progressivism.

143 / Launching the Second New Deal

The worst phase of the depression over by 1934, the normally conservative middle and upper classes began to judge the First New Deal by conventional standards and to turn receptive ears toward its critics. Herbert Hoover, for example, had taken to the American road to warn that the whole fabric of constitutional government was being destroyed by the steady encroachment of the federal government upon the rights of the states. The developments that turned the industrial and business classes decisively against the administration, however, stemmed mainly from the NRA. On the one hand, small businessmen rebelled against codes that favored big business. On the other, when the NRA tried to bring the code authorities under control, the great industrial leaders turned sharply against the administration. Moreover, practically all manufacturers, large and small, resisted when the National Labor Board endeavored to implement Section 7a of the NIRA.

The conservative revolt took shape in August 1934, with the formation of the American Liberty League, a combination of conservative lawyers and Democratic politicians led by Alfred E. Smith and John W. Davis and allied with certain big business interests, notably the Du Pont family. Dedicated to opposing New Deal bureaucracy and capricious presidential tyranny, the Liberty League championed state rights, "free enterprise," and the "American" system of the open shop. In their zeal to turn back the tide of progressivism, Liberty League orators entered the congressional campaign of 1934 to help elect conservatives of both parties.

Roosevelt at first viewed the revolt of the business community as the opposition of a small minority. Much more disturbing to him and his political advisers was the rising tide of opposition to the First New Deal program from disgruntled reformers and demagogic leaders. The frightening thing was the fact that the New Deal had obviously failed to bring hope to sharecroppers, tenant and subsistence farmers, the unemployed, and especially indigent old people. In their desperation, these lower class elements seemed ready to follow any crack-pot with a plan.

One of the first movements on the non-Communist Left was the campaign of the muckraking novelist, Upton Sinclair, to end poverty in California. Championing a radical program of high state income and inheritance taxes and a $50 monthly pension to indigent persons over sixty,[1] Sinclair won the Democratic gubernatorial nomination in California in 1934. His End Poverty in California movement, called EPIC, soon disintegrated; but its momentary success was a signal of mass dissatisfaction.

At the same time there came out of California a more important movement. It was the so-called Townsend Plan, the creation of the generous Dr. Francis E. Townsend of Long Beach, California, who proposed that the federal government pay $200 monthly to all unemployed persons over sixty. Townsend's proposal spread like wildfire among the destitute aged; by 1935 there were thousands of Old Age Revolving Pension, or Townsend, clubs, and the good doctor claimed 5,000,000 followers.

More disquieting to the administration were the movements being promoted from 1933 to 1935 by the Reverend Charles E. Coughlin and Senator Huey Pierce Long. A Roman Catholic priest in a Detroit suburb, Coughlin fell to discussing politics and economic issues in radio sermons around 1930; soon his animadversions against bankers and the Republican leadership were more popular than his religious messages. Advocating a program of far-

---

[1] Sinclair described his program in *I, Governor of California, and How I Ended Poverty* (Los Angeles, 1933). He sold almost 1,000,000 copies and partially financed his gubernatorial campaign from the proceeds.

reaching socialization of industry and credit, Coughlin at first supported the New Deal. However, he soon fell out with Roosevelt over monetary policies and turned his National Union for Social Justice against the New Deal in 1935. At the height of his influence Coughlin claimed 9,000,000 followers— an absurdly exaggerated estimate.

A much more dangerous menace to the American democracy was Huey P. Long, the Louisiana leader. Rising out of the poverty of the piney woods section of northern Louisiana, he won a reputation in the early 1920's, not because he was a mere demagogue of the anti-Negro, anti-Catholic type, but because he addressed himself realistically to the needs of the lower classes of his state. Elected Governor of Louisiana in 1928, Long redeemed his promises to the common people. Elected to the United States Senate in 1930, he continued to dominate the government of his state as completely as if he had remained at Baton Rouge. So powerful was his hold over the lower classes that in 1934–1935 he established a dictatorship, organized a private army of storm troopers, and could declare, "I am the law." Although he and his henchmen were enormously corrupt, Long was still the idol of the common people of Louisiana when an assassin's bullet cut short his career on September 8, 1935.

Long's significance on the national scene lay in the way in which he emerged as the chief agitator of lower class protest against the First New Deal compromise. Like Coughlin, Long was an ardent Roosevelt supporter in 1932. When Roosevelt refused to nationalize the banks, expropriate wealth, and knuckle under to Long's patronage demands in 1933, however, the Louisianan turned savagely against the administration and set out to wrest control of the Democratic party from Roosevelt. Organizing the Share Our Wealth Society in 1933, Long campaigned on a platform promising to make every man a king by giving every family a homestead worth $5,000 and an annual income of $2,500, and by confiscating large fortunes to provide this bounty to the poor.[2]

During the late months of 1934 and the early part of 1935 the President launched a program frankly designed to provide larger security and incomes for the masses. One of the really significant turning points in twentieth century American politics, this sudden leftward shift occurred, not because the President "planned it that way," but in response to the developments we have just discussed. In these circumstances Roosevelt converted challenge into opportunity, first, by accepting leadership of a new progressive coalition of farmers, workers, the lower middle classes, and the unemployed that came into existence during the congressional campaign of 1934, and, second, by reconstituting his program to satisfy the basic aspirations of these various groups.

The catalyst was the election of a Congress eager to implement a com-

---

[2] A survey published by the magazine *Fortune* in July 1935 revealed the extent to which Long's attack upon the wealthy reflected widespread popular opinion. When asked whether they believed the government should allow a man who had investments worth more than $1,000,000 to keep them, "subject only to present taxes," 45.8 per cent of the persons polled replied in the negative. In the Middle West 54.6 per cent and on the Pacific Coast 54 per cent of all persons queried replied in the negative.

prehensive reform program in November 1934. As the election results were in part interpreted as an emphatic mandate for a work relief program, the prestige of Harry L. Hopkins increased enormously. "Boys—this is our hour," Hopkins told his friends in the FERA soon after the election. "We've got to get everything we want—a works program, social security, wages and hours, everything—now or never."[3]

Soon after Thanksgiving, Hopkins joined Roosevelt at Warm Springs, Georgia, and apparently won his approval for "everything." Then, in his Annual Message to Congress on January 4, 1935, the President launched the Second New Deal. Dismissing the achievements of the past two years, he declared that the mandate of the people in the recent election was clear: The time had come to fulfill a bold new social mission and to subordinate profits and wealth to the general good. This he proposed to accomplish, first, by taking the government out of the business of giving cash and market baskets; second, by putting the 3,500,000 able-bodied persons on relief rolls to work in new programs of slum clearance, rural housing, rural electrification, and expanded public works; and, third, by inaugurating a comprehensive social security program to reduce the hazards of unemployment and old age.

144 / The WPA: the Second New Deal as the American Social Conscience

Advanced progressives hailed the President's full-fledged conversion to the cause of social justice, while Congress for the most part responded eagerly to the administration's suggestions from 1935 to 1937. The outcome of this converging of reform impulses was the enactment of a program that marked the full flowering of the humanitarian-progressive movement and the construction of at least the framework of the welfare state. We can best see what the Second New Deal intended and accomplished by looking at the details of its program.

The first item—the work relief program—was authorized by Congress on April 8, 1935, with the passage of the Emergency Relief Appropriation Act, providing nearly $5,000,000,000 to finance the program for the fiscal year 1935–1936. It was launched by the President on May 6, 1935, with the establishment of the Works Progress Administration and allied agencies. Secretary of the Interior Harold L. Ickes was made head of the WPA planning division, but to Harry Hopkins went the real power. He was made WPA administrator, directed to transfer unemployables and indigent persons to local relief rolls, and authorized to begin small work projects designed to put perhaps as many as 5,000,000 jobless men and women to work.

Actually, the number of workers on WPA rolls never reached this large figure. From 1935 to 1941 the average monthly number was 2,112,000, and the peak of WPA employment was 3,238,000 in November 1938. From

[3] Robert E. Sherwood, *Roosevelt and Hopkins, An Intimate History* (New York, 1948), p. 65; used by permission of Harper & Brothers, publishers.

1935 to 1941 the WPA spent $11,365,000,000 on some 250,000 projects ranging in size from large airports to the building of stone walls on university campuses. The bulk of WPA money, 78 per cent, to be exact, went for public construction and conservation. The balance was expended for a variety of community projects which, on the theory that professional people also had to eat, enrolled musicians, actors, writers, artists, and even historians.

In addition, Hopkins and his colleagues used their broad authority in ambitious experiments that well exemplified the humanitarian impulses of the Second New Deal. The first of these new agencies of social reform was the Resettlement Administration, which the President established as an independent agency under Tugwell in the Department of Agriculture in May 1935. Officials in the RA were eager to push bold schemes involving the rehabilitation of almost a million lower class farmers and the removal of 500,000 farm families from submarginal land. Congressmen, especially Southerners, however, suspected that the RA was bent upon collectivization and kept up such a steady attack that the agency's efforts never got beyond the experimental stage.[4]

Secondly, the President established the Rural Electrification Administration on May 11, 1935, to provide loans and WPA labor for the extension of power lines into rural areas not served by private companies. In spite of opposition by the private power interests, the REA made such a successful beginning that its authority and resources were greatly expanded in 1937.

Thirdly, with the establishment of the National Youth Administration on June 26, 1935, and a doubling of appropriations for the Civilian Conservation Corps, the administration embarked upon a long-range program to benefit unemployed young people. The NYA was designed to keep high school and college students off the labor market as well as to enable them to enlarge their knowledge and skills. By 1939–1940 some 750,000 high school, college, and graduate students were earning from $5 to $30 a month as typists, laboratory and library assistants, tutors, and the like.

The passage of the Emergency Relief Appropriation Act of 1935 and the creation of the WPA and its several adjuncts soon afterward spelled the rise to dominance in administration circles of Harry Hopkins and the triumph of the social worker over the businessman. Believing that it was government's duty to provide jobs if private industry could not,[5] Hopkins regarded the WPA not as a stopgap but as a means of fulfilling society's obligations to its citizens. In the second place, Roosevelt's approval of the work relief concept committed the administration to a program of pump-priming by deficit spending on a huge scale. Although Congress increased income and estate taxes in 1935, the administration did not attempt to redis-

---

[4] During its two years of independent existence, the RA purchased 5,000,000 acres of submarginal land and resettled 4,441 families on farms and in thirty-one homestead communities. In addition, it built three so-called Greenbelt towns, experiments in planned suburban communities for low-income city workers, near Washington, Cincinnati, and Milwaukee.

[5] Contemporary surveys of public opinion indicated that an overwhelming majority of Americans at the time shared Hopkins' conviction. In a *Fortune* poll, published in July 1935, for example, 76.8 per cent of all persons queried agreed that "the government should see to it that every man who wants to work has a job." Even 46.6 per cent of the prosperous and 69 per cent of the upper middle class persons replied in the affirmative.

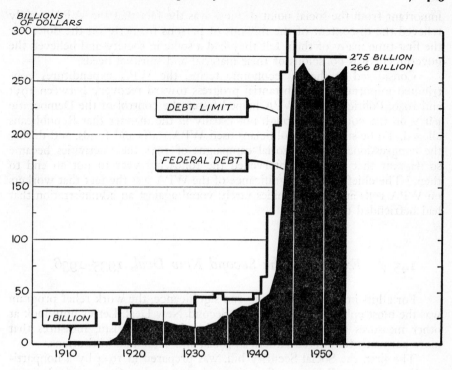

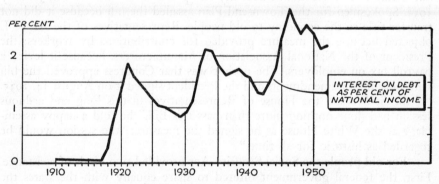

18. *The Growth of the National Debt, 1910–1953*

tribute the national income through drastic tax increases but financed the WPA program mainly through borrowing.[6]

The WPA's accomplishments, however, were substantial and to progressives far outweighed the costs. By rehabilitating millions of persons, it helped build a reservoir of trained manpower just before the time when the United States needed every skilled hand in a struggle for survival. Most

[6] During 1931 and 1932 the Hoover administration operated at a total deficit of $3,844,010,531; from 1933 through 1940 the Roosevelt administration accumulated a total deficit of $25,279,670,735. The gross national debt increased from $18,170,000,000 in 1929 to $23,350,000,000 in 1932 and to $52,848,000,000 in 1940.

important from the social point of view was the fact that the WPA greatly relieved the discontent of the millions of persons formerly on the dole. For the first time many of them felt they had a stake in society and believed the government was conscious of their material and spiritual needs.

Considered in sheerly economic terms, the WPA expenditures contributed importantly to substantial progress toward recovery between 1935 and 1940. Politically, the WPA helped fasten the control of the Democratic party on the country, although not usually in the manner that Republicans alleged. To be sure, local politicians used WPA staffs and funds, and during the congressional and senatorial campaigns of 1938 their activities became so flagrant that Congress intervened the following year to put an end to them.[7] The chief political significance of the WPA was the fact that workers on WPA rolls and their families rarely voted against an administration that had befriended them.

145 / *Expanding the Second New Deal, 1935–1936*

For all its immediate and long-run significance, the work relief program was the most ephemeral phase of the Second New Deal. Let us now look at other measures adopted at the high tide of progressivism, measures that more permanently altered American social and economic institutions.

The first, the Social Security bill, was prepared in 1934 by a nonpartisan Committee on Economic Security and presented to Congress in January 1935. Spokesmen for the Townsend Plan assailed the bill because it did not transfer title to the economy to old people. Representatives of the AF of L objected because the measure provided for contributions by workers; the President of the National Association of Manufacturers, because it levied a payroll tax on employers. The upshot was that Congress approved the bill with only minor amendments and the President signed it on August 14, 1935. "If the Senate and the House of Representatives in this long and arduous session had done nothing more than pass this Bill," he told a happy assemblage at the White House as he signed the measure, "the session would be regarded as historic for all time."

For old people the Social Security Act provided two kinds of assistance. First, the federal government offered to share equally with the states the burden of caring for persons over sixty-five who would have no opportunity to participate in the new old-age insurance program.[8] Second, the Act established a nation-wide system of old-age insurance, participation in which was compulsory except for public servants, domestic servants, farm and casual workers, merchant seamen, and employees of educational, religious, and

---

[7] With the passage of the Hatch Act, forbidding federal office-holders below the policy-making level from participating actively in political campaigns or soliciting or accepting contributions from WPA workers.

[8] The federal contribution was limited to $15 monthly per person but was increased to $20 in 1939. By 1940 some 2,000,000 persons were receiving assistance under this provision, and combined federal and state payments averaged $20 a month per person.

philanthropic institutions.[9] Benefit payments ranging from $10 to $85 a month would begin in 1942.

The Social Security Act nominally left the establishment of unemployment insurance systems to the states but gave the state governments no alternative but to cooperate. It levied an unemployment tax on employers beginning at 1 per cent of all payrolls in 1936 and rising to a permanent level of 3 per cent after 1937. However, employers might pay 90 per cent of the tax to approved state unemployment compensation commissions; and most of the balance paid directly into the federal Treasury would be returned to the states to finance the administration of their systems. On the other hand, states that failed to establish unemployment compensation systems would lose all the taxes paid by employers within their jurisdiction. Needless to say, within two years all the states had complied and provided a schedule of benefits that met minimum federal standards and afforded protection for some 28,000,000 workers.[10]

Nor was this all that the measure accomplished. It also provided for federal aid, on a matching basis, to the states for the care of the crippled, the blind, and dependent mothers and children and for public health services. Finally, it established a nonpartisan Social Security Board to administer the entire system.

Roosevelt and the authors of the Social Security Act knew that the measure was experimental and inadequate; but they were also confident the system would expand with the passage of time.[11] To the end of his life the President regarded Social Security as the New Deal's "supreme achievement." And who could gainsay him? Between 1935 and 1940, when the system was launched and strengthened, the administration and Congress effected a lasting revolution in American public policy. Discarding ingrained traditions of self-help and individual responsibility, they set the United States upon the high road leading to the welfare state.

During the early months of 1935 the question of new labor legislation also arose; but there was no such unanimity of administration and congressional opinion regarding wise labor policy as prevailed during the writing

[9] Employees and employers were required to pay at the rate of 1 per cent each on all wages under $3,000 a year from 1937 through 1939, at the rate of 1½ per cent each from 1940 through 1942, 2 per cent each from 1943 through 1945, 2½ per cent each from 1946 through 1948, and at the rate of 3 per cent each after 1948. The measure contemplated the accumulation of a reserve fund invested in government bonds, which would total some $47,000,000,000 by 1980 and make the system self-sustaining.

[10] Unemployment benefits varied in different states and sections. Maximum weekly payments ran from $15–$18 a week, while duration of payments ranged from twelve to twenty-six weeks in any single year.

[11] This, of course, is what did occur. In response to widespread criticisms, congressional leaders and the Social Security Board in 1937 undertook a study looking toward revision of the Social Security Act. The upshot was that Congress in 1939 completely overhauled the old-age retirement program by (1) extending the Act's coverage to include 1,600,000 additional workers, (2) advancing the date of the beginning of retirement benefits from 1942 to 1940, (3) increasing monthly payments to persons who had been insured for a short time, (4) providing benefits for wives and dependent children of retired workers and survivors' benefits for widows and dependent children when insured workers died before reaching sixty-five, and (5) continuing the old-age payroll tax of 1 per cent each on workers and employers until 1943.

of the Social Security bill. Senator Robert F. Wagner was working hard in Congress for passage of his labor disputes bill to give unions federal protection, but the President opposed the measure, saying that he preferred to obtain protection for labor through renewal of the NIRA.

Under administration pressure, the Senate voted to renew the NIRA and then, on May 16, 1935, approved the Wagner bill. Less than two weeks later the Supreme Court declared the code system of the NIRA unconstitutional; in response, the President at once reversed himself on the Wagner bill, persuaded House leaders to bring it to the floor, and signed the measure on July 5 after the House had speedily approved it.

What was this legislation that Roosevelt belatedly supported but soon made the cornerstone of his labor program? The Wagner, or National Labor Relations, Act reaffirmed the principles set forth in the now defunct Section 7a. But where Section 7a had been vague and weak, the Wagner Act was specific and strong. By making virtually impossible the organization of company unions and outlawing so-called "unfair practices,"[12] the measure deprived employers of their most formidable antiunion weapons. By establishing a nonpartisan National Labor Relations Board empowered to issue cease and desist orders and compel obedience from employers, the Act provided machinery for its own enforcement. Finally, by setting forth the explicit conditions under which unions should be entitled to recognition,[13] the Wagner Act threw the power of the federal government behind a union seeking to compel an employer to bargain in good faith.

Assuming that a strong labor movement was the surest safeguard of democracy in an industrial society and the best counterbalance to big business, Congress brought the power of the federal government to bear in the industrial struggle in order to redress the balance between the two opposing forces. Coming at a time when the advance guard of the AF of L were making plans to organize the basic industries, the Wagner Act and the NLRB straightway became the charter of liberty and shield of the American labor movement.[14]

Work relief, Social Security, and legislation to underwrite the labor movement were only the beginning of a new program designed to increase and strengthen public control over business and industry and to benefit the masses of people. The fact that the Supreme Court invalidated the NIRA just at the moment when the President and his advisers were formulating these new measures meant they could decide what features of the NRA experiment were worth salvaging.

Wisely refusing to press for enactment of a revised National Recovery bill, the President none the less saved several important components of the NRA program. We have seen how he abruptly espoused the Wagner Act in order to re-enact and reinforce Section 7a. In February 1935, after the Supreme Court had invalidated Section 9c of the NIRA, which established

[12] For example, interference with employees in the exercise of their guaranteed rights, discharge or blacklisting of employees for union activities, and discrimination against employees who brought charges against the company.

[13] A union was entitled to recognition by the employer as the sole bargaining agent when it won—usually in a secret election conducted by the NLRB—majority support among workers in an industry, company, shop, or craft.

[14] See below, pp. 428–432.

special controls for the oil industry, the President approved the Connally Act prohibiting the shipment in interstate commerce of oil produced in violation of interstate compacts. By the passage of the Guffey-Snyder Coal Conservation Act in August 1935, the administration salvaged the bituminous coal code and re-established the NRA coal code authority in a different form.[15] Another measure, the Alcohol Control Act of August 29, 1935, re-enacted the provisions of the NRA liquor code and vested enforcement in the Treasury Department. Refusing to approve a general wages and hours bill on the ground that such a measure was probably unconstitutional, Roosevelt instead supported and signed the Walsh-Healey Act on August 30, 1936. It attempted indirectly to establish fair labor standards for manufacturing and the construction industry.[16] To preserve the sections of the NRA codes that prohibited destructive competition, in 1936 and 1937 Congress enacted the Robinson-Patman Act, which outlawed differential pricing of commodities, and the Miller-Tydings Act, which legalized the setting of "fair trade" prices by manufacturers, below which a retailer could not sell.

To these measures for the public control of industry and business were added other more important substantive reforms during 1935 and 1936. We have seen how the Banking Act of 1935 established strong federal control over the Federal Reserve System and how the President obtained destruction of the public utility giants and strict federal control of the smaller holding companies.

In addition came a rash of measures from 1935 to 1940 that strengthened and extended the federal regulatory authority in many fields: the Federal Power Act of 1935, which enlarged the jurisdiction and rate-making authority of the Federal Power Commission; the Motor Carrier Act of 1935 and the Transportation Act of 1940, which brought trucking concerns and domestic water carriers under the regulation of the ICC; the Merchant Marine Act of 1936, which created a new Maritime Commission and authorized it to help create an American merchant marine; and the Civil Aeronautics Act of 1938, which established a Civil Aeronautics Authority, later called the Civil Aeronautics Board, to subject the operations and services of airlines to public control.

These were all measures of reform and regulation, to be sure; but they were not partisan in character and except for the Holding Company Act excited little opposition. More indicative of the Second New Deal's social

[15] This measure established a National Bituminous Coal Commission composed of representatives of management, labor, and the public and empowered to control production and prices of the raw material. The Act, moreover, guaranteed collective bargaining in the coal industry and stipulated that when wages and hours agreements were signed by the miners' union and producers of two-thirds of the national tonnage, such agreements should go into effect in the entire industry. In 1936 the Supreme Court declared the Guffey-Snyder Act unconstitutional, on the grounds that the labor provisions conferred legislative authority on the Coal Commission and that a tax levied by the Act on noncooperating producers resulted in an unconstitutional regulation of an industry that was not interstate in character. Omitting the provisions to which the Court had objected, Congress re-enacted the Guffey-Snyder Act in April 1937.

[16] The Walsh-Healey Act required the inclusion in all federal contracts involving the expenditure of $10,000 or more of provisions limiting hours to eight a day and forty a week, prohibiting child labor, and empowering the Secretary of Labor to set minimum wages.

and economic purposes was Roosevelt's campaign in 1935 to democratize the federal tax structure. In reply to his critics on the Left, on June 19, 1935, Roosevelt called upon Congress to check the growing concentration of economic power, reduce "social unrest and a deepening sense of unfairness," and encourage the wider distribution of wealth by increasing the tax burden on the upper classes and the large corporations. With astonishing alacrity Congress wrote most of the President's suggestions into the wealth tax bill, or the Revenue Act of 1935, and Roosevelt signed it on August 30. The measure left the normal income tax unchanged but increased the surtax to the highest rates in American history,[17] increased the federal estate tax to a maximum of 70 per cent, and provided for a graduated income tax on net corporation income.[18] Leaders of the business community denounced the Revenue Act of 1935 as a sophisticated version of the Share Our Wealth plan, but Roosevelt was undaunted.

146 / The Election of 1936

Republican leaders must have surveyed the political scene during the early months of 1936 with considerable dismay. Not since Andrew Jackson's day had the Democratic party been so firmly entrenched and so popular with the masses. Probably never before had there been such a dearth of able leadership in the GOP. There was Hoover, still revered by his friends; but all Republicans knew he would be a millstone around the party's neck if he were nominated. There was Senator William E. Borah of Idaho, a quadrennial candidate since 1912; but Borah was too old and erratic to suit the powers that controlled his party. There was Senator Arthur H. Vandenberg of Michigan, who had miraculously survived the Democratic landslide of 1934; but Vandenberg was not anxious to challenge the occupant of the White House. Finally, there was Governor Alfred M. Landon of Kansas, who had also survived the Democratic landslide of 1934 and had the support of William Randolph Hearst and his chain of newspapers.

When the Republican delegates assembled in Cleveland on June 9, 1936, they applauded Hoover's strictures against the New Deal without any thought of nominating him. Instead, they nominated Landon on the first ballot on June 11 and afterward named Frank Knox, publisher of the *Chicago Daily News*, as his running-mate. Their platform denounced the New Deal in the generalities of campaign oratory. But the Republican platform did not threaten to repeal the New Deal legislation, except to revise the corporation tax structure and the Reciprocal Trade Act, which empowered the President to make tariff agreements. On the contrary, by promising to provide better relief, farm subsidy, and labor programs the Republicans reaffirmed their own strong progressive tradition.

---

[17] The Revenue Act of 1935 increased the surtaxes only on net incomes over $50,000, rising in a graduated scale from a surtax of 31 per cent on net incomes over $50,000 to 75 per cent on incomes over $5,000,000.

[18] The Revenue Act of 1934 had levied a flat tax of 13¾ per cent on the net incomes of all corporations, large and small. The Act of 1935, on the other hand, levied a graduated tax of from 12½ to 15 per cent, depending on the size of the net corporation income.

The Democrats met in Philadelphia on June 23, 1936, in a convention that was riotous and triumphant. So prevalent was the good feeling that Roosevelt and Garner were nominated by a mighty shout on the first ballot and the southern Democrats, in a moment of exhilaration or perhaps intoxication, even agreed to abrogate the historic party rule that required a two-thirds majority for a presidential nomination.

The Democratic platform was a frank reiteration of the social ideals of the Second New Deal and a recital, with emphatic endorsement, of the good works of the Roosevelt administration. Declaring that "government in a modern civilization has certain inescapable obligations to its citizens," the platform promised enlargement of rural electrification and the farm program, public housing, additional legislation to protect workers, and vigorous enforcement of the antitrust laws against big business. The foreign policy planks, like those of the Republican platform, reflected the then dominant isolationist temper and the popular determination to avoid, as the Democrats said, "being drawn, by political commitments, international banking, or private trading, into any war which may develop anywhere."

Both candidates conducted dignified and strenuous campaigns. Landon spoke forcefully and made it clear he approved the basic features of the New Deal program; but he did not fire the public imagination or inspire popular confidence. On the other hand, Roosevelt was at his magnificent best as a campaigner and phrase-maker in this battle. His acceptance speech was a declaration of war against the "economic royalists," who had supposedly regimented and enslaved the people in an "industrial dictatorship," and a new call for dedication to the cause of democracy. "This generation of Americans," he concluded, "has a rendezvous with destiny. . . . We are fighting to save a great and precious form of government for ourselves and for the world." Taking nothing for granted, the President stumped the country as if his election were in doubt; and through all his speeches ran the strong themes of social and economic democracy. Frankly acknowledging that he had the support of the workers, farmers, young people, and the unemployed, he promised to continue the fight against "business and financial monopoly, speculation, reckless banking, class antagonism, sectionalism, war profiteering."

Two developments of the campaign were significant because they indicated long-range realignments. One was the development of a vigorous political consciousness among organized labor and the participation of the major unions in an all-out effort to return the Democrats to power. The leaders in labor's first important political crusade since 1924 were George L. Berry of the AF of L and John L. Lewis and Sidney Hillman, two spokesmen of the newly-formed CIO. They organized Labor's Non-Partisan League in April 1936, raised some $1,000,000, half of which came from Lewis' United Mine Workers, and turned their unions into momentary political machines. The second significant development in 1936 was the shift of a majority of Negro leaders and newspapers in the northern and mid-western states from the GOP to the Democracy. In 1936, for the first time in American history, a majority of Negro voters supported a Democratic candidate.

In spite of the fact that more than two-thirds of the metropolitan newspapers supported Landon, and the *Literary Digest* poll indicated the Republicans would win by a comfortable margin, it was obvious by mid-October that the Republican nominee simply did not have a chance. Even so, most observers were startled by the magnitude of the Democratic victory on November 3. Landon won 16,679,583 popular votes and carried only Vermont and Maine for a total of eight electoral votes. Representative William Lemke, radical farm leader from North Dakota, running on a Union party ticket supported by Dr. Townsend, Father Coughlin, and Huey Long's successor, the Reverend Gerald L. K. Smith, polled nearly 900,000 votes; the Socialist Norman Thomas and the Communist Earl Browder trailed far behind. In contrast, Roosevelt won 27,476,673 popular and 523 electoral votes and carried huge Democratic majorities with him in the greatest sweep since 1920. The verdict of the people was unmistakable: it was an emphatic mandate for the continuation of the program already well begun by the Second New Deal.

147 / *The Supreme Court Controversy*

Although during the presidential campaign of 1936 high Democratic spokesmen uttered veiled threats against the Supreme Court for overturning New Deal measures, the President gave no indication that he intended to bring the Court before the bar of public opinion. Nor was there any strong hint of an impending attack in Roosevelt's Annual Message of January 6, 1937, or in his second inaugural, delivered on January 20. Yet on February 5, 1937, he presented to Congress a plan for judicial reorganization, the purpose of which was nothing less than to bring the Supreme Court under popular control. Did he act out of sheer caprice or spite? Did he harbor dictatorial ambitions, as many of his opponents charged? We cannot understand Roosevelt's motive and purpose unless we understand also the gravity of the constitutional crisis that compelled him to take this dangerous step.

As one authority has put it, by the early months of 1937 "five willful Supreme Court Justices . . . had in fact contrived well-nigh complete absence of the power to govern."[19] In short, the Court's majority had nearly paralyzed the excutive and legislative branches. The responsibility for the situation lay primarily with the Court, not with the President or with Congress. Four of the justices—James C. McReynolds, George Sutherland, Willis Van Devanter, and Pierce Butler—were reactionaries who lived in a nineteenth century world of social Darwinism and liberty of contract. So consistently hostile were they to advanced progressive legislation that they were popularly called the "Four Horsemen." Somewhere between the reactionaries and the progressives stood the Chief Justice, Charles Evans Hughes, and Owen J. Roberts, who often voted with the "Four Horsemen." In a small minority were the three progressive justices, Louis D. Brandeis, Benjamin N. Cardozo, and Harlan F. Stone.

Before 1935 a majority of the Court seemed capable of recognizing an emergency when they saw one, but in January 1935, the process of judicial

[19] A. T. Mason, "Charles Evans Hughes: An Appeal to the Bar of History," *Vanderbilt Law Review*, VI (December 1952), 10.

nullification began. On January 7, in the so-called hot oil cases,[20] the Court invalidated Section 9c of the NIRA on the ground that it unconstitutionally conferred legislative authority upon the President in the regulation of the petroleum industry. More alarming to the administration was the Court's decision,[21] rendered on May 6 in a five to four verdict, which nullified the Railroad Retirement Act of 1934 on the grounds, first, that the government had deprived railway companies of property without due process of law by compelling them to contribute to pensions for their employees and, second, that Congress' control over interstate commerce did not warrant such interference in labor relations. If this were true, the Social Security bill then pending was also unconstitutional.

These two reversals of New Deal legislation were a prelude to "Black Monday," May 27, 1935, when the Court invalidated the Frazier-Lemke Farm Mortgage Act and the NIRA and also read a bit of constitutional law to the President himself. In Louisville Joint Stock Land Bank *v.* Radford, the Court declared that the Frazier-Lemke Act deprived creditors of property without due process of law. In Humphrey's Executor *v.* United States, the Court reprimanded the President for removing William E. Humphrey, a reactionary Republican, from the Federal Trade Commission and laid down a new constitutional rule of considerable importance.[22] The Court's most fateful decision on "Black Monday," however, was rendered in A. L. A. Schechter Corporation *v.* United States, in which all the justices agreed that the NIRA was unconstitutional, on the grounds that the statute conferred essential legislative authority on the President and that the corporation involved in the case was engaged only in intrastate commerce.

Stunned by the Schechter decision, the President, in a press conference on May 31, went to the root of the issue now before the country. He pointed out that the Court's objection to a plenary grant of legislative power to the Executive could be easily overcome. The danger, he added, lay in the Court's narrow view of interstate commerce as consisting only of goods in transit.[23] How could the federal government seek to remedy any national economic problem if this "horse and buggy" definition of interstate commerce prevailed?

After a period of anxious waiting, the Court answered the President's query by a series of epochal decisions that confirmed the Schechter doctrine. Speaking for himself, Hughes, and the "Four Horsemen" in the case of United States *v.* Butler on January 6, 1936, Justice Roberts held that the Agricultural Adjustment Act was unconstitutional. It was a strained decision, but its meaning was clear: the production of agricultural commodities was not interstate commerce, and Congress could not use the taxing power to regulate agriculture. Then, on May 18, 1936, came an even firmer reaffirmation of the Schechter doctrine, when Justice Sutherland, in Carter *v.* Carter Coal Company, invalidated the Guffey-Snyder Coal Conservation Act.

[20] Panama Refining Co. *v.* Ryan and Amazon Petroleum Corporation *v.* Ryan.

[21] Railroad Retirement Board *v.* Alton Railroad.

[22] Namely, that the independent regulatory commissions were arms of Congress, not of the Executive, and that the President could not remove their members except as Congress had stipulated.

[23] For this obsolete definition of interstate commerce Chief Justice Hughes had gone back to the notorious Knight decision of 1895.

Obviously, Sutherland asserted, the mining of coal was not interstate commerce. Congress, therefore, could not use the taxing power to regulate an industry over which it had no constitutional control. Having thus denied the federal government jurisdiction over manufacturing, mining, agriculture, and labor conditions, the conservative majority on June 1, 1936, went all the way and denied to the states the right to regulate hours and wages. This decision, rendered by Justice Butler in Morehead v. New York ex rel. Tipaldo, nullified a New York State minimum wage law for women and children by resurrecting the doctrine enunciated in Adkins v. Children's Hospital in 1923.[24]

By the summer of 1936, therefore, the country found itself in an intolerable constitutional situation. The Supreme Court had overturned several important New Deal measures; it seemed certain the justices would soon invalidate the Social Security and Wagner Acts; and the President and Congress knew they proceeded with further reform legislation only at the risk of additional judicial reprimands. Nor was this all. Staffed by conservatives who were as eager as their judicial superiors to prevent the extension of the public authority, the inferior federal courts were also engaging in a campaign of judicial nullification. Before 1937 they issued no less than 1,600 injunctions against federal administrative officials and for intermittent periods paralyzed such important agencies as the NLRB and the SEC.

After the people gave him their emphatic mandate on November 3, 1936, the President must have decided the reckoning could no longer be postponed. On February 5, 1937, therefore, he submitted to Congress a Judiciary Reorganization bill that empowered him to appoint a new federal judge whenever an incumbent failed to retire within six months after reaching the age of seventy. The number of additional judges would be limited to fifty, and not more than six of them could be named to the Supreme Court. In an accompanying message, Roosevelt explained why he desired to enlarge the federal courts. He pointed to the crowded dockets and delay in judicial business caused by insufficient and infirm personnel; described the confusion created by the hundreds of injunctions issued by inferior courts; and frankly asserted that the courts needed new blood and a modern outlook.

Assuming he could control the huge Democratic majorities in both houses, Roosevelt must have been stunned by the violent controversy that his measure provoked. Republicans and spokesmen for the Liberty League charged that the President wanted to destroy the Constitution and establish a personal dictatorship; the Chief Justice himself entered the fray, by addressing a public letter on March 21 to a Senate leader denying Roosevelt's allegation that the Supreme Court was behind in its work. Roosevelt must have expected and discounted this opposition, but he did not expect the enormous opposition that developed within his own party. In the Senate conservative Democrats like Carter Glass of Virginia and Walter F. George of Georgia joined progressives like Burton K. Wheeler of Montana in open rebellion.

For this nearly catastrophic rupture, Roosevelt was in large measure responsible, because he had not taken Democratic leaders into his confidence

[24] In this decision the Court had ruled that minimum wage laws violated the freedom of contract guaranteed by the Fourteenth Amendment.

before submitting the Judiciary Reorganization bill, and because he allowed Postmaster General Farley to use the patronage stick too bluntly after the controversy had begun. In any event, for the first time Roosevelt lost control of Congress; and when his chief spokesman in the Senate, Joseph T. Robinson of Arkansas, died at the height of the struggle on July 14, 1937, the President informed the new Senate Majority Leader, Alben W. Barkley of Kentucky, that he would accept a compromise to which all Democrats could agree.

It was not congressional opposition and Robinson's death alone, however, that caused Roosevelt and his friends to abandon the fight. The decisive factor was an extraordinary and sudden change in the opinions of the Supreme Court that occurred while the Court controversy raged and overnight transformed the supreme tribunal into a propounder of progressive legal doctrine. We may never know conclusively why this change occurred. Available evidence indicates that Chief Justice Hughes persuaded Justice Roberts to stand with the progressives in validating several important reform statutes then being tested. Only by such strategy, Hughes might have urged, could the Court save itself from reorganization and debasement at the hands of the Executive.

Whether this conjecture is correct, we cannot say; in any event, during the Court fight Hughes and Roberts acted more like high political strategists than consistent interpreters of the Constitution. On March 29, 1937, in the case of West Coast Hotel *v.* Parrish, the Court rendered judgment on a minimum wage statute of the State of Washington. A year before, Roberts had joined the "Four Horsemen" to invalidate a similar New York law. Now Roberts joined Hughes and the progressives to approve the Washington statute in sweeping language that left room for almost any reasonable form of state wages and hours legislation.

The crowning irony came on April 12, 1937, when the new progressive coalition upheld the National Labor Relations Act. Here the issue was essentially the same as the issues in the Schechter, Butler, and Carter Coal Company cases: Did the power of Congress to control interstate commerce include the power to control the actual production of commodities? Speaking for the majority, in National Labor Relations Board *v.* Jones and Laughlin Steel Corporation and several other cases, the Chief Justice in effect reversed the earlier decisions without openly admitting that any change in interpretation had occurred. Congress' control over interstate commerce was absolute and included the power to encourage and protect such commerce, Hughes declared. Because the peaceful movement of goods was essential to the life of the nation, he concluded, Congress might even prescribe the labor relations prevailing at the factories in which the goods were manufactured. Finally, on May 24, 1937, the Court approved the Social Security Act in three decisions[25] by Justices Stone and Cardozo that upheld the compulsory features of the unemployment and old-age retirement systems.

Thus the President had lost the proverbial battle and won the war by the time he abandoned the Judiciary Reorganization bill in mid-July 1937. Moreover, Justice Van Devanter, an implacable foe of New Deal legislation, retired on June 1, thus allowing Roosevelt to buttress the new progressive

---

[25] Carmichael *v.* Southern Coal Company, Charles C. Steward Machine Company *v.* Davis, and Helvering *v.* Davis.

majority on the supreme bench.[26] Now that the constitutional crisis was resolved in favor of broad interpretation, the advocates of compromise, Vice President Garner and Majority Leader Barkley, came forward with a new Judiciary bill that denied the President power to enlarge the courts but conceded badly needed procedural reforms. The Judicial Procedure Reform Act, which Roosevelt signed on August 26, 1937, empowered the Attorney General to participate in cases involving the constitutionality of federal statutes when they were first tried before district courts; made provision for moving such cases, when they went against the government, from district courts directly to the Supreme Court; and severely circumscribed the right of federal judges to stay the application of federal laws.

148 / Additions to the New Deal: 1937

Meanwhile, following the election of 1936 the President reaffirmed his determination to broaden and complete the reform structure of the Second New Deal. His Annual Message of January 6, 1937, and his second inaugural address of January 20 were clarion calls to Congress for aid to the millions of people in city and country on low incomes, the "one-third of a nation ill-housed, ill-clad, ill-nourished," over whom disaster hung like a pall. "The test of our progress," he declared in his inaugural, "is not whether we add more to the abundance of those who have much; it is whether we provide enough for those who have too little."

During the early months of 1937 Roosevelt presented his new program cautiously and in response to changing circumstances. Thus in his Annual Message of January 6 he merely asked Congress to consider measures for public housing, aid to tenant farmers, and broader social security coverage. On January 12 he submitted a plan for the reorganization of the Executive Department that had been drawn up by a committee of distinguished political scientists. On February 5 he added his plan for judiciary reorganization. This was as far as he could go until the constitutional crisis had been resolved; but after the Supreme Court executed its reversal in March and April 1937, Roosevelt moved quickly to round out his program. On May 24 he urged Congress to "extend the frontiers of social progress" by enacting legislation establishing minimum wages and maximum hours in American industry; and on July 12 he asked Congress to re-establish the AAA program.[27]

[26] Congress had enacted a Supreme Court Retirement Act, approved March 1, 1937, which permitted the justices to retire at full pay after reaching the age of seventy.

[27] After the Supreme Court's invalidation of the Agricultural Adjustment Act on January 6, 1936, Congress the following month adopted the Soil Conservation and Domestic Allotment Act, a hastily drawn and unsatisfactory substitute. Instead of using the outlawed processing tax to raise money to finance crop control, Congress simply appropriated $500,000,000 to be paid to farmers who diverted a part of their land from staple to soil-building crops.

The nation had been profoundly alarmed by the spectacle of millions of tons of topsoil being blown away in the parched Plains states, the great "Dust Bowl"; and the epic documentary film, "The Plow That Broke the Plains," had further dramatized the urgent need of saving American soil resources. Thus the conservation program of 1936 evoked widespread popular approval and support by the farmers, two-thirds of whom signed contracts with the Department of Agriculture. As a means of crop control, however, the Soil Conservation Act was woefully inadequate because under its provisions

This, then, was the administration's program to complete the Second New Deal. Unfortunately for the President, the Judiciary Reorganization bill consumed much of Congress' energies during the spring and early summer of 1937, disrupted the party's ranks, and gave conservative Democrats in both houses an excuse for defying the President's leadership on other questions. Combining with the Republican minority, these conservatives defeated the Executive Reorganization bill by charging it was a twin of the Judiciary Reorganization bill and another step toward presidential dictatorship.[28] The Senate approved the administration's wages and hours, or Fair Labor Standards, bill on July 31, 1937, but conservative Democrats and Republicans on the House rules committee combined to prevent the House from voting on the measure. And the President's proposal for a new agricultural act received scarcely any attention from the lawmakers.

Even so, the first session of the Seventy-Fifth Congress that sat from January to September 1937 left a memorable record of achievement: the Judicial Procedure Reform Act; the Guffey-Vinson Bituminous Coal Act, which re-enacted most of the provisions of the Guffey-Snyder Act; and, most important, the Bankhead-Jones Farm Tenancy Act and the Wagner-Steagall National Housing Act. As the last two measures were landmarks in the development of federal policy, let us look at them in some detail.

The Bankhead-Jones Farm Tenancy Act was the outgrowth of the investigations of the President's Committee on Farm Tenancy, which issued its report in February 1937. It revealed that more than half the farmers in the South, nearly a third in the North, and one-fourth in the West were sharecroppers or tenants; highlighted the poverty and misery of this important segment of the farm population; and took serious notice of a new group of the rural destitute—the hundreds of thousands of migratory farm workers and displaced cotton sharecroppers from the Southwest, the "Oakies," who were moving *en masse* to California in search of jobs.

To turn back the tide of tenancy the Committee suggested a remedy in keeping with the spirit of the Second New Deal. It proposed that the Resettlement Administration be reorganized as the Farm Security Administration, with authority to lend money to enable enterprising tenants to become landowners, refinance and rehabilitate small farmers who were in danger of losing their lands, promote withdrawal of submarginal land, and extend assistance to migratory workers. With the support of southern Democrats keenly responsive to the needs of small farmers and white tenants, the Bankhead-Jones Act, embodying the Committee's recommendations, became law on July 22, 1937.

---

the Agriculture Department had no power to compel cooperation by the recalcitrant minority. As the year 1936 was a time of severe drought in the corn and wheat belts, there were no grain surpluses in that area. As we will see, the return of good weather and apparent prosperity in 1937 stimulated the planting and production of huge cotton, wheat, corn, and tobacco crops and demonstrated the need for new and more effective controls.

[28] The Senate passed a revised reorganization bill in 1938 but conservatives in the House, led by the reactionary chairman of the rules committee, John J. O'Connor of New York, defeated it. Finally, in 1939 both houses approved a new administration Reorganization Act that deprived the President of power to reorganize the independent regulatory agencies but permitted him to appoint six administrative assistants and to reorganize and consolidate a number of lesser agencies.

From 1937 until the end of the Second World War,[29] the FSA was the social conscience of the Second New Deal in action on the rural front. It established some thirty camps that accommodated from 12,000 to 15,000 migratory farm workers and their families, helped farmers scale their debts, organized rural medical and dental care groups, sponsored cooperative leasing of land and purchase of machinery by tenants and small farmers, and carried on the homestead projects begun by the RA. By the middle of June 1944, moreover, the FSA had lent over $800,000,000 in short-term rehabilitation loans to 870,000 farm families. Finally, between 1937 and 1946 the FSA lent nearly $260,000,000 to 41,000 families—on a forty-year basis at 3 per cent interest—for the purchase of farms.

The Wagner-Steagall National Housing Act, approved September 1, 1937, represented the culmination of several years of planning and investigation by various agencies of the government. Large-scale public housing was one objective of the PWA from 1933 to 1937; and despite Secretary Ickes' caution, by 1937 the PWA Housing Division had constructed fifty-one public projects in thirty-six cities that provided new homes for 21,700 families. The housing program launched by the Wagner-Steagall Act of 1937, on the other hand, reflected the administration's determination to meet the housing problem comprehensively and not as part of a public works and recovery program. This measure established the United States Housing Authority in the Interior Department, with a capital of $1,000,000 and authority to borrow up to $500,000,000, increased to a total of $1,600,000,000 in 1940.

Instead of erecting apartment buildings and other units, as the PWA had done, the USHA worked through public housing agencies in all important cities—by lending up to 100 per cent of the costs of housing projects on a long-term basis, making annual subsidies to local agencies, and establishing standards of cost, construction, and eligibility of tenants.[30] All told, before 1941, when the USHA turned to the task of providing housing for defense workers, the agency had lent over $750,000,000 to local housing authorities for the construction of 511 projects with a total of 161,162 units. Obviously, it was only the beginning of what must be a long campaign to destroy slums and provide adequate housing for America's urban poor. Progressives and humanitarians, who did not expect the millennium to come overnight, were encouraged by the fact that so large a beginning had been made.

149 / *Recovery, Recession, and the Last Surge of Reform, 1937–1938*

From 1933 to 1936 health began to return to the ailing American economy, but the wounds of the depression were so deep that recovery was at

[29] In August 1946 Congress created a new Farmers' Home Administration and transferred to it the functions of the FSA.

[30] Residents of public housing projects, for example, had to be from among the lowest third of the income receivers. The average income of all families living in USHA projects on December 31, 1941, was $837 a year; the average rental of all USHA units was $12.64 a month.

best slow. National income rose from nearly $40,000,000,000 in 1932 to $42,489,000,000 in 1933, to $50,346,000,000 in 1934, and to $55,808,000,000 in 1936. The indices of production, employment, and payrolls in manufacturing[31] rose from 56, 62.3, and 38.3, respectively, in March 1933 to 104, 94.2, and 80.5, respectively, in December 1935. These statistics gave evidence of an unmistakable upward trend. Even so, the basic cogs of the economic machinery were still running at a feeble pace by 1936.

For a number of reasons—among them the removal of NRA restrictions on production, increased farm income as a result of the AAA program and the drought, and especially the impact of enormous federal expenditures for work relief beginning in the spring of 1935 and payment of the bonus in 1936—all the indices of economic activity began to rise sharply in the spring of 1936. From May 1936 to September 1937 the index of employment rose from 96.4 to 112.2—higher than the peak figure in 1929—while the payroll index increased from 84 to 109 and the index of industrial production rose from 101 to 117 during the same period.

Although the recovery from 1935 to the autumn of 1937 was accompanied by a speculative upsurge on the stock markets, the upswing was essentially sound[32] because based upon increased investment and production and larger purchasing power through higher wages and public spending. Instead of welcoming the return of prosperity and making certain the volume of credit was equal to business needs, however, the administration acted as if it feared prosperity. Assuming that another runaway boom was in the making, the Board of Governors of the Federal Reserve System increased the reserve requirements of member banks by 50 per cent early in 1937 and the Federal Reserve Banks bought government bonds on a large scale to prevent monetary and bank credit inflation. Moreover, the President made plans to cut drastically the work relief program, reduce other federal expenditures, and balance the budget by 1939. Thus between January and August 1937 WPA rolls were reduced approximately in half, from 3,000,000 to 1,500,000 workers.

Credit restrictions, reduced federal expenditures, and other factors combined in September and October 1937 to cause a severe slump in economic activity that set the indices tumbling and threatened to wipe out all the gains toward recovery the country had made since 1935. There was grave danger that price rigidity accompanied by widespread wage cutting would accentuate the downward spiral and that farm prices would fall to subdepression levels because of the extraordinarily large agricultural production in 1937. On October 12, 1937, therefore, Roosevelt called Congress into special session; and in a "fireside chat" and a message to the special session on November 15 he presented a program to halt the recession and complete the Second New Deal. That program included a new and comprehensive agricultural act, legislation to abolish child labor and establish minimum wages and maximum hours, revision of the antitrust laws to root out monopolistic control

---

[31] Monthly average, 1923–1925 = 100.

[32] It was not caused, for example, by monetary or bank credit inflation. The volume of money in circulation increased only slightly, from $5,567,100,000 in 1935 to $6,447,100,000 in 1937; total bank loans increased from $20,419,300,000 to $22,698,200,000 during the same period.

over prices, and reorganization of the Executive Department. He was willing, he added, to give businessmen an opportunity to increase production and end unemployment. "If private enterprise does not respond," he warned, "government must take up the slack."

Profoundly frightened by the prospect of returning depression during an election year, Democrats in Congress closed ranks and set to work with resolution and dispatch. The most urgent necessity was legislation to prevent the complete collapse of agricultural prices. Drought and soil conservation contracts had combined in 1936 to keep farm production at the lowest point since the First World War, except for the drought year of 1934. High prices stimulated tremendously increased plantings in 1937, however, and the return of good weather made possible the harvesting of the largest aggregate yield in American history.

To avert agrarian catastrophe, Congress enacted and the President signed on February 16, 1938, a new Agricultural Adjustment Act. To achieve control over production the measure provided for soil conservation payments up to $500,000,000 annually to farmers who cooperated with the Agriculture Department in restricting production to certain allotments. In addition, if the production of cotton, wheat, corn, tobacco, and rice exceeded normal requirements, marketing quotas might be applied if two-thirds of the producers of each crop voted to institute such controls. To achieve parity for agricultural prices, the Act of 1938 provided a number of devices. All farmers were eligible for soil conservation payments, but producers of cotton, rice, wheat, corn, and tobacco were granted even larger assistance. First, they were also eligible for parity, or price-adjustment, payments whenever Congress appropriated funds for this purpose.[33] Second, the Commodity Credit Corporation was authorized to make loans ranging from 52 to 75 per cent of the parity price—increased in 1941 to a maximum of 85 per cent—on the five leading staples. This provision not only established a floor below which prices could not fall but also enabled the Agriculture Department to store up surpluses in good years for use in years of drought and shortage.

A provision for the wider distribution of surplus farm products demonstrated that the administration had shifted from a philosophy of scarcity to a new policy of abundance. The Act authorized the Surplus Marketing Administration to buy food surpluses and distribute them to families on state relief rolls, to furnish food for school lunch programs, and in other ways to subsidize persons on relief and the WPA.[34] Finally, the measure provided a system of export subsidies to stimulate the sale of American agricultural products abroad.

Although the Second World War momentarily ended the farm problem, there can be little doubt that the second AAA brought stability to American agriculture during the interim years from 1938 to 1941. When the measure went into effect, huge surpluses threatened to depress prices to the level of 1932. By vigorous action on many fronts the Agriculture

[33] Congress appropriated $212,000,000 in 1938, $225,000,000 in 1939, and $212,000,000 in 1940 to bring farm income up to the parity level.

[34] The most interesting and widely used method was the so-called Food Stamp Plan, begun experimentally in Rochester, New York, in May 1939 and soon put into effect in all important cities. The Food Stamp Plan was an arrangement under which relief families received fifty cents' worth of free surplus food for every dollar they spent for food in any grocery store.

Department averted a rural depression in the critical years of 1938 and 1939 and helped farmers return to the near-prosperity level of 1937 by 1940.[35]

Meanwhile, the widespread wage cutting that occurred during the first months of the Recession of 1937 prompted the administration to muster all its strength to force the passage of the Fair Labor Standards, or wages and hours, bill. Since its passage by the Senate in July 1937 this measure had run afoul the opposition of many groups; and even after administration leaders prepared a new measure that won labor's support, the rules committee refused to allow the House to consider the bill. But extraordinary administration pressure coupled with a public appeal by the President on April 30 resulted in House approval of the bill on May 23, 1938.

The last of the great New Deal legislation, the Fair Labor Standards Act joined the Social Security and National Labor Relations Acts to round out a comprehensive structure of advanced labor legislation. In spite of certain necessary concessions, the Fair Labor Standards Act represented the culmination of perhaps the most important aspects of the social justice movement. First, it established a minimum wage of 25 cents an hour, to go into effect at once and to be gradually increased to 40 cents. Second, the Act limited hours of labor to forty-four a week, to be reduced within three years to forty a week, and provided for payment at the rate of time and a half for overtime work. Third, the measure forbade the shipment in interstate commerce of any goods manufactured in whole or in part by children under sixteen. Finally, it created a Wage and Hour Division in the Department of Labor to supervise the operation of the new law. Thus, although it left many workers unprotected, the Act abolished the worst sweatshops and ended the exploitation of children. By April 1939 nearly 13,000,000 workers were protected by the Wage and Hour Division; and when the minimum wage was increased from 25 to 30 cents in October 1939 some 700,000 workers, chiefly in the South, received immediate pay increases.

Meanwhile, the President waited to see whether the economy would recover without new efforts at pump priming. Instead of improving, the economic situation steadily worsened during the winter of 1937–1938, as the following table reveals:

1937	Index of Employment in Manufacturing	Index of Payrolls in Manufacturing	Index of Production
October	110.3	104.9	102
November	104.2	93.3	88
December	97.7	84.6	84
1938			
January	91.0	75.4	80
February	91.6	77.7	79
March	91.2	77.8	79

On April 14, 1938, therefore, the President sent a special message to Congress announcing a loosening of credit restrictions, demanding a drastic revival

[35] Cash farm income, including government payments, was $9,176,000,000 in 1937, $8,130,000,000 in 1938, $8,658,000,000 in 1939, and $9,120,000,000 in 1940.

of deficit spending, and calling upon business and labor to unite in a common war against the recession.

A frightened Congress hastily responded by making some $3,000,000,000 immediately available to expand the WPA, launching a huge public works program in conjunction with the states, and increasing the activities of the FSA, CCC, and other agencies. Almost at once, expanded bank credits and renewed pump priming reversed the tide of depression. Beginning in July and August 1938, the indices of manufacturing production, payrolls, and employment started upward, and recovery to the near-prosperity level of 1937 was almost complete by the end of 1939.

The last surge of New Deal reform was the inauguration by the administration and Congress in the spring and summer of 1938 of the most intense antitrust campaign since the presidency of William Howard Taft. Thurman Arnold of the Yale Law School, an ardent foe of monopoly, was appointed head of the Antitrust Division of the Department of Justice and given large new appropriations and increases in staff. Within a short time he had set in motion 215 major investigations and ninety-two test cases to sharpen federal antitrust policy. Secondly, on April 29, 1938, the President sent a special message to Congress calling for a thorough study of the concentration of economic power and its effect on the American system of free enterprise. "The liberty of a democracy," he warned, "is not safe if the people tolerate the growth of private power to a point where it becomes stronger than their democratic state itself."

Congress responded on June 16, 1938, by creating the Temporary National Economic Committee, composed of members of Congress and representatives of various Executive agencies. For seventeen months, from December 1, 1938, to April 26, 1940, the TNEC called some 552 witnesses, including bank presidents, corporation officials, and distinguished economists, and heard testimony that filled thirty-one volumes. In addition, TNEC economists wrote forty-three monographs covering almost every phase of American economic life.

The result was such a stock taking of the American economy as had never before been attempted. It seemed at first the administration contemplated some drastic new form of public control over business, industry, and finance. Such plans, however, did not long survive. After taking mountains of testimony, the TNEC submitted a final report on March 31, 1941, that was as timid as it was unoriginal. Failing to confront the challenge inherent in the fact of extraordinary concentration of economic power in the United States, the Committee recommended only traditional remedies like strengthening the antitrust laws and reform of the patent system. By the date of the publication of the final report, of course, the administration was more concerned with preparations for war than with sweeping reform of the economic system.

150 / *The Passing of the New Deal*

The administration's reform impulses and plans came to an abrupt halt in the early months of 1939 as the result of portentous developments in

Europe and Asia and political reversals at home. Hitler's triumph at Munich in September 1938 and his subsequent violation of the Munich Pact and partition of Czechoslovakia in March 1939 convinced Roosevelt that the Nazi menace to European and American democracy demanded a stronger foreign policy and preparation for possible conflict. Moreover, Japan's invasion of China in 1937 and threat of future expansion raised threats to American security in the Far East. In brief, the President saw clearly that a world-wide cataclysm impended in the near future and that his chief duty was now the protection of American security.

A firm defense of American interests, however, would almost inevitably require a radical alteration of the policy of nonintervention embodied in the neutrality legislation from 1935 to 1937. Such a reversal could not be accomplished unless Roosevelt had a strong majority in Congress; the difficulty was that the Democratic party was split wide open on foreign policy. Midwestern and western Democrats were ardent supporters of Second New Deal domestic policies; but, like their Republican counterparts, they were determined to avoid any action that might conceivably lead to American participation in a Second World War. Eastern Democrats generally supported progressive measures and, except for representatives of Irish-American districts, were willing to support a stronger foreign policy. Southern Democrats were the most vociferous champions of defense and cooperation with Britain and France; but they were growing acutely fearful that the administration's advanced reform measures would impinge upon race relations in their region. As a consequence of this division, Roosevelt might have to choose between continuing to work for domestic reform and isolation through a coalition of Midwesterners and Easterners on the one hand, or, on the other, constructing a new alliance of eastern and southern Democrats, who would support a strong foreign policy but demand an end to reform at home.

Political developments in 1938 emphasized this dilemma and revealed that the Second New Deal coalition of Midwesterners and Easterners was beginning to crumble. The first sign came in December 1937 and January 1938 during struggles in Congress over the proposed Ludlow Amendment and the Wagner-Van Nuys antilynching bill.[36] On January 6 the President addressed a strong plea to Congress for defeat of the Ludlow resolution, and the House defeated it by 209 to 188 on January 10, 1938. But Roosevelt must have perceived the significance of the alignment on the measure: three-fourths of the Republicans and a majority of midwestern and western Democrats combined in favor of the proposed amendment, while an overwhelming majority of southern and eastern Democrats voted against it. At the same

[36] Introduced by Representative Louis Ludlow, Democrat of Indiana, this proposed amendment required majority approval of a war resolution in a national referendum, except in the event of an invasion of the United States or its territories. It had the support of numerous church and pacifist groups and apparently of a large majority of the American people.

The Wagner-Van Nuys antilynching bill made lynching a federal crime and allowed the families of lynch victims to sue counties in which the lynching occurred for damages running to $10,000. It was supported by the National Association for the Advancement of Colored People and by liberal labor, church, and political groups in all sections except the South, where sentiment was divided.

time, the conflict over the antilynching bill came to a head in the Senate. Although he probably approved the measure in principle, Roosevelt said no word in condemnation when southern senators prevented a vote by filibuster.

The development that decisively compelled Roosevelt to make peace with the conservatives in order to build strength for his foreign policy was the failure of his campaign to purge conservative southern Democrats in the primary campaigns during the summer of 1938. Announcing his determination to participate in the Democratic primary campaigns on June 24, the President threw himself into the fight during the next two months. What Roosevelt said to Southerners was honest enough. Citing the *Report on Economic Conditions of the South,* issued on August 12, 1938, by a committee of leading southern educators, clergymen, editors, and businessmen, he declared that conditions that made the South "the Nation's No. 1 economic problem" could be remedied only with the cooperation of Southerners in united progressive action.

Instead of aiding the growing progressive element in the South, however, the President's intervention boomeranged to the benefit of the conservatives. In earlier primary campaigns in which Roosevelt had taken no part, two stanch southern progressives, Representative Lister Hill of Alabama and Senator Claude W. Pepper of Florida, won notable victories. In contrast, not a single southern conservative was dislodged by Roosevelt's attempted purge; in fact, it was the general consensus that only Roosevelt's opposition saved old Senator "Cotton Ed" Smith of South Carolina from defeat.

The outcome of the congressional elections in November, moreover, left Roosevelt no alternative but to end his civil war and draw his party together in a solid front. The Republicans made enormous gains in the Middle and Far West and by gaining seven seats in the Senate and eighty in the House became a formidable power for the first time since 1932. If he further antagonized the Southerners, whose support in foreign affairs he desperately needed, Roosevelt might well drive them into an alliance with the Republicans.

In his Annual Message to the Seventy-Sixth Congress on January 4, 1939, therefore, the President in effect announced the end of the great reform movement of the Second New Deal. Pleading only for a continuation of deficit spending until full recovery had returned, he asked for no new reform legislation and declared: "We have now passed the period of internal conflict in the launching of our program of social reform. Our full energies may now be released to invigorate the processes of recovery in order to preserve our reforms." The major theme of this address, in fact, was the enormity of the totalitarian threat to religion, democracy, and international peace.

Thus it was that the forward motion of progressivism came to a halt in the early uncertain months of 1939. And yet it would be erroneous to conclude that the failure of the "purge," the Republican revival, or even the increasing peril of the international situation alone accounted for the President's decision to abandon the fight for further reform legislation. More important was the fact that with one exception—the development of new regional hydroelectric projects like the Tennessee Valley Authority—the President and his party had brought to full completion by 1939 the progressive program first formulated by agrarian, social justice, and labor progressives from 1897 to 1917 and then enlarged in the 1920's and 1930's. In other words, progressives had nearly reached the limits of achievement within the framework of their ideology, which was essentially a faith in the middle way, in regulation and intervention on behalf of disadvantaged classes, rather than in socialistic ownership of the means of production. In the years after the Second World War progressives would find that their own ideological limitations made it difficult for them to do more than attempt to perfect the structure of the Second New Deal.

"As a Nation we have rejected any radical revolutionary program," Roosevelt observed in 1938. "For a permanent correction of grave weaknesses in our economic system we have relied on new applications of old democratic processes." And what student of American history could disagree with this judgment on the whole New Deal effort? The chief significance of the reform legislation of the 1930's was its essentially conservative character and the fact that it stemmed from half a century or more of discussion and practical experience and from ideas proposed as well by Republicans as by Democrats.

CHAPTER 20 / *THE NEW DEAL AND THE AMERICAN PEOPLE*

*P*ROGRESSIVES who had been in the vanguard of the reform movement might have been as much astonished as gratified in 1941 by the changes that had taken place in the American scene since 1932. Most important was the profound metamorphosis in popular attitudes toward the federal government that occurred in the four decades after 1900. By 1941 most Americans agreed that the federal government should be the most powerful organized force in their democracy: to farmers a guarantor of solvency, to workers a beneficent protector, to tenant farmers and the unemployed a friend in adversity, and to businessmen and bankers a powerful safeguard as well as a regulator.

Historians might argue that popular acceptance of progressive assumptions represented more a pragmatic response to obvious need than a reasoned acceptance of an elaborate ideology. None the less, historians were quick to perceive the significance of the institutional changes wrought by the New Deal legislation and the new spirit that permeated the American democracy by 1941. We have noted many of those changes in agriculture, industry, finance, and politics in the preceding two chapters. Now let us look at other and in the long run perhaps more important effects of the New Deal: the way in which the intellectual and political upheaval of the 1930's affected the labor movement; promoted the growth of bold concepts concerning the development of regional resources, constitutional interpretations, and the treatment of minority groups; and stimulated the expansion and maturing of the progressive ideology.

151 / *Labor's Civil War*

With the support of the federal government from 1933 to 1941, the labor movement experienced its most spectacular growth and finally won its old and hitherto elusive goal of the unionization of the mass industries. Unhappily for labor, however, this triumph was accomplished at the cost of a bitter civil war that split the ranks of organized labor and left deep scars for years to come.

The rupture grew out of a division among the leaders of the AF of L over immediate tactics and fundamental philosophy. After the death of Samuel Gompers in 1924, leadership in the union fell to more cautious men. Imbued with the conviction that craft unionism offered the only solid basis for the American labor movement, these conservative leaders abhorred the concept of industrial unionism, that is, the organization of all workers in a given industry into one big union rather than into a number of craft or trades unions. Experience proved, they argued, that industrial unions like the Knights of Labor and the IWW were inherently unstable and inevitably fell prey to radical agitators.

In opposition stood a small but aggressive minority among the leaders of the AF of L: John L. Lewis, gifted with a stentorian voice, a leonine appearance, and command of a virile Elizabethan vocabulary, who had built his United Mine Workers into the most powerful union in the United States by 1935; Sidney Hillman, one of the founders and president of the Amalgamated Clothing Workers; David Dubinsky, head of the International Ladies' Garment Workers; and Thomas McMahon, head of the United Textile Workers. These and other advanced spokesmen argued that the hope of the labor movement lay in meeting strength with strength by organizing mass industries on a mass, or industrial, basis and by attempting to bring the great body of Negro workers into the ranks of organized labor.

Under strong pressure from Lewis, Hillman, and Dubinsky, the AF of L convention at San Francisco in 1934 voted to charter so-called federal, or industrial, unions in the automobile, cement, aluminum, and other mass industries. But the conservatives had no intention of allowing the infant unions to grow into lusty giants and seize control of the AF of L. In fact, no sooner were the new unions launched than the craft unions began to raid them and draw off their members.

The struggle came to a head at the AF of L convention in Atlantic City in October 1935, when Lewis bluntly proposed that craft unions should have no jurisdiction over workers in the mass industries and made a ringing plea for a great campaign to organize the unskilled workers. The majority of the convention, however, rejected his resolution on October 16.

Soon afterward, on November 10, 1935, Lewis and other leaders of eight AF of L unions met in Atlantic City and formed the Committee for Industrial Organization, allegedly to help the AF of L unionize the basic industries. President William Green and the AF of L executive council struck back in January 1936 by ordering the CIO to disband. When the rebels defiantly welcomed new allies and laid plans for unionization campaigns, the AF of L executive council suspended ten unions in August 1936 and expelled them in March 1937. The following May, moreover, the executive council announced it would undertake an intensive organizational campaign of its own in the basic industries.

During the ensuing months occurred a bitter struggle for control of the masses of unorganized workers, and on almost every front the CIO triumphed. Beginning with 1,800,000 members in March 1937, the new union could claim a membership of nearly 3,750,000 six months later. When peace negotiations with the AF of L in October 1937 failed to yield an agreement satisfactory to Lewis, the rebel leaders finally declared their independence of the parent organization and soon afterward reorganized the CIO as the Congress of Industrial Organizations.

152 / The Triumph of the CIO

Meanwhile, the CIO had begun its offensive against the mass industries in June 1936 with the formation of the Steel Workers' Organizing Committee, or SWOC, under the command of Philip Murray, a lieutenant of Lewis in the UMW. For over seven months the SWOC campaigned in the steel industry, and everywhere discontented workers broke away from company unions and joined the CIO. In the past the company managers could always rely upon the military assistance of the states and the moral support of the federal government. In that year of New Deal grace, 1936, however, the Washington administration was openly friendly to the workers, while the Democratic Governor of Pennsylvania promised relief assistance if a strike should occur.

It soon became evident, however, that the leaders of United States Steel preferred surrender to a long and costly strike. Beginning in December 1936, Myron C. Taylor, chairman of the board of directors of the corporation, held a series of private conferences with John L. Lewis that led to a friendly understanding and agreement by officials of the corporation to recognize the SWOC. On March 2, 1937, therefore, Benjamin Fairless, president of the Carnegie-Illinois Steel Company, a United States Steel subsidiary, signed what was perhaps the most important contract in American labor history— important because it signified the surrender of the corporation that had taken leadership since 1901 in the movement to block unionization of the basic industries. Within a short time, all the rest of United States Steel's subsidiaries had signed similar contracts granting recognition, a 10 per cent wage increase, the forty-hour week, and time and a half for overtime work.

Heartened by this epochal victory, Murray and the SWOC expected the remainder of the steel companies, known collectively as Little Steel, to come quickly to terms. Several of the Little Steel companies, notably Inland Steel, made no effort to break the strike; but the leaders of the Bethlehem, Republic, and Youngstown Sheet and Tube companies fought back with all the force they could command. In Massillon, Ohio, Republic Steel officials organized a small army of deputies that killed two strikers in a wanton attack on July 11, 1937. In South Chicago police killed ten and wounded scores of strikers at the Republic Steel plant on Memorial Day, 1937.

So violent was Little Steel's counterattack that the SWOC's momentum was almost entirely halted. In July 1937 Inland Steel agreed to recognize the union; but the other companies held out. In pre-New Deal days this would probably have been the end of the story, at least until the workers organized for another bloody battle. Now, however, the workers' new ally, the federal government, went into action. First, a Senate sub-committee, headed by Robert M. La Follette, Jr., of Wisconsin, conducted a thorough investigation into all aspects of the strike during the spring and summer of 1938. It reported numerous violations of the Wagner Act and the civil liberties of the strikers by the steel companies, local police, and the National Guard;

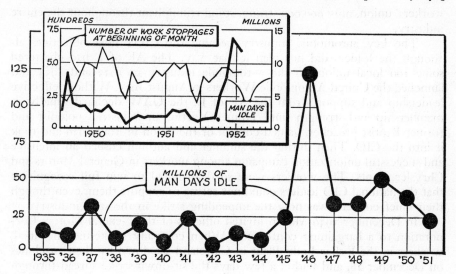

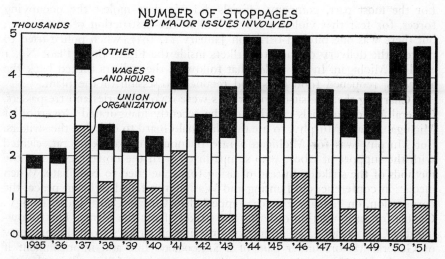

19. *Work Stoppages in the United States, 1935–1951*

discovered that the companies maintained corps of spies and *agents provocateurs;* and revealed that the same companies had collected arsenals of guns, tear gas, and ammunition for use against strikers.[1] Second, the National Labor Relations Board moved into the case upon appeal of the SWOC and compelled the Little Steel companies to recognize and bargain in good faith with the SWOC in 1941. By the end of that year, therefore, the steel

[1] It is only fair to add that in its investigations and report the La Follette sub-committee was grossly partial to the cause of the strikers. The sub-commitee, for example, made no effort to investigate the companies' plea that they were seeking merely to protect their own property and the right of nonunion members to work.

workers' union, now 600,000 strong, stood triumphant throughout the entire industry.

The key automobile industry became the CIO's next objective, although the leaders did not plan it that way. The AF of L had chartered some 100 local unions in the automobile industry in 1933 and 1934 and launched the United Automobile Workers in August 1935. Without effective leadership and support from the AF of L, the UAW declined rapidly in membership and strength until Homer Martin, an industrial unionist and former Baptist preacher, gained control of the union in May 1936 and took it into the CIO. Then during the summer and autumn ensued an intensive and successful unionization campaign among workers in General Motors and Chrysler plants. The workers were so determined to win full recognition that the national CIO leaders could not refuse to support them, even though their chief concern was now the impending strike in the steel industry.

In December 1936 Martin invited officials of the General Motors Corporation to a bargaining conference. When company spokesmen declined, workers in the Fisher Body Plant in Cleveland sat down by their machines on December 28, and within a few days the sit-down strike spread through key General Motors plants. There had been minor sit-down strikes before but none so well organized and on such a spectacular scale as this one. For the most part, company officials did not dare molest the occupying forces, for fear that violence would lead to the destruction of machinery; but there was one pitched battle on January 11, 1937, when police tried to prevent the delivery of food to strikers inside the Fisher Body Plant No. 1 at Flint, Michigan. In the *mêlée* that followed, the strikers turned back the attackers, reopened food lines, and retained possession of the plant.

Charging that the sit-down strikers were revolutionaries and trespassers, General Motors officials called upon the recently inaugurated Governor of Michigan, Frank Murphy, to use the National Guard to dislodge the strikers. But Murphy was for Michigan a rare phenomenon—a Democrat, elected with the support of labor, who sympathized with the objectives if not the methods of the strikers. Instead of using force, he tried to conciliate. When mediation conferences in Lansing and Washington failed to bring peace, the corporation, on January 29, 1937, appealed to Circuit Court Judge Paul V. Gadola for an injunction ordering the strikers from the plants. The following day Gadola signed an injunction ordering all strikers from the property of General Motors under pain of a $15,000,000 fine and imprisonment if they refused. "Unarmed as we are, the introduction of the militia, sheriffs, or police with murderous weapons will mean a blood bath of unarmed workers," the strikers replied. ". . . We have decided to stay in the plant." Judge Gadola ordered the sheriff to arrest the strikers; the sheriff refused and appealed to Governor Murphy. In turn, Murphy refused to use the National Guard and redoubled his efforts at mediation.

After days of tense negotiations, during which the President brought enormous pressure to bear upon General Motors officials, the corporation finally surrendered on February 11, 1937. In the settlement the UAW won all its demands except the closed shop—dismissal of the injunction proceedings, recognition of the UAW as the sole bargaining agent for the workers, and collective bargaining looking toward agreement on hours and wages. It was, obviously, a victory with momentous implications for the future of the labor movement in the United States.

Flushed with their victory over General Motors, the UAW leaders moved next against the smaller Chrysler Corporation and applied the sit-down and mass picketing techniques at eight Chrysler plants on March 8, 1937. When Judge Allan Campbell of Detroit ordered the arrest of CIO leaders and 6,000 sitting strikers, after they had defied his earlier injunction, the workers prepared to resist. But by this date public opinion throughout the country was growing alarmed by a wave of sit-down strikes in many branches of industry and was turning sharply against the new technique.[2] Announcing he would enforce the injunction, Governor Murphy at the same time succeeded in bringing Walter P. Chrysler and John L. Lewis together in high-level peace talks. The upshot was that Lewis called the strikers out of the plants on March 24 and the corporation surrendered on April 6 on the terms to which General Motors had recently agreed.

Henry Ford, who had always resisted the notion that workers should participate in the determination of company policies, proved to be the UAW's most formidable antagonist. Ford had the lowest wage scale of any of the major automobile producers in 1937; moreover, he had the most efficient "service department," a collection of labor spies and company police dedicated to destroying any incipient union. The UAW began an organizational campaign in the Ford Company soon after Chrysler capitulated, but it was badly managed and failed to win the workers in Ford's huge River Rouge plant. Among the smaller producers like Packard and Hudson, however, the UAW was consistently successful; by September 1937 the union had over 300,000 members and boasted bargaining agreements with every automobile producer except Ford.

Meanwhile, personal rivalry between factions headed by Homer Martin on the one side and Richard T. Frankensteen, R. J. Thomas, and Walter Reuther on the other came to a head in 1937–1938 and split the UAW. Backed by the CIO, Thomas and Reuther won the support of an overwhelming majority, whereupon Martin carried his followers into the AF of L. With the full support of the NLRB, the UAW-CIO went on to organize the Ford workers in the autumn of 1940 and the following spring conducted a strike that soon won complete recognition.

On numerous other labor fronts CIO unions won the right to speak for workers in most of the basic industries. In February 1936 an uprising of rubber workers in Akron, Ohio, led to the formation of the United Rubber Workers Union and the rapid conquest of the rubber industry by the CIO. The United Textile Workers Union organized the textile mills of the North and made a heroic but generally unsuccessful effort to penetrate the southern area in 1937 and 1938. On the Pacific Coast, Harry Bridges organized long-shoremen into a powerful CIO union. And so it went in dozens of other industries, until by the time the United States entered the Second World War the CIO had some 5,000,000 members, the AF of L had grown to a

---

[2] From September 1936 through May 1937 some 500,000 workers were engaged directly in sit-down strikes and forced the shutting down of other plants employing 600,000 workers. The high peak came in March 1937, when nearly 200,000 workers participated in sit-down strikes.

membership of 4,569,000, and independent unions could count an additional 1,000,000. Labor, in short, was well on its way toward achieving the organization of all important American industries and its long-sought goal of equality with management in the determination of labor policies. Off-setting and to a degree counterbalancing the power of big business now stood big labor, a new institution brought into being not merely by labor's own efforts but also because the federal government had thrown its moral and legal support to labor's side during the critical period of the CIO's life.

153 / *The TVA and the Concept of the Region*

Nothing the New Deal attempted so fired the imagination of progressives as the creation and development of the Tennessee Valley Authority. The greatest hydroelectric project in history, it harnessed the water resources of an area 40,000 square miles in size, made possible the utilization of vast quantities of electric power in a once impoverished region, and dramatically demonstrated man's ability to control the primeval forces of nature and repair the damage done to the good earth during two centuries of wasteful exploitation. Even more significant, however, was the way in which the TVA was conceived as a regional undertaking and operated by a nonpartisan agency as much responsible to the people of the region as to its superior, the federal government. As the first really significant experiment in public planning on a regional scale, the concepts and techniques developed by the TVA might well prove to be the New Deal's most important contribution to the theory and practice of government in the United States.

The reader will recall the struggle for control of Wilson Dam at Muscle Shoals, Alabama, in the 1920's and how Senator George W. Norris of Nebraska helped save the power resources of the Tennessee Valley for the American people.[3] Their plans for federal development thwarted by Presidents Coolidge and Hoover, progressives bided their time and enlarged their objectives. Their opportunity came with Roosevelt's nomination and election in 1932, for the new Democratic leader came out in support of public power projects that would serve as yardsticks for electric rates and make possible the wider consumption of power by the people. In January 1933 the President-elect visited the Tennessee Valley in company with Norris. Standing at the Wilson Dam, Roosevelt's fertile imagination must have been excited by the opportunities that unfolded.

Roosevelt converted these opportunities into objectives on April 10, 1933, when he asked Congress to establish a Tennessee Valley Authority, "a corporation clothed with the power of Government but possessed of the flexibility and initiative of a private enterprise," to plan for the full development of the natural resources of the valley. Congress responded quickly by creating the Tennessee Valley Authority, a corporation controlled by a three-man board and endowed with sweeping authority subject to the general supervision of the President and of Congress.

Fortunately, the TVA directors were men of broad vision and demo-

[3] See above, pp. 270-272.

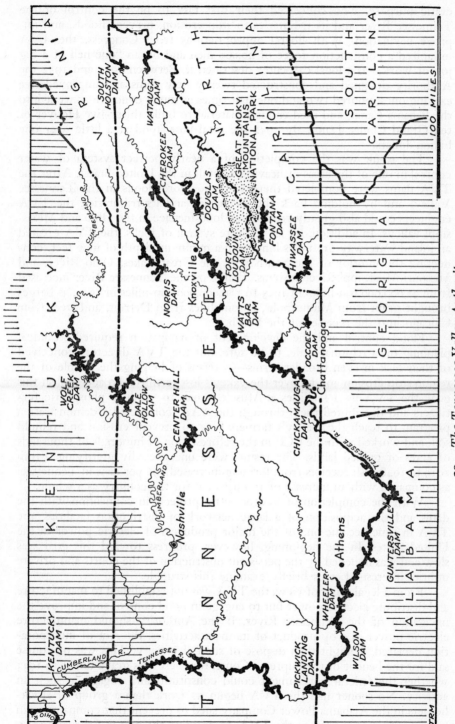

20. *The Tennessee Valley Authority*

cratic purpose, who conceived their first task to be the control of the Tennessee River and its tributaries to stop erosion, prevent floods, and improve navigation. With liberal appropriations from Congress, the TVA organized a construction force of 40,000 men and began "one hell of a big job of work," as a local carpenter described it. Between 1933 and 1952 the Authority designed and constructed twenty new dams and improved five existing ones; poured two and one half times as much concrete as went into the Panama Canal; and used enough material to build thirty-five Hoover or ten Grand Coulee Dams. By 1952 the total cost stood at a little over one billion dollars.

The result was the completion of a nearly perfect system of water control in one of the areas of heaviest rainfall in the United States. After the TVA dams were completed there were no more floods in the Tennessee Valley; and by holding back the Tennessee and its tributaries, the TVA engineers could also greatly reduce the flood menace in the Ohio and Mississippi valleys. In addition, by an intricate system of locks, the TVA created an inland waterway 652 miles long with a minimum depth of nine feet, connecting the interior of the South with the Great Lakes, Ohio River, and Missouri-Mississippi River systems. Traffic on the Tennessee River increased from 32,000,000 ton-miles in 1933 to 580,000,000 ton-miles in 1951, as barges brought grain from Minneapolis, automobiles from Detroit, and steel from Chicago into the recesses of the South.

Flood control and the development of navigation required technical planning on a regional scale, to be sure, but the TVA directors conceived of their task in even broader terms—in terms of helping the people of the region stop erosion and recover the valley's lost fertility. To accomplish this goal, the TVA used facilities at Muscle Shoals to produce phosphatic fertilizers and distributed them through the AAA; conducted a demonstration program to teach the Valley's farmers how to prevent erosion and rebuild soil; and worked with the CCC in the reforestation of hundreds of thousands of acres of gullied lands. The results were unexpectedly gratifying. From 1929 to 1948 cash receipts from farming increased 196 per cent in Tennessee, as compared with an increase of 170 per cent for the country as a whole.

With the completion of hydroelectric projects in connection with the dams and the acquisition of a large network of distribution facilities, the TVA in time became one of the major producers of electric power in the United States. In the beginning, however, progress toward this goal was slow and was impeded by the persistent obstruction of the courts and private utilities interests. Let us briefly examine this struggle.

From a legal point of view, the TVA was not established to manufacture and distribute electric power but to engage in flood control and improve the navigation of the Tennessee River. If the Authority should manufacture electric power as a by-product of its main activities, the Act of incorporation declared, it might then dispose of such electricity. This was of course said for the benefit of the Supreme Court, for there was grave doubt in 1933 whether the federal government could constitutionally engage in such an activity. No sooner had the TVA begun its work than a group of stockholders in the Alabama Power Company sued to prevent that company from selling certain properties to the TVA. In deciding the case in February 1935, the federal district judge in Birmingham ruled that the TVA had no right intentionally to manufacture and sell electric power and forbade seventeen municipalities from buying TVA power produced at Wilson Dam.

This judgment was reversed by the Supreme Court in Ashwander *v.* T. V. A. in February 1936. But in this decision the Supreme Court ruled only on the constitutionality of the sale of electricity produced at Wilson Dam. Seeing the loophole, nineteen utility companies brought suit against the TVA in May 1936, praying for an injunction forbidding the Authority to produce or distribute electric power except at Wilson Dam. The companies won a temporary injunction in December 1936, but the Supreme Court, in Tennessee Electric Power Co. *v.* T. V. A., summarily disposed of the case in January 1939 by ruling that the private companies had no right to complain of competition by the government. After this rebuff, the leader of the utility interests, Wendell L. Willkie, president of the Commonwealth & Southern Corporation, surrendered in August 1939 by selling the entire facilities of the Tennessee Electric Power Company to the TVA at his own price of nearly $79,000,000.

Commonwealth & Southern's withdrawal marked the end of private enterprise in the utilities field in the Tennessee Valley, for numerous smaller operating companies had either already sold out to TVA or soon followed Commonwealth & Southern's example. With the completion of new dams and the building of steam plants from 1940 to 1952, the TVA's revenues from the sale of electric power increased from $2,306,000 in 1938 to $95,000,000 in 1952, and the Tennessee Valley emerged as the largest producer of electric power among the regions of the United States. Over the period 1933–1951 total generating capacity in the valley increased from 800,000 kilowatts to nearly 3,541,000 kilowatts, while actual production of electricity increased from 1.5 billion to almost 18 billion kilowatt hours.

Convinced that the development of water, land, and hydroelectric resources on a regional scale would provide the basis for almost unlimited industrial expansion and the means of preventing floods, droughts, and erosion, President Roosevelt, on June 3, 1937, urged Congress to consider the creation of six additional regional authorities.[4] He was thinking, however, in terms more of future than of immediate development. Meanwhile, in a more limited way the administration pushed forward with other regional projects: Hoover Dam and the All-American Canal, completed in 1936 with the aid of PWA funds at a total cost of about $165,000,000, with an installed capacity of 1,835,000 horsepower; Grand Coulee Dam on the Columbia River in Washington, the largest masonry structure in the world, completed in 1942 at a cost of $435,734,000, with a total power capacity of 2,550,000 horsepower; and the great earthen Fort Peck Dam on the Missouri River in Montana, completed in 1939 and used principally for the purpose of flood control. Whether these projects should constitute the basis for new regional developments like the TVA would be one of the major issues confronting the American people in the years after 1945.

[4] In the following areas: the Atlantic Seaboard; the Great Lakes and the Ohio Valley; the Missouri River and the Red River of the North; in the drainage basins of the Arkansas, Red, and Rio Grande rivers; in the basin of the Colorado River; and in the Columbia River Valley.

154 / The New Deal in the Supreme Court

Although it was the last branch of the federal government to fall under New Deal influence, the Supreme Court after 1937 effected a profound and rapid revolution in constitutional interpretation. Sweeping away all doubt as to the constitutionality of advanced social and economic legislation, the New Deal Court became the chief practitioner of sociological jurisprudence, gave a larger degree of freedom to state and federal regulatory agencies than they had enjoyed before 1937, and added strong new safeguards for the protection of civil liberties, labor, and minorities. This revolution in American law occurred in the first instance because Roosevelt was privileged by virtue of his long tenure and the advanced age of incumbent judges to appoint virtually a new federal judiciary, from the district courts to the supreme tribunal. By 1941, for example, the President had appointed the Chief Justice and seven of the eight Associate Justices of the Supreme Court.

Convinced that the Constitution must serve the needs of an urbanized and industrialized democracy, the members of the "Roosevelt Court" completed and clarified the constitutional revolution begun by the unreformed Court in 1937. In a series of cases from 1938 to 1942 testing the constitutionality of the TVA's power operations, the Fair Labor Standards Act, the Holding Company Act of 1935, the second Railroad Retirement Act, the second Agricultural Adjustment Act, and other measures, the Court gave Congress virtually unlimited authority under the interstate commerce clause. Accepting the principle of stringent federal regulation, the new Court also gave to federal and state administrative agencies broad new freedom to act in the public interest—a reversal of the old Court's insistence on imposing judicial criteria on the regulatory agencies.

It was in the development of broad federal protection of religious, civil, and political liberty and defense against arbitrary police authority, however, that the New Deal Court made its most important contribution to constitutional interpretation. The basis for stern new safeguards had already been firmly laid by Chief Justice Hughes in the 1930's, in a series of decisions establishing the doctrine that because of the adoption of the Fourteenth Amendment no state could deprive a person of any of the basic rights guaranteed by the first ten Amendments.[5] The significant fact was the way in which the New Deal Court, with Hughes still its spokesman until his retirement in 1941, expanded the concept of basic liberties guaranteed by the Fourteenth Amendment.

To begin with, the Court reaffirmed Hughes' earlier condemnation of

[5] In Stromberg v. California and Near v. Minnesota, both rendered in 1931, Hughes invalidated a California statute forbidding the display of the red flag and a Minnesota censorship law, on the ground that the measures contravened fundamental civil rights guaranteed by the Fourteenth Amendment. In another decision in the second Scottsboro case in 1935—Norris v. Alabama—involving the conviction of seven Negroes for rape, moreover, Hughes reversed the conviction on the ground that Negroes had been excluded from the jury that convicted the Scottsboro boys. Such exclusion on the grounds of race, Hughes asserted, was a denial of the citizen's right to a trial by a jury of his peers.

so-called "Third Degree" methods of obtaining confessions by beating and torture and applied this ban as well against all subtler forms of torture. Again, after much hesitation, the Court majority in 1943 went to the defense of the Jehovah's Witnesses, a fanatical sect that disavowed loyalty to any earthly state, by ruling that local or state authorities could not require the children of Jehovah's Witnesses to salute the flag in school, since such action violated the Witnesses' religious scruples and liberty. The Court also nullified local ordinances requiring religious groups to obtain licenses to conduct open-air services or to distribute literature.

Inevitably, Negroes, who had most often been denied civil rights on account of race, benefited most from the Court's increased vigilance. As a result of decisions cited above, Negroes enjoyed a larger degree of personal safety and the right to a fair trial in which members of their race would participate. Perhaps more important was the way in which the new Court opened wide the gates to political and educational opportunities for Negroes and confirmed their right to live and travel as citizens of a great democracy, not as servants of a master class.

How the New Deal Court opened the polls to Negroes in the South illustrates the truth of the foregoing generalization. In Grovey v. Townsend, 1935, the Court had unanimously agreed that state party organizations, acting on their own initiative, could exclude Negroes from party primaries without violating the Fourteenth and Fifteenth Amendments. In 1944, however, in Smith v. Allwright, the New Deal Court reversed Grovey v. Townsend by declaring that because the party primary was an integral part of the electoral machinery of the state, Negroes could not be denied the right to participate in such elections because of race. When South Carolina tried to circumvent this ruling by removing all regulations for party primaries from its statute books, District Judge J. Waites Waring of Charleston refused to approve the subterfuge and ordered Democratic registrars to enroll qualified Negro voters in 1948. The Supreme Court upheld Waring's ruling by refusing to review the case. By thus taking a realistic view of southern political practices, the Court destroyed the white primary and hastened the day when Negroes would be citizens in fact as well as in theory.

On the educational front, moreover, the Court took the first step toward abandoning the legalism which, under the "separate but equal" concept, had permitted the southern states to deny equal opportunities to Negroes for three-quarters of a century. Speaking in 1938 in the case of Missouri *ex rel.* Gaines, Chief Justice Hughes set in motion the reversal that would end in repudiation of the theory that separate public schools, colleges, and universities for Negroes could in fact be equal. In the Gaines case the Court simply required the University of Missouri Law School to admit a Negro student because the state had not provided law school facilities for Negroes. This decision prompted many southern states immediately to establish law schools for Negroes. In 1950, however, in Sweatt v. Painter, the Court decreed that separate law school facilities could never be really equal and ordered the University of Texas to admit a Negro student who had refused to attend the state law school for Negroes in Houston. The effect of the Sweatt decision was to compel many southern state universities to admit Negroes to law, medical, and graduate schools. More important was the implication of the

Sweatt case, namely, that segregated public education on any level was unequal education.[6]

In other ways the Court moved to undermine the legal foundations of the caste system. In 1946 it invalidated a Virginia statute requiring segregated seating in interstate busses, decreed that such segregation was an undue burden on interstate commerce, and later applied the same criterion to interstate railway travel. Two years later, it struck a heavy blow at residential segregation by ruling that covenants forbidding the sale of real estate to persons on account of race or color were not enforceable in any courts. Reflecting an astute understanding of the realities of the American caste system and a determination to end Jim Crow as quickly as possible, these decisions heartened progressives and Negroes as no other development had done since the end of Reconstruction.

Nearly as important was a series of decisions that freed organized labor from the bonds imposed by the courts under the Sherman Antitrust Act. The fundamental issue was whether labor unions, in the conduct of industrial warfare, might employ methods that restrained interstate commerce. In Apex Hosiery Co. *v.* Leader, 1940, and United States *v.* Hutcheson, 1941, the Roosevelt Court formulated a new doctrine—that labor unions might restrain commerce when such restraint was incidental to the achievement of legitimate objectives. Reversing earlier decisions, the Apex and Hutcheson rulings gave organized labor its long-sought immunity from prosecution under the antitrust laws, except when unions sought directly to restrain commerce through monopolistic and restrictive practices or attempted to defy the government when it was an employer.[7]

Although the Roosevelt Court well deserved its reputation for progressivism, it was never a "rubber stamp" Court, as many New Deal critics averred. And it was far from being a unanimous or even a personally harmonious Court. By masterful mediation, Chief Justice Hughes had contrived to subordinate personal differences among the justices; but his successor, Harlan F. Stone, apparently failed to prevent differences of opinion from developing into violent personal antagonisms. In any event, by the time of Stone's death on April 22, 1946,[8] the Roosevelt Court had divided into two distinct and sometimes hostile factions. In the beginning, at least, divisions arose out of genuine differences of constitutional opinion. One faction, led by Justice Felix Frankfurter, was willing to give local authorities and state legislatures the benefit of the doubt in borderline cases involving civil rights; the other, whose chief spokesmen were Justices Hugo L. Black and William

[6] For subsequent developments culminating in the Court's sweeping outlawry of segregation in the public schools in 1954, see below, p. 604.

[7] For example, in United States *v.* United Mine Workers of America, 1947, the Court upheld a district court judge's injunction ordering John L. Lewis and the UMW to terminate a strike against the coal industry, then technically operated by the United States. In this important decision the Court ruled that the Norris Anti-Injunction Act did not apply when the United States was the employer. Again, in United States *v.* Petrillo, 1947, the Court upheld an Act of Congress of 1946 that made it unlawful for the musicians' union to attempt to compel radio stations to employ more musicians than they actually needed.

[8] President Truman appointed Fred M. Vinson of Kentucky to succeed Stone. Vinson died on September 8, 1953, and was succeeded by Governor Earl Warren of California, appointed by President Dwight D. Eisenhower.

O. Douglas, insisted upon a more rigid defense of civil rights based upon principles embodied in the Bill of Rights. On the other hand, in the area of state economic legislation Frankfurter and his friends evinced a readiness to impose judicial criteria while the Black-Douglas faction were willing to accept almost any form of state control over economic affairs. As the years passed these differences in interpretation were exacerbated by intemperate outbursts in which one faction accused the other of betraying civil liberties or of promulgating foolish doctrines. Unfortunate though this development was, it should not be allowed to obscure the fact that the New Deal Court sat during a critical period of peace and war and left a lasting impact on the American political system and ideology by its overhauling of constitutional interpretation concerning governmental power and civil and religious freedom.

155 / The Return of the Prodigals: Intellectuals and the New Deal

It is difficult to recount the impact of the New Deal on American intellectuals without seeming to exaggerate; yet reflection confirms the conviction that the hope of reform and redemption under Roosevelt's leadership stirred intellectuals as they had not been roused since 1917. Throwing off the torpor and cynicism that had ruined their influence and separated them from the middle classes in the 1920's, political thinkers, professors in various disciplines, editors, and socially-minded lawyers, clergymen, and writers reclaimed their high position as leaveners of progressivism and the chief interpreters of the American democratic tradition.

In a sense this was the natural response of a sensitive group to challenges to democracy raised at home by the depression and abroad by the rise of totalitarianism. The significant fact, however, was the way in which Roosevelt personally drew large numbers of intellectuals, particularly professors, into the service of the people and used them to construct his program of reform and rehabilitation.

This was true in the first two years of the New Deal, when the "Brains Trust" wrote much of the emergency legislation and when the President called into the public service men like William O. Douglas of the Yale Law School and Dean James M. Landis of the Harvard Law School to serve as chairmen of the SEC. It was true on a much broader scale when Roosevelt utilized the services of trained intellectual leaders to formulate and carry out the important measures of the Second New Deal. In fact, a recounting of the host of men and women who left university and foundation posts to launch and direct the Social Security, Farm Security, and kindred agencies would require more space than we could give.

Intellectuals working with the administration did more than formulate and direct. Organized in various President's committees on social security, farm security, executive reorganization, natural resources, the problem of southern poverty, and the like, they issued reports that stirred thoughtful Americans to the necessity for action in these fields. Working with the National Resources Planning Board, sociologists and economists surveyed the problem of population redistribution and other such subjects; working in conjunction with the TNEC, a large group of economists revealed the concentration of American wealth and of control in industry, exposed the quasi-monopolistic practices of big business, and pointed the way ahead to reform; cooperating with the special Senate sub-committee headed by Senator Gerald P. Nye, historians joined pacifists and progressives in exorcising war.

The result of these manifold labors was such a thoroughgoing examination of every phase of American economic and social life as the country had not experienced since the early years of the progressive period. In other words, professors and other intellectuals were the muckrakers of the 1930's and the catalysts of the latter reform movement. Their resources were greater and their audience was different from those of the earlier muckrakers, but their task and accomplishment were much the same. Little wonder it was, therefore, that a generation of intellectuals should have regarded the New Deal Era as a time bright with the hope of good things.

The 1930's were a time also when social scientists, under the impact of the depression crisis, discarded old concepts and matured new ones to justify a broad expansion of public authority. Following the trail blazed years before by the iconoclastic Thorstein Veblen, economists set to work to analyze American economic institutions critically and apart from *a priori* assumptions about the nature of economic activity. Almost unanimously these institutional economists taught the necessity of governmental control over and participation in economic affairs. The disciples of John Maynard Keynes, the British economist, for example, evolved a theory of governmental compensatory spending to prevent or end depressions and adduced intricate mathematical formulas to buttress an otherwise common-sense theory. To the degree that they recognized the interdependent character of the economy and the necessity for a larger measure of public participation in economic affairs, the institutional economists of the 1930's were collectivists. But like their earlier counterparts in the United States, they believed not in utopian socialism but in democratic capitalism controlled in the interest of all the people.

Working in an allied field and equally promoting the progressive tradition were a group of political scientists who abandoned the ivory tower of abstract principles to discover how and why the American political system actually functioned. It was the sociologists, however, who won the largest audience and had the most significant impact on the thoughtful American public. They were learned, sophisticated, and "scientific," to be sure; but like the muckrakers they performed the task, indispensable to the preservation of democracy, of laying bare the unpleasant facts of American social life.

The most important new developments in this field accurately reflected the major concerns of the Second New Deal—the South and the concept of the region, the Negro, and the problem of rural poverty. Led by Howard W. Odum and Rupert B. Vance of the University of North Carolina, southern sociologists set to the task of examining their region's institutions and social structure. This cathartic self-examination was too strong for many proud Southerners; to a growing body of young progressives, however, it seemed the first step toward a healthy reconstruction. Moreover, Southerners joined other sociologists in an almost frantic drive to understand and destroy the bases of racial prejudice. The culmination of this campaign was a cooperative study financed by the Carnegie Corporation of New York and synthesized by the Swedish sociologist, Gunnar Myrdal, in a huge volume entitled *An American Dilemma: The Negro Problem and Modern Democracy*, published in 1944.

What shall we say about the contribution intellectuals made? Progressive intellectuals in the New Deal era made their most lasting contribution by expanding the horizons of democratic ideology to encompass fundamentals that earlier progressives had often ignored. Assuming the essential soundness of the political institutional structure, New Deal progressives were able to give their major attention to the problems of economic justice and security, to the development of advanced concepts of civil liberty, and to fruitful experiments in compensatory spending and planning. The pioneers in the progressive movement had been principally concerned with constructing new forms for democracy and with bringing uncontrolled property under public control. It fell, therefore, to the latter-day progressives to broaden the horizons and objectives of the movement to include programs for the benefit of hitherto neglected disadvantaged groups: Negroes, the unemployed, tenants and sharecroppers, industrial workers, and the like. The dimensions of their accomplishment can be seen in the social and economic legislation of the Second New Deal; the significance of this accomplishment lay in the fact that the great majority of Americans, Republicans and Democrats alike, accepted and approved the new ideals of social welfare democracy.

156 /   *The Survival of the Democratic Tradition*

The 1930's were a time of severe testing for democracy throughout the world, as the forces of Fascism, Nazism, and racist militarism grew audacious and the democracies trembled in fear of future aggression and war. At the same time, the totalitarian powers used all the weapons of modern psychological warfare in a great campaign to capture the minds of men. And throughout the decade the American democracy was a vast free marketplace, where contenders peddled their ideological wares, often by deceit and cunning but always with such freedom as befits a democracy.

On one side were a crowd of fascist and Nazi-financed demagogues and their organizations, whose themes ranged from social justice to violent anti-Semitism. After Huey P. Long's death in 1935 the Reverend Charles E. Coughlin, Catholic priest of Royal Oak, Michigan, quickly emerged as the pre-eminent leader of the fascist forces. Discarding his social justice disguise in 1938, Coughlin came out frankly as a pro-Nazi and anti-Semite and formed the Christian Front in 1939 to unite the widely scattered anti-democratic organizations. By the autumn of 1939 the Christian Front had mobilized strong-arm gangs in cities throughout the country, and Coughlin counted his followers by the hundreds of thousands and his audience by the millions.

Working for the same objectives and using the same anti-Semitic, anti-Communist propaganda were a group of lesser fascist demagogues. There was, for example, the mystical megalomaniac, William Dudley Pelley, who organized the Silvershirt Legion, a counterpart of Hitler's Brown Shirts in 1933. Lawrence Dennis, author of *The Coming American Fascism* and other works, was the intellectual leader and principal adviser of the fascist groups. Long's chief organizer, the Reverend Gerald L. K. Smith of Shreveport, Louisiana, moved to Detroit, converted the "Share Our Wealth" organization into the Committee of One Million, and began a campaign against Jews, Negroes, and Communists. Smith's counterpart in the Middle West was the revivalist, the Reverend Gerald B. Winrod of Wichita, Kansas, who learned the secrets of the "international Jewish conspiracy" in Nazi Germany in 1934 and 1935 and who was as violently anti-Catholic as anti-Semitic. In the Northeast a naturalized German-American and veteran of Hitler's Munich beer-hall *putsch* in 1923, Fritz J. Kuhn, formed the *Amerikadeutscher Volksbund* in 1936; as *Bundesführer* he hailed the day when the swastika would replace the Stars and Stripes.

There were, besides, dozens of lesser evangels of fascism and religious hatred, who flooded America with Nazi propaganda, nurtured anti-Semitic passions, and formed an important component of the large isolationist faction after 1939. They had the support of a small but vocal element in Congress, and they reached a combined audience running into the millions. Potentially dangerous though they were, for a number of reasons they failed to subvert democracy or to become anything more than a lunatic fringe. This was true because most of them were sheer money-makers instead of conspirators working under the control of the Nazi government; because factionalism and personal rivalries prevented the little *führers* from uniting, and, above all, because practically the entire civil and religious leadership, Protestant and Catholic, recognized the rabble-rousers for what they were and effectively neutralized their propaganda.

Because it was better organized, used a more insidious propaganda, and was part of a vast international conspiracy controlled by the Soviet government, the Communist movement was a much more dangerous threat to the American democracy than were the fascist organizations we have just described. During the late 1920's the Communist party in the United States was torn by the struggle for power between Stalin and Trotsky then going on within the Soviet Union. After winning absolute power in Russia in 1927–1928, Stalin called the leaders of the American section to Moscow, removed the Trotskyites, and established a party hack, Earl Browder, as secretary general of the party.

The purging of the Trotsky element weakened American Communism at the time when the depression offered the party its greatest opportunity. Communists tried to bore into the AF of L unions and were turned back; they then organized rival but unsuccessful unions in the clothing, coal, textile, and other unions and thus earned the undying hatred of most American labor leaders. They also tried to organize the unemployed, and probably had a hand in the bonus riots in Washington in 1932. The net effect of all these efforts was only to confirm the dominant popular conviction that Communism was at war with American institutions. Party membership, which stood at 8,000 at the beginning of the depression, was only 12,000 in 1932 and, after two years of vigorous recruiting, only 24,000 in 1934. William Z. Foster, the party's presidential candidate in 1932, polled a mere 102,991 votes.

One of the chief causes for the Communist failure during the depression years was the fact that American comrades were never able to develop an ideology and a program of their own but were forced to follow tactics and the party line dictated by the Comintern, or Communist International. From 1928 to 1935 international Communism was in its so-called "third period," in which Stalin adhered to exaggerated notions of the world revolution in order to diminish Trotsky's influence. Convinced that the depression would culminate in the downfall of capitalism in the West, the Russian dictator declared war on labor unions and democratic leaders who seemed to offer the best hope of recovery and reform. In the United States this assault was directed chiefly at the New Deal, which the Communist party declared in 1934 was "the aggressive effort of the bankers and trusts to find a way out of the crisis at the expense of the millions of toilers . . . [and] a program of fascization and the most intense preparations for imperialist war."

Stalin obviously made a bad guess as to the outcome of the world depression; but the consequences of his policy were tragic in Germany, where Communist refusal to cooperate with the Social Democrats was a decisive factor in Hitler's rise to power in 1932–1933. Instead of collapsing, as Stalin expected, the German fascists soon won complete control of the Fatherland and began to prepare for an all-out struggle with Russia. Perceiving the enormity of the danger, Stalin effected a swift and complete reversal of policy, which he announced at the seventh Comintern meeting in Moscow in the summer of 1935. Hereafter Communists must take leadership in the movement to contain fascism by cooperating everywhere with democratic and "anti-fascist" forces in political parties, labor unions, and even church groups in so-called Popular Front movements.

This reversal gave Communists in the United States their first opportunity to try a policy of cooperation with and infiltration of progressive organizations. Quietly putting revolutionary doctrines and heroes in temporary storage, Communists now proclaimed the slogan, "Communism is Twentieth Century Americanism," disclaimed any intention of forcibly subverting the Constitution, and made a bold bid for the friendship of old-line groups. Their chief aim after 1935 was not the rapid expansion of party membership but the infiltration and control of labor unions, writers' groups, Popular Front organizations with mass memberships, and, finally, the federal government itself.

Communists scored their most important successes on the labor front. To be sure, they were in no way responsible for events that led to the split in the AF of L and the formation of the CIO in 1935. Lewis, Hillman, and other CIO leaders, however, needed thousands of trained organizers and accepted such support as the Communists could give without asking questions about Communist motives. The result was that by 1938 Communists controlled several major unions, including the electrical workers, the West Coast longshoremen, and the seamen, and were in strategic positions in the powerful UAW. Moreover, two fellow travelers if not party members, Lee Pressman and Len De Caux, were highly placed in the leadership of the CIO as general counsel and editor of the *C.I.O. News*. Even more important was the fact that during the critical struggle between the CIO and the AF of L from 1935 to 1940, the general counsel and a member of the NLRB, Nathan Witt and Edwin S. Davis, were strong Communist sympathizers if not card-bearing party members. They easily persuaded the Board to render opinions favorable to the CIO as against rival AF of L unions or employers.

To a large group of writers and a fractional minority of academic intellectuals, Communist doctrine and propaganda either appealed with the force of a new religion or else held out the hope of genuine cooperation to halt the spread of fascism and anti-Semitism at home and abroad. Sickened by the plight of the lower classes in the United States and inspired by the seeming material progress and social stability of the Soviet Union during the depression period, a number of distinguished American novelists, including Sherwood Anderson, Erskine Caldwell, and Granville Hicks, publicly supported Foster for President in 1932. From 1932 to 1935 left-wing writers and artists banded together in John Reed clubs to nurse the cult of proletarian literature; in 1935 the John Reed clubs metamorphosed into the League of American writers, which held annual conferences until 1939 and included a hard core of Communists and a host of momentary cooperators like Ernest Hemingway, Richard Wright, Archibald MacLeish, Upton Sinclair, and James T. Farrell. Banding together in the Group Theater, the Theater Union, and the Theater Collective, left-wing actors enjoyed the bohemian life and salved their social consciences by producing the plays of Clifford Odets, John Howard Lawson, Elmer Rice, and other "proletarian" playwrights.

The Communist leaders executed ambitious schemes to gain control of large segments of public opinion through the formation of other "front" organizations, in which distinguished non-Communist progressives lent their names and energies to bodies actually controlled by a Communist minority. The American League for Peace and Democracy, which claimed an affiliated membership of over 7,000,000, the American Student Union, and the American Youth Congress, which won the sponsorship of Mrs. Eleanor Roosevelt and pretended to speak for nearly 5,000,000 young people in various organizations, were two such "front" organizations.

On the political front from 1935 to 1939 the Communists pursued a two-pronged campaign: first to bore into and gain control of independent non-Communist political groups and, second, to build a powerful machine within the federal government to influence federal policies and to carry on political espionage. In both its aspects this campaign met with some success. During the campaign of 1936 the Communists put a ticket, headed by Browder, into the field; under cover, however, they worked hard for Roosevelt. Only in New York City, however, did the Communists gain any power in an important political party.[9]

More successful was the Communist effort to establish a conspiratorial underground in Washington. The leader of the principal group was Harold

[9] This was the American Labor party, formed by labor leaders and Socialists to support the Democratic cause in 1936. Communists entered the ALP at the outset but kept well under cover for a number of years. In 1944, however, Sidney Hillman, the CIO's chief political spokesman, joined forces with the Communists to capture the ALP and drive the anti-Communist right wing from control of the party. The right-wing group, headed by George S. Counts and David Dubinsky, thereupon seceded and formed the American Liberal party. The complete measure of Communist control of the American Labor party became evident after Hillman's death in 1946, when the devout admirer of Stalin, Representative Vito Marcantonio, became state chairman of the party.

Ware, who had managed a large collective farm in Russia in the early 1920's. Soon after Roosevelt's inauguration, Ware organized a Communist cell that included a number of party members strategically placed in various departments and agencies. Several of the conspirators and cooperators, notably Alger Hiss, Harry Dexter White, Julian Wadleigh, and Nathan Witt, rose to positions of high responsibility and carried from their offices thousands of documents to be photographed and passed on to the head of the Soviet underground, Colonel Boris Bykov. When Ware was killed in an automobile accident in 1935, Witt and later John Abt became leaders of the cell.

The American Communist movement began to lose strength in 1937, suffered mortal blows in 1938 and 1939, and had shrunk to its hard conspiratorial core by 1941. For this swift decline in prestige the American comrades had the actions of their Soviet masters and the fundamental democracy of the great body of American intellectuals to thank. Several thousand Americans, many of them non-Communists but imbued with the Popular Front psychology, fought on the Loyalist side in the Spanish Civil War from 1936 to 1939. At first hand many young idealists saw Communists at work, conspiring to control the Loyalist government and betraying and killing comrades-in-arms to achieve this goal. John Dos Passos, one of the most distinguished of the Popular Front novelists, was thus disillusioned by what he saw in Spain.

Also shattering to the illusions of a large body of American intellectuals who had regarded the Communist experiment with sympathetic interest were the purges, trials, and executions from 1936 to 1938 by which Stalin eliminated his closest friends and rivals and established a ruthless monolithic dictatorship. A commission of anti-Communist intellectuals headed by John Dewey made a thorough investigation of the trials, published their findings in 1938 under the title *Not Guilty*, and provoked a wild counterattack by the Communist and fellow-traveling left wing. The crowning disillusionment came, however, when the Soviet government signed a Non-Aggression Pact with Hitlerite Germany in August 1939. At once Communists changed from ardent "anti-fascists" into apologists for Nazism and vehement opponents of any form of support for Britain and France in their war against Germany. Thus events on the international scene ripped off the democratic disguise of American Communism and revealed the true character of the movement for all to see and know the truth.

Now that we have surveyed the rise and fall of American Communism in the 1930's, what shall we say about its significance, its strength, its hold over American intellectuals, and the danger it posed to the American democracy? In brief, how red was the so-called "Red Decade"?

The "Red Decade" was not as red as the above discussion might indicate. To begin with, few Americans accepted the Communist ideology, for historical materialism and a philosophy of class warfare were doctrines too strong for a people imbued with the Christian-democratic tradition. It must be remembered, also, that the Communists succeeded only to the degree that they were able to identify Communism with democracy and resistance to brutal aggression. Many Americans joined Writers' Leagues and Leagues Against War in the sincere belief that the Soviet Union was the only power willing to take effective measures to halt aggression and turn back the tide of anti-Semitism. Other Americans joined hands with Communists because they mistook the true character of Stalinism at home and abroad.

However, the significant fact was not the momentary error of these Americans but the proof, furnished by events of the 1930's, that Communism could not prosper when the channels of exposure and criticism were kept open. Through free debate and objective reporting of events, practically all Popular Front Americans recognized the character of international Communism and then rallied courageously to the defense of the democratic ideal. The American democracy survived in the face of the Communist assault, moreover, because the reforms of the Second New Deal healed the wounds of the body politic and gave proof that democracy could effect fundamental institutional changes without recourse to revolution, purges, and executions.

CHAPTER 21 / *THE UNITED STATES AND THE*
COLLAPSE OF THE
INTERNATIONAL STRUCTURE,
1931–1938

*A*ND now we come to that time of trouble when the forces of aggression in Europe and the Far East made a mockery of the peace structure so hopefully constructed during the Versailles Conference and the 1920's. Depression, fear, mutual suspicion, and a guilt complex arising from the alleged injustices of the Versailles settlement destroyed the democratic coalition, prevented the western democracies from finding a new *modus vivendi* for collective defense, and so paralyzed the peoples of Britain, France, and the United States that they were impotent in the face of the rising tide of aggression.

What an ironic circumstance—an overwhelming majority of the people of the world, with unrivaled resources and technology and a great superiority in military and naval power, unable to curb aggression because unwilling to run the risk of war! Why was this so? Perhaps an answer to this question will become evident as we review the events of the 1930's and relate the part the American people played in the unfolding tragedy.

157 / *Stimson, Hoover, and the Manchurian Crisis*

The first important assault upon the post-World War peace structure occurred in 1931–1932, when Japan occupied Manchuria and made war on China, and the western powers with interests in the Far East failed to cooperate in any effective measures to halt Japanese aggression. The background of the Manchurian episode can be briefly told. After the Russo-Japanese War the Japanese government enjoyed such large privileges in southern Manchuria that the province soon became an economic colony of the island empire, although it remained technically under Chinese political jurisdiction. Except during and immediately after the First World War, the Imperial government by and large attempted to protect its interests in Man-

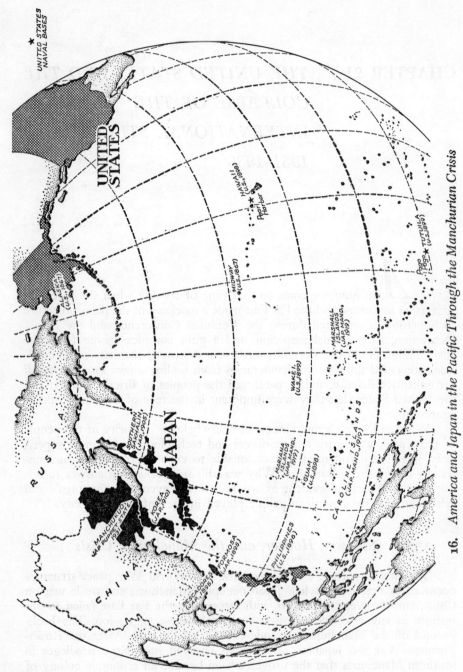

16.   *America and Japan in the Pacific Through the Manchurian Crisis*

churia by a policy of "friendship" with China and the great powers. Such a peaceful policy, however, would prevail only so long as China and the western powers acknowledged Japanese supremacy in Manchuria, for all Japanese, liberals and militarists alike, regarded the province as the economic life line of the Empire and the bulwark against Russian expansion.

Two developments in the 1920's excited Japanese fears for the safety of Manchuria and strengthened the clique who had long been clamoring for a "positive" policy of direct action. One was the resurgence of Soviet Russia as a Far Eastern power after Russian withdrawal from northern Manchuria and the Maritime Province following the Bolshevik revolution. In 1924 Sun Yat-sen, leader of the Chinese Nationalist party, the Kuomintang, joined forces with the Chinese Communists and the Soviet government in a drive to conquer and unite his country. Successful in this campaign, Sun's successor, Chiang Kai-shek, broke with the Chinese Communists in 1927 and next endeavored to oust the Russians from northern Manchuria. The result was an undeclared war between China and Russia in 1929, in which Soviet armies invaded northern Manchuria and compelled the Chinese to respect the Sino-Soviet treaty of 1924 providing for joint Chinese and Russian control of the Chinese Eastern Railway that ran from Siberia to Harbin and Vladivostok. At the same time, the Soviet government was busily engaged in constructing huge air and naval bases at Vladivostok, bases that pointed at the heart of Japan.

The return of Russian power to the Far East made the Japanese all the more determined to reinforce southern Manchuria as a barrier against Soviet expansion. But the development that incited Japan to "positive" action was the spread of Chinese nationalism into Manchuria and Chiang Kai-shek's attempt to control that province. By 1931 a number of minor incidents had increased the tension to the breaking point. Taking control of policy out of the hands of the Foreign Minister, the Japanese Army attacked and occupied Mukden, Changchun, and other Manchurian cities on September 18–19, 1931.

The blow was well timed, for Britain and the United States were then struggling to stave off international economic collapse. On September 21, 1931, China appealed to the League of Nations for protection, and the whole world turned to Britain and the United States. In general opposed to strong measures against Japan, the British waited to see what policy the Washington government would follow.

During the first weeks following the outbreak of the crisis, Secretary of State Henry L. Stimson pursued a cautious policy, on the assumption that strong American action might hinder the efforts of the Japanese Cabinet to bring the Army under control. On September 22 he called in the Japanese Ambassador and reminded him that the United States had a profound interest in protecting the integrity of China. On the other hand, the Secretary of State opposed the establishment of a commission of inquiry by the League Council, refused to agree that Japan had violated the Kellogg-Briand Pact, and warned the League Council that the United States would not cooperate in imposing economic sanctions against Japan.

While the Tokyo Foreign Office talked of direct negotiations with China and withdrawal, the Imperial Army drove steadily forward and consolidated its hold over all southern Manchuria. When the moderate Cabinet gave way in December to a Cabinet that supported the Army, and when Japanese forces on January 2, 1932, occupied Chinchow, the last Chinese stronghold in Manchuria, Stimson had to admit that his policy of peaceful persuasion had failed.

But what could the United States and the League of Nations do? Convinced that the Japanese militarists and imperialists had ruthlessly violated treaties and destroyed the entire security system erected at the Washington Conference, Stimson was now eager to rally Britain and America in defense of China, even if that meant economic sanctions and possible war. However, no statesman ever faced more discouraging obstacles in formulating a diplomatic program than did Stimson in late 1931 and early 1932. He had to content himself with expressing his government's abhorrence of Japanese aggression while he knew he could do nothing to bring the Japanese to book.

The reasons for Stimson's predicament are now well known. To begin with, evidence was overwhelming that the American people strongly condemned Japanese ruthlessness but even more strongly opposed any measures that might conceivably lead to war. The same public spokesmen—like Senator William E. Borah, the *Christian Century*, the *Nation*, and the *New Republic*—who were loudest in condemning Japan advised complete withdrawal of American forces from China. If this overwhelming popular resistance to warlike moves were not enough, then President Hoover's inflexible determination to avoid the risk of war would have proved an insurmountable barrier to forceful action. When Stimson suggested in October 1931 that the United States might have to cooperate with the League in imposing sanctions against Japan, Hoover was startled and concluded that his "able Secretary was at times more of a warrior than a diplomat." Through personal inquiry in London, the President learned that the British government would not support the United States in a strong policy. Convinced that the American people did not want war and that the imposition of sanctions would goad Japan into a war the United States might have to fight alone, Hoover sternly vetoed Stimson's plan for economic measures.

The President, however, was willing to allow his Secretary of State to use any weapons of moral coercion he could command, so that the United States at least would not seem to acquiesce in Japanese treaty violations. At Hoover's suggestion, therefore, Stimson revived the doctrine of nonrecognition of territorial and political changes effected by military force, which Bryan had first enunciated in 1915. First, however, Stimson turned to Britain and France for support. When London replied with a pointed rebuff, Stimson issued an identical warning to Japan and China on January 7, 1932: the American government would recognize no changes in the Far East brought about by force, which impaired the treaty rights of the United States and the independence and administrative integrity of China.

It was stern diplomacy and in the circumstances courageous, but it was not immediately successful. The British Foreign Office again refused to concur, while the Japanese Foreign Office replied with "elegant irony" on January 16 to the State Department. Then less than two weeks later, on January 28, the Japanese fleet and marines invaded Shanghai in retaliation against a Chinese boycott, wantonly bombarded the city, and killed thousands of civilians.

The Shanghai attack strengthened Stimson's hand but pointed up the fatal weakness of the weapons at his command. On the one hand, the British Foreign Secretary now joined Stimson in vigorous diplomatic condemnations of this new Japanese aggression. On the other, when Stimson suggested imposing economic sanctions, Hoover refused even more emphatically than before. Asserting that the Chinese could defend themselves, he declared it would be folly to fight for Asia. Thus again allowed to use only moral weapons, Stimson, in a long public letter to Senator Borah on February 23, 1932, set forth the American position in order to keep the record clear and to stipulate American policy for the future.

It was a triumph for Stimson's doggedly consistent stand when, on March 11, 1932, the Assembly of the League of Nations, with the Japanese representative abstaining, unanimously adopted a resolution incorporating almost verbatim the Bryan-Stimson doctrine of nonrecognition. Events in the Far Eastern crisis now moved to a swift conclusion: When a League commission of inquiry presented a report that named Japan as the aggressor, the League Assembly on February 24, 1933, called upon Japan to observe the Covenant and return Manchuria to China. The Japanese replied by withdrawing from the League, and the expansionists in control of the Imperial government set to work on plans for further territorial aggrandizement in the Far East.

Admitting that all his efforts to bring the Japanese to their senses had failed, Stimson concluded in retrospect none the less that his success in marshaling the opinion of the world against Japan and in obtaining the League's approval of the nonrecognition doctrine was perhaps the greatest achievement of his life. For the first time, in his view, since Wilson's day the United States had taken leadership more courageously than Britain and France in attempting to defend international peace. Without doing anything for the present to combat Japanese aggression, Stimson in company with the League had exposed that aggression for what it was—not a limited effort to protect legitimate interests but the first move in a bold plan to destroy Chinese independence. More important for the future was the fact that by reaffirming the American policy in the Far East set by Secretaries John Hay and W. J. Bryan and by refusing to acquiesce in Japan's absorption of China, Stimson and Hoover staked out a policy that would eventually culminate in war between their country and Imperial Japan.

158 / *The United States and the Collapse of European Stability, 1931–1933*

We have seen how President Hoover issued his plan for a one-year moratorium on all intergovernmental debt and reparations payments in the late spring of 1931, and how this move eased the strain on the international economy. The late summer or autumn of 1931 was clearly the time for the President to urge a mutual cancellation of all intergovernmental debt and reparations obligations. As Stimson argued at the time, such a move would have removed a huge incubus from the international economy, restored European confidence, and won for the United States a host of friends.

Hoover was personally willing to extend the moratorium until the worst of the depression had passed, but he regarded Europe's debts to the United States as sacred obligations and would never consent to cancel them or connect them officially with Germany's reparations obligations. In this matter he, not Stimson, spoke for the vast majority of Americans and for Congress, which by joint resolution on December 23, 1931, voiced its emphatic opposition to any reduction or cancellation of the war debts.

The truth was, however, that Germany could not pay reparations in 1932, and most of the European debtors were thus unable to meet their debt payments to America without running the risk of bankruptcy. Consequently the Europeans did what the circumstances demanded. Meeting in Lausanne, Switzerland, in June 1932, representatives of the western and central European powers reduced Germany's reparations obligations to $714,000,000 and tacitly agreed that this sum would never have to be paid. However, this final settlement would go into effect only when the nations in debt to the United States and one another had reached a "satisfactory settlement" of the war debts question. Instead of gracefully accepting the inevitable, as Stimson urged, Hoover condemned the Lausanne agreement and continued to apply diplomatic pressure on Europe.

The denouement of this story can be briefly told. Germany ceased reparations payments altogether after the Lausanne Conference; and when the time for the renewal of semiannual payments to the United States came in December 1932, Britain, Czechoslovakia, Italy, Finland, Latvia, and Lithuania met their obligations, while France, Greece, Poland, Belgium, Estonia, and Hungary defaulted. The following June 15, 1933, Britain, Italy, Czechoslovakia, Rumania, Lithuania, and Latvia made token payments, while the remaining debtors, except Finland, again defaulted. Congress replied on April 13, 1934, by passing the Johnson Act, which forbade any American citizen or corporation to lend money to any nation in default on its debt payments to the United States. When the Attorney General ruled that token payments did not meet the requirements of the Johnson Act, all of America's debtors except Finland defaulted in 1934 and afterward.

However, in the early months of 1933 there seemed to be some hope that American and western European leaders would unite in the forthcoming World Economic Conference to attack two other impediments to international economic recovery, high tariffs and unstable currencies. President Hoover had taken leadership in calling the conference and the new President, Roosevelt, promised cooperation. During late April and early May, Prime Minister Ramsay MacDonald of England, former Premier Édouard Herriot of France, and other spokesmen from Europe descended upon Washington for preliminary conversations with Roosevelt and his economic advisers. The upshot of these discussions was a firm American refusal to discuss suspension of war debt payments, agreement that the conference should meet in London in June 1933, and vague assurances by Roosevelt that the United States would cooperate in lowering tariff barriers and stabilizing currencies.

Once again an opportunity was given to the United States to take bold leadership in formulating a program to repair the ravages of the depression. Once again the American government refused the opportunity, because

Roosevelt had no intention of agreeing to the first necessary step, currency stabilization, unless the dollar had fallen sufficiently in value to stimulate a considerable price increase at home and an increase of American exports abroad. A large American delegation, headed by Secretary of State Cordell

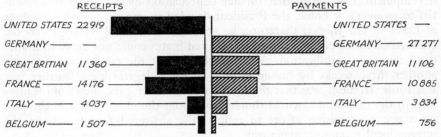

TOTAL RECEIPTS AND PAYMENTS
STIPULATED IN DEBT ADJUSTMENT AGREEMENTS
IN MILLIONS OF DOLLARS

RECEIPTS		PAYMENTS	
UNITED STATES 22 919		UNITED STATES —	
GERMANY — —		GERMANY — 27 277	
GREAT BRITIAN 11 360		GREAT BRITAIN 11 106	
FRANCE — 14 176		FRANCE — 10 885	
ITALY — 4 037		ITALY — 3 834	
BELGIUM — 1 507		BELGIUM — 756	

TOTAL DEBTS DUE UNITED STATES
ACCORDING TO FUNDING AGREEMENTS, 1923–1926

	MILLIONS OF DOLLARS	PRINCIPAL	INTEREST	MILLIONS OF DOLLARS	RATE PER CENT
GREAT BRITAIN	4 600			6 506	3.306
FRANCE	4 025			2 823	1.640
ITALY	2 042			366	0.405
BELGIUM	418			310	1.790
OTHER	438			617	—

TOTAL DEBTS AND PAYMENTS
TO JUNE 30, 1931

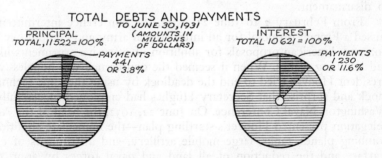

PRINCIPAL	(AMOUNTS IN MILLIONS OF DOLLARS)	INTEREST
TOTAL, 11 522 = 100%		TOTAL 10 621 = 100%
PAYMENTS 441 OR 3.8%		PAYMENTS 1 230 OR 11.6%

21. *The Intergovernmental Debt Situation on the Eve of the Lausanne Conference*

Hull, sailed for London on May 31, 1933; but they sailed in deepest ignorance of the President's intentions and in confusion among themselves. Hull believed his government should agree to lower its tariffs and peg the dollar at its then present value in gold; moreover, he thought Roosevelt agreed with him. On the other hand, a majority of the delegates opposed tariff reductions and were confused on stabilization.

The conference which opened on June 12 got off to a bad start when

Prime Minister MacDonald raised the war debts question. After a week of indecisive debate Roosevelt sent his economic adviser, Raymond Moley, to London with a tentative proposal to stabilize the dollar, then worth $4.00 to the British pound, at between $4.05 and $4.25 to the pound. But while Moley was on the high seas the dollar began to fall rapidly in value, until it reached $4.38 to the British pound on June 28. Having instructed Moley to drive a hard bargain with the British, Roosevelt was delighted by this development. Convinced that further depreciation of the dollar was essential to recovery at home, the President decided to end the agonizing debate at London. On July 3, therefore, he sent his "Bombshell Message" to the conference in which he declared the United States could not agree to immediate currency stabilization. Although Hull kept the conference alive for another three weeks by heroic efforts, all the delegates knew further talk was futile. Ironic it was that the President who later gave such bold leadership to the democratic world should have been the chief villain in the plot to wreck a promising effort to rebuild the shattered foundations of the international economic structure!

American economic unwisdom was matched in the political field by Washington's attitude concerning the important question of disarmament. From 1921 to 1926 various commissions of the League worked on the problem; and from 1926 to 1931 the United States joined the European powers in a League Preparatory Commission to draft a treaty for land disarmament. Despite French fears and hesitations, the World Disarmament Conference finally met at Geneva on February 2, 1932, amid alarming developments in Asia and Europe. Only a few days before the Japanese had attacked Shanghai, while in Germany the Nazi party, frankly committed to rearmament and repudiation of the Versailles Treaty, was growing daily. Yet the stronger the Nazis grew, the more inflexible the French became in their opposition to disarmament.

From February 2 to June 21, 1932, the conference intermittently discussed a French proposal for an international army and compulsory arbitration and American proposals for abolition of offensive armaments like tanks and bombing planes. When it seemed the conference was hopelessly mired, President Hoover tried to end the deadlock by using the same techniques of shock and surprise that Secretary Hughes had employed successfully at the Washington Naval Conference. On June 22, 1932, the head of the American delegation presented Hoover's startling plan—the immediate abolition of all bombing planes, tanks, large mobile artillery, and instruments of chemical warfare and the reduction of all land and naval forces by approximately one-third. Hoover's proposal revived the conference; and soon afterward the American, British, and French leaders promised revision of the Versailles Treaty and equality in land armaments to Germany. But these concessions came too late to save the future peace of Europe. Hitler became Chancellor of Germany on January 30, 1933; and although Roosevelt renewed Hoover's plea for action on May 16 and promised American participation in a new collective security system on May 24, Hitler withdrew his delegations from the World Disarmament Conference and the League of Nations on October 14, 1933.

One development in 1933—American recognition of the Soviet Union—

at first seemed a positive step in the direction of common action to prevent aggression. Since 1917 the Washington government had consistently refused to accord diplomatic recognition to the Moscow regime, chiefly because the Communist government refused to honor the debt of the earlier regime to the United States, confiscated American-owned property, denied religious freedom to Americans in the USSR, and waged covert warfare against American institutions through the Comintern and its branch in the United States. By 1933, however, international circumstances made an abrupt change in Russian policy imperative. In that year Russia feared a Japanese attack against the Maritime Province, and the Soviet authorities now wanted American friendship and the right to purchase supplies on credit in the United States should war with Japan occur.

On October 10, 1933, the President informed the Soviet government that he would receive a commissioner to explore "all questions outstanding between our countries"; and on November 7 the Russian Foreign Minister, Maxim Litvinov, arrived in Washington to open negotiations. The upshot was an agreement embodied in a formal exchange of notes on November 16, 1933. In return for American recognition, the Soviet government promised to abstain from carrying on propaganda activity in the United States, to guarantee religious freedom and fair trials to Americans in the Soviet Union, and to negotiate a settlement of the Czarist debt to the United States.

Ready to enter into full economic intercourse with the Soviet Union, the Washington administration established an Export-Import Bank on February 12, 1934, to facilitate exchange between the two countries. Hull's bright hopes of friendship and mutual accommodation were soon blasted, however, by Russian refusal to honor pledges given on November 16, 1933. Negotiations over a debt settlement failed because the Russians refused to acknowledge the interest on the debt; consequently the State Department blocked the extension of any credits to the Soviet Union. More damaging to Russian-American relations was the Kremlin's refusal to call off the dogs operating in the guise of the American Communist party. Until 1941 relations between the two governments were formally correct but hardly cordial.

159 / *The Good Neighbor Policy, 1933–1936*

Franklin D. Roosevelt and Cordell Hull came into control of American foreign policy at a time when the forces of international anarchy seemed about to engulf the New World as much as the Old. With courage and unflagging consistency they repudiated Wilsonian missionary interventionism, completed the Hoover-Stimson reversal of the Roosevelt Corollary, and then went on to construct an edifice of inter-American friendship and peace. Let us see how this so-called Good Neighbor policy[1] developed and what its larger consequences were.

[1] In his first inaugural Roosevelt dedicated the United States to the policy of the good neighbor in foreign affairs generally. A few weeks later, in an address on Pan-American Day, he reiterated the phrase and applied it specifically to the Latin American policy of the United States. The slogan at once caught the popular fancy and was thereafter associated only with the administration's Latin American policy.

Although Hughes, Stimson, and Hoover had taken the first steps, much remained to be done in 1933 to put the relations of the United States with its Latin American neighbors on a really cordial footing. For one thing, although the Hoover administration had tacitly repudiated the Roosevelt Corollary, it had steadfastly refused to surrender the alleged right to intervene in the internal affairs of the Caribbean republics. So long as the United States maintained this position, no Latin American could take seriously its professions of friendship.

Moreover, tragic circumstances were conspiring in Latin America in 1932 and early 1933 to present the new administration with perplexing difficulties in its search for unity and peace in the Western Hemisphere. In the first place, American trade with Latin America had declined from $2,079,-817,000 in 1929 to $573,814,000 in 1932. The effect was to blast the foundations of Latin American prosperity and cause wholesale economic disorganization, bankruptcy, and repudiation. Secondly, the peace of the New World was threatened by dissension from within as Roosevelt came into office, for in early 1933 the so-called Chaco War between Paraguay and Bolivia was raging intermittently in the jungles, a border conflict between Colombia and Peru threatened to explode into full-scale war, and unrest against the brutal dictatorship of Gerardo Machado was rising in Cuba.

Roosevelt's and Hull's determination to establish a genuine Pan-American accord was put immediately to test as a result of these and other developments. When the League of Nations offered to mediate the Peruvian-Colombian border dispute, for example, the State Department approved and in May 1933 appointed a member of the commission that settled the controversy a year later. Soon afterward, on August 7, 1933, the State Department concluded an agreement with Haiti for the withdrawal of American marines from the Negro republic by October 1, 1934. The real test of the new administration's sincerity came when a revolution against the Machado government broke out in Cuba in the spring of 1933. There were numerous demands for American intervention, but Roosevelt and Hull stubbornly resisted them. Without taking sides, the State Department stood by patiently until a second army *coup*, led by Fulgencio Batista, established a new government in late 1933 and early 1934.

These developments were a prelude to the Seventh Inter-American Conference that met in Montevideo, Uruguay, in December 1933. Hull was not sanguine over the prospect of establishing hemispheric solidarity at Montevideo, for anti-American feeling was still rife throughout Latin America, while Argentina and its Foreign Minister, Doctor Saavedra Lamas, seemed bent upon turning the conference into an anti-American affair. A few months before the Montevideo Conference was to open, Saavedra Lamas, in an obvious effort to embarrass the United States, invited all nations to join Argentina in signing an anti-war and nonaggression pact, one provision of which bound the signatories to refrain from any kind of intervention in the affairs of other states.

Arriving in Montevideo early in December 1933, Hull was greeted by an angry reception from the local press and deep hostility among many of the Latin American delegates. Determined to demonstrate American good will, Hull first called upon all the Foreign Ministers in their hotel suites. He next told the Argentinian Foreign Minister that the United States stood ready to renounce any right it once claimed to intervene in the affairs of sister states and would be happy to approve the Argentine nonaggression pact. Within a short time Saavedra Lamas gave his reply: Argentina would cooperate with the United States in working for peace and economic unity in the Western Hemisphere.

Hull's humble act of statesmanship assured the entire success of the conference, and the result of the newly found spirit of friendship was the signing of a number of important inter-American treaties. The most important of them was the Convention on Rights and Duties of States, which represented a sweeping triumph for Latin American jurisprudence on such important issues as recognition of *de facto* governments, the equality of states, nonintervention, the sovereignty of states in dealing with foreign nationals, the inviolability of territory, and territorial changes effected by forceful means.

The months following the Montevideo Conference were a critical period. Any refusal by the United States to observe the letter and spirit of the Convention on Rights and Duties of States would have destroyed all the progress thus far made. For the second time Cuba became the testing ground of the Good Neighbor's sincerity, for the Cubans demanded abrogation of the Cuban-American Treaty of 1903 that embodied the Platt Amendment and gave the United States a legal right to intervene in the internal and external affairs of the republic. After recognizing the government of Carlos Mendieta, who came to power with Batista's support on January 18, 1934, Hull hastened to make good his promises. On May 29, 1934, he signed a treaty formally abrogating the Platt Amendment and ending all special American rights in Cuba, except the right to maintain a naval base at Guantánamo.[2] In addition, Hull moved soon afterward to restore the basis of Cuban prosperity, the sugar trade, which had been hard hit by the Hawley-Smoot Tariff[3] and the depression. The tariff on Cuban sugar was reduced by 25 per cent in May and by an additional 40 per cent in August. As a result, American trade with Cuba increased nearly 100 per cent during the next year.

After the abolition of the Cuban quasi-protectorate there still remained three Caribbean countries—Haiti, the Dominican Republic, and Panama—in which the United States might legally intervene to protect property and maintain order. By special agreement with the Haitian government, American marines were withdrawn from Port-au-Prince on August 15, 1934, instead of on October 1, 1934, as the treaty of 1933 stipulated. Moreover, the Washington government allowed the Haitian-American Treaty of 1916, which had made Haiti a semi-protectorate of the United States, to expire in 1936 and relinquished its control over Haiti's financial affairs. In 1936 Panama and the United States concluded a treaty that ended the American

---

[2] Ratifications were exchanged on June 9, 1934, and the Cubans held a three-day festival to celebrate their full independence.

[3] American imports from Cuba declined in value from $207,421,000 in 1929 to $90,059,000 in 1931.

right to intervene in Panamanian affairs granted in the Panamanian-American Treaty of 1903.[4] The Dominican-American Treaty of 1924, which had continued the American receivership of the Dominican customs after the withdrawal of American troops and which did not expire until 1945, was abrogated by a new treaty between the two countries in 1940, and the receivership was ended in 1941.

Thus did the United States voluntarily surrender rights and privileges that few nations in the history of the world have willingly given up once they obtained them. No act of the Roosevelt administration better illustrated its good faith than the execution of this retreat from empire in the Caribbean region, for more was involved in this withdrawal than sheerly strategical considerations. By 1930 Americans had invested over $1,000,000,000 in Cuba, $87,000,000 in Santo Domingo, $29,000,000 in Haiti, $47,000,000 in Panama, and $13,000,000 in Nicaragua. Although none of these countries was noted for political stability, the United States gave up a treaty right to intervene for the protection of property interests because such a surrender had to be made in order to convince Latin America that the Good Neighbor meant what he had said at Montevideo.

It is only fair to add, however, that the Roosevelt administration was not motivated by sentimental altruism but rather by a desire to protect the security of the people of the United States. Convinced that the friendship of Latin America was essential to that security, Roosevelt and Hull adhered firmly to a policy of nonintervention, even when that policy involved possible capital losses by American citizens. Their action came none too soon, for events were swiftly unfolding in Europe and Asia that demanded concerted cooperation for peace by the American republics.

The Eighth Inter-American Conference was scheduled to meet in Lima, Peru, in 1938, but the international situation was so foreboding by 1936 that the State Department did not dare wait to sound a warning against potential Nazi aggression in the New World. At Roosevelt's suggestion, therefore, a special inter-American conference assembled at Buenos Aires in December 1936. As if to emphasize the seriousness of the international crisis heightened by the recent outbreak of civil war in Spain, the President went in person to Buenos Aires and opened the conference on December 1.

The delegates made easy progress on matters about which there was no disagreement. A new treaty—an Additional Protocol Relative to Non-Intervention—pledging the American republics not to intervene "directly or indirectly" in the affairs of neighboring states, for example, was signed by representatives of all twenty-one republics. On the overshadowing issue of mutual defense against aggression, however, Hull and the American delegation ran head on into the opposition of the Argentine Foreign Minister, Saavedra Lamas. On December 7 Hull presented the American plan. It envisaged the establishment of a permanent Inter-American Consultative Committee to determine whether a state of war existed among two or more

---

[4] A special article provided, however, that the two nations would consult with each other and take action to protect the Canal should war or aggression endanger its security. The United States Senate approved the treaty in 1939, but only after the Panamanian government had agreed that in emergencies the United States might act first and consult afterward.

Harry S. Truman

Franklin D. Roosevelt

Harry Hopkins

Harold L. Ickes

President Roosevelt and Vice President Wallace

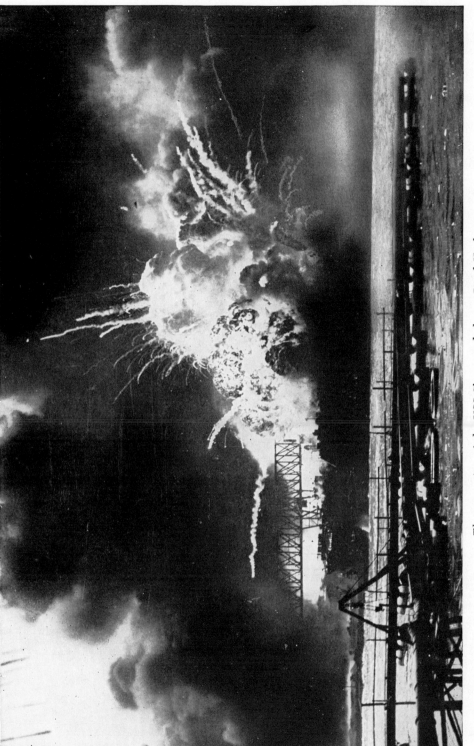

The magazine of the USS Shaw explodes at Pearl Harbor

The Yalta Conference: Prime Minister Churchill, President Roosevelt, Premier Stalin, and high ranking Allied Officers

ABOVE: *Surrender at Rheims*
BELOW: *Surrender in Tokyo Bay*

The mushroom cloud at Nagasaki, 1945

William Faulkner

George Gershwin

John L. Lewis

T. S. Eliot

ABOVE: *Candidate Eisenhower*
BELOW: *Candidate Stevenson receives congratulations from President Truman*

American republics; the imposition of a Pan-American embargo on credit and war materials in the event such a war did occur in the hemisphere; and consultation among the American republics in the event of any outside threat to hemispheric security. Bitterly opposing the American plan, Saavedra Lamas offered an alternative that envisaged close Pan-American cooperation with the League of Nations.

Rather than disrupt the conference, the American and Argentine delegations accepted a compromise offered by the Brazilians and embodied in the Convention for Collective Security and a Convention to Coordinate, Extend and Assure the Fulfillment of Existing Treaties. Omitting Hull's suggestion for a Permanent Consultative Commitee, these treaties pledged the signatories to consult with one another in the event war from within or without threatened the peace of the hemisphere; to refrain from hostile action against one another for six months while consultation was in progress; and to adopt a common neutrality in the event that war should break out. The Convention for Collective Security was weakened by the inclusion, at Argentina's insistence, of a reservation that gave each signatory freedom to refuse to join in mutual consultation in the event war outside the hemisphere threatened the peace of the Americas. Hull, none the less, was convinced the beginning toward a mutualization of the Monroe Doctrine had been made. Finally, as if to proclaim their unity and peaceful purposes, the delegates at Buenos Aires issued a Declaration of Principles of Inter-American Solidarity and Cooperation. It pledged the American republics to the peaceful settlement of all disputes and outlawed territorial conquest, collection of debts by force, and intervention by one state in the affairs of another.

Thus by the time Hitler's threats had ended hopes for peace in Europe, the Roosevelt administration had laid the groundwork for friendship and mutual defense in the Western Hemisphere. Considering the long background of mutual distrust, the Good Neighbor policy was a remarkable achievement. We will see in the following section, moreover, how the Washington administration reinforced political unity with measures of economic support and refused to use even the threat of force to protect American property interests in Latin America. Meanwhile, let us examine another phase of the American retreat from empire during the 1930's—the ironic way in which domestic self-interest combined with old anti-imperialistic impulses to impose independence upon the Filipinos.

Following the granting of near-autonomy to the Philippines by the Jones Act of 1916, President Wilson in 1920 recommended the granting of full independence to the islands. Committed to a more cautious policy, President Harding in 1921 sent a commission headed by General Leonard Wood and former Governor General W. Cameron Forbes to Manila to investigate. The commission advised that American withdrawal would constitute a "betrayal of the Philippine people . . . and a discreditable neglect of our national duty." Wood stayed on in the islands as Governor General and thoroughly antagonized the local leaders by his insistence upon prerogative. After Wood's death in 1927 the new Governor General, Henry L. Stimson, quickly won the confidence of the Filipino politicians.

Meanwhile, all Filipino leaders continued in the 1920's publicly to demand immediate independence and privately to wonder whether independence was worth losing the free American market for Philippine sugar and other agricultural products. By 1930 the Philippine-American trade had reached $183,000,000 in value, and almost two-thirds of the people of the islands were dependent upon it for the highest standard of living in the Orient. Moreover, after 1931 the fear of an expansive Japan caused Filipino leaders to count the blessings of American protection and to conclude that dominion status in an American Commonwealth was safer than a perilous independence.

Ironically, it was the depression that gave the greatest impetus to the movement for the independence that most Filipino leaders privately opposed by 1932. Western beet sugar growers, American investors in the Cuban sugar industry, southern cotton growers, and dairymen throughout the country were determined to end the competition from Philippine sugar and cocoanut oil. On January 17, 1933, their spokesmen in Congress adopted over Hoover's veto an Act for Philippine independence after a ten-year transition period, provided the Filipinos established a republican form of government. Objecting to the harsh provisions relating to trade and immigration, the Philippine legislature rejected the Act and sought instead dominion status. But Congress was adamant, and the Filipino leaders had to accept the Tydings-McDuffie Act of March 24, 1934, which was almost an exact replica of the Independence Act of 1933. Subsequently the Filipinos and President Roosevelt approved a Philippine Constitution drawn up by a constitutional convention in 1934 and 1935; Manuel Quezon became first President of the Commonwealth of the Philippines in 1935; and July 4, 1946, was set as the date for the launching of the Philippine Republic.

160 / *The Good Neighbor in Foreign Economic Policy*

During the first year of his presidency Roosevelt tried to ride two horses at the same time—by pursuing a thoroughly enlightened policy of cooperation, friendship, and restraint with foreign countries on the political level, on the one hand, and by experimenting with nationalistic economic measures, on the other. The President would obviously have to make up his mind and coordinate his political and economic foreign policies, either by pursuing a course of political and economic autarchy, such as Germany embarked upon in 1933, or else by stabilizing the dollar, lowering tariffs, and making serious efforts to reopen the channels of international trade.

From the beginning, Roosevelt's Secretary of State, Cordell Hull, was obsessed with the conviction that the United States could never find prosperity and friendship abroad unless it was willing to act like a good neighbor in foreign economic affairs. For almost a year he saw his suggestions for currency stabilization and a reciprocal trade program go unheeded while the proponents of economic nationalism had the President's ear. But he waited patiently, and by the end of 1933 Roosevelt was ready to stabilize the dollar and bring his little experiment in autarchy to an end.[5] With the

[5] In October 1936 the American, British, and French governments agreed to stabilize their currencies, to use large stabilization funds to maintain the value of these currencies in the international exchanges, and to adopt a common gold standard for purposes of international trade.

White House's blessing, moreover, Hull and his assistants set to work on a reciprocal trade bill in January 1934. It empowered the President to negotiate trade agreements, which would go into effect without congressional approval, and to raise or lower the existing Hawley-Smoot rates by as much as 50 per cent in order to obtain concessions from other countries. All tariff reductions made by the United States would apply to all nations that accorded the benefits of their lowest tariff rates to the United States. The Trade Agreements bill passed Congress easily and the President, with Hull at his side, signed the measure on June 12, 1934. "Each stroke of the pen," Hull afterward recalled, "seemed to write a message of gladness on my heart."

The State Department concluded its first trade agreement with Cuba on August 24, 1934, and soon afterward began negotiations with other nations. By the end of 1936 it had concluded trade agreements as well with Belgium, Sweden, Holland, Canada, France, Switzerland, Finland, and six Latin American nations. And American exports to these countries had increased 14 per cent during 1936, as compared with an increase in exports to other nations of only 4 per cent.

When Congress renewed the Trade Agreements Act for a second three-year period in 1937, Hull's chief objective became a trade agreement with Great Britain and a breakdown of the imperial preference barriers that Britain and the dominions had erected in 1932. He achieved some success in the signing of British-American and Canadian-American trade agreements at the White House on November 17, 1938. By the spring of 1940, when the Trade Agreements Act was renewed again, Hull had negotiated agreements with twenty-one nations, including all the leaders of the democratic bloc, which covered nearly two-thirds of the total foreign commerce of the United States.

Hand in hand with the reciprocal trade program went the execution of an economic policy to reconcile the broad political objectives of the Good Neighbor policy with the protection of American investments in Latin America. As we will see, absolute protection of the American property stake in Latin America was not possible within the framework of the Good Neighbor policy. Where immediate economic interests and long-range political objectives clashed, economic interests gave way; and in a sense "dollar diplomacy" worked in reverse.

To begin with, the Roosevelt administration merely continued Hoover's policy of refusing to use force or the threat of force to protect American investments in Latin America. Actually, the number of outright confiscations of American property in the 1930's were rare and were largely confined to Bolivia and Ecuador, both of which had irresponsible dictators during the period. Next, the Washington government established a second Export-Import Bank in March 1934 to stimulate foreign trade with Latin American and other countries. From 1934 through 1938 the bank lent some $66,000,000, most of which went to help stabilize Latin American currencies and exchange rates. Because of Hull's fierce opposition to barter deals, however, the bank never became an important direct factor in expanding the commerce of the Western Hemisphere.

This, in brief, was the Good Neighbor policy at work in the economic field; it was usually unspectacular and generally ignored by the public. One case, the Mexican expropriations of American-owned land and oil properties, however, exploded rather violently in the 1930's, involved the fate of property worth many millions of dollars, and put the principles of the Good Neighbor to severe test.

Beginning in 1934 the Mexican government of Lázaro Cárdenas undertook a program of expropriating the land holdings of American citizens in Mexico. Without ever questioning the right of Mexico to expropriate the land, Hull applied pressure on Mexico City to obtain only fair compensation to former owners. Friendly negotiations culminated in a settlement in 1941 by which the Mexican government agreed to pay $40,000,000 to settle all outstanding American agrarian claims. The land expropriations, however, were of minor importance as compared to the storm set off when the Mexicans moved against the British and American oil companies within their territory.

As we have seen earlier, the attempt of the Mexican Revolutionary government to claim ownership of foreign-held oil properties had provoked a near rupture in Mexican-American relations in the 1920's, a rupture healed in 1928 only when the Mexicans agreed that foreign oil companies might retain possession of properties acquired before 1917. Without openly repudiating this agreement, Cárdenas began a flanking movement aimed at the British and American companies soon after his accession in 1934. This campaign culminated in 1936, when the government-sponsored union of oil workers made demands that would have crippled, if not bankrupted, the companies. The companies refused to meet these extreme demands, and the Mexican government thereupon declared that an "economic conflict" existed and ordered them to comply. When the Mexican Supreme Court upheld the government's decree, the companies made a counter proposal, which Cárdenas approved. Just when it seemed the controversy was settled, the companies made the fatal mistake of demanding that Cárdenas put his approval in writing. Outraged by what he considered a slur on the national honor, the Mexican President on March 15, 1938, told his people that the government had decided to nationalize the oil industry and expropriate the property of the large foreign companies.

At once there arose in the United States and Britain enormous protest from the oil companies, whose spokesmen claimed the expropriated properties had a potential value of $450,000,000, and a demand in some quarters for forceful intervention. However, Hull calmly acknowledged that the Mexican government had an undoubted right to expropriate the oil property but insisted it also had a clear obligation to make prompt and adequate payment. Next, he began negotiations that culminated on November 19, 1941, in a general settlement of the oil and land claims,[6] in the conclusion of a Mexican-American trade agreement, and in a promise by the United States

---

[6] By the agreement on the oil issue, the United States and Mexico appointed a joint commission of experts to determine the value of the expropriated American oil properties. Both governments agreed, however, that oil in the ground was the property of the Mexican people. The joint commission reported on April 17, 1942, that the value of the expropriated American property was $23,995,991. The American companies grudgingly accepted the award after the State Department told them they must accept it or receive no compensation at all.

to help stabilize the *peso* and obtain loans through the Export-Import Bank.

Thus, instead of disrupting Mexican-American relations over the oil issue, Roosevelt and Hull turned the expropriation to the advantage of the people of the United States. By refusing to interfere in a controversy that was essentially Mexican in character, they won the lasting friendship of the Mexican people and a valuable ally during the Second World War, and convinced most Latin Americans that there were no strings attached to the Good Neighbor policy.

161 / American Disillusionment and the Triumph of Isolationism

Although he realized the consequences to the United States of the breakdown of the international system in Europe and Asia, Roosevelt was so acutely sensitive to political and popular pressures from 1932 to 1938 that he was more often the captive of public opinion than the audacious leader. There were signs during these years that the administration might have pursued a different course had the public been willing to approve collective action for peace. The important facts, however, were the determination of the American people to avoid international commitments and participation in all future wars and the administration's submission to the popular will.

As we have earlier observed, isolationism—the feeling of apartness coupled with a belief in the degeneracy of Europe and the unique virtue of American institutions and motives—had been one of the oldest and perhaps the dominant ideological force in American history. For a brief moment during the First World War the American people caught the internationalist vision, but then naively because an idealistic President made the fatal blunder of misrepresenting, or at least misunderstanding, the objectives for which the United States was fighting. Events at Versailles and in the European chancelleries afterward turned American idealism into disgust and confirmed traditional beliefs about Europe's congenital perversity.

Moreover, in the 1920's there developed among intellectuals a pervading guilt complex concerning American participation in the war and the peace conference. As European archives were opened, American historians set to work to discover the causes of the war; many concluded that Germany had been among the powers least responsible for the tragedy. This "new" history soon mushroomed into the cult of so-called revisionism. If Germany had not been primarily responsible for the war, the revisionists argued, then the Versailles Treaty was a monstrous fraud and injustice and the American people had been tricked into fighting for an unworthy cause.

This belief, popular among American intellectuals during the late 1920's, was fired by sensational exposures after 1932 and spread rapidly among the masses of people. In 1933 the House foreign affairs committee conducted an investigation of the arms traffic and its allegedly sinister influence in world politics. The following April the Senate approved a resolution for a special investigation of the munitions industry offered by Senator Gerald P. Nye, an extreme isolationist Republican from North Dakota.

When Nye himself was appointed chairman of the investigating committee, what ensued was not a restrained inquiry but rather a ruthless investigation to prove an old progressive thesis, that wars were always primarily economic in origin. It is useless now to say the committee's report grossly exaggerated the influence of bankers and businessmen and distorted the causes for America's entry into the First World War. The fact was that the committee's allegations set off a virtual wave of hysteria among thousands of thoughtful Americans, who resolved that such tragic mistakes should not happen again.

Thus the dominant temper of the American people in the mid-1930's was even more doggedly isolationist than before. A whole raft of books by scholars, journalists, and professional pacifists played upon the anti-war theme and reiterated the assertion that the American people could make their best contribution to the cause of peace by staying out of Europe's troubles and strengthening democracy at home. High school and college students were in revolt, organizing Veterans of Future Wars, joining pacifist movements like the Fellowship of Reconciliation, and vowing they would not fight if the nation went to war again. A wave of pacifism swept over the clergy. Little wonder it was that nearly two-thirds of the people questioned in a Gallup poll in April 1937 said American participation in the First World War had been a mistake.

So strong was the popular feeling by 1935 that neutrality legislation of some kind was inevitable; the only question was whether Congress would take control of foreign policy out of the President's hands. On August 20 Senator Pittman introduced a resolution prohibiting, "upon the outbreak or during the progress of war between, or among, two or more foreign States," the export of arms and munitions from the United States, making it unlawful for American ships to carry arms for or to any belligerent, and empowering the President to warn American citizens against traveling on belligerent ships. Under the Pittman Resolution the President had no discretion and no authority to discriminate in favor of the victims of aggression. The Senate passed the resolution on August 21. The best Hull could do was to persuade the House to amend the measure by limiting the life of the mandatory arms embargo provision to six months. Thus amended, the Pittman Resolution was quickly adopted by Congress and approved by the President with some misgiving on August 31, 1935.

162 / The United States and the Ethiopian Crisis, 1935–1936

While Congress sought to outlaw American participation in future wars, events in Europe and Asia began to unfold that spelled the end of international stability and would soon make a hollow mockery of America's vain pretensions. The year 1935 opened on an international situation dangerous for the peace of the world. In the Far East the Japanese were pushing forward with a penetration of northern China. In Europe Hitler was feverishly rearming Germany in defiance of the Versailles Treaty, while Mussolini was laying plans for the conquest of Ethiopia.

Hitler made the opening move on March 16, 1935, by denouncing all provisions of the Versailles Treaty for German disarmament and inaugurating conscription. Although they had the power to compel German compliance with the Treaty, the British, French, and Italian leaders contented themselves with a verbal protest. Then all hope for decisive Allied action faded when the British government concluded a treaty with the Nazis on June 18, 1935, conceding to Germany equality in submarines and the right to build a surface fleet 35 per cent the size of the Royal Navy.

Meanwhile, a skirmish between Italian and Ethiopian troops on December 5, 1934, had given Mussolini the pretext for picking a quarrel with the African empire. Rejecting the mediation of the League, Mussolini launched an invasion of Ethiopia from Eritrea and the Italian Somaliland on October 3, 1935. President Roosevelt applied an arms embargo two days later, and the State Department waited to see what the League would do. Under strong British pressure, the League Council condemned Italy as the aggressor on October 7; four days later the League Assembly voted to impose economic sanctions. And when the British moved their main fleet to the Mediterranean, it seemed that the stage was at last set for a real test of the collective security system.

Britain and France, however, preferred a compromise rather than a showdown. The League's sanctions against Italy went into effect on November 18; but the embargo did not include oil and coal. without which the Italian fleet and war machine could not function. Actually, had the League taken leadership the President and Secretary of State were prepared to cooperate in stern measures of economic coercion.[7] Fearing such action would drive Italy into alliance with Germany, the French Foreign Minister, Pierre Laval, blocked all suggestions for an oil embargo; and while the League debated, Mussolini completed his conquest of Ethiopia on May 9, 1936.

Meanwhile, consultation with Democratic leaders convinced Hull that Congress was determined to enact permanent neutrality legislation to supplant the Pittman Resolution, which would expire on February 29, 1936, and that the Senate would not give the President discretionary authority to apply the embargo only against aggressors. Hull accepted the situation and tried to make the most of it—by persuading Senator Pittman and Representative Sam D. McReynolds, chairman of the House foreign affairs committee, to introduce a neutrality bill extending the nondiscretionary arms embargo and adding provisions for a virtual embargo on the export of essential raw materials and the extension of credits to belligerents. Led by Senators Hiram Johnson, William E. Borah, and Gerald P. Nye, the isolationists counterattacked furiously, charging that Hull's measure was aimed at Italy and designed to strengthen the League system of sanctions. So effective was the attack that the Senate foreign relations committee refused even to report Hull's measure. Instead, Congress extended the provisions of the Pittman Resolution to May 1, 1937, and added amendments giving the President discretionary power in finding that a state of war existed,

[7] On November 15, 1935, for example, Hull announced the institution of a "moral," or voluntary, embargo against the shipment to Italy of coal, oil, cotton, and other raw materials in excess of normal Italian purchases in the United States.

prohibiting the extension of war loans and credits to belligerents, requiring the President to apply the neutrality legislation in the event other nations went to war after hostilities had begun, and exempting any American republic at war with a power outside the Western Hemisphere.

163 / *The United States and New Aggressions in Europe and Asia, 1936–1937*

Mussolini's successful defiance of the League revealed the fatal weakness of the Anglo-French bloc and cleared the road for new violations of the peace structure by Germany, Italy, and Japan. Indeed, at the height of the Ethiopian crisis, on March 7, 1936, Hitler denounced the Locarno treaties and sent his troops into the demilitarized Rhineland. Eight months later, on October 25, Hitler and Mussolini joined hands in the so-called Rome-Berlin Axis, which afterward metamorphosed into a political and military alliance between the two dictators. When the Germans and Japanese joined forces in an Anti-Comintern Pact on November 16, 1936, the stage was at last set for a new alliance of the militaristic-imperialistic nations to destroy the existing balance of power and establish fascist hegemony in the world.

Recognizing the new coalition as a dire threat to the security of their own regime, the leaders of the Soviet Union appealed to the western democracies for stern collective action to contain fascism. The leaders of Britain and France, however, feared the communist threat from within as much as the fascist danger from without; were obsessed by fear of a general war, which they would have to fight without even a modicum of support from the United States; and hopefully assumed that satisfaction of legitimate German and Italian complaints would preserve the peace of Europe. Had the American government been able to provide the necessary leadership and rally the Atlantic powers in this time of crisis the world might have been spared the worst tragedy in the history of mankind. Lacking American support, from 1936 to 1939 the dominant western powers stood by helplessly while Germany and Japan marched from one triumphant conquest to another.

No sooner had the Ethiopian crisis ended than Europe's peace was again threatened by the outbreak of civil war in Spain on July 18, 1936. In the beginning the conflict was simply a Spanish affair—a revolt of the army under General Francisco Franco, supported by the great landowners, the Roman Catholic Church, and the business classes, against a Popular Front government. However, Spain soon became an arena in which Spanish, Italian, and German fascists joined battle against an incompatible coalition of democrats and communists.

Before the civil war developed into this international contest, the British, French, German, Italian, Russian, and other European governments applied a seeming policy of strict nonintervention to prevent the Spanish cauldron from boiling into a general war. On September 9, 1936, representatives of twenty-seven European powers established a Non-Intervention Committee in London to prevent men and supplies from going to either side; and in March 1937 the Committee established a naval blockade of Spain.

But the Committee's efforts were totally futile, as the Italians, Germans, and Russians made a laughingstock of the blockade and the Italian government openly boasted of its aid to Franco.

In the meantime, the American government had joined the British and French in the policy of nonintervention. The Neutrality Act of 1936 did not apply to civil wars, it is true; but the State Department applied a "moral" embargo against the export of arms and war materials as a means of strengthening the Non-Intervention Committee. Then, when a dealer in secondhand airplanes sought to export some 400 airplane engines to the Loyalist government in December 1936, the administration hastily requested Congress to apply the arms embargo to Spain. A joint resolution granting the President's request passed with only one dissenting vote in both houses on January 6, 1937. Two days later it became law upon the approval of the President. Even after the true character of the civil war became evident and a large body of opinion favorable to the Loyalists, or the forces of the legitimate government, developed in the United States, the administration, fearful of alienating Catholic opinion, blocked all efforts at repeal of the joint resolution. Thus, with the indirect assistance of the western democracies and the open support of Germany and Italy, Franco destroyed the Spanish democracy and secured his dictatorship in 1939.

Moralists might debate and critics of the administration afterward denounce the American policy as a betrayal of the democratic cause. Actually, the administration could not have done otherwise, given the circumstances prevailing at home and in Europe at the time. The nonintervention policy was made in London and in Paris, not in Washington. The American people would not have countenanced aggressive support of the Loyalists and defiance of the international blockade. It was a situation in which Roosevelt and Hull had no alternative but to follow Britain and France in what was obviously a mistaken policy.

The overriding American determination to avoid entanglement in European troubles was again demonstrated in the late winter and spring of 1937, when Congress adopted a new and permanent neutrality law to supplant the temporary Act of 1936. Knowing he could not prevent legislation, Hull worked quietly and to a degree successfully to win larger discretion for the Executive in the enforcement of the new measure. Approved by Congress on April 29 and signed by Roosevelt on May 1, 1937, it authorized the President to determine when a state of war existed or when a civil war threatened the peace of the world. If the President should find that such international or civil wars existed, an embargo against the export of arms, ammunition, and credits should go immediately into effect. In addition, a "cash and carry" provision, to run for two years, empowered the President to require belligerents who purchased nonmilitary commodities in the United States to pay cash for such goods and to transport them in their own vessels.

It was a fateful time for a great nation thus to bind its hands, for at the very moment Congress approved the "permanent" Neutrality Act the Japanese were completing plans for a war against China and Hitler was contemplating the seizure of Austria and Czechoslovakia. Let us look briefly at these events that made war inevitable and American neutrality impossible.

After absorbing Manchuria and Outer Mongolia in 1932 and 1933, the Japanese Army began a campaign to penetrate the five northern provinces of China and detach them from the Nationalist government at Nanking. At the same time, the Nationalist leader, Chiang Kai-shek, consolidated his administrative power and strengthened his armed forces in preparation for the inevitable showdown. A clash between Chinese and Japanese troops near Peking on July 7, 1937, gave the Imperial Army an excuse for launching a full-scale campaign to conquer the northern provinces and bring Chiang to terms. Instead of submitting, however, the Chinese resisted courageously; and thus what the Japanese miltary leaders thought would be a mere "incident" quickly settled into a long and bloody war.

The Washington government was not surprised by this renewal of Japanese aggression, but it was in no position in the summer of 1937 to do anything to thwart it. On July 16 Hull circulated a note in which he implicitly condemned the Japanese and called upon the powers to reaffirm their allegiance to the principles of international morality. Next, on August 17, the President dispatched 1,200 marines to Shanghai to reinforce the 2,200 American soldiers already stationed in China.

In order to stir public support for a stronger policy, Hull persuaded the President to include a plea for international cooperation in an address he had agreed to deliver in Chicago on October 5. But Roosevelt went far beyond the draft prepared by the State Department, appealed to the American people to see the facts of international life, and implied that the peace-loving nations might have to quarantine aggressors to prevent the spread of international anarchy. Roosevelt hoped the slogan, "Quarantine the Aggressors," would catch the public fancy, as the phrases "New Deal" and "Good Neighbor Policy" had done. However, the quarantine speech stirred such violent reactions that it probably injured the movement for a larger degree of collective action.

The day following the President's address, October 6, the League Assembly adopted reports condemning Japanese aggression and suggesting that a conference of the signatories of the Nine Power Treaty consider proper measures of collective action. Fearing a Japanese threat to their far-flung interests in the Orient, the British strongly endorsed the suggestion. In Washington Hull also approved and recommended Brussels as the meeting place. What might have become the first great experiment in forceful cooperation against aggression, however, was wrecked before it could be launched—by the overwhelming American determination to avoid the risk of war, and by the President's refusal to defy this popular will. When press polls revealed a two to one congressional majority against cooperation with the League in applying sanctions against Japan, Roosevelt immediately retreated from the advanced position of his quarantine address. In a "fireside chat" on October 12, for example, he assured the people that the purpose of the Brussels Conference would be to settle the Sino-Japanese war by agreement and cooperation, obviously not by strong measures of economic warfare.

The truth probably was that the British and French leaders had no more heart for a policy that might lead to war than Roosevelt and Hull had. Seeing that the Brussels Conference would take no effective action, however, the

British Foreign Secretary, Anthony Eden, maneuvered to throw the onus for its failure on the United States. On November 2 Eden had a long talk at Brussels with the American delegate at the conference. Great Britain, Eden declared, was willing to stand shoulder to shoulder with the United States and would cooperate in any measures against Japan. But Britain would go only so far as the United States and would "base her policy upon American policy during the present crisis." When the conference opened the following day, moreover, other delegates demanded that the Americans take leadership in formulating a program of action. Impotent in the face of public opinion at home, the Washington government could not lead; and the conference broke up on November 24 after adopting a pious reaffirmation of the principles enunciated in the Nine Power Treaty.

The Japanese gave their answer on December 12, by bombing and sinking the United States gunboat *Panay* and three Standard Oil tankers in the Yangtze River near Nanking. The chief reaction in the United States was a loud demand for withdrawal of all American forces in China,[8] and Japan was allowed to apologize and pay an indemnity on December 23, 1937.

164 / *The President's Plan and Its Aftermath*

At the time he made his quarantine address, Roosevelt was contemplating some bold stroke—perhaps a meeting of the leaders of the great powers at sea—to prepare the way for the Brussels Conference. On October 6, 1937, Undersecretary of State Sumner Welles sent the President a memorandum embodying a program for action—the calling of a world conference in which the powers would seek to reconstruct international law and find a basis for political and economic cooperation. Roosevelt approved and contemplated calling in the diplomatic representatives on Armistice Day. He postponed action, however, when Hull strenuously opposed the plan on the grounds that Japan and the European dictators would of course pay lip service to peace and brotherhood and that their seeming concurrence would lull the democracies into a sense of false security.

Significant events in Europe soon afterward caused the President to take up his plan again. In November 1937 the British government embarked upon a policy aimed at appeasing Germany's legitimate grievances and establishing a new European accord. Lord Halifax, speaking for the Cabinet, described the new British policy in conversations with Hitler in Berlin; Hitler in turn promised sincere cooperation. Upon learning of this development, Roosevelt decided to launch his campaign for a new international *modus vivendi* in order to support Britain's attempt to come to an understanding with Germany.

First, however, on January 11, 1938, the President sent a secret message to Prime Minister Neville Chamberlain in which he described his plan. In delivering the message to the British Ambassador, Welles warned that "all the progress which had been made in Anglo-American co-operation during

[8] In a Gallup poll taken in January 1938, 70 per cent of the persons queried said they favored total American withdrawal from the Far East. Four months before only 54 per cent of the persons queried in a similar poll had favored such withdrawal.

the previous two years would be destroyed" if the British Cabinet did not cooperate.[9] Without consulting Foreign Secretary Eden, who was then abroad, Chamberlain replied on January 13 that the President's proposal would interfere with his, Chamberlain's, plan to appease Germany and recognize Italy's conquest of Ethiopia in return for certain guarantees. The news that Britain intended to condone Mussolini's conquest of Ethiopia dumbfounded the Washington administration, and Roosevelt and Hull both replied in terms of disgust.

In the meantime, upon his return to London Eden had put such pressure on Chamberlain that the Prime Minister informed the President on January 21, 1938, that the British government would cordially cooperate in his plan but could not take responsibility for its failure. Whether Roosevelt would have acted had circumstances not changed drastically soon afterward, we do not know. In any event, on February 20 Eden resigned primarily in protest over Chamberlain's Italian policy, while Hitler occupied and annexed Austria to Germany on March 12 and 13. As a consequence, the President's plan sank out of sight.

In view of the uncertain prospect for peace, the administration now began seriously to consider the naval and military impotence of the nation. Since 1933 the President and Congress had slightly augmented the army's feeble strength but had not provided enough new naval construction to maintain the fleet even at the strength authorized by the London Treaty of 1930. In December 1934 the Japanese had denounced the Washington Naval Treaty; late in 1935 and early in 1936 American, British, French, and Japanese delegates had met in London to discuss continuation of naval disarmament, and the Japanese had withdrawn when the Atlantic powers would not grant equality to the Imperial fleet.

A renewal of Japanese construction in 1937 and especially the outbreak of the Sino-Japanese War in the same year convinced the President that the time had come when the United States must look to its own resources for protection. On January 28, 1938, he sent a special message to Congress in which he urged additional military expenditures and an immediate increase of 20 per cent in expenditures for naval construction. Pacifists all over the country decried the President's request as beginning a new arms race. None the less, in May 1938 Congress approved the Vinson Naval Expansion Act authorizing the expenditure over the next decade of some $1,000,000,000 to create a navy presumably strong enough to meet the combined fleets of Japan, Germany, and Italy.

The adoption of the naval expansion bill was one sign, among others, of profound changes that were taking place in American opinion by the spring of 1938. The American people were still determined to avoid participation in Asia's and Europe's wars. Even so, most thoughtful Americans were beginning to perceive the enormity of the rising Nazi menace and were willing at least to admit the necessity for strong defenses against potential threats to the security of the Western Hemisphere.

[9] The quotation is from Winston S. Churchill, *The Gathering Storm* (Boston, 1948), pp. 251–252.

CHAPTER 22 / *THE SECOND ROAD TO WAR,*
1938–1941

*S*oon after his seizure of Austria in the late winter of 1938, Hitler brought Europe to the verge of war by his demand for the German-speaking Sudeten provinces of Czechoslovakia. By rejecting Russian cooperation and submitting to Hitler's demands during this so-called Munich crisis, the British and French postponed an inevitable war but lost a powerful ally. Hitler's hasty betrayal of his Munich pledges and his attack against Poland in September 1939 forced the two western democracies to stand up and fight to prevent Nazi power from overwhelming all of Europe.

During the hectic months before the outbreak of the war and afterward, until the fall of France in June 1940, the American government and people offered neither moral leadership nor decisive material support to the cause of freedom. But it is easy to criticize in retrospect and to forget how divided and distraught the American people were in this time of crisis, and how the administration could not lead where Congress and the people would not follow. The important fact was that once the Nazi menace to their own security became apparent, Americans, or a majority of them, rallied behind the President in a bold effort to rectify the mistakes of the past.

While the Washington government sought to help stem the Nazi tide in the West by measures short of war, it used stern diplomacy to turn back the rising tide of Japanese imperialism that threatened to engulf the Far East. At any time during the period from 1939 to December 1941 the American leaders could have come to terms with the Japanese government— by accepting Japanese control of China and Japanese demands for leadership in the Orient. The supreme tragedy was that by 1941 the situation had passed beyond the point of reasonable solution. As compromise on any terms that did not violate everything the American people had stood for in the Far East seemed impossible by 1941, the two nations reached the point where diplomacy could not harmonize fundamentally divergent objectives.

In the following chapter we will relate the way in which the American government and people haltingly at first, but boldly afterward, emerged from the chrysalis of isolation and assumed a position of decisive power in the affairs of mankind.

165 / From the Munich Crisis to the Outbreak of War

After the annexation of Austria, Hitler began a campaign for the incorporation of the German-speaking Sudeten provinces of Czechoslovakia into Greater Germany, prepared defenses along the French border, and made plans for a campaign in the East. Meanwhile, Prime Minister Chamberlain and his new Foreign Secretary, Lord Halifax, concluded that the best hope for peace lay in Czechoslovakia's granting autonomy to the Sudeten Germans. Chamberlain, therefore, attempted to mediate between the Czech government and Konrad Henlein, spokesmen of the Sudeten Germans. These negotiations failed because Henlein rejected autonomy and demanded the union of the Sudetenland with Germany.

When it seemed war was inevitable, Chamberlain flew to Germany for a personal meeting with Hitler on September 15, 1938. Informed that Germany would accept nothing less than cession of the Sudetenland, Chamberlain and the French Premier, Edouard Daladier, agreed that Czechoslovakia must surrender to the *Führer's* demands. The Czech leaders had no alternative but to submit. Then, when Hitler rejected Chamberlain's arrangement for the transfer of the disputed provinces, it seemed the British and French governments would accept war rather than further humble themselves.

The overwhelming majority of the people of western Europe and the United States, however, continued to hope for peace even in the blackest days of the September crisis. In response to promptings from Paris and London, Roosevelt appealed on September 26 to Chamberlain, Daladier, Hitler, and President Eduard Beneš of Czechoslovakia to compose their differences peacefully. The following day, moreover, he appealed to Mussolini to use his influence with Hitler for peace and dispatched a special message to Berlin. At the same time, in a last ditch appeal on September 27, Chamberlain suggested that Hitler, Daladier, Mussolini, and he meet personally to find a solution. The world was surprised when Hitler accepted and relieved when the four leaders met at Munich on September 29 and quickly agreed to a scheme for the dismemberment of the Czech Republic.

By a stroke of the pen, Chamberlain and Daladier confirmed Hitler's supremacy over his generals; made Germany absolutely dominant on the Continent; weakened the appeal of a western alignment for the Soviet leaders; and demonstrated their own incompetence as diplomats. In return, all they received was Hitler's unctuous promise that he would make no more territorial demands in Europe, would respect Czech sovereignty, and would settle all future disputes by peaceful negotiation.

Although he had acted as an unhappy partner in appeasement, Roosevelt at least was never guilty of believing that the Munich Agreement offered any hope for peace in Europe. On the contrary, he began soon afterward to reorient his domestic and foreign policies in preparation for the conflict that was bound to come.

To begin with, the President abandoned his "purge" of conservative Democrats, called a halt to the reform energies of the New Deal, and began a campaign for speedy rearmament in the autumn of 1938. When Hitler announced an expansion of German military strength on October 9, Roosevelt countered two days later by announcing a $300,000,000 increase in American spending for defense purposes and by calling upon his military advisers to plan for huge increases in aircraft production. In his Annual Message to Congress and his Budget Message on January 4 and 5, 1939, moreover, he asked for one and a third billion dollars for the regular defense establishment and an additional $525,000,000, most of it for airplanes. These appeals fell upon receptive ears, for the Munich tragedy had opened the eyes of millions of Americans to the Nazi danger to world peace, while violent anti-Jewish pogroms in Germany in November 1938 revealed anew the brutal character of the Nazi regime.[1] Thus Congress responded by increasing the military and naval budgets by nearly two-thirds and by authorizing the President to begin accumulating stockpiles of strategic raw materials for use if war occurred.

In addition, the Washington administration intensified its campaign to strengthen the collective security system in the Western Hemisphere. This was now a more urgent and difficult task than during the early years of the Good Neighbor policy, for the German government had begun a tremendous economic and propaganda campaign aimed at destroying American influence and establishing German hegemony in Latin America. Nazi agents had organized National Socialist parties among German immigrants in Brazil and Argentina, threatened economic reprisals against any Latin American nation that dared cooperate with the United States, and engaged in wholesale military espionage under the cover of German steamship and air lines.

Roosevelt and Hull therefore determined to form a solid hemispheric anti-Nazi front at the Pan-American Conference that opened at Lima, Peru, on December 9, 1938. As chairman of the American delegation and chief advocate of hemispheric solidarity, Hull had the cordial support of most of the Latin American governments. As during the Buenos Aires conference two years before, however, the Argentine delegation seemed determined either to dominate or wreck the proceedings. By marshaling a nearly solid Latin American opinion and by patient negotiations with the President and Foreign Minister of Argentina, Hull was able to obtain unanimous approval of the Declaration of Lima on Christmas Eve. In this pronouncement the twenty-one American republics affirmed their determination to consult with one another and resist jointly any Fascist or Nazi threat to the peace and security of the hemisphere.

During the uneasy months following Munich, the President's chief objective was repeal or drastic amendment of the Neutrality Act of 1937, in order to withdraw that measure's invitation to aggression. Anxious to avoid giving the isolationists an issue during the early months of 1939, Roosevelt moved for repeal of the arms embargo through negotiation rather than by direct attack. Hull was in constant communication with Key Pittman, chairman of the Senate foreign relations committee, urging him to take leadership in repealing the arms embargo, that "incitement to Hitler to

[1] It would be difficult to exaggerate the importance of the American reaction to this outbreak of terrorism against the Jews of Germany. Leaders of both parties joined in expressing the revulsion of the American people, while Roosevelt recalled Ambassador Hugh Wilson from Berlin in protest.

go to war." But Pittman warned that a repeal measure could not pass, and Roosevelt and Hull momentarily gave up the fight and concentrated instead on pushing measures for stronger defense.

Two months later, however, the international situation suddenly deteriorated to the point where war seemed inevitable. After spurring Slovak leaders to declare their independence of Prague, Hitler sent his armies into the Czech capital on March 15, 1939, and took control of what remained of unhappy Czechoslovakia. The dictator's cynical violation of an agreement upon which the ink was hardly dry caused such a profound revulsion of sentiment in Great Britain that Chamberlain was forced to abandon appeasement. Almost at once the Prime Minister began negotiating treaties guaranteeing the independence and territorial integrity of countries believed to be next in Germany's line of march, Poland, Rumania, Greece, and Turkey.

Reaction in Washington to Hitler's latest aggression was nearly as violent as in London. Speaking for the President on March 17, Acting Secretary of State Sumner Welles condemned Germany's "wanton lawlessness" and use of "arbitrary force." On the same day the President decided not to recognize the destruction of Czechoslovakia and to continue to deal with the Czech Minister in Washington. Accompanying this strong talk now went even stronger administration action to obtain revision of the neutrality statute. In order to win Senator Pittman's support, Roosevelt and Hull accepted a compromise measure—introduced by Pittman on March 20—that extended the "cash and carry" provision to include arms, ammunition, and other war materials.

In spite of the fact that the President ventured all his prestige in the fight to obtain either passage of the Pittman bill or outright repeal of the arms embargo, the campaign was to no avail. On May 19 Roosevelt called House leaders to the Executive Mansion and declared that repeal of the arms embargo might prevent war and would certainly make an Axis victory less likely if war occurred. In addition, he persuaded King George VI and Queen Elizabeth to pay a state visit to the United States in June in order to stimulate Anglo-American friendship. But Congress would not budge from its determined opposition to the President's demands.

After both houses had decisively refused to approve measures of revision, the President invited Senate leaders to the White House on July 18 for a frank discussion of the European situation. Upon ascertaining that all senators present but one thought revision of the Neutrality Act was impossible, Vice President Garner turned to Roosevelt and said: "Well, Captain, we may as well face the facts. You haven't got the votes, and that's all there is to it." The President replied that he had done his best and that the Senate would have to take the responsibility for refusing to act to protect the nation's security.

Meanwhile, Roosevelt and Hull worked as best they could to restrain Germany and Italy. On March 22, 1939, for example, the President warned the new Italian Ambassador that the United States would extend aid to Britain and France in the event war broke out and promised he would cooperate with Mussolini in any effort for peace. When the *Duce* occupied Albania on April 7, Roosevelt countered a week later by appealing personally to the two dictators to demonstrate that they did not want war. "Are you willing to give assurance that your armed forces will not attack or invade the territory or possessions" of Europe and the Middle East, the President bluntly asked. If Hitler and Mussolini were willing to give such assurances for a reasonable period, Roosevelt continued, he would take leadership in a movement for disarmament and equal access by Germany and Italy to the trade and natural resources of the world.

Broadcast everywhere, Roosevelt's message bolstered British and French courage and threw the German and Italian leaders into a paroxysm of rage. As it turned out, Roosevelt's message was a prelude to war, not the harbinger of peace the people of the world so desperately desired.

166 / *The Impact of the War upon the American People*

During the summer of 1939 the leaders of Europe engaged in last-minute negotiations in preparation for Armageddon. By signing the Munich Pact, Chamberlain and Daladier had not only isolated Russia but had also intensified Russian suspicions that they were trying to turn Hitler eastward against the Soviet Union. After the abandonment of appeasement, the British and French premiers appealed to the Kremlin for an alliance to contain Nazism. The Russians demanded as their price a guarantee of the security of all of eastern Europe and the Baltic states and acknowledgment of Russia's right in certain circumstances to occupy this broad zone stretching from Finland to Bulgaria.

While Chamberlain and Daladier were negotiating, Stalin and his new Foreign Minister, Vyacheslav Molotov, were simultaneously sounding out the possibilities of an agreement with Germany. Hitler was glad to make temporary concessions to prevent Russia from joining his adversaries in the West. The upshot of these negotiations was the signing of a Nazi-Soviet treaty of nonaggression in Moscow on August 23, 1939. The published terms provided simply that Russia and Germany would refrain from attacking each other; the secret provisions provided that in the event of a territorial re-arrangement in eastern Europe, Russia should have Finland, Estonia, Latvia, eastern Poland, and the Rumanian province of Bessarabia, while Germany might annex Lithuania[2] and western Poland.

Now safeguarded against the danger of a two-front war, Hitler increased his demands on Poland and mobilized his armies. Chamberlain warned that Britain would go at once to Poland's aid if Germany attacked but offered to discuss the Polish question, and Roosevelt added a new appeal for peace. Hitler responded by sending his armies into Poland on September 1; two days later Britain and France declared war on the Reich. Thus after four years of intolerable tension the chips were finally down for a last play.

Most Americans had seen that war was inevitable and took the outbreak of hostilities in stride. On September 5, 1939, the President issued an official proclamation of neutrality and put the Neutrality Act into force,[3] as he was

---

[2] By subsequent negotiation Germany exchanged Lithuania for Polish territory.

[3] Thus the arms embargo went into effect, causing an immediate cancellation of Anglo-French war orders worth $79,000,000. Belligerents, however, were free to buy raw materials and food, although the Johnson Act prevented the extension of credits to the British and French governments.

bound to do; but he did not make Wilson's mistake of asking the people to be impartial in thought as well as in deed. "This nation will remain a neutral nation," he declared on September 3, "but I cannot ask that every American remain neutral in thought as well. Even a neutral has a right to take account of facts. Even a neutral cannot be asked to close his mind or his conscience."

Moving swiftly to strengthen the defenses of the Western Hemisphere, the Washington administration on September 3 arranged for the calling of a conference of the Foreign Ministers of the American republics. Meeting at Panama City on September 23 amid an atmosphere of surprising unanimity, the conferees agreed upon common neutrality regulations and mutual consultation in the event a transfer of territory from one European power to another threatened the security of the New World. The most important work of the conference was the adoption of the Declaration of Panama, marking out a broad zone 300 miles wide around the Americas, excluding Canada and European colonies, into which the belligerents were forbidden to carry the war.

The President's primary objective, however, was still repeal of the arms embargo provision of the Neutrality Act. Calling Congress into special session, on September 21 he pleaded earnestly for repeal, but his main theme was the maintenance of American neutrality, for he shared the prevalent view that Britain and France could defeat Germany if only they could obtain the weapons of war. As if to demonstrate his belief that neutrality was desirable, he urged Congress to prohibit American ships from entering the European war zones and to apply the "cash and carry" principle to all European purchases in the United States.

Modest and thoroughly neutral though the President's request was, it stimulated isolationists to frenzied activity. In a radio broadcast, Senator Borah repeated the old American dictum that European wars were caused by "the unconscionable schemes of remorseless rulers" and warned that lifting the arms embargo would be tantamount to taking sides in a war in which American interests were not involved. Other isolationist leaders in Congress joined the attack, while the battle was squarely joined in the country at large. Pacifists, who argued that the only way to prevent war was to have nothing to do with the instruments of destruction, were joined by Communists, who charged that Britain and France were fighting to preserve imperialistic capitalism. Former President Hoover contributed the suggestion that the United States forbid only the export of offensive armaments. Colonel Charles A. Lindbergh, popular air idol of other days, warned that the American people had no stake in the war and should keep their hands clean. On the other side in support of the President was ranged a powerful new combination of southern and eastern Democrats in Congress joined by such preparationist Republicans as Stimson and Frank Knox, a vast majority of the business interests and the metropolitan press, and a large segment of the intellectual leadership of the country.

By the middle of October it was evident that the tide had turned in the President's favor. Meanwhile, Senator Pittman had drafted a new neutrality bill that lifted the arms embargo and imposed severe restrictions on American shipping. Pittman persuaded the foreign relations committee to report the measure favorably on September 28. After a month of debate, Congress approved the Pittman bill, and the President signed it on November 4, 1939. Although it afforded considerable advantage to the democratic allies, the Pittman Act—in its provisions prohibiting American ships to trade with belligerent countries and American citizens from traveling on belligerent vessels—reflected the high tide of the American determination to avoid controversies that had led to involvement in the First World War.

Meanwhile, Hitler's armies had overrun Poland before the French could mount an offensive on the Western Front and the Russians had shocked the world by joining the Germans in devouring Poland. During the months following the fall of Poland, until April 1940, the Germans built their offensive power for a drive in the West while the British and French acted as if the war could be won merely by waiting for the Nazi regime to collapse. This so-called "phony war" lulled Americans even more than the British and French into believing that the Germans could never win.

American attention was diverted from the western front in November and December 1939, when the Russians invaded Finland. A hot wave of anger swept over the American public, but the administration acted cautiously. Roosevelt indignantly denounced the "dreadful rape of Finland" and castigated the Soviet Union as "a dictatorship as absolute as any other dictatorship in the world"; the State and Treasury departments instituted an effective "moral" embargo on the export of war supplies to the Soviets; but beyond this action the administration would not go. Perceiving that the marriage between Germany and Russia was incompatible, Roosevelt and Hull simply refused to do anything to cement the alliance of the two totalitarian regimes.

Meanwhile, as the months passed without any eruption on the western front, the thoughts of Roosevelt and most Americans turned inevitably toward the peace they all desired. Their hope, however, exceeded the possibilities of the time. What they desired was a postwar world founded upon international justice and close cooperation for peace. To achieve new understanding and stimulate public discussion, the President and State Department cooperated with private foundations in launching studies and sponsoring public meetings. But what point was there in talking about peace so long as Hitler dominated the Continent, skeptics in the administration asked. Undaunted by such objections, in early February 1940 Roosevelt decided to send Sumner Welles to London, Paris, Rome, and Berlin to sound out the possibilities of a just and lasting settlement. Welles went on his mission and soon discovered what he and every informed person already knew—that Hitler would agree to no settlement which Britain, France, and the United States could approve, and that the ultimate decision must be made on the battlefield.

167 / The Menace of a Nazi Victory

The "phony war" ended on April 9, 1940, when Hitler sent his armies into Denmark and Norway and German airplanes and *Panzer* divisions struck hard at Belgium, Holland, and northern France on May 10. It is difficult to describe the terror that swept over the American people as Hitler's *Blitzkrieg* developed. All Americans except a few die-hard isolationists recognized that a Germany completely dominant in Europe would pose a dire threat to their peace and security. And now it was about to happen, the catastrophe that only a week before had seemed impossible. There was France, her poorly equipped armies reeling and scattering under the impact of Nazi power; there was the British expeditionary force, driven to the sea at Dunkirk and forced to execute a nearly impossible evacuation.

The immediate threat to American security was the possibility that Hitler might claim Iceland and Greenland, both of which commanded the American sea lanes to Britain, by virtue of his conquest of their mother country, Denmark. Roosevelt refused to order the occupation of Iceland but was obviously pleased when the British occupied it on May 10. Because of its proximity to the United States and Canada, however, Greenland could not be ignored. On April 18 Roosevelt declared that the island enjoyed the protection of the Monroe Doctrine. Refusing a request by Greenlanders that the United States assume a temporary protectorate, the Washington administration instead furnished military supplies and established a Greenland Patrol by the Coast Guard.

On May 10, 1940, the day before the Germans hurtled into the Low Countries, Chamberlain resigned and Winston Spencer Churchill, long the chief British opponent of appeasement, took the helm as Prime Minister with nothing to offer the people of the Empire but "blood, toil, tears, and sweat" and the hope of ultimate victory. When the *Blitzkrieg* was in its fifth day, Churchill sent a cable to Roosevelt in which he frankly acknowledged the likelihood of German conquest of Europe and asked the President to proclaim a state of nonbelligerency, to lend Britain forty or fifty old destroyers, and to supply several hundred aircraft and quantities of ammunition. Roosevelt had to reply that since Congress would have to approve a transfer of the destroyers the moment for such action was not opportune.

Before he received Churchill's urgent plea, however, Roosevelt had determined to ask Congress to hasten the nation's armament campaign.[4] This he did in a special message on May 16, 1940, in which he warned Americans that their own security would be gravely imperiled if an enemy should seize any outlying territory, and called for the production of 50,000 planes a year and large new expenditures for the armed forces. On May 31, moreover, after the Allied collapse on the western front, he asked Congress for an additional $1,000,000,000 for defense and for authority to call the National Guard and reserve personnel into active service.

Meanwhile, Roosevelt had been trying to bolster French morale and to dissuade Mussolini from joining Hitler. Deaf to such appeals, Mussolini rushed to join the Nazis in devouring the carcass of France on June 10. This act of aggression gave the President an opportunity to state in clear and ringing words the course the United States would follow. In an address at the University of Virginia on the day Italy entered the war, Roosevelt announced the end of American isolation and the beginning of a new phase of nonbelligerency, during which the United States would "extend to the

---

[4] The War Department had made plans for an increase in the army's strength to 500,000 men by July 1941, to 1,000,000 by January 1942, and to nearly 2,000,000 by July 1942; for the production of 50,000 aircraft a year; and for the production of vast numbers of tanks and guns.

opponents of force the material resources of this nation." Moreover, he voiced American indignation at Mussolini's treachery in the now famous indictment, "On this tenth day of June, 1940, the hand that held the dagger has struck it into the back of its neighbor."

This was the week in which France was tottering on the brink of ruin. After German armies entered Paris on June 12, the government of Paul Reynaud, who had succeeded Daladier as Premier on March 21, gave way on June 16 to a government headed by the aged Marshal Pétain, who surrendered to the Germans on June 22. The supreme moment of decision had now come for the President and his advisers. Hitler stood astride the Continent; Italian entry into the war seemed to presage early Axis control of the Mediterranean and North Africa; and the British army was stripped of virtually all its heavy equipment after the Dunkirk evacuation. Churchill had warned in repeated messages that the British Isles might be overrun without immediate American assistance and that a successor government might have to surrender the fleet in order to save the people of the kingdom. Should the Roosevelt administration assume the British were lost, abandon aid to them, and prepare to defend the Western Hemisphere? Or should it strip American defenses in the hope the British could survive?

Not only isolationists but many "realistic" Americans demanded adherence to the former course. They were joined by the Joint Planners of the War and Navy departments, who warned on June 27, 1940, that Britain might not survive and urged the President to concentrate on American defenses. It was the kind of advice that military leaders, who think in terms of the worst contingencies, have to give. But with the support of his new Secretaries of War and of the Navy, Henry L. Stimson and Frank Knox— whom he appointed on June 20 to gain Republican support for the defense effort—Roosevelt decided to gamble on Britain. Although he rejected Churchill's ambitious proposals for turning the United States into a gigantic arsenal for Britain, the President ordered the War and Navy departments to "scrape the bottom of the barrel" and turn over to private firms for re-sale to Britain all available guns and ammunition.[5] In addition, officials of the War, Navy, and Treasury departments conferred with a British Purchasing Mission and promised to deliver 14,375 aircraft by April 1942. Roosevelt's decision to gamble on British survival was the most momentous in his career to this time, for he acted in the certain knowledge that war with Germany was inevitable if Britain should go down.

168 / *The Great Debate*

The fall of France and the seeming imminence of British defeat shocked the American people with an almost indescribable fright and stimulated much wild talk of an immediate German invasion of the Western Hemisphere. Such panic soon subsided, however. More significant was the way in which the threat of Nazi victory intensified the great debate over American foreign

---

[5] From June to October 1940 some 970,000 rifles, 200,500 revolvers, 87,500 machine guns, 895 75 mm. guns, 316 mortars, and a huge quantity of ammunition were shipped to Britain.

policy that had been in progress since the Munich crisis. Upon the outcome of this controversy would depend the fate of the world.

Hitler's destruction of Czechoslovakia had convinced a small but influential minority of Americans that the United States would live in deadly peril if Nazism ever enveloped Europe. Soon after the outbreak of the war, these internationalists formed the Non-Partisan Committee for Peace through Revision of the Neutrality Law, with William Allen White of Kansas as chairman. By the end of October 1939, the Non-Partisan Committee had branches in thirty states; and its propaganda was a decisive factor in swinging public opinion behind repeal of the arms embargo provision. The Committee quietly disintegrated during the "phony war" but reorganized on May 17, 1940, as the Committee to Defend America by Aiding the Allies. Within a few months the Committee had over six hundred local branches and had taken leadership in a nation-wide campaign to combat isolationism and stimulate public support for the government's policy of all aid short of war.

The Committee's success was reflected in the transformation in public opinion that occurred during the summer of 1940. When the public opinion polls revealed in July that probably a large majority favored aid to Britain, the Committee next worked to generate public support for a transfer of destroyers to the British.[6] In mid-August a Gallup poll indicated that a majority of the people would approve if the President followed the Committee's lead. In addition, White and other Republican leaders in the Committee headed off the isolationist bloc in the Republican national convention and obtained a platform plank approving aid to "all peoples fighting for liberty."

It was inevitable that this movement to draw America closer to the war's orbit would not go unchallenged by the isolationist leaders. Although their ranks were considerably thinned by the fall of France, the isolationists—or noninterventionists, as they preferred to call themselves—were still a powerful if incongruous group by the autumn of 1940. They included pro-Nazi spokesmen like Father Coughlin, Gerald L. K. Smith, and William Dudley Pelley; subtle defenders of fascism like Anne Morrow Lindbergh, whose *The Wave of the Future* argued that Germany was bound to triumph; a large body of midwestern businessmen, whose main motive was hatred of the New Deal; Irish-Americans and Italian-Americans in the Northeast; old progressives like Senators Burton K. Wheeler and Gerald P. Nye, who still identified cooperation with England with the machinations of Wall Street; and many Protestant ministers and idealists, who had embraced a philosophy of nonresistance. The Hearst newspapers, the *Chicago Tribune*, the *New York Daily News*, the *Washington Times-Herald*, and other newspapers lent editorial support. Finally, there were the Socialists, led by Norman Thomas, who still thought of war in economic terms, and the Communists, who had become increasingly pro-Nazi after the signing of the Nazi-Soviet Non-Aggression Pact.

At the height of the debate over foreign policy in the summer and autumn of 1940 isolationists organized a number of committees, but the lead-

---

[6] It should be added that Roosevelt and White cooperated in this campaign. At a conference on June 29, 1940, for example, the President told White about the contemplated destroyer transfer and won White's and the Committee's support for the project.

ing opponent of aid to Britain was the America First Committee, incorporated in September 1940 with Robert E. Wood, chairman of the board of Sears, Roebuck, & Company, as national chairman. The America First movement soon included thousands of patriotic Americans who sincerely believed that defense of the Western Hemisphere and nonintervention in Europe's war was the only course of safety for the United States. But the America First Committee also had the support of all pro-Nazi groups in the country.

The debate between proponents of strong support for Britain and the noninterventionists did not end until Japanese bombs fell on Pearl Harbor, but it was evident long before this date that the former had won the battle for control of the American public mind. The public opinion polls showed

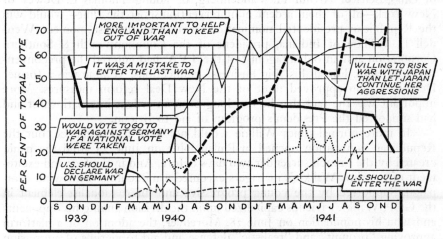

22. *American Public Opinion and the Issue of Intervention (Reproduced by permission of Professor Hadley Cantril and the Public Opinion Research Project of Princeton University)*

the metamorphosis that occurred: In September 1939 some 82 per cent of persons queried thought the Allies would win; by July 1940 only 43 per cent were sure Britain would win. More important, the proportion of Americans who believed a German victory would menace their security increased from 43 per cent in March 1940 to 69 per cent in July 1940. All through the period 1939–1941 an overwhelming majority of Americans queried indicated a desire to avoid active participation in the war. The important fact was that this same majority approved strong assistance to Britain; and by the spring of 1941 a majority of persons polled favored extending such aid even if it led to hostilities with Germany.

In this erosion of isolationist concepts and sentiments the President, administration leaders, and the Committee to Defend America played a significant role. An even more significant cause of the decline of isolationism, however, were the events that unfolded in Europe and the Far East from 1939 to 1941. The American people supported the administration in a strong policy and accepted the risk of war, not to defend obsolete neutral rights or to engage in a second crusade for democracy, but rather to defend their own security and freedom. The tragedy was that it required the momentary triumph of Hitler and the near defeat of the British Empire to awaken the American people to the simple facts of international life.

169 / The Presidential Election of 1940 and the World Crisis

Meanwhile, the crisis of the spring and summer had no less an impact upon the national conventions and presidential campaign of 1940 than upon popular attitudes regarding the American stake in an Allied victory. At the beginning of the year it seemed certain that either Senator Robert A. Taft of Ohio, Senator Arthur H. Vandenberg, or young Thomas E. Dewey of New York—all of them ardent noninterventionists at the time—would win the Republican presidential nomination. Almost at the last moment Wendell L. Willkie of Indiana, president of the Commonwealth & Southern Corporation and an old antagonist of the TVA, had entered the preconvention campaign. For all his "big business" connections, Willkie was a former Democrat who approved most of the New Deal reform measures. More important was the fact that he had long been an ardent internationalist and had supported the President's program of aid to Britain.

In more normal times Willkie would not have had a chance, but the Republican convention opened in Philadelphia on June 24 amid the panic created by the French surrender two days before. And in the fear and excitement of the time Willkie's managers executed a miraculous whirlwind campaign. Supported by the young progressive and internationalist element in the GOP, Willkie's friends capitalized upon the division among his opponents and won his nomination on June 28. Moreover, the adoption of a platform approving "prompt" and "realistic" defense and aid to victims of aggression was a second notable victory of the young internationalist group over the large die-hard isolationist bloc.

The nomination of the rugged, popular Willkie—the first colorful Republican candidate since 1904—compelled President Roosevelt to come to some decision concerning the Democratic nomination. Probably Roosevelt intended all along to run for a third term, for he made his nomination inevitable by refusing to support another candidate and by failing to discourage efforts in his own behalf. In any event, on July 16 he sent a message to the Democratic national convention, which had opened in Chicago the day before, saying he had no desire to remain in office and wanted the convention to be free to make a choice, but implying that he would accept the nomination if the convention insisted. Few of the party bosses wanted Roosevelt but there was nothing they could do except nominate him on the first ballot. The delegates rebelled, however, when the President insisted upon Secretary of Agriculture Henry A. Wallace as his running-mate; only by using the most ruthless methods was Roosevelt's spokesman, Harry Hopkins, able to force the Iowan upon an unwilling party.

The President delivered his acceptance speech by radio to the convention early in the morning of July 19, and then did not make another campaign address until September 11. In the meantime he gave all his energies to more urgent problems: military, air, and naval expansion, which he obtained easily from Congress; approval of the Burke-Wadsworth bill for selective service, which he won in September with Willkie's support; and defense of the northern reaches of the hemisphere, which he enhanced with the establishment in August of a Canadian-American Permanent Joint Board on Defense.

At the same time there was the danger that the Nazis would try to take control of the strategic French islands in the Caribbean, Guadeloupe and Martinique. The Washington government first warned Berlin against trying to seize the islands and then arranged for a conference of the Pan-American Foreign Ministers to meet at Havana on July 21, 1940, to consider counter measures. By extraordinary negotiations, Hull won unanimous approval at Havana on July 27 of a declaration that an attack on any American republic was an attack against all of them and a convention providing that an Inter-American Commission for Territorial Administration should take temporary control of any European possessions in the New World about to be transferred to another sovereignty. Following the Havana Conference, moreover, the Washington government began for the first time seriously to plan for the extension of large-scale economic and military aid to the Latin American countries.

The most urgent necessity confronting the administration during this summer of campaign and crisis, however, was devising some means of transferring forty or fifty destroyers[7] to Britain for anti-submarine operations and assistance in defense of the British Isles against the invasion that Hitler planned for mid-September of 1940. The chief difficulty was that Congress, on June 28, had adopted an amendment to the naval appropriations bill forbidding the President to transfer defense equipment to a foreign power unless the Army Chief of Staff and the Chief of Naval Operations first certified that the equipment was not essential to the national defense.

After the Nazis had begun a great air assault upon Britain preparatory to the invasion, Roosevelt found a way out of this dilemma. The upshot was an agreement signed in Washington on September 2, 1940, by which the United States gave fifty destroyers to the British government in return for a formal pledge that Britain would never surrender the fleet and for ninety-nine-year leases on air and naval bases in Newfoundland and the Caribbean. Because the agreement vastly enhanced the security of the Western Hemisphere, General George C. Marshall, Army Chief of Staff, and Admiral Harold R. Stark, Chief of Naval Operations, could in good conscience approve it, as the amendment of June 28 required. Churchill, however, revolted at the idea of a "deal" and insisted upon giving outright the leases for American bases in Newfoundland and Bermuda.

Isolationists were up in arms, but criticism in Congress was remarkably restrained. The truth was that a large majority of Americans approved, although the destroyer-bases agreement meant the end of formal neutrality and marked the beginning of a period of limited American participation in the war. Henceforth, the extent of that participation would bear a direct relation to German strength and the British needs.

---

[7] They were to be supplied from a reserve of 172 destroyers built during the First World War, which the Navy Department had reconditioned and returned to service.

While Roosevelt was thus engaged, Wendell Willkie had undertaken a one-man campaign against a silent opponent. Naively confident during the early weeks of the campaign, Willkie denounced Democratic inefficiency and played heavily upon the anti-third term theme. He was fatally handicapped, however, by his own basic agreement with most of Roosevelt's domestic and foreign policies. Around the first of October, Willkie apparently realized that he might be defeated. In desperation, badly wanting to win, he jettisoned his progressive, internationalist advisers and accepted the counsel of the Old Guard professionals, who "begged Willkie to abandon this nonsense about a bipartisan foreign policy—to attack Roosevelt as a warmonger—to scare the American people with warnings that votes for Roosevelt meant wooden crosses for their sons and brothers and sweethearts."[8]

The more Willkie played upon the war issue the more his campaign caught fire, and Democratic managers throughout the country were appalled lest the rising anti-war tide sweep the Republican candidate into the White House. Appeals poured into the White House, begging Roosevelt to tell the country that he stood for peace. In response, the President reversed his field. In a speech at Philadelphia on October 23 he assured the voters he had made no secret agreement to involve the United States in the war, "or for any other purpose." On October 28 he made a grand tour of New York City, climaxed by an evening address in the Madison Square Garden. Reviewing his long efforts to strengthen the nation's defenses, he warned that Americans could keep war from their shores only by stopping aggression in Europe. This, however, was the "realistic" way to preserve the peace that all Americans desired.

The Madison Square Garden address was in the main a forthright enunciation, but it neither reversed the rising Willkie tide nor quieted the fears of the Democratic politicians. On October 30 the President began a tour of New England, to be climaxed by a speech in Boston during the evening. All during the day he was inundated by telegrams warning that defeat impended unless he gave more explicit pledges to maintain peace. For once the great campaigner seemed unsure of himself and at the last minute included the following promise in his Boston address: "I have said this before, but I shall say it again and again and again: Your boys are not going to be sent into any foreign wars. . . . The purpose of our defense is defense." It was a categorical promise but an honest one. In the same speech Roosevelt made it clear that he considered defense of Britain defense of the United States as well; and obviously he had no intention of involving the country in a "foreign" war.

By the late evening of election day, November 5, it was evident the President had won again, although the margin of his victory was considerably smaller than it had been in 1936. He received 27,243,000 popular and 449 electoral votes, as compared with 22,304,400 popular and 82 electoral votes for Willkie. In addition, the Democrats retained large majorities in both houses of Congress. The Socialist and Communist candidates, Norman Thomas and Earl Browder, received 100,264 and 48,579 popular votes, respectively.

[8] Robert E. Sherwood, *Roosevelt and Hopkins, An Intimate History* (New York, 1948), p. 187; quoted by permission of Harper & Brothers, publishers.

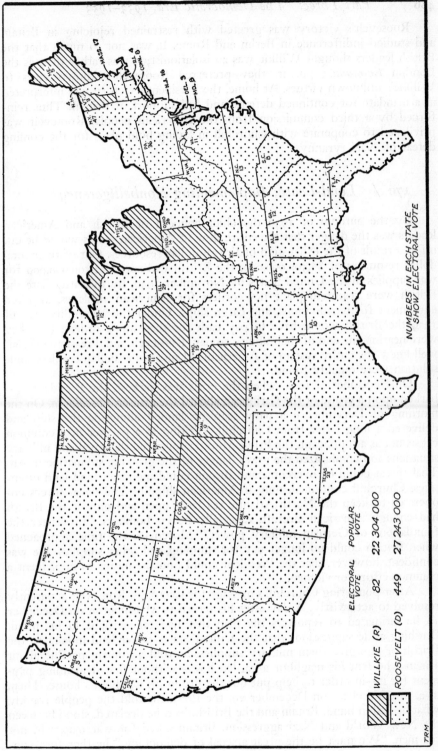

WILLKIE (R)

ROOSEVELT (D)

	ELECTORAL VOTE	POPULAR VOTE
WILLKIE (R)	82	22 304 000
ROOSEVELT (D)	449	27 243 000

NUMBERS IN EACH STATE
SHOW ELECTORAL VOTE

17. *The Election of 1940*

Roosevelt's victory was greeted with restrained rejoicing in Britain and studied indifference in Berlin and Rome. It was not so much that the British leaders thought Willkie was an isolationist; it was rather that, as the London *Economist* put it, they preferred Roosevelt's known vices to Willkie's unknown virtues. At home, the President's victory was interpreted as a mandate for continued defense and full support of Britain. Thus reinforced by a third commission from the American people, Roosevelt was privileged to cooperate with Churchill in laying bold plans for the coming defeat of Nazi tyranny.

170 / Lend-Lease: Implementing Nonbelligerency

By the autumn of 1940 the chief concern of British and American leaders was the danger that the entire flow of American goods would be cut off as a result of the exhaustion of British dollar resources. Out of their total dollar resources of $6,500,000,000, the British had spent $4,500,000,000 for war supplies in the United States by November 1940. By the latter date the British were ready to place new orders for American airplanes, armored equipment for ten divisions, and cargo ships. Under the Neutrality Act of 1939 the British would have to pay cash for these huge orders; but they were nearing the end of their ability to pay. Roosevelt and Treasury officials well knew the entire system of American aid must soon collapse unless some solution were quickly found.

On December 2, 1940, when the crisis was darkest, the President embarked upon a cruise of the Caribbean aboard the cruiser *Tuscaloosa*. On the morning of December 9 a navy seaplane landed alongside the ship and delivered a long letter from Churchill. Writing as a partner in a common cause, not as a supplicant, the Prime Minister reviewed the naval and military situations and emphasized the grave danger of the growing submarine threat. That threat could be overcome and Britain could mount air and land offensives, Churchill continued, only if American shipping and naval forces cooperated to keep the North Atlantic sea lanes open and only if the British had enough American aircraft, especially heavy bombers, "to shatter the foundations of German military power." Moreover, the time approached when Britain could no longer pay for shipping and other supplies. He was confident, however, that the President could find the means to implement a common effort for victory.

After pondering Churchill's message for two days, Roosevelt apparently resolved to act swiftly. A day after his return to Washington on December 16 he intimated to reporters the plan that had taken shape in his mind. Brushing aside suggestions that the United States either lend money to the British or else give them military supplies, he told a homely parable about a man who lent his neighbor a garden hose—without first demanding payment for it—in order to help put out the fire in his neighbor's house. Then, in a "fireside chat" on December 29, the President told the people frankly what he had in mind. Britain and the British fleet, he declared, stood between the New World and Nazi aggression. Britain asked for war materials, not for men. "We must be the great arsenal of democracy," he therefore concluded. ". . . I call upon our people with absolute confidence that our common cause will greatly succeed."

Public reaction was immediate and overwhelmingly favorable. In his Annual Message on January 6, 1941, Roosevelt reiterated the danger from Nazi aggression; asked Congress "for authority and for funds sufficient to manufacture additional munitions and war supplies of many kinds, to be turned over to those nations which are now in actual war with aggressor nations" and to be paid for not in dollars but in goods and services at the end of the war; and voiced a fervent hope for a postwar world built upon the four essential freedoms: freedom of speech and of worship, and freedom from want and fear.

Drafted by Treasury officials during the first week in January 1941, the Lend-Lease bill was approved by administration and congressional leaders on January 9 and introduced in Congress the following day. Immediately non-interventionists rallied to the attack, charging that the purpose of the bill was to take the country into war and, as the *Chicago Tribune* said, to "destroy the Republic." But administration spokesmen and a host of leaders from all walks of life countered effectively in the congressional hearings, and public opinion unmistakably supported them. The House approved the Lend-Lease bill on February 8, the Senate, on March 8, and the President, on March 11, 1941. The following day Roosevelt asked Congress for $7,000,-000,000 for Lend-Lease production and export; Congress complied two weeks later.

What the enactment of the Lend-Lease Act signified no man could doubt. "Our blessings from the whole British Empire go out to you and the American nation for this very present help in time of trouble," Churchill wrote to Roosevelt on March 9, 1941. "Through this legislation," the President told Congress on March 12, "our country has determined to do its full part in creating an adequate arsenal of democracy." Actually, Roosevelt's characterization was an understatement. The passage of the Lend-Lease Act converted the United States from a friendly neutral, which sometimes helped more than the rules of traditional neutrality demanded, into a full-fledged nonbelligerent, committed to pour out all its resources if need be to enable Britain to bring Germany to her knees. If there had ever been any doubts before that the American people would falter or refrain from taking the risk of war, those doubts were now resolved.

Having committed itself to underwriting a British victory, the Washington government could not sit by and watch Nazi submarines prevent the delivery of goods vital to German defeat. German depredations on British and neutral shipping from the beginning of the *Blitzkrieg* to the end of 1940 had been staggering enough,[9] but the spring of 1941 witnessed an even more powerful German attack. Extending the war zone on March 25, 1941, to include Iceland and the Denmark Strait between Greenland and Iceland, the Nazis sent swarms of new submarines into the North Atlantic that hunted their prey in "wolf packs," used surface vessels in daring raids, and threw a large part of the German air force into the battle to choke off the stream of supplies flowing from America to British ports. In March 1941 the Ger-

[9] British, Allied, and neutral shipping losses from May through December 1940 totaled 3,139,190 tons.

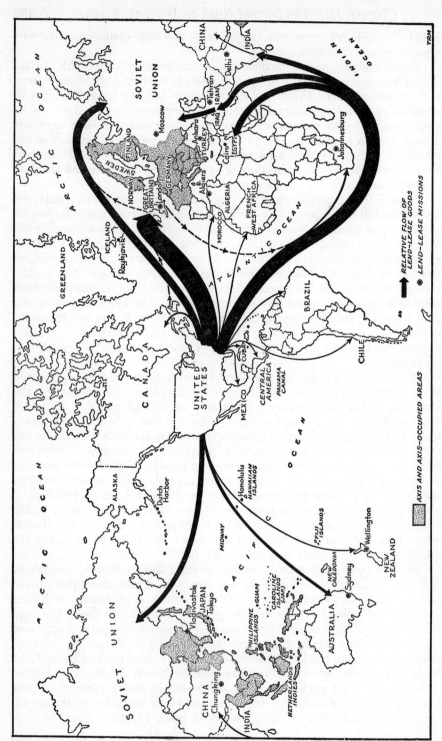

18. *Lend-Lease Supply Routes*

mans destroyed 537,493 tons of merchant shipping; in April, 653,960; in May, 500,063. As Churchill repeatedly warned, the outcome of the Battle of the Atlantic might well determine the entire course of the war.

For the President, therefore, the choice lay not between action and inaction but rather among various means of participating in the Battle of the Atlantic. First, on March 25 and April 2, 1941, he authorized American naval yards to repair British vessels; second, on March 28 he transferred ten Coast Guard cutters to the British fleet to assist in anti-submarine operations; third, on March 31 he had the Coast Guard seize thirty Axis and thirty-five Danish merchant ships in American ports. Bold though this action was, it was not enough; and Secretary Stimson urged Roosevelt to use his power as commander in chief to order the navy to convoy British and Allied merchant ships all the way from American to British ports.

The President rejected Stimson's advice but decided on April 10 to extend the American Neutrality Patrol far out into the Atlantic, to longitude 25° west, a line which passes between Brazil and the west coast of Africa in the south and slightly west of Iceland in the north. Within the area between the American coast and longitude 25° west, American naval vessels would search out, but not attack, Nazi submarines and warn British vessels of their presence.[10] In addition, on April 10 the President issued a proclamation removing the area of the Red Sea from the list of war zones forbidden to American ships.

Meanwhile, isolationists in Congress were raising the charge that Roosevelt had begun an undeclared naval war by ordering American vessels in the patrol area to convoy British ships and attack Nazi U-boats. Six days after a German submarine torpedoed an American freighter, the *Robin Moor*, in the South Atlantic on May 21, the President had a "fireside chat" with the people and told them what their navy was doing in the North Atlantic. Reiterating that German control of the Atlantic would imperil American security, he revealed that the Nazis were sinking ships twice as fast as British and American shipyards could replace them. The hope of victory, he continued, lay in increasing shipbuilding and in helping reduce losses on the seas. To accomplish the latter objective, he explained, "Our patrols are helping now to insure delivery of the needed supplies to Britain." He ended by warning that "all additional measures necessary to deliver the goods" would be taken, by calling upon industry and labor to redouble their efforts, and by declaring an unlimited state of national emergency.

171 / *The Invasion of Russia*

Ever since the Soviet Union sealed its pact of friendship with Hitlerite Germany and then seized eastern Poland, absorbed the Baltic states, launched an aggressive war against Finland, and afterward tore the province of Bessarabia from Rumania, an overwhelming majority of Americans had thought

[10] This is the substance of orders issued by Roosevelt to Admiral Ernest J. King on April 19–21, 1941. The navy began intensified patrol activities on April 24, 1941. Meanwhile, on April 9 the State Department concluded an agreement with the Danish Minister in Washington, authorizing the United States to build naval and air bases on Greenland

no better of the Russians than they thought of the Nazis. This anti-Russian tension, moreover, was increased during the period from August 1939 to June 1941 by the efforts of American Communists to cripple defense production through strikes in airplane factories and otherwise to impair American solidarity. Congressional vexation at such subversion took form in the spring of 1940 in the Smith Act, which made it unlawful for any group to advocate or teach the violent overthrow of government in the United States, or for any person to belong to such a group.

We now know that the Soviet leaders would have probably been prepared to come to agreement with Hitler for a division of Europe and the Middle East. Conversations between Hitler and Molotov in Berlin in November 1940 failed to bring agreement, but only because Hitler thought the Russians wanted too much. Enraged by Russian demands, Hitler, on December 18, 1940, ordered preparations for an invasion of Russia during the coming spring.

Hitler launched his attack against the Soviet Union in the early morning hours of June 22, 1941. The Washington government reacted circumspectly, for the American public at the time probably welcomed a showdown battle between the dictatorships, while Roosevelt's military advisers warned that Russia would collapse within three months and that any aid given to the Soviet armies would only fall into Hitler's hands.

Meanwhile, Roosevelt used the breathing space afforded by the German attack to strengthen home defenses and the American position in the North Atlantic. The most urgent defense necessity in the early summer of 1941 was the extension of the terms of service of the 900,000 men drafted in the preceding autumn, for the defense effort would practically collapse if the men were allowed to go home when their year's term expired. The President, therefore, allowed General Marshall to ask Congress on July 3 to extend the term of service and also to remove the provisions in the Selective Service Act of 1940 that prohibited sending draftees outside the Western Hemisphere. Marshall's request stirred a hornet's nest of opposition, not only from isolationists but from administration supporters in Congress as well. After Marshall explained that the army had no desire to send a new A.E.F. and pleaded that extension of the draft was essential to national security, however, the upper house extended the term of service by six months on August 7, 1941. In the House, on the other hand, the struggle was bitter and long in doubt until that body, on August 12, approved extension by a vote of 203 to 202.

While this controversy was in its first stage, the President moved decisively to strengthen American control of the North Atlantic sea lanes. Negotiations among Roosevelt, Churchill, and the Prime Minister of Iceland culminated in the occupation of Iceland by American marines on July 7, 1941, and the inauguration of United States naval escorts for convoys of American and Icelandic ships between the Atlantic Coast and Iceland on July 26. Thus by one stroke the character of American naval operations in the North Atlantic was drastically changed. Henceforward, the American navy would not merely patrol the area between Iceland and the United States but would destroy "hostile forces" that threatened American and Icelandic shipping in that broad expanse of water.

172 /   The Atlantic Conference and the Brink of War

On July 13, 1941, Harry Hopkins, Lend-Lease administrator and now Roosevelt's closest confidant, left Washington for London to pave the way for a personal meeting of the American and British leaders. Roosevelt not only wanted to meet his intimate friend by correspondence, the "Former Naval Person"; he also wanted the military and naval leaders of both countries to coordinate plans for future operations. At Roosevelt's explicit instruction, however, Hopkins warned Churchill that there should be no talk of economic or territorial deals or of American participation in the war. Churchill was delighted and agreed to come to a secret meeting "in some lonely bay or other" on August 9.

At Churchill's suggestion, Hopkins flew to Moscow for conversations with Stalin and other Soviet leaders concerning Russian hopes and needs. From Stalin he learned firsthand the news that the Russian armies would withstand the first Nazi onslaught and take the offensive during the coming winter; that the Kremlin would welcome Lend-Lease aid and facilitate its delivery; and that the Russian government desired above all American entry into the war and "would welcome the American troops on any part of the Russian front under the complete command of the American Army."

Hopkins was back in London in time to join Churchill and his party aboard the new battleship, *Prince of Wales,* for the journey to the rendezvous with Roosevelt off Argentia, Newfoundland. The President arrived aboard the cruiser *Augusta,* and the two leaders met on the American vessel on the morning of August 9.[11] During the conferences that followed, the British tried to get some commitment promising American belligerence if Japan attacked British possessions in the Far East. In this, as in all other matters discussed, Roosevelt and his advisers refused to make any commitments of a military or naval character.

The most important work of the Argentia meeting was the approval, after some stiff argument about Britain's imperial policy, by Roosevelt and Churchill on August 12 of the joint declaration known as the Atlantic Charter. The product of careful thought and patient negotiation, this document recorded Anglo-American agreement on "certain common principles" on which the two governments based "their hopes for a better future for the world"—no territorial aggrandizement, no territorial changes that did not accord with the wishes of the people involved, the right of all peoples to choose the form of government under which they lived, economic collaboration in the postwar world, and the right of all peoples to live in peace and in freedom from fear, want, and aggression.

News of the Argentia conference and the text of the Atlantic Charter were published in the press on August 15 and provoked isolationist editors and politicians to new outbursts. But the overwhelming majority of Americans believed Roosevelt's assurances that he had made no commitment to intervene actively and approved the idealistic aspirations embodied in the

[11] It was, incidentally, their second meeting. They had met casually in London on July 29, 1918.

Atlantic Charter. Obviously, the preponderant majority continued to approve giving aid to Hitler's enemies and to hope that the United States would not have to enter the "shooting war." Roosevelt probably shared these sentiments. Like the great majority of his fellow-countrymen, he continued to hope for peace while approving policies that must lead to war if American objectives were ever to be attained.

For example, soon after his return from Argentia the President set to the task of providing greater assistance to Russia, an undertaking made immensely difficult by the opposition of isolationists, the Catholic press, and many anti-Communist Americans. Although he was uncertain of public and congressional reaction, Roosevelt began discussions that led to an Anglo-American-Soviet conference in Moscow in late September 1941 and an agreement by which Britain and the United States promised to furnish $1,000,000,000 worth of aid to Russia before June 30, 1942. And when Congress voted a new $6,000,000,000 appropriation for Lend-Lease production and export and rejected an amendment forbidding extension of aid to Russia in October, Roosevelt declared the Soviet Union eligible for Lend-Lease assistance on November 7.

More significant for the immediate future, however, was Roosevelt's decision to ease further the British position in the North Atlantic. At the Atlantic Conference the President decided to allow British and Allied vessels to join American convoys between the United States and Iceland. This was done unofficially before the end of August, although orders to this effect were not issued until September 13.

While Roosevelt pondered the best way to break the news to the people, a German submarine attacked the destroyer *Greer* south of Iceland on September 4, after the *Greer* had joined a British airplane in trailing the U-boat. The incident gave the President the "provocation" he needed to justify a change of policy. In a radio address on September 11, he declared that the attack on the *Greer* was part of a Nazi plan to control the Atlantic, in preparation for an assault upon the Western Hemisphere. The time for active defense had come, he added; hereafter American ships and planes would protect all ships within the area between the United States and Iceland. Moreover, he continued, he had ordered the army and navy to shoot on sight at all German and Italian war vessels in the American patrol area.

The President's speech was in effect a declaration of an undeclared naval war against Germany—the inevitable outcome of the adoption of the Lend-Lease Act and the American decision to get supplies through the troubled waters to Great Britain. Not only did a large majority of Congress and the public approve this forward step; the majority also approved when Roosevelt, on October 9, 1941, finally asked Congress to revise the Neutrality Act of 1939 in order to permit the arming of American merchantmen and indirectly suggested that Congress permit American ships to enter war zones and belligerent ports. While debate on these proposals proceeded, a German submarine torpedoed the destroyer *Kearny* on the night of October 16–17, with the loss of eleven lives. A fierce debate in both houses ensued, and the isolationists made a determined last stand. But the Senate on November 7 and the House on November 13 voted to allow merchantmen to arm and to pass through the war zone to British ports.

Meanwhile, the undeclared naval war in the North Atlantic proceeded. On October 31 a submarine sank the destroyer *Reuben James*, with the loss of 115 lives, but there was no such general agitation for war as had followed German attacks on American ships in early 1917. The American people now clearly understood their immediate task—to deliver supplies to Britain and Russia regardless of the peril. They assumed that task not gladly, for they knew it involved the risk of war, but with grim determination and still fervent hope that somehow they could avoid full-scale participation.

173 / *Futile Negotiations with Japan, 1938–1941*

Between the adjournment of the Brussels Conference of 1938 and the outbreak of the German-Polish crisis in the spring of 1939, relations between the United States and Japan continued in a state of suspended hostility. During this period the military clique in the Imperial government were pressing for an alliance with Germany to offset Soviet and American power and undertaking extensive military operations against the Russian forces along the Manchurian border. The army's hopes for an alliance with the Nazis were momentarily blasted by the signing of the Nazi-Soviet Pact in August 1939; meanwhile, however, the Imperial government undertook a diplomatic campaign to force the British to recognize Japanese conquests in China. Faced with imminent war with Germany and denied any promise of American military aid, the Chamberlain government, on July 24, 1939, surrendered to Japanese demands by recognizing that the Japanese army was supreme in the areas it occupied.

The announcement of the Anglo-Japanese agreement of July 24 galvanized the American government's determination to play a stronger role in the Far East. On July 26, 1939, therefore, the President sent to Tokyo the necessary six months' notice of the possible abrogation of the Japanese-American commercial treaty of 1911. It was no idle warning but a stern threat that after January 26, 1940, the United States might deny to the Japanese access to the source from which they obtained more than half the raw materials, especially iron, steel, and oil, for their war machine.

The threat of full-scale war with Russia and economic retaliation by the United States restrained the extreme militarists in Japan and prevented the Imperial government from embarking upon new conquests following the outbreak of war in Europe. Instead, the Japanese ended the border clash with the Soviet forces in September and next launched a strenuous effort to liquidate the "China Incident." Moreover, in December 1939 the Japanese Foreign Office opened negotiations with the State Department to prevent the imposition of the threatened American embargo. When these talks ended in a stalemate because neither government would recede on the basic issue of China, the Washington administration simply reaffirmed its traditional position and declared that for the time being it would not end the export of American war supplies.

During the early months of 1940 Japanese-American official relations were relatively quiescent, especially after a new government under Admiral

Mitsumasa Yonai came to power in Tokyo on January 14, 1940. In the United States, however, public opinion was moving strongly toward the application of an embargo; in fact, sentiment in Congress was so vociferous that administration leaders suppressed it only with difficulty.

The State Department's policy of threatening economic retaliation might well have succeeded had not Germany's triumph in western Europe convinced the Japanese military leaders that the power of Britain, France, and the Netherlands was gone and that henceforth they would have to deal only with the United States. Excited by the opportunity to seize French Indo-China and the Netherlands East Indies and by the hope of an alliance with Germany, the army leaders and expansionists caused the fall of the moderate Yonai Cabinet on July 16, 1940, and created a new government headed by Prince Fumimaro Konoye, with the boastful Yosuke Matsuoka as Foreign Minister and the ardent expansionist, General Hideki Tojo, as Minister of War.

As its first step toward achieving a "new order in Greater East Asia," the new Cabinet demanded and after some negotiation obtained from the Vichy government the right to build airfields and station troops in northern Indo-China. As a second and more important step, Konoye, Tojo, and Matsuoka in early August 1940 approved a program envisaging the conquest of British, French, and Dutch Far Eastern possessions and agreed to sign a military alliance with Germany if Hitler approved these plans of conquest. Following the arrival of a new German Ambassador in Tokyo on September 7, the bargain was struck and sealed in Berlin on September 27, 1940.[12]

In response to these threats, the Washington government moved cautiously to apply such counter-pressure as would not provoke Tokyo to immediate war. First, on July 26, 1940, the United States applied an embargo on the export of aviation gasoline, lubricants, and prime scrap metal to Japan. Then, after the Japanese occupied northern Indo-China, the American government announced the extension of a new $25,000,000 loan to China on September 25[13] and the following day decreed an embargo on the export of all types of scrap iron and steel. This action was followed in December by a virtual embargo on the export of iron ore and pig iron, certain chemicals, certain machine tools, and other products. Encouraged by the firmer American policy, Churchill reopened the Burma Road, the chief supply route between Nationalist China and the outside world, on October 8, 1940.[14] The Japanese protested, but the Washington government's firm stand and rumors

[12] This was the Tripartite Agreement, or Triple Alliance, under which Japan recognized German and Italian leadership in Europe, Germany and Italy recognized Japan's leadership in the establishment of a "new order" in Greater East Asia, and the three signatories agreed to cooperate militarily, politically, and economically "if one of the three Contracting Powers is attacked by a Power at present not involved in the European War or in the Chinese-Japanese conflict."

[13] On November 30, 1940, after the Japanese had recognized a puppet Chinese government in Nanking, moreover, Roosevelt announced that the United States would extend a $100,000,000 loan to Nationalist China. This assistance, incidentally, came in the nick of time to save Chiang Kai-shek's government at Chungking from collapse.

[14] In response to Japanese threats, the British government had closed the Burma Road on July 12, 1940.

of Anglo-American naval cooperation in the Pacific[15] caused the Konoye government to beat a momentary diplomatic retreat.

By a policy of implicit threatening, therefore, the United States had prevented the Japanese from striking while Britain and America were in direst peril following the fall of France. Even so, it was evident by the beginning of 1941 that Matsuoka and his following of militarists and expansionists had been only momentarily checked. Indeed, the tragedy was that Japanese-American relations had by this time reached a point beyond which diplomacy could not operate. There was a large moderate element in Japan anxious to avoid war with the United States and willing to abandon hope of further expansion, if that were necessary to preserve the peace. But the American government would never come to friendly agreement unless the Imperial government also withdrew entirely from China and gave evidences of willingness to respect Chinese integrity. And no responsible group in Japan, however moderate and opposed to war with America, would submit to this fundamental American requirement for friendly relations.

Thus the essentially insoluble Chinese question was the real root of the discord; and the impossibility of agreement on this basic issue weakened the moderates and gave the militarists and expansionists an excuse for their alliance with Germany and their plans for the conquest of the Far East. In a speech before the Diet on January 26, 1941, Foreign Minister Matsuoka frankly stated the impossibility of reconciling Japanese aspirations with American policy. "There is nothing left but to face America," he declared. ". . . Japan must demand America's reconsideration of her attitude, and if she does not listen, there is slim hope for friendly relations between Japan and the United States."

Matsuoka's blunt talk, however, hid the fact that Japan was not yet prepared to engage the western democracies. There was still the danger that the Soviet Union would strike in the north if Japan turned southward; and there was still the faint hope that somehow the United States might be frightened into acquiescing in Japanese plans. In order to safeguard Japan's long exposed northern flank, Matsuoka made a pilgrimage to Berlin, Rome, and Moscow in March and April 1941. Hitler urged that Japan strike immediately at Singapore, and Foreign Minister Ribbentrop intimated that a German-Russian conflict was no longer inconceivable and promised that Germany would attack Russia if the Soviets attacked Japan after she was involved in war with Britain and America. Matsuoka was pleased but not

[15] Alarmed by the conclusion of the Tripartite Pact, the Washington government in the late autumn of 1940 also began to consider joint British, American, and Dutch planning for the defense of the Western Pacific. Discussions between Washington and London culminated in elaborate Anglo-American staff discussions from January 27 to March 27, 1941, and in British-American-Dutch-Commonwealth staff discussions in Singapore from April 21 to April 27, 1941. During both conferences, known respectively as ABC-1 and ADB, the American representatives refused to make political or military commitments. Instead, they simply joined potential allies in making tentative plans for common action in the event a Japanese attack forced the United States into the war.

It should be added that the American conferees at the ADB Conference named certain circumstances—notably a Japanese attack on British and Dutch possessions—in which the United States would enter the war. General Marshall and Admiral Stark, however, refused to approve the ADB report because it contained this commitment.

entirely satisfied by these assurances. His supreme objective—a pledge of Soviet neutrality—he obtained not in Berlin but in Moscow on April 13, in the form of a Neutrality Pact, by which Japan and Russia promised to remain neutral if either power were attacked by one or more countries.

Meanwhile, on the other side of the water, the Konoye government had begun secret discussions with the Washington government in a desperate effort to see if any ground for accommodation existed. Let us look at the complicated background and development of these negotiations. In December 1940 an American Catholic bishop and priest in Tokyo discussed the problem of Japanese-American relations with certain Japanese leaders. The upshot was that Premier Konoye asked them to convey a startling message to the President—that Japan would for all practical purposes nullify the Tripartite Pact, withdraw its troops from China, and discuss the problem of closer economic relations with the United States. The two Catholic emissaries delivered the message to the President in the latter part of January 1941; they were followed soon afterward by two unofficial Japanese representatives, who urged that Roosevelt and Konoye could come to a comprehensive agreement[16] in a personal meeting, after which the Emperor would dismiss Matsuoka. Although he doubted that Konoye could carry through, Hull began discussions on April 14 with the new Japanese Ambassador, Admiral Kichisaburo Nomura, who had meanwhile been brought into the secret discussions. Without rejecting the Japanese proposal, Hull countered on April 16 with a four-point program that embodied traditional American demands concerning China.

Encouraged by Hull's seeming willingness to negotiate, a Liaison Conference of Japanese leaders on April 21, 1941, decided to continue the discussions and to defer making reply to Hull's note of April 16 until the return of Matsuoka from Moscow. The Foreign Minister was infuriated by the negotiations that had proceeded during his absence. Japan's destiny lay with Germany and in expansion, he argued; strength, not weakness, would prevent the United States from interfering. He countered on May 7 with the suggestion that Japan and the United States sign a neutrality pact; Hull at once rejected the proposal as a *carte blanche* for Japanese seizure of British, French, and Dutch far eastern possessions. On May 12 Matsuoka next submitted to the State Department a revised and remarkable proposal for a comprehensive understanding, by which the United States would cut off aid to Britain, urge Chiang Kai-shek to come to terms with Japan, resume normal trade relations with Japan, and end its ban on Japanese immigration.

Although Matsuoka's proposal was obviously unacceptable, Roosevelt and Hull agreed to continue the negotiations, chiefly to buy time and in the hope that the moderate majority in the Tokyo Cabinet would depose the unruly Foreign Minister. On May 31 and more fully on June 6 and 21, therefore, Hull restated the American position and proposed that the Japanese agree that American aid to Britain was defensive in character and that

[16] As elaborated in a proposal brought to the State Department on April 9 by a messenger from the Imperial Army, the Japanese proposed withdrawal of Japanese troops from China by agreement between China and Japan, reaffirmation of the Open Door policy, merger of the Chinese Nationalist regime with the Japanese puppet government in Nanking, resumption of normal economic relations between Japan and the United States, and an American loan to Japan.

the Tripartite Pact would not apply if such aid led to a German-American clash. At this moment, when it seemed the opponents of war with the United States might gain the upper hand in Tokyo, the German attack on Russia removed the threat of Soviet interference and encouraged the Japanese leaders to decide to occupy all of Indo-China, perhaps preparatory to an attack on Singapore.

The German assault on Russia also momentarily disrupted the desultory Japanese-American talks then in progress. Matsuoka apparently wanted to end the negotiations altogether; but he carried his arrogance too far and was deposed on July 16 and replaced by the more moderate Admiral Teijiro Toyoda. As the Washington government knew from intercepted Japanese messages to Berlin,[17] the Cabinet shake-up, however, did not mean any immediate change in Japanese policy. In fact, on July 14 the Imperial government presented a demand to Vichy for the immediate occupation by Japanese forces of land, air, and naval bases in southern Indo-China.

The Washington government reacted swiftly and violently. The United States could only conclude that the occupation of southern Indo-China was the prelude to further Japanese conquests and could see no point in further discussions, Hull told Nomura on July 23, 1941. The following day, after Vichy had surrendered to the Japanese demands, the President received the Japanese Ambassador, hinted he was contemplating applying an embargo on the export of oil to Japan, and warned that a Japanese attack on the Dutch East Indies would result in serious consequences. On the other hand, Roosevelt continued, if Japan would withdraw from Indo-China he would take leadership in a movement to neutralize that French colony and would help Japan find access to raw materials.

The President, however, was done with mere parleying. On July 28 he impounded all Japanese funds in the United States, closed the Panama Canal to Japanese shipping, and called the Philippine militia into active service. Moreover, on August 1 he forbade the export to Japan of a number of vital materials, including oil that could be refined into aviation gasoline, while the British and Dutch governments applied similar sanctions.

This decisive retaliation put the Tokyo authorities in the dilemma of having to choose between a modified retreat or a desperate war with the United States. Although extremists welcomed the prospect of war, the naval leaders were reluctant and frankly admitted that the Empire would probably be defeated in a protracted conflict. The Cabinet, therefore, maneuvered to find a solution that would include both Japanese occupation of southern Indo-China and peace with the United States. On August 7 Premier Konoye proposed that the President meet him in personal conference to discuss means of relieving the tension. On August 17, upon his return from the Atlantic Conference, Roosevelt gave his reply: If Japan made any further aggressive moves the United States would take all necessary steps to safeguard American security. However, if the Japanese government sincerely desired to come to agreement along the lines already laid down by the United States, then the American government would be willing to resume the exploratory discussions disrupted by the Japanese occupation of Indo-China.

Faced squarely with the choice of war or agreement with the United

[17] Experts in the American government had earlier deciphered the Japanese diplomatic code.

States, Konoye now moved desperately to offset the pressure for war at home and to persuade the President to join him in a personal conference. On August 18 Foreign Minister Toyoda reiterated Konoye's proposal to Ambassador Joseph C. Grew, while Konoye ordered a ship to stand in readiness to take him to the meeting. Then on August 28 Nomura presented the Imperial government's reply to the American note of August 17: The Japanese government would withdraw its troops from Indo-China as soon as the "China Incident" was settled; it would undertake no expansion southward or make war on the Soviet Union unless attacked; and it agreed that the principles set forth in the American note were "the prime requisites of a true peace." In a subsequent note of clarification dated September 4, the Japanese government made perhaps its most important offer, namely, that Japan would not feel bound by the Tripartite Pact to go to war if the United States became involved in a defensive war with Germany.

Roosevelt was so pleased by the Japanese response that he was ready to give his immediate consent to the proposal for a conference. But Hull urged caution and insisted that the two governments agree upon the fundamental issue of China before the chiefs of state met. Despite warnings from Tokyo that only some bold stroke could restrain the war party, the President accepted the State Department's view that Japan would not attack and that a policy of continued firmness would force the Imperial government to surrender. Thus on September 3 Roosevelt replied that he would be glad to confer with Konoye, but that basic differences would have to be cleared up first.

In the circumstances, the President's reply spelled the doom, not only of the projected conference, but of peace as well. Whether the momentous decision was wise or foolish will be long debated by historians. Defenders of the administration have argued that agreement on important issues was impossible and that in any event Konoye could not have forced the army to make the concessions necessary to preserve the peace. On the other hand, Roosevelt's antagonists have maintained that the administration rejected Konoye's invitation in order to goad Japan into attacking the United States. At least on the point of the administration's intentions the records are full and revealing. They indicate that the President and State Department, far from desiring war, were convinced the Japanese could not undertake hostilities and would retreat in the face of a firm American policy. Subsequent events soon proved how mistaken this assumption was.

In view of the primacy of the Nazi danger and the likelihood that the United States would soon be drawn into the European war, American policy in the Far East should have been directed at one objective only—the maintenance of peace with Japan on any terms short of countenancing further Japanese aggressions in the southwest Pacific. Such a policy might have necessitated the unfreezing of Japanese assets, the lifting of the embargo on the export of oil and metals, and an easing of the pressure on Japan to withdraw immediately from China. There is considerable evidence that such concessions by the United States at this time—that is, early September 1941—would have enormously strengthened the Japanese moderates and might have sufficed to preserve the *status quo* and gain precious time.

Instead of making even slight concessions, however, Roosevelt and Hull continued to make demands for Japanese withdrawal from China, demands that were impossible in the circumstances. The time would come when the United States and Britain might demand a showdown on China.[18] But that time was after the defeat of Germany, when the two democracies were invincible, not in the late summer of 1941, when they were weak and wisdom demanded a policy of delay.

174 / *Pearl Harbor*

Events following the delivery of Roosevelt's reply of September 3 confirm the thesis that the effect of American policy was to strengthen the extremists and perhaps tip the balance in Tokyo in favor of the war party. On September 6, soon after receipt of the President's reply of September 3, an Imperial Conference met for a showdown on policy. The Army Chief of Staff urged immediate preparations, if not a decision, for war; the Navy Chief of General Staff agreed Japan might have to resort to hostilities to avoid economic destruction as a consequence of the American embargo. Emperor Hirohito, however, demanded that negotiations be continued in the hope of peaceful understanding. The Imperial Conference ended by agreement to continue military preparations, to be completed by the end of October, and for the last time to seek American acquiescence in the minimum Japanese program.[19]

Following the Imperial Conference, during the evening of September 6, Premier Konoye met secretly with Ambassador Grew and reiterated his desire for a personal meeting with Roosevelt. Soon afterward, on September 22 and 25, Konoye renewed his invitation, and Grew added a plea for acceptance. Hull replied on October 2, again declaring the two governments must agree on fundamental issues, principally China, before a general conference could succeed. To Konoye, Washington's final refusal spelled the doom of his efforts to prevent war. He and the navy leaders tried to persuade the army chieftains that Japan could not defeat America and must evacuate China as a prerequisite to peace. The army adamantly refused and insisted that there was no recourse but war. Then Konoye sent a special emissary to Washington to plead the absolute necessity for some kind of speedy

[18] From a sheerly strategic point of view, the continuation of the Sino-Japanese War served Anglo-American interests by keeping large Japanese forces occupied, draining Japanese resources, and deterring the Japanese from expanding into the southwestern Pacific. Perceiving the rather obvious fact that involvement in China in part prevented the Japanese from expanding northward, the Soviet leaders played a skillful game of preserving peace with Japan while at the same time sending a modicum of supplies to Nationalist China to make certain the Japanese would have to continue their now useless war in China.

[19] This the Imperial Conference defined as (1) Anglo-American agreement to close the Burma Road and cease all aid to Nationalist China, (2) Anglo-American agreement to make no offensive preparations in the Far East, and (3) Anglo-American agreement to resume normal trade relations with Japan. In return Japan would (1) agree not to use Indo-China as a base for offensive operations except against China, (2) withdraw troops from Indo-China after establishment of peace in the Far East, (3) guarantee the neutrality of the Philippines, (4) refrain from war against Russia unless attacked, and (5) agree to clarify Japanese obligations under the Tripartite Pact.

agreement. Japan was even willing to evacuate China, the messenger told Welles on October 13.

But the situation in Tokyo was passing out of Konoye's control. The Premier had a long conference with high military and naval officials on October 12 and argued in behalf of agreement to withdraw from China. But the War Minister, General Tojo, instantly vetoed the proposal. Further discussions revealed that the Premier and the army group had reached an impasse, and Konoye resigned on October 16. As his successor the Emperor named Tojo himself, after the General had promised he would continue negotiations.

Instead of propelling the Japanese immediately into war with England and America, the fall of the Konoye government only intensified the dissension in Tokyo between the army and the anti-war group. Supported by the navy, the Emperor demanded reconsideration of the program adopted at the Imperial Conference on September 6; and from mid-October through November 5 the debate proceeded. The new Foreign Minister, Shigenori Togo, tried to find a solution for the evacuation of China, but the army would not yield and insisted that war was preferable to the gradual economic ruin of the Empire. Togo did persuade the army to agree to one last effort at compromise with the United States; on November 5 the military chieftains agreed but won the Emperor's consent to preparations for immediate attack if the negotiations had yielded no agreement by about November 25. On the same day the army and navy issued war orders, to go into effect in early December.

Thus between November 7 and December 7 the futile negotiations proceeded anew in Washington. Without going into the repetitious details, it suffices to say that neither government retreated from its irrevocable position on the key issue of China, that Tokyo conducted the negotiations largely as a cover for attack, and that the American leaders continued the discussions mainly in the hope of deferring the conflict that they knew from intercepted Japanese messages was practically inevitable.

The utter hopelessness of the deadlock was further revealed after a special Japanese envoy, Saburu Kurusu, arrived at the White House on November 17. After talking with Roosevelt and Hull, Kurusu was unable to persuade his government to agree to a stop-gap proposal that the United States would accept, while Hull would not approve a temporary *modus vivendi*—actually, in Japanese eyes, an ultimatum—that Tokyo offered on November 20. The crisis came to an abrupt head on November 21, when the State Department intercepted a message from Tokyo to the Japanese Ambassadors extending the negotiations to November 29 but warning that after that date "things" would automatically begin to happen. Hull had prepared a counter *modus vivendi* for a ninety-day truce; however, he abandoned it on November 25, after receiving news of the movement of Japanese troopships off Formosa and strong protests from the Chinese and British governments. Instead, chiefly to keep the record clear, Hull called in Nomura and Kurusu on November 26, rejected the Japanese proposal of November 20, and then proceeded to read the text of a draft "Mutual Declaration of Policy" and "Steps to be taken by the Government of the United States and by the Government of Japan." The "Mutual

Declaration" was a reaffirmation of the principles Hull had long enunciated; the proposed agreement for "Steps to be taken" provided, however, for the Japanese evacuation not only of Indo-China but of China as well and the support of the Nationalist government by the Japanese.

Hull's note of November 26 was neither an ultimatum nor a basis for new discussions, for the Secretary knew diplomacy had failed and that hereafter the safety of the nation would rest in other hands. On November 24 the army and navy had warned its commanders in the Pacific area that a surprise Japanese attack on the Philippines and Guam was possible. This warning was repeated in even stronger terms on November 27. In Tokyo, also, responsibility and initiative had passed to the practitioners of war. On November 25 a carrier task force left the Kuriles to attack the great American naval base in Hawaii, Pearl Harbor, while large army forces in southern Indo-China were poised to strike at Malaya. The receipt of Hull's note of November 26 in Tokyo, therefore, merely confirmed the Japanese conclusion that the Empire had no alternative left but war. The Emperor approved war plans on November 29 and a declaration of war on December 1; moreover, the Foreign Office received word from Berlin that Germany would declare war against the United States as soon as Japan had struck.

The Washington leaders knew from intercepted messages only that the Japanese would attack somewhere soon. Although recognizing that an assault on the Philippines and Guam was possible, they concluded that Tokyo would avoid such direct provocation to the United States. Thus on the eve of war the American government were more concerned over what to do in the event of a Japanese attack on Malaya and the Dutch East Indies than with immediate defense of American territory. Although the Cabinet and American military and naval advisers agreed the United States must fight if Japan attacked the British and Dutch possessions, the President refused to give any definite assurances to these governments. When news of the movement of large Japanese forces against Malaya reached Washington on December 6, however, Roosevelt dispatched an urgent personal appeal to Hirohito, warning that the present tension could not last much longer and urging him to take some action to dispel the threat of war.

In the afternoon of Saturday, December 6, the Japanese reply to Hull's note of November 26 began to come into Washington over the wires. The first sections, which were decoded by early evening, revealed Japan's rejection of the note; the final section, which announced a termination of the negotiations, was in the President's hands by the morning of December 7. By the time Nomura and Kurusu were able to deliver the message to Hull the attack on Pearl Harbor had already occurred and first reports from the stricken base had reached Washington.

Meanwhile, American military and naval commanders in the Pacific had been duly but not strenuously warned that surprise Japanese attacks were likely. Like their superiors in Washington, however, they expected the Japanese to strike at Malaya, not at them. The commanders in Hawaii, Admiral Husband E. Kimmel and General Walter C. Short, were unconcerned as the "day of infamy" approached. Kimmel had concentrated virtually his entire fleet in Pearl Harbor; fearing sabotage, Short had disposed his airplanes and anti-aircraft guns in such a manner as to make effective defense impossible; and neither commander had established an effective air patrol. Thus the carrier task force under Admiral Chuichi Nagumo approached Hawaii from the northwest undetected and unknown.

At 7:55 a.m. on December 7, 1941, the first wave of Japanese airplanes, 189 in number, attacked airfields first and then the fleet anchored in the harbor. At 8:50 a second wave of 171 Japanese planes followed. The navy and marine corps were unable to get a single plane off the ground; an army fighter squadron at Haleiwa, which the Japanese overlooked, got a few planes into the air and destroyed several of the attackers; by the time of the second major assault a few anti-aircraft batteries were in action; and several naval craft were able to get into action and attack Japanese submarines. Otherwise, the Japanese were unopposed and raked and bombed at will. And when the last attacking planes turned toward their carriers at about 9:45 the great American bastion in the Pacific was a smoking shambles: practically every airplane on the island of Oahu either destroyed or disabled; all eight battleships in Pearl Harbor disabled—two of them, the *Oklahoma* and *Arizona*, destroyed or sunk; three cruisers and three destroyers heavily damaged or destroyed; and 2,323 men of both services dead. The cost to the Japanese was twenty-nine airplanes, five midget submarines, and one fleet submarine.

First reports of the attack came to Washington at about two in the afternoon, while later news told of other Japanese attacks on the Philippines, Hong Kong, Wake Island, Midway Island, Siam, and Malaya and of a Japanese declaration of war against the United States and Great Britain. After Cabinet meetings in the afternoon and evening, the President called congressional leaders to the White House and reviewed dispatches he had received. The following day, December 8, he appeared before the two houses, excoriated the "unprovoked and dastardly attack by Japan," and asked Congress to recognize the obvious state of war that existed. It was done within an hour and with only one dissenting vote in the House of Representatives. In his war message Roosevelt had deliberately avoided mention of Germany and Italy, in order to leave the decision for fullfledged war for the time being to Hitler. Delighted by the Pearl Harbor attack, Hitler responded to the Japanese request for a German declaration of war against the United States on December 11, and Mussolini at once followed suit. The President and Congress reciprocated during the afternoon of the same day.

Words fail to convey the shock and indignation the American people felt as they heard the news over their radios on the afternoon of Pearl Harbor day. They did not know their armed forces had suffered the most humiliating defeat in American history by a foreign foe or the desperate circumstances that impelled the Japanese to undertake a suicidal war. The American people only thought they had been treacherously attacked, and in their anger they forgot all the partisan quarrels and debates over foreign policy that had so long divided them and resolved with firm determination to win the war the Japanese had begun. The agony of doubt was over; the issue was now fully joined. The American people had embarked, not gladly upon a second crusade, but grimly upon a war for survival.

CHAPTER 23 / *THE SECOND WORLD WAR:*
THE AMERICAN HOME FRONT

*N*OT since the dark days of the Revolution had the American people confronted so dire a military menace or so staggering a task as during the Second World War. Within a few months after Japanese bombs fell on Pearl Harbor, the ensign of the Rising Sun floated triumphantly over all the outposts and bastions of the far Pacific region, while Hitler and his armies stood poised to strike at the Middle East and join forces with the Japanese in India.

It was perhaps fortunate that the American people in December 1941 little knew how long the war would last and what the costs would be. However, they had certain advantages that made victory possible: courageous allies, a unity unprecedented in American history, enormous resources and industrial capacity, superb political and military leadership, and, most important, the determination to win. These factors combined from 1941 to 1945 to achieve miracles of production that made earlier American war efforts look small by comparison.

The astonishing thing, however, was the fact that Americans could engage in total war without submitting to the discipline of total war at home. To be sure, the war intensified certain social tensions and created new problems of adjustment; but the mass of Americans took the war in stride, without emotional excitement or hysteria.

175 / *Mobilizing Manpower for War*

The adoption of the war resolutions by Congress found the United States in the midst of a sizable rearmament campaign, the momentum of which was daily increasing. Planners in the War and Navy departments had realistically faced up to the long-run requirements for the defeat of the Axis and presented a Victory Plan to the President in September 1941. In addition, thanks to the extension of the terms of service of the draftees of 1940, the American army in December 1941 was already a formidable defense force of about 1,600,000 men, a majority of whom had recently been seasoned in battle maneuvers.

All these preparations saved precious time. Meanwhile, soon after approving the war declarations, Congress ordered the registration of all men between the ages of twenty and forty-four for war service and of men between forty-five and sixty-five for potential labor service, and extended the terms of all servicemen to six months beyond the duration of hostilities. The drafting of men beyond the age of thirty-eight was soon abandoned; on the other hand, on November 13, 1942, the President signed an amendment to the Selective Service Act lowering the draft age to eighteen.

All told, the draft boards registered some 31,000,000 men, of whom 9,867,707 were inducted into service. Including volunteers, a total of 15,145,-115 men and women served in the armed services before the end of the war —10,420,000 in the army, 3,883,520 in the navy, 599,693 in the marines, and 241,902 in the Coast Guard. It was an immense mobilization, yet by European standards it was far from being a total one. By contrast, the Soviet Union mobilized 22,000,000 men and women, Germany, 17,000,000, and the British Empire, 12,000,000.

Housing and training the huge American force was a task of incredible size. First came the job of building new army and Air Forces camps, posts, and bases at home and expanding old ones. By the end of March 1943, when three-fourths of the army's home construction projects were completed, the army had provided housing for nearly 5,000,000 men in the United States. Then came the task of training men for combat in the jungles of New Guinea, the Bavarian Alps, and the deserts of Africa, as well as in the French and German countryside. "An infantryman, for example," General Marshall afterward wrote, "became proficient in his primary weapons and familiarized with the M1 rifle, the carbine, the hand grenade, the rifle grenade, the automatic rifle, the .30 caliber medium machine gun, the 60-mm mortar, and the two-man rocket launcher. These were the weapons that every infantry rifleman might be called upon to use." The training, of course, occurred in stages: thirteen weeks in basic training, twenty-six weeks' additional training after the soldier was assigned to a division, and a final thirteen weeks spent in maneuvers and field exercises.

Because the first offensive blows could be delivered from the air, the Army Air Forces were authorized at the outset of American participation to increase their strength to two and one-third million men and were given highest priority on manpower and materials. When the Japanese attacked Pearl Harbor the AAF had 292,000 men and 9,000 planes, 1,100 of them fit for combat, in service. When the Japanese surrendered in August 1945, the AAF had enlisted 2,300,000 men and women and had 72,000 planes in service. During the intervening years the AAF had accomplished one of the miracles of modern times.

By the end of the war the third branch of the army, the Services of Supply, had grown in strength to over 1,750,000 men and executed its unspectacular but prodigious task with a minimum of hardship to the civilian population. Between 1943 and 1945 alone, the Services of Supply operated a fleet of 1,537 ships, paid out over $22,000,000,000 in pay and allowances, processed more than $75,000,000,000 in army contracts, managed 3,700 posts or cantonments in the United States, transported 7,370,000 men and 101,750,000 tons of cargo, and administered a far-flung medical service.

Thanks to the wealth, technology, and industrial and agricultural capacity of his country, the American soldier was the best paid, best clothed, and by 1943 the best equipped fighting man in the world. In that year, for example, Americans achieved not only a quantitative but also a decided qualitative superiority in fighter planes and bombers. Even in areas of research in which the Germans had a head start, such as atomic fission, American scientists and engineers had won decisive advantages by 1945. On the battlefield the best American weapons were the light semi-automatic Garand rifle and the multiple-driven truck; they combined to give a superiority in firepower and mobility that the Germans were never able to overcome in spite of general equality in machine guns, mortars, rocket-launched missiles, and artillery.[1]

In the meantime, the navy, marines, and Coast Guard had grown from relative weakness after the Pearl Harbor disaster to dimensions of gigantic strength at the time of the Japanese surrender. On December 7, 1941, the navy had a complement of 337,349 men, in addition to 66,048 in the Marine Corps and 25,336 in the Coast Guard. By the summer of 1945, on the other hand, the navy's manpower had increased to 3,408,347 officers and men, the Marine Corps' to 484,631, and the Coast Guard's to 170,480. Before Japanese bombs disabled or sank part of the Pacific Fleet at Pearl Harbor, the navy had in operation some 4,500 ships, including seventeen battleships, seven fleet carriers, eighteen heavy and nineteen light cruisers, 200 destroyers and torpedo boats, and 114 submarines. By the end of 1945 the navy had grown to more than 91,000 ships of all sizes, including twenty-four battleships, two large cruisers, twenty-nine fleet carriers, seventy-three escort carriers, twenty-three heavy and forty-five light cruisers, 489 destroyers and torpedo boats, 500 escort vessels, and 274 submarines.

The magnitude of the job of supplying a fleet that operated in practically every ocean in the world staggers the imagination, and a few illustrations must suffice to indicate how the system worked. In 1940 the navy had one good advanced base, Pearl Harbor, in the Pacific. By the end of the war, however, it had constructed bases at Guam, Leyte-Samar in the Philippines, and Okinawa together capable of accommodating the entire fleet. And from the West Coast poured an ever-increasing stream of materials—it reached a volume of 600,000 tons a month in the early part of 1945—to supply the bases and flotillas in the Pacific.

Finally, there was the mobilization of women for war service: the Women's Auxiliary Corps, which grew in size to 100,000 and sent 17,000 WACs overseas; the navy's counterpart, the WAVEs, who numbered about 86,000 at the end of the war; and the Coast Guard's SPARs and the Marine Corps' Women's Reserve. Working as stenographers, clerks, technicians, cryptographers, and the like, the female contingents not only performed

---

[1] In certain categories, however, the Germans retained a marked advantage. The German 88-mm rifle, for example, was superior to the American 90-mm rifle. Use of a smokeless, flashless powder gave the German infantryman a great advantage over his American foe, who had to use powder that exposed his position every time he fired. Moreover, from 1943 to 1945 the American medium Sherman tank was no match for the heavy German Tiger and Panther tanks. Not until the production of the heavy Pershing tank in the winter of 1944–1945 were American armored divisions able to meet the German *Panzer* forces on equal terms.

indispensable functions but released over 200,000 men for service on the battle fronts.

176 / *The Price of Victory*

Measured in human costs, the price of victory in the Second World War came high to the American people—253,573 dead, 651,042 wounded, 114,205 prisoners, and 65,834 men missing. In all theaters from December 7, 1941, to the Japanese surrender, the army suffered 943,222 casualties—201,367 killed, 570,783 wounded, 114,205 prisoners, and 56,867 missing; the Navy, Marine Corps, and Coast Guard, 141,432 casualties—52,206 killed, 80,259 wounded, and 8,967 missing. Relative to total numbers, the 36,700 airmen who died in combat made the greatest sacrifice, but the infantry divisions, with only one-fifth the total army personnel, suffered 70 per cent of all army casualties. For the men who died, however, Americans and their allies exacted a fearful retribution. Germany and Italy suffered 373,600 dead and lost 8,108,983 prisoners to the Allies on the Western Front alone. The Japanese gave up 1,093,000 battle dead in areas outside China.

For their relatively low death lists, Americans in large measure could thank the medical corps of the several services. Although American soldiers lived and fought in deserts and jungles as well as in the temperate zones, the death rate from nonbattle causes was no higher than the rate for similar groups at home. And for the sick and wounded there was extraordinary care, while use of sulfa drugs, penicillin, and whole blood brought such healing and relief from wounds and shock as would not have been possible a decade before.

The result was to cut the rate of deaths from disease and battle wounds in half from the rate of the First World War. Almost 59 per cent of the soldiers wounded in the Second World War were returned to battle duty. Moreover, through increased use of psychiatry, the Medical Corps was able to return from 40 to 60 per cent of the battle-shock cases to combat and another 20 to 30 per cent to limited duty. Finally, for the maimed and psychologically ill, the army established twenty-five convalescent centers, which offered training in new skills and helped prepare the permanently disabled for useful civilian life.

177 / *"Scientists Against Time"*

In the last analysis the war was won as well in the laboratory and on the testing ground as on the battlefield. At the outset of the war, however, American scientists lagged far behind the Germans in research in atomic fission, jet propulsion, and rockets and behind the British in work on jet propulsion, radar, and other electronic devices. Alarmed by the prospect of his country entering the war scientifically unprepared, Dr. Vannevar Bush, president of the Carnegie Institution of Washington, persuaded the President in June 1940 to establish the National Defense Research Committee, with representatives from the defense departments, universities, and private

industry. Then, in June 1941, Roosevelt reorganized the government's research program by creating the Office of Scientific Research and Development. As Director of the OSRD, Bush had virtual dictatorial powers and
could approve or veto all projects or initiate research on his own initiative.

By the autumn of 1941 Bush and his colleagues had accomplished a full
mobilization of scientific personnel and facilities. Let us look briefly at some
of the most significant results of this great effort—the development of radar
and electronic devices, rockets for combat use, the proximity fuse, and,
finally, the atomic bomb.

Work on radar, or radio detection, had been in progress in the United
States, Britain, and Germany since the early 1930's, but it was the British
who first perfected radar and put it to large-scale use. Radar detection saved
the British Isles during the great German air assault of 1940–1941. Used in
patrol planes, radar sets enabled the British and American navies to bring
the German submarines under control.[2] Used in fighters, radar enabled the
air forces to launch powerful night interceptors; used in bombers, it provided a perfect bombsight. As the basis of a new method of fire-control,
radar gave eyes to guns as well as to airplanes and ships. By July 1945
the American armed services alone had received $3,000,000,000 worth of
radar equipment and $71,000,000 worth of Loran, a long-range navigational
aid.

The outbreak of the war in 1939 found research in the field of rocket
warfare well advanced in Britain and Germany and practically nonexistent
in the United States. With the help of British scientists and the support of
the Navy Department and the Army Ordnance Department, however,
NDRC scientists had a sizable research program under way by the end of
1941. One of the first results was the "bazooka," a tube rocket launcher
perfected in 1942, which could be operated by two infantrymen and discharged a rocket powerful enough to destroy a tank. Subsequently, scientists developed an incredible variety of rocket launchers and rockets for use
in land combat, in anti-aircraft operations, by airplanes, and in ship-to-shore
bombardments. What this meant in terms of increased fire power can perhaps best be illustrated by the fact that a single fighter plane carrying rockets
could discharge a salvo as heavy as a destroyer's, while "a squadron of
Grumman Hellcats carrying Tiny Tims [a 11.75-inch aircraft rocket] packs
a punch comparable to a broadside from a division of heavy cruisers."[3]

The Germans, on the other hand, made the greatest progress in research
in rocket missiles and scored their greatest success with the V-1 flying bomb
and the V-2, an enormous rocket that flew 3,400 miles an hour and carried
a warhead of one ton of explosives. First sent against the British Isles on
June 6, 1944, the V-1 traveled so slowly that the Allied anti-aircraft gunners
and fighters could shoot it down. However, no defense against the V-2,
except the capture of the sites from which it was launched, was ever found.

One of the most brilliant scientific achievements of the war was the
development, exclusively by the OSRD, of the proximity fuse. A miniature

---

[2] Perhaps even more effective in anti-submarine operations was so-called sonar, or
underwater sound detection apparatus, developed by the NDRC in conjunction with the
Harvard Underwater Sound Laboratory.

[3] James Phinney Baxter 3d, *Scientists Against Time* (Boston, 1946), p. 46.

radio set in the head of the shell that detonated it by proximity to the target, the proximity fuse was described by the Chief of the Army Ground Forces as "the most important innovation in artillery ammunition since the introduction of high-explosive shells." After overcoming incredible production difficulties, the American agencies involved conducted first large-scale successful tests in August 1942 and were able to get the fuse into mass production within a year. By the end of the war, production reached the rate of 2,000,000 a month and absorbed one-fourth the facilities of the entire American electronics industry. Proximity fuses were first used by the navy against Japanese aircraft in 1943 and next in quantity against German V-1 bombs in 1944. Fearing that the Germans would recover an unexploded shell and put the fuse into production, the Joint Chiefs of Staff did not allow the ground forces in Europe to use the new weapon until December 1944. Put into use against the Germans in their Ardennes counteroffensive, the proximity fuse compounded the effectiveness of American artillery and proved devastating against the German ground troops.

The mobilization of American scientists paid numerous other dividends —among them the development of more powerful explosives and fire bombs, of DDT and other weapons in the warfare against insects and vermin, of advanced techniques in the use of blood plasma and whole blood, of penicillin, and of new and deadly gases, which were never used. But the greatest triumph of American scientific and production genius was the development of the atomic bomb. As the perfection of this weapon marked an epochal turning point in history, let us look at the story of its production in some detail.

On January 26, 1939, the Danish physicist, Niels Bohr, startled a group of American physicists assembled in Washington by announcing that two Germans at the Kaiser Wilhelm Institute in Berlin had recently accomplished atomic fission in uranium. Nuclear physicists had long understood the structure of the atom and known that atomic fission was theoretically possible. But the deed had now been done, and the road was open for the development of a bomb more powerful and deadly than the world had ever dreamed of.

The grave danger was that the Nazis would use German scientific knowledge and industrial capacity to produce atomic bombs and literally conquer the world. In the summer of 1939, therefore, Professor Enrico Fermi of Columbia University, Professor Albert Einstein of the Institute for Advanced Study, and others indirectly persuaded the President to begin a small research program. It was not until 1940—when the President gave the NDRC control of atomic research—however, that work was begun in earnest. By the summer of 1941 research at Columbia, California, and other universities confirmed the possibilities of atomic fission through a chain reaction. The chief problem now was to find a fissionable element in sufficient quantity. Earlier experiments had proved that the uranium isotope, U-235, was fissionable; but since U-235 was an infinitesimal part of uranium, the chances were remote of ever accumulating enough of the element to manufacture atomic bombs. This problem was solved by Dr. Ernest Lawrence of the University of California at Berkeley, who used a huge cyclotron, or "atom smasher," to convert the plentiful uranium element, U-238, into a new element, plutonium, which was as fissionable as U-235 and much easier to obtain in quantity.

The next objective became the production of a chain reaction in uranium, that is, the almost simultaneous fission of the uranium atoms through a chain bombardment by neutrons. Under the direction of Dr. Arthur H. Compton, a group of physicists built the first atomic pile, or apparatus, under the stadium at Stagg Field of the University of Chicago. By an intricate process that passes the layman's understanding, these physicists produced the first controlled chain reaction on December 2, 1942.

From this time forward the production of an atomic bomb was possible, provided a means of production could be devised. But what a problem it was! "The technological gap," writes one physicist, "between producing a controlled chain reaction and using it as a large scale power source or an explosive is comparable to the gap between the discovery of fire and the manufacture of a steam locomotive." As production was outside the province of the OSRD, it turned control over to the Manhattan District of the Army Engineer Corps, headed by General Leslie R. Groves, on May 1, 1943.

Drawing upon the combined resources of the OSRD, universities, and private industries, Groves pushed the project with incredible speed. Oak Ridge, Tennessee, eighteen miles west of Knoxville, and Hanford, Washington, were selected as sites for two plutonium producing plants because of the availability of quantities of water and electricity. Work on the bomb itself was begun in the spring of 1943 at a laboratory built on a lonely mesa at Los Alamos, outside Santa Fe, New Mexico. Here, under the direction of Dr. J. Robert Oppenheimer, a group of American, British, and European scientists worked night and day to perfect the bomb.

Scientists at Los Alamos began the final assembly of the first atomic bomb on July 12, 1945, and tension mounted as the fateful day of testing drew near. Nearly $2,000,000,000 had been expended in an effort which yet might fail. The bomb was moved to the air base at Alamogordo and successfully detonated at 5:30 a.m. on July 16. A searing blast of light, many times brighter than the noonday sun, was followed by a deafening roar and a huge mushroom cloud; and relief mixed with a feeling of doom filled the minds of the men who watched the beginning of a new era in human history, the atomic age.

178 / *American Industry Goes to War*

The story of how changing agencies mobilized the American economy for staggering tasks is a tale full of confusion and chaos, incompetence and momentary failure, political intrigue and personal vendetta, but withal one of superb accomplishment on many home fronts. Before it was too late, government and American industry accomplished one of the economic miracles of modern times—the production of a stream of goods that not only provided a high standard of living at home but also supplied the American armed forces with all and the British, French, and Russians with a large part of the resources and *matériel* for victory.

During the first period of industrial mobilization, from August 1939 until about the end of 1941, the task was the comparatively easy one of utilizing idle plants and men to supply the inchoate American armed forces and the British. In August 1939 the President established the War Resources Board, headed by Edward R. Stettinius, Jr., of the United States Steel Corporation and composed mainly of big business executives, to advise the Assistant Secretary of War on industrial mobilization. Without effective authority to begin with, the War Resources Board soon fell victim to labor and New Deal critics, who charged it was dominated by Morgan and Du Pont interests.

This was, of course, the time of the "phony war," when Allied victory seemed assured and the necessity for total economic mobilization seemed remote. None the less, before its dissolution in October 1939, the War Resources Board prepared an industrial mobilization plan that envisaged giving dictatorial economic authority to a single administrator in the event the United States entered the war. Rejecting the Board's proposal, Roosevelt asked the former chairman of Wilson's War Industries Board, Bernard M. Baruch, to prepare another. Baruch in turn presented a plan that met all Roosevelt's objections to the Board's proposal and provided for a gradual but rational transition into a total war economy.

For reasons unknown, Roosevelt suppressed the Baruch plan and allowed the partial mobilization effort of 1939–1940 to drift aimlessly. The fall of France, however, ended the complacency in Washington and galvanized the President into action, inadequate though it was. Calling for vast new defense appropriations and the production of 50,000 planes a year, he re-established the Advisory Commission to the old and nearly defunct Council of National Defense on May 28, 1940. Composed of representatives of management, labor, agriculture, and consumers and headed by William S. Knudsen, president of the General Motors Corporation, the Commission was charged with the responsibility of getting defense production into high gear. In addition, on June 25 Congress authorized the RFC to finance the building of defense plants and, in the Revenue Act of October 8, 1940, allowed businessmen to write off the cost of construction through tax deductions over a five-year period.

Because it abdicated control over priorities to the Army-Navy Munitions Board, the Advisory Commission had lost control of the industrial mobilization by December 1940. Although he had decided to launch the nation upon a defense of the free world through Lend-Lease, Roosevelt still stubbornly refused to institute the kind of mobilization plan that Baruch had earlier suggested. Instead, on January 7, 1941, he established the Office of Production Management, headed by Knudsen and Sidney Hillman of the CIO, to cooperate with the President and defense secretaries in stimulating and controlling war production. In addition, an Office of Price Administration and Civilian Supply, established on April 11 and headed by Leon Henderson, would work to protect consumers' interests.

The various divisions of the OPM went to work to improve the priorities system, coordinate British and American orders, and especially to help automobile manufacturers prepare for conversion to the production of tanks and planes. What took place during the spring and summer of 1941, therefore, was a gradual shift from a peacetime to a wartime economy, with inevitable hardships as industries converted to defense production. As shortages of electric power, aluminum, steel, railroad rolling stock, and other materials grew, as the priorities system nearly broke down, and as internal bickering and public criticism mounted, Roosevelt attempted another superficial reorganization. On August 28, 1941, he suspended the OPM but left an OPM Council; created a Supplies Priorities and Allocation Board, headed by the Sears-Roebuck executive, Donald M. Nelson; and added other agencies, many of which overlapped in a confusing way. The central force in the new apparatus, however, was the Supplies Priorities and Allocations Board, for it had the power to determine and allocate requirements and supplies for the armed forces, the civilian economy, and the British and the Russians.

On January 16, 1942, the President at last attempted to establish a comprehensive economic mobilization, by creating the War Production Board, under Donald Nelson, to take supreme command of the economic home front. Nelson was an excellent technician, "big, jovial, and self-possessed"; but he failed to meet the test of leadership. He continued to allow the military departments to control priorities, with the result that he never established firm control over production. He permitted the great corporations to obtain a practical monopoly on war production, which caused a near scandal when the facts were disclosed by a special Senate committee headed by Harry S. Truman of Missouri. Finally, he allowed industrial expansion to get out of hand and occur in the wrong areas.

By the autumn of 1942 American industry was booming but chaos threatened. Alarmed by the prospect, Roosevelt brought Justice James F. Byrnes to the White House as head of the Office of Economic Stabilization on October 3 and gave him supreme command of the economic effort.[4] One of Byrnes' first moves was to force the adoption of a plan that established such complete control over the allocation of steel, aluminum, and copper that the priorities difficulty vanished almost at once. Then in May 1943 Roosevelt created the Office of War Mobilization, a sort of high command with control over all aspects of the economy, with Byrnes as Director or "Assistant President." Representative Fred M. Vinson of Kentucky succeeded Byrnes as head of the Office of Economic Stabilization. By the spring of 1943, therefore, the home front was at last well organized and under control.

179 / *The Miracle of Production*

In spite of all its shortcomings, the American industrial mobilization did succeed far beyond the expectations of most Americans. Few persons in 1939 could visualize the potentialities of full employment of manpower, resources, and capital and plant. Still fewer persons knew the proper formula

---

[4] Nelson remained as head of the WPB until August 1944, when the President sent him to China to advise Chiang Kai-shek on economic matters. He was succeeded by Julius A. Krug.

for shifting the economic machinery into high gear. It was the vast expansion of federal expenditures and the availability of billions of public capital for investment that invigorated the economy in 1940. And it was the continued high level of federal expenditures, coupled with a program of high taxes and the cooperation of labor and management, that effected the miracle of American production from 1941 to 1945.

We can gain some understanding of the total achievement by considering the general performance of the American economy from 1939 through 1945. Measured by depression standards, 1939 was a relatively prosperous year. Gross national product stood at $91,300,000,000—higher in real dollars than during the boom year of 1929. By 1945, on the other hand, the gross national product had risen, in 1939 dollars, to $166,600,000,000. From 1939 to 1945, moreover, the index of manufacturing production increased 96 per cent, of agricultural production, 22 per cent, and of transportation services, 109 per cent. Contrasted with the performance of the economy during the First World War, when the total national output increased hardly at all, this was a remarkable achievement.

The keys to success in the industrial effort were the conversion of practically the entire American durable goods industry to war production and the application of mass production techniques to the manufacture of instruments of warfare. The automobile and automotive parts industries, for example, converted entirely to war production after Pearl Harbor and alone turned out 20 per cent of the entire war production, while the electronics and appliance industries made radar equipment, proximity fuses, machine guns, materials for the atomic bomb, and a thousand other items of destruction.

In 1941 American war production was a mere trickle, only $8,400,-000,000 in value; in 1942 it totaled $30,200,000,000 in value and equaled that of Germany, Italy, and Japan combined; by 1944 American factories were producing twice the volume of the Axis partners. A few illustrations will give point to the generalizations. In 1939 the American airplane industry employed 46,638 persons and produced 5,865 planes. At the peak of production in 1944, the industry employed 2,102,000 persons and turned out 96,369 aircraft. All told, from Pearl Harbor to the end of the war, American factories produced 274,941 military aircraft, 34,500 of which went to the Allies under Lend-Lease.

But the war was won as well on the seas as in the air; and an essential ingredient of the Allied victory in the battle of supply was the production of merchant ships in the United States. The construction of merchant shipping, which had totaled only 1,000,000 tons in 1941, rose from 8,000,000 tons in 1942 to a peak of over 19,000,000 tons in 1943 and, as the need diminished, declined to nearly 16,500,000 tons in 1944 and nearly 8,000,000 tons from January through July of 1945. All told, from July 1, 1940, to August 1, 1945, American shipyards produced a total of 55,239,000 tons of merchant shipping—a tonnage equal to two-thirds the merchant marines of all the Allied nations combined.

Perhaps the most remarkable example of how American ingenuity and industry combined to effect miracles of production was the creation, almost overnight, of a new synthetic rubber industry. Japanese conquest of Malaya and the Netherlands East Indies deprived the United States of 90 per cent of its natural rubber supply at a time when the total stockpile of rubber in the United States amounted to only 540,000 tons and normal consumption exceeded 600,000 tons annually. As total imports during 1942 could not exceed 175,000 tons, the rubber shortage threatened to hobble the entire war effort.

For months Nelson and the WPB wrestled unsuccessfully with the problem, until Undersecretary of the Navy James V. Forrestal took the matter directly to Harry Hopkins and the President. The upshot was the appointment by Roosevelt on August 16, 1942, of a special committee headed by Bernard M. Baruch to investigate and recommend. Reporting on September 10, the Baruch committee warned that the war effort and civilian economy might collapse if a severe rubber shortage occurred; urged the institution of nation-wide gasoline rationing and a thirty-five-mile speed limit; and recommended the immediate construction of a vast industry to produce rubber synthetically from petroleum.

Roosevelt acted at once to implement the Baruch committee's proposals. Appointed Rubber Director in the WPB on September 15, 1942, William M. Jeffers, president of the Union Pacific Railroad, ruthlessly cut his way through the existing priorities system; and by the end of 1943 he had brought into existence a synthetic rubber industry that produced 762,000 tons in 1944 and 820,000 tons the following year. In addition, the Rubber Reserve Corporation and its successor, the Rubber Development Company, found enough natural rubber in Latin America, Ceylon, and Liberia to permit the manufacture of heavy tires and medical equipment.

180 / *The Greatest Tax Bill in History*

Americans accustomed to normal federal expenditures of about $8,000,-000,000 annually during the 1930's found it difficult to comprehend the magnitude of federal spending during the Second World War. During the fiscal years from 1941 to 1945 federal expenditures aggregated $321,212,-605,000—a sum roughly twice as large as all previous federal expenditures from 1789 to 1941 and ten times as great as during the First World War. A large part, some 41 per cent, of the money for the war effort came from tax receipts, which totaled nearly $131,000,000,000 during the fiscal years 1941–1945. The balance was raised by borrowing from individuals, banks, and corporations; such borrowing, in turn, increased the gross national debt from $49,000,000,000 in 1941 to $259,000,000,000 in mid-1945.

In order to reduce inflationary pressures and provide revenue without creating new money, Treasury officials made extraordinary efforts to induce individuals and nonbanking institutions to purchase war bonds. War bonds could be purchased almost anywhere and by payroll deduction, and from 1941 through 1945 individuals and nonbanking institutions purchased nearly $100,000,000,000 worth of war bonds.[5] To make up the balance of

[5] Individuals purchased some $40,000,000,000 worth of the popular series "E" bonds, designed especially for the small investor.

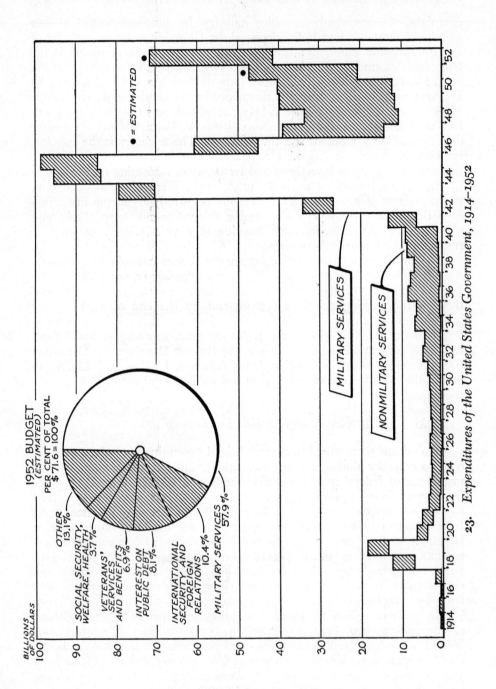

23. Expenditures of the United States Government, 1914–1952

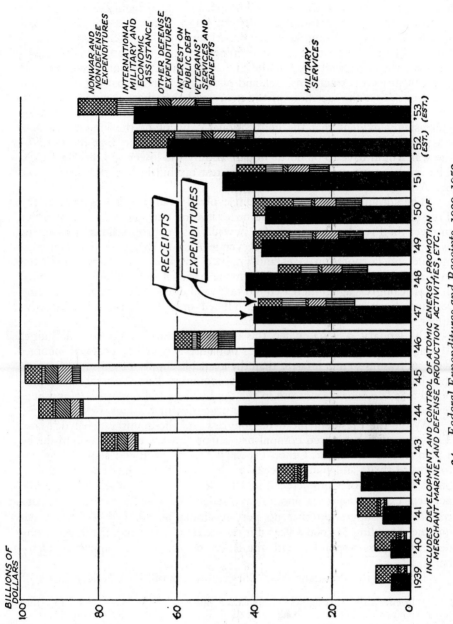

24. Federal Expenditures and Receipts, 1939–1953

INCLUDES DEVELOPMENT AND CONTROL OF ATOMIC ENERGY, PROMOTION OF MERCHANT MARINE, AND DEFENSE PRODUCTION ACTIVITIES, ETC.

the deficit, the Treasury had to call upon Federal Reserve and commercial banks to take an additional $87,500,000,000 in federal securities.[6]

Thus was money found to pay the huge direct costs of the Second World War to the American people. Meanwhile, the administration and Congress had joined hands in a determined campaign to broaden and revolutionize the tax structure. On the one hand, the President, Congress, and a vast majority of Americans, rich and poor alike, agreed that the few should not profit from the sacrifices of the many and that there should be no new millionaires as a result of the defense and war efforts. On the other, it became increasingly evident that the conventional concept of the income tax as a tax principally on wealth was hopelessly inadequate, and that the costs of the war would have to be borne in part also by the lower and middle classes. The result, as we will see, was "the greatest tax bill in history," paid by all the American people.

The administration's tax program evolved gradually in response to the Treasury's need for funds and the necessity for curbing inflation. In order to meet the President's requests for new defense appropriations in 1940, for example, Congress approved two Revenue Acts in that year that increased income and corporation taxes and imposed an excess profits tax graduated to a maximum of 50 per cent. When the national defense effort expanded in 1941, Congress again increased old taxes and devised new means of finding revenue. Even so, the income tax touched only the small minority with upper middle and upper class incomes.

By January 5, 1942, when the President presented his annual Budget Message to Congress, the nation was not only at war but personal incomes were increasing so much faster than the available supply of consumers' goods that inflation threatened to disrupt the economy. Roosevelt therefore proposed a $7,000,000,000 increase in the tax burden; and on April 27 and September 7, 1942, he appealed even more urgently for tax increases.

While the President pleaded, Congress and the country debated. Many Treasury officials favored compulsory saving but were never able to devise a plan that would work. Other Treasury experts proposed a spendings tax, to reward thrift and punish excessive spending. The NAM and the United States Chamber of Commerce urged taxation to the limit, including a 100 per cent excess profits tax and a heavy federal sales tax. The President contributed the suggestion that no person should be allowed to have a net income exceeding $25,000 a year during wartime. After months of agonizing delay, Congress responded with the Revenue Act of 1942, approved October 21.

It was, as the President said, "the greatest tax bill in American history,"

---

[6] "In effect, the banking system monetized this part of the federal debt. In return for government securities the banks created new checking deposits for the Treasury, which then spent the money into the income stream to purchase goods and services or to make transfer payments into the hands of business firms and individuals." Lester V. Chandler, *Inflation in the United States* (New York, 1951), p. 73; quoted by permission of Harper & Brothers, publishers.

This infusion of such vast quantities of federal securities was the chief factor in the great expansion of bank credits and the money supply that occurred during the war. Total bank loans and investments increased from $54,177,000,000 on December 31, 1940, to $140,277,000,000 on December 31, 1945; during the same period money in circulation increased from $7,848,000,000 to $26,746,000,000.

designed to raise more than $7,000,000,000 additional revenue annually, a sum exceeding total federal revenues in any peacetime year before 1941. Increasing the combined corporate income tax to a maximum of 40 per cent, the measure also raised the excess profits tax to a flat 90 per cent and provided for a postwar refund of 10 per cent of excess profits taxes paid. Moreover, the measure increased excise taxes and levied a host of new ones and stiffly increased estate and gift taxes. The revolutionary feature of the Revenue Act of 1942, however, was the way in which it broadened the income tax to tap low incomes as well as practically to confiscate large ones. In 1941 only 13,000,000 persons had paid federal income taxes; in contrast, some 50,000,000 persons were caught in the net cast by the Act of 1942.[7]

The difficulty of collecting income taxes from 50,000,000 persons by the conventional method of individual returns led to the adoption, in 1943, of a measure requiring employers to collect the tax by payroll deductions. Meanwhile, as personal incomes, governmental expenditures, and inflationary pressures mounted, the President, in his Budget Message of January 6, 1943, demanded a $16,000,000,000 increase in the federal tax load during the coming fiscal year. Although Treasury officials later lowered the request to $10,500,000,000, congressional leaders rebelled and adopted a Revenue Act in early February 1944 that yielded additional revenue of only $2,200,000,000, chiefly by increasing the excess profits tax to 95 per cent and by heavy increases in excise taxes. The President replied on February 22 with a veto so stinging that his spokesman in the Senate, Alben W. Barkley of Kentucky, resigned his post as Majority Leader. The Senate Democratic caucus promptly and unanimously re-elected Barkley, and an angry House and Senate overrode the veto by enormous majorities on February 24 and 25, 1944.

From this time forward administration and congressional leaders were concerned, not with increasing the tax burden, but with simplifying the withholding system and planning for the days of peace and reconversion that must soon come. In May 1944 Congress approved the Individual Income Tax Act, which repealed the Victory tax, substituted an increase in the normal tax, and allowed some 30,000,000 taxpayers with incomes under $5,000 to file a simplified tax return. In July 1945, moreover, Congress approved a Tax Adjustment Act to aid business during the reconversion period; it provided for refunds or reductions in corporation taxes during the next two years of about $5,500,000,000.

In retrospect, perhaps the most significant aspect of the tax program from 1941 to 1945 was the way in which it reflected the nation's conviction that a war for survival should not become a war for the enrichment of the few. There could be no "swollen fortunes" when the federal income tax reached a maximum of 94 per cent of total net income, to say nothing of

---

[7] Specifically, the Act of 1942 lowered exemptions to $500 for single persons and $1200 for married persons and increased the normal income tax from 4 to 6 per cent. On top of this normal tax, however, came a surtax ranging from 13 to 82 per cent and a Victory tax of 5 per cent, collected at the source on all incomes above $624 a year. The Act of 1942 promised that part of the Victory tax would be refunded after the war, but Congress revoked this pledge in 1944. In 1941 a married person with two dependents and a net income of $500,000 paid $344,476 in federal income taxes; under the Act of 1942 he paid $439,931. A married person with two dependents and a net income of $3,000 paid $58 in the first instance and $267 in the second.

state income and local property taxes. Indeed, as a consequence of extraordinary taxation, the nation's top 5 per cent of income receivers suffered their severest relative economic losses in the history of the country. Their share of disposable income declined from 25.7 per cent in 1940 to 15.9 per cent in 1944.[8] And with an excess profits tax of 95 per cent and corporation income taxes reaching a maximum of 50 per cent, there were few cases of "swollen profits." Net corporation income was $9,400,000,000 in 1941 and 1942, increased slightly in 1943 and 1944, and fell back to $8,500,000,000 in 1945. Dividends increased hardly at all during the same period.

181 / Combating Inflation on the Home Front

Aside from the mobilization of fighting men and the maintenance of a steady flow of materials to the battle fronts, perhaps the most important problem at home was the prevention of a runaway inflation that would compound the costs of the war and increase the burdens of many classes. To state the problem in its simplest terms, inflationary pressures existed after 1941 because the volume of disposable personal income greatly exceeded the supply of goods and services available for civilian consumption at the prevailing price level. Disposable personal incomes rose from $92,000,-000,000 in 1941 to $151,000,000,000 in 1945, but the supply of civilian goods and services, measured in constant dollars, rose from $77,600,000,000 to only $95,400,000,000 during the same period.

Because of the existence of the so-called "inflationary gap" between disposable incomes and available goods and services, the danger of inflation stalked the home front. Remembering how wholesale prices had risen some 170 per cent during and immediately after the First World War, administration leaders were determined such a catastrophe should not again occur. Moreover, they understood the enormous complexity of the problem and knew that economic stabilization could not be achieved by imposing a few direct controls. What ensued, therefore, was a comprehensive and fruitful experiment in stabilization that involved a broad extension of the federal authority over almost every aspect of economic life.

The most obvious and the first tried weapon against inflation was control of prices and rents. When he reorganized the defense mobilization machinery early in 1941, Roosevelt established an Office of Price Administration and Civilian Supply, headed by the explosive Leon Henderson, to work in conjunction with the Office of Production Management. Without real power, Henderson was helpless to control prices and the cost of living during 1941, by January 1942 retail prices were increasing at the rate of 2 per cent a month and threatening to rise at an even faster pace.

In response to the President's urgent plea for authority, Congress enacted the Emergency Price Control Act in January 1942. This measure empowered the Price Administrator to fix maximum prices and rents in special areas and to pay subsidies to producers if that were necessary to prevent

---

[8] The relative status of the top 1 per cent of income receivers declined even more. Their share of disposable income declined from 11.5 per cent in 1940 to 6.7 per cent in 1944.

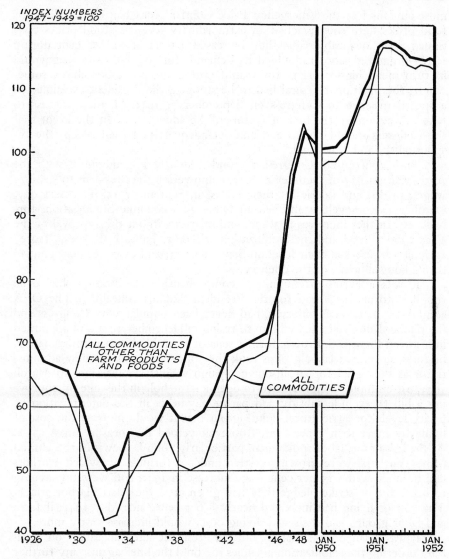

25.   *Wholesale Prices in the United States, 1926–1952*

price increases. On the other hand, the powerful farm bloc denied the Price
Administrator authority to control agricultural prices until they had reached
110 per cent of parity.

During the next three months the OPA launched a two-pronged campaign—to stabilize prices piecemeal and to establish a system of rationing
for tires, automobiles, gasoline, sugar and, somewhat later, shoes, fuel oil,
and coffee. Following the President's lead, moreover, on April 28 the OPA
issued its first General Maximum Price Regulation, which "froze" most
prices and rents at their level of March 1942.

Events soon revealed large loop holes in the stabilization program. The most obvious was the Emergency Price Control Act's ban on a ceiling for food prices until they reached an extraordinary level. As food prices continued their inexorable rise—they increased a total of 11 per cent during 1942—organized labor redoubled its demands for pay increases that would in turn mean higher prices for manufactured products. Somehow, somewhere, the inflationary spiral had to be stopped, the President exclaimed in a special message to Congress on September 7, 1942. "I ask Congress to take . . . action by the first of October," he added. ". . . In the event that the Congress should fail to act, and act adequately, I shall accept the responsibility, and I will act."

Thus confronted, Congress responded swiftly if grudgingly with the Anti-Inflation Act of October 2, 1942, empowering the President to stabilize wages, prices, and salaries at their levels on September 15. The next day, October 3, Roosevelt established an Office of Economic Stabilization; forbade any further increases in wages and salaries without the approval of the War Labor Board and the Stabilization Director, James F. Byrnes; "froze" agricultural prices at their level on September 15; and extended rent control throughout all areas of the country.

It was a heroic beginning at comprehensive stabilization, but even rougher storms lay ahead for the President and his colleagues. The OPA administrator, Leon Henderson, had never been popular with Congress and the public. Roosevelt allowed him to resign in December 1942 and appointed in his stead Prentiss S. Brown, former senator from Michigan. Unfortunately, business, farm, and labor groups took the appointment of the new administrator as the signal for an all-out campaign against stabilization. In March 1943, for example, Congress tried to open a large hole in the dike by approving a bill to exclude subsidy and parity payments in the determination of parity levels for agriculture. Pointing out that it would increase the cost of living by more than 5 per cent, Roosevelt vetoed the measure on April 2. At the same time, labor spokesmen, particularly John L. Lewis of the United Mine Workers, were growing restive under a formula by which workers had been allowed a 15 per cent wage increase in 1942, and were threatening to break the no-strike pledge they had given after the Pearl Harbor attack. The cost of living had increased nearly 8 per cent since May 1942; if farm and labor groups had their way living costs would increase vastly more.

It was a dangerous situation, but the President acted decisively on April 8 by ordering the stabilization agencies to "hold the line" against any further unwarranted price and wage increases. Nor was this all. When Lewis called a general coal strike on May 1 in defiance of the "hold the line" order, the President seized the coal mines and virtually ordered the miners back into the pits. Moreover, the OPA began an aggressive campaign to "roll back" food prices, which culminated in a 10 per cent reduction in the retail prices of meat, coffee, and butter on May 7. It was not the end of the battle against inflation, but the tide had turned. From the spring of 1943 until the end of the war the cost of living advanced less than 1.5 per cent. For the long period from September 1939 to August 1945 the cost of living increased by less than 29 per cent. Considering the power of organized pressure groups and a normal public vexation at the inconveniences of direct controls, the victory in the battle against inflation was remarkable indeed.

182 / Workers, Farmers, and the War Effort

The nearly insatiable demands of the American and Allied war machines created new opportunities for workers and solved most of the problems of the depression. The following statistics give the over-all picture: From the beginning of the defense effort in 1940 to the end of the war the number of civilian workers increased from about 46,500,000 to over 53,000,000. The chief factor in this expansion of the working force was the addition of about 7,000,000 workers from the reservoir of the unemployed. Their numbers, in turn, were augmented by 3,800,000 young persons, most of them children between the ages of fourteen and seventeen; nearly 2,000,000 women over thirty-five, who doffed aprons and put on overalls; about 1,000,000 elderly people, who left retirement to improve their own meager standards of living; and about 600,000 young war wives.

To all these workers, old and new, the war boom brought such prosperity as they had never known before. To state the matter briefly, between January 1941 and July 1945 the cost of living advanced some 30 per cent while weekly earnings of persons employed in manufacturing increased 70 per cent. Much of this increase occurred, however, because men worked longer—average hours per week increased from 40.6 in 1941 to 45.2 in 1944— and benefited from overtime pay.

The task of mobilizing this huge labor force, of restraining labor's natural desire for higher wages, of controlling irresponsible labor leaders who were willing to strike in defiance of the national interest, and, most important, of persuading labor and management to forget old antagonisms and join hands in the common effort—these were the administration's chief perplexities on the industrial relations front.

We might begin by pointing to the administration's least successful effort—its failure to achieve comprehensive control over manpower resources. In April 1942 the President created the War Manpower Commission and appointed former Governor Paul V. McNutt of Indiana to direct the flow of workers into war industries. Beginning with voluntary efforts, the WMC gradually evolved coercive measures that prohibited workers in defense industries from leaving their jobs without the approval of the United States Employment Service. The system worked reasonably well but did not solve the more important problem of recruiting new workers and shifting workers from nondefense to war industries. One solution, of course, was national service legislation to draft men for war work. Although the CIO and AF of L bitterly opposed such legislation, the manpower shortage seemed so critical by the end of 1943 that the President finally came out in support of a national service act in his Annual Message in January 1944. Following the German counteroffensive in December 1944, the House approved a labor draft bill; but the collapse of Germany occurred before the Senate could act on the measure.

Much more important and difficult was the task of preventing strikes and of reconciling labor's natural desires for economic advancement and union security with the general objective of winning the war without run-

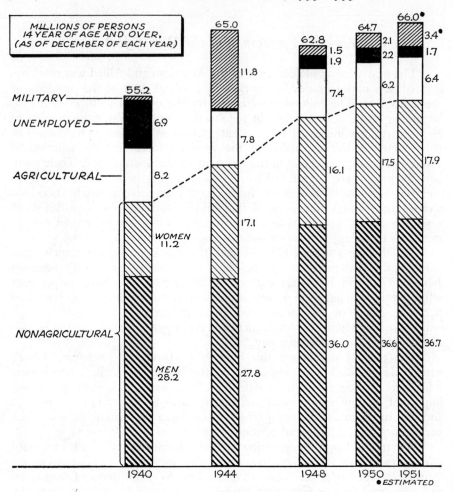

MILLIONS OF PERSONS
14 YEAR OF AGE AND OVER,
(AS OF DECEMBER OF EACH YEAR)

65.0

64.7

66.0•

62.8

3.4•

2.1

1.5
1.9

1.7

2.2

11.8

7.4

6.2

6.4

MILITARY——— 55.2

UNEMPLOYED——— 6.9

7.8

16.1

17.5

17.9

AGRICULTURAL——— 8.2

17.1

WOMEN
11.2

NONAGRICULTURAL

36.0

36.6

36.7

MEN
28.2

27.8

1940   1944   1948   1950   1951
•ESTIMATED

26. *The American Labor Force, 1940–1951*

away inflation. This gigantic and at times nearly impossible task was entrusted to the War Labor Board, created by the President on January 12, 1942, and composed of twelve members representing management, labor, and the public. Established to prevent labor disputes, the WLB soon discovered that mediation was impossible until it had constructed a complete edifice of labor policy. Inevitably, therefore, the WLB emerged as a powerful policy making body in the war economy.

To the leaders of the 10,500,000 organized workers in early 1942 the fundamental issue was the protection of the right of collective bargaining they had won during many a hard battle from 1933 through 1941. On this issue, the WLB stood firm in defense of labor's rights under the Wagner Act, even the right to the closed shop when a majority of workers voted in favor of it. Moreover, it applied a compromise—the so-called maintenance of membership plan—that protected unions in rapidly expanding war plants.

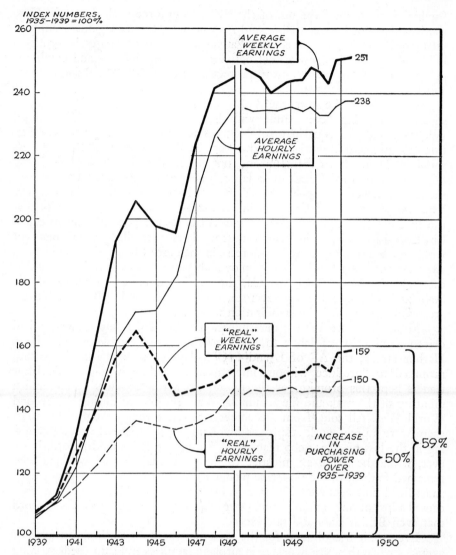

INDEX NUMBERS,
1935–1939 = 100%

AVERAGE WEEKLY EARNINGS — 251

AVERAGE HOURLY EARNINGS — 238

"REAL" WEEKLY EARNINGS — 159

— 150

"REAL" HOURLY EARNINGS

INCREASE IN PURCHASING POWER OVER 1935–1939 — 50%   59%

27. *Hourly and Weekly Earnings of Production Workers in Manufacturing in the United States, 1939–1950*

Under this arrangement unions retained their membership and the right to bargain for all workers during the life of a bargaining contract; on the other hand, new workers coming into an industry or plant were not required to join the union as a condition of employment. It was not all labor leaders wanted, but it gave them security against raids by employers and rival unions. In fact, under the aegis of the maintenance of membership plan, union membership expanded to nearly 15,000,000 by the end of the war.

Maintenance of membership, however, provided no answers to the two thorniest problems of wartime labor administration—inexorable demands for higher wages and the use of the strike to enforce such demands. Here the issue lay not between labor and management, for management enjoyed guaranteed profits and was usually anxious to increase wages in order to hold and attract labor, but rather between the public interest and combined private interests. In its attempt to protect the former, the WLB fought hard and not always successfully.

Throughout the war the WLB defended labor's right to enjoy a standard of living "compatible with health and decency" and endorsed union demands for equal pay for Negroes and women and for the elimination of sectional differentials. On the other hand, it also asserted that workers should be content to maintain and not improve their standard of living during wartime. In theory most labor leaders concurred; the trouble was they could never agree with the WLB on what that standard of living was. The rise in the cost of living during the early months of 1942 precipitated the first crisis. On July 16, 1942, the WLB responded with the so-called Little Steel formula, under which most workers were allowed a 15 per cent wage increase to offset a similar increase in the cost of living since January 1, 1941. On the other hand, when employers began to award pay increases that exceeded the Little Steel formula, the President, under authority of the Stabilization Act of October 2, 1942, empowered the WLB to forbid increases that imperiled the stabilization program.

Meanwhile, the WLB's determination to hold the line on wages had driven a minority of labor to irresponsible action. Soon after the Pearl Harbor attack, the AF of L and CIO had given a no-strike pledge and promised to "produce without interruption." Although responsible labor leaders kept this promise for the most part, a few reckless leaders and a minority of the rank and file accumulated a sorry record during the Second World War. All told, from December 8, 1941, through August 14, 1945, there were 14,731 work stoppages involving 6,744,000 workers and resulting in the loss of 36,301,000 man-days. To cite only the bald record, however, would be to do an injustice to the great majority of workers who remained faithful to the no-strike pledge. Most of the work stoppages were short-lived and occurred in defiance of union leadership. Moreover, they caused a loss of only one-ninth of 1 per cent of total working time—a record that even British labor did not exceed.

Even so, it was difficult for the mass of Americans to think in terms of averages when they saw workers in airplane factories and ship yards striking for higher pay or over comparatively trivial matters like union jurisdiction. In addition, two major incidents—a coal strike and the near occurrence of a nation-wide railroad strike in 1943—alarmed the American people. Refusing to appear before the WLB, John L. Lewis called a general coal strike on May 1, 1943. The President seized the mines, but the miners struck again on June 11 because the WLB would not break the Little Steel formula and grant high wage increases. When Roosevelt threatened to ask Congress to draft the miners they returned to work; but by the threat of a third strike Lewis forced the administration to surrender on his terms.[9]

[9] Under the agreement concluded between Lewis and Secretary of the Interior Ickes the miners received normal wage increases under the Little Steel formula; in addition, they received pay increases to compensate for reduced lunch periods and for time spent going to and from the pits.

Lewis's cynical defiance of the federal authority was more than Congress could bear. In hot resentment it approved and re-enacted over the President's veto on June 26, 1943, the Smith-Connally, or War Labor Disputes, Act. This measure empowered the President to seize any struck war plant and required unions to wait thirty days before striking and to hold a secret vote of the workers before a strike was executed. Actually, it was useless legislation which prevented no strikes and only gave an additional weapon, the strike threat, to labor leaders. More indicative of the rising anti-labor sentiment was the enactment by many state legislatures of laws to prevent certain union practices and to subject unions to a measure of public regulation.[10] We can say in summary, therefore, that although labor gained in union strength and improved living standards during the war, such gains were often purchased at the price of labor's greatest asset, the support of the American people at large.

For agriculture, the war boom brought new problems but also a stability and prosperity unknown since 1919. From 1940 to 1945 net cash income from farming increased from $2,300,000,000 to $9,458,000,000, or by more than 400 per cent. Under the stimulus of heady prosperity, farmers not only painted their houses and barns and enjoyed a higher standard of living; they also reduced their total mortgage and debt loads and added $11,000,-000,000 to their savings. At the same time, tenancy declined sharply in the nation as a whole, from a national average of 38.7 per cent in 1940 to 31.7 per cent in 1945.

Two factors—increased production and higher prices, both of them stemming from vastly increased demands at home and abroad—made possible this return of agriculture to its long-sought position of parity in the American economy. From 1940 to 1945 agricultural prices more than doubled and would have gone even higher had the President not thwarted the plans of the farm bloc in Congress. During the same period, moreover, the index of all farm production rose from 108 to 123, while increases in food crops were even more spectacular. Incredible though it sounds, this expansion was accomplished in spite of a declining farm population and without any significant increase in acreage planted and harvested.[11]

183 / *Public Opinion, Civil Rights, and War*

Never before had Americans gone to war with such determination and unity as during the Second World War. After the Pearl Harbor attack significant opposition to the war effort simply did not exist. And because disloyalty was rare, there were no volunteer leagues of patriots, no Com-

---

[10] For example, these laws forbade the closed shop, mass picketing, secondary boycotts, and the like, and required unions to file financial reports and obtain licenses for labor organizers.

[11] The total number of agricultural workers declined from 11,671,000 in 1940 to 10,873,000 in 1945. On the other hand, the index of productivity in agriculture increased from 112 in 1940 to 136 in 1945 because of increased use of tractors, trucks, and other machinery. Two factors making possible larger yields without significant increases in acreage were a large expansion in the use of fertilizers and the spread of hybrid corn.

mittees of Public Safety, no high powered propaganda campaigns and war madness.

This is not to say, however, that the government abandoned control over news and expressions of opinion[12] or was not ready to act ruthlessly to suppress dangerous dissent. At the President's command, for example, the Justice Department convened a special grand jury in Washington in July 1941 and laid before it and two succeeding grand juries voluminous evidence concerning the far-flung network of Nazi and fascist organizations in the United States. The upshot was the indictment under the Smith Act of thirty leading seditionists for conspiring to establish a Nazi government in the United States and to incite disloyalty among the armed forces. For over seven months in 1944 the trial proceeded until the presiding judge died, apparently a victim of the badgering of the defense attorneys. The seditionists were indicted a second time in 1945, and government attorneys rushed to Germany to obtain new evidence. In November 1946, however, the Circuit Court of Appeals of the District ended the fiasco by dismissing the indictment on the ground that the government's proceedings were a travesty on justice.

Because of judicial protection of civil liberty, the government was scarcely more successful when it tried to imprison individual champions of Nazism and opponents of the war. The critical test arose when the Justice Department invoked the Espionage Act against one Hartzel, who published a diatribe against American participation in the war in 1942 and mailed copies to army officers. In Hartzel *v.* United States, 1944, the Supreme Court made enforcement of the Espionage Act virtually impossible by declaring that the government had to prove specific intent to obstruct the war effort before it could obtain convictions under the law. Again, when the government obtained the conviction of twenty-four leaders of the German-American Bund for violations of the Espionage Act, the Court reversed the conviction on the ground of insufficient evidence of criminal

[12] Some kind of censorship, for example, was inevitable; and the day after the Pearl Harbor attack the President entrusted censorship of war news to the War and Navy departments and the FBI. Then, following passage by Congress of the first War Powers Act on December 18, 1941, the President established an Office of Censorship, with Byron Price, executive news editor of the Associated Press, as director. With the voluntary cooperation of newspapermen and radio announcers, Price maintained a press censorship that yielded to enemy agents no significant information about troop movements, the travels of Roosevelt and Churchill, the production of the atomic bomb, and the like.

To coordinate war news and conduct official propaganda at home and abroad, the President established the Office of War Information on June 13, 1942, with Elmer Davis, veteran correspondent and commentator, in charge. Thanks in part to Roosevelt's determination to avoid hysterical excesses and in part to Davis' restraining influence, the OWI happily never became a second Creel committee. Until Republican opposition to domestic propaganda caused the President to end that phase of the agency's work in 1943, the OWI produced motion pictures and published pamphlets and posters reminding Americans of their duty and depicting the dangers of an Axis victory. On the other hand, the agency did not spread manufactured atrocity stories—the truth was horrible enough— or attempt to engender hatred of the enemy. Indeed, such hatred, especially against the Japanese, already existed in full measure and was fanned by the radio, press, and motion pictures. Much more important was the work of the overseas branch of the OWI. Broadcasting daily programs to the Axis peoples, it used truth as its principal weapon in undermining the enemy's morale.

intent. And when the government brought denaturalization proceedings against German-born leaders of the Bund, the Court made it plain it would allow denaturalization and deportation only if the government could clearly prove that the defendants had taken the oath of allegiance to the United States with reservations.

Actually, the government knew that the assorted crack-pots who made up the Bund and other pro-Nazi organizations were no menace, for the FBI had penetrated these groups and placed their leaders under surveillance. Espionage and sabotage, however, were different matters, and in dealing with them the Justice Department moved swiftly and sternly. The FBI broke a small Nazi espionage ring in 1938, destroyed the major Nazi network in 1941, and was prepared to move against potential spies and saboteurs on the eve of American entrance into the war. And within less than three days after the Pearl Harbor attack the FBI had taken more than 1,700 enemy aliens into custody.[13] By such effective countermeasures the Justice Department completely destroyed the elaborate German intelligence and sabotage systems, with the result that not a single known act of sabotage was committed in the United States after December 7, 1941.

Thus deprived of its underground in America, the German High Command resorted to audacious plans. It trained two teams of saboteurs—they were Germans who had lived in America and American citizens of German descent—and sent them by submarines in May 1942 to destroy the American aluminum industry and blow up bridges and railroad facilities. One team landed on Long Island, the other on the Florida coast. Captured almost immediately by the FBI, the eight invaders were tried by special military commission, sentenced to death, and executed on August 8.[14] The father of one of the saboteurs, Hans Haupt of Chicago, was also convicted of treason for hiding his son and given life imprisonment; another German-American, Anthony Cramer, was convicted of treason for assisting one of the saboteurs.[15]

The one great blot on the administration's otherwise excellent civil liberties record during the war was the detention and forced removal of Japanese-Americans from the West Coast to internment camps in the in-

---

[13] All told, the Justice Department arrested some 16,000 enemy aliens during the war, one-fourth of whom were imprisoned.

[14] The President commuted the sentences of two saboteurs who gave evidence to life imprisonment and thirty years' imprisonment.

[15] In Cramer v. United States, 1945, the Supreme Court reversed Cramer's conviction on the ground that the government had not proved that he gave aid and comfort to the enemy within the meaning of the treason clause. However, the Court upheld Haupt's conviction in 1947.

Aside from Haupt and Cramer, only one other person was tried for treason during the war. He was a Detroit Bundsman, Max Stephan, who was sentenced to death in 1942 for helping a German prisoner of war escape; the President commuted his sentence to life imprisonment one day before the execution was to take place. During the war and afterward, however, the Justice Department obtained indictment of a number of turncoat Americans—among them Ezra Pound, the poet, Robert H. Best, a former foreign correspondent, Mildred Gillars, known to servicemen as "Axis Sally," and Mrs. Iva d'Aquino, better known as "Tokyo Rose"—who broadcast for the Axis during the war. Most of them were apprehended at the end of hostilities, convicted of treason, and sentenced to long prison terms. Pound, however, was declared insane and incarcerated in St. Elizabeth's Hospital in Washington.

terior of the country. The greatest single violation of civil rights in American history, it revealed the danger inherent in yielding supremacy to the military branch. The episode was not only tragic but also supremely ironic, for the evacuation, as subsequent events and investigations proved, was totally unnecessary.

The issue was not the arrest of Japanese subjects who were potential saboteurs, for they were rounded up immediately after the Pearl Harbor attack, but the loyalty of some 112,000 Nisei, or American citizens of Japanese ancestry. In the panic following December 7, 1941, the General Staff declared the West Coast a theater of war, and newspapers and political leaders in California began a widespread campaign for the removal of all Japanese-American citizens.

The demand was taken up in Washington by the congressional delegations from California, Oregon, and Washington and was seconded by the commanding general on the West Coast, John L. De Witt. On February 19, 1942, the President authorized the army to take control; soon afterward General De Witt ordered the removal of *all* Japanese-Americans from an area comprising the western third of Washington and Oregon, the western half of California, and the southern quarter of Arizona. Ruthlessly ejected from their homes, tens of thousands of Nisei were first herded into temporary stockades surrounded by barbed wire and then transported to ten relocation centers established by the War Relocation Authority in western deserts and in the swamplands of Arkansas. Eventually those persons suspected of disloyalty, some 18,000 of them, were confined in a camp at Tule Lake, California, while the remainder were allowed to find new homes or go to colleges in the Midwest and East. Some 36,000 Nisei chose resettlement during the war.

The most disappointing aspect of the whole affair, however, was the Supreme Court's refusal to vindicate the principle of civilian supremacy or defend elementary civil rights. In Korematsu *v.* United States, rendered in December 1944, a divided Court apologetically approved the evacuation on the ground that the military leaders were justified in taking extreme measures against persons on account of race to protect the national security, even though the situation was not serious enough to justify the imposition of martial law. The meaning of the decision was clear and foreboding: in future emergencies no American citizen would have any rights that the President and army were bound to respect when, *in their judgment*, the emergency justified drastic denial of civil rights.

184 / *Negroes and the Home Front*

The Second World War was a time of unrest and new striving on America's troubled frontier of Negro-white relations. There were race riots and national discriminations like continued segregation in the armed services and separation of Negro and white blood in Red Cross blood banks. In the South racial tensions rose to the danger point as Negroes acquired a measure of financial independence and social self-respect. Yet, withal, Negroes emerged from the war with a larger measure of economic and political security than they had ever enjoyed.

During the First World War increased racial tensions had produced mass riots, a wave of lynchings, and such degradation as Negroes had not suffered since about 1900. The social and economic upheavals of the Second World War increased tensions, to be sure, and sometimes with disastrous results. For one thing, the South was swept by rumors alleging that Negro men planned to appropriate white women when the white soldiers were gone; that Negro women had formed "Eleanor Clubs," named for Mrs. Roosevelt, and vowed never again to work in white kitchens; and that Negroes were gathering ice picks for a mass uprising. Southern fears were further stimulated by the presence in the armed services of nearly 1,000,000 Negroes and by the obvious determination of Negroes everywhere to fight rather than accept conventional insults. In the words of a southern sociologist, "The South and the Negro, in the early 1940's, faced their greatest crisis since the days of the reconstruction."[16]

The most dangerous racial tension, however, developed in industrial areas outside the South, as a result of the sudden immigration of nearly 1,000,000 southern Negroes in search of jobs and new social opportunities. There were numerous minor clashes in many cities, and New York escaped a major race riot in early 1944 only because of the quick action of its Mayor and police force. Tensions flared into large-scale rioting in Detroit, home of Gerald L. K. Smith and other Negro-baiters. A fight between a Negro and a white man on June 20, 1943, led to other clashes; and soon mobs of whites were roaming the Negro section, killing and burning as they went. By the time federal troops had restored order twenty-five Negroes and nine whites had been killed.

This was the dark side of an otherwise bright picture, for the Second World War was a time also of great advancement for American Negroes. In spite of rumors of riot, Negroes in the South enjoyed greater acceptance and security and larger political and economic opportunities than ever before in history. Lynching, long the extreme form of southern race control, became almost a historic phenomenon, as the number of Negroes thus done to death declined from five in 1942 to one in 1945. A distinguished body of southern leaders, Negro and white, met in Atlanta in 1944 and organized the Southern Regional Council to combat prejudice and misunderstanding by concerted action in communities and states. Equally significant was the growth during the war of an advanced equalitarian movement outside the South. Assuming the proportions almost of a crusade, this campaign against Jim Crow won many triumphs, the most important of which was a growing concern for civil rights by the major parties.

Negroes made greatest progress North and South during the war on the economic front. Of all groups they had suffered most during the depression; nor did the defense boom of 1940–1941 bring relief, as employers stubbornly refused to hire black workers. The administration moved slowly, until A. Philip Randolph, president of the Brotherhood of Sleeping Car Porters, called upon 50,000 Negroes to march upon Washington to protest

---

[16] Howard W. Odum, *Race and Rumors of Race* (Chapel Hill, N.C., 1943), p. 4.

the exclusion of black men from defense jobs. Randolph called off the threatened march; but he did so only after Roosevelt had issued his epochal Executive Order 8802 on June 25, 1941. It directed that Negroes be admitted to job training programs, forbade discrimination in work on defense contracts, and established a Fair Employment Practices Committee to investigate charges of discrimination on account of race.

In the face of bitter opposition, more from white workers than employers, the FEPC made progress slowly and performed its most effective service during 1942 and 1943 by conducting hearings on discrimination in most of the large cities of the country. However, when the President, in May 1943, reorganized the agency, expanded its budget, and directed that anti-discrimination clauses in contracts be enforced, the FEPC set to work in an effective way. Establishing fifteen regional offices, it heard some 8,000 complaints and conducted thirty public hearings from 1943 to 1946. The results were unexpectedly gratifying. By the end of 1944, when war production was at its height, nearly 2,000,000 Negroes were at work in aircraft factories, ship yards, steel mills, and other war plants in the South as elsewhere.[17]

To be sure, the millennium had not come for American Negroes when the war ended in August 1945. To men of good will, however, the steady enlargement of economic, social, and political opportunities for Negroes during the war years was perhaps the most encouraging development on the American home front. In 1945 Negroes could look forward to a postwar era full not only of struggle but also of hope for the coming of a new era in which they might stand erect as free men and citizens of the great democracy.

[17] In addition, New York, New Jersey, and Indiana established Fair Employment Practices Commissions, while many cities set up anti-discrimination boards.

CHAPTER 24 / *THE SECOND WORLD WAR: DIPLOMATIC AND MILITARY ASPECTS*

*I*N contrast to their limited participation in the First World War, the American people were privileged to play a leading and decisive role in the military operations that brought victory for the United Nations in 1945. In this chapter we will follow the Allies on the long and tortuous road from defeat to victory. Since the war was won not only in the factory and on the battlefield but around the conference table as well, we will also note how Roosevelt and Churchill forged the bonds of Anglo-American unity, drew the Russian leaders into close association, and gave such an effective demonstration of leadership as the world had rarely seen before.

185 / *The Formation of the Grand Alliance*

Soon after the Pearl Harbor attack, American and British leaders gathered in Washington to lay plans for combined conduct of the war. With his civilian and military advisers, Prime Minister Winston S. Churchill arrived in Washington on December 22, 1941, for a week of conferences known by the code name of ARCADIA and extended on the military level until January 14, 1942. This was a time when Allied military fortunes were at their lowest ebb since the fall of France, but negotiations proceeded smoothly and yielded complete agreement on all important points: American production goals for 1942 and 1943, pooling of Anglo-American munitions and their disposal by a joint Munitions Assignment Board, the immediate establishment of a Combined Chiefs of Staff in Washington and a joint British, American, and Dutch command in the Pacific, and, most important, strategy for the conduct of the war.[1]

[1] The immediate strategy envisioned American occupation of northern Ireland and a combined British-American invasion of North Africa, first called GYMNAST, perhaps in March 1942. As for long-range strategy, American and British leaders agreed that Germany was the chief enemy because she controlled industry and manpower superior to the Japanese. Therefore, the Allies should launch their first major offensives against the Continent and conduct holding operations in the Pacific until Nazi power had been bridled.

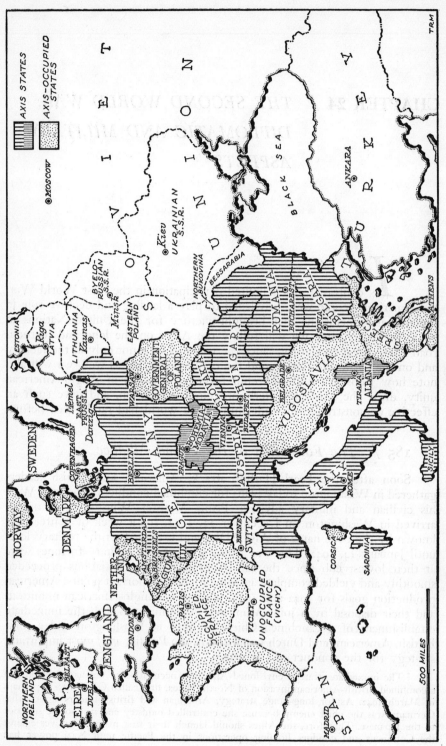

19. *Axis Europe, 1941*

On the diplomatic level, moreover, Roosevelt and Churchill worked in complete harmony for the formation of a grand coalition of the Allies. The fruit of their labor was the Declaration of the United Nations, signed at the White House on New Year's Day, 1942, by Roosevelt, Churchill, Maxim Litvinov for the USSR, and representatives of twenty-three other nations at war with the Axis. Reaffirming the principles set forth in the Atlantic Charter, the signatory powers pledged their full resources to the defeat of the Axis nations with which they were at war and promised one another not to make a separate peace.

The weakest link in the new Allied chain was Russia. By hearty cooperation, the USSR could hasten victory and help lay the groundwork for postwar cooperation; by making a separate peace, on the other hand, Russia could postpone the hope of Allied victory perhaps indefinitely. The President's and Prime Minister's most pressing diplomatic problem during the early months of 1942 was how to deal with Russian territorial ambitions in Europe and the Russian demand that Britain and the United States guarantee those ambitions in advance. The masters of the Kremlin presented the first installment of their demands during a visit of Foreign Secretary Anthony Eden to Moscow in December 1941, when Stalin requested Britain's immediate approval of Russia's absorption of the Baltic states and parts of Finland, Poland, and Rumania. Stalin, moreover, warned that the conclusion of a British-Soviet alliance would depend upon British endorsement of his territorial claims.

The issue came to a head when the Soviet Foreign Minister, Molotov, arrived in London on May 20, 1942, to press Russian territorial and military demands. Strengthened by a warning from Washington that the United States might publicly denounce any Anglo-Russian agreement conceding Stalin's ambitions, Churchill and Eden stood firm and persuaded Molotov to sign, on May 26, a general twenty-year Treaty of Alliance that included no references to boundaries. "This was a great relief to me," Churchill writes, "and a far better solution than I had dared to hope." As we will see, however, it was not the end but only the beginning of a long and bitter controversy that helped split the Grand Alliance after the war.

186 / *The Ebb Tide of Allied Military Fortunes*

So swift and far-reaching were the Axis victories during the first six months of 1942 that it seemed the United Nations had lost the war before they could begin fighting. Following air attacks on the far-flung British and American possessions on December 7, the Japanese launched sea-borne invasions of Hong Kong, Malaya, the Philippines, and lesser islands during the days following the Pearl Harbor attack. They were free to roam and strike almost at will, for the once mighty Anglo-American Pacific naval power was nearly gone by the end of 1941.

Guam, a lonely American outpost in the Marianas, fell to the Japanese on December 11, 1941; Wake Island, on December 23; and Hong Kong, on Christmas Day. Meanwhile, Japanese forces pressed forward in the conquest

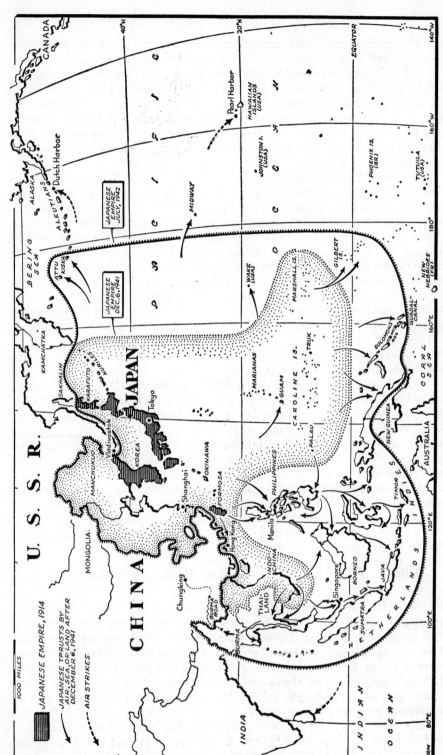

20. *The Tides of Japanese Expansion*

of Malaya, Burma, and the Philippines. Singapore, the great British naval base in the Far East, surrendered on February 15, 1942, to a Japanese force that came down from the north. Most of Burma fell in March and April 1942, while Ceylon and India were threatened by a large Japanese naval force that momentarily controlled the Indian Ocean and the Bay of Bengal in April.

In the Philippines General Douglas MacArthur, with a force of 19,000 American regulars, 12,000 Philippine Scouts, and 100,000 soldiers of the new Philippine army, fought a desperate delaying action. When Japanese troops threatened Manila, MacArthur withdrew his troops into the Bataan Peninsula for a hopeless but gallant last stand. MacArthur was transferred to Australia on March 17, 1942. His successor, General Jonathan Wainwright, withdrew to Corregidor and other forts off the tip of the peninsula and held out there until disease, starvation, and superior enemy forces made further resistance impossible. He surrendered his force of 11,574 men on May 6; some 37,000 troops left on the peninsula to cover his withdrawal had surrendered on April 9.

Meanwhile, by the end of December 1941 large new Japanese forces were poised in Malaya and the Philippines to strike at Borneo, the Celebes, New Guinea, and the Dutch East Indies, an area rich in oil, rubber, and tin. Only the small American Asiatic Fleet and a few Dutch and British cruisers stood athwart the path of Japanese conquest of the Indies. In the Battle of Macassar Strait, January 24, 1942, American destroyers executed a daring night attack against a Japanese convoy and forced it to turn back. But in the subsequent engagements, known as the Java Sea campaign, the Allies lost their entire naval force, except for four American destroyers that made their way to Australia. By the end of March 1942 the Japanese were in possession of the East Indies, had pushed into New Britain and the Solomon Islands, and were in position to strike at Port Moresby, the Allied stronghold in southern New Guinea, and at Australia itself.

While the Japanese were carving out an empire in the Southwestern Pacific, events almost as catastrophic for the Allies were transpiring in the Atlantic, on the eastern front in Russia, and in North Africa. In the Atlantic, German submarines came perilously close to winning the Battle of the Atlantic during 1942. Hitler's undersea raiders ranged up and down the Atlantic coast and penetrated the Caribbean and Gulf of Mexico. Moreover, Allied convoys carrying Lend-Lease supplies to Murmansk and Archangel in Russia had to run a murderous gauntlet of U-boats and land-based German bombers. Nearly one-fourth the ships that traveled this perilous Arctic route in 1942 were sunk. But everywhere Allied and neutral shipping losses mounted fearfully and aggregated nearly 8,000,000 tons during 1942. "The disaster of an indefinite prolongation of the war," to quote Churchill's phrase, threatened to upset Allied plans for military operations.

Meanwhile, the Germans had mounted a large offensive to drive through North Africa, cut the Suez Canal, and penetrate Arabia and the Middle East. On May 26 the German commander, General Erwin Rommel, the "Desert Fox," opened the campaign in Libya. After several sharp defeats, the British retreated into Egypt to El Alamein, only seventy-five miles from Alexandria, to regroup and reinforce the shattered Eighth Army. By July 1 the German

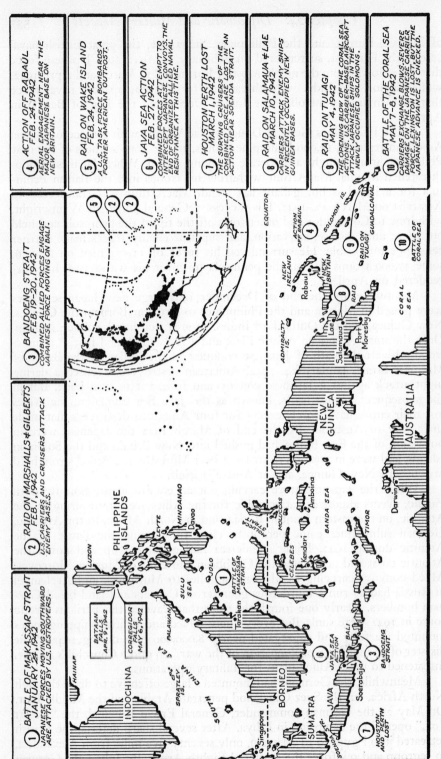

1 BATTLE OF MAKASSAR STRAIT
JANUARY 24, 1942
JAPANESE FORCES MOVING SOUTHWARD
ARE ATTACKED BY U.S. DESTROYERS.

2 RAID ON MARSHALLS ≠ GILBERTS
FEB. 1, 1942
U.S. CARRIERS AND CRUISERS ATTACK
ENEMY BASES.

3 BANDOENG STRAIT
FEB. 19-20, 1942
COMBINED ALLIED FORCES ENGAGE
JAPANESE FORCE MOVING ON BALI.

4 ACTION OFF RABAUL
FEB. 24, 1942
AERIAL ENGAGEMENT NEAR THE
MAJOR JAPANESE BASE ON
NEW BRITAIN.

5 RAID ON WAKE ISLAND
FEB. 24, 1942
A U.S. TASK FORCE BOMBARDS A
FORMER AMERICAN OUTPOST.

6 JAVA SEA ACTION
FEB. 27, 1942
COMBINED FORCES ATTEMPT TO
INTERCEPT JAPANESE CONVOYS. THE
END OF ORGANIZED ALLIED NAVAL
RESISTANCE AT THIS TIME.

7 HOUSTON PERTH LOST
MARCH 1, 1942
THE SURVIVING CRUISERS OF THE
COMBINED FORCE ARE LOST IN AN
ACTION NEAR SOENDA STRAIT.

8 RAID ON SALAMAUA ≠ LAE
MARCH 10, 1942
CARRIERS ATTACK ENEMY SHIPS
IN RECENTLY OCCUPIED NEW
GUINEA BASES.

9 RAID ON TULAGI
MAY 4, 1942
THE OPENING BLOW OF THE CORAL SEA
ACTIONS. U.S. CARRIER-BASED AIRCRAFT
ATTACK JAPANESE SHIPS IN THE
NEWLY OCCUPIED SOLOMONS.

10 BATTLE OF THE CORAL SEA
MAY 7-8, 1942
CARRIERS EXCHANGE BLOWS. SEVERE
DAMAGE IS DONE TO JAPANESE
FORCES. LEXINGTON IS LOST, BUT THE
JAPANESE ADVANCE IS CHECKED.

21. *The Defensive Phase in the Southwest Pacific*

lines were overextended and Rommel's *Afrika Corps* was too exhausted to press the offensive.

These military reversals during the spring and summer of 1942 cast a dark cloud over Anglo-American hopes of victory and had a nearly fatal impact on relations between Britain and America on the one hand and Russia on the other. For in the face of impending defeat, the Russians demanded relief in the West, in the form of a second front; and when that relief was not forthcoming they grew sullen and threatened to disrupt the Grand Alliance.

The issue of a second front in 1942 first arose prominently when Molotov arrived in Washington on May 29 for conferences mainly of a military nature with the President and his advisers. Stalin wanted, Molotov declared, an Anglo-American invasion of western Europe strong enough to draw forty German divisions from the eastern front. Without a second front in 1942, he continued, Germany might deal the USSR a mighty, crushing blow. "If you postpone your decision," he concluded in ominous words, "you will have eventually to bear the brunt of the war." Roosevelt turned to General Marshall for an answer. Marshall replied that there were enough men and supplies for the undertaking; the chief problem was to obtain adequate shipping for an expeditionary force without cutting off supplies to the Soviet Union.

Molotov returned to Moscow with only the President's promise that the United States would do everything possible to launch a cross-Channel invasion in 1942. As the Germans drove deeper into southeastern Russia and penetrated the Caucasus, the pressure from Moscow for relief in the West increased; and the President and his advisers began to consider the feasibility of an Anglo-American thrust at the northern coast of France, known by the code name SLEDGEHAMMER, as a means of averting total disaster in eastern Europe.

This was the issue that dominated the conferences among Roosevelt, Churchill, and their chiefs of staff that began in Washington on June 21, 1942. Churchill was frank and stubborn in his opposition to any limited diversionary attempt. He admitted the British would have six or eight divisions available for an invasion by September; and, he continued, if the Americans could guarantee the success of the undertaking the British would gladly cooperate. But were there not other ways in which combined Anglo-American forces could successfully attack, perhaps by an invasion of North Africa, the Prime Minister countered.

In the midst of these heated deliberations came the news of Rommel's threatened drive into Egypt. The impending collapse of the Allied military position in the entire Middle East diverted the conferees' attention from the coast of France to the imperiled area, enabled Churchill to drive home his arguments for a North African invasion, and caused the Prime Minister to hurry home to face his critics in the House of Commons.

During the last week of June 1942, the President and his military staffs moved swiftly to bolster British defenses in Egypt. But once this crisis had passed, Roosevelt decided to have the issue of the second front decided once and for all and sent Harry Hopkins, General Marshall, and Admiral Ernest J. King, the American naval commander, to London on July 16 to thrash the matter out with the British leaders. They joined General Dwight D. Eisenhower, now commander of the European Theater of Operations, and other Americans in London on July 18 for preliminary conferences. Marshall and Eisenhower were enthusiastic for an invasion of France, which they contemplated beginning on a limited scale until a large offensive could be mounted. But talks with British staff officers failed to budge the British from their adamant opposition; and American naval officers agreed that a cross-Channel operation in September or October would be dangerous. Informed of the stalemate, Roosevelt replied that the Americans should now insist upon offensive operations somewhere, preferably in North Africa. When it seemed the conferees would also postpone decision on GYMNAST, as the North African operation was first called, the President replied that plans must be made at once and that landings in North Africa should occur not later than October 30, 1942.

Enthusiastically approved by Churchill, Roosevelt's decision for a North African campaign ended the argument over SLEDGEHAMMER. There now remained only the task of preparing for TORCH—the new code name of the North African operation—and the unpleasant job of explaining to Stalin why his western Allies could not open a second front in 1942.

187 / The Tide Begins to Turn

If the spring and summer of 1942 were a time when the military fortunes of the Allies were at their lowest point, then events of the coming autumn would at least bring hope to the embattled United Nations. In the Pacific, the American navy and marines finally stemmed the onrushing tide of Japanese conquest and began their slow and painful progress along the road back to Tokyo. In North Africa, the Anglo-American Allies began a campaign that ended the Nazi threat to the Middle East and culminated in an invasion of Sicily and Italy in 1943. In Europe, the Russians finally held firm on the banks of the Volga and then began a counteroffensive that would not cease until the Soviet armies had spread through eastern Europe and conquered the capital of Nazidom.

During the high tide of Japanese expansion, from January through April 1942, the American Pacific Fleet, commanded by Admiral Chester W. Nimitz, had regrouped and given warning that it still existed. In January and February two carrier task forces executed raids on the Marshall and Gilbert Islands and Wake Island, while the following month planes from the carriers *Lexington* and *Yorktown* hit ports in New Guinea. A spectacular blow came on April 18, when medium bombers from the carrier *Hornet* raided Tokyo; but the most decisive engagement during this defensive phase was the Battle of the Coral Sea, May 7 and 8, when planes from the *Lexington* and *Yorktown* turned back a large Japanese force moving around the southeastern coast of New Guinea to attack Port Moresby.

The Battle of the Coral Sea ended the period when the Pacific Fleet was totally on the defensive. Assuming that the Americans had concentrated their naval forces in the South Pacific, the Japanese now sent a large armada and invasion force against Midway Island, an outpost guarding the Hawaiian Islands, in a bold effort to cut American communication lines in the Pacific and perhaps establish bases in the islands themselves. Anticipating this attack, Nimitz had moved his carriers and cruisers into the Central Pacific, and one of the most decisive battles of the Pacific war raged with incredible fury from June 3 to June 6. Dive bombers from Midway joined with dive bombers and torpedo planes from the *Enterprise, Hornet,* and *Yorktown* to sink four Japanese carriers, a heavy cruiser, and three destroyers and to damage one heavy cruiser and two destroyers. In contrast, the Americans lost only the *Yorktown* and a destroyer. The "first decisive defeat suffered by the Japanese Navy in 350 years," to quote Admiral King, the Battle of Midway removed the threat to the Hawaiian Islands and restored the balance of naval power in the Pacific. It was, moreover, convincing proof of the importance of air power, for warships did not exchange a single salvo during the engagement.

By midsummer of 1942 it was the Americans' turn to take the offensive. From April to July the Japanese had moved into the Solomon Islands and were building airfields which imperiled the Allied position in the South Pacific. Assembling a large South Pacific force of warships, transports, and marines in New Zealand, Admiral Robert L. Ghormley attacked Tulagi and Guadalcanal in the Solomons on August 7 and soon had won control of Tulagi and the main part of Guadalcanal. In the Battle of Savo Island during the evening of August 8, however, a Japanese cruiser and destroyer force surprised the Allies and sank four cruisers and damaged other ships. Not knowing the damage they had done, the Japanese then withdrew without attacking the Allied transports. But they soon returned with troops, and during the next six months the battle raged on Guadalcanal and for control of the air and seas in the Solomons area. The issue was long in doubt, as the Japanese enjoyed an advantage in land-based aircraft from their base in Rabaul and reinforced their troops on Guadalcanal by nightly runs on the so-called "Tokyo Express" down the slot from Bougainville to Guadalcanal. However, in a number of violent battles the American navy won control of the seas; the First Marine Division on Guadalcanal was relieved by larger army forces, which gradually overcame the Japanese invaders; and the Japanese withdrew on the night of February 7–8, 1943.

In the meantime, Allied planners and diplomats were at work preparing for TORCH, the Anglo-American offensive in North Africa. The British Eighth Army at El Alamein opened an offensive against Rommel's forces on October 24, 1942, and three Allied convoys converged west of Gibraltar soon afterward. Striking simultaneously on November 8 at Oran and Algiers in Algeria and Casablanca on the Atlantic coast of French Morocco, the Anglo-American forces encountered heavy French resistance only around Casablanca. Marshal Pétain, head of the Vichy French government, severed diplomatic relations with the United States on November 9 and called upon his forces in North Africa to fight the invaders. When the Germans invaded unoccupied France on November 11, however, Pétain's deputy in North Africa, Admiral Jean Darlan, took control of all French forces and con--

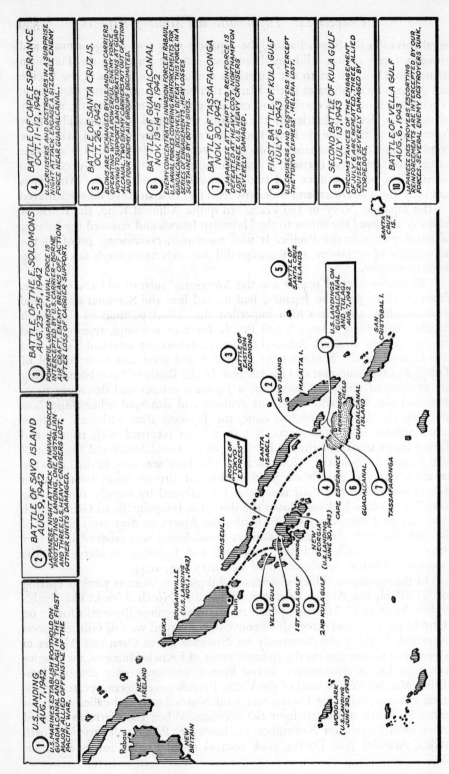

1. **U.S. LANDING**
   AUG. 7, 1942
   U.S. MARINES ESTABLISH FOOTHOLD ON GUADALCANAL AND TULAGI IN THE FIRST MAJOR ALLIED OFFENSIVE OF THE PACIFIC WAR.

2. **BATTLE OF SAVO ISLAND**
   AUG. 9, 1942
   JAPANESE NIGHT ATTACK ON NAVAL FORCES PROTECTING LANDING. ONE AUSTRALIAN AND THREE U.S. HEAVY CRUISERS LOST, OTHER UNITS DAMAGED.

3. **BATTLE OF THE E. SOLOMONS**
   AUG. 23-25, 1942
   POWERFUL JAPANESE NAVAL FORCE IS INTERCEPTED BY U.S. CARRIER-BORNE AIRCRAFT. ENEMY BREAKS OFF ACTION AFTER LOSS OF CARRIER SUPPORT.

4. **BATTLE OF CAPE ESPERANCE**
   OCT. 11-12, 1942
   U.S. CRUISERS AND DESTROYERS IN A SURPRISE NIGHT ATTACK DEFEAT A SIZEABLE ENEMY FORCE NEAR GUADALCANAL.

5. **BATTLE OF SANTA CRUZ IS.**
   OCT. 26, 1942
   BLOWS ARE EXCHANGED BY U.S. AND JAP CARRIERS OPERATING WITH A POWERFUL ENEMY FORCE MOVING TO SUPPORT LAND OPERATIONS AT GUADALCANAL. TWO ENEMY CARRIERS PUT OUT OF ACTION AND FOUR ENEMY AIR GROUPS DECIMATED.

6. **BATTLE OF GUADALCANAL**
   NOV. 13-14-15, 1942
   ENEMY CONCENTRATES INVASION FORCE AT RABAUL. U.S. NAVAL FORCES COVERING REINFORCEMENTS FOR GUADALCANAL ENCOUNTER ENEMY IN A SERIES OF ENGAGEMENTS. HEAVY LOSSES SUSTAINED BY BOTH SIDES.

7. **BATTLE OF TASSAFARONGA**
   NOV. 30, 1942
   A JAPANESE ATTEMPT TO REINFORCE IS DEFEATED AT HEAVY COST. NORTHAMPTON LOST, THREE U.S. HEAVY CRUISERS SEVERELY DAMAGED.

8. **FIRST BATTLE OF KULA GULF**
   JULY 6, 1943
   U.S. CRUISERS AND DESTROYERS INTERCEPT THE "TOKYO EXPRESS". HELENA LOST.

9. **SECOND BATTLE OF KULA GULF**
   JULY 13, 1943
   CIRCUMSTANCES OF THE ENGAGEMENT OF JULY 6 ARE REPEATED. ONE ALLIED CRUISER SEVERELY DAMAGED BY ENEMY TORPEDOES.

10. **BATTLE OF VELLA GULF**
    AUG. 6, 1943
    JAPANESE DESTROYERS ESCORTING REINFORCEMENTS ARE INTERCEPTED BY OUR FORCES. SEVERAL ENEMY DESTROYERS SUNK.

22.   *The Offensive-Defensive Phase in the Southwest Pacific*

cluded an armistice agreement with the Allied supreme commander, General Eisenhower, that recognized Darlan's control and promised the cooperation of some 50,000 French colonial troops in North Africa.[2]

American and British policy had diverged since the fall of France. Britain had given moral and material support to General Charles de Gaulle as the leader of the French forces carrying on resistance outside France and as representative to some extent of the growing underground resistance in France itself. The Americans, on the other hand, had regarded the De Gaullist movement as a minor military auxiliary. Roosevelt, in fact, was to continue to resist the political claims of De Gaulle's movement until after the liberation of France, when the reaction of the French people was unmistakable.

During the two weeks following the conclusion of the Darlan agreement, American and British units from Algiers engaged in a race with the Germans for control of Tunisia, then occupied by small French forces. As the Germans reached the province in large numbers first and poured additional men, tanks, and planes into North Africa, the ensuing campaign became a crucial test of strength. From February 11, 1943, when the fighting began in earnest, until May 12, when the last German and Italian troops surrendered, the Allies—General Sir Bernard Montgomery's British Eighth Army in the east and Eisenhower's combined Anglo-French-American armies in Tunisia—gradually closed the jaws of a gigantic vise on the Germans. The result was a military disaster which cost the Axis fifteen divisions and 349,206 men killed and captured, 250 tanks, over 2,300 airplanes, and 232 ships. In contrast, the Allies suffered only 70,000 casualties in a campaign that hardened their troops and opened the Mediterranean once again to Allied shipping.

In the meantime, Roosevelt, Churchill, their political advisers, and the American and British Chiefs of Staff met at Casablanca for a full-dress conference in January 1943. For three days before Roosevelt arrived on January 14, the Chiefs of Staff considered plans for operations after the Tunisian campaign had ended. These discussions were continued after Roosevelt and Churchill arrived. The upshot was a decision, first, to invade Sicily in order to secure complete control of the Mediterranean and advanced air bases and, second, to defer the invasion of France at least until 1944, although General Marshall argued strenuously for a cross-Channel invasion in 1943.

In Casablanca, Roosevelt and Churchill inevitably became involved in the complexities of French politics. After Darlan's assassination on December 24, 1942, the Free French group headed by General Charles de Gaulle in London and the supporters of General Giraud, most of whom had served under Vichy, were contending for the right to speak for the French people. All the President wanted was the cooperation of the two factions in the common cause of liberation and agreement that the French people should decide the question of sovereignty after the war was over. To obtain this

[2] Eisenhower's agreement with Darlan nearly cost him his post as supreme commander. The Americans had brought with them General Henri H. Giraud, who had escaped from German captivity, in the hope that he could command the loyalty of all French forces in North Africa. When Giraud failed to win that support, Eisenhower recognized Darlan because he was the *de facto* French chief of state. None the less, liberal groups in the United States and Britain were outraged by what they charged was American collaboration with the worst reactionary elements in the Vichy regime.

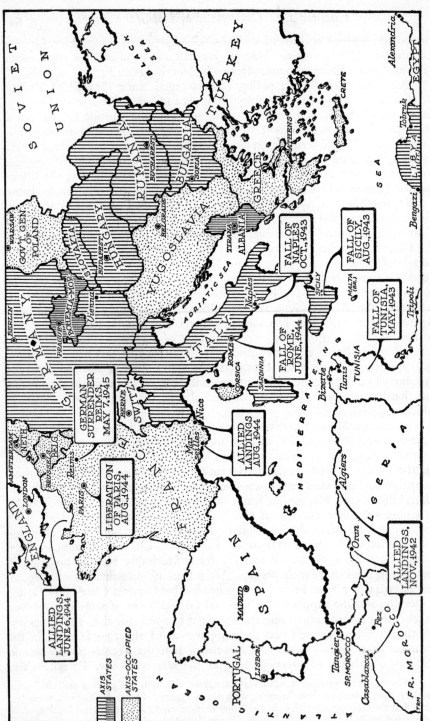

23. *Western Fronts, 1942–1945*

cooperation, Roosevelt and Churchill persuaded the austere and sensitive De Gaulle to come to Casablanca on January 22, meet with Giraud, and work out plans for future cooperation.

The work of the conference completed, on January 24 Roosevelt and Churchill held a joint press conference at Casablanca in which they reviewed their work and looked forward to victories ahead. But more important was Roosevelt's declaration, made after previous consultation with Churchill, that the Allies would insist upon the unconditional surrender of the Axis enemies. "It does not mean the destruction of the population of Germany, Italy, and Japan," he explained, "but it does mean the destruction of the philosophies in those countries which are based on conquest and the subjuga-tion of other people." Whether the decision to demand unconditional sur-render was one of the "great mistakes of the war," because it strengthened the German popular will to resist and closed the door to negotiations by an anti-Hitler faction, we will leave to critics and defenders of the policy to debate.

188 / 1943: the United Nations on the Offensive

The Anglo-American victory in Tunisia in May 1943 marked the be-ginning of new and more powerful air, sea, and land offensives by the United Nations in almost every sector of the globe. In brief, the tide had already definitely turned, and henceforward progress toward victory was steady if often slow and costly.

The decisive turning point of the European war in 1943 occurred when the Russians held Stalingrad from September to November 1942 against furious German attacks and then launched a counteroffensive that destroyed or captured a large German army in the blazing city on February 2, 1943. From this point on, the Soviet armies pressed forward along the entire length of the eastern front. By October 1943 the Red armies had driven across the Don Basin deep into the Ukraine and stood on the east bank of the Dnieper River, poised for a winter offensive that would drive through the Ukraine into Rumania. One decisive factor in the Soviet victories was the stream of Lend-Lease supplies from the United States that grew from a trickle in 1941 to a mighty torrent in 1943, after the development of new supply routes obviated the necessity of using the perilous North Atlantic route to Murmansk.[3]

The year 1943 also witnessed the turning of the tide in the Battle of the Atlantic, "the dominating factor all through the war." By the spring of 1943 the Germans had more than one hundred U-boats constantly at sea, but the Anglo-American Allies had finally found the means to victory—aggressive offense through new methods of detection, air patrols both from land bases

---

[3] The new supply routes ran through Iran into southern Russia. From October 1941 to January 1944 Lend-Lease supplies worth $4,250,000,000 went from the United States to Russia. They included 7,800 planes, 4,700 tanks and tank destroyers, 70,000 trucks, and huge quantities of ammunition; equipment for an oil refinery and a tire factory; and large quantities of food and clothing.

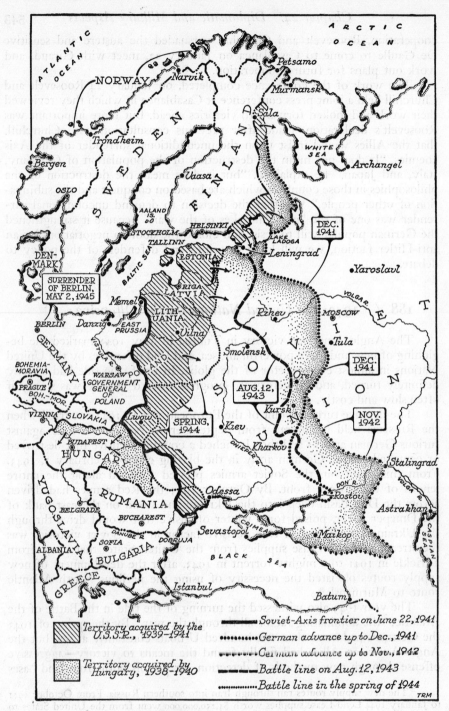

ATLANTIC
OCEAN

ARCTIC
OCEAN

NORWAY

Narvik

Petsamo

Murmansk

Sala

WHITE
SEA

Trondheim

DEC.
1941

Archangel

Bergen

S W E D E N

F I N L A N D

Vaasa

OSLO

AALAND
IS.
OO

Yaroslavl

STOCKHOLM

HELSINKI

TALLINN

BALTIC SEA

LAKE
LADOGA

Leningrad

DEN-
MARK

ESTONIA

RIGA

LATVIA

VOLGA R.

SURRENDER
OF BERLIN,
MAY 2, 1945

Memel

LITH-
UANIA

Rzhev

MOSCOW

BERLIN

Danzig

EAST
PRUSSIA

Vilna

Tula

GERMANY

Smolensk

DEC.
1941

VISTULA R.

S

O

Orel

BOHEMIA-
MORAVIA

WARSAW

PO

AUG. 12,
1943

PRAGUE

BOH.

MOR.

GOVERNMENT
GENERAL
OF POLAND

Kursk

V

I

NOV.
1942

VIENNA

SLOVAKIA

Lwow

SPRING,
1944

Kiev

U

N

Kharkov

O

BUDAPEST

DNIEPER R.

Stalingrad

H U N G A R Y

Odessa

DON R.

VOLGA R.

R U M A N I A

Rostov

Astrakhan

BELGRADE

CASPIAN SEA

YUGOSLAVIA

BUCHAREST

CRIMEA

Maikop

DANUBE R.

DOBRUJA

Sevastopol

ALBANIA

SOFIA

B U L G A R I A

BLACK SEA

GREECE

Istanbul

Batum

TRM

Territory acquired by the
U.S.S.R., 1939–1941

⸺⸺⸺ Soviet-Axis frontier on June 22, 1941

•••••• German advance up to Dec., 1941

••••••• German advance up to Nov., 1942

Territory acquired by
Hungary, 1938–1940

– – – Battle line on Aug. 12, 1943

••••••• Battle line in the spring of 1944

24. Eastern Front, 1941–1945

and escort carriers, and fast destroyers and destroyer escorts. The turning point came from March through May 1943, when U-boat sinkings in the Atlantic declined from 514,744 tons to 199,409 tons and the number of submarines destroyed rose from twelve to forty. Henceforward Allied control of the Atlantic and Mediterranean grew increasingly secure, in spite of desperate German efforts to break the Allied defenses. From August 1943 through March 1944 Allied shipping losses averaged not more than 150,000 tons monthly; by May 1944 they had declined to 27,297 tons; and during the summer of 1944, when the invasion of France was launched, not a single Allied ship was torpedoed in the North Atlantic. And for decreasing results the Germans paid such a high price—237 submarines sunk in 1943, 241 in 1944, and 153 during the first four months of 1945—as to make their undersea campaign a useless drain on their resources and manpower.

In the Pacific, Allied power increased so swiftly from March 1943 to March 1944 that the naval and military commanders, Admiral Nimitz and General MacArthur, were able not only to overwhelm or neutralize the Japanese bastions in the South Pacific but also to launch new offensives that pierced the outer perimeter of the Japanese defenses.

The objective of the first great Allied offensive was Rabaul in New Britain Island, the most important Japanese air and naval base in the South Pacific area. The Allied attack was two-pronged. First came a tortuous drive by American, Australian, and New Zealand ground forces, paratroops, and the American Fifth Air Force under MacArthur's command along the northern coast of New Guinea. By February 1944 the enemy had been cleared from the eastern part of the island. Meanwhile, in June 1943 American army and marine divisions began a drive through the central and northern Solomon Islands that carried to New Georgia on June 30, Bougainville on November 1, and the Green Islands on February 15, 1944. Finally, with the occupation of the Admiralty Islands north of New Guinea on February 29, 1944, Rabaul was cut off from communication with the Japanese base of Truk, and its encirclement was complete. Hereafter, the Allied commanders were content to reduce Rabaul to impotence through aerial bombardment, without attempting to capture it.

While the Allies were thus securing their hold on the South Pacific, the United States Navy launched two major offensives in the Central Pacific that cracked the outer rim of Japanese defenses in that area. Under the command of Admiral Raymond A. Spruance, a new Central Pacific Force that included marine and army units attacked Tarawa and Makin Islands in the Gilberts on November 20, 1943. Makin was lightly garrisoned and fell quickly; but the Second Marine Division that invaded Tarawa after an inadequate bombardment met fierce resistance from Imperial Marines and had to fight for every inch of ground until the last defenders were wiped out on November 24. Striking next at the Marshall Islands between February 1 and 19, 1944, army and marine divisions rooted out Japanese defenders on Kwajalein, Roi, Namur, and Eniwetok. With Japanese defenses in this outer rim shattered, the American navy steamed into the enemy's interior defenses in daring raids against Truk on February 16 and against Saipan in the Marianas, only 1,350 miles from Tokyo, on February 21, 1944. In May

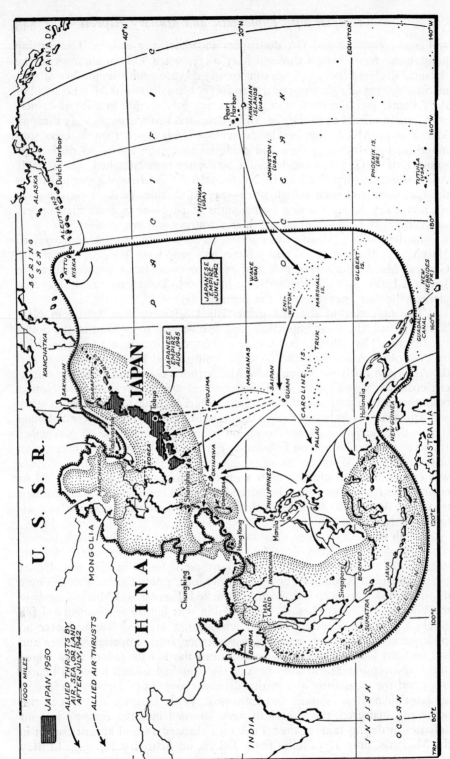

25. *The Allied Offensives in the Pacific*

and August 1943, meanwhile, combined sea and ground forces far to the north had reconquered the Aleutian islands of Attu and Kiska, occupied by the Japanese in June 1942 after the fateful Battle of Midway.

189 / *Planning for Victory and the Surrender of Italy*

No sooner had the Anglo-American Allies taken the offensive than they began to look forward to victory and the problems of an uncertain postwar future. In March 1943 Roosevelt, Hull, and Hopkins began exploratory discussions in Washington with the British Foreign Secretary, Anthony Eden. The President was reluctant to approve Russia's absorption of the Baltic states and parts of Finland and Poland, but he agreed there was probably nothing the United States and Britain could do to dislodge the Russians from territory they had occupied. Roosevelt and Eden emphatically agreed that Germany should be completely disarmed and broken into a number of states. In addition, they talked in a general way about the organization of a postwar security agency, the United Nations.

Determined to avoid Wilson's mistake of ignoring congressional leaders, Roosevelt and Hull assiduously drew them into discussions of plans for a United Nations. Since Pearl Harbor there had been considerable debate in Congress and the press looking toward American leadership in a postwar organization, and by the spring of 1943 the public demand for strong American leadership in planning for the future was obviously overwhelming. None the less, it was a tribute to Roosevelt's and Hull's discreet labors when the House of Representatives on September 21 and the Senate on November 5 approved by overwhelming majorities the Fulbright and Connally Resolutions pledging the United States to membership in an international organization, "with power adequate to establish and to maintain a just and lasting peace."

Meanwhile, Churchill and his advisers arrived in the United States on May 11, 1943, for another grand conference on war strategy, known as TRIDENT. In brief, the conferees agreed that the British should seize the Azore Islands to provide new air and naval facilities,[4] approved plans for a tremendous increase in the aerial bombardment of Germany, instructed Eisenhower to plan for an invasion of Italy after the conquest of Sicily was complete, set May 1, 1944, as the date for OVERLORD—the new code name for the invasion of France—and mapped detailed plans for offensive operations in the Pacific.

Soon after the TRIDENT conference the war in the Mediterranean erupted again according to the Allied schedule. After intensive aerial preparation, a huge Anglo-American armada disgorged 160,000 troops, 600 tanks, and 1,800 guns on the beaches of Sicily on July 10, 1943. By August 17 the British Eighth Army under General Montgomery and the American Seventh, under General George S. Patton, had routed the Italian and German defenders and overrun the island. It was an important turning point, for a group of conspirators persuaded the King of Italy, Victor Emmanuel III,

---

[4] The British Cabinet, however, won permission from the Portuguese government to establish these bases and thus the projected invasion never came off.

to connive at the deposition and arrest of Mussolini on July 25[5] and formed a new government under Marshal Badoglio, who proceeded at once to open negotiations looking toward the surrender of Italy.

This sudden turn of events raised perplexing new difficulties for Roosevelt and Churchill—whether to negotiate with the Badoglio government, as Eisenhower and other Allied leaders requested, or to demand unconditional surrender in accordance with the Casablanca declaration. The situation was so uncertain that the President, the Prime Minister, and their respective entourages met in Quebec on August 17, 1943, for a conference known by the code name of QUADRANT.

The new Italian government made secret contact with the Allies. The Italians were anxious to surrender but insisted that the Allies protect Rome, the King, and the government from the Germans, who had meanwhile taken control of most of Italy. Roosevelt and Churchill agreed to send an air-borne division to capture the airfields around Rome, and the armistice was signed on September 3. By the time preparations for an air-borne assault on Rome were completed, however, the Germans had surrounded the city in force and had seized the airfields.

Meanwhile, on September 3, the British Eighth Army crossed the Straits of Messina and began the invasion of the Italian mainland, known as operation AVALANCHE. A week later a British air-borne division seized the large Italian naval base at Taranto, while the United States Fifth Army, under the command of General Mark Clark, landed in the Gulf of Salerno south of Naples. In spite of furious German counterattacks, the Fifth Army occupied Naples on October 7 and pushed northward to the Volturno River. Meanwhile, British forces had cleared the central and eastern sections of the Italian boot; and by January 1, 1944, Allied forces had pushed to a winter line south of Cassino.

Although a long and bloody campaign for Italy still impended, the Italian surrender and the successful invasion of Italy yielded large dividends to the Anglo-American Allies. It brought the surrender of the Italian fleet and guaranteed complete Allied control of the Mediterranean, gave the Allies advanced air bases from which to bomb the Balkans and Central Europe, consumed some of Hitler's best divisions, and, most important, gave the British and Americans the incalculable advantage of being on the offensive.

190 / *Slow Progress Toward Accord with Russia*

After approving final plans for the Italian surrender, the conferees at Quebec turned to other urgent, if less immediate, problems. For example, they reaffirmed May 1, 1944, as the date for OVERLORD; agreed to launch an invasion of the Toulon-Marseilles area in southern France in conjunction with OVERLORD; and established a Southeast Asia Command in Burma under Lord Louis Mountbatten. Moreover, Hull and Eden discussed postwar plans for Germany and approved the draft of a Four-Power Declaration—to be submitted to the coming conference of foreign ministers in

[5] On September 12, 1943, a German parachute force rescued Mussolini, who established a new Fascist "government" under German protection at Lake Como.

Moscow—pledging America, Britain, Russia, and China to work for the establishment of an effective postwar security organization. After the conferees finished their work on August 24, Churchill accompanied Roosevelt back to Washington and stayed with him intermittently during the next three weeks, during which time the Badoglio government surrendered and the Allies began their invasion of the Italian mainland.

Soon afterward, Secretary Hull made the arduous air journey to Moscow for the conference of Foreign Ministers that opened in the Russian capital on October 18. Before this time no one in Washington or London knew what Russian postwar ambitions were, except for the territorial demands that Stalin had outlined to Eden in December 1941. In Moscow from October 18 to 30, 1943, however, Hull, Molotov, and Eden discussed immediate and postwar problems with so little disagreement that it seemed the future collaboration of the three major powers was assured. They agreed, for example, upon a plan for the postwar treatment of Germany that the State Department had prepared and the President had tentatively approved; indeed, Molotov declared it expressed Stalin's views and had his complete endorsement.[6] They agreed, moreover, that Austria should be reconstituted an independent nation and regarded as a liberated and not an enemy state, while Hull persuaded Stalin and Molotov to sign the Four-Power Declaration. In addition, during a state dinner on October 30, Stalin told Hull the welcome news that Russia would join the war against Japan after the defeat of Germany. Finally, the conferees approved the draft of a three-power declaration on war crimes, which was issued over the signatures of Roosevelt, Stalin, and Churchill in Moscow on November 1. It promised swift and terrible punishment, not only for the leaders of the Nazi government but as well for all Germans guilty of atrocities.

In spite of ominous Soviet-American differences over Poland,[7] the Moscow Conference was a resounding success. To be sure, no one knew absolutely whether Russia would cooperate with the West in the postwar era, but such cooperation seemed now not only possible but even probable. As one milestone along the road to Allied unity, the conference prepared the way for the next—a personal meeting of the Big Three at Teheran.

[6] As this plan eventually became the cornerstone of Allied postwar policy toward Germany, it would be well to examine it in some detail. It called for the unconditional surrender of Germany by whatever government exercised power at the end of the war. An Inter-Allied Control Commission would supervise the surrender and occupation of Germany by Soviet, American, and British troops. During the occupation the Control Commission would undertake to destroy all vestiges of Nazism and take necessary steps to encourage the establishment of a democratic government and to restore freedom of religion, speech, the press, and political activity. Moreover, Germany should be denied a standing army and general staff and prohibited from manufacturing any war materials or aircraft of any kind. The Hull plan was vague on future German boundaries, except to say that East Prussia should be separated from the Reich. Finally, Germany should be required to pay reparations in goods, equipment, and manpower, but not in money.

[7] The Kremlin had severed diplomatic relations with the Polish Government-in-Exile in London, because the Poles had demanded that the International Red Cross investigate a German charge that the Russians had murdered 8,000 to 10,000 Polish officers in 1939 and buried their bodies near Smolensk. Moreover, the Russians were beginning to deal with a group of Polish Communists in the Soviet Union. At Moscow Hull urged the Russians to restore relations with the Polish government in London, but Molotov made it clear the Kremlin would deal only with a Polish government it could control.

It had long been Roosevelt's ambition to meet personally with the leader of the Russian people, and before the Moscow Conference he had invited Stalin to join him and Churchill at Ankara, Bagdad, or Basra in Iraq. Pleading he could not go far from Russia because he must maintain personal control over his High Command, Stalin replied that he would go only to Teheran for the conference. When further pleading failed to move Stalin from his decision, the President agreed to go to the Iranian capital.

On November 13, 1943, the President and his advisers left Hampton Roads on the new battleship *Iowa* for a long journey first to Cairo, for conferences with Churchill, Chiang Kai-shek, Lord Mountbatten, and General Stilwell on the situation in Burma and China. Most of the discussions at Cairo from November 23 to 27 revolved around the beginning of an Allied drive in Burma, to open supply lines to China, and a Chinese offensive in northern China.[8]

On November 27 the President and his party flew from Cairo to Teheran. For security reasons, Roosevelt moved into a villa in the Russian compound the next day. During the next four days the Big Three thrashed over practically all outstanding military and political problems—military operations in Italy; the question of an Anglo-American invasion of the Istrian peninsula and of southeastern Europe, raised by Churchill; and Anglo-American plans for offensive operations in the Pacific, during discussions of which Stalin again promised that Russia would join the war against Japan after Germany's surrender.

The Russians, however, were most concerned about the launching of OVERLORD and seemed desperately anxious to pin Roosevelt and Churchill to a definite time and place for the great invasion. Stalin pressed Roosevelt to name a supreme commander for OVERLORD and implied he would believe the operation would be launched only when the President had named the commander. Roosevelt had long wanted General Marshall, for whom he had warm affection and respect, to have the honor of leading the liberation of Europe; but he wisely refused to follow the impulse to give Stalin an immediate answer. As it turned out, Roosevelt and his advisers concluded that Marshall could not be spared to direct OVERLORD, because he was the only man who could coordinate in Washington the far-flung military operations both in the Pacific and in Europe. On his way home from Teheran, therefore, the President had a long talk with Eisenhower and told him he would be named supreme commander of OVERLORD.

The Big Three talked not merely about OVERLORD but as well about the future of Germany and plans for postwar collaboration. Now they seemed to favor partition; emphasizing the danger of future German resurgence, Stalin added that he did not think the State Department plan

[8] The Allies opened this campaign in December 1943, when General Stilwell's Chinese divisions moved from Ledo against Japanese forces in northern Burma and British forces moved down the southwestern coast of Burma in January 1944. Japanese counterattacks against Chittagong and Imphal, both in India, were eventually repulsed but delayed British liberation of Rangoon and southern Burma until the spring of 1945. To the north, however, Stilwell's American and Chinese forces were more successful and assured completion of the new supply line to China, the Ledo Road, which was opened in January 1945.

submitted at the Moscow Conference was severe enough. Roosevelt outlined his plan for a future United Nations organization, which would assume responsibility for preventing wars and aggression. During all these conversations the utmost frankness and usually a spirit of cordiality prevailed. In fact, the President was convinced he had broken through the wall of suspicion and distrust surrounding Stalin, won Russian trust and friendship, and laid the basis for fruitful collaboration in the future. His feeling was well expressed in the concluding sentences of the Declaration of Teheran, issued on December 1: "We came here with hope and determination. We leave here, friends in fact, in spirit, and in purpose."

After a final dinner on December 2, the President said good-by to Stalin, paid a short visit to American troops of the Persian Gulf Command, and then went to Cairo for conferences with Churchill and the President and Foreign Minister of Turkey, relative to Turkey's entrance into the war. In addition, from December 4 to 6 the two Allied leaders and the Combined Chiefs of Staff held conferences of tremendous military importance. Thus, as the year 1943 drew to a close the Allies were on the offensive on all fronts, Allied unity existed in fact as well as in name, and the Anglo-American leaders were completing plans for the final assaults against Germany and Japan.

191 / *The Allied Air Offensives in Europe, 1940–1945*

After the failure of the German air *Blitz* against England in 1940–1941, superiority in the air passed to the British. From 1940 to the spring of 1942, the RAF Bomber Command conducted a limited number of night raids against selected industrial and transportation targets in Germany. Results, however, were so unsatisfactory that the new chief of the Bomber Command, Sir Arthur Harris, executed a complete change in British bombing tactics— a change from the target system to mass bombing of industrial areas in order to disrupt the German economy and cause the German people to lose the will to fight. The first 1,000-plane RAF raid, against Cologne on May 30, signaled the beginning of the new campaign; it was followed in 1942 by others against centers in the Ruhr, Bremen, Hamburg, and other German cities. It was only a small beginning, for less than 50,000 tons of bombs fell on Axis Europe in 1942, and German war production and civilian morale were not visibly impaired.

Meanwhile, the United States Eighth Air Force had established bases in England in early 1942 and joined in the air war on August 17, 1942. As the offensive power of the Eighth Air Force grew and was reinforced by the Ninth Air Force of fighters and the Fifteenth Air Force of bombers, the Americans became a powerful factor in the air campaign during the summer of 1943. While the British continued their devastating night attacks, the Americans used their heavier armored Flying Fortresses and Liberators in daring daylight raids—until extremely heavy losses in a raid on Schweinfurt on October 14, 1943, convinced the American commanders that further large daylight operations must await the production of long-range fighters to protect the bombers. All told, American and British bombers dropped 206,188 tons of bombs on targets in Europe in 1943.

A new phase in the air campaign began in February 1944 with the arrival in England of the P-51 long-range fighters, which made possible the resumption of daylight raids; the introduction of radar bombsights, which greatly increased the accuracy of night bombing; the use of increasingly heavy bombs; and the rapid build-up of the Eighth and Fifteenth Air Forces. On February 23, 1944, the Americans began a systematic campaign to destroy the German aircraft industry. In March the attack shifted to French and Belgian marshaling yards, railroads, and bridges. Then, after the invasion of France, the American AAF and the British RAF began a coordinated and relentless "round-the-clock" assault upon German synthetic oil and chemical plants. In February 1945 some 8,000 to 9,000 Allied planes turned to the task of paralyzing the German transportation system. Finally, in April the air forces joined the advancing Allied armies in reducing the German nation to utter impotence and ruin.[9]

The over-all dimensions of the Anglo-American air effort in Europe are so enormous as to stagger the imagination: 1,442,280 bomber and 2,686,799 fighter sorties, which dropped 2,697,473 tons of bombs on Germany and Nazi-occupied Europe and cost the Allies some 40,000 planes and 158,000 personnel. But to what effect? Did the results justify the enormous expenditure of war materials and use of manpower that the air operations required? Fortunately, the intensive investigations of the United States Strategic Bombing Survey, conducted in the immediate postwar period, have supplied definite answers to these questions. In general, Anglo-American strategic bombing, especially in the last year of the war, was decisive in three particular ways: in destroying or impeding the development of German productive capacity, in nearly paralyzing the German transportation systems in France, Belgium, and the Reich, and in causing a breakdown of morale among the German people. To state the matter briefly, by March 1945 the entire German economy was so near collapse as a consequence of Allied air raids that German war production would have practically ceased by May 1945 and the German armies would have had to cease fighting by June or July even without the Allied invasion of Germany. All told, Allied bombs dropped on Germany killed 305,000 persons and wounded 780,000 others, destroyed or damaged 5,500,000 homes, and deprived 20,000,000 persons of essential utilities. By the beginning of 1944, according to a poll taken by the Strategic Bombing Survey immediately after the war, some 77 per cent of the German people were convinced the war was lost; and by May 1945 most Germans had lost all will to continue the uneven struggle.

[9] The increasing fury of the air assault can be read in the following statistics of tonnage of bombs dropped on Axis Europe in 1944 and 1945:

Year	Quarter	Total tonnage dropped
1944	First	114,360
	Second	333,556
	Third	403,808
	Fourth	349,810
1945	First	369,687
	April	111,462

192 / *Victory in Europe: To the Westwall*

On January 15, 1944, General Dwight D. Eisenhower, Supreme Commander, Allied Expeditionary Forces, arrived in London with orders from Roosevelt and Churchill to "enter the continent of Europe and, in conjunction with the other Allied Nations, undertake operations aimed at the heart of Germany and the destruction of her armed forces."

Never was so stupendous a task defined in so few words! The Combined Chiefs of Staff and various technical staffs in Britain and America had been hard at work on plans for OVERLORD since 1942. In Eisenhower's headquarters in London planning for the actual invasion and subsequent operations proceeded apace after mid-January 1944. The prelude to OVERLORD began on March 6, with the shift in the strategic air offensive to France and Belgium. The effect of this assault was to paralyze almost completely the invasion area and the region through which the Germans would have to move reinforcements and supplies.

Now approached the appointed time, June 5, 1944,[10] for which the world waited. Delayed a day by a sudden storm, the great invasion armada put out to sea early in the morning of June 6. The Germans expected the invasion to come in the Pas de Calais area, where the English Channel is narrowest. Instead, the Allies struck at five beaches along a sixty-mile stretch of the Cotentin Peninsula in Normandy. First came furious air and naval bombardments of the invasion area and beaches; next came the landing of three air-borne divisions behind the German lines a few minutes after midnight on June 6; finally, at 7:30 in the morning the sea-borne troops hit the beaches. German resistance was generally light; but on Omaha Beach the American invaders met a fierce defense, suffered heavy casualties, and overcame the Germans, as General Omar N. Bradley has written with superb repetition, only by "guts, valor, and extreme bravery."

Hampered by constant air attacks that made it impossible to move reinforcements by day, and thinking the Normandy invasion was a screen for a larger invasion in the Pas de Calais, the German commanders, Field Marshals Erwin Rommel and Karl von Rundstedt were never able to bring up their reserve divisions in time to prevent the Allies from securing and capturing a bridgehead in Normandy. Within two weeks after D-Day the Allies had landed more than 1,000,000 troops with enormous quantities of supplies in a broad sector along the Normandy coast, captured Cherbourg, Caen, and St. Lô, "eaten the guts out of the German defence," and were poised for a grand sweep through northern France.

On July 25 the battle of the "break-through" began, with a lightning-like thrust by General Patton's Third Army into Brittany and a break-through to Avranches and Falaise by the American First Army and the British Second Army. Soon the battle for Normandy turned into the battle for France. Under orders to "stand firm," the German Seventh Army in the area between Falaise and Argentan was surrounded and destroyed or

[10] The date for the launching of OVERLORD was postponed from May 1 to the more unfavorable first week in June 1944 because of a shortage of landing craft.

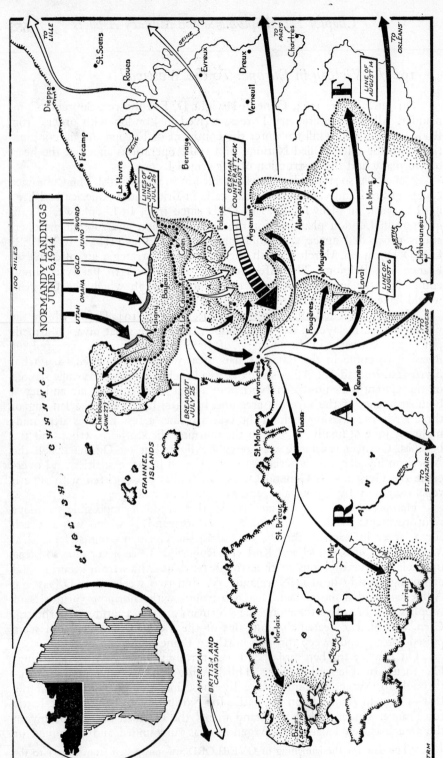

26. *The Normandy Landings and the Break-through*

captured during a furious battle from August 19 to 23. While the remaining German armies scurried to the Westwall, or Siegfried Line, the Allies completed the liberation of France in *Blitzkrieg* fashion. Paris was lightly garrisoned and fell to French troops on August 25. Ten days earlier the American Seventh Army invaded southern France between Toulon and Cannes and joined in the race for the German frontier. And by September 15 American and British armies had captured Brussels and Antwerp, freed Luxembourg, crossed the German border at Aachen, and stood poised all along the western front for the invasion of Germany.

While the Anglo-American armies liberated France and Belgium, the armies of the United Nations were pressing hard on other fronts. After seeking vainly to break the German Gustav Line in Italy, the Allies, on January 22, 1944, tried to turn the German flank by landings at Anzio and Nettuno on the west coast of Italy, only thirty-six miles from Rome. But the Germans counterattacked so furiously that the operation failed. In the spring, however, the British Eighth Army and the American Fifth Army pushed northward, joined the beleaguered divisions on the Anzio beachhead, and captured Rome on June 4, 1944. Under heavy Allied pressure and harassment, the Germans retreated hastily to their Gothic Line, which ran across Italy some 150 miles north of Rome, where they managed to stabilize the fighting around September 1, 1944.

Meanwhile, during the spring of 1944 the Russians, now reinforced and adequately equipped, began offensives along the entire eastern front fully as important in the Allied strategy as the Anglo-American sweep across France. One Russian drive on the northern sector forced Finland to sue for an armistice on August 25. The greatest Russian offensive, however, opened on June 23 to coincide with the Anglo-American drive in the West. After capturing the German stronghold of Vitebsk, Soviet armies broke through to the Baltic on August 1. In the central sector, five Russian armies rolled into Poland, reached the Vistula River in late July, captured Warsaw on January 17, 1945, and reached the Oder River, only forty-five miles from Berlin, the following month. Farther to the south, two Red armies overran Rumania in August 1944; marched into Bulgaria; captured Belgrade on October 20, and then moved against Budapest, which fell after a long struggle in February 1945.

By the autumn of 1944, therefore, it was obvious to the Allies and to most Germans that the German military situation was hopeless. Her armies reeling and scattering under heavy Allied blows on all fronts, her railroads and industries crumbling under an increasing rain of bombs from the sky, her once proud navy and air force reduced to helplessness, Germany was now a beleaguered fortress awaiting final destruction because her fanatical master preferred complete destruction to unconditional surrender. Foreseeing inevitable ruin under Hitler's leadership, some high German officers in cooperation with certain anti-Nazi groups, perfected plans to take control of the German government and assassinate Hitler. Their agent left a time bomb in Hitler's headquarters on July 20, 1944; thinking Hitler was dead, the conspirators proceeded to take first steps to seize control of the army and government. Unfortunately, Hitler was only injured by the bomb's blast. With the support of loyal troops, he rounded up the opposition, executed about 5,000 persons after drumhead trials, and sent another 10,000 enemies of Nazidom to concentration camps. In consequence, the war would proceed to its bitter end.

193 / The Campaign and Election of 1944

We must interrupt our story of events in Europe in 1944 to give some attention to the political scene in the United States, for the year of OVER-LORD was also the time when the American people faced the quadrennial task of determining the control of their federal and state governments.

From the beginning of the American defense and war efforts the President strove hard and on the whole successfully to draw Democrats and Republicans together in a common effort. Politics of course persisted, but on issues involving prosecution of the war and the erection of a postwar security structure Democrats and Republicans worked in genuine collaboration. As we will see, moreover, even on domestic issues party lines were blurred and often meaningless.

During the congressional campaign of 1942 the Republicans made a hard fight to win control of the legislative branch. In the elections on November 3 they failed to win control of Congress but made such sweeping gains that the GOP's victory in 1944 seemed at least possible.[11] Especially significant for the future was the election of Thomas E. Dewey as the first Republican Governor of New York since 1920 and the fact that in 1943 Republican governors would rule in twenty-six states that cast 342 of the 531 electoral votes.

Actually, what occurred in the federal and state elections in November 1942 was not merely a Republican revival but also a strong conservative upsurge. The significance of the upheaval became apparent after the organization of the Seventy-Eighth Congress in January 1943, when many southern Democrats joined Republicans to form a majority coalition and seize control of legislative policy from the administration's hands. In all matters relating to the war and to postwar policies, this coalition gave the President aggressive support. In domestic matters, however, they proceeded as fast as they could to destroy certain parts of the New Deal and to remind the President that Congress still existed.

While the conservative coalition and the President engaged in frequent verbal duels during the winter and early spring of 1944, the politicians in both camps began their preparations for the coming national conventions and presidential campaign. Wendell L. Willkie was still the titular head of his party; moreover, since 1940 he had emerged as an advanced internationalist and a progressive of genuine conviction. But Willkie had no support among the party leaders and had become so closely identified with the Roosevelt administration as to lose his status as the leader of the opposition. He withdrew from the preconvention campaign after suffering an impressive defeat in the Wisconsin presidential primary in April. Meanwhile, Willkie's

[11] The Democrats elected 222 and the Republicans 209 members of the House—a Republican gain of forty-seven seats. The Republicans, moreover, gained nine seats in the Senate.

chief rival, Governor Dewey, was fast emerging as the new Republican leader. Ambitious and able, Dewey had many assets: youth and vigor, a reputation for efficiency, moderate liberalism, and, most important, proved ability as a vote-getter in the crucial Northeast.

After Willkie's withdrawal, Dewey had to contend only with the favorite sons, the most important of whom, Governor John W. Bricker of Ohio, was put out of the serious running by William Allen White's quip that he was "an honest Harding." When the Republican convention met in Chicago on June 26, Dewey was nominated on the first ballot by a vote of 1,056 to 1, while Bricker was pacified by the vice presidential nomination. The convention adopted a platform that was aggressively internationalist and essentially progressive in tone.[12]

By the early summer of 1944 the Democratic leaders found themselves in the predicament of men with no control over their party's presidential nomination. Many old-line bosses and most southern conservatives bitterly resented Roosevelt's leadership and preferred to nominate some conservative. But Roosevelt again frustrated his enemies by waiting until July 11, only a week before the Democratic convention opened, to say he would accept a fourth nomination. "All that is within me," he wrote in a public letter to National Chairman Robert E. Hannegan, "cries out to go back to my home on the Hudson River. . . . But as a good soldier . . . I will accept and serve."

The President's announcement settled the matter, for obviously the rank and file of Democrats wanted him to run; and no party leader dared deny him the opportunity of leading his people from war into peace. The great and crucial struggle, therefore, revolved around the nomination of a vice presidential candidate, for Roosevelt was in uncertain health and a Democratic Vice President elected in 1944 might well become the next President of the United States.

The battle for the succession was bitter and created divisions in the party that persisted for years afterward. Vice President Henry A. Wallace enjoyed the support of the advanced progressive wing and large elements in the CIO but had the almost unanimous opposition of the party bosses, Southerners, and many moderates who suspected that he was temperamentally unfit for the presidency and hopelessly inept in political leadership. Roosevelt endorsed Wallace publicly but refused to insist upon his nomination. In fact, the President had apparently promised the succession to Byrnes and actually tried to obtain the nomination for the South Carolinian.

The President's plans, however, were upset on the eve of the convention by the intervention of a newcomer in high Democratic councils, Sidney Hillman, a vice president of the CIO and former co-director of the defense

[12] Although the Republican platform roundly condemned the administration's alleged inefficiency, waste, excessive centralization, and destruction of private enterprise, on all major issues it admitted that the Republicans had no fundamental quarrels with their opponents. Embodying the declaration issued at the conference of Republican leaders at Mackinac Island on September 7, 1943, the platform was as internationalist as any One World devotee could have desired. Although condemning Democratic inefficiency in the administration of welfare legislation, the Republicans promised to continue and strengthen the labor, social security, and agricultural reforms of the New Deal. All in all, the GOP platform was the most significant endorsement of the Roosevelt policies yet written.

effort. Alarmed by the rising tide of anti-labor sentiment and the failure of workers to go to the polls in 1942, Hillman organized the Political Action Committee of the CIO in 1943, not only to rally workers and progressives, but also to win new bargaining power for labor within the Democratic party. By the spring of 1944 he had built the PAC into a machine so powerful that it frightened the labor-baiting Representative Martin Dies from the Texas Democratic primary campaign and was instrumental in defeating two other members of Dies' un-American activities committee for renomination.

Now Hillman used his power in a more spectacular way. In conferences with and by letters to the President, he virtually vetoed Byrnes' nomination, on the grounds that the South Carolinian was unacceptable to labor and to northern Negroes. When Edward J. Flynn, Democratic leader of New York, warned that Byrnes was also unacceptable to Catholics because he had left the fold and joined the Episcopal church, the President concluded that his assistant must give way to a compromise candidate. He therefore declared that Senator Harry S. Truman or Justice William O. Douglas would be acceptable running-mates; and he agreed with Hillman that the PAC should shift its support from Wallace to Truman when it became obvious that Wallace could not be nominated. In any event, Roosevelt declared in his final instructions to National Chairman Hannegan, the party managers must "clear it with Sidney," that is, must win Hillman's approval for any vice presidential candidate.

The issue was settled during the three days before the Democratic convention opened in Chicago on July 19, 1944. After Hillman declared he would fight Byrnes' nomination to the bitter end, the President, on July 17, asked the South Carolinian to withdraw. Byrnes' withdrawal narrowed the field to Wallace, who still enjoyed the PAC's seeming support, and Truman, upon whom the administration and party leaders had finally agreed. During the balloting for the vice presidency on July 19 and 20, Wallace led on the first ballot and Truman won on the third, as the leaders had planned. A short time before, the convention had nominated the President on the first ballot; a short time after the fight over the vice presidency it adopted a platform that promised a continuation of progressive policies at home and vigorous American leadership abroad in the postwar era.

During the ensuing summer and autumn Dewey campaigned hard under tremendous handicaps—smashing Allied victories in Europe and the Pacific, the high degree of economic stabilization that prevailed on the home front by this time, a general disposition against changing governments in the midst of the world crisis, and, most important, Dewey's own general agreement with basic administration policies, which compelled him to make his criticisms on a captious level. Dewey's chief advantage was Roosevelt's failing health and a growing suspicion that perhaps the President was incapable of managing affairs of state. This suspicion became more marked after he delivered an address at Bremerton, Washington, and was halting and ineffective. However, Roosevelt came back in a speech before the Teamsters' Union in Washington on September 23 that convinced millions of voters that he was still the champion campaigner. He followed this masterpiece with strenuous tours and speeches in Chicago, Wilmington, Delaware, New York City, and New England.

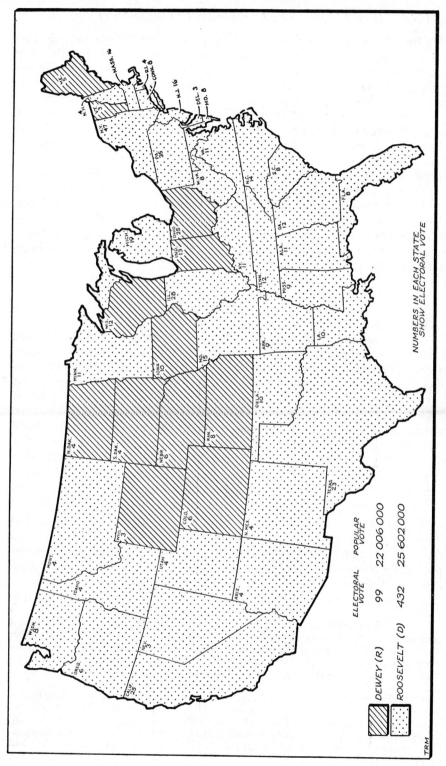

NUMBERS IN EACH STATE
SHOW ELECTORAL VOTE

	ELECTORAL VOTE	POPULAR VOTE
DEWEY (R)	99	22 006 000
ROOSEVELT (D)	432	25 602 000

27. *The Election of 1944*

TRM

By this aggressive campaign and by committing himself squarely to a full resumption of progressive policies in the postwar era, the President recovered the prestige and support he had seemingly lost earlier in the campaign. Almost as decisive as the President's campaign was the PAC's work in ringing door bells and getting workers to the polls. In the election on November 7, Roosevelt received 25,602,505 popular and 432 electoral votes; Dewey, 22,006,278 popular and ninety-nine electoral votes. Although they lost one seat in the Senate, the Democrats gained twenty seats in the House, all but four of them in the large cities, and captured governorships in Ohio, Massachusetts, Missouri, Idaho, and Washington. In view of the urgent international tasks ahead, the most important outcome of the election was not the continuation of Democratic control but rather the fact that Americans of both parties were now irrevocably committed to assume the leadership in world affairs they had so often rejected before 1941. For better or for worse, there could be no turning back on the high road to international responsibility.

194 / *Yalta: the High Tide of Allied Unity*

The progress of the Allied and Russian advances against the German fortress raised the danger that war in Europe might end before the three great powers had come to definite agreement on plans for future collaboration in Europe. Indeed, there was little evidence that the American leaders yet knew even their own minds on the most important aspect of postwar planning, a policy for the control of Germany.[13] More disturbing, however, were signs of growing Allied dissension that threatened to split the Grand Alliance and prevent the organization of a postwar United Nations. For one thing, at a conference at Dumbarton Oaks in Washington in September 1944, British, American, and Russian delegates agreed upon the basic structure of the United Nations but could not agree upon certain fundamental aspects of voting procedure. For another, during the autumn and winter of 1944–1945 the State Department and the British Foreign Office engaged in heated controversies over the organization of a new Italian government and the methods and objectives of British intervention in Greece. The most potentially dangerous source of trouble was the question of Russian policy in eastern Europe and especially in Poland.

Thus the President's thoughts inevitably turned toward another meeting

[13] American confusion on this aspect of postwar policy was revealed during a heated controversy in the Washington administration in the late summer of 1944. The conflict revolved around the so-called Morgenthau Plan, prepared by Harry Dexter White in the Treasury Department and presented by Secretary of the Treasury Henry Morgenthau, Jr. The Morgenthau Plan proposed to give parts of Germany to Poland, Russia, Denmark, and France and to divide the remaining rump, strip it of all industrial capacity, and convert it into a large "goat pasture." Although the plan was born of vengeance, Roosevelt approved it over the violent opposition of Hull and Secretary of War Stimson. Moreover, at a conference with Churchill in Quebec from September 11 to 16, 1944, the President was so insistent that Churchill reluctantly agreed to consider the Morgenthau Plan as a basis for postwar German policy. Yet within six weeks the President had dropped the plan altogether.

of the Big Three to discuss matters that could be settled only on the high level. Churchill and Stalin were agreeable, although Stalin insisted he could not leave Russia because he was personally directing the Russian armies. The three leaders, therefore, soon agreed upon Yalta in the Crimea as the place and early February 1945 as the time of the conference.

Since the Yalta meeting would obviously be the last Big Three conference before the surrender of Germany, the President, the new Secretary of State, Edward R. Stettinius, Jr.,[14] and the State Department went to unusual pains, first, to formulate an American program and, second, to come to firm agreement with the British before the Big Three met. Stettinius took his staff to Marrakech in French Morocco for a briefing session from January 26 to 29, 1945; then they went on to Malta for full and rewarding conferences with Churchill and Eden on January 31 and February 1. Roosevelt arrived with his party aboard the cruiser *Quincy* the following day, and it was soon evident that the recent Anglo-American difficulties had not impaired his intimate relationship with Churchill. Stettinius was much encouraged, moreover, by the great improvement in the President's physical appearance. He appeared more cheerful and calm than at the time of his fourth inaugural and "always . . . mentally alert and fully capable of dealing with each situation as it developed."

The Anglo-American-Russian conferees assembled at Yalta on February 3 and 4, 1945, for the opening of the conference called ARGONAUT on the latter day. From February 4 through 11 the Big Three discussed almost every conceivable problem related to the future of Europe, Asia, and the United Nations. In addition, the foreign ministers and military and naval leaders of the three powers worked behind the scenes smoothing out minor differences and laying the groundwork for major understandings. It was easily the most harmonious tripartite conference, for Stalin and Molotov seemed determined to meet their guests at least halfway. Without following the conferees in their long deliberations, let us now summarize their major agreements and decisions.

a. *Germany*. The discussions relating to Germany revolved around the questions of dismemberment, reparations, future Allied control, and French participation in the Inter-Allied Control Commission. The conferees approved dismemberment in principle and agreed to consider details in future negotiations. However, they agreed that northern East Prussia, including Königsberg, should go to Russia; that Poland should annex the southern half of East Prussia; that Russia should annex certain former eastern Polish provinces; and that Poland should receive territory in eastern Germany as compensation.[15] As for reparations, the Russians proposed exacting a total bill of $20,000,000,000, half of which should be paid to the USSR. Roosevelt and Churchill would not approve any fixed sum but agreed to accept the

[14] Cordell Hull resigned because of ill health on November 21, 1944, after thirteen and a half years as Secretary of State.

[15] Roosevelt and Churchill refused to agree to a definite cession of this territory to Poland. At the Potsdam Conference in July, however, the American and British leaders agreed that the Poles should occupy the region between the Oder-Neisse rivers and the old eastern German boundary, pending settlement of the boundary by a future peace conference. The Poles at once proceeded to incorporate the territory, expel the German population, and settle the region with Poles.

Russian proposal as the basis for future negotiations and to establish a Reparations Commission with headquarters in Moscow. Early in the meetings the Russians withdrew their objection to French participation in the occupation of Germany and near the end of the conference Stalin agreed also that France should have a seat on the Control Commission. As the several occupation zones had already been drawn by the European Advisory Commission, there was no discussion of this matter at Yalta.

b. *The Governments of Poland and Eastern Europe.* The Polish question did not disrupt the conference, as some observers feared it might; but it was the source of more controversy than any other issue before the conferees. As we have seen, Roosevelt and Churchill approved certain changes in Poland's eastern boundary and agreed that Poland should be compensated for loss of territory in the east by annexing parts of eastern Germany. It was at least a practical solution, one that seemed eminently just at the time.

The crucial question involved the future control of Poland. Arguing that they could not tolerate the existence of a Poland unfriendly to the USSR, Stalin and Molotov insisted that Britain and the United States recognize the Soviet-sponsored Lublin Provisional government, which the Kremlin had recognized. Roosevelt and Churchill adamantly refused. Then Stalin suggested that the Lublin government be enlarged to include some of the leaders of the London Government-in-Exile, supported by the western powers. When Roosevelt and Churchill again refused, Stalin finally agreed that the Lublin government should be reorganized to include democratic leaders at home and abroad and that free elections should be held at an early date to determine the future government of the country. Roosevelt made it clear that the British and American Ambassadors in Warsaw would determine whether this pledge had been honestly kept.

As for the other so-called liberated countries of eastern Europe, the three powers pledged themselves to assist the peoples of these countries to establish, through free elections, democratic governments responsive to the popular will.[16]

c. *The Organization of the United Nations.* In the discussions over the organization of the United Nations, the Russians conceded practically everything for which the Americans had fought at the Dumbarton Oaks Conference. First, they accepted the American formula for voting in the Security Council.[17] Second, the Soviets withdrew their demand for sixteen

---

[16] It should be added that in October 1944 Churchill and Eden had had conferences with Stalin in Moscow over the future of the Balkans. They agreed that during the coming months Russia should have predominance in Rumania and Bulgaria, that Britain should have predominance in Greece, and that the two countries would share responsibility in Yugoslavia and Hungary. Churchill tried to make it clear, however, that the arrangement provided merely a temporary *modus vivendi* to prevent a conflict of British and Russian forces during the period of German withdrawal and should not be construed to authorize interference in the domestic affairs of the Balkan states. In any event, the Yalta agreements superseded the Churchill-Stalin agreement.

[17] The main issue here was whether the permanent members of the Security Council, that is, the great powers, should have the right to veto the consideration of disputes to which they were a party. The Americans fought against use of the veto in such circumstances and overcame Russian objections at Yalta. However, the right of the great powers to use the veto in all important matters was not involved, for Americans and Russians alike insisted upon having a veto over any proposed action by the Security Council.

votes in the General Assembly and received in return additional representatives and votes for the Ukraine and White Russia.[18] Third, Stalin agreed to Roosevelt's proposal that all nations at war with Germany by March 1, 1945, might become members of the United Nations—an important concession that enabled the United States to strengthen its position in the General Assembly through a full Latin American representation.

d. *The Far East.*   By secret agreement between the Americans and Russians, which Churchill approved but did not help make, and which was not published until February 11, 1946, Stalin agreed to bring Russia into the war against Japan within two or three months after the surrender of Germany. In return, the President approved the transfer of the Kurile Islands from Japan to Russia, recognized Russian control of Outer Mongolia, and agreed that Russia should recover all rights and territory lost at the end of the Russo-Japanese War.[19] In return, Stalin agreed to recognize Chinese sovereignty over Manchuria and to conclude a treaty of friendship and alliance with the Nationalist government of China.

What shall we say about the Yalta agreements? Did they represent, as many critics afterward charged, base appeasement of Russia, betrayal of the peoples of Poland and eastern Europe, and useless surrender to Communism in the Far East by a mentally incompetent President who was hoodwinked by the wily Stalin? Or were they wise, necessary, and "realistic," as defenders of the President have replied?

We can dispose of the charge that Roosevelt was mentally incompetent by pointing out that all the participants agree that it is untrue. Roosevelt was obviously tired at Yalta and exhausted afterward by the strain of the grueling sessions and of his long journeys. But there is no evidence that he was not in full possession of his mental faculties during the conference itself.[20]

Roosevelt and Churchill undoubtedly knew the risks they were running and the dangers inherent in the agreements on Poland and eastern Europe. They knew also that they had no alternative but to accept a compromise and hope the Russians would honor it—because the Russians were already in eastern Europe and the United States and Britain did not then possess sufficient military power in Europe to drive the Soviet armies out, and, more important, because neither the Anglo-American peoples nor soldiers would have tolerated even the suggestion of a long and bloody war to save Poland or Rumania from Communist domination. These were all historical realities with which Churchill and Roosevelt had to reckon in the late winter of 1945. In spite of them, they obtained important concessions from Stalin; and future conflicts with the Soviet Union developed because the Russians

---

[18] In return, Stalin and Churchill agreed the United States might have three votes in the General Assembly if it so desired.

[19] This commitment involved (a) the transfer of the southern half of Sakhalin from Japan to Russia, (b) internationalization of the port of Darien and the safeguarding of "the preeminent interests of the Soviet Union in this port," (c) restoration of the Russian lease on Port Arthur as a naval base, and (d) joint Soviet-Chinese operation of the Chinese Eastern Railroad and the South Manchuria Railroad.

[20] It might be well in passing to consider the charge that Alger Hiss, who was a member of the State Department staff at Yalta and had been an agent for the Soviet spy ring in the 1930's, was the principal author of the Yalta agreements. It has never been demonstrated that Hiss had any influence in determining any important decisions at the conference.

lowered the Iron Curtain in violation of, not in accordance with, the Yalta agreements.

We now know that Roosevelt concluded the secret Far Eastern agreement with Stalin because he and his military advisers were egregiously mistaken about Japan's capacity to continue large-scale resistance and, consequently, about the necessity of bringing Russia into the Pacific war. No one yet knew whether the atomic bomb would explode or the damage it would do. Lacking intelligence reports from Japan, the American military leaders did not know that the Japanese Kwantung Army in Manchuria had been gravely weakened or that Japan was near collapse because of air raids and the submarine blockade. Acting on the advice of his military advisers, Roosevelt made the agreement with Stalin, he thought, in order to prevent the death of perhaps 1,000,000 American men in bloody campaigns in Japan and on the Asiatic mainland. To avert this catastrophe, the President virtually let Stalin name his own price for Soviet participation. Actually, however, Soviet Far Eastern policy was neither determined nor defined at Yalta. It is a fair assumption that the Russians would have entered the war against Japan and re-established themselves as a major Far Eastern power whether the Americans liked it or not.[21]

Critics of the Yalta agreements tend to forget that the Russians, also, made substantial concessions. They agreed to participate in a United Nations that would certainly be controlled by the Anglo-American bloc; to give France a share in the control of Germany; and to respect the integrity of the peoples of eastern Europe. They seemed determined to act reasonably and to meet Churchill and Roosevelt halfway on all important issues. Roosevelt and Churchill, therefore, acted in the only manner that was historically possible. As Churchill put it, "Our hopeful assumptions were soon to be falsified. Still, they were the only ones possible at the time."[22]

195 / *Victory in Europe: Triumph and Tragedy*

We come now to the portentous events of the spring of 1945, when the triumph of the onrushing Allied and Russian armies was overshadowed by the larger tragedy of ruthless Soviet domination of eastern Europe and the failure of the American leadership to understand and perhaps act in time to restrain Communist imperialism.

The British and American armies approached the Siegfried Line in September 1944. Having rejected General Montgomery's plan for concentrating on an all-out thrust across the north German plain, Eisenhower made an effort to turn the northern flank of the German defenses by landing three air-borne divisions to capture bridges across the Meuse, Waal, and Rhine rivers. This effort failed when the British 1st Airborne Division was unable

---

[21] It might be added, also, that Chiang Kai-shek, who was not informed until much later of the details of the Far Eastern agreement, was delighted by the Russian promise of a treaty of alliance because he thought it meant Soviet neutrality in the Nationalist government's war with the Chinese Communists.

[22] W. S. Churchill, *Triumph and Tragedy* (Boston, 1953), p. 402; by permission of Houghton Mifflin Company, publishers.

28. *Allied Offensives to the Rhine, 1944–1945*

to hold a bridge across the Rhine at Arnhem, and the Allies were denied the opportunity to make a rapid drive across the north German plain. Instead, they brought up reinforcements for a winter campaign through the heavy German defenses manned by armies now regrouped and strengthened.

While American and British armies were probing along the length of the Siegfried Line, Hitler laid plans for one final gamble—a counteroffensive through the weak center of the Allied lines in the Ardennes Forest, which he hoped would split the enemy's forces and carry to Liége and perhaps Antwerp. Bad weather in late November and early December enabled Von Rundstedt, the German commander, to bring up his forces in secret. They struck furiously in the Ardennes on December 16 and scored heavily until Allied counterattacks forced them to withdraw. By the end of January 1945 the Battle of the Bulge, as the German offensive is commonly known, was over. Hitler's gamble had cost him his last reserves of aircraft and some of his best divisions.

In fact, the German army in the west was so weakened by ruinous losses in the Ardennes counteroffensive that it could no longer prevent the Allied armies from advancing to the Rhine. In the north, forces under Field Marshal Montgomery captured Cleves on February 12; Cologne, on the left bank of the Rhine, fell to the American First Army on March 6; to the south, troops of the French First and the American Third and Seventh armies cleared the Saar and Palatinate areas by March 25. Meanwhile, by an unbelievable stroke of good luck, American troops captured the Ludendorff Bridge across the Rhine at Remagen on March 7 before it could be demolished and quickly established a bridgehead on the other side of the river.

While the Anglo-American armies were poised along the Rhine for a final drive into the heart of Germany and Russian armies were massed on the Oder River for an assault upon Berlin, new tensions between the western democracies and Russia gave warning of troubled times ahead. For one thing, in February 1945 the Russians had ruthlessly imposed a Communist government on Rumania. For another, Anglo-American negotiations with a German general for surrender of German forces in Italy caused Stalin to address a letter to Roosevelt virtually accusing him and Churchill of treacherously negotiating for the surrender of all German forces in the West so that the British and American armies could occupy Berlin before the Russians captured the city.

Even more ominous, however, were Russian actions in Poland. Not only had the Russians refused to honor the Yalta agreement to reorganize the puppet Lublin government; they also refused to allow American and British observers to enter Poland and proceeded to liquidate the leaders of the democratic parties in that unhappy country. It was plain, therefore, that Stalin would tolerate no Polish government he could not completely control; indeed, he admitted as much in correspondence with Churchill. By mid-March, when the Polish dispute was nearing the point of open rupture, Roosevelt was so weak that he had lost his grasp and could not take leadership in opposing Soviet violations of the Yalta agreements. Actually, Poland was irretrievably lost to Communist imperialism, as Stalin's blunt replies to Churchill's vigorous protests revealed.

Poland was lost, but not yet Prague and Berlin, if the Allies had resolved to act quickly and send their armies hurtling across Germany. Churchill perceived clearly that "Soviet Russia had become a mortal danger to the free world"; and all through April and early May he pleaded with his American colleagues to push rapidly toward the two central European capitals. Even more important, he proposed that the Allies stay in force on this forward eastern line until the Russians had honored their earlier promises.[23]

American responsibility for the failure to take advantage of this unparalleled opportunity to seize strong outposts in Central Europe can best be demonstrated by an elaboration of military and political events. On March 24 the combined Anglo-American armies began their crossing of the Rhine, and by April 1 Montgomery's forces in the north and Bradley's in the center had converged to encircle the Ruhr and trap more than 250,000 German troops. Nothing now stood between the Anglo-American Allies and Berlin and Prague. But Eisenhower chose instead to send his extra divisions to capture the so-called National Redoubt—the Alpine area of Bavaria and western Austria, which Hitler had presumably prepared for a final stand—and then to drive for a junction with the Russians in the Leipzig-Dresden area along the line of the River Elbe, at which point the Allied armies would halt.

Having made his decision, Eisenhower relayed it to Stalin directly on March 28 without consulting Churchill or Roosevelt. Stalin was pleased; Churchill was so distressed that he appealed personally to Roosevelt to join him in ordering the Supreme Commander to move against Berlin. "I deem it highly important," the Prime Minister wrote to Eisenhower on April 2, "that we should shake hands with the Russians as far to the east as possible." Eisenhower, however, argued that his plan was sound on military grounds; and he had the firm support of other American field generals and of Marshall in Washington. "I could see no political advantage accruing from the capture of Berlin that would offset the need for quick destruction of the German army on our front," Bradley writes. "As soldiers we looked naïvely on this British inclination to complicate the war with political foresight and non-military objectives."[24]

Yet by April 11 the vanguard of the American army had reached the Elbe, only fifty-three miles from Berlin, while the Russians were still on the banks of the Oder. Churchill now redoubled his pleading, but his voice was no longer heard in Washington. Tired and unable longer to stand at the helm, Roosevelt wanted rest and recovery, not a new quarrel with his generals and the Russians. Early in April he went to Warm Springs to renew his strength before opening the San Francisco Conference of the United Nations on April 25. On April 12 he complained of a terrific headache, lost consciousness, and died at 4:35 p.m. of a massive cerebral hemorrhage.

[23] Roosevelt and Churchill had made no agreement anywhere to stop their armies at any certain point. At Yalta they and Stalin had approved the occupation zones drawn earlier; but Churchill was prepared not to retreat from the Soviet zone until the Russians lived up to the agreement on Poland and consented to a real integration of the occupation administration in Germany.

[24] Omar N. Bradley, *A Soldier's Story* (New York, 1951), pp. 535-536; by permission of Henry Holt and Company, publishers.

Roosevelt's growing weakness and death came at a fateful time in the history of the world. The new President, Harry S. Truman, had been utterly unprepared by his predecessor. Relying upon the best advice he had—the advice of Marshall, Eisenhower, and the State Department—Truman supported the Supreme Commander's decision to halt his armies at the Elbe and to move against, as it turned out, the phantom in the National Redoubt instead of driving to Berlin and Prague. Informing Stalin of this decision on April 21, Eisenhower sent Patton into Bavaria the next day. By the first of May, however, Eisenhower could have captured Prague with ease; and Churchill again pleaded for action that "might make the whole difference to the post-war situation in Czechoslovakia." Eisenhower then decided to send Patton into Prague and so informed the Soviet High Command but drew back after receiving a vehement protest from Stalin. Thus while the Americans waited the Russians occupied Prague on May 9.

Meanwhile, Hitler remained in Berlin, confident a miracle would yet save the Third Reich. He was heartened by Roosevelt's death and certain the western Allies and Russia would soon turn against each other. But *Götterdämmerung* was near at hand. On April 15 Marshal Gregory K. Zhukov began a massive offensive across the Oder that reached the suburbs of Berlin a week later. American and Russian troops met on the Elbe near Torgau on April 27. The following day Italian Partisans captured and shot Mussolini. In his bunker in Berlin, Hitler married Eva Braun and appointed Admiral Karl Doenitz his successor on April 29; the next day he committed suicide, and his body was burned in the garden of the Reichschancellery.

All that now remained was to end the war as quickly as possible. On May 2 nearly 1,000,000 German troops in northern Italy and Austria surrendered. Two days later German troops in northwest Germany, Holland, Schleswig-Holstein, and Denmark laid down their arms. Then, at Eisenhower's headquarters in Rheims, Colonel General Alfred Jodl surrendered unconditionally the remnants of the Germany army, air force, and navy at 2:41 a.m. on May 7. All hostilities ceased at midnight May 8, 1945. Churchill did not exaggerate when he wrote: "The unconditional surrender of our enemies was the signal for the greatest outburst of joy in the history of mankind." But the rejoicing throngs in Britain and America knew only of the triumph and nothing of the tragedy that overshadowed the world. "I moved amid cheering crowds," Churchill remembers, "or sat at a table adorned with congratulations and blessings from every part of the Grand Alliance, with an aching heart and a mind oppressed by forebodings."[25]

196 / Victory in the Pacific

By the early summer of 1944 American military, naval, and air power in the Pacific was overwhelmingly preponderant—the American navy, for example, was now five times stronger than the Imperial fleet—and the time had come for a series of hammer blows that would strike at the heart of the enemy.

[25] The quotations are from W. S. Churchill, *Triumph and Tragedy,* pp. 548 and 456; used by permission of the Houghton Mifflin Company, publishers.

Assembling a huge force of ships, aircraft, and troops, Admiral Raymond A. Spruance moved against the strongly-held Marianas, about 1,350 miles south of Tokyo. In rapid succession the three principal islands in the group, Saipan, Tinian, and Guam, fell quickly before the overpowering assault. Meanwhile, as Americans were invading Saipan a large Japanese force of five battleships, nine aircraft carriers, and other ships sailed from the Philippines to intercept the invaders. On June 19, 1944, over 500 Japanese airplanes attacked and slightly damaged a battleship and two carriers. But the Japanese lost 402 airplanes and pilots, the core of their naval aviation; and pursuing American submarines and aircraft caught up with the Japanese fleet on June 20 and, in the first Battle of the Philippine Sea, sank three carriers and two destroyers and severely damaged one battleship, four carriers, and other craft.

Moving with irresistible momentum, American naval and amphibious forces attacked the Western Caroline Islands in September, overpowering fierce resistance on Peleliu, Angaur, and Ngesebus islands and neutralizing the main Japanese garrisons on the islands of Babelthuap and Yap.

While the navy was clearing the Central Pacific sea lanes to the Philippines, farther south General MacArthur was making final preparations for an invasion of the islands. First came an Allied drive in April and May 1944 that cleared the northern coast of New Guinea; next, amphibious offensives against Wakde, Biak, Noemfoor, and other islands off the northwestern coast of New Guinea that cleared the lower approaches to the Philippines; and, finally, capture of Morotai Island in September, which put the Southwest Pacific Forces within striking distance of the Philippines.

As prelude to the great invasion, during September and October 1944 land-based bombers and planes from carriers of the Third Fleet scourged Japanese airfields and installations in Mindanao, Luzon, and Formosa, operations that practically destroyed Japanese airpower in the area and disrupted Japanese sea communications. Then, on October 20, the Americans returned to redeem their pledge to liberate the Philippines—with an invasion of Leyte Island by the Sixth Army, the Seventh Fleet under Admiral Thomas C. Kinkaid, and the Third Fleet under Admiral William F. Halsey.

In the certain knowledge that American conquest of the Philippines would spell the doom of the Empire, because it would cut communications between Japan and Indo-China, Malaya, and the East Indies, the Japanese admirals made one last desperate effort to destroy the American invaders in Leyte Gulf. The three major naval engagements that ensued between October 24 and 25, 1944—the Battle of Surigao Strait, the Battle off Samar, and the Battle off Cape Engaño, collectively known as the Battle for Leyte Gulf—ended disastrously for the Japanese. In this greatest naval battle in history the Japanese lost practically their entire fleet—three battleships, four carriers, nine cruisers, and eight destroyers.

With the threat of Japanese naval intervention forever ended, MacArthur could now press forward with his overwhelming campaign in the Philippines. While the invasion of Leyte was at its height, he launched an attack against Mindoro in December and then attacked Luzon from Lingayen Gulf in early January 1945. Not until July 5, 1945, however, were the Japanese rooted out of the mountains of northern Luzon and out of Mindanao and dozens of smaller islands. All told, the Japanese lost over 400,000 men and 9,000 planes in the entire Philippines campaign.

The American conquest of the Marianas, the Western Carolines, and the Philippines blasted the inner rim of Japanese defenses; cut communications between the home islands and Indo-China, Malaya, and the East Indies; reduced the Japanese navy to the size of a single task force; and afforded the Americans advanced bases from which they could finally bomb the homeland of the Empire.

The air war against Japan began on June 15 and 16, 1944, when a force of large new B-29 Superfortresses of the Twentieth Air Force, operating from bases in China, attacked steel works in Kyushu. Although the Twentieth Air Force made subsequent raids on Japan and Manchuria, its operations were limited because all its supplies and bombs had to be flown over the Himalayan Hump from India. The turning point in the air war came with the capture of the Marianas, for Saipan, Guam, and other islands afforded bases from which Superfortresses could attack Japan in strength. Later the capture of Okinawa yielded bases for American fighter planes and fighter-bombers that joined in the increasing aerial assault.

All told, American planes dropped about 160,000 tons of bombs on the Japanese home islands from November 1944, when the bombardment from the Marianas began, to September 1945, when the war ended. From November 1944 to March 1945 the air commanders concentrated their attack against Japanese aircraft factories. Then, on March 9, the Air Force began a new and terrible phase of its campaign—a firebomb attack on Tokyo that destroyed sixteen square miles of the city and caused 185,000 casualties, followed soon afterward by similar fire raids on Nagoya, Osake, and Kobe. Thereafter the Air Force alternated saturation bombing of some sixty-six civilian areas with attacks on industrial and military targets.

Although the tonnage of bombs dropped on Japan was about one-ninth the tonnage dropped on Germany, the physical destruction in Japan almost equaled that in Germany. American bombs killed 330,000 Japanese civilians and injured nearly 500,000 others; moreover, they destroyed 2,510,000 buildings and 40 per cent of the built-up areas of sixty-six cities. The effects on the Japanese war economy were equally devastating. By July 1945 air attacks had reduced the productive capacity of Japanese oil refineries by 83 per cent, of aircraft engine plants by 75 per cent, of electronics and communication equipment plants by 70 per cent, and of munitions factories by some 30 per cent. For a nation with an industrial capacity only 10 per cent that of its chief enemy, these losses were fatal.

Let us now turn back to the last phase of the relentless American drive by land and sea toward Japan. While MacArthur was bringing the Philippines campaign to its climax, marine divisions invaded Iwo Jima, 750 miles south of Japan, on February 19, 1945. The Japanese defenders had made the island virtually one vast pillbox; they fought so courageously that the Iwo Jima operation was the bloodiest in the history of the United States Marine Corps. By March 16, however, the entire island, with its two airfields, was in American hands. Next came a larger attack, beginning April 1, by marine and army forces against Okinawa, a large island in the Ryukyus only 350 miles southwest of Japan. The Japanese and American leaders both knew that the fall of Okinawa would spell the early doom of the Empire. The defenders, therefore, fought fanatically during the battle that raged from April 1 to June 21 and lost nearly 111,000 dead and 9,000 prisoners. The most spectacular aspect of the Japanese defense was the unrelenting and often effective *kamikaze,* or suicide, attacks by Japanese aircraft against American warships and transports. All told, the Japanese lost some 4,000 aircraft, 3,500 of them in *kamikaze* attacks, during the Battle of Okinawa.

After the fall of Okinawa the only question was whether Japan would collapse from within before the Americans had launched their final invasion of the island empire. We have noted the terrible devastation wrought by the Superfortresses. In February 1945 they were joined by the thousands of planes of the Third Fleet and in April by fighter-bombers from Iwo Jima and Okinawa, which struck repeatedly at airfields and other targets in the home islands. In mid-July American battleships and heavy cruisers joined in the attack by shelling steel works, synthetic oil plants, and other industrial targets on the mainland and by heavy attacks upon Japanese shipping. But Japan was suffering most from a combined sea, air, and mine blockade that reduced her once large merchant fleet to ineffectiveness and deprived her people of food and her industries of vital raw materials.[26]

Indeed, since the autumn of 1943 it had been evident to certain Japanese leaders that they were fighting a losing battle and that the Imperial government should seek peace, even at the cost of giving up China, Korea, and Formosa. On July 18, 1944, soon after the American invasion of the Marianas, a moderate group led principally by the naval chieftains forced Tojo to resign and established a new Cabinet under General Kuniaki Koiso. An important element in the new government, led by Navy Minister Mitsumasa Yonai and allied with officials in the Imperial Court, were determined to end the war as quickly as possible. In February 1945 the Emperor threw his full support to the peace party; on April 8, after the invasion of Okinawa, he appointed Baron Kantaro Suzuki as Premier and ordered him to end the war. Suzuki, however, did not control the army, which was determined to fight to the bitter end and threatened to revolt if the Cabinet moved for peace. Thus in May the Cabinet began secret discussions with the Russian Ambassador, Jacob Malik, looking toward Russian mediation. In June and early July, moreover, the Emperor intervened openly and through his Ambassador in Moscow asked the Soviet government to end the war.

This was the situation when Truman, Churchill, Clement Attlee, soon to be Churchill's successor, and Stalin met at Potsdam in mid-July 1945 for the last conference of the Big Three. Knowing the atomic bomb was a reality and that its use might avert the necessity of a long and bloody campaign in Japan and China, Truman and Attlee on July 26 issued the Potsdam Declaration calling upon Japan to surrender or face "the utter devastation of the Japanese homeland."

In Tokyo the leaders of the Suzuki government agreed to accept the

[26] Japan entered the war with 6,000,000 tons of merchant shipping and constructed an additional 4,100,000 tons between 1941 and 1945. Of this total of 10,100,000 tons, the Japanese lost 8,900,000—54.7 per cent to submarines, 16.3 per cent to carrier-based planes, 14.5 per cent to land-based planes, 9.3 per cent to mines laid by B-29s, 4 per cent to marine accidents, and less than 1 per cent to surface gunfire.

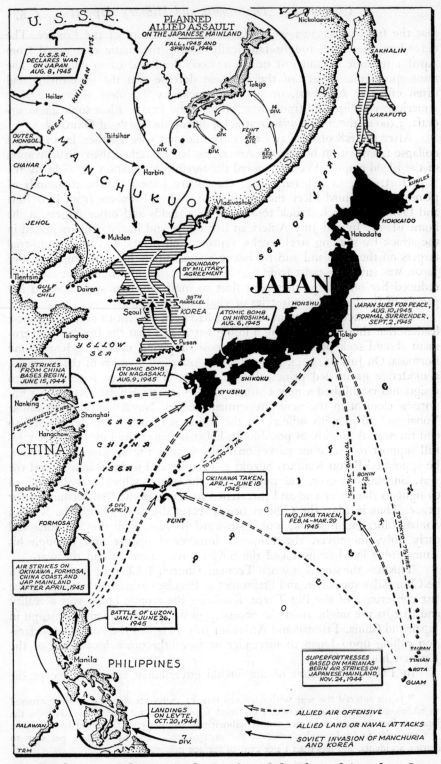

29. *Final Stages of the War in the Pacific and the Planned Assault on Japan*

Potsdam Declaration but could not persuade the army leaders to surrender. When Suzuki, on July 28, declared for home consumption that the Potsdam Declaration was "unworthy of public notice," President Truman and his advisers decided to use the atomic bomb to end Japan's agony. Thus on August 6 a lone B-29 flew over Hiroshima and dropped the first atomic bomb used in warfare. It leveled 4.4 square miles of the city and killed between 70,000 and 80,000 persons. Still the Japanese army refused to surrender. Then, on August 9, news came to Tokyo that Russia had entered the war and the Americans had dropped a second atomic bomb on Nagasaki. When hurried conferences failed to yield agreement to accept the Potsdam ultimatum, the Emperor made the decision for peace; and the following day the Cabinet informed the Washington government that it accepted the Potsdam terms, provided the status of the Emperor were not changed.

When Washington replied on August 11 that the Emperor must be subject to the Supreme Commander of the Allied Powers, the military and naval chieftains in Tokyo balked. But the Emperor insisted, and on August 14 the Suzuki government formally accepted the Allied demands. The Emperor at once prepared records of an Imperial Rescript ordering his armed forces to surrender; and the Cabinet, after suppressing an insurrection of army fanatics, sent emissaries to General MacArthur to arrange the details of surrender. On September 2 a great Allied fleet entered Tokyo Bay and soon afterward Foreign Minister Mamoru Shigemitsu and a representative of the Imperial General Staff signed the articles of surrender on board the battleship *Missouri*. General MacArthur and representatives of the Allied powers accepted on behalf of their respective governments.

CHAPTER 25 / THE AMERICAN ECONOMY, 1930–1953

*I*T is a forbidding task to relate in one chapter the rise of the American people from the slough of depression to the pinnacle of economic strength. It is an even more formidable task to attempt to describe the economic society in which Americans lived at mid-century. Yet it is a story worth the telling, for we cannot meet the problems of the future unless we understand the past and present. And the future is already here.

197 / The American People, 1930–1953

Studying the steady decline in the birth rate since the 1860's, demographers in the 1930's took a gloomy view of the future of population growth in the United States. On the basis of seemingly irrevocable trends, they projected curves that forecast further steady decline in rate of growth until a peak population had been reached between 1960 and 1980. Demographic developments of the 1930's seemed fully to justify these predictions. From 1930 to 1940 the population of the United States increased from 122,775,046 to only 131,669,275 souls. The rate of increase for the decade of 7.2 per cent was less than half the rate of the preceding decade and about one-third the rate from 1900 to 1910. The virtual ending of European immigration contributed to the decline, but the chief factor was the acceleration of the decline in the birth rate—from 23.7 per 1,000 in 1920 to a low of 16.6 in 1933.

Population experts found abundant reasons for the decline in the birth rate after the First World War—urbanization, greater education of the masses, the so-called emancipation of women, higher living standards, and then the depression of the thirties. The trouble was the sum of their reasons did not equal the whole; and a demographic revolution occurred in the 1940's that cast a grave doubt on the validity of their previous assumptions. After hovering at around 17.0 in the middle 1930's, the birth rate increased slightly between 1937 and 1940. Then came a sharper increase with the draft and war, and a momentary decline in 1944–1945, because of the absence of millions of men in Europe and Asia. However, as veterans returned to build homes and begin families, the birth rate began to soar—from 23.3 per 1,000 in 1946 to a peak of 25.8 in 1947 and back to a level of about 24.0 from 1948 to 1952. Meanwhile, the population of the United States increased 14.5 per cent between 1940 and 1950 and reached a total of 150,697,361 souls by the latter date.

Certainly the war and postwar prosperity, which seemed to offer secure futures to young Americans, was an important factor in this remarkable change. But prosperity does not alone explain the increase, for during the earlier period of the 1920's prosperity had been accompanied by a steady decline in birth rates, while the depression alone was not responsible for the further decline after 1929. Even more important was a pervading change in social values—a growing conviction that families of three and four children were "normal" and desirable, in contrast to the socially correct family of one and two children in the thirties. Whatever the causes, the results of the rise in the birth rate after 1940 were wonderful to behold—an annual crop of babies that warmed the hearts of manufacturers of washing machines and diapers,[1] and a whole new set of calculations concerning America's future social and economic needs and capacities. Whether the future would bring further significant changes in the birth rate, no one could say, although by 1953 the unchastened demographers were again at work on their projections.[2]

Along with the increase in birth rates and total population went continued improvement in the health of the American people from 1930 to 1950. New medical and surgical techniques, new drugs—like sulfanilamide, penicillin, antibiotics, and cortisone—more effective public health services, and wider consumption of vitamins, fresh vegetables, and milk all combined to render impotent many ancient enemies of mankind. The use of penicillin, for example, made possible the virtual eradication of venereal diseases. The use of sulfa drugs, penicillin, and other antibiotics reduced the number of deaths from influenza and pneumonia from 102.5 per 100,000 in 1930 to 35.2 in 1950. Typhoid, diphtheria, malaria, and childbirth fever practically disappeared, while more Americans died from automobile accidents in 1950 than from tuberculosis, which had been the second greatest single cause of death fifty years before. Consequently, the death rate decreased from 11.3 per 1,000 in 1930 to 9.6 in 1950,[3] while the average life expectancy for white males increased from forty-six years in 1901, to fifty-eight years in 1930, to nearly sixty-six years in 1950. Thus Americans in the 1940's were growing older and younger at the same time. But as they grew older they faced new perils as the diseases of old age—heart diseases, cancer, arteriosclerosis, and mental illnesses—took an increasing toll and moved into first rank as the undisputed enemies of American life.

---

[1] Over 3,750,000 babies were born in 1951, as compared with a paltry 2,200,000 in 1930.

[2] Actually, it would seem that the American population would continue to grow at an increasing rate for some time to come. The net reproduction rate, or intrinsic rate of natural increase, is a better index than the crude birth rate. During the 1930's the net reproduction rate hovered around 981, which meant that the American population was not in the long run reproducing itself. From 1944 to 1949, however, the net reproduction rate was 1,385—the highest point at any time since 1900.

[3] Even more spectacular and gratifying was the decrease in the death rate among Negroes, from 16.3 per 1,000 in 1930 to 11.2 in 1950.

30. *Population Change, 1940–1950*

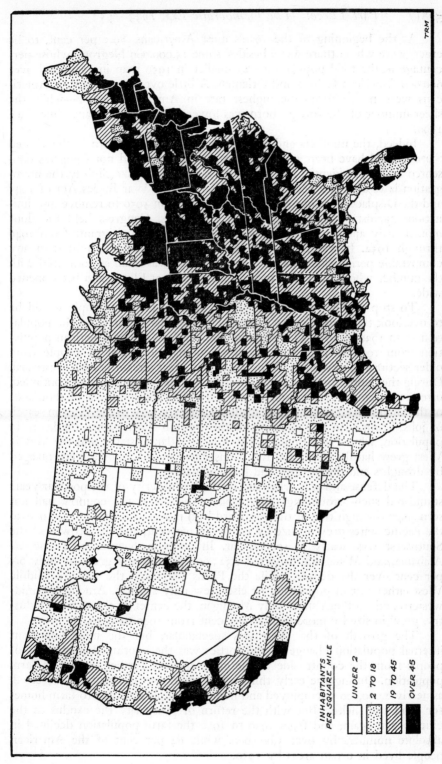

31. *Population Density in 1950*

INHABITANTS
PER SQUARE MILE

UNDER 2

2 TO 18

19 TO 45

OVER 45

At the beginning of the 1950's most Americans, 89.5 per cent, to be exact, were white; there were, besides, some 15,000,000 Negroes, whose percentage in the total population was smaller in 1950 than in 1790, and over 600,000 American Indians and Orientals. A little over 93 per cent of Americans were native-born—the highest rate in American history—while the sheer number of the foreign-born was lower in 1950 than at any time since 1890.

Indeed, the numbers and percentage of the foreign-born in the United States would have been appreciably smaller in 1950 had not Congress consented under presidential and public pressure to liberalize slightly the immigration laws after the Second World War. By the War Brides Act of 1945 and the Displaced Persons Act of 1948, amended in 1950 to remove discriminations against southern and eastern Europeans, Congress held the door momentarily ajar and admitted some 854,000 quota immigrants from 1946 through 1952. It was the largest number of immigrants admitted in any comparable period since the early 1920's, but it was small as compared with the number who would have come had the gates at Ellis Island been opened wide.

To stop at this point in our survey of the American people would be to overlook the revolutionary internal changes that occurred in the population from 1930 to 1950. One striking characteristic of the American population from 1930 to 1950 was the never-ending movement of people from older sections to new ones. Before 1930 one great stream headed westward. During the depression decade, westward migration diminished but continued, often in a tragic way, as displaced sharecroppers and hundreds of thousands of the unemployed and destitute made their weary way to the West in search of jobs. From 1930 to 1940 most of the western states gained markedly in population, while New England, the Middle Atlantic states, and the Middle West grew hardly at all, and the Plains states and Oklahoma were ravaged by droughts and dust storms and lost population.

The defense and war crises and the high prosperity of the postwar years stimulated such astounding movements of people as the country had not seen since the high tide of the westward land movement. From 1940 to 1950 the Pacific states grew in size by nearly 49 per cent, and the growth of the Southwest was nearly as spectacular. In contrast, Kentucky, Tennessee, Alabama, and Mississippi exported 1,325,000 persons and grew by only 6.5 per cent over the decade, while the Plains states and the western Middle West either lost in population or else grew only slightly. Among the midwestern and northern states only Michigan, the center of the defense industry, grew in size by more than 20 per cent from 1940 to 1950.

The growth of the West was spectacular, but the most important internal population change of the forties was the continued movement of people from the countryside to the cities and the further decline in farm population. During the early thirties this trend was momentarily reversed, as nearly 2,000,000 unemployed and homeless people returned to farm homes for food and shelter. But with the return of prosperity the exodus to the cities began again; and from 1940 to 1950 the farm population declined in absolute numbers by over 5,000,000, while 64 per cent of the American people lived in urban areas by 1950.

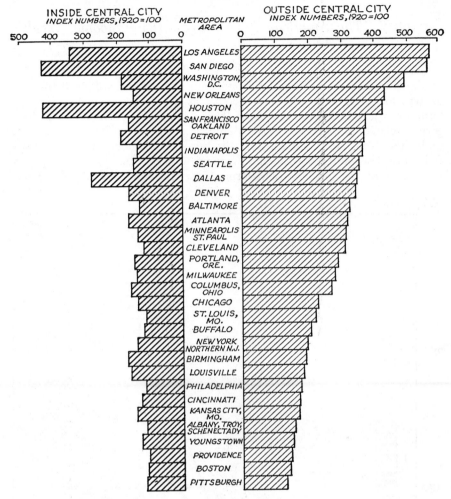

INSIDE CENTRAL CITY
INDEX NUMBERS, 1920 = 100

METROPOLITAN AREA

OUTSIDE CENTRAL CITY
INDEX NUMBERS, 1920 = 100

28. *The Growth of the Suburbs, 1920–1950. (This chart shows the comparative growth of central cities and their suburbs from 1920 to 1950.)*

The most significant phenomenon of urban growth was the further expansion of the suburban areas adjacent to the central cities of the so-called metropolitan districts. In 1930 there were ninety-six metropolitan districts, with 44.6 per cent of the total population of the United States. By 1950 there were 168 such districts, in which 84,500,680 people, or 56.1 per cent of the population, lived.

One other important internal population trend remains to be noted here —the acceleration of the movement of Negroes from the South to the North and other sections. In spite of the migrations of the First World War and the twenties, 80 per cent of American Negroes lived south of the Mason and Dixon line in 1930. By 1950, on the other hand, almost 5,000,000 Negroes, or nearly one-third the total number, lived outside the South.

198 / *The American People, 1930–1953: Income, Wealth, and Industry*

The years from the onset of the Great Depression to the inauguration of Eisenhower were a time of retrogression and despair, followed by such growth in industry, wealth, and incomes as the American people had not hitherto experienced, even during the boom times of the 1920's. As we have earlier related the impact of the depression, the beginnings of recovery under the New Deal, and the revitalization of the economy by the huge federal outlays between 1940 and 1945, a few generalizations will suffice to remind us of the general trends from 1933 through 1945. Briefly stated,

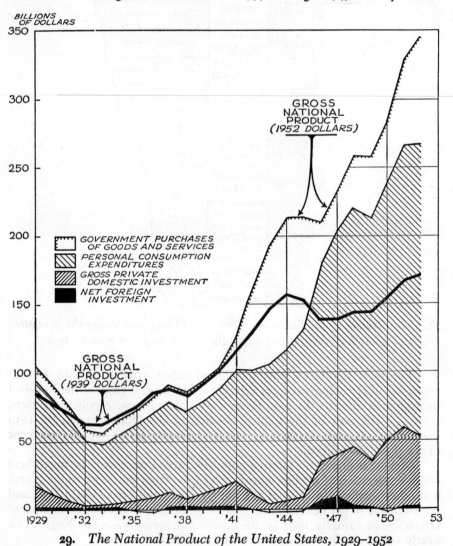

29. *The National Product of the United States, 1929–1952*

recovery from the depression was already fairly complete before the great defense spending of 1941 opened a new era in American economic history. The gross national product, measured in constant 1953 dollars, declined from $175,900,000,000 in 1929 to $123,400,000,000 in 1933 and then gradually increased to $205,700,000,000 in 1940. At the same time, per capita disposable income,[4] measured in 1953 dollars, declined from $1,059 in 1929 to $728 in 1933 but recovered steadily to $1,130 by 1940.

Actually, the recovery of the late thirties was only the prelude to a startling upswing during the war years 1941–1945. In 1945 the gross national

[4] That is, income left after taxes and Social Security payments.

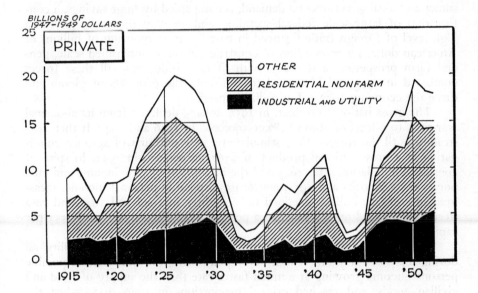

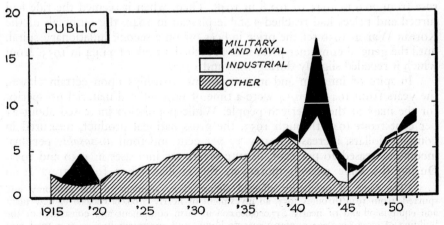

30. *Private and Public Construction in the United States, 1915–1952*

product, in 1953 dollars, aggregated nearly $320,000,000,000; disposable personal income, measured by the same standard, stood at $1,508; unemployment was at an almost irreducible minimum; and individuals and corporations had accumulated savings of $48,500,000,000 and state and local governments surpluses totaling more than $10,000,000,000.

Even so, as the war drew to a close in 1945, economists and public leaders were obsessed by the fear of economic storms ahead when private industry converted from war to civilian production. Rarely had learned predictions been so far from the mark, for in the mid-summer of 1945 the nation stood on the verge, not of a postwar depression, but of an era of unprecedented economic expansion and lasting achievement. Pent-up consumer and local governmental demand, accompanied by huge savings, a continuation of large-scale federal spending and an easy monetary policy, a high level of foreign trade financed in part by an outpouring of billions of American dollars, a resumption of construction on an intensified scale, general farm prosperity, and the growth of new industries—all these forces combined in 1945 and afterward to confound the prophets of gloom and drive the economy forward at a dizzy speed.

The gross national product, in 1953 dollars, declined from its abnormal war peak to a level of about $283,000,000,000 in 1946 and 1947. It then rose steadily until the Korean War stimulated a new outburst of activity culminating in a gross national product of $367,000,000,000 in 1953. In spite of considerable inflation after 1945 and the imposition of new income and corporate taxes in 1950 and 1951, aggregate disposable personal income, measured in constant dollars, declined only slightly in 1946 and 1947 and rose steadily afterward until it reached a peak of $248,000,000,000, or $1,553 per capita, in 1953.[5]

To be sure, inflation was a constant threat to economic stability all during the postwar years. It first developed during the war, with disposable personal income growing at a much faster rate than the supply of food and civilian goods, and reached critical proportions in 1946–1947, when the federal price control program collapsed and a series of strikes pushed prices inexorably higher. The general consumer price index (1947–1949 = 100) rose from 76.9 in 1945 to 102.8 in 1948. Then, when it seemed the tide had turned and prices had reached a stable plateau in 1949, the outbreak of the Korean War in 1950 set the price indices off on a second inflationary spiral. until the general consumer price index reached a peak of 114.4 in 1953, from which it receded slightly during 1954 and 1955.

In spite of inflation and its consequent hardships upon certain classes, the years from 1945 to 1954 were a time of unparalleled material prosperity for the mass of the American people. While population increased about 21 per cent from 1946 through 1953, the gross national product, measured in constant dollars, increased nearly 37 per cent and total *disposable* personal income increased 20 per cent, despite severe tax increases in 1950 and 1951. During the same period, moreover, the civilian labor force grew from

[5] The tonic of prosperity affected almost every segment of the economy and spurred, from 1946 through 1953, an investment of nearly $200,000,000,000 in new plant and equipment and of nearly $37,000,000,000 in farm equipment and construction; the building of over 8,000,000 nonfarm private homes and apartment houses, at a total cost of nearly $75,000,000,000; and the building of thousands of schools, hospitals, and other public nonmilitary facilities, at a total cost of nearly $48,000,000,000.

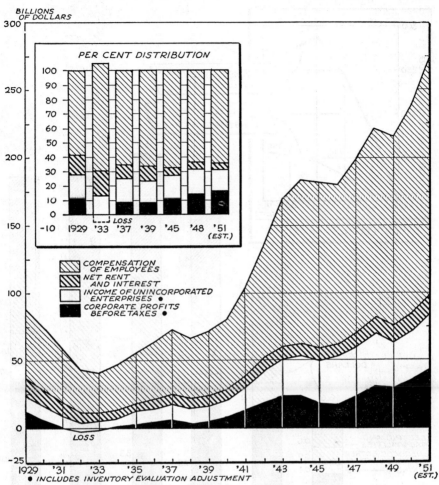

31. *The National Income of the United States, 1929–1951*

55,251,000 to nearly 62,000,000 persons, and the number of business firms increased from 3,487,000 to nearly 4,250,000.

Being general, the foregoing generalizations fail to indicate the relative status of the important groups in the economy and the significant shifts in income distribution that occurred after 1940. As we have seen in an earlier chapter, farmers experienced incredible prosperity during the war years 1940–1945, when net farm income, measured in 1935–1939 dollars, almost doubled from $4,386,000,000 to $8,358,000,000. Measured in these same dollars, net farm income increased slightly in 1946 and 1947 but in 1948 began a downward plunge that apparently had not ended by 1953, when it aggregated $5,730,000,000.[6]

[6] It is true that the number of farms declined slightly after 1945 and that the farm population declined from 26,147,000 in 1947 to 23,276,000 in 1951; but the decline was not severe enough to compensate for the more rapid decline in real farm income. Measured in constant dollars, net income per farm declined from a high of $1,495 in 1947 to $1,040 in 1953.

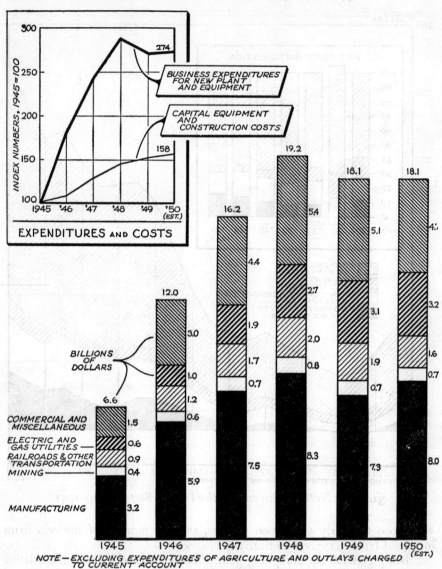

32. Postwar Expansion in the United States: Expenditures for New Plant and Equipment, 1945–1950

In other words, the real income of farmers decreased one-third after 1947 while the real income of most other Americans was on the rise. The chief cause of agrarian distress after 1947, however, was not declining prices, for aggressive federal price supports for major staples and dairy products kept gross farm income either above or at the parity level. The chief cause was the rising costs of equipment, machinery, labor, and taxes, which reduced the farmer's net share of his gross income from 49 per cent in 1946 to 35.6 per cent in 1953.

In contrast to the plight of the farmers was the steady improvement, in spite of inflation and higher taxes, of the economic status of most workers in industry, mining, construction, transportation, and other fields. This was true, basically, because from 1940 to 1953 employment and income expanded faster than the population and the increase in prices and taxes. For example, the net spendable real income of the average industrial worker with three dependents increased some 40 per cent from 1939 through 1951, as compared with a rise in real labor income of 26 per cent during the prosperous decade 1919–1929.

The period 1939–1953 was also a time of dynamic change in the pattern of industrial production. The following table illustrates the major changes in that pattern from 1939 to 1951:

THE TEN LEADING AMERICAN INDUSTRIES, 1939 AND 1951

	1939			*1951*	
Rank	Industry	Value Added by Manufacturing (in millions of dollars)	Rank	Industry	Value Added by Manufacturing (in millions of dollars)
1.	Food and kindred products	$3,485	1.	Machinery, except electrical	$11,219
2.	Primary metal industries	2,169	2.	Food and kindred products	10,579
3.	Machinery, except electrical	2,037	3.	Transportation equipment, including automobiles	9,789
4.	Chemicals and allied products	1,819	4.	Primary metal industries	9,769
5.	Textile mill products	1,818	5.	Chemicals and allied products	8,165
6.	Printing and publishing	1,765	6.	Fabricated metal products	7,139
7.	Transportation equipment, including automobiles	1,773	7.	Electrical machinery	5,753
8.	Fabricated metal products	1,401	8.	Textile mill products	5,421
9.	Apparel	1,386	9.	Printing and publishing	5,289
10.	Electrical machinery	941	10.	Apparel	4,699

These statistics of dollar value added by manufacture convey a crude sense of the fundamental shifts in industrial production, but they obscure the dynamic growth of certain segments of the industrial economy, which we will examine in a later section. They also fail to indicate one of the most important developments in recent American history—the startling growth of industry in the South after 1939, which transformed that region in a

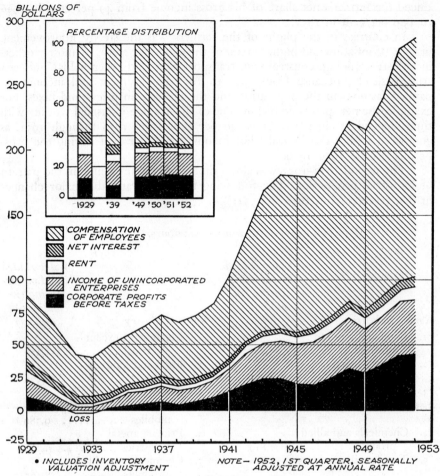

33. *The Distribution of the National Income, 1929–1952*

dozen different ways. In 1939 all the southern states combined accounted for about 12 per cent of the value added by manufacturing in the United States; by 1951 the southern share had risen to 18 per cent of the total.

What was the economic condition of the American people in 1953, at the end of thirteen years of almost uninterrupted expansion and prosperity? The answer one gives depends in large measure upon the economic goals he sets for a democratic society. The goal of most Americans is an expanding economy that affords a rising standard of living for the masses without destroying the incentives to unusual talent and industry. The best, certainly the most elemental, measurement of progress toward this goal is the distribution of the national income among the major groups of income receivers. In the period after 1939 the seemingly inexorable tide of concentration of incomes in fewer and fewer hands was at last reversed, and the nation made greater progress toward the democratic economic goal than during any earlier comparable period at least since the Civil War. The following tables best illustrate the generalization:

PERCENTAGE OF MONEY INCOME, BEFORE AND AFTER TAXES, RECEIVED BY EACH
FIFTH OF THE NATION'S FAMILIES, RANKED BY SIZE OF INCOME, 1941 AND 1947

| | Per cent of total money income | | | |
| | Before tax | | After tax | |
Family units ranked by income	1941	1947	1941	1947
Lowest fifth	3.5	4.0	3.7	4.3
Second fifth	9.1	9.8	9.5	10.4
Third fifth	15.3	15.4	15.9	16.2
Fourth fifth	22.5	22.6	23.2	22.8
Highest fifth	49.6	48.2	47.7	46.3

PERCENTAGE DISTRIBUTION OF FAMILIES BY MONEY INCOME LEVEL, 1941 AND 1947

| | Per cent of all family units | | | |
| | 1941 | | 1947 | |
Money income classes	Before tax	After tax	Before tax	After tax
Under $500	14	14	4	4
$500–$1,000	17	17	8	9
$1,000–$1,500	15	16	} 17	18
$1,500–$2,000	15	15		
$2,000–$3,000	21	22	17	19
$3,000–$4,000	9	9	17	17
$4,000–$5,000	4	3	12	12
$5,000–$7,500	} 5	4	15	13
$7,500–$10,000			5	4
$10,000 and over			5	4

PERCENTAGE OF DISPOSABLE INDIVIDUAL INCOME RECEIVED BY—

Year	Top 1 per cent	Top 5 per cent
1919	12.2	24.3
1929	18.9	33.5
1940	11.5	25.7
1945	7.4	16.8
1946	7.8	17.9

To be sure, Americans had not achieved the millennium by 1953 nor even yet begun to reach the limits of economic fulfillment. Poverty still existed. In 1951 over 17 per cent of all American families and 39 per cent of the Negro families received less than $1,500 annual income;[7] millions of old persons suffered heavily during the inflation; and there still remained

---

[7] It should be pointed out, however, that of all major groups in the United States Negroes made the greatest relative economic progress after 1940. From 1940 to 1950 the number of Negro farm owners increased 20 per cent, the number of Negro farm laborers decreased 15 per cent, the number of Negroes in domestic service severely declined, and the number of Negroes employed in industry, government, and trade increased at a spectacular rate.

some 1,300,000 families on marginal and eroded farms, with annual cash incomes less than $1,000. The fact remains, however, that by 1953 the majority of Americans were no longer living in poverty or near subsistence. Here was surely one of the most significant economic and social revolutions of modern times.

199 / *The Further Technological Revolution*

In large measure responsible for the economic progress of the United States since the Great Depression was a further revolution in technology that increased the productivity of labor in mines and factories and on the farms, emancipated the housewife from numerous drudgeries, destroyed unskilled labor's ancient slavery to the pick and shovel, and culminated in the development of new industries and inventions that made Jules Verne look like a good prophet of the shape of things to come. In an earlier chapter we have discussed the principal factors in the first technological revolution of the period 1900–1930—the increasing horsepower per worker, application of the principles of scientific management to industrial and business operations, the assembly line technique of mass production, the use of interchangeable parts, and research and development of new inventions and techniques. These were also the chief components of the further technological revolution after 1930; the chief differences between the two phases were differences in degree and speed.

If the true measure of the technological revolution is horsepower, then the extent of the revolution after 1930 was startling indeed. Total energy produced from mineral fuels and water power doubled from 1933 to 1951; the production of electric power alone increased nearly 500 per cent, while the increase of horsepower in automobiles, airplane engines, farm and industrial tractors, diesel locomotives, and a thousand gadgets was incalculable but enormous.

There was, besides, the spread of scientific management to practically every business and industry and, more important, the wider application of the assembly line method of mass production. The further use of the assembly line and interchangeable parts proceeded slowly during the depression years and then came to full flowering during the defense and war crises from 1940 to 1945, especially in the shipbuilding and airplane industries. Moreover, the introduction of electronic measuring devices enabled automatic machine tools to produce engines of almost perfect quality and practically eliminated the need for hand tooling.

Another significant factor in the technological revolution after 1940 was a rapid acceleration in research devoted to industrial and military needs. From its first important beginnings during the First World War, industrial research developed slowly in the twenties and expanded rapidly even during the depression years. But this was merely the beginning of what would soon become perhaps the most important American enterprise. With the organization of the National Defense Research Committee in 1940 and the Office of Scientific Research and Development in 1941, the federal government entered the field in a decisive way. From 1941 to 1945 the number of professional scientists employed in research grew from 87,000 to 119,000 and expenditures from $900,000,000 to $1,520,000,000. Once the war ended, however, both private and public research continued to expand. By 1953, 192,000 scientists—about one-fourth of all scientists and engineers in the country—were engaged in research projects, expenditures for which aggregated some $4,000,000,000.

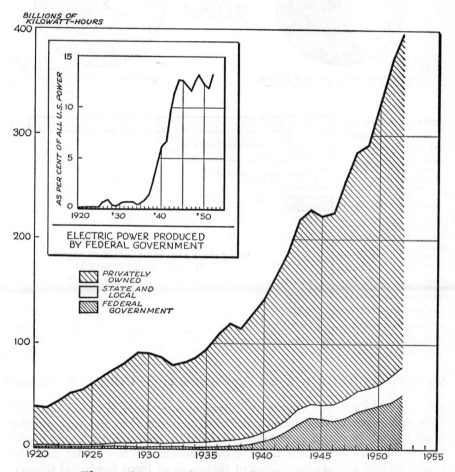

34. *Electric Power Production in the United States, 1920–1952*

The far-reaching and pervasive impact of the technological revolution after 1930 is at once obvious and impossible to measure fully. We can, however, partially measure one of its most important results, the increase in the productivity of labor in several fields. During the 1930's productivity in industry increased about 20 per cent. We have no general estimate for the gain in productivity in manufacturing for the period after 1939, but a crude idea of the increase can be gained by pointing out that between 1939 and 1953 the volume of industrial production increased some 130 per cent, while the number of workers increased only 45 per cent. The most spectacular,

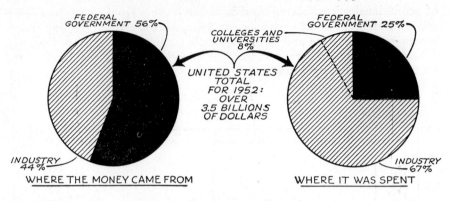

WHERE THE MONEY CAME FROM   WHERE IT WAS SPENT

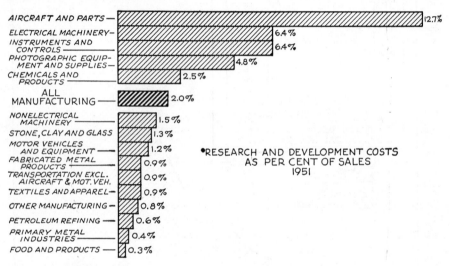

35. *Spending for Research and Development in the United States in 1952*

although not the largest, increase occurred in agriculture. Between 1929 and 1935 output per worker actually declined; between 1939 and 1949, on the other hand, it increased 34 per cent, as the horse and mule gave way to the tractor and new inventions like the corn picker, the hay loader, and the cotton picker[8] displaced hundreds of thousands of hired hands and tenants.

200 / *The Rise of New Industries*

In the 1920's the rise of the automobile, chemical, radio, aviation, and motion picture industries was beginning to cause a significant revolution in the American way of life. That revolution proceeded apace but unevenly in

---

[8] The manufacture of the cotton picker, which seems destined to revolutionize southern agriculture, did not begin commercially until 1949. By the autumn of 1952 about 11,500 cotton pickers were in use.

the depressed thirties; it came to full flowering in the postwar era, as mass production reached a level that would have been considered fantastic in the 1920's.

The Continued Pre-eminence of the Automobile. The automobile continued to enjoy its pre-eminence as the chief single dynamic factor in the American economy. Production of passenger cars and trucks declined from the prosperity peak figure of 5,358,000 in 1929 to 1,371,000 in 1932; returned to a prosperity level of nearly 5,000,000 in 1937; and then ceased almost altogether during the war years. Pent-up consumer demand in the postwar era, on the other hand, stimulated unprecedented production which culminated in the manufacture in 1950 of 8,003,000 cars and trucks.

From 1930 to 1951 the number of automobiles and trucks on the highways increased from 26,532,000 to 51,292,000. And with this increase went the steady growth of the petroleum industry, filling stations, and garages; the expenditure of billions of dollars for the construction and maintenance of highways—nearly $4,000,000,000 in 1951 alone; and a vast expansion of tourist courts and motels to serve the millions of Americans who took annually to the roads.[9] It is not too much to say that the economy would have collapsed if by some magic the automobile had been removed from the American scene.

The Age of Chemicals. Although the automobile clung tenaciously to its title to leadership in the American economy, the most significant development of the late thirties and the postwar era was the growth of the chemical industry and its sudden spawning of countless new and related industries. Indeed, by 1950 the chemical industry in all its aspects was "the premier industry" of the United States, a "great, yeasty force at the center of the economy," which produced at least one-fifth the total national industrial product.

It was born for the most part during the First World War, when the United States was cut off from German supplies and domestic manufacturers and the federal government first turned on a large scale to the production of organic chemicals, dyes, and nitrogen. With tariff protection, domestic manufacturers secured their independence in the twenties and were turning out a product valued at $3,232,556,000 by 1929. After a slight decline during the depression, production began to climb again in 1936 and rose steadily afterward. By 1939 the chemical industry turned out a total product valued at nearly $4,000,000,000.

Before 1940 the American chemical industry concentrated almost exclusively upon old-line products—rayon and organic chemicals for industrial, farm, and medicinal uses. However, the manufacture of nylon, a synthetic yarn derived chemically from coal, air, and water, by Du Pont in December 1939 was the harbinger of the new chemical age that lay beyond the horizon. By 1951 the basic chemical industry—and the following sta-

---

[9] A few statistics will illustrate the economic significance of the industries that serve the automobile owner. In 1951 the manufacturers of tires and tubes employed 92,244 workers, who added $753,633,000 in value by manufacture. In 1948 there were 95,544 garages and service shops that employed 117,252 workers; 118,253 service stations that employed 285,954 persons and sold products valued at $6,483,301,000; and 25,919 tourist camps and motels.

tistics give an incomplete picture, because they account only for the production of basic raw materials—employed 703,000 workers and added $8,164,-512,000 in value to products by manufacture. It was an increase since 1939 of 140 per cent in workers employed, of 330 per cent in value added by manufacture, and of 170 per cent in actual volume of production. The most significant development in the field after 1939, however, was the sudden growth of a whole complex of new synthetic industries—plastics, synthetic rubber, synthetic fibers, detergents, drugs, insecticides, and so on—built upon chemical processes and production.

The Electrical Era. As we have seen, the fivefold increase in the manufacture of electric power from 1930 to 1951 was one of the prime forces spurring the progress of the further technological revolution. The most significant development in the field, however, was the consequent growth of two relatively new industries, appliances and electronics, which vitalized the American economy in the thirties and forties as the automobile industry had done in the twenties and together effected profound changes in the American way of life.

Still in its infancy in 1930, the electrical appliance industry concentrated on conventional items and was just beginning to venture into large-scale production of refrigerators and stoves. Progress during the thirties was slow, and even by 1939 the entire value of electrical appliances manufactured was only $145,700,000. Then, after the Japanese surrender, the appliance age suddenly materialized. Overnight, it seemed, a host of new products came on the market in an unending stream. There were air conditioners, electric blankets, dehumidifiers, electric and gas clothes dryers and automatic washing machines, home freezers, electric dishwashers and garbage disposal units, power lawn mowers, and a hundred other such gadgets.[10]

Even more startling was the sudden burgeoning of the electronics industry during and after the war. As the editors of *Fortune* observed in July 1951, "Electronics has in progress more revolutions of profound impact upon industrial society than any technology" and would "someday crowd the dynamically expanding chemical industry as premier industry in the second half of the century."

During the 1930's the electronics industry produced mainly radios, radio parts, and communications equipment, and its product value barely exceeded $500,000,000 in 1939. With revolutionary new discoveries during the war and immediately afterward, the industry came of age and by 1951 turned out a product valued at some $2,500,000,000. So numerous and baffling were the new inventions that we can only mention the most important of them: power rectifiers and electronic controls, gauges, selectors, and counters; micro-wave relay systems for the transmission of sound and television waves; electronic computers—the "mechanical brains"—which could perform elaborate tasks of computation and even correct their own mistakes; and the transitor, which was a simple substitute for the vacuum tube.

The prime mover in the electronics revolution was television, the per-

[10] By January 1953, for example, 1,253,000 homes had dishwashers and food waste units, 32,217,000 had electric washing machines, nearly 5,000,000 had home freezers, and nearly 3,000,000 had clothes dryers.

fection of which from 1945 to 1948 gave rise to the fastest growing major industry in the postwar era. Production of television sets increased from 7,000 in 1947 to 6,000,000 in 1952; and by January 1953 there were nearly 20,000,000 sets in use. At the same time there occurred a parallel growth of television stations from ten in 1946 to 108 in 1951 and of television revenues from $658,000 to $235,700,000.

New Metals and Fuels. The primary development in the metals field after 1940 was the rise of new or relatively new metals. The production of the most important of these, aluminum, swelled from 286,642 tons in 1940 to 1,129,489 in 1951. In addition, there was magnesium, another lightweight metal, production of which grew some twenty times between 1940 and 1953, and titanium, an entirely new metal in 1949, which seemed well on the way toward displacing lead in the manufacture of paint.

Two important changes in fuels from 1930 to 1950, the introduction of fuel oils and the widespread use of natural gas for home and business heating, stimulated the economy, changed living habits, and revived the construction and maintenance of pipe line systems. While residential consumption of coal declined from 265,000,000 tons in 1929 to 76,531,000 in 1951, the sales of fuel oil to home and business users increased from a value of $125,925,000 in 1939 to $732,119,000 in 1948 and the value of natural gas consumed by domestic, commercial, and industrial users increased from $415,519,000 in 1930 to $2,118,675,000 in 1951.

Satisfying the postwar demand for natural gas, moreover, gave rise to such an outburst of pipe line construction as the country had never seen before. In fact, so frenzied was the activity in this field that virtually a great new industry came rapidly into being after 1945. Total expenditures for pipe lines in 1950, for example, exceeded $1,000,000,000; and by the following year there were more than 300,000 miles of lines "big and small, snaking beneath U. S. soil."

The Aviation Transport Industry Comes of Age. Although it was firmly established in 1930, the American air transportation industry was still in a primitive and experimental stage of development. However, rapid technological change from 1930 to 1950 made possible man's nearly complete conquest of the air. The slow and inefficient Ford tri-motor aircraft gave way to the all-metal monoplaned Douglas DC-3 in the mid-thirties; then came the production of the huge Boeing flying boat on the eve of the war and, in the postwar era, a number of sleek new four-engined airliners— among them, the Douglas DC-4, DC-6, and DC-7, the Boeing Stratocruiser, and the graceful Lockheed Constellation and Super Constellation—carrying up to 100 passengers. Concurrent developments in electronics, moreover, enabled pilots to fly as easily at night as in daytime and to land safely even when the ceiling was zero.

Expansion in air transportation service occurred in direct ratio to technological change. In 1934, when twenty-four American air lines flew 572,265 passengers over some 51,000 miles of route, air travel was still a novelty and, to most people, a hazardous adventure. By 1952 air travel at home and overseas was not only commonplace but also a real threat to the railroads and shipping lines. Thirty-five scheduled air carriers flew routes at home and abroad totaling 188,442 miles; carried 27,377,551 passengers and a quarter billion ton-miles of freight; employed 95,753 persons; and collected over a quarter billion dollars in revenues.

201 / Concentration and Competition in the American Economy

It would little profit a democratic society if economic growth were accompanied by inexorable concentration of wealth and ownership of the means of production in the hands of an irresponsible few. Was the inevitable tendency of capitalism toward monopoly, restricted production at high prices, and the aggrandizement of economic and political power by the few? In brief, from 1930 to 1950 the seemingly inevitable movement toward concentration was either halted or else reversed for the first time since the 1870's. This is a broad generalization and an important one, but the general and specific data support it. Thus, the proportion of the total corporate assets owned by the 139 largest manufacturing concerns fell from 50 per cent in 1931 to 45 per cent in 1947. In addition, the data regarding the share of production in specific industries controlled by the largest producers from 1935 to 1947 reveals, if anything, that the small producers gained at the expense of the largest corporations.[11]

We can gain additional support for our generalization by pointing to the significant slowing down of the movement toward concentration of control in American industry that took place after 1929. The far-reaching merger movement of the twenties practically ceased in the thirties. During and after the war the concentration movement gained some momentum but did not reach significant proportions.[12]

What shall we say about the nature of the American economy at mid-century? Were the forces of monopoly stronger than the forces of competition? Large segments of the economy—agriculture, mining, construction, trade, finance, and services—remained competitive, and sometimes fiercely so, in 1950. Government, transportation, communications, and utilities were inherently monopolistic. Manufacturing, however, was more complicated and more difficult to describe. In 1947, the 113 corporations with assets each in excess of $100,000,000 owned 46 per cent of all manufacturing plant, property, and equipment and 40 per cent of the total manufacturing assets

---

[11] A few examples must suffice to illustrate this point. In 1935 the Aluminum Company of America produced all primary aluminum; in 1947 it produced 57.8 per cent of the output. The three largest automobile companies produced 86 per cent of the automobiles in 1935 and 78 per cent in 1948. It should be added, however, that in many important branches of industry there was no appreciable change in the share of the large producers from 1935 to 1947.

[12] Between 1940 and 1947 more than 2,450 independent manufacturing and mining companies, with aggregate assets of $5,200,000,000, disappeared through mergers. The important point is, however, that big business grew mainly through normal expansion and only very slightly through the acquisition of competitors. From 1940 to 1947 the super-corporations, that is, corporations with assets of more than $100,000,000 each, increased their assets 6 per cent by mergers and yet doubled in wealth during this period.

in the United States. Many important industries—like automobiles, aluminum, tires, meat products, cigarettes, liquors, and copper smelting and refining—were dominated by three or four large producers.[13] Thus on the surface oligopoly—that is, control by the few—seemingly prevailed in most important branches of manufacturing.

However, there is grave danger in arriving at *a priori* conclusions from obvious facts. For one thing, the forty-nine industries in each of which four companies sold 75 per cent or more of the total product together accounted for only 8 per cent of the manufacturing output. In the second place, the dominance of an industry by four or eight large concerns did not necessarily signify the absence of competition, as an examination of the development of the automobile, steel, agricultural implements, oil, and other industries would reveal.

Indeed, there seems little reason to doubt the conclusion of Richard B. Heflebower, one of the wisest students of this problem: "Competition outweighs monopoly by a wide margin in the American economy today." At mid-century historic price competition remained a powerful force in distribution and in many branches of industry characterized by a large number of producers. So-called oligopolistic growth since 1900 had usually meant the growth of large rivals at the relative expense of corporations once totally dominant in their respective fields. And often the decline of price competition had been offset by the rise of competition in quality and design of products and in advertising. Moreover, the rise of powerful combinations of retailers, themselves not monopolies, had operated to restore competition not only among retailers but as well among the so-called manufacturing oligopolies. By manufacturing, or threatening to manufacture, products themselves, combinations like Sears Roebuck, Montgomery Ward, A & P, and numerous other chains had restored vigorous competition in most consumers' goods. As one economist has put it, "The formula for competition is simple: add one part of Sears Roebuck to twenty parts of oligopoly." Finally, technological change in American industry had been too rapid and far-reaching since 1930 to permit would-be monopolists to stand still and attempt to exercise an imperial sway.

Nor should we ignore the role the federal government played after 1929 in the development of an expansive and essentially competitive economy. From 1929 to 1952 the federal government metamorphosed into incomparably the most powerful economic force in the nation. It took control of the money supply and interest rates out of the hands of private bankers; emerged as the single greatest spender, with far-reaching control over contracts and prices; entered the capital markets through the RFC, the Export-Import Bank, and a hundred other agencies; broke the aluminum monopoly and destroyed the utility holding company empires; assumed a large share of the responsibility for industrial research; entered the fields of production in electricity, synthetic rubber, and atomic energy; and encouraged business

---

[13] In 1947 there were forty-nine industries in which four large firms produced 75 per cent of the output. The steel industry was dominated by eight large producers; eight manufacturers owned 55.2 per cent of the assets of the electrical machinery industry; three manufacturers sold 67.2 per cent of the agricultural implements.

enterprise through programs of subsidization, chiefly by allowing depreciation for tax purposes.

In addition, after the end of the ill-fated NRA experiment, the Washington government began the most concerted and successful antitrust campaign since the heyday of the crusade under Theodore Roosevelt and Taft.[14] Along with an expansion in the work of the Antitrust Division of the Justice Department and the Federal Trade Commission went a virtual revolution in judicial opinion concerning restraint of trade that finally gave the federal government power to destroy, not only monopoly, but oligopoly as well. In a series of decisions from 1911 to 1927 the Supreme Court had laid down the rule that a corporation was not illegal under the Sherman law merely because it was large. This doctrine prevailed until 1945, when Justice Learned Hand of the Court of Appeals delivered a verdict in United States *v.* Aluminum Company of America.[15] The government had asked for Alcoa's dissolution on the grounds that the company was a monopoly, *ipso facto,* because it controlled 90 per cent of the production of bar aluminum and had used illegal methods to maintain its predominance. Affirming the allegations of past unfair trade practices, Hand declared that Alcoa was a monopoly because its control of the market was so large as to give it the benefits of a monopoly.

An even more significant decision was the one rendered by the Supreme Court in American Tobacco Company *v.* United States in 1946. In 1940 the Antitrust Division had instituted criminal proceedings against the American Tobacco, R. J. Reynolds, and Liggett and Myers tobacco companies, alleging that the big three had conspired to control the price of leaf tobacco and cigarettes. In the subsequent court hearings the government was able to prove that the companies had paid and charged identical prices for the two products, but it failed to prove that the defendants had conspired to maintain common prices. Brushing aside the companies' pleas that they had never conspired to set prices, the Court sustained the conviction of the District Court. The crime of monopoly, the Supreme Court declared in its epochal decision, consisted as much in the possession of power to suppress competition and raise prices as in the commission of illegal acts. Moreover, the Court added, the government did not have to prove the existence of collusion to set prices if such collusion could be reasonably inferred from market conditions.

In the Tobacco decision the government finally won the power for which it had been struggling at least since Taft's administration—the power to strike at oligopolies as well as monopolies. It did not follow that the government desired or intended to force the atomization of the American industrial structure. What was important was the fact that the government now possessed effective recourse against the most common oligopolistic practice in the American economy, collusion to eliminate price competition.

The government scored another legal triumph in the immediate postwar era in the successful culmination of its long battle against the basing-point

[14] See above, p. 422.
[15] The Supreme Court had failed to obtain a quorum to hear the case and allowed Justice Hand to render the decision.

system of pricing.[16] In a series of decisions from 1945 to 1948, but most notably in decisions in 1948 involving the steel and cement industries, the Supreme Court dealt a deathblow to this instrument for the elimination of price competition. Finally, in 1950 Congress also took a hand by plugging an old loophole in the Clayton Act and prohibiting the purchase of the assets of one corporation by another, when such purchase would tend to lessen competition or lead to monopoly.

202 / *Organized Labor in the Postwar Era*

The years from 1945 to 1953 were a time of tumult but also of growth in numbers and strength for organized labor in the United States. From 1945 through 1952 union membership increased from a total of 14,621,000 to about 17,000,000; and by the latter date unions had enrolled about 57 per cent of all workers susceptible of organization and were firmly established in all major fields of manufacturing, mining, transportation, and construction.

These statistics buttress the conclusion that organized labor finally won security and equality of bargaining power with management in the postwar era. Indeed, by 1953 there were numerous signs that both labor and management had passed beyond the stage of industrial warfare into a new era of cooperation and mutual accommodation. But conflict on an unprecedented scale in the industrial and political arenas preceded the coming of peace.

The war's end found the leaders of organized labor resentful against a stabilization program that they thought had deprived workers of deserved wage increases; fearful of inflation, large-scale unemployment, and depression in the reconversion period; and yet determined not only to hold but also to enlarge the gains labor had made since 1940. The inevitability of industrial strife was demonstrated by the failure of the National Labor-Management Conference, which met in Washington at the President's request from November 5 through 30, 1945, to formulate a program for averting strikes.

The fundamental issue in the autumn of 1945, however, was substantive, not procedural: could management grant wage increases large enough to guarantee workers the same "take home" pay after a return to the normal forty-hour week, without necessitating price increases? When the Office of War Mobilization and the President agreed in October that industry could grant a general 24 per cent wage increase without endangering either profits or the price control program, the stage was set for the opening of the first and decisive round.

The wave of strikes began soon after the Japanese surrender, but the crucial stage came from November 1945 to January 1946, when 180,000 auto workers in the General Motors plants, some 200,000 electrical workers, and 750,000 steel workers struck for a 30 per cent wage increase. In contrast to the riotous strikes of the mid-thirties, these postwar strikes were mild

[16] This was the system of adding freight charges from a certain base point to the point where the sale was made, regardless of where the product was manufactured. A good example was the "Pittsburgh-plus" system used in determining the price of steel products. Buyers of steel in Chicago had to pay freight charges on steel from Pittsburgh to Chicago, even though the steel involved was actually produced in Gary, Indiana, only a few miles away.

affairs because management and labor eschewed violence and appealed to the public for support. The young leader of the auto workers, Walter P. Reuther, for example, declared that his union would ask no more than General Motors could afford to give and demanded that the corporation open its books to public scrutiny. When presidential fact-finding boards recommended wage increases of 19½ cents an hour, General Motors and leaders in the steel and electrical machinery industries compromised on an increase of 18½ cents an hour, thereby setting the pattern of wage increases for most of American industry.

In the late winter of 1946 an uneasy peace settled over the industrial front, as new and more violent eruptions impended in the coal and railroad industries. Determined not to be outdone by his rivals, John L. Lewis, president of the United Mine Workers, was demanding not only the 18½ cent hourly increase but also a number of other so-called "fringe" benefits, to be met by payment of a certain royalty on coal tonnage by the operators. When the operators refused, miners throughout the country walked out of the pits on April 1, 1946, and the government seized the mines soon afterward.

During the subsequent negotiations Lewis won most of his demands and signed a contract with Secretary of the Interior Julius A. Krug on May 29, 1946. In the following October, however, Lewis demanded an increase in wages and welfare benefits and threatened to call a second strike if the government did not surrender by November 20. When negotiations failed to bring agreement, the government, on November 18, 1946, obtained a temporary restraining injunction from Judge Alan T. Goldsborough of the District Court in the District of Columbia. When Lewis defied the injunction, Goldsborough fined him and the UMW $10,000 and $3,500,000, respectively, for contempt on December 4. Lewis then ordered the miners back to work pending the reversal of Goldsborough's decision that he confidently expected. In March 1947 the Supreme Court reduced the $3,500,000 fine to $700,000, provided the union purge itself of contempt, but upheld the conviction. Lewis then withdrew the strike order; but when the mines were returned to their owners in the following June, he won a new contract that conceded all his demands.

Meanwhile, the country had been rocked by a nation-wide railroad strike and events that followed in its wake. When the failure of protracted brotherhood-management negotiations over wages and working rules led the Engineers and Trainmen to call a strike, the President seized the railroads on May 17, 1946, and offered a compromise settlement that eighteen unions accepted. The Engineers and Trainmen, however, would not yield and walked out on May 23. Now for the first time in its history was the nation threatened by almost total paralysis. After the strikers had ignored his appeal to return to work, on May 25 the President asked Congress for drastic, almost dictatorial, power to save the country.[17] Actually, the leaders of the

[17] Specifically, Truman requested Congress to empower him to declare a state of national emergency whenever a strike imperiling the national safety occurred in a vital industry under federal control. Workers who persisted thereafter in striking would lose all employment and seniority benefits and would be drafted into the army. Moreover, union leaders would be fined and imprisoned if they persisted in strike activities.

Engineers' and Trainmen's brotherhoods had given in three minutes before Truman appeared before the joint session. The House approved a measure embodying the President's demands, but the Senate refused to act once the danger had passed.

The autumn of 1946 witnessed a second squaring off between labor and management, induced in large measure by price increases that wiped out all of labor's gains during the preceding year. There were numerous small strikes but no major ones, because the big unions resorted more to persuasion and appeals to public opinion than to direct action. Negotiations in the major industries were protracted but not bitter; the break came in mid-April 1947, when the automobile and steel companies conceded a fifteen-cent hourly wage boost and set the pattern for the balance of industry.

The peaceful wage settlements of the spring of 1947 marked a decisive turning point in labor relations during the postwar era. There afterward occurred third, fourth, and fifth rounds of wage increases, but management evinced a willingness to increase wages so long as the increases could be passed on to consumers in the form of higher prices. The number of workers involved in strikes, which stood at an all-time high of 4,600,000 in 1946, declined to 2,170,000 in 1947 and to 1,960,000 in 1948. And with returning peace came a new spirit of mutual accommodation and epochal innovations in collective bargaining contracts.[18]

However, the increased inflation and economic activity that followed the outbreak of the Korean War in 1950 stimulated further wage demands, strikes in which 4,843,000 workers were involved, and the inevitable wage increases. Congress made a gesture toward economic stabilization by approving the Defense Production Act, which empowered the President to establish price and wage controls, in August 1950. But the President's authority was so circumscribed that the Economic Stabilization and Wage Stabilization boards that he established in January 1951 could do little more than oversee and approve price and wage increases.

The last great strike of the Democratic era occurred while the two major parties were in the midst of preparations for the national conventions of 1952 and ended in a significant testing of the presidential authority. After a breakdown in wage negotiations in the steel industry threatened to lead to a nation-wide strike, President Truman seized the steel plants on April 8,

---

[18] The two-year contract between General Motors and the UAW, concluded in 1948 and renewed for a five-year period in 1950, contained two of the most important innovations in collective bargaining in the postwar era. The General Motors contract provided, first, for an upward or downward revision of wage rates every three months according to a schedule based upon the consumers' price index and, second, for automatic annual wage increases ranging from 2 to 2½ per cent, in order to give workers the benefit of increases in productivity. By 1951 over 1,000,000 other workers shared the benefits of the so-called escalator clause and the annual improvement provision. Another major innovation in bargaining contracts was the widespread adoption of so-called welfare provisions. Although the musicians' union and the UMW won such provisions in 1944 and 1946, respectively, the important turning point in industry came in October 1949, when a brief strike by the steel workers won pensions and health insurance for workers in the steel industry in lieu of a wage increase. By 1950 more than 8,500,000 workers were covered by pension plans to supplement the Social Security system and perhaps as many enjoyed the benefits of medical and life insurance purchased by their employers.

1952, in order to prevent an interruption of the flow of steel to defense plants. The workers got a wage increase from the government, until the Supreme Court intervened on June 2 by ruling that the seizure was illegal in the absence of statutory authority. The President then withdrew and a strike ensued for fifty-four days, until both sides compromised their differences in an agreement signed at the White House on July 24, 1952.

Although organized labor attained unprecedented power and the status of an established institution during the postwar era, it also suffered heavy losses in popular support and adverse state and federal legislation.[19] For this anomalous development, management's campaign to enlarge employers' rights and restrict union prerogatives was only in small part responsible. The chief responsibility lay with the leaders of the labor movement. Their efforts to break the economic stabilization program during the war, their undemocratic procedures and refusal to accept responsibility for the fulfillment of contracts, and their failure to move decisively against "feather-bedding" and racketeering in the unions all contributed to the profound change in public sentiment that occurred after 1940. But the chief cause of the change was the growing popular conviction that big labor, irresponsible and uncontrolled, could pose as dire a menace to the general interest as could uncontrolled and irresponsible big business.

The Democrats nominally controlled the Seventy-Ninth Congress that sat during 1945 and 1946, but control of legislative policies lay with a coalition of conservative Democrats and Republicans determined to rectify the alleged unbalance established by the Wagner Act. Their first solution was the Case bill, approved by the House on February 7 and by the Senate on May 25, 1946, but successfully vetoed by the President on June 11.[20] On the other hand, in 1946 and 1947 Truman approved a series of bills to outlaw a number of allegedly unfair union practices—"feather-bedding," especially in the musicians' union; racketeering or interference with interstate commerce; and union demands for payment for past portal-to-portal work time.[21]

After the Republican sweep in the congressional elections of 1946 the conservative coalition in the Eightieth Congress moved quickly to accomplish a thoroughgoing revision of the Wagner Act. The Hartley bill, approved by the House on April 17, 1947, was sweeping, severe, and vindictive—an obvious effort to break the labor movement. Led by Robert A. Taft of Ohio, the anti-labor forces in the Senate were equally determined to reduce union power but were unable to win approval for their most ambitious objectives, notably the prohibition of industry-wide bargaining. The Taft-Hartley, or Labor-Management Relations, bill, approved by both houses in June 1947, therefore, represented a compromise between what

[19] In 1947, for example, more than thirty states enacted legislation prohibiting secondary boycotts, jurisdictional strikes, and sometimes strikes in vital industries.

[20] The Case bill provided for "cooling-off" periods before important strikes could occur, outlawed secondary boycotts and union interference with interstate commerce, and allowed employers to sue unions for breach of contract.

[21] The Portal-to-Portal Act of 1947 was adopted in response to the Supreme Court's ruling in the so-called Mt. Clemens Pottery case in June 1946. In this decision the Court ruled that workers were entitled to pay for time spent in preparing for their job as well as for time spent going to their jobs after they had reached the place of their employment. At once unions filed thousands of suits to recover back pay under the ruling.

the foes of organized labor wanted and labor's friends were willing to concede.[22]

Whether the Taft-Hartley Act was a wise attempt to restore balance to the field of industrial relations or whether, as President Truman declared in his unsuccessful veto message on June 20, 1947, it contained "seeds of discord which would plague this nation for years to come," we will not attempt to say. The power of the unions grew during the years following the measure's adoption, while management demonstrated even greater willingness after 1947 than before to accept unions and work with them in good faith.

In restrospect, we can see that organized labor not only grew in bargaining power in spite of the Taft-Hartley Act but also passed from awkward adolescence into at least the first stage of maturity after 1947. Symbolic of the change that occurred within the labor movement was the rise of what one sociologist has called the "new men of power"—a young and socially-minded union leadership better trained in law and labor economics than in the art of industrial warfare. The election of Walter P. Reuther as president of the CIO after the death of Philip Murray in 1952 was a notable victory for the progressive element in that union. Symbolic also of labor's maturing was the notable lessening of tension between unions and management, as union leaders adopted the objectives of "welfare capitalism" and made a determined and successful effort to purge their ranks of Communists and racketeers.[23]

203 / Americans and Their "Mixed" Economy at Mid-Century

What, then, was this American economy at mid-century? Was it capitalistic in the traditional sense? Was it a welfare economy fatally weakened by a "creeping socialism"? Confused by a welter of conflicting claims and charges, the ordinary American groped in darkness for understanding.

Much of the popular confusion stemmed from the effort to apply old economic and political theories to new economic and political conditions. In 1952 it was futile to attempt to describe the American economy in terms of conventional capitalism; only reactionary Americans and the Kremlin's

[22] It outlawed the closed shop and certain "unfair" union practices—refusal to bargain in good faith, secondary boycotts, jurisdictional strikes, exaction of pay for work not performed, and the like; permitted employers to sue unions for breach of contracts, to petition the NLRB for elections to determine the bargaining agents, and to speak out during organizational campaigns; and provided for "cooling-off" periods and use of the injunction by the President in strikes imperiling the national health or safety. The measure, moreover, required unions to register with and submit annual financial reports to the Secretary of Labor, prohibited union contributions to political parties, and prohibited the certification of unions until their officers had filed affidavits that they were not Communists.

[23] The AF of L had never tolerated Communist infiltration. The CIO, which had allowed such infiltration in the late thirties and during the war, finally expelled the electrical workers' union, the farm equipment workers' union, and nine other Communist-dominated unions in 1949 and 1950 and set about to organize new CIO unions in the industries involved.

propagandists would make such an effort. It was equally futile to attempt to impose a socialistic pattern upon an economic system as complex and dynamic as the American.

By the end of the Democratic era the American economy was neither capitalistic nor socialistic, competitive nor monopolistic, business controlled nor laboristic. It was a "mixed" economy, a combination of many elements. Manufacturers, bankers, and businessmen still retained control over a large share of the important economic decisions. Yet their control was restrained or shared by other important groups—the federal and state governments, labor unions, farm groups, and organized consumers. The American economy was indubitably a "free" economy, yet political agencies and not the market determined the price of agricultural commodities; manufacturers were not "free" to ride roughshod over workers or determine wage and hours policies. The United States was not a "welfare state" in the European sense, yet the federal and state governments sponsored far-reaching programs of social security and assistance to the poor.

In retrospect, we can see that the institutional reforms of the New Deal and underlying forces at work since 1933 transformed a monolithic economic society dominated by the business-financial elements into a virtually new economic society of great countervailing forces, as one economist has called them—industry, business, banking, finance, organized labor, and agriculture—each of them struggling for a larger share of the national income, each appealing to the political power.

Americans in the middle of the twentieth century might not understand the subtleties of their contemporary economic order, but the great majority would agree that it was a far better economic society than the monolithic order of 1929. In other words, the vast majority of Americans, regardless of political faith, liked their "mixed" economy and desired government to continue to assume responsibility for making it work.

CHAPTER 26 / SOCIAL AND CULTURAL TRENDS, 1933–1953

*F*ROM 1933 to 1953 the American people ran almost the whole gamut of human experience, from depression and despair to prosperity and hope, from peace to war and back to dubious peace and uncertain war again. It is of course impossible to encompass the total American social and cultural experience during these two turbulent decades within the confines of a single chapter, but we can gain some insight into the meaning and significance of the changes that occurred by looking at specific manifestations of social and cultural development, for in every case the microcosm reflected the whole.

204 / Social Trends from Depression to Prosperity

The most sweeping and important changes in the American social scene were stimulated in the first instance by the demographic and economic revolutions of the Democratic era from 1933 to 1953. The decline of the agricultural and rural populations, which we noted in the preceding chapter, was not as rapid as the destruction of the rural way of life of long hours, backbreaking toil, and primitive living conditions by science and technology. Even more important was the complete triumph of the city over the country and small town in customs, manners, and habits of thought.

From 1933 to 1953 the growth of the large cities was dwarfed by the development, especially in the postwar era, of the small cities and suburban areas. From 1940 to 1950 the central cities of the metropolitan districts grew by only 13.9 per cent while the outlying suburbs grew by 35.5 per cent. Everywhere along the fringes of cities there grew large planned communities of small single-family homes with their own shopping centers, and former city dwellers not only found a new way of life in suburbia but also became increasingly conservative as property owners and members of integrated communities.

The effect of prosperity was greatly to enlarge the middle classes at the same time that high taxes reduced the wealthy to a relatively low estate. The result was to create a society in which the great mass of industrial workers and their leaders thought and acted as members of the middle class, not as an impoverished proletariat, and in which skilled workers often enjoyed higher incomes than most teachers and white collar workers.

What changes time wrought as this drive toward equality gained powerful momentum after 1939! By 1953 the effects were evident on all sides—in the gradual disappearance of city slums, blighting poverty, the old leisure class, and the servant class, and the relative decline of what was once called High Society.

The drive toward equality had its greatest impact in changing old American attitudes and practices toward large groups formerly outside the main stream of social life—southern and eastern Europeans, Jews, Negroes, and other minority groups. Only an ignorant optimist would claim that Americans had reached a state of social blessedness by mid-century. The significant fact, however, was that the American society had made greater progress toward the democratic ideal during the two decades 1933–1953 than during any comparable period at least since Reconstruction. By the postwar period practically all leaders in church, school, press, labor, law, and government had joined in a campaign to square American practices with professions. It was a crusade on many levels, but it operated most spectacularly in the troubled area of Negro-white relations.

To begin with, white Americans in all sections evinced greater willingness to integrate Negroes into the main stream of life. In addition, legal, political, and religious attacks tore huge holes in the walls of caste after 1933. By 1953 the federal government had obliterated discrimination in the federal service and was on the way toward destroying segregation in the armed services. Although all efforts to obtain a federal fair employment practices act had failed, ten non-southern states and many cities had outlawed discrimination in hiring and established commissions with powers of enforcement. The Supreme Court had joined the battle by opening the polls in the South to Negro voters, wiping out all vestiges of Jim Crowism in interstate travel, and outlawing restrictive covenants that forbade the sale of real estate to Negroes. Also in response to the Supreme Court's decree, Negro students were enrolled in twelve southern state universities and in four southern state colleges in the autumn of 1953; and fear that the Court would abolish segregation on the lower levels of education spurred the southern states to make desperate efforts in the postwar period to afford equal public school facilities for Negro children.[1]

Meanwhile, what happened to American customs, manners, and morals during the years of depression, war, and postwar fear and crisis? It is difficult to generalize about the social attitudes and behavior of millions of people, and yet there were significant changes. To begin with, there were numerous evidences that the American people, or at least the vocal minority directly involved, recovered the equilibrium they had lost in their search for new

[1] In an epochal decision on May 17, 1954, the Supreme Court declared that segregation on account of race in the public schools was a violation of the Fifth and Fourteenth Amendments. It is too early to say what the effects of this ruling will be, but the decision will probably mean the immediate abolition of segregation in public schools in the District of Columbia and in non-southern states; gradual elimination of segregation in the public schools of the Upper South; and considerable strain and tension in the Lower South.

moral standards in the 1920's. Even before the Great Depression struck, the revolt against the Christian moral code had largely spent its force. By the mid-thirties the revolt had almost completely fizzled and was being nurtured only by professional intellectuals and bohemians.

While most Americans learned to live with sex without losing their heads about it,[2] they also enlarged and made permanent the revolution in *mores* governing the family that had begun after the First World War. Discarding the Christian code governing family relationships, most middle class Americans in the 1920's adopted a new code that exalted happiness as the supreme objective of marriage, permitted divorce for often trivial reasons, and, above all, gave women and children equality with men in family relationships. The general acceptance of these concepts during the thirties and forties signified that they had become a cornerstone of American social life. The number of divorces per 100 marriages increased from nine in 1914 to an apparently stable level of around seventeen from 1936 through 1941. Then with the war came hasty marriages and a startling increase in the divorce rate, which culminated in a peak of nearly thirty-one divorces for every 100 marriages in 1945. The rate declined slightly afterward, but not greatly; and by 1950 nearly one-fourth as many people were breaking the marriage bonds as were getting married.

Defenders of the family often bewailed the prevalence of divorce without understanding the causes of the phenomenon—the weakening of religious sanctions against divorce, the widespread conviction that unhappy marriages were better dissolved than endured, the increased economic independence of women and, above all, the fact that public and private organizations had taken over many of the functions associated with the rearing of children.

The tempo of American life slowed markedly during the depression, as unemployment and lessened incomes forced millions of Americans to retrench and give attention to the elemental tasks of living. But with the defense and war crises the tempo of life accelerated in an incredible way. Millions of men and women, many of whom had never been outside their counties, were suddenly dispersed to remote corners of the globe. Millions of civilians left the shelter of communities in which they had been reared to work in war industries. Indeed, the wonder is that the social system withstood the shock so well, without major riots or upheavals.

Prosperity in the postwar era further accelerated the tempo of life and heightened certain tensions. The return of millions of veterans put an almost unbearable strain on housing facilities. But this was a momentary tension, for by 1952 the supply of new houses and apartments had largely relieved the strain. More significant was the way in which the tempo of American life increased during the postwar era as the result of the proliferation and integration of private activities. By 1951 there were at least 200,000 organizations of every conceivable kind and purpose in cities, towns, and

---

[2] Evidence that Americans had long since passed beyond the hysteria of the twenties came in full measure with the publication in 1948 and 1953 of Alfred C. Kinsey's *Sexual Behavior in the Human Male* and *Sexual Behavior in the Human Female*. Courageously and, he thought, scientifically, Kinsey made the first serious effort to determine the sexual patterns of the American people. If his findings were sensational, the public reaction was sober; and criticism was directed not at Kinsey's investigations but rather at his techniques.

countryside: labor unions, Parent-Teachers' Associations, church groups, Community Chests, organizations of farmers and businessmen, all of them institutionalizing and integrating voluntary activities. The philanthropic agencies alone mobilized 2,000,000 volunteers and raised $3,000,000,000 for good works in 1949.

Surveying the American scene in the middle of the twentieth century, Americans might well have been encouraged by the progress their generation had made toward the eradication of social and economic injustices and the lessening of racial tensions. Yet in the midst of plenty and apparent progress there was gloom and fear of the future.

A good measure of the prevailing pessimism at mid-century stemmed from the experiences of the adult generation and from profound changes in recent religious thought. The depression had left deep scars and bitter memories, and millions of older Americans in the postwar period lived in fear that prosperity could not last. The Second World War and revelations of Nazi and Communist cruelty ended fatuous dreams of automatic moral improvement, while the threat that a third world conflagration would bring mass if not total extermination hung like a pall over the minds of men in the postwar years.

It was enough to make even the most optimistic shudder, but it was not all. In the thirties the American democracy had survived the assaults of demagogues of the right and left and of purveyors of racial and religious prejudices; during the war Americans had found a kind of unity and domestic peace through mutual sacrifice. But in the postwar era old and new threats to democracy arose at home. A wave of corruption swept over the nation, engulfing leaders in private organizations and in government on every level. Stimulated by ambitious demagogues, fear of Communist infiltration seized millions of Americans and spurred a fierce attack on civil liberties and nonconformity unprecedented since the early 1920's. There were ugly recrudescences of hostility between Catholics and Protestants over the issues of religious freedom and state support of parochial schools. Worst of all during the prosperity years, organized crime and racketeering became big businesses again and threatened the integrity of state and local government, while other threats—increased juvenile delinquency, alcoholism, and bootlegging of narcotics to young people—menaced the social order.

And yet full-scale revelations of these darker phases of American life brought new public and private efforts at amelioration as well as consternation. For example, the special Senate committee to investigate crime in interstate commerce, commonly known as the Kefauver Committee, dramatized the glaring shame of the cities as Lincoln Steffens had done in a journalistic fashion fifty years before and provoked a wave of crime investigations and popular uprisings against politicians allied with racketeers in many cities and states. As for the liquor problem, there was actually less drinking per capita in 1952 than in 1915; the problem simply seemed larger because of the increased attention given it by scientists, educators, and organizations like Alcoholics Anonymous and because of the spread of so-called social drinking. And if juvenile delinquency and narcotic addiction increased in the postwar period, then state and city agencies also redoubled their efforts to eradicate the causes as well as the outward manifestations of these twin evils.

205 / *Main Currents in American Fiction, 1933–1953*

During the years between the Great Depression and the inauguration of Eisenhower, American fictional writing reflected the violent crosscurrents of thought and the challenges to democracy that confused the American mind. To begin with, the rebel spokesmen of the Lost Generation, who had joyously discarded the genteel tradition and joined in warfare against what they considered smug idealism and prudish cant, lived on into the thirties and forties. By 1933, however, their revolt had lost much of its meaning, and the standards of a new rebellion were being unfurled by other insurgents. There was the tragic spectacle of F. Scott Fitzgerald, perhaps the most sensitive and talented writer of the Lost Generation, caught in the moral and cultural collapse of which he had written so poignantly. His final works, *Tender Is the Night*, 1934, and *The Last Tycoon*, 1941, were artistically distinguished but revealed a neurotic mind sickened by the corruption that he thought damned American life.

Ernest Hemingway and Sinclair Lewis gave further evidence of the bewilderment that confused and enfeebled the survivors of the Lost Generation after 1930. Hemingway had been the most robust and literarily the most influential of the American writers of the twenties. In a series of stories —*Death in the Afternoon*, 1932, *Winner Take Nothing*, 1933, and *The Green Hills of Africa*, 1935—Hemingway violated his own literary standards and nearly renounced human values. Then, fired by the challenge of fascism, he replied in 1940 with his most popular novel, *For Whom the Bell Tolls*. In the place of repudiation he now substituted devotion to a cause, the fight of the Spanish Loyalists. But his political ideology was confused and his characters were out of place; and *For Whom the Bell Tolls* marked the end of the Lost Generation, not its rebirth.

In a different way, the work of Sinclair Lewis after 1930 illustrated the deterioration of the Lost Generation. So long as Lewis held a mirror to the absurdities of middle class thought and manners he was superbly effective. But after 1930 he searched for new themes and evidenced less tension with society. His *It Can't Happen Here*, 1935, depicted the rise and triumph of fascism in America and forecast the salvation of democracy by the middle class. In other novels from 1943 to 1947 he returned to old themes and took up a new one, racial prejudice; but withal he demonstrated, as one critic has observed, "a continuous decline of powers and an irritable indecision concerning the meaning of what he is doing."

In contrast, the thirties and forties saw the rise of William Faulkner of Oxford, Mississippi, who had begun his literary career in the twenties but who had been culturally too isolated to be a member of the Lost Generation. From his lonely outpost Faulkner sought to find the meaning of life through a reconstruction of the southern past, through the heroes and villains and plain people caught in the vortex of a society in dissolution. From reading his earlier novels—like *The Sound and the Fury*, 1929, *Light in August*, 1932, and *Absalom! Absalom!*, 1935—it is difficult for the layman to know whether Faulkner rejected completely the value structure of the past or used a powerful symbolism to reaffirm old values. But in his later works—*Go Down, Moses*, 1942, *Intruder in the Dust*, 1948, *Requiem for a Nun*, 1951, and *A Fable*, 1954—Faulkner's purpose at last became clear. It was to reaffirm the eternal worth of human beings and the dignity of the human spirit.

In the meantime, the 1930's witnessed an astounding rebirth of the social and economic novel in America that equaled if it did not exceed the outpouring of the years before the First World War. The mass of human suffering during the depression stimulated despair, while the hope of salvation either through the destruction or reform of capitalism stimulated both a cathartic analysis of the American system and a political climate in which such analysis could flourish.

The most loquacious and perhaps the most bitter critic of American capitalism among the fictional writers of the thirties was John Dos Passos, who had made his literary debut in the twenties. In his trilogy, *U. S. A.*—*The Forty-Second Parallel*, 1930, *Nineteen-Nineteen*, 1932, and *The Big Money*, 1936—Dos Passos used a variety of literary techniques like the "newsreel," brief biographies, and episodic fiction to reconstruct the panorama of American life from 1900 to 1929. In a second trilogy—*Adventures of a Young Man*, 1939, *Number One*, 1943, and *The Grand Design*, 1948—Dos Passos continued the story through the depression and the New Deal.

Writing in the same vein but on a less panoramic scale and perhaps with less bitterness was James T. Farrell, whose *Young Lonigan*, 1932, *The Young Manhood of Studs Lonigan*, 1934, and *The Judgment Day*, 1935, recounted the moral and spiritual disintegration of a lower middle class Irish neighborhood in south Chicago. Farrell wrote social literature without seeking to ride an economic theme; what gave the *Studs Lonigan* trilogy its harshness was the language of the street that Farrell employed.

John Steinbeck protested the injustices of an economic system that allegedly degraded workers and sharecroppers to the level of animal existence. His greatest work, *The Grapes of Wrath*, 1939, was a moving odyssey of the flight of a sharecropper family, the unforgettable Joads, from Oklahoma to California. In this and other novels Steinbeck emerged as a social novelist of the first rank and also as the writer who best understood the tragedy of the lower classes of his time.

The bitterest critics of the depression decade were the so-called "proletarian" writers—Marxists, Communists, and fellow-travelers—who used the novel as propaganda to hasten the conversion of the middle classes to revolutionary ideals. The politically devout among them magnified the sins of capitalism, glorified the "little people," and heralded the coming triumph of the disinherited. The "deviationists" used proletarian themes but would not surrender their artistic integrity to the commissars of Union Square. To a varying degree, Dos Passos, Farrell, and Steinbeck were proletarian writers and the most distinguished members of the group. The Negro naturalist, Richard Wright, was briefly a party member; his *Native Son*, 1940, and *Black Boy*, 1945, showed considerable genius if a strong penchant for unrelieved violence. The majority of proletarian writers, however, were important for their economic and social criticism, not for their literary accomplishments.

Not all the writers of the thirties were angry and raucous. There were survivors from the genteel past: Willa S. Cather, who published one of her most important books, *Shadows on the Rock*, in 1931 and one of her most poignant tales, *Sapphira and the Slave Girl*, in 1940; Ellen Glasgow, who continued her satires on life in Virginia; and the southern short story writers, Elizabeth Madox Roberts and Katherine Anne Porter. And there were three new novelists, Pearl S. Buck, John P. Marquand, and Robert Penn Warren, who enriched the literature of the thirties and forties and helped keep alive the traditions of graceful writing and moral purpose.

Judged sheerly by popular standards, the most important literary development after 1930 was the emergence of the historical novel as a mature literary form. Many of the historical novelists of the thirties and forties romanticized the past but succeeded because they were good storytellers. On the other hand, a large minority, including Margaret Mitchell, Kenneth Roberts, Walter Edmonds, Conrad Richter, and Samuel Shellabarger, were careful students of history who illustrated the timelessness of human experience. Margaret Mitchell's masterpiece, *Gone With the Wind*, 1936, for example, was an epic of individuals and a civilization destroyed and struggling to live again.

By the Second World War it was evident that a great era in American literature had ended. It began with the revolt of the naturalists before 1917, flowered in the twenties with the rise of the Lost Generation, and culminated in the thirties in the literature of the people and the search for a symbolic expression of human tragedy in the writings of William Faulkner, Robert Penn Warren, and other mature authors. But what new school would take their places? What would become of American literature after the old gods were dead?

Viewing the literary scene at mid-century, the historian could give neither answers nor assurances of a new literary revival. Indeed, it seemed the wellsprings of fiction were drying up, that the young authors of the postwar period were neither as talented nor as clear of purpose as their forbears had been thirty years before. There was, to be sure, an outburst of war fiction, as if the war gave a momentary excuse for writing. There were the neo-Hemingways, to borrow a name—Alfred Hayes, John Horne Burns, Norman Mailer, and Irwin Shaw—who wrote powerfully of war's horrors and brutality. But they were too intense and "stultified and frozen in a helpless attitude of horror" to be effective; and they did not give promise of founding a school. There were other young writers, like John Hersey, Herman Wouk, and James Michener, who found courage and nobility in the great tragedy. But none of these, whether despairing or hopeful, had given promise by 1953 that they could carry beyond the war theme.

This indecision, this inability to find intellectual and moral bearings was reflected as well in other young writers in the postwar era, who exploited new themes and invented new symbols but failed to establish communication with a large reading public. One of the most gifted of the postwar writers, Ross Lockridge, Jr., whose *Raintree County*, 1948, gave promise of richer development, cut himself off by suicide. What was the trouble? Were young writers entirely at odds with their civilization and yet afraid to revolt? Whatever the causes, the decline of fictional writing in the postwar era did not augur well for the future of American literature.

206 / *The Flowering of Poetry and the American Drama*

There were crosscurrents and new moods in American poetical writing after the brilliant renaissance of the period 1910–1927. Some of the old masters and practitioners of more conventional forms survived in the thirties and forties. For example, the dean of American poets, Edwin Arlington Robinson, confirmed his supremacy during the period between the completion of his Arthurian trilogy in 1927 and his last work, *King Jasper,* published in 1935. His death in that year deprived America of her greatest poet since Walt Whitman. Robert Frost, whose reputation was already well established by 1930, continued to write with deceiving simplicity about nature and man's struggles. Indeed, if anything he improved his style and broadened his vision to include inquiries into the nature of man and of God. Carl Sandburg, another of the "new" poets of the earlier renaissance, affirmed his faith in American destiny in *The People, Yes,* published in 1936. But two other poetic rebels, Edgar Lee Masters and Vachel Lindsay, had passed from the literary scene by the thirties.

These poets of the people had few followers in the thirties and forties. There was Stephen Vincent Benét, who continued to voice American democratic idealism in *Litany for Dictatorships,* 1936, *Nightmare at Noon,* 1940, and *Western Star,* published in 1943, the year of his untimely death. Moreover, the challenge of depression at home and the rise of fascism abroad stimulated a brief outburst of democratic and leftist poetry in the 1930's. Muriel Rukeyser's *Theory of Flight,* 1935, and *U. S. 1,* 1938; Kenneth Fearing's *Poems,* 1935; and Archibald MacLeish's *Public Speech,* 1936, *America Was Promises,* 1939, and other works, were poetic counterparts of the fictional "literature of the people."

Despite these survivals of social poetry, the most important fact about American poetic thought and writing was the growing influence of the imagist school established by Ezra Pound before the First World War and dominated by Thomas Stearns Eliot, an American expatriate living in London, after 1920. Eliot secured his supremacy among the young poets in *The Waste Land,* 1921. Converted to Anglo-Catholicism in the late twenties, he turned to religious themes; and his later notable poems, *Ash Wednesday,* 1930, and *Four Quartets,* 1943, and his plays, *Murder in the Cathedral,* 1935, and *The Cocktail Party,* 1950, sought to convey the meaning in life and the universe.

By mid-century the revolt against the romantic poetic tradition had long since become a mature movement with elaborate standards. We can now see that the emphasis upon imagery, symbolism, and intellectualization produced a "new" poetry which, in its attempt to recreate the complexity of human experience, often went beyond the ability of the average reader to enjoy and comprehend. But many great poets, especially those who wrestled with philosophical problems, have done this. The significant contribution of the modern poets was, in the words of one historian of the school, the triumph of "sincerity over sham, of naturalness over affectation, of a striking turn toward precision, analysis, and structure; of a wider range of conception and idea; of a deeper apprehension of meaning."[3]

We have earlier seen how a host of young playwrights, notably Eugene O'Neill, created an American drama in the decade following the Armistice. O'Neill's creative energies waned in the early thirties and leadership passed to other playwrights. Indeed, so voluminous, varied, and excellent was the outpouring after 1930 that it seemed the drama had become the chief form of American literary expression. Maxwell Anderson, who had made his literary debut earlier in the twenties, turned to writing historical tragedies in poetic verse. His *Elizabeth the Queen*, 1930, *Mary of Scotland*, 1933, and *Valley Forge*, 1934, established him as perhaps the leading American dramatist of the 1930's. S. N. Behrman and Philip Barry continued to enliven the stage with penetrating social satires that often said more than audiences understood. In *Green Pastures*, 1930, Marc Connelly depicted Negro folkways and religious thought in one of the most beautiful plays of the decade. In *Our Town*, 1938, and *The Skin of Our Teeth*, 1942, Thornton Wilder expressed human values and the theme of man's survival in spite of evil, ignorance, and war.

These and a host of other playwrights celebrated the foibles and folly as well as the enduring values of American life, but they were creative artists rather than social critics. Of greater significance to the social historian of the thirties was the work of a large group of playwrights who used the stage as a sounding board for all kinds of ideologies and social and political protest. There were, most notably, the leftists—Elmer Rice, John Howard Lawson, and especially Clifford Odets, the most frankly Marxian of them— who joined together in the Theater Union and the Group Theater and wrote fierce denunciations of the sins of capitalism. The most talented playwright of this group, Lillian Hellman, demonstrated great power in her *The Children's Hour*, 1934, and then turned to propaganda in *The Little Foxes*, 1939, *Watch on the Rhine*, 1941, and *The Searching Wind*, 1944. Of different political faith was Robert Sherwood, who best reflected the changing temper of the non-Marxist intellectual during the thirties. His *The Petrified Forest*, 1934, reflected the pessimism of its day and the view that reason was ineffectual as compared with brute force; his *Idiot's Delight*, 1936, was one of the most eloquent pieces of anti-war propaganda during the high tide of pacifist sentiment. In response to the challenges of Nazism and Communism, however, Sherwood replied with two ringing affirmations of faith in man and democracy—*Abe Lincoln in Illinois*, 1938, and *There Shall Be No Night*, 1940.

From the pinnacle of great achievement in the 1930's American dramatic output declined steadily in the forties and early fifties. There were musical plays and light comedies galore in the war and postwar years, but only two new playwrights of any literary consequence, Tennessee Williams and Arthur Miller. Williams' *The Glass Menagerie*, 1944, *A Streetcar Named Desire*, 1947, *Summer and Smoke*, 1948, and *Camino Real*, 1953, revealed rare ability to probe the tormented mind. Miller's *All My Sons*, 1947, and

[3] Louise Bogan, *Achievement in American Poetry, 1900–1950* (Chicago, 1951), p. 106; used by permission of Henry Regnery Company, publishers.

The Death of a Salesman, 1949, proved that the dramatic voice of protest against materialism was not dead in the postwar era. But two good play-wrights do not make a dramatic revival. Whether television, with its large financial rewards for quick plays, was responsible for the postwar decline; or whether playwrights, like fictional writers, were floundering in their search for new themes, we cannot say. In any event, there were few hopeful signs at mid-century of any important rebirth of the drama in the United States.

207 / Art, Architecture, and Music

The thirties and forties saw the full maturing of American endeavor in the fine arts. Indeed, development of artistic efforts and public appreciation was so rapid that one observer could conclude in 1954 that the American people at mid-century were obsessed by a passion for art and "culture." There were many signs that this was not a rash observation: the growth of symphony orchestras in medium-sized cities and the phenomenal success of summer music "festivals," for example, or the universality of musical train-ing in the public schools and colleges in every section; the growth of art museums on university campuses and in regional centers; the success of *Life* magazine's sophisticated series on western thought and culture; the wide-spread acceptance of modern architectural forms in the postwar era; and in a thousand other such manifestations too numerous to mention here.

The dominant trend among American artists during the post-Armistice decade had been a movement away from realism toward abstraction, cubism, and surrealism. However, the impact of the depression, the conflict of ideolo-gies, and the threat of war stimulated a strong revival of artistic realism dedicated to the people.[4] The most significant manifestation of this attempt to restore art to the people was the development of an aggressively "Ameri-can" school that drew its inspiration from the region and sought to portray every aspect of American life on canvas.

The three leaders of the new regional school were John Steuart Curry, Grant Wood, and Thomas Hart Benton, whose scenes of life in Kansas, Iowa, and Missouri recalled the grandeur as well as the reality of midwestern life. But the names of the "American" school were legion: artists of the calm New England countryside, of southwestern desert desolation, of Negro life, of decaying plantations, of the Bowery and Skid Row and the chaos of city life, of workers, farmers, and other plain people. The great artistic redis-covery of America gained new momentum, moreover, when the WPA estab-lished an Arts Division in 1935, hired thousands of artists, good and bad, to paint murals in postoffices and courthouses, and sponsored various projects of instruction in art and the handicrafts.

Then there was a second large and more vocal group among the Ameri-can realistic school, who combined attachment to the local scene with devo-

---

[4] To be sure, the abstract painters and surrealists survived in the thirties, as was evidenced by the work of Walter Quirt, George L. K. Morris, and Stuart Davis. But they suffered a relative decline in artistic influence and found it increasingly difficult to justify their work in social terms.

tion to radical ideologies. From 1936 to 1940 leaders of the *avant-garde* met in annual Artist Congresses and turned out a flood of propaganda on canvas, the main themes of which were the oppression of labor, lynching and abuse of the Negro, and wicked capitalists conspiring to oppress the people and drive the world to war. There were, for example, William Gropper's and Joseph Hirsch's savage caricatures of American politicians, Robert Gwathmey's pictures of the South, Ben Shahn's scenes of capitalistic-police oppression in the coal regions. As one authority has observed, "Too many of these lynchings, prairie wagons, and barroom carousels possessed an energy that was simply of the nerves and muscles."[5]

The war years saw the mobilization of American artists of all political faiths in the common cause. The postwar era witnessed a decline in art as propaganda but no less concern with the American scene than in the thirties. There was, moreover, a revival of interest in primitivism and, most important, abundant evidence of the continued power and strength of the artistic revival in the United States.

Meanwhile, the motion picture reached new heights of maturity as a popular art form in the 1930's and 1940's. After the perfection of Technicolor in 1935 there were no technical developments of importance until the introduction of three-dimensional movies and Cinerama in 1952. But there was considerable improvement in technique, form, lighting, the use of music, and general quality of acting, as Hollywood continued to attract most of the best actors and actresses in America and Europe by the lure of fabulous salaries. Moreover, during the thirties Walt Disney perfected the animated cartoon and demonstrated its versatility in full-length productions like "Snow White and the Seven Dwarfs" in 1938 and "Fantasia" in 1940.

When the final history of the motion pictures is written the 1930's will rank as Hollywood's golden decade, at least during the first half century of the industry's existence. There were films for every taste and mood, ranging from superb comedies like "It Happened One Night," 1934, and "The Philadelphia Story," 1940, to epic dramas like "Mutiny on the Bounty," 1936, and "Gone With the Wind," 1939. Charles Laughton, Paul Muni, Walter Huston, James Stewart, Victor McLaglen, Frederic March, Gary Cooper, and a whole galaxy of stars raised motion pictures to new artistic heights. For lovers of nonsense there were the incomparable Marx brothers, whose series had not been equaled for sheer hilarity by 1953. For devotees of social satire there were Charlie Chaplin's "City Lights," 1931, "Modern Times," 1936, and "The Great Dictator," 1940, and Orson Welles' caricature of William Randolph Hearst, "Citizen Kane," 1941.

The thirties were a memorable motion picture decade, above all, because Hollywood for a brief time addressed itself to serious social questions and became almost an echo of the American social conscience. During a time when democracy was everywhere under attack, Paul Muni recalled the traditions of democracy and justice in "Juarez" and "The Life of Emile Zola," while Raymond Massey embodied the living Emancipator in "Abe Lincoln in Illinois." In addition, a whole series—"I Am a Fugitive from a Georgia Chain Gang," "Dead End," "Black Legion," "The Grapes of Wrath," and

[5] Oliver W. Larkin, *Art and Life In America* (New York, 1949), p. 450; quoted by permission of Rinehart and Company, publishers.

"Fury," for example—revealed the cancerous growths in the body of American social life. Finally, the federal government contributed two memorable documentary films, "The River" and "The Plow that Broke the Plains," which depicted America's wastage of human and natural resources and pointed the way toward social redemption through democratic collective action.

During the war years, however, Hollywood discreetly abandoned social themes and turned to the production of films to entertain and inspire, or to educate the American people to an understanding of the Nazi menace and their new international responsibilities. During the war period there also occurred a marked revival of religious movies, the most notable of which were "The Song of Bernadette" and "Going My Way."

In the postwar era Hollywood faced new dangers and crises the direst in the history of motion pictures. The most serious menace to the film's integrity was the determination of a vocal minority to scourge Hollywood of alleged Communists and to prevent the production of any films that attempted seriously to grapple with social questions. The campaign of suppression promptly frightened producers from certain controversial social themes and gave leadership in the social protest film to the Italians, who produced the most meaningful films during the postwar era. After 1945 Hollywood turned more and more to musical comedies, romantic extravaganzas, westerns, and trivial productions; but it would be unfair to say that American producers lost all integrity or courage in the postwar era. They turned to new social themes as old ones lost their relevance for the contemporary generation. Thus "Crossfire" and "Gentlemen's Agreement" explored the depths of anti-Semitism; "The Lost Week-End" and "Snake Pit" dealt courageously with the plight of alcoholics and the mentally ill. "Pinkie," "Intruder in the Dust," "Lost Boundaries," and "Home of the Brave" confronted the explosive subjects of race prejudice and miscegenation; and "The Best Years of Our Lives," "High Noon," and "A Place in the Sun" symbolized the plight of the individual in a world of craven and corrupt men.

Meanwhile, the two decades from 1930 to 1950 saw the culmination of a revolution in American architecture no less significant than the revolution that occurred in other fields, as the modern functional school founded by Louis Sullivan and Frank Lloyd Wright finally came to dominance among American architects and found wider acceptance by the rank and file of the people. It is true that progress in the movement to free Americans from their prison walls of stone and cement must have seemed painfully slow to the pioneers. As late as the mid-thirties modern homes were still architectural curiosities; the federal government was pouring hundreds of millions of dollars into massive marble mausoleums in Washington and elsewhere; and the Gothic or colonial style still prevailed in the construction of college and public school buildings.

Slowly, however, American architectural ideas and practices began to change in the 1930's. The first important sign that the tide had turned toward functionalism came from 1930 to 1939, with the construction of Rockefeller Center and the McGraw-Hill and Daily News skyscrapers in New York City and of modern garden-type apartment projects throughout the country by the Federal Housing Authority. Moreover, Hitler's lash or the fear of tyranny drove many of Europe's best functional architects to America before 1939; they were not only a generative force in themselves but also helped strengthen liaison with other European functionalists. The most important turning point in the thirties was the planning and construction of the New York World's Fair of 1939–1940, which gave the functionalists an opportunity to introduce advanced design to millions of Americans. Especially noteworthy was Norman Bel Geddes' General Motors Building with its "Futurama" of a new America.

With the resumption of public and private construction on a large scale after the war, the functional architects were able finally to begin the revolution in building of which they had so long dreamed. In private home design the Cape Cod and Georgian gave way not so much to the completely functional design as to a modified form, the so-called ranch type. In the construction of public school and university buildings, the old styles gave way completely to new buildings with huge windows, spacious grounds, and movable interiors and furniture. Apartment buildings, new skyscrapers, and even churches that embodied the functional principles of design went up all over the land.

One of the happiest cultural developments in the period 1930–1950 was the flowering of the musical tradition in the United States. Popular support for symphony orchestras, music schools, and so-called classical music gave the lie to the old charge that educated Americans as a group did not know or appreciate the great music of the past, while American composers of serious music gave further proof of the vitality of the musical tradition in the United States. Nor was this all; in the fields of jazz, swing, and folk music Americans reigned incontestably supreme, as the two decades after 1930 witnessed the full maturing of these forms. By mid-century, the day had passed when Americans would look to Europe for approval and leadership in this important area of artistic endeavor.

The distinguished group of serious composers who began their work after the First World War continued to compose in the classical tradition and were joined in the thirties by a larger company. Notable among the new American composers were two romanticists of great virtuosity, Samuel Barber and William Schuman; William Grant Still, who drew upon the American Negro past for haunting melodies; and Aaron Copland, the most prominent of the group. The war and postwar years saw the rise of a younger serious musical generation—among them being Douglas Moore, Virgil Thompson, and Gian-Carlo Menotti—who gave promise of carrying serious American music to even new heights of excellence. "If future achievements maintain the pace of the past twenty years," one authority observed in 1952, "it may not be long before American composers occupy the position in world music held by the Germans and Austrians one hundred years ago, the French and Russians fifty years ago, and now in possession of the British composers of our time."[6]

Equally heartening was the growth of American jazz, swing, folk music, and the musical drama during this period. Authentic jazz gained recognition

[6] John Culshaw, *A Century of Music* (New York, 1952), p. 204; quoted by permission of Roy Publishers.

at home and in Europe as a significant musical form, but the most important popular musical development of the thirties was the evolution of swing music, a refinement of jazz through elaborate arrangement and the use of larger orchestras. There were dozens of swing leaders in the thirties and forties, but the "King of Swing" was the incomparable Benny Goodman, whose clarinet set the viscera of jitterbugs afire.

The period under discussion also saw the steady growth of America's most popular folk music, the love ballad and the popular song. Year in and year out the song writers voiced the hopes and fears and the wisdom and nonsense of the American people, but the American tradition of folk music found its strongest exponents during this period in George Gershwin and Richard Rodgers and Oscar Hammerstein II. Gershwin climaxed his long career in 1935 with the writing of *Porgy and Bess*, based upon a play about Negro life in Charleston by Du Bose Heyward, which was perhaps the greatest American opera, one destined to be sung as long as men love music. Richard Rodgers had written a number of successful musicals with his librettist, Lorenz Hart, in the twenties and thirties, but collaboration between them had become nearly impossible by the time Hart died in 1943. In 1942 Rodgers found a new and more congenial partner in Oscar Hammerstein II. The result of their collaboration was a series of musical dramas—among them, *Oklahoma!*, *Carousel*, *South Pacific*, and *The King and I*—that caused a grateful nation to hail them as America's own Gilbert and Sullivan.

208 / Crises in American Education, 1933-1953

The following generalizations illustrate the main trends in American public education: From 1930 to 1950 the number of pupils enrolled in public schools decreased slightly from 25,678,000 to 25,111,000, but the decrease was more than offset by the growth in the number of students enrolled in private elementary and secondary schools. Total expenditures for public education expanded during the same two decades from $2,317,000,000 to nearly $6,000,000,000 and expenditure per student increased from $90.22 in 1930 to $231.05 in 1950. Finally, there were encouraging increases in the length of school term, average daily attendance, and in teachers' salaries.

These general statistics, however, obscure the crises and challenges through which American schools passed during the two decades following the election of Franklin D. Roosevelt. Never before, it seemed, had American public education been beset by so many dangers. First came the depression and general recovery by 1940. Then came the war and new crises in the public schools. Crowding in defense areas caused incredible strains, and in many areas authorities used abandoned buildings and put the schools on double shift. School buildings fell into disrepair as it became impossible to find building materials and other equipment. But the worst problem of all was the exodus of men and women from the teaching profession. By 1945 some 350,000 teachers, or more than one-third the number employed in 1941, had left for higher paying jobs in business, industry, and government. In many instances school administrators hired whomever they could find, and by 1945 109,000 teachers were employed on emergency certificates. But it was not enough: "Schools were closed or were conducted on short terms; many subjects included in the high school curriculum had to be abandoned for lack of adequately prepared teachers."[7]

The situation got considerably worse in the postwar era before the tide began to turn. Surveying the national educational scene in late 1946 and early 1947, the educational reporter for the *New York Times* revealed the dimensions of the postwar crisis in American education. The result of these and other disclosures was to generate such a crusade for education as the country had not witnessed since the 1920's. Groups like the NAM, the Chamber of Commerce, the AF of L, and the CIO joined powerful teachers' lobbies and citizens' committees in nearly every American community to demand increased school appropriations and new buildings. The results were encouraging if not wholly adequate to meet the crisis. By 1950 there was a surplus of high school teachers and the shortage among elementary teachers was rapidly diminishing. The average teacher's salary and expenditure per pupil had increased much more rapidly than the cost of living—from $1,995 and $124.27, respectively, in 1946 to $3,010 and $231.05, respectively, in 1950; and in certain areas, notably the South, the increases had been even more spectacular.

For colleges and universities the two decades from 1930 to 1950 were a time of phenomenal growth and development over the long period. For example, enrollment in such institutions increased from 1,100,737 to 2,659,021 and expenditures grew from $632,249,000 to $2,123,275,000 between 1930 and 1950. But between the beginning and the end of this period one crisis after another confronted higher education. There was first the depression, which hit colleges and universities a heavy blow. No sooner had they recovered lost ground than they faced an even worse crisis when enrollments plummeted downward during the war. Then came the shock of a sudden increase in the number of students after the Japanese surrender, as veterans enjoying liberal public support returned to college or entered for the first time. As enrollments increased from 1,155,272 in 1944 to 2,659,021 in 1950, the strain on housing, classroom, and library facilities became well-nigh unbearable.

The gravest danger to American higher education in the postwar era came not from overcrowding and deterioration of standards, but from the consequences of popular alarm regarding alleged Communists among the ranks of college and university teachers. Actually, there was little controversy over the question whether Communists should be allowed to teach, either in the public schools or state colleges and universities. By the end of 1953 the Association of American Universities, the National Education Association, and the American Federation of Teachers had all taken firm stands against the employment of Communist teachers. The grave danger to academic freedom in the postwar era, in higher education as well as among the public schools, stemmed instead from powerful campaigns in many states and cities aimed at driving nonconformist and progressive teachers from the classroom by identifying dissent and progressivism with Communism.

[7] I. L. Kandel, *The Impact of the War Upon American Education* (Chapel Hill, N.C., 1948), p. 7; quoted by permission of the University of North Carolina Press, publishers.

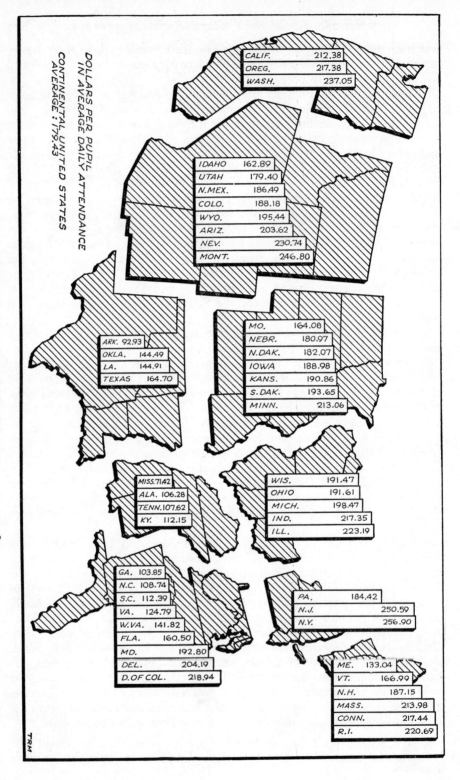

DOLLARS PER PUPIL
IN AVERAGE DAILY ATTENDANCE

CONTINENTAL UNITED STATES
AVERAGE : 179.43

CALIF.	212.38
OREG.	217.38
WASH.	237.05

IDAHO	162.89
UTAH	179.40
N.MEX.	186.49
COLO.	188.18
WYO.	195.44
ARIZ.	203.62
NEV.	230.74
MONT.	246.80

ARK.	92.93
OKLA.	144.49
LA.	144.91
TEXAS	164.70

MO.	164.08
NEBR.	180.97
N.DAK.	182.07
IOWA	188.98
KANS.	190.86
S.DAK.	193.65
MINN.	213.06

MISS.	71.42
ALA.	106.28
TENN.	107.62
KY.	112.15

WIS.	191.47
OHIO	191.61
MICH.	198.47
IND.	217.35
ILL.	223.19

GA.	103.85
N.C.	108.74
S.C.	112.39
VA.	124.79
W.VA.	141.82
FLA.	160.50
MD.	192.80
DEL.	204.19
D. OF COL.	218.94

PA.	184.42
N.J.	250.59
N.Y.	256.90

ME.	133.04
VT.	166.99
N.H.	187.15
MASS.	213.98
CONN.	217.44
R.I.	220.69

TRM

36. *Expenditures for Public Education, 1947–1948*

After the exposure of a far-flung Communist espionage network in the United States in 1948–1949, many states and cities imposed test oaths on teachers and established committees to examine textbooks for subversive materials. The University of Oklahoma virtually excluded any but native-born citizens from its staff; Kansas, Massachusetts, and Pennsylvania authorized schools to dismiss teachers for disloyalty; and Maryland, New York, and New Jersey forbade teachers to join certain proscribed organizations.

However well-intentioned these efforts were, their chief effect was not to expose the infinitesimally small number of Communists in the classrooms but to impeach the integrity of the overwhelming majority of teachers and to cast a pall of fear over the schools. As conformity and blind acceptance of the *status quo* became synonymous in many minds with "Americanism," fear of being called a Communist drove thousands of teachers either into silence or to extremes of orthodoxy.[8]

Although crises kept intruding during the two decades of turmoil from 1930 to 1950, the period was a time of continuing thoughtful inquiry into the philosophy, methods, and goals of higher education that culminated in a sweeping postwar victory for the proponents of an integrated curriculum designed to afford a general education for American undergraduates. Leadership in the revolt against the intellectual chaos of the free elective system came in the thirties from Robert M. Hutchins, president of the University of Chicago. The revolt came to a head with the publication of the Harvard committee's *General Education in a Free Society* in 1945. A milestone in the development of educational philosophy in the United States, the Harvard report was an eloquent plea for greater emphasis upon general education that would acquaint students with the whole of human experience rather than with isolated fragments. As Harvard, Yale, and Princeton led the way in curriculum changes in the postwar period, dozens of other institutions followed suit.

In numerous other ways this searching self-examination of American higher education provoked changes in the postwar era. There was, for example, widespread recognition of the importance of Judaism and Christianity in the development of western civilization, and this in turn gave rise to the establishment of religion departments in numerous institutions that had once gladly abandoned the study of religion. When a *New York Times* survey in 1943 revealed that most college students were appallingly ignorant of their country's history, several states required students in state-supported colleges and universities to take courses in American history. Recognition of Amer-

[8] The dangers inherent in reckless assaults upon academic freedom and in the imposition of indiscriminate test oaths were illustrated by a tragic controversy that nearly wrecked the University of California and rocked academic circles in the United States from 1949 to 1952. In order to protect the University from attacks by certain demagogues in the legislature, the president and regents imposed a loyalty oath of their own on March 25, 1949. Forty-nine professors, among them the most distinguished scholars and teachers in the University, were discharged when they refused to sign the oath on the ground that it impeached their loyalty and integrity and affronted their dignity. In the battle that ensued the University of California suffered not only the loss of other professors who resigned in protest or refused to accept appointment but the respect of the entire academic world as well. Eventually, in 1951 and 1952, the regents rescinded the oath and reinstated the discharged professors who had not gone elsewhere. But the damage was already done.

ica's new international responsibilities after 1941 stimulated a flowering of international studies, especially of "general area" programs relating to Russia and the Far East.

Looking back over the development of higher education in the United States since 1900, Americans at mid-century might feel inclined to boast. Within fifty years they had freed themselves from cultural dependence upon Europe and built a system of higher education on the whole unexcelled anywhere else in the world. But the most significant fact of all was that the expansion of higher educational opportunities had gone hand in hand with steady improvement in standards. The American people were nearer than ever to the great goal of universal higher education for all men and women who could meet the standards imposed.

209 / *The Return to Religion*

During the twenty years from 1930 to 1950 religious bodies continued to grow in membership and material resources. From 1926 to 1951 total church membership in the United States increased from 54,576,346, or 46 per cent of the total population, to 88,673,005, or 57 per cent. But the general statistics obscure the important trends in growth. The depression years from 1929 to 1939 were a time of such precipitous decline as to lead certain observers to conclude that the church was a dying institution. The onset of war and the return of full prosperity abruptly reversed the downward plunge in church membership and influence in 1940–1941; and during the following decade the return to religion constituted one of the most significant social and intellectual movements in the United States.

Among the various religious bodies only the Jewish congregations, which did little better than hold their own, failed to record substantial gains. All Protestant denominations grew faster than the general population; but the significant growth occurred among the bodies that made an aggressive appeal to the lower middle and lower classes. The Baptists, particularly the southern wing, made the most striking gains, increasing in numbers from 8,262,287 in 1936 to 17,065,572 in 1951. Moreover, the various holiness bodies on the social frontier of Protestantism—the Church of the Nazarene, the several Churches of God, the Pentecostal Assemblies, and the Foursquare Gospel Movement—also grew rapidly and gave evidences of changing from fringe sects into established denominations.

By mid-century it was evident that the United States, more than ever before in the twentieth century, was a predominantly Protestant country. From 1936 to 1951 Roman Catholics increased in numbers from 19,914,937 to 29,241,580, or at a rate of 47 per cent for the fifteen year period. This was indeed a substantial expansion, but the total Protestant membership increased by 65 per cent during the same period, and the proportion of Catholics in the total church population declined from 36 per cent in 1936 to 33 per cent in 1951.

As significant as the sheer fact of growth in church membership was the way in which the social character of the churches apparently changed during the late thirties and forties. If we accept the assumption that Protestantism was the religion of the middle and upper classes before 1940 and that Catholicism was the religion at least of the city masses, then the realignment of the class structure among the major denominations that took place in the forties was nothing less than revolutionary. A survey made in 1945–1946 revealed that the "lower classes" constituted 56 per cent of the membership in all major bodies—66 per cent among the Catholics, 68 per cent among the Baptists, 53 per cent among the Lutherans, and 52 per cent among the Methodists. But even among the so-called upper class denominations, the Episcopalians, Presbyterians, and Congregationalists, the lower class members were a large minority. A second survey revealed that 44 per cent of all American church members were urban manual workers, 17 per cent were farmers, 20 per cent were white collar workers, and 19 per cent were from the business and professional classes. By mid-century, therefore, the American churches, Protestant and Catholic alike, had long since ceased to be strongholds of social snobbery and middle class conservatism and had become in large measure the spiritual homes of all people. The implications of this fact for the future development of the American democracy were as far-reaching as they were obvious.

The causes for the return to religion were complex and often obscure. Prosperity after 1939 was in part responsible, but prosperity alone does not explain the phenomenon. It was plain to all who would see that the most important factor was the profound change in popular attitudes toward man, society, and God that took place during the late thirties and afterward. In brief, there occurred a metamorphosis from a prevailing optimism and humanism to a profound despair of man and his works, as the mass destruction of the Second World War, the revelations of Nazi and Soviet inhumanity, and the fear of future annihilation destroyed public faith in automatic human progress and caused millions of Americans to seek understanding and hope in religion.

The most important development in American religious thought after 1929—the decline of liberalism and humanism and the rise of so-called neo-orthodoxy—was in part a manifestation of the general disillusionment. A child of the nineteenth century belief in progress through automatic evolution, Protestant liberalism represented an attempt to reconcile Christianity with modern science and scholarship that denied the infallibility of the Scriptures. Frankly embracing evolution and the higher criticism, many liberals abandoned theological exegesis for a social gospel that emphasized man's capacity for improvement. Hopeful and optimistic, liberalism looked toward the early establishment of the Kingdom of God among men. It is impossible to measure precisely the extent to which liberalism affected Protestant beliefs in the twentieth century, although one survey in the late twenties revealed that liberal ideas prevailed among a large minority of ministers and among a large majority of seminary students.

Meanwhile, however, a conservative counterattack was forming in Europe and slowly spreading to America. Surveying the wreckage of the First World War and the failure of the League of Nations in the twenties and early thirties, the German and Swiss Calvinist theologians, Karl Barth, Emil Brunner, and Paul Tillich, indicted liberalism for glorifying man instead of God and for forgetting that man's sin produced perpetual crises in history. Modernists in so far as higher criticism and evolution were concerned, Barth, Brunner, and Tillich were also thoroughly orthodox in their emphasis upon the sovereignty and majesty of God, the sinfulness of man, and the sufficiency of biblical revelation.

Only faintly heard in the United States during the confident twenties, these European theologians of crisis gained many American followers in the thirties and forties. The most important theologian of the new school in the United States was Reinhold Niebuhr of the Union Theological Seminary in New York City. His *Moral Man and Immoral Society*, 1932, *Beyond Tragedy*, 1937, and *The Nature and Destiny of Man*, 1941–1943, epitomized the neo-orthodox indictment of shallow liberalism and pointed the return to historic concepts of God and Man.

There were many liberals who refused to go the whole way with the neo-orthodox theologians but who also confessed that liberalism had obviously failed in the face of crisis. In 1935, for example, Harry Emerson Fosdick, pastor of the Riverside Church in New York City, repudiated humanism and called for a return to biblical theology. In addition, the thirties and forties saw a marked revival of interest in the writings of Luther and Calvin; the discovery of the Danish mystic, Sören Kirkegaard; and a stronger emphasis upon the Atonement and the concept of the Church as the Body of Christ.

While this reconstruction of American Protestant thought was taking place, there was no diminution in the social energies of Protestantism, for the neo-orthodox leaders were as much champions of social righteousness as heralds of prophetic religion. But there was a considerable shift in Protestant thought after 1930 concerning the Church's social mission. Many leaders in the early social gospel movement conceived of the Church's mission almost exclusively in social terms and hopefully thought they could effect an immediate Christianization of the social order. Leaders in the movement after 1930, on the other hand, were much less optimistic and thought of the Church more as the saving remnant in an immoral society than as the remaker of the social order.

Meanwhile, there were numerous signs during the decades 1930–1950 that the forces drawing Protestants together continued to be far stronger than the old antagonisms and differences keeping them apart. In fact, there was such a striking decline of denominationalism and so strong a development of neighborhood churches as to warrant the generalization that denominational cliquishness scarcely existed among large numbers of Protestants by mid-century. The only disruptive elements in Protestantism after 1929 were the extreme fundamentalists, who insisted upon complete acceptance of historic creeds, and a lunatic fringe that included a wide variety of apostles of discord.

More than offsetting the disruptive forces was a powerful ecumenical movement toward either organic union or close fellowship among the major Protestant bodies. In 1931, for example, the Congregational and Christian churches combined; in 1939 the three main Methodist bodies healed old wounds and formed the largest single Protestant denomination; and movements for union within the Presbyterian and Lutheran bodies seemed to hold the promise of success in the postwar era. Throughout the thirties, moreover, the Federal Council of Churches of Christ in America continued to speak for a large majority of American Protestant churches. In 1941 the Federal Council combined with eight important interdenominational agencies; and in 1950 the entire structure was reorganized and reintegrated into the National Council of the Churches of Christ, which included every important Protestant denomination except the southern Baptists and the Missouri Synod Lutherans. The final and most heartening outgrowth of the ecumenical spirit was the World Council of Churches, organized in Amsterdam in 1948 after years of preparation, which combined practically all the non-Roman Catholic churches of the world into a working fellowship.

The return to religion during the years after 1939 confounded cynics and encouraged persons who regarded organized religion as an indispensable cornerstone of democracy. On the other hand, many thoughtful Americans were dismayed by an unhappy development in the religious field in the postwar era—the strong revival of old Protestant-Catholic antagonisms. There was a long background of mutual misunderstanding, but the most disturbing issues in the postwar era were federal aid to education and public support for parochial schools.

In many northern and midwestern states, public authorities furnished bus transportation, textbooks, and lunches to children attending parochial schools. As a consequence, Protestants charged that Catholics were working slowly toward full public support of parochial schools. During debates over federal aid to education in the postwar era, moreover, Catholics opposed any federal assistance to the states unless aid to children attending parochial schools was also included. Protestants in turn replied that Catholics were in principle opposed to public schools and had joined with reactionary groups to destroy the entire system of public education.

Protestant alarm at alleged Catholic aggressions took shape in the formation in 1948 of Protestants and Other Americans United for Separation of Church and State. The distinguished leaders who formed this group were not themselves religious bigots; but their propaganda was inevitably anti-Catholic, and it was a powerful factor in encouraging anti-Catholic antagonisms. The most vocal spokesman in the postwar Protestant crusade was Paul Blanshard, whose *American Freedom and Catholic Power,* 1949, and *Communism, Democracy, and Catholic Power,* 1952, stirred one of the liveliest controversies of the decade, especially after school boards in Newark and New York City banned *The Nation* from the public schools because it printed Blanshard's articles.

Several Catholic spokesmen answered Blanshard and other Protestant critics moderately; but many distinguished Catholic leaders, including Francis Cardinal Spellman of New York, poured oil on the flames by charging that Protestant critics and opponents of public aid to parochial schools were Ku Kluxers, bigots, or subversives. Although the worst phase of the controversy had apparently passed by 1953, the tension and bitterness remained to disturb the American social scene at mid-century.

CHAPTER 27 / *POLITICS AND PROBLEMS*
OF THE TRUMAN ERA

*N*ot in many years had the American political scene seemed so confused as during the period between the end of the Second World War and the election of 1952. The Democratic party was torn by struggles over civil rights, labor policy, and measures to combat the postwar inflation and was weakened by a growing popular conviction that the Truman administration was riddled with corruption and tainted with Communism. Although out of power in Washington except for a brief period during 1947 and 1948 when they controlled Congress, the Republicans were beset by difficulties as perplexing if not as apparent as those that plagued their opponents. Torn by divisions between internationalists and neo-isolationists and progressives and reactionaries, weakened by a long absence from power, and showing evidences of reckless irresponsibility, the GOP gave no brighter promise of uniting the country and providing constructive leadership than did the Democrats.

Yet never before had the problems confronting the American people been so great. But what shall we say of the achievements of the postwar period? The following chapter will attempt to answer that question. It must suffice to say here that, in spite of seeming chaos and undoubted intense partisanship, the American people and their leaders met the challenges of their time more courageously and with greater wisdom than their grandfathers had done during Reconstruction and their fathers had done during the decade following the Armistice.

210 / *Harry S. Truman and the Progressive Movement*

At 7:09 p.m. on April 12, 1945, a distraught man stood in the White House and took the oath as President of the United States. Franklin D. Roosevelt had died a few hours before, and now leadership was entrusted to his Vice President, Harry S. Truman. For Roosevelt, as for Lincoln, death was a merciful deliverer, sparing him from a host of troubles at the moment of his greatest triumph. For Truman, Roosevelt's passing meant a new life of trial and yet such opportunity as rarely comes to a son of man.

"Who the hell is Harry Truman?" Admiral William D. Leahy had asked when Roosevelt told him of the vice presidential nominee in the summer of 1944. That same question was repeated often if less profanely during the days of mourning that followed the war President's death. Who was this man to whom Fate had entrusted the leadership of the American people?

Born on May 4, 1884, at Grandview, in Jackson County, Missouri, Harry S. Truman was the grandson of pioneers from Kentucky and grew up a son of the Middle Border in Grandview, Independence, and Kansas City. Afflicted with poor eyesight, he found compensation in music and books; denied his ambition to go to West Point and become a soldier, he worked as a bank clerk and farmer after being graduated from high school in 1901. When war came he went to France with his National Guard field artillery regiment and rose to the rank of major through hard work and courageous service on the western front.

In 1919 Truman married his childhood sweetheart and entered the clothing business in Kansas City with his former sergeant. Ruined by the postwar recession in 1922, Truman accepted nomination as county judge, or county commissioner, of eastern Jackson County from the Pendergast Democratic machine of Kansas City. Defeated for re-election in 1924 in part because of his opposition to the Ku Klux Klan, Truman returned to the courthouse in Independence as presiding judge in 1927. During the next seven years he rebuilt the county's roads and courthouse, helped plan a system of parkways for Kansas City, and earned a reputation as an able and incorruptible administrator.

Nominated for the United States Senate in 1934 with the help of the Pendergast machine, Truman won easily in the Democratic landslide in the autumn elections. In Washington, however, he was known as the "Gentleman from Pendergast"; and when his patron, Tom Pendergast, was sentenced to federal prison in 1939 for income tax evasion, it seemed Truman's political career was also blasted. He surprised his friends as well as his enemies in 1940, however, by winning the Democratic senatorial nomination on his own—by winning the votes of workers, farmers, and Negroes in a campaign prophetic of his more famous battle eight years later.

Truman returned to Washington in December 1940 with increased political stature, destined, it seemed, not for greatness but for a long and honorable career in the upper house. Then came the defense crisis and his first opportunity to render national service. Appalled by the waste in defense spending and the neglect of small business by the army in the awarding of contracts, he obtained appointment in 1941 as chairman of a special Senate committee to investigate the defense effort. From 1941 to 1945 the Truman Committee, as the group was called, worked assiduously to prevent waste and favoritism. Even more important was the way in which Truman's fairness and insistence upon constructive criticism won for him the admiration of President Roosevelt and the vice presidential nomination in 1944.

Even so, the country knew little of the character of Harry S. Truman when he entered the White House in April 1945. Because he was uncommonly modest in demeanor, unpretentious in physical appearance, and obviously lacking in Roosevelt's histrionic abilities and patrician touch, many Americans assumed that Truman was the epitome of the average man.

Never had the popular judgment been more mistaken, for in most aspects the new President was extraordinary indeed.

He was extraordinary in his personal warmth and charm, in a breadth of learning that often astonished scholars, and in his ability to understand difficult situations. He was extraordinary in his personal honesty and integrity. When he failed in business, for example, he refused to go into bankruptcy and paid his debts instead. Although he had the support of a corrupt political organization, he never allowed the machine to use him or misappropriated a single dollar of county funds. He was extraordinary in his devotion to duty and the general interest, and in his capacity for hard work. He was extraordinary in his hatred of pretense, his feeling for the underdog, and his broad sympathy that tolerated no racial or religious distinctions. But above all he was extraordinary in his courage—whether in defying the Ku Klux Klan in his home county, on the hustings fighting a seemingly lost battle, in dismissing a renowned general, or in leading his country in bold pursuit of peace and security.

There were, however, other traits that weakened Truman's force as a personal leader. President during a period of intense partisanship, he had a capacity for descending to the lower level of political warfare. Although usually cautious in matters of state, he was often rash and impulsive in personal matters and given to name-calling in public. Although absolutely honest himself, he was so much a professional politician, who accepted the game as he found it, that he gave the appearance of being unable to see dishonesty in others. This weakness came out especially in his loyalty to the Pendergast machine and in his refusal to reappoint the federal district attorney who had helped uncover the corruption in Kansas City.

Many of Truman's weaknesses stemmed in the beginning from his undue modesty and feeling of inadequacy for the great tasks ahead. "I don't know whether you fellows ever had a load of hay or a bull fall on you," he told reporters on April 13, 1945. "But last night the moon, the stars and all the planets fell on me." He had inherited a Cabinet and administration of strangers; and in his loneliness he turned at first to friends in the Senate and gathered around him a group of intimates, known as the Missouri Gang.

In time, to be sure, Truman found himself as President, built his own administration, and drew into his Cabinet, the federal agencies, and the diplomatic service many able and distinguished public servants. There would have been a lowering of the tone of the public service after the war, moreover, had Roosevelt lived, for corruption permeated city, state, and federal politics and administration, Republican as well as Democratic. And yet the conclusion is inescapable that Truman in some measure contributed to the deterioration of public morality by trusting too much and refusing to move hard and fast against corruption in high places. Because of this failure he contributed also to the Democratic defeat in 1952, as we will later see.

Even so, historians in the future will probably be kinder to Truman than were many Americans in his own day. They will forgive him his personal excesses, just as they earlier forgave Lincoln his, and remember Truman's strength and courage and how in large matters he put the national interest above personal and party advantage. They will remember his contributions, the most important of which was a far-sighted foreign policy in Europe. They will remember, too, the difficulties of his tasks and the way in which he grew in leadership.

In spite of early tribulations, Truman became not only leader of his own party but also the true heir of Bryan, Wilson, and the two Roosevelts in perpetuating and developing the progressive tradition in the United States. In the conviction that the President must be the one national spokesman and defender of the general interest, he preserved the Executive branch against certain congressional assaults and even strengthened the office of President. In a period of postwar reaction, he fought hard and for the most part successfully to prevent a normal reaction from developing into a general repudiation of progressive ideals and practices.

Truman's most significant contribution, however, was the way in which he joined progressives in extending the horizons and enlarging the goals of the American progressive movement. This was a task of considerable difficulty, for at the end of the war progressives were divided, confused, and uncertain. Some, like the spokesmen of the CIO and the non-Communist followers of Henry A. Wallace, in a varying degree demanded the institution of a full-fledged collectivistic state, with widespread nationalization and comprehensive planning and economic controls. Others, especially many Southerners, demanded an end to further reform. Allying himself with neither extreme, Truman not only consolidated and extended the New Deal structure but also extended the frontiers of progressivism in the direction of civil rights, public health, and public power. As we will see, his Fair Deal opened new vistas ahead for progressives and provided a program for the future.

211 / *Demobilization, Reconversion, and a New Federal Structure*

As we have seen in an earlier chapter,[1] the immediate postwar years were a time of inflation and widespread labor unrest but withal of tremendous economic expansion and prosperity. They were a time also of growing international tension, which caused the problems of foreign policy to intrude into all the calculations of the executive and legislative leaders of the United States. Looking back over the tumult of the years 1945–1947, the historian is astonished by the constructive things that were done in spite of the apparent chaos in Washington.

The first order of national business in 1945 and 1946 was demobilization of the armed forces and conversion of the economy from a war to a peace footing. Even before the Japanese surrendered, it was apparent to the new President and his military advisers that the world was entering an uncertain period of potential conflict and that the national security demanded the retention of large armed forces during the period of realignment and emergence of a postwar power structure. And yet the dimensions of the Soviet threat to peace were not clear in the autumn of 1945, while the popular and congressional demand for speedy and drastic demobilization was so overwhelming that probably no administration could have resisted it. As one

[1] See above, pp. 582, 597–601.

writer has observed, "That rush to disarm in late 1945 was surely one of the most expensive economies—in terms of life and effort as well as of money—in which the United States ever indulged."[2] But it was inevitable.

In May 1945 the army began a limited demobilization, and with the collapse of Japan both armed services began discharging men as rapidly as possible. When the army slowed demobilization in January 1946, there were riots among enlisted men abroad and frenzied protests at home. By appealing for patience and support, the President and the Army Chief of Staff, General Eisenhower, quieted the storm. None the less, demobilization had to proceed inexorably in response to public and congressional demand. When it was completed by midsummer of 1946 the great wartime army and navy had been reduced to 1,500,000 and 700,000 men, respectively.

Time and again in 1946 and afterward until the Korean War the President and his military advisers pointed out the elemental fact that American armed strength was barely sufficient to meet the country's minimum international responsibilities, much less provide for security in the event of new aggressions. To be sure, Congress grudgingly extended a weak Selective Service from July 1, 1946, to May 31, 1947, and reinstituted Selective Service on a broader basis a year later. At the same time, the men on Capitol Hill refused to approve the administration's plan for universal military training and insisted upon even further reductions in armed strength from 1946 to 1948. Although there were momentary increases after the Communists seized power in Czechoslovakia and the Berlin blockade heightened Soviet-American tension in 1948, the President and his new Secretary of Defense, Louis Johnson, joined the economy forces in Congress in 1949 to effect new reductions that brought American armed strength to a postwar low point in the spring of 1950. By the eve of the Korean War they had imposed a $13,000,000,000 ceiling on defense expenditures and reduced the army to 600,000 men and ten active divisions.

Meanwhile, the country had confronted the problems of reconversion. One major problem—assistance for the millions of veterans—was solved thoroughly and without a show of partisanship. Determined that veterans should have generous help in finding jobs, adjusting to civilian life, and recovering lost educational opportunities, Congress in June 1944 had enacted the Servicemen's Readjustment Act, with good reason called the "G.I. Bill of Rights,"[3] and from 1945 through 1952 a grateful nation generously poured out its resources to help its former servicemen. Expenditures of the Veterans' Administration rose from $828,392,000 in 1944 to a peak of nearly $10,000,-000,000 in 1950 and then declined to about $6,000,000,000 in 1951 and 1952. From 1945 through 1952 the government gave $13,548,765,000 for education and training alone and nearly $4,000,000,000 for unemployment benefits and self-employment help; in addition, the Veterans' Administration guar-

---

[2] Walter Millis (ed.), *The Forrestal Diaries* (New York, 1951), p. 110; quoted by permission of the Viking Press, publishers.

[3] It provided large sums for new veterans' hospitals and vocational rehabilitation for the wounded in body and spirit; guaranteed unemployment compensation of $20 weekly for a year to veterans who could not find work; provided substantial assistance to veterans in the purchase of homes, farms, and businesses; and offered free tuition, books, and subsistence to veterans for job training and four years of college or university education.

anteed or insured nearly $16,500,000,000 in veterans' loans for homes, farms, and businesses and operated a chain of some 150 hospitals that served an average daily number of 108,038 patients in 1950.

Nor was there much partisan controversy in 1945 and 1946 over the desirability of tax reductions and assistance to industry in its conversion to civilian production. In November 1945, for example, Congress responded to public pressure by reducing taxes nearly $6,000,000,000, while during 1945 and 1946 the administration disposed of most of the government-owned war plants, which represented a total investment of $15,000,000,000 and accounted for some 20 per cent of the nation's industrial capacity.

The overshadowing domestic fear in 1944 and 1945 was the dread of a catastrophic postwar depression that might end in national bankruptcy and world chaos. The government's success in marshaling industry and labor during the war stimulated advanced progressives to conceive bold ideas. Repudiating the theory that the nation must inevitably careen through alternating periods of "boom and bust," progressives like Henry A. Wallace and spokesmen of the CIO talked of "60,000,000 jobs" and proposed that the federal government assume the responsibility of planning for full employment through indirect stimulation of purchasing power and, if necessary, sufficient compensatory spending to prevent recession. Approved by Roosevelt, the promise of "full employment" after the war became the major Democratic domestic pledge during the presidential campaign of 1944. Reaffirmed by President Truman in the late summer of 1945, the proposal for a planning measure stimulated the first full-fledged debate on postwar domestic policy.

The administration's plan was embodied in the Full Employment bill submitted by Senator James E. Murray, Democrat from Montana, in the autumn of 1945. It proposed that the President and his staff should prepare an annual national production and employment budget—an estimate of the investment and production necessary to maintain full employment—and that a congressional Joint Committee on the National Budget should assume responsibility for "federal investment and expenditure as will be sufficient to bring the aggregate volume . . . up to the level required to assure a full employment volume of production."

To conservatives, approval of the Murray bill could mean nothing less than committing the federal government to a permanent program of deficit spending through partisan agencies. They countered by proposing the establishment of a nonpartisan National Economic Commission to advise the President and Congress on the state of the economy and measures necessary, as one conservative put it, "to foster private enterprise . . . and promote a high and stable level of employment."

Although conservatives and progressives disagreed on means, the significant aspect of the debate over the Murray bill was the fact that both groups agreed that the chief responsibility for economic stabilization lay with the federal government. The outcome was the adoption in February 1946 of a compromise measure, the Employment Act, which affirmed national responsibility for prosperity without prescribing an inflexible formula to achieve it. The Act created, first, a three-man Council of Economic Advisers, presumably expert and nonpartisan, who should constantly study the economy for signs of weakness and advise the President and Congress on means of promoting the national economic welfare, and, second, a congressional Joint Committee on the Economic Report to study and propose stabilization measures.

A milestone in the development of American progressivism, the Employment Act established machinery, as the first chairman of the Council of Economic Advisers has written, for "mobilizing all our organizational resources, public and private, within our system of free enterprise, for a sustained high level of national production and the correspondingly high level of national income."[4] Future experience would reveal that even "experts" on the Council could disagree and that the ultimate decisions had to be made by political agencies. None the less, under the Employment Act investigation and planning for the national welfare became for the first time systematic and geared to the administrative and legislative machinery.

Even more urgent than the adoption of the Employment Act was the problem of constructing a postwar policy for the development of atomic energy. On the first basic issue of control, most Republicans and Democrats agreed that national security demanded the retention of an absolute governmental monopoly on all aspects of research and production of fissionable materials, at least until effective international machinery had been established to prevent the manufacture of atomic bombs. On the second basic issue of control of the atomic energy program at home, however, a heated controversy ensued when a special Senate committee set to work on an atomic energy bill in the autumn of 1945. The chairman of the committee, Senator Brien MacMahon of Connecticut, drafted a measure establishing exclusive civilian control through an Atomic Energy Commission and won the support of most progressives, scientists, and religious and educational leaders. On the other hand, Senator Arthur H. Vandenberg of Michigan suggested giving military and naval leaders a full voice in determining atomic energy policies and won the overwhelming support of the Senate committee.

The controversy came to a head in March and April 1946, after the committee adopted Vandenberg's amendment to the MacMahon bill providing for military participation. So violent was the public reaction that Vandenberg and his supporters agreed to a compromise amendment establishing a Military Liaison Committee to work with the Commission but placing exclusive control over policies in civilian hands. Thus the Atomic Energy Act, approved by the President on August 1, 1946, preserved governmental monopoly on fissionable materials, vested complete control of research and production in the hands of a five-man Atomic Energy Commission, and gave to the President alone the power to order the use of the atomic bomb in warfare.

One problem—the unification of the armed services—was entirely nonpartisan but gave rise to one of the bitterest controversies of the postwar era. Almost everyone, including the military and naval spokesmen, agreed that the Pearl Harbor disaster and wasteful competition by the services during the war had already proved the need for common control and direction of the defense establishment. But violent disagreement arose on almost every practical suggestion for unification, chiefly because the generals and the

[4] Edwin G. Nourse, *The 1950's Come First* (New York, 1951), p. 8; by permission of Henry Holt and Company, publishers.

army's friends in Congress favored unification and the admirals and the navy's champions feared that army domination of a unified defense structure would result in elimination of the Marine Corps and favoring land-based air forces at the expense of sea power.

From the end of 1945 until the summer of 1947, the partisans of the two services maneuvered and skirmished. Fortunately, the Secretary of the Navy, James V. Forrestal, supported unification and held rebellious admirals in check, while the President skillfully mediated. The result of the give and take was the National Security Act of July 26, 1947, which overhauled and strengthened the defense structure. It created a single Department and Secretary of Defense with Cabinet rank and supervision over the Secretaries of the Army, Navy, and Air Force; established a Joint Chiefs of Staff representing the three services, who should prepare defense plans and consider matters of strategy; and created a National Security Council, a National Security Resources Board, and a Central Intelligence Agency, charged with over-all responsibility for advising the President and Congress on measures to promote the national security.

As the first Secretary of Defense, James V. Forrestal, soon discovered, it was easier to erect the façade of a new defense structure than to compel genuine unification of the forces.[5] Even so, the adoption of the National Security Act was one of the great accomplishments of the Truman era. If it had done nothing more than establish an independent Air Force and provide the framework in which gradual unification could occur, the measure would have justified all the labor that went into its writing and adoption.

There was little partisan bickering and considerable agreement among all leaders in the government on the need for a thoroughgoing overhaul of the federal administrative and legislative structures, which had often grown without pattern during the New Deal and war periods. The most significant step toward executive reorganization came in 1947, when Congress approved and the President appointed a distinguished commission on executive reorganization headed by former President Herbert Hoover. Undertaking a comprehensive study of the complicated executive machinery, it issued eighteen reports, embodying recommendations for many consolidations, in the early months of 1949.[6]

---

[5] Forrestal broke under the strain, resigned on March 2, 1949, and committed suicide soon afterward in a moment of depression.

[6] Among the most important recommendations were the reduction of the number of federal departments and agencies from sixty-five to twenty-three, the establishment of a Department of Welfare, to consolidate federal activities in the fields of public health, education, and social welfare, and thoroughgoing reorganization of the Post Office Department. In the Reorganization Act of June 20, 1949, Congress authorized the President to submit plans for reorganization, which would go into effect unless Congress specifically disapproved. Between 1949 and 1950 Truman submitted thirty-six reorganization plans, all of which were allowed to go into effect except a plan to establish a Department of Welfare. Defeated in 1950 by Republicans and southern Democrats, who feared approval might imply acquiescence in the President's proposal for national health insurance, this plan was approved by Congress early in 1953 in response to a suggestion by President Eisenhower. After investigations in 1951 revealed widespread corruption in the Bureau of Internal Revenue, moreover, Congress the following year approved the President's plan to draw all officials of that Bureau, except the Commissioner, from the Civil Service ranks.

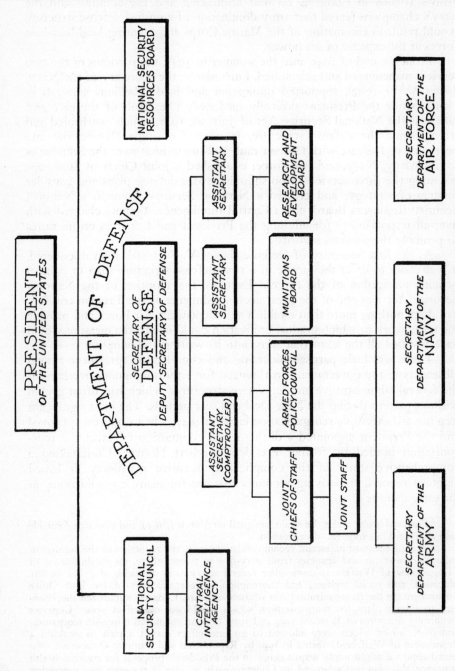

37. Organization for National Security in the Postwar Era

Largely at the President's insistence, Congress approved another major governmental change in 1947. Effected by the Presidental Succession Act of that year, it changed the line of the presidential succession after the Vice President from the Secretary of State and other Cabinet members to the Speaker of the House and the President *pro tempore* of the Senate, then followed by the Secretary of State and other Cabinet members. A final constitutional alteration was the Twenty-Second Amendment, which forbade election to the presidency for more than two full terms or the re-election of a President for more than one term if he had served more than two years of an unfinished term. Passed by the Republican Eightieth Congress in 1947 and approved by the thirty-sixth state on February 26, 1951, the Amendment came too late to achieve its major purpose—to prevent the re-election of Franklin D. Roosevelt; and it specifically exempted Truman from its interdiction. None the less, it also reflected a widespread conviction that the powers of the presidency were too great to justify the risk of having another perpetual President.

212 / *Truman's Struggles with Congress, 1945–1948*

If the President and his Democratic colleagues united with Republicans in Congress to accomplish many far-reaching changes in the immediate postwar era, they also engaged in bitter controversies over other aspects of economic and social policy—the continuation of New Deal programs for aid to agriculture and public health and housing, for example, or the questions of economic controls and revision of federal labor policies. By his gestures of friendship toward congressional leaders during the first months of his presidency, Truman encouraged conservatives to believe that he planned to preside over the liquidation of the progressive movement. This brief "honeymoon" came to an end on September 6, 1945, when the President sent his first important domestic message to the Capitol. Cutting loose from alleged conservative ties, he called for a full revival of progressive policies—extension of Social Security, increase in the minimum wage, a program for national health insurance, a renewal of the New Deal's war against slums, new regional developments like the TVA, a full employment bill, executive reorganization, and extension of wartime economic controls through the reconversion period.

Truman's chief problem in dealing with the Seventy-Ninth Congress, which sat during 1945 and 1946, was finding majority support for his legislative program. On many nonpartisan issues he succeeded with relative ease; on others he won compromise solutions that conservatives could approve. On advanced measures of welfare and civil rights he made no headway against the Republicans and southern Democrats who often controlled the two houses during 1945 and 1946. On the issues of economic controls and revision of federal labor policy,[7] Truman fought and lost his hardest battles with the conservative coalition.

Soon after the Japanese surrender, the President and Office of Price

---

[7] For Truman's controversy with Congress over labor policy in 1946, see above, pp. 600–601.

Administration announced they would undertake "continued stabilization of the national economy" by a gradual relaxation of wartime controls over prices, wages, and scarce commodities. During the last months of 1945 and the first half of 1946 the OPA was able to end most rationing, to continue priorities on scarce industrial materials, and to hold wholesale prices to an increase of only 7 per cent and the general cost of living to an increase of 3 per cent. At the same time, inflationary pressures were mounting powerfully to burst the bonds of price controls. Consumers with extra billions were buying in black markets; organized labor was driving for higher wages; and manufacturers and farmers had combined with Republican leaders in Congress to demand an end to all controls.

A bitter battle raged in Congress over extension of the OPA during the spring of 1946, and on June 27 the conservative coalition presented the President with a Price Control bill that extended the OPA for one year but severely weakened the agency's power and commanded it to decontrol prices "as rapidly as possible." Instead of acquiescing in the inevitable compromise, Truman vetoed the bill on June 29 and allowed price controls to end altogether on July 1. As Congress debated a new measure, prices rose wildly in the severest inflation since 1942. To be sure, on July 25, 1946, Congress approved a second Price Control bill extending price and rent controls for one year, but the damage was already done; and the new measure was, if anything, weaker and even more confusing than the bill that Truman had vetoed. The President gave up the fight after the Republican victory in the congressional elections in November 1946. On November 9 he ended all controls on wages and prices, except on rents, sugar, and rice; and the OPA began winding up its affairs a month later.

The wild inflation occurred just at the moment when the GOP leaders were beginning their campaign to capture Congress in the autumn elections. All during the late summer and early autumn, Republican campaigners and advertisements played up the theme of confusion and failure in the price control program. When the decontrol board, established by the Price Control Act, restored price ceilings on meat on August 21, for example, farmers simply withheld beef from the market and embattled housewives waited in line in vain for hamburger at any price. This episode gave the Republicans their most telling slogan, "Had Enough?"

In addition to the rising consumer resistance to price controls, numerous other signs pointed to an overwhelming Republican victory in November 1946. Truman had embittered organized labor by his drastic bridling of John L. Lewis and his stern action in breaking the railroad strike in the spring of 1946; at the same time, he had lost the support of conservatives by his vigorous advocacy of welfare and civil rights legislation. New Dealers, on the other hand, were disgruntled by two incidents that threatened to disrupt the Democratic party in 1946. The first was the dramatic resignation of the old curmudgeon, Harold L. Ickes, as Secretary of the Interior, following a disagreement over the appointment of Edwin Pauley as Undersecretary of the Navy. The second was Truman's firing of Secretary of Commerce Henry A. Wallace, soon after the former Vice President, on September 12, 1946, publicly attacked the administration's policy of stiffening resistance to Russian demands. But the Democratic party's chief liability in the autumn of 1946 was Truman himself, for the President had given millions of Americans an impression of total ineptitude.

Few observers were surprised, therefore, when the GOP won control of the House and Senate for the first time since 1930 and captured governorships in twenty-five of the thirty-two non-southern states on November 5, 1946, What was surprising, however, was the dimension of the landslide and the sharp decrease in the urban Democratic vote that occurred. Indeed, it was obvious that the machines in cities like Boston, New York, and Chicago, had been seriously weakened by prosperity and the movement of people into the suburbs. It was obvious, also, that the hitherto solidly Democratic labor bloc had momentarily disintegrated.

The significance of the Republican triumph soon became evident after the Eightieth Congress convened on January 3, 1947. There were many new faces and an entirely new conservative leadership in the two houses, but above them all, at least in consideration of domestic matters, stood Robert A. Taft of Ohio, chairman of the Republican policy committee in the Senate, champion of the business interests, and trenchant foe of advanced progressivism.

All through 1947 and the early months of 1948 the Republican leaders in Congress and the President and his Democratic allies sparred in preparation for the coming presidential campaign, and the noise emanating from Washington might have led a superficial observer to conclude that effective government was impossible in the melee. And yet there was often considerable difference between appearance and reality. In foreign policy during 1947–1948 the President and Congress cooperated to achieve a record unsurpassed during any comparable period in American history; and in many areas of domestic policy there was substantial agreement.

Even so, there were sharp differences over fundamental policies, the most important of which was labor legislation. Although he had moved severely against certain arrogant labor leaders in 1946 to vindicate the national sovereignty, Truman fought hard to defeat the Taft-Hartley Act.[8] Adopted over his veto in June 1947, it constituted the most important conservative triumph of the postwar era. A second matter of long controversy was ways and means of combating inflation. The President pleaded against further tax reduction, which he said would only increase inflationary pressures; but the Republicans in July 1947 adopted a measure over his veto that gave greatest relief to persons on low and middle class incomes. When prices continued to rise during the summer and autumn, Truman called Congress into special session on November 17, 1947, to consider a ten-point anti-inflation program. Responding with the Anti-Inflation bill of December 1947, the Republican leaders carefully avoided giving the President any effective power. In March 1948 Congress extended rent controls for another year; at the same time, it added to inflationary pressures by adopting, over Truman's veto, another measure of tax reduction, the third since the end of the war. The President and Congress fought their last battles before the

[8] See above, p. 601.

campaign of 1948 over housing and agricultural policies; the result was the triumph of the powerful real estate lobby in Washington and the adoption of a temporary agricultural act in June 1948.[9]

213 / The Election of 1948

Not for two decades had Republicans been so confident as during the early months of 1948. Among the Republican hopefuls, the most energetic candidate was former Governor Harold E. Stassen of Minnesota, who won widespread popular support by his frank support of progressive policies at home and vigorous American leadership in world affairs. In spite of his victories in the Wisconsin and Nebraska presidential primaries in early April, Stassen never had a chance against the party leaders. They preferred Robert A. Taft, whose conservatism had won the support of a large part of the business community, particularly in the Middle West. Taft's chances, however, were fatally weakened by his isolationist record before 1942, his lukewarm support of postwar internationalism, and above all by the popular feeling that he was cold and such a poor campaigner that he could never win.

In their natural desire to win, the Republican leaders rejected Taft and turned to General Dwight D. Eisenhower. When Eisenhower refused to be a candidate, they turned again to their titular leader, Governor Thomas E. Dewey of New York, who had gained a reputation as a progressive and strong internationalist. Meeting in Philadelphia on June 21, 1948, the Republican national convention nominated Dewey on the third ballot; named Governor Earl Warren of California as his running-mate; and adopted a brief platform that approved the New Deal reform structure and the postwar bipartisan foreign policy and promised further tax reductions, greater efficiency, and civil rights, welfare, and public housing legislation.

In the meantime, civil wars were apparently destroying the Democratic party. After his dismissal as Secretary of Commerce in September 1946, Henry A. Wallace had assumed the editorship of the *New Republic* and tried to rally New Dealers behind an advanced collectivistic program and against the administration's policy of resistance to Soviet imperialism. Organizing the Progressive Citizens of America in 1947, Wallace appealed especially to idealistic young people. When he announced, on December 29, 1947, that he would run for President on a third-party ticket, observers predicted he would poll from 5,000,000 to 8,000,000 votes and blast Democratic chances in 1948.

While the nation watched to see what dimensions the Wallace rebellion would assume, progressive leaders in the Democratic party maneuvered desperately to avoid having to choose between Truman and Wallace. Through

[9] Truman and moderate Republicans led by Senator Taft supported the Taft-Ellender-Wagner bill, which would have inaugurated a broad program of public housing designed to benefit lower income groups. All the Republican majority would allow, however, was a measure, adopted June 19, 1948, which provided only governmental credit for veterans' homes and cooperative housing projects. As for agriculture, Congress in June 1948 approved a measure continuing support of farm prices at 90 per cent of parity through 1949, to be followed by a program of flexible supports ranging from 60 to 90 per cent of parity.

their organization, Americans for Democratic Action, they tried alternately to force Truman to retire and to find a winning candidate in Justice William O. Douglas or General Eisenhower. The powerful Democratic leaders, Frank Hague of Jersey City, Edward Flynn of New York, and Jacob Arvey of Chicago, also joined the movement to oust Truman and draft Eisenhower. As if to make certain the rupture of the party, southern Democrats were up in arms against the President's civil rights program, threatening to bolt the party if the convention adopted a strong civil rights plank in the platform.

It was, therefore, a gloomy and contentious Democratic convention that assembled in Philadelphia from July 12 to 15, 1948. Determined to write a program for the future, the ADA progressives, led by Mayor Hubert Humphrey of Minneapolis and supported by the large city leaders, adopted a platform that reaffirmed the progressive tradition. Then, after a bitter fight on the floor, the convention adopted a civil rights plank demanding establishment of an FEPC and enactment of federal anti-lynching and anti-poll tax laws. Finally, early in the morning of July 15 a harassed convention named Truman for President because it had no other choice. As his running-mate the President chose Alben W. Barkley, President *pro tempore* of the Senate, after Justice Douglas had declined to run.

What Democratic leaders feared the most, a rupture in the party, ocurred soon after the Philadelphia convention adjourned. Meeting in Philadelphia from July 22 to 25, the rebel left wing organized the Progressive party, adopted a platform demanding gradual nationalization of basic industries, an end to segregation, and reorientation of foreign policy toward friendship with Russia, and nominated Wallace for President and Senator Glen Taylor of Idaho, "the singing cowboy," for Vice President. It was, actually, the high point of Wallace's strength, for the convention revealed what many persons had earlier suspected: that the Progressive party organization was controlled by Communists and fellow travelers, and that Wallace had allowed himself to be used in a Communist attempt to disrupt the progressive ranks. Few progressives went to the third-party convention; only one or two former New Deal leaders remained in the new party; and the more Wallace campaigned the more support he lost.

Meanwhile, the southern rebellion had also erupted. Meeting at Birmingham on July 17, 1948, the so-called "Dixiecrats" waved Confederate flags, formed the States' Rights Democratic party, and nominated Governor J. Strom Thurmond of South Carolina and Governor Fielding L. Wright of Mississippi on their "national" ticket. As opponents of the President's civil rights program and of the expansion of the federal authority, the "Dixiecrats" made a powerful appeal to southern white sentiments and won control of the Democratic party in Alabama, South Carolina, Mississippi, and Louisiana. By failing to organize an all-southern rebellion, however, they missed their chief objective, namely, to throw the election into the House of Representatives where they could wield the balance of power.

The rebellion of the left and right wings of the Democracy simply enhanced the supreme confidence of the Republican leaders. Governor Dewey conducted a mild and dignified campaign in which he repeated old strictures against alleged Democratic incompetence but made it clear that he approved all the basic aspects of Democratic domestic and foreign policy. Encouraged by the Gallup Poll, which showed him far in the lead, Dewey did not bestir himself unduly, except to make plans for his inauguration. And, it should be added, the mass of newspapers and magazines shared Dewey's confidence. The magazine *Life*, for example, printed its last issue before the election with a picture of the "next President" on the cover.

Indeed, apparently the only man in the country who thought Truman could win was the President himself. At the Democratic convention he startled the country by announcing he would call the Eightieth Congress into special session and give the Republicans an opportunity to enact their platform into law. And when Congress met from July 26 to August 7 without passing any important legislation, Truman went to the country in perhaps the most strenuous personal campaign in American history. Traveling more than 30,000 miles, he made 351 speeches, many of them "whistle-stop" talks in railroad yards from the rear platform of his car, to an estimated 12,000,000 people. Castigating the "do-nothing" Eightieth Congress, he urged a bold and full resumption of progressive policies: repeal of the Taft-Hartley Act, strong civil rights protection for minority groups, national health insurance, new antitrust legislation, federal aid to education, broadening of social security benefits, an increase in the minimum wage, and continued high parity support for farm prices. Moreover, he went into Harlem to become the first presidential candidate ever to appeal in person for Negro votes.

The American people admired the President's courage in fighting hard alone and assumed Dewey was bound to win. As one writer observed in the *New Yorker*, Americans seemed willing to give Truman anything but the presidency. But he knew better than the pollsters and commentators, and he went to bed on election night, November 2, 1948, confident and serene. In the most surprising political upset in American history, Truman won 24,105,695 popular and 304 electoral votes; Dewey, 21,969,170 popular and 189 electoral votes; Thurmond, 1,169,021 popular and 38 electoral votes; and Wallace, 1,156,103 popular votes. Moreover, the Democrats won control of the next Congress by majorities of ninety-three in the House and twelve in the Senate.

How did it happen, this political upheaval that no one on election eve had thought was possible? Republican critics of Dewey like the *Chicago Tribune* charged that his ineffectual campaign had failed to rouse the voters and was the chief cause of the Republican defeat. But in a careful survey one analyst later proved that Dewey had polled about the maximum normal Republican vote and that Truman would have been the gainer by a larger turnout on election day.

Truman and the Democrats retained control of the federal government for a number of reasons. The country was at peace, prosperous, and relatively united on foreign policy. The Democrats could thus stand as champions of a happy *status quo* and depict their opponents as the advocates of unnatural change. Moreover, by their firm support of civil rights legislation and repeal of the Taft-Hartley Act, Truman and progressive Democrats recaptured labor support and won an almost solid Negro allegiance. Ironically enough, the Wallace and "Dixiecrat" rebellions probably assured

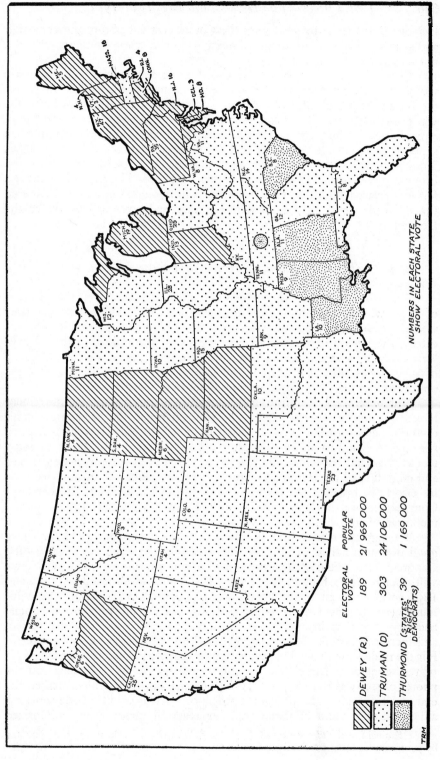

NUMBERS IN EACH STATE
SHOW ELECTORAL VOTE

	ELECTORAL VOTE	POPULAR VOTE
DEWEY (R)	189	21 969 000
TRUMAN (D)	303	24 106 000
THURMOND (STATES' RIGHTS DEMOCRATS)	39	1 169 000

32. *The Election of 1948*

Democratic victory, by removing the Communist issue from the campaign and assuring Negroes and other minority groups that the southern wing did not dominate the Democracy.

In the last analysis, however, the decisive factor in the Democratic victory was the unexpected behavior of the farmers in the Middle West and the Border States, all of which except Indiana went for Truman. Since the war farmers had feared and expected a depression. In 1948 farm prices began a precipitous decline, yet the Republicans promised not continued high price supports but "flexible" supports that could mean disaster in the rural areas. Truman, on the other hand, promised maintenance of a program that had brought prosperity. "I talked about voting for Dewey all summer," one Iowa farmer declared, "but when the time came I just couldn't do it. I remembered the depression and all the good things that had come to me under the Democrats."[10]

214 / *The Fair Deal: Revival of Progressivism*

Truman, obviously, was a new political creature after the election of 1948, while progressives were happier than they had been at any time since 1936. Not only did they have a champion in the White House dedicated to the cause of further reform; they also would have in the Eighty-First Congress a host of new and vigorous leaders. Surveying the wreckage of their hopes, chastened Republican leaders agreed with Dewey that the only hope for the GOP lay in a frank espousal of progressivism.

Not since 1936, therefore, had the future of the progressive movement looked brighter than when Harry S. Truman began the presidency in his own right and formally launched what he called the Fair Deal in his Annual Message to Congress on January 20, 1949. In these and subsequent messages to Congress and appeals to the people he repeated his proposals of the past and consolidated them into a comprehensive program. Let us now see how his efforts to broaden the horizons of progressivism fared at the hands of Congress before the Korean crisis set the nation upon the path of partial mobilization and war.

To state the matter briefly, Truman won less than he asked for and a good deal more than cynics thought he could get from the Eighty-First Congress. In the field of foreign policy he won notable victories, which we will discuss in the following chapters. For labor, he obtained, in 1949 and 1950, an amendment to the Fair Labor Standards Act increasing the minimum wage from 40 to 75 cents an hour and amendments to the Social Security Act that brought 10,000,000 new beneficiaries into the system and increased benefits for retired workers by an average of 77.5 per cent. For the millions who lived in rented homes and apartments, he won extension of rent control to March 31, 1951. His greatest victory for labor and the poorer classes was the Housing Act of 1949, adoption of which marked the end of a bitter struggle that had raged since 1945. Providing large sums for aid to cities in slum clearance and for research, this measure authorized

[10] Samuel Lubell, *The Future of American Politics* (New York, 1952), p. 161; quoted by permission of Harper & Brothers, publishers.

the construction of 810,000 units for low-income families during the next six years.

In other ways, moreover, the President and Congress cooperated to effect a substantial expansion of the economic and welfare activities of the federal government. Although he failed to win approval for the St. Lawrence Seaway, a Missouri Valley Authority, and other regional projects, Truman obtained large increases for the Reclamation Bureau's ambitious hydroelectric, water-control, and irrigation program in the West. He won, also, increased appropriations for the TVA, the Rural Electrification Administration, and the Farmers Home Administration, which since the war had continued the work of the Farm Security Administration in extending loans to farmers for rehabilitation and farm ownership. Finally, in June 1950 the President gained approval of a new Displaced Persons bill to admit some 400,000 European refugees and replace the measure of 1948, which he had labeled "anti-Catholic and anti-Semitic."

However, in striving to achieve labor's most important goal—repeal of the Taft-Hartley Act—the President, the AF of L, and the CIO tried too hard and failed. Congress and the public were obviously unwilling to give up many features of the measure that organized labor condemned as a "slave labor" law. On the other hand, the Senate, with the approval of Senator Taft, adopted a series of amendments that revised the measure substantially in labor's favor. Gambling on the future, Truman and his labor allies ruined the opportunity by rejecting the compromise and demanding nothing less than complete repeal of the Taft-Hartley Act.

On other important Fair Deal measures, the President and his friends pushed too hard too fast. The administration's program for agriculture, the Brannan Plan,[11] was farsighted and probably the best solution of the farm problem; but it aroused charges of regimentation and socialism and provoked the bitter opposition of the spokesmen of the large farmers. In spite of the failure of the Brannan Plan, the administration could claim that the Agricultural Act approved by Congress in October 1949 not only redeemed Democratic pledges but also reaffirmed a progressive policy for agriculture. This measure continued rigid price supports at 90 per cent of parity through 1950 and provided for a system of "flexible" price supports ranging from 75 to 90 per cent of parity afterward.

In other and more controversial projects of Fair Deal reform, Truman encountered bitter opposition and defeat. His proposal for national health insurance provoked the American Medical Association to undertake a gigantic campaign of newspaper advertising and lobbying that defeated the plan. The administration's plan for federal aid to education had substantial biparti-

---

[11] Proposed by Secretary of Agriculture Charles Brannan in April 1949, this plan represented the first serious effort since 1938 to eliminate the weaknesses in federal farm policy. It proposed to guarantee to farmers maintenance of a "farm income standard," or a dollar income as high as the average of the preceding ten years. To accomplish this goal, Brannan proposed to continue the program of price supports through loans and storage of nonperishable commodities. But for perishable commodities like meat, eggs, and dairy products, Brannan suggested a new method of distribution and maintenance of parity income—the immediate sale of all such commodities at whatever price the market would bring, followed by federal payments to the farmer to make up the difference between what he received and the official support price.

san support, but it ran afoul the opposition of the Roman Catholic Church, because it did not include certain subsidies to children enrolled in parochial schools.

It was in the field of civil rights, however, that the President suffered his most discouraging defeats. On December 5, 1946, he had appointed a Committee on Civil Rights, composed of distinguished Southerners, Negroes, and leaders in church and education throughout the country, to investigate and recommend "more adequate and effective means and procedures for the protection of the civil rights of the people of the United States." The following year the Committee issued its report, *To Secure These Rights*, which exposed the operation and consequences of the caste system and called for the inauguration of a systematic federal-state program to root out injustices based on race—by strengthening of the Civil Rights Section of the Justice Department and use of the FBI in cases involving violations of civil rights, enactment of anti-lynching and anti-poll tax laws, establishment of a permanent FEPC, and other such measures.

Year in and year out President Truman appealed to Congress to implement the Committee's recommendations; but he was never able to overcome the threat of a southern filibuster in the Senate. However, he had other if more limited recourses; and through them he struck a series of hard blows at the caste system. He strengthened the Civil Rights Section, began the practice of having the Justice Department assist private parties in civil rights cases, invited Negroes to the inaugural reception and ball in 1949, appointed the first Negro as Governor of the Virgin Islands and judge of the federal courts, and, most important, in 1948 set under way the abolition of segregation in all government departments and in the armed services.

Looking back over the administration's achievements during the eighteen months between the beginning of Truman's second term and the outbreak of the Korean War, the historian must wonder at how much, not how little, the Fair Deal accomplished during this period of prosperity and relative social and economic contentment. One fact of supreme importance was obvious at mid-century: regardless of party affiliation, the vast majority of Americans were so fundamentally progressive in temper and assumptions regarding the proper role of government that their differences involved only the degree and speed of further movement toward the progressive state.

215 /   *The Second Red Scare*

By the fateful day in June 1950, when the North Korean Communists invaded South Korea, the American people were convulsed by fear of Communist infiltration of their government and institutions. This second Red Scare, so reminiscent of the hysteria of the years after the First World War, would grow to larger proportions before it began to ebb and would leave in its backwash a residue of personal and partisan bitterness unparalleled since the days of Reconstruction. For this reason its effects were tragically disruptive during a time when the American people desperately needed unity of will and purpose. The unhappy fact was, however, that, unlike the Red Scare of 1919 and 1920, the popular fear of Communist infiltration following the Second World War was in some measure justified. And because the fear was present and in part well grounded, millions of Americans turned receptive ears to demagogues who sought to gain personal power and destroy freedom in politics, the press, and education by using the Communist issue.

In an earlier chapter we reviewed the rise and decline of Communism in the United States during the 1930's and noted the success of underground party members in infiltrating into some key positions in the federal government.[12] That infiltration continued unabated during the war. As one writer has put it, "During the war years, Communists and fellowtravelers had entered the government in droves. . . . During wartime, most government agencies had considered Communist affiliations to be unimportant. In the Office of Strategic Services, it was common knowledge that the employment of pro-Communists was approved at very high levels provided they were suited for specific jobs."[13]

Although the FBI undertook its first comprehensive investigation of Communist organizations and the departments in Washington began their own disjointed and often ineffective investigations in 1945 and 1946, two events—the *Amerasia* case and the exposure of a Soviet spy ring in Canada —gave the impetus for a full-scale drive to root Communists out of the American government.

Early in 1945 the Office of Strategic Services discovered that certain of its most secret documents had fallen into the hands of Philip J. Jaffe, editor of *Amerasia*, a Communist-sponsored monthly magazine established for the purpose of influencing American policy in the Far East. On March 11, 1945, OSS officers raided the *Amerasia* offices and discovered huge piles of diplomatic and military documents. A few days later jurisdiction was given to the FBI, which easily established an intimate connection between Jaffe and his associates and Soviet and Chinese Communist officials. Knowing it could not make a strong case, because it had taken evidence illegally, the Justice Department none the less prosecuted Jaffe and his co-conspirators in order to destroy their ring. Jaffe and an accomplice subsequently received light fines for conspiring to receive government property illegally.

A much more important factor in awakening the American people and government to the menace of Communism from within was the report issued in 1946 by a Canadian royal commission appointed to investigate charges of Communist espionage. The commission proved that the Communist party in Canada was an arm of the Soviet government; exposed the operation of several Soviet spy rings; and revealed that at least twenty-three Canadians in "positions of trust," one of them a member of Parliament, another a leading atomic scientist, were agents of the Communist ring and had sent atomic secrets and samples of uranium to Moscow.

These revelations spurred the FBI and security officers of the various Washington departments to a full-scale drive against Communists. Then, on March 22, 1947, President Truman issued an Executive Order inaugurating a comprehensive investigation of all federal employees by the FBI and the Civil Service Commission. Some features of the program evoked strong op-

---

[12] See above, pp. 442–446.
[13] Nathaniel Weyl, *The Battle Against Disloyalty* (New York, 1951), p. 180; used by permission of Thomas Y. Crowell, publishers.

position from liberals, who charged that the government had introduced the principle of "guilt by association" and had failed to provide adequate safeguards against discharge on account of rumors and unknown accusers. On the whole, however, the administration moved with regard for justice and civil rights during its loyalty probe from 1947 to 1951.

By the early months of 1951 the gigantic task had been completed. The Civil Service Commission had cleared more than 3,000,000 federal employees; the FBI had made some 14,000 full-scale investigations of doubtful cases; over 2,000 employees had resigned; and 212 persons had been dismissed on the ground that there was reasonable doubt as to their loyalty. Nor was this all. In August 1950 the President approved a measure authorizing heads of ten so-called "sensitive" departments and agencies to dismiss persons who were not necessarily disloyal but who were deemed to be bad security risks. Persons thus accused might demand a hearing by the security board of their own agency but were denied the right of appeal to a review board.

In spite of the thoroughness, even the severity, of the administration's loyalty probe,[14] it was not enough to quiet the popular alarm or to prevent the Republicans from exploiting the issue of Communism in government. This was true, not only because demagogues played upon the issue, but also because a number of sensational trials and exposures after 1947 revealed the former full extent of the Communist infiltration, the way in which the American Communist party served as an arm of the Kremlin, and the devastating effectiveness of the Soviet espionage ring in delivering to Moscow secrets vital to the security of the American people and the rest of the free world. It was true, moreover, because the President and a large body of public leaders were drawn into a compromising position in one of the most celebrated and tragic cases in American history—the trial of Alger Hiss, ostensibly for perjury but actually for Soviet espionage.

A member of the Ware Group, the most important Communist cell in Washington, during the New Deal era, Hiss had risen rapidly through various departments to a position of considerable trust in the State Department and had in a sense become the epitome of the able young civil servant. Among a host of friends he could count a Justice of the Supreme Court and a future Secretary of State. He resigned from the State Department in 1947 to accept the presidency of the Carnegie Endowment for International Peace of New York City.

Whittaker Chambers, a former Soviet agent, had denounced Hiss and other Communists to the State Department in 1939 but had failed to offer proof or even to describe the espionage network of which Hiss was a member. Convinced subsequently that democracy and Communism were engaged in a death grapple, Chambers told his story to the House un-American activities committee in 1948; and when Hiss sued for libel, Chambers produced microfilms of sixty-five State Department documents that he said Hiss had passed to him in early 1938. Called before a federal grand jury in New York, Hiss denied that he had ever delivered State Department documents to

---

[14] Perhaps the best testimony to the effectiveness of the program was the failure of the Justice Department, security officials in the various departments, and congressional committees to find any Communists in the government after the Republicans came to power in 1953.

Chambers. He was then indicted for perjury and convicted on January 21, 1950, after a first trial had ended in a hung jury.

Hiss' personal tragedy was awful enough; more tragic, however, was the way in which he betrayed the President, who in the autumn of 1948 denounced the House committee's investigation as a "red herring," and a large body of distinguished public leaders who testified to his integrity. Indeed, it is not too much to say that the Hiss trials, more than any other event of the postwar era, contributed to the growing public conviction that the Roosevelt and Truman administrations had been and were still oblivious to the danger of Communist subversion at home.

One effect of the Hiss trials was to rehabilitate the House un-American activities committee, which had long been the whipping boy of liberals, and to spur it to new investigations in 1949 and 1950. At the same time, in 1949, the country was shocked by the arrest, trial, and conviction of Judith Coplon, a young employee in the Justice Department, for passing vital information on the FBI's counterespionage system to a Soviet agent. However, the event that set off nearly a wave of hysteria in the United States in 1950 was the revelation that a group of Anglo-American agents had succeeded in delivering full information on the manufacture of the atomic bomb to the Soviet government from 1943 to 1947.[15]

Revelation of the fact that the atomic spy ring was not broken up until five years after it had accomplished its mission raised new fears in the minds of millions of Americans and set the stage for the spectacular rise of Joseph R. McCarthy of Wisconsin and the burgeoning of a full-scale anti-Communist hysteria in the United States. Elected to the Senate in 1946 after defeating the distinguished Robert M. La Follette, Jr., for the Republican nomination, McCarthy had already acquired considerable reputation for moral callousness, doubtful integrity, and utter ruthlessness by 1950. In search of an issue to rehabilitate his ebbing political fortunes, he chose Communism and Communist infiltration of the government in January 1950. By his indiscriminate and reckless attacks during the next three years he won clear title as the most unprincipled man in public life since Aaron Burr and the most successful demagogue since Huey Long. At the same time, he did more than any other living American to confuse and divide the people and discredit his country's good name abroad.

On February 9, 1950, McCarthy opened his campaign, many persons thought, to win control of the Republican party, by charging that he had the names of 205, or fifty-seven, Communists in the State Department. Unable to point out a single Communist then in the Department, McCarthy countered by naming Owen Lattimore of the Johns Hopkins University and an expert on the Far East as the head of "the espionage ring in the

---

[15] All during the war Soviet agents made fantastic attempts to obtain information about all phases of the atomic energy program. Army intelligence and FBI agents frustrated most of these efforts but failed to discover the most important atomic spy ring. It was led by Dr. Klaus Fuchs, a German-born physicist and naturalized British subject, who had been sent to Los Alamos in 1944 to help make the atomic bomb and who succeeded in delivering apparently complete information on the bomb to Soviet agents. The American people learned the shocking and frightening news of his betrayal when Fuchs was arrested in February 1950 and promptly confessed to British authorities, and when the FBI soon afterward arrested Fuchs' accomplices in the United States.

State Department." When J. Edgar Hoover, head of the FBI, affirmed that there was no evidence to substantiate this charge,[16] a special Senate committee headed by Millard Tydings of Maryland gave Lattimore a clean bill of health. Such failure only stirred McCarthy to more frenzied attacks. He turned next against Philip C. Jessup, American representative in the General Assembly of the United Nations, charging savagely that this distinguished public servant had Communist connections; against Senator Tydings, whom he helped defeat for re-election in the autumn of 1950; and finally against Generals George C. Marshall and Dwight D. Eisenhower, whom he accused on June 15, 1951, of assisting the Russians in their drive for world domination.

McCarthy's smear campaign and use of the "big lie" tactic, so reminiscent of the methods of Adolf Hitler, filled many men with loathing, but millions of Americans were so frightened by the revelations of Communist espionage and infiltration that they turned receptive ears to his propaganda. Moreover, leaders in the Republican party encouraged the Wisconsin demagogue and used him with apparently telling effect in the congressional campaign of 1950. There would be a reckoning after the inauguration of the Republican administration in 1953, to be sure; but for a time it seemed the great GOP had at least approved of "McCarthyism."

216 / Communism, the Courts, and Congress

"McCarthyism" was only the most violent manifestation of the anti-Communist fear that engulfed the United States from 1948 to 1953. In a varying degree the hysteria affected the press, schools, churches, the courts, and Congress. It created an atmosphere of fear and above all stimulated the conviction that it was safer to conform than to disagree with the majority. To be sure, many bold voices pleaded for sanity and preservation of civil liberties, and there were signs by 1953 that the hysteria was beginning to ebb. Meanwhile, however, the government had carried through and the courts had approved a program to destroy the Communist movement that greatly diminished traditional American civil liberty.

The Truman administration opened the drive in 1948 by obtaining the indictment of eleven high-ranking Communist leaders for conspiring, in violation of the Smith Act of 1940, to *teach* the violent overthrow of the United States. The government had prepared its case thoroughly; and during the trial that lasted more than nine months in 1949 it proved its charges by the testimony of a number of former Communists and agents planted in the Communist party by the FBI. The defense, on the other hand, failed either to convince the public that the trial was unfair or to harry the long-suffering trial judge into insanity or suicide. Convicted and sentenced to varying terms in prison, the Communist leaders appealed to the Court of Appeals, where the conviction was upheld. The case, Dennis *v*. United States, then came before the Supreme Court for final review.

[16] Apparently the only serious charge brought against Lattimore was the allegation that he consciously sought to influence American Far Eastern policy in order to further Soviet interests. The Senate Internal Security Committee, which reopened the Lattimore case during 1951 and 1952, made this accusation and obtained an indictment charging Lattimore with perjury and seeking to further Soviet interests.

In one of the most important decisions in its history, the Court upheld the constitutionality of the Smith Act and confirmed the conviction of the eleven Communists by a vote of six to two on June 4, 1951. The charge levied against them was not conspiracy to overthrow the government by force, but conspiracy to teach or advocate revolution. Speaking for the majority, Chief Justice Vinson reconciled the conviction with the right of free speech by invoking the "clear and present danger" doctrine and by affirming that the government had proved the Communist threat was sufficiently substantial to justify conviction under this doctrine.

Soon afterward, the Justice Department obtained the conviction and imprisonment of some forty regional, state, and Hawaiian Communist leaders for violating the Smith Act. Although the Communist party itself survived, by 1953 the Communist movement in the United States was nearly destroyed, its apparatus broken and its leaders scattered and in prison.

Troubled by this jailing of people, not for acts of violence or even conspiracy to commit such acts, but for teaching and advocating violent overthrow of the government, defenders of the Anglo-American traditions were shocked, furthermore, by two Supreme Court decisions in 1951 and 1952 that seemed to condone police censorship and state suppression of free speech on broad grounds.[17] Indeed, many persons wondered whether the Court had not been sucked into the vortex of the reaction against Communism.

Congress, too, reacted violently in 1950 by approving over the President's veto the McCarran Internal Security bill, which was easily the severest measure since the Sedition Act of 1918 and one of the most confused. It required Communist organizations to register with the Attorney General and to furnish complete membership lists and financial statements, but specifically declared that membership or officeholding in a Communist organization was not, *per se*, a crime. In a second breath, the Act made it illegal knowingly to conspire to perform "any act" that would "substantially" contribute to the establishment of a totalitarian dictatorship in the United States; forbade the employment of Communists in defense plants or the granting of passports to Communists; authorized the government to intern Communists in the event of war; and established a bipartisan Subversive Activities Control Board to assist the Attorney General in exposing subversive organizations.

If, as the President charged in his veto message, the internal security provisions of the McCarran Act were mainly blundering and ineffective, then the provisions relating to immigation, deportation, and naturalization struck a serious blow at American security. By forbidding the entry into the United States of any person who had once been a member of a totalitarian organiza-

---

[17] In the cases of Feiner *v.* New York and Beauharnais *v.* Illinois. Feiner had been arrested for disorderly conduct while making a soapbox speech in Syracuse, New York, during the campaign of 1948. The shocking aspect of the Supreme Court's verdict, which upheld the conviction, was the implication that the police were justified in arresting any person who *in their opinion* was provoking a riot. Beauharnais was head of the anti-Negro White Circle League of Chicago and was convicted of violating an Illinois statute forbidding the libeling of any person or group on account of race, color, creed, or religion. In upholding the conviction by a five to four majority, the Court specifically approved the new theory of "group libel" and thus further enlarged the state's control over speech and expression.

tion, for example, the measure deprived the American government of its most effective means of inducing Russian and other Communist leaders to break with their governments and come into the free camp. Little wonder it was, therefore, that the Justice Department, the Defense Department, and the Central Intelligence Agency, as well as the President, opposed the McCarran bill.

Congressional determination to strike at Communism was reflected again two years later, when the two houses in June 1952 passed over Truman's veto the McCarran-Walter Immigration and Nationality bill. By permitting the naturalization of Asiatics living in the United States and the admission of some 2,000 Orientals annually on a quota basis, the measure rectified an old injustice. On the other hand, the President and many liberals thought its provisions for the exclusion and deportation of aliens and the control of American citizens abroad were unnecessarily harsh and subversive of the fundamental rights of citizens.

Obviously, the obsessive fear of Communism in the postwar era provoked not merely hysteria among the American people but also caused their leaders and judges to approve programs and measures that were, to say the least, contrary to the nation's traditions of civil liberty. Where would it all lead and when would it end, this uncontrolled fear, this "McCarthyism," this indiscriminate alarm unbefitting a great, free, and powerful democracy? Thoughtful men at mid-century did not know the answer.

CHAPTER 28 / VAIN STRUGGLES FOR A BRAVE NEW WORLD, 1945–1949

*A*FTER the German and Japanese surrenders, the American people thanked God the awful carnage was over and that a new world order would banish fears and rivalries upon which wars bred. Events following the war, however, soon made a mockery of these hopes. Unapparent though it was to most Americans in 1945, the Allied victory had raised a new menace—the threat of Soviet expansion—almost as great as the Nazi danger had been. For with the collapse of Germany and Japan the most effective counterbalances to Soviet power were destroyed, and the American people found themselves confronted with the alternatives of either allowing the Russians to fill the power vacuums in Europe and the Far East or of building new aggregations to offset a balance favorable to Russia.

In due time the American people would learn that perils and hardships inevitably accompany leadership in world affairs. The grave danger during the period 1945–1949 was, however, that Americans were still so inexperienced and naive as to expect prompt and easy solutions, and that they would abandon leadership when their hopes were frustrated, as they had done in 1919 and 1920. Let us now see what triumphs and failures awaited the American people and their leaders during the postwar years, and how they groped toward effective leadership in world affairs.

217 / The Brave New World

From the beginning of American participation in the Second World War, President Roosevelt and Secretary of State Cordell Hull worked diligently to achieve the primary objective of their postwar policy, the creation of an effective international organization to prevent aggression and preserve the peace. In the United States they found an almost unanimous response; abroad they found disagreement only upon details; and at the Dumbarton Oaks Conference in 1944 and the Yalta Conference in early 1945 the leaders of the three great powers resolved their differences, approved the structure of the new agency, and convoked an international conference to meet in San Francisco in April 1945 to draft a charter for the United Nations.

It seemed for a time in March and April 1945 that Anglo-American and Russian disagreement over Poland might disrupt the conference before it could meet. But when President Truman made it clear to Foreign Minister Molotov on April 22, 1945, that the United States intended to take leadership in forming an international organization whether or not the Moscow government cooperated, the Russians abruptly changed their attitude. Thus the conference opened on schedule on April 25, and representatives of forty-six nations met to transform a wartime alliance into a permanent structure for world peace.

The San Francisco Conference, however, was an inauspicious beginning for the reign of universal brotherhood. From its beginning nearly to its end on June 26, the American and Russian delegates wrangled over questions large and small; and on one occasion President Truman saved the conference from disruption only by appealing personally to Stalin. In the end, the Charter of the United Nations that was signed on June 26, ratified by the United States Senate on July 28, and promulgated on October 24, 1945, embodied a minimum of concessions to Soviet demands and every important objective for which the United States had contended. In all its strengths and weaknesses, therefore, the Charter was mainly an American document— Woodrow Wilson's League Covenant embellished and revised. What structures did it establish to promote peace in the brave new world?

The legislature of the United Nations was a two-house body. There was the General Assembly, in which each member nation might have as many as five delegates but only one vote—except Russia, which had three votes— empowered to discuss any question and to recommend to the Security Council on any matter within the scope of the Charter, except in the case of a dispute already on the Council's agenda. A "town meeting of the world," the Assembly was conceived as a sounding board for the small nations. Initiative and authority in fundamental matters were given, instead, to the Security Council, composed of representatives of five powers[1] with permanent seats and six other members elected by the General Assembly. Questions of procedure might be settled by the vote of any seven members, but all permanent members had to approve action on any substantive question.

The Charter created elaborate additional apparatus to deal with other matters. There was a Secretariat, headed by a Secretary- General, to perform routine tasks of administration, and an International Court of Justice endowed with such jurisdiction as member states chose to grant. There were also dozens of subsidiary and allied independent agencies: the United Nations Economic and Social Council, with its own numerous commissions; the Trusteeship Council, established to supervise old League mandates and territories taken from Japan and Italy at the end of the Second World War; the International Monetary Fund, with total resources of nearly $9,000,000,000 for currency stabilization and the expansion of world trade; and the International Bank for Reconstruction and Development, with subscribed capital of $9,100,000,000, to facilitate long-term productive investment in war-ravaged and economically backward areas. There was, finally, the United Nations Relief and Rehabilitation Administration, eventually given nearly

[1] The United States, Great Britain, Russia, France, and China.

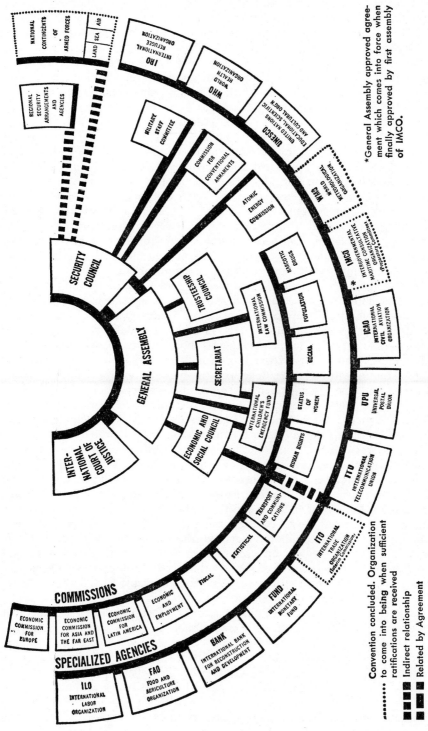

NATIONAL CONTINGENTS OF ARMED FORCES

LAND · SEA · AIR

REGIONAL SECURITY ARRANGEMENTS AND AGENCIES

IRO INTERNATIONAL REFUGEE ORGANIZATION

WHO WORLD HEALTH ORGANIZATION

UNESCO UNITED NATIONS EDUCATIONAL SCIENTIFIC AND CULTURAL ORGN.

WMO WORLD METEOROLOGICAL ORGANIZATION

IMCO *INTERGOVERNMENTAL CONSULTATIVE MARITIME ORGANIZATION (Preparatory Commission)

MILITARY STAFF COMMITTEE

COMMISSION FOR CONVENTIONAL ARMAMENTS

ATOMIC ENERGY COMMISSION

NARCOTIC DRUGS

POPULATION

ICAO INTERNATIONAL CIVIL AVIATION ORGANIZATION

SECURITY COUNCIL

TRUSTEESHIP COUNCIL

INTERNATIONAL LAW COMMISSION

SOCIAL

STATUS OF WOMEN

UPU UNIVERSAL POSTAL UNION

GENERAL ASSEMBLY

SECRETARIAT

INTERNATIONAL CHILDREN'S EMERGENCY FUND

HUMAN RIGHTS

ITU INTERNATIONAL TELECOMMUNICATION UNION

INTER-NATIONAL COURT OF JUSTICE

ECONOMIC AND SOCIAL COUNCIL

TRANSPORT AND COMMUNI-CATIONS

ITO INTERNATIONAL TRADE ORGANIZATION (Interim Commission)

STATISTICAL

FISCAL

FUND INTERNATIONAL MONETARY FUND

COMMISSIONS

ECONOMIC COMMISSION FOR EUROPE

ECONOMIC COMMISSION FOR ASIA AND THE FAR EAST

ECONOMIC COMMISSION FOR LATIN AMERICA

ECONOMIC AND EMPLOYMENT

BANK INTERNATIONAL BANK FOR RECONSTRUCTION AND DEVELOPMENT

SPECIALIZED AGENCIES

ILO INTERNATIONAL LABOR ORGANIZATION

FAO FOOD AND AGRICULTURE ORGANIZATION

*General Assembly approved agreement which comes into force when finally approved by first assembly of IMCO.

Convention concluded. Organization to come into being when sufficient ratifications are received

Indirect relationship

Related by Agreement

38.   The United Nations

$4,000,000,000 to provide food and clothing for the war-stricken peoples of Europe and Asia from 1945 to 1947.

It was an imposing structure, one calculated to fit every need and please all but the most extreme nationalists. But it was a structure for world confederation and cooperation, not for effective world government. On paper the United Nations Charter inaugurated an era of universal peace, for all members agreed to follow the path of arbitration rather than choose the road to war. And yet the United Nations was weak precisely because it lacked power sufficient to its task. Like the American union established by the Articles of Confederation, the United Nations was an association of sovereign states, with no authority except such as the leading members condescended to let it use. Established primarily to prevent future wars, the United Nations could be blocked in performing this elemental function by the veto of one of the permanent members of the Security Council. In other words, the United Nations would be powerless to prevent aggression by one of its leading members. In this respect, it was a weaker peace instrument than the League of Nations had been. Nor was there much hope of reform and reorganization, for the Charter gave the permanent members of the Security Council the right to veto any proposed amendments.

In their fear of isolationist sentiment at home and compelling desire to bring Russia into the new world order, the American leaders, notably Roosevelt and Hull, insisted upon establishing an agency that would not impair national sovereignty and could function effectively only so long as all the great powers agreed. Thus, the veto was more an American than a Russian invention; the provision in Article 51 for "regional" defensive associations, the creation of which later emphasized the weakness of the United Nations as a peace agency, was included at American insistence.

However, these inherent weaknesses of the United Nations were only dimly perceptible as the American people set to the task of helping create a new and better world in 1945. To the first and most urgent task, that of relief for war-ravaged areas, the American people and their government responded with commendable generosity. Through UNRRA, the United States contributed some $2,700,000,000 in food and supplies to the peoples of China and central and eastern Europe. In addition, the American army assumed the burden of relief in Japan and the American zone of Germany, while the American Red Cross, church groups, and private organizations added several hundred million dollars' worth of clothing and food. Nor was this all. Through the sale on credit of surplus property and Lend-Lease supplies and the extension of credits by the Export-Import Bank, the Washington government made some $4,700,000,000 available for additional relief and reconstruction, chiefly to western Europe.

To the second task, the reconstruction of foreign trade, the American government addressed itself with considerable boldness and success in the immediate postwar years. The fundamental problem was Europe's continued dependence upon the United States for food, supplies, and industrial equipment and her inability to pay in full, either in dollars, goods, or services, because of the abrupt termination of Lend-Lease assistance at the end of the war. In 1946 and 1947, for example, foreigners accumulated deficits of $7,704,000,000 and $11,478,000,000, deficits so staggering that world trade would have collapsed without decisive support by the United States. Before 1948 the Washington government solved the problem by a series of stop-gap expedients: UNRRA and other aid, loans by the Export-Import Bank, a credit loan of $3,750,000,000 to the British government in 1946, and the like. The world economy was not much healthier in 1948 than it had been in 1945; on the other hand, stop-gap aid sufficed to prevent the collapse of the international economic structure until a comprehensive reconstruction program could be matured and launched.

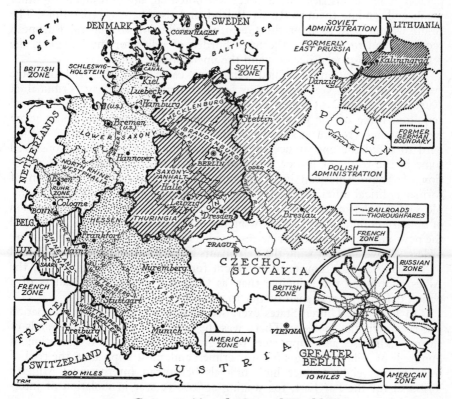

33. *Germany After the Second World War*

The third and perhaps the most difficult task in building the brave new world was the reconstruction and reform of Germany and Japan and the punishment of individuals allegedly responsible for the war. It was an undertaking for which the American people were unprepared, and in retrospect many of the occupation policies seemed unwise, unnecessarily harsh, and, above all, utopian. Not even during the bitterest days of Reconstruction had the American government practiced such terrible vengeance upon former enemies; not even during the heyday of Wilsonian missionary interventionism had the United States embarked upon such a stupendous task of reforming other nations.

American occupation policy in Germany was determined in the beginning by the desire to visit condign punishment and then to remake the

German people and institutions over in the image of an American model. All the four occupying powers were pledged to destroy Nazism and to help build new democratic governments and institutions, but the American occupation authorities outshone all the others in zeal. By the middle of 1949, when "denazification" was completed, military authorities and German tribunals had punished 1,635 major and some 600,000 minor Nazi offenders. At the same time, the Americans cooperated with the other powers in limiting German steel production to a low level, in destroying not only armament plants but also industries with a direct war potential, and in dismantling other plants and sending them to Russia, Poland, and elsewhere as reparations. The result was in part to limit the German contribution to general European recovery and to aggravate the huge burden of relief for the homeless, the refugees and displaced persons, and the unemployed.

The culmination of Allied vengeance came with the trial of some twenty-two high Nazi officials by an International Military Tribunal at Nuremberg from November 21, 1945, to October 1, 1946. The Tribunal acquitted three of the defendants and convicted nineteen, of whom seven were sentenced to prison and the balance were sentenced to death.[2] Trying hard to avoid the appearance of a kangaroo court, the Tribunal observed some of the forms of justice. Even so, the trial violated nearly every tradition of Anglo-American jurisprudence. The conviction and execution of former political officials for planning and waging aggressive war, for example, violated the ancient prohibition against *ex post facto* laws. The execution of military commanders for following the orders of their superiors established the new and impossible doctrine that soldiers might be punished for obeying orders. Above all, by trying the defendants in a special military court instead of allowing regular courts to try them for war crimes and atrocities, the Allies established the principle that, as Churchill put it, "the leaders of a nation defeated in war shall be put to death by the victors."

In Japan the United States exercised complete control over occupation and reconstruction policies. There was the inevitable purge of thousands of alleged militarists and supporters of aggression; the trial and execution of hundreds of military leaders for war crimes; and, most important, the trial of some twenty-eight former high officials before an International Military Tribunal for the Far East, for waging aggressive war in violation of international law.[3]

At the same time, the Supreme Commander for the Allied Powers, General Douglas MacArthur, and his subordinates came not merely to punish but also to reform. Attempting to destroy institutions and customs that had served the Japanese people for thousands of years, they sought to create a new political, economic, and social order with roots deep in the American utopian traditions. Including the renunciation even of defensive war, complete demilitarization, land distribution, an antitrust campaign in

---

[2] The death sentence was executed by the hanging of eight defendants. One of them, Martin Bormann, was never apprehended and was presumed to be dead; another, Hermann Goering, cheated the hangman by committing suicide.

[3] This "trial" began in Tokyo on June 3, 1946, and ended on April 16, 1948. On November 11, 1948, the Tribunal found all defendants guilty and sentenced seven of them, including two former Premiers of Japan, to death by hanging. The sentences were executed in Tokyo on December 23, 1948.

the Populist tradition, and the inauguration of social democracy, MacArthur's program aimed at nothing less than the creation of the perfect state and society. A few "reactionaries" protested; a few "realists" suggested that the utter destruction of Japanese power would only serve the interests of the Soviet Union by creating a power vacuum in the Far East; but the vast majority of Americans hailed the building of this new and better America in the far Pacific.

218 / The Breakup of the Grand Alliance, 1945–1947

Until his death President Roosevelt worked hard to remove Soviet suspicions and create an atmosphere of mutual trust in which genuine collaboration could develop. In spite of increasing evidences of Russian bad faith and imperialistic ambitions, in spite of warnings by the American Ambassador in Moscow, W. Averell Harriman, and his assistant, George F. Kennan, that such collaboration was impossible, President Truman and his new Secretary of State, James F. Byrnes,[4] continued Roosevelt's search for understanding during 1945 and 1946. Perhaps it was well they made the effort, for in their striving and failure they awakened a vast majority of Americans to the enormity of the Soviet danger to the free world.

Russian action in establishing a Communist government in Rumania, bitter Allied dissension over the creation of a government for Poland, and Stalin's cynical charge that Roosevelt and Churchill were conspiring to make a separate peace with Germany had raised grave doubts as to the permanence of the Grand Alliance by the spring of 1945. When the rift widened at the San Francisco Conference, President Truman sent Harry Hopkins to Moscow in May 1945 to join Harriman in frank talks with Stalin. In an angry mood, the Russian leader accused the American government of insulting the USSR at San Francisco and of ending Lend-Lease aid abruptly after the German surrender in order to apply strong pressure on the Soviet government. Reassured by Hopkins, Stalin mellowed in conversation and agreed to admit non-Communist Poles to the Polish government and to meet with President Truman and Prime Minister Churchill at Potsdam in July for a full discussion of outstanding problems.

Truman, Stalin, Churchill, and Clement Attlee, Churchill's successor as head of the new Labour government, assembled in Potsdam, outside shattered Berlin, on July 17, 1945, for the last meeting of the chiefs of state of the Grand Alliance. The conferees quickly agreed to issue a Declaration demanding the immediate surrender of Japan and to establish a Council of Foreign Ministers to prepare peace treaties for Italy and the Balkan states that had joined in Hitler's attack against Russia. There was, however, almost interminable disagreement over the sensitive issues—reparations and the implementing of the Yalta Declaration on Liberated Countries. Under strong pressure from Truman and Churchill, the Russians finally agreed to allow Anglo-American observers in Rumania, Hungary, Bulgaria, and Finland to move about freely. In return, the American and British leaders approved

---

[4] President Truman appointed Byrnes Secretary of State on June 30, 1945, to succeed Edward R. Stettinius, Jr.

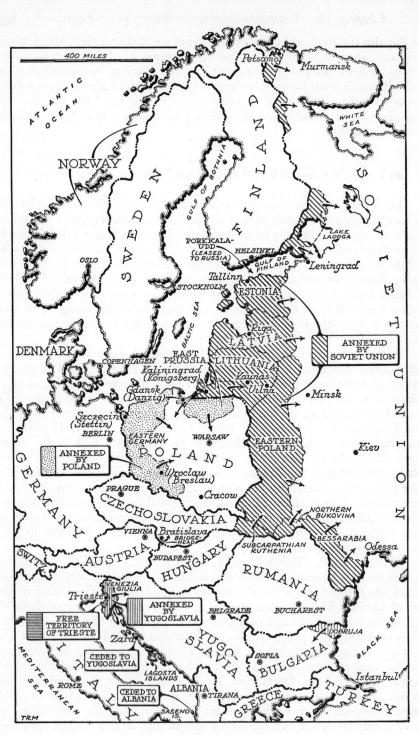

34. *Eastern Europe: Territorial Changes, 1939–1947*

Polish occupation and administration of German territory east of the Neisse River, until a peace conference could settle the fate of German boundaries. The reparations issue had been earlier and unsuccessfully discussed by the Reparations Commission in Moscow. At Potsdam, Stalin accepted Secretary Byrnes' proposal that each power obtain reparations from its own zone and that the Allied powers should transfer 15 per cent of the capital equipment in the Western Zone to Russia in exchange for food, coal, and other raw materials. Unsettled issues, like the Russian demand for virtual control of the Dardanelles and Italy's North African colony of Tripolitania, were deferred for future discussion.

For seventeen months following the Potsdam Conference, Byrnes and his advisers struggled in the face of mounting obstacles to come to firm agreement with the Russians on all outstanding problems—a united policy for Germany, peace treaties for Italy and the central European and Balkan countries, and international agreement for disarmament and control of atomic energy. Imbued with Roosevelt's conviction that American cooperation with the Soviet Union was the indispensable cornerstone of postwar peace, Byrnes sought to overcome Russian suspicion through concession and compromise. He tried to find understanding, and in his failure he prepared the way for a bolder policy of firm support of western Europe and stern resistance to further Soviet aggrandizement.

The point of greatest potential conflict between the West and Russia was the future of Germany and whether that axis of Europe should become a prize or a pawn in a portentous rivalry. In order to destroy the German threat to French and Russian security and to the future peace of the world, Roosevelt had envisaged and seemingly won Stalin's cordial support for united Allied action in demilitarizing and thus neutralizing Germany for years to come. At London in September 1945 and at Moscow during the following December, Byrnes urged the Russians to join in a twenty-five-year alliance to prevent the resurgence of German militarism. When Truman, Stalin, and the British and French Foreign Ministers approved, Byrnes proceeded hopefully to prepare the treaty, only to encounter insuperable Russian opposition in the spring of 1946. Byrnes' successor, George C. Marshall, again raised the proposal in April 1947 and again encountered violent Soviet opposition. By the time the permanent disruption of the Grand Alliance had occurred in the spring of 1947, therefore, Russian policy was clear. It was to keep Germany permanently divided until the entire nation came under Soviet control.

Byrnes also worked with unflagging zeal to find agreement on the peripheral issues of peace treaties for Austria, Italy, Hungary, Rumania, and Bulgaria. The Russians stubbornly refused to approve an Austrian treaty, as such action would have compelled them to withdraw from a vital outpost in central Europe and would have destroyed their excuse for retaining troops in Hungary and Rumania. On the other hand, the Secretary of State finally succeeded in winning peace treaties for Italy, Hungary, Rumania, and Bulgaria.

Completed at New York in December 1946 and signed at Paris on February 10, 1947, these treaties confirmed western Allied supremacy in Italy and North Africa and Soviet predominance in Hungary and the Balkans.

It was perhaps the only settlement possible, but it ended in American recognition of Soviet control of southeastern Europe and marked the beginning of an intense policy of "sovietization" of that area. On the other hand, it should be added that while most Americans regretted Byrnes' retreat from the Yalta agreements on eastern Europe, they were probably not willing at this time to support a firmer policy. And even had the people been willing to support a strong policy, American military weakness and strategic disadvantages would have made firmer action impossible.

On the other overshadowing issue of 1945–1946—international disarmament and control of atomic energy—the President, the Secretary of State, and their advisers formulated a new plan to relieve the world's anxiety over atomic warfare and lay the foundations for future peace. With sole possession of atomic bombs from 1945 until the Russians detonated their first in the summer of 1949, the American leaders might have pursued policies of "atomic imperialism," that is, policies of threat and coercion. Instead, they came forward with what was easily the most revolutionary and probably the boldest disarmament proposal of modern history—the plan submitted to the United Nations Atomic Energy Commission by Bernard M. Baruch on June 14, 1946. Drafted mainly by Dean G. Acheson and David E. Lilienthal, the Baruch plan proposed the creation of an International Atomic Development Authority, which would eventually own, control, and operate all uranium and thorium mines and production facilities and alone conduct research in atomic explosives. The Authority might permit use of atomic energy for peaceful purposes but would have full authority, unrestrained by the veto, of inspection and punishment of violators of the law controlling atomic energy.

It was breath taking, this proposal to create what might have become the most powerful agency in the world; but it was more than the Russians believed they could safely approve. Recognizing that the Authority would inevitably be controlled by the United States and its friends, they countered with a proposal simply to outlaw the manufacture and use of the atomic bomb and to vest enforcement in the Security Council, in which they might veto the punishment of violators of the agreement. The Russians subsequently made important concessions by accepting the principle of unlimited international inspection but would never give up the power to veto punishment of violators. Unwilling to accept any compromise that impaired the principle of effective international control, the American government rejected the Soviet overtures and in effect ended all serious hopes for atomic disarmament.

The failure of the Baruch plan in 1946 and afterward was only the most important manifestation of the larger failure of the United States and the Soviet Union to find a basis for common action on Germany, general disarmament, and creation of armed forces for the United Nations. Perhaps the Americans might have benefited by extending material aid to the Russians for civilian reconstruction after the abrupt cession of Lend-Lease; perhaps they tried to move too boldly and quickly and in so doing deepened Russian distrust and confirmed Russian suspicions that the United States meant to dominate the world. On the other hand, it seems fair to say that the Russian leaders, because of their ignorance, isolation, or desire to extend their own power, rejected American friendship and wrecked the world's best hopes for a future free of the threat of war.

219 / *The Chinese Tragedy*

In Asia the Chinese Communist victory of 1949 upset the balance of power in the world and wrecked all American hopes for peace and stability in the Far East. The Communist victory in China also had a supremely ironic quality. For half a century the American government and people had sought to maintain Chinese independence and give the Chinese people what they regarded as the benefits of western civilization, democracy, and Christianity. Among all the major powers in the Far East, the United States had been the least imperialistic and self-seeking, and had defended Chinese integrity even to the point of a long and bloody war with Japan. Yet in 1950, only five years after the Japanese surrender, the American people found themselves at war with a Chinese government that hated and reviled them as China's most dangerous enemies. The dimensions of the tragedy are apparent but the causes are sometimes obscure.

We must begin our story with some consideration of events in the Far East after the Japanese attack on Pearl Harbor, for the stage was set for the Communist triumph during the period 1941 to 1945. By the end of 1941 the Nationalist government headed by Chiang Kai-shek was exhausted and nearly fatally weakened after four years of seemingly hopeless resistance to the Japanese. Driven out of its richest and most industrialized provinces, isolated in Chungking, and cut off from outside help after the Japanese conquest of Burma, the Nationalist government managed to survive after 1941 only because the Japanese concluded that the final destruction of Chiang's government was not worth the effort.

Prevented from implementing its plans for large-scale operations on the Chinese mainland by the Japanese conquest of Southeast Asia, the American government did its best from 1941 to 1944 to keep China in the war. The extension of a half-billion-dollar credit in 1942, the sending of a growing trickle of supplies by air over the treacherous Himalayan Hump, and the dispatch of military advisers to Chungking were manifestations of American good will, but they were totally inadequate to the main task of strengthening and supplying the Chinese armies. That task could be accomplished only after an Allied drive through northern Burma had opened a land route to Chungking; and military necessities elsewhere prevented the Anglo-American planners from launching this undertaking until 1944 and early 1945. In January 1945 Allied armies in Burma broke the siege of China and opened a supply route from India to Kunming, but by this date the war was nearly over and the Nationalist government had been terribly weakened.

Meanwhile, as the lifeblood drained from the Chungking regime, Roosevelt and his advisers matured plans to strengthen China after the war and establish her as one of the great powers of the world. At Cairo and Teheran Roosevelt won Churchill's and Stalin's seeming approval of the Cairo Declaration, issued on December 1, 1943, which promised the return of Manchuria and Formosa to China. At Yalta in early 1945 the President won a permanent seat on the Security Council for China and Stalin's promise of support for the Nationalist government. These were great plans but dangerous ones, unless the Soviet government honored its promises and the United States was prepared to support and strengthen the Nationalists. Yet even while the leaders talked at Yalta, China stood on the verge of a civil war, the outcome of which would be to make China a great power but one allied with the Soviet Union and dedicated to the destruction of American influence in the Far East.

All through the war, Chiang Kai-shek faced not only the outward menace of Japanese invasion but also the internal threat of Communist subversion and conquest. Driven out of southern China in 1934–1935, the Chinese Communists had fought their way to Yenan, in the province of Shensi in northwest China, and there had established a precarious government, harassed but never conquered by the Nationalist forces. An attempt to unify the Chinese forces after the Japanese invasion in 1937 broke down, and the Communists grew stronger and rejected Chiang's appeals that they submit to the central government and join in a common defense of the motherland. The Communists were so strong by the beginning of 1944, in fact, that Chiang had diverted 400,000 of his best troops from the fighting fronts in order to contain the threatened Communist tide.

This was the situation in early 1944, when the Allied need for manpower in Burma and the beginning of a new Japanese offensive in China caused the American government to undertake a policy looking toward the unification of all Chinese forces. Reassured by Stalin and Molotov that Russia had no interest in controlling China and that, in any event, the Chinese Communists were not *bona fide* Communists, the President sent Vice President Wallace to Chungking in June 1944 to urge Chiang to come to terms with his enemies in order to make possible the use of all Chinese forces, both Nationalists and Communists, against the common enemy. A short time later Roosevelt sent General Patrick J. Hurley as his personal representative to Chiang. Going by way of Moscow, Hurley learned from Molotov that the Kremlin was not interested in or responsible for the Chinese comrades and would take no part in the civil war.

But the more American leaders urged Chiang to come to agreement with his enemies, the more stubbornly did he insist that the Chinese Communists were revolutionaries bent upon the domination of China. And the more Chiang refused to approve unification upon any basis except the military submission of Yenan, the stronger the conviction grew in American circles that Chiang and his government were unreasonable, corrupt, incompetent, and unrepresentative of the Chinese people.

Although he rejected coalition with the Communists, Chiang allowed American newspaper reporters and official observers to go to Yenan in the spring of 1944. Naive rather than dishonest, the reporters sent back glowing reports about the Communists, while American Foreign Service representatives in Yenan confirmed the newspapermen's reports that the Communists were primarily agrarian reformers, extraordinarily efficient, and above all devoted to the cause of democracy in China. At the same time, these observers emphasized the obvious shortcomings of the Chungking regime so heavily that "The main effect of their reporting was . . . to weaken faith in the power of the Generalissimo [Chiang] and his group to govern China."[5]

A rational American policy toward China would have been difficult at best as the showdown between the Communists and Nationalists approached in 1945. Such a policy, however, was rendered almost impossible because of the incredibly irresponsible way in which the Washington administration was then doing business in China. The two chief American officials in that country—General Hurley, who became Ambassador in December 1944, and General Albert C. Wedemeyer, who succeeded General Joseph W. Stilwell as Chiang's Chief of Staff and commander of American forces in China in October 1944—tried hard to work with Chiang and to mature a program of effective support of the Nationalists. The Foreign Service experts in China, on the other hand, argued that the Nationalist government was hopelessly corrupt and tyrannical and that the Communists would prevail because they were genuinely representative of the people. They appealed over Hurley's head to Washington, urging that the United States should either compel Chiang to come to terms with the Communists or else, if he refused, join hands with the Yenan regime.

When Roosevelt supported Hurley in a showdown in Washington in March 1945, the American policy toward China became reasonably clear. The United States would continue to support Chiang and the Nationalists but would also seek to arrest the civil war by bringing the Nationalists and Communists together in some coalition government. It was a policy that had Hurley's cordial support, for the Ambassador, like most other Americans, was convinced that Russia would not intervene in China and that in any event the Chinese Communists were neither genuine Communists nor allied with Moscow.[6]

To carry forward this policy of conciliation and unification, Hurley set more intensively to the task of mediation upon his return to Chungking in May 1945. In addition, in Moscow Harry Hopkins received from Stalin an unequivocal pledge of support for the Nationalist government. Then the war in the Pacific suddenly ended, and the American government had to re-examine its position and redefine its policy in China. Quickly it came to Chiang Kai-shek's assistance in the first task ahead—accepting the surrender of Japanese forces and occupying key ports and cities throughout China proper before the Communists could occupy them. Thus during September and October 1945 the American Army Air Forces moved three Chinese armies from the interior to eastern and northern provinces, while the United States Navy later transported an additional 400,000 Nationalist troops by water to Manchurian ports. Moreover, some 55,000 American marines occupied strategic cities like Tsingtao, Tientsin, and Peiping until the Nationalist troops could take over. By the end of 1945, therefore, American and Chinese troops had accepted the surrender of Japanese forces everywhere in China but

[5] Herbert Feis, *The China Tangle* (Princeton, 1953), p. 259.

[6] Hurley's views were "confirmed" in Moscow by Stalin and Molotov in April 1945. It is only fair to add, however, that the American Ambassador, W. Averell Harriman, and his assistant, George F. Kennan, were not deceived by Stalin's assurances and warned the State Department against taking them seriously.

Manchuria, and Chiang controlled the important cities of the southern and eastern provinces and of Manchuria.

Even so, the situation was fraught with danger. The Chinese Communists were powerfully entrenched in many parts of northern China and Manchuria and were secretly receiving huge quantities of former Japanese arms from the Russian occupation forces in Manchuria. The Nationalist armies were fearfully overextended, while Chiang's political agents were often inexperienced, inefficient, and corrupt. Moreover, before their withdrawal from Manchuria in February 1946, the Russians stripped that province of some $2,000,000,000 worth of industrial and railroad equipment, thus leaving the area useless to assist in the rebuilding of China. Worst of all, it was obvious that China stood on the brink of full-scale civil war, the outcome of which might well decide the fate of Asia.

Clearly, this was a crucial moment of decision in Washington. Should the United States occupy China and Manchuria, at least with token forces, and give full material assistance to the Nationalists in their war against Yenan? Should it seek to halt the civil war through mediation and threaten to withdraw support if Chiang refused to cooperate? Or should it withdraw from China altogether and let the two opposing forces decide the fate of their country? These were the choices confronting the American leaders in the late autumn of 1945. Had they then realized the full consequences of a Communist victory they might have chosen the unpleasant course of military support of the Nationalists, short of large-scale participation by American troops. Instead, in order to avert the risk of American participation in a Chinese war they tried the easy solution of mediation and withdrawal if mediation failed.

This policy was not adopted because of any lack of reliable information concerning the probable outcome of a struggle between the Nationalists and Communists fighting by themselves. In a series of messages in late November 1945, General Wedemeyer warned that the task of unifying and pacifying China was too great for Chiang and his generally incompetent government to accomplish. Numerous other military observers confirmed Wedemeyer's analysis and agreed that abandoning Chiang meant abandoning China to the Communists. And yet there was no disposition in Washington or the country at large to follow the course of wholeheartedly supporting and attempting to control Chiang's allegedly reactionary, inefficient, and corrupt regime in a war against what many persons thought was the honest, efficient, and democratic Communist regime. In fact, the administration's determination to avoid participation in the civil war was overwhelming and enjoyed almost universal support in the United States.

Thus in late November and early December 1945 the Washington leaders agreed upon a policy. It was to send General Marshall to China to press for a truce and to conduct mediation looking toward the establishment of some form of coalition government in which both the Kuomingtang, or Nationalist, and Communist parties would be represented and would compete peacefully for power. Marshall was thus instructed on December 9, and on December 15 the President explained the outlines of American policy to the world.

Marshall arrived in Chungking at the end of December 1945 and set to work at once to cooperate with Chiang and the Communists in finding a formula for peace and unity. For several months it almost seemed he would succeed, as the opposing groups approved a cease-fire and a plan for governmental reorganization. Actually, Marshall merely delayed the inevitable full-scale war—inevitable because neither side would trust the other or yield on essential points—during a time when delay worked greatly to the advantage of the Communists. He abandoned his mission in January 1947 with a blast at both the reactionaries in the Nationalist government and the Communists and with the declaration that the hope of Chinese salvation lay with a liberal group who were without power and prestige in the Kuomingtang.

While Marshall returned to Washington to become Secretary of State the war in China began in earnest. At the outset the Nationalists were well-equipped[7] and greatly superior in numbers to the Communists. But the Communist forces had the edge in training, discipline, and leadership and the advantage of operating from interior lines of communication, while the Nationalist commanders were content to occupy isolated cities and seemed totally unable to wage aggressive campaigns. By mid-1947 the tide was beginning to turn, as waves of defeatism swept through the Nationalist armies and Chiang's government at Nanking lost further popular support through its failure to curb inflation, to suppress the war lords and bandits, or to govern competently.

With the end of Marshall's mission and the resumption of the civil war in January 1947, the Washington government had to decide quickly how to meet the new situation in China. Convinced that the Nationalist armies were adequately equipped and that they could do nothing further without running a serious risk of full-scale participation in the conflict, the American leaders simply withdrew all their military forces, except a small contingent of marines at Tsingtao, and refused to extend any large new assistance to Chiang's government in 1947.

When the Communist drive gained dangerous momentum in the early months of 1947, however, the President sent General Wedemeyer back to China in July to investigate and recommend. With unusual perception the General explained the dangers of the Chinese situation in a report on September 19, 1947. While admitting that the "reactionary leadership, repression and corruption" of the Kuomingtang had caused the people to lose faith in Chiang's government, he held out the hope of genuine reform, provided the United States gave effective moral and material support to Nanking. Wedemeyer then proceeded to say what others before him had either not understood or had not had the courage to say: Communist control of China would imperil American interests in and the peace of the Far East, because the Chinese Communists were the agents of Soviet expansion and the Kremlin's instruments for achieving domination of the Far East. How could the United States prevent the Communist tide from overwhelming China? First, Wedemeyer answered, by insisting that the United Nations take control of Manchuria to prevent that province from falling into the Soviet orbit. Second, by inaugurating a large program of "moral, advisory, and material" assistance

[7] They had obtained the arms and equipment of some 1,235,000 Japanese soldiers and received from the United States in 1945–1946 some $700,000,000 worth of Lend-Lease supplies in addition to large quantities of surplus military equipment.

to China "to protect United States strategic interests against militant forces which now threaten them."

In retrospect we can see that Wedemeyer offered the only possible means of stemming the Communist tide in the Far East. Such action as he proposed might not have sufficed. Indeed, most historians agree that the Nationalist government was doomed, that only full-scale American military participation could have averted a Communist victory, and that the American people would not have tolerated sending large ground forces to China. Yet these are unproved hypotheses. The administration not only refused to sanction Wedemeyer's report; it also kept it secret until the Communists had driven Chiang from the Chinese mainland and failed even to try to rally the American people to the peril of a Chinese Communist victory.

Instead of taking unprecedented measures to save China, the President and his advisers seemed overborne by a sense of helplessness and despair. At Truman's request,[8] Congress appropriated $400,000,000 for aid to China in April 1948, it is true; but in asking for this piddling amount, only $125,000,000 of which could be spent for military supplies, Secretary Marshall declared that there was nothing the United States could do to "make the present Chinese Government capable of reestablishing and then maintaining its control throughout all of China." And in granting this assistance Congress made it plain that it assumed no responsibility for the Nationalist regime.

Of course the small assistance under the China Aid Act of 1948 was too little too late to save the situation. After their capture of Mukden in October 1948, the Communists swept on to victory with incredible speed, assisted by the rapid disintegration of the Nationalist government and armies. In April 1949 the Communists crossed the Yangtze and quickly captured Hankow, Shanghai, Canton, and other southern ports and cities. Chiang retired to Chungking in October and fled by air with the remnants of his government to Formosa in December. Meanwhile, Mao Tze Tung and Chou En-lai had established the People's Republic of China at Peking, declared their friendship for the USSR, and begun an intensive campaign to drive American officials, missionaries, and citizens from China and to rally Asiatics in a great campaign to end American influence in the Far East.

220 / *The Decline of the Good Neighbor Policy*

Heartwarming evidences of the success of the Good Neighbor policy came within a few days after the Japanese struck at Pearl Harbor, as twelve Latin American governments either declared war upon or broke diplomatic relations with the Axis. "We were now to gather the fruits of patient cultivation at the conferences of Montevideo, Buenos Aires, Lima, Panama, and Havana," Hull afterward wrote, "and of our innumerable measures to apply and solidify the doctrine of the Good Neighbor."[9]

Two days after the Pearl Harbor attack the State Department invited

---

[8] Actually, the President asked for $570,000,000 for aid to China over a fifteen-month period.

[9] Cordell Hull, *The Memoirs of Cordell Hull* (2 vols., New York, 1948), II, 1139; quoted by permission of the Macmillan Company, publishers.

the other American republics to send delegates to Rio de Janeiro on January 15, 1942, to consider the necessity for joint action. Despite the sullen opposition of the Argentine spokesmen, who were more friendly to Germany than to the United States, the chief of the American delegation at Rio, Sumner Welles, won the approval of a resolution calling upon the American republics to demonstrate hemispheric unity by breaking with the Axis powers and cooperating with their northern neighbor. Following the Rio Conference all Latin American governments that had not already taken the step, except Argentina and Chile, either severed relations with or declared war upon the Axis powers.[10]

As the war progressed, moreover, the American republics joined hands in genuine collaboration for the common defense. Brazil participated in the campaign against the German U-boats, provided airfields for the "air ferry" to Africa, and sent a division to the Italian front. And because of its large assistance, Brazil received the lion's share—$331,651,000 out of a total of $459,422,000—of American Lend-Lease aid to Latin America. Even so, most of the other Latin American republics did what they could, by sending vital raw materials, offering air bases, and joining with American agents to root out Axis influences.

The one important exception and the source of greatest danger to inter-American solidarity was Argentina, whose leaders not only refused to break with the Axis but also maintained intimate relations with Nazi agents and were openly sympathetic to the German cause. In June 1943 a group of army officers seized control of the Buenos Aires government and launched a campaign to destroy the democratic opposition; and when a new President, General Edelmiro Farrell, came to power in February 1944, the American government undertook to persuade the other American republics to withhold recognition and several months later froze Argentina's gold assets in the United States.

In order to ease the fear in Latin America that the United States might take even stronger unilateral action against Argentina, the State Department called a special conference of the American states at war to meet in Mexico City in February 1945. After inviting the Argentine nation to declare war on the Axis and return to the inter-American fold, the delegates on March 3, 1945, approved the Act of Chapultepec, which completed the mutualization of the Monroe Doctrine by declaring that any attack upon the territory or sovereignty of any single American state would be met by the combined forces of all of them. Rather than lose the friendship of Latin America and her chance for membership in the United Nations, the Argentine government soon afterward declared war on Germany and Japan, ratified the Act of Chapultepec, and received the diplomatic recognition of the United States.

For a brief time it seemed the breach had been healed, especially when the American delegation at the San Francisco Conference joined the Latin American representatives in winning membership in the United Nations for Argentina. At the very moment when it seemed the chief threat to hemispheric solidarity had passed, however, the American Ambassador in Buenos Aires, Spruille Braden, and the State Department had already set in motion an ill-fated campaign to overturn the Argentine government.

[10] Chile broke relations in January 1943; Argentina, in January 1944.

There were good reasons for the State Department's distrust of the Farrell government in Buenos Aires, for it had suppressed free speech, opposition parties, and the press. The Washington government, however, did more than stand by in silent disapproval; it did the unusual thing of attempting to destroy the militaristic regime in Buenos Aires. When Uruguay on November 22, 1945, accused Argentina of preparing aggression against her neighbors and called for inter-American consultation to consider this threat to hemispheric peace, Secretary Byrnes publicly approved. In addition, Ambassador Braden was at work in Buenos Aires with the leaders of the democratic opposition, and by speeches and public statements he virtually called upon the *Argentinos* to change their government as the price for retaining American friendship.

The leader of the anti-democratic forces, Colonel Juan D. Perón, answered Braden's challenge by demanding a national election and by announcing on December 14, 1945, that he would be a candidate for the presidency. Then on February 12, 1946, just two weeks before the election, the State Department issued a so-called Argentine Blue Book accusing the militaristic clique of "aid to the enemy, deliberate misrepresentation and deception in promises of hemispheric cooperation, subversive activity against neighboring republics, and [forming] a vicious partnership of Nazi and native totalitarian forces." American faith in Argentina could be restored, the Blue Book warned, only when the Argentine people were represented by a government that commanded "full faith and confidence at home and abroad."

It was stern but ill-fated diplomacy, this intervention in the political affairs of a sovereign, suspicious, and proud people. In what was probably a fair presidential election on February 24, 1946, the *Argentinos* gave a large majority to Perón and a clear answer to their northern neighbor. The State Department had no alternative but to recall Braden and accept the verdict; at the same time, it refused to cooperate with the movement then under way to construct a regional defense association and declared that the United States would wait for evidences of the good faith of the new Perón government.

During the remainder of 1946 relations between the United States and Argentina remained in such a state of intolerable tension as to imperil the entire structure of hemispheric unity. Most Latin American governments disliked the Perón regime; but they disliked American intervention in Argentine affairs even more and dreaded the possibility of such interference in their own internal affairs at some future date. In the face of mounting criticism at home and in Latin America, President Truman and Secretary Marshall agreed that the now pointless feud must end. On June 3, 1947, therefore, the President announced that his government was ready to begin discussions looking toward the conclusion of a hemispheric defense pact.

In response, delegates from all the twenty-one American republics gathered at Rio de Janeiro on August 15, 1947, to consider the establishment of enforcement machinery for the Act of Chapultepec. The chief accomplishment of the conference was the Inter-American Treaty of Reciprocal Assistance, signed in the Brazilian capital on September 2, 1947. It obligated all signatories to sever diplomatic and economic relations with a violator, internal or external, of the Act of Chapultepec, when two-thirds of the member states thus voted; but no party to the treaty would be required to use its armed forces without its consent. In addition, the treaty specified a broad security zone around the North and South American continents, including Greenland and Alaska, and declared that any armed attack anywhere within this zone would constitute an attack against all American republics.

From March 30 to May 2, 1948, moreover, a ninth Inter-American Conference assembled at Bogotá to reorganize the political machinery of the hemispheric system. Interrupted by an outbreak that the Colombian government said was Communist-inspired, the conference none the less drafted a charter for the Organization of American States, which gave full constitutional status to the inter-American system;[11] a Pact of Bogotá, providing for the peaceful settlement of disputes; and an agreement on economic cooperation that pledged all signatories to treat foreign capital fairly and not to expropriate foreign-owned property without just compensation.

The mutual defense and political structures thus erected at Rio and Bogotá were certainly signs that the Good Neighbor policy had been thoroughly mutualized. Even so, we cannot say that hemispheric solidarity increased in actual practice from 1945 to 1952. For one thing, the postwar era was a time of severe economic dislocation in Latin America, caused mainly by Latin America's inability to sell as much to the United States as it wished to buy and by the failure of American investors to help remedy the large "dollar gap" that threatened to disrupt inter-American trade. Burdened by its huge financial commitments to Europe, the Washington government gave scant attention to this problem. For another, the postwar era was a time of political unrest in Latin America unprecedented since the depression, as leaders of the downtrodden and illiterate masses and representatives of the privileged classes, usually military cliques, contended for power.

Perhaps the chief cause of the decline of the Good Neighbor policy in the postwar period was the fact that Latin America ceased to be of prime importance in American foreign and economic policies, at least after the end of the Argentine affair in 1947. The Good Neighbor policy had been the cornerstone of American foreign policy and almost a popular obsession in the 1930's, supported alike by internationalists and isolationists. As the United States assumed large new responsibilities after 1945, on the other hand, the direction of American foreign policy and popular interest inevitably shifted to Europe and Asia, and this shift provoked bitter criticism throughout the Latin American area.

Huge American purchases of raw materials following the outbreak of the Korean War momentarily solved Latin America's economic problems, it is true; small amounts of American aid under the Mutual Security Act made possible the extension of some technical assistance; and the Export-Import and World banks furnished slight funds for internal development. Even so, by 1952 Latin American economic, political, and social institutions remained so fundamentally unstable that the Good Neighbor policy of superficial

---

[11] The charter established three representative bodies within the Organization—the Inter-American Conference, the Meeting of Consultation of Foreign Ministers, and the Council of the Organization—and constituted the Pan-American Union in Washington as its permanent secretariat.

political and military cooperation would no longer suffice to preserve the peace of the hemisphere.

221 / Beginnings of Containment: the Truman Doctrine

In the spring of 1947 there occurred a change in American foreign policy that may well rank in importance with the promulgation of the Monroe Doctrine or the decision to enter the two world wars of the twentieth century. After struggling patiently for nearly two years to find friendly accommodation with Russia on crucial international problems, the Truman administration undertook a bold program aimed at nothing less than halting the further expansion of Soviet power in Europe. This, in brief, was the so-called Truman Doctrine of containment, designed in the beginning only to prevent Communist-Soviet subversion of Greece and Turkey but soon afterward enlarged to include the defense of western Europe against a Communist attack from within and without.

Precisely when the President concluded that friendship and genuine collaboration with Russia was impossible, we cannot say. Certainly he never fully shared Roosevelt's illusions about the chances of successful cooperation; and as early as January 1946 he was fully aware of the danger of Soviet expansion into Iran, Turkey, Greece, and the Mediterranean. The failure of Secretary Byrnes' policy of compromise to win agreement in 1946 on the major issues of peace treaties for central Europe and disarmament would have compelled, in any event, a considerable reorientation of American foreign policy. But the policy of containment did not stem merely from irritation and disappointment over Russian behavior. It was a radical new departure grounded upon certain harsh assumptions and devised to meet the specific threat of Soviet control of the eastern Mediterranean.

By the spring of 1947 many leaders in the United States and Great Britain had abandoned the assumptions of collaboration and had concluded that cooperation was at best difficult, at worst, impossible. In the Truman administration there were, for example, Admiral Leahy and Secretary Forrestal, who argued courageously for the re-establishment of American naval power in the Eastern Mediterranean in order to thwart Russian expansion in that area. There was former Prime Minister Winston S. Churchill, who warned the free world of the peril of Soviet aggression in a much criticized speech at Fulton, Missouri, on March 5, 1946. There was, also, Ambassador W. Averell Harriman, who admonished the State Department of Soviet plans and ambitions from his lonely outpost in Moscow. And of course there was the President himself. By the beginning of 1947 he was done with a policy of endless concessions.

However, it was George F. Kennan, Counselor of the American Embassy in Moscow, who first fully and frankly elaborated the assumptions behind the policy of containment. On February 9, 1946, Stalin declared that international peace was impossible "under the present capitalist development of world economy" and called upon the Russian people to prepare for "any eventuality." Soon afterward, in an eight-thousand-word dispatch to the State Department, Kennan sought to make clear the character, tactics, motivation, and ambitions of the Soviet state and the international Communist movement. After exploring the historical background of Russian distrust of the West, Kennan pointed up the immediate danger: "We have here a political force committed fanatically to the belief that with the U. S. there can be no permanent *modus vivendi*, that it is desirable and necessary that the internal harmony of our society be disrupted, our traditional way of life be destroyed, the international authority of our state be broken, if Soviet power is to be secure."[12]

If it were true, as Kennan and others asserted, that the leaders of the Soviet Union and their minions throughout the world were imbued with the conviction that Communism and democracy were at war with each other and at work to promote the violent overthrow of non-Communist governments, then how could the American government and people best meet the threat of Soviet imperialism and subversion through infiltration? Again it was Kennan who best summarized what numerous other Americans were thinking in early 1947. In an anonymous article in the July 1947 issue of *Foreign Affairs* he elaborated the doctrine of containment: The United States could live at peace with the Soviet Union only by building its own strength and by erecting effective counterweights within its resources in order to contain Communist power at least in Europe. "It is clear," he wrote, "that the main element of any United States policy toward the Soviet Union must be that of a long-term, patient but firm and vigilant containment of Russian expansive tendencies. . . . To avoid destruction the United States need only measure up to its own best traditions and prove itself worthy of preservation as a great nation."

Disillusioned and disgusted by Russian obstruction and hostility, Truman and his new Secretary of State, George C. Marshall,[13] were suddenly impelled in the late winter of 1946–1947 toward an open policy of containment by the threat of Soviet expansion in the eastern Mediterranean area and the Middle East. During the war the Russians had attempted to create a puppet regime in the Iranian province of Azerbaijan and had withdrawn their troops early in 1946 only after the United States protested sharply and the Security Council threatened to investigate. In spite of this withdrawal, the Russian threat to Iran had by no means passed by early 1947. Even more threatening to peace was the extraordinary Russian pressure on Turkey for the cession of certain territory and the right to build naval bases in the Bosporus. From 1945 to 1947 the Soviet Foreign Office pressed these demands on the Ankara government, while Russian propaganda warned of the dire consequences of Turkish refusal to yield. In brief, it seemed the Communist leaders were determined to achieve a historic Russian objective —control of the Straits and the eastern Mediterranean.

Another dire threat to the security of this area was the possibility that Communist-Soviet forces would capture Greece and thus outflank Turkey and imperil the entire Middle East. From late 1944 to early 1947 the British supported a rightist Greek government in a protracted and bloody effort to suppress the Communist-led faction known as the EAM. Supported diplo-

---

[12] Quoted in Walter Millis (ed.), *The Forrestal Diaries* (New York, 1951), pp. 138–139; used by permission of the Viking Press, publishers.

[13] President Truman appointed Marshall Secretary of State on January 7, 1947.

matically by the Soviet Union and given arms and bases of operation by Bulgaria, Yugoslavia, and Albania, the EAM held large areas of northern Greece and fought tenaciously to drive the British and the rightist government from Athens.

On February 24, 1947, the British Ambassador informed the Washington government that Great Britain could no longer bear the burden of resistance to Communist expansion in the eastern Mediterranean area and would soon have to withdraw entirely from Greece. It was a declaration that marked the end of historic British supremacy in one of the most strategic areas in the world, and the President's response marked a fateful turning point in the history of American foreign policy. Going before Congress on March 12, 1947, he asked for $400,000,000 in order that the United States might render effective assistance to Greece and Turkey and thereby protect the security of the Middle East. But even more important was his bold enunciation of the so-called Truman doctrine, which went far beyond Kennan's concept of containment: "I believe that it must be the foreign policy of the United States to support free peoples who are resisting attempted subjugation by armed minorities or by outside pressures. . . . The free peoples of the world look to us for support in maintaining their freedoms. If we falter in our leadership, we may endanger the peace of the world—and we shall surely endanger the welfare of our own Nation."

The meaning of the President's pronouncement was clear and shocking to the American people, then inadequately prepared to assume such enormous new responsibilities in Europe and the Near East. But amid a barrage of charges that it was supporting British imperialism and needlessly provoking the Soviet Union, the administration stood firm. And with the crucial help of Senator Arthur Vandenberg of Michigan, chairman of the Senate foreign relations committee, who had changed from an isolationist into a vigorous internationalist during the war, the President won the support of a Republican Congress for his Greek-Turkish Aid bill in May 1947. Thus, as one writer has expressed it, "Congress took the plunge and, in taking it, confirmed a new departure in American foreign policy. The United States served notice that henceforward, to deny further strategic advantages to Russia, it would act to bolster up nations and governments resisting Soviet pressure and penetration."[14]

During the years ahead the United States did not falter in its task to save Greece from Communist domination and to strengthen the Turkish bastion on the Soviet southern flank. All told, the Washington government spent some $659,000,000 under the Greek-Turkish aid program from 1947 to 1950. The American task in Turkey was quickly and inexpensively accomplished, as the Turkish government was honest, efficient, and undisturbed by internal warfare. Thus with some $350,000,000 in aid to the Ankara government from 1947 to 1953, the United States was able to help the Turks achieve economic stability and to modernize their sizable army without the slightest show of friction on either side.

The Greek problem, on the other hand, proved to be immensely diffi-

[14] John C. Campbell *et al., The United States in World Affairs, 1947–1948* (New York, 1948), p. 48; quoted by permission of the Council on Foreign Relations, New York City.

cult. During most of the period after 1947 the American government found itself in the embarrassing position of defending democracy in Greece by supporting a reactionary government that refused to do anything effective to attack the basic economic and social evils that stirred the masses to revolt. Indeed, the chief critics of American policy in Greece have argued that the American government intervened too little, not too much, in the internal affairs of that impoverished country.

In any event, with the help of an American military mission and enormous military supplies from the United States a reorganized Greek army undertook a determined campaign in late 1948 to end the civil war. After clearing the Peloponnesus area of guerillas, the army turned northward toward the stronghold of the EAM. The success of the army's campaign was assured when Yugoslavia broke with the Soviet bloc in 1948 and abandoned support of the Greek Communists in the summer of 1949. By October 1949 the long civil war was over, and the Greek people could now turn to the urgent problems of domestic reconstruction.

Thus the Truman Doctrine succeeded in accomplishing its first major objectives. American aid to Turkey won for the United States and western Europe a powerful ally on Russia's southern flank and prevented Russian power from bursting into the eastern Mediterranean or threatening the Middle East. American aid to Greece saved that country from certain Communist conquest and at least gave the Greeks an opportunity to solve their internal problems in their own way.

222 / *To Save Western Europe: the Marshall Plan*

As winter turned into spring in 1947 there were alarming signs that the Greco-Turkish situation was merely a reflection of a more momentous crisis that threatened all of non-Communist Europe. In a varying degree Britain, France, Italy, and the other nations of western Europe were staggering under nearly impossible burdens of reconstruction, careening from one economic crisis to another, and facing the grim prospect of violent social upheaval if they failed to accomplish miracles of recovery.

From the German surrender to March 1947 the American government and people had kept western Europe from near starvation and economic collapse by an outlay of some $11,000,000,000 in UNRRA aid, loans, credits, and assistance of various kinds. But this huge outpouring had helped Europeans mainly to find dollars to pay for food, clothing, and other elemental necessities, not to build a sound recovery. As the months passed in 1947, the situation grew worse, not better, until it was clear that the cessation of large-scale American aid might mean the possible triumph of Communism in France and Italy.

In a little-noticed speech at Cleveland, Mississippi, on May 8, 1947, Undersecretary of State Dean Acheson pointed up the necessity of strengthening governments that were "seeking to preserve their independence and democratic institutions and human freedoms against totalitarian pressures, either internal or external." Then, in an address at Harvard University on June 5, Secretary Marshall responded to suggestions of Kennan and the

Policy Planning Staff of the State Department and pointed up the solution. The European governments, he declared, should work out a comprehensive reconstruction program and tell America how it might best help in achieving lasting recovery. "Any government willing to assist in the task of reconstruction," he promised, "will find full cooperation on the part of the United States."

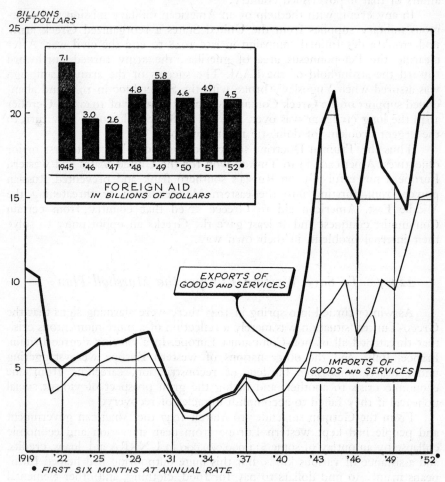

39. *Foreign Trade and Foreign Aid, 1919–1952*

What the Secretary envisaged was nothing less than the rebuilding of the western European economy in order to provide a more stable social order. There was the danger that the Russian and eastern European governments might wreck the plan in Congress before it could be started by accepting the American offer of help. By June 1947, however, that danger was remote, for since 1945 the Russians had been hard at work consolidating their economic control over eastern Europe, which they would not relinquish; and only two months before Marshall's speech they had revealed their determination to prevent the solution of Europe's most urgent problem, the unification and economic rehabilitation of Germany. Therefore, Marshall must have known he could safely issue his invitation to all the European nations and thereby throw upon the Soviet Union the onus for refusing to cooperate.

In any event, the showdown came soon after Marshall made his memorable address, when the Foreign Ministers of Britain, France, and Russia met in Paris on June 27, 1947, to consider a proper reply. The upshot was that the British and French spokesmen, Ernest Bevin and Georges Bidault, voiced the overwhelming enthusiasm and gratitude of western Europe, while Foreign Minister Molotov expressed the sullen opposition of the Communist bloc and left the meeting when he could not disrupt it. Then, on July 12, representatives from Britain, France, Italy, Turkey, and the other non-Communist nations of Europe met in Paris and appointed a Committee of European Economic Cooperation, which two months later submitted a master recovery plan calling for $22,400,000,000 in assistance and loans from the United States. By the autumn of 1947, therefore, the lines were drawn for "a struggle which was to be waged with weapons of politics and propaganda as well as with loans, grants and trade agreements."[15] That struggle was already particularly acute in France and Italy, where the Communists, driven from coalition Cabinets early in the spring, were working hard to destroy moderate governments by accusing them of abetting American imperialism and building up Germany in order to gain American dollars.

Meanwhile, the lines were also being drawn in the United States between the champions of the European Recovery Program, as the Marshall Plan was called, and an incongruous company of opponents. When the President, on December 19, 1947, submitted the draft of an Economic Cooperation bill calling for $17,000,000,000 in aid during the next four years, the debate began in earnest. Opponents of the measure were fatally handicapped by Communist opposition and soon overwhelmed by a coalition that included the important farm organizations, the AF of L and the CIO, the NAM, and numerous other pressure groups. Any doubts that Congress would approve the Economic Cooperation bill were ended in February 1948, when a Communist minority in Czechoslovakia seized control and destroyed a democracy for which millions of Americans felt strong emotional attachment.

In Congress the main burden of leadership fell upon Senator Vandenberg, who wisely insisted upon eliminating the provision for authorization of the full commitment and upon reducing the first appropriation from $6,800,000,000 for the first fifteen months to $5,300,000,000 for the first twelve months. Then, after the hearings had ended, Vandenberg opened debate in the Senate on March 1, 1948, with an address that brought senators and spectators to their feet in applause. "The greatest nation on earth either justifies or surrenders its leadership," he declared. "We must choose. . . . The iron curtain must not come to the rims of the Atlantic either by aggression or by default."

The Senate approved the bill by a huge majority on March 13. Then, while the House dallied, the President and Secretary of State began a public

[15] John C. Campbell *et al.*, *The United States in World Affairs, 1947-1948*, p. 444.

campaign to point up the dangers of Soviet expansion and the immediate menace of a Communist victory in Italy if the House had not acted before the Italian elections on April 18. Under almost irresistible popular pressure, the House approved the measure on March 31 and the President signed it on April 3, 1948. If there had ever been any doubts that the American government and people would falter because the task of saving western Europe seemed too great, those doubts were now ended. The launching of the European Recovery Program meant that hereafter the destinies of the American people were inextricably intertwined with the destinies of the free peoples who stood on the dangerous frontier between a world in chains and a world struggling for a new birth of freedom.

From April 1948 until it was supplanted by the Mutual Security Agency in December 1951, the Economic Cooperation Administration joined hands with the Committee of European Economic Cooperation to carry forward one of the most ambitious and successful reconstruction programs in history. While the American government gave some $12,000,000,000 in assistance through the ECA during this period, it was the CEEC that took the initiative and furnished the chief direction. Results were astonishing even by the end of 1950, before the American rearmament campaign following the outbreak of the Korean War gave a further stimulus to economic activity in the western world. For the Marshall Plan countries as a whole from 1947 through 1950, gross national product increased 25 per cent, industrial production, 64 per cent, and agricultural production, 24 per cent. In most categories recovery was not only complete but went far beyond the prewar levels.

223 / The Berlin Crisis and the North Atlantic Treaty

We have thus far viewed the launching and operation of the European Recovery Program partially out of the context of other great events that were impelling the western nations toward closer unity and driving the Soviet Union into opposition and a desperate campaign to consolidate its control over eastern Europe. As we will see, the ERP was only the most important aspect of a determined American effort to unite western Europe and to draw this productive region closer within the American orbit. As we will also see, the success of this effort provoked Soviet countermeasures that drove the United States and its European friends into outright military alliance and a common effort to construct strong defenses against a possible Soviet thrust to the Atlantic.

The success of all plans for western European unity would depend upon the ability of European and American statesmen to agree upon a plan for rehabilitating Western Germany and drawing it into the western community. Until the end of 1947 American, British, and French leaders continued to plead for the unification and neutralization of Germany; but at the Moscow and London meetings of the Council of Foreign Ministers in March-April and November-December 1947 the Russians made it clear they would approve no agreement on Germany that did not give them a large voice in the control of the Ruhr Valley, the industrial heart of Europe.

After the failure of the London Conference, the western Allied powers had to face the harsh reality that agreement with Russia was impossible and that their only alternative was to agree upon their own plan for Germany. Difficult at best, this undertaking had to be accomplished without arousing French fears of German resurgence and without driving France either into the arms of the extreme nationalists or into the Communist camp. And yet the effort had to be made, for German recovery was the key to European recovery, and the defense of western Germany was the key to the defense of western Europe.

British and American leaders, therefore, wasted little time after the London Conference in preparing new plans for western Germany. In February 1948 they consolidated their zones and created a German government with limited authority at Frankfort. In June, at London, they won French approval for a plan to establish a West German federal government with limited sovereignty, for sweeping currency reform in the three western zones, and for measures to include West Germany as a full partner in the ERP and to increase German foreign trade. Subsequently, the Germans organized state governments in October 1948, adopted a constitution for a German Federal Republic on May 8, 1949, and elected a federal Diet that met at Bonn in September and organized a full-fledged constitutional government.

Soviet reaction to the Marshall Plan and the western Allied measures for uniting and rehabilitating West Germany was immediate, and so violent as to threaten the peace of the world. To begin with, in October 1947 the Soviet leaders formed the Cominform to unite eastern Europe in a campaign of complete "sovietization," that is, a final destruction of all anti-Communist elements in the countries east of the Iron Curtain. Through the Communist parties and Communist-controlled trades unions in Italy and France, the Kremlin next launched a campaign of strikes and violence that impeded but did not prevent substantial Italian and French recovery. In February 1948 the Soviet government engineered the *coup* that overthrew the coalition government in Prague and established a totalitarian Communist regime in Czechoslovakia. On the other hand, Soviet efforts to control the Communist government of Yugoslavia headed by Marshal Tito backfired in a violent break between Belgrade and Moscow and the subsequent alignment of Yugoslavia with the West.

The climax of the Kremlin's campaign to thwart the Marshall Plan and the unification of Germany was the Berlin blockade. Beginning on April 1, 1948, the Soviet authorities began to restrict movement of people and freight from the western zones into Berlin, then under four-power control but isolated in the eastern zone of Germany. This action provoked violent controversies in the Allied Kommandatura, the four-power control council for the German capital, and eventuated in Soviet withdrawal from that body on July 1. Meanwhile, in retaliation against Allied introduction of the new West German currency in Berlin, Soviet authorities on June 23 had halted all traffic to Berlin from the western zones.

Soviet propaganda made no effort to conceal the objectives of the Berlin blockade—either to force the Allies from their advanced position behind the Iron Curtain or else to compel them to abandon their plans for West

German unification. Yet allied withdrawal from Berlin would signify surrender in the face of superior force, the end of Allied influence in the rest of Germany, and a diplomatic victory for the Soviet Union with catastrophic implications throughout the world. Free men everywhere turned to Washington for leadership in this first test of strength between the West and the Soviet Union.

The thought of retreat apparently never troubled the mind of the stubborn Missourian in the White House. When army leaders raised the question of withdrawal on June 28, Truman "interrupted to say that there was no discussion on this point, we were going to stay." Rejecting the suggestion that the army send armed convoys and fight its way into Berlin if need be, the President instead approved a bolder plan—to supply West Berlin by air and thereby to force the Russians to make the decision for peace or war. Soon afterward he approved the sending of two groups of B-29 bombers to English bases—an obvious warning to the Kremlin; at the same time he moved cautiously and refused to give the Military Establishment physical possession of atomic bombs because, as he said, he did not propose "to have some dashing lieutenant colonel decide when would be the proper time to drop one."

While the siege of Berlin proceeded from June 1948 to mid-May of 1949 the British R.A.F. and the United States Air Force accomplished a miracle of supply. By September 1948 the airlift was carrying a daily average of 4,000 tons of supplies, including huge quantities of coal, to the western sectors of Berlin. All told, British and American planes made 277,264 flights and carried nearly 2,500,000 tons of supplies, enough to sustain the outpost.

The airlift cheered free men as no other event since the end of the war had done, but it was no permanent solution. That solution must come through diplomacy. Thus in July 1948 the American, British, and French governments opened negotiations that forced the Soviet government to admit that it had instituted the blockade in retaliation against Allied policy in western Germany. In a full-dress meeting with Stalin, Molotov, and the British and French Ambassadors in Moscow on August 2, the American Ambassador, Walter Bedell Smith, warned the Russian leaders that the western powers would not be bullied and that the Soviet threat "could not be allowed to succeed." Stalin was seemingly conciliatory, but efforts at compromise during the next few months foundered upon Russian insistence that the western Allies abandon their plans for the unification of western Germany without Soviet participation and the Allied refusal to discuss this larger issue so long as the Berlin blockade was in effect.

In the end the Russians yielded and lifted the blockade on May 12, 1949, in return for Allied agreement to hold a meeting of the Council of Foreign Ministers in Paris on May 23. It was a small price to pay for so large a victory in what was by this time called the cold war between the West and the East. The Paris conference yielded no important agreement on Germany but revealed considerable Soviet indecision and obvious unity among the Allied powers. As the new American Secretary of State, Dean Acheson, observed upon his return to Washington, "the position of the West has grown greatly in strength, and . . . the position of the Soviet Union in regard to the struggle for the soul of Europe has changed from the offensive to the defensive."

It was a masterful understatement, for by the time Acheson spoke the western European nations and the United States were united in a military alliance and had launched plans for the common defense of the Atlantic community. Let us now see how the deadly peril of Communist aggression first drove western Europe together and then impelled the American government to abandon its historic tradition against alliances and to join hands with its friends for defense of the free world.

The first major thrust toward Atlantic unity was the Marshall Plan, the implementing of which reflected a dramatic reversal of economic nationalism and a determination by American and western European statesmen to create an integrated economic community free from artificial barriers to trade and investment. The second thrust toward unity came at the height of the debate over the ERP. In a momentous speech before the House of Commons on January 22, 1948, the British Foreign Secretary, Ernest Bevin, announced his country's readiness to join some western European union. At Brussels two months later, on March 17, representatives of Britain, France, the Netherlands, Belgium, and Luxembourg signed a fifty-year treaty of economic cooperation and military alliance; and on the following April 17 the Foreign Ministers of this so-called Brussels Union established elaborate machinery to speed the processes of economic and military collaboration. The following year, on January 28, 1949, a new institution, called the Council of Europe, was founded, which included not only the Brussels powers but Italy, Ireland, Denmark, Norway, Sweden, the Saar, and the German Federal Republic as well.[16]

After taking first steps to coordinate military plans and resources, the leaders of western Europe turned to Washington for the support promised in the Vandenberg Resolution, adopted by the Senate on June 11, 1948, which implicitly promised American cooperation with a western European alliance. Negotiations looking toward an Atlantic alliance began in the American capital in July 1948 and culminated in the completion of a draft treaty during the following December. Signed in Washington on April 4, 1949, by representatives of the United States, Britain, France, Italy, the Netherlands, Belgium, Canada, Iceland, Luxembourg, Denmark, Norway, and Portugal, this, the North Atlantic Treaty, was the culmination of American and European efforts to create a counterweight to Soviet power in western Europe. The Treaty declared that an armed attack against any member in Europe, North America, or the Algerian Department of France would be considered an attack against all signatories; and it looked forward to the creation of joint military forces. Thus in September 1949 Congress approved the Mutual Defense Assistance Act, which appropriated $1,000,-000,000 for arms and equipment for the signatories and an additional $211,000,000 for Greece and Turkey.

The most significant aspect of these momentous events, however, was

[16] The most important outcome of this drive toward European union in the economic field was the approval of the so-called Schuman Plan, originated by Jean Monnet of France and pressed by Robert Schuman, French Foreign Minister. Signed on March 19, 1951, by representatives of France, Germany, Italy, the Netherlands, Belgium, and Luxembourg, the treaty implementing the Schuman Plan established a High Authority to pool all coal and steel resources, production, and distribution of the signatories.

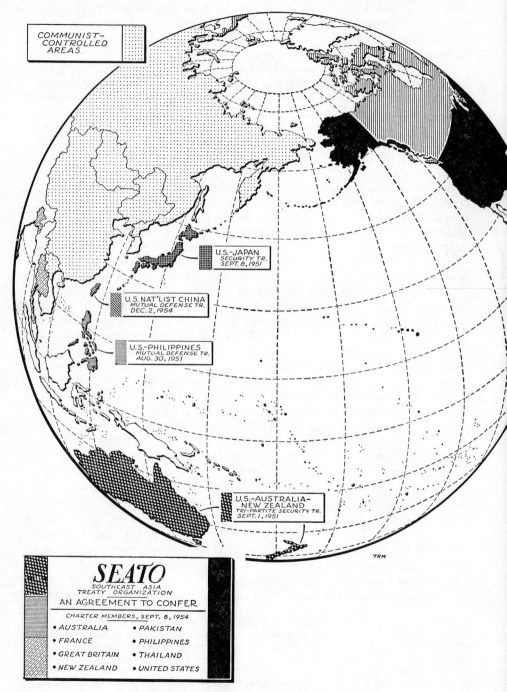

Pacific

COMMUNIST-
CONTROLLED
AREAS.

U.S.–JAPAN
SECURITY TR.
SEPT. 8, 1951

U.S. NAT'LIST CHINA
MUTUAL DEFENSE TR.
DEC. 2, 1954

U.S.–PHILIPPINES
MUTUAL DEFENSE TR.
AUG. 30, 1951

U.S.–AUSTRALIA-
NEW ZEALAND
TRI-PARTITE SECURITY TR.
SEPT. 1, 1951

TRM

SEATO
SOUTHEAST ASIA
TREATY ORGANIZATION
AN AGREEMENT TO CONFER
CHARTER MEMBERS, SEPT. 8, 1954

• AUSTRALIA	• PAKISTAN
• FRANCE	• PHILIPPINES
• GREAT BRITAIN	• THAILAND
• NEW ZEALAND	• UNITED STATES

35. *The American Security System in the East*

Atlantic

COMMUNIST-
CONTROLLED
AREAS

WEST GERMANY
BY LONDON TREATY
OCT. 3, 1954

GREECE AND
TURKEY
OCT. 22, 1951

NATO
NORTH ATLANTIC
TREATY ORGANIZATION
A MILITARY ALLIANCE

CHARTER MEMBERS, APRIL 4, 1949

- BELGIUM
- CANADA
- DENMARK
- FRANCE
- GREAT BRITAIN
- ICELAND
- ITALY
- LUXEMBOURG
- NETHERLANDS
- NORWAY
- UNITED STATES

TRM

36. *The American Security System in the West*

the fact that the signing of the North Atlantic Pact reflected an overwhelming American determination to do the things necessary to protect western Europe from Soviet attack. President Truman and Secretary Acheson had wisely drawn Republican as well as Democratic senators into the negotiations leading to the preparation of the Treaty. Consequently, when debate on the Treaty opened in the Senate on July 5, 1949, a solid bipartisan phalanx overwhelmed the opposition and ratified the Pact without reservation on July 21 by a vote of 82 to 13.

CHAPTER 29 / THE KOREAN CRISIS AND THE END OF THE DEMOCRATIC ERA, 1949–1953

*T*HE FOUR years between the signing of the North Atlantic Treaty and the inauguration of Dwight D. Eisenhower were a time of mounting international crises, domestic tension, and moral challenge rarely paralleled before in the experience of the American people. Catapulted into leadership of what was commonly called the free world, they and their leaders now had to demonstrate whether they could lead courageously and wisely in a seemingly endless struggle for peace and security. American policy won a series of victories in western Europe from 1949 to 1952. In the Far East, on the other hand, the Communist victory in China upset the precarious balance of power and set the stage for the direst menace to peace in the postwar era—the North Korean and Chinese assault upon South Korea. Let us now review the events of this troubled period and see how Americans met the challenges that they raised.

224 / Prelude to the Korean Crisis

All during late 1949 and early 1950 the American people were convulsed and confused by a bitter debate over foreign policy in general and over the failure of American policy in the Far East in particular. In spite of the marked development of a neo-isolationism, especially in the Midwest, and growth of the conviction that the United States could not continue to pour billions into Europe, the administration continued to enjoy large bipartisan support in all sections and in Congress for its policy of assistance to western Europe, as was evidenced by the approval of the North Atlantic Treaty and the enactment of the Mutual Defense Assistance Act in 1949. In addition, during the following year the President mustered considerable Republican support in obtaining a $35,000,000 appropriation to launch his "bold new program" of preventing the spread of Communism by rendering technical assistance to underdeveloped areas.

Even so, by the first months of 1950 there were numerous signs that the Republican leaders were eager to burst the bonds of unity imposed by the bipartisan policy and preparing to use foreign policy as a major issue in the congressional elections of 1950. The Republican leader on foreign policy in the Senate, Arthur H. Vandenberg, was so disturbed by the threatened rebellion that he violated his doctor's orders after a severe lung operation and returned to Washington in January 1950 to head off the revolt. He succeeded momentarily; but his great services were ended by renewed illness that removed him from his post and took his life on April 18, 1951. Long before he died, his Republican colleagues had raised a violent storm over China that was for a time subdued by the Korean crisis and then afterward was renewed on an even greater scale when the Chinese intervened in Korea.

Following the establishment of the Chinese People's Republic allied with the Soviet Union in September 1949 and the withdrawal of Chiang Kai-shek to Formosa, the Washington government was compelled to formulate a policy to meet the new situation in the Orient. The administration would perhaps have recognized the Peking regime, as Britain, India, and other powers did, had not the Chinese Communists launched a violent campaign in the autumn of 1949 to drive American diplomatic agents, missionaries, and private interests from China. As the months passed, anti-Communist sentiment in the United States grew enormously; and by the beginning of 1950 a so-called China lobby and a large number of Republicans had begun a tremendous campaign to discredit the administration and compel it to extend military assistance and naval protection to the Chinese Nationalists on Formosa.

Meanwhile, the State Department had washed its hands of responsibility for the Chinese débâcle by releasing a white paper that accused the Nationalists of blame for their defeat. Moreover, on January 5, 1950, the President reaffirmed his determination not to be drawn into the Chinese civil war, even if such a policy resulted in the capture of Formosa by the Chinese Communists. Then, a week later Secretary of State Dean Acheson announced what was in effect a new American policy in the Far East.[1] The American government, he declared, desired only to help the peoples of Asia realize their democratic aspirations. The United States would protect a "defensive perimeter" that ran from the Aleutians to Japan, the Ryukus, and the Philippines, but it could not attempt to defend other areas—Korea, Formosa, and Southeast Asia—from military attack. Aggression in this area, Acheson concluded, would have to be met by the people attacked and by the United Nations.

Acheson's speech only exacerbated the Republican attack, which took a violent turn as Senators Joseph R. McCarthy, Kenneth S. Wherry, Robert A. Taft, and other GOP spokesmen opened a campaign to drive the Secretary from office and prove that the State Department was riddled with Communists and fellow travelers who, as Taft put it, had "surrendered to every demand of Russia . . . and promoted at every opportunity the Communist cause in China." So violent was this campaign that it wrecked the bipartisan foreign policy, made the formulation of a rational Far Eastern policy impossible at the very time when it was most desperately needed,

[1] Acheson had succeeded Marshall on January 21, 1949.

and raised grave doubts abroad whether the United States was capable of wise leadership.

The months preceding the outbreak of the Korean War were a time of trouble and soul-searching in the United States as well because thoughtful men began to wonder whether the world at mid-century was heading straight for destruction. The President's revelation on September 23, 1949, that the Russians had detonated an atomic bomb upset all assumptions upon which American defensive strategic plans had been based since 1945. It also renewed a fierce debate in high administration circles over the development of a hydrogen or tritium bomb, potentially 1,000 times more powerful than the atomic bombs that destroyed Hiroshima and Nagasaki. When the President announced on January 31, 1950, that he had ordered the Atomic Energy Commission to proceed with work on the hydrogen bomb, thoughtful Americans were stunned by the gloomy prospects ahead even while they agreed their government had no other recourse. Acheson tried to quiet the mounting fear but admitted that the American people were entering a new era of "total diplomacy," in which their patience and wisdom would be put to severe and numerous tests.

225 / The Korean Crisis

Not many months after Acheson spoke there occurred the invasion of South Korea, which threatened the peace of the world and sorely taxed the courage and capacities of the American people before it had ended. The background of this story can be briefly told. Although Roosevelt and his advisers had decreed that Korea should be freed from Japanese control at the end of the war, they gave no thought to a postwar policy for Korea, in spite of the fact that Japan and Russia had fought one war for control of this strategic peninsula and that Russian dominance there after 1945 would gravely threaten the future security of Japan. When Russian troops entered northern Korea on August 10, 1945, and American forces occupied southern Korea on September 8, the two governments agreed to divide their occupation zones at the thirty-eighth parallel, which ran north of the Korean capital of Seoul.

In their early postwar naiveté, the American leaders assumed that the Korean people would proceed to organize a government and that the occupation forces would thereupon be withdrawn. At the Moscow Conference in December 1945, the Russians approved a plan to create a Korean government under the guidance of a Joint American-Soviet Commission. But the Russian representatives on the Commission blocked all efforts at the unification of the country and at the same time proceeded to establish a Communist "people's government" in North Korea and to train and equip an army of some 150,000 men.

The United States then appealed in protest to the United Nations Assembly, which established a Temporary Commission on Korea in November 1947. The Commission visited Seoul in January 1948 and, after being denied entry into the Soviet zone, held elections in South Korea for a constituent assembly. The assembly met in July 1948, adopted a constitution for a new Republic of Korea, and elected Syngman Rhee as President. Soon afterward, the United Nations Assembly, the United States, and other non-Communist powers recognized the South Korean regime as the only lawful government of Korea. The United States, in addition, withdrew its last troops from South Korea in June 1949 and gave substantial assistance to Rhee's government during 1949 and the first months of 1950.

This, in general, was the situation when North Korean forces crossed the thirty-eighth parallel in an all-out invasion of South Korea at 4 a.m., Korean time, on June 25, 1950. Precisely what part the Soviet government played in planning the invasion or what its objectives were, we cannot now say. It seems likely, however, that the withdrawal of American troops from South Korea and Acheson's statement that Korea lay outside America's "defense perimeter" in the Far East, caused the men in the Kremlin to conclude that the United States would not fight to prevent Soviet control of the entire Korean peninsula.

News of the invasion reached Washington at 9:26 p.m., Washington time, on June 24. After hurried conferences with his staff at the State Department at about midnight, Secretary Acheson called the President, then in Independence, Missouri, who agreed that Acheson should bring the matter before the Security Council of the United Nations at once. By the following afternoon, when the Security Council met in emergency session, it was fully evident that the North Koreans had launched not a border raid but a full-scale war. With the Russian representative absent,[2] the Council by a vote of 9 to 0 adopted a resolution condemning the invasion as aggression and demanding the withdrawal of Communist troops from South Korean territory.

Soon afterward the President arrived in Washington and went straight to the Blair House, the temporary presidential mansion, for a full-dress conference with his civilian and military advisers. The upshot of this meeting was Truman's decision to order the Seventh Fleet to neutralize Formosa and to direct General Douglas MacArthur, American commander in Tokyo, to furnish arms and limited air support to the South Koreans. All during the following day, Monday, June 26, the President conferred with intelligence and army officials. Intelligence agents, it should be added, knew next to nothing concerning the strength of the North Korean forces or the object of their assault. Then in the evening Truman called his advisers to Blair House and after hearing their views announced that American naval and air forces in the Far East would render full assistance to the South Koreans. "Everything I have done in the last five years," he declared, "has been to try to avoid making a decision such as I have had to make tonight."[3]

Events moved swiftly to a climax after the second Blair House conference. During the following morning of June 27 the President called congressional leaders of both parties to the White House and told them of his

---

[2] The Russians had boycotted the Security Council since the preceding January, because the Council had refused to seat a delegate from the Chinese Communist government.

[3] Beverly Smith, "Why We Went to War in Korea," *Saturday Evening Post*, CCXXIV (Nov. 10, 1951), 80.

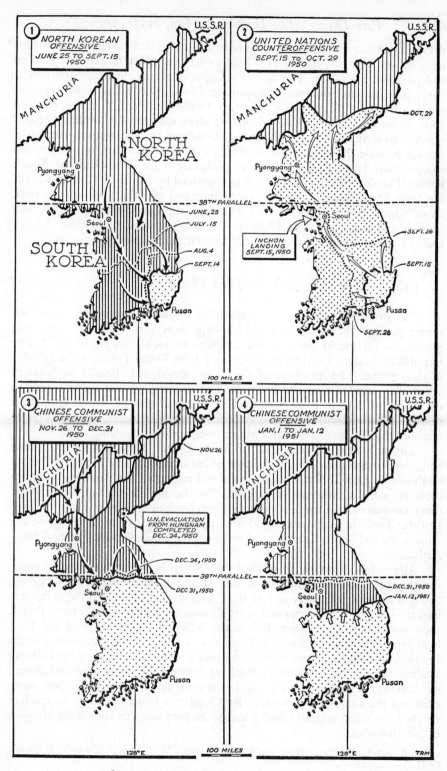

37. *The Korean War, June 25, 1950—January 12, 1951*

decision to resist the Communist invasion and of his determination to attempt to rally the United Nations in a bold collective effort to repel aggression and preserve the peace. The Security Council met in the afternoon and at 10:45 p.m. adopted an American-sponsored resolution calling upon member nations to render all necessary assistance to the Republic of Korea. And on June 29 and 30, after it had become evident that the Communists would quickly overrun the peninsula unless American troops stopped them, the President made the hardest decision of all—to send two divisions of ground troops from Japan to Korea and to authorize a naval blockade of North Korea. The decision, incidentally, was approved by the Joint Chiefs of Staff, the State Department, General MacArthur, and all other military advisers, all of whom assumed that limited American support would suffice to turn the tide and that Russia and China would not intervene. Obviously, the full costs of the intervention were neither known nor assessed in advance.

226 / The Korean War: First Phase

The President's decision to intervene in the Korean struggle was, as one writer put it, "like a gust of wind blowing away a fog of uncertainty and gloom. . . . Here at last was the courage to tackle an aggressor."[4] The Republican leaders, Governor Dewey and John Foster Dulles, were effusive in their praise. The members of the House stood and cheered on June 28 when they learned that the President had ordered air and naval forces to defend South Korea. Even Senator Taft declared that he would vote for a resolution authorizing the use of American forces in Korea, even though he opposed the President's acting without congressional consent.

Throughout the free world and in the United Nations, moreover, men and governments rallied to the support of South Korea. The Security Council established a United Nations Command and requested the American government to name a commander in chief. By the middle of September some nineteen nations had made a military contribution; and by the end of 1950 British, Turkish, Australian, and Philippine troops were fighting beside Americans and South Koreans under the supreme commander, General Mac-Arthur.

Meanwhile, however, it seemed that North Korean troops would over-run the entire Korean peninsula before American power could be decisively brought to bear. By September 12 the Communists had pressed the defenders into the southeastern corner and were threatening to drive them from Pusan, their remaining supply port. But as the Allied defenses stiffened and then held firm, MacArthur brought in large new American reinforcements to turn the tide. Opening a United Nations offensive on September 15 with a daring landing on the North Korean flank at Inchon, he soon captured Seoul, overran southern Korea, and enveloped and destroyed or captured more than half the Communist invaders. By October 1 United Nations forces had reached the thirty-eighth parallel and were preparing to launch an invasion of North Korea.

4 Albert L. Warner, "How the Korea Decision Was Made," *Harper's Magazine,* CCII (June 1951), 104.

At home the American people watched breathlessly during the first two months of North Korean supremacy and went on a buying spree that caused violent price increases and momentary scarcities. But the most significant impact of the Korean incident upon the American people was the way in which it awakened them to the peril of new and more portentous Soviet aggressions, perhaps against the Middle East, perhaps against western Europe. And it was obvious that the peril was great precisely because the United States and western Europe were unprepared to meet it with any effective counterforce. As one contemporary put it, "The vital question was whether time still remained to create the armed strength which alone might deter the Kremlin from undertaking further and even more dangerous adventures."[5]

Thus the chief issue before Congress and the administration was not whether the United States should prepare to meet unseen dangers but how it should prepare. Resisting demands for an all-out mobilization, the President and Congress moved swiftly to set a limited mobilization under way. In August 1950 Congress approved the basic legislation, the Defense Production Act, which announced the American determination to "oppose acts of aggression and . . . to develop and maintain whatever military and economic strength is found to be necessary to carry out this purpose." This measure empowered the President to institute allocations and priorities, authorize tax incentives to encourage defense production, build industrial plants, and impose limited price and sweeping credit controls. During September, Congress appropriated an additional $12,600,000,000 for the defense establishment, approved plans to double the armed forces from 1,500,000 to 3,000,000 men by the middle of 1951, adopted a revenue bill designed to raise nearly $4,500,000,000 in additional income and corporate taxes, and appropriated over $5,000,000,000 for military assistance, chiefly to western Europe.

The President moved cautiously in the late summer and early autumn of 1950 to get a limited, orderly mobilization under way. Assuming that the Korean War would soon be ended, he did not establish special mobilization machinery or invoke the price control provisions of the Defense Production Act. Assuming also that the greatest danger to the world was a Soviet invasion of western Europe, the Washington government during the summer and autumn of 1950 embarked upon a bold program to stimulate western European rearmament and create a unified North Atlantic Treaty Organization army with sizable German units included. With the promise of huge new Mutual Defense assistance, Britain, France, and the other NATO countries announced plans for rearmament, while the North Atlantic Council met in Brussels on December 18 and 19, 1950, and approved plans for unifying all NATO forces under the command of General Eisenhower. Before 1954, however, the American proposal for limited German rearmament foundered upon French opposition.

During this summer and autumn of fear and crisis the American people were convulsed by one of the bitterest congressional campaigns in American history. Without openly repudiating the Korean intervention, Republican spokesmen charged that Truman and Acheson had blundered so badly as

[5] Richard P. Stebbins *et al.*, *The United States in World Affairs, 1950* (New York, 1951), p. 244; used by permission of the Council on Foreign Relations.

to make the Korean War inevitable. They warned of further inflation, socialization, and aggrandizement of federal power if the Truman policies were not abandoned. But the main Republican issue was Communism—the alleged Democratic failure to recognize and cope with Communist infiltration, or actual Communist influence in the State Department. Not all Republican leaders emulated the example of McCarthy, who engineered the defeat of the veteran Democratic senator from Maryland, Millard Tydings, or so obviously appealed to the popular fear as did Representative Richard M. Nixon in his successful campaign in California for election to the Senate. Even so, almost everywhere Republican campaigners highlighted the issue with considerable success.

Although the Democrats retained narrow control of both houses in the election of November 7, 1950, the results were actually a smashing reversal for the administration and in a sense a popular repudiation of the President himself. Two Fair Deal stalwarts in the Senate—Frank P. Graham of North Carolina and Claude W. Pepper of Florida—had been defeated earlier in the primaries by anti-Truman conservatives, and a whole host of the President's friends followed them into retirement after November 7. On the other hand, the Democrats' most spectacular effort during the campaign—the combined Democratic and union labor drive to unseat Senator Taft in Ohio—failed so dramatically as to make Taft a leading contender for the Republican presidential nomination in 1952.

The Republican triumph of 1950 went deeper than the victory of a few of its leaders and the defeat of some distinguished Democrats. More important were the underlying if less spectacular developments and results of the election—the return of the agrarian Middle West to the Republican fold; the obvious success of the Communist and inflation issues; and the fact that in the House contests the Republicans polled a larger vote than the Democrats. Indeed, as the year 1950 drew to a close many signs pointed toward a Republican victory in 1952.

227 / *The Korean Crisis Threatens a Third World War*

Following their capture of Seoul on September 26, 1950, the United Nations forces quickly cleared South Korea and drove to the thirty-eighth parallel, where they momentarily halted until the General Assembly, on October 7, called upon MacArthur to take all necessary steps to establish United Nations control throughout all Korea. Only a few days before, the Foreign Minister of the Chinese People's Republic had warned that the Chinese would not "supinely tolerate seeing their neighbors being savagely invaded by imperialists"; on October 3, moreover, he had told the Indian Ambassador in Peking that "if the U. S. or U. N. forces crossed the Thirty-eighth Parallel, China would send troops to the Korean frontier to defend North Korea." But few leaders in the free world took the threat seriously. At a conference on Wake Island on October 15, for example, MacArthur assured the President that there was little danger of Chinese intervention and promised a great slaughter if the Chinese armies entered the fight.

During October 1950 MacArthur's troops drove triumphantly north-ward toward the Yalu River that separates Korea from Manchuria. Then, when it seemed North Korean resistance had entirely collapsed, advanced American troops encountered large units of Chinese troops some fifty miles south of the Yalu on about October 30. Subsequent reconnaissance revealed what MacArthur should have earlier discovered, that the Chinese had massed armies of some 850,000 men in Manchuria and moved advanced units into northern Korea.

The entire western world waited during the early weeks of November to see what the future would bring. While Chinese "volunteers" skirmished defensively, the Security Council heard representatives of the Peking gov-ernment demand prompt American withdrawal from Korea. But in Korea, on November 24, MacArthur launched a final great United Nations offensive to drive the Chinese "volunteers" beyond the Yalu and end the war before Christmas. It was a nearly fatal strategical blunder, for MacArthur drove his men into a huge trap. The Chinese counterattacked on November 26 and split the center of the United Nations line held by Republic of Korea troops. The United States Eighth Army on the eastern flank withdrew in an orderly retreat toward the thirty-eighth parallel, but the X Corps on the northwestern flank was isolated and cut off. After two weeks of desperate fighting, the First Marine Division, the 3rd and 7th infantry divisions, and the ROK Capital Division fought their way to the port of Hungnam, from which they were evacuated and transferred to the main United Nations defensive line north of the thirty-eighth parallel. It was one of the most spectacular operations in the history of modern warfare.

The Washington government, in the meantime, had gravely accepted the challenge and begun to prepare the United States and the United Nations for a possible general war. "This new act of aggression," Secretary Acheson declared of the Chinese intervention on November 29, "has created . . . a situation of unparalleled danger. . . . No one can guarantee that war will not come." On December 1 the President denounced the Chinese inter-vention as unprovoked aggression; in a nation-wide broadcast on Decem-ber 15 he outlined a vast new mobilization program; and the following day he declared a state of national emergency and announced the establishment of an Office of Defense Mobilization and the beginning of production and stabilization controls.

During the next two years the American mobilization effort proceeded on the whole smoothly and successfully under the direction of Charles E. Wilson, former president of the General Electric Company. Although it opposed the President on nearly every other score, Congress granted his requests for unprecedented peacetime appropriations for the Military Estab-lishment, civilian defense, and tremendous new military assistance to the NATO countries.[6] The result was a sudden and spectacular increase in the military strength of the United States and its allies; by the end of 1952 the

[6] Congress appropriated nearly $57,000,000,000 for national defense and almost $7,500,000,000 for Mutual Security assistance during 1951–1952 and nearly $47,000,000,000 for national defense and some $6,500,000,000 for Mutual Security purposes during 1952–1953.

NATO countries had brought into being military forces probably capable of withstanding a Soviet invasion of western Europe.

228 / *The Second "Great Debate" and the MacArthur Affair*

It would be pleasant for the historian to record that the American people and their leaders met the new perils raised by the Chinese intervention and the threat of Soviet aggression calmly, wisely, and in firm conjunction with their European allies. The truth is, however, that the American people nearly lost their heads, the Truman administration nearly lost control of foreign policy, and the United States almost lost its allies as a result of the "great debate" and events that followed the Chinese intervention.

The "great debate" began on November 10, 1950, when, in reply to the President's announcement that he would send additional divisions to Europe, Senator Taft proposed a re-examination of the nation's foreign and military policies and raised the question whether defense of western Europe was essential to American security. The high point of the discussion came on December 20, when former President Hoover voiced the convictions of a large group of neo-isolationists. The United States, he declared, should defend the Atlantic and Britain and the Pacific to Japan; but it should withdraw troops from the western European nations and withhold further support until they had organized and equipped sufficient forces to withstand a Russian assault.

The debate exploded with exceptional bitterness in Congress on January 8, 1951, when Senator Wherry offered a resolution declaring that "no ground forces of the United States should be assigned to duty in the European area for the purposes of the North Atlantic Treaty pending the adoption of a policy with respect thereto by Congress." Administration and military spokesmen replied frankly that defense of western Europe was essential to the defense of the United States; General Eisenhower returned from his command post in Paris and reported to Congress that the western European nations could build a strong anti-Russian barrier if the American people did not desert them. Even so, the debate raged and the issue was long in doubt, especially after a majority of House Republicans on February 15 signed a manifesto endorsing Hoover's proposals. The resolution of the conflict came on April 4, 1951, when the Senate reaffirmed American commitments under the North Atlantic Treaty, approved the sending of four additional divisions to Europe to serve under Eisenhower's command, but warned the President not to send additional troops without "further Congressional approval."

The furor of the debate over troops for Europe was nothing as compared to the fury that burst upon the country following the President's recall of General MacArthur from his command in Tokyo. Indeed, few episodes in American history have been so extraordinary or revealing as was the MacArthur affair, for it brought to a head the Republican campaign against Truman and Acheson and the bitter conflict over the Far Eastern and European policies of the United States.

The episode began soon after the outbreak of the Korean War and in the beginning involved the relations of the United States and Chiang Kai-shek's government on Formosa. Following an ostentatious and unauthorized visit to Formosa in July 1950, MacArthur, about August 28, addressed a message to the annual convention of the Veterans of Foreign Wars in which he called for the incorporation of Formosa into the American security system and talked about "offensive strategy" in the Far East. On October 15 Truman met MacArthur on Wake Island, again explained that he had no intention of becoming involved in the Chinese civil war, and warned the General that he must make no more provocative statements.

For a time MacArthur was silent, but following the Chinese intervention in Korea he opened a campaign aimed at forcing the administration to permit him to bomb Chinese bases in Manchuria. On December 6 the President replied, forbidding the release by civilian or military officials of any statement on foreign policy without prior approval by the State Department. During the following weeks, when it seemed the Chinese and North Koreans might drive the United Nations forces from Korea, the President and Joint Chiefs of Staff deliberated the question of what policy to adopt should such a catastrophe occur. On December 29, 1950, MacArthur suggested that the United States blockade the Chinese coast, bombard the Chinese mainland by air and by sea, and support a Nationalist invasion of China from Formosa. The Joint Chiefs replied that such retaliatory measures could not then be permitted; at the same time they began to prepare for similar desperate measures should the United Nations armies be driven from Korea.

Events in Korea during the next few weeks decided the issue. The American Eighth Army, now under the command of General Matthew B. Ridgway, halted the Chinese-North Korean assault and began a limited offensive of its own on January 26, 1951. Now that it was evident the United Nations could remain in Korea, the President and Joint Chiefs quickly agreed upon a policy—to conduct a limited war for the limited objective of defending and establishing the integrity of South Korea. Such a policy would avert the danger of a general war with China—"the wrong war, at the wrong place, at the wrong time, and with the wrong enemy," General Omar N. Bradley, chairman of the Joint Chiefs, later called it, which might require a shifting of all available manpower and resources to the Far East and thus invite a Russian attack on western Europe. Limited and essentially defensive operations in Korea would not destroy the Chinese Communist regime, the President and Joint Chiefs agreed. At the same time, such operations could inflict such terrible punishment on the Chinese and North Korean forces that they would have to abandon their aggression and by so doing would acknowledge defeat and the vindication of the principle of collective security.

MacArthur, however, was temperamentally incapable of accepting the President's decision, and in his conviction that blundering political leaders were depriving his people of victory the General resorted to desperate measures. After the Joint Chiefs informed him that the President was about to attempt to settle the Korean conflict by diplomacy, MacArthur replied with a public statement on March 25, 1951, aimed at preventing a peaceful settlement. Then, in reply to a letter from Joseph W. Martin, Jr., of Massachusetts, Republican minority leader in the House, the General called for a war to defeat Communism in the Far East. "We must win," he concluded. "There is no substitute for victory."

By the day on which Martin read MacArthur's letter to the House, April 5, the country was convulsed by a frenetic Republican campaign to force the administration to adopt MacArthur's proposals for a victory offensive in Korea and possible war against China. The publication of MacArthur's letter to Martin was an open challenge to the President's foreign policy by a military commander who had joined hands with the administration's foes. Reluctantly but resolutely the man from Independence took the inevitable step: On April 10, 1951, he relieved MacArthur of his commands in Japan and Korea and appointed General Ridgway as his successor. "I could do nothing else and still be President of the United States," Truman wrote on April 10. "Even the Chiefs of Staff came to the conclusion that civilian control of the military was at stake and I didn't let it stay at stake very long."[7]

It was a courageous act, this recall of a General who was the greatest living American in millions of American eyes, but for a time it seemed all the furies of hell were abroad in the country. Words are inadequate to describe the anger of the Republicans, the China lobby, and a vast majority of the newspapers and commentators. With a large entourage MacArthur returned to his native land for the first time in a decade. Across the country—in San Francisco, Chicago, New York, and Washington—he made triumphal tours and received the adulation of millions of cheering people. And on April 19 he addressed a joint session of Congress and appealed for support for stern action against the Chinese.

While the nation reverberated from the din of the political strife, congressional leaders agreed that the Senate Armed Services Committee should investigate MacArthur's recall and review American Far Eastern policy. From May 3 to June 25, 1951, the committee heard more than 2,000,000 words of testimony from MacArthur, Bradley, Acheson, and dozens of other military and civilian officials. Under judicious control, the committee acted neither like partisans, prosecutors, nor circus performers but rather like men who wanted only to learn the truth. And as the hearings ground on, the country recovered its senses and at least the majority of thoughtful Americans understood and probably approved the administration's policy.

In retrospect, we can see that the MacArthur affair cleared the air of popular confusion over Far Eastern policy. As Secretary of Defense George C. Marshall, Secretary Acheson, and General Bradley sought to make clear, the United States would neither adopt the MacArthur program nor evacuate Korea but would continue to "inflict the greatest number of casualties . . . in order to break down not only the morale but the trained fabric of the Chinese Armies." The unification of Korea remained a political and diplomatic objective; but as unification had never been a military objective, the United Nations would accept a compromise that provided for Communist withdrawal north of the thirty-eighth parallel. In brief, the United States would fight only a limited war in Korea for limited objectives in order to avert the risk of a third World War.

[7] William Hillman, *Mr. President* (New York, 1952), p. 133.

229 / Decision in Korea: Truce and Armistice

While the MacArthur affair erupted at home, the Washington government carried forward plans and measures to convince the Chinese Communists that aggression did not pay. Secretary Acheson won approval in the United Nations of an embargo against the shipment of arms, munitions, and critical raw materials to China on May 18, 1951; moreover, Acheson made it clear that the United States would strenuously oppose the Peking regime's effort to obtain admission to the United Nations and would prevent Communist seizure of Formosa. On the military front in Korea, the United Nations forces repulsed two great Chinese offensives in April and May with staggering losses to the attackers. By the middle of June 1951, therefore, it was obvious that the American policy was succeeding. The Communists had suffered an estimated 1,162,500 casualties; the best Chinese armies had been decimated; and China was isolated diplomatically and economically from the free world and had no hope of forcing a military decision.

Moreover, the Chinese intervention confirmed the American government's determination to conclude a peace treaty with Japan that would not only restore sovereignty to that conquered Empire but also make it the cornerstone of a new American security system in the far Pacific area. Under the direction of John Foster Dulles, Republican adviser to the State Department, negotiations looking toward a peace settlement proceeded smoothly with the former allied Pacific powers during 1950 and 1951. To be sure, the Russians objected, but their opposition only strengthened Anglo-American-Commonwealth unity and facilitated the meeting of a peace conference in San Francisco and the signing of a "peace of reconciliation" between Japan and forty-eight other nations and commonwealths on September 8, 1951. The treaty stripped Japan of its overseas empire but in all other respects was extraordinarily generous, for it imposed no restrictions upon the future development of the Japanese economy, levied no reparations, and recognized Japan's right to rearm.

A short time before, the American government had taken the first steps toward building a security system in the Pacific comparable to the NATO system in the Atlantic and Mediterranean areas. On August 30, 1951, the United States and the Philippines concluded a Mutual Defense Treaty; two days later, the United States, Australia, and New Zealand signed a Tripartite Security Treaty; finally, on the same day the Japanese Peace Treaty was signed at San Francisco, September 8, 1951, the American and Japanese governments concluded a Security Treaty that granted to the United States the right to maintain land, sea, and air bases in Japan.[8]

[8] After the American disappointment at the substantial French withdrawal in the face of Communist forces in Indo-China in the spring of 1954, the movement for a collective security system in the Pacific culminated in the signing in Manila on September 8, 1954, of the South East Asian Defense Treaty by representatives of Britain, America, France, Australia, New Zealand, Pakistan, the Philippines, and Siam. Without providing for automatic collective action and excluding China, Formosa, and Indo-China, the pact pledged the signatories to act jointly to preserve the peace of the Pacific, to cooperate in programs to advance economic and social well-being, and to settle disputes by peaceful means.

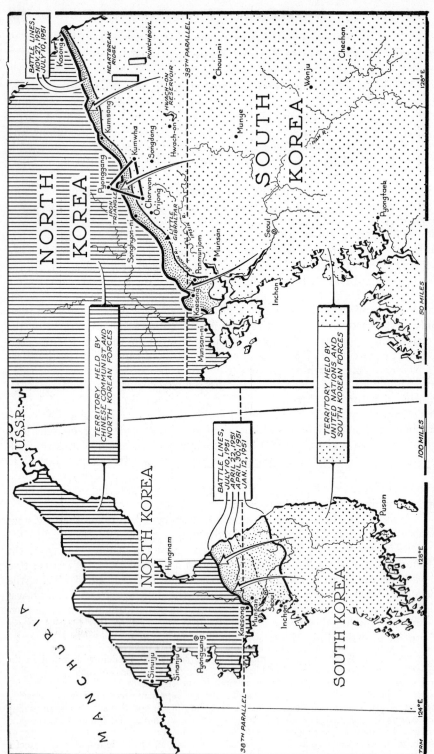

38. *The Korean War, January 12, 1951–July 10, 1951*

While the American government was thus beginning to marshal the Pacific countries in a broad anti-Communist front, the first sign of Communist retreat in the Far East came on June 23, 1951, when Jacob A. Malik, head of the Russian delegation in the United Nations, declared that the Korean conflict could be ended if the belligerents began discussions looking toward a "cease-fire and an armistice providing for the mutual withdrawal of forces from the 38th parallel." When leaders in Moscow endorsed the suggestion, General Ridgway opened truce negotiations with Chinese and North Korean officials at Kaesong on July 10. While the negotiators haggled at truce headquarters at Kaesong and later at Panmunjon, the United Nations forces conducted only defensive operations to hold their line north of the thirty-eighth parallel. We now know that the strengthened United Nations armies could have cleared the decimated Communist forces from North Korea in the summer of 1951 and that the Russians proposed truce talks chiefly to avert this catastrophe to their cause. Whether the Washington leaders knew this fact at the time, we cannot say. In any event, they instructed Ridgway and his successor, General Mark W. Clark, to maintain an impregnable defensive position and to prevent a large build-up of offensive Communist power through unrelenting air assaults upon North Korea.

Meanwhile, the truce negotiations proceeded amid charges and counter-charges on both sides. The first break came on November 27, 1951, when the Communists yielded their demand for United Nations withdrawal southward to the thirty-eighth parallel and accepted the American demand for an armistice demarcation line that coincided with the military line at the time an armistice was signed. Then, when it seemed the chief stumbling block to an armistice had been removed, the Communist and United Nations negotiators reached an impasse over the question of repatriation of prisoners of war. The Communists demanded the forcible delivery by the United Nations of some 83,000 Chinese and North Koreans who had signified they would resist such repatriation. When the Americans adamantly refused, the Communists broke off discussions in October 1952.

The Communists waited to resume negotiations until the inauguration of a Republican administration committed to ending the Korean War. In March and April they agreed to exchange wounded prisoners of war; and on April 26, 1953, armistice talks began again in earnest. The new Eisenhower administration now encountered fierce opposition, not from the Communists, who conceded all essential United Nations demands, but from Syngman Rhee, doughty President of the Republic of Korea, who threatened to withdraw his troops from the United Nations command and resume hostilities if his allies approved an armistice that left Chinese troops in North Korea. At the showdown, however, the South Korean President gave in and agreed to support the armistice even though he would not sign it; in return, the American government promised to train and equip a South Korean army of twenty divisions, to extend some $1,000,000,000 in economic aid, and to conclude a mutual security pact to protect South Korea against further Communist aggression.

Negotiations ground to a successful conclusion at Panmunjon with the signing of an elaborate armistice measure on July 27, 1953, which conceded every important objective for which the American people and their allies had been fighting.[9] Thus ended the Korean War, which had cost the United States billions of dollars and 25,604 dead, 103,492 wounded, and over 10,000 missing, most of whom were probably dead. Only the future could tell whether the American government and people, having made the indispensable effort in Korea to preserve the peace, and having succeeded in this difficult undertaking, would meet future crises with comparable courage. There were signs by mid-1953 that they understood neither the magnitude of their achievement nor the concept of a limited war that did not end in smashing victory.

230 / Challenges to Democratic Supremacy

After the outbreak of the Korean War, there were signs of mounting popular discontent with administration policies at home and abroad. Whether the disparate and often mutually hostile forces of opposition and discontent could coalesce behind a common platform and leader and successfully challenge Democratic supremacy in 1952, no observer could safely predict at the beginning of the preconvention campaigns. The significant fact was, however, that for one reason or another probably a majority of the American people desired a change of government by the early months of 1952.

To begin with, not since Alfred E. Smith's nomination in 1928 had the South been so restive and resentful. Indeed, practically the entire white South was on the verge of revolt against the President's civil rights program and in a state of tense fear lest the Supreme Court abolish segregation in the public schools. In addition, Democratic leaders and private interests in Texas, Oklahoma, Louisiana, and Florida were near rebellion because of presidential and northern Democratic opposition to southern and southwestern demands for state ownership of off-shore oil lands and exclusive state regulation of the natural gas industry.

This was also the time when Senator McCarthy launched and pressed his campaign to expose alleged Communist infiltration in high places in Washington. Other Republican leaders were less abusive than the Wisconsin demagogue, but they joined his attack by charging that Roosevelt had "sold out" to Stalin at Yalta and asserting that Communist sympathizers in the State Department had facilitated the Communist victory in China. By the spring of 1952 these powerful attacks had succeeded in planting in millions of American minds the suspicion that the Democratic party was tainted with treason and Communism.

[9] Specifically, the agreement established a demilitarized zone along a boundary that coincided with the military line and a joint United Nations-Communist Military Armistice Commission and a Neutral Nations Supervisory Commission to enforce a cease-fire and prevent violations of the armistice. To supervise the repatriation of prisoners of war and the release of prisoners who refused to return to their home lands, the agreement established a Neutral Nations Repatriation Commission, composed of representatives of Sweden, Switzerland, Poland, Czechoslovakia, and India. India, moreover, would furnish troops to take charge of the prisoners of war. Finally, the signatories recommended to their respective governments the meeting, within three months, of a political conference "to settle through negotiation the question of the withdrawal of all foreign forces from Korea, the peaceful settlement of the Korean question, etc."

An even more significant factor in generating opposition to Democratic rule, because its impact fell upon a larger number of people, were the revelations of widespread corruption in Washington during 1951 and the early months of 1952. An investigation of the Reconstruction Finance Corporation by a Senate committee in 1951 revealed corrupt influences in the granting of loans and exposed a ring of so-called "five per centers." Then soon afterward came the sensational and nationally televised investigation by a special Senate committee, headed by Estes Kefauver of Tennessee, into organized crime in the United States. It exposed embarrassing connections between the Democratic city machines in the North and the crime syndicates. Finally, in late 1951 and early 1952, came the crowning blow—the revelation that the Bureau of Internal Revenue was literally riddled with corruption and that the Assistant Attorney General in charge of income tax evasion cases had accepted large gifts, including two mink coats for his wife, from "fixers" and persons accused of income tax fraud.

Such revelations were of course good grist for the Republican propaganda mill, even though the scandals of the Truman era were insignificant as compared to the corruption that riddled the Grant and Harding administrations. But even more damaging to Democratic prestige was the way in which the President failed to take dramatic leadership in driving the corrupters from the government and from Washington. To be sure, he reorganized the RFC and the Bureau of Internal Revenue; but he acted slowly and, it seemed, reluctantly. Truman finally launched a housecleaning of other departments early in 1952. But the affair turned into a farce because his Attorney General, J. Howard McGrath, would not allow the special investigator to question employees of the Justice Department about the sources of their incomes. The investigator resigned when Truman upheld McGrath; Truman dismissed McGrath on April 3, 1952, and appointed James P. McGranery as Attorney General. And McGranery quietly abandoned the project of a special investigation.

Economic developments following the Korean War also contributed to the general growing dissatisfaction. There was an inevitable inflation following the outbreak of hostilities—wholesale prices, for example, increased 13 per cent from June 1950 to January 1952—followed by new rounds of wage demands and a sharp increase in the number of work stoppages. Although per capita disposable income, measured in constant dollars, continued to rise in spite of tax increases in 1950 and 1951, certain groups—persons living on fixed incomes and relatively fixed salaries, for example, or farmers, whose costs increased more rapidly than income—suffered considerable hardship.

Ironically, however, it was the American participation in the Korean War that generated the greatest popular discontent. Almost the entire nation had cheered when the President intervened, it is true, but disillusionment and a kind of unknowing despair swept through large elements of the country following the Chinese intervention and the administration's refusal to take desperate measures to end the war quickly. Few Americans actually wanted to run the risk of a third World War, but millions of them could not comprehend the concept of limited war and were certain there must be some quick and easy way out of the stalemate. While the truce talks ground on to no seeming end or purpose, casualties mounted and a tide of peace sentiment threatened to engulf the administration and the party in power.

231 / *The End of the Democratic Era: the Campaign and Election of 1952*

While charges and fear of corruption, Communism, inflation, and bungling in the Far East generated a powerful longing for a change of government, Republican leaders got a campaign underway in late 1951 and early 1952 to capture the presidency and Congress. Since his smashing re-election to the Senate in 1950, Senator Robert A. Taft had emerged more than ever as the unchallenged Republican leader in Congress, the spokesman of conservatives and neo-isolationists in the country at large, and the pre-eminent foe of the President's foreign and domestic policies. With the support of powerful business interests, conservative-isolationist newspapers like the *Chicago Tribune,* and Republican state organizations in the South and Middle West, Taft opened an all-out campaign to win the presidential nomination and wrest control of the GOP from the eastern internationalist leaders who had controlled the party since 1940.

On the other hand, the eastern wing, led by Governor Dewey of New York and the men in control of Republican organizations in New England, Pennsylvania, New Jersey, and Maryland, was powerful and enjoyed a working alliance with West Coast GOP leaders. In domestic policies they were moderately progressive and committed to preserving the New Deal reform structure; in foreign policy they were committed to support of the United Nations and the free world in the struggle against Communism. Their chief task in heading off the growing Taft movement was that of finding a leader who could defeat the Ohioan and then go on to win the presidency in the autumn.

At first it seemed an impossible undertaking. Former Governor Harold E. Stassen, now president of the University of Pennsylvania, was eager for the leadership but unacceptable to the eastern Republicans. Their most obvious spokesman, Governor Dewey, was disqualified by virtue of his defeat in 1948. The eastern Republicans turned, therefore, to General Eisenhower, president of Columbia University on leave and supreme commander of NATO forces in Europe, and implored him to run. Eisenhower reluctantly agreed to enter the preconvention campaign and accept the nomination if it were offered to him only in order, as he told intimate friends, to prevent Taft's nomination and the triumph of isolationism in the Republican party.

The Republican maneuvers began in January 1952, when Eisenhower's manager, Senator Henry Cabot Lodge, Jr., of Massachusetts, entered the General's name in the New Hampshire presidential primary and Taft and his friends opened a campaign to win the South and Middle West. Although Eisenhower won easily in New Hampshire, Pennsylvania, and New Jersey, Taft won such impressive victories in Wisconsin, Nebraska, and elsewhere in the Midwest that Eisenhower resigned as supreme commander in western

Europe, returned to the United States on June 1, and three days later entered the campaign in person with a speech at his home town of Abilene, Kansas.

Not since William H. Taft and Theodore Roosevelt battled for control of the GOP in 1912 had Republicans waged such a bitter and narrowly contested prenomination campaign. Taft and Eisenhower each garnered about 500 delegates; the nomination would go, therefore, to the candidate who won control of Minnesota and California, committed to favorite sons, and especially of contested delegations with sixty-eight votes from Texas, Georgia, and Louisiana.

The Taft forces controlled the Republican National Committee when the Republican convention opened in Chicago on July 7, 1952. But in the critical struggle for the contested delegates they were outmaneuvered by Dewey and Lodge, who won in a bitter battle on the convention floor and were thereby able to nominate Eisenhower on the first ballot on July 11. It was an impressive victory but a potentially fatal one, for Taft and his embittered supporters were threatening to bolt the ticket. Upon Eisenhower's success in closing the breach would depend the fate of the party in the coming campaign. Meanwhile, the convention had nominated Senator Richard M. Nixon of California for the vice presidency and adopted a platform broad enough to accommodate both wings of the GOP.[10]

The Democrats also went through a long and bitter campaign to determine control of their party and the naming of a presidential ticket. By January 1952 there were a host of Democratic contenders—Senator Richard B. Russell of Georgia, Vice President Alben W. Barkley of Kentucky, W. Averell Harriman of New York, Senator Robert S. Kerr of Oklahoma, and Senator Estes Kefauver of Tennessee. But of all the Democratic claimants it was Kefauver who made the most vigorous campaign and scored the earliest successes by his open opposition to the Truman administration.

In spite of the Tennessee senator's success in scattered presidential primaries, power in the Democratic party rested in the hands of the leaders of the northern and midwestern state organizations and in large measure with the President himself. During the early months of the preconvention campaign Truman played a cautious game in order to head off a Kefauver boom. However, on March 30, 1952, Truman announced that he would not run again; and soon afterward he began a campaign among Democratic leaders to draft Governor Adlai E. Stevenson of Illinois for the leadership of the Democracy. But Stevenson was a rarity in the annals of American political history—a man who did not want to be President—and until the eve of the Democratic convention he insisted that he was not a candidate.

Truman and the party leaders, therefore, turned to Barkley and promised to support him for the nomination. Barkley went to Chicago for the

---

[10] It promised reductions in federal expenditures and taxes, extension of the Social Security system, maintenance of high farm price supports, and exclusive state control of the so-called tide lands; condemned corruption in government; approved the Taft-Hartley Act but promised substantial revision favorable to labor; approved in principle an FEPC but declared that the states should have primary control of race relations; denounced the President's alleged usurpation of the war-making power by intervening in Korea without congressional consent; and announced a new policy of the "liberation" of peoples under Soviet domination, which would replace the allegedly futile policy of containment.

Democratic national convention "with the assurances of party leaders from President Truman down, that Adlai Stevenson would not take the presidential nomination and that . . . [he] would be the convention's choice."[11] But on the eve of the convention a group of "certain self-anointed political labor leaders," including Walter Reuther and Jack Kroll of the CIO and George M. Harrison of the AF of L, told Barkley he was too old to run and asked him to withdraw. Although they spoke without authority they gained their objective.

When the Democrats assembled in national convention on July 21, 1952, the Kefauver forces made a gallant but futile effort to challenge the control of the President and his friends. After Barkley's withdrawal the Truman leaders turned again to Stevenson, who consented to run, and nominated him on the third ballot on July 25. In addition, the convention named Senator John J. Sparkman of Alabama as Stevenson's running-mate and adopted a platform demanding repeal of the Taft-Hartley Act, enactment of a full civil rights program, including a compulsory FEPC, and maintenance of high price supports for farmers and promising a continuation of the Truman administration's policies in Asia and full support of the NATO nations.

During the next three months the Democrats fought hard to turn back the tide of accumulated discontent that threatened to overwhelm them. After accepting the nomination, Stevenson acted not like a reluctant candidate but like a man who wanted to win. And in a series of addresses, unparalleled for literary excellence since Wilson's day, he tried to tell the American people that there was no easy road to peace and security. Beginning as a moderate progressive on domestic issues, the Illinoisan was drawn inevitably into a full espousal of Fair Deal progressivism. By demanding repeal of the Taft-Hartley Act and continuation of high agricultural price supports, he appealed for labor and farm support and won the open endorsement of the CIO and AF of L but not of the powerful farm organizations. By going into the heart of the South and championing advanced civil rights legislation, he won the overwhelming allegiance of Negroes. By his high seriousness and obvious intellectual capacities he drew most intellectuals to his side.

However, it was not enough to withstand the tremendous Republican assault from all quarters and on nearly every conceivable issue. In his speeches in August and early September, Eisenhower launched a "great crusade" for honest and efficient government at home and for "freedom in the world." Taking up the theme of the liberation of captive peoples, first developed by John Foster Dulles and included in the Republican platform, Eisenhower condemned the Truman administration's "appalling and disastrous misman-agement" of foreign affairs and promised a surer road to peace than the policy of containment had been. On domestic issues he talked in generalities broad enough to please almost all classes and interests.

During the early weeks of the campaign, Eisenhower struck a posture of national leadership above the din of party battle. He soon persuaded himself, however, that the hope of national salvation lay as much in the sweeping triumph of the Republican party as in his own election; and

[11] Alben W. Barkley, "That Reminds Me—," *Saturday Evening Post*, CCXXVI (June 5, 1954), 30.

midway in the campaign he shifted his ground in order to insure Republican unity and victory. First, in order to conciliate the conservative element, Eisenhower invited Senator Taft to New York City and there, on September 12, 1952, submitted in writing to Taft's terms of surrender and won the Ohioan's promise of hearty cooperation.[12] Second, soon after the New York conference Eisenhower opened a strongly partisan attack upon the Truman administration and the President personally; at the same time, he made it clear he agreed with Taft that one objective of his administration would be to destroy such products of "creeping socialism" as the TVA and the government's hydroelectric projects in the Northwest. Third, Eisenhower established himself aggressively as leader of his party by supporting all Republican candidates, including his bitter enemies, Senator McCarthy and Senator William Jenner of Indiana, for election.

Eisenhower's most important shift, however, occurred in October, when he took up the Korean issue in a supreme effort to capitalize upon the overriding popular obsession for peace. Without ever specifically denying that the President had acted wisely by intervening, he attempted to prove that the Korean War had been the direct outcome of Truman's own blundering and charged that the United States had walked into a Soviet trap by agreeing to begin cease-fire negotiations in 1951. Then, at Detroit on October 24, he struck the high note of his campaign by promising to bring the Korean War to "an early and honorable end." "That job," he continued, "requires a personal trip to Korea. I shall make that trip. Only in that way could I learn how best to serve the American people in the cause of peace. I shall go to Korea."

Meanwhile, a united Republican party had begun one of the most powerful and best financed campaigns in the history of the country. Utilizing all the techniques of advertising through television, radio, and the press, Republican spokesmen pressed an attack that sent the Democrats reeling into an ineffective defense. Practically all Republican campaigners used the Communist issue; a few of them like McCarthy went so far as to charge that Stevenson was tainted with Communist associations. Even more devastating was the Republican attack on American participation in the Korean War. So vigorous and persistent was this offensive that the Democrats were unable to defend their record, much less make a successful counterattack of their own.

All signs pointed to a Republican victory, but the pollsters were unsure of themselves and Eisenhower and his campaigners fought hard to avert a last-minute swing to Stevenson. That swing did not occur, and on November 5, 1952, Stevenson polled 27,314,987 popular votes and carried only North Carolina, West Virginia, Kentucky, South Carolina, Georgia, Ala-

---

[12] Taft had earlier made it clear that he regarded Eisenhower as another Dewey, as a "me-too" candidate who would carry the GOP to defeat by agreeing substantially with the Democrats on all important points. At the New York conference of September 12, 1952, Eisenhower agreed that the main isssue of the campaign was "liberty against creeping socialization" and promised to defend the basic principles of the Taft-Hartley Act and to treat Taft's followers fairly in dispensing the patronage. The two men, Taft explained after the conference, disagreed on foreign policy; but, he added, "I think it is fair to say that our differences are differences of degree."

NUMBERS IN EACH STATE
SHOW ELECTORAL VOTE

	ELECTORAL VOTE	POPULAR VOTE
EISENHOWER (R)	442	33 824 000
STEVENSON (D)	89	27 315 000

39. *The Election of 1952*

TRM

bama, Mississippi, Louisiana, and Arkansas, for a total of eighty-nine electoral votes. In contrast, Eisenhower won 33,824,351 popular votes and carried thirty-nine states with a total electoral vote of 442.

What did it mean, this smashing victory by a party out of power for two decades? Did it signify merely the personal triumph of a great General, admired and beloved by Americans of all classes and sections? Or did it signify a repudiation of the progressive past and the beginning of a new conservative supremacy in American politics?

To begin with, Eisenhower's election was the perhaps inevitable personal triumph of a man who seemed to embody all the qualities that Americans most admired—honesty, simplicity, personal goodness, and decency; whose rise from humble origins gave testimony once again to the strength of the American democracy; and who had comported himself with dignity and earned the reputation of a leader of men since the North African campaign. In addition, the Republican candidates won because they were the opposition at a time when discontent with certain federal policies was great enough to destroy normal voting habits and break the Democratic coalition of farmers, workers, the lower middle classes, and Southerners. Many southern Democrats, including the Governors of Texas and South Carolina, voted as much against Truman's civil rights program and for state ownership of the tide lands as for Eisenhower. Many Democratic workers defected because as Catholics and persons of eastern European ancestry they were particularly susceptible to the Republican anti-Communist campaign and denunciation of the Yalta agreements. Midwestern farmers voted Republican, in part, because Eisenhower simply outbid the Democrats for their support. The lower middle classes and persons on fixed and Social Security incomes were obsessed by the fear of further inflation.

But all observers agreed that the one compelling national issue that had the greatest impact upon the greatest number of voters, because it crystallized the accumulated discontent, was the Korean War. "In marking their ballots for Eisenhower," one analyst has written, "many persons, of course, hoped to bring their sons and husbands back home. Still, the election should not be interpreted as a vote for peace at any price. It was more a vote of impatience with the frustrating state of neither war nor peace."[13]

And yet we can easily exaggerate the meaning of the popular verdict by emphasizing only Eisenhower's triumph and the issues that divided the parties. The astonishing phenomenon was the continued strength of the Democratic party. In spite of Eisenhower's personal popularity, widespread discontent with the Truman policies, and the power of the Republican offensive, the Republicans managed to elect only a majority of eight in the House and, because of the defection of Senator Wayne Morse of Oregon from the GOP, to break even in the Senate. As Eisenhower ran far ahead of most other Republican candidates, it is a safe assumption that he carried the slight Republican majority in Congress along with him into office. Nor could reactionaries or neo-isolationists claim that the election signified a repudiation either of progressivism at home or of the Truman policies abroad. Actually, the differences between the parties and the candidates on funda-

[13] Samuel Lubell, "Who Elected Eisenhower?" *Saturday Evening Post*, CCXXV (Jan. 10, 1953), 74.

mental issues was slight as compared to their substantial agreement on the necessity of preserving the great New Deal reform structure and American security through a continuation of the alliance-assistance system inaugurated after 1945.

The change of government took place between November 5, 1952, and January 20, 1953, as the President and President-elect forgot campaign animosities and worked together to facilitate the transfer of power. To redeem his promise, Eisenhower flew to Korea on December 2, made a brief tour of inspection, and after consulting with the military commanders declared he had no "panacea" to end the stalemate. Then on January 20, 1953, came the inauguration of the new administration and the day for which Republicans had waited for twenty years.

No man could say whether the event marked a new beginning for the GOP and the end of the long period of Democratic supremacy. One fact, however, was certain: the future was dark and full of danger for the world. For while Americans voted in November 1952 an AEC and Defense Department task force detonated the first hydrogen bomb in an explosion sufficiently powerful to level a great city. Whether such force would be used for mankind's advancement or destruction would be the great challenge confronting the people of the United States and of the world as they entered a new and frightening age—the thermo-nuclear age of potential mass destruction or of achievement unparalleled in the history of the world.

SUGGESTED ADDITIONAL READING

1. AMERICAN POLITICS FROM THEODORE ROOSEVELT TO HERBERT HOOVER

A. *Aspects of the Progressive Revolt, 1897–1917*

The best general account is Harold U. Faulkner, *The Quest for Social Justice, 1898–1914* (1931), but see Russel B. Nye, *Midwestern Progressive Politics* (1951), C. Vann Woodward, *Origins of the New South, 1877–1913* (1951), Eric F. Goldman, *Rendezvous with Destiny* (1953), and Benjamin P. De Witt, *The Progressive Movement* (1915), for special phases. John Chamberlain, *Farewell to Reform* (1932), is a stimulating but often shallow criticism.

Still the classic accounts of the progressive revolt in the cities and states are Lincoln Steffens' *The Shame of the Cities* (1904) and *The Struggle for Self-Government* (1906), which should be read with *The Autobiography of Lincoln Steffens* (1931) and the following memoirs of leaders in city and state reform: Tom L. Johnson, *My Story* (1911); Brand Whitlock, *Forty Years of It* (1925 edn.); Robert M. La Follette, *La Follette's Autobiography* (1913); Frederic C. Howe, *Confessions of a Reformer* (1925); and Josephus Daniels, *Tar Heel Editor* (1939) and *Editor in Politics* (1941). Ransom E. Noble, Jr., *New Jersey Progressivism Before Wilson* (1946), and George E. Mowry, *The California Progressives* (1951), are pioneer state studies. Among the biographies of city and state leaders, the following range far beyond the scope of this section: Alpheus T. Mason, *Brandeis: A Free Man's Life* (1946); Belle C. and F. La Follette, *Robert M. La Follette* (2 vols., 1953); Walter Johnson, *William Allen White's America* (1947); and Aubrey L. Brooks and H. T. Lefler (eds.), *The Papers of Walter Clark* (2 vols., 1948–1950).

There is need for a broad study of the social justice movement. Don D. Lescohier, "Working Conditions," and Elizabeth Brandeis, "Labor Legislation," in John R. Commons *et al.*, *History of Labor in the United States* (4 vols., 1918–1935), vol. III, contain much of the basic information. Josephine C. Goldmark, *Impatient Crusader: Florence Kelley's Life Story* (1953), records the work of one of the pioneers. See also the following memoirs by leaders in the movement: Jane Addams, *Twenty Years at Hull-house* (1910) and *The Second Twenty Years at Hull-house* (1930); Lillian D. Wald, *The House on Henry Street* (1915); and Edward A. Ross, *Seventy Years of It* (1936).

On the muckrackers there is a rich literature: Cornelius C. Regier, *The Era of the Muckrakers* (1932); Louis Filler, *Crusaders for American Liberalism* (1939); Daniel Aaron, *Men of Good Hope* (1951); and Lloyd R. Morris, *Postscript to Yesterday* (1947). The writings of the muckrakers and the literature of revolt are discussed in this volume, Sections 35–36.

We have no general history of intellectual progressivism, but Henry S. Commager, *The American Mind* (1950); Joseph Dorfman, *Thorstein Veblen and His America* (1934); and Goldman, *Rendezvous with Destiny*, and Mason, *Brandeis*, both cited above, provide invaluable insight. For the most important contributions by the intellectual progressives, see Section 37 of this volume.

The literature on Socialism and left-wing unionism is large and excellent: Donald D. Egbert and S. Persons (eds.), *Socialism and American Life* (2 vols., 1952); Howard H.

Quint, *The Forging of American Socialism* (1953); Ira Kipnis, *The American Socialist Movement, 1897–1912* (1952); Paul F. Brissenden, *The I. W. W.* (1919); and Ray Ginger, *The Bending Cross, A Biography of Eugene Victor Debs* (1949).

B. *The Republican Era, 1901–1913*

There is no good political history of the Republican era. Matthew Josephson, *The President-Makers* (1940), covers the period in detail but is often inaccurate and biased. Mark Sullivan, *Our Times, the United States, 1900–1925* (6 vols., 1926–1935), vols. I–IV, is racy and informative. For legislative issues and battles see Frank W. Taussig, *Tariff History of the United States* (1931 edn.), and Sidney Ratner, *American Taxation* (1942), for tariff and tax struggles; Henry R. Seager and C. A. Gulick, Jr., *Trust and Corporation Problems* (1929), for antitrust policy; Gifford Pinchot, *Breaking New Ground* (1947), for the story of the conservation movement; and William Z. Ripley, *Railroads: Rates and Regulation* (1912), for the best account of the development of federal railroad regulation.

Our best sources for the politics of this period are biographies and related works. Henry F. Pringle, *Theodore Roosevelt* (1931), is still the best biography, but no student should overlook Elting E. Morison and J. M. Blum, *The Letters of Theodore Roosevelt* (8 vols., 1951–1954), and John M. Blum, *The Republican Roosevelt* (1954), for new information and insights. H. F. Pringle, *The Life and Times of William Howard Taft* (2 vols., 1939), covers the entire period and beyond. For other political leaders in the period, see Philip C. Jessup, *Elihu Root* (2 vols., 1938); Richard W. Leopold, *Elihu Root and the Conservative Tradition* (1954); Merlo J. Pusey, *Charles Evans Hughes* (2 vols., 1951); Nathaniel W. Stephenson, *Nelson W. Aldrich* (1930); John A. Garraty, *Henry Cabot Lodge* (1953); Francis B. Simkins, *Pitchfork Ben Tillman* (1944); Paxton Hibben and C. H. Grattan, *The Peerless Leader* [Bryan] (1929); Claude G. Bowers, *Beveridge and the Progressive Era* (1932), and Hermann Hagedorn, *Leonard Wood* (2 vols., 1931). George E. Mowry, *Theodore Roosevelt and the Progressive Movement* (1946); Kenneth W. Hechler, *Insurgency* (1940); and A. T. Mason, *Bureaucracy Convicts Itself: The Ballinger-Pinchot Controversy of 1910* (1941), are excellent for the rise of the insurgents and the rupture of the GOP.

C. *The Wilson Era*

The only general works on the period 1912–1921 are Frederick L. Paxson, *The American Democracy and the World War* (3 vols., 1936–1948), and Arthur S. Link, *Woodrow Wilson and the Progressive Era* (1954). For aspects of domestic history, see Carter Glass, *An Adventure in Constructive Finance* (1927), Henry P. Willis, *The Federal Reserve System* (1923), and J. Laurence Laughlin, *The Federal Reserve Act* (1933), for the background and writing of the Federal Reserve bill; and John D. Clark, *The Federal Trust Policy* (1931), for the writing of the Clayton and Federal Trade Commission bills.

The most voluminous and sometimes the best literature on the Wilson era are the biographies and memoirs of the leaders of that period. Herbert C. F. Bell, *Woodrow Wilson and the People* (1945), is the best short biography. Ray S. Baker, *Woodrow Wilson: Life and Letters* (8 vols., 1927–1939), is most useful as a source of Wilson's letters, while R. S. Baker and W. E. Dodd (eds.), *The Public Papers of Woodrow Wilson* (6 vols., 1925–1927), prints Wilson's speeches and public papers. An indispensable source is Charles Seymour (ed.), *The Intimate Papers of Colonel House* (4 vols., 1926–1928). A. S. Link, *Wilson: The Road to the White House* (1947), J. M. Blum, *Joe Tumulty and the Wilson Era* (1951), and Frank Freidel, *Franklin D. Roosevelt, The Apprenticeship* (1952), shed new light on Wilson's background and the formulation of his policies.

Most of the leaders of the Wilson administration wrote memoirs to establish their importance in a critical period. Among the more important are J. Daniels, *The Wilson Era—Years of Peace, 1910–1917* (1944); Mary B. Bryan (ed.), *The Memoirs of William Jennings Bryan* (1925); William G. McAdoo, *Crowded Years* (1931); David F. Houston, *Eight Years with Wilson's Cabinet* (2 vols., 1926); and Joseph P. Tumulty, *Woodrow Wilson As I Know Him* (1921).

D. *Demobilization and the Politics and Problems of the Twenties*

For general histories, none of which is comprehensive, see Paxson, *The American Democracy and the World War*, vol. III, and Sullivan, *Our Times*, vols. V–VI, cited above, which cover demobilization and the Harding era; H. U. Faulkner, *From Versailles to the New Deal* (1950), a brief survey; Preston W. Slosson, *The Great Crusade and After, 1914–1928* (1930); and James R. Mock and E. Thurber, *Report on Demobili-*

zation (1944). Karl Schriftgiesser, *This Was Normalcy* (1948), tells the political story from 1920 to 1928 from the Democratic-progressive point of view.

Valuable for Republican politics and policies of the twenties are Samuel H. Adams, *Incredible Era: The Life and Times of Warren Gamaliel Harding* (1939), a scathing account; William A. White, *A Puritan in Babylon* (1938), a superb biography of Coolidge; W. A. White, *Autobiography* (1946); Pusey, *Hughes*, cited above; Herbert Hoover, *Memoirs* (3 vols., 1951–1952), vol. II. The literature on Democratic politics in the twenties is sparse. F. Freidel, *Franklin D. Roosevelt: The Ordeal* (1954), is significant and perceptive; James M. Cox, *Journey through My Years* (1946), is good for the campaign of 1920; and H. F. Pringle, *Alfred E. Smith* (1927), is still the best biography of the leading Democrat of the period.

There is an abundant and fast-growing literature on the problems of the post-Armistice decade. For the first Red Scare, Zechariah Chafee, Jr., *Free Speech in the United States* (1941), is indispensable, but see also Frederick L. Allen, *Only Yesterday, An Informal History of the Nineteen-Twenties* (1931), and Arthur G. Hays, *Let Freedom Ring* (1928). Major aspects of postwar intolerance and bigotry are related by John M. Mecklin, *The Ku Klux Klan* (1924); Walter Lippmann, *American Inquisitors* (1928); Ernest S. Bates, *This Land of Liberty* (1930); Bessie L. Pierce, *Public Opinion and the Teaching of History in the United States* (1926); and Howard K. Beale, *Are American Teachers Free?* (1936). The facts and significance of the greatest legal *cause célèbre* of the twenties are related in Felix Frankfurter, *The Case of Sacco and Vanzetti* (1927), and G. Louis Joughin and E. M. Morgan, *The Legacy of Sacco and Vanzetti* (1948). Norman F. Furniss' judicious *The Fundamentalist Controversy, 1918–1931* (1954) replaces Maynard Shipley's muckraking *The War on Modern Science* (1927). For the origins of the twentieth century prohibition movement, see Peter H. Odegard, *Pressure Politics, the Story of the Anti-Saloon League* (1928), an understanding work; Ernest H. Cherrington, *The Evolution of Prohibition in the United States* (1920), by a leader in the Anti-Saloon League; and Virginius Dabney, *Dry Messiah: The Life of Bishop Cannon* (1949), often unfair to the leading southern prohibitionist. The failure of the "noble experiment" is recounted in two popular works, Charles Merz, *The Dry Decade* (1931), and Herbert Asbury, *The Great Illusion, an Informal History of Prohibition* (1950).

For three major legislative issues of the twenties—tariff, taxes, and federal policy toward the electric power industry—see Taussig, *Tariff History*, and Ratner, *American Taxation*, both cited above, and George W. Norris, *Fighting Liberal* (1945). Ernest H. Gruening, *The Public Pays* (1931); Stephen Raushenbush, *The Power Fight* (1932); and Carl D. Thompson, *Confessions of the Power Trust* (1932), are highly condemnatory of the private utilities. The Farm Bloc, the revival of insurgency, and the Progressive party of 1924 are amply treated in Nye, *Midwestern Progressive Politics*, cited above; Theodore Saloutos and J. D. Hicks, *Agrarian Discontent in the Middle West, 1900–1939* (1951), a superb study; Arthur Capper, *The Agricultural Bloc* (1922), by the leader of the Farm Bloc; Kenneth C. MacKay, *The Progressive Movement of 1924* (1947); Claudius O. Johnson, *Borah of Idaho* (1936); and Norris, *Fighting Liberal*, White, *Autobiography*, and the La Follettes, *La Follette*, all cited earlier.

E. *The Supreme Court and Social and Economic Policy, 1897–1929*

Charles Warren, *The Supreme Court in United States History* (2 vols., 1937), is a general survey, but Louis B. Boudin, *Government by Judiciary* (2 vols., 1932), gives more attention to the Supreme Court and social and economic legislation. Alfred H. Kelly and W. A. Harbison, *The American Constitution* (1948), and Carl B. Swisher, *American Constitutional Development* (1943), are briefer surveys but adequate for the general reader. In addition, there are some excellent biographies of leaders in the Court for this period: Pringle, *Taft*, Pusey, *Hughes*, and Mason, *Brandeis*, already cited; Max Lerner (ed.), *The Mind and Faith of Justice Holmes* (1943); Samuel J. Konefsky, *Chief Justice Stone and the Supreme Court* (1945); and Joel F. Paschal, *Mr. Justice Sutherland* (1951), a superb study of the Court's leading exponent of *laissez faire*.

2. AMERICAN POLITICS FROM HOOVER TO EISENHOWER, 1928-1953

A. *Hoover and the Great Depression*

The literature on the Hoover administration is large but not entirely free from partisan overtones. Charles A. and Mary R. Beard, *America in Midpassage* (1939), is detailed; C. A. Beard and G. H. E. Smith, *The Old Deal and the New* (1940), is brief. Both works are basically unfriendly to Hoover. William S. Myers and W. H. Newton, *The Hoover Administration* (1936), and Ray L. Wilbur and A. M. Hyde, *The Hoover Policies* (1937), make a strenuous defense. Hoover's *Memoirs*, vol. III, cited above, claims much and concedes nothing, while W. S. Myers (ed.), *The State Papers of Herbert Hoover* (2 vols., 1934), provides basic source material.

For special aspects of Hoover's domestic policies, see Saloutos and Hicks, *Agrarian Discontent*, and Ratner, *American Taxation*, cited above; Josephine C. Brown, *Public Relief, 1929-1939* (1940); and Rexford G. Tugwell's *Mr. Hoover's Economic Policy* (1932), a searching criticism.

For vivid accounts of the impact of the depression on American life, thought, and politics, see Dixon Wecter, *The Age of the Great Depression, 1929-1941* (1948); Frederick Lewis Allen, *Since Yesterday, The Nineteen-Thirties in America* (1940); and Gilbert V. Seldes, *Years of the Locust (America, 1929-1932)* (1933). Broadus Mitchell, *Depression Decade* (1947), analyzes the causes and problems of the depression in a general way, but the following monographs are useful for specific aspects: the Brookings Institution, *The Recovery Problem in the United States* (1936); Charles S. Johnson *et al.*, *The Collapse of Cotton Tenancy* (1935); Maurice Levin *et al.*, *America's Capacity to Consume* (1934); and Edwin G. Nourse *et al.*, *America's Capacity to Produce* (1934).

B. *Franklin D. Roosevelt and American Politics*

The literature on the era of Franklin Roosevelt, already richer than that dealing with any other comparable period in American history since 1865, is constantly growing. The student might profitably begin with Samuel I. Rosenman (ed.), *The Public Papers and Addresses of Franklin D. Roosevelt* (13 vols., 1938-1950), which contains voluminous notes and commentaries. There is yet no good general history of the New Deal period. Denis W. Brogan, *The Era of Franklin D. Roosevelt* (1950), and Basil Rauch, *The History of the New Deal, 1933-1938* (1944), are brief general surveys with a strong New Deal bias. C. A. and M. R. Beard, *America in Midpassage*, cited earlier, is detailed, verbose, and without perspective. D. Wecter, *Age of the Great Depression*, cited above, is good for the social impact of New Deal policies, but B. Mitchell, *Depression Decade*, cited earlier, sometimes sounds as if the author were lecturing from a Socialist soap-box. Samuel Lubell, *The Future of American Politics* (1952), shrewdly analyzes the impact of the New Deal on party loyalties and the party structure, while Matthew Josephson, *Sidney Hillman: Statesman of American Labor* (1952), is useful for understanding the New Deal's impact on labor politics.

Biographies of Roosevelt and the memoirs of his friends and enemies are numerous enough to fill a special volume, and we will mention only the most important of them. We might begin with the most important, Robert E. Sherwood, *Roosevelt and Hopkins* (1948), a fascinating biography-memoir of Harry L. Hopkins, Roosevelt's closest adviser from 1935 to 1945. The first two volumes of F. Freidel's definitive and objective biography have already been cited; the author has additional volumes in preparation. John Gunther, *Roosevelt in Retrospect* (1950), is the best brief biography, John T. Flynn, *The Roosevelt Myth* (1948), is the most hostile; and Harold F. Gosnell, *Champion Campaigner, Franklin D. Roosevelt* (1952), is the best political biography.

Some of our best sources for the New Deal era are the memoirs of Roosevelt's friends and enemies. Cordell Hull, *Memoirs* (2 vols., 1948); S. I. Rosenman, *Working with Roosevelt* (1952); Frances Perkins, *The Roosevelt I Knew* (1946); Eleanor Roosevelt, *This Is My Story* (1937) and *This I Remember* (1949); Charles Michelson, *The Ghost Talks* (1944); and Edward J. Flynn, *You're the Boss* (1947), recount the brighter side. James A. Farley's *Behind the Ballots* (1938), was written under the Rooseveltian spell, but his *Jim Farley's Story* (1948), reveals considerable bitterness. Harold L. Ickes, *Secret Diary* (3 vols., 1953–1954), is waspish and sheds light on the personal vendetta in the Roosevelt circle, especially the rivalry between Ickes and Hopkins. Raymond B. Moley, *After Seven Years* (1939), is critical and indispensable for understanding the First New Deal.

c. *Aspects of the New Deal*

1. *Financial Reform and the Problem of Recovery.* Ferdinand Pecora, *Wall Street Under Oath* (1939), and J. T. Flynn, *Security Speculation* (1934), demonstrate the need for financial reform. Marriner S. Eccles, *Beckoning Frontiers: Public and Personal Recollections* (1951), tells the story of the writing of the Banking Act of 1935, while Marion L. Ramsay, *Pyramids of Power: The Story of Roosevelt, Insull and the Utility Wars* (1937), James C. Bonbright, *Public Utilities and National Power Policies* (1940), and William O. Douglas, *Democracy and Finance* (1940), cover the Holding Company Act of 1935 and the effort to regulate the securities exchanges.

The Treasury's monetary policies and the administration's experiments in "pump-priming" are adequately discussed in G. Griffith Johnson, Jr., *Treasury and Monetary Policy, 1933–1938* (1939); Henry H. Villard, *Deficit Spending and the National Income* (1941); John K. Galbraith and G. G. Johnson, Jr., *The Economic Effects of the Federal Public Works Expenditures, 1933–1938* (1940); and Arthur E. Burns and D. S. Watson, *Government Spending and Economic Expansion* (1940). The best study of the NRA is Leverett S. Lyon *et al.*, *The National Recovery Administration* (1935); but see also Hugh S. Johnson, *The Blue Eagle from Egg to Earth* (1935), and Donald R. Richberg, *The Rainbow* (1936), for accounts by two NRA administrators, and Merle Fainsod and L. Gordon, *Government and the American Economy* (1941), for an incisive analysis. For the work of the RFC, see Jesse H. Jones, *Fifty Billion Dollars: My Thirteen Years with the RFC, 1932–1945* (1951).

2. *The New Deal and Relief, Social Security, and Public Housing.* Mitchell, *Depression Decade*, cited above, includes an excellent summary of these phases of New Deal policy. Good surveys are Grace Abbott, *From Relief to Social Security* (1941); Donald S. Howard, *The WPA and Federal Relief Policy* (1943); Paul H. Douglas, *Social Security* (1939); and Seymour E. Harris, *The Economics of Social Security* (1941). Frances Perkins tells the story of the writing of the Social Security Act in *The Roosevelt I Knew*, cited above, while Harry Hopkins describes the work-relief program in *Spending to Save* (1936). Nathan Straus, *Seven Myths of Housing* (1944), is a good survey of the New Deal's housing program.

3. *The New Deal and Agriculture, 1933–1941.* Saloutos and Hicks, *Agrarian Discontent*, and Nye, *Midwestern Progressive Politics*, cited earlier, are excellent for the farm problem in 1932 and 1933. For the AAA and its program, see Henry A. Wallace, *New Frontiers* (1934); Russell Lord, *The Wallaces of Iowa* (1947); John D. Black, *Parity, Parity, Parity* (1942); and E. G. Nourse *et al.*, *Three Years of the Agricultural Adjustment Administration* (1937). Arthur F. Raper and I. DeA. Reid, *Sharecroppers All* (1941); Thomas J. Woofter, Jr., and E. Winston, *Seven Lean Years* (1939); and Howard Kester, *Revolt Among the Sharecroppers* (1936), describe the plight of tenants, sharecroppers, and submarginal farmers during the thirties.

4. *The South, the Concept of the Region, and the TVA.* Howard W. Odum, *Southern Regions of the United States* (1936), and Rupert B. Vance, *Human Geography of the South* (1935 edn.) and *All These People, the Nation's Human Resources in the South* (1945), are comprehensive. National Emergency Council, *Report on Economic Conditions of the South* (1938), was the basis for Roosevelt's statement that the South was the nation's "economic problem No. 1." V. O. Key, Jr., *Southern Politics in State and Nation* (1949), is a superb study. H. W. Odum and H. E. Moore, *American Regionalism* (1938), is the pioneer work in developing the regional concept. For the TVA, see C. Herman Pritchett, *The Tennessee Valley Authority: A Study in Public Administration* (1943), a dispassionate study, and David E. Lilienthal, *TVA: Democracy on the March* (1953 edn.), a spirited defense.

5. *Opposition to the New Deal.* There is, unfortunately, no study of Republican politics in the 1930's, but Lubell, *Future of American Politics*, cited above, analyzes the causes for the GOP's weakness, while H. Hoover's *The Challenge to Liberty* (1934) and *Addresses Upon the American Road* (1938) reflect the conservative Republican reaction to the New Deal. A good study of the American Liberty League is badly needed. For

non-Communist left-wing opposition to the New Deal, see Harnett T. Kane, *Louisiana Hayride* (1941), a study of Huey P. Long, and works and speeches by Long, Upton Sinclair, and the Reverend Charles E. Coughlin. Egbert and Persons, *Socialism and American Life*, cited earlier. contains the best survey of the rise and decline of Communism in the United States 'n the thirties. Eugene Lyons, *The Red Decade, the Stalinist Penetration of America* (1941), gives an exaggerated picture of Communism's triumph, but Wilson Record, *The Negro and the Communist Party* (1951), is thorough and balanced. Nathaniel Weyl, *Treason, the Story of Disloyalty and Betrayal in American History* (1950) and *The Battle Against Disloyalty* (1951), are also excellent, not only for Communism but also for Nazi and pro-Nazi activities in the United States during the 1930's. Whittaker Chambers, *Witness* (1952); Benjamin Gitlow, *I Confess* (1940) and *The Whole of Their Lives* (1948); Fred E. Beal, *Proletarian Journey* (1937); Hede Massing, *This Deception* (1951); and Louis F. Budenz, *Men Without Faces: The Communist Conspiracy in the U. S. A.* (1950), are memoirs by disillusioned former leaders in American Communism. Leon G. Turrou, *Nazi Spies in America* (1939); Harold Lavine, *Fifth Column in America* (1940); and John R. Carlson, *Undercover* (1943), are valuable for fascist and pro-Nazi groups.

6. *The Supreme Court Controversy and the New Deal Court.* M. J. Pusey, *The Supreme Court Crisis* (1937) and *Hughes*, cited earlier, make an ingenious but unconvincing defense of the Chief Justice and should be balanced with Samuel Hendel's more scholarly *Charles Evans Hughes and the Supreme Court* (1951), Paschal, *Sutherland*, cited above, and Mason, *Brandeis*, cited above. For contemporary accounts, journalistic and scholarly, see Robert H. Jackson, *The Struggle for Judicial Supremacy* (1941); Edward S. Corwin, *Court Over Constitution* (1938); and Drew Pearson and R. S. Allen, *Nine Old Men* (1936). E. S. Corwin, *Constitutional Revolution, Ltd.* (1941), recounts the conversion of the Supreme Court to progressive concepts in 1937 and afterward. For the New Deal Court, see C. H. Pritchett, *The Roosevelt Court* (1948); Charles P. Curtis, Jr., *Lions Under the Throne* (1947); Wesley McCune, *The Nine Young Men* (1947); S. J. Konefsky, *Chief Justice Stone*, cited above, and (ed.), *The Constitutional World of Mr. Justice Frankfurter* (1949); and John P. Frank, *Mr. Justice Black* (1949).

D. *Politics and Problems of the Truman Era, 1945–1953*

The literature on the Truman era is scanty and usually marred by partisan bias. Among the biographies of Truman, Jonathan Daniels, *The Man of Independence* (1950), is the best but carries the story only to 1949. William Hillman (ed.), *Mr. President* (1952), contains brief excerpts from Truman's diaries and letters. Morris B. Schnapper (ed.), *The Truman Program* (1949), is a collection of Truman's speeches on all major Fair Deal policies. Robert S. Allen and W. V. Shannon, *The Truman Merry-Go-Round* (1950), is highly critical. Walter Millis and E. S. Duffield (eds.), *The Forrestal Diaries* (1951), is an indispensable source, especially revealing on military and naval policies. Arthur H. Vandenberg, Jr. (ed.), *The Private Papers of Senator Vandenberg* (1952), deals mainly with foreign affairs but reveals the tensions that divided the Republican party. For the campaign and election of 1948, see Arthur M. Schlesinger, Jr., *The Vital Center* (1949); Lindsay Rogers, *The Pollsters* (1949); William S. White, *The Taft Story* (1954); and Schnapper, *The Truman Program;* Lubell, *The Future of American Politics*, Goldman, *Rendezvous with Destiny*, and Key, *Southern Politics*, all cited earlier. White, *The Taft Story*, cited above, Kevin McCann, *Man From Abilene* (1952), and Adlai E. Stevenson, *Major Campaign Speeches, 1952* (1953), are useful for the campaign of 1952, but the best analysis is S. Lubell, "Who Elected Eisenhower," *Saturday Evening Post*, January 10, 1953.

For economic issues in the postwar era, the best single volume is George A. Steiner, *Government's Role in Economic Life* (1953). Lester V. Chandler, *Inflation in the United States, 1940–1948* (1950), is comprehensive and clearly written. On the writing and significance of the Employment Act of 1946, see E. G. Nourse, *The 1950's Come First* (1951) and *Economics in the Public Service* (1953), and S. E. Harris, *Economic Planning* (1949). For the mobilization following the outbreak of the Korean War, see L. V. Chandler and D. H. Wallace (eds.), *Economic Mobilization and Stabilization* (1951), S. E. Harris, *The Economics of Mobilization and Inflation* (1951), and Steiner, *Government's Role in Economic Life*, cited above.

Charles W. Tobey, *The Return to Morality* (1952); Paul H. Douglas, *Ethics in Government* (1952); Blair Bolles, *How to Get Rich in Washington* (1952); H. Hubert

Wilson, *Congress: Corruption and Compromise* (1951); and K. Schriftgiesser, *The Lobbyists* (1951), describe the causes and consequences of corruption during the Truman era. The President's Committee on Civil Rights, *To Secure These Rights* (1947); Robert K. Carr, *Federal Protection of Civil Rights* (1947); Milton R. Konvitz, *The Constitution and Civil Rights* (1947); and Morroe Berger, *Equality by Statute* (1952), highlight the postwar drive for an FEPC, anti-lynching, and other civil rights measures.

The literature on Communism, civil rights, and so-called McCarthyism is large and steadily growing. On Communism in the United States, see the works cited above in *Opposition to the New Deal* and Herbert A. Philbrick, *I Led Three Lives* (1952); Oliver R. Pilat, *The Atom Spies* (1952), and Morris L. Ernst and D. L. Loth, *Report on the American Communist* (1952). Allistair Cooke, *A Generation on Trial* (1950), is a balanced analysis of the Hiss trials and their consequences. R. K. Carr, *The House Committee on Un-American Activities, 1945-1950* (1952), Clair Wilcox (ed.), *Civil Liberties Under Attack* (1951); Alan Barth, *The Loyalty of Free Men* (1951); Max Lowenthal, *The Federal Bureau of Investigation* (1950); Carey McWilliams, *Witch Hunt: The Revival of Heresy* (1950); Francis Biddle, *The Fear of Freedom* (1951); and Walter Gellhorn, *Security, Loyalty, and Science* (1950) and *The States and Subversion* (1952), condemn the excessive fear of internal Communism and call for a reaffirmation of faith in democracy. C. H. Pritchett, *Civil Liberties and the Vinson Court* (1954), is a superb summary. Most of the works just cited deal with McCarthyism, but see also Jack Anderson and R. W. May, *McCarthy* (1952); Joseph R. McCarthy, *McCarthyism, the Fight for America* (1952); and William F. Buckley, Jr. and L. B. Bozell, *McCarthy and His Enemies, the Record and Its Meaning* (1954).

3. THE UNITED STATES AND ITS WORLD RELATIONS, 1898–1953

A. *The War with Spain, Imperialism, and the United States and Europe and Asia, 1901–1914*

Samuel F. Bemis (ed.), *The American Secretaries of State and Their Diplomacy* (10 vols., 1927-1929); S. F. Bemis, *A Diplomatic History of the United States* (1950 edn.); and Thomas A. Bailey, *A Diplomatic History of the American People* (1950 edn.), are good surveys for readers deficient in background.

Walter Millis, *The Martial Spirit* (1931), is a popular history of the War with Spain. Valuable supplements are Julius W. Pratt, *Expansionists of 1898* (1936); Marcus M. Wilkerson, *Public Opinion and the Spanish-American War* (1932); Harold and M. Sprout, *The Rise of American Naval Power* (1939); and Theodore Roosevelt, *Autobiography* (1913).

There is no good book-length study of the controversy over imperialism, but J. W. Pratt, *America's Colonial Experiment* (1950), is a splendid survey of the rise, governing, and decline of the American colonial empire, while Robert E. Osgood, *Ideals and Self-Interest in America's Foreign Relations* (1953), includes a thoughtful analysis of the impact on American thought of the rise of the United States to world power. For special aspects, see David A. Lockmiller, *Magoon in Cuba: A History of the Second Intervention, 1906-1909* (1938); W. Cameron Forbes, *The Philippine Islands* (2 vols., 1928); Francis B. Harrison, *The Corner-Stone of Philippine Independence* (1922); and Charles C. Tansill, *The Purchase of the Danish West Indies* (1932).

We lack any general study of American relations with Europe from 1901 to 1914. Garraty, *Lodge,* Leopold, *Root,* Jessup, *Root,* Pringle, *Roosevelt and Taft,* all cited above, Tyler Dennett, *John Hay* (1933), and Allan Nevins, *Henry White: Thirty Years of American Diplomacy* (1930), are valuable for the diplomacy of the Roosevelt-Taft period, although Dennett overrates Hay and is unfair to Roosevelt. Richard R. Heindel, *The American Impact on Great Britain, 1898-1914* (1940); Lionel M. Gelber, *The Rise of Anglo-American Friendship, . . . 1898-1906* (1938); and Clara E. Schieber, *The Transformation of American Sentiment toward Germany, 1870-1914* (1923), are monographs of merit.

In contrast to the paucity of good works on American-European relations from 1901 to 1914 stands a large body of general and monographic studies dealing with the United States and the Far East during the same period. A. Whitney Griswold, *The Far*

Eastern Policy of the United States (1938); Edwin O. Reischauer, *The United States and Japan* (1950); and John K. Fairbank, *The United States and China* (1948), are the best surveys, but George F. Kennan, *American Diplomacy, 1900–1950* (1951), makes some provocative observations. For important monographs, see T. Dennett, *Roosevelt and the Russo-Japanese War* (1925); T. A. Bailey, *Theodore Roosevelt and the Japanese-American Crisis* (1934); Eleanor Tupper and G. E. McReynolds, *Japan in American Public Opinion* (1937). Pringle, *Taft*, cited above, Herbert Croly, *Willard Straight* (1924), and Thomas W. Lamont, *Henry P. Davison* (1933), are useful for Taft's "dollar diplomacy" in the Far East, while L. Ethan Ellis, *Reciprocity, 1911* (1939), relates Taft's ill-fated effort to win a reciprocal trade agreement with Canada. The most concise survey of Wilson's Far Eastern policy before 1917 is in A. S. Link, *Woodrow Wilson and the Progressive Era*, cited earlier, but see also Tien-yi Li, *Woodrow Wilson's China Policy, 1913–1917* (1952).

B. *The United States and Latin America, 1900–1933*

S. F. Bemis, *The Latin American Policy of the United States* (1943), covers the entire period and is the only detailed survey. For general works on the United States and the Caribbean, see Wilfrid H. Calcott, *The Caribbean Policy of the United States, 1890–1920* (1942); Dexter Perkins, *Hands Off: A History of the Monroe Doctrine* (1941), *The Monroe Doctrine, 1867–1907* (1937), and *The United States and the Caribbean* (1947); Howard C. Hill, *Roosevelt and the Caribbean* (1927); and Pratt, *America's Colonial Experiment*, cited above. Pringle, *Roosevelt*, cited above, Dwight C. Miner, *The Fight for the Panama Route* (1940), and William D. McCain, *The United States and the Republic of Panama* (1937), are good for the Panama incident and the building of the Canal. Link, *Woodrow Wilson and the Progressive Era*, cited above, has the best summary of Wilson's Caribbean and Mexican policies, but see also George M. Stephenson's *John Lind of Minnesota* (1935) for details on Wilson's campaign against Huerta.

The decline of American intervention in Mexico and the Caribbean area in the 1920's has been well related by Bemis, *Latin American Policy of the United States*, cited above; Howard F. Cline, *The United States and Mexico* (1953); Pusey, *Hughes*, cited earlier; Harold Nicolson, *Dwight Morrow* (1935); and Alexander de Conde, *Herbert Hoover's Latin-American Policy* (1951).

C. *The First Road to War, 1914–1917*

Among the general studies, Charles Seymour, *American Diplomacy during the World War* (1934) and *American Neutrality, 1914–1917* (1935), are the best. Seymour (ed.), *The Intimate Papers of Colonel House*, cited earlier, includes materials indispensable to understanding Wilson's policies. Link, *Woodrow Wilson and the Progressive Era*, cited above, is also a useful summary that agrees for the most part with Seymour's interpretation. Edwin M. Borchard and W. P. Lage, *Neutrality for the United States* (1937), and C. C. Tansill, *America Goes to War* (1938), emphasize American unneutrality but miss some important issues. C. Hartley Grattan, *Why We Fought* (1929), and Walter Millis, *Road to War: America, 1914–1917* (1935), are journalistic studies that students still enjoy.

Special studies on this subject abound, and we will mention only a few of them: Armin Rappaport, *The British Press and Wilsonian Neutrality* (1950); Horace C. Peterson, *Propaganda for War* (1939), which overrates the influence of Allied propaganda; George S. Viereck, *Spreading Germs of Hate* (1930), excellent for German propaganda activities; Carl Wittke, *German-Americans and the World War* (1936); and Clifton J. Child, *The German-Americans in Politics, 1914–1917* (1939).

R. E. Osgood, *Ideals and Self-Interest in America's Foreign Relations*, cited earlier, presents an incisive analysis of American reactions to the challenges of the First World War. For the preparedness controversy and the peace movement from 1914 to 1917, see H. Hagedorn, *The Bugle that Woke America* (1940), a study of Theodore Roosevelt and the preparedness crisis; Outten J. Clinard, *Japan's Influence on American Naval Power, 1897–1917* (1947); H. Hagedorn, *Leonard Wood*, cited earlier; E. E. Morison, *Admiral Sims and the Modern American Navy* (1942); Merle Curti, *The American Peace Crusade* (1929) and *Bryan and World Peace* (1931); and J. Addams, *Peace and Bread in Time of War* (1922).

Almost all the biographies and memoirs cited in preceding sections have chapters on the background of America's first intervention. To these should be added Robert Lansing, *War Memoirs of Robert Lansing* (1935); J. Daniels, *The Wilson Era—Years of*

War and After, 1917–1923 (1946); Burton J. Hendrick, *The Life and Letters of Walter H. Page* (3 vols., 1924–1926); Stephen Gwynn (ed.), *Letters and Friendships of Sir Cecil Spring Rice* (2 vols., 1929); James W. Gerard, *My Four Years in Germany* (1917); and Johann H. von Bernstorff, *My Three Years in America* (1920) and *Memoirs* (1936).

D. *Wilson, the Versailles Conference, and the Great Betrayal*

The early American movement for a League of Nations is related by Ruhl J. Bartlett, *The League to Enforce Peace* (1944), the background of the Peace Conference by Seymour, *American Diplomacy during the World War*, cited above, and by Harry R. Rudin, *Armistice, 1918* (1944). R. S. Baker, *Woodrow Wilson and World Settlement* (3 vols., 1922), is a friendly account; T. A. Bailey, *Woodrow Wilson and the Lost Peace* (1944), is more critical. Two British analyses, John M. Keynes, *Economic Consequences of the Peace* (1919), and Harold Nicholson, *Peacemaking, 1919* (1933), are highly critical of Wilson's leadership and policies, but see Étienne Mantoux, *The Carthaginian Peace* (1952), for a spirited reply to Keynes. Russell H. Fifield, *Woodrow Wilson and the Far East* (1952), relates Wilson's struggles with Japan at Versailles. Among the personal literature, Edward M. House and C. Seymour (eds.), *What Really Happened at Paris* (1921), and Robert Lansing, *The Peace Negotiations, a Personal Narrative* (1921), are the most important, but see also Nevins, *Henry White*, cited above; Frederick Palmer, *Bliss, Peacemaker* (1934); and Stephen Bonsal, *Unfinished Business* (1944).

The best accounts of Wilson's failure in the Treaty fight at home are T. A. Bailey, *Woodrow Wilson and the Great Betrayal* (1945), and Denna F. Fleming, *The United States and the League of Nations, 1918–1920* (1932). Bailey emphasizes Wilson's guilt for the failure of the Treaty; Fleming emphasizes Lodge's role. Blum, *Tumulty*, Garraty, *Lodge*, Johnson, *Borah*, Leopold, *Root*, Jessup, *Root*, and Seymour, *Intimate Papers of Colonel House*, all cited above, have significant chapters on the Treaty fight.

E. *The Twenties: Futile Search for Isolation*

The most comprehensive general history of American foreign policy in the 1920's is D. F. Fleming, *The United States and World Organization, 1920–1933* (1938). Fleming's *The United States and the World Court* (1945) is specialized but discusses an issue that persisted throughout the entire period. A. Nevins, *The United States in a Chaotic World* (1950), is a brief but satisfactory survey.

The postwar naval race, Japanese-American tension, the American Siberian intervention, and Russo-American relations from 1918 to 1933 are discussed by H. and M. Sprout, *Toward a New Order of Sea Power* (1940); William S. Graves, *America's Siberian Adventure, 1918–1920* (1931); Frederick L. Schuman, *American Policy toward Russia Since 1917* (1928); Robert P. Browder, *The Origins of Soviet-American Diplomacy* (1953); and William A. Williams, *American-Russian Relations, 1781–1947* (1952).

For the Washington Naval Conference and further efforts at naval disarmament, see Pusey, *Hughes*, Sprout and Sprout, *Toward a New Order of Sea Power*, and Griswold, *Far Eastern Policy of the United States*, all cited above; and Merze Tate, *The United States and Armaments* (1948), and Raymond L. Buell, *The Washington Conference* (1922). Robert H. Ferrell, *Peace In Their Time* (1952), is an excellent account of the American peace crusade of the twenties and the negotiation of the Kellogg-Briand Pact. Rodman W. Paul, *Abrogation of the Gentlemen's Agreement* (1936), is good for the Japanese-American crisis of 1924. For American international economic policy during the twenties, see Nevins, *The United States in a Chaotic World*, cited above; Herbert Feis, *The Diplomacy of the Dollar: First Era, 1919–1932* (1950); and Harold G. Moulton and L. Pasvolsky, *World War Debt Settlements* (1926) and *War Debts and World Prosperity* (1932).

W. S. Myers, *The Foreign Policies of Herbert Hoover* (1940), and Council on Foreign Relations, *Survey of American Foreign Relations, 1928–1931* (4 vols., 1928–1931) and *The United States in World Affairs, 1931–1933* (3 vols., 1932–1934), cover the general aspects of Hoover's foreign policy.

F. *The United States and the Collapse of the International Structure, 1931–1936*

The literature on the first important challenge to the postwar treaty structure, Japan's invasion of Manchuria in 1931, is voluminous and many-sided in interpretation. Among the works already cited, Griswold, *Far Eastern Policy;* Fleming, *United States and World Organization;* and Council on Foreign Relations, *Survey of American Foreign Relations, 1931 and 1932*, are most useful. Robert Langer, *Seizure of Territory: The Stimson Doctrine* (1947); Sara R. Smith, *The Manchurian Crisis, 1931–1932* (1948); and

Reginald Bassett, *Democracy and Foreign Policy, the Sino-Japanese Dispute, 1931–33* (1952), are significant contributions. Hoover defends his failure to take stern action in his *Memoirs,* vol. III, cited above, while Stimson explains his differences with Hoover frankly in Henry L. Stimson and M. Bundy, *On Active Service in Peace and War* (1948). Richard N. Current, *Secretary Stimson* (1954), is a severe criticism.

The shifting pattern of Franklin D. Roosevelt's international economic policies comes out clearly in R. B. Moley, *After Seven Years,* and C. Hull, *Memoirs,* both cited earlier. Hull also relates in detail the development of the reciprocal trade program, but see in addition R. L. Buell, *The Hull Trade Program* (1938); H. Feis, *The Changing Pattern of International Economic Affairs* (1940); and A. Nevins, *The New Deal and World Affairs* (1950), a brief survey of the entire period 1933–1945.

Hull, *Memoirs,* and Sumner Welles, *The Time for Decision* (1944), are basic sources for the Good Neighbor policy by its two chief architects. Edward O. Guerrant, *Roosevelt's Good Neighbor Policy* (1950), is a brief analysis, but see also S. F. Bemis, *Latin American Policy of the United States,* cited earlier. Cline, *The United States and Mexico,* cited above, should be read with J. Daniels, *Shirt-Sleeve Diplomat* (1947), for Mexican-American controversies and conciliation in the 1930's.

There is no good history of the anti-war crusade of the 1930's, but the volumes of *The United States in World Affairs* for the years 1934 to 1939 contain a wealth of information on public opinion, while T. A. Bailey, *The Man in the Street* (1948), has relevant chapters. For the enactment and significance of the neutrality legislation, see Borchard and Lage, *Neutrality for the United States,* cited above; James M. Seavey, *Neutrality Legislation* (1939); and Elton Atwater, *American Regulation of Arms Exports* (1941).

G. *The Second Road to War, 1937–1941*

Although only a decade and a half have passed since the outbreak of the Second World War, we now have a body of literature on the background of American participation that excels the writing on the causes of American entry into the First World War. Basic sources for the period 1937–1941 are *The Public Papers and Addresses of Franklin D. Roosevelt,* cited above; State Department, *Peace and War: United States Foreign Policy, 1931–1941* (1943); Hull, *Memoirs,* cited above; and Winston S. Churchill, *The Gathering Storm* (1948) and *Their Finest Hour* (1949).

The general works fall roughly into three major groups—"official" histories, "revisionist" studies, and books by authors with no particular axe to grind. Among the "official" histories, which glorify Roosevelt and ignore his mistakes, are B. Rauch, *Roosevelt, from Munich to Pearl Harbor* (1950); Sherwood, *Roosevelt and Hopkins,* cited above; and the sources cited in the preceding paragraph, except the Churchill volumes. The leading "revisionist" was Charles A. Beard, whose *American Foreign Policy in the Making, 1932–1940* (1946) and *President Roosevelt and the Coming of the War, 1941* (1948) deserve serious consideration. C. C. Tansill, *Backdoor to War* (1952), another "revisionist" study, is more a diatribe than an historical work. For a convenient summary of "revisionist" arguments and writings, see Harry E. Barnes (ed.), *Perpetual War for Perpetual Peace* (1953). The two outstanding works in the objective group and among the finest products of American historical scholarship are William L. Langer and S. E. Gleason, *The Challenge to Isolation, 1937–1940* (1952) and *The Undeclared War, 1940–1941* (1953). H. Feis, *The Spanish Story, Franco and the Nations at War* (1948), and Hans L. Trefousse, *Germany and American Neutrality, 1939–1941* (1951), are useful special studies.

All the general sources and works cited above deal with the background of the rupture in Japanese-American relations, but the Langer and Gleason volumes contain the fullest accounts. H. Feis, *The Road to Pearl Harbor* (1950), is also excellent and objective. W. Millis, *This Is Pearl!* (1947), is a sound popular account. George E. Morgenstern, *Pearl Harbor, the Secret History of the War* (1947), a "revisionist" study, deserves consideration. Joseph C. Grew, *Ten Years in Japan* (1944) and *Turbulent Era, a Diplomatic Record of Forty Years, 1904–1945* (2 vols., 1952), are the memoirs of the American Ambassador in Tokyo in the 1930's.

For the first Great Debate over American policy toward the war, we now have adequate studies for both the internationalist and isolationist organizations—Walter Johnson, *The Battle against Isolation* (1944), a study of the Committee to Defend

America by Aiding the Allies, and Wayne S. Cole, *America First, the Battle against Intervention, 1940–1941* (1953), a study of the America First Committee.

H. *The Diplomacy of the Second World War, 1941–1945*

Sherwood, *Roosevelt and Hopkins,* cited above, recounts the intimate diplomacy of the Grand Alliance and reprints many of the basic documents, as does Hull's *Memoirs,* cited earlier. Even more important, however, are W. S. Churchill's *The Grand Alliance* (1950), *The Hinge of Fate* (1950), *Closing the Ring* (1951), and *Triumph and Tragedy* (1953). Chester Wilmot, *The Struggle for Europe* (1952), the best one-volume history of military and diplomatic operations, is highly critical of Roosevelt's policies. Also critical of the unconditional surrender doctrine, the Yalta agreements, and other such policies is Hanson W. Baldwin, *Great Mistakes of the War* (1950).

Ray S. Cline, *Washington Command Post* (1951), Mark S. Watson, *Chief of Staff* (1950), and S. McKee Rosen, *Combined Boards of the Second World War* (1951), reveal how considerations of military strategy affected Anglo-American diplomacy from 1941 to 1945. H. Feis, *The China Tangle* (1953), is a superb account of American wartime relations with China. W. L. Langer, *Our Vichy Gamble* (1947), and Carlton J. H. Hayes, *Wartime Mission in Spain, 1942–1945* (1945), recount the State Department's efforts to retain French friendship and keep Franco out of the war. For the Yalta Conference, see Sherwood, *Roosevelt and Hopkins,* already cited; Churchill, *Triumph and Tragedy,* already cited; Edward R. Stettinius, Jr., *Roosevelt and the Russians* (1949); James F. Byrnes, *Speaking Frankly* (1947); and S. Welles, *Seven Decisions that Shaped History* (1951). Toshikazu Kase, *Journey to the Missouri* (1950), is an account of the struggle of Japanese moderate leaders to end the war.

I. *The Brave New World, the Cold War, and the Korean Crisis, 1945–1953*

There are hundreds of reports, journalistic surveys, and "tracts for the times" and few broad or even specialized historical studies of American foreign relations from 1945 to 1953. However, the student will find Council on Foreign Relations, *The United States in World Affairs, 1945–1952* (7 vols., 1947–1953), thorough in coverage and objective in tone. They constitute the basic literature for this period.

For the United Nations and American international economic policies from 1945 to 1948, see Abraham H. Feller, *United Nations and World Community* (1952); Raymond F. Mikesell, *United States Economic Policy and International Relations* (1952); Brian Tew, *International Monetary Cooperation, 1945–1952* (1952); and Clair Wilcox, *A Charter for World Trade* (1949). Hajo Holborn, *American Military Government* (1947); Drew Middleton, *The Struggle for Germany* (1949); and Benjamin U. Ratchford and W. D. Ross, *Berlin Reparations Assignment* (1947), are useful for American occupation policies in Germany. There has been no good study of the Nuremberg trial, but see R. H. Jackson, *The Case Against the Nazi War Criminals* (1946) and *The Nuremberg Case* (1947), for a justification of the proceedings. J. Gunther, *The Riddle of MacArthur* (1951); Edwin M. Martin, *Allied Occupation of Japan* (1948); and Russell Brines, *MacArthur's Japan* (1948), reveal the dimensions of the American experiment in Japan.

The causes of the disruption of the Grand Alliance have been told many times. Churchill, *Triumph and Tragedy;* Sherwood, *Roosevelt and Hopkins;* and Wilmot, *The Struggle for Europe,* all cited earlier, discuss the beginnings of tension between the western democracies and the Soviet Union. Byrnes, *Speaking Frankly,* cited above, relates Secretary Byrnes' futile struggle for understanding and friendship. There are a few glimpses of Truman's private views in Hillman, *Mr. President,* and detailed discussions of the growing tension in Millis (ed.), *The Forrestal Diaries,* and Vandenberg (ed.), *The Private Papers of Senator Vandenberg,* all cited previously. G. F. Kennan, *American Diplomacy, 1900–1950,* cited above, contains an incisive chapter on the Truman Doctrine and Kennan's own influential articles on containment. For the Berlin crisis, see Lucius D. Clay, *Decision in Germany* (1950); Frank L. Howley, *Berlin Command* (1950); and Walter B. Smith, *My Three Years in Moscow* (1950).

The debate over the failure of American policy in China has stimulated the printing of most of the basic documents and the writing of some first-rate scholarly studies on recent American policy in the Far East. Department of State, *United States Relations with China* (1949), is the White Paper that presents the official version and the documents. H. Feis, *The China Tangle,* cited above, goes only through the end of the Marshall mission. Kenneth S. Latourette, *The American Record in the Far East, 1945–1951* (1953), covers American policy in the entire area and takes the position that the United States could not have prevented the Communist triumph. Robert C. North, *Moscow and the Chinese Communists* (1953), is more critical.

For the Cold War, see the works cited for the causes of the disruption of the Grand Alliance, especially the volumes in *The United States in World Affairs* series. S. E. Harris, *The European Recovery Program* (1948), is a brief survey; Theodore H. White, *Fire in the Ashes* (1953), is a moving record of American success in the Cold War in western Europe. Halford L. Hoskins, *The Atlantic Pact* (1949), and D. Middleton, *Defense of Western Europe* (1952), recount the movement toward Atlantic unity and the development of plans for mutual defense after 1949.

American policies in the Middle East after 1945 are discussed in Leften S. Stavrianos, *Greece: American Dilemma and Opportunity* (1952); Ephraim A. Speiser, *The United States and the Near East* (1947); L. V. Thomas and R. N. Frye, *The United States and Turkey and Iran* (1951); and James G. McDonald, *My Mission in Israel, 1948–1951* (1951).

The United States in World Affairs, 1950–1953, is the best source for the Korean crisis. See also Richard H. Rovere and A. M. Schlesinger, Jr., *The General and the President* (1951), for the MacArthur affair, and Mark W. Clark, *From the Danube to the Yalu* (1954), for events of the last months of the Korean War and the protracted armistice negotiations.

4. THE AMERICAN PEOPLE DURING TWO WORLD WARS

A. *The American Military and Naval Contributions in the First World War*
The best summaries of military operations are John J. Pershing, *Final Report* (1919), and Leonard P. Ayres, *The War with Germany* (1919). J. J. Pershing, *My Experiences in the World War* (2 vols., 1931), and James G. Harbord, *The American Army in France, 1917–1919* (1936), are candid memoirs by two American commanders. There are a number of general and special studies of the American naval contribution. George T. Davis, *A Navy Second to None* (1940); H. and M. Sprout, *The Rise of American Naval Power*, cited above; and Donald W. Mitchell, *History of the Modern American Navy* (1946), are general accounts that cover the First World War. Useful special works and memoirs are Thomas G. Frothingham, *The Naval History of the World War* (3 vols., 1924–1926); Richard H. Gibson and M. Prendergast, *The German Submarine War, 1914–1918* (1931); J. Daniels, *Our Navy at War* (1922); E. E. Morison, *Admiral Sims*, cited above; and William S. Sims, *The Victory at Sea* (1920).

B. *The American Home Front, 1917–1918*
F. L. Paxson, *American Democracy and the World War*, vol. II, cited earlier, is the best general summary, but M. Sullivan, *Our Times*, vol. V, cited above, and John B. MacMaster, *The United States in the World War* (2 vols., 1918–1920), contain valuable information on social and economic life during the period of American belligerency. As yet we have no good general study of politics during the First World War, but F. Palmer, *Newton D. Baker: America at War* (2 vols., 1931), and Daniels, *The Wilson Era, Years of War and After*, Blum, *Tumulty*, Baker, *Wilson*, vols. VII and VIII, Ginger, *The Bending Cross*, Freidel, *Roosevelt*, vol. I, Ratner, *American Taxation*, Hoover, *Memoirs*, vol. II, and McAdoo, *Crowded Years*, all cited earlier, are useful.

John M. Clark, *The Costs of the World War to the American People* (1931), is an economic summary. Bernard M. Baruch, *American Industry in War* (1941 edn.), discusses the problems of industrial mobilization, while Grosvenor B. Clarkson, *Industrial America in the World War* (1923), relates the work of the War Industries Board.

For special studies, see Alexander D. Noyes, *The War Period of American Finance, 1908–1925* (1926); Walker D. Hines, *War History of American Railroads* (1928); Edward N. Hurley, *The Bridge to France* (1927); Frank M. Surface and R. L. Bland, *American Food in the World War and Reconstruction Period* (1931); George Creel, *How We Advertised America* (1920) and *Rebel at Large* (1947); J. R. Mock and C. Larson, *Words that Won the War: The Story of the Committee on Public Information, 1917–1919* (1939); Wittke, *German-Americans and the World War*, cited above; Ray H. Abrams,

Preachers Present Arms (1933); Chafee, *Free Speech in the United States,* cited earlier; and Norman Thomas, *The Conscientious Objector in America* (1923). Weyl, *The Battle Against Disloyalty* and *Treason,* both cited earlier, contain good accounts of German espionage and sabotage in the United States, but see also Henry Landau, *The Enemy Within* (1937), and Franz von Rintelen, *The Dark Invader* (1933).

c. *The American Military Effort, 1941–1945*

Historians, generals, and journalists have written hundreds of volumes on virtually all aspects of the American military effort in the Second World War, and the list that follows is a selection of the works most useful to the general reader.

Among the general studies, Churchill's volumes, previously cited, include brilliant summaries of all major operations. Wilmot, *The Struggle for Europe,* cited above, is incomparable for Allied operations in Europe. Roger W. Shugg and H. A. De Weerd, *World War II* (1946), and Fletcher Pratt, *War for the World* (1950), are briefer surveys. Walter Millis (ed.), *The War Reports* (1947), reprints the official reports of the army, air, and naval supreme commanders. Sherwood, *Roosevelt and Hopkins,* and Stimson, *On Active Service,* both cited earlier, reveal administration thought on war plans and operations.

For accounts by American military leaders, see Dwight D. Eisenhower, *Crusade in Europe* (1948); Omar N. Bradley, *A Soldier's Story* (1951); Henry H. Arnold, *Global Mission* (1949); George S. Patton, *War As I Knew It* (1947); Joseph W. Stilwell, *The Stilwell Papers* (1948); Jonathan M. Wainwright, *General Wainwright's Story* (1946); Robert L. Eichelberger and M. Mackaye, *Our Jungle Road to Tokyo* (1950); Walter Krueger, *From Down Under to Nippon* (1953); and M. W. Clark, *Calculated Risk* (1950).

Samuel A. Stouffer *et al., The American Soldier* (2 vols., 1949), is a scholarly survey of the impact of the war upon the American fighting man. For more popular observations, see Ernie Pyle, *Here Is Your War* (1943), *Brave Men* (1944), and *G. I. Joe* (1945).

D. *The United States Navy and the Second World War*

The definitive history of the American navy during the Second World War— Samuel E. Morison, *History of United States Naval Operations in World War II* (14 vols., 1947–   ), is nearing completion. Among the special studies, the following are significant: Jeter A. Isely and P. A. Crowl, *The U. S. Marines and Amphibious War* (1951), and James A. Field, *The Japanese at Leyte Gulf* (1947). For significant personal literature, see Ernest J. King and W. M. Whitehill, *Fleet Admiral King* (1952); William D. Leahy, *I Was There* (1950); Millis (ed.), *The Forrestal Diaries,* cited earlier; and William F. Halsey, *Admiral Halsey's Story* (1947).

E. *Problems of the Home Front, 1941–1945*

D. W. Brogan, *The Era of Franklin D. Roosevelt,* cited above, covers the period hurriedly. Jack Goodman (ed.), *While You Were Gone: A Report on Wartime Life in the United States* (1946), contains some good essays. John Dos Passos, *State of the Nation* (1944); William F. Ogburn (ed.), *American Society in Wartime* (1943); and Reuben Hill, *Families Under Stress* (1949), deal with aspects of the war's impact on the American society.

The story of American industrial mobilization has been told by spokesmen of various groups but not by an impartial historian. Donald M. Nelson, *Arsenal of Democracy* (1946), and Civilian Production Administration, *Industrial Mobilization for War, History of the War Production Board . . . , 1940–1945* (1947), are "official" histories. Eliot Janeway, *The Struggle for Survival* (1951), is extremely critical of the administration's effort. Bruce Catton, *The War Lords of Washington* (1948), condemns big business leadership, while Harry A. Toulmin, Jr., *Diary of Democracy: The Senate War Investigating Committee* (1947), describes the work of the Truman Committee. Frederic C. Lane *et al., Ships for Victory* (1951), is excellent for the shipbuilding program; E. R. Stettinius, Jr., *Lend-Lease, Weapon of Victory* (1944), is good for the export of *matériel;* and James P. Baxter, 3rd, *Scientists Against Time* (1946), is a superb account of American scientific achievement during wartime.

For studies of the administration's stabilization efforts, see Byrnes, *Speaking Frankly,* L. V. Chandler, *Inflation in the United States,* and L. V. Chandler and D. H. Wallace (eds.), *Economic Mobilization and Stabilization,* all cited above; S. E. Harris, *Inflation and the American Economy* (1945); and Harvey C. Mansfield *et al., A Short History of OPA* (1948). Walter W. Wilcox, *The Farmer in the Second World War* (1947), is excellent, while Randolph E. Paul, *Taxation for Prosperity* (1947), recounts wartime tax struggles with considerable objectivity.

E. S. Corwin, *Total War and the Constitution* (1947), and F. Biddle, *Democratic Thinking and the War* (1944), discuss the impact of war upon American civil liberties. C. McWilliams, *Prejudice: Japanese-Americans, Symbol of Racial Intolerance* (1944), is a devastating indictment of the removal of Japanese-Americans from the West Coast, but see also Dorothy S. Thomas and R. S. Nishimoto, *The Spoilage* (1946), and D. S. Thomas *et al.*, *The Salvage* (1952), for a scholarly study of the evacuation and particularly its effect upon Japanese-Americans. C. H. Pritchett, *The Roosevelt Court*, cited above, gives detailed attention to the courts and civil rights during the war.

5. THE AMERICAN PEOPLE AND THEIR ECONOMIC INSTITUTIONS, 1897–1953

A. *The American People: Demographic Changes and Wealth*

Warren S. Thompson, *Population Problems* (1953 edn.), is the best recent survey. Earlier and more comprehensive demographic studies are President's Research Committee, *Recent Social Trends in the United States* (2 vols., 1933); W. S. Thompson and P. K. Whelpton, *Population Trends in the United States* (1933); National Resources Committee, *Problems of a Changing Population* (1938); Walter F. Wilcox, *Studies in American Demography* (1940); and R. B. Vance, *Research Memorandum on Population Redistribution* (1938). However, the best sources for decennial demographic changes are the summary volumes of the *Census*.

There are a number of excellent studies of wealth, income, and income distribution in the United States since the 1890's. For discussions in the broad context of economic development, see H. U. Faulkner, *The Decline of Laissez Faire, 1897–1917* (1951); George Soule, *Prosperity Decade: From War to Depression, 1917–1929* (1947); and B. Mitchell, *Depression Decade*, cited earlier. Robert F. Martin, *National Income in the United States, 1799–1938* (1939), is an excellent statistical summary. Charles B. Spahr, *An Essay on the Present Distribution of Wealth* (1896); Willford I. King, *The Wealth and Income of the People of the United States* (1915); and Wesley C. Mitchell *et al.*, *Income in the United States, . . . 1909–1919* (2 vols., 1921–1922), discuss income distribution from the late nineties to the twenties. For the changing patterns in income distribution since 1920, see President's Conference on Unemployment, *Recent Economic Changes in the United States* (2 vols., 1929); Frederick C. Mills, *Economic Tendencies in the United States* (1932); M. Leven *et al.*, *America's Capacity to Consume*, cited above; E. G. Nourse *et al.*, *America's Capacity to Produce*, cited earlier; and Simon Kuznets, *National Income* (1946) and *Shares of Upper Income Groups in Income and Savings* (1953).

B. *The Problems of Labor, 1897–1953*

There are brief discussions in Faulkner, *Decline of Laissez Faire*, Soule, *Prosperity Decade*, and Mitchell, *Depression Decade*, all cited above, and in Foster R. Dulles, *Labor in America* (1949). However, the third and fourth volumes of J. R. Commons *et al.*, *History of Labour*, cited above, are the best general works for the period 1896–1932.

For studies of unionization and labor struggles, see Lewis L. Lorwin, *The American Federation of Labor* (1933); Leo Wolman, *The Growth of American Trade Unions, 1880–1923* (1924) and *Ebb and Flow in Trade Unionism* (1936); Robert R. R. Brooks, *When Labor Organizes* (1937) and *Unions of Their Own Choosing* (1939); Herbert Harris, *American Labor* (1939) and *Labor's Civil War* (1940); Edward Levinson, *Labor on the March* (1938); Joel I. Seidman, *American Labor from Defense to Reconversion* (1953); Louis Adamic, *Dynamite, the Story of Class Violence in America* (rev. edn., 1934); Samuel Yellen, *American Labor Struggles* (1936); Interchurch World Movement, Commission of Inquiry, *Report on the Steel Strike of 1919* (1920) and *Public Opinion and the Steel Strike* (1921); and R. R. R. Brooks, *As Steel Goes* (1940).

Most of the general works just cited have chapters on wages, hours, working conditions, and the health of American workers. For specialized studies, however, see Solomon Fabricant, *Employment in Manufacturing, 1899–1939* (1942); Paul H. Douglas, *Real Wages in the United States, 1890–1926* (1930); and Robert M. Woodbury, *Workers' Health and Safety* (1927).

The history of the labor movement since the 1890's is writ large in the memoirs and biographies of its leaders. Samuel Gompers, *Seventy Years of Life and Labor* (2 vols., 1925), is one of the great autobiographies in American literature. Elsie Glück, *John Mitchell, Miner* (1929), illuminates the career of a wise leader. James A. Wechsler, *Labor Baron: A Portrait of John L. Lewis* (1944), and Saul D. Alinsky, *John L. Lewis: An Unauthorized Biography* (1949), present radically different portraits of the stormy petrel of the twentieth century labor movement. M. Josephson, *Sidney Hillman*, cited earlier, is an important if uncritical contribution, while Charles A. Madison, *American Labor Leaders* (1950), is also useful. C. Wright Mills, *The New Men of Power* (1948), and Eli Ginzberg, *The Labor Leader* (1948), are sociological studies of the rise of a new labor leadership since the enactment of the Wagner Act.

c. *Government and Labor*

All the general and many of the special studies cited in the preceding section include discussions of the development of public policy and judicial interpretation concerning labor unions. For judicial interpretation, the following monographs are excellent: F. Frankfurter and N. Greene, *The Labor Injunction* (1930); Edward Berman, *Labor and the Sherman Act* (1930); Charles O. Gregory, *Labor and the Law* (1946); and Elias Lieberman, *Unions Before the Bar* (1950). A. S. Link, *Woodrow Wilson and the Progressive Era*, cited earlier, has a discussion of the labor policies of the Wilson administration, but for labor during the First World War, see Pringle, *Taft*, cited above, and Alexander M. Bing, *War-time Strikes and Their Adjustment* (1921). Carroll R. Daugherty, *Labor Under the N.R.A.* (1934), is a contemporary survey. Harry A. Millis and E. C. Brown, *From the Wagner Act to Taft-Hartley* (1950), covers the development of federal policy from 1935 to 1946, but Seidman, *American Labor from Defense to Reconversion*, cited above, is more comprehensive. For postwar labor policies, state and federal, see Charles C. Killingsworth, *State Labor Relations Acts* (1948); Millis and Brown, cited above; Emily C. Brown, *National Labor Policy* (1950); and Fred A. Hartley, Jr., *Our New National Labor Policy* (1948).

D. *The Changing Tides of Immigration*

Carl Wittke, *We Who Built America* (1939), and George M. Stephenson, *History of American Immigration, 1820–1924* (1926), are standard surveys, but J. R. Commons, *Races and Immigrants in America* (1907), is still useful. Oscar Handlin, *The Uprooted* (1951), and L. Adamic, *From Many Lands* (1940) and *A Nation of Nations* (1945), highlight the impact of the uprooting upon the immigrants and the immigrant contribution to American life.

Most of the works on immigration policy reflect the controversial aspects of the issue. Roy L. Garis, *Immigration Restriction* (1927), and William S. Bernard, *American Immigration Policy* (1950), are thorough and objective. Reflecting the conviction that the national interest demanded severe restriction are Jeremiah W. Jenks and W. J. Lauck, *The Immigrant Problem* (1926 edn.); Henry P. Fairchild, *Immigration* (1933 edn.) and *The Melting Pot Mistake* (1926); and Frank J. Warne, *The Immigrant Invasion* (1913) and *The Tide of Immigration* (1916). For another controversial aspect, see Sidney L. Gulick, *The American-Japanese Problem* (1914); Y. Ichihashi, *Japanese in the United States* (1932); and McWilliams, *Prejudice: Japanese-Americans*, cited earlier. Bernard, *American Immigration Policy*, cited above, and President's Commission, *Whom Shall We Welcome?* (1953), are the best surveys of immigration policy since 1945.

E. *The Growth of American Industry, 1897–1953*

Faulkner, *Decline of Laissez Faire*, Soule, *Prosperity Decade*, and Mitchell, *Depression Decade*, all cited above, include chapters on the growth of industry from 1897 to 1941, while chapters from Harold F. Williamson (ed.), *The Growth of the American Economy* (1951 edn.), bring the story to 1950.

For developments in the late nineteenth century and early twentieth century, see Thomas C. Cochran and W. Miller, *The Age of Enterprise* (1942); Louis M. Hacker, *The Triumph of American Capitalism* (1940); Victor S. Clark, *History of Manufactures in the United States* (3 vols., 1929), vol. III; and B. J. Hendrick, *The Age of Big Business* (1921). Edmund E. Day and W. Thomas, *The Growth of Manufactures, 1899 to 1923* (1928); the President's Conference, *Recent Economic Changes*, cited above; S. Fabricant,

The Output of Manufacturing Industries, 1899–1937 (1940); and National Resources Committee, *The Structure of the American Economy* (2 vols., 1939–1940), are more specialized. Editors of Fortune, *U.S.A., the Permanent Revolution* (1951), is excellent for the rise of new industries in the period after 1945, while B. and G. S. Mitchell, *The Industrial Revolution in the South* (1930), and Calvin B. Hoover and B. U. Ratchford, *Economic Resources and Policies of the South* (1951), are excellent for the growth of industry in the South since the 1890's.

Biographies are often the most palatable form of economic history for the general reader. F. L. Allen, *The Great Pierpont Morgan* (1949), and Lewis Corey, *The House of Morgan* (1930), reveal different points of view about the leading financier of the twentieth century. A. Nevins, *Study in Power: John D. Rockefeller, Industrialist and Philanthropist* (2 vols., 1953), is as much a history of the American oil industry as a biography of its master builder. A. Nevins, *Ford, the Times, the Man, the Company* (1954), is a saga of the rise of the automobile in the twentieth century. For leaders in iron and steel, moreover, see B. J. Hendrick, *The Life of Andrew Carnegie* (2 vols., 1932); Ida M. Tarbell, *The Life of Elbert H. Gary* (1925); and George Harvey, *Henry Clay Frick, the Man* (1928).

F. *Concentration and Competition in the American Economy*

The best survey of the concentration movement in American industry from 1870 to the 1920's is Seager and Gulick, *Trust and Corporation Problems*, cited earlier, but Arthur R. Burns, *The Decline of Competition* (1936), G. Warren Nutter, *The Extent of Enterprise Monopoly in the United States, 1899–1939* (1951), Adolf A. Berle, Jr. and G. C. Means, *The Modern Corporation and Private Property* (1932), and Federal Trade Commission, *The Merger Movement* (1948), are excellent general surveys. John Moody, *The Truth About the Trusts* (1904), is the best source for the merger movement from 1897 to 1903. James C. Bonbright and G. C. Means, *The Holding Company* (1932), analyzes the chief instrument of consolidation in the 1920's. Harry W. Laidler, *Concentration of Control in American Industry* (1931), describes the extent of concentration in 1930, while Clair Wilcox, *Competition and Monopoly in American Industry* (1940), and David Lynch, *Concentration of Economic Power* (1946), describe the situation in the late thirties.

For developments during and after the Second World War, see J. K. Galbraith, *American Capitalism* (1952); Federal Trade Commission, *The Merger Movement*, cited above, *Interlocking Directorates* (1951), and *The Concentration of Productive Facilities* (1949); and Wassily W. Leontief, *Studies in the Structure of the American Economy* (1953). Thurman W. Arnold, *The Bottlenecks of Business* (1940); Walton H. Hamilton, *Antitrust in Action* (1940); and Corwin D. Edwards, *Maintaining Competition* (1949), are excellent for the philosophy and achievements of the second antitrust crusade from 1938 to 1952.

G. *Financial Institutions and Developments Since the 1890's*

The best survey for the general reader, F. L. Allen, *The Lords of Creation* (1935), gives special attention to the financial leaders. Faulkner, *Decline of Laissez Faire*, Soule, *Prosperity Decade*, Mitchell, *Depression Decade*, and Williamson (ed.), *Growth of the American Economy*, give considerable attention to financial institutions and policies from 1897 to 1950. An indispensable general work for the serious student is Geroge W. Edwards, *The Evolution of Finance Capitalism* (1938).

Among the specialized works, Louis D. Brandeis, *Other People's Money, and How the Bankers Use It* (1914), summarizes the findings of the Pujo Committee in 1913; Henry L. Staples and A. T. Mason, *The Fall of a Railroad Empire* (1947), the story of Morgan and the New Haven Railroad, is a case study in banker mismanagement; W. Z. Ripley, *Main Street and Wall Street* (1927), discusses banking developments in the 1920's, while F. Pecora, *Wall Street Under Oath*, and J. T. Flynn, *Security Speculation*, cited earlier, highlight the bankers' contributions to the stock market crash of 1929. S. E. Harris, *Twenty Years of Federal Reserve Policy* (2 vols., 1933), and Paul M. Warburg, *The Federal Reserve System* (2 vols., 1930), are excellent for monetary policies before the New Deal.

H. *The Technological Revolution*

Excellent surveys and special studies are Harry Jerome, *Mechanization in Industry* (1934); National Resources Committee, *Technological Trends and National Policy* (1937); L. L. Lorwin, *Technology in Our Economy* (1941); S. Fabricant, *Labor Savings in American Industry, 1899–1939* (1945); Spurgeon Bell, *Productivity, Wages, and National Income* (1940); and G. J. Stigler, *Trends in Output and Employment* (1947).

6. SOCIAL AND INTELLECTUAL MAIN CURRENTS IN AMERICAN LIFE, 1897–1953

A. *Social Trends and Changes*

Faulkner, *The Quest for Social Justice*, Slosson, *The Great Crusade and After*, and Wecter, *The Age of the Great Depression*, all cited earlier, are excellent general works that cover the years from 1897 to 1941. L. R. Morris, *Postscript to Yesterday*, cited above, and *Not So Long Ago* (1949), cover the same ground but emphasize manners and ideas; M. Sullivan, *Our Times*, cited earlier, contains a wealth of social history, while F. L. Allen, *The Big Change: America Transforms Itself, 1900–1950* (1952), surveys the half century in a panoramic fashion.

President's Committee, *Recent Social Trends in the United States*, cited earlier, is the best general work for the period 1919–1932, but also excellent for changing social patterns in the twenties are F. L. Allen, *Only Yesterday*, cited above; Robert S. and H. M. Lynd, *Middletown* (1929); Harold E. Stearns (ed.), *Civilization in the United States* (1922); E. H. Gruening (ed.), *These United States* (2 vols., 1923–1924); Ben B. Lindsey and W. Evans, *Revolt of Modern Youth* (1925); and James T. Adams, *Our Business Civilization* (1929). For the impact of the depression and the New Deal, see Allen, *Since Yesterday*, already ctied; Ruth Lindquist, *The Family in the Present Social Order* (1931); R. S. and H. M. Lynd, *Middletown in Transition* (1937); H. E. Stearns (ed.), *America Now*, (1938); and White House Conference, *Children in a Democracy* (1940). Francis E. Merrill, *Social Problems on the Home Front* (1948), is an excellent analysis of social tensions and changes during the Second World War.

Sociologists, social psychologists, foreign observers, and other scholars have written a multitude of works on the postwar social scene in the United States. Harold J. Laski, *The American Democracy* (1948), is the commentary of a British Socialist. John W. Chase (ed.), *Years of the Modern* (1949); D. Wecter *et al.*, *Changing Patterns in American Civilization* (1949); Editors of Fortune, *U.S.A., the Permanent Revolution*, cited earlier; Jacques Barzun, *God's Country and Mine* (1954); and Graham Hutton, *Midwest at Noon* (1946), comment on the changing *mores*. David Riesman, *The Lonely Crowd* (1950) and *Faces in the Crowd* (1952), are penetrating studies of mass behavior. National Conference on Family Life, *The American Family* (1948), and Ruth S. Cavan, *The American Family* (1953), are the best surveys for the postwar era.

Among the specialized works on aspects of social change, see Sophonisba P. Breckinridge, *Women in the Twentieth Century* (1933); Agnes Rogers, *Women Are Here to Stay* (1949); H. Asbury, *Sucker's Progress, an Informal History of Gambling* (1938); F. R. Dulles, *America Learns to Play* (1940); G. J. Stigler, *Domestic Servants in the United States, 1900–1940* (1946); David L. Cohn, *Combustion on Wheels, an Informal History of the Automobile Age* (1944) and *The Good Old Days*, (1940); Kenneth E. Boulding, *The Organizational Revolution* (1953); Sidney H. Ditzion, *Marriage, Morals, and Sex in America* (1953); and Alfred C. Kinsey, *Sexual Behavior in the Human Male* (1948) and *Sexual Behavior in the Human Female* (1953).

B. *Currents of American Thought*

Herbert W. Schneider, *A History of American Philosophy* (1946); M. Curti, *The Growth of American Thought* (1951 edn.); and Ralph H. Gabriel, *The Course of American Democratic Thought* (1940), discuss important developments since the 1890's. H. S. Commager, *The American Mind*, cited earlier, is also general in scope. Richard Hofstadter, *Social Darwinism in American Thought, 1860–1915* (1944); Morton G. White, *Social Thought in America* (1949); and J. Dorfman, *The Economic Mind in American Civilization* (3 vols., 1946–1949), are all indispensable if specialized. Joseph W. Krutch, *The Modern Temper* (1929), and W. Lippmann, *A Preface to Morals* (1929), summarize the intellectual discontent of the 1920's.

For representative American philosophers, see Schneider, *American Philosophy*, cited above, and Ralph B. Perry, *The Thought and Character of William James* (1935);

Sidney Hook, *John Dewey* (1939); and the writings of James, Dewey, Josiah Royce, and George Santayana.

c. *The Growth of American Education, 1897–1953*

Of all the major fields of American history, the history of education is most neglected. Among the general surveys, Ellwood P. Cubberley, *Public Education in the United States* (1934 edn.); Stuart G. Noble, *A History of American Education* (1938); and Edgar W. Knight, *Education in the United States* (1951 edn.), are the best. Isaac L. Kandel (ed.), *Twenty-Five Years of American Education* (1924), has excellent chapters on development during the quarter century after 1897. For the twenties, see President's Committee, *Recent Social Trends*, cited earlier. Malcolm W. Willey (ed.), *Depression, Recovery, and Higher Education* (1937); David S. Hill and F. J. Kelly, *Economy in Higher Education* (1933); I. L. Kandel, *The End of An Era* (1941); and Hollis P. Allen, *The Federal Government and Education* (1950), are useful for the depression and the impact of federal aid in the 1930's, I. L. Kandel, *The Impact of the War Upon American Education* (1948), for the Second World War period.

There is no general study of educational developments since 1945, but the following highlight the postwar crises: Benjamin Fine, *Our Children Are Cheated: The Crisis in American Education* (1947); James B. Conant, *Education in a Divided World* (1948); Ernest O. Melby, *American Education Under Fire* (1951); E. O. Melby and M. Puner, *Freedom and Public Education* (1953); Arthur E. Bestor, Jr., *Educational Wastelands* (1953); and Albert Lynd, *Quackery in the Public Schools* (1953).

The development of educational philosophies and the debate over general education are revealed in M. Curti, *The Social Ideas of American Educators* (1935); John Dewey, *Democracy and Education* (1916); George S. Counts *et al.*, *The Social Foundations of Education* (1934); Robert M. Hutchins, *Higher Learning in America* (1936) and *Education for Freedom* (1943); Alexander Meiklejohn, *Education Between Two Worlds* (1942); and Harvard Committee, *General Education in a Free Society* (1945).

For the development of American scholarship since 1897, see M. Curti (ed.), *American Scholarship in the Twentieth Century* (1953), and the following biographies and memoirs: Henry James, *Charles W. Eliot* (2 vols., 1930); Henry A. Yeomans, *Abbott Lawrence Lowell* (1948); Nicholas M. Butler, *Across the Busy Years* (2 vols., 1939); J. R. Commons, *Myself* (1934); Richard T. Ely, *Ground Under Our Feet* (1938); Alvin S. Johnson, *Pioneer's Progress* (1952); Arthur F. Burns, *Wesley Clair Mitchell* (1952); and Samuel Tenenbaum, *William Heard Kilpatrick* (1951).

d. *American Religious Institutions and Thought Since 1897*

William W. Sweet, *The Story of Religion in America* (1939), covers the twentieth century, but more detailed are H. W. Schneider, *Religion in 20th Century America* (1952), and Willard L. Speery, *Religion in America* (1945). Theodore Maynard, *The Story of American Catholicism* (1941), is also useful.

Charles H. Hopkins, *The Rise of the Social Gospel in American Protestantism, 1865–1915* (1940); Aaron I. Abell, *The Urban Impact on American Protestantism, 1865–1900* (1943); and Henry F. May, *Protestant Churches and Industrial America* (1949), are excellent for the awakening of the church's social conscience. Charles S. Braden, *These Also Believe* (1949), is an account of the sects along the frontier of Protestantism. Ralph L. Roy, *Apostles of Discord* (1953), is a study of Protestant bigotry and fundamentalism at mid-century. For the renewal of Protestant-Catholic antagonisms and the struggle over religion in the schools in the postwar years, see Roy, *Apostles of Discord*, just cited; Conrad H. Moehlman, *The Wall of Separation between Church and State* (1951); Paul Blanshard, *American Freedom and Catholic Power* (1949) and *Communism, Democracy, and Catholic Power* (1951); and James M. O'Neill, *Catholicism and American Freedom* (1952).

Gerald B. Smith (ed.), *Religious Thought in the Last Quarter-Century* (1927), and Arnold S. Nash (ed.), *Protestant Thought in the Twentieth Century* (1951), are good surveys, but no student should overlook the work of the leading neo-orthodox theologian, Reinhold Niebuhr, especially *Moral Man and Immoral Society* (1932) and *The Nature and Destiny of Man* (2 vols., 1941–1943), and the synthesis of latter-day liberal thought, Henry N. Wieman *et al.*, *Religious Liberals Reply* (1947).

e. *American Literature, 1897–1953*

For significant work in fiction, poetry, and drama, see the relevant sections in this volume. The following list includes only general works and omits biographies and critical studies of individual writers.

The basic general history is Robert E. Spiller *et al.*, *Literary History of the United States* (1953 edn.), which contains discussions of virtually every American writer worthy of mention, lengthy essays on the major writers, and a good general bibliography. For general works on fictional writing, see Frederick J. Hoffman, *The Modern Novel in America, 1900–1950* (1951), a brief but incisive survey; Walter F. Taylor, *The Economic Novel in America* (1942), useful for the literature of protest; Alfred Kazin, *On Native Grounds* (1942), excellent for American naturalism; Granville Hicks, *The Great Tradition* (1935), a survey of left-wing and proletarian writers; and F. J. Hoffman, *Freudianism and the Literary Mind* (1945).

Among the special and period studies, the following are helpful: Van Wyck Brooks, *The Confident Years, 1885–1915* (1952); Malcolm Cowley, *Exile's Return: A Literary Odyssey of the 1920's* (1951); Wilbur M. Frohock, *The Novel of Violence in America, 1920–1950* (1950); Maxwell D. Geismar, *The Last of the Provincials: The American Novel, 1915–1925* (1947); John W. Aldridge, *After the Lost Generation* (1951); and Leo Gurko, *The Angry Decade* (1947).

For the growth of literary criticism in the twentieth century, see F. J. Hoffman *et al.*, *The Little Magazine* (1946); Irene and A. Cleaton, *Books & Battles* (1937); Charles I. Glicksberg (ed.), *American Literary Criticism, 1900–1950* (1952); and especially William V. O'Connor, *An Age of Criticism, 1900–1950* (1952). Alan S. Downer, *Fifty Years of American Drama, 1900–1950* (1951), and Louise Bogan, *Achievement in American Poetry, 1900–1950* (1951), cover the main currents in their respective fields.

F. *Art, Architecture, and Music*

Oliver W. Larkin, *Art and Life in America* (1949), is a splendid general history that relates the American achievement in painting, architecture, sculpturing, and photography to the main currents of thought and politics. Another excellent if more specialized survey is Virgil Barker, *American Painting, History and Interpretation* (1950). John I. H. Baur, *Revolution and Tradition in Modern American Art* (1951), emphasizes recent trends, while Thomas H. Benton, *An Artist in America* (1937), sets forth the philosophy of the "American" school.

James M. Fitch, *American Building* (1948), and Larkin, *Art and Life in America*, cited above, are excellent for main trends in American architecture and especially for the social and intellectual forces that shaped it. Carl W. Condit, *The Rise of the Skyscraper* (1952), discusses the Chicago pioneers who developed the skyscraper form. For vigorous enunciations of the functional philosophy, see Frank L. Wright, *Modern Architecture* (1931) and *Autobiography* (1932), and Lewis Mumford (ed.), *Roots of Contemporary American Architecture* (1952) and *The Culture of Cities* (1938).

John T. Howard, *Our American Music* (1946 edn.), and John Culshaw, *A Century of Music* (1952), review the American achievement in the field of so-called serious music, while Aaron Copland, *Our New Music* (1941), defends the modern school. For ragtime, jazz, and other popular music since 1900, there is a large and excellent literature: Sigmund Spaeth, *A History of Popular Music in America* (1948); Rudi Blesh and H. Janis, *They All Played Rag-time* (1950); R. Blesh, *Shining Trumpets* (1946); William C. Handy, *Father of the Blues* (1941); Douglas Gilbert, *Lost Chords* (1942); Robert Goffin, *Jazz* (1944); Winthrop Sargeant, *Jazz* (1946); Eddie Condon, *We Called It Music* (1947); and Deems Taylor, *Some Enchanted Evenings* (1953).

G. *Main Trends in American Journalism, 1897–1953*

Frank L. Mott, *American Journalism* (1950 edn.) is a comprehensive survey. James E. Pollard, *The Presidents and the Press* (1947), covers a little known aspect of presidential and journalistic history. Oswald G. Villard, *Some Newspapers and Newspaper-men* (1923) and *The Disappearing Daily* (1944), are excellent for twentieth century developments, while Simon M. Bessie, *Jazz Journalism* (1938), is a good account of tabloid newspapers. Commission on Freedom of the Press, *A Free and Responsible Press* (1947), and M. L. Ernst, *The First Freedom* (1946), discuss developments since the 1930's, particularly the consolidation movement and the impact of pressure groups on newspaper policies.

Biographies and memoirs of editors and newspapermen help to recreate the history of American journalism since the 1890's. See, for example, L. Steffens, *Autobiography*, and

G. Creel, *Rebel at Large*, both cited earlier; Oliver Carlson and E. S. Bates, *Hearst, Lord of San Simeon* (1936); Ferdinand Lundberg, *Imperial Hearst* (1936); Willis F. Johnson, *George Harvey* (1929); John L. Heaton (comp.), *Cobb of the "World"* (1924); R. S. Baker, *American Chronicle* (1945); and O. G. Villard, *Fighting Years, Memoirs of a Liberal Editor* (1939).

H. *The American Negro from Serfdom to Citizenship*

In no field of American history or sociology is there a more rewarding literature than in the area of the Negro and race relations in the United States. General histories abound, but the best are John H. Franklin, *From Slavery to Freedom: A History of American Negroes* (1947), and E. Franklin Frazier, *The Negro in the United States* (1949). Gunnar Myrdal, *An American Dilemma* (2 vols., 1944), is a massive, penetrating study of all phases of the race question. Arnold M. Rose, *The Negro in America* (1948), is an abridgment of Myrdal's volumes. F. B. Simkins, *A History of the South* (1953), E. F. Frazier, *The Negro Family in the United States* (1939), and C. S. Johnson, *Patterns of Negro Segregation* (1943), are other general studies.

For Negro movements and the Negro in politics since 1900, see William E. B. Du Bois, *Dusk of Dawn* (1940); Robert L. Jack, *History of the National Association for the Advancement of Colored People* (1943); Walter White, *A Man Called White* (1948); Elbert L. Tatum, *The Changed Political Thought of the Negro, 1915–1940* (1951); Henry L. Moon, *Balance of Power, the Negro Vote* (1948); and V. O. Key, Jr., *Southern Politics*, cited above.

Louise V. Kennedy, *The Negro Peasant Turns Cityward* (1930), and Ira DeA. Reid, *The Negro Immigrant* (1939), are excellent for the black migration from the South during and after the First World War; Walter White, *Rope & Faggot* (1929), and A. F. Raper, *The Tragedy of Lynching* (1933), for lynching in the twentieth century; and Horace R. Cayton and G. S. Mitchell, *Black Workers and the New Unions* (1939), and Herbert R. Northrup, *Organized Labor and the Negro* (1944), for the integration of Negroes into the ranks of organized labor.

Bernard H. Nelson, *The Fourteenth Amendment and the Negro Since 1920* (1946), and C. H. Pritchett, *The Roosevelt Court* and *Civil Liberties and the Vinson Court*, both cited earlier, discuss in ample detail the broadening of Negro rights. Harry S. Ashmore, *The Negro and the Schools* (rev. edn., 1954), is thorough and covers the Supreme Court's decision of May 17, 1954, outlawing segregation in the public schools.

For general developments in the period after 1945, Arnold M. Rose, *The Negro in Postwar America* (1950), is the best survey, but see also Bucklin Moon, *The High Cost of Prejudice* (1947); Frank S. Loescher, *The Protestant Church and the Negro* (1948); Dwight W. Culver, *Negro Segregation in the Methodist Church* (1953); J. Saunders Redding, *On Being Negro in America* (1951); and Carl T. Rowan, *South of Freedom* (1952).

INDEX

Export-Import Bank, 455, 461, 595, 652, 667
Exports: amount and character of (1900–14), 54 (1919–30), 285; capital as, 54–5; decline in (1929–32), 358; gold exports forbidden, 1933, 385–386

Fable, A, 608
Factory Investigating Commission, 57
Fair Deal, 640–2
Fair Employment Practices Committee (FEPC), 530, 637, 642
Fair Labor Standards Act, 421; amended, 640
Fair Labor Standards bill, 417
Fairless, Benjamin, 428
Falaba, 180
Fall, Albert B., and Teapot Dome scandal, 251–3
"Fantasia," 613
Far East: American investment in, 54; balance of power in, 280–2; colonies in, 16; dollar diplomacy in, 153–6; opposition to war in, 450; Roosevelt policy in, 150–3; Taft policy in, 155–6; Wilson policy in, 161, 277; Yalta discussions of, 563
Farewell to Arms, A, 324
Farley, James A.: and patronage, 414; Postmaster General, 384; as Roosevelt's campaign manager, 378
Farm Bloc: legislation, 260, 263–5; organization of, 256, 263; and surplus products, 265; and tax bills, 262
Farm Bureau Federation: and agricultural crisis, 1921, 256; and domestic allotment plan, 397
Farm Credit Administration, 397
Farm Holiday Association, 396, 397
Farm problem, 1861–1900, 7–8; 1920–28, 263–7; 1933–5, 396–9; 1940–53, 583–5. *See also* Agriculture
Farm Security Administration (FSA), 417–18, 422, 641
Farmer-Labor party, 257
Farmers: and crop-control measures, 1933, 397–9; and deflation, 1920–1, 301; income of, 206, 263, 264, 399, 419, 525, 583–5; and mortgage foreclosures, 396–7, 399; and Populist party, 10; tenant (1910–4), 24 (1937), 416, 417 (1940–5), 525; for Truman, 640. *See also* Agriculture, Farm problem
Farmers' Alliances, 8, 10
Farmers' Home Administration, 418 *n*, 641
Farmers Loan and Trust Company, 50
Farrell, Edelmiro, 665; government of, 666–7
Farrell, James T., 444, 608
Fascism: demagogues of, 441–2; and Ku Klux Klan, 340, 342; Western Hemisphere unites against, 473, 476
Faulkner, William, 325, 607–8, 609
Fearing, Kenneth, 610
"Feather-bedding," 600
Federal Bureau of Investigation (FBI): and *Amerasia* case, 643; and Communists in government, 643–4
Federal commodity loan system, 11

Federal Council of Churches of Christ in America, founding of, 35, 36; indicts capitalism, 363; and Protestant unity, 34–5, 623
Federal Deposit Insurance Corporation, 386 *n*
Federal Emergency Relief Act, 394
Federal Emergency Relief Administration (FERA), 394–5, 403
Federal Farm Board, 366–7
Federal Farm Loan Act, 134
Federal Farm Loan Banks, 134 *n*, 265
Federal Farm Loan Board, 134 *n*
Federal Home Loan Bank Act, 372
Federal Housing Administration (FHA), establishment of, 388; garden-type apartments of, 614
Federal income tax: becomes law, 107; declared unconstitutional, 104; fraud accusations in, 697; "greatest in history," 1942, 516–18; increased by Roosevelt, 410, under Wilson, 129; in Populist platform, 11; Supreme Court decision on, 116; wartime increase in, 205–7
Federal Land Banks, 265, 372
Federal Power Act, 409
Federal Power Commission: enlarged powers of, 1935, 409; first established, 1920, 237, 269; new, 1930, 269
Federal Radio Commission, 275
Federal Reserve Act, 130; overhauled by Banking Act of 1935, 387
Federal Reserve Banks, 372
Federal Reserve Board, 130; and stock speculation, 1929, 355–6
Federal Reserve Board of Governors, 387
Federal Reserve System, 130
Federal Trade Commission: as business arbiter, 314; forerunner of, 95; investigates meat-packing industry, 264; regulates business activities, 133; shift in attitude of, 315; and Supreme Court rulings, 275
Federal Trade Commission Act, 275, 314
Federalists, 4
Feiner *v.* New York, 647 *n*
Feis, Herbert, 661 *n*
Fellowship of Reconciliation, 464
Felton, Rebecca L., 320 *n*
Ferguson, Miriam A., 320 *n*
Fermi, Enrico, 508
Figures of Earth, 324
Final Report of the Commission on Industrial Relations, 56 *n*
Finance: and Civil War greenbacks, 9–10; concentration of power in, 45; corporations in, 46; empires in, 49–52; European, 1931, 353, 354, 369–70; international, 283–7; reforms in, First New Deal, 385–90; trends in, 1919–29, 315–17. *See also* Capital, Capitalism
Financier, The, 40, 77, 324
Finland, 477
First World War, 1914–18, 175–234; American neutrality in, 175–8; British blockade in, 177; cost of, 205, 216; financing of, 205–7; intellectual attitude toward, 463–4; isolationism after, 479–82; labor

A NOTE ON THE TYPE

This book was set on the Linotype in Janson, a recutting made direct from the type cast from matrices (now in possession of the Stempel foundry, Frankfurt am Main) made by Anton Janson some time between 1660 and 1687.

Of Janson's origin nothing is known. He may have been a relative of Justus Janson, a printer of Danish birth who practiced in Leipzig from 1614 to 1635. Some time between 1657 and 1668 Anton Janson, a punch-cutter and type-founder, bought from the Leipzig printer Johann Erich Hahn the type-foundry that had formerly been a part of the printing house of M. Friedrich Lankisch. Janson's types were first shown in a speci-men sheet issued at Leipzig about 1675. Janson's successor, and perhaps his son-in-law, Johann Karl Edling, issued a specimen sheet of Janson types in 1689. His heirs sold the Janson matrices in Holland to Wolffgang Dietrich Erhardt of Leipzig.

Composed, printed, and bound by KINGSPORT PRESS, INC., *Kingsport, Tennessee.*

Designed by HARRY FORD.